Contemporary Business 2006

Contemporary
Business
2006

Louis E. Boone
University of South Alabama

David L. Kurtz
University of Arkansas

THOMSON

SOUTH-WESTERN

Australia · Canada · Mexico · Singapore · Spain · United Kingdom · United States

THOMSON

SOUTH-WESTERN

Contemporary Business 2006

Louis E. Boone and David L. Kurtz

VP/Editorial Director:
Jack W. Calhoun

VP/Editor-in-Chief:
David Shaut

Senior Publisher:
Melissa S. Acuña

Acquisitions Editor:
Melissa S. Acuña

Senior Developmental Editor:
Rebecca von Gillern

Marketing Manager:
Nicole Moore

Production Editor:
Amy Hackett

Technology Project Editor:
Pam Wallace

Web Coordinator:
Karen Schaffer

Manufacturing Coordinator:
Diane Lohman

Production House:
LEAP Publishing Services, Inc.

Compositor:
GGS Information Services, Inc.

Printer:
QuebecorWorld
Versailles, Kentucky

Art Director:
Stacy Shirley

Cover and Internal Designer:
Knapke Design
Cincinnati, Ohio

Cover Image:
The Beast® roller coaster located at Paramount's
Kings Island™ near Cincinnati, Ohio

Photography Manager:
Deanna Ettinger

Photo Researcher:
Charlotte Goldman

Library of Congress Control Number:
2004117232

For more information about our products,
contact us at:
Thomson Learning Academic Resource
Center
1-800-423-0563

Thomson Higher Education
5191 Natorp Boulevard
Mason, OH 45040
USA

Asia (including India)
Thomson Learning
5 Shenton Way
#01-01 UIC Building
Singapore 068808

Australia/New Zealand
Thomson Learning Australia
102 Dodds Street
Southbank, Victoria 3006
Australia

Canada
Thomson Nelson
1120 Birchmount Road
Toronto, Ontario
MIK 5G4
Canada

Latin America
Thomson Learning
Seneca, 53
Colonia Polanco
11560 Mexico
D.F. Mexico

UK/Europe/Middle East/Africa
Thomson Learning
High Holborn House
50/51 Bedford Row
London WC1R 4LR
United Kingdom

Spain (including Portugal)
Thomson Paraninfo
Calle Magallanes, 25
28015 Madrid, Spain

*To the 3.4 million students around the globe who began their
business studies using* Contemporary Business *in their classes*

and

To the Text and Academic Authors Association, which awarded
Contemporary Business
*The William Holmes McGuffey Award for Excellence and Longevity,
the first business textbook ever to
receive this prestigious award.*

Boone&Kurtz

Dear Students:

We are pleased that you have decided to use this new edition of Contemporary Business. We hope that you will see the value in our concerted effort to keep this text to a reasonable length while including all of the topics that are so important to you. We have tried not to fall into the trap of too many chapters and far too many pages for any student to read in the time available for a one-term course. Our length objectives are to provide you with a "right-sized" text and to make certain that every page contains up-to-the-minute coverage that is complete, well written, and accompanied by learning materials that serve as industry benchmarks for quality and completeness. Even better is the fact that you can purchase a brand new copy of the text for about the same price as a used copy of last year's hardcover version.

Contemporary Business 2006 contains every chapter and every page of the hardcover edition and has been updated to include important business and marketing developments occurring since publication of the original edition. In fact, with the two additional comprehensive cases and videosÑPeter Pan Business Lines and Fallon WorldwideÑthere's even more here than in the hardcover version.

We also hope that you'll enjoy the free audio reviews that accompany the text. The four CDs allow you to review classroom-reading assignments anywhere, anytime. You can listen to them while exercising, in your car, or even while walking across campus on your way to class.

You can also find many interesting study helps at the Interactive Study Center on our Web site (http://boone.swlearning.com). It's easy to use and contains invaluable information on careers and all the latest business news.

As authors, we are particularly gratified that Contemporary Business has served for many years as the benchmark in overall quality and ranks as the global leader in sales. It has been an honor to be recognized by our fellow U.S. and Canadian authors who voted Contemporary Business the first basic business text to receive the prestigious McGuffey Award for Textbook Excellence. Best of all, we're delighted to be able to provide this updated text at this price.

Sincerely,

Gene Boone

Dave Kurtz

Preface

Contemporary Business 2006 is replete with changes, up-to-the-minute updates, and improvements. New business terms, technological breakthroughs, and industry developments appear on every page. As expected, you'll learn more about:

Offshoring

RFID (radio frequency identification)

Blogs

VOIP (voice-over Internet protocol)

Leadership Lessons from *The Apprentice*

The Vanishing Mass Market

Why Hybrids Are Hot

The Morphing of Malls

GPS: Civilian and Military Problem-Solver

Dumping: China's Low-Priced Furniture Exports

Segway: How a Sure Thing Failed

Video Phones and Privacy

And this is what users of the text have come to expect from this award-winning text on which so many other introductory business texts pattern themselves. Instructors know the book will be current, complete, and focused on providing the teaching and learning resources to help them win teaching awards and assist their students in making that A. After all, from the very first edition, *Contemporary Business* has been a book of firsts. No introductory business text in print has been used by as many students—either in the U.S. or abroad. And the best just got better.

Contemporary Business FIRSTS

Previous users will recognize that the significant improvements and up-to-the-minute currency of *Contemporary Business 2006* is the latest installment of a trend we established way back in the first edition—to move the introductory business course into the 21st century with a series of "firsts." As authors and instructors, we knew that keeping several steps ahead of the competition was the reason *Contemporary Business* became the best selling basic business text. We plan to keep it that way.

Consider our record of providing instructors and students with "firsts":

- The first business text written specifically for the student—rather than the professor—featuring a clear, concise style that students readily understand and enjoy. This decision was made by the authors in response to the overly long, all too boring, and much too definition-focused textbooks of the day and led to an avalanche of other books striving to emulate our approach.
- The FIRST introductory business text based on marketing research and written the way instructors actually teach the course.
- The FIRST business text to integrate computer applications—and later, Internet assignments—into each chapter.
- The FIRST business text to employ extensive pedagogy—such as opening vignettes and boxed features—to breathe life into the exciting concepts and issues facing contemporary business.
- The FIRST business text to offer end-of-chapter cases written by the authors and then filmed by professional producers with text concepts included in each chapter video.
- The FIRST business text to utilize multimedia technology to integrate all components of the introduction to business ancillary program, videos, overhead transparencies, and PowerPoint CD-ROMs for both instructors and students—enabling instructors to custom create lively lecture presentations.

Key Features of the New Edition

The new edition of *Contemporary Business* is packed with innovations. By now you know that the book will be filled with the very latest developments in every aspect of business. When the European Union made a huge expansion from 15 to 25 members, that expansion and its impact on global markets had to be discussed, which it is in Chapter 4 along with such topics as the SARS epidemic that temporarily derailed the burgeoning Chinese economy.

Here are some of the exciting features of the new edition.

Major Expansion of Text Coverage of Business Ethics

Following closely on the heels of the 9/11 tragedy was an ethical disaster of historic proportions by some high-profile corporations. Leaders of such corporate giants as Enron, WorldCom, Arthur Andersen, and Tyco quickly turned from heroes to villains in the wake of disclosures of legal and ethical misdeeds covered up by auditors with conflicts of interest and indirectly aided by corporate boards exhibiting a shocking lack of corporate governance. The result was an almost daily reporting of scandals, bankruptcies, job losses, Congressional investigations, and news coverage of arrested executives taking the so-called "perp walk" in front of TV cameras, a form of humiliation previously reserved for drug and violent crime offenders. Former top executives were indicted on civil and criminal charges, with some serving jail time.

In addition to hundreds of millions of dollars lost by investors who were misled by company announcements and incorrect financial reports and the job losses of thousands of innocent employees at these firms, the ethical misdeeds tarnished the image of business in the minds of the general public. In a shift as rapid and far-reaching as the 2003 blackouts that affected 50 million Americans in Canada and parts of the U.S., the vision of business careers sank to new depths. A Harris Poll founded that just 16 percent of parents want their children to become CEOs, down from 28 percent the year earlier.

In the wake of the recent crisis in business ethics, business programs in colleges and universities are examining their curricula and evaluating the extent and quality of their coverage of ethical issues. A number of universities, including Rutgers University and Ohio State University, are either adding new courses or expanding existing elective courses in ethics. Still others advocate the integration of ethics throughout the courses that comprise their business core curriculum. Many of the latter currently conduct extensive review of course content to determine the adequacy of current coverage.

Contemporary Business 2006 provides instructors and students with a thorough treatment of ethical issues affecting business, both from a macro perspective and in relation to specific business functions. The value of business ethics is introduced in Chapter 1 and then followed by a detailed analysis in Chapter 2, which focuses specifically on ethical and social responsibility issues. Laws passed in response to these ethical abuses, including the Sarbanes-Oxley Act, are discussed in detail in the "Legal Framework for Business" appendix that follows Chapter 4, and its implications for managers are outlined in Chapter 8. Portions of the law that impact accounting practices are described in Chapter 15, and finance-related implications are covered in Chapter 17.

Here are a few examples that illustrate this coverage:

- "Business Leaders Pay with Jail Terms for Ethical Misdeeds" (Chapter 2 opening vignette)
- "The Year of the Whistleblower" (Chapter 2 Hits & Misses feature)
- "New Rules for Accountants" (Chapter 16 Best Business Practices feature)
- "MCI Returns: The Company Formerly Known as WorldCom" (Chapter 16 Hits & Misses feature)
- "Enron: A Lesson for Every Investor" (Chapter 18 opening vignette)

Every chapter includes a special experiential feature called Solving an Ethical Controversy. This feature is designed to facilitate class debates of current ethical issues. Each begins with a brief background and is followed by a series of pros and cons designed to elicit class discussion of the issues. Examples of these features in this 2006 edition include:

- "Protecting Your Privacy—and Identity—in a World of Technological Evesdroppers"
- "Fighting File-Sharing: Music and Movies"
- "Executive Pay: How Much Is Too Much?"
- "Business Behind Bars"
- "The New Drug War"
- "Is Marketing to Kids Ethical?"
- "Does Spam Threaten the Future of E-Mail?"
- "Going Private: Is Being a Public Company Worth the Hassle?"

Impact of War and Continuing Concerns about Terrorism

The impact of the terrorist attacks of September 11, 2001, continues to permeate the business world. The airline industry, devastated by passenger defections following 9/11 and the soaring fuel prices of recent years, is still struggling to recover. And the industry is far different than before—with fewer flights; major carriers, such as United, operating under bankruptcy protections; and regional upstarts, such as JetBlue and Southwest, succeeding against the giants. Hybrids are increasingly the choice of fuel price-conscious auto purchasers, and sales of SUVs—especially the Hummer—have slowed as the cost of a fill-up has increased.

War and terrorism continue to impact business in various ways, and their looming effects pervade most of the chapters. New laws passed to reduce consumer security concerns and lessen the threat to marketers are introduced in the legal environment section of Chapter 3. Several terrorism-related features are included in the new edition:

- "Succeeding in the Shadow of Ground Zero" (Case 1.1 in Chapter 1)
- " 'The Money's Too Good and the Need Too Great'—Accepting the Risk of Working Overseas" (Chapter 9 opening vignette)
- "Security Nation" (Chapter 15 opening vignette)
- "GPS: High-Tech Problem Solver in Both Civilian and Military Markets" (Best Business Practices feature in Chapter 15)

Federal budget surpluses were turned into major deficits due to a combination of factors: a short economic slowdown, followed by an economic recovery that pushed unemployment rates back below the 5.5 percent level; federal tax cuts; a continuing military presence in Iraq and Afghanistan; and a rebuilding effort in the billions of dollars. These events are discussed in numerous chapters, with a special focus in Chapter 3, "Economic Challenges Facing Global and Domestic Business."

A Shorter Text

The common complaint among both instructors and students is that business texts are much too long to be covered in a single term. And introductory business texts are the most frequent subjects of this criticism. After all, the typical text is between 22 and 24 chapters long and stretches on for more than 700 pages. At the same time, they quickly state that they do not want a watered-down version of a text in the form of an "essentials" edition.

In preparing this new edition, we have worked diligently to create a "right-sized" text of approximately 600 pages and 18 chapters that offers the rigor and comprehensiveness instructors expect while still being short enough to cover in a single term. In the new 2006 edition, we have accomplished this objective. We think you will agree.

A New, More Strategic Focus

"More strategic, less descriptive." In response to numerous instructors who made such complaints about the overly descriptive nature of the typical introduction to business text, the *Contemporary Business 2006* has made a number of changes. First, Chapter 5 contains sections on business planning and the development of a business plan. In addition, Chapter 8 includes a detailed discussion of strategic planning as part of the discussion of managerial duties. A new appendix, "Developing a Business Plan," provides additional strategic tools for the reader.

Two Cases for Every Chapter

Many reviewers of the previous edition requested alternative cases to provide more flexibility for different assignments from one academic term to the next. The new 2006 edition includes two case assignments for every chapter. For example, Case 14.1, "Wow! It's Yao!," which examines the popularity of the 7′ 5″ Chinese NBA star and his success in product endorsements, is accompanied by Case 14.2, "FUBU—For Us, By Us," which focuses on the success of the urban clothing company. The second chapter case of every chapter is accompanied by a professionally created video to augment the written case materials.

Peter Pan Bus Lines and *Fallon Worldwide*: Two New Comprehensive Cases and Video Alternatives

Contemporary Business 2006 provides added flexibility for instructors who want to make use of more than one comprehensive case by providing two new alternatives. Peter Pan Bus Lines is an all-new, custom-produced case that gives the instructor a choice of using different cases to provide students more comprehensive—and more challenging—assignments than the more narrowly focused end-of-chapter video cases. This case describes the impact of the 9/11 terrorist attacks on the firm's business plan and how management and other company employees developed and implemented new plans aimed at reducing the likelihood of terrorist attacks. The case focuses on such topics as the need for flexibility in planning; marketing efforts to increase travel during the post-9/11 period; human resource training; and the creation of marketing of intangible services from industries offering tangible products.

A second comprehensive case alternative, Fallon Worldwide, describes the growth of this well-known Minneapolis-headquartered advertising agency into international markets so that it could continue to provide world-quality services to clients that were becoming global competitors. The case is also an excellent illustration of how American firms succeed in one of their major global markets: consumer and business services.

Either of these cases could serve as an excellent wrap-up for the course during one of the class meetings during the final week of the term.

18 All New Videos!

Professionally written and produced, the new video case package provides intriguing, relevant, and current real-world insight into the modern marketplace. Tied directly to chapter concepts, the videos highlight how real-world organizations struggle with the challenges of the 21st century marketplace. Each video is a user-friendly 8 to 10 minutes long and contains on-screen questions for the viewer at two locations. Three discussion questions linking video materials to chapter concepts are included approximately halfway through the case, and an additional three questions are found at the end of the video. Each video is supported by a written case with applications questions. They include:

- Case 1.2 Cannondale Keeps Satisfied Customers Rolling
- Case 2.2 Timberland Walks the Walk
- Case 3.2 FedEx Hits the Ground Running
- Case 4.2 ESPN Broadcasts Sports Around the World
- Case 5.2 Fresh Samantha: A Juicy Business
- Case 6.2 The Geek Squad to the Rescue!
- Case 7.2 Elderly Instruments Stays Young on the Internet
- Case 8.2 Buffalo Zoo's Leader Talks to the Animals—and People, Too
- Case 9.2 Fannie Mae: Making Dreams Come True
- Case 10.2 Communication Is Key at Le Meridien
- Case 11.2 Cannondale Produces World-Class Bicycles
- Case 12.2 Goya Foods Serves Many Markets
- Case 13.2 Monopoly: America's Love of Rags-to-Riches Game Is Timeless

- Case 14.2 FUBU: For Us, By Us
- Case 15.2 Cannondale Puts Technology and Information to Work
- Case 16.2 Chicago-Style Pizza Finds a Nationwide Market
- Case 17.2 Developing a Financial Strategy for a Retail Chain
- Case 18.2 Morgan Stanley Fights the Battle of the Bulls and Bears

Greater Emphasis on the Applied, "How To" Approach

The most common student suggestion for improving all business textbooks can be summed up as, "Give more real-life information that I can apply." In *Contemporary Business 2006*, we do just that. Brand-new features cover topics as current as this morning's news, including:

- "Business Discovers Blogs" (Chapter 6 Hits & Misses feature)
- "Online Grocers Are Ready to Deliver" (Chapter 7 opening vignette)
- "The Next Internet Business Targets" (Chapter 7 Best Business Practices feature)
- "Make-or-Break Leadership Lessons from *The Apprentice*" (Chapter 8 opening vignette)
- "McDonald's Reinvents Itself in a Low-Carb, Atkins Diet World" (Chapter 12 Best Business Practices feature)
- "How Kodak Is Reinventing Itself in the Digital Age" (Chapter 13 opening vignette)

Additional "how to" features that move the student beyond memorization and focus on applications are found in these locations:

- End-of-chapter Projects and Applications, Experiential Exercises, "Nothing But Net" Internet assignments, and two cases in every chapter.
- "Business Tool Kits" placed throughout the text. Examples include:
     Making Meetings Worthwhile
     Managing Your Time
     Preparing an Electronic Résumé
     Dressing for an Interview
     The Fine Art of Delegation

Additional Features of the New Edition

Contemporary Business 2006 is packed with innovations. Here are some of the exciting new features:

NEW!   The value of diversity—both in the workforce and in the marketplace—is an important focus of this edition. The rapid growth of the Hispanic American and African American populations is discussed in Chapters 1 and 5 and throughout the marketing chapters of Part 4. Other overall population segments, including Asian Americans and Native Americans, are also examined. Examples of special features include:

- "Wal-Mart's Gender Problem" (Chapter 2 Hits & Misses feature)
- "Diversity Training Programs and Multiculturalism" (Chapter 4 Business Tool Kit feature)
- "Providing Work-Life Benefits: Costs and Payoffs in Attracting and Retaining Top Performers" (Chapter 9 Best Business Practices feature)
- "Home Depot and Ikea Focus on the Hispanic Market" (Chapter 12 Hits & Misses feature)
- "Goya Foods" (Chapter 12 video case)
- "CPA Firm's People-Friendly Policies Excel at Attracting, Promoting, and Retaining Women" (Chapter 16 opening vignette)

NEW!   Two new features have been added to let students test their comprehension of business concepts in every chapter in a "dry run" environment before exams. Each chapter now contains eight or nine Concepts Checks at the end of each section. Consisting of two or three questions, the checks are designed for use by students as they read through a chapter assignment. In addition, students can take complete self-tests to determine how well they have learned chapter concepts by going to the Web site before they take a class exam.

EARLY COVERAGE! "Launching Your Business Career" has been completely rewritten and moved to the front of the textbook as a Prologue. In an environment characterized by increased student interest in improving their career potential, this special Prologue offers practical insights to help students prepare for a successful business career. Students also can access specific career information on the text Web site.

NEW! "A Guide to Your Personal Finances" has been added as Appendix B. With a focus on explaining how students can apply many of the business concepts discussed in the text to their personal finances, this appendix provides the most detailed and complete coverage of this topic of any introductory business in print.

NEW! All opening vignettes, Best Business Practices, Business Hits & Misses, and ethical controversy features are new to this edition.

Unparalleled Resource Package

Like each previous edition, *Contemporary Business 2006* is filled with innovations. The result: the most powerful basic business package available.

Since the first edition of this book was published, Boone & Kurtz has exceeded expectations of instructors—quickly becoming the benchmark for other texts—with its precedent-setting learning materials. We have continued to improve on our signature package features—equipping students and instructors with the most comprehensive collection of learning tools, teaching materials, and innovative resources available. As expected, this new edition continues to serve as the industry benchmark by delivering the most extensive, technologically advanced, user-friendly package on the market.

For the Professor

Test Bank and *Examview* Testing Software

Consisting of over 4,800 questions—the largest number of any introductory business text—the test bank meets your every need in testing students on chapter content. Each chapter of the test bank is organized following the chapter objectives, and every question is categorized by type of question (including application, comprehension, and knowledge-based multiple-choice, true/false, and essay) and text page reference. The *Examview Testing Software* is a Windows-based software program that is both easy to use and attractive. You will be amazed at how far testing software has advanced!

Instructor's Manual

Completely revised! Each chapter of the IM begins with an introduction to the chapter and a concise guide to changes in the new edition. Following this easy transition guide, instructors will find a complete set of teaching tools. Each chapter contains the following teaching tools:

- *Annotated chapter objectives:* a quick summary of each objective for the instructor that also shows how it relates to the rest of the chapter materials.
- *Detailed lecture outline:* suggestions for use of other supporting appropriate lecture materials, including additional examples, articles, activities, discussion suggestions, transparencies, and PowerPoint presentation slides.

The Instructor's Manual also includes complete solutions to all end-of-chapter questions, teamwork projects, experiential exercises, *Nothing But Net* Internet assignments, and the two end-of-chapter cases.

Media Instructor's Manual

This special Media Instructor's Manual includes everything you'll need to help you utilize to the fullest all of the media products that accompany *Contemporary Business 2006.* Each chapter includes a comprehensive guide for incorporating each of the media elements available for this product:

- The 18 video cases
- The six Krispy Kreme continuing case segments, each related to a different part in the text
- E-lectures
- The PowerPoint presentation

The media IM accomplishes this by equipping you with a guide for using technology in your classroom; a guide to the PowerPoint presentation software; a guide for the best use of E-lectures; and a complete guide for each of the 18 video cases. Each video case guide includes learning goals, chapter concepts spotlighted in the video, a video case synopsis, as well as video case questions and suggested answers.

Transparency Acetates with Teaching Notes

More than 200 full-color transparency acetates are available to support *Contemporary Business 2006.* The transparencies consist of important figures and ads from the text as well as special content acetates outlined specifically for *Contemporary Business 2006.* The transparency acetates are accompanied by a complete set of teaching notes describing how best to use them in a classroom lecture or discussion.

PowerPoint Presentation Software

After reviewing competitive offerings, the authors are convinced that the *Contemporary Business 2006* PowerPoint presentation is the best you'll find. It provides a complete teaching experience for instructors and a memorable learning experience for students. Each chapter of the presentation contains chapter objectives, the main concepts of the chapter outlined and explained after each chapter objective, many figures from the text to enhance student learning, and embedded Web links and video links that give students a strong, complete visual presentation of the chapter's main concepts. Each chapter ends with a clearly presented summation of the chapter objectives and key business concepts.

Instructor's Resource CD-ROM

It's so easy to organize your support materials when they're all in one place! New with this edition of the text is an Instructor's Resource CD-ROM that contains all of the key instructor supplements: Instructor's Manual, Test Bank, *Examview Testing Software,* and Media Instructor's Manual.

WebTutor Advantage on Blackboard and/or WebCT

WebTutor Advantage puts you ahead of the game in providing online course management for you and online learning for your students. It contains all of the interactive study guide components that you could ever want and three valuable technology-oriented additions you never thought you'd get! Included in our *WebTutor Advantage* offerings for *Contemporary Business 2006* are:

- Chapter objectives
- A chapter outline
- Electronic lectures (E-lectures)
- Applying Business Concepts—Critical Thinking Exercises
- Chapter quizzing

- Infotrac exercises
- Video cases with questions
- Threaded discussion questions for online discussions
- Links to the text Web site: http://boone.swlearning.com

Video Cases

Would this be *Contemporary Business 2006* without a brand new custom video package containing a video case for every chapter in the text? Of course not! And these videos will exceed your every expectation. Each of the 18 videos has been professionally produced and is tied directly to the key concepts in the chapter. Each video is new and highlights businesses as small as online musical instruments retailer Elderly Instruments and as large as global sports broadcaster ESPN. Each gives students a glimpse into how managers actually work, strategize, and meet challenges in the real world. The video-creation process begins with written cases prepared by the authors and contained in the text. Each is a significant improvement over corporate public relations-type cases used by competing texts.

Guides to the video cases can be found in the Media Instructor's Manual. Answers to the discussion and applications questions can be found in both the Instructor's Manual and the Media Instructor's Manual.

Krispy Kreme Continuing Video Case

This feature has been completely updated for *Contemporary Business 2006* to reflect the fast-growing donut company's expansion beyond its Southeastern roots to new markets throughout the U.S., Canada, and into such global markets as Australia and the United Kingdom. In addition, it examines changes in the firm's original business plan in response to the growing popularity of low-carb diets. The written and video case elements are divided into seven sections and appear at the end of each Part in *Contemporary Business*.

The written case segments, created by the authors, including learning concepts and discussion questions. Answers to these questions can be found in the Instructor's Manual and in the Media Instructor's Manual.

For the Student

Study Guide

Completely updated for the new 2006 edition, the Study Guide contains the following features for each chapter in the text:

- A chapter overview that briefly discusses the chapter objectives
- A complete chapter outline
- A self-quiz
- Applying Business Concepts, a section containing short scenarios for students to analyze by answering questions presented to them

Each chapter ends with a *Surfing the Net* section in which students are provided with online resources related to the chapter concepts.

Audio Chapter Reviews on CD-ROM

Every *Contemporary Business 2006* chapter now comes with an audio review! These audio reviews are provided on CD-ROM for student use. Listen to them while you're exercising, while you're walking around campus, and—heck, listen to them on the way to class as a preview of what you'll be learning that day! Just listen to them, because they'll supply you with a good summary of the chapter objectives and the major concepts in a chapter. Step to the head of the class, because they'll get you prepared in a completely new way!

Technology Products for Both Instructors and Students

Boone & Kurtz Web Site

The Boone & Kurtz Web site offers a complete array of supplementary materials for both instructors and students. Instructors will find many ways to enhance their courses using the *Instructor's Resources,* where they will find the major text supplements in electronic format for viewing or downloading.

Students will find a Web site designed specifically for *Contemporary Business 2006* that includes both a *Student Resources* section and an *Interactive Study Center.* The Student Resources section consists of downloadable files for the PowerPoint presentation as well as information about study aids that can help you ace your course. The Interactive Study Center, a dynamic online learning center, consists of interactive quizzes, crossword puzzles, career information, and more in-depth work including:

- *Infotrac Exercises.* The InfoTrac database gives students direct access to the real world of business through academic journals, business and popular magazines, newspapers, and a vast assortment of government publications. Internet exercises created for use with our text can be found in the Interactive Study Center portion of our Web site. They provide learning exercises related to specific articles or industries, as well as give guidance on how to conduct original research based on materials found in Infotrac.
- *Internet Resources.* These resources direct you to extensive support for business topics discussed in the text. Here you'll find articles, exercises, company data and company profiles, as well as a special feature on time management. This features includes advice and guidelines on effectively managing your work and leisure time as a student.
- *Internet Applications.* These online business exercises use some of the links from the new edition and test you on chapter concepts.

Acknowledgments

Our work to make *Contemporary Business 2006* the unrivaled textbook choice for the introductory business course was aided by the invaluable suggestions and contributions of dozens of people who teach the introductory business course on a regular basis and are in the best position to comment on what works best—and what doesn't work at all. Every recommendation made a difference in the creation of the new edition. Our special thanks go out to Focus Group participants who met with us in cities throughout the nation to critique business books, make suggestions, and—through their inputs—aid us immeasurably in our efforts to ensure that *Contemporary Business* continues to be the benchmark against which other texts must attempt to measure up:

Jamil Ahmad
Los Angeles Trade—Technical College

Sylvia Allen
Los Angeles Valley College

Kenneth F. Anderson
Borough of Manhattan Community College

Andrea Bailey
Moraine Valley Community College

Norman E. Burns
Bergen Community College

Diana Carmel
Golden West College

Barbara Ching
Los Angeles City College

Scott Colvin
Naugatuck Community College

Ron Colley
South Suburban College

Peter Dawson
Collin County Community College

Dr. Richard L. Drury
Northern Virginia Community College

John A. Fawcett
Norwalk Community College

Dr. Barry Freeman
Bergen Community College

Richard Ghidella
Fullerton College

Ross Gittell
University of New Hampshire

Clark Hallpike
Elgin Community College

Carnella Hardin
Glendale College—Arizona

Britt Hastey
Los Angeles City College

Dave Hickman
Frederick Community College

Nathan Himelstein
Essex County College

Scott Homan
Purdue—West Lafayette

Howard L. Irby, Jr.
Bronx Community College

Robert Ironside
North Lake College

Charlotte Jacobsen
Montgomery College

Bruce Johnson
College of the Desert

Judith Jones
Norwalk Community College

Marce Kelly
Santa Monica College

Gregory Kishel
Cypress College—Santa Ana College

Patricia Kishel
Cypress College

Andy Klein
DeVry

Mary Beth Klinger
College of Southern Maryland

John S. Leahy
Palomar College

Delores Linton
Tarrant County College—Northwest Campus

Hugh McCabe
Westchester Community College

Tricia McConville
Northeastern University

Stacy Martin
Southwestern Illinois College

Theresa Mastrianni
Kingsborough Community College

Bob Matthews
Oakton Community College

Rebecca Miles
Delaware Tech

Linda Morable
Richland College

Linda Mosley
Tarrant County College

Carol Murphy
Quinsigamond Community College

Andrew Nelson
Montgomery College

Greg Nesty
Humboldt College

Linda Newell
Saddleback College

Emmanuel Nkwenti
Pennsylvania College of Technology

Paul Okello
Tarrant County College

Lynn D. Pape
Northern Virginia Community College—Alexandria Campus

Charles Pedersen
Quinsigamond Community College

John Pharr
Cedar Valley—Dallas County Community College District

Sally Proffitt
Tarrant County College Northeast

Jeff Podoshen
DeVry

Jude A. Rathburn
University of Wisconsin—Milwaukee

Levi Richard
Citrus College

Joe Ryan
Valley College

Althea Seaborn
Norwalk Community College

John Seilo
Orange Coast Community College

Pat Setlik
Harper College

Richard Sherer
Los Angeles Trade—Technical College

Gerald Silver
Purdue University—Calumet

Leon Singleton
Santa Monica College

Malcolm Skeeter
Norwalk Community College

Robert Smolin
Citrus College

Darrell Thompson
Mountain View College

Sandra Toy
Orange Coast College

Phil Vardiman
Abilene Christian University

Sal Veas
Santa Monica College

Gina Vega
Merrimack College

Michelle Vybiral
Joliet Junior College

S. Martin Welc
Saddleback College

Rick Weidmann
Prince George's Community College

Steve Wong
Rock Valley College

A number of other colleagues at colleges and universities throughout the U.S. also provided invaluable recommendations for improving the new edition. They include:

Susan Borkowski
La Salle University

Felipe Chia
Harrisburg Area Community College

Robert Ewalt
Bergen Community College

Al Fundaburk
Bloomsburg University

Janice Keil
Bloomsburg University

Noel McKeon
Florida Community College—DTC

Richard Paradiso
Thomas Nelson Community College

Maurice Sampson
Community College of Philadelphia

Phyllis Shafer
Brookdale Community College

Susan Thompson
Palm Beach Community College

Lila Waldman
Bloomsburg University

Gloria Walker
Florida Community College at Jacksonville

Thanks also to all of our colleagues who have assisted us in previous editions in our continuing efforts to make the best business text even better. The new edition continues to reflect so many of their recommendations. Among the hundreds of reviewers and focus group participants who contributed to the book during previous editions, we acknowledge the special contributions of the following:

Alison Adderly-Pitman
Brevard Community College

David Alexander
Angelo State University

Kenneth Anderson
Mott Community College

Charles Armstrong
Kansas City Kansas Community College

Donald B. Armstrong
Mesa College

Nathaniel Barber
Winthrop University

Alan Bardwick
Community College of Aurora

Keith Batman
Cayuga Community College

Robb Bay
Community College of Southern Nevada

Charles Beem
Bucks County Community College

Carol Bibly
Triton College

Daniel Biddlecom
Erie Community College—North Campus

Joseph Billingere
Oxnard College

Larry Blenke
Sacramento City College

Paula E. Bobrowski
SUNY Oswego

Charlane Bomrad Held
Onandaga Community College

Brenda Bradford
Missouri Baptist College

Steven E. Bradley
Austin Community College

Willie Caldwell
Houston Community College

Barney Carlson
Yuba College

Maria Carmen Guerrero-Caldero
Oxnard College

Bonnie Chavez
Santa Barbara City College

Felipe Chia
Harrisburg Area Community College

Rowland Chidomere
Winston-Salem State University

Marie Comstock
Allan Hancock College

Ronald C. Cooley
South Suburban College

Suzanne Counte
Jefferson College

Robert Cox
Salt Lake Community College

Pam Crader
Jefferson College

Norman B. Cregger
Central Michigan University

Dana D'Angelo
Drexel University

Dean Danielson
San Joaquin College

Kathy Daruty
Los Angeles Pierce College

David DeCook
Arapahoe Community College

Richard L. Drury
Northern Virginia Area Community College—Annandale

Linda Durkin
Delaware County Community College

Lance J. Edwards
Otero Junior College

William Ewald
Concordia University

Carol Fasso
Jamestown Community College

Jodson Faurer
Metropolitan State College at Denver

Jan Feldbauer
Austin Community College

Sandie Ferriter
Harford Community College

Steven H. Floyd
Manatee Community College

Nancy M. Fortunato
Bryant and Stratton

John G. Foster Jr.
Montgomery College—Rockville

William D. Foster
Fontbonne College

Blane Franckowiak
Tarrant County Community College

Edward Friese
Okaloosa-Walton Community College

Atlen Gastineau
Valencia Community College—West Campus

Milton Glisson
North Carolina A&T State University

Bob Googins
Shasta Community College

Robert Gora
Catawba Valley Community College

Don Gordon
Illinois Central College

Gary Greene
Manatee Community College

Blaine Greenfield
Bucks County Community College

Stephen W. Griffin
Tarrant County Community College

Annette L. Halpin
Beaver College

Michael Hamberger
Northern Virginia Area Community College—Annandale

Neal Hannon
Bryant College

Douglas Heeter
Ferris State University

Paul Hegele
Elgin Community College

Chuck Henry
Coastline Community College

Thomas Herbek
Monroe Community College

Tom Heslin
Indiana University, Bloomington

Joseph Ho
College of Alameda

Alice J. Holt
Benedict College

Vince Howe
University of North Carolina, Wilmington

Eva M. Hyatt
Appalachian State University

Kathy Irwin
Catawba Valley Community College

Gloria M. Jackson
San Antonio College

Ralph Jagodka
Mount San Antonio College

Chris Jelepis
Drexel University

Steven R. Jennings
Highland Community College

Geraldine Jolly
Barton College

Dave Jones
LaSalle University

Don Kelley
Francis Marion University

Bill Kindsfather
Tarrant Conty Community College

Charles C. Kitzmiller
Indian River Community College

B. J. Kohlin
Pasadena City College

Carl Kovelowski
Mercer Community College

Ken Lafave
Mount San Jacinto College

Rex Lambrecht
Northeastern Junior College

Fay D. Lamphear
San Antonio College

Bruce Leppine
Delta College

Thomas Lloyd
Westmoreland County Community College

Jim Locke
Northern Virginia Area Community College—Annandale

Paul Londrigan
Mott Community College

Kathleen J. Lorencz
Oakland County Community College

John Mack
Salem State College

Paul Martin
Aims College

Lori Martynowicz
Bryant and Stratton

Michael Matukonis
SUNY Oneonta

Virginia Mayes
Montgomery College—Germantown

Joseph E. McAloon
Fitchburg State College

James McKee
Champlain College

Michael McLane
University of Texas, San Antonio

Ina Midkiff
Austin Community College

Rebecca Mihelcic
Howard Community College

Richard Miller
Harford Community College

Joseph Mislivec
Central Michigan University

Kimberly K. Montney
Kellogg Community College

Gail Moran
Harper College

Linda S. Munilla
Georgia Southern University

Kenneth R. Nail
Pasco-Hernando Community College

Joe Newton
Buffalo State College

Janet Nichols
Northeastern University

Frank Nickels
Pasco-Hernando Community College

Sharon Nickels
St. Petersburg Junior College

Nnamdi I. Osakwe
Livingstone College

Tibor Osatreicher
Baltimore City Community College

George Otto
Truman College

Thomas Paczkowski
Cayuga Community College

Alton Parish
Tarrant County Community College

Jack Partlow
Northern Virginia Area Community Colelge—Annandale

Jeff Penley
Catawba Valley Community College

Robert Pollero
Anne Arundel Community College

Alton J. Purdy
Solano Community College

Surat P. Puri
Barber Scottia College

Angela Rabatin
Prince George's Community College

Linda Reynolds
Sacramento City College

Brenda Rhodes
Northeastern Junior College

Merle Rhodes
Morgan Community College

Pollis Robertson
Kellogg Community College

Robert Ross
Drexel University

Benjamin Sackmary
Buffalo State College

Martin St. John
Westmoreland County Community College

Catherina A. Sanders
San Antonio College

Lewis Schlossinger
Community College of Aurora

Gene Schneider
Austin Community College

Raymond Shea
Monroe Community College

Nora Jo Sherman
Houston Community College

Leon J. Singleton
Santa Monica College

Jeff Slater
North Shore Community College

Candy Smith
Folsom Lakes College

Solomon A. Solomon
Community College of Rhode Island

R. Southall
Laney College

E. George Stook
Anne Arundel Community College

James B. Stull
San Jose State University

Bill Syverstein
Fresno City College

Thomas Szezurek
Delaware County Community College

Daryl Taylor
Pasadena City College

John H. Teter
St. Petersburg Junior College

Gary Thomas
Anne Arundel Community College

Michael Thomas
Henry Ford Community College

Frank Titlow
St. Petersburg Junior College

Roland Tollefson
Anne Arundel Community College

Sheb True
Loyola Marymount University

Robert Ulbrich
Parkland College

Ariah Ullman
SUNY Binghamton

Sal Veas
Santa Monica College

Steven Wade
Santa Clara University

Dennis Wahler
San Jacinto Evergreen Community College District

W. J. Walters
Central Piedmont Community College

Timothy Weaver
Moorpark College

Richard Wertz
Concordia University

Darcelle D. White
Eastern Michigan University

Jean G. Wicks
Bornie State University

Tom Wiener
Iowa Central Community College

Dave Wiley
Anne Arundel Community College

Richard J. Williams
Santa Clara University

Joyce Wood
Northern Virginia Community College

Gregory Worosz
Schoolcraft College

Martha Zennis
Jamestown Community College

We would also like to express our appreciation to our research and editorial staff, especially Karen Hill and Mikhelle Taylor. Their untiring efforts on our behalf are most appreciated. We also acknowledge—and thank—Dr. Douglas Hearth, our colleague at the University of Arkansas, who participated in making the *Contemporary Business* supplements an outstanding and innovative teaching and learning package. We would also like to thank Sal Veas and Marce Kelly at San Diego State for their outstanding efforts on the PowerPoint presentations and the Collaborative Learning Handbook—these two supplements make our package hard to beat! Finally, this book would never have become a reality without the outstanding efforts of the South-Western/Thomson editorial, production, and marketing teams. Our Business Editor Melissa Acuña, Developmental Editor Rebecca von Gillern; Marketing Manager Nicole Moore; Production Editor Amy Hackett; and Technology Editors Kristen Meere, Pam Wallace, and Karen Schaffer did a wonderful job.

Louis E. Boone
David L. Kurtz

About the Authors

Gene Boone was born about the time World War II began and had a relatively quiet childhood until 1956 when he received a 45 rpm RCA Victor recording of *Heartbreak Hotel* by Elvis Presley. Within a year, he had discovered Buddy Holly, Little Richard, and Chuck Berry—and he wanted more. So he decided to combine high school with a two-year gig as a part-time DJ at a local radio station. Talk about soft jobs—play music you want to hear and get paid for it! Play lists didn't exist in those days, and as long as irate listeners didn't call in and demand that the station manager fire you, you could play anything you liked. A diverse group of fellow DJs introduced him to artists who were quickly added to his growing list of favorites: blues greats John Lee Hooker and B.B. King; the haunting, poetry-like songs of Simon & Garfunkel; the unique vocal blending of the Everly Brothers, whose work impacted the groups who led the British Invasion of the 1960s; and the riveting, soulful music by the son of an Arkansas cotton farmer—a man named Johnny Cash.

But few people make a lifelong career out of spinning tunes at a small-time radio station, so following graduation, he started looking for something fun that paid a bit more. College professor sounded like a cool occupation that would keep him indoors and, perhaps, help him meet women (assuming they considered tweed jackets attractive). Nobody told him until it was too late that it was going to take another eight years in college to achieve his ambition—eight more years!—but he struggled through it. He's happy he did, because he was able to affect (at least a little) the lives of thousands of his young, middle age, and older students in a half-dozen universities throughout the United States, as well as in Australia, England, and Greece. These gigs proved to be almost as much fun as the first.

But his love of music, which had never died, was rekindled during an evening section of a business class several decades ago at the University of Southern Mississippi in which one of his students—sitting on the back row—would soon make music that linked him forever to tequila-flavored drinks and talking tropical birds. Short in stature and soft-spoken, Jimmy Buffett hardly looked the part of a pop music star, but over the decades, he consistently demonstrated just how much he had learned about business and marketing in that fall semester course.

xxii *About the Author*

During his high school days, no one in Salisbury, Maryland, would have mistaken **Dave Kurtz** for a scholar. In fact, he was a mediocre student, so bad that his father steered him toward higher education by finding him a succession of back-breaking summer jobs. Thankfully, most of them have been erased from his memory, but a few linger, including picking peaches, loading watermelons on trucks headed for market, and working as a pipe fitter's helper. Unfortunately, these jobs had zero impact on his academic standing. Worse yet for Dave's ego, he was no better than average as a high-school athlete in football and track.

But four years at Davis E. Elkins College in Elkins, West Virginia, turned him around. Excellent teachers helped get Dave on sound academic footing. His grade point average soared—enough to get him accepted by the graduate business school at the University of Arkansas, where he met Gene Boone. After graduate school, the two became career co-authors, with over 50 books between them. Gene and Dave also got involved in several entrepreneurial ventures.

Today, Dave Kurtz is back teaching at the University of Arkansas after duty tours in Ypsilanti, Michigan, Seattle, and Melbourne, Australia. He is the proud grandfather of five "perfect" grandkids and a sportsman with a golfing handicap too high to mention. Dave, his wife Diane, two demanding Yorkies, and a neurotic schnauzer live in Rogers, Arkansas, where he teaches at the Sam M. Walton College of Business in nearby Fayetteville.

Brief Contents

Contents

Chapter 6

Starting Your Own Business: The Entrepreneurship Alternative   194

Opening Vignette
Fanning the Entrepreneurial Flames at Apple with the iPod   195

Business Tool Kit
The Pros and Cons of Owning Your Own Business   207

Business Tool Kit
Creativity and the Creative Process   210

Solving an Ethical Controversy
Entrepreneurs Behaving Badly: What Can Be Done? What Should Be Done?   214

Hits & Misses
Segway: Has a "Sure Thing" Failed?   217

Best Business Practices
Entrepreneur Creates Three Companies That Make the *Fortune* 1000   219

Chapter 7

Electronic Commerce: The Internet and Online Business   228

Opening Vignette
Online Grocers Are Ready to Deliver   229

Business Tool Kit
Conducting Online Research   235

Part 3

Management: Empowering People to Achieve Business Objectives 263

Chapter 8

Management, Leadership, and the Internal Organization 264

Chapter 9

Human Resource Management, Motivation, and Labor–Management Relations   294

Part 4   Marketing Management   381

Part 5

Managing Technology and Information 487

Chapter 15

Using Technology to Manage Information 488

Part 6   Managing Financial Resources   543

Prologue

Launching Your Business Career

After a rocky start in the first few years of the 21st century, the U.S. economy is back on solid footing again. And the U.S job market, while still less than ideal, seems to be picking up as well. Unemployment rates have dropped to 5.4 percent, and mass layoffs of earlier years are down. Where once recent college graduates faced a long, grim job search, they are now seeing brighter prospects. A recent job outlook survey by the National Association of Colleges and Employers (NACE) found that employers expect to hire 13 percent more college graduates compared with the previous year. And starting salaries are expected to rise slightly also. The average starting annual salary for new business graduates is trending upward, with nearly 3 percent growth over the previous year, to $38,188. The largest jump in starting salaries occurred in the information systems field, with an uptick of 8.2 percent, to $43,053.[1]

With the U.S. economy growing steadily at a pace around 3 or 4 percent and consumer spending up, the prospects for businesses overall are improving. Only the threat of rising oil costs casts a cloud over the economic picture.[2] The U.S. worker productivity rate—how much an employee produces for every hour of work—dropped from a recent high of 3.9 percent to 1.9 percent annually, according to the U.S. Department of Labor. The drop in productivity suggests that for employers to keep pace with the economic growth, they will have to hire more workers—good news for college graduates.[3] Hiring in the U.S. is expected to be strongest in the Midwest (up more than 26 percent), followed by the Northeast and West (up 15 percent each). The South should see the smallest gain at nearly 6 percent.[4] Milwaukee-based Web site CollegeGrad.com's surveys of the job market for entry-level employees reveal that the strongest job prospects are in government agencies, professional services such as accounting and insurance, and technology companies. Figure 1 shows the top 10 entry-level employers.[5]

Companies are planning their hiring strategies carefully to get and keep the most productive, creative employees and avoid the cost of rehiring. So soon-to-be college graduates still need to be on their toes. But creativity has never been in short supply among college business students, and by the time you finish this class—and college—you will be well equipped to take on the challenge. You'll be able to think of your hunt for employment as a course itself, at the end of which you will have a job. And you will be on your way toward a rewarding career.

During the next few weeks, you will be introduced to all the functional areas of business. You will learn how firms are organized and operated. You'll find out who does what in a company. Gradually, you will identify areas of employment that you may wish to pursue. And you'll learn about many individual companies—large and small: who founded them, what products they offer, how they serve their customers, and what types of decisions they make.

Employer and Projected 2004 Entry-Level Hires

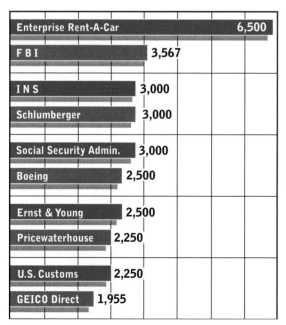

Employer	Hires
Enterprise Rent-A-Car	6,500
FBI	3,567
INS	3,000
Schlumberger	3,000
Social Security Admin.	3,000
Boeing	2,500
Ernst & Young	2,500
Pricewaterhouse	2,250
U.S. Customs	2,250
GEICO Direct	1,955

FIGURE 1

Major U.S. Employers of Entry-Level Job Seekers

Source: Data from "Top Entry-Level Employers," CollegeGrad.com, Milwaukee, http://www.collegegrad.com, accessed January 5, 2005.

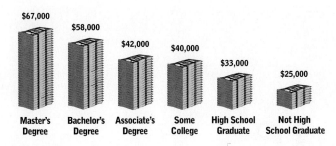

FIGURE 2

Average Annual Earnings Compared with Education

Source: Data from U.S. Census Bureau, as cited in Dan Seligman, "The Story They All Got Wrong," *Forbes*, November 25, 2002, p. 126.

Selecting a career is an important life decision. It sets you on a path that will influence where you live, how much money you earn, and what you do every day. And whether your goal is to operate a farm or to rise high in the ranks of a major corporation, you'll need to understand the principles of business. That's why *Contemporary Business* begins by discussing the best way to approach career decisions and how to prepare for an *entry-level job*—your first permanent employment after leaving school. We then look at a range of business careers and discuss employment opportunities in a variety of fields.

Education will improve your prospects of finding and keeping the right job. In addition, with more education, you are likely to earn more and meet the requirements needed for advancement to more responsible and higher paying positions. Education comes in many forms. In addition to taking classes, try to gain related experience, either through a job or participation in campus organizations. Cooperative education programs, internships, or work-study programs can also give you hands-on experience while you pursue your education. These work experiences will often set you apart from other job seekers in the eyes of recruiters—people who hire employees.

Most likely, every one of you will be responsible for making a living once you leave school. Education will influence that as well. As the U.S. Census Bureau data shown in Figure 2 reveal, the average annual earnings for a full-time worker with a degree is at least 68 percent higher than the average for someone without a high school diploma. On average, the holder of a bachelor's degree earns $58,000 annually, and a person with an associate's degree earns $42,000. The high school dropout may beat the odds with skill and luck but, on average, commands a salary of $25,000. But don't mistake these average earnings for starting salaries. Like all other summary figures, these numbers reflect the average annual compensation for all people with a certain educational level. In addition to earnings for entry-level employees, they also reflect the higher compensation levels typically received by senior personnel with decades of experience. But while a degree may help you get in the door for job interviews from employers who refuse to consider applicants with less academic credentials, it does not guarantee success; you have to achieve that yourself.

They Said It

You can get all A's and flunk life.

—*Walker Percy (1916–1990)*
American author

Internships: A Great Way to Acquire Business Experience

Many business students complete one or more internships prior to finishing their academic careers. Many arrange internships during the summer when they are less likely to enroll in additional courses, but others may complete them by taking a semester off from college. These opportunities give you hands-on experience in a business environment, whether it's banking or manufacturing. Not only does an internship teach you how a business runs, but it can also show you whether you want to pursue a career in a particular industry. You might spend a summer interning in an investment firm and graduate from college with your job search focused on investment banking. Or you might decide that financial services is not the industry for you.

Although internships generally pay little or nothing, they have been described as a critical link in bridging the theory–practice educational gap. They help to carry students between their academic present and their professional future, so it is important to make the most of your internship. Since so many companies make permanent job offers to impressive interns, career counselors advise that it is just as important to excel at your internship as it is in your coursework or future job. Here are some tips to a successful internship experience:

- *Be professional.* Dress for your future career and be punctual.
- *Stand out.* Work hard and show initiative so that you make a good impression.
- *Get evaluated.* Ask your employer how you are doing to learn about your strengths and weaknesses.
- *Have an open mind.* Show that you are willing to learn.

- *Be social.* Talk with and socialize with your boss and other staff members.
- *Build your résumé.* In addition to your internship, gather work and life experience through volunteer work, extracurricular activities, and summer study programs.
- *Keep in touch.* After you leave your internship, update people on what you are currently doing so that you stay in the mind of prospective employers.[6]

In addition, internships can serve as critical networking and job-hunting tools. In some instances, they lead to future employment opportunities, allowing students to demonstrate technical proficiency while providing cost-effective employee training for the company. An excellent source of information about the nation's outstanding internships can be found at your local bookstore—*America's Top 100 Internships* by Oldman and Hamadeh. New editions are published annually by Villard Books.

Courtesy of Principal Financial Service, Inc.

Find a job—or an industry— you love.

Self-Assessment for Career Development

You are going to spend a lot of time during your life working, so why not find a job—or at least, an industry—that interests you? To choose the line of work that suits you best, you must first understand yourself. Self-assessment can be a painful experience, since it involves answering some tough questions. It means looking in the mirror and viewing your strengths and weaknesses clearly. Remember, however, it does pay off by helping you find a career that will be enjoyable, meaningful, and rewarding. You may decide that a high salary is important—say, if you plan to support a large family, pursue an expensive lifestyle, or want to set aside a hefty sum for retirement. You may decide that helping others is your most important goal. Or you may discover that having a job involving a lot of travel suits you best. Self-assessment will help you determine all of these things and more.

The number of resources offering help in choosing your career is staggering. They include school libraries, career guidance and placement offices, counseling centers, and online job search services. You may also wish to talk with recent graduates who are working in fields that interest you. Don't be afraid to contact friends or neighbors of your parents, either. Many adult professionals will be happy to talk with you about their jobs.

As another option, you might arrange an informational interview, a session with a company representative designed to gather more information about a firm or an occupation, rather than to apply for a job. If you are interested in a particular firm, for example, perhaps you could arrange an interview with someone who works there to find out what it is really like. If you are curious about working in a certain field but are not completely sure it is for you, make an appointment with someone who does that job to find out what it really involves. Colleges often have databases of graduates who are working in various fields and willing to talk with students on an informational basis, so be sure to start your search right at your own school.

The Self-Assessment Process

Let's look at what's involved in a basic self-assessment process. The steps in this career inventory are as follows:

1. *Outline your career goals.* What kind of job would you like to have, and where do you see yourself in five years? Ten years? What kind of preparation is needed to reach your goals? Write your goals down so you can refer to them later.
2. *Consider your career interests.* What do you want from your work? John Holland of the University of Missouri has developed a game that matches individual interests and skills with similar careers. You can learn more about Professor Holland's game by visiting the following Web site: `http://www.career.missouri.edu/holland`.
3. *List your skills and specific talents.* It is important to determine your aptitude for specific careers. Your school's career development office has information on various tests that can help determine your aptitude for specific careers. Most placement centers can often administer career and personality inventories or will make other arrangements for you to take them.
4. *Briefly sketch out your educational background.* List the schools, colleges, and special training programs you have attended and any studies you plan to complete before starting full-time employment. Make a candid assessment of how your background matches up with the current job market.
5. *List the jobs you have held, both paying and volunteer, and the responsibilities of each position.* Analyze what you liked and disliked about each.
6. *Consider your hobbies and personal interests.* Many people have turned hobbies and personal pursuits into rewarding careers.[7] Jake Burton earned a bachelor's degree in economics, but decided to pursue an entrepreneurial career. He had grown up skiing and had watched snowboarding soar in popularity among winter sports enthusiasts. So he moved to Burlington, Vermont, and started Burton Snowboards, his own snowboard manufacturing company. His business has flourished, and Jake is known for his successful efforts to advance the sport.[8]

> ## They Said It
>
> The best career advice given to the young is, "Find out what you like doing best and get someone to pay you for doing it."
>
> —*Katharine Whitehorne (b. 1928)*
> *British columnist*

Job Search Guidelines

Once you have narrowed your choice of career possibilities to two or three that seem right for you, get your job search under way. Since the characteristics that made these career choices attractive to you are also likely to catch the attention of other job seekers, you must expect competition. Locate available positions that interest you; then be resourceful! Your success depends on gathering as much information as possible. Register at your school's career center. Establish an applicant file, including letters of recommendation and supporting personal information. Most placement offices send out periodic lists of new job vacancies, so be sure to get your name and address on the mailing list—and include your e-mail address. Become familiar with the process by which your career planning office allocates limited interview slots with attractive employers.

Preparing Your Job Credentials

Most placement or credential files include the following information:

1. Letters of reference from people who know you well—instructors and employers
2. Transcripts of coursework to date
3. A personal data form to report factual information
4. A statement of career goals

Career center personnel will provide special forms to help you develop your file. Often, these forms can be completed online. Prepare the forms carefully, since employers are always interested in your written communication skills. Keep a copy of the final file for later use in preparing similar information for other employment sources. Check back with the career center to make sure your file is in order, and update it whenever necessary to reflect additional academic accomplishments and added work experiences.

Letters of reference are very important. Before you contact each person, think carefully about the way in which the person knows you and how that knowledge could contribute to a job application. For instance, could a swimming coach or music instructor vouch for your hard work and determination? Could a former employer describe how punctual you are and how well you get along with people? Try to include someone from your school's business faculty on your list of references or at least one of your current instructors. Always ask people personally for letters of reference. Be prepared to give them brief outlines of your academic preparation, along with information concerning your job preferences and career objectives. This information will help them prepare their letters quickly and efficiently. It also shows that you are serious about the task and respect their time. Remember, however, that these people are very busy. Allow them at least a couple of weeks to prepare their reference letters; then follow up politely on missing ones.

Finding Employment through the Internet

The Internet now plays an important role for both employers and job seekers. Companies of all sizes are posting their job opportunities on the Web, both on their own sites and on specialized job sites, such as Monster.com and HotJobs.com. Both of these sites offer job postings, résumé hints, a place to post résumés, and career management advice. You'll also find salary comparisons and tips on successful interviewing.[9] If this sounds easy, keep in mind that these sites may receive hundreds of thousands of hits each day from job hunters, which means you have plenty of competition. This doesn't mean you shouldn't use one of these sites as part of your job search; just don't make it your sole source. Savvy job seekers often find that their time is better spent zeroing in on niche boards offering more focused listings. Information systems applicants can check out Dice.com, while sales applicants can look to Salesgiant.com.

In addition, an increasing number of companies now post job openings right on their own Web sites. Some offer virtual tours of what it is like to work for the firm. For example, the Enterprise Rent-a-Car Web site features profiles of young assistant managers.

Newspapers, the source for traditional classified want ads, also post their ads on the Web. Job seekers can even visit sites that merge ads from many different newspapers into one searchable database, such as CareerPath (http://www.careerbuilder.com). Some sites go a step further and create separate sections for each career area. For example, entire sections may be devoted to accounting, marketing, and other business professions. Searches can then be narrowed according to geographical location, entry level, company name, job title, job description, and other categories.

Job seekers can also connect with employers by posting their résumés on job sites. As an added service, many sites offer guidance in the preparation of a résumé. Employers search the résumé database for prospects with the right qualifications. One commonly used approach is for an employer to list one or more *keywords* to select candidates for personal interviews—for example, "field sales experience," "network architecture," or "auditing"—and then browse the résumés that contain all the required keywords. Employers also

Courtesy of Southern Company

Energy firm Southern Company advertises for skilled workers in print but includes its Web address so that candidates can go there to learn more about available careers at the various subsidiaries of this southeastern U.S. energy supplier.

scan résumés into their human resource database, and then when a manager requests, say, 10 candidates, the database is searched by keywords that have been specified as part of the request. Job seekers are responding to this computer screening of applicants by making sure that relevant keywords appear on their résumés.

Perhaps surprisingly, many job seekers still bypass the Web during their search, despite the growing number of companies choosing to advertise jobs on the Internet. According to one survey, more than three of five people looking for a job during the past five years found one through networking, 16 percent through a newspaper ad, and only 7 percent found a job on the Internet.[10] However, this is likely to change as job seekers and companies learn how to communicate more efficiently via the Internet.

The *Contemporary Business* Web site hosts a comprehensive job and career assistance section. The site is updated frequently to include the best job and career sites for identifying and landing the career you want, as well as current strategies for getting the best results from your Web-based career search activities.

Finding Employment through Other Sources

We've already mentioned the importance of registering at your college's career planning or placement office. If you have completed formal academic coursework at more than one institution, you may be able to set up a placement file at each. In addition, you may want to contact private and public employment services available in your location or in the area where you would like to live.

Private Employment Agencies   These firms often specialize in certain types of jobs—such as marketing, finance, sales, or engineering—offering services for both employers and job candidates that are not available elsewhere. Many private agencies interview, test, and screen job applicants so potential employers do not have to do so. Job candidates benefit from the service by being accepted by the agency and because the agency makes the first contact with the potential employer.

A private employment agency usually charges the prospective employer a fee for finding a suitable employee. Other firms charge job seekers a fee for helping find them a job. Be sure that you understand the terms of any agreement you sign with a private employment agency.

State Employment Offices   Don't forget to check the employment office of your state government. Remember that in many states, these public agencies process unemployment compensation applications along with other related work. Because of the mix of duties, some people view state employment agencies as providing services for semiskilled or unskilled workers. However, these agencies do list jobs in many professional categories and are often intimately involved with identifying job finalists for major new facilities moving to your state. In addition, many of the jobs listed at state employment offices may be with the state or federal government itself. These jobs can pay well. An economist with the National Marine Fisheries may earn up to $73,000 a year, and a financial manager with the Department of the Army may earn up to $104,000.[11]

Other Sources   A variety of additional sources can help you to identify job openings. Newspaper employment advertisements, especially Sunday editions of metropolitan newspapers, often prove to be rich sources of job leads. As noted earlier, newspapers may also post their classifieds on the Internet. Trade journals or magazines may list job openings, both in print and on the Web. College instructors and administrators, community organizations, family members, neighbors, and friends may also provide job leads. Talking with these individuals, even informally, may lead you to someone who is looking to hire a new employee. Don't be afraid to let people know you are searching.

Learning More about Job Opportunities

Carefully study the various employment opportunities you have identified. Obviously, you will like some more than others, but you can examine a variety of factors when assessing each job possibility:

1. Actual job responsibilities
2. Industry characteristics
3. Nature of the company

4. Geographical location
5. Salary and opportunities for advancement
6. Contribution of the job to your long-range career objectives

Too many job applicants consider only the most striking features of a job, perhaps its location or the salary offer. However, a comprehensive review of job openings should provide a balanced perspective of the overall employment opportunity, including both long-run and short-run factors.

Building a Résumé

Regardless of how you locate job openings, you must learn how to prepare and submit a *résumé,* a written summary of your personal, educational, and professional achievements. The résumé is a personal document covering your educational background, work experience, career preferences and goals, and major interests that may be relevant. It also includes such basic information as your home and e-mail addresses, as well as your telephone number. It should not include information on your age, marital status, race, or ethnic background.

Your résumé is usually your formal introduction to an employer, so it should present you in the best light, accenting your strengths and potential to contribute to a firm as an employee. However, it should never contain embellishments or inaccuracies. You don't want to begin your career with unethical behavior, and an employer is bound to discover any discrepancies in fact—either immediately or during the months following your employment. Either event typically results in short-circuiting your career path.

> *They Said It*
>
> A résumé is a balance sheet without any liabilities.
>
> —*Robert Half (1918–2001)*
> *American personnel-agency executive*

Organizing Your Résumé

The primary purpose of the résumé is to highlight your qualifications for a job, usually on a single page. An attractive layout facilitates the employer's review of your qualifications. You can prepare your résumé in several ways. You may use narrative sentences to explain job duties and career goals, or you may present information in outline form. A résumé included as part of your credentials file at the career center on campus should be quite short. Remember, too, to design it around your specific career objectives.

Figures 3, 4, and 5 illustrate different ways to organize your résumé—by *reverse chronology,* or time; by *function*; and by *results.* Regardless of which format you select, you will want to include the following: a clearly stated objective, work or professional experience, education, personal interests, and volunteer work. While all three formats are acceptable, one study showed that 78 percent of employers preferred the reverse chronological format—with the most recent experience listed first—because it was easiest to follow.[12]

Tips for Creating a Strong Résumé

Your résumé should help you stand out from the crowd, just as your college application did. A company may receive hundreds or even thousands of résumés, and you want yours to be on the top of the stack. So here are some do's and don'ts from the pros:

Do

- State your objective clearly. If you are applying for a specific job, say so. State why you want the job and why you want to work at a particular company.
- Use terms related to your field so that an electronic scanner—or busy human resource manager—can locate them quickly.
- Provide facts about previous jobs, internships, or volunteer work, including results or specific achievements. Include any projects or tasks you undertook through your own initiative.
- Highlight your strengths and skills.
- Write clearly, concisely, and to the point. Keep your résumé to a single page.
- Proofread your résumé carefully.

FELICIA SMITH-WHITEHEAD
4265 Poplar Lane
Cleveland, Ohio 44120
216-555-3296
FeliciaSW@aol.com

OBJECTIVE

Challenging office management position in a results-oriented company where my organizational and people skills can be applied; leading to an operations management position.

WORK EXPERIENCE

ADM Distribution Enterprises, Cleveland, Ohio   2004–Present
Office Manager of leading regional soft-drink bottler. Coordinating all bookkeeping, correspondence, scheduling of 12-truck fleet to serve 300 customers, promotional mailings, and personnel records, including payroll. Installing computerized systems.

Merriweather, Hicks & Bradshaw Attorneys, Columbus, Ohio   2002–2004
Office Supervisor and Executive Secretary for Douglas H. Bradshaw, Managing Partner. Supervising four clerical workers and two paraprofessionals, automating legal research and correspondence functions, and assisting in coordinating outside services and relations with other firms and agencies. Promoted from Administrative Assistant to Office Supervisor.

Conner & Sons Custom Coverings, Cleveland, Ohio   1997–2002
Secretary in father's upholstery and awning company. Performing all office functions over the years, running the office when the owner was on vacation.

EDUCATION
Telecom Systems, Word Processing Seminar Series, Certificate   2004
McBundy Community College, Office Management,   2003
    Automated Office Systems, Associate's Degree
Mill Valley High School, Honors, Certificate   2001

COMPUTER SKILLS

Familiar with Microsoft Office and Adobe Acrobat

LANGUAGE SKILLS

Fluent in Spanish (speaking and writing)
Adequate speaking and writing skills in Portuguese

PERSONAL

Member of various community associations; avid reader; enjoy sports such as camping and cycling; enjoy volunteering in community projects.

FIGURE 3
Chronological Résumé

Don't

- Offer any misleading or inaccurate information.
- Make vague statements, such as "I work well with others" or "I want a position in business."
- Include a salary request.
- Make unreasonable demands, such as a private office or company car.
- Highlight your weaknesses.
- Submit a résumé with typos or grammatical errors.
- Include pictures or graphics or use fancy type fonts.[13]

Take your time with your résumé; it is perhaps the most important document you'll create about yourself during your career. If you need help, go to your school's career center. If you are dealing with an employment agency, a counselor there should be able to help as well.

Keep in mind that you will probably have to modify your résumé at times to tailor it to a particular company or job. Again, take the time to do this; it may mean the difference between standing out and being lost in a sea of other applicants.

Your Cover Letter

In most cases, you won't just send a résumé to a firm without an accompanying letter. A *cover letter* should introduce you, explain why you are submitting a résumé (cite the specific job opening if possible), and let the recipient know where you can be reached for an interview. Your letter should also thank the recipient for his or her time and consideration. A cover letter should be presented in traditional business format. Of course, be sure to proofread your letter before sending it.

Submitting through Automated Systems

Most large organizations have moved to automated (paperless) résumé processing and applicant-tracking systems. As a result, if you write and design a technology-compatible résumé and cover letter, you'll enjoy an edge over an applicant whose résumé and cover letter can't be added to a database. Also, remember that résumés are often transmitted electronically and then placed in a company database with an automated applicant-tracking system. In fact, a recent survey of employers revealed that almost half preferred to receive résumés via e-mail. Five years earlier, that number was only 4 percent.[14] Figure 6 lists tips for creating a good electronic résumé.

The Job Interview

Congratulations! You've prepared an effective résumé, and you've been contacted for an interview. An interview is more than a casual conversation. During an interview, at least one company manager will learn about you, and you'll learn more about the company and the job. Although you may feel nervous about the interview, you can control some of its outcome by doing your homework: planning and preparing for this important encounter with your potential employer. If you haven't already done so, research the company to learn everything you can about the firm, its industry, the products it offers, its competitors, and its customers (are they individual consumers, other businesses, or both?). Try to find the answers to the following basic questions:

1. How was the company founded?
2. What is its current position in the industry? What is its financial status?
3. In which markets does it compete? What goods or services does it offer?
4. How is the firm organized?
5. Who are its competitors? Who are its customers?
6. How many people does it employ?
7. Where are its production facilities and offices located?

Enrique Garcia
Five Oceanside Drive, Apt. 6B
Los Angeles, CA 90026
215-555-7092
EGARCIA@hotmail.com

OBJECTIVE
Joining a growth-oriented company that values highly productive employees. Seeking an opportunity that leads to senior merchandising position.

PROFESSIONAL EXPERIENCE

Administration
Management responsibilities in a major retailing buying office, coordinated vendor-relation efforts. Supervised assistant buyers.

Category Management
Experience in buying home improvement, and sport and recreation categories.

Planning
Chaired a team charged with reviewing the company's annual vendor-evaluation program.

Problem Solving
Successfully developed a program to improve margins in the tennis, golf, and fishing categories.

WORK EXPERIENCE

Senior Buyer for Southern California Department Stores	2003–Present
Merchandiser for Pacific Discount Stores, a division of Southern California Department Stores	2001–2003

EDUCATION

Bachelor's Degree California State University—San Bernardino	1999–2001
Associate's Degree Los Angeles City College	1997–1999

FIGURE 4
Functional Résumé

This information is useful in several ways. First, it helps to give you a feeling of confidence during the interview. Second, it can keep you from making an unwise employment decision. Third, it can impress an interviewer, who may be trying to determine your interest level. However, don't try to offer the interviewer advice about how the company should conduct its business unless you are asked.

Where do you find this company information? Your school's career center, the public library in mid-size and large cities, and most employment agencies should have information on prospective employers. Business instructors at your college may also provide tips. Most firms now have their own Web sites that give at least basic information about the company. Finally, you may want to talk off-the-record with someone you know who works for the company. Who knows? That person may later become a valuable reference for you during the application process.

ANTONIO PETTWAY
2527 N.W. 47th Street
St. Louis, MO 63166
314-555-2394
apettway@sbcglobal.net

OBJECTIVE
To apply my expertise as a construction supervisor to a management role in an organization seeking improvements in overall production, long-term employee relationships, and the ability to attract the best talent in the construction field.

PROFESSIONAL EXPERIENCE

DAL Construction Company, St. Louis, Missouri   2003–Present
Established automated, on-site recordkeeping system improving communications and morale between field and office, saving 400 work hours per year, and reducing the number of accounting errors by 20 percent. Developed a crew selected as "first choice crew" by most workers wanting transfers. Completed five housing projects ahead of deadline and under budget.

St. Louis County Housing Authority, St. Louis, Missouri   2001–2003
Created friendly, productive atmosphere among workers enabling first on-time job completion in 4 years and one-half of usual materials waste. Initiated pilot materials delivery program with potential savings of 3.5 percent of yearly maintenance budget.

Jackson County Housing Authority, Kansas City, Missouri   2001
Produced information pamphlets increasing applications for county housing by 22 percent. Introduced labor-management discussion techniques saving jobs and over $21,000 in lost time.

Payton, Durnbell & Associates Architects, Kansas City, Kansas   2000–2001
Developed and monitored productivity improvements saving 60 percent on information transfer costs for firm's 12 largest jobs.

EDUCATION
Central Missouri State University, Business   1998–2000

COMPUTER SKILLS
Adobe Illustrator and AutoCAD

PERSONAL
Highly self-motivated. Willing to relocate. Avid reader and writer.

FIGURE 5
Results-Oriented Résumé

Tips for Successful Interviewing

An interview is your personal introduction to the company. You want to make a good impression, but you also want to find out whether you and the firm make a good fit. Although the interviewer will be asking most of the questions, you will want to ask some as well. People who conduct interviews say that the most important qualities candidates can exhibit are self-confidence, preparedness, and an ability to communicate clearly.

When you are contacted for an interview, find out the name(s) of the person or people who will be interviewing you. It's also appropriate to ask whether the initial interview will be with a human resource manager, with the person to whom you would be reporting on the job, or with both. Many people who conduct initial job interviews work in their firms' human resource divisions. These interviewers can make recommendations to managers and supervisors about which individuals to employ. Managers who head the units in which an applicant will be employed may get involved later in the hiring process. Some hiring decisions come from human resource personnel together with the immediate supervisor of the prospective employee. Often, however, immediate supervisors make the decision alone or in combination with input from senior employees from the department who will be colleagues of the new hire. Although the human resource department rarely has sole hiring authority, it is very important to take this initial interview seriously and present yourself professionally because this person will likely determine whether the interview process goes further.

In a typical format, the interviewer tries to talk as little as possible, giving you a chance to talk about yourself and your goals. You want to present your thoughts clearly and concisely, in an organized fashion, without rambling on to unrelated topics. The interviewer may wait until you are finished or prompt you to talk about certain subjects by asking questions. Be as specific as possible when answering questions. The questions that interviewers ask often include the following:

- "Why do you want this job?"
- "Why do you want to work in this field?"
- "Where do you see yourself five years from now? Ten years?"
- "What are your strengths? What are your weaknesses?"
- "Why should I hire you?"
- "Are you considering other jobs or companies?"[15]

At some point, the interviewer will probably ask whether you have any questions of your own. It's a good idea to come prepared with some questions, but others may arise during the interview. Try to keep your list concise; ask three or four of your most important questions. Here is a sample of appropriate questions for the initial interview:

- "Could you clarify a certain aspect of the job responsibilities for me?"
- "What qualifications are you looking for in a candidate?"
- "Do people who start in entry-level jobs at this company tend to develop their careers here?"
- "In what ways could I perform above and beyond the job requirements?"

The questions you ask reflect just as much about you as the answers you give to the interviewer's questions. "[Interviewers] are listening to the questions the applicant asks as an indicator of how deeply they've thought about our company, our job, and our industry. [Based on these questions], they judge how intuitive applicants are, how creative, and how insightful they are," notes employment expert and author Pierre Mornell.[16]

At some point during your conversation, the interviewer may give you an idea of the salary range for the job. If not, he or she will do so during a subsequent interview. Or you may ask about the range, but do not ask exactly how much you will be paid if you get the job. When you receive this information, keep in mind that typically there may be little or no negotiation of an entry-level salary. Here are a few other questions not to ask: When will I be promoted? How much vacation and sick time do I get? When is my first raise? How much will it be?[17]

A successful first interview will probably lead to an invitation to come back for another interview. Depending on the type of job, you might be asked to take some skills tests. For instance, if you are entering a training program for a financial institution, you might be required to take some math-oriented tests. If you are applying for a job as a sales representative, you may be given a test that assesses your personality traits. In some instances, you might even be allowed to take a test online from your own home.

Employment Decisions

Employers still considering you to be a viable job candidate now know a lot about you. You should also know a lot about the company. The primary purpose of further interviews is to determine whether you can work effectively within the organization.

If you create a positive impression during your second or later interviews, you may be offered a job. If you are offered more than one, congratulations! If you have to make a decision between offers, try to select the one that most closely matches your career objectives, even if the salary is less or the benefits not quite as attractive. The point of an entry-level job is to set you on the path toward your career. If you receive a few rejections, persevere. Each job application and each interview add to your experience, giving you more polish as a job candidate. You will find a job if you keep trying.

1. Use a plain font. Use a standard serif typeface, such as Courier or Times. Simplicity is key.
2. Use 11- to 14-point type sizes.
3. Keep your line length to no more than 65 characters (letters, spaces, and punctuation).
4. Do not use graphics, bullets, lines, bold, italics, underlines, or shading.
5. Use capital letters for your headings.
6. Justify your text to the left.
7. Use vertical and horizontal lines sparingly. Lines may blur your type.
8. Omit parentheses and brackets, even around telephone numbers. These can blur and leave the number unreadable.
9. Use white paper and black type.
10. Use a laser-quality printer.
11. Print on one side of the paper only.
12. Don't compress space between letters. Use a second page rather than pack everything into one page and risk having it scan unclearly.
13. Do not staple pages of a résumé together.
14. Use industry "buzz words." Searches often look for industry jargon.
15. Place your name as the first text on the résumé. Do not put anything else on that line.
16. Fax résumés on the "fine mode" setting. It is much easier to read than the "standard mode" setting.
17. Do not fold your résumé. A crease makes scanning—and retrieving—difficult.
18. If you are sending your résumé in the body of e-mail, do not distinguish between pages, as the full e-mail will download into the database as one sheet.
19. Don't send a résumé as an e-mail attachment unless you are specifically instructed to do so. Many employers discard unsolicited attachments.

Source: Reprinted from Mary Dixon Werdler, "Translate Your Résumé for Electronic Eyes," http://www.jobweb.com, accessed February 1, 2002. Copyright National Association of Colleges and Employers.

FIGURE 6 **Creating an Electronic Résumé**

Nontraditional Students

At one time, colleges and universities served a market made up mostly of 18- to 22-year-olds. This was the primary age group that sought to break into the job market. A quick glance around your class is likely to convince you that this is no longer the case. In fact, you may not fall into this category at all.

More adults are returning to school to complete academic programs, and more workers who already have associate's or bachelor's degrees are returning to college to update or increase their education. These people are often referred to as *nontraditional students*. Although the term covers any student who does not fit into the 18- to 22-year-old age group (the so-called traditional clients of higher education), it is actually inaccurate, since older students have become the norm on many campuses. In any case, nontraditional students usually have two other characteristics: They work, either full time or part time, and college is often only one of their daily responsibilities. They may be married, have children, own homes, and even run their own businesses.

Most nontraditional students come from one of the following groups:

1. *Homemakers.* Full-time homemakers may return to school to refresh or continue an interrupted education, with the goal of entering the workforce as family obligations diminish or for economic reasons.
2. *Veterans.* Another major segment of nontraditional students enters school after discharge from the military.
3. *Displaced workers.* Workers who have lost their jobs because of an economic downturn, a business closing, or a change in technology may return to school for retraining. The difficult economy of recent years produced jobless rates that approached 6.5 percent and sent thousands of laid-off workers back to college to get their degrees.[18]
4. *Older, full-time employees.* These workers may enter school to seek additional education to enhance career prospects or for personal satisfaction.

Challenges Faced by Nontraditional Students

Nontraditional students often face different challenges than do younger students. One is scheduling. Often, older students must juggle the responsibilities of work, school, and family. They may have to study at odd times: during meals, while commuting, or after putting the kids to bed. Nontraditional students may also be trying to change careers, so they must learn skills in a different field.

Nontraditional students also have a very important advantage over traditional college students: experience. Even experience in an unrelated field is a plus. Older students know how businesses operate. Often, they have developed useful skills in human relations, management, budgeting, and communications. Also, through observing other people's mistakes and living through their own, they have often learned what not to do.

Like other students, nontraditional students need to review their accomplishments, skills, likes, and dislikes. The same exercises and resources suggested earlier can help both traditional and older students to assess their strengths and determine their career goals.

Types of Careers

As the business environment changes, so do business sectors and jobs. For instance, entire fields of industry have evolved because of the Internet. Others have diminished or changed dramatically. There's a good chance you'll pursue a career in an industry that didn't even exist when your parents were mapping out their own careers. Anything dealing with e-commerce is one example. This field goes far beyond companies that operate solely on the Internet. "There's a lot more to e-business than dot-coms," notes Claudia Santin, dean of students at the University of Miami's business school. "It's another means of connecting the global marketplace." This means that a whole new generation of recent graduates can help businesses bridge the gap between traditional brick-and-mortar companies and the Internet. "The vast majority of e-business—at least 60 percent—is transformation, taking a brick-and-mortar company and using the power of the Web to do their business more effectively," says

Charles Newman, a professor of business at Florida International University. "Increasing productivity, establishing closer relationships with customers. That's what the buzz is all about."[19] Internet marketing is also on the rise; in fact, it has become a standard topic in many business classrooms. "Students recognize that the Internet is a powerful communications vehicle with the ability to segment and target very specific customer groups," remarks one business student. "To market effectively, all channels of contact with existing and potential customers need to be fully and appropriately utilized."[20] Whether or not you decide to make marketing your career, it makes good business sense to learn all you can about marketing and the Internet.

As technology continues to drive growth and change in many industries, you are likely to find yourself at least considering a technology-related field. You might find yourself working in the biotech industry, which employs more than 100,000 U.S. workers. There are the large pharmaceutical firms like Merck and Pfizer; specialized research-based companies like Amgen and Genentech; and even smaller biotech firms that research diseases and foods, develop new medicines, or manufacture the machines that make these medicines or deliver them into a patient's system. Firms like these need people who understand the principles of business and can communicate effectively with diverse populations that include patients, doctors, researchers, hospital administrators, and other businesspeople.[21] Other fast-growing tech industry jobs include software application and systems engineers and systems administrators.[22]

Maybe you want to enjoy the benefits of working in one of the new technology fields, but you aren't oriented toward science or the way computers run. No problem—business still needs you. You might land a job as a sales representative for any of these companies; you might decide to become a Web writer and editor, providing editorial content for Internet and intranet sites, polishing it for style, consistency, and clarity; or you might enjoy marketing, supporting the business objectives of your company.

Another industry that has experienced dramatic growth and change is that of security—ranging from security guards, to the sales and installation of residential alarm systems, to the development of highly complex computer security programs.[23] In the aftermath of the terrorist attacks of September 11, 2001, and the 2003 war with Iraq, companies that deal with any type of security issues are bound to need employees. You could be one of them.

Several traditional fields are currently enjoying a resurgence of demand. If you're interested in finance but a little leery of the Wall Street roller coaster, consider mortgage banking. Mortgage rates have dipped so low that the demand for new and refinanced mortgages on homes has skyrocketed. "Mortgage banking and anything having to do with residential home construction are still very hot areas of the [job] market," says John Challenger, CEO of Challenger, Gray & Christmas, an employment outplacement firm. Countrywide Financial plans to hire 800 to 1,000 home-loan sales consultants as soon as possible, boosting its current sales force of 2,500. "Frankly, as we fill those positions and continue to make inroads in the purchase market, we'll likely add more," says a company spokesperson.[24]

These examples are a tiny sample of the types of careers available to you. But if you follow the steps for self-assessment listed earlier in this prologue, register with your school's career planning office, talk with graduates and older friends, research industries and companies, read newspapers and business magazines, pay attention to advertisements for different companies and products, and watch the news on television and online, you'll become aware of the many types of careers that people pursue every day.

Salaries

As you gain more information about industries and specific companies where you might want to work, naturally you'll want to know how much you can expect to earn. Your pay will determine your standard of living, the length of time it will take to pay off school loans, and other important factors in your life. If you are paid a *salary,* you will receive a set amount of money each week, every two weeks, or once a month. People usually quote salaries in yearly amounts, such as $25,000 a year or $40,000 a year. If you are paid in *wages,* your pay is usually calculated by the hour, such as $10 per hour. Even if you start on an hourly wage, as you move up in your career you will graduate to being paid on a salary basis. Typically, workers who are employed on an hourly wage are eligible to earn overtime pay, but salaried employees are not. However, salaried employees generally earn more than do hourly employees. If you land a job in sales, you may be paid a *commission,* or percentage of each sale you make. Many salespeople are paid a set *base salary* plus commissions.

Table 1   Typical Compensation for Business-Related Positions

Retail		Finance	
Senior salesperson	$21,900	Assistant cash manager	$51,700
Entry-level assistant sales manager	$39,400	Accountant	$53,700
Intermediate-level account manager	$58,500	Cash manager	$61,000
Manufacturing		**Construction**	
Logistics analyst	$44,300	Urban planner	$54,000
Purchasing manager	$74,300	Construction administrator	$55,000
Plant manager	$97,000	**Sales**	
Hospitality		Entry-level sales rep	$37,700 (base salary)
Executive housekeeper	$30,274		$14,300 (bonuses and commissions)
Catering sales manager	$36,050		$52,000 (total)
Resident manager	$41,200		
Front office manager	$48,000		

Sources: Phillip Longman and Adam Martin, "What Are You Worth?" *Business 2.0,* March 2003, pp. 88–89; Christine Galea, "2002 Salary Survey," *Sales & Marketing Management,* May 2002, p. 34.

They Said It

Money makes the world go 'round.

—*John Kander (b. 1927) and Fred Ebb (b. 1933)*
American songwriters

When a firm contacts you with a job offer, you'll receive information about the amount you will be paid. Salaries vary from industry to industry and from region to region. Table 1 shows a sample of average salaries for a variety of positions in different industries. Some of these are entry-level positions, and others are further up the career ladder. Remember, the offer you receive may be less or more than the salaries listed here depending on the specific job, the industry, the company, and the region in which you live.

A Long-Range View of Your Career

As we said earlier, choosing a career is an important life decision. A career is a professional journey—regardless of whether you want to run an art gallery or a hospital, whether you are fascinated by language or math, whether you prefer to work with animals or people. In the end, you hope to contribute something good to society while enjoying what you do—and make a reasonable living at it.

Throughout your career, it is important to stay flexible and continue learning. Challenging new skills will be required of managers and other businesspeople during these first decades of the 21st century. Remain open to unexpected changes and opportunities that can help you learn and develop new skills. Keep in mind that your first job will not be your last. But tackle that first job with the same enthusiasm you'd have if someone asked you to run the company itself because everything you learn on that job will be valuable at some point during your career.

Finally, if you haven't already started your career search, begin now. Do this by talking with various resources, lining up an internship, looking for a part-time job on or off campus, or volunteering for an organization. Register with the campus career center long before you graduate. Then, when you reach your final semester, you'll be well on your way to beginning the career you want.

We are confident that this textbook will present a panorama of career options for you. Whatever you decide, be sure it is right for you. As the old saying goes, "You pass this way just once." Enjoy the journey!

Additional Information Sources

More Career Information on the *Contemporary Business* Web Site

More career information is available to students using *Contemporary Business* at the following Web site: http://boone.swlearning.com.

The "Management Careers" section on the Web site enables you to learn more about business careers and to locate currently posted job opportunities. The site provides a vast number of career resources such as links to job sites, career guidance sites, and the like. Also, many links include extensive career information and guidance, such as interviewing techniques and tips for résumé writing.

DID YOU KNOW?

1. Of new college grads, 10 percent hold their first job for less than a year, and 25 percent move to another job within five years.
2. On average, men still earn 35 percent more than women for comparable jobs.
3. Railroad brake and switch operators, phone operators, utility meter readers, farmers and ranchers, and insurance processing clerks are among the fastest declining jobs.
4. The metropolitan area encompassing Fayetteville, Springdale, Bentonville, and Rogers, Arkansas, currently has one of the fastest job growth rates in the nation.

Projects and Applications

1. Prepare your own résumé following the procedures outlined earlier in this section. Ask your instructors, friends, and relatives to critique it. Then revise and proofread it.
2. Arrange for an informational interview with someone in your community who is working in a profession that interests you. (Write, call, or e-mail to request an appointment. The interview should take no more than 15 to 20 minutes. Come prepared with questions to ask.) Report to your class about what you learned.
3. Discuss how you would answer each of the questions listed on page xlvi that interviewers most often ask.
4. Select a partner and take turns interviewing each other for a job in front of the class. (Use the interview questions mentioned earlier.) After completing the interviews, ask the class to give you feedback on how you looked and acted during your interview. Would they advise you to do or say anything differently?
5. Pick a Web site dealing with careers. Select an employment field and prepare a report on what you learned from the Web site. What jobs are available? From your perspective, were they in desirable locations? What did these jobs pay? Did the information in the Web site agree or conflict with your initial perceptions of the job?

Part 1
Business in a Global Environment

Chapter 1
Business: 2006 and Beyond

1 Distinguish between business and not-for-profit organizations and identify the factors of production.

2 Describe the private enterprise system and explain how competition and entrepreneurship contribute to the system.

3 Identify the six eras of business and explain how the relationship era influences contemporary business.

4 Describe how technology is changing the way businesses operate and compete.

5 Relate the importance of quality and customer satisfaction to efforts to create value for customers.

6 Explain how productivity affects competitiveness in the global market.

7 Describe the major trends in the workforce that challenge managers' skills for managing and developing human resources.

8 Identify the skills that managers need to lead businesses in the new century.

9 Discuss the importance of good business ethics and social responsibility in business decision making.

Pixar: Creative Use of Resources—and a Profitable Partnership—Produce a Hit

It appeared to be a match made in heaven—a partnership comprised of the Walt Disney Co., an American cultural icon associated with the very beginnings of animated films and Pixar, a start-up organization with a seemingly can't-miss combination of factors of production to die for. Pixar was counting

on Disney's sophisticated distribution network experience and marketing clout to make sure that its films would appear on thousands of movie theater screens. Disney expected Pixar to create at least one or two blockbuster hits. So, a deal was struck: for a 50/50 split of ticket receipts, Disney would handle the distribution of seven Pixar animated films. If everything worked out well, the partners could discuss continuing the arrangement for additional films. If the result of the experiment was a string of flops, everyone could walk away.

But as film after film was released, the word "flop" was never spoken as each new release seemed to exceed the success of its successor. First came *Toy Story*, then *A Bug's Life*. These hits were followed by blockbusters *Toy Story II*, *Monsters, Inc.*, *Finding Nemo*, and *The Incredibles*. The latter film generated almost $71 million at the box office its opening weekend, shattering all previous Disney records, including the previous year's $70.3 million for *Finding Nemo*.

© AFP/Getty Images

Although the original agreement calls for one additional film, Pixar seemed determined to prove that companies "grow up" just like people do and announced that it was leaving Disney to strike out on its own with a new distribution partner. Pixar proved to be a hit by almost every artistic and financial standard. In fact, in its short life it has already become the most successful film studio of all time, with 17 Oscars to its credit, and is widely seen as the wave of the future in animation. How did Pixar capitalize on its strengths to reach the top of the industry in a few short years?

It has employees, it has financial capital, and it has raw materials. In this case, however, the raw materials are not tangible items like steel, cloth, chemicals, or tons of flour and a special "secret" recipe. Pixar's raw materials include the imagination of its carefully nurtured creative staff, with which it fashions its unique screenplays and characters, and the rapidly evolving animation technology that allows it to turn those stories into brilliant cinematic reality.

Although a company as young as Pixar, with so few films released to date, could easily be in a very precarious financial position, the animation high flyer operates with exceptionally high profits, no debt, and a reserve of about $500 million in cash. It handles its financial resources with great skill, earning profits of $125 million last year and growing more stable with every film it has released. It has yet to make a flop. DVDs and movie tie-in items like toys and books are a rich source of supplemental revenue for the firm. In fact, DVD sales of existing films like *Toy Story* and *Monsters, Inc.* already bring in about 20 percent of the firm's revenues, a figure that's expected to rise to almost 70 percent in a few years as new generations of families discover these now-classic films. The video of *Finding Nemo*, for example, has already sold well over 40 million copies.

Pixar has its eye on costs, too. The major reason for its break with Disney was its desire to work out a more favorable distribution deal with a new partner that will be satisfied with less than the 50 percent of box office that Disney earned from

Pixar's first seven films. But until it makes the break with Disney, Pixar will continue to benefit from the larger company's expertise in distribution and the invaluable cachet of using the Disney name when marketing its films.

Even its animation expertise is derived in part from parent Disney. Many of Pixar's most gifted animators were trained in the Disney studios and brought the company's legendary story development process and technical innovation with them. Also among its employees are the same computer scientists who worked out the technological principles behind computer-generated animation, known as CG.

With the kind of entrepreneurial and can-do spirit that Pixar has, it has established itself as *the* brand name in animation, an industry where for generations the concepts of branding began and ended with the Disney name. Says one industry analyst of Pixar, "This is all they do, and they do it well." In fact, Pixar has plans for expanding its young brand. It has already inked a deal with THQ, the videogame maker, to make videogames based on some of its existing films, and it has granted exclusive rights to THQ for games based on four more films to be released beginning in 2006.[1]

Chapter Overview

The early years of the 21st century have seen both tragedy and triumph. The combination of terrorism, recession, and war, along with a growing U.S. budget deficit that replaced the recent surplus, has shaken consumer confidence. Americans who had been riding high on a decade-long wave of prosperity are suddenly closing their wallets, both to retailers and the stock market. Changes that occurred during this period include:

- Unemployment, which had been at its lowest level in over a quarter century, rose sharply, reaching 6 percent in 2003. Workers in the airline and tourism industries were laid off in response to the 9/11 terrorist attacks, the war with Iraq, and rising gas prices, but the hardest-hit businesses were the airline and telecom industries.
- Gasoline prices soared above $2 a gallon as a combination of events—domestic production slowdowns resulting from powerful hurricanes in the Gulf of Mexico, labor unrest in Nigeria, attacks on Iraqi pipelines by terrorist insurgents, and growing demands for additional oil imports by China and Japan—pushed oil prices temporarily to a recent $55 per gallon.
- Rates for home mortgages dropped below 6 percent, while interest earned on savings accounts hovered around 1 percent.

Business growth opens doors of opportunity for those who are prepared to put ideas into action. John C. Diebel's idea was to put modern computing power into telescopes for amateur astronomers. He started his own company, Meade Instruments, to build and sell telescopes, adapting features of expensive telescopes to more affordable models. Before long, Meade's new telescope had captured more than half the market for telescopes sold to hobbyists.[2] Meade, which was once a fledgling new company, has now become a strong competitor in its field. Not only do new companies put ideas into action, but well-known and trusted names do so as well. Bruce Roth, vice president of chemistry at pharmaceutical giant Pfizer, invented the chemical compound that is more widely known under its trade name—Lipitor. Lipitor, which lowers cholesterol, has become the best-selling prescription drug in history. Within a few years, it could top $10 billion a year in sales.[3]

In the new century, everyone faces new challenges posed by the technological revolution, which is changing the rules of business. The combined power of telecommunications and computer technology is creating inexpensive, global networks that transfer voice messages, text, graphics, and data within seconds. These sophisticated technologies create new products, and they demand new approaches to marketing existing products. Technology is also speeding the rate of change in the business world, where new discoveries rapidly outdate inventions created just months before. Even promotional messages can illustrate the impact of technology.

Innovative technologies are also globalizing today's business world. Businesses can now easily manufacture, buy, and sell across national borders. You can order a Big Mac in Boston or Bulgaria, and Japanese and Korean companies manufacture most of the consumer electronics products sold in the U.S. This rapidly changing business landscape compels businesspeople to react quickly to shifts in consumer tastes and other market dynamics. Success requires creativity, split-second decision making, and innovative vision. Whether you decide to start your own business, as John Diebel did, work for a small family-run business, or sign on with a large international corporation, your achievements will depend on your ability to keep pace with the constant changes in today's world. These changes include a new focus on business ethics, in the wake of the collapse of such giants as Enron, Arthur Andersen, HealthSouth, and WorldCom, and the problems at cable television giant Adelphia Communications, drug company ImClone Systems, and diversified manufacturer Tyco International.

Contemporary Business explores the strategies that allow companies to compete in today's interactive marketplace and the skills that you will need to turn ideas into action for your own career success. This chapter sets the stage for the entire text by defining business and revealing its role in society. The chapter's discussion illustrates how the private enterprise system encourages competition and innovation while preserving business ethics.

What Is Business?

What image comes to your mind when you hear the word *business?* Some people think of their jobs, others think of the merchants they patronize as consumers, and still others think of the millions of firms that make up the world's economy. This broad, all-inclusive term can be applied to many kinds of enterprises. Businesses provide the bulk of employment opportunities as well as the products that people enjoy.

Business consists of all profit-seeking activities and enterprises that provide goods and services necessary to an economic system. Some businesses produce tangible goods, such as automobiles, breakfast cereals, and computer chips; others provide services such as insurance, dental care, auto rentals, and entertainment ranging from Six Flags theme parks and Broadway plays to music concerts.

Business drives the economic pulse of a nation. It provides the means through which standards of living improve. At the heart of every business endeavor is an exchange between a buyer and

To achieve their growth objectives, both large and small companies need to put ideas into action. A major business of management consulting and technology services company, Accenture, focuses on helping other companies "turn innovation into results."

business all profit-seeking activities and enterprises that provide goods and services necessary to an economic system.

profits rewards for
businesspeople who take the
risks involved to offer goods
and services to customers.

seller. A buyer recognizes a need for a good or service and trades money with a seller to obtain that product. The seller participates in the process in hopes of gaining profits—a critical ingredient in accomplishing the goals necessary to maintain constant improvement in standards of living.

Profits represent rewards for businesspeople who take the risks involved in blending people, technology, and information to create and market want-satisfying goods and services. In contrast, accountants think of profits as the difference between a firm's revenues and the expenses it incurs in generating these revenues. More generally, however, profits serve as incentives for people to start companies, expand them, and provide consistently high-quality competitive goods and services.

Consider, for example, the role of profits among companies offering goods and services on the Internet. Few large firms saw the Internet as a business opportunity in its early years, but as customers began getting comfortable with the experience, online profitability began to look like a real possibility. Thousands of Internet companies—dot-coms—appeared virtually overnight, only to disappear just as quickly due to lack of planning, mismanagement, too-rapid growth, and zero profits. Today, a few original Internet survivors such as eBay, along with newer Internet companies such as hotels.com, are continuing to post profits.[4]

Although the quest for profits is a central focus of business, businesspeople also recognize their social and ethical responsibilities. To succeed in the long run, companies must deal responsibly with employees, customers, suppliers, competitors, government, and the general public.

Not-for-Profit Organizations

What do the Smithsonian Institute, the U.S. Postal Service, the American Heart Association, and C-SPAN have in common? They are all classified as **not-for-profit organizations,** businesslike establishments that have primary objectives other than returning profits to their owners. These organizations play important roles in society by placing public service above profits. Not-for-profit organizations operate in both the private and public sectors. Private-sector not-for-profits include museums, libraries, trade associations, charitable and religious organizations, and most colleges and universities. In addition, government agencies, political parties, and labor unions are classified as not-for-profit organizations.

A good example of a not-for-profit organization is New York's Metropolitan Museum of Art. Like profit-seeking businesses, the Met must generate funds to cover its operating costs. Revenues come from a number of sources, including individual donations, memberships, government grants, gift-shop sales, and special fund-raising drives. Such events provide added value to museum members and attract thousands of occasional and first-time visitors, who may

FIGURE 1.1

The Nature Conservancy: Not-for-Profit Organization Fighting to Save 200 of the World's Last Great Places

To a visitor, it's a barren desert.
To our supporters, it's bustling with life.

If you know the land like we do, you'll know that even the most arid landscapes are full of life. That's why The Nature Conservancy works with people like you to preserve special places close to your heart and home. Help us save the Last Great Places around the world. Visit nature.org or call 1-888-2 JOIN TNC.

The Nature Conservancy®
Saving the Last Great Places

nature.org

Courtesy of the Nature Conservancy

become members. Not-for-profit organizations use business concepts and functions ranging from human resource management to advertising, as illustrated by the promotional message for the Nature Conservancy's Last Great Places campaign to save high-priority wilderness sites, shown in Figure 1.1.

Not-for-profit organizations are a substantial part of the U.S. economy. More than 1.5 million non-government not-for-profits currently operate in the U.S. They control more than $1 trillion in assets and employ more people than the entire federal government and all 50 state governments combined. In addition, millions of volunteers work for them in unpaid positions. Not-for-profits secure funding from both private sources, including donations, and government sources. They are commonly exempt from federal, state, and local taxes.

Although they focus on goals other than generating profits, managers of not-for-profit organizations face many of the same challenges dealt with by executives who head profit-seeking businesses. A major challenge is obtaining the funding they need to provide their services. Public television and radio stations, for instance, have become more creative in soliciting donations. In addition to the old standby of pledge drives urging viewers or listeners to send in $100 and receive a tote bag, DVD, or videocassette, public broadcasters focus on building longer-term relationships with their members. In Boston, about 6 percent of the people who contribute to WGBH send in at least $300 a year. Of course, all of these big donors were once first-time members. The relationship-building process begins with a thank-you note for the donation and a subscription to the station's monthly viewing guide. Midlevel and large contributors get special attention from the station. These donors are invited to seminars, luncheons, program premieres, and other opportunities for face-to-face contact with the station's staff.

These events are designed to obtain feedback and cement member loyalty to the station. WGBH even applies research techniques, gathering data about viewers. Invitations are targeted according to each group's likely interests. The success of events is evaluated in terms of participants' subsequent donations and other indicators of their involvement with the station.[5]

As in the world of profit-seeking businesses, the new century is bringing changes to the not-for-profit sector. An aging and increasingly diverse population may require not-for-profits to find new ways of delivering services. Government funding is also declining, a trend that is forcing not-for-profit executives to develop new cost-cutting methods. Faced with increased competition for limited funding, not-for-profits also have to boost their effectiveness at marketing and fund-raising, a lesson that public broadcasting has already been applying. Some not-for-profits sell merchandise or have even set up profit-generating arms to provide goods and services that people are willing and able to pay for. College bookstores sell everything from sweatshirts to coffee mugs with school logos imprinted on them, while the Sierra Club and the Appalachian Mountain Club both have full-fledged publishing programs. These changes and others require leaders with strong business skills and experience. Consequently, many of the concepts discussed in this book apply to not-for-profit organizations as much as to profit-oriented firms.

Factors of Production

Capitalism, like other economic systems, requires certain inputs for effective operation. Economists use the term **factors of production** to refer to the four basic inputs: natural resources, capital, human resources, and entrepreneurship. Table 1.1 identifies each of these inputs and the type of payment received by firms and individuals who supply them.

Natural resources include all productive inputs that are useful in their natural states, including agricultural land, building sites, forests, and mineral deposits. For example, the sawmill operated by Willamette Industries in the little town of Dallas, Oregon, takes 2,500-pound second-growth logs from Oregon's hillsides and cuts them into boards. Other companies use natural resources after they have been processed by companies like Willamette. Natural resources are the basic inputs required in any economic system.

Capital, another key resource, includes technology, tools, information, and physical facilities. *Technology* is a

factors of production
four basic inputs for effective operation: natural resources, capital, human resources, and entrepreneurship.

Table 1.1	Factors of Production and Their Factor Payments	
Factor of Production	**Corresponding Factor Payment**
Natural resources	Rent
Capital	Interest
Human resources	Wages
Entrepreneurship	Profit

broad term that refers to such machinery and equipment as production lines, telecommunications, and basic inventions. Information, frequently improved by technological innovations, is another critical success factor because both managers and operating employees require accurate, timely information for effective performance of their assigned tasks. Technology plays an important role in the success of many businesses. Sometimes technology results in a new product, such as the device introduced by OmniSonics that uses sound waves rather than drugs or tools to clear blocked arteries in heart patients. The new method is not only effective, but it also results in no damage to artery walls.[6]

Sometimes technology helps a company improve a product, such as the global positioning satellite systems (GPS) found in some automobiles and a key component in the recent war with Iraq. Precise data from the 27 orbiting satellites made possible the precise targeting of cruise missiles and smart bombs and made GPS—along with the Internet—two of the U.S. Department of Defense's greatest dual-use technology successes.[7]

And sometimes technology helps a company operate more smoothly by tracking deliveries, providing more efficient communication with suppliers, analyzing sales figures, compiling marketing data, and training employees. Convergy's 100 sales reps participate in online training sessions two or three times a week (depending on their needs), using a system that combines online presentations with a conference call. The customer service and electronic communications billing company posted sales far above many of its competitors during the recent recession, a feat that top managers attribute partly to the efficient training program. "What it's enabled us to do is keep our sales force educated all year long about what the latest product features and benefits are," says Mary Kay Nedrich, director of sales training and development.[8]

Technology is an important component of a company's capital.

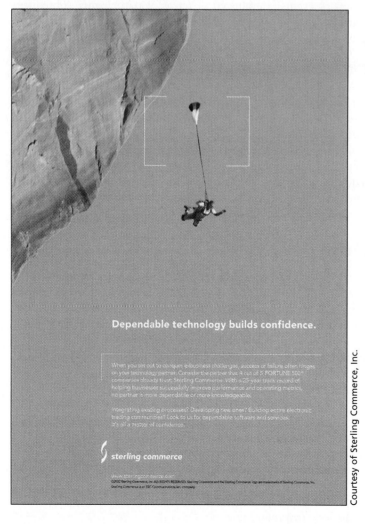

Dependable technology builds confidence.

sterling commerce

Money is necessary to acquire, maintain, and upgrade a firm's capital. A company's funds may come from investments by its owners, profits plowed back into the business, or loans extended by others. Money then goes to work building factories; purchasing raw materials and component parts; and hiring, training, and compensating workers. People and firms that supply capital receive factor payments in the form of interest.

Human resources represent another critical input in every economic system. Human resources include anyone who works, from the chief executive officer (CEO) of a huge corporation to a self-employed auto mechanic. This category encompasses both the physical labor and the intellectual inputs contributed by workers. With the widespread use of computer technology, most companies now rely on their employees as a source of ideas and knowledge as well as physical effort. Some companies may solicit employee ideas through an online "suggestion box" or in staff meetings, while others, such as Electronic Arts, which develops video games, use unconventional methods to tap their employees' creativity. Workers are encouraged to wander through an 81-foot-wide outdoor maze to get their mental juices flowing; if that doesn't do the trick, they can grab an espresso or play volleyball.[9] The competitive edge gained through effective, well-trained human resources is significant because competitors cannot easily match another company's talented, motivated employees in the way it can buy the same computer system or purchase the same grade of natural resources.

Figure 1.2 emphasizes the importance of human resources to organizational goals and the need for employees to maintain and update their skills. Pfizer, the pharmaceutical giant behind such blockbuster drugs as Lipitor, Viagra, and Zoloft, relies on the skills, knowledge, creativity, and passion of its employees to achieve success. "At Pfizer, the people we're proud to call colleagues are some truly exceptional individuals dedicated to helping people live longer, healthier, and happier lives," says the ad.

FIGURE 1.2
Importance of Human Resources

Entrepreneurship is the willingness to take risks to create and operate a business. An entrepreneur is someone who sees a potentially profitable opportunity and then devises a plan to achieve success in the marketplace and earn those profits. Consider Gene Cage's business, Papa Geno's Herb Farm, located in rural Roca, Nebraska. Its fragrant natural resources are not hard to identify: the soil and seedlings for dill, basil, lavender, and dozens of other herbs that Geno's sells to customers through its Web site and those of other online retailers who specialize in the worldwide sale of herbs. Some of these online merchants have also become sources of funds and technological capital; one recently invested $1 million in Papa Geno's. It also assisted the herb grower by providing access to its information system and helped Papa Geno's in developing sales forecasts. That way, it would be able to count on Papa Geno's as a reliable supplier. Herb entrepreneur Cage has embraced Internet technology and his alliances with online merchants because of their ability to bring him customers from around the globe and to fill orders at a lower cost than through traditional channels like catalogs. Cooks and gardeners who visit Papa Geno's Web site find special offers such as free recipes, newsletters, and even free plants. However, combining an old-fashioned business like raising herbs with modern technology presents a problem in the area of human resources. It is not easy to find people with expertise in both horticulture and the Internet and then convince them to move to a rural area like Roca. So Cage offers generous benefits and acts as a mentor to his 17 full-time employees. They are helping Cage grow his company faster than any herb.[10] The next section looks at how the factors of production are allocated and used within the private enterprise system, the economic system in which U.S. businesses currently operate.

Concept Check

1. Distinguish between a profit-oriented business and a not-for-profit organization.
2. Identify four types of capital.

BUSINESS TOOL KIT

Choosing the Right Career

Choosing the right career can be challenging for college students. Some may already know what they want to be when they grow up; others don't have a clue. It really helps to do some research and map out your career goals and aspirations so that you know what to work toward in your search for the right career field. The following is a list of tips on how to narrow down your potential career options and select the right career.

1. Evaluate your personal interests, values, personality, and lifestyle. Are you a people person, or do you prefer solitary work? Do you prefer living in a city, a suburb, or the country? What are your hobbies? Believe it or not, your local library or bookstore has career guides for every type of person, with titles ranging from *Outdoor Careers* and *Careers for Nonconformists* to *Careers for Bookworms and Other Literary Types.*

2. Utilize the resources around you. Every school has a career counselor or advisor office as well as a career center that can help you narrow down your interests and even assist you in finding your first job. These departments also offer many aptitude tests and resources to help you locate the perfect career.

3. Use the current *Occupational Outlook Handbook* or take a look at the Web site of the U.S. Department of Labor's

Bureau of Labor Statistics (http://www.bls.gov) for job information and career outlooks. These government sources give you specific information about different career fields: the skills, training, and experience you will need to enter the field; wages, work hours, and benefits; supply and demand; size; projected growth; and many more facts.

4. Take the time to talk to everyone around you about their careers, especially professionals already working in fields that pique your interest, professors who teach related courses, the students themselves—even friends and family who might have interesting careers. Get their feedback on what *they* see you doing; sometimes those around you have a better perspective on these issues than you do.

5. Brainstorm and write down all of your abilities, skills, talents, and interests. This includes volunteer work you've done, community projects, church involvement, extracurricular activities, and the like. Most of all, remember to follow your passion! Whatever you are passionate about, you will enjoy doing it for many years to come.

Sources: "Choosing the Right Career," Employment Resources for Humboldt County Web site located at http://www.thejobmarket.org/jobseekers/choose_index.phtml; Cassandra Hayes, "Choosing the Right Path," *Black Enterprise Magazine,* April 2001, p. 42.

The Private Enterprise System

private enterprise system economic system that rewards businesses for their ability to identify and serve the needs and demands of customers.

competition battle among businesses for consumer acceptance.

No business operates in a vacuum. All operate within a larger economic system that determines how goods and services are produced, distributed, and consumed in a society. The type of economic system employed in a society also determines patterns of resource use. Some economic systems, such as communism, feature strict controls on business ownership, profits, and resources to accomplish government goals.

In the U.S., businesses function within the **private enterprise system,** an economic system that rewards businesses for their ability to perceive and serve the needs and demands of consumers. A private enterprise system minimizes government interference in economic activity. Businesses that are adept at satisfying customers gain access to necessary factors of production and earn profits.

Another name for the private enterprise system is **capitalism.** Adam Smith, often identified as the father of capitalism, first described the concept in his book *The Wealth of Nations,* published in 1776. Smith believed that an economy is best regulated by the invisible hand of **competition,** the battle among businesses for consumer acceptance. Smith thought that competition among firms would lead to consumers receiving the best possible products and prices because less efficient producers would gradually be driven from the marketplace.

They Said It

People compete until their last breath.

—*Michael Eisner (b. 1942)*
Former Chairman and CEO, Walt Disney Co.

This invisible hand concept is a basic premise of the private enterprise system. In the U.S., competition regulates much of economic life. To compete successfully, each firm must find a basis for **competitive differentiation,** the unique combination of organizational abilities and approaches that sets a company apart from competitors in the minds of consumers. New Jersey-based Commerce Bancorp, whose branches serve customers in Delaware, New Jersey, New York, and Pennsylvania, has differentiated itself from its competitors by doing away with so-called bankers' hours and bulletproof tellers' windows. The firm encourages its employees to think of themselves as retailers who are there to serve customers. "It's all about the customer," says Commerce branch manager Regina McGee. "If you don't have customers, you don't have a job."[11]

Businesses operating in a private enterprise system face a critical task of keeping up with changing marketplace conditions. Firms that fail to adjust to shifts in consumer preferences or ignore the actions of competitors leave themselves open to failure. For a success story, consider SCP Pool Corp., the world's largest swimming pool supply company. In just 25 years, it grew from a single location in suburban New Orleans to 200 service centers throughout North America and Europe staffed by 2,400 SCP employees. When the economy slowed during the early years of this century, many consumers cut back on spending, particularly on items that were perceived to be luxuries, like built-in swimming pools, turning instead to less costly forms of entertainment. But CEO Manuel Perez de la Mesa was undaunted by this change in preference. "This is a middle-class product," he explains. "People didn't realize that 76 percent of pool owners actually earn less than $75,000 a year." So SCP launched an awareness campaign—called Backyard Escape—about the benefits of backyard pools, including marketing kits for pool contractors, a Web site, an online brochure, and a contractor directory. SCP marketers say that the campaign has actually helped the company expand its market.[12]

Throughout this book, our discussion focuses on the tools and methods that 21st-century businesses apply to compete and differentiate their goods and services. We also discuss many of the ways in which market changes will affect business and the private enterprise system in the years ahead.

Basic Rights in the Private Enterprise System

Certain rights critical to the operation of capitalism are available to citizens living in a private enterprise economy. As shown in Figure 1.3, these include the rights to private property and profits, freedom of choice, and competition.

The right to **private property** is the most basic freedom under the private enterprise system. Every participant enjoys the right to own, use, buy, sell, and bequeath most forms of property, including land, buildings, machinery, equipment, patents on inventions, and various intangible properties.

The private enterprise system also guarantees business owners the right to all profits—after taxes—they earn through their activities. Although a business is not assured of earning a profit, its owner is legally and ethically entitled to any income it generates in excess of costs.

Freedom of choice means that a private enterprise system relies on the potential for citizens to choose their own employment, purchases, and investments. They can change jobs, negotiate wages, join labor unions, and choose among many different brands of goods and services. People living in the capitalist nations of North America, Europe, and other parts of the world are so accustomed to this freedom of choice that they sometimes forget its importance. A private enterprise economy maximizes individual human welfare and happiness by providing alternatives. Other economic systems sometimes limit freedom of choice to accomplish government goals, such as increasing industrial production.

The private enterprise system also permits fair competition by allowing the public to set rules for competitive activity. For this reason, the U.S. government has passed laws to prohibit "cutthroat"

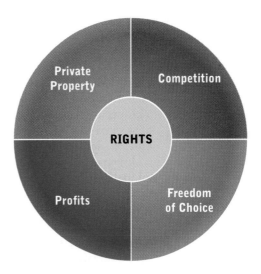

FIGURE 1.3
Basic Rights within a Private Enterprise System

competition—excessively aggressive competitive practices designed to eliminate competition. It also has established ground rules that outlaw price discrimination, fraud in financial markets, and deceptive advertising and packaging.

The Entrepreneurship Alternative

entrepreneur risk taker in the private enterprise system.

One of the exciting career options offered by capitalism is entrepreneurship. In fact, the entrepreneurial spirit beats at the heart of private enterprise. An **entrepreneur** is a risk taker in the private enterprise system. Individuals who recognize marketplace opportunities are free to use their capital, time, and talents to pursue those opportunities for profit. The willingness of individuals to start new ventures drives economic growth and keeps pressure on existing companies to continue to satisfy customers. If no one were willing to take economic risks, the private enterprise system wouldn't exist.

By almost any measure, entrepreneurial spirit fuels growth in the U.S. economy. Of the businesses operating in the U.S. economy during the course of a year, about one in seven first started operating during the past 12-month period. These newly formed businesses are also the source of many of the nation's new jobs each year. Every year, they create more than one of every five new jobs in the economy. Most measures of entrepreneurship look at the smallest or youngest businesses on the assumption that they are the enterprises in which entrepreneurship is most significant. These companies are a significant source of employment or self-employment. Of the 20 million U.S. businesses currently in operation, 15 million are self-employed people without any employees. Nearly 12 million U.S. employees currently work for a business with fewer than 10 employees.[13] Besides creating jobs and selling products, entrepreneurship provides the benefits of innovation. In contrast to more established firms, start-up companies tend to innovate most in fields of technology that are new and uncrowded with competitors, thereby making new products available to businesses and consumers.

Entrepreneurs often find novel ways to use natural resources, technology, and other factors of production. Nathaniel Weiss found a creative application for technology: a package of hardware and software that translates music played on a guitar into sheet music. His product, called G-vox, became a hit among guitarists because it saved them the long process of transcribing the solos and songs they wrote. With publicity in guitar magazines, Weiss was able to sell G-vox in small music stores and through mail order. He then expanded on this success by developing G-vox products that work with other instruments and that not only transcribe music but also play the sounds of other instruments, so musicians can hear how they sound together with other instruments being played. These products are particularly useful for teaching. Weiss succeeded because he not only had good product ideas but also worked with others to make his ideas a success. He negotiated a deal with Fender and then teamed up with publisher McGraw-Hill to develop more products for the educational market. Thanks to Weiss's creativity and his ability to collaborate with others, G-vox Interactive Music has grown to 50 employees, and its size has been doubling every year. G-vox constantly updates its products, and consumers can currently order new versions of its Encore, Music Time Deluxe, and Master Tracks Pro products online at the company Web site.[14]

Entrepreneurship is also important to existing companies in a private enterprise system. Large firms often encourage entrepreneurial thinking, hoping to benefit from enhanced flexibility, improved innovation, and new market opportunities. Jim Throneburg runs his family's North Carolina sock manufacturing firm, Thorlo. The company has been around for a long time, and Throneburg makes certain it continually innovates and changes. A few decades ago, he noticed that American consumers had begun buying different athletic shoes for different sports. "If the shoe changed for function, I figured I needed to design a sock that complemented the shoe," he recalls. His figuring resulted in a thick-soled hiking sock and later a padded sock for the military. Since then, Thorlo has created more than 25 varieties of sport socks. Throneburg invests heavily in research—in search of new markets and new technologies. Thorlo has spent millions on developing new yarns and designs, and the firm responds to requests from its customers for new products. "Everything that's not labor and material is R&D [research and development] as far as I'm concerned," notes Throneburg.[15]

They Said It

A dream doesn't become reality through magic; it takes sweat, determination, and hard work.

—Gen. Colin Powell (b. 1937)
U.S. Secretary of State

As the next section explains, entrepreneurs have played a vital role in the history of American business. They have helped to create new industries, developed successful new business methods, and improved U.S. standing in global competition.

Concept Check

1. What is an alternative term for private enterprise system?
2. What is the most basic freedom under the private enterprise system?
3. What is an entrepreneur?

Six Eras in the History of Business

In the roughly four centuries since the first European settlements appeared on the North American continent, amazing changes have occurred in the size, focus, goals, and use of technology of U.S. businesses. As Table 1.2 indicates, U.S. business history is divided into six distinct time periods: (1) the Colonial period, (2) the Industrial Revolution, (3) the age of industrial entrepreneurs, (4) the production era, (5) the marketing era, and (6) today's relationship era. The next sections describe how events in each of these time periods have influenced U.S. business practices.

The Colonial Period

Before the U.S. Declaration of Independence from Great Britain in 1776, Colonial society emphasized rural and agricultural production. Colonial towns were small compared with European cities, and they functioned as marketplaces for farmers, craftspeople, bankers, and lawyers. The economic focus of the nation centered on rural areas, since prosperity depended on the output of farms and plantations. The success or failure of crops influenced every aspect of the economy.

Colonists depended on England for manufactured items as well as financial backing for their infant industries. Even after the Revolutionary War (1776–1783), the U.S. maintained close economic ties with England. British investors continued to provide much of the financing for developing the U.S. business system, and this financial influence continued well into the 19th century.

The Industrial Revolution

The Industrial Revolution began in England around 1750, moving business operations from an emphasis on independent, skilled workers who specialized in building products one by one to a factory

Table 1.2   Six Eras in Business History

Era	Main Characteristics	Time Period
Colonial	Primarily agricultural	Prior to 1776
Industrial Revolution	Mass production by semiskilled workers, aided by machines	1760–1850
Industrial entrepreneurs	Advances in technology and increased demand for manufactured goods, leading to enormous entrepreneurial opportunities	Late 1800s
Production	Emphasis on producing more goods faster, leading to production innovations like assembly lines	Prior to 1920s
Marketing	Consumer orientation, seeking to understand and satisfy needs and preferences of customer groups	Since 1950s
Relationship	Benefits derived from deep, ongoing links with individual customers, employees, suppliers, and other businesses	Began in 1990s

system that mass-produced items by bringing together large numbers of semiskilled workers. The factories profited from the savings created by large-scale production, bolstered by increasing support from machines over time. As businesses grew, they could often purchase raw materials more cheaply in larger lots than before. Specialization of labor, limiting each worker to a few specific tasks in the production process, also improved production efficiency.

Influenced by these events in England, business in the U.S. began a time of rapid industrialization. Agriculture became mechanized, and factories sprang up in cities. During the mid-1800s, the pace of the revolution was increased as newly built railroad systems provided fast, economical transportation. In California, for example, the combination of railroad building and the gold rush fueled a tremendous demand for construction.

The Age of the Industrial Entrepreneur

Building on the opportunities created by the Industrial Revolution, entrepreneurship increased in the U.S. during the late 19th century. In 1900, Arthur R. Wilson and several partners paid $10,000 in gold coins for a 27-acre parcel of granite-rich land in California. This natural resource was the basis for Granite Rock Co., which provided the material for roads and buildings in California's booming economy. The company, now called Graniterock, evolved in response to technological, competitive, and marketplace demands and continues to survive in the 21st century.

Inventors created a virtually endless array of commercially useful products and new production methods. Many of them are famous today:

- Eli Whitney introduced the concept of interchangeable parts, an idea that would later facilitate mass production on a previously impossible scale.
- Robert McCormick designed a horse-drawn reaper that reduced the labor involved in harvesting wheat. His son, Cyrus McCormick, saw the commercial potential of the reaper and launched a business to build and sell the machine. By 1902, the company was producing 35 percent of the nation's farm machinery.
- Cornelius Vanderbilt (railroads), J. P. Morgan (banking), and Andrew Carnegie (steel), among others, took advantage of the enormous opportunities waiting for anyone willing to take the risk of starting a new business.
- Cleveland bookkeeper John D. Rockefeller saved and borrowed to finance his own dry goods trading business. The business thrived, and Rockefeller decided to go into oil refining. By age 31, he was well on his way to becoming one of the richest men in the world. The company he founded in 1868, the Standard Oil Co., was declared a monopoly by the U.S. government in 1911 and ordered to be broken up into more than 30 small units. Today, its descendants continue as multibillion-dollar global businesses and are key components of such multinational oil giants as ExxonMobil, BP, ChevronTexaco, and ConocoPhillips.[16]

The entrepreneurial spirit of this golden age in business did much to advance the U.S. business system and raise the overall standard of living of its citizens. That market transformation, in turn, created new demand for manufactured goods.

The Production Era

As demand for manufactured goods continued to increase during the early years of the 20th century, businesses focused even greater attention on the activities involved in producing those goods. Work became increasingly specialized, and huge, labor-intensive factories dominated U.S. business. Assembly lines, introduced by Henry Ford, became commonplace in major industries. Business owners turned over their responsibilities to a new class of managers trained in operating established companies. Their activities emphasized efforts to produce even more goods in quicker processes.

During the production era, business focused attention on internal processes rather than external influences. Marketing was almost an afterthought, designed solely to distribute items generated by production activities. Little attention was paid to consumer wants or needs. Instead, businesses tended to make decisions about what the market would get. If you wanted to buy a Ford Model T automobile, your color choice was black—for decades the only color produced by the factory.

The Marketing Era

The Great Depression of the early 1930s changed the shape of U.S. business yet again. As incomes nose-dived, businesses could no longer automatically count on selling everything they produced. Managers began to pay more attention to the markets for their goods and services, and sales and advertising took on new importance. During this period, *selling* was often synonymous with *marketing*.

Demand for all kinds of consumer goods exploded after World War II. After nearly five years of doing without new automobiles, appliances, and other items to contribute to the war effort, consumers were buying again. At the same time, however, competition also heated up. Soon businesses began to think of marketing as more than just selling; they envisioned a process of determining what consumers wanted and needed and then designing products to satisfy those needs. In short, they developed a **consumer orientation.**

Businesses began to analyze consumer desires before beginning actual production. Consumer choice skyrocketed. Today's automobiles no longer come just in black; instead, car buyers can choose from a wide range of colors and accessories.

Businesses also discovered the need to distinguish their goods and services from those of competitors. **Branding,** the process of creating an identity in consumers' minds for a good, service, or company, is an important tool used by marketing-oriented companies. A **brand** can be a name, term, sign, symbol, design, or some combination that identifies the products of one firm and differentiates them from competitors' offerings.

One of the early masters of branding was Ray Kroc, who bought a small restaurant and built it into the famous McDonald's restaurant chain. Kroc insisted that every one of his restaurants follow the same operating procedures and offer similar menu items, reinforcing the nationwide image of the growing restaurant franchise in consumer minds across the country. Today, the golden arches are among the best-known company symbols in the world.

The marketing era has had a tremendous effect on the way business is conducted today. Even the smallest business owners recognize the importance of understanding what customers want and the reasons they buy.

brand name, term, sign, symbol, design, or some combination that identifies the products of one firm and differentiates them from competitors' offerings.

The Relationship Era

Contemporary business has entered a new age, driven by advances in information technology. Powerful computers, online connections, and other technologies are helping businesses to form deep, direct links with their customers, employees, and suppliers. During this new era, the *relationship era,* business has begun to focus on developing and leveraging relationships for mutually beneficial returns. Graniterock—introduced in the section on the industrial entrepreneur—invites customers to visit its Web site, not just to order products, but to calculate materials requirements, subscribe to its quarterly newsletter, and learn about its commitment to quality. By interacting with Graniterock on its Web site, customers forge stronger ties than they would by simply viewing the occasional advertisement and calling to place orders for granite or ready-mix concrete.[17]

Businesses gain several advantages by developing ongoing connections with customers. Since it is much less expensive to serve existing customers than to find new ones, businesses that develop long-term customer relationships can reduce their overall costs. Long-term relationships with customers enable businesses to improve their understanding of what customers want and prefer from the company. As a result, businesses enhance their chances of sustaining real advantages through competitive differentiation.

Relationships have helped Dell, Inc. maintain a competitive edge as personal computers become less of an innovation and more of a commodity. The company developed its reputation for excellence by offering customized personal computers (PCs), sold over the telephone and delivered within days. Consumers and businesspeople alike can call Dell, specify the size of hard drive, modem speed, monitor dimensions, and other features, and the company builds the computer to order. Today, customers can also place customized orders by clicking on options at the company's Web site. Dell further cements that relationship by including on-site service as part of the computer purchase.

For large and small business customers, Dell takes the relationship building further. When customers buy more than $50,000 worth of products from Dell each year, the company assigns a manager to service the account, assisting the buyer in placing orders and solving any problems that might arise. The account managers get to know their customers and phone them with information about products that can help them improve their results. Dell uses high-tech as well as high-touch to stay close to its customers. Through its Web site, the company offers a service called Premier Page. Companies that set up a Premier Page can not only place orders there but can also track order status and details of past purchases and arrange to have Dell install software on their computers, even their own customized programs. Customers can use their Premier Page to connect to technical support instantly.[18]

Dell is just one of the thousands of both small and large businesses to discover that the relationship era is an age of connections. Connections—between businesses and customers, employers and employees, technology and manufacturing, and even separate companies—are fueling economic growth. The world economy is increasingly interconnected, as businesses expand beyond their national boundaries. In this new global economy, techniques for managing networks of people, businesses, information, and technology are of paramount importance to business success.

Each new era in U.S. business history has forced managers to reexamine the tools and techniques they formerly used to compete. Tomorrow's managers will need creativity and vision to stay on top of rapidly changing technology and to manage complex relationships in the global business world of the fast-paced 21st century.

Concept Check

1. During which era could customers buy only black Model Ts?
2. During which era was the idea of branding developed?

Managing the Technology Revolution

The relationship era is driven by new technologies that are changing nearly every aspect of people's lives. To succeed in the 21st century, business leaders must understand how technology is changing the shape of not just business, but the world as a whole.

This insight can begin with a definition of **technology** as a business application of knowledge based on scientific discoveries, inventions, and innovations. In business, technology can streamline production, creating new opportunities for organizational efficiency. Technological innovation has played a part throughout business history. During the Colonial era, scientific discoveries about agriculture increased farm production. During the Industrial Revolution, factories allowed mass production of goods. During the production era, assembly lines streamlined manufacturing. Today, a factory may rely on automated machinery to produce finished products. In an office, computers may simplify the process of managing the information involved in running a business.

Technological breakthroughs such as supercomputers, laser surgery, and cars powered by electricity and natural gas result in new goods and services for consumers, improved customer service, reduced prices, and more comfortable working conditions. Technology can make products obsolete, just as contact lenses and laser surgery reduced the eyeglass market, and DVDs are rapidly replacing videocassettes. Technology also opens up new business opportunities. First there was the creation of DVDs; now there is the creation of self-destructing DVDs. Companies like Flexplay and SpectraDisc have developed versions of "disposable" DVDs, in which a time-release chemical eventually renders the discs unusable. Both companies believe that their technology of nonreturnable, limited-life discs will solve the problem of late fees and stock disappearing from the shelves of rental stores.[19]

Changes in technology can also create whole new industries and new ways of doing business. Perhaps the most significant of these changes is the Internet.

The Internet

Internet worldwide network of interconnected computers that, within limits, lets anyone with a PC or other computing device send and receive images and data anywhere.

The **Internet** is a worldwide network of interconnected computers that, within limits, lets anyone with access to a PC or other computing device send and receive images and data anywhere. The roots of the Internet began when the U.S. Department of Defense created a secure military communications system in 1969. Over time, other government and business computer networks were also created and interlinked. In 1986, the National Science Foundation facilitated comprehensive connections among many of these computer networks by dedicating five supercomputers that allowed all of the various networks to communicate with each other.

In 1993, Internet usage began to spread to individual users with the development of the **World Wide Web** (or **Web**), an interlinked collection of graphically rich information sources within the larger Internet. The Web has opened new opportunities for organizations and individuals to communicate their messages to the world on Web sites. More than half of all U.S. households have at least one computer, most of which are connected to the Internet. In addition, many people access the Internet through Web-enabled phones and other handheld devices. Businesses and individuals communicate over the Internet via *e-mail,* instantly sending messages, documents, and pictures around the globe. E-mail is the most widely used Internet application.

What does the Internet mean to business? First, it represents a huge community of prospective customers. Hundreds of millions of people use the Internet. Although the U.S. still has the largest concentration of users, China, the United Kingdom, and Germany are close behind. Women make up about 45 percent of users worldwide, and the fastest-growing age group on the Internet is seniors.[20] Many of those people currently connected to the Internet are spending money online. Retail sales online reached $72 billion during one recent year, representing a 41 percent increase; in contrast, traditional retail sales rose to $2.25 trillion, representing a 4.2 percent increase.[21] The Internet is also a major source of jobs. A recent study found that the number of Internet-related jobs had reached the 2.5 million mark and continues to grow.

The opportunities brought by the Internet are particularly significant for low-income developing nations. Even in countries where phone lines and computers are rare, people are accessing the Internet with cellphones and at Internet cafes and public access centers sponsored by government and charitable organizations. At the I-Cafe in remote Ulan Bator, Mongolia, a newspaper reporter recently found students looking for scholarships to U.S. universities and a trader corresponding via e-mail with a partner in Russia. The trader, Tamir Hyadborjigin, uses the Internet to find and communicate with trading partners, including the Russian company, which supplies leather-processing equipment, and a California company from which he plans to import vitamins to sell in Mongolia. Besides negotiating purchases over the Web, Hyadborjigin plans to set up a Web site to sell leather products in other countries.[22]

The Internet facilitates direct, interactive relationships between businesses and their customers. Instead of relying on intermediaries such as retailers, agents, and brokers to reach customers, businesses can now connect directly with the people who buy and use their products. People now book over $5 billion in airline tickets at self-service Web sites like Travelocity and Expedia. Travel agents must now find ways to use the Internet to better serve their customers. Vacationers who are interested in a repeat trip to Disney World can register at Waltdisneyworld.com, type in the date of their last visit to the park—along with other information such as birthdays and children's ages—and receive a personalized account of what has changed at the park since their last visit.[23]

The Internet's interactive capability also allows businesses to customize their products and communications for individual customers around the world. Catalog marketer Lands' End was the first business to use its Web site to let shoppers specify their physical characteristics that are then used to design three-dimensional models of themselves. They can try clothes from the Web site on the model and rotate the model 360 degrees to show how the clothes look on a person with those dimensions.[24] Chapter 7 describes in greater detail how the Internet works and how companies are applying Internet technology to forge relationships with customers.

Concept Check

1. Describe three ways in which business benefits from technology.
2. What is the most widely used Internet application?

From Transaction Management to Relationship Management

As business enters the 21st century, a significant change is taking place in the ways companies interact with customers. Since the Industrial Revolution, most businesses have concentrated on building and promoting products and then hoping that enough customers would buy them to cover costs and earn acceptable profits, an approach called **transaction management.**

In contrast, in the relationship era, businesses are taking a different, longer-term approach to their interactions with customers. Firms now seek ways to actively nurture customer loyalty by carefully managing every interaction. They earn enormous paybacks for their efforts. A company that retains customers over the long haul reduces its advertising, sales, and account initiation costs. Since customer spending tends to accelerate over time, revenues also grow. Companies with long-term customers often can avoid the costly reliance on price discounts to attract new business, and they find that many new customers come from loyal customer referrals.

relationship management collection of activities that build and maintain ongoing, mutually beneficial ties between a business and its customers and other parties.

Increasingly, business focuses on **relationship management,** the collection of activities that build and maintain ongoing, mutually beneficial ties with customers and other parties. At its core, relationship management involves gathering knowledge of customer needs and preferences and applying that understanding to get as close to the customer as possible. American Skiing Co. (ASC) has suffered through a few snowless winters—and some missed opportunities. Now, the company is launching a massive effort to get in touch with current skiers as well as people who might become skiers. ASC owns seven resorts across the country, from Sunday River in Maine to Steamboat in Colorado to the Canyons in Utah. Each resort has its own identity and loyal following. ASC is determined to enhance those identities, secure a loyal following, and develop new customers. "We have the best snow, the best service, the best lifts, and the best programs," claims John Urdi, vice president of sales and marketing for ASC's Attitash Bear Peak in New Hampshire. "We just have to reiterate that and reintroduce it to the skiing public." Under its new plan, ASC will make greater investments in database technology and collect and use gathered information to learn more about customers, conduct consumer research, and develop more programs to attract families and children. Each of these initiatives is designed to build relationships with skiers—and potential skiers—of all ages.[25]

Because so many companies have begun to rely on different types of technology during the past decade, customers often feel left out in the cold—phones are answered by computers and business processes are automated. Sometimes it's impossible to reach a human being to ask a question or make a complaint. Some smart companies are now turning the trend around, moving back toward human interaction and gaining a competitive edge by doing so. Paul Estenson, CEO of E Group, a marketing services company based in Minneapolis, believes in developing real relationships with his customers. At his company, every call is answered by an employee and addressed immediately. "We're in a last-minute, we-want-it-yesterday industry, where our customers have specific needs to be addressed immediately," he explains. "If we miss a call or procrastinate on a voice message, our customers call our competition—we can't afford that. We answer every call and service the customer right then and there." A recent survey showed that 90 percent of E Group's customers were pleased with the personal attention they received.[26]

EGroup develops relationships with consumers by promising to deliver personalized Web searches.

Courtesy of EGroup, Inc.

Strategic Alliances and Partnerships

Businesses are also finding that they must form partnerships with other organizations to take full advantage of available opportunities. A **partnership** is an affiliation of two or more companies with the shared goal of assisting each other in the achievement of common goals. One such form of partnership between organizations is a **strategic alliance,** a partnership formed to create a competitive advantage for the businesses involved.

Some of the most widely reported strategic alliances today involve partnerships between dot-com businesses—those formed to sell goods and services on the Internet—and traditional retailers that have experience selling to consumers through stores or catalogs. The traditional retailers contribute their expertise in buying the right amount of the right merchandise, as well as their knowledge of distribution—accepting orders and warehousing and transporting the goods. Often, they also provide a more familiar brand name. The dot-com businesses contribute their knowledge of the Internet, ability to provide the latest technology, and the fast pace of a start-up enterprise. Bloomingdale's, Home Depot, Dell, Inc., IBM, and Motorola all have one thing in common: an arrangement with eBay in which they sell excess or outdated merchandise—everything from laptops to tractors to clothes—on the Internet auction site. With this agreement between retailers and the Web marketing giant, everyone wins: Consumers get good prices, the retailers get 45 cents on the dollar instead of the 20 cents they'd earn in a clearance or liquidation sale, and eBay gets a cut.[27]

Sometimes Internet companies make alliances with each other. AOL recently asked Google to become AOL's exclusive search engine, in return for which AOL would distribute Google's ads to its 35 million subscribers.[28] Traditional companies make alliances as well. American Skiing Co., mentioned earlier, is increasing its marketing alliances with companies like Pepsi and ExxonMobil to attract more customers. For instance, consumers who fill up at Mobil stations three times during the winter can receive a $10 coupon for use toward a lift ticket at an ASC ski resort.[29]

Concept Check

1. What is the difference between transaction management and relationship management?
2. Why do companies form strategic alliances?

Creating Value through Quality and Customer Satisfaction

Today's savvy consumers want the satisfaction of acquiring more than ordinary goods and services. Their demands extend beyond just low prices. Firms seeking to tighten bonds with customers must provide value to customers to earn their long-term loyalty.

Value is the customer's perception of the balance between the positive traits of a good or service and its price. Customers who think that they have received value—that is, positive benefits for a fair price—are likely to remain satisfied and continue their relationships with a firm. But when customers perceive an inequitable balance between benefits and price, they become dissatisfied and start looking for opportunities outside their relationships with the business. Value is also an important way to differentiate goods and services from competing offerings. A firm that provides real value to customers often enjoys superior advantages and wider opportunities in the marketplace. Although many business strategists argue that being first to enter a market offers assurance of success, recent history shows examples of first movers losing out to companies that offered greater value. More people buy their personal computers from companies like Dell, which customize their offerings, than from industry pioneers like IBM.[30]

Customers' value perceptions are often tied to **quality,** the degree of excellence or superiority of a firm's goods and services. Technically, quality refers to physical product traits, such as durability and performance reliability. Figure 1.4 emphasizes the high-quality design and performance of the Toyota Camry, quoting reviews from reputable sources such as *The New York Times* and *The Detroit News.* However, quality also includes **customer satisfaction,** the ability of a good or service to meet or exceed buyer needs and expectations. In the realm of online shopping, quality includes not just the characteristics of the products sold but the ability of online sellers to protect credit card purchasers from theft or misuse of their card number and to deliver the products advertised within the promised time.

Technology wields a double-edged sword for customer satisfaction. On the one hand, using technology can give a business the ability to improve interactions with

value customer's perception of the balance between the positive traits of a good or service and its price.

customer satisfaction ability of a good or service to meet or exceed a buyer's needs and expectations.

> ## They Said It
>
> Quality in a product . . . is not what the supplier puts in. It is what the customer gets out and is willing to pay for. . . . Customers pay only for what is of use to them and what gives them value.
>
> *—Peter Drucker (b. 1909)*
> *American business philosopher and author*

FIGURE 1.4
The Importance of Quality

Courtesy of Toyota Motor Sales, U.S.A., Inc. Photography by Terry Heffernan and Peter Rodger.

customers. On the other hand, technologies like online communications, computerized engineering, and satellite communications have led customers to expect more from firms with which they do business. Customers are no longer content to wait for replies to their questions or complaints. They expect instant responses and personalized attention to their needs. They now insist on products that can perform expanded functions with improved reliability. Firms that do not keep up with customer expectations lose customers to rivals that do. Stephen and Bo Kline, owners of Typhoon, a small chain of Thai restaurants in the Pacific Northwest, have learned how to harness technology to improve their customers' dining experience. Wait staff at Typhoon carry handheld computers containing software developed by Vectron Systems, enabling them to take dinner orders at each table and transmit them directly to the kitchen. Using the new system can cut as much as

15 minutes off the waiting time per table, meaning that customers receive their dinners more quickly, which increases their satisfaction.[31] It is clear that businesses in all industries face a common challenge of finding new ways to add value to customer interactions through increased customer satisfaction and quality.

Concept Check

1. Define the term value.
2. Describe the different aspects of quality.

Competing in a Global Market

Businesses can no longer limit their sights to events and opportunities within their own national borders. The world's economies are developing increasing interdependence. To remain competitive, companies must continually search for both the most efficient manufacturing sites and the most lucrative markets for their products.

International trade is currently expanding at an annual rate of more than 3 percent.[32] The U.S. is the leading player in this global market: U.S. exports of merchandise account for 12 percent of the world's exports, and U.S. exports of commercial services represent more than 18 percent of the world's services exports.[33] Major trading partners—led by Canada, Mexico, Japan, and China—are shown in Figure 1.5. Emerging economies in Latin America, Eastern Europe, and Asia are presenting tremendous opportunities for trade. Rising standards of living in these areas have created increasing customer demand for the latest goods and services.

The prospects of succeeding in the global marketplace appeal to U.S. businesses, which can find huge markets outside North America. Of the world's 6 billion residents, just 5 percent reside in the United States. U.S. giants such as The Coca-Cola Co. and Microsoft have proved that they can duplicate their domestic success abroad. As shown in Figure 1.6, eight of the world's top-10 brands have U.S. origins. The only non-U.S. brands to make the top 10 are Nokia (Finland) and Mercedes (Germany).

Going global has been a significant opportunity for Wal-Mart. Wal-Mart is already the largest employer in 21 states in the U.S., with sales that represent more than 2 percent of the nation's gross

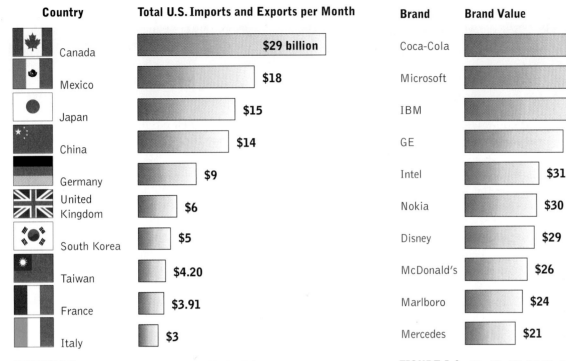

FIGURE 1.5 Top-10 Trading Partners with the U.S.

Source: U.S. Census Bureau, "Top Ten Countries with which the U.S. Trades," accessed at the Census Bureau Web site, http://www.census.gov/foreign-trade/top/dst/current/balance.html, January 15, 2004.

FIGURE 1.6 The World's 10 Most Valuable Brands

Source: Data from Interbrand Corp. and J.P. Morgan Chase & Co., in "The Best Global Brands," *BusinessWeek,* August 5, 2002, http://www.businessweek.com.

national product. But the company is also expanding across the world at a rapid rate, with 4,000 stores in nine countries, where consumers can purchase local foods and brands at great prices. The process of growth is complicated for the superpower, but its philosophy is simple. According to CEO Lee Scott: "Simply put, our long-term strategy is to be where we're not."[34]

Many U.S. businesses are also finding that imported goods made by foreign manufacturers can create new opportunities to satisfy the needs of domestic consumers. One of these businesses is Papa Geno's Herb Farm, described earlier in this chapter. Papa Geno's buys specialty herbs from the best suppliers, a strategy that sometimes requires overseas travel. The company buys lavender from a farmer in Provence in southern France. Every year, two employees from Papa Geno's fly to France "with cash stuffed in their underwear" to sit down at the farmer's kitchen table, share a bottle of wine, and reach a deal with her. For other companies, foreign suppliers are attractive because of their prices. An important reason the electronics industry is booming in Mexican cities like Guadalajara and Monterrey is that the costs of making circuit boards and assembling computers and electronic gadgets are much lower there. This trend provides a source of low-cost goods for U.S. consumers, as well as business opportunities for companies.

Naturally, the Internet has broadened horizons for companies of all sizes. Small businesses now have access to the world market, as do the firms that serve those businesses. As illustrated in Figure 1.7 on page 23, Federal Express offers online services to assist businesses in estimating duties and taxes, as well as access to customs forms and documents.

The U.S. is an attractive market for foreign competitors because of its size and high standard of living. Foreign companies like Matsushita and Sun Life of Canada operate production, distribution, service, and retail facilities here. Foreign ownership of U.S. companies has increased as well. MCA is a well-known firm with foreign parents. Foreign investment in the U.S. means additional competitive pressures for domestic firms.

Productivity: Key to Global Competitiveness

Global competitiveness requires nations, industries, and individual firms to work efficiently at producing goods and services. As discussed earlier, firms need a number of inputs, or factors of production, to produce goods and services.

BEST BUSINESS PRACTICES

Ending the Reign of Ma Bell

"Our industry and our business is going to change more in the next 5 years than it has during the last 20 combined," says Duane Ackerman, CEO of BellSouth Corp.

Those words describe what may be the end of an era for traditional local phone companies and the demise of the business model that has served them since the turn of the 20th century. When the U.S. court system restructured the monopoly in the phone industry in 1996 and separated long-distance carrier AT&T (known as Ma Bell) from its four regional carriers (created in the first breakup of AT&T in 1984 and known as the Baby Bells), competitors rode into the telecommunications market on a wave of technological and business innovation that shows no sign of slowing down.

Technologies such as cable and wireless communications brought new phone carriers onto the scene, and cell phone usage proliferated. Suddenly there was no longer an advantage to being physically wired into consumers' homes, which had given the phone companies their seemingly invincible business edge. Now new carriers like Sprint and MCI could offer phone service. Cable TV and satellite companies began to offer not only high-speed Internet access but also phone service. Internet providers got into the act with both wireless and Internet phone service. Tiny Internet-and-phone start-ups with low overhead are finding ways to become profitable even with very few—and strictly local—customers.

"Anyone who wants to go into the phone business can do it," says Bryan Martin, CEO of 8x8 Inc., which offers its Santa Clara, California, customers unlimited local and long-distance calls, along with video calls, for $29.95 a month. The bundle goes by the brand name "Packets."

And since they can keep their old home numbers, customers are only too happy to save money on the bundled services these firms can offer, for instance, Cablevision System Corp.'s package of television, broadband, and Internet phone service, available in New York City for 30 percent below the industry average. As the tab for buying these services separately approaches $200 for many households, customers are dropping their phone service in ever-increasing numbers. Since 2001, the Baby Bells have seen a drop of about 18 percent in the number of their local phone customers, and they are continuing to lose about 4 percent of their local customer base every year. Cable and Internet companies around the country are picking up the slack.

AT&T soon began to offer local service, while the Baby Bells, like Verizon, added long distance and cell phone service. The Bells are even gearing up to offer TV service on their broadband Internet lines. Their offerings will be priced to compete, but it will be tough to get back the customers who have already taken the opportunity to move on.

QUESTIONS FOR CRITICAL THINKING

1. What are some of the business advantages new telecom competitors have over AT&T and the Baby Bells?
2. New union contracts make it harder for the Bells to reduce their staffs. What impact do you think this will have on their competitiveness?

Sources: Nick Pachetti, "You're Wired!" *Money*, September 2004, pp. 102–108; Shawn Young, "A Price War Hits Internet Calling," *The Wall Street Journal*, August 26, 2004, pp. D1, D3; Ken Brown and Almah Latour, "Phone Industry Faces Upheaval as Ways of Calling Change Fast," *The Wall Street Journal*, August 25, 2004, pp. A1, A8; Jyoti Thottam, "The Internet Is Calling," *Time*, August 23, 2004, pp. 42–43.

productivity relationship between the number of units produced and the number of human and other production inputs necessary to produce them.

Productivity describes the relationship between the number of units produced and the number of human and other production inputs necessary to produce them. So, productivity is a ratio of output to input. When a constant amount of inputs generates increased outputs, an increase in productivity occurs.

Total productivity considers all inputs necessary to produce a specific amount of outputs. Stated in equation form, it can be written as follows:

$$\text{Total productivity} = \frac{\text{Output (goods or services produced)}}{\text{Input (human/natural resources, capital)}}$$

Many productivity ratios focus on only one of the inputs in the equation: labor productivity or output per labor-hour. An increase in labor productivity means that the same amount of work produces more goods and services than before.

Productivity is a widely recognized measure of a company's efficiency. In turn, the total productivity of a nation's businesses has become a measure of its economic strength and standard of living. Economists refer to this measure as a country's **gross domestic product (GDP)**—the

FIGURE 1.7
Operating in the Global Market

sum of all goods and services produced within its boundaries. The GDP is based on the per-capita output of a country—in other words, total national output divided by the number of citizens. As Figure 1.8 shows, the U.S. GDP remains the highest in the world, almost double that of second-ranked China.

Some economists argue that this measure doesn't necessarily prove that the U.S. is the most productive or competitive nation in the world. They point out that Americans actually work longer hours and take fewer vacations than do workers in other countries. And continued economic growth in countries such as China, Japan, and India has raised questions about the global competitiveness of the U.S. Some experts suggest that U.S. managers focus too much on short-term goals and devote insufficient attention to developing long-range plans for worldwide competition. Plant closings, business failures, and employee layoffs are seen as signs of the need to invest more in long-term research, development, and innovation to remain competitive in the global market.

Still, the U.S. had a productivity growth over the last decade, before falling off somewhat during the economic slowdown. Much of the credit for growth goes to technology. During the past two decades, thousands of American companies invested heavily in information technology, and economists believe those investments are paying off in the first decade of the 21st century. Several companies that have led the productivity wave through technology are Wal-Mart, Amazon.com, and Lands' End.[35] Other countries that have made similar investments in technology also have been enjoying productivity gains, including Australia and four European nations: Denmark, Finland, Ireland, and Norway. In these countries, information technology has enabled companies to innovate faster and maintain customer relationships and partnerships around the globe. By contrast, most of the traditionally high-productivity European countries such as Germany have been struggling with productivity. Some experts believe this is partly because many European companies have lagged in applying technology to improve service sector productivity.[36]

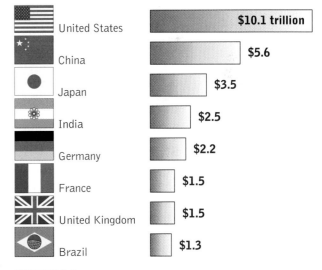

United States — $10.1 trillion
China — $5.6
Japan — $3.5
India — $2.5
Germany — $2.2
France — $1.5
United Kingdom — $1.5
Brazil — $1.3

FIGURE 1.8
Nations with the Highest Gross Domestic Products
Source: *CIA: The World Factbook,* "Field Listing—GDP," April 12, 2003, accessed at the Central Intelligence Agency Web site, http://www.cia.gov/cia/publications/factbook/fields/2001.html.

Concept Check
1. Why is the U.S. an attractive market for foreign competitors?
2. What is productivity?

Developing and Sustaining a World-Class Workforce

A skilled and knowledgeable workforce is an essential resource for keeping pace with the accelerating rate of change in today's business world. Employers need reliable workers to foster strong ties with customers and partners. They must build workforces capable of the productivity needed to compete in global markets. Business leaders are also beginning to realize that the brainpower of employees plays a vital role in a firm's ability to stay on top of new technologies and innovations.

A world-class workforce can be the foundation of a firm's competitive differentiation, providing important advantages over competing businesses. Building a world-class workforce is a difficult task, though, and it is made all the more complex by the changing characteristics of workers as well as the effects of recent business history.

Preparing for Changes in the Workforce

In the coming decades, companies will face several trends that challenge their skills for managing and developing human resources: aging of the population, shrinking labor pool, growing diversity of the workforce, the changing nature of work, and new employer–employee relationships.

Aging of the Population
Members of the baby boom generation, people born between 1946 and 1965, are nearing the peaks of their careers, and the oldest of them have begun to retire. So, employers must deal with issues arising from reliance on older workers, such as retirement, disability programs, retraining, and insurance benefits. By 2030, the number of Americans who are age 65 or older will reach 71 million—nearly double what it is today. These seniors will represent nearly 20 percent of the U.S. population.[37] As these individuals leave the workforce, they will attract the attention of businesspeople eager to earn profits by serving their needs. A similar trend is occurring on a global scale. The worldwide population of seniors is expected to double by 2030 as well, from 420 million to 973 million.[38] These figures represent challenges for businesses and the societies they serve. Fifty years ago, the world had 12 people of working age to support each person who was 65 or older; today, there are 9 people to support each senior. By the year 2050, there will only be 4 workers for every senior.[39]

Because of these changes, companies are increasingly seeking—and finding—talent at the extreme ends of the working age spectrum. Teenagers are entering the workforce sooner, and some seniors are staying longer—or seeking new careers after retiring from their primary careers. Companies that once encouraged early retirement are now developing incentives to keep workers on longer.

Shrinking Labor Pool
During the final decades of the 20th century, cost cutters at many large companies eliminated jobs as a way to reduce expenses and boost profits. Now managers face the opposite problem: a shrinking labor pool. Some economists predict that the U.S. workforce could fall short by as many as 10 million by the year 2010. More sophisticated technology has intensified the challenge by requiring workers to have more advanced skills. Although the pool of college-educated workers has doubled in the last 20 years, from 20 million to 40 million, the demand is still greater than the supply of these individuals.[40]

The challenge of a shrinking labor pool is especially great in developed nations, where the birthrate has shrunk to less than the rate of deaths. Particularly in Europe, the population of some countries is expected to decline over the first half of this century. The same forecasts predict continued growth in the U.S. population because immigration more than makes up for the low birthrate. In the future, as in the past, immigrants will provide a significant share of the nation's labor and entrepreneurship to the U.S. One estimate predicts that 85 percent of the population growth of 18- to 24-year-olds will be from minorities and immigrant families during the next decade.[41]

Increasingly Diverse Workforce
Reflecting these immigration trends, the U.S. workforce is growing more diverse. In the last 10 years, California and Florida received the most immigrants, although Colorado, North Carolina, and Kentucky received the greatest *percentage* of growth in foreign-born residents. Many of these individuals are looking for jobs, and companies are willing to train them. Managers must also learn to work effectively with diverse ethnic groups, cultures, and lifestyles

to develop and retain a superior workforce for their company.

To benefit from diversity, executives of many companies develop explicit strategies to encourage and manage multiculturalism. Office Depot, illustrated in Figure 1.9, has a well-developed diversity program for employees. As another example of commitment to diversity, MasterCard recognizes the importance of having a diverse workforce to meet its customers' needs. All MasterCard employees receive diversity training and participate in career development programs designed to help them fulfill their potential.[42] "By being diverse, we can better operate and compete for business globally," says the ad. "We can also build stronger relationships with our employees, customers, and strategic partners around the world."

The Changing Nature of Work

Not only is the U.S. workforce changing, but so is the very nature of work. Manufacturing no longer accounts for most of U.S. annual output. Instead, 60

Windows of opportunity open and close quickly...

But that is how you do your best work. You adapt fast to change and growth, and that is why Office Depot is the ideal company for your career. Office Depot is committed to creating an inclusive environment where people are valued and respected. *Your success* at Office Depot has no limit...It's up to you!

For more information about careers at Office Depot, please visit our website at www.officedepot.com. Office Depot is an Equal Opportunity Employer, M/F/D/V. A smoke/drug free environment.

Office DEPOT
What you need. What you need to know.

Courtesy of Office Depot

FIGURE 1.9
Office Depot: Developing a Diverse Workforce

percent of this nation's GDP comes from services such as banking and communications. This change will lead U.S. employers to rely heavily on service workers with sharp knowledge skills, as well as manufacturing and technological skills. Different work lifestyles, such as telecommuting, are also becoming common in business life. Many employers allow job flexibility so employees can meet family and personal needs along with job-related needs. Employers are also hiring growing numbers of temporary and part-time employees.

Another business tool for staffing flexibility is **outsourcing,** contracting with another business to perform tasks or functions previously handled by internal staff members. In addition to reducing the continuing costs of hiring and training new employees, outsourcing can make a firm more competitive. Businesses concentrate on the functions that provide competitive differentiation and delegate others that do not add to customer value, such as the details of developing information systems, providing employee benefits, or collecting late payments.

A staffing revolution in which services are being outsourced has occurred in the U.S. military.[43] But while KP duty fades into memory, outsourcing has created problems for many corporations and even some state governments (see the "Hits & Misses" box on page 27).

The New Employer–Employee Partnership

Employees are no longer likely to remain with a single company throughout their entire careers. To handle the challenges of a changing workforce and to gain competitive advantage by fully utilizing employee talents, many employers are trying to form new types of relationships with employees. They know that after the highly publicized layoffs of the past two decades, employees do not expect loyalty in the form of long-term employment. Consequently, employees feel less obligation to remain loyal and spend their entire career at the same company. So employers are trying to build a new kind of relationship—among equals. They emphasize creating an employer-employee partnership that recognizes and encourages workers'

> *They Said It*
>
> You know it's going to be hell when the best rapper out there is a white guy and the best golfer is a black guy.
>
> —*Charles Barkley (b. 1963)*
> *American basketball star*

Today's soldier is a business-boosted warrior. Soldiers like this one in Kuwait get more and more backup from private companies who perform services previously the responsibility of men and women in uniform.

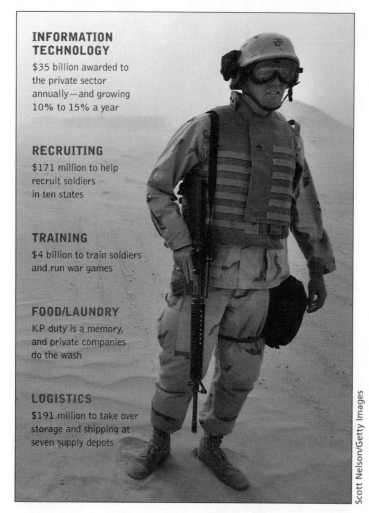

INFORMATION TECHNOLOGY

$35 billion awarded to the private sector annually—and growing 10% to 15% a year

RECRUITING

$171 million to help recruit soldiers in ten states

TRAINING

$4 billion to train soldiers and run war games

FOOD/LAUNDRY

KP duty is a memory, and private companies do the wash

LOGISTICS

$191 million to take over storage and shipping at seven supply depots

Scott Nelson/Getty Images

important contributions to providing value and satisfying customers.

To forge the partnerships that support this new kind of commitment, employers emphasize listening to and respecting their employees. They share financial data and reward employees with company stock so that they participate in the firm's success. In addition, the new employer–employee partnership often includes the employer helping employees to develop their knowledge and skills so that they are more valuable to their current employer—and in the job market down the line.

Reaping the Benefits of Diversity

As discussed previously, today's workers come from many different ethnic, lifestyle, and age groups. Enlightened business leaders recognize the gain they receive from encouraging all of their employees to contribute their unique perspectives, skills, and experiences.

Diversity, blending individuals of different ethnic backgrounds, cultures, religions, ages, genders, and physical and mental abilities, can enrich a firm's chances of success. Several studies have shown that diverse employee teams and workforces tend to perform tasks more effectively and develop better solutions to business problems than homogeneous employee groups. This difference is due in part to the varied perspectives and experiences that foster innovation and creativity in multicultural teams.

Since nearly every business serves a diverse group of customers, diversity in its workforce can improve management's understanding of customer needs and relationships with customer groups, as discussed earlier in the MasterCard International example. MasterCard is used by customers in 210 countries and territories around the world, so developing a workforce that can understand different cultures, speak different languages, and come up with solutions tailored to meet the needs of a diverse customer base makes good business sense.[44]

Also, practical managers know that attention to diversity issues can help them avoid costly and damaging legal battles. Employee lawsuits alleging discrimination are now among the most common legal issues employers face. Losing a discrimination lawsuit can be very costly, yet in a recent survey, a majority of executives from racial and cultural minorities said they had seen discrimination in work assignments.

Concept Check

1. *What is the new employer–employee relationship?*
2. *How can having a diverse workforce benefit a company?*

Wanted: A New Type of Manager

Today's companies look for managers who are intelligent, highly motivated people with the ability to create and sustain a vision of how an organization can succeed. The 21st-century manager must also apply critical-thinking skills and creativity to business challenges and steer change.

HITS & MISSES

Offshoring: Exporting America

"There is almost no limit on the technology that can take jobs overseas. Anyone in any field who has ever thought, 'Gee, I could just as easily do this job from home,' or who has smiled at the thought of working from a laptop on a beach should understand that his or her replacement 'could just as easily do this job' from Bangalore."

Many U.S. workers, particularly if they are unemployed, identify with the fear expressed in this quotation from reader mail addressed to a popular business columnist. And Congress is listening. The House recently voted to prevent U.S. firms from getting federal loans if they evade taxes by relocating overseas, and many states have tried, usually without success so far, to place limits on companies that outsource jobs to cheaper English-speaking labor in locations such as India, New Zealand, and Eastern Europe. Several state governors proposed executive action to forbid the awarding of state contracts to companies that shipped jobs overseas, and legislators in more than 40 states introduced almost 100 bills intended to preserve state funds only for contractors who certify their work would be done in the U.S. However, along with many corporations, more than half the states already outsource work, including to overseas call centers, and the attraction of low costs has helped keep much antioffshoring legislation from passing. The gover-

nors of California and Massachusetts are among those who have vetoed such laws, though the governors of Missouri and Arizona have banned offshoring for state contracts.

However, to workers abroad, like Maumita Biswas of southern India, a job at a call center working for a U.S. corporation is an economic windfall that puts her in the top 20 percent of Indian wage-earners. Thanks to her salary of $2,500 a year, Biswas and her family can now afford U.S. clothing, cosmetics, CDs, videos, and other products, "and that sends money back to the U.S.," she says.

QUESTIONS FOR CRITICAL THINKING

1. Do you think keeping costs to consumers down by outsourcing jobs is a good business strategy? Why or why not?
2. Would your opinion change if you knew that only about 5 percent of information technology jobs have gone overseas?

Sources: Jim Hopkins, "Drugmakers Shift More Production Outside USA," *USA Today*. October 19, 2004, pp. B1, B2; Julie Schmit, "States Try to Keep Jobs in the USA," *USA Today*, August 31, 2004, p. B1; "House Blocks Loans to Offshore Firms," *Mobile Register*, July 16, 2004, p. A4; J.D. Heyman et al., "Is This Woman a Threat to the American Worker?" *People*, July 12, 2004, pp. 109–112; Anne Fisher, "Think Globally, Save Your Job Locally," *Fortune*, February 23, 2004, p. 60.

Importance of Vision

An important managerial quality needed in the 21st century is **vision,** the ability to perceive marketplace needs and what an organization must do to satisfy them. For example, not many people imagine paper when they think of the information economy. Most people think of cellphones and laptop computers. But not entrepreneur Norm Brodsky. Brodsky has found that the more information people create and gather with their computers, the more backup copies they print. He already runs a successful records storage business, and on a tip from a supplier, he and two partners investigated a new line of work: secure document shredding. He quickly determined that destroying confidential records was a young and growing industry, with customers willing to pay a premium to maintain the security of their documents even as they are shredded. Some businesses drive a portable shredder directly to customers, and others collect documents in locked containers and shred all the customers' documents in bulk. By considering an unlikely source of business growth, Brodsky and his partners launched a fast-growing and highly profitable company.[45]

The need for vision isn't limited to entrepreneurs. Dick Notebaert is credited for bringing telecommunications firm Qwest back from the brink of bankruptcy, which is an achievement in itself; but to turn the company around, its CEO needs vision. The former head of Ameritech began his own quest to save Qwest by renegotiating loans and selling off assets such as Qwest's Yellow Pages. Next, he traveled around the country to Qwest's different offices, making sure to connect with employees who, understandably, were worried about their company and their jobs. Then he set out to repair the company's image and position it as a strong alternative to competitors. Notebaert believes that Qwest's long-distance business, historically a money-loser, will become profitable in the long run. He is looking for

They Said It

When I am president, and with your help, we're going to repeal every benefit, every loophole, every reward that entitles any Benedict Arnold company or CEO to take the money and the jobs overseas and stick the American people with the bill."

—*John Kerry (b. 1943) 2004 presidential candidate (on receiving an endorsement from the AFL-CIO)*

BUSINESS TOOL KIT

Dressing for an Interview

Congratulations . . . you've got a job interview! If this is your first professional job interview, there are a few basic things you should know before stepping out of your house. You should always dress your best for an interview, and it makes sense to err on the side of conservative. For a professional job interview, take the time and effort to buy a good quality "interview" suit. Here are a few tips on how to dress appropriately for an interview.

1. Solid colors and conservative suits go a long way toward making you look professional. Although this may not be your style and you may feel creatively stifled in such conservative garb, it's always best to express your individuality in different, subtler ways. A tasteful scarf or an interesting tie can give the interviewer a small peek into the window of your soul.

2. You should have no visible piercings, tattoos, or green hair if you're interviewing for a job in a corporate environment. Most mainstream companies are still looking for young, bright talent . . . who can fit into a corporate environment. Those tattoos and piercings are best left hidden or disguised when interviewing for a professional position.

3. Don't wear T-shirts, cutoffs, shorts, sandals, or sweat suits. Remember, the key word is *professional* even if the interviewer tells you that it's a "business casual" environment. Casual does *not* mean you can show up to work in your pajamas and slippers, and it certainly doesn't mean you can interview in them!

4. Be well groomed and have a neat, professional hairstyle. Subtlety applies to perfume and aftershave as well; you don't want the defining moment of your interview to be the sneezing fit the interviewer has.

5. Believe it or not, some interviewers base much of their opinion of you on the condition of your shoes. Be sure they are of good quality, clean, polished, low heeled, and well cared for. And as far as hosiery goes, it's best to stick with neutral hosiery for women (no runs in your stockings) and black dress socks for men.

Sources: "Checklist—Dressing for an Interview," September 11, 2002, West Texas A&M University, Career and Counseling Services Web site, located at http://wtcareer.wtamu.edu/cs/student/wear.htm; Alison Doyle, "Dressing for Success: How to Dress for an Interview," December 2001, about.com's Guide for Job Searching, located at http://jobsearch.about.com/library/weekly/aa120201a.htm.

They Said It

Never lose hope in your dreams. For without dreams, life is a broken-winged bird that cannot fly.

—*Langston Hughes (1902–1967) American poet*

alliances with satellite-TV and cellular companies to help fill gaps in Qwest's current capabilities. And he believes fervently—while industry watchers are skeptical, especially in the face of a scandal that involved the sales commissions of several managers—that Qwest can make it alone, without a merger.[46]

Importance of Critical Thinking and Creativity

Critical thinking and creativity are essential characteristics of the 21st century workforce. Today's businesspeople need to look at a wide variety of situations, draw connections between disparate information, and develop future-oriented solutions.

Critical thinking is the ability to analyze and assess information to pinpoint problems or opportunities. The critical-thinking process includes activities like determining the authenticity, accuracy, and worth of information, knowledge, and arguments. It involves looking beneath the surface for deeper meaning and connections that can help to identify critical issues and solutions.

Creativity is the capacity to develop novel solutions to perceived organizational problems. Although most people think of it in relation to artists, musicians, and inventors, that indicates a very limited definition. In business, creativity refers to the ability to see better and different ways of doing business. A computer engineer who solves a glitch in a software program is executing a creative act; so is a mailroom clerk who finds a way to speed delivery of the company's overnight packages. Companies must constantly find innovative ways to communicate with and attract new customers, while keeping the interest of established customers. About 10 years ago, Coach was a stodgy division of Sara Lee Corp.

that was best known for its sturdy briefcases and handbags—tailored, but hardly stylish. Designs just weren't keeping up with current trends, so leather goods shoppers drifted off to competitors such as Ralph Lauren and Donna Karan. Sales plummeted. "We were about to hit a wall," recalls CEO Lew Frankfort. Recognizing that the company needed a shot of creativity, Frankfort hired former Tommy Hilfiger designer Reed Krakoff as Coach's new creative director. Krakoff turned to his favorite artists for inspiration in design: Alexander Calder, Le Corbusier, and others. He even reached back to some of the hipper Coach designs of the 1960s and 1970s. "I had to take these ideas and make them fun— young in spirit," Krakoff explains. With Krakoff's guidance, Coach began producing trendier designs in new materials—lighter weight leathers, fabric, and even nylon. In addition, company marketers conducted consumer surveys to find out what consumers wanted. Shoppers noticed and began buying the new bags, wallets, belts, and other goods. Today, Coach introduces a new collection every month—to the delight of its now-loyal customers.[47]

Some practice and mental exercise can cultivate the ability to think creatively. Here are some exercises and guidelines that foster creativity:

- In a group, brainstorm by listing ideas as they come to mind. Build on other people's ideas, but don't criticize them. Wait until later to evaluate and organize the ideas.
- Think about how to make familiar concepts unfamiliar. A glue that doesn't stick very well? That's the basis for 3M's popular Post-it notes.
- Plan ways to rearrange your thinking with simple questions like "What features can we leave out?" or by imagining what it feels like to be the customer.
- Cultivate curiosity, openness, risk, and energy as you meet people and encounter new situations. View these encounters as opportunities to learn.
- Treat failures as additional opportunities to learn.
- Get regular physical exercise. When you work out, your brain releases endorphins, and these chemicals stimulate creative thinking.
- Pay attention to your dreams and daydreams. You might find that you already know the answer to a problem.

Creativity and critical thinking must go beyond generating new ideas, however. They must lead to action. In addition to creating an environment where employees can nurture ideas, managers must give them opportunities to take risks and try new solutions.

Ability to Steer Change

Today's managers must guide their employees and organizations through the changes brought about by technology, marketplace demands, and global competition. Managers must be skilled at recognizing employee strengths and motivating people to move toward common goals as members of a team. Throughout this book, real-world examples demonstrate how companies have initiated sweeping change initiatives. Most, if not all, have been led by managers comfortable with the tough decisions that today's fluctuating conditions require. Lew Frankfort of Coach and Dick Notebaert of Qwest are good examples of individuals who are able to recognize the need for change and make the decisions necessary to achieve that change.

Factors that require organizational change can come from both external and internal sources; successful managers must be aware of both. External forces might include feedback from customers, developments in the international marketplace, economic trends, and new technologies. Internal factors might arise from new company goals, emerging employee needs, labor-union demands, or production problems.

Concept Check

1. Why is vision an important managerial quality?
2. What is the difference between creativity and critical thinking?

Managing Ethics and Social Responsibility

In recent years, stories about misconduct by businesses and their employees have become all too common. The collapse of Enron and WorldCom took with them thousands of jobs as well as the life savings of their employees and caused a ripple effect throughout the stock market—investors no longer trusted top executives, who were charged with mismanaging company funds. Top executives at Tyco were discovered to have evaded taxes and looted the company. Even the squeaky clean image of Martha Stewart was tarnished by charges that she engaged in insider stock trading. And *Time* named three women who had blown the whistle on their own organizations—Sherron Watkins of Enron, Cynthia Cooper of WorldCom, and Colleen Rowley of the FBI—as its 2003 Persons of the Year.[48]

These and other corporate scandals have caused the American public to lose confidence in top executives in general. According to one survey, only 17 percent of Americans currently rate business executives highly, representing an 8 percent decline from the previous year. The survey revealed that nurses remain the top-rated professionals for ethics and honesty, while advertisers (9 percent), telemarketers (6 percent), and car salespeople (5 percent) rank at the bottom of the scale.[49] These examples are a wake-up call to businesspeople, demonstrating the importance of ethics and social responsibility in all business activities.

Business ethics refers to the standards of conduct and moral values involving right and wrong actions arising in the work environment. Poor ethical standards can lead to public image problems, costly lawsuits, high levels of employee theft, and a host of other expensive problems. In contrast, ethical decision making fosters trust, a vital element of strong relationships with customers, employees, and other organizations. It is particularly important for top executives to demonstrate ethical behavior, since employees often follow their example. In addition, Internet technology has given rise to a whole new realm of ethics related to workers' rights to privacy.

Strong company and individual ethics are often the cornerstone of visionary companies. Drug manufacturer Johnson & Johnson has maintained a strong code of ethics for more than 50 years. These ethical standards form a framework for decision making throughout the company. When bottles of the firm's best-seller Tylenol were found to have been laced with poison in the 1980s, executives did not hesitate to recall the product or deal openly with the media because their actions were guided by deeply ingrained principles.

Companies like Shell enhance their image and relationship with society by participating in social responsibility programs. In this case, Shell has formed an alliance with The Ocean Conservancy to clean up debris along coastlines around the world.

COLLECTING 12.58 MILLION POUNDS OF TRASH ISN'T A WALK ON THE BEACH. ACTUALLY IT IS.

Through a strong commitment to sustainability, Shell and The Ocean Conservancy are reducing marine debris on coastlines around the world.
Shell is one of the largest worldwide participants in The Ocean Conservancy's International Coastal Clean-up with over 1,300 employees volunteering in the U.S. alone.
The result? Globally, over 12 million pounds of trash were collected in the largest one-day volunteer marine clean-up in the world.

And by doing so, we've taken an important step toward the preservation of marine life.
To find out more about The Ocean Conservancy and the International Coastal Clean-up, go to www.oceanconservancy.org. For details on this and other Shell sustainable development activities, go to www.shell.com.

Courtesy of Shell International Ltd.

Working hand-in-hand with business ethics is **social responsibility,** a management philosophy that highlights the social and economic effects of managerial decisions. Businesses demonstrate their social responsibility in a variety of ways. Sports outfitter Patagonia is widely known for its commitment to social responsibility. The company's objectives include treating employees well and supporting environmentalism. For example, part of Patagonia's written mission is to support grass-roots environmental activism by donating 10 percent of the company's annual profits to hundreds of grass-roots environmental groups. One of its ongoing programs is support of the Arctic National Wildlife Refuge. On the company's Web site, customers can write directly to their congresspeople in support of this cause. In addition, Patagonia is donating time and money to the cause. Its reputation for social responsibility has helped Patagonia establish a positive image in the minds of consumers.[50]

SOLVING AN ETHICAL CONTROVERSY

The New Drug War

The costs of prescription drugs in the U.S. are among the highest in the world, much higher than prices in Canada, which regulates drug prices as part of its national health care system. Not surprisingly, a growing number of Americans send an estimated $1 billion a year in Canadian drugs to patients south of the border. But the U.S. drug makers who supply Canada have cut their shipments to many Canadian drugstores that regularly sell to U.S. consumers. After all, they argue, someone has to pay the high costs of research and testing involved in new drug breakthroughs—and it is illegal for individuals to import drugs into the U.S. Many Canadians worry that this new demand is likely to overwhelm its drug supplies. In the meantime, one in seven U.S. families report having trouble paying their medical bills, even though two-thirds of them have health insur-ance. So the appeal of lower prices in Canada is likely to continue.

Should U.S. consumers be allowed to purchase pre-scription drugs from Canada at a lower price than they pay at home?

PRO
1. Uninsured patients are at particular risk for having to forego needed medication they cannot afford.
2. Some cities and states, such as Illinois and Wisconsin, are already helping their residents purchase cheaper Canadian drugs.

CON
1. U.S. drug companies are already working to lower the prices of prescription drugs, particularly to the uninsured.
2. It is too easy for counterfeit or low-quality drugs to cross the border unde-tected.

SUMMARY
Both Canada and the U.S. already import some drugs from other countries, and Canada maintains quality by imposing its own manufacturing standards on overseas plants it uses. Michigan Congressman, John Dingell, proposes allowing the gov-ernment to negotiate with drug compa-nies for lower prices. Other possible solu-tions include price controls on U.S. drugs and revisions to the patent laws, which grant drug makers a 17-year monopoly on new products and keep prices high.

Sources: Colin McClelland, "Canadians Call on Ottawa to Ban Cross-Border Drug Shopping," *USA Today*, October 20, 2004, p. B1; "Americans Going to Canada for Flu Shots," http://www.usatoday.com/news/health, October 20, 2004; Julie Appleby, "Drugmakers Spend More on Dividends than Research," *USA Today*, October 11, 2004, p. B1.

Chapter 2 explores business ethics, social responsibility, and the influence of business on society as a whole in detail. Because this is such an important issue, each chapter also presents a feature high-lighting a current ethical controversy in business. See the "Solving an Ethical Controversy" box for a discussion of prescription drug pricing issues.

What Makes a Company Admired?

Every year, publications and organizations publish lists of companies that are "most admired." What characteristics make a company admirable? Most people would mention solid profits, stable growth, a safe and challenging work environment, high-quality goods and services, and business ethics and social responsibility. As you read this text, you'll be able to make up your own mind about why companies should—or should not—be admired. *Fortune* publishes a list of the most-admired U.S. companies each year, which is the result of a survey of 10,000 executives and business observers. The companies on the list have survived through difficult economic times, offer goods and services that consumers need or want, and employ top executives with good business ethics. General Electric ranked number 1 recently; interestingly, GE ranked No. 1 on the worldwide list as well. The company has also frequently ranked in the top spots on the *Financial Times* list of U.S. and global companies. The 120-year-old company, now headed by CEO Jeff Immelt, has weathered its share of tough times. But he stresses the importance of his company's "culture of integrity." Immelt recently began broadcasting executive meetings over GE's Web site so that shareholders and customers could learn more about the company. "We want to be touched and felt and viewed and discovered," he explains. "I think that plays to our strengths."51

Concept Check

1. *Define* business ethics *and* social responsibility.
2. *Why is it important for a company to behave responsibly?*

Did You Know?

1. Approximately one-third of the world's inhabitants eat with knives and forks, another third with chopsticks, and the final third with their hands.

2. To meet the shopping needs of its customers who work different time periods, Wal-Mart keeps 1,400 of its stores open 24 hours a day.

3. The thumb and forefinger circle *okay* sign used in the U.S. signifies money in Japan, zero in France, and is a vulgar gesture in Latin America.

4. In the United Kingdom, the hood of a car is called a *bonnet* and the trunk a *boot*. Windshields are called *windscreens*, flashlights are *torches*, and undershirts are known as *vests*. Even words have different spellings: color is spelled *colour*, tire becomes *tyre*, and theater is *theatre*.

What's Ahead

As business speeds along in the 21st century, new technologies, population shifts, and shrinking global barriers are altering the world at a frantic pace. Businesspeople are catalysts for many of these changes, creating new opportunities for individuals who are prepared to take action. Studying contemporary business will help you to prepare for the future.

Throughout this book, you'll be exposed to the real-life stories of many businesspeople. You'll learn about the range of business careers available and the daily decisions, tasks, and challenges that they face. By the end of the course, you'll understand how marketing, accounting, and human resource management work together to provide competitive advantages for firms. This knowledge can help you become a more capable employee and enhance your career potential.

Now that this chapter has introduced some basic terms and issues in the business world of the 21st century, Chapter 2 takes a detailed look at the ethical and social responsibility issues facing contemporary business. Chapter 3 deals with economic challenges. Chapter 4 focuses on the challenges and opportunities faced by firms competing in global markets.

Summary of Learning Goals

1 **Distinguish between business and not-for-profit organizations and identify the factors of production.**

Business consists of all profit-seeking activities that provide goods and services necessary to an economic system. Not-for-profit organizations are businesslike establishments, but their primary objectives—instead of profits—involve social, political, governmental, educational, or similar functions. The four basic factors of production are natural resources, capital, human resources, and entrepreneurship.

2 **Describe the private enterprise system and explain how competition and entrepreneurship contribute to the system.**

The private enterprise system is an economic system that rewards firms based on how well they match and counter competitors' goods and services. Competition in the private enterprise system ensures success for firms that satisfy consumer demands. Entrepreneurs are the risk takers in the private enterprise system. If no one takes risks, no successful businesses emerge, and the private enterprise system will not function.

3 Identify the six eras of business and explain how the relationship era influences contemporary business.

The six historical eras are the Colonial period, the Industrial Revolution, the age of the industrial entrepreneur, the production era, the marketing era, and the relationship era. In the relationship era, businesspeople focus on developing and sustaining long-term relationships with customers and other businesses.

4 Describe how technology is changing the way businesses operate and compete.

Technology is the business application of knowledge based on scientific discoveries, inventions, and innovations. New technologies allow businesses to provide new goods and services for consumers, improve customer service, lower prices, and enhance working conditions. However, technology is also changing the shape of some industries, sometimes creating entirely new industries. Technology also opens new questions about business ethics and social responsibility.

5 Relate the importance of quality and customer satisfaction to efforts to create value for customers.

Today's savvy consumers are looking for goods and services with positive traits offered at fair prices, the essence of value. A customer's perception of value is tied to quality, the degree of excellence or superiority of a firm's goods and services. Quality also includes customer satisfaction, the ability of a good or service to meet or exceed buyer needs and expectations. If customers feel they have received value—that is, quality for a fair price—they are likely to remain satisfied and continue their relationships with a firm.

6 Explain how productivity affects competitiveness in the global market.

Global competitiveness requires nations and companies to work efficiently at producing goods and services. Productivity describes the relationship between the number of units produced and the human and other production inputs needed to produce them. Productivity is a widely used measure of a company's efficiency. In turn, the total productivity of a nation's businesses has become a measure of its economic strength, standard of living, and ability to compete.

7 Describe the major trends in the workforce that challenge managers' skills for managing and developing human resources.

The major trends in today's workforce are aging of the population, shrinking labor pool, increasingly diverse workforce, changing nature of work, and the new employer-employee partnership.

8 Identify the skills that managers need to lead businesses in the new century.

Managers in the new century need vision, the ability to perceive marketplace needs and how their firm can satisfy them. Critical-thinking skills and creativity allow managers to pinpoint problems and opportunities and plan novel solutions. Finally, managers are dealing with rapid change, and they need skills to help steer their organizations through shifts in external and internal conditions.

9 Discuss the importance of good business ethics and social responsibility in business decision making.

Business ethics are the standards of conduct and moral values involving right and wrong actions in the workplace. Businesses that set high ethical standards avoid public image problems, costly lawsuits, customer mistrust, and other expensive problems. They can also offer guidelines for executives and employees to apply in making decisions. Social responsibility is a management philosophy that highlights the social and economic effects of business decisions and actions. Socially responsible firms seek to give back to their communities, customers, and employees.

Business Terms You Need to Know

business 5

profits 6

factors of production 7

private enterprise system 10

competition 10

entrepreneur 12

brand 15

Internet 16

relationship management 18

value 19

customer satisfaction 19

productivity 22

Other Important Business Terms

not-for-profit organizations 6

natural resources 7

capital 7

human resources 8

entrepreneurship 9

capitalism 10

competitive differentiation 11

private property 11

consumer orientation 15

branding 15

technology 16

World Wide Web 17

transaction management 17

partnership 18

strategic alliance 19

quality 19

gross domestic product (GDP) 23

outsourcing 25

diversity 26

vision 27

critical thinking 28

creativity 28

business ethics 30

social responsibility 30

Review Questions

1. In what ways are not-for-profit organizations a substantial part of the U.S. economy? What challenges will not-for-profits face in the next decade or two?

2. Identify and describe the four basic inputs that make up factors of production. Give an example of each factor of production that a utility company might use.

3. What is a private enterprise system? What are the four rights that are critical to the operation of capitalism? Why would capitalism have difficulty functioning in a society that does not assure these rights for its citizens?

4. How has technology affected business throughout its six historical eras, including the relationship era?

5. What is relationship management? How might a strategic alliance between a motorcycle dealer and a local radio station benefit both firms?

6. How do companies create customer value through quality and customer satisfaction?

7. Why is productivity so important to a company's competitiveness? To a nation's competitiveness?

8. Identify the major changes in the workforce that will affect the way managers build a world-class workforce in the 21st century. Why is brainpower so important?

9. Identify four qualities that the "new" managers of the 21st century must have. Why are these qualities important in a competitive business environment?

10. Give a brief example of at least one company you know that practices good business ethics and social responsibility.

Projects and Applications

1. The entrepreneurial spirit fuels growth in the U.S. economy. Choose a company that interests you—one you have worked for or dealt with as a customer—and read about the company in the library or visit its Web site. Learn what you can about the company's early history: Who founded it and why? Is the founder still with the organization? Do you think the founder's original vision is still embraced by the company? If not, how has the vision changed?

2. Brands distinguish one company's goods or services from its competitors. Each company you purchase from hopes that you will become loyal to its brand. Some well-known brands are McDonald's, Coca-Cola, Hilton, and Old Navy. Choose a type of good or service you use regularly and identify the major brands associated with it. Are you loyal to a particular brand? Why or why not?

3. The Internet has already begun to change many industries. Think of an industry you are familiar with that has changed—or will change—because of the Internet. De-scribe the changes. Do you think that the Internet has improved the industry's relationship with its customers? Why or why not?

4. More and more businesses are forming strategic alliances to become more competitive. Think of an alliance between two firms you are familiar with (or between a business and a not-for-profit organization) that could be beneficial to both and explain the benefits.

5. Social responsibility is an important part of managerial thinking at many companies. To find out more, research one of the following companies (or select one of your own) and describe its social responsibility programs:
   a. Timberland
   b. Recreational Equipment Inc. (REI)
   c. Procter & Gamble
   d. American Express
   e. Merck

Experiential Exercise

Background: This chapter describes how the nature of the workforce is changing: the population is aging, the labor pool is shrinking, the workforce is becoming more diverse, the nature of work is changing, and employers are forging new partnerships with their employees.

Directions: To better understand how companies respond to changes in the workforce, select a company to research.

1. Form teams of two to three students. Each team will then select a company and research how that company is responding to changes in the workforce. Teams may choose one of the following companies (or select their own):
   a. Wal-Mart   e. Charles Schwab
   b. Boeing   f. Starbucks
   c. Marriott   g. Adobe Systems
   d. Nordstrom

2. Once teams have completed their research, they may be asked to present their findings to the class.

NOTHING BUT NET

1. **Understanding Internet terminology.** The Internet seems to have a language all its own. To help novice surfers better understand the Internet, several Web sites have glossaries of Internet terms. Visit the site listed here and define the following terms:

bookmark	frames
cache	HTML
CGI	spiders
cookie	

   http://www.lib.berkeley.edu/TeachingLib/
   Guides/Internet/Glossary.html

2. **Search engines.** The Internet contains literally hundreds of thousands of different Web sites and billions of pages. Sometimes finding what you want can be a lengthy and frustrating process. One tool to help you find what you're looking for is a search engine. Type in a word or a phrase and the search engines will find sites

   that match. One of the most popular search engines is Google (http://www.google.com). Visit this site and choose a key term from the chapter, along with a company name—such as Gap, *New York Times,* General Mills, Annie's Homegrown, or Visa. Prepare a brief report on your experience.

3. **Accessing the *Contemporary Business* Web site.** Accompanying *Contemporary Business* is a Web site (http://boone.swlearning.com) that contains helpful tools and information. Visit the Web site and list three topics discussed there that interest you. Explain why you would like to learn more about these topics.

   Note: Internet Web addresses change frequently. If you don't find the exact sites listed, you may need to access the organization's or company's home page and search from there.

Case 1.1

Succeeding in the Shadow of Ground Zero

On September 12, 2001, Richard Cohn and Ibrahim Merchant stood in front of what used to be their bustling, popular restaurant. The sunny outdoor terrace was strewn with debris and coated with dust and ash. The dining room inside looked like a war zone. Tables and chairs were toppled everywhere, broken glass littered the floor, and a blanket of ash had turned to gray mud because the pipes in the kitchen had burst. "It was so creepy," recalls Cohn. "It had gone from a paradise to the aftermath of a nuclear war." In fact, the partners' restaurant, called South-West NY, was part of the biggest crime scene in U.S. history. It was located in the World Financial Center, a complex just across the street from what had once been the Twin Towers of the World Trade Center. Thirty-seven thousand people had worked at the World Financial Center, and many of them had been loyal patrons of SouthWest NY. For the first few days after the tragedy, all Cohn and Merchant could feel was despair.

But soon Cohn, who was born in New York and is Jewish, and Merchant, who is a Muslim from Pakistan, decided that their business must somehow reopen. They had invested $3 million in the enterprise, but the decision involved more than that. "We didn't want the terrorists to destroy what was left of downtown," explains Merchant. Reopening was much more difficult than mopping up the kitchen and dining room and replacing the furniture. The partners first had to lay off most of their staff because they couldn't possibly meet a payroll. But within a couple of months, they were able to rehire to fill the 45 jobs at the restaurant, and three months later SouthWest opened its doors again. But there were no customers. Tourists avoided the area around the Trade Center, which was still under cleanup. Many companies had left the area forever. Those who had lived in apartments nearby were still struggling to reclaim their residences—and weren't particularly interested in dining out. "Many people thought we were crazy [to reopen at all]," says Merchant.

Gradually, however, customers began to drift in. First came employees from Merrill Lynch, one of the first major businesses to return to the World Financial Center. As spring unfolded and more people returned to work at the Center, the trickle of customers became a steady stream. On a sunny day, the terrace of SouthWest NY is filled with diners again, with some patrons waiting as much as 45 minutes for a table.

The World Financial Center has not returned to capacity, just as much of the area surrounding the site of the World Trade Center has not. Downtown Manhattan is different. But business owners like Merchant and Cohn believe it is important to revitalize the area in every way possible. Two partners, from very different backgrounds, have managed to rebuild their business from the ashes—literally.

Sources: "A Year Later," *Brandweek*, September 9, 2002, pp. 1–10; Lucette Lagnado, "Staying Put Downtown," *The Wall Street Journal*, September 6, 2002, p. B1; "Manhattan Small Business Owners Hurt by 9/11," *USA Today*, August 27, 2002, http://www.usatoday.com.

Video Case 1.2

Cannondale Bicycle Co.

This video case appears on page 602. A recently filmed video, designed to expand and highlight the written case, is available for class use by instructors.

Chapter 2
Business Ethics and Social Responsibility

1 *Explain the concepts of business ethics and social responsibility.*

2 *Describe the factors that influence business ethics.*

3 *List the stages in the development of ethical standards.*

4 *Identify common ethical dilemmas in the workplace.*

5 *Discuss how organizations shape ethical behavior.*

6 *Describe how businesses' social responsibility is measured.*

7 *Summarize the responsibilities of business to the general public, customers, and employees.*

8 *Explain why investors and the financial community are concerned with business ethics and social responsibility.*

Business Leaders Pay with Jail Terms for Misdeeds

In the last few years, the media have brought us startling pictures of a number of top executives in handcuffs—and headed to court—for legal and ethical violations that harmed their investors, their employees, their customers, and the public image of business. The past two years have seen the 'buzzards come

home to roost' as a long and growing list of offenders have decided to plead guilty to charges that collectively added up to an unparalleled series of ethical and legal misdeeds. In addition, a growing number of CEOs and other members to top management have been found guilty and sentenced to jail terms. Among the most highly publicized cases is ImClone Systems, a biotechnology firm tainted by improper stock sales. Its CEO, Sam Waksal, was charged with tipping off family members and his friend, domestic diva Martha Stewart, of an impending stock price plunge. Waksal is in jail; Stewart and her stockbroker are both serving light sentences.

Meanwhile John Rivas, founder and CEO of Adelphia Communications, has joined his own son, Timothy, who served as chief financial officer for the firm, in earning a prison sentence for conspiracy, bank fraud, and securities fraud.

Bernard Ebbers, former CEO of World-Com, has been indicted on fraud and conspiracy charges related to an accounting scandal at the firm. State and federal authorities continue to investigate his case; Ebbers is pleading innocent. The company has struggled out of bankruptcy as MCI Inc.

Even not-for-profit organizations have their share of ethical woes. Dick Grasso, former head of the New York Stock Exchange, is the target of both a lawsuit and an investigation into his annual salary: an almost unheard of $140 million in salary and bonuses for the head of a not-for-profit organization.

© Don Emmert/AFP/Getty Images

Dennis Kozlowski, former CEO of Tyco International, and Mark Swartz, the company's former chief financial officer, have been indicted on 38 felony counts of stealing $170 million from the firm and acquiring an additional $430 million through illegal stock sales. Their trials are scheduled for 2005. Kozlowski allegedly managed to pay himself and Swartz nearly $96 million in unapproved bonuses, to negotiate near-immunity from firing, and to arrange for generous retirement benefits by undermining the board's oversight role and heavily filtering the information that reached its members.

Halliburton Company has been fined $7.5 million by the Securities and Exchange Commission, and two former financial officials have been charged in what the SEC says was an improper change in accounting practices that allowed the firm to report higher earnings than it could otherwise have done.

Perhaps the biggest scandal of all is the spectacular financial losses that brought down energy trader Enron Corp. following suspected fraud by several of its top executives, including former CEO and founder, Kenneth Lay, Richard Causey, former head of accounting, and Jeffrey Skilling, who was briefly CEO before the company's collapse. Lay has blamed former chief financial officer Andrew Fastow for "betraying" his trust. Fastow has pleaded guilty, as did his wife Lea, who also worked for Enron. Both will serve prison terms. In exchange for being allowed to serve their sentences sequentially (the Fastows have two young sons), Fastow has agreed to assist in the ongoing investigations. Prosecutors expect Fastow's testimony to help convict Lay on charges ranging from bank and securities fraud to insider trading. Lay insists he did not know what was going on in the firm before it filed for bankruptcy and reported losses of $1 billion. "I cannot take responsibility for criminal conduct that I was not aware of," Lay told CNN. "Enron was a company with about 30,000 employees in about 30 different countries." The problem with Lay's "I didn't

know" defense, according to Professor Larry Soderquist of Vanderbilt University Law School, is that "fraud was Enron's most important product." Top executives who dealt with Lay on a daily basis were the alleged engineers of the fraud that formed the basis of the company's skyrocketing profitability. Observers are asking how it is possible to earn millions for running a company and not know where and how its profits have been earned.[1]

Chapter Overview

The dark cloud of scandal visited the boardrooms of dozens of U.S. corporations during the first years of the 21st century. Ethical failures in a number of large or well-known firms led to lawsuits, indictments, fines, guilty pleas, jail sentences for high-profile executives, the financial failures of several powerful U.S. businesses, job losses for thousands of former employees at these firms, and the loss of billions of dollars in investors' savings, which had been held as stock shares in these companies. Other troubled firms included Global Crossing, HealthSouth, the investment firm Crédit Suisse First Boston, and even the venerable auction house, Sotheby's. Enron's auditor, highly respected public accounting firm Arthur Andersen, declared bankruptcy after information spread about its failure to disclose accurate information to shareholders and regulatory officials—to say nothing of its shredding of Enron documents. The image of the CEO—and business in general—suffered as the evening news carried dramatic pictures of the so-called *perp walk*—parading indicted and handcuffed corporate executives before the media in an exercise previously reserved for local criminals. Following a series of disclosures in congressional investigations and from civil and criminal investigations by state attorneys general, in 2002 Congress enacted the **Sarbanes-Oxley Act** to correct these abuses by adding oversight for the nation's major companies and a special oversight board to regulate public accounting firms that audit the financial records of these corporations.

They Said It

A small personal matter has been blown out of all proportion, and with such venom and gore.

—Martha Stewart (b. 1941)
American entrepreneur
(on learning of her sentence of 5 months in jail and 5 months of house arrest, following her conviction for obstruction of justice in the ImClone stock scandal)

As we discussed in Chapter 1, the underlying aim of business is to serve customers at a profit. But most companies try to do more than that, looking for ways to give back to customers, society, and the environment. When does a company's self-interest conflict with society's and customers' well-being? And must the goal of seeking profits conflict with upholding high principles of right and wrong? In response to the second question, a growing number of businesses of all sizes are answering no.

Concern for Ethical and Societal Issues

business ethics
standards of business conduct and moral values.

An organization that wants to prosper over the long term cannot do so without considering **business ethics,** the standards of conduct and moral values governing actions and decisions in the work environment. Businesses also must take into account a wide range of social issues, including how a decision will affect the environment, employees, and customers. These issues are at the heart of social responsibility, the philosophies, policies, procedures, and actions directed toward the enhancement of society's welfare as a primary objective. In short, businesses must find the delicate balance between doing what is right and doing what is profitable.

In business, as in life, deciding what is right or wrong in a given situation does not always involve a clear-cut choice. As Figure 2.1 shows, businesses have many responsibilities—to customers, to employees, to investors, and to society as a whole. Sometimes conflicts can arise in trying to serve the different needs of these separate constituencies. The ethical values of executives and individual employees at all levels can influence the decisions and actions a business takes. Throughout your own business career, you will encounter many situations in which you will need to weigh right and wrong before making a decision or taking action. So, we begin our discussion of business ethics by focusing on individual ethics.

Customers   Employees   Investors   Society

FIGURE 2.1
Constituencies to Which Businesses Are Responsible

Business ethics are also shaped by the ethical climate within an organization. Codes of conduct and ethical standards play increasingly significant roles in businesses in which doing the right thing is both supported and applauded. This chapter demonstrates how a firm can create a framework to encourage—and even demand—high standards of ethical behavior and social responsibility from its employees. The chapter also considers the complex question of what business owes to society and how societal forces mold the actions of businesses. Finally, it examines the influence of business ethics and social responsibility on global business.

Concept Check

1. To whom do businesses have responsibilities?
2. If a firm is meeting all its responsibilities to others, why do ethical conflicts arise?

The New Ethical Environment

Over the past five years, business ethics have been in the spotlight as never before. High-profile investigations, lawsuits, arrests, and even convictions, as well as business failures due to fraud and corruption, have created a long string of headline news. While these events have brought about rapid change in many areas and new laws to prevent them from happening again, they have also obscured for many people the fact that most companies and their leaders are highly ethical.[2] A recent CNN/USA Today/Gallup poll found that only 17 percent of U.S. respondents rated business executives highly, down from 25 percent a year earlier.[3] And 94 percent of respondents to a *BusinessWeek Online* survey felt that misdeeds by companies such as Enron and WorldCom were a "very serious" or "somewhat serious" problem.[4]

Yet the vast majority of business owners and managers have built and maintained enduring companies without breaking the rules. As Joseph Neubauer, CEO of Aramark Worldwide Corp., points out and most executives are aware, "It takes a lifetime to build a reputation, and only a short time to lose it all." Companies that show high earnings and steady sales growth over time were led by CEOs who personified the best in management practices. These leaders may not be household names, but they and hundreds of other mainstream business executives are highly respected for their integrity, honesty, and business ethics. One example of a firm with a longstanding commitment to ethical practice is Johnson & Johnson, the giant multinational manufacturer of health-care products. The sixth most admired company in the world, according to *Fortune,* Johnson & Johnson has abided by the same basic code of ethics, its well-known Credo, for more than 50 years. The Credo, reproduced in Figure 2.2, remains the ethical standard against which the company's employees periodically evaluate how well their firm is performing. Management is pledged to address any lapses that are reported.[5]

It is clear, though, that not all companies successfully set and meet high ethical standards. Thousands of employees who lost their jobs due to management misdeeds and millions of investors who saw their savings melt away as the value of their investments in these rogue companies either plummeted or vanished entirely felt betrayed lately, spurring Congress, regulatory agencies, and businesses everywhere to take new steps to rectify problems and prevent them from occurring in the future. A survey of about 125 companies in 22 countries found, for instance, that more than three out of four

Our Credo

We believe our first responsibility is to the doctors, nurses and patients, to mothers and fathers and all others who use our products and services. In meeting their needs everything we do must be of high quality. We must constantly strive to reduce our costs in order to maintain reasonable prices. Customers' orders must be serviced promptly and accurately. Our suppliers and distributors must have an opportunity to make a fair profit.

We are responsible to our employees, the men and women who work with us throughout the world. Everyone must be considered as an individual. We must respect their dignity and recognize their merit. They must have a sense of security in their jobs. Compensation must be fair and adequate, and working conditions clean, orderly and safe. We must be mindful of ways to help our employees fulfill their family responsibilities. Employees must feel free to make suggestions and complaints. There must be equal opportunity for employment, development and advancement for those qualified. We must provide competent management, and their actions must be just and ethical.

We are responsible to the communities in which we live and work and to the world community as well. We must be good citizens — support good works and charities and bear our fair share of taxes. We must encourage civic improvements and better health and education. We must maintain in good order the property we are privileged to use, protecting the environment and natural resources.

Our final responsibility is to our stockholders. Business must make a sound profit. We must experiment with new ideas. Research must be carried on, innovative programs developed and mistakes paid for. New equipment must be purchased, new facilities provided and new products launched. Reserves must be created to provide for adverse times. When we operate according to these principles, the stockholders should realize a fair return.

FIGURE 2.2
Johnson & Johnson's Credo

Source: "Our Company: Our Credo," Johnson & Johnson Web site, http://www.jnj.com.

are setting up ethics standards and codes, up from less than half in 1991. Cropping up more frequently in such ethical guidelines are not just issues already covered by law, such as contracts, employment discrimination, and safety, but also broader ethical concerns about the environment, child labor, and human rights.[6] With passage of the Sarbanes-Oxley Act of 2002, which establishes new rules and regulations for securities trading and accounting practices, a company is also required to publish its code of ethics, if it has one, and inform the public of any changes made to it. The new law may actually motivate even more firms to develop written codes and guidelines for ethical business behavior.

In addition to the growing number of firms currently creating their own ethical codes, others have proceeded to implement them through the seven steps specified during the 1990s when the federal government created the U.S. Sentencing Commission to institutionalize ethics compliance programs that would establish high ethical standards and end corporate misconduct.[7] The requirements for such programs are shown in Table 2.1.

The current ethical environment of business also includes the appointment of new corporate officers specifically charged with deterring wrongdoing and ensuring that ethical standards are met. These ethics compliance officers, whose numbers are rapidly rising, are responsible for conducting employee training programs that help spot potential fraud and abuse within the firm, investigating sexual harassment and discrimination charges, and monitoring any potential conflicts of interest. Some also ensure that financial reporting of the financial statements is accurate.[8] This last responsibility is more important than ever, now that the Sarbanes-Oxley Act requires financial officers and CEOs to personally certify the validity of companies' financial statements.

Table 2.1   Minimum Requirements for Ethics Compliance Programs

- Standards and procedures, such as codes of ethics, capable of detecting and preventing misconduct
- High-level personnel responsible for ethics compliance programs
- No substantial discretionary authority given to individuals with a propensity for misconduct
- Effective communication of ethical code requirements through ethics training programs
- Establishment of systems to monitor, audit, and report misconduct
- Consistent enforcement of ethical codes and punishment
- Continuous improvement of the ethics compliance program

Source: U.S. Sentencing Commission, *Federal Sentencing Guidelines Manual.* St. Paul, MN: West Publishing, 1984, Ch. 8.

BUSINESS TOOL KIT

The Basics of Business Ethics

Business ethics are big business these days. The downfall of such corporate giants as Enron, WorldCom, and Global Crossing demonstrates the power of decisions made *not* based on ethical values. Doing the right thing still matters in business, so developing your own personal arsenal of ethics before facing sticky situations at work can go a long way. Knowing your limitations of what you will and won't do in any certain situation helps both your decision making and your value as an employee. Here are a few tips on developing your own personal code of ethics at work:

1. Evaluate your personal moral and/or religious system for absolutes. Oftentimes, what you've been taught at home about ethics and fair play will resonate in the business world as well.

2. Role-play iffy ethical situations and gauge your response. If asked by a manager to shred documents after hours, what would you do? If offered a job at a company that has sweatshops in Malaysia, would you take the job? Realize that right and wrong in the business world are not always clear-cut, so it's best to evaluate a situation before you respond to it.

3. Today's headlines illustrate that ethics come from the top. If your company's top management or CEO doesn't place an obvious emphasis on ethics, seek out their posi-

tion on the subject. If one is not already in place, use your own personal set of ethics to encourage your department in developing a professional set of ethics for the company.

4. When you are faced with an ethical dilemma, there are three questions you should ask yourself, according to the authors of *The Power of Ethical Management:* Is it legal? Is it balanced? How will it make me feel about myself? Authors Kenneth Blanchard and Norman Vincent Peale believe that asking these three questions gives you a more balanced approach to the dilemma, especially if it falls into that "gray" area.

5. If one is offered at your school, consider taking a business ethics course. Many colleges and businesses schools are now offering a required class on the legal, ethical, and political aspects of business. If you are a business major, it would be wise for you to take a course in ethics before you graduate to the "real world" of right and wrong.

Sources: Matthew Phillips, "College Courses Offer Basics for Dealing Ethically in Business," *The Business Review: Albany Edition,* accessed February 23, 2003; Paul Singer, "Business Schools Add Ethics in Wake of Corporate Scandals," *Associated Press State & Local Wire,* August 16, 2002, accessed at http://www .kellogg.northwestern.edu/news/hits/020816ap.htm; "Business Ethics: The Foundation of Effective Leadership," http://www.onlinewbc.gov/docs/ manage/ethics.html, accessed August 10, 2001.

Individuals Make a Difference

In today's business environment, individuals can make the difference in ethical expectations and behavior. As executives, managers, and employees demonstrate their personal ethical principles—or lack of ethical principles—the expectations and actions of those who work for and with them can change.

What is the current status of individual business ethics in the U.S.? Although ethical behavior can be difficult to track or even define in all circumstances, evidence suggests that some individuals act unethically or illegally on the job. A poll of U.S. employees found that 30 percent knew of or suspected unethical behavior in their companies. In another poll, the main types of unethical behavior observed by employees were lying, withholding information, abusing or intimidating employees, inaccurately reporting the amount of time worked, and discrimination. Each year, U.S. organizations lose more than $400 billion to fraud, or an average of $9 per day per employee.[9]

Technology seems to have expanded the range and impact of unethical behavior. For example, anyone with computer access to data has the potential to steal or manipulate the data or to shut down the system, even from a remote location. Often, the people who hack into a company's computers are employees, and some observers consider employee attacks to be the most expensive. They often result in the theft of intellectual property, such as patented or copyrighted information. Computer technology also helps people at one company attack another. Steven Cade, whose business, La Jolla Club Golf Co., specializes in child-sized golf clubs, recently admitted to using the Internet to spread deceptive

Stage 1: Preconventional

Individual is mainly looking out for his or her own interests. Rules are followed only out of fear of punishment or hope of reward.

↓

Stage 2: Conventional

Individual considers the interests and expectations of others in making decisions. Rules are followed because it is a part of belonging to the group.

↓

Stage 3: Postconventional

Individual follows personal principles for resolving ethical dilemmas. He or she considers personal, group, and societal interests.

FIGURE 2.3
Stages of Moral and Ethical Development

> *They Said It*
>
> I would rather be the man who bought the Brooklyn Bridge than the one who sold it.
>
> —*Will Rogers (1879–1935)*
> *American humorist*

messages about a much larger competitor, Callaway Golf Co. Cade admitted he used 27 different false names to post these messages online.

Nearly every employee, at every level, wrestles with ethical questions at some point or another. Some rationalize questionable behavior by saying, "Everybody's doing it." Others act unethically because they feel pressured on their jobs or have to meet performance quotas. Yet, some avoid unethical acts that don't mesh with their personal values and morals. To help you understand the differences in the ways individuals arrive at ethical choices, the next section focuses on how personal ethics and morals develop.

Development of Individual Ethics

Individuals typically develop ethical standards in the three stages shown in Figure 2.3: the preconventional, conventional, and postconventional stages. In the preconventional stage, individuals primarily consider their own needs and desires in making decisions. They obey external rules only because they are afraid of punishment or hope to receive rewards if they comply.

In the second stage, the conventional stage, individuals are aware of and act in response to their duty to others, including their obligations to their family members, coworkers, and organizations. The expectations of these groups influence how they choose between what is acceptable and unacceptable in certain situations. Self-interest, however, continues to play a role in decisions.

The postconventional stage, the final stage, represents the highest level of ethical and moral behavior. The individual is able to move beyond mere self-interest and duty and take the larger needs of society into account as well. He or she has developed personal ethical principles for determining what is right and can apply those principles in a wide variety of situations.

An individual's stage in moral and ethical development is determined by a huge number of factors. Experiences help to shape responses to different situations. A person's family, educational, cultural, and religious backgrounds can also play a role, as can the environment within the firm. Individuals can also have different styles of deciding ethical dilemmas, no matter what their stage of moral development.

To help you understand and prepare for the ethical dilemmas you may confront in your career, let's take a closer look at some of the factors involved in solving ethical questions on the job.

On-the-Job Ethical Dilemmas

In the fast-paced world of business, you will sometimes be called on to weigh the ethics of decisions that can affect not just your own future but possibly the futures of your fellow workers, your company, and its customers. As already noted, it's not always easy to distinguish between what is right and wrong in many business situations, especially when the needs and concerns of various parties conflict.

Consider the situation decision makers at pharmaceutical companies face. Under worldwide pressure to make life-saving drugs affordable in developing countries, the drug industry faces the possibility that it might have to drastically lower prices on expensive new drugs. Or under a "health care crisis" trade rule set by the World Trade Organization, drug makers might have to allow countries to develop their own cheap generic versions of drugs that are legally still under patent protection. During the anthrax scare that followed the 9/11 terrorist attacks, the U.S. and Canadian governments threatened to violate drug makers' patents themselves to make an anthrax antidote affordable. While they are still conscious of their responsibility to shareholders who expect the companies to be profitable, some drug firms are now taking the initiative to act against diseases. Merck has been treating 25 million people a year for river blindness at no cost, and after years of such efforts, it may soon eradicate this debilitating disease. Five drug companies have joined with United Nations agencies to cut the prices of HIV drugs. Aventis and Bristol-Myers Squibb are working with the World Health Organization to distribute a drug that failed to treat cancer but is a powerful antidote to sleeping sickness. The Swiss firm Novartis is giving away a drug combination that could eradicate leprosy and is selling a new malaria drug to developing countries at cost. But says Novartis CEO Daniel Vasella, "I need to justify what I am doing to my shareholders."[10]

As these examples illustrate, solving ethical dilemmas is not easy. In many cases, each possible decision can have unpleasant consequences and positive benefits that must be evaluated. The ethical issues that confront managers of drug companies are just one example of many different types of ethical questions encountered in the workplace. Figure 2.4 identifies four of the most common ethical challenges that businesspeople face: conflict of interest, honesty and integrity, loyalty versus truth, and whistleblowing.

FIGURE 2.4
Common Business Ethical Challenges

Conflict of Interest   A **conflict of interest** exists when a businessperson is faced with a situation in which an action benefiting one person or group has the potential to harm another. Conflicts of interest may pose ethical challenges when they involve the businessperson's own interests and those of someone to whom he or she has a duty or when they involve two parties to whom the businessperson has a duty. Lawyers, business consultants, or advertising agencies would face a conflict of interest if they represented two competing companies: A strategy that would most benefit one of the client companies might harm the other client. Similarly, a real estate agent would face an ethical conflict if he or she represented both the buyer and seller in a transaction. In general, the buyer benefits from a low price, and the seller benefits from a high price. Handling the situation responsibly would be possible, but it would also be difficult. A conflict may also exist between someone's personal interests and those of an organization or its customers. An offer of gifts or bribes for special treatment creates a situation in which the buyer, but not necessarily his or her company, may benefit personally.

conflict of interest
situation in which a business decision may be influenced by the potential for personal gain.

Ethical ways to handle conflicts of interest include (1) avoiding them and (2) disclosing them. Some companies have policies against taking on clients who are competitors of existing clients. Most businesses and government agencies have written policies prohibiting employees from accepting gifts or specifying a maximum gift value of, say, $50. Or a member of a board of directors or committee might abstain from voting on a decision in which he or she has a personal interest. In other situations, people state their potential conflict of interest so that the people affected can decide whether to get information or help they need from another source instead.

Honesty and Integrity   Employers highly value honesty and integrity. An employee who is honest can be counted on to tell the truth. An employee with **integrity** goes beyond truthfulness. Having integrity means adhering to deeply felt ethical principles in business situations. It includes doing what you say you will do and accepting responsibility for mistakes. Behaving with honesty and integrity inspires trust, and as a result, it can help build long-term relationships with customers, employers, suppliers, and the public. Employees, in turn, want their managers and the company as a whole to treat them honestly and with integrity. One ethical issue concerning employees that has surfaced recently involves insurance policies. Many companies, especially banks, have built up huge tax-free investments by taking out life insurance policies on employees without their knowledge. When an employee or retiree died, the company collected the insurance, and that person's survivors never knew about it. New rules require firms to obtain employee permission, however, and employees are winning more lawsuits in so-called "janitor's insurance" cases.[11]

Unfortunately, violations of honesty and integrity are widespread. Some people misrepresent their academic credentials and previous work experience on their résumés or job applications. Others steal from their employers by taking home supplies or products without permission or by carrying out personal business during the time they are being paid to work. Many employees lie to protect themselves from punishment or to make their performance look better than it really is. Following the merger of CUC International and HFS to form Cendant, a major provider of travel (trip.com and CheapTickets), auto rentals (Avis and Budget), and real estate (Century 21, Coldwell Banker, ERA) services, managers from HFS began to find financial discrepancies. They discovered that the top managers at CUC had for years been reporting incorrect financial data about the company, claiming $500 million in profits that were purely fictional. CUC's former head, Walter Forbes, said he didn't know about the misbehavior and wasn't responsible for it. He resigned in

whistleblowing
employee's disclosure to government authorities or the media of illegal, immoral, or unethical practices committed by an organization.

exchange for a severance package worth $47.5 million. Others have challenged Forbes's statements of ignorance, and Cendant has taken Forbes to court in an attempt to force him to repay the entire amount.[12]

Companies need to deal honestly and fairly with their employees also. Otherwise, they can encounter costly problems (see the "Hits & Misses" box).

Loyalty versus Truth   Businesspeople expect their employees to be loyal and to act in the best interests of the company. But when the truth about a company is not favorable, an ethical conflict can arise. Individuals may have to decide between loyalty to the company and truthfulness in business relationships. People resolve such dilemmas in various ways. Some place the highest value on loyalty, even at the expense of truth. Others avoid volunteering negative information but answer truthfully if someone asks them a specific question. People may emphasize truthfulness and actively disclose negative information, especially if the cost of silence is high, as in the case of operating a malfunctioning aircraft or selling tainted medicine. Two investigators for Los Alamos National Laboratory in New Mexico, home of some of the U.S.'s most sensitive defense secrets, reported the loss of $2.7 million worth of missing computers and other property and the abuse of lab-issued credit cards (with which one employee had tried to buy a car). An investigation by the Department of Energy found that even if the lab was not guilty of covering up such "blatant acts of criminality," it had at least subjected the two men to intimidation and pressure to keep quiet, including issuing a series of memos urging employees to "resist the temptation to 'spill your guts.'" "I believe in being dedicated to your boss," said one of the two men, "but there's a line you don't cross, and they crossed that line and began to perceive wrong as right."[13]

Whistleblowing   When an individual does encounter unethical or illegal actions at work, the person must decide what action to take. Sometimes it is possible to resolve the problem by working through channels within the organization. If that fails, the person should weigh the potential damages to the greater public good. If the damage is significant, a person may conclude that the only solution is to blow the whistle. **Whistleblowing** is an employee's disclosure to government authorities or the media of illegal, immoral, or unethical practices. The two men who reported the theft of property at Los Alamos were whistleblowers.

A whistleblower must weigh a number of issues in deciding whether to come forward. Resolving an ethical problem within the organization can be more effective, assuming higher level managers cooperate. A company that values ethics will try to correct a problem, and staying at a company that does not value ethics may not be worthwhile. In some cases, however, people resort to whistleblowing because they believe the unethical behavior is causing significant damage that outweighs the risk that the company will retaliate against the whistleblower. Those risks have been real in the past. About half of whistleblowers who responded to a survey by the National Whistleblower Center said they were fired for reporting illegal conduct, and most of the other respondents said they had been harassed or unfairly disciplined at work after reporting wrongdoing at their firms.[14] The two men who blew the whistle at Los Alamos were fired, though they have since been rehired to help in the investigation at the lab.

State and federal laws protect whistleblowers in certain situations, such as reports of discrimination, and the Sarbanes-Oxley Act of 2002 now requires that firms in the private sector provide procedures for anonymous reporting of accusations of fraud. Under the act, anyone who retaliates against an employee for taking concerns of unlawful conduct to a public official can be prosecuted. Whistleblowers who still experience dramatic retribution for their actions have recourse thanks to the act—those who have been fired, demoted, threatened, or harassed have 90 days to file a complaint with the U.S. Department of Labor.

Obviously, whistleblowing and other ethical issues arise relatively infrequently in firms with strong organizational climates of ethical behavior. The next section examines how a business can develop an environment that discourages unethical behavior among individuals.

Concept Check

1. What role can an ethics compliance officer play in a firm?
2. What are honesty and integrity and how do they differ?
3. How can loyalty and truth come into conflict for an employee?

HITS & MISSES

Wal-Mart's Gender Problem

It's a landmark lawsuit intended to prove Wal-Mart discriminates against its female workers on pay. And it's been made a class-action suit, covering women who worked at the giant retailer anywhere in the U.S. since late 1998—a group that could reach 1.8 million, or the size of Philadelphia's entire population. The outcome will be tremendously influential and potentially extremely costly for Wal-Mart. (Home Depot settled a class-action sex-bias suit a few years ago for $104 million.)

Based on settlements of similar lawsuits against firms like The Coca-Cola Co., Lucky Stores, Cracker Barrel, and State Farm Insurance, an adverse ruling could cost Wal-Mart hundreds of millions of dollars and bring its pay and promotion decisions under outside scrutiny and supervision for a decade or more.

The crux of the suit is the claim that women employees, who make up 65 percent of Wal-Mart's hourly-paid workforce, earn 5 to 15 percent less than men in comparable jobs, even when the women have higher job-performance ratings and more seniority. Another complaint raised in the suit, brought by two current and four former employees, is that fewer women than men are promoted to management positions.

Company officials insist the firm does not discriminate and says any complaints of bias represent isolated cases. It has been working to create a new wage structure to increase the pay of some workers and tie executive bonuses to results such as the promotion of more females to management positions. But the claimants are asking for more, including a court-appointed watchdog to monitor employment practices as well as back earnings and punitive damages.

Other retailers will be watching the case closely. Retailing is one of the top 20 occupations for women in the U.S.

QUESTIONS FOR CRITICAL THINKING

1. Some observers in the retail industry believe the Wal-Mart case will prompt other companies to review their own employment practices, while others say most retailers have already ensured that they pay equal money for equal performance. If you were a Wal-Mart competitor, would you review your pay scales and promotion policies as a result of this suit? Why or why not?
2. What do you think are some advantages and disadvantages of having a court-appointed monitor to oversee ethical practices in a firm?

Sources: Adam Geller, "World's Largest Private Employer Finds Union at Back Door," *Mobile Register*, October 17, 2004, pp. F1, F5; Stephanie Armour, "Wal-Mart in Record Sex-Bias Lawsuit," *USA Today*, June 23, 2004, p. A1; Stephanie Armour and Lorrie Grant, "Wal-Mart Suit Could Ripple through Industry," *USA Today*, June 23, 2004, p. B4; Ann Zimmerman, "Wal-Mart Plans Changes to Wages, Labor Practices," *The Wall Street Journal*, June 7, 2004, p. B3.

How Organizations Shape Ethical Conduct

No individual makes decisions in a vacuum. Choices are strongly influenced by the standards of conduct established within the organizations where people work. Most ethical lapses in business reflect the values of the firms' corporate cultures.

As shown in Figure 2.5, development of a corporate culture to support business ethics happens on four levels: ethical awareness, ethical reasoning, ethical action, and ethical leadership. If any of these four factors is missing, the ethical climate in an organization will weaken.

Ethical Awareness

The foundation of an ethical climate is ethical awareness. As we have already seen, ethical dilemmas occur frequently in the workplace. So, employees need help in identifying ethical problems when they occur. Workers also need guidance about how the firm expects them to respond.

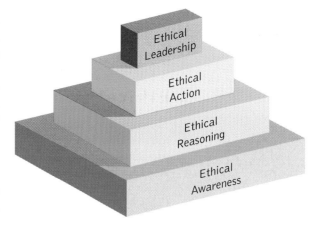

FIGURE 2.5
Structure of an Ethical Environment

Citibank encourages consumers to use their credit wisely. The company uses its Web site to educate credit card users about the "rules" of credit and ways to spend responsibly, prevent fraud, protect their identity, understand different types of credit, apply for credit, budget wisely, and use credit bureau reports.

Courtesy of Citigroup, Inc.

code of conduct formal statement that defines how the organization expects and requires employees to resolve ethical issues.

One way for a firm to provide this support is to develop a **code of conduct,** a formal statement that defines how the organization expects and requires employees to resolve ethical questions. Johnson & Johnson's Credo, presented earlier, is such a code. At the most basic level, a code of conduct may simply specify ground rules for acceptable behavior, such as identifying the laws and regulations that employees must obey. Other companies use their codes of conduct to identify key corporate values and provide frameworks that guide employees as they resolve moral and ethical dilemmas.

Canada-based Nortel Networks, an international telecommunications giant with customers in 150 countries, uses a code of conduct to define its values and help employees put them into practice. The code of conduct defines seven core values that Nortel requires as it strives to become known as a company of integrity. The code also defines standards for conduct among employees and between employees and the company's shareholders, customers, suppliers, and communities. Employees are expected to treat one another with respect, including respect for individual and cultural differences, protect the company's assets, and fulfill whatever commitments they make. The code of conduct also states that each employee is responsible for behaving consistently with its standards and for reporting possible violations of the code. Nortel provides each employee with a copy of this code of conduct and also posts it on its Web site.[15]

Other firms incorporate similar codes in their policy manuals or mission statements; some issue a code of conduct or statement of values in the form of a small card that employees and managers can carry with them. Harley-Davidson has developed a brief code of ethics that employees can apply both at work and in their personal lives. It reads: "Tell the truth, keep your promises, be fair, respect the individual and encourage intellectual curiosity."

Sometimes companies can express ethical awareness through their advertising, as in the Citibank ad shown above.

Ethical Reasoning

Although a code of conduct can provide an overall framework, it cannot detail a solution for every ethical situation. Some ethical questions have black-and-white answers, but others do not. Businesses must provide the tools employees need to evaluate the options and arrive at suitable decisions.

Many firms have instituted ethics training programs. More than 50 percent of the employees surveyed in one study reported that their companies provide training in the subject. Lockheed Martin Corp. has developed a training program in the form of interactive lessons that employees can access online. The sessions include cases performed by actors, plus tests in the form of multiple-choice questions. They cover a variety of business-related topics, from security to sexual harassment. The company also keeps tabs on which employees have completed which training sessions. In addition, Lockheed Martin uses a game called the Ethics Challenge, in which the players use cards and tokens to read about and resolve ethical quandaries based on real-life situations. Everyone in the company, from hourly workers to the chairman, is required to play the Ethics Challenge once per year.

Many authorities debate whether ethics can actually be taught, and one recent study suggests that a corporate ethics program to deter theft had the greatest impact on employees least likely to steal from the company in the first place.[16] But training can give employees an opportunity to practice applying ethical values to hypothetical situations as a prelude to applying the same standards to real-world situations.

Ethical Action

Codes of conduct and ethics training help employees to recognize and reason through ethical problems. In addition, firms must also provide structures and approaches that allow decisions to be turned into ethical actions. Texas Instruments gives its employees a reference card to help them make ethical decisions on the job. The size of a standard business card, it lists the following guidelines:

- Does it comply with our values?
- If you do it, will you feel bad?
- How will it look in the newspaper?
- If you know it's wrong, don't do it!
- If you're not sure, ask.
- Keep asking until you get an answer.

Goals set for the business as a whole and for individual departments and employees can affect ethical behavior. A firm whose managers set unrealistic goals for employee performance may find an increase in cheating, lying, and other misdeeds, as employees attempt to protect themselves. In today's Internet economy, the high value placed on speed can create a climate in which ethical behavior is sometimes challenged. Ethical decisions often require careful and quiet thought, and such thought seems to be nearly impossible in a business that is moving at warp speed.

Some companies encourage ethical action by providing support for employees faced with dilemmas. One common tool is an employee hotline, a telephone number that employees can call, often anonymously, for advice or to report unethical behavior they have witnessed. Nortel Networks, for example, operates a Business Ethics Advice Line. Employees from around the world can contact the advice line via phone or e-mail to ask for advice in applying the code of conduct in specific situations. Ethics compliance officers at some firms, as mentioned previously, are responsible for guiding employees through ethical minefields.

Ethical Leadership

Executives must not only talk about ethical behavior but also demonstrate it in their actions. This principle requires employees to be personally committed to the company's core values and be willing to base their actions on them. In a recent survey, employees questioned about ethical leadership said they felt less pressure to commit misconduct in their organizations when leaders and managers behaved ethically. They also reported being more satisfied with their organizations overall. Consistent with these findings, another large-scale study found that when employees think their employer's ethics program was designed primarily to protect upper management from being blamed for misconduct, the program actually promotes unethical behavior.[17]

One important way for business leaders to model ethical behavior is to admit when they are wrong and correct their organization's mistakes and problems. The Red Cross, already under scrutiny for its use of funds, was widely criticized for announcing plans to divert some of the nearly $1 billion raised under the auspices of a special 9/11 Liberty Fund. The charity said it would create a blood bank and upgrade its telecommunications equipment with some of the money. The fund had been created for the aid of victims of the 9/11 terrorist attacks, and most people made donations to it for that specific purpose. When the public protested, the Red Cross abandoned plans to divert the money and pledged to use all of the Liberty Fund for its original purpose, as well as to revamp its fund-raising practices so that such problems do not recur. "We made some large mistakes," said chairman David McLaughlin at a news conference.[18]

BEST BUSINESS PRACTICES

High Gas Prices Fuel the Move to Hybrids

The U.S. is captive to its dependence on imported oil. Easy-to-work oil fields are drying up, and although new ones are discovered every year, worldwide demand is growing even faster, pushed along in part by rapidly developing economies like China's.

U.S. consumers are used to high gasoline prices, but recent price spikes have led many to consider hybrid cars that blend internal combustion engines with battery-backed electric motors, resulting in incredible mileage. Says one marketing analyst, "The industry seems to be overcoming the image of hybrids as being little two-seaters with skinny tires."

In fact, the public is so eager to take a hybrid for a test drive that sales for the Toyota Prius jumped from 299 to nearly 4,400 in a single year, threatening to outstrip supply. "Clearly, the extraordinary response to Prius took us by surprise," said a Toyota senior vice president. The Prius started as a compact car but has been extensively made over as a midsize sedan with a slightly higher price tag—and a long waiting line.

Honda has been making the hybrid Insight for several years and is adding a hybrid model of its popular Civic, with 30 percent better mileage than its namesake, and a new hybrid Accord, with a V-6 engine that ups its own mileage by using less gas at cruising speed.

Ford has entered the market with the first hybrid SUV, the four-cylinder Escape, which the company calls the "cleanest and most fuel-efficient SUV on the road." While Ford plans to make about 20,000 cars per year, customers will have to wait for the Escape, as well. Only a few thousand will be available at a time.

Toyota is also entering the luxury SUV market with the Lexus RX400h, with what's called a "major expansion" of hybrid technology—and a backlog of orders 9,000 units long.

Drivers seem to be sending a message by accepting high prices and long waiting lines for these gas-saving cars, many of which are selling out each year's production. The auto industry is listening. "You really don't start to see the economic advantages [of hybrid ownership] for several years," says one analyst. "But people are willing to pay the premium to make an environmental statement." The average driver will need about six years to recover the higher sticker price of his or her new hybrid car, assuming stable gasoline prices. Despite some potential challenges in making as many cars as the public is ready to buy, many manufacturers feel it's crucial to make the switch to environmentally friendly cars. "We think of it as enlightened self-interest," says the president of Toyota Motor Corp. Those who ignore the public's desire for cars that save fuel and reduce pollution "won't be in business" in the future.

QUESTIONS FOR CRITICAL THINKING

1. Makers of hybrid cars have stressed great mileage in their marketing, but they have also started making sure that the cars are becoming roomier inside, with easier maintenance and lower emissions. What market forces have shaped these changes?

2. What more do you think car manufacturers can do to position themselves as environmentally responsible firms?

Sources: Chester Dawson, "How Hybrids Are Going Mainstream," *Business-Week*, November 1, 2004, p. 41; James R. Healey, "Accord Hybrid the Best One Yet," *USA Today*, September 24, 2004, p. 9D; Akweli Parker, "Ford to Sell First American Hybrid," *Mobile Register*, August 1, 2004, p. F1.

They Said It

We're not going to see $1 a gallon ever again.

—*Jason Schenker (b. 1977)*
Wachovia Corp. economic analyst

However, ethical leadership should also go one step further and charge each employee at every level with the responsibility to be an ethical leader. Everyone should be aware of transgressions and be willing to defend the organization's standards. The Nortel Networks guidelines specifically communicate these responsibilities. The company tells employees, "You have a responsibility to ask questions when you have doubts about the ethical implications of any given situation or proposed course of action" and "You have a responsibility to report any concerns about business practices within the corporation that may violate this Code of Business Conduct."[19] As noted earlier, Nortel also provides employees with the tools for carrying out these responsibilities.

Perhaps one of the best measures of ethical leadership is whether a company focuses on the welfare of its customers and investors and how well it can perform in the long run. Auto manufacturers, for instance, have been developing hybrid cars, which get great gas mileage and so help protect the environment. Customers are clamoring to buy the new vehicles, as the "Best Business Practices" box explains.

Unfortunately, not all organizations are able to build a solid framework of business ethics. Because the damage from ethical misconduct can powerfully affect a firm's stakeholders—customers, investors, employees, and the public—pressure is exerted on businesses to act in acceptable ways. But when businesses fail, the law must step in to enforce good business practices. Many of the laws that affect specific industries or individuals are described in other chapters in this book. For example, legislation affecting international business operations is discussed in Chapter 4. Laws designed to assist small businesses are examined in Chapter 5. Laws related to labor unions are described in Chapter 9. Legislation related to banking and the securities markets is discussed in Chapters 17 and 18. Finally, for an examination of the legal and governmental forces designed to safeguard society's interests when businesses fail at self-regulation, see the Appendix to Part 1, "The Legal Framework for Business," beginning on page 138.

Concept Check

1. What is a code of conduct?
2. How does ethical leadership contribute to ethical standards throughout a company?

Acting Responsibly to Satisfy Society

A second major issue affecting business is the question of social responsibility. In a general sense, **social responsibility** is management's acceptance of the obligation to consider profit, consumer satisfaction, and societal well-being of equal value in evaluating the firm's performance. It is the recognition that business must be concerned with the qualitative dimensions of consumer, employee, and societal benefits as well as the quantitative measures of sales and profits, by which business performance is traditionally measured. Businesses may exercise social responsibility because such behavior is required by law, because it enhances the company's image, or because management believes it is the ethical course of action.

Historically, a company's social performance has been measured by its contribution to the overall economy and the employment opportunities it provides. Variables such as wage payments often serve to indicate social performance. Although profits and employment remain important, today many factors contribute to an assessment of a firm's social performance, including providing equal employment opportunities; respecting the cultural diversity of employees; responding to environmental concerns; providing a safe, healthy workplace; and producing high-quality products that are safe to use.

A business is also judged by its interactions with the community. To demonstrate their social responsibility, many corporations highlight charitable contributions and community service in their annual reports and on their Web site. Procter & Gamble, for instance, contributes millions of dollars through the Procter & Gamble Fund, corporate contributions, product donations, individual facilities' gifts, and other types of giving. The company donates products to America's Second Harvest, a network of food banks. It donates to universities and research organizations patents that do not fit the company's strategic plans but may offer commercial potential, thereby providing revenue to the organizations that apply the patents.[20]

Some firms measure social performance by conducting **social audits,** formal procedures that identify and evaluate all company activities that relate to social issues such as conservation, employment practices, environmental protection, and philanthropy. The social audit informs management about how well the company is performing in these areas. Based on this information, management may take steps to revise current programs or develop new ones.

Outside groups may conduct their own evaluations of businesses. Various environmental, religious, and public interest groups have created standards of corporate performance. Reports on many of these evaluations are available to the general public. The Council on Economic Priorities produces publications such as *The Better World Investment Guide,* which recommends basing investment decisions on companies' track records on various social issues, including environmental impact, nuclear weapons contracts, community outreach, and advancement of women and minorities. Other groups publicize their evaluations and include critiques of the social responsibility performance of firms. The Center for Science in the Public Interest evaluates the healthfulness of the food marketed to consumers.[21]

Many firms find that consumers evaluate their social track records through their purchase decisions in retail stores. Some consumer groups organize boycotts of companies they find to be socially irresponsible. In a **boycott,** consumers refuse to buy a company's goods or services. Mail Abuse Prevention System (MAPS) offers a new twist on the old-fashioned boycott: a service that blocks incoming e-mail from companies that it believes have sent spam. The company compiles the Real-Time Blackhole List, a list of reported spammers, and for those who subscribe, it deletes mail from those sources or returns

social responsibility
management's acceptance of the obligation to consider profit, consumer satisfaction, and societal well-being of equal value in evaluating the firm's performance.

To the
General
Public

To
Customers

**Business's
Social
Responsibilities**

To
Employees

To Investors
and the
Financial
Community

FIGURE 2.6
Responsibilities of Business

it to the sender. Bouncing the messages back not only spares the receiver, but it can also swamp the sender's Web site so that it effectively shuts down during the onslaught. Companies that place online marketing messages treat MAPS with kid gloves. MessageMedia, for example, says it has refused to work with clients who do not adhere to MAPS guidelines because a misstep by one of its clients could land MessageMedia on the list.[22]

As Figure 2.6 shows, the social responsibilities of business can be classified according to its relationships to the general public, customers, employees, and investors and other members of the financial community. Many of these relationships extend beyond national borders.

Responsibilities to the General Public

The responsibilities of business to the general public include dealing with public health issues, protecting the environment, and developing the quality of the workforce. Many would argue that businesses also have responsibilities to support charitable and social causes and organizations that work toward the greater public good. In other words, they should give back to the communities in which they earn profits. Such efforts are called *corporate philanthropy.* Figure 2.7 summarizes these four responsibilities, which are discussed in the sections that follow.

Public Health Issues   One of the most complex issues facing business as it addresses its ethical and social responsibilities to the general public is public health. Central to the public health debate is the question of what businesses should do about dangerous products like tobacco, alcohol, and handguns. Tobacco products represent a major health risk, contributing to heart disease, stroke, and cancer among smokers. Families and coworkers of smokers share this danger as well, since their exposure to secondhand smoke increases their risks for cancer, asthma, and respiratory infections. Recently, courts have agreed with this assessment of smoking as a health risk, and tobacco companies have been assessed heavy fines to compensate for their actions. In 1998, Altria (then known as Philip Morris) and three other tobacco companies agreed to a $206 billion settlement with 46 states. Two years later, a Florida jury ordered the tobacco industry to pay $145 billion in punitive damages to Florida smokers who had developed illnesses associated with long-term smoking. Altria, whose products represent one of every two cigarettes sold in the U.S., was ordered to pay about half the entire amount. Faced with the prospect of even more legal action, the tobacco companies have spent tens of millions of dollars on socially responsible activities and causes, such as youth smoking prevention programs, food banks, and medical assistance in developing countries. But not everyone is buying the sincerity of the tobacco industry's attempts at social responsibility. In 2003, the U.S. Department of Justice filed a countersuit, demanding that the nation's biggest cigarette makers be ordered to forfeit $289 billion in "ill-gotten gains"—profits derived from a half century of "fraudulent" and dangerous marketing practices.[23]

FIGURE 2.7
Business Responsibilities to the General Public

Public Health Issues
AIDS
Smoking
Alcohol Abuse
Drug Abuse

Protecting the Environment
Avoiding Pollution
Recycling
Green Marketing
Environmentally
  Friendly Technologies

Corporate Philanthropy

Monetary Donations
  to Charitable and
  Social Organizations
Support for Employee
  Volunteer Efforts
Donations of Goods to
  Charitable and
  Social Organizations

Developing the Quality of the Workforce
On-the-Job Training
Education Benefits
Operating Where
  Jobs Are Needed
Valuing Diversity

Substance abuse, including alcohol abuse, is another serious public health problem worldwide. Motor vehicle accidents are a major killer, and drunk drivers cause many serious crashes. Alcohol abuse has also been linked to such major diseases as cirrhosis of the liver. Other risks to public health and safety come from fatty foods, television violence, and motorcycles.

Of particular concern is the impact of such products on vulnerable groups. Alcohol ads appeal to teenagers. Absolut vodka ads have even become collector's items for many teens, raising concerns that the company is encouraging underage drinking. Many consumers view alcohol advertising, whether aimed at adults or young people, as socially irresponsible. Some brewers have tried to counter these views by sponsoring advertising campaigns that promote moderation.

Businesses also face challenges when dealing with the consequences of diseases like AIDS, which is especially dangerous because, on average, five years pass between a person's first exposure to HIV and actual development of the disease. During this period, people may not show any symptoms, and they probably don't even know they have the virus, but they are still carriers who can transmit the disease to others. This large pool of unknown carriers contributes greatly to the rapid spread of the disease.

The onslaught of AIDS has forced companies to educate their workers about how to deal with employees and customers who have the deadly disease. Health care for AIDS patients can be incredibly expensive, straining the ability of small companies to pay for health-care coverage. Do companies have the right to test potential employees for the AIDS virus and avoid this expense? Some people believe that this screening would violate the rights of job applicants; others feel that a firm has a responsibility not to place AIDS patients in jobs where they could infect members of the general public. These are difficult questions. In resolving them, a business must balance the rights of individuals against the rights of society in general.

Protecting the Environment   Businesses consume huge amounts of energy, which increases the use of fossil fuels like coal and oil for energy production. This activity introduces carbon dioxide and sulfur into the earth's atmosphere, substances that many scientists believe will result in dramatic climate changes during the 21st century. Meanwhile, the sulfur from fossil fuels combines with water vapor in the air to form sulfuric acid. The acid rain that results can kill fish and trees and pollute ground water. Wind can carry the sulfur around the entire globe. Sulfur from U.S. factories is damaging Canadian forests, and pollution from London smokestacks has been found in the forests and lakes of Scandinavia. Other production and manufacturing methods leave behind large quantities of waste materials that can further pollute the environment and fill already bulging landfills. Some products themselves, particularly electronics, are difficult to reuse or recycle. Junked parts can introduce poisons like lead, cadmium, and mercury into ground-water supplies.[24]

For many managers, finding ways to minimize the **pollution** and other environmental damage caused by their products or operating processes has become an important economic, legal, and social issue. The solutions can be difficult, and expensive. It costs computer makers about $20 to recycle each old computer, for instance.[25] Drivers may face high costs, too. Hybrid cars use a combination of gas and electricity to power their engines and promise much higher fuel efficiency than conventional autos. As gasoline prices reached the previously unheard of $2 per gallon mark, sales of U.S. hybrids reached 5,000 a month. Most of the purchasers chose the $20,000 Honda Civic hybrid, which gets about 48 miles per gallon, 30 to 50 percent better than the gas-powered version. Other hybrid auto purchasers chose the $20,000 Toyota Prius or the $21,000 Honda Insight. However, the fuel saving isn't cheap. Experts figure that adding the electric system to the car also adds about $3,500 to the sticker price.[26]

The more exotic Hy-wire, a hydrogen-powered prototype that cost General Motors $5 million to build, can reach 100 miles an hour with only water vapor as exhaust. But even though Toyota, Honda, and BMW have similar prototypes in the works, cutting costs enough to market the vehicles and earn a profit continues to be a major stumbling block.[27]

Despite the difficulty, however, companies are finding they can be environmentally friendly and profitable, too. Over the past quarter century, 3M has reduced emissions of hazardous wastes, mainly by finding alternatives to toxic solvents. The changes have saved the company hundreds of millions of dollars. And the $3.1 million that Dow Chemical has spent to reduce toxic emissions at its Midland, Michigan, plant actually resulted in savings of $5.4 million a year. These kinds of savings come from

They Said It

Canada is a country whose main exports are hockey players and cold fronts. Canadian imports are baseball players and acid rain.

—*Pierre Trudeau (1919–2000)*
former prime minister of Canada

The Toyota Prius boasts both an electric motor with a battery that never needs recharging and a "super-efficient" gasoline engine. This hybrid power system is fuel efficient and less polluting to the environment. The car gets its energy economy from a system that knows which fuel source to use at which time.

Courtesy of Toyota

sources like greater efficiency, reduced operating costs, and less money spent on complying with regulations.[28]

Another solution to the problems of pollutants is **recycling**—reprocessing used materials for reuse. Recycling can sometimes provide much of the raw material that manufacturers need, thereby conserving the world's natural resources and reducing the need for landfills. Several industries are developing ways to use recycled materials. Recycling firms in Asia, like NTT DoCoMo and J-Phone, are buying used cell phones in bulk from wireless carriers, crushing and melting them, and extracting platinum, silver, and even gold. It takes about 125,000 phones to produce a one-kilo gold bar worth $10,000. In the U.S., phones are recycled for their batteries, while larger appliances like TVs and VCRs are mined for reusable metals.[29]

Many environmentalist groups have realized that working in partnership with companies can help them achieve their goals. One such organization, Environmental Defense, worked with McDonald's to streamline the fast-food company's waste output and has begun similar partnerships with FedEx and Starbucks, among others.

Greenpeace is working with European firms to replace polluting refrigerants with a more environmentally friendly substance called Greenfreeze, and The Coca-Cola Co. and Unilever have committed to join and support the campaign.[30]

Many consumers have favorable impressions of environmentally conscious businesses. To target these customers, companies often use **green marketing,** a marketing strategy that promotes environmentally safe products and production methods. A business cannot simply claim that its goods or services are environmentally friendly, however. In 1992, the FTC issued guidelines for businesses to follow in making environmental claims. A firm must be able to prove that any environmental claim made about a product has been substantiated with reliable scientific evidence. In addition, as shown in Figure 2.8, the FTC has given specific directions about how various environmental terms may be used in advertising and marketing.

Concern had developed, though, that consumers themselves, while supportive of green products in theory, have been less willing to put their money where their sentiments are. Philips Electronics NV, for instance, increased sales by more than 10 percent for its economically friendly fluorescent light bulbs after it stopped calling them EarthLight and promoted their seven-year life span instead. Gerber Products Co. switched from glass baby-food bottles to plastic after nearly three of four baby-food shoppers said they preferred the convenience of plastic, even though plastic

recycling reprocessing of used materials for reuse.

green marketing marketing strategy that promotes environmentally safe products and production methods.

If a business says a product is...	The product or package must...
Biodegradable	break down and return to nature in a reasonably short period of time.
Recyclable	be entirely reusable as new materials in the manufacture or assembly of a new product or package.
Refillable	be included in a system for the collection and return of the package for refill. If consumers have to find a way to refill it themselves, it is not *refillable*.
Ozone Safe/Ozone Friendly	must not contain any ozone-depleting ingredient.

FIGURE 2.8
FTC Guidelines for Environmental Claims in Green Marketing

can't be recycled. About four in ten consumers surveyed by Roper ASW said they don't buy "green" products because they are afraid they won't perform as well. Said one, "I know the environment is going downhill, but you go in the store and buy the closest thing to your hand—something you've used before that you know works."[31]

Sometimes the new technologies themselves raise controversy. An example is **genetic engineering,** a type of biotechnology that involves altering crops or other living things by inserting genes that provide them with a desirable characteristic, such as nutritional value or resistance to pesticides. One of the most controversial of these genetically modified (GM) crops has been corn engineered to make *Bacillus thuringiensis* (Bt), a type of bacteria that acts as a natural insecticide. The potential value of such a crop is that it reduces the need for chemical pesticides. Critics warn that it could be an ecological disaster. If most corn makes Bt, caterpillars could become resistant to it, requiring more pesticide use in the long run. In addition, some research has suggested that exposure to the corn is deadly to monarch butterfly caterpillars. Critics also fear that introducing genes from one type of plant into another—for example, daffodil genes have been used to add beta carotene to rice—may create products with hidden allergens that could trigger a dangerous allergic reaction in susceptible people.

Some consumers, especially in Europe, have resisted buying GM foods, and the European Union has maintained a controversial moratorium on approving new GM crops.[32] Both U.S. and foreign farmers are uncertain whether to adopt the technology because consumer resistance could make the crops worthless in the marketplace. Already, some food processors are willing to pay premium prices for food that has not been genetically engineered. Frito-Lay asked its corn suppliers to plant only unmodified seeds, and Wild Oats Market and Whole Foods Market are eliminating GM ingredients from their store brands. An agreement negotiated under the United Nations Convention on Biodiversity allows countries to ban imports of GM seeds, animals, and crops and to require labels on living GM goods, such as animals and whole grains, saying that they may contain GM organisms. Taco Bell recently recalled its taco shells distributed through supermarkets due to concerns about adverse consumer reactions when it discovered that GM corn had been used. Still, biotech food has become part of U.S. agriculture. About one-third of the corn and almost half the soybeans currently grown in the U.S. have been genetically engineered to either include an insecticide or resist herbicides used to kill weeds around the crops. The companies that provide these technologies are hoping that sentiment will become more favorable when food producers begin offering products engineered to provide health benefits, such as eggs with reduced cholesterol.[33]

Developing the Quality of the Workforce
In the past, a nation's wealth has often been based on its money, production equipment, and natural resources. A country's true wealth, however, lies in its people. An educated, skilled workforce provides the intellectual know-how required to develop new technology, improve productivity, and compete in the global marketplace. It is becoming increasingly clear that to remain competitive, U.S. business must assume more responsibility for enhancing the quality of its workforce, including encouraging diversity of all kinds, as Eastman Kodak does.

Used with permission of Eastman Kodak Company.

Diversity determines a company's success.

Eastman Kodak Company is committed to becoming a truly diverse corporation. Embracing the ideals of diversity enables us to better meet the needs of our customers, employees, suppliers, and the communities in which we live and work. All of which ensures our continued success in the global marketplace.

At Kodak ... Diversity Includes You.

Eastman Kodak celebrates the company's ideals of maintaining diversity among its workforce "to better meet the needs of our customers, employees, suppliers, and the communities in which we live and work." The message also directs minority-owned suppliers to a section of the company's Web site.

In developed economies like that of the U.S., most new jobs require college-educated workers. Companies find it more economical to hire overseas workers for low-skilled tasks because wages are lower in developing nations. With demand greatest for workers with advanced skills, the difference between the highest-paid and lowest-paid workers has been increasing. Among full-time workers in the U.S., the top 10 percent earn an average of $1,200 per week, compared with just $275 for the average worker in the bottom 10 percent. Twenty years ago, a college graduate on average earned 38 percent more than someone with only a high school diploma, but today the typical college graduate earns 71 percent more.[34] Clearly, education is essential to the well-being of the workforce. Businesses must encourage students to stay in school, continue their education, and sharpen their skills. Companies must also encourage employees to learn new skills and remain competitive.

Organizations also face enormous responsibilities for helping women, members of various cultural groups, and those who are physically challenged to contribute fully to the economy. Failure to do so is not only a waste of more than half the nation's workforce but also devastating to a firm's public image. Some socially responsible firms also encourage diversity in their business suppliers. Retail giant JCPenney's Partnership Program is designed to foster relationships with minority- and women-owned businesses—an effort the company has worked at for more than 30 years.

Through a commitment to developing employee diversity, ChevronTexaco has successfully rebounded from a racial discrimination lawsuit. When information that the company's top managers had engaged in racist behavior became public, the company (then known simply as Texaco) was embarrassed, and its stock price tumbled. It quickly agreed to settle the lawsuit and crafted a plan to place more value on diversity among employees. Recruiting methods were revised to reach a more diverse pool of applicants, and scholarship programs were launched to develop talented minorities interested in key careers like the physical sciences and international business. The company set specific goals for hiring and promoting qualified minority employees, and to achieve those goals, it included women and minorities on human resource committees and established mentoring programs. Within three years, the company had increased its recruiting of minorities to more than four of every 10 new hires, and minorities accounted for one of every five promotions.

Concern Worldwide is a not-for-profit corporation that employs about 3,000 people in nearly 30 developing countries, all working to eliminate hunger and poverty. The ad agency that designed this ad to raise public awareness and ask the public for financial support for Concern Worldwide donated its services, and the magazine in which the ad appeared donated the space.

corporate philanthropy act of an organization giving something back to the communities in which it earns profits.

Corporate Philanthropy

As Chapter 1 pointed out, not-for-profit organizations play an important role in society by serving the public good. They provide the human resources that enhance the quality of life in communities around the world. To fulfill this mission, many not-for-profit organizations rely on financial contributions from the business community. Firms respond by donating billions of dollars each year to not-for-profit organizations. This **corporate philanthropy** includes cash contributions, donations of equipment and products, and supporting the volunteer efforts of company employees. Recipients include cultural organizations, adopt-a-school programs, community development agencies, and housing and job training programs.

Corporate philanthropy can have many positive benefits beyond the purely altruistic rewards of giving, such as higher employee morale, enhanced company image, and improved customer relationships. After the 9/11 terrorist attacks, major firms made donations that totaled over $120 million. Discover Card raised $5 million for the relief efforts by contributing portions of card member charges. DuPont donated another $5 million. The American Heroes Fund, a not-for-profit organization created by fashion clothing and jewelry marketer Polo Ralph Lauren, received $4 million from its parent organization. In an effort to maximize the benefits of corporate giving in an era of downsizing, businesses have become more selective of the causes and charities they choose to support. Many seek to align their marketing efforts with their charitable giving. For example, many companies make contributions to the Olympics and create advertising that features the company's sponsorship. This is known as *cause related marketing.*

Another form of corporate philanthropy is volunteerism. In their roles as corporate citizens, thousands of businesses encourage their employees to contribute their efforts to projects as diverse as Habitat for Humanity, the United Way, and Red Cross blood drives. In addition to making tangible contributions to the well-being of fellow citizens, such programs generate considerable public support and goodwill for the companies and their employees. In some cases, the volunteer efforts occur mostly during off-hours for employees. In other instances, the firm permits its workforce to volunteer during regular working hours. Nortel Networks offers a combination of grants, use of company facilities, and limited time off work for volunteers in the locations where it has facilities, from Atlanta to Paris to Beijing. Regional teams work with selected local community organizations to develop programs that address math, science, and technology education; health care and human services issues; and needs specific to their area. Community involvement for each city is coordinated by an employee who makes sure the efforts are in line with company guidelines.[35] Sometimes companies help by contributing resources to promote worthy causes, such as Concern Worldwide's mission to help poverty stricken people around the world.

Responsibilities to Customers

Businesspeople share a social and ethical responsibility to treat their customers fairly and act in a manner that is not harmful to them. Consumer advocate Ralph Nader first pioneered this idea in the late 1960s. Since then, **consumerism**—the public demand that a business consider the wants and needs of its customers in making decisions—has gained widespread acceptance. Consumerism is based on the belief that consumers have certain rights. The most frequently quoted statement of consumer rights was made by President John F. Kennedy in 1962. Figure 2.9 summarizes these consumer rights. Numerous state and federal laws have been implemented since then to protect these rights.

consumerism public demand that a business consider the wants and needs of its customers in making decisions.

The Right to Be Safe   Contemporary businesspeople must recognize obligations, both moral and legal, to ensure the safe operation of their products. Consumers should feel assured that the products they purchase will not cause injuries in normal use. **Product liability** refers to the responsibility of manufacturers for injuries and damages caused by their products. Items that lead to injuries, either directly or indirectly, can have disastrous consequences for their makers.

Many companies put their products through rigorous testing to avoid safety problems. Still, testing alone cannot foresee every eventuality. Companies must try to consider all possibilities and provide adequate warning of potential dangers. When a product does pose a threat to customer safety, a responsible manufacturer responds quickly to either correct the problem or recall the dangerous product. For example, the Betesh Group toy manufacturer recently recalled its Busy Bug stuffed toy after it discovered that children could chew off—and choke on—the bug's fabric antennas. A warning went out to discount department stores to pull the toys, and the company set up a toll-free hotline to answer consumer questions and concerns.[36]

The Right to Be Informed   Consumers should have access to enough education and product information to make responsible buying decisions. In their efforts to promote and sell their goods and services, companies can easily neglect consumers' right to be fully informed. False or misleading advertising is a violation of the Wheeler-Lea Act, a federal law enacted in 1938. The Federal

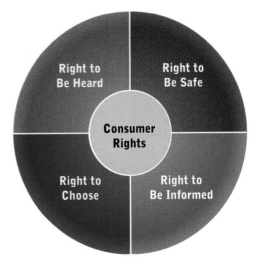

FIGURE 2.9
Consumer Rights as Proposed by President Kennedy

BUSINESS TOOL KIT

Being Considerate of One's Coworkers

Let's face it—as a new college graduate, you will not be getting the corner office with a view. More likely you will be introduced to the world of cubicles and the common work area where everyone can hear each other's phone conversations, work-related discussions, and everything else that transpires between the cubicle walls. Being a team player means being considerate of your coworkers, so here are some tips for playing it cool while at work.

1. No loud radios or CDs—keep volume low or use headphones if you have to have a radio at your desk. The same goes for conversations and phone calls; use your "inside" or library voice in order to not disturb those working. In addition, if you carry a cell phone, make sure that the volume is turned to low or on vibrate so as not to disturb others.

2. Avoid using the speaker phone unless it's for a conference call. Nothing is more irritating to your coworkers than having to listen to all of your conversations or on-hold music through a speaker phone. And although it might be tempting, try not to listen to others' personal phone calls. You don't want anyone listening to yours, do you?

3. Keep general areas tidy, put things back where they belong, and refill or replace when something runs out. This is especially true if there is a community coffeepot! And don't forget that the community kitchen is just that—

a *community* kitchen that the whole office uses. Don't steal lunches or anything else that doesn't belong to you.

4. If you borrow something, return it. Good manners are part of good business communications, and they need to be practiced in the office as well as at home and in public places. You will foster good working relationships with all of your colleagues, which can only help you in your job.

5. Good manners extend to the use of the community fax or copy machine. Try to save big jobs for early or late in the day so you don't monopolize the copier and irritate anyone who only needs to make one copy.

6. Don't shout over your cubicle walls, even if it's a business-related question. Make the effort to get up, walk around, and address your colleague in a normal tone of voice so as to not disturb your other work mates. Maybe your colleague will think twice and do the same next time!

Sources: "Office and Cubicle Etiquette," http://www.business-person .com/etiquette/Officeetiquette.html, accessed January 13, 2004; Bob Rosner, "The Cubicle Lifestyle," http://more.abcnews.go.com/sections/ business/dailynews/ww0227/ww0227.html, accessed February 27, 2003; Jacqueline Blais, "Mind Your Manners Even If You're at Work," *USA Today,* January 17, 2000, pp. B1, B5.

Trade Commission (FTC) and other federal and state agencies have established rules and regulations that govern advertising truthfulness. These rules prohibit businesses from making unsubstantiated claims about the performance or superiority of their goods or services. They also require businesses to avoid misleading consumers. Businesses that fail to comply face scrutiny from the FTC and consumer protection organizations. In one case, the FTC responded to complaints by filing charges against Star Publishing Group, which under the name National Consumer Services placed want ads promising as much as $800 per week for starting a home-based business. Consumers who called the toll-free number in the ad reached a recording selling a guide to start a business that the recording falsely implied would involve government work.

The Food and Drug Administration (FDA), which sets standards for advertising conducted by drug manufacturers, recently eased restrictions for prescription drug advertising on television. In print ads, drug makers are required to spell out potential side effects and the proper uses of prescription drugs. Because of the requirement to disclose this information, prescription drug television advertising was limited. Now, however, the FDA says drug ads on radio and television can directly promote a prescription drug's benefits if they provide a quick way for consumers to learn about side effects, such as displaying a toll-free number or Internet address. The FDA also monitors "dietary supplements," including vitamins and herbs. These products may make claims about their general effect on health but may not claim to cure a disease, unless the company

They Said It

Suddenly our name
is not so cool.

—*statement released by the band Anthrax*

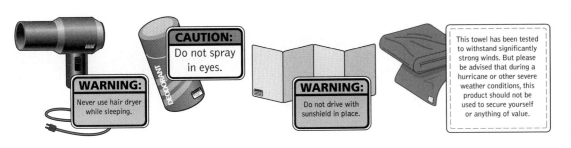

FIGURE 2.10
Wacky Warning Labels
The number of product liability lawsuits has skyrocketed. To protect themselves, businesses have become more careful about including warnings on products. However, some companies may go overboard, as demonstrated by these actual product warning labels.

has presented the FDA with research and received the agency's approval. For instance, a product may say it helps the body maintain a healthy immune system but not that it fights colds.

The responsibility of business to preserve consumers' right to be informed extends beyond avoiding misleading advertising. All communications with customers—from salespeople's comments to warranties and invoices—must be controlled to clearly and accurately inform customers. Most packaged-goods firms, personal computer makers, and other makers of products bought for personal use by consumers include toll-free customer service numbers on their product labels so that consumers can get answers when they have questions about a product.

To protect their customers and avoid claims of insufficient disclosure, businesses often include warnings on products. As Figure 2.10 shows, sometimes these warnings go far beyond what a reasonable consumer would expect.

The Right to Choose   Consumers should have the right to choose which goods and services they need and want to purchase. Socially responsible firms attempt to preserve this right, even if they reduce their own sales and profits in the process. Brand-name drug makers have recently gone on the defensive in a battle being waged by state governments, insurance companies, consumer groups, major employers like General Motors and Verizon, and unions. These groups want to force down the rising price of prescription drugs by ensuring that consumers have the right and the opportunity to select cheaper generic brands. The Federal Trade Commission has even sued drug companies that it says paid generic drug competitors to keep their products off the market long after the patents on brand-name drugs have expired.[37]

Since the long-distance telephone industry has been deregulated, some customers have also been the victims of fraud. Several unscrupulous long-distance carriers have duped customers into switching their service through an unsavory practice called *slamming.* The firms get customers to sign contest-entry forms that contain less-than-obvious wording saying they agree to be switched. Yet another issue involves the use—and abuse—of computers to track their owners' habits and preferences, as the "Solving an Ethical Controversy" box describes.

The Right to Be Heard   Consumers should be able to express legitimate complaints to appropriate parties. Many companies expend considerable effort to ensure full hearings for consumer complaints. The eBay auction Web site assists buyers and sellers who believe they were victimized in transactions conducted through the site. It deploys a 200-employee team to work with users and law enforcement agencies to combat fraud. The company provides all users with insurance coverage of up to $200 per transaction, with a $25 deductible. It operates a feedback forum, where it encourages users to rate one another. The auction site operates a software program that tracks individuals' bidding performance, looking for patterns associated with fraudulent behavior. And when it receives complaints of fraud, eBay forwards them to the FTC. So, although eBay cannot prevent all instances of fraud, it does provide an environment in which buyers and sellers feel protected.[38]

Responsibilities to Employees

As Chapter 1 explained, one of the most important business resources is the organization's workforce. Companies that are able to attract skilled and knowledgeable employees are better able to meet the challenges of competing globally. In return, businesses have wide-ranging responsibilities to their employees, both here and abroad. These include workplace safety, quality of life issues, avoiding discrimination, and preventing sexual harassment and sexism. Today, they also have to accommodate office workers who fear working in tall buildings.

Protecting Your Privacy—and Identity—in a World of Technological Eavesdroppers

Invasions of spyware, software that hides itself inside a computer without the user's knowledge or permission, are growing exponentially. *Consumer Reports* believes about a third of computer users have been forced to deal with programs, inadvertently downloaded from the Internet, that bring blizzards of pop-up ads, slow operating systems, and even crash computers. Spyware can also open the door to identity theft.

Less malicious technology called "cookies" allows marketers to keep track of Web sites users visit and offer pop-up ads based on the surfers' interests. The latest form of tracking lets marketers follow users around the Web, offering targeted ads wherever they browse.

Marketers are interested in software that allows customization and targeted messages. "If someone spends an awful lot of time on mutual fund pages, clearly they are interested in mutual funds. Why not have ... mutual fund advertising follow them?" says the executive vice president of sales at MarketWatch.com, Inc.

But privacy advocates are concerned that so-called behavioral targeting is worrisome in that it allows the information gathered to be recorded.

Should marketers be allowed to harvest personal information from your computer to better target their ads?

PRO
1. Targeted marketing provides an important and efficient information benefit for the consumer.
2. Services can be designed to require user authorization for the collection of information and the appearance of pop-up ads.

CON
1. Consumers should not have to pay for software to protect their computers from an onslaught of advertising.
2. Only the most savvy computer users know how to deal with cookies and spyware; the rest are being victimized because they lack the tools to protect their privacy.

SUMMARY
Spyware remains a problem, but there may be room for a legitimate form of targeted online advertising. Dotomi, Inc. (started by the creator of ICQ, the popular chat program), allows users to opt in to customized advertising from such marketers as American Express, Avis, Blockbuster, and Office Depot. A combination of banner ads and e-mail marketing, Direct Messaging lets users select the brands whose ads they allow. As an industry spokesperson points out, "It customizes ads in a way that no one has before, without violating privacy."

Sources: Jeanette Borzo, "Banner Ads Get Personal," *Business 2.0*, October 2004, p. 58; Toddi Gutner, "What's Lurking in Your PC?" *BusinessWeek*, October 4, 2004, pp. 108–110; Patrick Norton, "Stomping Out Spyware," *Ziff-Davis News*, September 15, 2004, http://story.news.yahoo.com; Anick Jesdanun, "Ads Follow You Around the Web," *Mobile Register*, July 4, 2004, p. 5F.

Workplace Safety   A century ago, few businesses paid much attention to the safety of their workers. In fact, most business owners viewed employees as mere cogs in the production process. Workers—many of whom were young children—toiled in frequently dangerous conditions. In 1911, 146 people, mostly young girls, died in a fire at the Triangle Shirtwaist Factory in New York City. Contributing to the massive loss of life were the sweatshop working conditions at the factory, including overcrowding, blocked exits, and a lack of fire escapes. The horrifying tragedy forced businesses to begin to recognize their responsibility for their workers' safety.

The safety and health of workers while on the job is now an important business responsibility. The Occupational Safety and Health Administration (OSHA) is the main federal regulatory force in setting workplace safety and health standards. These mandates range from broad guidelines on storing hazardous materials to specific standards for worker safety in industries like construction, manufacturing, and mining. OSHA tracks and investigates workplace accidents and has the authority to fine employers who are found liable for injuries and deaths that occur on the job. As Figure 2.11 shows, workplace injuries and illnesses declined during the 1980s and

They Said It

Pete, please don't do anything foolish. Please take care of yourself and don't be a hero. I don't need a Medal of Honor winner. I need a son. Love, Mom

—*letter engraved on Vietnam War Memorial in New York City*

1990s. Even though rates of injury and illness are lower in service industries than in goods-producing industries, the four industries with highest injury rates are all service providers: restaurants, hospitals, nursing homes, and retail stores. Most reports to OSHA involve injuries, most of which involve disorders arising from making the same motion over and over, such as carpal tunnel syndrome.[39]

Although businesses occasionally complain about having to comply with too many OSHA regulations, ultimately management must set standards and implement programs to ensure that workers are safe in the workplace. The Jewel-Osco food-drug chain, the Midwest division of Albertson's, shows employees training videos about safe practices. The videos teach about fire safety, germs transmitted in blood, and actions to take if the store is robbed. The store makes special efforts to protect teenage employees. They are expected to read and sign a statement that they will not use any machinery, lift equipment (including the elevator), or meat slicers. Use of power equipment is limited by law to employees 18 years of age or older, and those employees must undergo training before the store permits them to use the equipment. Laws also extend extra protection to teenage workers by limiting the number of hours they work and the number of trips they may make away from their primary place of employment each day. Protection of young workers is especially significant because almost one workplace injury in three involves employees with less than a year's experience.[40]

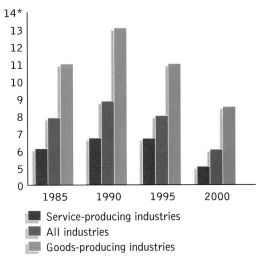

FIGURE 2.11
Rates of Workplace Injuries and Illnesses
Source: U.S. Department of Labor, Bureau of Labor Statistics, "Injuries, Illnesses, and Fatalities," http://www.bls.gov/iif/oshwc/osh/os/osnr0013.txt, accessed February 24, 2003.

Quality of Life Issues   Balancing work and family is becoming harder for many employees. They find themselves squeezed between working long hours and handling child-care problems, caring for elderly parents, and solving other family crises. A "sandwich generation" of households, those caring for two generations—their children and their aging parents—has arisen. As the population ages, the share of American households providing some type of care to a relative or friend age 50 years or older is expected to double to more than two in five in the early years of the 21st century. At the same time, as married women spend more time working outside the home, they have fewer hours per week to spend on family. The employees juggling work with life's other demands aren't just working mothers. Childless couples, single people, and men all express frustration with the pressures of balancing work with family and personal needs.

Helping workers find solutions to these quality of life issues has become an important concern of many businesses, but finding answers isn't always easy. Some companies offer flexible work arrangements to support employees. Other firms offer benefits such as subsidized child care or on-site education and shopping to assist workers trying to balance work and family.

Another solution has been to offer **family leave** to employees who need to deal with family matters. Under the Family and Medical Leave Act of 1993, businesses with 50 or more employees must provide unpaid leave annually for any employee who wants time off for the birth or adoption of a child, to become a foster parent, or to care for a seriously ill relative or spouse. The law requires that employers grant up to 12 weeks of leave each year. This unpaid leave also applies to an employee who has a serious illness. Workers must meet certain eligibility requirements. Employers must continue to provide health benefits during the leave and guarantee that employees will return to equivalent jobs. The issue of who is entitled to health benefits can also create a dilemma as companies struggle to balance the needs of their employees against the staggering costs of health care.

The Family and Medical Leave Act gives employees the right to take time off, but because the leave is unpaid, many workers find that they cannot afford to use this right. The U.S. Department of Labor recently issued a ruling authorizing states to experiment with unemployment compensation as part of their unemployment insurance programs. States that elect to participate in this experiment can authorize partial wage replacement to parents who take approved leave. In states where it is available, the unemployment compensation would be available to employees at companies of any size, so long as they meet the state's eligibility requirements for unemployment compensation. The Department of Labor plans to evaluate whether parents who receive the benefits are more likely to remain in the workforce over the long run.[41]

Ensuring Equal Opportunity on the Job   Businesspeople face many challenges managing an increasingly diverse workforce in the 21st century. By 2050, ethnic minorities and immigrants will make up nearly half the U.S. workforce. Technological advances are expanding the ways people with physical disabilities can contribute in the workplace. Businesses also need to find ways to responsibly recruit and manage older workers and workers with varying lifestyles. In addition, beginning with Lotus Development Corp. in 1982, companies have begun to extend benefits equally to employees, regardless of sexual orientation. In particular, that means the company offers benefits like health insurance to unmarried domestic partners if it offers them to spouses of married couples. Companies that now offer these gender-neutral benefits include Boeing, Citigroup, Disney, General Mills, and Prudential. This treatment reflects the view that all employee groups deserve the right to work in an environment that is nondiscriminatory.

To a great extent, efforts at managing diversity are regulated by law. The Civil Rights Act (1964) outlawed many kinds of discriminatory practices, and Title VII of the act specifically prohibits discrimination in employment. As shown in Table 2.2, other nondiscrimination laws include the Equal Pay Act (1963), the Age Discrimination in Employment Act (1968), the Equal Employment Opportunity Act (1972), the Pregnancy Discrimination Act (1978), the Civil Rights Act of 1991, and numerous executive orders. The Americans with Disabilities Act (1990) protects the rights of physically challenged people. The Vietnam Era Veterans Readjustment Act (1974) protects the employment of veterans of the Vietnam War.

Perhaps the next round of protection will extend to the level of genetics. As scientists make progress in decoding the human genome, some people worry that employers will discriminate based on genetic characteristics, such as a gene that predisposes a person to cancer or some other costly disease. In fact, the executive branch of the federal government is now prohibited from discriminating on the basis of genetic information. When he signed the order, former President Clinton stated that he hoped it would serve as a challenge to businesses and other government agencies to adopt similar policies.[42]

The **Equal Employment Opportunity Commission (EEOC)** was created to increase job opportunities for women and minorities and to help end discrimination based on race, color, religion, disability, gender, or national origin in any personnel action. To enforce fair-employment laws, it investigates charges of discrimination and harassment and files suit against violators. The EEOC can also help employers set up programs to increase job opportunities for women, minorities, people with disabilities, and persons in other protected categories.

Fair treatment of employees is more than a matter of complying with EEOC regulations, however. Like white male employees, women and people of color want opportunities to excel and rewards for excellence. They also want to be treated with respect. A minority employee who misses out on a plum assignment may miss out on the big raise that goes with it. As the employee's salary grows more slowly, managers may eventually begin to use the size of the salary as an indicator that the employee contributes less to the organization. Chapter 9 takes a closer look at diversity and employment discrimination issues as part of a discussion of human resource management.

Age Discrimination   The Age Discrimination in Employment Act of 1968 (ADEA) protects individuals who are 40 years of age or older, prohibiting discrimination on the basis of age and denial of benefits to older employees. A recent settlement between the EEOC and the California Public Employees' Retirement System (Calpers) suggests that age bias cases are being closely watched. The settlement, the largest to date, will pay an estimated $250 million to over 1,700 retired firefighters, police, and other law officers whose disability payments were based on their age at hiring. The policy was deemed discriminatory.[43]

sexual harassment
inappropriate actions of a
sexual nature in the
workplace.

Sexual Harassment and Sexism   Every employer has a responsibility to ensure that all workers are treated fairly and are safe from sexual harassment. **Sexual harassment** refers to unwelcome and inappropriate actions of a sexual nature in the workplace. It is a form of sex discrimination that violates the Civil Rights Act of 1964, which gives both men and women the right to file lawsuits for

Table 2.2   Laws Designed to Ensure Equal Opportunity

Law	Key Provisions
Title VII of the Civil Rights Act of 1964 (as amended by the Equal Employment Opportunity Act of 1972)	Prohibits discrimination in hiring, promotion, compensation, training, or dismissal on the basis of race, color, religion, sex, or national origin.
Age Discrimination in Employment Act of 1968 (as amended)	Prohibits discrimination in employment against anyone aged 40 years or over in hiring, promotion, compensation, training, or dismissal.
Equal Pay Act of 1963	Requires equal pay for men and women working for the same firm in jobs that require equal skill, effort, and responsibility.
Vocational Rehabilitation Act of 1973	Requires government contractors and subcontractors to take affirmative action to employ and promote qualified disabled workers. Coverage now extends to all federal employees. Coverage has been broadened by the passage of similar laws in more than 20 states and, through court rulings, to include persons with communicable diseases, including AIDS.
Vietnam Era Veterans Readjustment Act of 1974	Requires government contractors and subcontractors to take affirmative action to employ and retain disabled veterans. Coverage now extends to all federal employees and has been broadened by the passage of similar laws in more than 20 states.
Pregnancy Discrimination Act of 1978	Requires employers to treat pregnant women and new mothers the same as other employees for all employment-related purposes, including receipt of benefits under company benefit programs.
Americans with Disabilities Act of 1990	Makes discrimination against the disabled illegal in public accommodations, transportation, and telecommunications; stiffens employer penalties for intentional discrimination on the basis of an employee's disability.
Civil Rights Act of 1991	Makes it easier for workers to sue their employers for alleged discrimination. Enables victims of sexual discrimination to collect punitive damages; includes employment decisions and on-the-job issues such as sexual harassment, unfair promotions, and unfair dismissal. The employer must prove that it did not engage in discrimination.
Family and Medical Leave Act of 1993	Requires all businesses with 50 or more employees to provide up to 12 weeks of unpaid leave annually to employees who have had a child or are adopting a child, or are becoming foster parents, who are caring for a seriously ill relative or spouse, or who are themselves seriously ill. Workers must meet certain eligibility requirements.

intentional sexual harassment. More than 15,000 sexual harassment complaints are filed with the EEOC each year, of which about 12 percent are filed by men. Thousands of other cases are either handled internally by companies or never reported.

Two types of sexual harassment exist. The first type occurs when an employee is pressured to comply with unwelcome advances and requests for sexual favors in return for job security, promotions, and raises. The second type results from a hostile work environment in which an employee feels hassled or degraded because of unwelcome flirting, lewd comments, or obscene jokes. The courts have ruled that allowing sexually oriented materials like pinup calendars and pornographic magazines at the workplace can create a hostile atmosphere that interferes with an employee's ability to do the job. Employers are also legally responsible to protect employees from sexual harassment from customers and clients. The EEOC's Web site informs employers and employees of criteria for identifying sexual harassment and how it should be handled in the workplace.

Preventing sexual harassment can be difficult because it involves regulating the conduct of individual employees. Ford Motor Co. unsuccessfully tried to end sexual harassment in Chicago-area factories over the course of several years. Beginning in 1994, female workers reported to the EEOC that they had been subjected to offensive language, name-calling, and unwanted touching by coworkers and supervisors. After a two-year investigation, the EEOC agreed and reached a settlement with Ford. Then a group of women in another Ford factory complained of similar mistreatment. The company fired 10 employees and took disciplinary actions against others. Nevertheless, a group of women complained that the problems continued. After months of negotiations, Ford agreed to spend $7.5 million to compensate the victims and $10 million to train employees and managers in appropriate behavior. The company also agreed to triple the number of female supervisors in the factories and to make prevention of sexual harassment a requirement for granting raises and promotions to plant managers.[44]

To avoid sexual harassment problems, many firms have established policies and employee education programs aimed at preventing such violations. An effective harassment prevention program should include the following measures:

- Issue a specific policy statement prohibiting sexual harassment
- Develop a complaint procedure for employees to follow
- Create a work atmosphere that encourages sexually harassed staffers to come forward
- Investigate and resolve complaints quickly and take disciplinary action against harassers

Unless all these components are supported by top management, sexual harassment is difficult to eliminate.

Sexual harassment is often part of the broader problem of **sexism**—discrimination against members of either sex, but primarily affecting women. One important sexism issue is equal pay for equal work. On average, U.S. women earn 77 cents for every dollar earned by men. In the course of a working lifetime, this disparity adds up to a gap of $420,000. The percentage of women who hold managerial and professional positions has grown to 49 percent, compared with 41 percent in 1983, but that trend has not necessarily reduced the pay gap. In terms of pay, full-time female managers in some industries, like entertainment and communications, have actually lost ground since 1995 compared with men, according to the U.S. General Accounting Office. Female doctors earn just 62 cents for every dollar earned by male doctors, and female financial managers earn 61 cents for every dollar earned by male financial planners. In general, women and men start with similar salaries, and the differences develop over time, with men typically paid more than women who have comparable experience.[45]

In some extreme cases, differences in pay and advancement can become the basis for sex discrimination suits, such as those filed against Wal-Mart Stores. Recently granted class-action status, these suits may become the largest sex discrimination case in U.S. history. The plaintiffs in the cases say that men dominate management jobs, while women hold more than 90 percent of the low-wage cashier jobs and earn less than male Wal-Mart employees even when they hold the same jobs and other differences are accounted for. Wal-Mart could face a costly settlement; similar suits filed by thousands of female employees of Home Depot Inc. cost the firm $104 million in penalties.[46]

Responsibilities to Investors and the Financial Community

Although a fundamental goal of any business is to make a profit for its shareholders, investors and the financial community demand that businesses behave ethically as well as legally. When firms fail in this responsibility, as we saw in the story that opened this chapter, thousands of investors and consumers can suffer.

State and federal government agencies are responsible for protecting investors from financial misdeeds. At the federal level, the Securities and Exchange Commission (SEC) investigates suspicions that publicly traded firms engaged in unethical or illegal behavior. For example, it investigates accusations that a business is using faulty accounting practices to inaccurately portray its financial resources and profits to investors. Regulation FD ("full disclosure"), a five-year-old SEC rule, requires that publicly traded companies make announcements of major information to the general public, rather than first disclosing the information to selected major investors. The agency also operates an Office of Internet Enforcement to target fraud in online trading and

Concept Check

1. What is social responsibility and why do firms exercise it?
2. How can businesses respond to consumer concerns about the environment?
3. What are quality of life issues? How can firms help employees address these needs?

online sales of stock by unlicensed sellers. Recall that the Sarbanes-Oxley Act of 2002 also protects investors from unethical accounting practices. Chapter 18 discusses securities trading practices further.

What's Ahead

The decisions and actions of businesspeople are often influenced by outside forces such as the legal environment and society's expectations about business responsibility. Firms also are affected by the economic environments in which they operate. The next chapter discusses the broad economic issues that influence businesses around the world. Our discussion will focus on how factors such as supply and demand, unemployment, inflation, and government monetary policies pose both challenges and opportunities for firms seeking to compete in the global marketplace.

DID YOU KNOW?

1. A global survey of managers showed the environment as the No. 1 issue for the early years of the 21st century.
2. About 1.8 million tons of waste from used PCs, televisions, and other high-tech products are created in the U.S. each year.
3. When it comes to such qualities as ethics and honesty, nurses are the highest-rated professionals. Ranked at the bottom are advertisers, telemarketers, and car salespeople.
4. Singapore has strict laws against littering, spitting, and the importation of chewing gum.
5. Of the population of highly industrialized nations, 15 percent is over the age of 65, compared with less than 5 percent for the typical developing nation.

Summary of Learning Goals

1   Explain the concepts of business ethics and social responsibility.
Business ethics refers to the standards of conduct and moral values that govern actions and decisions in the workplace. Businesspeople must take a wide range of social issues into account when making decisions. Social responsibility refers to management's acceptance of the obligation to consider profit, consumer satisfaction, and societal well-being of equal value in evaluating the firm's performance.

2   Describe the factors that influence business ethics.
Among the many factors shaping individual ethics are personal experience, peer pressure, and organizational culture. Individual ethics are also influenced by family, cultural, and religious standards. Additionally, the culture of the organization where a person works can be a factor.

3   List the stages in the development of ethical standards.
In the preconventional stage, individuals primarily consider their own needs and desires in making decisions. They obey external rules only from fear of punishment or hope of reward. In the conventional stage, individuals are aware of and respond to their duty to others. Expectations of groups, as well as self-interest, influence behavior. In the final, postconventional stage, the individual can move beyond self-interest and duty to include consideration of the needs of society. A person in this stage can apply personal ethical principles in a variety of situations.

4   Identify common ethical dilemmas in the workplace.
Conflicts of interest exist when a businessperson is faced with a situation where an action benefiting one person has the potential to harm another, as when

the person's own interests conflict with those of a customer. One type of behavior that generates a conflict of interest is bribery. Honesty and integrity are valued qualities that engender trust, but a person's immediate self-interest may seem to require violating these principles. Loyalty to an employer sometimes conflicts with truthfulness. Whistleblowing is a possible response to misconduct in the workplace, but the personal costs of doing so are high.

5

Discuss how organizations shape ethical behavior.

Employees are strongly influenced by the standards of conduct established and supported within the organizations where they work. Businesses can help shape ethical behavior by developing codes of conduct that define their expectations. Organizations can also use this training to develop employees' ethics awareness and reasoning. They can foster ethical action through decision-making tools, goals consistent with ethical behavior, and advice hotlines. Executives must also demonstrate ethical behavior in their decisions and actions to provide ethical leadership.

6

Describe how businesses' social responsibility is measured.

Today's businesses are expected to weigh their qualitative impact on consumers and society, in addition to their quantitative economic contributions such as sales, employment levels, and profits. One measure is their compliance with labor and consumer protection laws and their charitable contributions. Another measure some businesses take is to conduct social audits. Public-interest groups also create standards and measure companies' performance relative to those standards. Consumers may boycott groups that fall short of social standards.

7

Summarize the responsibilities of business to the general public, customers, and employees.

The responsibilities of business to the general public include protecting the public health and the environment and developing the quality of the workforce. Additionally, many would argue that businesses have a social responsibility to support charitable and social causes in the communities in which they earn profits. Business also has a social and ethical responsibility to treat customers fairly and protect consumers upholding the rights to be safe, to be informed, to choose, and to be heard. Businesses have wide-ranging responsibilities to their workers. They should make sure that the workplace is safe, address quality of life issues, ensure equal opportunity, and prevent sexual harassment.

8

Explain why investors and the financial community are concerned with business ethics and social responsibility.

Investors and the financial community demand that businesses behave ethically as well as legally in handling their financial transactions. Businesses must be honest in reporting their profits and financial performance to avoid misleading investors. The Securities and Exchange Commission is the federal agency responsible for investigating suspicions that publicly traded firms have engaged in unethical or illegal financial behavior.

Business Terms You Need to Know

business ethics 40	code of conduct 48	green marketing 54	sexual harassment 62
conflict of interest 45	social responsibility 51	corporate philanthropy 56	
whistleblowing 46	recycling 54	consumerism 57	

Other Important Business Terms

Sarbanes-Oxley Act 40

integrity 45

social audit 51

boycott 51

pollution 53

genetic engineering 55

product liability 57

family leave 61

Equal Employment
Opportunity Commission
(EEOC) 62

sexism 64

Review Questions

1. What do the terms *business ethics* and *social responsibility* mean? Cite an example of each. Who are the main constituents that businesses must consider?

2. Identify and describe briefly the three stages in which individuals typically develop ethical standards. What are some of the factors that determine the stage of moral and ethical development an individual occupies at any given time?

3. What are the four most common ethical challenges that businesspeople face? Give a brief example of each.

4. What are the four levels of development of a corporate culture to support business ethics? Describe each briefly.

5. How do organizational goals affect ethical behavior? How might these goals interfere with ethical leadership? Give an example.

6. What basic consumer rights does the consumerism movement try to ensure? How has consumerism improved the contemporary business environment?

7. What are some of the major factors that contribute to the assessment of a company's social performance?

8. Identify the major benefits of corporate philanthropy.

9. What are some of the responsibilities that firms have to their employees?

10. How does a company demonstrate its responsibility to investors and the financial community?

Projects and Applications

1. Write your own personal code of ethics, detailing your feelings about ethical challenges such as lying to protect an employer or coworker, favoring one client over another, misrepresenting credentials to an employer or client, and using the Internet for personal purposes while at work. What role will your personal ethics play in deciding your choice of career and acceptance of a job?

2. "Everybody exaggerates when it comes to selling products, and customers ought to take that with a grain of salt," said one advertising executive recently in response to a complaint filed by the Better Business Bureau about misleading advertising. "Don't we all have a brain, and can't we all think a little bit, too?" Do you agree with this statement? Why or why not?

3. Imagine that you work for a company that makes outdoor clothing, such as L. L. Bean, Timberland, or Patagonia.

Write a memo describing at least four specific ways in which your company could practice corporate philanthropy.

4. Imagine that you are the human resource management director for a company that is trying to establish and document its responsibilities to its employees. Choose one of the responsibilities described in the chapter—such as workplace safety—and write a memo describing specific steps your company will take to fulfill that responsibility.

5. Suppose that you own a small firm with 12 employees. One of them tells you in confidence that he has just learned he is HIV positive. You know that health-care costs for AIDS patients can be disastrously high, and this expense could drastically raise the health insurance premiums that your other employees must pay. What are your responsibilities to this employee? To the rest of your staff? Explain.

Experiential Exercise

Ethical Work Climates

Answer the following questions by circling the number that best describes an organization for which you have worked.

Questions	Disagree				Agree
1. What is the best for everyone in the company is the major consideration here.	1	2	3	4	5
2. Our major concern is always what is best for the other person.	1	2	3	4	5
3. People are expected to comply with the law and professional standards over and above other considerations.	1	2	3	4	5
4. In this company the first consideration is whether a decision violates any law.	1	2	3	4	5
5. It is very important to follow the company's rules and procedures here.	1	2	3	4	5
6. People in this company strictly obey the company policies.	1	2	3	4	5
7. In this company people are mostly out for themselves	1	2	3	4	5
8. People are expected to do anything to further the company's interests, regardless of the consequences.	1	2	3	4	5
9. In this company people are guided by their own personal ethics.	1	2	3	4	5
10. Each person in this company decides for himself or herself what is right and wrong.	1	2	3	4	5

Add up your score: _____

These questions measure the dimensions of an organization's ethical climate. Questions 1 and 2 measure caring for people; questions 3 and 4 measure lawfulness; questions 5 and 6 measure adherence to rules; questions 7 and 8 measure emphasis on financial and company performance; and questions 9 and 10 measure individual independence. *Questions 7 and 8 are reverse scored* (1 = 5, 2 = 4, 3 = 3, 4 = 2, and 5 = 1). A total score above 40 indicates a very positive ethical climate. A score between 30 and 39 indicates an above-average ethical climate. A score between 20 and 29 indicates a below-average ethical climate, and a score of less than 20 indicates a very poor ethical climate.

Go back over the questions and think about changes that you could have made to improve the ethical climate in the organization. Discuss with other students what you could do as a manager to improve ethics in future companies you work for.

Source: Richard L. Daft, *Management*, Sixth Edition. Mason, OH: South-Western Publishing, 2004, used by permission. The exercise is based on Bart Victor and John B. Cullen, "The Organizational Bases of Ethical Work Climates," *Administrative Science Quarterly*, 33 (1988), pp. 101–125.

NOTHING BUT NET

1. **Best places to work.** Every year *Fortune* magazine compiles a list of the 100 best companies to work for. Visit the magazine's Web site (http://www.fortune.com) and review the most recent year's list of the 100 best companies. Which made the top 10? What criteria does the magazine use when compiling its list?

2. **Community involvement.** Being a good corporate citizen means being involved in the community. Visit the two Web sites listed here and read about how several companies with major operations in your state are involved in community improvement. Prepare a brief oral report to your class about your findings.

   http://www.dow.com/about/corp/social/social.htm

   http://www.jnj.com/community/index.htm

3. **Protecting the environment.** Many companies are in the forefront of the environmental movement. Visit the Web site of a company you believe is committed to environmentally friendly business practices. Write a report on that firm's efforts. Examples include companies such as the following:

   http://www.ford.com/en/goodworks/environment/default.htm

   http://www.patagonia.com/enviro/main_enviro_action.shtml

   http://www.starbucks.com/aboutus/csr.asp

   Note: Internet Web addresses change frequently. If you don't find the exact sites listed, you may need to access the organization's or company's home page and search from there.

Case 2.1

Strategy for Competing with Microsoft: Fight or Flight?

Everybody should compete with Microsoft once in their lifetime," says Netscape's Marc Andreesen of his old rival, "so they have stories to tell their grandchildren. And then don't do it anymore."

The recent settlement of the U.S. Department of Justice's antitrust suit against Microsoft Corp. surprised some who had expected harsher penalties for the software giant. Found guilty of creating and maintaining a monopoly with its Windows operating system, Microsoft had fought the suit on the grounds that inextricably bundling its Internet browser with its Windows operating system was necessary for technical reasons. It now must make amends in various ways. It must reimburse the plaintiff states $25 million in legal fees; it must allow PC makers to install and promote non-Microsoft browsers, multimedia players, and other products; it cannot retaliate against those who do so; and (in settling a related suit brought by California) it must provide consumers and businesses who purchased certain Microsoft products with vouchers worth $5 to $29 toward computer products of any manufacture, up to a total of $1.1 billion. Sixteen other states and the District of Columbia have brought suits similar to California's.

But the federal settlement stopped short of forcing the company to split itself in two and softened penalties contemplated by the first judge in the case. U.S. District Judge Colleen Kollar-Kotelly's decision was based, she said, on the states' failure to show that Microsoft's devastatingly competitive business strategies hurt consumers even as they forced rival browser companies out of the market. She declined to force the firm to give up its intellectual property by licensing its Office software or providing an open-source license for its browsers. Further suits against Microsoft, Time Warner, and the European Union's antitrust unit are still pending.

Microsoft founder Bill Gates called the antitrust settlement "a good compromise" and pledged to honor the agreement. "We're committed to moving forward as a responsible leader in an industry that is constantly, constantly changing," said the firm's CEO, Steve Ballmer. On the other hand, the end of the case leaves Microsoft cash-rich and free to pursue any other market it chooses, such as handheld devices, servers, applications software, video gaming, technology consulting, and Internet services. "They're absolutely more dangerous now," says Ken Wasch, president of the Software & Information Industry Association.

Meanwhile, Marc Andreesen, having lost the browser war he waged against Microsoft, has taken his new startup, Opsware Inc., into market niches that Gates's company hasn't yet touched.

QUESTIONS FOR CRITICAL THINKING

1. Was it ethical for Microsoft to force users of its Windows operating system to use its Internet browsers as well by bundling the programs together and preventing PC manufacturers from making other software available to computer buyers? Was Microsoft's behavior toward its rivals ethical? Why or why not?

2. Should Microsoft change its business practices to protect itself against future antitrust suits? How? Who would benefit from such changes?

Sources: "Billion-dollar Deal Is a Decent Outcome," *The San Jose Mercury News,* January 20, 2003, http://www.bayarea.com/mld/mercurynews; Clint Swett, "Don't Expect Too Much from Microsoft Accord," *The Sacramento Bee,* January 14, 2003, http://www.sacbee.com; David Ho, "Judge Denies Appeal in Microsoft Ruling," *Associated Press,* January 13, 2003; Tom Bemis, "Microsoft Settles Calif. Suits for $1.1 Bil," *CBS MarketWatch.com* January 10, 2003, http://www.cbs.marketwatch.com; Steve Hamm, "What's a Rival to Do Now?" *BusinessWeek,* November 18, 2002, pp. 44–46.

Video Case 2.2

Timberland

This video case appears on page 603. A recently filmed video, designed to expand and highlight the written case, is available for class use by instructors.

Chapter 3
Economic Challenges Facing Global and Domestic Business

Learning Goals

1 Distinguish between microeconomics and macroeconomics.

2 Explain the factors that drive demand and supply.

3 Compare the three major types of economic systems.

4 Describe each of the four different types of market structures in a private enterprise system.

5 Identify and describe the four stages of the business cycle.

6 Explain how productivity, price-level changes, and employment levels affect the stability of a nation's economy.

7 Discuss how monetary policy and fiscal policy are used to manage an economy's performance.

8 Describe the major global economic challenges of the 21st century.

Cracking the DeBeers Diamond Monopoly

DeBeers, the giant London and South African–based company that once controlled 80 percent of total sales of rough, uncut diamonds sold around the world, long held a near-monopoly in the mining and marketing of industrial diamonds, a $500 million a year industry. These stones are used for cutting

and polishing in a wide variety of industries, including manufacturing and construction equipment.

Known as "the Syndicate," DeBeers used a variety of methods to maintain its tight control over a business steeped in tradition. The company hoarded diamonds in huge quantities, keeping prices high by parceling out small quantities at a time. It was also able to determine who could buy uncut stones, how many, and of what quality, and it controlled the fate of the all-important cutting centers where the stones were polished. It sold rough diamonds directly to only a few selected buyers (called *sightholders*), and even with them, DeBeers used highly restrictive business methods, such as offering boxes of gems under take-it-or-leave-it terms, cutting off the supplies of any sightholders who protested the tactics.

In 1994 the U.S. Justice Department charged DeBeers with conspiring to fix prices for industrial diamonds in the U.S. and elsewhere, and while the case dragged on for years, other cracks in the monopoly's walls appeared. Some sightholders rebelled and began buying rough diamonds directly from the governments of diamond-producing countries such as Russia, Canada, and Australia (all of which have opened new diamond mines), bypassing DeBeers in defiance of long-standing exclusive agreements they had with the firm. DeBeers had to fight for a share of the huge diamond reserves discovered in Canada, proving once and for all how severely its once-important industry relationships had been damaged.

© EPA/Landov

Within a few short years, DeBeers's share of the rough-diamond market had dropped from 80 to 60 percent, helped in part by the appearance of these new sources it could not control.

In the meantime, under the restrictions of the Justice Department suit, DeBeers executives were unable to contact U.S. customers or travel to the U.S., the world's most lucrative diamond market for both industrial use and jewelry, because they risked arrest if they did so. The company continued its relationships with U.S. buyers by working through intermediaries, but it lost some of its marketing clout and legitimacy. "They haven't been able to set foot in a market that represents half the world's diamond market," said the research director of an industry publication. "DeBeers could not call you in this country, they couldn't send you an e-mail, they couldn't mail you anything."

And, finally, one more threat to DeBeers's ability to remain the near-exclusive supplier of diamonds to the world appeared on the horizon—cultured (artificial) diamonds, made by increasingly sophisticated manufacturing processes in ever-higher quality.

So when DeBeers finally settled the case against it by pleading guilty, accepting a $10 million fine, and admitting to conspiracy committed in 1991 and 1992, few in the diamond business were very surprised. Some even thought that

DeBeers's concern about the encroachment of artificial diamonds might have accelerated the settlement, a suggestion the company denies. One spokesperson for DeBeers commented, "It was apparent by 2000 that diamonds were beginning to lose out to other luxury goods. Our sales were flat, and other luxury goods were taking off."

However, the chairman of Apollo Diamonds, which makes synthetic diamonds for both the jewelry and technology markets, observes that "DeBeers may recognize that market dynamics are going to change with the introduction of cultured diamonds. It does . . . seem coincidental that their settlement comes at the same time that Apollo Diamonds is entering the market with cultured diamonds."

In addition to the fine, DeBeers was required to reform its business practices to ensure that the market remains competitive. The company also agreed to join an industry effort to prevent trade in diamonds from being used to pay for brutal conflicts in African countries.[1]

Chapter Overview

Business firms exist to facilitate the exchange of goods and services and thereby make a profit for their owners. There is growing sentiment among the world's economies that free exchange, unlike the restricted market DeBeers once controlled, offers the highest profits for firms and the widest choices of products for consumers.

When we examine the exchanges that companies and societies make as a whole, we are focusing on the *economic systems* operating in different nations. These systems reflect the combination of policies and choices a nation makes to allocate resources among its citizens. Countries vary in the ways they allocate scarce resources.

Economics, the social science analyzing the choices made by people and governments in allocating scarce resources, affects each of us, since everyone is involved in producing, distributing, or simply consuming goods and services. In fact, your life is affected by economics every day. When you decide what goods to buy, what services to use, or what activities to fit into your schedule, you are making economic choices.

The choices you make often are international in scope. Consider, for example, someone who decides to buy a new set of automobile tires. Along with such U.S. companies as Goodyear, the person might consider buying a non-U.S. brand like Michelin or Pirelli. If he or she buys the Michelin tires, this one person with a single purchase has become involved in international trade by choosing to buy from a French supplier. In recent years, U.S. firms have begun emphasizing the American origin of their goods and services in their marketing communications in an effort to appeal to consumers' desire to support the U.S. economy. A recent promotional message from Goodyear utilizing such appeals is shown in Figure 3.1. Businesses also make economic decisions when they choose how to use human and natural resources, invest in machinery and buildings, and form partnerships with other firms.

Economists refer to the study of small economic units, such as individual consumers, families, and businesses, as **microeconomics.** On a broader level, government decisions about the operation of the country's economy also affect you, your job, and your financial future. A major feature of the Sarbanes-Oxley Act of 2002 was to place strict limits on the consulting services that accounting firms can provide for a company whose financial records they audit. The new law affected the entire accounting profession, including the need for accountants and the request for their services. The subsequent sale of major public accounting firm PricewaterhouseCooper's consulting services to IBM was a result of the new limitations.[2] The study of a country's overall economic issues is called **macroeconomics** (*macro* means large). This discipline addresses such issues as how an economy maintains and allocates resources and how government policies affect people's standards of living. Chapter 1 described the increasing interdependence of nations and their economies. Reflecting that interdependence, macroeconomics examines not just the economic policies of individual nations but the ways in which those individual policies affect the overall world economy. Microeconomics and macroeconomics are interrelated disciplines. Macroeconomic issues help to shape the decisions that individuals, families, and businesses make every day.

In this chapter, we introduce economic theory and the economic challenges facing individuals, businesses, and governments in the global marketplace. We begin with the microeconomic concepts of supply and demand and their effect on the prices people pay for goods and services. Next we explain the various types of economic systems, along with tools for comparing and evaluating their performance. Then we examine the ways in which governments seek to manage economies to create stable business environments in their countries. The final section in the chapter looks at some of the driving economic forces that are affecting people's lives during the first decade of the 21st century.

economics social science that analyzes the choices made by people and governments in allocating scarce resources.

microeconomics study of small economic units, such as individual consumers, families, and businesses.

macroeconomics study of a nation's overall economic issues, such as how an economy maintains and allocates resources and how government policies affect the standards of living of its citizens.

demand willingness and ability of buyers to purchase goods and services.

supply willingness and ability of sellers to provide goods and services.

Microeconomics: The Forces of Demand and Supply

A good way to begin the study of economics is to look at the economic activities and choices of individuals and small economic units such as families and firms. These economic actions determine both the prices of goods and services and the amounts sold. Microeconomic information is vital for a business because the survival of the firm depends on selling enough of its products at prices high enough to cover expenses and earn profits. This information is also important to consumers, whose well-being may depend on the prices and availability of needed goods and services.

At the heart of every business endeavor is an exchange between a buyer and a seller. The buyer recognizes that he or she has a need or wants a particular good or service and is willing to pay a seller to obtain it. The seller wants to participate in the process because of the anticipated financial gains from selling the good or service. So, the exchange process involves both demand and supply. **Demand** refers to the willingness and ability of buyers to purchase goods and services at different prices. The other side of the exchange process is **supply,** the willingness and ability of sellers to provide goods and services for sale at different prices. Understanding the factors that determine demand and supply, as well as how the two interact, can help you understand many actions and decisions of individuals, businesses, and government. This section takes a closer look at these concepts.

FIGURE 3.1
Focusing on U.S.-Made Vehicles and Tires

Courtesy of the Goodyear Tire and Rubber Company

Factors Driving Demand

For most people, economics amounts to a balance between their unlimited wants and limited financial means. Because of this dilemma, each person must make choices about how much money to save and how much to spend, as well as how to allocate spending among all the goods and services competing for attention. This continuing effort to address unlimited wants with limited means caused one writer to refer to economics as "the dismal science."

Even though you may be convinced that the Nissan Xterra shown in Figure 3.2 can take you rock climbing, mountain biking, and backpacking—and haul all the necessary gear—your spouse might have dreams of a new Infiniti, which its advertisers call "the muscle car with brains." The Nissan Xterra retails for around $27,000, while the Infiniti's sticker is roughly $42,000. Eventually, you may win because the Xterra costs less, allowing you and your spouse to spend more money on other needs, such as a larger apartment or your own home.

Demand is driven by a number of factors that influence how people decide to spend their money, including price. It may also be driven by outside circumstances or larger economic events, such as those described in the Hits and Misses box. Diversified Optics, a small manufacturer of optical devices located in Salem, New Hampshire, experienced dramatically increased demand for its products—night scopes and night vision binoculars the military uses during combat and other activities—during the recent war with Iraq.[3]

In general, as the price of a good or service goes up, people buy smaller amounts. In other words, as price rises, the quantity demanded declines. At lower prices, consumers are generally willing to buy more of a good. A **demand curve** is a graph of the amount of a product that buyers will purchase at different prices. Demand curves typically slope downward, meaning that lower and lower prices attract larger and larger purchases.

Over the past few years, a steep decline in prices for DVD players has been matched by strong growth in demand among viewers who recognize the superior picture quality provided by the new format. These price cuts have been accompanied by additional incentives in the form of lower prices on DVDs—sometimes even lower than the videocassette version of films—and huge increases in shelf space at rental outlets like Blockbuster. To attract purchasers who resist the format switch because of their VHS video collections, DVD suppliers have offered a combination player capable of playing either version.

FIGURE 3.2
Building Demand for a Product

HITS & MISSES

Waging War on the Gas Guzzlers

If you're even a little familiar with Americans' ardor for bigger and heavier automobiles, it shouldn't come as a surprise that it took nothing less than a "perfect storm" of converging factors to start cooling the U.S.'s love affair with huge gas-guzzling vehicles. While the country is far from shaking off its dependence on foreign oil supplies, recent months have brought gasoline prices over $2 a gallon, which nearly doubled the cost of filling up the average car and brought a full tank into the $60 to $80 range for owners of the biggest SUVs like General Motors's Hummer.

Drivers also began to wake up to the consequences for the country at large of increased dependence on imported fuel, including worrying about balance of payments issues and the need to maintain difficult trade alliances with governments and organizations that are otherwise hostile to many U.S. interests. For instance, OPEC, the oil-producing cartel, routinely restricts oil output to force wholesale prices of crude oil up worldwide. Although domestic oil refiners are producing oil at record levels, it is still not enough to meet current domestic demands.

Not least of the storm winds gathering around gas guzzlers is a growing concern about the environmental effects of squandering a dwindling resource. Creating more pollution and drilling for oil in ecologically sensitive areas are unwelcome future options, even to some who prefer gas guzzlers to more efficient vehicles like the new hybrid cars. And in the shorter term, prices of raw materials—chemicals, plastics, and auto parts—and of consumer items such as carpet, tires, electronics, and paint all depend on the price of oil. So, higher oil prices, driven by unchecked gas consumption, reverberate throughout the economy.

Months of declining sales of General Motors's $50,000 Hummer 2 might provide some evidence that drivers are rejecting gas guzzlers at last. The heavy, oversized military-style vehicle has recently begun spending more days on the selling lot than other luxury cars, taking an average of 62 days to sell compared with 31 days about a year ago. GM is giving dealers incentives of $2,000 to $3,000, and dealers are passing $1,500 cash back to buyers (with dealer financing). Meanwhile, at the GM factory, there are plans to offer a midsize SUV, the Hummer 3, for thousands of dollars less. GM sees the slowing of H2 sales as a demand problem based on demographics. Teenagers find the Hummer exciting, and the other group attracted to it consists of buyers in their late 40s and 50s who want to feel young. According to one industry analyst, GM's problem is that there are too few Hummer buyers in those two groups to maintain high sales volume.

But the car's puny nine miles per gallon is even worse than buyers expected, and in the wake of complaints about its pathetic mileage comes dissatisfaction with the combat-style vehicle's cheaply designed and cramped interior.

QUESTIONS FOR CRITICAL THINKING

1. Given slackening demand, what challenges do manufacturers and retailers of gas-guzzling SUVs face?
2. Do you think slowing sales of the Hummer represent consumers' short-term frustration with gasoline prices or a long-term change in driving preferences? Explain your answer.

Sources: James R. Healey, "Bush Plans Could Mean Cheaper Fuel," *USA Today*, November 5, 2004, p. B1; Joan Lowy, "Experts Say High Gas Prices May Be Here to Stay," *Mobile Register*, October 31, 2004, p. F6; Barrington Salmon, "Oil's Slippery Slope," *USA Today*, October 18, 2004, p. Bf; Sharon Silke Carte, "GM Adds Incentives as Hummer Sales Decline," *The Wall Street Journal*, August 18, 2004, p. D2.

Gasoline provides another good example of how demand curves work. The left side of Figure 3.3 shows a possible demand curve for the total amount of gasoline that people will purchase at different prices. When gasoline is priced at $2.09 a gallon, drivers may fill up their tanks once or twice a week. At $2.59 a gallon, many of them may start economizing. They may make fewer trips, start carpooling, or ride buses to work. So, the quantity of gasoline demanded at $2.59 a gallon is lower than the amount demanded at $2.09 a gallon. The opposite happens at $1.59 a gallon. Some drivers may decide to top off their tanks more often than they would at a higher price; they may also decide to take cross-country vacations or drive to school instead of taking the bus. As a result, more gasoline is sold at $1.59 a gallon than at $2.09 a gallon. These relationships are played out in real life all the time. As you undoubtedly know, gas prices soared as oil prices rose prior to war with Iraq. Consumers

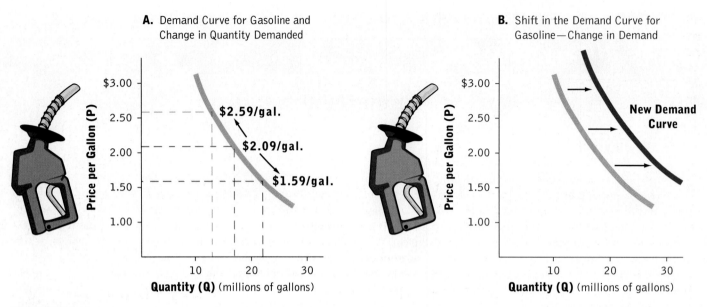

A. Demand Curve for Gasoline and Change in Quantity Demanded

$2.59/gal.
$2.09/gal.
$1.59/gal.

Price per Gallon (P)

Quantity (Q) (millions of gallons)

B. Shift in the Demand Curve for Gasoline—Change in Demand

New Demand Curve

Price per Gallon (P)

Quantity (Q) (millions of gallons)

FIGURE 3.3
Demand Curves for Gasoline

complained—some states even launched investigations into gasoline pricing practices—and they also cut back on their driving.

Economists make a clear distinction between changes in the quantity demanded at various prices and changes in overall demand. A change in quantity demanded, such as the change that occurs at different gasoline prices, is simply movement along the demand curve. A change in overall demand, on the other hand, results in an entirely new demand curve.

As American households' incomes have risen—aided in many cases by two incomes—and their transportation tastes have changed, many American consumers have chosen to purchase sport-utility vehicles (SUVs), which consume large amounts of gasoline. At the same time, in developing countries like India and China, consumers have been able to afford cars for the first time. These changes have increased the demand for gasoline at all prices.[4] The right side of Figure 3.3 shows how the increased demand for gasoline worldwide has created a new demand curve. The new demand curve shifts to the right of the old demand curve, indicating that overall demand has increased at every price. A demand curve can also shift to the left when the demand for a good or service drops. However, the demand curve still has the same shape.

Although price is the underlying cause of movement along a demand curve, many factors can combine to determine the overall demand for a product—that is, the shape and position of the demand curve. These influences include customer preferences and incomes, the prices of substitute and complementary items, the number of buyers in a market, and the strength of their optimism regarding the future. Changes in any of these factors will produce a new demand curve.

Take a change in income as an example. As consumers have more money to spend, firms can sell more products at every price. This means the demand curve has shifted to the right. The price of complementary goods also can influence demand. If the price of gasoline remains high, we would expect the demand for SUVs to fall as some consumers switch to more fuel-efficient forms of transportation, creating demand for a different type of vehicle. Millennium Cell, a New Jersey-based firm that has developed a hydrogen fueling system for cars, is hoping that this demand takes hold. "If we can get the oil man to say the word 'hydrogen,' that's significant progress," says Stephen Tang, president of the firm.[5] Table 3.1 describes how a demand curve is likely to respond to each of these changes.

For a business to succeed, management must carefully monitor the factors that may affect demand for the goods and services it hopes to sell. In setting prices, firms often try to predict how the chosen levels will influence the amounts they sell. The Coca-Cola Co. experimented with smart vending machines, adjusting their prices to such variables as the weather. If the temperature was hot outside, the machines could automatically raise the price. If the vending machine contains too many cans of

Table 3.1   Expected Shifts in Demand Curves

Factor	Demand Curve Shifts to the Right *if:*	to the Left *if:*
Customer preferences	increase	decrease
Number of buyers	increases	decreases
Buyers' incomes	increase	decrease
Prices of substitute goods	increase	decrease
Prices of complementary goods	decrease	increase
Future expectations become more	optimistic	pessimistic

root beer and restocking was five days away, the machine could lower the price of root beer. Organizations also try to influence overall demand through advertising, free samples and presentations at retail stores, sales calls, product enhancements, and other marketing techniques.

Factors Driving Supply

Important economic factors also affect supply, the willingness and ability of firms to provide goods and services at different prices. Just as consumers must make choices about how to spend their incomes, businesses must also make decisions about how to use their resources to obtain the best profits.

Obviously, sellers would prefer to command high rather than low prices for their product offerings. A **supply curve** graphically shows the relationship between different prices and the quantities that sellers will offer for sale, regardless of demand. Movement along the supply curve is the opposite of movement along the demand curve. So as price rises, the quantity that sellers are willing to supply also rises. At progressively lower prices, the quantity supplied decreases. In Figure 3.4, a possible supply curve for gasoline shows that increasing prices for gasoline should bring increasing supplies to market, as oil companies are motivated by the possibility of earning growing profits.

Businesses require certain inputs to operate effectively in producing their output. As discussed in Chapter 1, these *factors of production* include natural resources, capital, human resources, and entrepreneurship. Natural resources include

Courtesy of America's Dairy Farmers and Milk Processors

Beauty mark.

Milk has vitamin A and niacin to help keep skin looking smooth and healthy.

got milk?

For more than a decade, America's Dairy Farmers and Milk Processors, the milk industry's trade association, has tried to increase overall demand for its products with its famous "Got Milk?" promotional campaign. Celebrities adorned with milk "moustaches" are used to attract attention to their advertising messages.

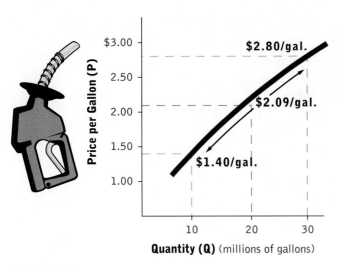

FIGURE 3.4
Supply Curve for Gasoline

everything that is useful in its natural state, including land, building sites, forests, and mineral deposits. Human resources include the physical labor and intellectual inputs contributed by managers and operative employees. Capital refers to resources such as technology, tools, information, physical facilities, and financial capabilities. The fourth factor of production, entrepreneurship, is the willingness to take risks to create and operate a business.

Factors of production play a central role in determining the overall supply of goods and services. A change in the cost or availability of any of these inputs can shift the entire supply curve, either increasing or decreasing the amount available at every price. For example, if the cost of raw materials—natural resources—rises, producers may respond by lowering production levels, shifting the supply curve to the left. On the other hand, if an innovation in the production process allows them to turn out more products using fewer raw materials than before, the change reduces the overall cost of the finished products, shifting the supply curve to the right. Table 3.2 summarizes how changes in various factors can affect the supply curve.

A rightward shift in the supply curve for electricity in recent years is the result of a glut of new generating plants. Responding to periodic supply emergencies and encouraged by such remarks as Vice President Dick Cheney's warning that the only way to avert a nationwide energy crisis is to open more than one new power plant per week for the next 20 years, such electricity producers as Mirant, AES, Calpine, and NRG Energy began to start up new generating units at three times that rate. The resulting oversupply contributed to price reductions for electricity.[6]

How Demand and Supply Interact

Separate shifts in demand and supply have obvious effects on prices and the availability of products. In the real world, changes do not alternatively affect demand and supply. Several factors often change at the same time—and they keep changing. Sometimes such simultaneous changes in multiple factors cause contradictory pressures on prices and quantities. In other cases, the final direction of prices and quantities reflects the factor that has changed the most.

Figure 3.5 shows the interaction of both supply and demand curves for gasoline on a single graph. Notice that the two curves intersect at *P*. The law of supply and demand states that prices (*P*) are set by the intersection of the supply and demand curves. The point where the two curves meet identifies the **equilibrium price,** the prevailing market price at which you can buy an item.

If the actual market price differs from the equilibrium price, buyers and sellers tend to make economic choices that restore the equilibrium level. So how do we explain the shortages of vaccines to protect against such diseases as tetanus, diphtheria, whooping cough, measles, mumps, and chicken pox? Why do many of the 75 million adults seeking vaccination against influenza often encounter delays in

Table 3.2	Expected Shifts in Supply Curves	
	Supply Curve Shifts	
Factor	**to the Right** *if:*	**to the Left** *if:*
Costs of inputs	decrease	increase
Costs of technologies	decrease	increase
Taxes	decrease	increase
Number of suppliers	increases	decreases

obtaining flu shots? The answer lies with the federal government, which pays vaccine makers between 38 and 60 percent of the going price for these vaccines in the global marketplace. The result is a reduction in product supply. In recent years, the number of commercial makers of the vaccine DTAP dropped from four to two, and the number of tetanus vaccine manufacturers dropped from two to one. Also, current suppliers operate on razor-thin profit margins with just enough production capability and inventory to meet demand—assuming everything goes smoothly. Any unexpected demand results in shortages and delays.[7]

In other situations, suppliers react to market forces by reducing prices. McDonald's Japan, which operates 3,900 restaurants, saw sales plummet following a strong aversion to beef by customers concerned about the brain-destroying illness called "mad cow disease," which originated in the U.K. and was recently discovered in western Canada. Although McDonald's Japan uses Australian beef, sales declined as much as 18 percent below sales of the previous year. So, the firm's management made a pricing decision to increase demand for their supply of beef. They sliced burger prices from 80 yen to 59 yen, or about 50 cents. In addition, they added a more diverse menu of salads and soups to keep customers coming to McDonald's—even if they didn't want a burger at all.[8]

As pointed out earlier, the forces of demand and supply can be affected by a variety of factors. One important variable is the larger economic environment. The next section explains how macroeconomics and economic systems influence market forces and, ultimately, demand, supply, and prices.

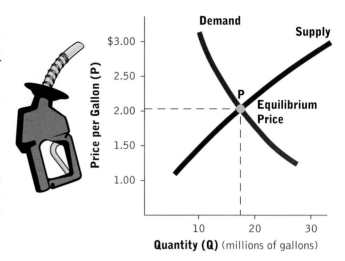

FIGURE 3.5
Law of Supply and Demand

Concept Check

1. What is the difference between changes in quantity demanded at various prices and change in overall demand?
2. What is an equilibrium price?

Macroeconomics: Issues for the Entire Economy

The political and economic choices made in recent years by North Korean leader Kim Jong Il have influenced the daily lives of North Koreans since the death of his father a decade ago. When recent famines killed an estimated 2 million of that nation's 22 million people, the U.S. built goodwill in the formerly isolationist land by donating 1.5 million tons of grain. Although other nations have tried cooperative efforts to increase North Korea's production of consumer goods and to convince them to seek peaceful solutions to problems, it is difficult and expensive to ship goods among North Korea's neighbors because of the different gauges of rail systems. In addition, North Korea's buildup of weapons is likely to deter aid from other countries.[9]

Every country faces decisions about how to best use the four basic factors of production. Each nation's policies and choices help to determine its economic system. But the political, social, and legal environments differ in every country. So, no two countries have exactly the same economic system. In general, however, these systems can be classified into three categories: private enterprise systems, planned economies, or combinations of the two, referred to as *mixed economies*. As business becomes an increasingly global undertaking, it is important to understand the primary features of the various economic systems operating around the world.

Capitalism: The Private Enterprise System and Competition

Most industrialized nations operate economies based on the **private enterprise system,** also known as *capitalism* or a *market economy*. A private enterprise system rewards businesses for meeting the needs and demands of consumers. Government tends to favor a hands-off attitude toward controlling business ownership, profits, and resource allocations. Instead, competition regulates economic life, creating opportunities and challenges that businesspeople must handle to succeed.

private enterprise system economic system that rewards businesses for their ability to identify and serve the needs and demands of customers.

Table 3.3   Types of Competition

Characteristics	Pure Competition	Monopolistic Competition	Oligopoly	Monopoly
Number of competitors	Many	Few to many	Few	No direct competition
Ease of entry into industry by new firms	Easy	Somewhat difficult	Difficult	Regulated by government
Similarity of goods or services offered by competing firms	Similar	Different	Similar or different	No directly competing products
Control over price by individual firms	None	Some	Some	Considerable in a pure monopoly; little in a regulated monopoly
Examples	Small-scale farmer in Indiana	Local fitness center	Boeing aircraft	Rawlings Sporting Goods, exclusive supplier of major league baseballs

The relative competitiveness of a particular industry is an important consideration for every firm because it determines the ease and cost of doing business within that industry. Four basic degrees of competition take shape in a private enterprise system: pure competition, monopolistic competition, oligopoly, and monopoly. Table 3.3 highlights the main differences among these types of competition.

Pure competition is a market structure, like that of small-scale agriculture, in which large numbers of buyers and sellers exchange homogeneous products, so no single participant has a significant influence on price. Instead, prices are set by the market itself as the forces of supply and demand interact. Firms can easily enter or leave a purely competitive market because no single company dominates. Also, in pure competition, buyers see little difference between the goods and services offered by competitors.

Agriculture is probably the best example of pure competition. The grain grown and sold by one farmer is virtually identical to that sold by others. As the weather affects the supply of wheat, soybeans, and cotton, the price for these commodities rises or falls according to the law of supply and demand. Although such factors as weather and acreage set aside each year to grow wheat determine supply, demand also plays a role in prices for commodities. Growing international demand for U.S. wheat has been strong enough to keep prices for that crop steady, even though production has increased.

Monopolistic competition is a market structure, like that for retailing, in which large numbers of buyers and sellers exchange relatively well-differentiated (heterogeneous) products, so each participant has some control over price. Sellers can differentiate their products from competing offerings on the basis of price, quality, or other features. In an industry that features monopolistic competition, it is relatively easy for a firm to begin or stop selling a good or service. The success of one seller often attracts new competitors to such a market. Individual firms also have some control over how their individual goods and services are priced.

An example of monopolistic competition is the market for pet food. Consumers can choose from private-label (store brands) and brand-name products in bags, boxes, and cans. Producers of pet food and the stores that sell it have wide latitude in setting prices. Consumers can choose the store or brand with the lowest prices, or sellers can convince them that a more expensive offering is worth more because it offers better nutrition, more convenience, more information, or other benefits.

An **oligopoly** is a market situation in which relatively few sellers compete and in which high start-up costs form barriers to keep out new competitors. In some oligopolistic industries, such as paper and steel, competitors offer similar products. In others, such as aircraft and automobiles, they sell different models and features. The huge investment required to enter an oligopoly market tends to discourage new competitors. The limited number of sellers also enhances the control these firms exercise over price. Competing products in an oligopoly usually sell for very similar prices because substantial price competition would reduce profits for all firms in the industry. So, a price cut by one firm in an oligopoly will typically be met by its competitors. However, prices can vary from one market to another, as from one country to another.

Cement is a product for which an oligopoly exists. Mexican-based Cemex SA is the third-largest cement manufacturer in the world and the largest seller of cement in both the U.S. and Mexico. It holds 60 percent of the market share in Mexico. Cement is usually sold in bulk in the U.S., like a commodity. However, it is sold as a branded product in Mexico. Cemex's prices are too high for many Mexican families to afford, which often means they must put plans for home building on hold. Since Cemex is also Mexico's largest seller of concrete, which is made

Courtesy of Nestlé Purina PetCare Company

Purina **ONE** cat food may be more expensive than some other brands, but many cat fanciers choose it because it contains ingredients designed to combat a common health problem in felines. Advertisers often highlight the differences in their products from competitors. Monopolistic competition relies on differentiation of products in a market.

with cement, those prices remain high as well. Although large construction companies in the U.S. can force cement manufacturers to drop their prices, Mexican construction companies are smaller and have little clout, so they end up paying higher prices.[10]

The final type of market structure is a **monopoly,** in which a single seller dominates trade in a good or service for which buyers can find no close substitutes. A pure monopoly occurs when a firm possesses unique characteristics so important to competition in its industry that they serve as barriers to prevent entry by would-be competitors. Thanks to a deal with Major League Baseball to supply all 30 MLB teams, Rawlings Sporting Goods has the entire market for major league baseballs. As the opening vignette explained, from the 1930s to the 1990s, De Beers enjoyed a near monopoly in the market for diamonds by virtue of owning or buying any rough diamonds it could throughout the world. The company at one time controlled 80 percent of the world's diamond supply. Recent discoveries of diamond reserves outside De Beers's control, coupled with a lawsuit and a promise to stop buying diamonds sold to raise money for armed conflicts in the African nations of Angola, Sierra Leone, and the Democratic Republic of Congo, have reduced the company's share of the market to 60 percent.

Many firms create short-term monopolies when research breakthroughs permit them to receive exclusive patents on new products. In the pharmaceuticals industry, drug giants like Merck and Pfizer invest billions in research and development programs. When the research leads to successful new drugs, the companies can enjoy the benefits of their patent: the ability to set prices without fear of competitors undercutting them. Once the patent expires, drugs like allergy medicine Claritin may be sold to consumers without a prescription.

Because a monopoly market lacks the benefits of competition, the U.S. government regulates monopolies. Besides issuing patents and limiting their life, the government prohibits most pure monopolies through antitrust legislation such as the Sherman Act and the Clayton Act. The U.S. government has applied these laws against monopoly behavior by Microsoft and by disallowing proposed

© AP/Wide World Photos

Rawlings is the only supplier of baseballs for Major League Baseball and the NCAA.

mergers of large companies in some industries. In other cases, the government permits certain monopolies in exchange for regulating their activities.

With *regulated monopolies,* a local, state, or federal government grants exclusive rights in a certain market to a single firm. Pricing decisions—particularly rate-increase requests—are subject to control by regulatory authorities such as state public service commissions. An example is the delivery of first-class mail, a monopoly held by the United States Postal Service (USPS). The USPS is a self-supporting corporation wholly owned by the federal government. Although it is no longer run by Congress, postal rates are set by a Postal Commission and approved by a Board of Governors. The federal government wants the USPS to be profitable, and a special commission has been created with the mission of overhauling the organization with the goal of turning its 30,000 offices around the country into revenue producers.[11]

During the 1980s and 1990s, the U.S. government favored a trend away from regulated monopolies and toward **deregulation.** Regulated monopolies that have been deregulated include long-distance and local telephone service, cable television, cellular phones, and electrical service. Long-distance companies like AT&T and MCI are now allowed to offer local service. The idea is to improve customer service and reduce prices for telephone customers through increased competition. But the four regional "Baby Bells," which are the four largest phone companies in the U.S., currently control 90 percent of the market. It will take time and money for any competitors to make a dent in these markets.[12]

Deregulation of electric utilities began when California opened its market in 1998. By 2002, when the giant Houston-based energy firm Enron collapsed, about half the states were on board. In those states, private companies could compete with utilities to sell electricity and natural gas. However, California's disastrous energy deregulation, during the early years of the 21st century, brought a temporary halt to this trend. California joined investors reeling from watching the stock of bankrupt energy trader Enron plunge from $90 a share to less than 9 cents three years later.[13]

Planned Economies: Communism and Socialism

In a **planned economy,** government controls determine business ownership, profits, and resource allocation to accomplish government goals rather than those set by individual businesses. Two forms of planned economies are communism and socialism.

The writings of Karl Marx in the mid-1800s formed the basis of communist theory. Marx believed that private enterprise economies created unfair conditions and led to worker exploitation because business owners controlled most of society's resources and reaped most of the economy's rewards. Instead, he suggested an economic system called **communism,** in which all property would be shared equally by the people of a community under the direction of a strong central government. Marx believed that elimination of private ownership of property and businesses would ensure the emergence of a classless society that would benefit all. Each individual would contribute to the nation's overall economic success, and resources would be distributed according to each person's needs. Under communism, the central government owns the means of production, and the people work for state-owned enterprises. The government determines what people can buy because it dictates what is produced in the nation's factories and farms.

A number of nations adopted communist economic systems during the early 20th century in an effort to improve the quality of life for their citizens and to correct abuses they believed to be present in their previous systems. In practice, however, communist governments often give people little or no freedom of choice in selecting jobs, purchases, or investments. Communist governments often make mistakes in planning the best uses of resources to compete in the growing global marketplace. Government-owned monopolies often suffer from inefficiency.

Consider the former Soviet Union, where large government bureaucracies controlled nearly every aspect of daily life. Shortages became chronic because producers had little or no incentive to satisfy customers. The quality of goods and services also suffered for the same reason. When Mikhail Gorbachev became the last prime minister of the dying Soviet Union, he tried to improve the quality of Soviet-made products. Effectively shut out of trading in the global marketplace and caught up in a treasury-depleting arms race with the U.S., the Soviet Union faced severe financial problems. Eventually, these economic crises led to the collapse of Soviet communism and the breakup of the Soviet Union itself.

A second type of planned economy, **socialism,** is characterized by government ownership and operation of major industries. Socialists assert that major industries are too important to a society to be left in private hands and that government-owned businesses can serve the public's interest better than can private firms. For instance, these countries might operate their health-care industry under a socialist system. However, socialism also allows private ownership in industries considered less crucial to social welfare, like retail shops, restaurants, and certain types of manufacturing facilities.

What's Ahead for Communism?   Many formerly communist nations have undergone dramatic changes in recent years. Some of the most exciting developments have occurred in the republics that formerly composed the Soviet Union. These new nations have restructured their economies by introducing Western-style private enterprise systems. By decentralizing economic planning and sweetening incentives for workers, they are slowly shifting to market-driven systems.

Economic reforms in the former communist countries haven't always progressed smoothly. Although many have opened their arms to Western entrepreneurs and businesses, these investors have often encountered difficulties such as official corruption, crime, and the persistence of bloated bureaucracies. Reducing the power of government-operated monopolies has also proved a difficult challenge.

Today, communism exists in just a few countries, like the People's Republic of China, Cuba, and North Korea. Even these nations show signs of growing openness toward some of the benefits of private enterprise as possible solutions to their economic challenges. Since 1978, China has been shifting toward a more market-oriented economy. The national government has given local government and individual plant managers more say in business decisions and has permitted some small private businesses. Households now have more control over agriculture, in contrast to the collectivized farms introduced with communism. In addition, Western products such as McDonald's and Coca-Cola have been making their way into Chinese consumers' lives.

Another symbol of China's changing economic strategy accompanied the 1997 return of Hong Kong to Chinese rule. China's government promised that Hong Kong's businesses will continue to operate in a private enterprise economic system. The addition of this prosperous city has helped China to achieve the world's second-largest gross domestic product (GDP).[14]

Mixed Market Economies

Private enterprise systems and planned economies adopt basically opposite approaches to operating economies. In practice, though, most countries implement **mixed market economies,** economic systems that display characteristics of both planned and market economies in varying degrees. In nations generally considered to have a private enterprise economy, government-owned firms frequently operate alongside private enterprises.

Table 3.4   Comparison of Alternative Economic Systems

System Features	Capitalism (Private Enterprise)	Planned Economies		
		Communism	Socialism	Mixed Economy
Ownership of enterprises	Businesses are owned privately, often by large numbers of people. Minimal government ownership leaves production in private hands.	Government owns the means of production with few exceptions, like small plots of land.	Government owns basic industries, but private owners operate some small enterprises.	A strong private sector blends with public enterprises.
Management of enterprises	Enterprises are managed by owners or their representatives, with minimal government interference.	Centralized management controls all state enterprises in line with 3- to 5-year plans. Planning now is being decentralized.	Significant government planning pervades socialist nations. State enterprises are managed directly by government bureaucrats.	Management of the private sector resembles that under capitalism. Professionals may also manage state enterprises.
Rights to profits	Entrepreneurs and investors are entitled to all profits (minus taxes) that their firms earn.	Profits are not allowed under communism.	Only the private sector of a socialist economy generates profits.	Entrepreneurs and investors are entitled to private-sector profits, although they often must pay high taxes. State enterprises are also expected to produce returns.
Rights of employees	The rights to choose one's occupation and to join a labor union have long been recognized.	Employee rights are limited in exchange for promised protection against unemployment.	Workers may choose their occupations and join labor unions, but the government influences career decisions for many people.	Workers may choose jobs and labor-union membership. Unions often become quite strong.
Worker incentives	Considerable incentives motivate people to perform at their highest levels.	Incentives are emerging in communist countries.	Incentives usually are limited in state enterprises but do motivate workers in the private sector.	Capitalist-style incentives operate in the private sector. More limited incentives influence public-sector activities.

France has blended socialist and free enterprise policies for hundreds of years. The nation's banking, automobile, utility, aviation, steel, and railroad industries have traditionally been run as nationalized industries, controlled by the government. Meanwhile, a market economy flourishes in other industries. Over the past two decades, the French government has loosened its reins on state-owned companies, inviting both competition and private investment into industries previously operated as government monopolies.

The proportions of private and public enterprise can vary widely in mixed economies, and the mix frequently changes. Like France, dozens of countries have converted government-owned and operated companies into privately held businesses during the past two decades in a trend known as **privatization.** Governments may privatize state-owned enterprises to raise funds and to improve their economies, believing that private corporations can manage and operate the businesses more cheaply and efficiently than government units can.

Table 3.4 compares the alternative economic systems on the basis of ownership and management of enterprises, rights to profits, employee rights, and worker incentives.

Concept Check

1. Which economic system is the U.S. economy based on?
2. What are the two types of planned economies?

Evaluating Economic Performance

Ideally, an economic system should provide two important benefits for its citizens: a stable business environment and sustained growth. In a stable business environment, the overall supply of needed goods and services is aligned with the overall demand for those goods and services. No wild fluctuations in price or availability complicate economic decisions. Consumers and businesses not only have access to ample supplies of desired products at affordable prices but also have money to buy the items they demand.

Growth is another important economic goal. An ideal economy incorporates steady change directed toward continually expanding the amount of goods and services produced from the nation's resources. Growth leads to expanded job opportunities, improved wages, and a rising standard of living.

Flattening the Business Cycle

In reality, a nation's economy tends to flow through various stages of a business cycle: prosperity, recession, depression, and recovery. No true economic depressions have occurred in the U.S. since the 1930s, and most economists believe that society is capable of preventing future depressions through effective economic policies. Consequently, they expect a recession to give way to a period of economic recovery. Figure 3.6 shows the four stages of the business cycle.

recession cyclical economic contraction that lasts for six months or longer.

Both business decisions and consumer buying patterns differ at each stage of the business cycle. In periods of economic prosperity, unemployment remains low, strong consumer confidence about the future leads to record purchases, and businesses expand to take advantage of marketplace opportunities. The decade-long run of economic prosperity in the U.S. from the early 1990s to 2001 was one of the longest in a century.

During a **recession**—a cyclical economic contraction that lasts for six months or longer—consumers frequently postpone major purchases and shift buying patterns toward basic, functional products carrying low prices. Businesses mirror these changes in the marketplace by slowing production, postponing expansion plans, reducing inventories, and often cutting the size of their workforces. During past recessions, people facing layoffs and depletions of household savings have sold cars, jewelry, and stocks to make ends meet. During the most recent recession, they did this as well but with a twist: They turned to eBay. There, they sold everything from old books to kitchen knickknacks. Rick Steinberg, Jr., of Stockton, California, lost his job and found himself in urgent need of $1,100 for car repairs so he could expand his job hunt to the San Francisco area. He turned to a prized possession: his collection of medieval Lego figures featuring warriors, swordsmen, and smiling peasants. In a yard sale, the tiny toys would have brought next to nothing. But on eBay, Steinberg fetched $2,000. "It's like I had stocks and I'm cashing them in," said Steinberg.[15]

> ## *They Said It*
>
> It's a recession when your neighbor loses his job; it's a depression when you lose your own.
>
> —*Harry S. Truman (1884–1972)*
> *33rd president of the United States*

Should the economic slowdown continue in a downward spiral over an extended period of time, the economy falls into depression. Many Americans have grown up hearing stories from their great-grandparents who lived through the Great Depression of the 1930s. However, some companies can actually manage to prosper during poor economic times. Businesswoman Maria de Lourdes Sobrino, founder of Lulu's Dessert, has survived three recessions and continues to remain optimistic about the future.

In the *recovery* stage of the business cycle, the economy emerges from recession and consumer spending picks up steam. Even though businesses often continue to rely on part-time and other temporary workers during the early stages of a recovery, unemployment begins to decline, as business activity accelerates and firms seek additional workers to meet growing production demands. Gradually, the concerns of recession begin to disappear, and consumers start purchasing more discretionary items such as vacations and new computer equipment (see the

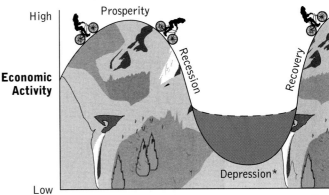

FIGURE 3.6
Four Stages of the Business Cycle
*Most economists believe that sufficient government tools are available to prevent the occurrence of a major depression. Thus, a recession would be followed by an economic recovery.

BUSINESS TOOL KIT

Basic Computer Skills Needed in the Global Age

College is a place where your horizons are broadened and your brain is wrinkled. It is also the place to get acquainted with or further develop basic computer skills. Be sure to learn these basics even if they aren't required in college—you will need them in the professional world. Everyday technology tools such as those listed below will keep you productive and computer savvy. Computers are as essential as pencil and paper in today's global world, so using a computer keyboard, accessing the Internet, and operating software proficiently will give you a definite edge. Here are some of the essential applications to learn:

1. **Word processing software.** Software that uses a computer to type, store, retrieve, edit, and print various types of documents. The most common word processing programs are Microsoft Word and WordPerfect.

2. **Corporate e-mail systems.** *E-mail* is short for electronic mail, which facilitates the rapid transmission of messages both inside and outside the organization. E-mail has many advantages over snail mail, but remember that e-mailed messages are *not* private. Your company has the right to monitor your e-mail usage, so be sure to use e-mail for work-related purposes only. Many companies use Microsoft Outlook or Lotus Notes.

3. **Desktop publishing software.** A system that allows you to use different typefaces, specify various margins and justifications, and embed illustrations and graphs directly into the flow of text. Many firms use desktop publishing systems to create and print newsletters, reports, form let-

ters, brochures, and advertising materials. Two examples of desktop publishing software are Microsoft Publisher and Quark Xpress.

4. **Spreadsheet applications.** Software programs that create the computerized equivalent of an accountant's worksheet, allowing the user to manipulate variables and see the impact of alternative decisions on operating results. Lotus 1-2-3, Microsoft Excel, and Quattro Pro are three of the more popular spreadsheet programs.

5. **Computerized presentation software.** A type of business software that enables users to create highly stylized images for slide shows and reports. You can create various types of charts and graphs with presentation tools such as Microsoft's PowerPoint and Corel's Presentations.

6. **Internet.** Worldwide network of interconnected computers that lets anyone with access to a personal computer—equipped with a modem and Internet connection—send and receive images and data anywhere.

7. **World Wide Web.** Collection of resources on the Internet that offers easy access to text, graphics, sound, and other multimedia resources.

8. **Additional company software.** Any type of proprietary company software that your organization will train you to operate, such as inventory, accounting, graphics, banking, electronic timesheet, and other types of programs.

Sources: "Advice on Developing Computer Skills," http://www.epinions.com, June 26, 2003; Diana Carew, "Computer Skills Key to 21st Century Literacy," *Community College Week,* November 11, 2002, p. S3; Kathleen Melymuka, "Charlotte's Web of Educational Help," *Computerworld,* September 11, 2000, p. 50.

Best Business Practices box). It is important to note that recovery doesn't necessarily take place at a steady pace. As one economic journalist puts it, "One hour brings good news, the next bad." But the National Bureau of Economic Research usually declares when a recession begins and when it ends.[16]

Economists observe several indicators to measure and evaluate how successfully an economic system provides both stability and growth. These variables include productivity as measured by GDP, rate of inflation or deflation, and employment levels.

Productivity and the Nation's Gross Domestic Product

productivity relationship between the goods and services produced in a nation each year and the inputs needed to produce them.

An important concern for every economy is **productivity,** the relationship between the goods and services produced in a nation each year and the inputs needed to produce them. In general, as productivity rises, so does an economy's growth and the wealth of its citizens. In a recession, productivity stagnates or even declines.

As Chapter 1 explained, a commonly used measure of productivity is a country's **gross domestic product (GDP),** the sum of all goods and services produced within a nation's boundaries each year.

BEST BUSINESS PRACTICES

Breaking Microsoft's Stranglehold on Computer Operating Systems

Over the past couple of decades, through innovation and acquisitions, Microsoft has built a near-monopoly with its ubiquitous Windows operating system, giving it tremendous power in the personal computer marketplace and earning widespread complaints by captive users of the system. Now a new challenger is gaining strength, backed by the likes of IBM, Hewlett-Packard, and other hardware manufacturers, some of whom are spending big bucks to promote it. Linux, an alternative and, some say, a more user-friendly and responsive operating system, is free to users and—better yet—it's an open system. That means that technical users of the program can make changes in it to meet their specific needs, an advantage Windows doesn't offer.

The creators of Linux have been pushing the product, not to make a profit—it is, after all, free of cost—but to ensure that the marketplace for computer operating systems remains a creative and competitive one rather than the near-monopoly Microsoft's business practices have created. And it looks as though Linux might be making inroads.

Created initially in 1991 by Linus Torvalds, then a college student in Finland, Linux developed through the free contributions of thousands of programmers around the world, whose creative input Torvalds has organized and distributed. Although it began as a favorite among users outside the corporate world, the operating system is now the backbone of data centers at firms like Charles Schwab & Co. and Sabre Holdings.

IBM is heavily invested in Linux, spending billions to cofound the nonprofit that now manages Linux's development, opening Linux training centers in developing countries,

nurturing new users as big as the city government of Munich, and dedicating its own programmers to writing free Linux code. "No one wants to be monopolized and controlled," says the general manager of IBM's Linux division. "Customers have been dominated by a single vendor. Linux gives you a chance to unlock that. We've got 50 more deals like Munich going right now."

Another new Windows competitor is Mozilla, which offers an open-source Internet browser called Firefox that is rapidly gaining a reputation for being fast and, more important, substantially less vulnerable to virus attacks than Windows's Internet Explorer (IE). IE is a particular target of virus writers, with attacks aimed at it rising by 500 percent last year, according to the security software maker Symantec.

Microsoft has issued software fixes for its current operating systems and browsers, and it is offering big customers like foreign governments earlier involvement in programming decisions as well as training, support, and lower prices. But most observers believe that these cracks in the monopoly can only widen as time passes.

QUESTIONS FOR CRITICAL THINKING
1. Do you think competition in the market for computer operating systems is a good thing for PC users? Why or why not?
2. Can Microsoft protect its market share? How?

Sources: Andy Reinhardt, "Not So Fast, Linux," *BusinessWeek*, November 8, 2004, pp. 60–61; Steve Hamm, "A World Without Microsoft," *BusinessWeek*, November 8, 2004, p. 132; Cassell Bryan-Low, "Microsoft Notches Open-Source Win with UK Accord," *The Wall Street Journal*, August 18, 2004, p. B8.

Economists calculate per-capita GDP by summing the total output of all goods and services produced within a country and then dividing that output by the number of citizens. GDP is an important indicator for measuring a country's business cycle, since a shrinking GDP indicates a recession. As the economy again begins to expand, GDP reflects this growth.

In the U.S., GDP is tracked by the Bureau of Economic Analysis (BEA), a division of the U.S. Department of Commerce. Current updates and historical data on the GDP are available at the BEA's Web site (http://www.bea.doc.gov).

Price-Level Changes

Another important indicator of an economy's stability is the general level of prices. For most of the 20th century, economic decision makers concerned themselves with **inflation,** rising prices caused by a combination of excess consumer demand and increases in the costs of raw materials, component parts, human resources, and other factors of production. Excess consumer demand generates what is known as *demand-pull inflation;* rises in costs of factors of production generates *cost-push inflation.* America's

inflation rising prices caused by a combination of excess consumer demand and increases in the costs of raw materials, human resources, and other factors of production.

SOLVING AN ETHICAL CONTROVERSY

When a Bargain Isn't a Bargain

Every consumer loves a bargain. There's nothing like the thrill of finding something really great at a really low price—whether it's a designer coat, an airfare, or a new washing machine. But in the first years of the 21st century, prices on such items as clothing, furniture, long-distance telephone services, automobiles, lodging, appliances, and airfares remained unchanged or even declined instead of increasing—sometimes at double-digit rates. Some industries simply experienced a slowdown in price hikes. Consumers loved it, but economists warned that price drops could actually lead to an even weaker economy.

Should businesses continue to cut prices to attract customers?

PRO
1. Consumers deserve every break they can get, especially during a recession. Price drops help everyone.
2. Lower prices encourage consumers to spend more, thus circulating more money through the economy.

CON
1. Consistent price declines mean smaller profits, which can force businesses to cut costs—and jobs—wherever possible.
2. Price cuts could slow economic recovery and push the economy into a spiral of deflation, which hasn't occurred in the U.S. since the 1930s and the Great Depression.

SUMMARY
With more supply than demand for certain products—such as airline tickets, banking services, computers, and many retail goods—companies have actually cut back on their supply by closing factories, stores, and offices. Consumers have gotten used to low prices and are insisting on them. Industry observers have pointed out for several years that the overall number of retail stores in the U.S. is excessive. Many of them predict a shakeout in which weaker companies will not survive. "We have too many businesses," says Paul Kasriel, chief economist for Northern Trust Corp., "and they can't all make it."

Sources: Jodie T. Allen, "Watch Out Below," *U.S. News & World Report,* May 26, 2003, pp. 36–38; Robert J. Samuelson, "The Bogeyman of Deflation," *Newsweek,* May 19, 2003, p. 42; Rich Miller, "Commentary: If Deflation Sets In, the Fed Has a Problem," *BusinessWeek Online,* January 27, 2003, http://www.businessweek.com.

most severe inflationary period during the last half of the 20th century peaked in 1980, when general price levels jumped almost 14 percent in a single year. In extreme cases, an economy may experience *hyperinflation*—an economic situation characterized by soaring prices. In 1993, for example, Ukrainian consumers, living through the confusion of their first year as an independent nation following the collapse of the Soviet Union, saw the price of food, clothes, and housing soar 50 times what they had paid the previous year!

Inflation devalues money as persistent price increases reduce the amount of goods and services people can purchase with a given amount of money. This is bad news for people whose incomes do not keep up with inflation or who have most of their wealth in investments paying a fixed rate of interest. Inflation can be good news to those whose income is rising or those with debts at a fixed rate of interest. A homeowner during inflationary times is paying off a fixed-rate mortgage with money that is worth less and less each year. Over the last decade, inflation helped a strong stock market to drive up the number of millionaires from 2 million in 1991 to over 7 million. But because of inflation, being a millionaire does not make a person as rich as it once did. In terms of buying power, $1 million today equals $173,000 four decades ago. Put another way, to live like a 1960s millionaire, you would need almost $6 million.

When increased productivity keeps prices steady, it can have a major positive impact on an economy. In a low-inflation environment, businesses can make long-range plans without the constant worry of sudden inflationary shocks. Low interest rates encourage firms to invest in research and development and capital improvements, both of which are likely to produce productivity gains. Consumers can purchase growing stocks of goods and services with the same amount of money, and low interest rates encourage major acquisitions like new homes and autos.

Recent Fears about Deflation In recent years, concerns have switched from inflation to the opposite occurrence: **deflation.** Unlike during inflationary times, deflation is a period of falling prices. To many, such an economic environment sounds positive. In Japan, where deflation has been a reality for several years, shoppers pay less for a variety of products. Monthly rents on a tiny 100-square-meter house in Tokyo have declined from an average of $2,241 to $2,193 in just four years. A Big Mac that cost $2.40 four years ago can now be purchased for $2.13. A high-quality men's suit carries an average price of $353. Four years ago, the same suit would have been priced at $425.[17]

Americans have not experienced a general pattern of falling prices in 70 years. During the Great Depression of the 1930s, the negative image of deflation was born. The weak economy triggered a deflationary spiral in which companies cut jobs and slashed prices as the economy continued to slow. The result was an ever-weakening economy, staggering rates of unemployment (a 25% unemployment rate at one point), and lower prices. Even shoppers with jobs and purchasing ability began to put off making purchases to wait for even better deals later.

The recent experiences with deflation show a different pattern. Some costs have fallen: interest rates on homes, clothing costs (especially children's clothing), price tags on furniture, and prices of computer equipment and other high-tech consumer items. But other costs have risen. These include healthcare costs, childcare and other service expenses, tuition fees, heating costs, and shipping expenses for businesses.[18]

The notion of deflation as a negative economic indicator is discussed in the Solving an Ethical Controversy box. A wave of consumer pessimism about the future could drive down demand and prices as people postpone purchases, increase savings, and restrict spending to wait out the expected crisis. Businesses would lose money on the lower-priced goods or be stuck with inventories they are unable to sell.

These trends would likely prompt management decision makers to scale back production plans. The results could include layoffs, declines in the value of personal investments such as homes, and short-term interest rates hovering near zero.

Measuring Price Level Changes In the U.S., the government tracks changes in price levels with the **Consumer Price Index (CPI),** which measures the monthly average change in prices of goods and services. The federal Bureau of Labor Statistics (BLS) calculates the CPI monthly based on prices of a "market basket," a compilation of the goods and services most commonly purchased by urban consumers. Figure 3.7 shows the categories included in the CPI market basket. Each month, BLS representatives visit thousands of stores, service establishments, rental units, and doctors' offices all over the U.S. to price the multitude of items in the CPI

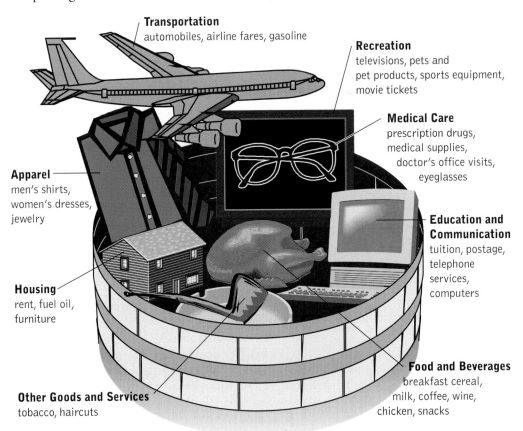

FIGURE 3.7
Contents of the CPI Market Basket
Source: Information from Bureau of Labor Statistics, "Consumer Price Indexes: Frequently Asked Questions," January 20, 2004, http://www.bls.gov/cpi.

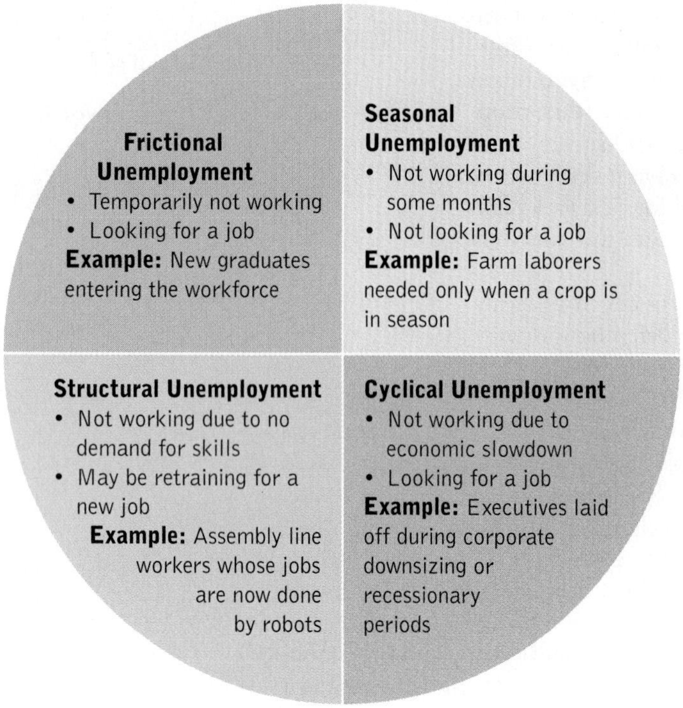

Frictional Unemployment
- Temporarily not working
- Looking for a job

Example: New graduates entering the workforce

Seasonal Unemployment
- Not working during some months
- Not looking for a job

Example: Farm laborers needed only when a crop is in season

Structural Unemployment
- Not working due to no demand for skills
- May be retraining for a new job

Example: Assembly line workers whose jobs are now done by robots

Cyclical Unemployment
- Not working due to economic slowdown
- Looking for a job

Example: Executives laid off during corporate downsizing or recessionary periods

FIGURE 3.8
Four Types of Unemployment

market basket. They compile the data to create the CPI. So, the CPI provides a running measurement of changes in consumer prices. The recent economic downturn saw apparel and hotel prices drop 2 percent, telephone services 4 percent, and personal computers a whopping 21 percent.[19]

The CPI is not a perfect measure of inflation. Critics complain that it may actually overstate inflation by not fully accounting for changes in the goods that people buy. If breakfast cereal gets more expensive, many consumers will switch to toast, and the amount they spend will not increase as fast as a simple measure of cereal's price would suggest. The CPI also does not directly measure the change in costs to businesses. A **Producer Price Index (PPI)** is another economic indicator used to track prices. A PPI looks at prices from the seller's perspective. The Bureau of Labor Statistics computes three major categories of PPIs:

1. The PPI for *finished goods* measures the prices sellers obtained for items that will not undergo further processing, including goods sold to consumers and machinery sold to businesses.
2. The PPI for *intermediate goods* measures the prices sellers obtained for items that will require further processing, including ingredients for food products, components to be assembled into finished goods, and boxes for shipping items.
3. The PPI for *crude goods* measures the prices sellers obtained for raw materials to be used in making parts or finished goods.

Employment Levels

People need money to purchase the goods and services produced in an economy. Because most consumers earn that money by working, the number of people in a nation who currently have jobs is an important indicator of both overall stability and growth. People who are actively looking for work but unable to find jobs are counted in unemployment statistics.

Economists refer to a nation's **unemployment rate** as an indicator of its economic health. The unemployment rate is usually expressed as a percentage of the total workforce who are actively seeking work but are currently unemployed. The total labor force includes all people who are willing and available to work at the going market wage, whether they currently have jobs or are seeking work. The U.S. Department of Labor, which tracks unemployment rates, also includes so-called *discouraged workers* in the total labor force. These individuals want to work but have given up looking for jobs, for various reasons.

Unemployment can be grouped into the four categories shown in Figure 3.8: frictional, seasonal, cyclical, and structural. *Frictional unemployment* applies to members of the workforce who are temporarily not working but are looking for jobs. This pool of potential workers includes new graduates, people who have left jobs for any reason and are looking for others, and former workers who have decided to return to the labor force. *Seasonal unemployment* is the joblessness of workers in a seasonal industry. Construction workers and farm laborers typically must contend with bouts of seasonal unemployment when wintry conditions make work unavailable.

Cyclical unemployment includes people who are out of work because of a cyclical contraction in the economy. During periods of economic expansion, overall employment is likely to rise, but as growth slows and a recession begins, unemployment levels commonly rise. At such times, even workers with good job skills may face temporary unemployment. Figure 3.9 shows the percentage of job losses in several industries during the most recent recession. The national unemployment rate soared during this period, reaching a peak of 6 percent before begging to decline. Cyclical unemployment may hit certain groups harder than others. During the recent recession, the unemployment rate for African Americans hit a high of 11 percent, and the rate for Hispanic Americans reached 7.8 percent.

Structural unemployment applies to people who remain unemployed for long periods of time, often with little hope of finding new jobs like their old ones. This situation may arise because these workers lack the necessary skills for available jobs or because the skills they have are no longer in demand. For instance, technological developments have increased the demand for people with computer-related skills but have created structural unemployment among many types of manual laborers.

> **Concept Check**
>
> 1. What is the difference between a recession and a depression?
> 2. Distinguish between inflation and deflation.

Managing the Economy's Performance

As recent years have vividly demonstrated, a national government can use both monetary policy and fiscal policy in its efforts to fight unemployment, increase business and consumer spending, and reduce the length and severity of economic recessions. The Federal Reserve System reduced interest rates 11 times during a single year at the beginning of the downturn, thus reducing the cost of borrowing for businesses and households. At the same time, the federal government enacted a major tax cut and greatly increased spending in an effort to assist business sectors hurt by the aftermath of the terrorist attacks and to enhance national security and military preparedness.

Monetary Policy

A common method of influencing economic activity is **monetary policy,** government action to increase or decrease the money supply and change banking requirements and interest rates to influence spending by altering bankers' willingness to make loans. An *expansionary monetary policy* increases the money supply in an effort to cut the cost of borrowing, which encourages business decision makers to make new investments, in turn stimulating employment and economic growth. By contrast, a *restrictive monetary policy* reduces the money supply to curb rising prices, overexpansion, and concerns about overly rapid economic growth.

In the U.S., the Federal Reserve System ("the Fed") is responsible for formulating and implementing the nation's monetary policy. It is currently headed by Chairman Alan Greenspan and a Board of Governors, with each of the members appointed by the president. All national banks must be members of this system and keep some percentage of their checking and savings funds on deposit at the Fed.

The Fed's Board of Governors uses a number of tools to regulate the economy. By changing the required percentage of checking and savings accounts that banks must deposit with the Fed, the governors can expand or shrink funds available to lend. The Fed also lends money to member banks, which in turn make loans at higher interest rates to business and individual borrowers. By changing the interest rates charged to commercial banks, the Fed affects the interest rates charged to borrowers and, consequently, their willingness to borrow.

Fiscal Policy

Governments also influence economic activities through taxation and spending decisions. Through revenues and expenditures, the government implements **fiscal policy,** the second technique that officials use to control inflation, reduce unemployment, improve the general welfare of citizens, and encourage economic growth. Increased taxes may restrict economic activities, and lower taxes and increased government spending usually boost spending and profits, cut unemployment rates, and fuel economic expansion.

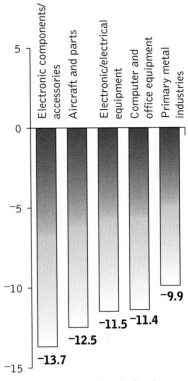

FIGURE 3.9

Top Job Losses by Industry in the Recent Recession

Source: Data from "Top Industry Job Losses," *USA Today,* September 4, 2002, p. B1.

> *They Said It*
>
> I am concerned about the economy. I was the first one laid off.
>
> —*Al Gore (b. 1948)*
> *vice president of the United States, 1993–2001, and former presidential candidate*

monetary policy government action to increase or decrease the money supply and change banking requirements and interest rates to influence bankers' willingness to make loans.

fiscal policy government spending and taxation decisions designed to control inflation, reduce unemployment, improve the general welfare of citizens, and encourage economic growth.

BUSINESS TOOL KIT

Balancing Your Budget: Money Management Skills for College Students

How well do you manage money? Do you have a job, receive a paycheck, and budget for your needs and wants? Or do you get spending money from your parents or relatives for textbooks, food, and fun? Either way, creating a realistic spending plan is a vital skill to learn during the college years. How you manage money now affects how you will manage money in the future, and, in today's economy, it's important to get a head start.

First, know where your money is coming from (income) and where your money is going (expenditures). Benjamin Franklin once said, "Beware of little expenses; a small leak will sink a great ship." Tracking your money is easy; simply keep a written record of every dime you make and spend. Get a notebook, divide each page into two columns—income and expenditures—and keep track of bills you pay, checks you write, withdrawals you make from ATM machines, soft drinks you buy, and so on. Budgeting software is available, but a simple notebook and pencil will work to start. When you keep a written budget, your finances are always organized, you know where your money is going, and you've established a useful habit that will hold you in good stead as you accumulate additional money and assets over the years.

Second, set some financial goals—even if they seem basic. "Paying off my credit card balance each month" is a great goal to shoot for, so write it down. Banking somewhere that offers free checking, depositing $50 a month into your savings account, and packing a lunch instead of buying it twice a week are all good goals that can aid you in your saving

and budgeting plans. In addition, write down your long-term goals, such as paying off your student loans in half the time, saving for a down payment on a house, or investing in the stock market. These will give you something concrete to shoot for as you work your way through college and beyond.

Keep in mind that the college years are usually when people start accumulating credit cards and credit card debt. Take a stroll on your campus and look at all the ads, flyers, and brochures offering credit cards to students—and *beware*. Establishing a solid credit history is a good thing; starting your first job out of college in debt is not. If you're concerned about establishing a credit history, remember that school loans count as "credit" on your credit report and are offered at a much lower interest rate than other types of loans.

The basic premise in establishing a budget is to learn how to live within your means. Develop a realistic budget for your necessities and your lifestyle; develop a spending plan that takes into account your long-term financial goals; and know where every penny goes so you can work toward meeting those goals. The rule is simple: Save more and spend less. If you follow this basic rule, whether in college or afterward, you will always be a good manager of your money.

Sources: Louis E. Boone, David L. Kurtz, and Douglas Hearth, *Planning Your Financial Future*, 3rd edition (Mason, OH: Thomson/South-Western), 2003; Gail Vaz-Oxlade, "Uh-oh, It's the 'B' Word," *Chatelaine*, May 2002, p. 54; Anne Papmehl, "In Praise of Budgeting: The Purpose of a Personal Budget Is to Enhance, not Diminish, Your Quality of Life," *CMA Management*, February 2002, pp. 48–49; Reasie A. Henry, Janice G. Weber, and David Yarbrough, "Money Management Practices of College Students," *College Student Journal*, June 2001, p. 244.

budget organization's plan for how it will raise and spend money during a given period of time.

They Said It

The principle of the [tax law] is pretty simple—we believe the more money people have in their pockets the more likely it is somebody is going to find work in America.

*—George W. Bush (b. 1946)
43rd president of the United States*

Two huge tax cuts designed to provide an economic stimulus for ending the lingering inflation were passed during the early years of this century. The most recent of these was enacted into law in 2003. Although almost every taxpayer benefited from the third-largest tax cut in U.S. history, wealthy households and those with children received the biggest boost. The recent stimulus package reduced tax rates in every income category, cut taxes on dividends and *capital gains* (profits resulting from sales of stocks and other items owned for a year or more), and raised to $1,000 from $600 the tax credit for dependent children under age 17, among other items.

Each year, the president proposes a **budget** for the federal government, a plan for how it will raise and spend money during the coming year, and presents it to Congress for approval. A typical federal budget proposal undergoes months of deliberation and many modifications before receiving approval. The federal budget includes a number of different spending categories, ranging from defense and social security to interest payments on the national debt. The decisions about what to include in the budget have a direct effect on various sectors of the economy. During a recession, the federal government may approve major spending on interstate highway repairs to improve transportation and increase employment in the construction industry.

The primary sources of government funds to cover the costs of the annual budget are taxes, fees, and borrowing. Both the overall amount of these funds and their specific combination have major effects on the economic well-being of the nation. One way governments raise money is to impose taxes on sales and income. Increasing taxes reduces people's and businesses' incomes, leaving them with less money to spend. Such a move can reduce inflation, but overly high taxes can also slow economic growth. So, governments try to establish a level of taxation that enables them to provide the services that citizens want without slowing economic growth too severely. Figure 3.10 shows a breakdown of where each dollar of U.S. federal tax revenue comes from and how the federal government spends your tax dollars.

> ### They Said It
>
> Three groups spend other people's money: children, thieves, politicians. All three need parental supervision.
>
> —*Dick Armey (b. 1940) former American politician*

FIGURE 3.10

Where Federal Tax Revenues Come from and How Your Tax Dollars Are Spent

Amounts indicate the sources of $1 of tax revenue.

Individual income taxes	Social-insurance taxes*	Corporate income taxes	Gift, estate, excise, and miscellaneous taxes
53 cents	**35 cents**	**8 cents**	**4 cents**

*includes Social Security, Medicare, Medicaid, disability

Source: Data from "The Tax File," *Newsweek,* April 15, 2002, p. 40.

How Your Tax Dollars Are Spent

Spending $2.1 trillion

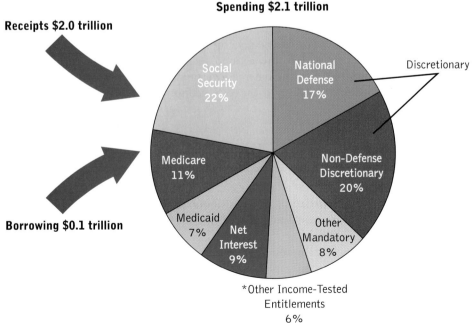

Receipts $2.0 trillion

Borrowing $0.1 trillion

Social Security 22%
National Defense 17%
Discretionary
Medicare 11%
Non-Defense Discretionary 20%
Medicaid 7%
Net Interest 9%
Other Mandatory 8%
*Other Income-Tested Entitlements 6%

*Income-tested entitlements are those for which eligibility is based on earnings.

Source: "A Citizen's Guide to the Federal Budget: Fiscal Year 2003," Budget of the United States Government, http://www.whitehouse.gov/omb, accessed October 28, 2003.

Taxes don't always generate enough funds to cover every spending project the government hopes to undertake. When the government spends more than the amount of money it raises through taxes, it creates a **budget deficit.** To cover the deficit, the U.S. government has borrowed money by selling Treasury bills, Treasury notes, and Treasury bonds to investors. All of this borrowing makes up the **national debt.** Currently, the national debt is nearly $6.5 trillion.[20] If the government takes in more money than it spends, it is said to have a **budget surplus.**

Although the federal government had carried a large deficit for the last half of the 20th century, a **balanced budget**—in which total revenues raised by taxes equaled total proposed spending for the year—was achieved by 1998. This feat was accomplished through a combination of income tax receipts due to the prosperous, technology-driven economy of the 1990s and spending cuts in such areas as defense and welfare. But the balanced budget proved to be temporary, as the government increased defense and security spending in response to the terrorist attacks of 2001 and the war with Iraq. The weakened economy also produced lowered tax revenues. As a result, federal spending once again exceeded revenues.[21]

They Said It

Christmas is a time when kids tell Santa what they want and adults pay for it. Deficits are when adults tell the government what they want— and their kids pay for it.

—*Richard Lamm (b. 1935)*
former governor of Colorado

Achieving a balanced budget—or even a budget surplus—does not erase the national debt, which must be paid off. U.S. legislators continually debate how fast the nation should use revenues to reduce its debt. For households, reducing or eliminating debt is usually beneficial. But for the federal government, the decision is more complex. When the government raises money by selling Treasury bills, it makes safe investments available to investors worldwide. If foreign investors cannot buy Treasury notes, they might turn to other countries, reducing the amount of money flowing into the United States. U.S. government debt has also been used as a basis for pricing riskier investments. If the government issues less debt, the interest rates it commands would be higher, raising the overall cost of debt to private borrowers. In addition, the government uses the funds from borrowing, at least in part, to invest in such publicly desirable services as education and scientific research. To the extent that the economy needs such public services, debt reduction may not always be the most beneficial use of government funds. However, others argue that paying down the national debt will free up more money to be invested by individuals and businesses.

The U.S. Economy: A Roller Coaster Ride

During the first six years of the 21st century, the economy was battered by a combination of an economic recession, the second war with Iraq in a decade, and the lingering impact of international terrorism on the economy. The federal government made active use of both fiscal and monetary policy to stimulate the economy and encourage economic recovery. Today, American businesses, the federal government, and economists are continuing to watch over many aspects of the U.S. economy. A few important factors to monitor are:

They Said It

One American out of work is too many Americans out of work.

—*George W. Bush (b. 1946)*
43rd president of the United States

- *Unemployment.* During the 1990s, more than 19 million new jobs were created, 1 million of which were in high-paying high-tech industries. After a recent surge in the unemployment rate to 6.3 percent, the rate has fallen to 5.4 percent.
- *Inflation and deflation.* Worries about inflation, which often plague an uncertain economy, were replaced by concerns over deflation, until modest inflation returned.
- *Productivity.* U.S. productivity has risen strongly and continues to do so. Some companies are reaping the benefits of investing in information technology and automation. Retailers are finding ways to sell more products with fewer employees.
- *Consumer spending.* As consumers regain their confidence and spend more, the economy should grow faster. The less they spend, the slower economic growth will be.[22]

Concept Check

1. What is the difference between an expansionary monetary policy and a restrictive monetary policy?
2. What are the three primary sources of government funds?
3. Does a balanced budget erase the federal debt?

Global Economic Challenges of the 21st Century

Businesses face a number of important economic challenges in this new century. As the economies of countries around the globe become increasingly interconnected, governments and businesses must compete throughout the world. Although no one can predict the future, both governments and businesses will likely need to meet several challenges to maintain their global competitiveness. As Table 3.5 indicates, five key challenges exist: (1) the economic impact of the continuing threat of international terrorism, (2) the shift to a global information economy, (3) the aging of the world's population, (4) the need to improve quality and customer service, and (5) efforts to enhance the competitiveness of every country's workforce.

Creating a Long-Term Global Strategy

No country is an economic island in today's global economy. Not only is an ever-increasing stream of goods and services crossing national borders, but a growing number of businesses have become true

Table 3.5 Global Economic Challenges

Challenge	Facts and Examples
International terrorism	Assistance in locating and detaining known terrorists by dozens of nations following the 2001 terrorist attacks
	Cooperation in modifying banking laws in most nations in an effort to cut off funds to terrorist organizations
	Severe declines in tourism in Mideast countries following continued acts of violence
Shift to a global information economy	By 2006, half of all American workers will hold jobs in information technology or in industries that intensively use information technology, products, and services.
	Software industry in India is growing more than 50 percent each year.
	Internet users in Asia and Western Europe will more than double during the next five years.
Aging of the world's population	Median age of the U.S. population is 35 plus, and by 2025, over 62 million Americans will be 65 or older—nearly double today's number. This will increase demands for health care, retirement benefits, and other support services, putting budgetary pressure on governments.
	As baby boomers, now beginning to reach their mid-50s, begin to retire, businesses around the globe will need to find ways to replace their workplace skills.
Improving quality and customer service	In today's global marketplace, every company will have to achieve world-class performance in product quality and customer service.
Enhancing competitiveness of every country's workforce	Leaner organizations (with fewer supervisors) require employees with the skills to control, combine, and supervise work operations.
	Employers must provide training necessary to develop the increased skills they require of their workforce.
	Government investment in education and training in Ireland has attracted such international giants as Dell Inc., Microsoft, and Intel to its shores and resulted in low unemployment, strong growth, and an average income about equal to Britain.

multinational firms, operating manufacturing plants and other facilities around the world. As global trade and investments grow, events in one nation can reverberate around the globe. For instance, forecasts of record sales by the U.S. computer industry were proven incorrect one year when a major earthquake in Taiwan interrupted the production of key components like computer chips and motherboards. Producers of personal computers delayed the launch of new models and worried about maintaining expected profit levels. Buyers had grown accustomed to steady declines in computer prices, and computer makers had to rethink business strategies that had been based on a world of falling chip prices.

Despite the risks of world trade, global expansion can offer huge opportunities to U.S. firms. With U.S. residents accounting for less than 1 in every 20 of the world's 6 billion people, growth-oriented American companies cannot afford to ignore the world market. U.S. businesses also benefit from the lower labor costs in other parts of the world, and some are finding successful niches importing goods made by foreign manufacturers. Still, it is extremely important for U.S. firms to keep track of the foreign firms that make their products; in the heat of competition among those firms for American business, substandard and sometimes abusive working conditions have begun to emerge in foreign factories in places like Vietnam, Thailand, and the Philippines.[23] In addition, the huge purchasing power of the U.S. makes this market desirable for foreign companies.

U.S. firms must also develop strategies for competing with each other overseas. In the huge but fragmented snack-chip industry, Frito-Lay International currently claims 30 percent of the market outside North America, which is eight times more than its closest competitor, Procter & Gamble, has captured. Coca-Cola still edges out Pepsi as the top-selling cola worldwide.[24]

Concept Check

1. Why is virtually no country an economic island these days?
2. Describe two ways in which global expansion can benefit a U.S. firm.

DID YOU KNOW?

1. With the exception of Vermont, every U.S. state operates under laws requiring a balanced budget.
2. The cost of living for an international manager is highest in Tehran, Tokyo, and Abidjan. Low-cost cities are Warsaw, Harare, New Delhi, and Mexico City.
3. One of every seven American families earns more than $100,000 a year.

What's Ahead

Global competition is a key factor in today's economy. In Chapter 4, we focus on the global dimensions of business. We cover basic concepts of doing business internationally and examine how nations can position themselves to benefit from the global economy. Then we describe the specific methods used by individual businesses to expand beyond their national borders and compete successfully in the global marketplace.

Summary of Learning Goals

1 Distinguish between microeconomics and macroeconomics.

Microeconomics is the study of economic behavior among individual consumers, families, and businesses whose collective behavior in the marketplace determines the quantity of goods and services demanded and supplied at different prices. Macroeconomics is the study of the broader economic picture and how an economic system maintains and allocates its resources; it focuses on how a government's monetary and fiscal policies affect the overall operation of an economic system.

2 Explain the factors that drive demand and supply.

Demand is the willingness and ability of buyers to purchase goods and services at different prices. Factors that drive demand for a good or service include customer preferences, the number of buyers and their incomes, the prices of substitute goods, the prices of complementary goods, and consumer expectations about the future. Supply is the willingness and ability of businesses to offer products for sale at different prices. Supply is determined by the cost of inputs and technology resources, taxes, and the number of suppliers operating in the market.

3 ### Compare the three major types of economic systems.

The major economic systems are private enterprise economy, planned economy (such as communism or socialism), and mixed market economy. In a private enterprise system, individuals and private businesses pursue their own interests—including investment decisions and profits—without undue governmental restriction. In a planned economy, the government exerts stronger control over business ownership, profits, and resources to accomplish governmental and societal—rather than individual—goals. Communism is an economic system without private property; goods are owned in common, and factors of production and production decisions are controlled by the state. Socialism, another type of planned economic system, is characterized by government ownership and operation of all major industries. A mixed market economy blends government ownership and private enterprise, combining characteristics of both planned and private enterprise economies.

4 ### Describe each of the four different types of market structures in a private enterprise system.

Four basic models characterize competition in a private enterprise system: pure competition, monopolistic competition, oligopoly, and monopoly. Pure competition is a market structure, like that in small-scale agriculture, in which large numbers of buyers and sellers exchange homogeneous products, so no single participant has a significant influence on price. Monopolistic competition is a market structure, like that of retailing, in which large numbers of buyers and sellers exchange differentiated products, so each participant has some control over price. Oligopolies are market situations, like those in the steel and airline industries, in which relatively few sellers compete and high start-up costs form barriers to keep out new competitors. In a monopoly, one seller dominates trade in a good or service, for which buyers can find no close substitutes. Privately held local water utilities and firms that hold exclusive patent rights on significant product inventions are examples.

5 ### Identify and describe the four stages of the business cycle.

The four stages are prosperity, recession, depression, and recovery. Prosperity is characterized by low unemployment and strong consumer confidence. In a recession, consumers often postpone major purchases, layoffs may occur, and household savings may be depleted. A depression occurs when an economic slowdown continues in a downward spiral over a long period of time. During recovery, consumer spending begins to increase and business activity accelerates, leading to an increased number of jobs.

6 ### Explain how productivity, price-level changes, and employment levels affect the stability of a nation's economy.

As productivity rises, so do an economy's growth and the wealth of its citizens. In a recession, productivity stalls or possibly declines. Changes in general price levels—inflation, price stability, or deflation—are important indicators of an economy's general stability. The U.S. government measures price-level changes by the Consumer Price Index. A nation's unemployment rate is an indicator of both overall stability and growth. The unemployment rate shows the number of people actively seeking employment who are unable to find jobs as a percentage of the total labor force.

7 ### Discuss how monetary policy and fiscal policy are used to manage an economy's performance.

Monetary policy encompasses a government's efforts to control the size of the nation's money supply. Various methods of increasing or decreasing the overall money supply affect interest rates and therefore affect borrowing and investment decisions. By changing the size of the money supply, government can encourage growth or control inflation. Fiscal policy involves decisions regarding government revenues and expenditures. Changes in government spending affect economic growth and employment levels in the private sector. However, government must also raise money, through taxes or borrowing, to finance its expenditures. Since tax payments represent funds that might otherwise have been spent by individuals and businesses, any taxation changes also affect the overall economy.

8 ### Describe the major global economic challenges of the 21st century.

Businesses face five key challenges in the 21st century: (1) the threat of international terrorism, (2) the shift to a global information economy, (3) the aging of the world's population, (4) the need to improve quality and customer service, and (5) efforts to enhance the competitiveness of every country's workforce.

Business Terms You Need to Know

economics 72	demand 73	recession 85	monetary policy 91
microeconomics 72	supply 73	productivity 86	fiscal policy 91
macroeconomics 73	private enterprise system 79	inflation 87	budget 92

Other Important Business Terms

demand curve 74	deregulation 82	gross domestic product (GDP) 86	budget deficit 94
supply curve 77	planned economy 82	deflation 89	national debt 94
equilibrium price 78	communism 82	Consumer Price Index (CPI) 89	budget surplus 94
pure competition 80	socialism 83	Producer Price Index (PPI) 90	balanced budget 94
monopolistic competition 80	mixed market economy 83	unemployment rate 90	
oligopoly 80	privatization 84		
monopoly 81			

Review Questions

1. Distinguish between macroeconomics and microeconomics. Give at least one example of issues addressed by each.

2. Draw supply and demand graphs that estimate what will happen to demand, supply, and the equilibrium price of pizza if these events occur:
   a. A widely reported medical report suggests that eating cheese supplies a significant amount of the calcium needed in a person's daily diet.
   b. Consumer incomes decline.
   c. The price of flour decreases.
   d. The state imposes a new tax on restaurant meals.
   e. The biggest competitor leaves the area.
   f. The price of hamburgers increases.

3. What are the three major types of economic systems in existence today? Give an example of each. What are the pros and cons of each?

4. Describe the four different types of competition in the private enterprise system. In which type of competition would each of the following businesses be likely to engage?
   a. a 100-acre Wisconsin dairy farm
   b. Arby's
   c. Southwest Airlines
   d. the U.S. Postal Service
   e. Volkswagen of America
   f. Dell, Inc.

5. What are the four stages of the business cycle? In which stage do you believe the U.S. economy is now? Why?

6. What are the effects of inflation on an economy? What are the potential effects of deflation?

7. Describe the four types of unemployment. Which type might signify that an economy is in a downturn?

8. Explain the difference between monetary policy and fiscal policy. What are the benefits of paying down the national debt? What might be the negative effects?

9. What are four economic factors that American businesses, the federal government, and economists will be watching closely as the 21st century unfolds?

10. Identify the five key challenges that governments and businesses worldwide will be facing in the new century.

Projects and Applications

1. Describe a situation in which you have had to make an economic choice in an attempt to balance your wants with limited means. What factors influenced your decision?

2. Suppose you come up with a great idea for a new product. It might be a new form of transportation, clothing made of a new type of fabric, or a new way to record and play back music. You decide to start a company based on this new product, and you are determined to succeed. What steps might you take to develop overall demand for your product?

3. Think of a company that you admire or to which you are a loyal customer. It might be a music store, a clothing manufacturer, a particular grocery store, a restaurant chain, or even a dot-com that you'd like to work for someday. Consider the fact that the firm you selected enjoys many freedoms in the private enterprise system. How might your company have to change if it wanted to expand into a country with a mixed market—or even a planned—economy?

4. In the past, many proposals have been made for privatizing certain federal or state-run agencies such as Social Security, Medicare, and the U.S. Postal Service. Do you favor privatization of some of these agencies? Why or why not?

5. Consider your economic lifetime so far. What stages of the business cycle have you experienced? In what ways have these stages affected your—and your family's—lifestyle? (You might want to talk with your parents, grandparents, and other relatives about their views.)

Experiential Exercise

Background: In this chapter, you learned about the various types of competition: pure competition, monopolistic competition, oligopoly, and monopoly. Each type of competition can be distinguished in terms of number of competitors, ease of entry into the industry, similarity of goods or services offered by competing firms, and control over prices.

Directions: Visit a large general merchandise retailer—such as a Target or Wal-Mart store.

1. Choose five different goods sold by the retailer and make a list of them. Note also one or two major competitors (if there are any) on the shelves nearby.

2. When you get home, classify each of the goods in terms of the competitive environment. Be sure to note the characteristics you used to make each classification.

3. Create a chart illustrating your findings. Include each of the goods, its competitors, its classification of competitive environment, and the characteristics you used to make the classification.

4. Present your chart to the class.

NOTHING BUT NET

1. **Gross domestic product.** As discussed in the chapter, GDP represents the total value of goods and services produced by a nation's economy. In the U.S., the Bureau of Economic Analysis, a unit of the U.S. Department of Commerce, compiles statistics on U.S. GDP. Visit the Web site http://www.bea.doc.gov/bea and click "Gross Domestic Product." Answer the following questions:

   a. What is the current level of GDP? By how much has GDP changed over the prior quarter?

   b. Distinguish between nominal GDP and real GDP.

   c. What are the four general components of GDP? Which one of the four is the largest? Which one grew the fastest? Which component grew the slowest?

2. **Unemployment.** Each month, the Bureau of Labor Statistics releases data on unemployment. Access the most recent month's employment report. What is the current unemployment rate? How is it measured? By how much did the unemployment rate change? Which demographic groups had the highest and lowest rates of unemployment? http://www.bls.gov (click "Employment and Unemployment")

3. **Electric utility deregulation and Enron.** Electric utilities are among the most heavily regulated companies in the U.S. Over the past few years, there has been a movement toward deregulating the industry. However, in light of the collapse of giant utility broker Enron, several states and the federal government have begun to rethink the pace and scope of utility deregulation. Visit the Web sites listed here or search the Web with a search engine and prepare a report on the current status of utility deregulation.

   http://www.citizen.org (search the site for articles about utility deregulation)

   http://www.cato.org (search the site for articles about utility deregulation)

   http://www.eei.org/issues (click "electricity policy")

   Note: Internet Web addresses change frequently. If you don't find the exact sites listed, you may need to access the organization's or company's home page and search from there.

Case 3.1

How Terrorism Affects Demand

When terrorism strikes, people fear for their safety as well as the safety of loved ones. If the terrorism continues beyond a single act—as it did when two snipers killed 10 and wounded 3 people in the suburbs of Washington, DC, in the fall of 2002—people stay inside. They don't shop, they don't eat at restaurants, and they don't travel. They go to work, but if they happen to work at a gas station, restaurant, movie theater, or shopping mall, they'll notice that not too many customers are showing up. That's what happened to the business owners during the weeks of those sniper attacks outside Washington: Demand for local goods and services fell dramatically.

"People are staying home, being with their families—they are not out shopping," said David Edgerley, head of the Montgomery County (Maryland) Economic Development Office. He noted that retail business in his county was probably down 25 percent. Individual stores reported that sales were down 50 percent. Washington, DC, and its surrounding communities are usually bustling with tourists, but during the sniper attacks, many tourist activities—particularly school group tours—were canceled. A hotel in Fairfax, Virginia, reported that canceled reservations cost it more than $85,000. A Pennsylvania-based tour-bus company said that 20 school groups had canceled trips to Washington. "Business is terrible," said Richard J. Navari, managing partner at a 210-room Comfort Inn in the area. Twelve school groups, representing $80,000 in business, canceled their reservations for October. That's on top of the $400,000 of business the same hotel lost after the terrorist attack on the Pentagon on September 11, 2001. MartzGroup, a Pennsylvania-based tour company that runs trips to Washington, estimated a loss of $100,000 because of trip cancellations and rescheduling. "This is something that has traumatized the region," said William A. Hanbury, president and CEO of the Washington Convention and Tourism Corp. "We can't continue to let this happen or it will begin to damage the economy." As often happens, some businesses actually experienced an increase in demand because of the circumstances. Online merchants such as Peapod, which delivers groceries to consumers'

homes, had a surge in business. The company had to hire new drivers and find more trucks to keep up with the increased demand. Although customers had to wait a bit longer for their deliveries, they seemed to prefer the slight inconvenience to shopping at grocery stores themselves. Drugstore.com also reported an increase in sales of 9 to 14 percent, as consumers ordered over-the-counter items like shampoo and toothpaste online instead of visiting their local pharmacy. Takeout Taxi was another company that enjoyed increased demand. The firm delivers food from 125 restaurants to customers in Montgomery County and continued to do so throughout the attacks. Orders increased 20 percent, and drivers noted that their tips were higher. Owner Richard Baran explained, "People really appreciate that our drivers are doing this."

The snipers were eventually caught, and despite huge fall-offs in Washington visitors to the Cherry Blossom Festival half a year later, life eventually returned to normal. People began to shop again, and visitors slowly returned to the area. But Washington, DC, and its suburbs had suffered a blow from which it would take time to recover. "We're just thinking very positively," said Gayle Marrocco, owner of Pumpkinville, a popular pumpkin patch outside Leesburg, Virginia. She is hoping to see thousands of schoolchildren turn out to pick their pumpkins when the fall crop is ready.

QUESTIONS FOR CRITICAL THINKING

1. What steps might businesses have taken after the sniper attacks were over to get their customers to return? What steps might businesses like Peapod and Takeout Taxi have taken after the conclusion of the attacks to maintain the increased demand for their goods and services?

2. What other types of natural disasters or social crises might affect demand in a community or region?

Sources: Susan Horsburgh and Susan Schneider Simison, "Gun Fighter," *People*, June 2, 2003, pp. 79–80; Laura Cohn, "In the Sniper Zone, Deliveries Rise," *BusinessWeek*, November 4, 2002, p. 12; Denise Pappalardo, "Online Merchants Offer Users an Alternative," *ComputerWorld*, October 25, 2002, http://www.computerworld.com; Michael Barbaro and Dana Hedgpeth, "Fear Hurts Business," *Washingtonpost.com*, October 16, 2002, http://www.washingtonpost.com.

Video Case 3.2

FedEx

This video case appears on page 604. A recently filmed video, designed to expand and highlight the written case, is available for class use by instructors.

Chapter 4
Competing in Global Markets

Global Battle for the Chinese Auto Market

There was a time when a visitor to China could look down any wide avenue and see a virtual fleet of black bicycles belonging to office and factory workers. The few autos on the roads belonged to government officials, or they served as taxis and delivery vehicles.

But with the huge growth of China's middle class, which now numbers some 250 to 300 million people who have the luxury of disposable income, demand for cars is rising rapidly. Aside from U.S. and European carmakers, among those clamoring for a share of this growing car market in China are Chinese firms that hope not only to capture home markets but also to become international players, distributing their products around the world.

Despite a few years of strong growth in auto sales, China still has only about eight cars for every 1,000 people—compared with 940 for every 1,000 in the U.S. But most automakers believe that growth will continue in China, perhaps becoming the world's second largest auto market in just a few years. The U.S. is currently the largest, with 17 million new cars sold each year. China's recent entry into the World Trade Organization has paved the way for foreign automakers like GM and Volkswagen to offer their own financing programs in China for the first time, which will make sales even easier. Many observers believe that a recent slowdown in sales was due to the Chinese government's effort to slow consumer spending, not by a drop in real demand. GM, in fact, considers China to be its most important market outside the U.S., and one of the cars it is marketing most heavily there is the Cadil-

© Michael Reynolds/EPA/Landov

lac, which carries a $63,000 price tag and is closely associated by the Chinese with presidents and movie stars. The market for luxury cars like the Cadillac is made up mostly of China's wealthiest entrepreneurs, and GM is focusing its efforts on appeals to their desire to be daring and adventurous, leading the pack. "We want to make sure we differentiate Cadillac from the top German brands like Mercedes and BMW," says the brand director of Shanghai GM. "We want to position the brand as something different and very bold."

Meanwhile, competition for GM and all foreign manufacturers is rising from a nearby quarter. Now a partner of both GM and Volkswagen in China, Shanghai Automotive Industry Corp. (SAIC) already owns half the joint auto manufacturing operation it runs in Shanghai and pockets half the profis. After more than doubling in size since 2000, SAIC has become one of the world's 500 largest companies, and its chairman and CEO is optimistic about growth: "The size of the industry is such that even if the growth rate slows down, there's a huge amount of demand. It's probably a once-in-a-lifetime opportunity that you don't want to be shy on." The company has aggressive expansion plans and expects to increase production every year. Its three-part plan includes working with its partners GM and VW to more than double their production over the next few years; buying a major stake in South Korea's Sanyong Motor, which makes SUVs, thus gaining entry to the Korean market; and developing and marketing its own passenger car in China, beginning with 1.5 million vehicles in 2007. "With the increase in private buyers," says SAIC's president, "the market potential is very huge."

The desire of Japanese auto companies to convert their domestic products into regional and global brands is already in the works in a number of other industries. By building their own brands into household names, Chinese companies should be able to generate additional profits for everything from their beer and herbal medicines to computers and refrigerators. Appliance maker Haier already sells its air conditioners, refrigerators, and freezers successfully through chains like Wal-Mart, Home Depot, and Target. The company, which already manufactures some of its products in the United States, expects to become a world-class supplier and double its U.S. sales over the next five years. Legend, China's best-selling computer maker with more than a third of the domestic market, has increased its research and development budget and plans to branch out into digital cameras and audio players. Li-

Ning Sports Good Co., the country's largest brand of sporting goods, is sponsoring teams in international competitions, using brand exposure to try to reach global status within the next 10 years. The idea is to match the success of the Japanese and Koreans, who have built up brand recognition and value in names such as Sony, Samsung, and Sanyo.

Other export-minded Chinese businesses are turning to such Western marketing mainstays as sponsorships. Aiming both at consumers back home and at Chinese Americans, Beijing Yanjing Beer Group spent $6 million over the past five years to sponsor the Houston Rockets, where 7' 2" star Yao Ming has made things Chinese hypercool. Says Chris Walton, CEO of MindShare in Shanghai, "I fully expect companies in the categories of automobiles, airlines, real estate, finance, insurance, and food to . . . join the likes of Haier and Legend in the next . . . 10 years." Economically, China plans to make its products—including automobiles—names heard around the world.

In fact, industry analysts expect China's car market to reach five to eight million new cars a year by 2012. Another projection for the future, from a British industry consultant, says that "teenagers in Europe or the U.S. will be considering a Shanghai Auto car within the next decade."[1]

Chapter Overview

Consider for a moment how many products you used today that came from outside the U.S. Maybe you drank Brazilian coffee with your breakfast, wore clothes manufactured in Honduras or Malaysia, drove to class in a German or Japanese car fueled by gasoline refined from Venezuelan crude oil, and watched a movie on a television set assembled in Mexico for a Japanese company like Sony. A fellow student in Portugal may be wearing Levi's jeans, using a Gateway or Dell computer, and drinking Coca-Cola.

Like Volkswagen, Levi Strauss, Dell, Sony, and The Coca-Cola Co., most U.S. and foreign companies recognize the importance of international trade to their future success. As Chapter 1 explained, economic interdependence is increasing throughout the world as companies seek additional markets for their goods and services and the most cost-effective locations for production facilities. No longer can businesses rely only on sales in domestic markets. Today, foreign sales are essential to U.S. manufacturing, agricultural, and service firms as sources of new markets and profit opportunities. Foreign companies also frequently look to the U.S. when they seek new markets.

Thousands of products cross national borders every day. The computers that U.S. manufacturers sell in Canada are **exports,** domestically produced goods and services sold in markets in other countries. **Imports** are foreign-made products purchased by domestic consumers. Together, U.S. exports and imports make up 26 percent of the U.S. gross domestic product (GDP). U.S. exports exceed $973 billion each year, and annual imports total $1.4 trillion. That total amount is nearly double the nation's imports and exports just a decade ago.[2]

Transactions that cross national boundaries may expose a company to an additional set of environmental factors such as new social and cultural practices, economic and political environments, and legal restrictions. Before venturing into world markets, companies must adapt their domestic business strategies and plans to accommodate these differences.

This chapter travels through the world of international business to see how both large and small companies approach globalization. First, we consider the reasons nations trade, the importance and characteristics of the global marketplace, and the ways nations measure international trade. Then we examine barriers to international trade that arise from cultural and environmental differences. To reduce these barriers, countries turn to organizations that promote international trade and multinational agreements designed to encourage trade. Finally, we look at the strategies firms implement for entering global markets and how they develop international business strategies.

They Said It

No nation was ever ruined by trade.

—*Benjamin Franklin (1706–1790)*
American statesman and philosopher

exports domestically produced goods and services sold in other countries.

imports foreign goods and services purchased by domestic customers.

Why Nations Trade

As domestic markets mature and sales growth slows, companies in every industry recognize the increasing importance of efforts to develop business in other countries. Wal-Mart opens stores in Mexico, Boeing sells jetliners in Asia, and moviegoers in Britain flock to see the latest episode of *Star Wars* from Lucasfilm Ltd. These are only a few of the thousands of U.S. companies taking advantage of large populations, substantial resources, and rising standards of living abroad that boost foreign interest in their goods and services. Likewise, the U.S. market, with the world's highest purchasing power, attracts thousands of foreign companies to its shores.

International trade is vital to a nation and its businesses because it boosts economic growth by providing a market for its products and access to needed resources. Companies can expand their markets, seek growth opportunities in other nations, and make their production and distribution systems more efficient. They also reduce their dependence on the economies of their home nations.

International Sources of Factors of Production

Business decisions to operate abroad depend on the availability, price, and quality of labor, natural resources, capital, and entrepreneurship—the basic factors of production—in the foreign country. Indian colleges and universities produce thousands of highly qualified computer scientists and engineers each year. To take advantage of this talent, many U.S. computer software and hardware firms have set up operations in India. Oracle, the world's second-largest software company, is tripling the size of its Indian research facility. The firm's Indian Development Center, located in Hyderabad, already employs 2,200 professionals, working on a variety of e-business applications.[3]

Trading with other countries also allows a company to spread risk because different nations may be at different stages of the business cycle or in different phases of development. If demand falls off in one nation, the company may still enjoy strong demand in other nations. Companies such as Toyota and Sony have long used international sales to offset weak domestic demand.

Size of the International Marketplace

In addition to human and natural resources, entrepreneurship, and capital, companies are attracted to international business by the sheer size of the global marketplace. Only 1 in 5 of the world's 6 billion-plus people lives in a relatively well-developed country. The share of the world's population in the less developed countries will increase over the coming years because developed countries have lower birthrates. Some long-range predictions, however, suggest that worldwide birthrates could decline over the next 50 to 75 years.[4]

As developing nations expand their involvement in global business, the potential for reaching new groups of customers dramatically increases. Firms looking for new sales are inevitably attracted to giant markets like China and India, with populations of 1.2 billion and 1 billion each. However, people alone are not enough to create a market. Consumer demand also requires purchasing power. As Table 4.1 shows, population size is no guarantee of economic prosperity. Of the 10 most populous countries, only the U.S. appears on the list of those with the highest per-capita GDPs.

Though people in the developing nations have lower per-capita incomes than those in the highly developed economies of North America and Western Europe, their huge populations do represent lucrative markets. Even when the high-income segments of those populations amount only to small percentages of all households, their sheer numbers may still represent significant and growing markets.

Also, many developing countries have posted high growth rates of annual GDP. For instance, over the past few years, U.S. GDP has grown at an annual rate of about 3.5 percent. By contrast, GDP growth in less developed countries such as China, Malaysia, Mexico, and South Korea has exceeded 7 percent annually.[5] These markets represent opportunities for global businesses, even though their per-capita incomes lag behind those in more developed countries. Dozens of international firms are currently establishing operations in these and other developing countries to position themselves to benefit from local sales driven by expanding economies and rising standards of living. Wal-Mart Stores is one of those companies. Over the last few years, the retail giant has opened dozens of new stores in developing countries from China to Brazil. In Mexico alone, Wal-Mart operates 600 stores with annual sales of $10 billion.

Table 4.1   The World's Top 10 Nations Based on Population and Wealth

Country	Population (in Millions)	Country	Per-Capita GDP (in U.S. Dollars)
China	1,284	Luxembourg	$43,400
India	1,046	United States	$36,300
United States	281	Bermuda	$34,800
Indonesia	232	San Marino	$34,600
Brazil	176	Switzerland	$31,100
Pakistan	148	Norway	$30,800
Russia	145	Cayman Islands	$30,000
Bangladesh	133	Aruba	$28,000
Nigeria	130	Denmark	$28,000
Japan	127	Canada	$27,700

Sources: Data from U.S. Census Bureau, International Database, "World's 50 Most Populous Countries: 2002," http://www.census.gov, accessed February 17, 2003; U.S. Central Intelligence Agency, "GDP—Per Capital," *World Factbook 2002*, December 9, 2002, http://www.cia.gov.

DaimlerChrysler promotes its international operations to demonstrate how much of the world it considers a home base for business. Both developed and developing nations are represented in the flag created for the ad, and the copy points out that "there are over 200 countries we call home."

Major World Markets

The major trading partners of U.S. firms include the country's northern and southern neighbors, Canada and Mexico. Other important global partners include Japan, China, Germany, and the United Kingdom. It is not a coincidence that these countries represent the world's major market regions: North America, Western Europe, the Pacific Rim, and Latin America. The most globalized nation in the world is, surprisingly enough, Ireland.

The regions containing the most important global trading partners of the U.S. also encompass such emerging markets as India, Malaysia, and Vietnam. As Figure 4.1 shows, many of the world's most attractive emerging markets are located around the Pacific Rim and in Latin America.

FIGURE 4.1
Major Emerging Markets for the 21st Century

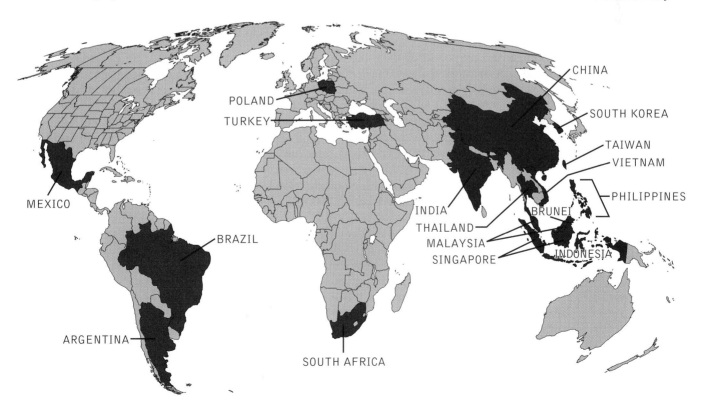

HITS & MISSES

Staying Alive in a Competition against Low-Priced Imports

U.S. shoppers have recently noticed a big influx of inexpensive wooden furniture from China. The items are better quality than past cheap imports, thanks to new factories, price competition among Chinese manufacturers, low-cost labor, and advice about design and manufacturing from U.S. consultants. Manufacturers of Chinese-made furniture have made their products their country's biggest export, surpassing the combined annual volume of toys, televisions, car parts, and shoes.

In fact, Chinese products now make up over a third of the U.S. wood furniture market. U.S. consumers looking for mid-priced furniture are buying up $1,000 leather sofas and $2,500 to $3,500 eight-piece dining rooms from trusted retailers like Ethan Allen, Bassett, and Macy's, bypassing U.S.- and European-made products that cost hundreds of dollars more. They're happy with the prices, the styling, and the quality. In the meantime, about 50 U.S. wood furniture plants have closed and thousands of workers have been laid off.

Some U.S. manufacturers, like Rowe Furniture Inc. of Virginia, are fighting back against the imports with wider choices, rapid production, and quick delivery. "I want to show American manufacturers that there are other ways to compete than letting manufacturing go," says Rowe's president and chief operating officer. Other companies, like Furniture Brands International Inc. of North Carolina, have become importers themselves.

Others, such as a coalition of 14 companies that have petitioned U.S. trade officials for help, are crying foul. They accuse Chinese manufacturers of dumping—the sale of exported products at lower prices than they are sold for in domestic markets—and are asking for antidumping taxes to be imposed on the imports. It remains to be seen how strong a case they have and whether such duties, if imposed, can be set high enough to make a difference on the selling floor. In the meantime, one U.S. consumer said of his recently purchased $595 solid-wood entertainment center from China, "It's absolutely beautiful."

QUESTIONS FOR CRITICAL THINKING

1. Do you think the Chinese manufacturers are engaged in dumping? Why or why not?

2. Is it fair to expect U.S. consumers to pay more for products than they have to? Why or why not?

Sources: Chuck Salter, "When Couches Fly," *Fast Company*, July 2004, pp. 80–81; Dan Morse, "In North Carolina, Furniture Makers Try to Stay Alive," *The Wall Street Journal*, February 20, 2004, pp. A1, A6; Dan Morse and Katy McLaughlin, "China's Latest Export: Early American," *The Wall Street Journal*, July 17, 2003, pp. D1, D2.

Absolute and Comparative Advantage

Few countries can produce all the goods and services their people need. For centuries, trading has been the way that countries can meet the demand. If a country can focus on producing what it does best, it can export surplus domestic output and buy foreign products that it lacks or cannot efficiently produce. The potential for foreign sales of a particular good or service depends largely on whether the country has an absolute advantage or comparative advantage.

A country has an *absolute advantage* in making a product for which it can maintain a monopoly or that it can produce at a lower cost than any competitor. For centuries, China enjoyed an absolute advantage in silk production. The fabric was woven from fibers recovered from silkworm cocoons, making it a prized raw material in high-quality clothing. Demand among Europeans for silk led to establishment of the famous *Silk Road*, a 5,000-mile link between Rome and the ancient Chinese capital city of Xian.

Absolute advantages are rare these days. But some countries manage to approximate absolute advantages in some products. Because many oil deposits are in the Middle East, these countries have a degree of control over oil supplies, which they sometimes manipulate to affect their income. Climate differences can give some nations or regions an advantage in growing certain plants. Saffron, perhaps the world's most expensive spice at around $40 per ounce, is the stigma of a flowering plant in the crocus family. It is native to the Mediterranean, Asia Minor, and India. Today, however, saffron is cultivated primarily in Spain, where the plant thrives in the soil and climate. Attempts to grow it in other parts of the world have generally been unsuccessful.[6]

A nation can develop a *comparative advantage* in a product if it can supply it more efficiently and at a lower price than it can supply other goods, compared with the outputs of other countries. China is profiting from its comparative advantage in producing furniture (see the Hits & Misses box). On the other hand, Japan has maintained a comparative advantage in producing electronics by preserving efficiency and technological expertise. By ensuring that its people are well educated, a nation can also develop a comparative advantage in providing skilled human resources.

Canon has adopted a strategy for research and development based on various nations' comparative advantage in engineering knowledge. Rather than basing all of Canon's research at its Tokyo headquarters, the company operates regional headquarters in Europe and the Americas, each focused on a different area of expertise. In the U.S., engineers concentrate on digital and networking technology, whereas Canon engineers in France focus on telecommunications.

Concept Check

1. What are the major world markets with which the U.S. trades?
2. Distinguish between absolute advantage and comparative advantage.

Measuring Trade between Nations

Clearly, engaging in international trade provides tremendous competitive advantages to both the countries and individual companies involved. Any attempt to measure global business activity requires an understanding of the concepts of balance of trade and balance of payments. Another important factor is currency exchange rates for each country.

A nation's **balance of trade** is the difference between its exports and imports. If a country exports more than it imports, it achieves a positive balance of trade, called a *trade surplus.* If it imports more than it exports, it produces a negative balance of trade, called a *trade deficit.* The U.S. has run a trade deficit every year since 1976. Despite being the world's top exporter, the U.S. has an even greater appetite for foreign-made goods. The trade deficit recently set an all-time record high of more than $435 billion.[7]

As Figure 4.2 shows, U.S. exports have been growing, but imports have been growing faster. Because imports exceed exports, the trade balance shown in the shaded area is a deficit. Trade deficits with two countries—China and Japan—account for over half the deficit.

A nation's balance of trade plays a central role in determining its **balance of payments**—the overall flow of money into or out of a country. Other factors also affect the balance of payments, including overseas loans and borrowing, international investments, profits from such investments, and foreign aid payments. Figure 4.3 illustrates the components of a country's balance of payments. To calculate a nation's balance of payments, subtract the monetary outflows from the monetary inflows. A positive balance of payments, or a *balance of payments surplus,* means more money has moved into a country than out of it. A negative balance of payments, or *balance of payments deficit,* means more money has gone out of the country than entered it.

balance of trade
difference between a nation's exports and imports.

balance of payments
difference in money flows into or out of a country.

Major U.S. Exports and Imports

The U.S., with combined exports and imports of over $2 trillion, leads the world in the international trade of goods and services. As listed in Table 4.2, the leading categories of goods exchanged by U.S. exporters and importers range from machinery and vehicles to scientific and telecommunications equipment. Strong U.S. demand for imported goods is partly a reflection of the nation's prosperity and diversity.

Although the U.S. imports more goods than it exports, the opposite is true for services. U.S. exporters sell more than $280 billion in services annually. Much of that money comes from travel and tourism—money spent by foreign nationals visiting the United States. U.S. service exports also include business and technical services such as engineering, financial services, computing, legal services, and entertainment, as well as royalties and licensing fees. Major service exporters include

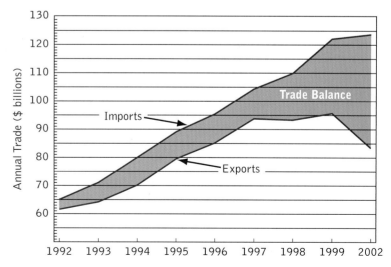

FIGURE 4.2

U.S. International Trade in Goods and Services

Source: Data from U.S. Census Bureau, Foreign Trade Division, "U.S. International Trade in Goods and Services Highlights: Goods and Services Deficit Decreases," accessed at http://www.census.gov/indicator/www/ustrade.html, January 14, 2004.

Monetary Inflows	Monetary Outflows
• Payments for exported goods and services	• Payments for imported goods and services
• Expenditures by foreign travelers	• Expenditures by residents traveling outside the country
• Income from foreign investments earned by domestic residents	• Investments by residents in foreign securities and real estate
• Investments from foreign sources	• Payments to foreign governments
• Payments from foreign governments	

FIGURE 4.3
Components of the Balance of Payments

America Online, Citibank, Walt Disney, Allstate Insurance, and Federal Express, as well as retailers such as The Gap, Office Depot, and Costco.

Businesses in many foreign countries want the expertise of U.S. financial and business professionals. Entertainment is another major growth area for U.S. service exports. In 2005, Disney, which already operates theme parks in France and Japan, opened a theme park on Hong Kong's Lantau Island. The company invested $318 million for a 43 percent share of the new Magic Kingdom and its three hotels. It also earns fees for managing the theme park and has announced plans to build one in Shanghai as well.

With annual imports exceeding $1 trillion, the U.S. is by far the world's leading importer. American tastes for foreign-made goods—which show up as huge trade deficits with the consumer-goods exporting nations of China and Japan—also extend to European products. The 25 countries of the European Union (EU) ship more than $220 billion of merchandise, including Audi cars, Roquefort cheese, and high-tech machinery, to U.S. buyers.

Exchange Rates

exchange rate value of one nation's currency relative to the currencies of other countries.

A nation's **exchange rate** is the rate at which its currency can be exchanged for the currencies of other nations. Each currency's exchange rate is usually quoted in terms of another currency, such as the number of Mexican pesos needed to purchase one U.S. dollar. Almost 12 pesos are needed to exchange for a dollar. A Canadian dollar can be exchanged for approximately 70 cents in the U.S. The euro, the currency used in many of the EU countries, has made considerable moves in exchange value during its few years in circulation—ranging from less than 90 cents when it was first issued to around $1.18 in Amer-

Table 4.2	Top 10 U.S. Exports and Imports		
Exports		**Imports**	
Electrical machinery	$89 billion	Vehicles	$157 billion
Vehicles	$57 billion	Electrical machinery	$85 billion
Computers and office equipment	$49 billion	Computers and office equipment	$75 billion
Airplanes	$48 billion	Clothing	$64 billion
Power-generating machinery	$36 billion	Telecommunications equipment	$63 billion
Miscellaneous manufactured articles	$35 billion	Miscellaneous manufactured articles	$58 billion
General industrial machinery	$34 billion	Power-generating machinery	$36 billion
Scientific instruments	$31 billion	General industrial machinery	$33 billion
Telecommunications equipment	$30 billion	Organic chemicals	$29 billion
Specialized industrial machinery	$27 billion	Transport equipment	$24 billion

Source: Data from U.S. Department of Commerce, International Trade Administration, Office of Trade and Economic Analysis, "U.S. Manufacturers Trade 1996–2001: Top Ten Product Exports Imports Balances in 2001 by Two-Digit SITC Product Groups," accessed at http://www.ita.doc.gov, January 15, 2004.

Exchange Rate Basics

The exchange rate is used throughout the world economic system. It is important to learn how it works because we live in a global community and the value of currency is an important economic thermometer for every country. Foreign exchange rates are influenced by a number of factors, including domestic economic and political conditions, central bank intervention, balance-of-payments position, and speculation over future currency values.

The *exchange rate* is basically the price of a currency when traded for another currency. In other words, for those in the U.S., the exchange rate is how much of another currency one would need to equal a U.S. dollar. For example, with the current Canadian exchange rate, approximately 70 cents equals one U.S. dollar. Currency values fluctuate depending on the supply and demand for each currency in the international market.

Business transactions are usually conducted in the currency of that particular region. When business is conducted in Japan, transactions are likely to be in yen. In the United Kingdom, transactions are in pounds. With the adoption of the euro in Europe, the number of foreign currencies in that region has been reduced (the euro is the common currency adopted by the members of the European Union, which includes Belgium, Denmark, France, Germany, Greece, Italy, Ireland, Luxembourg, the Netherlands, and the United King-

dom). Other countries' currencies include the Australian dollar, the Indian rupee, the Italian lira, the Mexican peso, the Taiwanese dollar, and the South African rand.

If you happen to have Internet access, you can find currency converters such as those located at http://beginnersinvest.about.com/cs/currencycalc/index.htm, which can help in your dollar-for-dollar conversions. It also helps to understand how much spending power a U.S. dollar has in other countries. For example, as of June 2003, one U.S. dollar is worth 72 cents in British pounds; $1.17 in euros; $2.28 in German marks; $7.80 in Hong Kong dollars; and 92 cents in Irish punts.

The foreign currency market is the largest financial market in the world, with a daily volume in excess of 1.5 trillion U.S. dollars. Because this is 50 times the size of the transaction volume of all the equity markets put together, this makes the foreign exchange market the most liquid and efficient financial market in the world.

Sources: Kim Clark and Anna Mulrine, "Where Dollars Walk Tall," *U.S. News & World Report,* April 28, 2003, p. d2; Federal Reserve Bank of San Francisco, "Ask Doctor Econ," June 2001, http://www.frbsf.org/education/activities/drecon/2001/0106.html, accessed June 13, 2003; Joshua Kennon (site guide), "Investing for Beginners," http://beginnersinvest.about.com/mbody.htm, accessed June 13, 2003; OANDA FXTrade Web site, http://fxtrade.oanda.com/faq/trading_faq.shtml, accessed June 12, 2003; Phil Weiss, "That Slippery Foreign Currency," January 10, 2001, http://www.fool.com/portfolios/rulemaker/2001/rulemaker010110.htm, accessed June 12, 2003.

ican currency in recent years. European consumers and businesses now use the euro to pay bills by check, credit card, or bank transfer. Euro coins and notes are also used in many EU-member countries.

Currency values fluctuate, or "float," depending on the supply and demand for each currency in the international market. In this system of *floating exchange rates,* currency traders create a market for the world's currencies based on each country's relative trade and investment prospects. In theory, this market permits exchange rates to vary freely according to supply and demand. In practice, exchange rates do not float in total freedom. National governments often intervene in the currency markets to adjust the exchange rates of their own currencies. In recent years, the euro has fluctuated greatly in value, from a high of $1.19 to a low of about 80 cents.

Nations influence exchange rates in other ways as well. They may form currency blocs by linking their exchange rates to each other. Many governments practice protectionist policies that seek to guard their economies against trade imbalances. For instance, national governments sometimes take deliberate action to devalue their currencies as a way to increase exports and stimulate foreign investment. **Devaluation** describes a fall in a currency's value relative to other currencies or to a fixed standard. In Brazil, a recent currency devaluation made investing in that country relatively cheap, so the devaluation was followed by a flood of foreign investment. Pillsbury bought Brazil's Brisco, which makes a local staple, *pao de queijo,* a cheese bread formed into rolls and served with morning coffee. Other foreign companies invested in Brazil's construction, tourism, banking, communications, and other industries. For an individual business, the impact of currency devaluation depends on where that business buys its materials and where it sells its products. St. Jude Medical does about a quarter of its business in Western Europe. Recent declines in the dollar–euro exchange rate made its products more competitively priced with those of competing medical providers, boosting revenues and profits.

Exchange rate changes can quickly create—or wipe out—a competitive advantage, so they are important factors in decisions about whether to invest abroad. If the euro's value plunges relative to the U.S. dollar, American exports to Europe bring home fewer dollars at the new exchange rate. In Europe, a declining euro means that a price of 10 euros is not worth as much, so companies are pressured to raise prices, possibly fueling inflation. At the same time, the falling euro makes European vacations more affordable for American tourists because their dollars are worth more relative to the euro.

Currencies that owners can easily convert into other currencies are called *hard currencies*. Examples include the euro, the U.S. dollar, and the Japanese yen. The Russian ruble and many central European currencies are considered soft currencies because they cannot be readily converted. Exporters trading with these countries often prefer to barter, accepting payment in oil, timber, or other commodities that they can resell for hard-currency payments.

Concept Check

1. Compare balance of trade and balance of payments.
2. Explain the function of an exchange rate.
3. What happens when a currency is devalued?

Barriers to International Trade

All businesses encounter barriers in their operations, whether they sell only to local customers or trade in international markets. Countries such as Australia, Germany, and New Zealand regulate the hours and days retailers may be open. Besides complying with a variety of laws and exchanging currencies, international companies may also have to reformulate their products to accommodate different tastes in new locations. Frito-Lay exports cheeseless Chee-tos to Asia, and Domino's Pizza offers pickled ginger pizzas at its Indian fast-food restaurants.

In addition to social and cultural differences, companies engaged in international business face economic barriers as well as legal and political ones. Some of the hurdles shown in Figure 4.4 are easily breached, but others require major changes in a company's business strategy. To successfully compete in global markets, companies and their managers must understand not only how these barriers affect international trade but also how to overcome them.

Social and Cultural Differences

The social and cultural differences among nations range from language and customs to educational background and religious holidays. Understanding and respecting these differences are critical in the process leading to international business success. Businesspeople with knowledge of host countries' cultures, languages, social values, and religious attitudes and practices are well equipped for the marketplace and the negotiating table. Acute sensitivity to such elements as local attitudes, forms of address, and expectations regarding dress, body language, and timeliness also helps them to win customers and achieve their business objectives.

Language English is the second most widely spoken language in the world, followed by Hindustani, Spanish, Russian, and Arabic. Only Mandarin Chinese is more commonly used. It is not uncommon for students abroad for whom English is not their first language to spend eight years of elementary and high school in English language classes. Understanding a business colleague's primary language may prove to be the difference between closing an international business transaction and losing the sale to someone else. Company representatives operating in foreign markets must not only choose correct and appropriate words but also translate words correctly to convey the intended meanings. Firms may also need to rename products or rewrite slogans for foreign markets.

Potential communication barriers include more than mistranslation. Companies may present messages through inappropriate media, overlook local customs and reg-

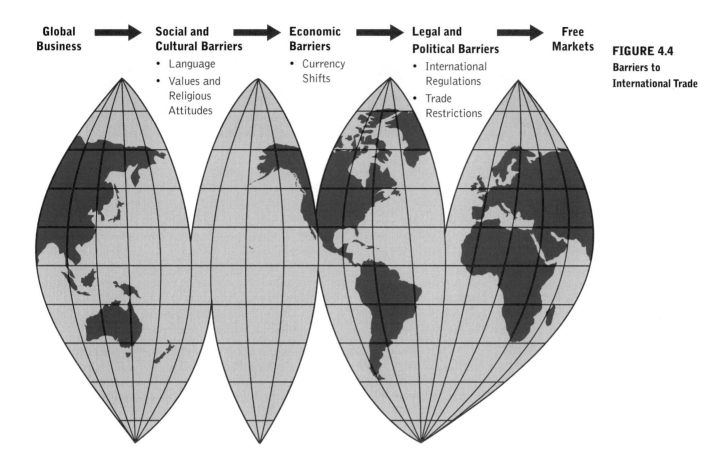

Global Business ➡ Social and Cultural Barriers
- Language
- Values and Religious Attitudes

➡ Economic Barriers
- Currency Shifts

➡ Legal and Political Barriers
- International Regulations
- Trade Restrictions

➡ Free Markets

FIGURE 4.4
Barriers to International Trade

ulations, or ignore differences in taste. Cultural sensitivity is especially critical in cyberspace. Web site developers must be aware that visitors to a site may come from anywhere in the world. Some icons that seem friendly to U.S. Internet users may shock people from other countries. A person making a high-five hand gesture would be insulting people in Greece; the same is true of making a circle with the thumb and index finger in Brazil and a two-fingered peace sign with the back of the hand facing out in Great Britain. Even colors can pose problems. In the Middle East, people view green as a sacred color, so a green background on a Web page would be inappropriate there.

Gift-giving traditions employ the language of symbolism. For example, in Latin America, knives and scissors should not be given as gifts because they represent the severing of friendship. Flowers are generally acceptable, but Mexicans use yellow flowers in their Day of the Dead festivities, so they are associated with death.[8]

Values and Religious Attitudes   Even though today's world is shrinking in many ways, people in different countries do not necessarily share the same values or religious attitudes. Marked differences remain in workers' attitudes between traditionally capitalist countries and those adopting new capitalist systems and even among traditionally capitalist countries.

U.S. society places a higher value on business efficiency and low unemployment than European society, where employee benefits are more valued. The U.S. government does not regulate vacation time, and employees typically receive no paid vacation during their first year of employment, then two weeks' vacation, and eventually up to three or four weeks if they stay with the same employer for many years. In contrast, the EU mandates a minimum paid vacation of four weeks per year, and most Europeans get five or six weeks. In these countries, a U.S. company that opens a manufacturing plant would not be able to hire any local employees without offering vacations in line with that nation's business practices.

The attractiveness of such a liberal vacation benefit for workers in EU nations like Germany is featured in the promotional message shown in Figure 4.5. The quality of the German highway system and lengthy vacations provided for German workers are used by Porsche North American marketers to humorously highlight the pleasure of owning and driving a Porsche® 911® Turbo.

BUSINESS TOOL KIT

Global Etiquette: Learning About Differences

Committing a faux pas in class or at the dinner table in your home is one thing; committing a faux pas in a foreign country may mean the end of your business relationship. Each culture has its own set of rules and customs, and before you head out to dinner with your foreign business associates or venture into their country for a meeting, you need to learn all you can about global etiquette and what is and isn't appropriate in that particular culture.

For instance, colors can signify different meanings to different cultures—in China, white and green are considered unlucky colors. Although fast-food giant McDonald's offered a veggie burger for the large Hindu population in India (India considers the cow to be a sacred animal), McDonald's also continued to offer its beef hamburgers for the large Muslim minority in the country. Hindus demonstrated in giant numbers, accusing McDonald's of being the world's largest killer of cattle. Cultural mistakes or misreadings such as this one can be costly both to businesses and to employees.

Here are some additional little-known facts about other countries and their customs:

1. You may offend your Japanese hosts if you refill your own teacup at dinner or forget to refill theirs.
2. Smiling in public in Romania is not appropriate; the locals will think you are odd.
3. In Thailand, do not gesture much with your hands—you may find yourself the source of ridicule.
4. In Canada, when making the victory sign with the index and middle fingers outstretched, be sure not to hold your palm inward, as the gesture suddenly becomes obscene.
5. Never use first names until your Costa Rican colleague suggests you do so.
6. In parts of the Middle East, you should never use your left hand when you offer someone your business card (most Middle Easterners consider the left hand unclean).
7. In South Korea, don't write a person's name in red ink; this is an indication that the person is deceased.

Most importantly, learn the basic vocabulary and historical background of the country and region, as well as the proper use of greetings and introductions. Pay attention to your physical gestures, facial expressions, dress code, and dining and drinking habits. It could save you a lot of embarrassment and possibly make or break your career.

Sources: Dean Foster Associates, "Cultural Snapshots: Japan," http://www.worldroom.com/pages/career/article23.phtml, accessed June 13, 2003; Etiquette International, "F*I*R*S*T *G*E*T *G*O*O*D," http://www.etiquetteintl.com/Articles/FirstGetGood.aspx, accessed June 13, 2003; Maureen Rauscher, "Guide to Global Etiquette," http://www.worldroom.com/pages/career/article23.phtml, accessed June 13, 2003; Monster.com's Global Etiquette section, http://international.monster.com/workabroad/archives/etiquette/, accessed June 13, 2003.

U.S. culture values national unity, with tolerance of regional differences. The U.S. is viewed as a national market with a single economy. European countries that are part of the 25-member EU are trying to create a similar marketplace. However, many resist the idea of being European citizens first and British, Danish, or Dutch citizens second. British consumers differ from Italians in important ways, and U.S. companies that fail to recognize this variation will run into problems with brand acceptance.

Disagreements between the U.S. and France about the war in Iraq produced concerns among international businesses ranging from Disneyland Paris to Perrier sparkling water about the possible revenue impact of consumers voicing their political opinions through their purchase behavior. In moves reminiscent of World War I when patriotic Americans began eating *liberty* cabbage instead of sauerkraut, a number of restaurants—including Washington, D.C., government cafeterias that serve members of the House of Representatives—began to serve freedom fries instead of French fries. An estimated 40 percent of U.S. households began to boycott a variety of French products, including French wines and products ranging from Dannon to L'Oréal. And many boycotted the wrong product, assuming that American products like Estée Lauder, Grey Poupon, Vidal Sassoon, and Yoplait were French. After receiving reports of restaurants replacing its French's mustard with Heinz, Wayne, New Jersey–based Reckitt Banckiser even issued a public statement to assure its customers of the product's American origins. It also pointed out that almost every jar of French's is manufactured in Springfield, Missouri.[9]

> *They Said It*
>
> French's would like to say there is nothing more American than French's mustard. The only thing French about French's Mustard is the name.
>
> —*press release from condiments maker R. T. French amid anti-French protests in the U.S.*

Religion plays an important role in every society, so businesspeople also must cultivate sensitivity to the dominant religions in countries where they operate. Understanding religious cycles and the timing of major holidays can help prevent embarrassing moments when scheduling meetings, trade shows, conferences, or events such as the dedication of a new manufacturing plant. People doing business in Saudi Arabia must take into account Islam's month-long observance of Ramadan, when work ends at noon. Friday is the Muslim Sabbath, so the Saudi workweek runs from Saturday through Thursday. Furthermore, Muslims abstain from alcohol and consider pork unclean, so gifts of pigskin or liquor would be offensive.

Economic Differences

Business opportunities are flourishing in densely populated countries such as China and India, as local consumers eagerly buy Western products. Although such prospects

FIGURE 4.5
Vacation Benefits for Employees in EU Countries

PORSCHE, CARRERA, 911, the Porsche Crest and the shape of the PORSCHE 911 automobile are registered trademarks of Dr. Ing. h.c. F. Porsche AG. Used with permission of Porsche Cars North America, Inc. Copyrighted by Porsche Cars North America, Inc.

might tempt American firms, managers must first consider the economic factors involved in doing business in these markets. A country's size, per-capita income, and stage of economic development are among the economic factors to consider when evaluating it as a candidate for an international business venture.

Infrastructure   Along with other economic measures, businesses should consider a country's **infrastructure.** Infrastructure refers to basic systems of communication (television, radio, print media, and telecommunications), transportation (roads and highways, railroads, and airports), and energy facilities (power plants and gas and electric utilities). With widespread access to personal computers (PCs), the U.S. led the way in the use of Internet technology. Other countries are catching up; for example, consumers in Brazil can order a General Motors sedan online at a local dealership.[10]

Many consumers in Western Europe, Japan, and Hong Kong own cell phones. Even most of their children have their own phones: More than 8 in 10 Japanese high schoolers, 7 in 10 Scandinavian teens, and the majority of British teens have their own cell phones, compared with one in three U.S. teens.[11] The availability of this technology makes these countries fertile soil for Internet businesses that adapt to wireless communication. European cell phones had built-in digital cameras years ago, and now they offer other options such as MP3 digital music players, FM radios, text messaging, and wireless Internet access.[12]

Financial systems also provide a type of infrastructure for businesses. In the U.S., buyers have widespread access to checks, credit cards, and debit cards, as well as electronic systems for processing these forms of payment. In many African countries, such as Ethiopia, local businesses do not accept credit cards, so travelers to the capital city, Addis Ababa, are warned to bring plenty of cash and traveler's checks.

Currency Conversion and Shifts   Despite growing similarities in infrastructure, businesses crossing national borders encounter basic economic differences: national currencies. Although many countries buy and sell in U.S. dollars, firms may trade in the local currency—the Mexican peso, Indonesian rupee, Swiss franc, Japanese yen, and English pound.

Foreign currency fluctuations may present added problems for global businesses. As explained earlier in the chapter, the values of the world's major currencies fluctuate in relation to each other. Rapid and unexpected currency shifts can make pricing in local currencies difficult. Shifts in exchange rates can also influence the attractiveness of various business decisions. A devalued currency may make a nation less desirable as an export destination because of reduced demand in that market. However, devaluation can make the nation desirable as an investment opportunity because investments there will be a bargain in terms of the investor's currency.

Political and Legal Differences

Like social, cultural, and economic differences, legal and political differences in host countries can pose barriers to international trade. All forms of tobacco advertising have been banned in Malaysia for 10 years, and the government is taking steps to ban all forms of cigarette brand promotion as well, including sponsorship of sporting events. Scenes that depict smoking in movies and television shows may also be edited out of existing programming.[13] To compete in today's world marketplace, managers involved in international business must be well versed in legislation that affects their industries.

Some countries impose general trade restrictions. Others have established detailed rules that regulate how foreign companies can operate. The one consistency among all countries is the striking lack of consistent laws and regulations governing the conduct of business.

Political Climate   An important factor in any international business investment is the stability of the political climate. The political structures of many nations promote stability similar to that in the U.S. Other nations, such as Indonesia, Congo, and Bosnia, feature quite different—and frequently changing—structures. Host nations often pass laws designed to protect their own interests, often at the expense of foreign businesses.

In recent years, the political structures of Russia, Turkey, the former Yugoslavia, Hong Kong, and several central European countries including the Czech Republic and Poland have seen dramatic changes. Such political changes almost always bring changes in the legal environment. Hong Kong's new status as part of China is an example of an economy where political developments produced changes in the legal and cultural environments. Since the collapse of the Soviet Union, Russia has struggled to develop a new market structure and political processes. Russian President Vladimir V. Putin has strengthened law enforcement to help legitimate businesses by cracking down on the organized-crime figures who have built business empires on a pattern of bribery and extortion. With the recent announcement that British Petroleum would invest nearly $7 billion in a new Russian oil company, many believe other foreign investors will soon follow.[14]

Firms can face many challenges when expanding to foreign markets. Citibank recruits local professionals who understand the political, social, and cultural environment for their management training program.

© AP/Wide World Photos

Legal Environment   When conducting business internationally, managers must be familiar with three dimensions of the legal environment: U.S. law, international regulations, and the laws of the countries where they plan to trade. Some laws protect the rights of foreign companies to compete in the U.S. Others dictate actions allowed for U.S. companies doing business in foreign countries.

The *Foreign Corrupt Practices Act* forbids U.S. companies from bribing foreign officials, political candidates, or government representatives. This act prescribes fines and jail time for U.S. managers who are aware of illegal payoffs. Until recently, many countries, including France and Germany, not only accepted the practice of bribing foreign officials in countries where such practices were customary but allowed tax deductions for these expenses. The U.S., France, Germany, and 31 other countries recently signed the Organization for Economic Cooperation and Development Anti-Bribery Convention. This agreement makes offering or paying bribes a criminal offense and ends the deductibility of bribes.[15]

Still, corruption continues to be an international problem. Its pervasiveness, combined with U.S. prohibitions, creates a difficult obstacle for Americans who want to do business in many foreign countries. Chinese pay *huilu*, and Russians rely on *vzyatka*. In the Middle East, palms are greased with *baksheesh*. Figure 4.6 compares 102 countries based on surveys of perceived corruption. This Corruption Perceptions Index is computed by Transparency International, a Berlin-based international organization that rates the degree of corruption observed by businesspeople and the general public.

The growth of online business with the unfolding information age has introduced new elements to the legal climate of international business. Patents, brand names, trademarks, copyrights, and other intellectual property are difficult to police, given the availability of information on the Internet. However, some countries are adopting laws to protect information obtained by electronic contacts. Malaysia imposes stiff fines and long jail terms on those convicted of illegally accessing computers and using information that passes through them.

Sometimes legal issues abroad, particularly human rights concerns, can become issues for U.S. courts to decide. Some U.S. firms have had to deal with suits brought in connection with the actions of foreign governments in the countries where they do business, as discussed in the Solving an Ethical Controversy box.

FIGURE 4.6
Corruption in Business and Government

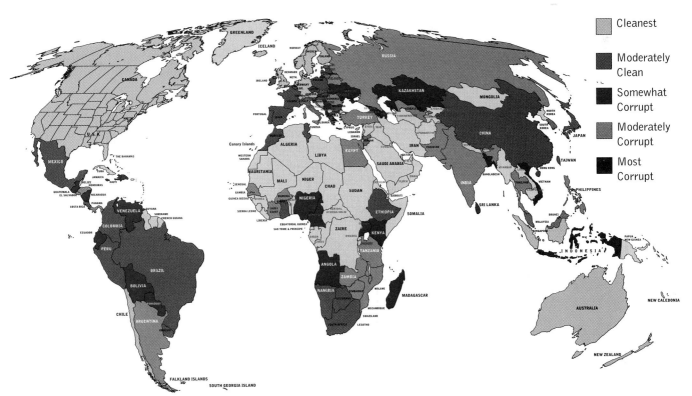

Legend:
- Cleanest
- Moderately Clean
- Somewhat Corrupt
- Moderately Corrupt
- Most Corrupt

Source: Data from Transparency International, "Transparency International 2002 Corruption Perceptions Index," accessed at the Internet Center for Corruption Research, http://www.gwdg.de, January 16, 2004.

SOLVING AN ETHICAL CONTROVERSY

How Responsible Is Unocal?

A lawsuit against Unocal Corp. of California charges that the firm knew about and approved of the military government of Myanmar's (formerly Burma) forcing peasants to build a pipeline for the firm, holding workers at gunpoint, and torturing and killing resisters. The company denies the charges, but the case has sparked a dozen similar suits that have large multinational corporations worried. The suits may be strengthened by a centuries-old law allowing foreigners to use U.S. courts to remedy illegal acts committed abroad. The Coca-Cola Co. is being sued by a Colombian labor union for allegedly hiring paramilitary units responsible for the murder of union organizers. In a suit brought by South Africans, IBM, Citigroup, and others are accused of alleged profiteering under the now-outlawed policies of apartheid. ExxonMobil faces a suit alleging that it hired Indonesian troops who committed human rights abuses.

Should U.S. multinationals be held liable for the human rights abuses of foreign governments?

PRO

1. Corporate managers should accept responsibility for illegal actions undertaken on their behalf or paid for with their resources.
2. Multinationals should improve the lives and working conditions of employees abroad, including safeguarding their human rights.

CON

1. Corporate management cannot be responsible for events they are unaware of and cannot control.
2. Multinationals are in the business of producing goods and services, not interfering in other countries' legal and social policies.

SUMMARY

Companies named in the suits are under pressure from some groups to cut their business ties with countries where violations occurred. Meanwhile, corporate lobbyists have been asking the Department of Justice to have such suits dismissed on the grounds that they could disrupt the fight against terrorism. Experts on both sides agree that 1,000 U.S. and foreign companies could face similar suits in the future.

Sources: "The Story You Haven't Heard About: The Yadana Project in Myanmar," http://www.unocal.com/myanmar/, accessed February 14, 2003; Human Rights Watch, "Corporations and Human Rights," http://www.hrw.org/about/initiatives/corp.html, accessed February 14, 2003; Paul Magnusson, "Making a Federal Case Out of Overseas Abuses," *BusinessWeek*, November 25, 2002, p. 78.

They Said It

Do not mistake bribe-taking for corruption.

—*Vladimir Rushaylo (b. 1952)*
Secretary, Russian Security Council, denying
allegations that many Russian officials are corrupt

International Regulations To regulate international commerce, the U.S. and many other countries have ratified treaties and signed agreements that dictate the conduct of international business and protect some of its activities. The U.S. has entered into many *friendship, commerce, and navigation treaties* with other nations. Such treaties address many aspects of international business relations, including the right to conduct business in the treaty partner's domestic market. Other international business agreements involve product standards, patents, trademarks, reciprocal tax policies, export controls, international air travel, and international communications.

In 2000, Congress granted China full trade relations with the U.S. China agreed to lower trade barriers, including subsidies that held down the prices of food exports, restrictions on where foreign law firms can open offices, and taxes charged on imported goods. In exchange for China's promise to halve these taxes, called *tariffs*, the U.S. granted Chinese businesses equal access to U.S. markets enjoyed by most other countries.

Many types of regulations affect the actions of managers doing business in international markets. Not only must worldwide producers and marketers maintain required minimum quality levels for all the countries in which they operate, but they must comply with numerous specific local regulations. Britain prevents advertisers from encouraging children to engage in such unhealthy behavior as eating frequently throughout the day or replacing regular meals with candy and snack foods. Malaysia's Censorship Board prohibits nudity and profanity on TV. Germany and France allow publishers to set prices that retailers charge for their books. Because companies like Amazon.com adhere to the fixed prices,

German customers looking for English-language books can get better prices by buying at the U.K. Web site, even with the extra shipping costs.

A lack of international regulations or enforcement can generate its own set of problems. Software piracy offers an example. China is especially notorious for piracy. When the China Ministry of Culture approved a series of Rolling Stones concerts in Beijing and Shanghai as part of the British rock group's 40th anniversary world tour, it failed to approve four of the Stones' most famous hits—"Brown Sugar, "Beast of Burden," "Honky Tonk Woman," and "Let's Spend the Night Together." "Don't feel too sorry for Chinese Stones fans, though," stated a reporter for *Rolling Stone* magazine. "Thanks to the country's multimillion-dollar bootleg industry, most of the band's catalog is available for around 50 to 60 cents per CD."[16] Illegally copied U.S. software, music, and movies cost American firms billions of dollars in lost revenues.

Others copy consumer goods ranging from shampoo to cigarettes. Britt Kiefer's Soft Toy Concepts can't afford to skip the annual Hong Kong Toys & Games Fair, where Kiefer makes nearly half her sales for the year. But eager would-be counterfeiters come equipped with everything from pencil and paper to Palm Pilots for drawing toy plans. "It's a bit scary here," Kiefer admits.[17]

Types of Trade Restrictions

Trade restrictions such as taxes on imports and complicated administrative procedures create additional barriers to international business. They may limit consumer choices while increasing the costs of foreign-made products. Trade restrictions are also imposed to protect citizens' security, health, and jobs. A government may limit exports of strategic and defense-related goods to unfriendly countries to protect its security, ban imports of insecticide-contaminated farm products to protect health, and restrict imports to protect domestic jobs in the importing country.

Other restrictions are imposed to promote trade with certain countries. Still others protect countries from unfair competition. Table 4.3 summarizes major arguments for and against trade restrictions.

Regardless of the political reasons for trade restrictions, most take the form of tariffs. In addition to tariffs, governments impose a number of nontariff—or administrative—barriers. These include quotas, embargoes, and exchange controls.

Tariffs   Taxes, surcharges, or duties on foreign products are referred to as **tariffs.** Governments assess two types of tariffs—revenue and protective tariffs—both of which make imports more expensive for domestic buyers. Revenue tariffs generate income for the government. Upon returning home, U.S. leisure travelers who are out of the country more than 48 hours and who bring back goods purchased abroad must pay import taxes on their value in excess of from $600 to $1,200, depending on the country of origin. This duty goes directly to the U.S. Treasury. The sole purpose of a protective tariff is to raise the retail price of imported products to match or exceed the prices of

tariff tax imposed on imported goods.

Table 4.3 Arguments for and against Trade Restrictions	
For	**Against**
Protect national defense and citizens' health	Raise prices for consumers
Protect new or weak industries	Restrict consumer choices
Protect against a practice called *dumping*, in which products are sold for less abroad than in the home market, competing unfairly with domestic goods	Cause retaliation by other countries, which limits export opportunities for businesses
Protect domestic jobs in the face of foreign competition	Result in loss of jobs from international business
Retaliate for another country's trade restrictions	Cause inefficient allocations of international resources

similar products manufactured in the home country. In other words, protective tariffs seek to level the playing field for local competitors.

Of course, tariffs create a disadvantage to companies that want to export to the countries imposing the tariffs. In addition, governments do not always see eye to eye on the reasons behind protective tariffs. So they do not always have the desired effect. The U.S. recently imposed tariffs on steel imports that were intended to improve market conditions for U.S. steel producers and give them a chance to modernize their production facilities. The tariffs have instead increased worldwide production because the price of steel became attractively high; production in Brazil was up by more than a third, for example. And U.S. firms that rely on imported steel have lobbied for exemptions to keep down their costs. "With this steel being excluded [from the tariff], it probably saved some jobs here," said Etta Wicker, office manager of Alabama manufacturer International Knife & Saw. "When you talk about [costs] going up 30 to 40 percent, that was going to hit us hard."[18]

Nontariff Barriers
Nontariff, or administrative, trade barriers restrict imports in more subtle ways than tariffs. These measures may take such forms as quotas on imports, unnecessarily restrictive standards for imports, and export subsidies. Because many countries have recently substantially reduced tariffs or eliminated them entirely, they increasingly use nontariff barriers to boost exports and control flows of imported products.

Quotas limit the amounts of particular products that countries can import during specified time periods. Limits may be set as quantities, such as number of cars or bushels of wheat, or as values, such as dollars' worth of cigarettes. Governments regularly set quotas for agricultural products and sometimes for imported automobiles. Although the U.S. government had previously imposed about 1,000 quotas related to clothing imports from various countries, many of them were lifted by 2005.

Quotas help to prevent **dumping**, a practice that developed during the 1970s. In one form of dumping, a company sells products abroad at prices below its cost of production. In another, a company exports a large quantity of a product at a lower price than the same product in the home market and drives down the price of the domestic product. Three U.S. coat-hanger manufacturers recently asked the government to limit imports of Chinese wire hangers because the foreign suppliers continually cut prices each time the domestic producers reduced their prices to compete with the Asian exporters. The domestic producers also presented evidence showing that Chinese market share in the U.S. had jumped from 3 to 12% in just three years.[19] Dumping benefits domestic consumers in the importing market, but it hurts domestic producers. It also allows companies to gain quick entry to foreign markets.

More severe than a quota, an **embargo** imposes a total ban on importing a specified product or even a total halt to trading with a particular country. Embargo durations can vary to accommodate changes in foreign policy. The U.S. government recently restored diplomatic relations with Iran and lifted its embargo on carpets, dried fruits, pistachios, and caviar imported from that country. Pistachios represent Iran's third-largest export, but the U.S. may not resume its place as a major buyer of the nuts. Since the first sack of pistachio seeds was sent from Iran to California, the state has developed its own pistachio crop. California growers say they still have an advantage because of high duties imposed on imported pistachios during the 1980s when Iranian companies were accused of dumping the nuts on the U.S. market. U.S. growers also insist they have developed a superior product in the meantime.

In addition to restoring relations with Iraq following the 2003 war, the U.S. removed an embargo on that nation's biggest import: oil. However, it also banned imports for two years from Norinco, a major Chinese industrial conglomerate, for selling missile parts to Iran.[20]

Another form of administrative trade restriction is **exchange controls.** Imposed through a central bank or government agency, exchange controls affect both exporters and importers. Firms that gain foreign currencies through exporting are required to sell them to the central bank or another agency. Importers must buy foreign currencies to pay for their purchases from the same agency. The exchange control authority can then allocate, expand, or restrict foreign exchange to satisfy national policy goals.

They Said It

Ignorant people in preppy clothes are more dangerous to America than oil embargoes.

—V. S. Naipaul (b. 1932)
Trinidad-born author

Concept Check
1. How might values and attitudes form a barrier to trade, and how can they be overcome?
2. What is a tariff? Whom does it protect?
3. Why is dumping a problem for companies marketing goods internationally?

Reducing Barriers to International Trade

Although tariffs and administrative barriers still restrict trade, overall the world is moving toward free trade. Several types of organizations ease barriers to international trade, including groups that monitor trade policies and practices and institutions that offer monetary assistance. Another type of federation designed to ease trade barriers is the multinational economic community, such as the European Union. This section looks at the roles these organizations play.

Organizations Promoting International Trade

For the more than 50 years of its existence, the **General Agreement on Tariffs and Trade (GATT),** an international trade accord, sponsored a series of negotiations, called *rounds,* that substantially reduced worldwide tariffs and other barriers. Major industrialized nations founded the multinational organization in 1947 to work toward reducing tariffs and relaxing import quotas. The last set of negotiations—the Uruguay Round—cut average tariffs by one third, in excess of $700 billion, reduced farm subsidies, and improved protection for copyright and patent holders. In addition, international trading rules now apply to various service industries. Finally, the new agreement established the **World Trade Organization (WTO)** to succeed GATT. This organization includes representatives from 145 countries, and others have applied to join. Two recent applicants approved for membership during the past three years are China and Taiwan.

World Trade Organization   Since 1995, the WTO has monitored GATT agreements among the member nations, mediated disputes, and continued the effort to reduce trade barriers throughout the world. Unlike provisions in GATT, the WTO's decisions are binding on parties involved in disputes.

The WTO has grown more controversial in recent years as it issues decisions that have implications for working conditions and the environment in member nations. Concerns have been expressed that the WTO's focus on lowering trade barriers encourages businesses to keep costs down through practices that may increase pollution and human rights abuses. Particularly worrisome is the fact that the organization's member countries must agree on policies, and developing countries tend not to be eager to lose their low-cost advantage by enacting stricter labor and environmental laws. Other critics fret that if well-funded U.S. giants like fast-food chains, entertainment companies, and Internet retailers are free of constraints on entry into foreign markets, they will wipe out smaller foreign businesses serving the distinct tastes and practices of other countries' cultures.

Trade unions in developed nations complain that the WTO's support of free trade makes it easier to export manufacturing jobs to low-wage countries. According to the U.S. Department of Commerce, about a million U.S. jobs are lost each year as a result of imports or movement of work to other countries, and the pace of the migration has increased in the last few years. They are not always minimum-wage jobs either. The Kodak plant in Rochester, New York, the largest employer in the area, recently shut down one of its plants and laid off 500 people after announcing that their jobs in the manufacture of single-use cameras were moving to China and Mexico.[21] Very little production of shoes or clothing remains in the U.S.; shirt-maker C. F. Hathaway recently closed its last domestic plant.[22] And high-tech jobs are beginning to move abroad as well, to India, China, and other countries.[23] Although free trade can also contribute to economic growth and change, including the creation of new jobs, all these concerns about WTO policy have led to protest demonstrations—sometimes violent—beginning with the WTO meeting in Seattle a few years ago.

World Bank   Shortly after the end of World War II, industrialized nations formed an organization to lend money to less developed and developing countries. The **World Bank** primarily funds projects that build or expand nations' infrastructure such as transportation, education, and medical systems and facilities. The World Bank and other development banks provide the largest source of advice and assistance to developing nations. Often, in exchange for granting loans, the World Bank imposes requirements intended to build the economies of borrower nations.

The World Bank has come under fire for making loans with conditions that ultimately hurt the borrower nations. When developing nations are required to balance government budgets, they are

World Trade Organization (WTO)
135-member international institution that monitors GATT agreements and mediates international trade disputes.

sometimes forced to cut vital social programs. One World Bank official agrees that the critics are right in some situations: "Some of the conditions set were too harsh . . . and made tough economic conditions worse."[24] In addition, environmental and human rights activists maintain that the World Bank should consider the impact of its loans on the environment and the treatment of workers.

International Monetary Fund Established a year after the World Bank, the **International Monetary Fund (IMF)** was created to promote trade through financial cooperation and, in the process, eliminate barriers. The IMF makes short-term loans to member nations that are unable to meet their budgetary expenses. It operates as a lender of last resort for troubled nations. In exchange for these emergency loans, IMF lenders frequently extract significant commitments from the borrowing nations to address the problems that led to the crises. These steps may include curtailing imports or even devaluing currency. Throughout its existence, the IMF has worked to prevent financial crises by warning the international business community when countries encounter problems meeting their financial obligations. Often, the IMF lends to countries to keep them from defaulting on prior debts and to prevent economic crises in particular countries from spreading to other nations. However, like the WTO and World Bank, the IMF has come under criticism. One criticism is that economic problems sometimes arise because banks and other businesses become insolvent, not because of government policies. IMF bailouts or restrictions on government spending then don't address the real economic problems plaguing some troubled economies.[25] The IMF has responded by developing plans to help debtor governments restructure their financial and legal processes.

Another concern is that IMF lending has placed many poor nations in an impossible position. Some countries owe far more money than they can ever hope to repay, and the debt payments make it impossible for their governments to deliver desperately needed services to their citizens. The nations of sub-Saharan Africa are hard-pressed to deal with the ravages of AIDS, yet their debt exceeds their GDP and is three times as high as their total annual exports. Critics maintain that situations like these can only be improved by forgiving the debt. Canceling $1.3 billion of Uganda's debt payments permitted that nation to cut school tuition and almost double the number of children enrolled in primary school. The arguments in favor of debt forgiveness are primarily humanitarian, but the major argument against it is that it will merely encourage nations to borrow with no intent to repay their loans.

North American Free Trade Agreement (NAFTA) 1994 agreement among the U.S., Canada, and Mexico to break down tariffs and trade restrictions.

International Economic Communities

International economic communities reduce trade barriers and promote regional economic integration. In the simplest approach, countries may establish a free-trade area in which they trade freely among themselves without tariffs or trade restrictions. Each maintains its own tariffs for trade outside this area. A customs union sets up a free-trade area and specifies a uniform tariff structure for members' trade with nonmember nations. In a common market, or economic union, members go beyond a customs union and try to bring all of their trade rules into agreement.

One example of a free-trade area is the **North American Free Trade Agreement (NAFTA)** enacted by the U.S., Canada, and Mexico. Other examples of regional trading blocs include the MERCOSUR customs union (joining Brazil, Argentina, Paraguay, Uruguay, Chile, and Bolivia), and the 10-country Association of South East Asian Nations (ASEAN). To ensure continuing success in meeting its goal of creating peace, stability, and prosperity, ASEAN holds annual meetings at which members review developments and give directives for meeting economic and political challenges.

They Said It

Interdependence re-creates the world in the image of a global village.

—*Marshall McLuhan (1911–1980)*
Canadian educator and author

NAFTA

NAFTA became effective in 1994, creating the world's largest free-trade zone with the U.S., Canada, and Mexico. With a combined population of over 416 million and a total GDP of $12 trillion, North America represents one of the world's most attractive markets. The U.S.—the single largest market and one of the world's most stable economies—dominates North America's business environment. Although fewer than 1 person in 20 lives in the U.S., the nation's more than $10 trillion GDP represents over one-fourth of total world output.[26]

Canada, our neighbor to the north, is far less densely populated but has achieved a similar level of economic development. In fact, Canada's economy is booming and has been growing at a faster rate than the U.S. economy in recent years.[27] About two-thirds of Canada's GDP is generated in the services section, and three of every four Canadian workers are engaged in service occupations. The country's per-capita GDP places Canada in the top 10 nations in terms of its people's spending power. Canada's economy is fueled by trade with the U.S., and its home markets are strong as well. The U.S. is Canada's biggest trading partner, making up 86 percent of the country's exports and 74 percent of its imports. U.S. business is also attracted by Canada's human resources. For instance, all major U.S. automakers have large production facilities in Canada.

South of the border, Mexico is moving from developing nation to industrial nation status, thanks largely to NAFTA. The U.S.–Mexican border is home to about 1,200 **maquiladoras,** foreign-owned businesses that manufacture products for export. At their peak in the first years of this century, these manufacturing operations employed more than 450,000 Mexicans in industries ranging from electronics to auto parts. Nearly half of Mexico's merchandise exports originated here, and most of the goods went to the U.S. But a combination of a strengthened peso and the loss of many of the tax and tariff exemptions that contributed to their early success has resulted in substantial reductions in output and employment. The surviving *maquiladoras* are currently trying to adapt to a new environment in which highly skilled and better-paid workers use advanced technology to produce world-class products for export.[28]

By eliminating all trade barriers and investment restrictions among the U.S., Canada, and Mexico over a 15-year period, NAFTA opens more doors for free trade. The agreement also eases regulations governing services, such as banking, and establishes uniform legal requirements for protection of intellectual property. The three nations can trade with one another without tariffs or other trade barriers, simplifying shipments of goods across the partners' borders. Standardized customs and uniform labeling regulations create economic efficiencies and smooth import and export procedures.

Trade among the partners has increased steadily, with U.S. exports to Mexico growing at almost twice the rate of exports to other countries. Since NAFTA went into effect, Mexican exports grew from $52 billion to about $150 billion, and foreign direct investment in Mexico has grown dramatically.[29] U.S. observers are split on whether NAFTA has helped or hurt the environment and labor conditions. Critics say producers have moved operations to Mexico to avoid stricter pollution controls and labor laws. Advocates of NAFTA argue that Mexico has improved conditions to trade with the U.S. and Canada. Mexicans are also of two minds. Farmers—about one quarter of the Mexican workforce—are especially concerned that they may suffer under increased competition from their more efficient U.S. counterparts.[30]

European Union

Perhaps the best-known example of a common market is the **European Union (EU).** The EU combines 25 countries, more than 450 million people, and a total GDP exceeding $12 trillion to form a huge common market.[31] As Figure 4.7 shows, ten central European countries and former Soviet republics— Cyprus, Malta, Estonia, Latvia, Lithuania, Hungary, Poland, the Czech Republic, Slovakia, and Slovenia—became the latest EU members in 2004.[32]

European Union (EU)
25-nation European economic alliance.

The EU's goals include promoting economic and social progress, introducing European citizenship as a complement to national citizenship, and giving the EU a significant role in international affairs. To achieve its goal of a borderless Europe, the EU is removing barriers to free trade among its members. This highly complex process involves standardizing business regulations and requirements, standardizing import duties and taxes, and eliminating customs checks so that companies can transport goods from England to Italy or Poland as easily as from New York to Boston.

Unifying standards and laws can contribute to economic growth. But just as NAFTA sparked fears in the U.S. about free trade with Mexico, some people in Western Europe worried that

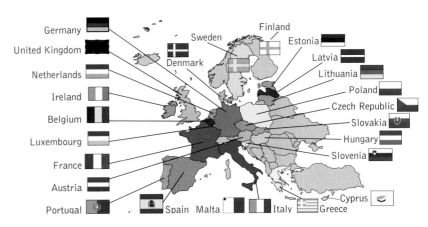

FIGURE 4.7
The 25 Nations of the European Union

The introduction of the euro was an event of enormous cultural and financial significance. This public service ad from the European Central Bank shows the seven euro banknotes; the larger the note, the higher the denomination. The eight euro coins, not pictured here, each have a common side and a national side that differs from country to country. All notes and coins are accepted in each of the participating countries of the European Union—Austria, Belgium, Finland, France, Germany, Greece, Ireland, Italy, Luxembourg, the Netherlands, Portugal, and Spain.

© AP/Wide World Photos

Concept Check

1. What international trade organization succeeded GATT and what is its goal?
2. Compare and contrast the goals of the World Bank and the International Monetary Fund.
3. Identify the current members of NAFTA and briefly explain how it works.
4. What are the goals of the European Union and how do they promote international trade?

opening trade with such countries as Poland, Hungary, and the Czech Republic would cause jobs to flow eastward to lower-wage economies.

The EU also introduced the euro to replace currencies like the French franc and Italian lira. For the 12 member states that have already adopted the euro, potential benefits include eliminating the economic costs of currency exchange and simplifying price comparisons. Businesses and their customers now make check and credit card transactions in euros and use euro notes and coins in making cash purchases.

Going Global

While expanding into overseas markets can increase profits and marketing opportunities, it also introduces new complexities to a firm's business operations. Before making the decision to go global, a company faces a number of key decisions, beginning with the following:

- Determining which foreign market(s) to enter
- Analyzing the expenditures required to enter a new market
- Deciding the best way to organize the overseas operations

These issues vary in importance depending on the level of involvement a company chooses. Education and worker training in the host country would be much more important for a bank planning to open a foreign branch or an electronics manufacturer building an Asian factory than for a firm that is simply planning to export American-made products.

The choice of which markets to enter usually follows extensive research focusing on local demand for the firm's products, availability of needed resources, and ability of the local workforce to produce world-class quality. Other factors include existing and potential competition, tariff rates, currency stability, and investment barriers. A variety of government and other sources are available to facilitate this research process. A good starting place is the *CIA World Factbook,* which contains country-by-country information on geography, population, government, economy, and infrastructure.

U.S. Department of Commerce counselors at the agency's district offices offer a full range of international business advice, including computerized market data and names of business and government contacts in dozens of countries. As Table 4.4 shows, the Internet provides access to many resources for international trade information.

Levels of Involvement

After a firm has completed its research and decided to enter a foreign market, it can choose one or more entry strategies shown in Figure 4.8:

- Exporting or importing

Table 4.4   International Trade Research Resources on the Internet

Web Site and Address	General Description
Asia, Inc. http://www.asia-inc.com	Business news in Asia, featuring articles on Asian countries from India to Japan
Europages http://www.europages.com	Directory of and links to Europe's top 500,000 companies in 33 European countries
Emerging Markets Directory http://www.emdirectory.com	Links to sites with information about the emerging markets of Asia, Latin America, Europe, Africa, and the Middle East
World Trade Organization http:www.wto.int	Details on the trade policies of various governments
CIA World Factbook http://www.cia.gov/cia/ publications/factbook	Basic facts about the world's nations, from geography to economic conditions
STAT-USA http://www.stat-usa.gov	Extensive trade and economic data, information about trends, daily intelligence reports, and background data (access requires paid subscription to the service)
U.S. Commercial Service http://www.buyusa.gov	Information about Commerce Department counseling services, trade events, and U.S. export regulations
U.S. Business Advisor http://www.business.gov	One-stop access to a range of federal government information, services, and transactions
U.S. State Department http://www.travel.state.gov/ travel/warnings.html	Listing of the State Department's latest travel warnings about conditions that may affect safety abroad, supplemented by the list of consulate addresses and country information

- Entering into contractual agreements like franchising, licensing, and subcontracting deals
- Direct investment in the foreign market through acquisitions, joint ventures, or establishment of an overseas division

Although the company's risk increases with the level of its involvement, so does its overall control of all aspects of producing and selling its goods or services.

Companies frequently combine more than one of these strategies. Web portal Yahoo! used joint ventures with local firms to gain a quick presence in Japan, Britain, France, Germany, and South Korea. Only after developing experience as an international company has Yahoo! begun to engage in direct investment by creating foreign subsidiaries. Waiting to develop expertise before moving overseas is risky for online businesses, though, because Web sites are so easy for competitors to copy. Alando, an auction Web site based in Germany, looks remarkably like eBay. Rather than fight the company, eBay entered Germany by acquiring Alando.

Importers and Exporters

When a firm brings in goods produced abroad to sell domestically, it is an

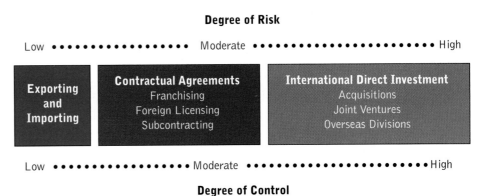

Degree of Risk

Low •••••••••••• Moderate •••••••••••••••••••• High

Exporting and Importing	**Contractual Agreements** Franchising Foreign Licensing Subcontracting	**International Direct Investment** Acquisitions Joint Ventures Overseas Divisions

Low •••••••••••••••• Moderate ••••••••••••••••••••••High

Degree of Control

FIGURE 4.8
Levels of Involvement in International Business

BUSINESS TOOL KIT

Diversity Training Programs and Multiculturalism

In the ever-expanding global workplace, many organizations are offering diversity training programs to their employees. These programs are a good way to start educating employees about diversity, multiculturalism, and other cultural issues that affect the workplace. Diversity training aims to educate employees about the different cultures, languages, attitudes, and perceptions that may surround them in the global workplace. Although there is no across-the-board standard content, most diversity training programs address the following subjects:

1. The overall business objective is to improve employee retention, satisfaction, and productivity by increasing diversity awareness.

2. Diversity programs encourage employees to think beyond the issues of race and consider other issues such as religion, nationality, and gender. Other topics addressed in diversity training include language, holidays, learning styles, sexual harassment, sensitivity training, work-life issues, cross-cultural communication, and even people's weight and hobbies. The objective is to learn how to appreciate and respect people of different cultural backgrounds, ages, religious practices, and sexual orientation.

3. Training helps increase people's awareness of their own stereotypes regarding other cultures and races. The goal of diversity training is to promote understanding and acceptance rather than to just point fingers and place blame.

4. The events of September 11 have increased the sensitivities of the diverse workforce, bringing about more discrimination claims and lawsuits because of racial or cultural misunderstandings in the workplace. Budgets for diversity training have increased because of this need for education from the highest level of management to the lowest position in the company.

5. Most importantly, senior management needs to support diversity training programs, or else employees will not support them. Each company should be specific about why it, as an organization, believes in diversity training.

Diversity training programs bring these and many other issues to the attention of employees, managers, and customers alike. Not only do employees become educated about the differences that surround them, the company's bottom line is helped by the increased employee retention, employee and customer satisfaction, and mutual understanding of differences.

Sources: Daniel Vasquez, "California Realtors, Homebuilders Seek Out Cultural Diversity Training," *Knight Ridder/Tribune Business News,* May 13, 2003; Nextel Communications Inc., "Nextel Diversity Training Produces an ROI of 163%," *Managing Training & Development,* February 2003, p. 1; Vicki Lee Parker, "Workers at North Carolina Companies Undergo Diversity Training," *Knight Ridder/Tribune Business News,* January 13, 2003; Thomas Tennant, "The New Face of Diversity Training," *Corporate Meetings & Incentives,* January 1, 2003; Michael D. Lee, "Post-911 Training," *T&D Magazine,* September 2002, pp. 32–36.

importer. Conversely, companies are exporters when they produce—or purchase—goods at home and sell them in overseas markets. An importing or exporting strategy provides the most basic level of international involvement, with the least risk and control.

Roots, a Canadian clothing manufacturer, has used its success as the chosen outfitter of the U.S. Olympic team to plan an expansion of its U.S. stores from just seven to more than 300. The company already has 150 stores across Canada and earns $300 million in annual sales. It will roll out its U.S. expansion over about five to eight years.

Exports are frequently handled by special intermediaries called *export trading companies.* These firms search out competitively priced local merchandise and then resell it abroad at prices high enough to cover expenses and earn profits. When a retail chain like Dallas-based Pier One Imports wants to purchase West African products for its store shelves, it may contact an export trading company operating in a country such as Ghana. The local firm is responsible for monitoring quality, packaging the order for transatlantic shipment, arranging transportation, and handling the customs paperwork and other steps required to move the product from Ghana to the U.S.

Firms engage in exporting of two types: indirect and direct. A company engages in *indirect exporting* when it manufactures a product, such as an electronic component, that becomes part of another product that is sold in foreign markets. The second method, *direct exporting,* occurs when a company seeks to sell its product in markets outside its own country. Often the first step for companies entering foreign markets, direct exporting is the most common form of international business. Firms that find success in exporting their products may then move on to other entry strategies.

In addition to reaching foreign markets by dealing with export trading companies, novice exporters may choose two other alternatives: export management companies and offset agreements. Rather than simply relying on an export trading company to assist in locating foreign products or foreign markets, an exporting firm may turn to an *export management company* for advice and expertise. These international specialists help the first-time exporter complete paperwork, make contacts with local buyers, and comply with local laws governing labeling, product safety, and performance testing. At the same time, the exporting firm retains much more control than would be possible with an export trading company.

An *offset agreement* matches a small business with a major international firm. It basically makes the small firm a subcontractor to the larger one. Such an entry strategy helps a new exporter by allowing it to share in the larger company's international expertise. The small firm also benefits in such important areas as international transaction documents and financing, while the larger company benefits from the local expertise and capabilities of its smaller partner.

Countertrade   A sizable share of international trade involves payments made in the form of local products, not currency. This system of international bartering agreements is called **countertrade.**

A common reason for resorting to international barter is inadequate access to needed foreign currency. To complete an international sales agreement, the seller may agree to accept part of the purchase cost in currency and the remainder in other merchandise. Since the seller may decide to locate a buyer for the bartered goods before completing the transaction, a number of international buyers and sellers frequently join together in a single agreement.

Countertrade may often be a firm's only opportunity to enter a particular market. Many developing countries simply cannot obtain enough credit or financial assistance to afford the imports that their people want. Countries with heavy debt burdens also resort to countertrade. Russian buyers, whose currency is often less acceptable to foreign traders than the stronger currencies of countries like the U.S., Germany, Great Britain, and Japan, may resort to trading local products ranging from crude oil to diamonds to vodka as payments for purchases from foreign companies unwilling to accept Russian rubles. Still other countries, such as China, may restrict imports. Under such circumstances, countertrade may be the only practical way to win government approval to import needed products.

Contractual Agreements   Once a company, large or small, gains some experience in international sales, it may decide to enter into contractual agreements with local parties. These arrangements can include franchising, foreign licensing, and subcontracting.

Franchising   Common among U.S. companies, franchising can work well for companies seeking to expand into international markets, too. A **franchise,** as described in detail in Chapter 5, is a contractual agreement in which a wholesaler or retailer (the franchisee) gains the right to sell the franchisor's products under that company's brand name if it agrees to the related operating requirements. The franchisee can also receive marketing, management, and business services from the franchisor. While these arrangements are common among leading fast-food brands such as Pizza Hut, McDonald's, and KFC, other kinds of service providers also often look to franchising as an international marketplace option.

The Howard Johnson hotel chain is using franchising to expand into Europe. Its franchise agreement with a U.K. business called Premier Hotels calls for Premier to develop 40 hotels in Austria, Belgium, Germany, Luxembourg, the Netherlands, Portugal, Spain, and Switzerland. Premier already operates Howard Johnson hotels in Great Britain. Calling on the experience of a European firm makes sense because chain hotels are relatively uncommon in Europe. At the same time, the franchising arrangement enables the hotels to tap into the Howard Johnson's reservation system, which also includes specialized management software.[33]

Foreign Licensing   In a **foreign licensing agreement,** one firm allows another to produce or sell its product, or use its trademark, patent, or manufacturing processes, in a specific geographical area. In return, the firm gets a royalty or other compensation.

Licensing can be advantageous for a small manufacturer anxious to launch a well-known product overseas. Not only does it get a market-tested product from another market, but little or no investment is required to begin operating. The arrangement can also allow entry into a market otherwise closed to imports due to government restrictions.

Licensing brands is a huge international business, generating $26 billion annually for their owners. General Motors (GM) started engaging in licensing almost by accident. The company had been

HITS & MISSES

The Americanization of Toyota

What more can the world's most profitable car maker achieve? With revenues at an all-time high, Toyota recently reported an operating profit of about $2,000 per vehicle, compared with $18 for GM and a loss of almost $200 for Ford.

Also the most efficient company in the auto industry, Toyota isn't resting on its laurels. Now that it has achieved one of its major goals by capturing 10 percent of the world's auto market, it has set itself an even more ambitious goal, to achieve 15 percent of the market and so move up from second-largest to the world's largest car company. Along the way to its recent success, it has incorporated many U.S. business models and strategies, such as quicker and less conservative decision making, into its traditional Japanese corporate culture.

Another change is that some new models now debut in the U.S. and are then introduced to the domestic Japanese market, instead of the other way around. The company has also adopted more aggressive marketing techniques, creating new market segments, such as for SUV crossover vehicles like the popular RAV4 and Lexus RX330, in order to achieve the advantage of "getting there first." And with the introduction of the Scion, Toyota became the first car maker to target a new model specifically at the young buyer. Gone is the slow, cau-

tious approach that led the firm to produce underpowered and undersized cars that failed to meet sales expectations. "We are a different player than we were five to ten years ago," says one of the firm's senior managing directors. "We are willing to get into any segment where the customer will benefit. . . . Americanization is going on in every facet of our business."

With North America now contributing 70 to 80 percent of the company's profits worldwide, thanks to larger and more powerful cars designed for U.S. drivers, Toyota's focus on U.S. business methods seems well timed.

QUESTIONS FOR CRITICAL THINKING

1. Some observers believe that Toyota's plans for growth while holding costs steady may undercut its long-time strategic advantage, quality. How do you think Toyota can protect its reputation for quality under rapid growth?
2. Why do you think "Americanization" is important to Toyota's growth?

Sources: Norihiko Shirouzu and Sebastian Moffett, "As Toyota Closes in on GM, Quality Concerns Also Grow," *The Wall Street Journal*, August 4, 2004, pp. A1, A2; Alex Taylor III, "The Americanization of Toyota," *Fortune*, December 8, 2003, pp. 165–170; Brian Bremner and Chester Dawson, "Can Anything Stop Toyota?" *BusinessWeek*, November 17, 2003, pp. 114–122.

spending millions of dollars a year on lawsuits against companies that were placing GM brands on clothing. Then General Motors management realized that caps and T-shirts bearing the Corvette logo could be a source of profits, not a drain on the legal department. GM has since negotiated over 1,200 licensing agreements to place its brands on goods from cologne to clothing, generating over $1 billion a year in revenues. Most licensed brands are American, but Europeans have been jumping on the licensing bandwagon.

Subcontracting The third type of contractual agreement, **subcontracting,** involves hiring local companies to produce, distribute, or sell goods or services. This move allows a foreign firm to take advantage of the subcontractor's expertise in local culture, contacts, and regulations. Subcontracting works equally well for mail-order companies, which can farm out order fulfillment and customer service functions to local businesses. Manufacturers practice subcontracting to save money on import duties and labor costs, and businesses go this route to market products best sold by locals in a given country.

A key disadvantage of subcontracting is that companies cannot always control their subcontractors' business practices. Several major U.S. companies have been embarrassed by reports that their subcontractors used child labor to manufacture clothing.

International Direct Investment Investing directly in production and marketing operations in a foreign country is the ultimate level of global involvement. Over time, a firm may become successful at conducting business in other countries through exporting and contractual agreements. Its managers may then decide to establish manufacturing facilities in those countries, open branch offices, or buy ownership interests in local companies (see the Hits & Misses box).

In an *acquisition,* a company purchases another existing firm in the host country. An acquisition permits a largely domestic business operation to gain an international presence very quickly. Wal-Mart enjoyed an 86 percent increase in foreign sales after it acquired ASDA, a British supermarket chain with annual revenues of $14 billion. In another acquisition, British- and Dutch-based consumer products and foods giant Unilever recently acquired an Indonesian maker of Bangso soy sauce and Sariwangi, Indonesia's best-selling tea. Indonesia is the world's fourth-most-populous nation, so its local markets are highly prized. Since entering the country, Unilever has been selling its bottled Lipton iced tea from motorcycle saddlebags in remote villages and urging Indonesians to brush their teeth twice a day with Pepsodent toothpaste. (Indonesians typically brush once a day.) Unilever's efforts are gaining ground—such tactics account for 72 percent of its sales in this Asian country. The company plans to invest an additional $500 million to increase the market shares of seven local Unilever brands over the next 10 years.[34]

Joint ventures allow companies to share risks, costs, profits, and management responsibilities with one or more host country nationals. To compete against the likes of Korea's Samsung and Boise's Micron Technologies, German computer chip maker Infineon Technologies has entered into a joint venture with Taiwan's Nanya Technology Corp. The two companies are sinking $2.2 billion into their 50-50 venture and are building a new manufacturing plant together in Taipei. Such an arrangement allows Infineon to share the risk in the volatile chip market, splitting the cost of the new factory with its Taiwanese partner while also sharing the profits.[35]

By setting up an *overseas division,* a company can conduct a significant amount of its business overseas. This strategy differs from that of a multinational company in that a firm with overseas divisions remains primarily a domestic organization with international operations. Gateway, for instance, sells 10 percent of its computer products in Europe, the Middle East, and Africa. To serve these regions, the company operates a call center in Dublin, offering technical support and customer service. A call center in Ireland lets Gateway take advantage of low taxes, a skilled multilingual workforce, and Ireland's advanced telecommunications infrastructure. When Gateway set up the call center, it also got financial help from the Irish Development Authority. The call center also gives Gateway the advantage of being closer to its growing base of customers on the other side of the Atlantic.[36]

From Multinational Corporation to Global Business

A **multinational corporation (MNC)** is an organization with significant foreign operations. As Table 4.5 shows, firms headquartered in the U.S. dominate the list of the world's largest multinationals. Among the top 20 MNCs, only Japan rivals the U.S. dominance.

Since the 1960s, when the first concerns surfaced about their influence on international business, MNCs have undergone a number of dramatic changes. For one, despite the continuing dominance of U.S. companies, America can no longer claim most of the top slots. Today's MNC is just as likely to be based in Japan (Sony, Nissan, and Matsushita), Germany (DaimlerChrysler, Volkswagen), or Switzerland (Nestlé, Crédit Suisse). Additionally, MNCs integrate capital, technologies, and even ideas from their various global operations. These operations no longer function as distant market outposts.

Many U.S. multinationals, including Nike and Wal-Mart, have expanded their overseas operations because they believe that domestic markets are peaking and foreign markets offer greater sales and profit potential. Other MNCs are making substantial investments in developing countries in part because these countries provide low-cost labor compared with the U.S. and Western Europe. In addition, many MNCs are locating high-tech facilities in countries with large numbers of technical school graduates, such as India.

As MNCs contribute to a global economy, they reap the benefits of the global marketplace. Consumers in countries as geographically and culturally distant as Saudi Arabia and Canada shave with Gillette's razor blades, wash clothes with Procter & Gamble's Tide detergent, and use computers with Intel chips inside.

Sources of Export Assistance

Regardless of the global business strategy that a firm chooses, it may require export assistance. Companies can tap a variety of resources for this help. The U.S. Department of Commerce maintains a toll-free information hot line (1-800-USA-TRADE) that describes various federal export programs. The

multinational corporation (MNC) firm with significant operations and marketing activities outside its home country.

Table 4.5   The World's 10 Largest Marketers

Rank and Company	Business	Country of Origin	Revenues (in Billions)
1. Wal-Mart Stores	diversified retail	United States	$220
2. ExxonMobil	oil and gas	United States	$192
3. General Motors	automobiles	United States	$177
4. British Petroleum	oil and gas	United Kingdom	$174
5. Ford Motor	automobiles	United States	$162
6. DaimlerChrysler	automobiles	Germany	$137
7. Royal Dutch/Shell	oil and gas	United Kingdom/Netherlands	$135
8. General Electric	diversified finance	United States	$126
9. Toyota Motor	automobiles	Japan	$121
10. Citicorp	diversified finance	United States	$112

Source: Data from Paola Hjelt, "Fortune Global 5 Hundred," *Fortune,* July 22, 2002, p. F1.

Web site of the Commerce Department's International Trade Administration (http://www.ita.doc.gov) also provides links to trade information, as well as Country Commercial Guides.

Companies can also seek advice from trade counselors at the Commerce Department's 68 district offices, who can offer information about exporting, computerized market data, and names of contacts in more than 60 countries. Some of these services are free; others are reasonably priced.

As Figure 4.9 shows, U.S. companies—the most active in international direct investments—allocated over half their $1,381 billion in total direct investment to Europe. The U.S. market is also a popular investment location for foreign investors, which recently invested over $1,321 billion in projects ranging from factories to dot-com enterprises.

Concept Check

1. Name three possible entry strategies for beginning overseas business operations.
2. What is countertrade?
3. Compare and contrast licensing and subcontracting.
4. Describe joint venturing.

FIGURE 4.9
Destinations and Sources of Direct Investment Dollars

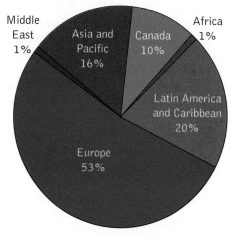

Destinations of Direct Investments by U.S. Companies

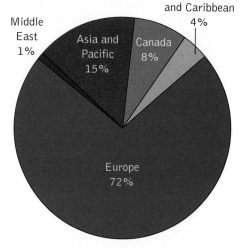

Sources of Foreign Direct Investment in the United States

Note: Numbers may not add to 100 due to rounding.

Source: Bureau of Economic Analysis International Accounts Data, "Foreign Direct Investment in the U.S." and "U.S. Direct Investment Abroad," July 9–10, 2002, http://www.bea.doc.gov.

Developing a Strategy for International Business

In developing a framework within which to conduct international business, managers must first evaluate their corporate objectives, organizational strengths and weaknesses, and strategies for product development and marketing. They can choose to combine these elements in either a global strategy or a multidomestic strategy.

Global Business Strategies

A **global business** (or *standardization*) **strategy** specifies a standardized, worldwide product and marketing strategy. The firm sells the same product in essentially the same manner throughout the world. Many companies simply modify their domestic business strategies by translating promotional brochures and product-use instructions into the languages of the host nations. Toyota adapts its marketing not only to international markets but to groups within nations. The company's new Scion model is aimed at U.S. youth.[37]

A global marketing perspective can be appropriate for some goods and services and certain market segments that are common to many nations. The approach works for products with nearly universal appeal and for luxury items like jewelry. But Coca-Cola marketers, for instance, have discovered how carefully they must tailor Coke's marketing themes in Asia, where despite their similar fashion sense, teens are often far more conservative than in the West. Rebellion and anger are not as important as respecting religious mores and doing well in school, so in Singapore Coca-Cola toned down some of its images of unruly teens to reach a broader youth market.[38] Scientific equipment, on the other hand, is not bound by geographical differences.

Multidomestic Business Strategies

Under a **multidomestic business** (or *adaptation*) **strategy,** the firm treats each national market in a different way. It develops products and marketing strategies that appeal to the customs, tastes, and buying habits of particular national markets. Companies that neglect the global nature of the Internet can unwittingly cause problems for potential customers by failing to adapt their strategy. European consumers, for instance, were hesitant to adopt online ordering of products ranging from books to railroad tickets. But in the last few years, Internet use in Western Europe has grown dramatically. Companies as diverse as the European divisions of Amazon.com, Egg PLC of London, an

global business strategy offering a standardized, worldwide product and selling it in essentially the same manner throughout a firm's domestic and foreign markets.

multidomestic business strategy developing and marketing products to serve different needs and tastes of separate national markets.

Photo courtesy of Hitachi, Ltd.

To capture these enhanced pictures of a human brain (under the rainbow) and a flower petal and pollen grain (at the lower left), a scientist in any country in the world could use the same magnetic resonance imaging (MRI) instrument or electron microscope. Hitachi's ad points out that the microscopes have many uses in fields that range from semiconductors to biotechnology; these instruments—as well as other technical and medical devices—do not need to be tailored to users' home country or native language. So, Hitachi's "Global Vision" can probably be marketed around the world with relative ease.

Concept Check

1. What is a global business strategy? What are its advantages?
2. What is a multidomestic business strategy? What are its advantages?

DID YOU KNOW?

1. At the height of the SARS epidemic, Chinese public health officials handed out "spit bags" to people in Beijing who couldn't resist the traditional habit of spitting in streets and on sidewalks.

2. Chevrolet's new Borrego concept car is a poor concept, at least as far as names go. In Spanish-speaking countries, the word is spelled *borego* and has three possible meanings. The first is yearling or sheep; the second is simpleton; the third is hoax or false news.

3. Americans are likely to encounter some of the world's most challenging cuisines in China, with rats either deep fried or as ka-bobs; in North Africa, a meal might include locusts and grasshoppers—fried, roasted, stewed, or made into dumplings.

4. Among the world's most populous cities are Mexico City, 24 million people; São Paulo, more than 23 million; and Calcutta, 16 million.

5. In India and Bulgaria, shaking your head sideways means yes, but nodding means no.

online financial services company, and the French national railroad have seen the numbers of visitors to their Web sites climbing, along with Internet revenues. "The Web is a lot more practical, functional, and comfortable," says a French marketing executive who used the Internet to purchase rail travel online.[39]

What's Ahead

Examples in this chapter indicate that both large and small businesses are relying on world trade, not just major corporations. Chapter 5 examines the special advantages and challenges that small-business owners encounter. In addition, a critical decision facing any new business is the choice of the most appropriate form of business ownership. Chapter 5 also examines the major ownership structures—sole proprietorship, partnership, and corporation—and assesses the pros and cons of each. The chapter closes with a discussion of recent trends affecting business ownership, such as the growing impact of franchising and business consolidations through mergers and acquisitions.

Summary of Learning Goals

1

Explain the importance of international business and the main reasons nations trade.

The U.S. is both the world's largest importer and the largest exporter, although less than 5 percent of the world's population lives within its borders. With the increasing globalization of the world's economies, the international marketplace offers tremendous opportunities for U.S. and foreign businesses to expand into new markets for their goods and services. Doing business globally provides new sources of materials and labor. Trading with other countries also reduces a company's dependence on economic conditions in its home market. Countries that en-

courage international trade enjoy higher levels of economic activity, employment, and wages than those that restrict it. The major world markets are North America, Western Europe, the Pacific Rim, and Latin America. Emerging markets such as China and Brazil will become increasingly important to U.S. businesses over the next decade.

2

Discuss the relationship of absolute and comparative advantage to international trade.

Nations usually benefit if they specialize in producing certain goods or services. A country has an absolute advantage if it holds a monopoly or produces a good or service at a lower cost than other nations. It has a comparative advantage if it can supply a particular product more efficiently or at a lower cost than it can produce other items.

3

Describe how nations measure international trade and the significance of exchange rates.

Countries measure the level of international trade by comparing exports and imports and then calculating whether a trade surplus or a deficit exists. This is the balance of trade, which represents the difference between exports and imports. The term *balance of payments* refers to the overall flow of money into or out of a country, including overseas loans and borrowing, international investments, profits from such investments, and foreign aid. An exchange rate is the value of a nation's currency relative to the currency of another nation. Currency values typically fluctuate, or "float," relative to the supply and demand for specific currencies in the world market. When the value of the dollar falls compared with other currencies, the cost paid by foreign businesses and households for U.S. products declines, and demand for exports may rise. An increase in the value of the dollar raises the prices of U.S. products sold abroad, but it reduces the prices of foreign products sold in the U.S.

4

Identify the major barriers that confront global businesses.

Businesses face several obstacles in the global marketplace. Companies must be sensitive to social and cultural differences, such as languages, values, and religions, when operating in other countries. Economic differences include standard of living variations and levels of infrastructure development. Legal and political barriers are among the most difficult to judge. Each country sets its own laws regulating business practices. Trade restrictions like tariffs and administrative barriers also present obstacles to international business.

5

Explain how international trade organizations and economic communities reduce barriers to international trade.

Many international organizations seek to promote international trade by reducing barriers. The list includes the World Trade Organization, World Bank, and International Monetary Fund. Multinational economic communities create partnerships to remove barriers to flows of goods, capital, and people across the borders of member nations. Two major economic agreements are the North American Free Trade Agreement and the European Union.

6

Compare the different levels of involvement used by businesses when entering global markets.

Exporting and importing, the first level of involvement in international business, involves the lowest degree of both risk and control. Companies may rely on export trading or management companies to assist in distribution of their products. Contractual agreements such as franchising, foreign licensing, and subcontracting offer additional, flexible options. Franchising and licensing are especially appropriate for services. Companies may also choose local subcontractors to produce goods for local sales. International direct investment in production and marketing facilities provides the highest degree of control but also the greatest risk. Firms make direct investments by acquiring foreign companies or facilities, forming joint ventures with local firms, and setting up their own overseas divisions.

7

Distinguish between a global business strategy and a multidomestic business strategy.

A company that adopts a global (or standardization) strategy develops a single, standardized product and marketing strategy for implementation throughout the world. The firm sells the same product in essentially the same manner in all countries in which it operates. Under a multidomestic (or adaptation) strategy, the firm develops a different treatment for each national market. It develops products and marketing strategies that appeal to the customs, tastes, and buying habits of particular national markets.

Business Terms You Need to Know

exports 105

imports 105

balance of trade 109

balance of payments 109

exchange rate 110

tariff 119

World Trade Organization (WTO) 121

North American Free Trade Agreement (NAFTA) 122

European Union (EU) 123

multinational corporation (MNC) 129

global business strategy 131

multidomestic business strategy 131

Other Important Business Terms

devaluation 111

infrastructure 115

quotas 120

dumping 120

embargo 120

exchange controls 120

General Agreement on Tariffs and Trade (GATT) 121

World Bank 121

International Monetary Fund (IMF) 122

maquiladoras 123

countertrade 127

franchise 127

foreign licensing agreement 127

subcontracting 128

joint ventures 129

Review Questions

1. How does a business go about deciding whether to trade with a foreign country? What are the key factors for participating in the information economy on a global basis?

2. According to Table 4.1, which country or countries represent attractive markets for foreign businesses? Why?

3. What is the difference between absolute advantage and comparative advantage? Give an example of each.

4. Can a nation have a favorable balance of trade and an unfavorable balance of payments? Why or why not?

5. Identify several potential barriers to communication when a company attempts to conduct business in another country. How might these be overcome?

6. Identify and describe briefly the three dimensions of the legal environment for global business.

7. What are the major nontariff restrictions affecting international business? Describe the difference between tariff and nontariff restrictions.

8. What is NAFTA? How does it work?

9. How has the EU helped trade in Europe?

10. What are the key choices a company must make before reaching the final decision to go global?

Projects and Applications

1. When Britain transferred Hong Kong to China in 1997, China agreed to grant Hong Kong a high degree of autonomy as a capitalist economy for 50 years. Do you think this agreement will hold up? Why or why not? Consider China's economy, population, infrastructure, and other factors in your answer.

2. The tremendous growth of online business has introduced new elements to the legal climate of international business. Ideas, patents, brand names, copyrights, and trademarks are difficult to monitor because of the boundaryless nature of the Internet. What steps could businesses take to protect their trademarks and brands in this environment? What steps might countries take? Do you think such steps should even be taken? Why or why not?

3. The WTO monitors GATT agreements, mediates disputes, and continues the effort to reduce trade barriers throughout the world. However, widespread concerns have been expressed that the WTO's focus on lowering trade barriers may encourage businesses to keep costs down through practices that may lead to pollution and human rights abuses. Others argue that human rights should not be linked to international business. Do you think environmental and human rights issues should be linked to trade? Why or why not?

4. The IMF makes short-term loans to developing countries that may not be able to repay them. Do you agree that the IMF should forgive these debts in some cases? Why or why not?

5. Describe briefly the EU and its goals. What are the pros and cons of the EU? Do you predict that the EU alliance will hold up over the next 20 years? Why or why not?

Experiential Exercise

Background: *Fortune* magazine has published "The Fortune Global 500," a statistical snapshot of the world's largest corporations, every year since 1990. This exercise is designed to (a) help you learn more about this important list, (b) see how much you already know about the biggest global businesses, and (c) learn some new things about global business.

Directions: Your instructor will direct you to either work alone or as a member of a group to answer these questions. Use the most recent edition of "The Fortune Global 500," which is published in *Fortune* magazine normally in late July or early August, or go to *Fortune*'s online version at http://www.fortune.com/fortune/global500.

1. On what is the Global 500 ranking based (for example, profits, number of employees, sales revenues)?

2. Among the world's 10 largest corporations, list the countries represented with the number of companies from each country.

3. Identify the top-ranked company along with its Global 500 ranking and country for each industry classification listed in the following table:

Global 500 Rank	Industry Classification	Company	Country
	Food and Drug Stores		
	Industrial and Farm Equipment		
	Petroleum Refining		
	Utilities: Gas and Electric		
	Telecommunications		
	Pharmaceuticals		

4. _____ is the Global 500 company with the greatest assets.

5. _____ is the Global 500 company with the highest profits.

6. Each of the 500 corporations is identified by industry. In the following table, list the five top-ranked industries based on the number of companies in that industry that made the Global 500 list:

Rank	Industry Classification	Number of Companies
1		
2		
3		
4		
5		

7. In the following table, list the three industries with the fewest companies represented on the Global 500 list and list at least one company from each industry in column two:

Industry Classification	Company

8. In the following table, identify the top two employers in the world—the two companies employing more people than any other company:

Company	Industry	Employees	Country

9. Identify the two largest beverage companies in the world. Fill in their names and other information requested in the following table:

Global 500 Rank	Company	Sales Revenues

10. Which country has the greatest representation in the "Electronics, Electrical Equipment" industry classification? Which has the greatest representation in "Banks: Commercial and Savings"?

NOTHING BUT NET

1. **Going global.** One of the most successful internationally focused companies is Switzerland-based Nestlé. Check out the company's Web site and list five interesting facts about Nestlé.

   http://www.nestlé.com

2. **International Monetary Fund (IMF).** Visit the Web site of the International Monetary Fund (IMF). Prepare an oral report to your class on the IMF's organizational structure and the services it provides to member countries.

   http://www.imf.org

3. **Introduction of the euro.** Euro coins and currency have replaced the national currencies of a number of the 25 countries that make up the European Union (EU). The introduction has not been without some bumps. Use a search engine to find the latest information and news related to the introduction of the euro. Prepare a brief report outlining the current situation, some of the issues facing the euro, and the member countries of the European Monetary Union. The Web site listed here provides a good starting point.

   http://fullcoverage.yahoo.com/fc/world/European_Monetary_Union

   Note: Internet Web addresses change frequently. If you don't find the exact sites listed, you may need to access the organization's or company's home page and search from there.

Case 4.1

Global Growth Is Key to Starbucks and McDonald's Business Plans

Charlie Bell, president of McDonald's in Europe, notes that if you took a picture of one of the chain's Paris restaurants, "you wouldn't think it was a McDonald's." Why does that make Bell happy? Because McDonald's is recognizing that quick service in look-alike settings is no longer the international formula for success. Parisian McDonald's franchises feature hardwood floors, exposed brick, armchairs, and music videos. Elsewhere in France, there are no Golden Arches or plastic fixtures. The new muted colors, varied interiors, and video games create an ambience where management hopes consumers will linger to eat. And sales are finally on the rise. The company's expansion plans in France and the rest of Europe include the acquisition of upscale food chains and tailored menus featuring chicken-on-focaccia, espresso, and brioche.

McDonald's also plans to continue expanding in China by opening more than 100 restaurants a year. It already operates in more than 500 locations in 70 Chinese cities. The rapid expansion "is something we would like to sustain for an extended period of time," according to Tony Chen, McDonald's public affairs director for China. "This is one of our most profitable markets."

Starbucks is moving abroad with similar speed. In 1999, the coffee chain had about 280 stores overseas; today, in the early stages of its international expansion, the number has grown to more than 1,200. The company plans to double the number of stores worldwide—including expansion in the U.S. and Canada—over the next few years. It already operates in Vienna, Zurich, Madrid, Berlin, Jakarta, and the Middle East—and Greece, Mexico, and Puerto Rico are next. Sales and profits are rising steadily, and Starbucks stock has increased more than 2,200 percent in value over the last decade. Overseas stores are company-owned but operated with local partners who share in the profits.

Starbucks will face some challenges as it grows abroad, including European cities in which existing coffee bars are an ingrained part of the local culture. Tight regulations and generous employee benefits are also the norm, and the chain's premium prices may meet some resistance. Imitators are already cropping up, particularly in Starbucks's second biggest overseas market, England. But for the moment, the coffee is sweet, the concept is hip, and the expansion rolls forward.

QUESTIONS FOR CRITICAL THINKING

1. Why is expansion in Europe and China so important to McDonald's? Do you think McDonald's will face the same market saturation it is experiencing at home, where new-store openings have been drastically reduced and scores of existing outlets have closed? Why or why not?

2. What can Starbucks do to ensure that cultural differences do not impede its overseas expansion?

Sources: Carol Matlack and Pallavi Gogoi, "What's This? The French Love McDonald's?" *BusinessWeek,* January 13, 2003, p. 50; Leslie Chang, "McDonald's Still Plans Growth in China, Despite Cuts in U.S.," *The Wall Street Journal,* November 14, 2002, p. B10; Stanley Holmes et al., "Planet Starbucks," *BusinessWeek,* September 9, 2002, pp. 100–109; Shirley Leung, "Armchairs, TVs, and Espresso—Is It McDonald's?" *The Wall Street Journal,* August 30, 2002, pp. A1, A6.

Video Case 4.2

ESPN

This video case appears on page 605. A recently filmed video, designed to expand and highlight the written case, is available for class use by instructors.

Part 1 Appendix

The Legal Framework for Business

Jackpot Justice

In a society that includes three of every four lawyers on earth and allows them to share in any lawsuit awards they win for their clients, where three-fourths of all obstetricians have been sued, and where juries routinely award millions of dollars to plaintiffs in suits against corporations, businesses face a special risk over which they often have little control—the risk of being sued. In the week following pharmaceutical giant Merck's withdrawal of its prescription pain-reliever Vioxx from the market, its stock price dropped 27 percent, and the company lost $27 billion in shareholder value. This was partly in response to the loss of revenue from Merck's second-best-selling drug, and partly because of the hundreds of lawsuits filed that week. Hundreds—perhaps even thousands—of these lawsuits are expected and are likely to cost Merck up to $18 billion. Suits against business are nothing new, nor are they always frivolous or unjustified. But when even a single lawsuit can overwhelm a multimillion-dollar insurance company—such as the firm that insured asbestos maker Congoleum—forcing it out of business, executives begin to wonder whether, and how, they can protect themselves. What decisions can they make that will take the unknowns in the legal environment into account?

After succeeding with its $400 billion lawsuit against the tobacco companies, in 2004, the federal government filed another, this time for $280 billion. Perhaps there was nothing the tobacco companies could have done to fend off the $280 billion lawsuit. Tobacco causes cancer and is addictive, and the industry now concedes that its products are harmful. Asbestos makers face a similar situation, with lawsuits so common they are settled by cripplingly expensive formulas, which require the company to file

for temporary bankruptcy. However, not all companies embroiled in asbestos suits are equally culpable, and some claimants are genuinely ill. But the gulf between them and other plaintiffs is so great that lawyers for those few who have asbestos-related illnesses have actually joined their former adversaries, asbestos makers and insurance companies, to oppose other claimants and push for legal reform.

The U.S. Chamber of Commerce recently released a study showing that 10 states, including Mississippi, West Virginia, and Alabama, are the "least friendly to business," with juries in corporate lawsuits giving out the biggest awards, while 10

© Royalty-Free/CORBIS

other states, such as Delaware, Nebraska, and Virginia, were among those "friendliest to business." The rankings are based on juries' fairness and judges' impartiality and competence, among other characteristics. If they are reliable, they may suggest that location could become a factor in a firm's legal environment. Already some states have limited the damages that may be awarded in medical malpractice cases and have made it tougher to win defective-product suits against companies in the state.

Congress, too, is considering legislation to try to stem the tide of consumer *class-action suits*—a class-action suit groups a number of small plaintiffs, often hundreds or thousands of them, to allow for efficient processing. But many companies facing such suits complain that plaintiffs' lawyers shop around for sympathetic courts, resulting in "a giant speed trap astride the nation's litigation highways," according to Professor Lester Brickman of Cardozo School of Law. Besides resulting in huge awards that eventually hurt consumers themselves, because businesses must pass along their increased costs to survive, such company-hostile locations often force firms to settle the case instead of fighting it. "It's the Barbary Coast," says Professor Brickman. "You have to pay ransom. If you go to trial, you court corporate death."

One proposal before Congress would allow defendants in class-action suits to move the cases from state to federal courts, where the rules are more restrictive. A consumer advocate noted, however, that "federal courts are a judicial hellhole for consumers," pointing out that a federal circuit court of appeals in Chicago ruled that those harmed in accidents caused by defective Firestone tires did not constitute a class, limiting the bargaining power of the claimants.

The general counsel for the American Tort Reform Association (ATRA) is in favor of such restrictions. "Certain state courts certify class actions that are not true class actions," he says. "They don't have enough facts in common." Another factor worrying companies and their legal staffs is the fact that when permissive state courts are allowed to define "class" loosely, the presiding local judge in a case may end up with a remarkable amount of power over major firms. The suit against Intel over its Pentium 4 processor, for instance, classes hundreds of thousands of consumers into a group who claim they were led to believe the computer chip gave better performance than its predecessors. A judge in Illinois's suburban Madison County will decide the case. "One judge in one county shouldn't essentially be regulating or setting policy for an industry, or for one product that's being sold coast to coast," says the vice president and general counsel of Altria Group.[1]

Overview

The first four chapters of the text show how important the legal environment is to business, government, and the general public and how changes occur to rectify problems. The corporate governance failures discussed in Chapter 2—and throughout the text—continue to be addressed in the aftermath of corporate malfeasance, prison sentences for executives like ImClone's CEO, Sam Waksal, civil and criminal charges against several other business leaders, the bankruptcies of such wrongdoers as Enron and WorldCom, and the passage of new laws designed to end abuses by unethical business executives. These events also led to new regulations restricting investment advisors, accountants, and board members in their oversight responsibilities. A business environment of greed, excess, and social responsibility failures was modified as a result of the demands of ethical business leaders, government officials, investors, and the general public.

On a more personal level, you may have experienced actions you felt should be addressed. On average, the typical e-mail user receives more junk e-mail (called *spam*) than actual messages. Also, those annoying telephone solicitations became so pervasive that a do not call law was enacted in 2003, making it illegal to call anyone listed on the federal don't call roster maintained by the Federal Trade Commission.

Legal issues affect every aspect of business. In fact, most of the remaining chapters will discuss legislation that specifically affects the business functions analyzed in each chapter. Already, an overview of the legal environment was presented in Chapter 2, and legislation affecting international operations was covered in Chapter 4. Chapter 5 covers laws designed to assist small businesses. Laws related to human resource management and labor unions are examined in Chapter 9. Laws affecting business operations, such as environmental regulations and product safety, are one of the topics in Chapter 13, and marketing-related legislation is examined in Chapter 14. Finally, legislation pertaining to banking and the securities markets is discussed in Chapters 17 and 18. In this appendix, we provide an overall perspective of legislation at the federal, state, and local levels and point out that, while business executives may not be legal experts, they do need to be knowledgeable in their specific area of responsibility. A good dose of commonsense also helps to avoid potential legal problems.

Despite business's best efforts, legal cases do arise in all aspects of business: contractual relationships, employment law, the environment, and other areas. The U.S. is clearly the world's most litigious society. Take, for example, the experience of just one major U.S. firm: At any one time, Wal-Mart is involved in up to 10,000 legal cases. Tort costs nationwide have surged to 2.3 percent of U.S. GDP, and some insurance industry experts believe that lawsuits related to tobacco, asbestos, medical malpractice, mold, investments, and even the fat content of food will bring the annual cost of litigation to $1,000 per citizen within just a few years.[2]

This appendix looks at the general nature of business law, the court system, basic legal concepts, and finally, the changing regulatory environment for U.S. business. Let's start with some initial definitions and related examples.

Legal System and Administrative Agencies

judiciary branch of the government charged with deciding disputes among parties through the application of laws.

The **judiciary,** or court system, is the branch of government charged with deciding disputes among parties by applying laws. This branch consists of several types and levels of courts, each with a specific jurisdiction. Court systems are organized at the federal, state, and local levels. Administrative agencies also perform some limited judicial functions, but these agencies are more properly regarded as belonging to the executive or legislative branch of government.

At both the federal and state levels, **trial courts**—courts of general jurisdiction—hear a wide range of cases. Unless a case is assigned by law to another court or to an administrative agency, a court of general jurisdiction will hear it. The majority of cases, both criminal and civil, pass through these courts. Within the federal system, trial courts are known as *U.S. district courts,* and at least one such court operates in each state. In the state court systems, the general jurisdiction courts are often called *circuit courts,* and states typically provide one for each county. Other names for general jurisdiction courts are superior courts, common pleas courts, or district courts.

> *They Said It*
>
> When you go into court, you are putting your fate into the hands of 12 people who weren't smart enough to get out of jury duty.
>
> —*Norm Crosby (b. 1927)*
> *American comedian*

State judiciary systems also include numerous courts with lower, or more specific, jurisdictions. In most states, parties can appeal the decisions of these lower courts to the general jurisdiction courts. Examples of lower courts are probate courts—which settle the estates of deceased persons—and small-claims courts—where people can represent themselves in suits involving limited amounts of money.

Appeals of decisions made at the general trial court level are heard by **appellate courts.** Both the federal and state systems have appellate courts. The appeals process allows a higher court to review the case and correct any lower court error indicated by the appellant, the party making the appeal.

Appeals from decisions of the U.S. circuit courts of appeals can go all the way to the nation's highest court, the U.S. Supreme Court. Appeals from state courts of appeal are heard by the highest court in each state, usually called the *state supreme court.* In a state without intermediate appellate courts, the state supreme court hears appeals directly from the trial courts. Parties not satisfied by the verdict of a state supreme court can appeal to the U.S. Supreme Court and may be granted a hearing if they can cite grounds for such an appeal and if the Supreme Court considers the case significant enough to be heard. In a typical year, the Supreme Court hears roughly 100 of the 7,000 cases filed with it.

While the great majority of cases are resolved by the system of courts described here, certain highly specialized cases require particular expertise. Examples of specialized federal courts are the U.S. Tax Court for tax cases and the U.S. Court of Claims, which hears claims against the U.S. government itself. Similar specialized courts operate at the state level.

Administrative agencies, also known as bureaus, commissions, or boards, decide a variety of cases at all levels of government. These agencies usually derive their powers and responsibilities from state or federal statutes. Technically, they conduct hearings or inquiries rather than trials. Examples of federal administrative agencies are the Federal Trade Commission (FTC), the National Labor Relations Board, and the Federal Energy Regulatory Commission. Examples at the state level include public utility commissions and boards that govern the licensing of various trades and professions. Zoning boards, planning commissions, and boards of appeal operate at the city or county level. The FTC has the broadest power of any of the federal regulatory agencies. It enforces laws regulating unfair business practices, and it can stop false and deceptive advertising practices.

Types of Law

Law consists of the standards set by government and society in the form of either legislation or custom. This broad body of principles, regulations, rules, and customs that govern the actions of all members of society, including businesspeople, is derived from several sources. **Common law** refers to the body of law arising out of judicial decisions, some of which can be traced back to early England.

law standards set by government and society in the form of either legislation or custom.

Statutory law, or written law, includes state and federal constitutions, legislative enactments, treaties of the federal government, and ordinances of local governments. Statutes must be drawn precisely and reasonably to be constitutional, and thus enforceable. Still, courts must frequently interpret their intentions and meanings.

With the growth of the global economy, a knowledge of international law becomes crucial. **International law** refers to the numerous regulations that govern international commerce. Companies must be aware of the domestic laws of trading partners, trade agreements such as NAFTA, and the rulings of such organizations as the World Trade Organization. For example, UPS once brought a case against the Canadian postal service, contending that Canada violated NAFTA by subsidizing the parcel delivery service of its post office.

In a broad sense, all law is business law because all firms are subject to the entire body of law, just as individuals are. In a narrower sense, however, **business law** consists of those aspects of law that most directly influence and regulate the management of various types of business activity. Specific laws vary widely in their intent from business to business and from industry to industry. The legal interests of Internet firms, for example, differ from those of hotel chains.

State and local statutes also have varying applications. Some state laws affect all businesses that operate in a particular state. Workers' compensation laws, which govern payments to workers for injuries incurred on the job, are an example. Other state laws apply only to certain firms or business activities. For example, states have specific licensing requirements for businesses, such as law firms, funeral homes, and hair salons. Many local ordinances also deal with specific business activities. Local regulations on the sizes and types of business signs are commonplace.

> *They Said It*
>
> The minute you read something that you can't understand, you can almost be sure it was drawn up by a lawyer.
>
> —*Will Rogers (1879–1935) American actor and humorist*

business law aspects of law that most directly influence and regulate the management of business activity.

Regulatory Environment for Business

The emphasis in government regulation of business has changed over time. Sometimes the pendulum swings toward increasing regulation of business practices, and sometimes it swings toward deregulation. But the goal of both types of legislation is protection of healthy competition. Let's look at these issues and the legislation that characterized them.

Antitrust and Business Regulation

John D. Rockefeller's Standard Oil monopoly precipitated antitrust legislation. Breaking up monopolies and restraints of trade was a popular issue in the late 1800s and early 1900s. In fact, President Theodore Roosevelt always promoted himself as a "trustbuster." The highly publicized Microsoft case is a recent example of antitrust litigation.

The 1930s saw the passage of several laws designed to regulate business. Actually, the rationale for many of these laws was protecting employment. Remember that the world was in the midst of the Great Depression during the 1930s. So the government was very concerned about keeping its citizens employed. And recently, the government became concerned with international business transactions and their effects on U.S. business practices, particularly the sources of funds. The major federal antitrust and business regulation legislation includes the following:

Law	What It Did
Sherman Act (1890)	Set a competitive business system as a national policy goal. The act specifically banned monopolies and restraints of trade.
Clayton Act (1914)	Put restrictions on price discrimination, exclusive dealing, tying contracts, and interlocking boards of directors that reduced competition or might lead to a monopoly.
Federal Trade Commission Act (1914)	Established the FTC with the authority to investigate business practices. The act also prohibited unfair methods of competition.
Robinson-Patman Act (1936)	Outlawed price discrimination in sales to wholesalers, retailers, or other producers. The act also banned pricing designed to eliminate competition.
Wheeler-Lea Act (1938)	Banned deceptive advertising. The act gave the FTC jurisdiction in such cases.
USA Patriot Act (2001)	Limited interactions between U.S. and foreign banks to those with "know your customer" policies; allowed the U.S. Department of the Treasury to freeze assets and bar a country, government, or institution from doing business in the U.S.; gave federal authorities broad powers to monitor Internet usage and expanded the way data are shared among different agencies.

Business Deregulation

Deregulation was a child of the 1970s whose influence continues today. Many formerly regulated industries were freed to pick the markets they wanted to serve. The deregulated industries were also allowed to price their products without the guidance of federal regulations. For the most part, deregulation led to lower consumer prices. In some cases, it also led to a loss of service, as many smaller cities with inadequate commercial air carrier service can attest. Following are several major laws related to deregulation:

Law	What It Did
Airline Deregulation Act (1978)	Allowed airlines to set fares and pick their routes.
Motor Carrier Act and Staggers Rail Act (1980)	Permitted the trucking and railroad industries to negotiate rates and services.
Telecommunications Act (1996)	Cut barriers to competition in local and long-distance phone, cable, and television markets.
Gramm-Leach-Bliley Act (1999)	Permitted banks, securities firms, and insurance companies to affiliate within a new financial organizational structure; required them to disclose to customers their policies and practices for protecting the privacy of personal information.

Consumer Protection

Consumer protection is another major goal of business law, and many laws have been passed in this area. Although we cite just the major federal laws, it is important to note that much of this legislation was passed at the state and local levels. The major federal laws related to consumer protection include the following:

Law	What It Did
Federal Food and Drug Act (1906)	Banned adulteration and misbranding of foods and drugs involved in interstate commerce.
Consumer Credit Protection Act (1968)	Required disclosure of annual interest rates on loans and credit purchases.
National Environmental Policy Act (1970)	Established the Environmental Protection Agency to deal with various types of pollution and organizations that create pollution.
Public Health Cigarette Smoking Act (1970)	Prohibited tobacco advertising on radio and television.
Consumer Product Safety Act (1972)	Established the Consumer Product Safety Commission with authority to specify safety standards for most products.
Nutrition Labeling and Education Act (1990)	Stipulated detailed information on the labeling of most foods.

Employee Protection

Chapters 2 and 9 cover many of the issues employers face in protecting their employees from injury and harm while on the job. Some of the relevant laws in this area include the following:

Law	What It Did
Fair Labor Standards Act (1938)	For hourly (nonexempt) workers, provided payment of the minimum wage and overtime pay for time worked over 40 hours in a workweek, restricted the employment of children, and required employers to keep records of wages and hours.
OSHA Act (1970)	Required employers to provide workers with workplaces free of recognized hazards that could cause serious injury or death and required employees to abide by all safety and health standards that apply to their jobs.
Americans with Disabilities Act (1991)	Banned discrimination against the disabled in public accommodations, transportation, and telecommunications.
Family and Medical Leave Act (1993)	Required covered employers to grant eligible employees up to 12 workweeks of unpaid leave during any 12-month period for the birth and care of a newborn child of the employee, placement with the employee of a son or daughter for adoption or foster care, care of an immediate family member with a serious health condition, or medical leave for the employee if unable to work because of a serious health condition.
Economic Recovery and Assistance for American Workers Act (2002)	Provided up to 13 weeks of additional unemployment benefits for workers who have exhausted their regular benefits of 26 weeks.

Investor Protection

Chapters 16, 17 , and 18 describe the institutions subject to investor protection laws and some of the recent events that have brought the Sarbanes-Oxley law into being. Following is a summary of other legislation to protect investors:

Law	What It Did
Securities Exchange Act (1934)	Created the Securities and Exchange Commission with the authority to register, regulate, and oversee brokerage firms, transfer agents, clearing agencies, and stock exchanges; the SEC also has the power to enforce securities laws and protect investors in public transactions.
Bank Secrecy Act (1970)	Deterred laundering and use of secret foreign bank accounts; created an investigative paper trail for large currency transactions; imposed civil and criminal penalties for noncompliance with reporting requirements; improved detection and investigation of criminal, tax, and regulatory violations.
Sarbanes-Oxley Act (2002)	Established a five-member accounting oversight board subject to Securities and Exchange Commission oversight; prohibited CPA firms from providing some types of consulting services for their clients; required corporate executives to attest to the validity of the company's financial statements.

Cyberspace and Telecommunications Protection

Computers and widespread use of the Internet and telecommunications have dramatically expanded the reach of businesses. They have also raised some thorny issues such as computer fraud and abuse, online privacy, and cyberterrorism. The Napster music-downloading case demonstrated how the Internet is creating a whole new arena of regulatory decisions. Some cases like Microsoft's antitrust case are based on laws on the books for years. Other Internet-related regulation is based on more contemporary legislation. Following are some of the major laws enacted to regulate cyberspace and telecommunications:

Law	What It Did
Computer Fraud and Abuse Act (1986)	Clarified definitions of criminal fraud and abuse for federal computer crimes and removed legal ambiguities and obstacles to prosecuting these crimes; established felony offenses for unauthorized access of "federal interest" computers and made it a misdemeanor to engage in unauthorized trafficking in computer passwords.
Children's Online Privacy Protection Act (1998)	Authorized the FTC to set rules regarding how and when firms must obtain parental permission before asking children marketing research questions.
Identity Theft and Assumption Deterrence Act (1998)	Made it a federal crime to knowingly transfer or use, without lawful authority, a means of identification of another person with intent to commit, aid, or abet any violation of federal, state, or local law.
Anticybersquatting Consumer Protection Act (1999)	Prohibited people from registering Internet domain names similar to company or celebrity names and then offering them for sale to these same parties.
Homeland Security Act (2002)	Established the Department of Homeland Security; gave government wide new powers to collect and mine data on individuals and groups, including databases that combine personal, governmental, and corporate records, including e-mails and Web sites viewed; limited information citizens can obtain under the Freedom of Information Act; gave government committees more latitude for meeting in secret.
Amendments to the Telemarketing Sales Rule (2003)	Created a national "do not call" registry, which prohibits telemarketing calls to registered telephone numbers; restricted the number and duration of telemarketing calls generating dead air space with use of automatic dialers; cracked down on unauthorized billing; and required telemarketers to transmit their caller ID information. Telemarketers must check the do not call list quarterly, and violators could be fined as much as $11,000 per occurrence. Excluded from the registry's restrictions are charities, opinion pollsters, and political candidates.

The Core of Business Law

The cornerstones of U.S. business law are contract law and the law of agency; the Uniform Commercial Code, sales law, and negotiable instruments law; property law and the law of bailment; trademark, patent, and copyright law; tort law; bankruptcy law; and tax law. The sections that follow set out the key provisions of each of these legal concepts.

Contract Law and Law of Agency

Contract law is important because it is the legal foundation on which business dealings are conducted. A **contract** is a legally enforceable agreement between two or more parties regarding a specified act or thing.

contract legally enforceable agreement between two or more parties regarding a specified act or thing.

Contract Requirements   As Figure 1 points out, the four elements of an enforceable contract are agreement, consideration, legal and serious purpose, and capacity. The parties must reach agreement about the act or thing specified. For such an agreement, or contract, to be valid and legally enforceable, each party must furnish consideration—the value or benefit that a party provides to the others with whom the contract is made. Assume, for example, that a builder hires an electrical contractor to wire a new house. The wiring job and the resulting payment are the considerations in this instance. In addition to consideration, an enforceable contract must involve a legal and serious purpose. Agreements made in a joking manner, related purely to social matters, or involving the commission of crimes are not enforceable as legal contracts. An agreement between two competitors to fix the prices for their products is not enforceable as a contract because the subject matter is illegal.

> *They Said It*
>
> A verbal contract isn't worth the paper it's written on.
>
> —*Samuel Goldwyn (1882–1974)*
> *American motion picture producer*

The last element of a legally enforceable contract is capacity, the legal ability of a party to enter into agreements. The law does not permit certain persons, such as those judged to be insane, to enter into legally enforceable contracts.

Contracts govern almost all types of business activities. Examples of valid contracts are purchase agreements with suppliers, labor contracts, franchise agreements, and sales contracts.

Breach of Contract   A violation of a valid contract is called a **breach of contract.** The injured party can go to court to enforce the contract provisions and, in some cases, collect **damages**—financial payments to compensate for a loss and related suffering.

agency legal relationship whereby one party, called a principal, appoints another party, called an agent, to enter into contracts with third parties on the principal's behalf.

Law of Agency   All types of firms conduct business affairs through a variety of agents, such as partners, directors, corporate officers, and sales personnel. An **agency** relationship exists when one party, called a *principal,* appoints another party, called the *agent,* to enter into contracts with third parties on the principal's behalf.

The law of agency is based on common law principles and case law decisions of state and federal courts. Relatively little agency law has been enacted into statute. The law of agency is important because the principal is generally bound by the actions of the agent.

The legal basis for holding the principal liable for acts of the agent is the Latin maxim *respondent superior* ("let the master answer"). In a case involving agency law, the court must decide the rights and obligations of the various parties. Generally, the principal is held liable if an agency relationship exists and the agent has some type of authority to do the wrongful act.

Uniform Commercial Code

Most U.S. business law is based on the Uniform Commercial Code—usually referred to simply as the UCC. The UCC covers topics like sales law, warranties,

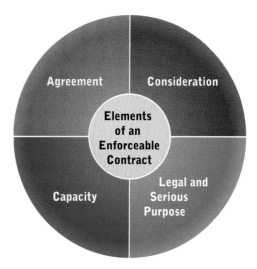

FIGURE 1
Four Elements of an Enforceable Contract

and negotiable instruments. With the exception of Louisiana, which uses the Napoleonic Code, all the states have adopted the UCC. Even Louisiana has adopted some provisions of the UCC.

sales law law governing the sale of goods or services for money or on credit.

Sales law governs sales of goods or services for money or on credit. Article 2 of the UCC specifies the circumstances under which a buyer and a seller enter into a sales contract. Such agreements are based on the express conduct of the parties. The UCC generally requires written agreements for enforceable sales contracts for products worth more than $500. The formation of a sales contract is quite flexible because certain missing terms in a written contract or other ambiguities do not prevent the contract from being legally enforceable. A court will look to past dealings, commercial customs, and other standards of reasonableness to evaluate whether a legal contract exists.

Courts will also consider these variables when either the buyer or the seller seeks to enforce his or her rights in cases in which the other party fails to perform as specified in the contract, performs only partially, or performs in a defective or unsatisfactory way. The UCC's remedies in such cases consist largely of monetary damages awarded to injured parties. The UCC defines the rights of the parties to have the contract performed, to have it terminated, and to reclaim the goods or place a *lien*—a legal claim—against them.

Warranties   Article 2 of the UCC also sets forth the law of warranties for sales transactions. Products carry two basic types of warranties: An express warranty is a specific representation made by the seller regarding the product, and an implied warranty is only legally imposed on the seller. Generally, unless implied warranties are disclaimed by the seller in writing, they are automatically in effect. Other provisions govern the rights of acceptance, rejection, and inspection of products by the buyer; the rights of the parties during manufacture, shipment, delivery, and passing of title to products; the legal significance of sales documents; and the placement of the risk of loss in the event of destruction or damage to the products during manufacture, shipment, or delivery.

negotiable instrument commercial paper such as checks that is transferable among individuals and businesses.

Negotiable Instruments   The term **negotiable instrument** refers to commercial paper that is transferable among individuals and businesses. The most common example of a negotiable instrument is a check. Drafts, certificates of deposit, and notes are also sometimes considered negotiable instruments.

Article 3 of the UCC specifies that a negotiable instrument must be written and must meet the following conditions:

1. It must be signed by the maker or drawer.
2. It must contain an unconditional promise or order to pay a certain sum of money.
3. It must be payable on demand or at a definite time.
4. It must be payable to order or to bearer.

Checks and other forms of commercial paper are transferred when the payee signs the back of the instrument, a procedure known as *endorsement*.

Property Law and Law of Bailment

Property law is a key feature of the private enterprise system. Property is something for which a person or firm has the unrestricted right of possession or use. Property rights are guaranteed and protected by the U.S. Constitution.

As Figure 2 shows, property can be divided into three basic categories. Tangible personal property consists of physical items such as equipment, supplies, and delivery vehicles. Intangible personal property is nonphysical property like mortgages, stocks, and checks that are most often represented by a document or other written instrument, although it may be as vague and remote as a computer entry. Students probably are familiar with certain types of intangible personal property such as checks and money orders. Other less-known examples are important to the businesses or individuals that own and use them: bonds, notes, letters of credit, and warehouse receipts.

A third category of property is real property, or real estate. All firms have some interaction with real estate law because of the need to buy or lease the space in which they operate. Some companies are created to serve these real estate needs. Real estate developers, builders, contractors, brokers, appraisers, mortgage companies, escrow companies, title companies, and architects all deal with various aspects of real property law.

The law of bailment deals with the surrender of personal property by one person to another when the property is to be returned at a later date. The person delivering the property is known as the *bailor,* and the person receiving the property is the *bailee.* Some bailments benefit bailees, others benefit bailors, and still others provide mutual benefits. Most courts now require that all parties practice reasonable care in all bailment situations. The degree of benefit received from the bailment is a factor in court decisions about whether parties have met the reasonable care standards.

Bailment disputes are most likely to arise in business settings such as hotels, restaurants, banks, and parking lots. A series of rules have been established to govern settlement of such disputes. The law focuses on actual delivery of an item. For example, the proprietor of a restaurant is not liable for theft or damage to a coat a patron hangs on a hook or on the back of a chair. The reason: The patron has made no actual delivery to the restaurant's proprietor. On the other hand, if the restaurant has a coat-check room and the patron receives a claim check, the coat has been delivered, and the proprietor is liable for theft or damage to the coat.

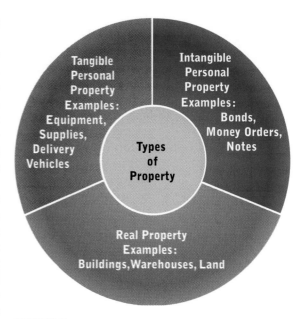

FIGURE 2
Three Basic Types of Property

Trademarks, Patents, and Copyrights

Trademarks, patents, and copyrights provide legal protection for key business assets by giving a firm the exclusive right to use those assets. A **trademark** consists of words, symbols, or other designations used by firms to identify their offerings. The Lanham Act (1946) provides for federal registration of trademarks. Trademarks are a valuable commercial property. For instance, Coca-Cola is considered the world's most widely recognized trademark.

If a product becomes too well known, its notoriety can create problems. Once a trademark becomes a part of everyday usage, it loses its protection as a legal trademark. Consider the fate of aspirin, cola, nylon, kerosene, linoleum, and milk of magnesia. All these product names were once the exclusive property of their manufacturers, but they have passed into common language, and now anyone can use them. Companies often attempt to counter this threat by advertising that a term is actually a registered trademark. A recent Supreme Court ruling sent a lawsuit regarding the name of a Kentucky lingerie shop—Victor's Little Secret—back to the appeals court level. Victoria's Secret had sued the firm under the Federal Trademark Dilution Act, claiming that the other shop's name would confuse shoppers. The Supreme Court said that the international lingerie firm did not clearly show its brand had been tarnished, but it still has the chance to do so under the appeal.[3]

A **patent** guarantees an inventor exclusive rights to an invention for 17 years. Copyrights and patents have a constitutional basis; the U.S. Constitution specifies that the federal government has the power "to promote the progress of science and useful arts, by securing for limited times to authors and inventors the exclusive rights to their respective writings or discoveries." Patent owners often license others to use their patents for negotiated fees.

A **copyright** protects written material such as this textbook, designs, cartoon illustrations, photos, computer software, and so on. This class of business property is referred to as *intellectual property.* Copyrights are filed with the Library of Congress. Congress recently extended copyright protection for creative material by an additional 20 years, covering artistic works for the lifetime of the creator plus 70 years; for companies, the time is 95 years. The extension, which was backed primarily by The Walt Disney Company to protect its exclusive rights to Mickey Mouse, was upheld by the Supreme Court.[4] Curiously, Disney finds itself on the other side of an ongoing copyright suit regarding Winnie the Pooh. In a case that has now dragged on for more than a dozen years, Stephen Slesinger Inc., which acquired the rights to the character and stories of AA Milne in 1929, maintains that Disney has short-changed it on millions of dollars in royalties from the sale of merchandise, videos, DVDs, and other electronic products based on Winnie the Pooh. The outcome of that case is yet undetermined.[5]

Law of Torts

A **tort** (French for "wrong") refers to a civil wrong inflicted on another person or the person's property. The law of torts is closely related to the law of agency because a business entity, or principal, can be held liable for torts committed by its agents in the course of business dealings. Tort law differs from both criminal and contract law. While criminal law is concerned with crimes against the state or society, tort law deals with compensation for injured persons who are the victims of noncriminal wrongs.

Tort cases are often extremely complex and frequently result in considerable monetary awards or judgments. In Durham, North Carolina, jurors awarded a woman $5 million in a medical malpractice suit against a dentist who botched the extraction of her wisdom teeth. The woman suffered nerve damage, a damaged jaw joint, continual pain, and other severe health complications. In another case from North Carolina, a jury awarded a patient's family $4.5 million in a wrongful death suit. The suit charged the surgeon with misdiagnosing a ruptured appendix and going on vacation without arranging for the patient to be monitored.[6]

Types of Torts   A tort may be intentional, or it may be caused by negligence. Assault, slander, libel, and fraud are all examples of intentional torts. Businesses can become involved in such cases through the actions of both owners and employees. A security guard who uses excessive force to apprehend an alleged shoplifter may have committed a tort. Under agency law, the guard's employers, such as a shopping mall or individual retailer, can be also held liable for any damages or injury caused by the security guard.

The other major group of torts results from negligence. This type of tort is based on carelessness rather than intentional behavior that causes injury to another person. Under agency law, businesses can also be held liable for the negligence of their employees or agents. The delivery truck driver who kills a pedestrian while delivering goods creates a tort liability for his or her employer if the accident results from negligence.

Product Liability   An area of tort law known as **product liability** has been developed by both statutory and case law to hold businesses liable for negligence in the design, manufacture, sale, or use of products. Some states have extended the theory of tort law to cover injuries caused by products, regardless of whether the manufacturer is proven negligent. This legal concept is known as *strict product liability*.

The business response to product liability has been mixed. To avoid lawsuits and fines, some recall defective products voluntarily; others decide to fight recall mandates if they feel the recall is not justified. Upon receiving reports of 26 infants being injured when its Magic Start Crawl 'n Stand toy tipped over, Playskool recalled 300,000 of its toys, which had been sold in Wal-Mart stores.[7]

Bankruptcy Law

bankruptcy legal nonpayment of financial obligations.

Bankruptcy, the legal nonpayment of financial obligations, is a common occurrence in contemporary society. The term *bankruptcy* is derived from *banca rotta,* or "broken bench," referring to the medieval Italian practice of creditors breaking up the benches of merchants who did not pay their bills.

Federal legislation passed in 1918 and revised several times since then provides a system for handling bankruptcies. Bankruptcy has two purposes. One is to protect creditors by providing a way to seize and distribute debtors' assets. The second goal, which is almost unique to the U.S., is also to protect debtors, allowing them to get a fresh start.

Federal law recognizes two types of bankruptcy. Under voluntary bankruptcy, a person or firm asks to be judged bankrupt because of inability to repay creditors. Under involuntary bankruptcy, creditors may request that a party be judged bankrupt.

Personal Bankruptcies   Personal bankruptcy law has recently been revised to encourage more individuals to repay their debts rather than have them erased. Bankruptcy law offers individuals two primary options: Chapter 13 bankruptcy or Chapter 7 bankruptcy. Chapter 13 of the bankruptcy law—the wage earner plan—allows a person to set up a five-year debt repayment plan. Debtors often end up repaying only a portion of what they owe under Chapter 13. The court considers the bankrupt party's current income in determining the repayment schedule.

Chapter 7 sets out a liquidation plan under which a trustee sells the bankrupt person's assets and divides the proceeds among creditors. Changes to bankruptcy law have made it more difficult for individuals to file for Chapter 7 bankruptcy. Debtors must generally participate in credit-counseling programs before they file for bankruptcy protection. In addition, bankruptcy judges use a complex formula to decide whether an individual's debts can be eliminated. Both these provisions are expected to reduce the number of people qualifying for Chapter 7 bankruptcy.

Chapter 7 exempts limited amounts of selected property from the claims of creditors. These exemptions include retirement accounts, pensions, and limited levels of household furnishings, clothes, books, tools of one's trade, and prescribed health needs. Previous exemptions from full repayment of auto loans have been removed, and the amount of home equity that can be shielded from creditors has been greatly reduced.

Business Bankruptcies   Businesses can also go bankrupt. The specific provision under which they do this, Chapter 11, allows a firm to reorganize and develop a plan to repay its debts. Chapter 11 also permits prepackaged bankruptcies, in which companies enter bankruptcy proceedings after obtaining approval of most—but not necessarily all—of their creditors. Often, companies can emerge from prepackaged bankruptcies sooner than those that opt for conventional Chapter 11 bankruptcy proceedings. After emerging from its filing for Chapter 11 bankruptcy protection in 2002, discount retailer Kmart made a remarkable comeback that culminated in its recent merger with Sears—at one time the largest corporation in the U.S. Although both stores will continue to operate separately, shoppers can expect to find such Sears brands as Craftsman tools, Kenmore appliances, and Lands' End clothing at Kmart and such Kmart mainstay brands as Martha Stewart, Jaclyn Smith, and Joe Boxer at Sears.[8]

Financially strapped firms sometimes seek a merger with another firm. When lagging sales and higher costs of raw materials pushed home-product manufacturer Rubbermaid to the brink of bankruptcy, it merged with Freeport, Illinois-based Newell Inc. to become Newell Rubbermaid.[9] Given the potential liabilities, potential acquirers often require that the troubled company file under Chapter 11. This action is intended to avoid further litigation.

Tax Law

A branch of law that affects every business, employee, and consumer in the U.S. is tax law. A **tax** is an assessment by a governmental unit. Federal, state, and local governments and special taxing authorities all levy taxes.

Some taxes are paid by individuals and some by businesses. Both have a decided impact on contemporary business. Business taxes reduce profits, and personal taxes cut the disposable incomes that individuals can spend on the products of industry. Governments spend their revenue from taxes to buy goods and services produced by businesses. Governments also act as transfer agents, moving tax revenue to other consumers and transferring Social Security taxes from the working population to retired or disabled persons.

Governments can levy taxes on several different bases: income, sales, business receipts, property, and assets. The type of tax varies from one taxing authority to another. The individual income tax is the biggest source of revenue for the federal government. Many states rely heavily on revenue generated from sales taxes. In addition to sales taxes, some cities collect taxes on earnings. Finally, many community college districts get the bulk of their revenue from real estate or property taxes.

tax assessment by a governmental unit.

They Said It

If it isn't the sheriff, it's the finance company. I've got more attachments on me than a vacuum cleaner.

—*John Barrymore (1882–1942)*
American actor

They Said It

I am convinced that if most members of Congress did their own taxes, we would have had tax reform long ago.

—*Bill Archer (b. 1928)*
American politician

DID YOU KNOW?

1. Among many Middle Easterners, signing a contract is much less significant than giving your word.

2. When U.S. negotiators *table* a proposal, they intend to delay their decision on it. In Britain, *tabling* means taking immediate action.

3. In Illinois, it is illegal to use a firearm to hunt bullfrogs.

4. Molest a butterfly and you break a local law in Pacific Grove, California.

Business Terms You Need to Know

judiciary 140	contract 145	negotiable instrument 146
law 141	agency 145	bankruptcy 148
business law 141	sales law 146	tax 149

Other Important Business Terms

trial courts 140	international law 141	patent 147
appellate courts 140	breach of contract 145	copyright 147
common law 141	damages 145	tort 148
statutory law 141	trademark 147	product liability 148

Projects and Applications

1. Many firms incorporate in Delaware. Such choices are at least partially because Delaware regularly updates its corporate laws. A recent update permits the roughly 500,000 corporations registered in Delaware to hold electronic annual meetings. Delaware also allows annual meetings to be held via the Web, e-mail, or fax. What is your opinion of the First State's novel approach to corporate governance? What advantages and disadvantages occur to you?

2. U.S. companies have long had to comply with the Sherman Act's and Clayton Act's provisions about restraint of trade, price discrimination, and monopolies. The United Kingdom has similar, but even stronger, rules. The Competition Act sets up the Office of Fair Trading (OFT) and grants it the power to investigate industrial cartels, price fixing, restrictions on customers or markets, no-compete agreements, and exclusive purchasing arrangements. The OFT also has the power to seize documents without notice and to levy hefty fines. While often compared with the U.S.'s Sherman Act, the UK law is really closer to the European Union's competition law. How might the Competition Act benefit UK businesses and consumers? What, if any, downside do you see?

3. Use the Internet to select and research a state or federal business-related law enacted during the past year. Why was this legislation passed? What were the arguments for and against it? How do you think the new law will affect businesses? Consumers? Society in general?

4. In lieu of professional fees—typically billed on an hourly basis—some attorneys accept cases on a contingency basis. The attorney earns nothing if he or she loses the case. If the case results in an award, the attorney collects a contingency fee, which is typically 30 percent or more of the total award. Use the Internet to research the arguments for and against contingency fees.

5. The 1998 national tobacco settlement required tobacco companies to pay $206 billion over 20 years to 46 states to pay health costs related to cigarette smoking. Then Philip Morris, part of Altria Group, recently lost a $10.1 billion class-action lawsuit in Illinois after a judge found it deceived consumers when it claimed that its light cigarettes were less harmful. To appeal the Illinois suit, the company had to post a $12 billion bond. The company said it could not afford to post such a huge amount, stating that the amount should be lowered or it could declare bankruptcy.[10] The 45 other states are naturally concerned that if the company declares bankruptcy, Philip Morris will not pay its share of the national settlement. Consider the competing interests in these suits and debate the case from each party's viewpoint: the original 46 states and their settlement, Illinois smokers who thought switching to light cigarettes would be less harmful to their health, and Altria/Philip Morris. Should Altria be allowed to declare bankruptcy? Go online to see what has happened in the cases and compare those results with your positions.

Part 1   Krispy Kreme Continuing Case

Krispy Kreme: A Business for Every Taste

Krispy Kreme is an American success story, complete with ups and downs. Although the company's founder, Vernon Carver Rudolph, didn't invent the doughnut, he gave the little pastry a unique twist that quickly became a favorite of every person who tried one. Doughnut legend says that the Dutch settlers brought fried dough cakes to the New World sometime around the 1600s. The cakes contained nuts baked into their centers, so early colonists combined the words *dough* and *nut* to create the word *doughnut*, which became part of the American vocabulary. In 1847, a boy named Hanson Gregory suggested that his mother slice a circular hole in the middle of her fried cakes so that they would brown evenly, and the modern doughnut was born.

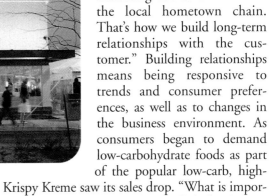

Ninety years later, Vernon Rudolph bought a doughnut shop in Kentucky from a French chef who passed along a secret recipe for a yeast-raised doughnut as part of the deal. Within a few years, Rudolph moved his business to Winston-Salem, North Carolina, where he opened the first Krispy Kreme bakery. As word spread about the tasty, airy doughnuts—which Rudolph had been selling just to grocery markets—customers began to stop by the shop and ask if they could buy the fresh, warm doughnuts directly from the bakery. So Rudolph created his first retail shop by simply cutting a hole in the wall of the bakery and serving warm, freshly prepared doughnuts to consumers.

Rudolph's Krispy Kremes have survived through the production era, the marketing era, and on into the relationship era in the history of business. In the 1950s, the company began to mechanize the doughnut-making process, instead of relying totally on hand cutting, so that more doughnuts could be produced in a shorter period of time. Although Rudolph died in 1973, his business continued to expand and grow as Krispy Kreme developed an identity for its brand and began franchising its shops. Today, more than 400 stores dot the U.S. landscape, and the firm has begun to expand overseas as well, to Australia, Canada, Mexico, and the United Kingdom. Much of the expansion has been achieved through franchise agreements—contracts between Krispy Kreme and entrepreneurs who want to operate Krispy Kreme stores. Krispy Kreme out-

lets crank out more than 7.5 million doughnuts each day, or about 3 billion a year. Although Krispy Kreme's signature product is its Hot Original Glazed doughnut fresh off the line, customers can enjoy about 20 doughnut varieties along with coffee and other beverages.

Throughout its history, Krispy Kreme has focused on building relationships with its customers. Even as the firm expands across the country and around the world, its managers want to be certain that Krispy Kreme fans feel that their shop is part of their home. "That's our goal," says Steve Bumgarner, field marketing coordinator. "To be the local hometown chain. That's how we build long-term relationships with the customer." Building relationships means being responsive to trends and consumer preferences, as well as to changes in the business environment. As consumers began to demand low-carbohydrate foods as part of the popular low-carb, high-protein diet, Krispy Kreme saw its sales drop. "What is important now is what we are going to do about it," declared CEO Scott Livengood. The firm announced plans to develop a low-sugar, low-carb doughnut and also decided to slow down its rapid growth into new markets until sales picked up again. In order to compete with Starbucks's popular coffeehouses, executives have also begun experimenting with plans to create comfortable places for consumers to sit and sip Krispy Kreme's own brand of coffee while savoring their doughnuts.

Despite changes in the business environment, Krispy Kreme's fans remain loyal. Visitors to the local Krispy Kreme shop can overhear comments such as, "They're more than doughnuts; they're like heaven," and "They melt in your mouth," from fans waiting in line for the taste of the warm confection from the doughnut maker. In Wichita, Kansas, 75 people camped out overnight so they could be the first inside when the doors to a new Krispy Kreme store opened at 5:30 A.M. Other store openings are greeted with local fanfare and media attention.

In a business environment scarred by ethical lapses, how a top executive sets a company's standards of conduct and moral values; conveys them to its employees, customers, and franchise partners; and applies them to business decisions can greatly affect the success of the firm. While Krispy Kreme was enjoying tremendous publicity—including having the city of Fresno, California, declare an official Krispy Kreme Day upon the opening of a new store—potential problems were brewing. When the firm repurchased several franchises, the Securities and Exchange Commission launched an inquiry into the way these transactions were reported in the firm's accounting records. CEO Scott Livengood countered that "Krispy Kreme has no higher priority than the confidence of our shareholders, customers, and employees. We are confident in our practices."

Since employees are often involved in communicating the shared moral values to friends and others they interact with outside the company, they must be knowledgeable concerning their employer's ethical standards. This ethical awareness is strengthened through personal experiences of how the organization treats its employees and its customers. As pointed out in Chapter 2, business ethics are shaped by individual, organizational, legal, and societal forces. Despite ongoing challenges, Krispy Kreme executives say they remain committed to ethical standards in the way their company conducts business. In a letter to shareholders in a recent annual report, Scott Livengood writes of his company's continued dedication to shared values:

We are committed to building an organization based on common values that resonate with the best in the human spirit. They include: integrity, authenticity, passion, learning, sharing, and positive expectation. We believe our commitment to these values will encourage creativity, responsibility, and community. We also believe the manner in which we accomplish our goals is as important as what we accomplish.

Krispy Kreme is well known for its commitment to social responsibility. In fact, the concept is part of its business strategy. Some industry experts believe that one of the company's most valuable marketing efforts comes through its fund-raising programs, in which nonprofit groups and charitable organizations purchase doughnuts at half price from Krispy Kreme, sell them to the public at full price, and pocket the profits for good

causes. Krispy Kreme fund-raisers have been held to raise money for graduations, proms, school trips, and band uniforms. "We helped raise some $43 million for various causes in our last fiscal year," reports Stanley Parker, senior vice president of marketing. "We get e-mails all the time from people who sold our doughnuts as kids, years ago, to raise money for baseball uniforms or to go on a field trip." The company's "Good Grades" program gives out free doughnuts to students who achieve As on their report cards. And when the Krispy Kreme shop opened in Fresno, the shop's franchisee donated part of the proceeds from the day's sales to Foster Friends, a charity that works with foster children who have special needs. "We want our company to establish deep roots in the community," notes an executive with one of the largest Krispy Kreme franchises in California.

QUESTIONS

1. Describe the characteristics of Krispy Kreme that illustrate its passage through three different eras in business history.

2. Why is it important for a company's top managers to communicate ethical standards through the organization? How do you think Krispy Kreme's executives should handle the SEC inquiry?

3. Describe the role that social responsibility plays in decision making at Krispy Kreme.

4. In which foreign markets do you think Krispy Kreme might be most successful? Why?

Sources: Company Web site, http://www.krispykreme.com, accessed January 10, 2005; David Stires, "Krispy Kreme Is in the Hole—Again," *Fortune*, November 1, 2004, pp. 42–43; Eric Dash, "SEC Steps Up Inquiry on Krispy Kreme," *The New York Times*, October 9, 2004, http://www.nytimes.com; Robert Barker, "Why Krispy Kreme Is Worth a Bite," *BusinessWeek*, September 27, 2004, p. 130; Christopher Palmeri and Amy Borrus, "What's Really Inside Krispy Kreme?" *BusinessWeek*, August 16, 2004, p. 72; Paul Nowell, "Low-Carb Craze Catches Up with Krispy Kreme," *USA Today,* May 26, 2004, p. 6B; Andy Sewer, "The Hole Story: How Krispy Kreme Became the Hottest Brand in America," *Fortune,* July 7, 2003, pp. 52–62.

Part 2
Starting and Growing Your Business

Chapter 5
Options for Organizing Small and Large Businesses

Learning Goals

1 Distinguish between small and large businesses and identify the industries in which most small firms are established.

2 Discuss the economic and social contributions of small business.

3 Compare the advantages and disadvantages of small businesses.

4 Describe how the Small Business Administration assists small-business owners.

5 Explain how franchising can provide opportunities for both franchisors and franchisees.

6 Summarize the three basic forms of business ownership and the advantages and disadvantages of each form.

7 Identify the levels of corporate management.

8 Describe recent trends in mergers and acquisitions.

9 Differentiate among private ownership, public ownership, and collective ownership (cooperatives).

Adding Bricks to the eBay Business Model

EBay's CEO, Meg Whitman, recently noted that her company has almost 105 million registered users, which means the online auction site handles more trades per day than the New York Stock Exchange. In fact, eBay moves more than $900 worth of goods every second.

But despite that volume, only one in eight registered users has actually put a product up for sale on the site. Many of them simply don't have the experience to handle an online sale, including taking professional-quality pictures or writing a description of their merchandise or collectible, setting a fair and realistic price, and arranging to accept payment and ship goods—nor do they have the time to learn. Perhaps they're too busy to deal with the details, or they already tried to sell the item through classified ads and failed. And some sellers don't have a computer with which to access the eBay site. But rather than risk not finding a buyer in the limited market of a garage sale or consignment shop, more and more sellers are stopping in at the nearest eBay neighborhood drop-off store. The store does all the rest, giving the item exposure to millions of buyers on eBay, tracking the bids, collecting the purchase price, and packaging the item and shipping it to the buyer. All the seller has to do is accept the check at the end of the process, minus a percentage of the winning buyer's bid.

"It's the 21st century pawn shop," says the owner of one drop-off store. And while individuals have been selling goods on eBay for about 10 years, new businesses that piggyback on the auction phenomenon are growing rapidly. Some are independent storefronts, like Online Auction Service & Internet Specialists in Hicksville, New York, which opened a few years ago and has sold everything from unwanted wedding gifts to hundreds of pounds of pillow stuffing and a horse carriage from the film *Amistad*. A Kawasaki dealer who uses the store's services to sell used motorcycles says that even unwanted models fetch high prices on eBay. "They just come right in and bing, bang, boom, it's done," he said.

Most middlemen warehouse the items sellers bring them, but Adam Hersch of Manhattan and his employees go to clients' locations rather than asking sellers to take the bus or subway to them. Even after his commission, Hersch says, the seller receives "about the same as what you'd get if you did it yourself. Even if it's a little less, I take all the hassle away."

Sellers are so eager to have the hassle taken away that drop-off services have grown into a major franchised business. AuctionDrop is growing in California and plans to expand to the New York area; QuickDrop, with nine locations in seven states, has set an 18-month growth goal of 200 locations in 38 states. "This is the future of e-commerce on the Internet, no question," says QuickDrop cofounder Jack Reynolds.

iSold It is the highest-volume competitor and is now selling franchises in 43 states. Other chains include Auction-Wagon and Pictureitsold. All auction middlemen charge their clients about the same commission—generally starting at about 30 percent of the final selling price—and, on the seller's behalf, pay eBay's fees as well. Elise Wetzel, founder of iSold It, says, "You can do it yourself, but who has the time and the knowledge? We're giving people access that they don't have right now. It's a value-added service." In fact, some of the drop-off stores will even help clients set

© David McNew/Getty Images

their asking prices, assessing the condition of the item in question, making sure it works, and researching similar items before starting the bidding online.

Most middlemen charge nothing to list the item, and if it doesn't sell, the client can take it back or donate it to charity. But their success rate is high. Nearly half of AuctionDrop's customers are repeat clients, for instance. On the other hand, most drop-off operators are savvy about what sells and what doesn't—and what is profitable. "If it costs you more than [$15 to sell], you'll go out of business," says Randy Adams, cofounder of AuctionDrop. "Digital cameras,

musical instruments—these items sell well. Average selling price . . . is the single most important aspect of this business." Some chains will reject items they don't feel they can sell.

Meanwhile, eBay isn't complaining about the mushrooming of stores that help sellers get their merchandise into auction. Even Meg Whitman has brought items to AuctionDrop. And although some experts are dubious about whether eBay would be wise to consider buying any of the drop-off chains, the last time an eBay piggyback took off, it was called PayPal. eBay recently bought the company.[1]

Chapter Overview

If you have ever thought of operating your own business, you are not alone. In fact, on any given day in the U.S., more people are trying to start new businesses than are getting married or having children. However, before entering the world of contemporary business, an entrepreneur needs to understand its framework.

Like the owners of eBay drop-offs, every business owner must choose the form of legal ownership that best meets the company's needs. Several variables affect the choice of the best way to organize your business:

- How easily can you set up this type of organization?
- How much financial liability can you afford to accept?
- What financial resources do you have?
- What strengths and weaknesses do you see in other businesses in the industry?
- What are your own strengths and weaknesses?

They Said It

Successful people have control over the time in their life. A shoemaker who owns his own shop gets up one morning and says, "I'm not opening." That's a successful guy.

—*Rod Steiger (1925–2002)*
American actor

We begin this chapter by focusing on small-business ownership, including the advantages and disadvantages of small-business ventures. We also look at the services provided by the U.S. government's Small Business Administration. The role of women and minorities in small business is discussed in detail, as well as global opportunities for small-business owners. We then provide an overview of the three forms of private business ownership—sole proprietorships, partnerships, and corporations. Next, we explore the structures and operations typical of larger companies and review the trends in business with a fresh look at mergers, acquisitions, and joint ventures. The chapter concludes with an explanation of public and collective ownership.

Most Businesses Are Small Businesses

Although many people associate the term *business* with corporate goliaths like ExxonMobil, Ford, PepsiCo, Pfizer, Microsoft, and Wal-Mart, nine of 10 firms with employees have fewer than 20 people on staff, and 98 percent have fewer than 100 employees. The vast majority of U.S. businesses have no payroll at all: Over 14 million people in the U.S. are earning business income without any employees.[2] Almost half the sales in the U.S. are made by small businesses.[3]

Small business is also the launching pad for entrepreneurs from every sector of the diverse U.S. economy. One third of the nation's 17 million small businesses are owned by women. Hispanic-owned businesses account for 4 percent of all U.S. businesses with fewer than 100 employees. African Americans own another 3.6 percent, and Asian Americans 3.5 percent.[4]

What Is a Small Business?

How do you distinguish a small business from a large one? Are sales the key indicator? What about market share or number of employees? The Small Business Administration (SBA), the federal agency most directly involved with this sector of the economy, considers a **small business** to be a firm that is independently owned and operated and is not dominant in its field. The SBA also considers annual sales and number of employees to identify small businesses for specific industries.

small business firm that is independently owned and operated, not dominant in its field, and meets industry-specific size standards for income or number of employees.

- Most manufacturing businesses are considered small if they employ fewer than 500 workers.
- To be considered small, wholesalers must employ no more than 100 workers.
- Most kinds of retailers and other services can generate up to $5 million in annual sales and still be considered a small business.
- An agricultural business is generally considered small if its sales are no more than $500,000 a year.[5]

The SBA has established size standards for specific industries. These standards, which range from $500,000 to $25 million in sales and from 100 to 1,500 for employees, are available at the SBA's "Size Standards" Web page, http://www.sba.gov/size.

An excellent example of a small business—and its founder-owner—can be found in a 97-year-old former Lutheran church in Maynard, Massachusetts. Ron Labbe's Studio 3D is the world's only one-stop shop for all things 3-D. His biggest seller is 3-D glasses. When Polaroid dropped the product, Labbe moved quickly, buying the remaining inventory of 750,000 pairs at 2.5 cents each. Today, they're hot sellers at 25 cents apiece.[6]

Since government agencies offer a number of benefits designed to help small businesses compete successfully with larger firms, operators of small businesses are interested in determining whether their

© Ron Labbe/Studio 3D

Studio 3D founder Ron Labbe's photographic experiences qualify him as an expert in things 3-D. He worked on a 3-D issue of *Sports Illustrated*, helped to launch the Magic Eye 3-D illusions found on millions of cereal boxes and posters, and has made 3-D slides in operating rooms.

companies meet the standards for small-business designation. If it qualifies, a company may be eligible for government loans or for government purchasing programs that encourage proposals from smaller suppliers.

Typical Small-Business Ventures

For decades, small businesses have competed against some of the world's largest organizations, as well as multitudes of other small companies. One of these fearless competitors is Dublin, California-based Sanrise Group, started by David Schneider to help businesses store the explosion of Internet data and solve today's data-storage chaos. Imitating Dell's original model of selling built-to-order PCs directly to customers, Sanrise designs preconfigured data-storage equipment to match specific business customer needs and ships it worldwide within 30 days. Not only does the equipment match customers' needs, but it also saves them 30 to 40 percent in storage costs, while letting them avoid the months often involved between order and delivery and setup. To continue to serve its 600-plus customers and compete with larger, better financed rivals, Sanrise raised a whopping $115 million from several major outside investors. Revenues are soaring, too, and are expected to reach $100 million soon.[7]

The past 15 years have seen a steady erosion of small businesses in many industries as larger firms have bought out small independent businesses and replaced them with larger operations. Drugstore retailers have been tremendously affected, as thousands of small neighborhood pharmacies have been replaced by retail giants like Walgreen's, CVS, and Rite Aid. The number of independent pharmacies has plummeted 30 percent over the past 10 years.[8] But as Table 5.1 reveals, the businesses least likely to be gobbled up and consolidated into larger firms are those that sell services, not things; rely on consumer trust and proximity; and keep their overhead costs low.

For centuries, most nonfarming small businesses have been concentrated in retailing and the service industries. As Figure 5.1 indicates, small businesses provide the majority of jobs in the construction, agricultural services, wholesale trade, services, and retail trade industries. Small service businesses can be as high-touch as a country inn or hair stylist, or as high-tech as Sanrise Group.

Retailing is another important industry for today's small businessperson. General merchandising giants like Sears, Target, and Wal-Mart may be the best-known retailing firms, but small privately owned retail stores far outnumber them. Small-business retailing includes stores that sell shoes, jewelry, office supplies and stationery, clothing, flowers, drugs, convenience foods, and thousands of other products. People wishing to form their own business have always been attracted to retailing because of the ability to start a firm with limited funds, rent a store rather than build a custom facility, create a Web site, and use family members to staff the new business.

Powell's Books, based in Portland, Oregon, is one of the most successful retail bookstores in the U.S. In contrast to so-called "Big Box" book superstores like Barnes & Noble and Books-A-Million that use

Table 5.1   David vs. Goliath: Business Sectors Most Dominated and Least Dominated by Small Firms

Most Likely to Be a Small Firm	Fewer Than 20 Workers	Least Likely to Be a Small Firm	Fewer Than 20 Workers
Dentists	98%	Hospitals	4%
Home builders	97	Paper mills	22
Florists	97	Nursing homes	23
Hair salons	96	Oil pipelines	25
Auto repair	96	Electric utilities	39
Funeral homes	95	Railroad car makers	44

Source: *USA Today* analysis of U.S. Small Business Administration data; reported in Jim Hopkins, "Big Business Can't Swallow These Little Fish," *USA Today,* March 27, 2002, pp. B1, B2.

their huge buying power to secure lower prices for large orders and Amazon.com's well-known high-tech, stock-everything strategy, Powell's competes by specializing in used, sometimes hard-to-find books. Through its seven bookstores and its Web site (Powells.com), Powell's serves customers who like buying from an independent store instead of one of the larger chains and who don't mind paying extra to find something special to read. Their different strategies permit the two competitors to benefit one another. Powell's buys returned books from Amazon.com at a discount and sells them as used. Amazon fills orders for out-of-print books through Powell's. This strategy will never make Powell's the largest bookseller, but that is just fine with the retailer's founder, Michael Powell.[9]

Small business also plays a significant role in agriculture. Although most farm acreage is in the hands of large corporate farms, the majority of farmers still operate as small businesses. Most U.S. farms are owned by individual farmers or families, not partners or shareholders.[10] The family farm is a classic example of a small-business operation. It is independently owned and operated, with relatively few employees, relying instead on the labor of family members. But today's small farmers must be able to combine savvy business and marketing techniques to thrive, as has California-based Earthbound Farm, an organic grower.

Almost half of small businesses in the U.S. are **home-based businesses**—firms operated from the residence of the business owner. Between 1960 and 1980, fewer people worked at home, largely because the number of farmers, doctors, and lawyers in solo practices was declining. But since then, the number of people working at home has more than doubled. A major factor in this growth is the increased availability of personal computers with access to the Internet and other communications devices such as fax machines and cell phones. As computer technology evolves at a rapid pace and more workers prefer the flexibility of working from alternative locations, the Census Bureau predicts that the number of home-based businesses will grow even faster during the early decades of the 21st century.[11]

Operating home-based businesses can help owners keep their costs low. Without having to lease or maintain separate office or warehouse space, a home-based business owner can pour precious funds into the business itself. But financing a small business can be challenging, as discussed in the Hits & Misses box. Some home-based business owners have even discovered the benefits of selling their goods through eBay, the online auction site. Andrew and Tracy Hortatsos, owners of ShadeSaver.com, sell 50 percent of their retail sunglasses through eBay. "It was probably the single most important thing we stumbled upon as far as allowing our business to grow," says Andrew Hortatsos.[12] The cost of operating from home through eBay is far less than the cost of leasing, staffing, and maintaining a retail store at a high-traffic shopping mall, not to mention the far greater number of consumers eBay reaches.

Other benefits of a home-based business include greater flexibility and freedom from the time and expense of commuting. Drawbacks include isolation and less visibility to customers—except, of course, if your customers visit you online. In that case, they don't care where your office is located.

Many small-business start-ups are more competitive because of the Internet. An estimated three of every five small businesses have an online presence. But the Internet does not automatically guarantee success, as illustrated by the thousands of dot.com failures during the early years of e-commerce. Setting up a Web site can be relatively inexpensive and gives a business the potential to reach a huge marketplace. Tiny Salem Five Cents Savings Bank, a Massachusetts firm with only nine branches, has a significant presence on the Internet. It established that presence by acting quickly in the mid-1990s, when Internet banking was still an innovation. Consumers liked the new service and low fees, and before long, Salem Five had attracted thousands of new customers. When bigger banks began adding Internet service, Salem Five changed its online name from salemfive.com to directbanking.com and honed its focus to New England, where the bank already had a good reputation to build on. It continues to

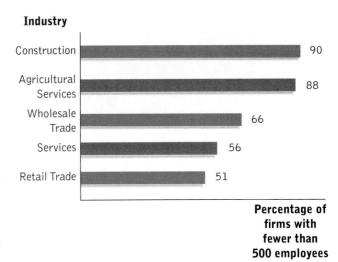

FIGURE 5.1

Major Industries Dominated by Small Businesses

Source: Data from Office of Advocacy, U.S. Small Business Administration, "Small Business Profile: United States," accessed from the SBA Web site, http://www.sba.gov/advo/stats, January 14, 2004.

> *They Said It*
>
> Size certainly matters, and not always in a positive way.
>
> —*Michael Powell (b. 1941) founder and owner, Powell's Books*

HITS & MISSES

"Put It on My Credit Card"

Everyone knows that credit cards are a double-edged sword. They're easy and convenient to use, on the one hand, but they are also a risky way to borrow more money than you can quickly pay back. With interest rates and penalties high, many consumers have learned to be wary of forgetting about budgeting and saying, "Put it on my credit card."

But what about small-business owners? Struggling to establish themselves and finding financing tough to obtain, many entrepreneurs use their personal credit cards as an important source of financing in the early years of their businesses, and even beyond. A National Small Business Association and Arthur Andersen survey reports that only 6 percent of all small businesses were operating with SBA loans, and a mere 2 percent had found venture capital to fund their start-ups. About half of small businesses in the survey used credit cards to pay for either starting or expanding their operations. The National Federation of Independent Business reports that smaller firms with sales under $500,000 and firms under 10 years old are the most likely to use credit cards for working capital.

Diana Frerick is a case in point. She has used credit cards more than once to finance start-ups in the karaoke business, most recently to open Karaoke Star Store & Stage, an equipment retailer that now has 14 employees and more than $2 million in revenues. "I thank God for credit cards," she says. "They're the easiest way to get money."

Matt Jung and Chip George had a less positive experience. "We had no assets," says Jung of their start-up. "We were taking anything we could get." After relying on credit to buy raw materials and finance operating costs for their beanbag chair company, Comfort Research, they found themselves deep in debt despite rapid growth and revenues of $2 million. It took years to pay off the debt and accumulated interest. "It's a very expensive way to borrow money," says Jung of his experience with credit cards. "I think they should be a last resort."

Steve Rotermund, who ruined his personal credit to keep his passenger-jet cleaning company afloat several years ago, still has trouble buying consumer goods on credit. His advice to fellow entrepreneurs is, "Try to get money other ways if you can. Anything is better than credit cards."

Nevertheless, when used wisely, small-business credit cards can be convenient for entrepreneurs. "A credit card with a $10,000 limit could provide you with enough working capital to purchase equipment or furniture, or pay for a marketing campaign," says the executive director of the National Association of Women Business Owners. Paying attention to the interest rate and other details can help business owners make wise decisions about credit, as can setting up a separate fund to fall back on if the business falters. Many financial institutions offer small-business cards with no annual fees and zero interest for the first six months. "What the small-business owner needs to do is compare," says an economist with the SBA.

QUESTIONS FOR CRITICAL THINKING

1. How do you think using credit cards for financing a small business resembles using them for personal items like clothing or entertainment? How does it differ?
2. Many financial institutions bundle other services with credit cards offered to small-business owners. Which ones would matter to you if you were looking for business credit?

Sources: Jonathan D. Epstein, "New York–Based Bank Launches Free Checking for Small Firms," *Buffalo News,* October 4, 2004, accessed at EBSCOhost http://web12.epnet.com; Danielle Knight, "Where to Find the Money," *U.S. News & World Report,*" August 2, 2004, p. 67; Barbara Whitaker, "Purchasing: For Buyers Who Have No Time, Tips for Choosing a Credit Card," *The New York Times,* September 12, 2004, http://www.nytimes.com; Bobbie Gossage, "Charging Ahead," *Inc.,* January 2004, pp. 42–44.

They Said It

You may not think you're going to make it. You may want to quit. But if you keep your eye on the ball, you can accomplish anything.

—*Hank Aaron (b. 1934)*
American baseball legend

Concept Check

1. Why are small-business owners interested in determining whether their companies can be designated small businesses by the SBA?
2. Identify three industries in which small businesses are common.

innovate and has opened branches with automated-teller machines and Internet kiosks offering videoconferencing with bank representatives. High technology coupled with concern for customer service keeps Salem Five in business even as the biggest banks spend millions of dollars on advertising.[13]

American business history is filled with inspirational stories of great inventors who launched companies in barns, garages, warehouses, and attics. For young visionaries like Apple Computer founders Stephen Jobs and Steve Wozniak, the logical option for transforming their technical idea into a commercial reality was to begin work in a family garage. The impact of today's entrepreneurs, including home-based businesses, is discussed in more depth in Chapter 6.

Contributions of Small Business to the Economy

Small businesses form the core of the U.S. economy. Businesses with fewer than 500 employees generate 47 percent of total U.S. sales and over half the nation's gross domestic product. Nine of every 10 U.S. businesses are small businesses. In addition, small businesses employ 53 percent of the nation's private nonfarm workforce.[14] One business that started small but has been growing is Guitar Center. The retail chain has created unique and lasting links with its customers, as discussed in the Best Business Practices box.

Creating New Jobs

Small businesses make tremendous contributions to the U.S. economy and to society as a whole. One impressive contribution is the number of new jobs created each year by small businesses. Three of every four new jobs created over the last 10 years were at companies with fewer than 500 employees. A significant share of these jobs was created by the smallest companies—those with four or fewer employees. Small firms are dominant factors in many of the industries that have added the most jobs: engineering and management services, construction trade contractors, wholesale trade, amusement and recreation, social services, and restaurants.[15]

In an economy slowed by recession, a sizable number of new jobs are created by entrepreneurs who decide to launch new business ventures. During the first years of the 21st century, employers hired 20 percent fewer new college graduates than before the recession began. Instead of spending his final year at Texas A&M University job hunting, James Ewing launched Northgate Vintage, a retail store that offers vintage clothing. "In my classes, everybody is talking about how hard it is to find a job," says Ewing. "I don't have to worry about that because I can focus on this."[16]

Even if you never plan to start your own business, you will probably work for a small business at some point in your career. Not only do small firms employ about half of all U.S. workers, but they are more likely than large firms to employ the youngest (and oldest) workers. In addition, as detailed in a later section of this chapter, small businesses offer significant opportunities to women and minorities.

Small businesses also contribute to the economy by hiring workers who traditionally have had difficulty finding jobs at larger firms. Compared with large companies, small businesses are more likely to hire former welfare recipients.[17] Driven in part by their limited budgets, small businesses may be more open to locating in economically depressed areas, where they contribute to rehabilitating neighborhoods and reducing unemployment.

Creating New Industries

The small-business sector also gives entrepreneurs an outlet for developing their ideas and perhaps for creating entirely new industries. Many of today's successful high-tech firms—Microsoft, Cisco Systems, Yahoo!, and Dell—began as small businesses.

The growth of such new businesses not only provides new goods and services but also fuels local economies. The high-tech companies in California's Silicon Valley created a need for many support services. A company called iQuantic provides human resources consulting to Silicon Valley clients, and to be close at hand, it located in a former mattress factory in San Francisco. By locating in San Francisco's run-down Mission District, iQuantic brought money into that neighborhood.[18]

Another contribution of small business is its ability to provide needed services to the larger corporate community. The movement toward corporate downsizing that began in the early 1990s created a demand for other businesses to perform activities previously handled by company employees. Outsourcing such activities as security, employee benefits management, maintenance, and logistics created opportunities that were often filled by employees of small businesses.

BEST BUSINESS PRACTICES

Guitar Center: Hitting All the Right Notes

What musician could resist a music store where you can "come in and try anything and hang out as long as you want"? That's the Guitar Center, a successful chain of about 130 music stores across the country and an additional 19 American Music Group (AMG) outlets. Not surprisingly, Guitar Center specializes in guitars, with models in every price range from a $99 Fender Squier to a vintage 1958 Fender Stratocaster for nearly $40,000. But the store also offers drums, amplifiers, keyboards, and other instruments, as well as audio and recording equipment, parts, accessories, books, magazines, videos, and music software. It appeals to musicians and music lovers of all ages. "It's an inviting place," said one 40-something customer. And a 14-year-old agreed, "This is the best place for guitars I've ever seen."

The country's largest music equipment dealer, Guitar Center Inc. posts net income of nearly $37 million a year. It attracts not only crowds of customers—1,400 people came to the recent grand opening of a new store—but also hundreds of potential employees. About 300 people showed up before a recent opening to apply for the store's 15 available jobs, and management's ability to handpick the most knowledgeable people to work in Guitar Center is just one component of the chain's success. Competitive savvy is another.

"They beat the competition on selection, they beat the competition on service, and they beat them on price, the three legs of the stool that really drive store choice," said an industry analyst. Guitar Center also advertises widely. Says one competitor about Guitar Center, "What your customer base does is go down there and check it out. Heck, I went down there and checked it out. They've got one of everything."

The chain is expanding rapidly, building on a strategy of growth begun in the 1970s, and added 14 new stores in one recent year, with about as many more still to come. In its high-ceilinged interiors are glass-walled rooms set aside for customers to try instruments, and some music lovers drop in regularly, often without buying anything. Product seminars and guest appearances by musical artists also draw customers to the store, where open space complements the massive displays of product offerings. Service is a priority, backed up by Guitar Center's online store.

The performance of the American Music Group has not been quite as strong as Guitar Center's. "The AMG business model is taking longer to develop than the company had anticipated," said one analyst, and expansion plans for AMG were recently put on hold. Unlike Guitar Center, AMG must appeal to band instructors and their parents, and some competitors say the company's business model—the "big-store" concept that made Wal-Mart a runaway success, using the store's buying power to leverage a wider variety and lower prices—won't work in that market, where long-term relationships are important.

QUESTIONS FOR CRITICAL THINKING

1. Competitors claim that Guitar Center's "guaranteed" lowest prices are possible because they often don't include the price of an instrument case. Do you think this pricing strategy could backfire? Why or why not?

2. Why do you think Guitar Center's big-store model has been less successful in its American Music Group stores?

Sources: "Guitar Center" company profile, http://www.monster.com, accessed October 1, 2004; company Web site, http://www.guitarcenter.com, accessed October 1, 2004; Alex Veiga, "Leading the Band," *Mobile Register,* May 9, 2004, pp. F1, F5; Lee Davidson, "'A Music Store for Musicians,'" *Mobile Register,* May 9, 2004, pp. F1, F5.

Small businesses might begin with a shift in consumer interests and preferences and then blossom into a whole new industry. A generation ago, no one would have called cheerleading an industry. But today's cheerleaders aren't just yell leaders, bouncing around on the sidelines and calling out encouragement to their favorite team. Instead, they are competitive, athletic teams in their own right, often logging more practice time and travel miles than the football team. They get recruited by college scouts and compete for national championships. Various businesses have grown up around the new cheerleading trend—training camps, costume and uniform suppliers, publications. The magazine *American Cheerleader* was launched in 1994 and now claims 200,000 in circulation, with a readership of 1 million.[19]

Attracting New Industries

Community leaders realize the importance of small businesses to their cities, and successful revitalization programs have improved conditions in depressed areas by attracting new industries. A federal program called the New Markets Initiative has been proposed to target areas where more than 20 percent of residents live in poverty or where the median income is significantly below the statewide average. Businesses in those areas would be eligible for government-guaranteed loans, as well as tax incentives, such as tax credits and exemption from paying tax on certain gains.[20]

Businesses need more than government incentives, however. They also need access to the necessary resources, including qualified workers, reasonably priced facilities, and strong markets. Other influences on location decisions include the availability of government-funded worker-training programs, sources of financing, and positive attitudes shown by city officials and local community groups.

Concept Check

1. What percentage of the nation's nonfarm workforce do small businesses employ?
2. What resources do small businesses need to survive in depressed areas?

Advantages of a Small Business

Small businesses are not simply smaller versions of large corporations. They differ greatly in forms of organization, market positions, staff capabilities, managerial styles, organizational structures, and financial resources. But these differences usually seem like strengths to small-business owners, who find many advantages in operating small businesses rather than working within large, powerful, multinational corporations. As Figure 5.2 indicates, the four most important advantages are innovation, superior customer service, lower costs, and opportunities to fill isolated niches.

Innovation

To compete effectively with giant corporations backed by massive resources, small firms often have to find new and creative ways of conducting business. Although the DVD rental market is dominated by behemoth Blockbuster, Reed Hastings knew that there just had to be a better way. Perhaps it was that $40 late fee he had to pay when he forgot to return *Apollo 13,* but Hastings recalls asking himself, "How come movie rentals don't work like a health club, where whether you use it a lot or a little, you get the same charge?" And from that question, Netflix.com, the first successful online DVD rental service, was born.

Today, the 41-year-old Californian heads a company with more than 1,000,000 subscribers, a DVD library of 15,000 titles, and revenue approaching $50 million. DVDs are shipped to subscribers and returned by them using the U.S. Postal Service. Why not use the Internet as a distribution method? Hastings explains, "We recognized the mail is a very efficient network. It costs us 37 cents to mail the DVD. That's 100 times cheaper than sending it over the Internet."[21]

Small businesses are often fertile ground in which to plant innovative ideas for new goods and services. As a chemist in the pharmaceutical industry, Thomas E. D'Ambra saw many exciting ideas neglected because his employer lacked the resources to pursue them. D'Ambra decided that a market existed for a company that would offer research services on a contract basis to firms in the industry. His start-up business, Albany Molecular Research, focused on research and development for new drugs on a contract basis. Today, the company employs 200 chemists and tackles research projects for such industry giants as DuPont Pharmaceuticals and Eli Lilly. With his customers facing a continued shortage of talented chemists, D'Ambra foresees a strong future for Albany Molecular.[22]

In a typical year, small firms will develop twice as many product innovations per employee as larger firms. They also obtain more patents per sales dollar than do larger businesses. In addition, the fact that small firms are a richer source of innovations is even more evident than these statistics show because large firms are more likely to patent their discoveries.[23] Key 20th century innovations that were developed by small businesses include the airplane, audiotape recorder, double-knit fabrics, optical scanner, personal computer, soft contact lens, and

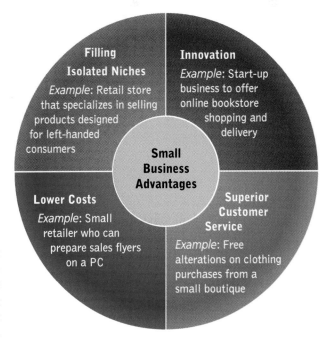

FIGURE 5.2
Advantages of Small-Business Ownership

In competing with rivals like DHL, FedEx, and UPS, U.S. Postal Service management has begun to focus on specific customer groups like small businesses and work with them to design mutually beneficial services. Netflix.com's decision to use the U.S. Postal Service to distribute its DVDs was based on analyses of cost and service quality.

the zipper. One area of innovation that is likely to occupy small businesses during the early years of the 21st century is security—whether it's the protection of information or the protection of people.

Superior Customer Service

A small firm often can operate with greater flexibility than a large corporation, allowing it to tailor its product line and the services it offers to the needs of its customers. Greg Rosenberg, co-owner of Beverly's Pet Center in Pembroke Pines, Florida, understands the importance of serving customers well. Surrounded by pet supply giants like PetsMart and Pet Supplies Plus, Beverly's decided to focus on two things: pets and customers. "We run a clean shop and train our employees to know what they're talking about," says Rosenberg. When they visit the store, kids get to play with the puppies, munch free popcorn, cheer at the hamster races, and scare themselves at the edge of Beverly's 4,000-gallon shark pond. It's an experience that the giant discounters just can't match. In fact, when the local PetsMart abandoned its location a few miles away, Beverly's moved in.[24]

Low Costs

Small firms may be able to provide goods and services at prices that large firms cannot match. Small businesses usually minimize their **overhead costs**—costs not directly related to providing specific goods and services—which allows them to earn profits on lower prices. Many small businesses avoid rent and utility expenses by operating out of the owners' homes. In addition, these firms often carry little or no inventory, further reducing total operating costs.

A typical small business sets up a lean organization with a small staff and few support personnel. The lower costs of maintaining a small permanent staff can provide a distinct advantage for a small business. Instead of hiring high-income attorneys and accountants as permanent staff members, small-business owner-managers typically hire these professionals when needed for special projects or as outside consultants. This approach typically helps to hold down payroll costs for the small business.

Another source of cost savings is the quantity and quality of work performed by the business owner. Entrepreneurs typically work long hours with no overtime or holiday pay. In addition, their family members may contribute services at little or no pay as bookkeepers, laborers, receptionists, production assistants, and delivery personnel.

> *They Said It*
>
> In the end, a vision without the ability to execute is probably a hallucination.
>
> —*Stephen M. Case (b. 1958)*
> *Cofounder, America Online*

Filling Isolated Market Niches

Large growth-oriented businesses tend to focus on major segments of the overall market. The growth prospects of market niches are simply too limited and the expenses involved in serving them too great to justify the time and effort. Because high overhead costs force large firms to set minimum sizes for their target markets, small underserved market niches have always attracted small businesses that are willing and able to serve them.

Schylling Toys celebrated its 30th birthday in 2005. The family-owned company specializes in toy revivals from the past—toys made of wood, tin, and other natural elements that today's children still enjoy. Jack-in-the-boxes, porcelain tea sets, and wooden pull and wind-up toys are just a few of the 400 classic items in the Schylling catalog. But managers Jack, Dave, and Tom Schylling realized that their little $20-million toy company would always be small potatoes compared with industry giants Mattel and Hasbro. Then Dave had a dramatic idea: Why not contact Warner Brothers and try to license rights to a few products based on the *Harry Potter* books that the industry leaders weren't likely to pursue? So the brothers proposed to pay a royalty on the sales of these items, and Warner agreed. Next, they produced a *Harry Potter* toy catalog and made a distribution deal with Starbucks. The Schyllings never strayed from their core business as a specialty toy maker, yet the success of the *Harry Potter* deal put them in a whole different league.[25]

In addition to filling smaller niches, certain types of businesses prefer to work with small organizations. Many service businesses illustrate this point. In a small medical practice or accounting firm, you are more likely to know who is providing the service you receive. Finally, economic and organizational factors may dictate that an industry consist primarily of small firms. Upscale restaurants and personal shopping services are typically small-business operations, keeping the owners in close contact with their customers.

Concept Check

1. How are small businesses able to offer superior customer service?
2. How do small businesses keep costs down?
3. Why are small businesses able to fill isolated market niches?

Disadvantages of a Small Business

Although small businesses bring a number of strengths to the competitive marketplace, they also have disadvantages in competing with larger, more established firms. A small business may find itself especially vulnerable during an economic downturn, since it may have accumulated fewer resources than its larger competitors to cushion a sales decline.

The primary disadvantages facing today's small businesses include management shortcomings, inadequate financing, and government regulations. These issues—quality and depth of management, availability of financing, and ability to wade through government rules and requirements—are so important that firms with major deficiencies in one or more areas may find themselves in bankruptcy proceedings. As Figure 5.3 shows, almost one new business in four will permanently close its doors within two years of opening them, and 62 percent will fail within the first six years of operation. By the tenth year, 82 of every 100 businesses will have gone under. Although highly motivated and well-trained business owner-managers can overcome these potential problems, they should thoroughly analyze whether one or more of these problems may threaten the business before deciding to launch the new company.

Management Shortcomings

Among the most common discoveries at a postmortem examination of a small-business failure is inadequate management. Business founders often possess great strengths in specific areas such as marketing or interpersonal relations, but they may suffer from hopeless deficiencies in others like finance or order

FIGURE 5.3
Rate of Business Failures

Source: Dave Marcum, Steve Smith, and Mahan Khalsa, *BusinessThink*. Hoboken, NJ: John Wiley & Sons, 2002, p. 1; Joyce M. Rosenberg, "Biggest Small-Business Mistake? No Planning," *Mobile Register*, April 28, 2002, p. F3.

fulfillment. Large firms recruit specialists trained to manage individual functions; small businesses frequently rely on small staffs who must be adept at a variety of skills.

An even worse result frequently occurs when people go into business with little, if any, business training. Some new businesses are begun almost entirely on the basis of what seems like a great idea for a new product. Managers assume that they will acquire needed business expertise on the job. All too often, the result is business bankruptcy.

If you are seriously contemplating starting a new business, heed some words of warning. First, learn the basics of business. Second, recognize your own limitations. Although most small-business owners recognize the need to seek out the specialized skills of accountants and attorneys for financial and legal assistance, they often hesitate to turn to consultants and advisers for assistance in areas such as marketing, where they may lack knowledge or experience.

Founders of new businesses frequently struggle with an all too common ailment: the so-called "rose-colored-glasses syndrome." Filled with excitement about the potential of newly designed products, they may neglect important details like marketing research to determine whether potential customers share their excitement. Individuals considering launching a new business should first determine whether the proposed product meets the needs of a large enough market and whether they can convince the public of its superiority over competing offerings.

Inadequate Financing

Another leading cause of small-business problems is inadequate financing. Often, first-time business owners start up with the assumption that their firms will generate enough funds from the first month's sales to finance continuing operations. Building a business takes time, though. Employees must be trained, equipment purchased, deposits paid for rent and utilities, and marketing dollars spent to inform potential customers about the new firm and its product offerings. Even a one-person, home-based business has start-up expenses—such as a new computer or additional phone lines—especially if the entrepreneur has already left his or her full-time job to pursue a business dream. Unless the owner has set aside enough funds to cover cash shortfalls during the first several months in which the business is becoming established, the venture may collapse at an early stage.

After surviving the cash crunch that often accompanies the first months of operation, a business must confront another major financial problem: uneven cash flows. For most small and large businesses, cash inflows and outflows do not display even patterns; instead, they fluctuate greatly at different times of the year. Small retail outlets generate much of their annual sales revenues during the December holiday period. Florists make most of their deliveries during three holidays: Valentine's Day, Easter, and Mother's Day. Large firms may build up sufficient cash reserves to weather periods of below-average sales, or they can turn to banks and other lenders for short-term loans; business start-ups often lack both cash balances and access to sources of additional funds.

But small firms rely less on debt for financing than large businesses do, with less than half of small companies borrowing money at least once during the course of a year.[26] And many small-business owners have found an unlikely solution for quick, short-term loans: credit cards. As Figure 5.4 shows, credit cards, despite their relatively high interest rates, are an important source of financing for small businesses. The heaviest users of credit cards for business financing are tiny firms with fewer than 10 employees. If a small-business owner has a good credit record with a consumer credit card,

FIGURE 5.4

Sources of Small-Business Financing
*Trade credit is purchasing goods or equipment from a supplier who finances the purchase by delaying the date of payment for those goods.
†A line of credit is an agreement between a bank and a borrower, indicating the maximum amount of credit the bank will extend to the borrower.
‡Total exceeds 100 percent because businesses typically use more than one source of financing.

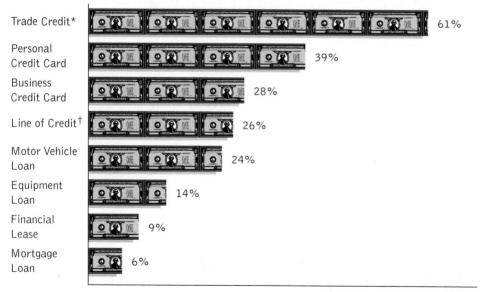

Trade Credit*	61%
Personal Credit Card	39%
Business Credit Card	28%
Line of Credit†	26%
Motor Vehicle Loan	24%
Equipment Loan	14%
Financial Lease	9%
Mortgage Loan	6%

Percentage of Businesses Using Source‡

Source: Data from Office of Advocacy, U.S. Small Business Administration, "The Facts about Small Business," p. 9, accessed from the SBA Web site, http://www.sba.gov/advo, January 14, 2004.

BUSINESS TOOL KIT

Obtaining Financing for a Small Business

When it comes to obtaining financing for your business, you have alternatives besides setting up a lemonade stand. Funding for the earliest stages of a business is called *seed capital* and usually comes from savings and credit cards. However, be sure to explore all of your alternatives before taking on too much personal debt.

- *Mom and Dad.* Who else believes in you and your idea wholeheartedly? Ask other relatives as well, especially those looking for a good financial investment. As with any business dealings, be professional and provide a written agreement between you and a parent, sibling, or relative—and always keep your word.
- *Banks and credit unions.* Banks and other financial institutions offer small-business loans with varying terms and generally provide five types of small-business credit: lines of credit, term loans, leasing, real estate financing, and credit cards. When you approach a bank or credit union for a loan, be aware that you will need to have a solid business plan to convince them that you are a good credit risk.
- *Small Business Administration (SBA) loans.* The Basic 7(a) Loan Guaranty Program is the SBA's most popular loan program; the SBA also offers a Certified Development Company (504) Loan Program, which offers a more long-term approach. Go to http://www.sba.gov for more information.
- *Angel investors.* Angel investors—individuals with money to spare and a taste for vicarious entrepreneurship—are another option when a business needs only $250,000 to $750,000 in start-up capital. Good sources for locating "angels" include banks, local chambers of commerce, and local or regional business journals.
- *Venture-capital funding.* Venture capitalists (VCs) invest through money management funds or make direct capital investments in a growing business. VCs are not the best source of financing if you're looking for only $10,000 to $50,000, and the terms they offer entrepreneurs are not always good. Also, they will have specific performance requirements and can play an intimate role in developing and expanding your business, so make sure you partner with a VC that shares your vision and values.

Entrepreneurs also have a wide variety of nonbank financing options, including commercial finance companies, credit unions, life insurance companies, and credit card firms. Other options include taking out a second mortgage on your home, partnering with a larger company, securing a community development loan, and finding other people who may be willing to make cash investments in your company in exchange for a share of ownership.

Sources: Rod Kurtz, "From One Company to Another: Start-ups," *Inc.,* June 2003; Harris Collingwood, "The Private-Capital Survival Guide," *Inc.,* March 2003; Helen Langan, "Searching for Business Financing," *Utah Business,* November 2002, p. 48.

---

he or she will have relatively easy approval for a corporate credit card. Even if the business owner doesn't have the best credit history, he or she will be more apt to win approval on a credit card than on a traditional business loan.[27] As discussed later in this chapter, small-business owners may have other sources of financing as well.

Inadequate financing can compound management shortcomings by making it more difficult for small businesses to attract and keep talented people. Typically, a big company can offer a more attractive benefits package and a higher salary. During the wave of dot-com start-ups, many people decided to take a chance and work for these companies, which often offered stock options—the right to buy stock in a firm at a lower price—in place of higher salaries or better benefits. If a company succeeded, its employees could become very rich. If it failed, its workers were not only left without profits, but they were often left without jobs.

With less money to spend on employees, successful small companies need to be more creative. Ronald Richey, who runs Precision Plastics, an injection-molding plant in Columbia City, Indiana, watched one-fifth of his employees quit each year. Lacking sufficient employees to operate the factory, he had to keep some of his machinery idle every week. Richey tried better communication and hiring temporary workers, but nothing worked. Then he thought of an innovative arrangement: If employees would work five six-hour shifts without lunch breaks, he would pay them 40 hours' wages each week for 30 hours of work. Two weeks into the new plan, turnover plummeted—and quality improved. Even with what is effectively a higher pay scale, Precision's profits have grown.[28]

Government Regulation

Small-business owners often complain bitterly about excessive government regulation and red tape. Paperwork costs alone account for billions of small-business dollars each year. A large company can better cope with requirements for forms and reports. These firms may decide that it makes economic sense to hire or contract with specialists in specific types of regulation, such as employment laws and workplace safety regulations. Small businesses often struggle to absorb the costs of government paperwork because of their more limited staff and budgets. Some small firms close down for this reason alone.

Recognizing the burden of regulation on small businesses, Congress sometimes exempts the smallest companies from certain regulations. Except for manufacturers, companies with 10 or fewer employees are exempt from some data-collection requirements of the Occupational Safety and Health Administration. Most small-business owners comply with employment and other laws, believing that such compliance is ethically correct and fosters better employee relations than trying to determine which regulations don't apply to a small business. To help small businesses comply with employment laws, the U.S. Department of Labor provides forms and guidelines at its "eLaws Advisors" Web page, http://www.dol.gov/elaws/. Employers can also file these forms online.

Taxes are another burdensome expense for a small business. In addition to local, state, and federal income taxes, employers must pay taxes covering workers' compensation insurance, Social Security payments, and unemployment benefits. Although large companies have similar expenses, they generally have more resources to cover them.

> **Concept Check**
>
> 1. What are the two most important things new business owners should learn about managing a business?
> 2. What are some sources for small-business financing?
> 3. How does government regulation affect small businesses?

Increasing the Likelihood of Business Success

In spite of the challenges just discussed, many small businesses do succeed. How can a prospective owner gain the many advantages of running a smaller firm while also overcoming the disadvantages? Most successful entrepreneurs believe that two recommendations are critical:

- Develop a business plan.
- Use the resources provided by such agencies as the Small Business Administration, local business incubators, and other sources for advice, funding, and networking opportunities.

Creating a Business Plan

Perhaps the most important task a would-be business owner faces is creating a business plan. An effective business plan can mean the difference between a company that succeeds and one that fails. A **business plan** is a written document that provides an orderly statement of a company's goals, the methods by which it intends to achieve these goals, and the standards by which it will measure achievements.

Plans give the organization a sense of purpose. They provide guidance, influence, and leadership, as well as communicate ideas about goals and the means of achieving them to associates, employees, lenders, and others. In addition, they set standards against which achievements can be measured. Planning usually works best when an entire organization participates in the process. Planning can include good ideas presented by employees and can also communicate information while making everyone feel a part of the team.

Although no single format best suits all situations, a good small-business plan will include a detailed time frame for achieving specific goals, projections of money flows (both income received by the business and funds disbursed to pay expenses), and units for measuring achievement (sales, profits, or changes in market share). A business plan should also cover the methods by which the firm will achieve specific goals, procedures it will follow, and values that define important standards for conduct. Perhaps most important, the plan should always be open to revision.

business plan written document that provides an orderly statement of a company's goals, the methods by which it intends to achieve those goals, and the standards by which it will measure achievements.

BUSINESS TOOL KIT

Managing Your Time

Learning how to effectively manage your time begins long before your first professional job. Part of the college experience involves developing good time management skills to juggle schoolwork, social activities, athletics, rest, and family obligations. Here are a few universal time management techniques:

1. Start by deciding which of your tasks or appointments are most important. In college, this includes studying for tests, writing papers, and completing projects. In the professional world, this might take the form of finishing a report, preparing a presentation, or making an important phone call.

2. Plan your week ahead of time and distribute your tasks evenly so that you don't fall behind. This is especially important when you have multiple tasks to complete. Seeing them all in a broad context will help you be more realistic.

3. Once you make a plan, stay with it. Distractions will certainly arise, so be sure you are realistic in how much time you allocate to each task. Now is a good time to develop discipline.

4. Work in places where you are most productive. For some, a dorm room is the best place to study; for others, a quiet library or empty classroom works best. The same principle holds true in the business world. If you have a project that needs your total attention, get away from your cubicle and find an empty conference room or arrange with your supervisor to work at home.

5. If you need extra help in managing your time, get it. Check out electronic schedulers, palm devices, or time management courses. If you rely on an electronic scheduler, though, be sure to schedule time for updating the scheduler.

6. Pay particular attention to how much time you spend on the Internet. Surfing the Web can waste a lot of valuable time. If necessary, keep a record or evaluate the History section of your browser. Set a time usage limit, and when that time is up, move on to something else.

7. Don't forget to leave room in your schedule for a little R&R or "staring at the wall" time. Working on hobbies, reading, watching movies, and hanging out with friends are as important as meeting all your deadlines—maybe more so. Don't forget that everyone needs downtime . . . even those who are time management experts!

Sources: "Reclaim Your Day from the Internet," *Essential Assistant*, May 2003, p. 6; Ihor Dlaboha, "Managing Your Time: Effectiveness Tops Efficiency," *ID: The Information Source for Managers and DSRs*, February 2002, p. 28.

Before writing a business plan, a business owner should answer some questions:

- How would you explain your idea to a friend? How does your idea differ from those behind existing businesses?
- What purpose does your business serve?
- What is the state of the industry you are entering?
- Who will your customers or clients be?
- How will you market the firm's goods or services?
- How much will you charge?
- How will you finance your business?
- How will you measure your firm's success or failure at specific time intervals?
- What credentials qualify you to run this business?

The name of a proposed business deserves special attention. Does the name reflect the firm's goals? Is it already registered by someone else? Does it convey any hidden meanings to other people? What does it mean phonetically in other languages? Is it offensive to any religious or ethnic groups? Recently, some established companies have changed their names to better reflect their businesses or correct public misperceptions. Tobacco products giant Philip Morris was aware that its corporate name carried a negative image among millions of nonsmokers—as well as a stock price considerably lower than other firms generating similarly high earnings. And with the addition of Kraft Foods, it knew that the name

Although the business plan for the formation of Compaq Computer has been widely reported to have been drawn on a table napkin during a restaurant meal, 21st century plans are used for a number of critical purposes in a business launch. They are likely to be considerably longer and involve time, thought, and inputs from numerous people involved in forming the new enterprise.

no longer reflected accurately the extent of the company's product lines. In 2003, Philip Morris selected a new name, a name completely unrelated to its products: Altria. The results of such name changes have sometimes been humorous. Tricon Global Restaurants, owner of Pizza Hut, Taco Bell, and KFC, acquired Long John Silver's and A&W food chains and thought that it needed to get rid of the "tri" part of its name. After much debate, it settled on its new name: Yum! Brands.

It is important to do research before starting a business. Trade journals are excellent sources of industry-related information. The Small Business Development Centers (SBDC) on many college campuses, the Small Business Administration in Washington, DC, many local chambers of commerce, and your local library can also assist in this research. An entrepreneur may gain useful insights by talking to suppliers in the industry and to local licensing authorities. How many similar businesses have succeeded? How many have failed? Why? What risks are specific to your industry? What markups are typical in the industry's pricing structure? What are common levels of expenses and profit percentages? Another way to gather information is to shop the competition.

A business plan typically includes the following components:

- An *executive summary* that briefly answers the who, what, why, when, where, and how questions for the business
- An *introduction* that includes a general statement of the concept, purpose, and objectives of the proposed business
- Separate *financial* and *marketing* sections that describe the firm's target market and marketing plan as well as detailed financial forecasts of need for funds and when the firm is expected to achieve breakeven—the level of sales at which revenues equal costs
- *Résumés of principals*—especially in plans written to obtain financing

Within its sections, a business plan should also cover some other topics. It should indicate whether the firm will be organized as a sole proprietorship, partnership, or corporation, and it should identify when it will need to hire employees. Other important facts are job descriptions for employees; the lines of authority in the business; a risk management plan, including detailed information on insurance; a list of suppliers with methods for assessing their reliability and competence; and a policy for extending credit to customers. Business plans are discussed in more detail in Appendix C, "Developing a Business Plan," and on the *Contemporary Business* Web site.

Since business plans are essential tools for securing outside funds, the financial section requires particular attention to detail. If the plan becomes part of a request for financing, the lender will examine the owner's management skills and experience, the major risks associated with the enterprise, available collateral, and the firm's ability to repay the loan. Potential outside investors are more likely to evaluate its potential for profits and growth and place less emphasis on downside risks.

They Said It

Rich people plan for four generations. Poor people plan for Saturday night.

—*Gloria Steinem (b. 1934)*
American feminist and journalist

In addition to cash flow, a business plan should project a detailed *profit-and-loss statement*. It must also state all assumptions it makes about the conditions under which the firm will operate. The assembled plan should be neat and easy to use. It should include a table of contents so that readers can turn directly to the parts that most interest them. Also, the format should be attractive, easy to read, and professional.

Small Business Administration

Small businesses can also benefit from using the resources provided by the **Small Business Administration (SBA).** The SBA is the principal government agency concerned with helping small U.S. firms, and it is the advocate for small businesses within the federal government. Over 3,000 employees staff the SBA's Washington headquarters and its regional and field offices. The primary operating functions of the SBA include providing financial assistance, aiding in government procurement matters, and providing management training and consulting.

Small Business Administration (SBA) federal agency that assists small businesses by providing management training and consulting, financial advice, and support in securing government contracts.

Financial Assistance from the SBA   Contrary to popular belief, the SBA seldom provides direct business loans. Its major financing contributions are the guarantees it provides for small-business loans made by private lenders, including banks and other institutions. Direct SBA loans are available in only a few special situations, such as natural disaster recovery and energy conservation or development programs. Even in these special instances, a business applicant must contribute a portion of the proposed project's total cost in cash, home equity, or stocks to qualify.

The SBA also guarantees **microloans** of less than $25,000 to start-ups and other very small firms. Microloans may be used to buy equipment or operate a business but not to buy real estate or pay off other loans. These loans are available from nonprofit organizations located in most states. Other sources of microloans include the federal Economic Development Administration, some state governments, and certain private lenders, such as credit unions and community development groups.

Small-business loans are also available through SBA-licensed organizations called **Small Business Investment Companies (SBICs).** SBICs use their own capital, supplemented with government loans, to invest in small businesses. Like banks, SBICs are profit-making enterprises, but they are likely to be more flexible than banks in their lending decisions. Well-known companies that used SBIC financing when they were start-ups include Apple Computer, Callaway Golf Co., America Online, Federal Express, Intel, and Sun Microsystems.

Another financial resource underwritten by the SBA is the *Angel Capital Electronic Network (ACE-Net),* which matches entrepreneurs looking for start-up capital with potential investors willing to exchange their money and advice for partial ownership of the company. Entrepreneurs post information about their businesses on ACE-Net's Web site, where potential investors can review it. Interested parties contact the firms. The goal is to help businesses seeking smaller amounts of capital than those typically handled by bigger investment firms. Some of these investors are easily identified by the names of their investment firms, such as California-based Angel Strategies and New Mexico-based The Gathering of Angels. But the recent economic downturn saw even investors being forced to tighten their belts. During the early years of the early 21st century, investors who continued to supply funds to small businesses scaled back their expectations for return on investment, but they still insisted that entrepreneurs make every effort to bring home strong sales and profits.[29]

Other Specialized Assistance   Although government purchases represent a huge market, small companies have difficulty competing for this business with giant firms, which employ specialists to handle the volumes of paperwork involved in preparing proposals and completing bid applications. Today, many government procurement programs specifically set aside portions of these orders for small companies; an additional SBA role is to assist small firms in securing these contracts. With **set-aside programs,** certain government contracts (or portions of those contracts) are restricted to small businesses. Every federal agency with buying authority must maintain an Office of Small and Disadvantaged Business Utilization to ensure that small businesses receive a reasonable portion of government procurement contracts. To help connect small businesses with government agencies, the SBA's Web site offers the Procurement Marketing & Access Network (PRO-Net&trade), which includes a search engine for finding business opportunities as well as a chance for small businesses to provide information about themselves.

FIGURE 5.5
Boeing: Taking a Proactive
Position in Encouraging
Small, Minority, and
Women-Owned Businesses
to Become Subcontractors
on Company Projects

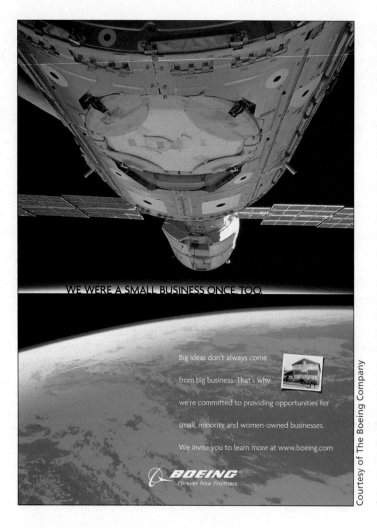

WE WERE A SMALL BUSINESS ONCE, TOO.

Big ideas don't always come
from big business. That's why
we're committed to providing opportunities for
small, minority and women-owned businesses.
We invite you to learn more at www.boeing.com

BOEING
Forever New Frontiers

Courtesy of The Boeing Company

Set-aside programs are also common in the private sector, particularly among major corporations. Figure 5.5 illustrates how the Boeing Co. encourages owners of small, minority, and women-owned businesses to join the thousands of other subcontractors working with the aerospace firm on the thousands of major projects it is involved with.

In addition to help with financing and government procurement, the SBA delivers a variety of other services to small businesses. It provides information and advice through toll-free telephone numbers and its Web site. Through the Service Corps of Retired Executives (SCORE), volunteers share business advice based on their years of experience. The SBA also offers hundreds of publications at little or no cost, and it sponsors popular conferences and seminars. But the agency does not have unlimited funds. "We must work within budget parameters," says former SBA head Hector Barretto, Jr. "We do not have blank checks to write. The SBA is at a crossroads."[30]

Business Incubators

business incubator
organization that provides
low-cost, shared facilities on
a temporary basis to small
start-up ventures.

In recent years, local community agencies interested in encouraging business development have implemented a concept called a **business incubator** to provide low-cost shared business facilities to small start-up ventures. A typical incubator might section off space in an abandoned plant and rent it to various small firms. Tenants often share clerical staff, computers, and other business services. The objective is that, after a few months or years, the fledgling business will be ready to move out and operate on its own.

Hundreds of business incubator programs operate nationwide. About half are run by not-for-profit organizations, including industrial development authorities. The remainder are divided between college- and university-sponsored incubators and business-run incubators.[31] These facilities offer management support services and valuable management advice from in-house mentors. Operating in an incubator gives entrepreneurs easy access to such basic needs as telephones and human resource experts. They also can trade ideas with one another.

Large Corporations Assisting Small Businesses

Corporate giants often devise special programs aimed at solving small-business problems. In doing so, they are not acting out of humanitarian interests. Instead, they recognize the size of the small-business market, its growth rate and buying power, and the financial rewards for firms that support small businesses. Figure 5.6 highlights a unique savings program offered by OPEN: The Small Business Network℠ from American Express. OPEN: The Small Business Network is designed to help small-business funders better manage cash flow. Through the OPEN Network, for example, customers can now more easily manage their accounts through an online tool called the "financial dashboard." These customers can also access a wide range of flexible payment options, including charge and credit cards and loans and leases, and network with their peers through a free program called OPEN Dialogue^sm.

Another way that small businesses get help from other companies is by forming an alliance to achieve mutual goals. When Amazon.com wanted to begin offering medicines and other health and beauty aids online, it didn't want to warehouse its own toothpaste and Tylenol. Instead, the company formed an alliance with drugstore.com. Under this arrangement, Amazon purchased a 40 percent share of drugstore.com and agreed to provide the smaller start-up with advice and visibility by featuring the online drug retailer on the Amazon Web site. Most drugstore.com employees are assigned a mentor from Amazon. The mentors help solve problems as they arise and recommend suppliers, such as a service that helped drugstore.com catalog the 16,000 items it stocks. Amazon's CEO, Jeff Bezos, says drugstore.com's employees were "better prepared for their launch than we were by a factor of about a million."[32]

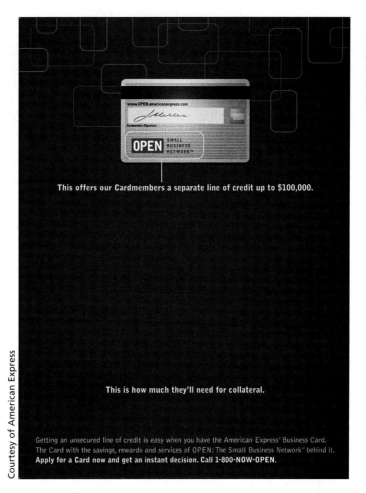

Courtesy of American Express

This offers our Cardmembers a separate line of credit up to $100,000.

This is how much they'll need for collateral.

Getting an unsecured line of credit is easy when you have the American Express® Business Card. The Card with the savings, rewards and services of OPEN: The Small Business Network™ behind it. **Apply for a Card now and get an instant decision. Call 1-800-NOW-OPEN.**

FIGURE 5.6
American Express: A Large Firm Providing Specialized Financial Services for Small Businesses

Teaming up with much bigger partners may involve risks for a small business, however. A small company loses some of the control and potential rewards it might otherwise keep, and its partner's reputation—good or bad—can reflect on the small business. Paisley Consulting, a 43-person small business based in Cokato, Minnesota, developed an internal-auditing software product called AutoAudit. Paisley's CEO Tim Welu was at first thrilled with his company's alliance with then–Big Five accounting giant Arthur Andersen, which promoted Paisley's software to its clients worldwide. Then the Enron and WorldCom scandals broke, and Andersen's endorsement no longer looked so rosy. Welu said of the debacle, "No one would ever have guessed there was any danger in being associated with Andersen." Luckily, the company had a termination clause in its agreement, which allowed it to free itself after 120 days notice. Welu notes that there was one upside to his association with the now-defunct firm: Many former Andersen employees landed jobs with the remaining Big Four firms, and they were knowledgeable about his software. So, word of Paisley's software has spread—but definitely not in the way the owner first imagined.[33]

Concept Check
1. Why is the name of a new business so important?
2. Why do larger corporations assist smaller companies?

Small-Business Opportunities for Women and Minorities

The thousands of new business start-ups each year include growing numbers of women-owned firms as well as new businesses launched by African Americans, Hispanics, and members of other minority groups. The numbers of women-owned and minority-owned businesses are growing much faster than the overall growth in U.S. businesses. The people who start these companies see small-business ownership and operation as an attractive and lucrative alternative to working for someone else.

Women-Owned Businesses

In the U.S. today, more than 9 million women-owned firms provide jobs for almost 28 million people. Almost two of every five U.S. businesses are owned by women, compared with one-fourth to one-third of businesses worldwide. One of every eight of these businesses is owned by minority women.[34]

Women, like men, have a variety of reasons for starting their own companies. Some are driven by an idea they believe can help others. Some have a unique business idea that they want to bring to life, like Jerusha Stewart, an African American businesswoman who founded iSpiritus Soul Spa, an online and offline store that sells personal growth and well-being products.[35] Others decide to strike out on their own when they lose their jobs or become frustrated with the bureaucracies in large companies. In other cases, women leave large corporations when they feel blocked from opportunities for advancement. Sometimes this occurs because they hit the so-called *glass ceiling*, discussed in Chapter 8. Because women are more likely than men to be the primary caregivers in their families, some may seek self-employment as a way to achieve flexible working hours so they can spend time with their families.

The fastest growth among women-owned firms is occurring in the construction, wholesale trade, transportation and communications, agribusiness, and manufacturing industries.[36] One woman who created a successful manufacturing business is Karen Alvarez of Dublin, California. She got her original product idea when she was grocery shopping with her children and one child fell from the shopping cart. To prevent such accidents, which occur to thousands of children every year, Alvarez developed the Baby Comfort Strap, a simple padded strap that parents use to buckle a small child to a cart or stroller. She consulted experienced retailers and manufacturers for help in developing packaging, pricing, and testing. When the Baby Comfort Strap proved to be a reliable seller, Alvarez began a successful strategy to generate publicity about the proneness of shopping carts to result in injuries to small children. This led to widespread awareness of the problem—and about how the Baby Comfort Strap could resolve it. This publicity worked, and Alvarez was able to set up distribution throughout the U.S.[37]

> *They Said It*
>
> Whatever women do, they must do twice as well as men to be thought half as good. Luckily, this is not difficult.
>
> —*Charlotte Whitton (1896–1975)*
> *Mayor of Ottawa*

As the number of female small-business owners has grown, they have also been able to establish powerful support networks in a relatively short time. Many nationwide business assistance programs serve women exclusively. Among the programs offered by the Small Business Administration are the Women-Owned Business Procurement program, which teaches women how to market to the federal government; the Women's Network for Entrepreneurial Training, which matches experienced female entrepreneurs with women trying to get started; and dozens of Women's Business Centers, which offer training and counseling in operating a business. Springboard Enterprises is a nonprofit organization based in Washington, DC, that promotes entrepreneurship and acquisition of capital for women entrepreneurs. Amy Millman, president of Springboard, assesses the small-business environment for women this way: "If you are an entrepreneur, it is always the right time to launch a business. There is great opportunity [if you] focus on the fundamentals. Remember, there is no free lunch."[38] In addition, women can find encouragement, advice, and mentors by joining organizations like the National Foundation for Women Business Owners (NFWBO) and Independent Means. The latter organization targets young women interested in starting a business.

Minority-Owned Businesses

Business ownership is also an important opportunity for America's racial and ethnic minorities. A recent study reported that more than two of every three African Americans surveyed said they would like to eventually run their own business.[39] In recent years, the growth in the number of businesses owned by African Americans, Hispanics, and Asian Americans has far outpaced the growth in the number of U.S. businesses overall. Figure 5.7 shows the percentages of minority ownership in major industries. The relatively strong presence of minorities in the services and retail industries is especially significant because these industries contain the greatest number of businesses.

Hispanics are the nation's largest group of minority business owners, followed by Asian American, African American, and Native American owners. The Small Business Administration attributes some of this pattern to recent growth in immigrants from Latin America and Asia along with the increase in their disposable income. In the last decade, disposable income for Latin Americans has grown 160 per-

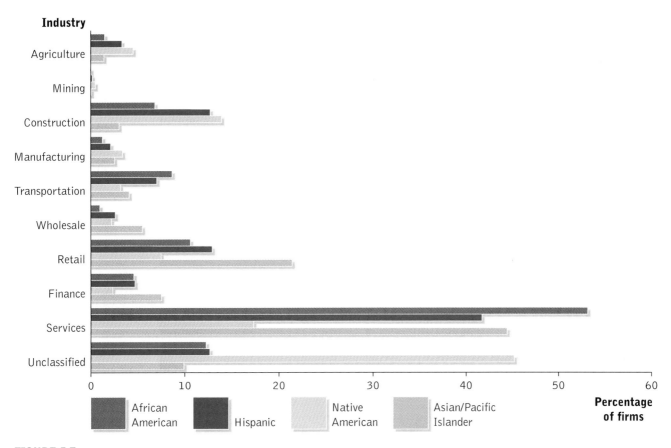

Industry

Percentage of firms

Legend: African American | Hispanic | Native American | Asian/Pacific Islander

FIGURE 5.7

Types of Businesses Owned by Racial and Ethnic Minorities

Source: Data from Office of Advocacy, U.S. Small Business Administration, "Minorities in Business," November 2001, p.17, accessed at the SBA Web site, http://www.sba.gov/advo, January 14, 2004.

cent, nearing $600 billion nationally.[40] Historically, large numbers of U.S. immigrants have started businesses. Most African American business owners were born in the U.S., compared with half of Hispanic owners and one third of Asian owners. The wave of Asian immigrants in the past two decades was followed by nearly 600,000 U.S. companies started by Chinese, Asian Indians, Pacific Islanders, and other Asians. David Chu, who came to New York City from Taiwan when his family

chased the immigrant dream of a better life in the U.S., is an outstanding example of a small-business success. After attending the Fashion Institute of Technology, Chu cofounded Nautica, a major apparel maker that employs 3,500 workers.[41]

Even more growth lies ahead for Hispanic-owned businesses during this decade, especially as trade between the U.S. and Latin

© AP/Wide World Photos

David Chu's Nautica—one of almost 600,000 U.S. firms launched by Asians in the past 20 years—offers upscale apparel for men and women. Separate Nautica companies specialize in jeans and children's clothing.

franchising contractual agreement that specifies the methods by which a dealer can produce and market a supplier's good or service.

America increases under NAFTA. Also, businesses owned by Hispanics and Asian Americans are more likely to export than are U.S. businesses in general.[42]

Despite their progress, minority business owners still face considerable obstacles. Minority entrepreneurs tend to start businesses on a smaller scale and have more difficulty finding investors than other entrepreneurs. They rely less on bank credit than do other business owners, possibly because they have a harder time getting loans from banks. The difference is especially pronounced in the case of African American entrepreneurs. Only 15 percent of black-owned businesses borrow from banks, less than half the rate for small businesses overall. Studies have found evidence that African American applicants from equally creditworthy companies are more likely to be denied loans than applicants of other races.[43]

The Franchising Alternative

They Said It

The road to success is dotted with many tempting parking spaces.

—*Anonymous*

A major factor in the growth of small business is a unique approach called franchising. **Franchising** is a contractual business arrangement between a manufacturer or another supplier and a dealer. The contract specifies the methods by which the dealer markets the good or service of the supplier. Franchises can involve both goods and services; some well-known franchises are Burger King, Subway, Fantastic Sam's, The UPS Store, Re/Max, and Blockbuster Video.

Starting a small, independent company can be a risky, time-consuming endeavor, but franchising can reduce the amount of time and effort needed to expand. The franchisor has already developed and tested the concept, and the brand may already be familiar to prospective customers.

Jani-King's position as the world's leading commercial cleaning franchise company with more than 9,000 franchise owners worldwide is, to a large extent, due to the continuing training and support provided by its regional support offices. Franchise fees are not fixed but are based on the amount of initial business offered by the local regional support office.

Courtesy of Jani-King The King of Clean

The Franchising Sector

Franchising started just after the U.S. Civil War, when the Singer Co. decide to build its business by franchising retail sewing-machine outlets. The concept became increasingly popular after 1900 in the automobile industry. Automobile travel led to demand for local auto sales and service outlets as well as gasoline, oil, and tire retailers. Auto manufacturers created systems of franchised distributors and then set up local retailers in each retail location—auto dealers, gas stations, tire stores, and auto-parts retailers. Dunkin Donuts, Meineke Muffler, and Super 8 Motels also set up their distribution systems through a network of local and regional franchises.

Today, the franchising concept continues its rapid growth. U.S. franchises generate sales of $1 trillion annually and employ over 8 million people. According to *Entrepreneur,* the No. 1 franchise is Subway, with Curves for Women (exercise centers for women) coming in second. 7-Eleven, McDonald's, Jani-King, and Taco Bell are also on *Entrepreneur's* top 10 list.[44] Areas in which strong growth is likely to continue include children's educational services like Sylvan Learning Centers, housecleaning services like Merry Maids, and lawn-care specialists like Lawn Doctor, which help time-starved but cash-rich consumers take care of their homes. In addition, the aging of the population bodes well for businesses catering to older Americans.[45] Compared with U.S. businesses in general, firms owned by African Americans and Asian-owned businesses are more likely to be franchises.[46] Figure 5.8 shows six of the hottest industries in which franchising growth is currently occurring.

Franchising overseas is also a growing trend for franchisors and franchisees who want to expand into foreign markets. It seems that anywhere you go in the world, you can get a McDonald's burger. But other international franchises like Best Western, Pak Mail, Pizza Hut, and 7-Eleven are almost as common.

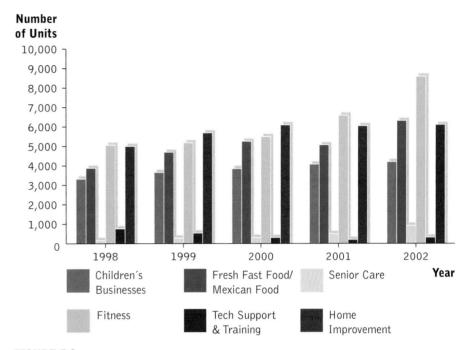

FIGURE 5.8
The Latest Trends in Franchising by Industry
Source: Data from "*Entrepreneur's* 24th Annual Franchise 500," *Entrepreneur,* January 2003, p. 82.

Some people get into franchising because they can operate their business from home, another continuing trend. Examples of these franchises include The Maids, TruGreenChemLawn, The Home Team Inspection Service, and ServiceMaster Clean.[47]

Franchising Agreements

The two principals in a franchising agreement are the franchisee and the franchisor. The individual or business firm purchasing the franchise is called the **franchisee,** a small-business owner who contracts to sell the good or service of the supplier—the **franchisor**—in exchange for some payment (usually a flat fee plus royalties expressed as a percentage of sales by the franchisee). The franchisor typically provides building plans, site selection help, managerial and accounting systems, and other services to assist the franchisee. The franchisor also provides name recognition for the small-business owner who becomes a franchisee. This public image is created by their familiarity with the franchise in other geographical areas and by advertising campaigns, all or part of which is paid for by contributions by the franchisees.

The franchisee purchases both tangible and intangible assets from the franchisor. A franchisor may charge a management fee in addition to its initial franchise fee and a percentage of sales or profits. Another may require contributions to a promotional fund. Total costs can vary over a wide range. A new McDonald's franchise costs $500,000, but total start-up costs can run anywhere from $1 million to $2 million. In contrast, a Subway franchise can cost in the range of $52,000 to $155,000.[48]

Franchise agreements often specify that the franchisee will receive materials, equipment, and training from the franchisor. Charmain and Charles Smith bought a Fruitfull Frozen Fruit Bars franchise from Happy & Healthy Products for $28,000, financing much of the purchase price with an SBA-backed loan. Charmain, with a decade of experience in the food service business, runs the franchise. Her husband, who also has a full-time job as a corporate financial executive, provides accounting and other services. The basic agreement with Happy & Healthy Products provides the franchisees with 10 freezers, two pallets of frozen fruit and yogurt bars, and a week of training, which covers sales and the company's products and equipment. The franchisee then sells the product to retailers to be stocked either in Fruitfull freezers or the retailer's own freezers. The Smiths' franchise has 43 such accounts in Georgia, including Kroger supermarkets, a chain of health clubs, and school cafeterias. The owners expect that before long, they will have 100 accounts with revenues of $75,000 to $100,000.[49]

Benefits and Problems of Franchising

As with any other business, a franchise purchaser bears the responsibility for researching what he or she is buying. Poorly financed or poorly managed franchise systems offer opportunities no better than those in poorly financed or poorly managed independent businesses. Although franchises are more likely than independent businesses to succeed, many franchises do go out of business. The franchising concept does not eliminate the risks of a potential small-business investment; it simply adds alternatives.

Advantages of franchises include a prior performance record, a recognizable company name, a business model that has proven successful in other locations, a tested management program, and business training for the franchisee. An existing franchise has posted a performance record on which the prospective buyer can base comparisons and judgments. Earlier results can indicate the likelihood of success in a proposed venture. In addition, a widely recognized name gives the franchisee a tremendous advantage; auto dealers, for instance, know that their brand-name products will attract particular segments of the market. A tested management program usually allows the prospective franchisee to avoid worrying about setting up an accounting system, establishing quality control standards, or designing employment application forms. In addition, most franchisors offer valuable business training. McDonald's teaches the basics of operating a franchise at its Hamburger University in Oak Brook, Illinois. Franchise operators quickly learn to meet customer expectations by following strict guidelines for how many seconds to cook the french fries and what words to use when serving customers. By following the franchisor's standards and building on an existing brand name, franchise operators typically can generate profits faster than an independent business owner.

Shelton Jefferson benefited from franchising when he wanted to expand his company. On his own, he had built a computer networking business. His own knowledge and experience were enough to lead the company as it provided the necessary hardware and software for computer networks, but customers were asking for training as well. Because Jefferson lacked expertise in providing training, he bought a franchise from a computer education company called The Fourth R. The franchisor helped him build computer training into a $500,000 component of his overall business.[50]

On the negative side, franchise fees and future payments can be a very expensive cost category. Like any business, a franchise may well be unprofitable during its first months and at times thereafter. Payments to the franchisor can add to the burden of keeping the business afloat until the owner begins to earn a profit.

Another potential drawback stems from the fact that the franchisee is linked to the reputation and management of the franchise. If customers are unhappy with their experience at one franchised sandwich shop, they might avoid stopping at another one several miles away, even if the second one is owned and operated by someone else. So a strong, effective program of managerial control is essential to maintain a franchise brand's effectiveness. Before signing on with a franchisor, potential franchisees carefully study its financial performance and reputation and talk with current franchise owners. Sources of information include the information provided by the franchisor, as well as state consumer protection agencies, the Better Business Bureau, and the Federal Trade Commission. The FTC's Web site includes advice for franchisees and reports of complaints against franchisors. Potential franchisees also should study the franchise agreement carefully to make sure they can succeed within the limitations of the agreement. In some instances, franchisors will decide to pursue additional sales by establishing new distribution outlets, which may compete directly with established franchisees. In today's online business environment, it is important to ask: Does the franchisor retain the right to sell the same products online that the franchisee is trying to sell through a local outlet? Such online competition might be less of a problem for a Mexican food franchise than for a franchise that provides secretarial services.

It is important to understand that even a franchise goliath like McDonald's can suffer from problems. Although the burger giant still serves 46 million people every day and has 30,000 restaurants in 121 countries, its profits have fallen in recent years in the wake of intense competition from Burger King, Wendy's, and other fast-food outlets offering added variety and enhanced quality. As a result, the burger chain that its regular customers call Mickey D's has decided to close stores that have not performed well and to slow down plans for expansion in other areas. In addition, McDonald's has been fighting a price war with Burger King by instituting its Dollar Menu, offering various sandwiches and side orders for $1 each. Finally, it plans to alter its hamburger recipe to give it a fresher, more pleasing taste. While no one is predicting that the Golden Arches will fall, all of these changes affect franchisees. Ultimately, most likely the best-managed franchises will survive, and the weaker ones will fail.[51]

Finally, some people are more suited to the demands of operating a franchise than others. Any person who is considering buying a franchise must think first about whether he or she has the right personality for the endeavor. Chapter 6 features an in-depth discussion of the basic characteristics that entrepreneurs should bring to their new endeavors.

Concept Check
1. Distinguish between franchisor and franchisee.
2. Name some of the largest franchises.

Small Business Goes Global

As recently as five years ago, only about 3 percent of small U.S. businesses with employees were involved in exporting.[52] For a small business, it is daunting to confront the global challenges, including cultural, legal, and economic barriers, described in Chapter 4. But even with this tiny percentage of small businesses engaged in exporting, small businesses play a key role in international trade. Over 95 percent of U.S. exporters are businesses with fewer than 500 employees, and they sell more than one of every four dollars' worth of all U.S. exports. Small businesses with Asian or Hispanic owners are most likely to export.[53] Also, with electronic commerce and the Internet, a small business now can enter new markets almost as easily as getting a Web address and setting up a home page.

Global Environment for Entrepreneurs

Although domestic interest in launching new business is strong, the U.S. is far from the top as the leading nation in terms of entrepreneurial activity. Based on the percentage of adults who either launched a new business last year or who currently operate a company less than 43 months old, the top prize goes to Mexico, where almost one adult in five meets the definition. Australia and New Zealand are tied for second place, following by Korea, Brazil, and Ireland. The U.S., with one adult in eight qualifying as an entrepreneur, is currently in seventh place.[54]

Growth Strategies for Small Businesses

Some small businesses generate much of their annual revenue from overseas sales, and the global reach of the Internet forces online companies to recognize these international markets quickly. The previous chapter identified the major online trade and exporting resources, and Chapter 7 will discuss in more detail how the Internet is contributing to the globalization of business. But globalization doesn't necessarily mean bigger. In some cases, companies are finding that staying small in overseas markets is more profitable. With two-thirds of companies operating in the global market earning less than $1,500 annually each, firms are recognizing that producing more affordable products for local markets is a viable business approach. Jordan Kassalow, a Brooklyn-based optometrist who ran a program for preventing eye disease in Africa, India, and Central America, noticed a need for affordable, nonprescription glasses—the kind you can buy at any drug store in the U.S. Most of Kassalow's patients couldn't afford to pay for an eye examination, much less prescription glasses. So he founded a company called Scojo Vision, which now sells nonprescription glasses in India, Guatemala, Haiti, and El Salvador for about $2 a pair. The company is training local entrepreneurs and providing them with loans of about $75 each for a kit containing eye charts, brochures, and glasses so they can start their own small businesses.[55]

Concept Check
1. Which nation is the leader in entrepreneurial activity?
2. What is a licensing agreement?

Alternatives for Organizing a Business

Whether small or large, every business fits one of three categories of legal ownership: sole proprietorships, partnerships, and corporations. As Figure 5.9 shows, sole proprietorships are the most common form of business ownership. However, the simple *number* of firms organized according to each model may overstate the importance of sole proprietorships and understate the role of corporations in generating revenues, producing and marketing goods and services, creating jobs, and paying taxes. After all,

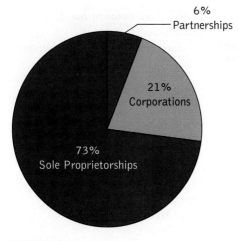

6%
Partnerships

21%
Corporations

73%
Sole Proprietorships

FIGURE 5.9

Forms of Business Ownership

Source: Data from U.S. Census Bureau, "Statistics about Business Size (including Small Business) from the U.S. Census Bureau," accessed from the Census Bureau Web site, http://www.census.gov/epcd/www/smallbus.html, January 14, 2004.

sole proprietorship form of business ownership in which the company is owned and operated by one person.

a corporate giant such as Wal-Mart, with annual sales of more than $220 billion, has a huge impact on the nation's economy, exceeding the collective effect of thousands of small businesses organized as proprietorships.

Each form offers unique advantages and disadvantages, as outlined in Table 5.2. To overcome certain limitations of the traditional ownership structures, owners may also use three specialized organizational forms: S corporations, limited-liability partnerships, and limited-liability companies. Along with the basic forms, this section will also briefly examine each of these alternatives.

Sole Proprietorships

The most common form of business ownership, the **sole proprietorship** is also the oldest and the simplest because no legal distinction separates the sole proprietor's status as an individual from his or her status as a business owner. Although sole proprietorships are common in a variety of industries, they are concentrated primarily among small businesses such as repair shops, small retail outlets, and service providers, such as painters, plumbers, and lawn-care operations.

Sole proprietorships offer advantages that other business entities cannot. For one, they are easy to form and dissolve. (Partnerships are also easy to form, but difficult to dissolve.) A sole proprietorship offers management flexibility for the owner, along with the right to retain all profits after payment of personal income taxes. Retention of all profits and responsibility for all losses give sole proprietors the incentive to maximize efficiency in their operations.

Minimal legal requirements simplify entering and exiting a sole proprietorship. Usually, the owner must meet only a few legal requirements for starting one, including registering the business or trade name—to guarantee that two firms do not use the same name—and taking out any necessary licenses. Local governments require that certain kinds of licenses be obtained before opening restaurants, motels,

Table 5.2   Comparing the Three Major Forms of Private Ownership

Form of Ownership	Number of Owners	Liability	Advantages	Disadvantages
Sole proprietorship	One owner	Unlimited personal liability for business debt	1. Owner retains all profits 2. Easy to form and dissolve 3. Owner has flexibility	1. Unlimited financial liability 2. Financing limitations 3. Management deficiencies 4. Lack of continuity
Partnership	Two or more owners	Personal assets of any operating partner at risk from business creditors	1. Easy to form 2. Can benefit from complementary management skills 3. Expanded financial capacity	1. Unlimited financial liability 2. Interpersonal conflicts 3. Lack of continuity 4. Difficult to dissolve
Corporation	Unlimited number of shareholders; up to 75 shareholders for S corporations	Limited	1. Limited financial liability 2. Specialized management skills 3. Expanded financial capacity 4. Economies of large-scale operations	1. Difficult and costly to form and dissolve 2. Tax disadvantages 3. Legal restrictions

retail stores, and many repair shops. Some occupational licenses require firms to carry specific types of insurance, such as liability coverage.

The ease of dissolving a sole proprietorship is an attractive feature for certain types of enterprises. This advantage is particularly important for temporary businesses set up to handle just a few transactions. For example, a part-time concert promoter could create a business to organize a single concert at a local arena.

Ownership flexibility is another advantage of a sole proprietorship. The owner can make management decisions without consulting others, take prompt action when needed, and keep trade secrets where appropriate. You've probably heard people say, "I like being my own boss." This flexibility leads many business owners to prefer the sole proprietorship organization form.

A disadvantage of the sole proprietorship form is the owner's financial liability for all debts of the business. Also, the business must operate with financial resources limited to the owner's personal funds and money that he or she can borrow. Such financing limitations can keep the business from expanding. Another disadvantage is that the owner must handle a wide range of management and operational tasks; as the firm grows, the owner may not be able to perform all duties with equal effectiveness. Finally, a sole proprietorship lacks long-term continuity, since death, bankruptcy, retirement, or a change in personal interests can terminate it.

These limitations can make potential customers nervous about buying major goods or services from a sole proprietorship. In cases where they know the form of organization being used by their supplier, they may worry that the sole proprietor will not be around long enough or have the resources to fulfill the agreement. Douglas D. Troxel wanted to offer his services as a consultant on mainframe computers, but big companies wouldn't sign contracts with him because he was operating as a sole proprietorship in his independent consulting business. So Troxel formed a corporation, named Serena Software in honor of his children, Sergie and Athena. His corporation began to land bigger jobs, generating enough funds for Troxel to hire a chief executive with marketing expertise. The new CEO, Richard A. Doerr, developed a marketing program with newer and more popular software applications, helping the company grow beyond $75 million in annual sales while Troxel kept customers happy by maintaining a close watch over product quality.[56]

Partnerships

Another option for organizing a business is to form a partnership. The Uniform Partnership Act, which regulates this ownership form in most states, defines a **partnership** as an association of two or more persons who operate a business as co-owners by voluntary legal agreement. The partnership was the traditional form of ownership for professionals offering services, such as physicians, lawyers, and dentists. Today, most of these service providers have switched to other organizational forms to limit personal liability.

partnership form of business ownership in which the company is operated by two or more people who are co-owners by voluntary legal agreement.

Like sole proprietorships, partnerships are easy to form. The legal requirements consist of registering the business name and taking out the necessary licenses. Partnerships also offer expanded financial capabilities in cases where each partner invests money. They also usually increase access to borrowed funds compared with sole proprietorships. Another advantage is the opportunity for professionals to combine complementary skills and knowledge. In the earlier example of Charmain and Charles Smith's Fruitfull Frozen Fruit Bars franchise, the two franchise owners each contribute important skills. Charmain has experience as a manager in the food service business, and Charles has a financial background.

Like sole proprietorships, most partnerships have the disadvantage of unlimited financial liability. Each partner bears full responsibility for the debts of the firm, and each is legally liable for the actions of the other partners. Partners must pay the partnership's debts from their personal funds if it ceases operations and its debts exceed its assets. Breaking up a partnership is also a much more complicated undertaking than dissolving a sole proprietorship. Rather than simply withdrawing funds from the bank, the partner who wants out must find someone to buy his or her interest in the firm.

In many states, partners can minimize some of these risks by organizing as a limited liability partnership. In many respects, such a partnership resembles a general partnership, but laws limit the liability of the partners to the value of their investments in the company.

The death of a partner also threatens the survival of a partnership. A new partnership must be formed, and the estate of the deceased is entitled to a share of the firm's value. To ease the financial strains of such events, business planners recommend life insurance coverage for each partner, combined with a buy–sell agreement. The insurance proceeds can be used to repay the deceased partner's heirs and allow the surviving partner to retain control of the business.

Partnerships are also vulnerable to personal conflicts. Personal disagreements may quickly escalate into business battles. Good communication is the key to resolving conflicts before they damage a partnership's chances for success or even destroy it.

Corporations

corporation business that stands as a legal entity with assets and liabilities separate from those of its owner(s).

A **corporation** is a legal organization with assets and liabilities separate from those of its owner(s). Although even the smallest business can choose the corporate form of organization, most people think of large companies when they hear the term corporation. In truth, many corporations are extremely large businesses.

A few years ago, Wal-Mart, whose annual worldwide sales are currently above the $220 billion mark, passed long-time No. 1-ranked General Motors to become the largest U.S.-based corporation in terms of sales. More recently, ExxonMobil moved into second place, pushing GM down to No. 3, but still a notch above its rival, Ford Motor Co. The list of the 10 largest U.S. corporations contains three more manufacturers: General Electric, IBM, and Altria, as well as banking firm Citigroup, telecommunications provider Verizon Communications, and international petroleum giant ChevronTexaco, which—like ExxonMobil—moved up the list following mergers. Annual revenues for each of the 10 companies currently total more than $67 billion. Global leader Wal-Mart generates sales of over $1 billion every 33 hours![57]

The corporate ownership form offers considerable advantages. First, because a corporation acquires the status of a separate legal entity, its stockholders take only limited financial risk. If the firm fails, they lose only the money they have invested. Protection also applies to legal risk. Class-action suits filed against automakers, cigarette makers, and drug manufacturers are filed against the companies, not the owners of those companies. The limited risk of corporate ownership is clearly reflected in corporate names throughout the world. While many U.S. and Canadian corporations include the Inc. designation in their names, British firms use the Ltd. abbreviation to identify their limited liability. In Australia, the abbreviation for proprietary limited—Pty. Ltd.—is frequently included in corporate names.

Corporations offer other advantages. They can draw on the specialized skills of many employees, unlike the typical sole proprietorship or partnership, for which managerial skills are usually confined to the abilities of their owners and a small number of employees. Corporations gain access to expanded financial capabilities based on the opportunity to offer direct outside investments such as stock sales.

The large-scale operation permitted by corporate ownership also results in a number of advantages for this legal form of organization. Employees can specialize in their most effective tasks. A large firm can generate internal financing for many projects by transferring money from one part of the corporation to another. Long manufacturing runs usually promote efficient production and allow the firm to charge highly competitive prices that attract customers.

One disadvantage for a corporation is the double taxation of corporate earnings. After a corporation pays federal, state, and local income taxes on its profits, its owners (stockholders) also pay personal taxes on any distributions of those profits they receive from the corporation in the form of dividends. One of the key components of the 2003 tax cut was the reduction of federal taxes of corporate dividends to 15 percent. Prior to passage of the economic stimulus legislation, people in the highest income bracket would pay more than 38 percent of any dividends received in federal taxes.

Corporate ownership also involves some legal issues that sole proprietorships and partnerships do not encounter. The number of laws and regulations that affect corporations has increased dramatically in recent years.

To avoid double taxation of business income while achieving or retaining limited financial liability for their owners, a number of firms have implemented modified forms of the traditional corporate and partnership structures. Businesses that meet certain size requirements, including ownership by no more than 75 shareholders, may decide to organize as **S corporations,** also called *subchapter S corporations.* These firms can elect to pay federal income taxes as partnerships while retaining the liability limitations typical of corporations. However, in recent years, the IRS has begun to focus on auditing S corporations, looking for those whose owners might be using artificially low pay as a method for reducing their taxes. So, while there are certain tax benefits for S corporations, such as those that came with the Job Creation and Worker Assistance Act of 2002, S corporations are now under closer scrutiny than they were in the past.[58]

Business owners may also form **limited liability companies (LLCs)** to secure the corporate advantage of limited liability while avoiding the double taxation characteristic of corporations. An LLC is governed by an operating agreement that resembles a partnership agreement, except that it reduces each partner's liability for the actions of the other owners. Professional corporations—such as law offices, accounting firms, and physicians—use a similar approach with the abbreviation PC shown at the end of the name of the business.

Changing Legal Structures to Meet Changing Needs

Before deciding on an appropriate legal form, someone planning to launch a new business must consider dozens of factors, such as these:

- Personal financial situations and the need for additional funds for the business start-up and continued operation
- Management skills and limitations
- Management styles and capabilities for working with partners and other members of top management
- Concerns about exposure to personal liability

Although the legal form of organization is a major decision, new business owners need not treat it as a permanent decision. Over time, changing conditions such as business growth may prompt the owner of a sole proprietorship or a group of partners to switch to a more appropriate form.

Concept Check

1. What is a partnership?
2. What factors should new business owners consider when choosing a legal structure?

Organizing and Operating a Corporation

One of the first decisions in forming a corporation is determining where to locate its headquarters and where it will do business. This section describes the various types of corporations and considers the options and procedures involved in incorporating a business.

Types of Corporations

Corporations fall into three categories: domestic, foreign, or alien. A firm is considered a **domestic corporation** in the state where it is incorporated. When a company does business in states other than the one where it has filed incorporation papers, it is registered as a *foreign corporation* in each of those states. A firm incorporated in one nation that operates in another is known as an **alien corporation** where it operates. Some firms—particularly large corporations with operations scattered around the world—may operate under all three of these designations. Others, such as consulting giant Accenture, appliance maker Helen of Troy, equipment manufacturer Ingersoll-Rand, and scandal-ridden Tyco, have come under heavy criticism for incorporating overseas to avoid paying U.S. taxes. This issue is discussed in the Solving an Ethical Controversy box.

The Incorporation Process

Suppose that you decide to start a business, and you believe that the corporate form offers the best way to organize it. Where should you set up shop? How do you establish a corporate charter? The following paragraphs discuss the procedures for creating a new corporation.

Where to Incorporate   Location is one of the most important considerations for any small-business owner. Although most small and medium-sized businesses are incorporated in the states where they do most of their business, a U.S. firm can actually incorporate in any state it chooses. The founders of large corporations, or of those that will do business nationwide, often compare the benefits provided in various states' laws to corporations in various industries.

The favorable legal climate in Delaware and the speed and simplicity of incorporating there have prompted a large number of major corporations to organize as Delaware corporations. Over half of the

SOLVING AN ETHICAL CONTROVERSY

The Rush to Incorporate Overseas

Everyone wants a bargain. And everyone, consumers and companies alike, would be happier to pay fewer taxes. But in the past few years, there has been a trend toward incorporating overseas—where U.S. companies can in effect become alien corporations when they come home to do business in their own country. Why go to all the trouble of establishing headquarters in Bermuda as diversified companies like Ingersoll-Rand and scandal-ridden Tyco did? Answer: To avoid millions in U.S. tax payments. That's because foreign companies pay U.S. taxes only on their domestic income, while U.S. companies pay taxes on worldwide income.

Should U.S. companies be allowed to incorporate overseas in order to receive tax benefits?

PRO

1. Federal tax laws put U.S. businesses at a disadvantage. "If the tax laws were different, we wouldn't have moved in the first place," explains Ingersoll CEO Herbert Henkel.

2. As more companies conduct business overseas, they should be allowed to incorporate wherever tax laws are most beneficial.

CON

1. If U.S. companies want to receive the benefits of being American corporations, they should pay U.S. taxes. "It's simply outrageous that there's this corporate rush to put up a shingle in Bermuda and still put a USA stamp on their products," says Congressman Richard Neal.

2. In addition to depriving the federal budget of needed revenues that other individual and business taxpayers must make up, the legal tax dodge of overseas incorporation gives these de facto U.S. corporations a competitive advantage over other firms in their industries who pay U.S. taxes on their total revenues.

SUMMARY

Some legislators have already moved to create roadblocks to overseas incorporations, while others are moving to change U.S. tax laws. Some companies, such as toolmaker Stanley Works, have backed down from plans to move their headquarters to Bermuda.

Sources: Brett Nelson, "Whipping Post," *Forbes*, January 6, 2003, p. 54; Curt Anderson, "U.S. Scrutinizes Bermuda Tax Shelters," *AP Online*, March 13, 2002, http:// www.bernie.house.gov; David Cay Johnston, "U.S. Corporations Are Using Bermuda to Slash Tax Bills," *New York Times*, February 18, 2002, http://www.nytimes.com.

FIGURE 5.10

Traditional Articles of Incorporation

- Name and Address of the Corporation
- Corporate Objectives
- Type and Amount of Stock to Issue
- Expected Life of the Corporation
- Financial Capital at the Time of Incorporation
- Provisions for Transferring Shares of Stock among Owners
- Provisions for Regulating Internal Corporate Affairs
- Address of the Business Office Registered with the State of Incorporation
- Names and Addresses of the Initial Board of Directors
- Names and Addresses of the Incorporators

companies in *Fortune* magazine's list of the top 500 companies have set up operations there. This popularity has led to incorporations becoming a $400 million government-run industry in Delaware.

The Corporate Charter Each state mandates a specific procedure for incorporating a business. Most states require at least three *incorporators*—the individuals who create the corporation—which opens incorporation possibilities to small businesses. Another requirement demands that a new corporation adopt a name dissimilar from those of other businesses; most states require that the name must end with the words *Company, Corporation, Incorporated,* or *Limited* to show that the owners have limited liability. Figure 5.10 lists 10 elements of the articles of incorporation that most states require for chartering a corporation.

The information provided in the articles of incorporation forms the basis on which a state grants a **corporate charter,** a legal document that formally establishes a corporation. After securing the charter, the owners prepare the company's bylaws, which describe the rules and procedures for its operation.

Corporate Management

Depending on its size, a corporation will have some or all of the ownership and management levels illustrated in Figure 5.11. At the top of the figure are **stockholders.** They acquire shares of stock in the corporation and so become part owners of it. Some companies, such as family businesses, are owned by relatively few stockholders, and the stock is generally unavailable to outsiders. In such a firm, known as a *closed,* or *closely held, corporation,* the stockholders also control and manage all activities. In contrast, an open corporation, sometimes called a *publicly held corporation,* sells stock to the general public, establishing diversified ownership, and often leading to larger operations than those of a closed corporation.

Stock Ownership and Stockholder Rights
Publicly held corporations usually hold annual stockholders' meetings. During these meetings, managers report on corporate activities, and stockholders vote on any decisions that require their approval, including elections of officers.

Stockholders' role in the corporation depends on the class of stock they own. Shares are usually classified as common or preferred stock. Although owners of **preferred stock** have limited voting rights, they are entitled to receive dividends before common-stock holders. If the corporation were dissolved, they would have first claims on assets, once debtors were repaid. Owners of **common stock** have voting rights but only residual claims on the firm's assets, which means they are last to receive any income distributions (dividends). Since one share is typically worth only one vote, small stockholders generally have little influence on corporate management actions. The various types of common and preferred stock are described in detail in Chapter 18.

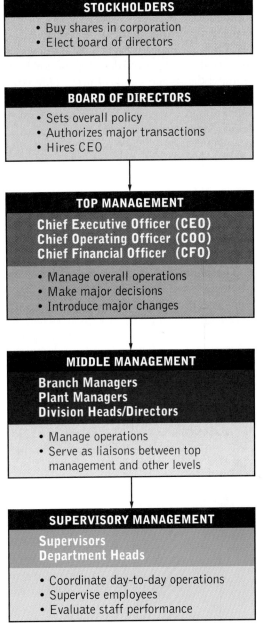

FIGURE 5.11

Levels of Management in a Corporation

stockholder person or organization who owns shares of stock in a corporation.

Board of Directors
Stockholders elect a **board of directors**—the governing body of a corporation. The board sets overall policy, authorizes major transactions involving the corporation, and hires the chief executive officer (CEO). Most boards include both inside directors (corporate executives) and outside directors—people who are not employed by the organization. Sometimes, the corporation's top executive also chairs the board. Generally, outside directors are also stockholders.

board of directors elected governing body of a corporation.

Corporate Officers and Managers
The CEO and other members of top management, such as the chief operating officer (COO), chief information officer (CIO), and chief financial officer (CFO), make most major corporate decisions. Managers at the next level down the hierarchy, middle management, handle the ongoing operational functions of the company. At the first tier of management, supervisory personnel coordinate day-to-day operations, assign specific tasks to employees, and often evaluate workers' job performance. The activities and responsibilities of managers at various levels in the organization are described in detail in Chapter 8.

In the past, top managers of corporations have had nearly free rein in the way they guide their companies. The firm's CEO has traditionally played a major role in nominating candidates for board membership and often served jointly as board chairman and CEO. Recent corporate and accounting scandals were traced to a shocking lack of business ethics coupled with illegal acts of members of top management and a failure of the corporate boards to fulfill their obligations to the firm's investors in providing adequate oversight. These failings among a number of large corporations prompted Congress to pass the Sarbanes-Oxley Act of 2002, which tightened requirements of corporate boards and required CEOs and CFOs of major corporations to certify in writing the accuracy of the firm's financial statements. New criminal penalties were established for corporate wrongdoers. This far-reaching legislation focusing on improving corporate governance and increasing the accountability of corporate boards, top executives, and accounting firms was introduced in the "Legal Framework for Business" appendix following Chapter 4. Its impact on business will be also be discussed in the management, accounting, and finance chapters later in the text.

Employee-Owned Corporations

Another alternative in creating a corporation is **employee ownership,** in which workers buy shares of stock in the company that employs them. The corporate organization stays the same, but most stockholders are also employees.

The popularity of this form of corporation is growing. Since the mid-1970s, the number of employee ownerships plans has grown sevenfold—to approximately 11,400. But the number of employees participating in such plans today is nearly 34 times as many—nearly 9 million people.[59] Several trends are behind the growth in employee ownership. One is that employees want to share in whatever wealth their company earns. Another is that managers want employees to care deeply about the company's success so that they will contribute their best effort. Since human resources are so essential to the success of a modern business, employers want to build their employees' commitment to the organization. Some of the country's most successful public corporations, including Procter & Gamble, Lowe's, and Southwest Air, have embraced employee ownership and watched their stock values hold up better than other companies in a slow economy. Employee-owned firms are discussed in more detail in Chapter 9.

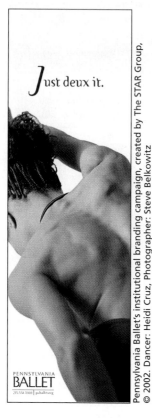

FIGURE 5.12
Promotion for a Not-for-Profit Corporation

Pennsylvania Ballet's institutional branding campaign, created by The STAR Group,
© 2002. Dancer: Heidi Cruz, Photographer: Steve Belkowitz

*J*ust deux it.

PENNSYLVANIA
BALLET

Not-for-Profit Corporations

The same business concepts that apply to firms whose objectives include earning profits also apply to **not-for-profit corporations**—firms pursuing objectives other than returning profits to owners. About 1.5 million not-for-profits operate in the U.S., including charitable groups, social welfare organizations, and religious congregations. This sector includes museums, libraries, religious and human-service organizations, private secondary schools, health-care facilities, symphony orchestras, zoos, and thousands of other groups such as government agencies, political parties, and labor unions.

A good example of a not-for-profit corporation is the Pennsylvania Ballet. This Philadelphia-based organization has been at the forefront of dance in America since its founding in 1963 and is widely regarded as one of the premier ballet companies in the nation. The promotion shown in Figure 5.12 emphasizes the athleticism involved in dance and is designed to increase consumer awareness of the company and its 40 full-time dancers, increase individual and season-ticket sales, attract individual and corporate donations, and make readers aware of its Web site (http://www.paballet.org). Visitors to the site learn about upcoming performances and can purchase tickets, buy gift certificates, and shop online at the gift shop.[60]

Most states have laws that set out separate provisions dealing with the organizational structures and operations of not-for-profit corporations. These organizations do not issue stock certificates, since they pay no dividends to owners, and ownership rarely changes. They are also exempt from paying income taxes.

Concept Check

1. Name the three categories of corporations.
2. What is the stockholders' role in a corporation?
3. What is an employee-owned corporation?

When Businesses Join Forces

Today's corporate world features many complex unions of companies, not always in the same industry or even in the same country. Many well-known firms have changed owners, become parts of other corporations, split into smaller units, or experienced financial bankruptcy in the wake of recent accounting and ethical scandals. Current trends in corporate ownership include mergers and acquisitions and joint ventures.

Mergers and Acquisitions (M&A)

In recent years, merger mania has hit U.S. corporations. Petroleum giants became even larger due to such megamergers as BP Amoco and ExxonMobil. Growth was also the primary motivation behind pharmaceutical giant Pfizer's purchase of rival Pharmacia Corp. for $60 billion in stock. The acquisition meant that the world's largest drug company added the arthritis medication Celebrex to its list of blockbuster drugs that includes Lipitor (cholesterol), Viagra (erectile dysfunction), and Zoloft (depression). The two companies also produce a number of over-the-counter products. Pfizer's lines include everything from Listerine mouthwash and Rolaids tablets to Visine eye drops, while Pharmacia makes the Rogaine hair products and the Nicorette smoking-cessation line.[61] Although M&A activity plunged during the recent recession, more than 9,000 mergers and acquisitions continue to take place annually. Consider just a few: America Online and Time Warner, Viacom and CBS, Hewlett-Packard and Compaq Computer, Sears and Kmart.

The terms *merger* and *acquisition* are often used interchangeably, but their meanings differ. In a **merger,** two or more firms combine to form one company; in an **acquisition,** one firm purchases the property and assumes the obligations of another. Acquisitions also occur when one firm buys a division or subsidiary from another firm. Many mergers and acquisitions cross national borders, as managers attempt to enter new markets and improve global competitiveness for their companies. Recently, Britain's Diageo, the world's largest producer of alcoholic beverages, sold its Burger King division to three U.S. companies. Even though the fast-food chain was second in size only to McDonald's, Diageo decided to concentrate on its drink labels such as Johnnie Walker scotch, Smirnoff vodka, and Guinness stout.[62]

Mergers can be classified as vertical, horizontal, or conglomerate. A **vertical merger** combines firms operating at different levels in the production and marketing process—the combination of a manufacturer and a large retailer, for instance. A vertical merger pursues one of two primary goals: (1) to assure adequate flows of raw materials and supplies needed for a firm's products or (2) to increase distribution. Software giant Microsoft Corp. is well known for acquiring small firms that have developed products with strong market potential. Large petroleum companies often try to reduce the uncertainty of their future petroleum supplies by acquiring successful oil and gas exploration firms.

A **horizontal merger** joins firms in the same industry that wish to diversify, increase their customer bases, cut costs, or offer expanded product lines. Cendant, which already owned the car-rental firm Avis, recently purchased the Budget rental car company for $107 million, making Cendant the second-largest rental car company behind Enterprise.[63]

A **conglomerate merger** combines unrelated firms. The most common reasons for a conglomerate merger are to diversify, spur sales growth, or spend a cash surplus that might otherwise make a firm a tempting target for a takeover effort. Conglomerate mergers may join firms in totally unrelated industries. A company well known for its conglomerate mergers is GE, which owns television broadcaster NBC and cable programmers CNBC and MSNBC (in a venture with Microsoft), along with its businesses such as appliances, aircraft engines, and industrial products. Experts debate whether conglomerate mergers are beneficial. The usual argument in favor of such mergers is that a company has management expertise it can use to succeed in a variety of industries. However, the stock of an acquiring company often falls in price when it makes an acquisition, suggesting that investors doubt the value of this strategy. One recent pattern that emerged was that the most successful mergers—those that produced high returns for buyers a year after the merger—were those that took place in well-established industries. Some of these include Northrop Grumman and Litton Industries (aerospace and defense), Westwood One and Metro Networks (media), and Devon Energy and Pennzenergy (oil and gas).[64]

merger combination of two or more firms to form one company.

acquisition procedure in which one firm purchases the property and assumes the obligations of another.

Joint Ventures: Specialized Partnerships

A **joint venture** is a partnership between companies formed for a specific undertaking. Sometimes a company enters into a joint venture with a local firm or government, sharing the operation's costs, risks, management, and profits with its local partner. A joint venture also may enable companies to solve a mutual problem. Four U.S. pipeline companies entered into a joint venture to provide better service to the oil refineries that use their services. Their venture, called Transport4, created an online resource at which oil companies can schedule use of the pipelines and track the delivery of petroleum, which often must pass through more than one company's pipelines to reach its destination. Transport4 collects orders and schedules petroleum shipments through the four pipeline companies' systems. It frees customers from calling each company to negotiate and renegotiate schedules. As discussed in the previous chapter, joint ventures also offer particularly attractive ways for small firms to conduct international business, since they bring substantial benefits from partners already operating inside the host countries.

Concept Check

1. Distinguish between a merger and an acquisition.
2. What is a joint venture?

Public and Collective Ownership

Most business organizations are owned privately by individuals or groups of people, but municipal, state, and national governments own some firms. In addition, groups of people collectively own some companies. Public ownership is common in many industries, both in the U.S. and abroad.

Public Ownership

One alternative to private ownership is some form of **public ownership,** in which a unit or agency of government owns and operates an organization. In the U.S., local governments often own parking structures and water systems. The Pennsylvania Turnpike Authority operates a vital highway link across the Keystone State. The federal government operates Hoover Dam in Nevada to provide electricity over a large region.

Government-Owned Corporations

Sometimes public ownership results when private investors are unwilling to invest in what they consider a high-risk project. This situation occurred with the rural electrification programs of the 1930s, which significantly expanded utility lines in sparsely populated areas. At other times, public ownership has replaced private ownership of failed organizations. Certain functions, such as municipal water systems, are considered so important to the public welfare that government often implements public ownership to protect its citizens from problems. Finally, some nations have used public business ownership to foster competition by operating public companies as competitive business enterprises. In Bogota, Colombia, the government runs a TV and radio network, Instituto Nacional de Radio & Television, that broadcasts both educational and commercial programs. Public ownership remains common abroad, despite a general trend toward privatization.

Customer-Owned Businesses: Cooperatives

Another alternative to traditional private business ownership is collective ownership of a production, storage, transportation, or marketing organization. Such collective ownership establishes an organization referred to as a **cooperative** (or **co-op**), whose owners join forces to collectively operate all or part of the functions in their industry.

Cooperatives allow small businesses to obtain quantity purchase discounts, reducing costs and enabling the co-op to pass on the savings to its members. Marketing and advertising expenses are shared among members, and the co-op's facilities can also serve as a distribution center.

Cooperatives are frequently found in small farming communities, but they also serve the needs of large growers of specific crops. For instance, Blue Diamond Growers is a cooperative that represents

California almond growers. Retailers have also established co-ops. Ace Hardware is a cooperative of independently owned hardware stores. Financial co-ops, such as credit unions, offer members higher interest rates on deposits and lower interest rates on loans than other profit-seeking institutions could provide.

Concept Check
1. What is public ownership?
2. Where are cooperatives typically found?

What's Ahead

The next chapter shifts the book's focus to the driving forces behind new-business formation: entrepreneurs. It examines the differences between a small-business owner and an entrepreneur and identifies certain personality traits typical of entrepreneurs. The chapter also details the process of launching a new venture, including identifying opportunities, locating needed financing, and turning good ideas into successful businesses. Finally, the chapter explores a method for infusing the entrepreneurial spirit into established businesses—intrapreneurship.

DID YOU KNOW?

1. Today, only one in 10 U.S. families is a one-income family.
2. The mergers and acquisitions frenzy of 1995 to 2001 was five times greater than any previous M&A boom in U.S. economic history.
3. Encore Software Ltd. has come out with Simputer, a handheld device that recognizes Indian speech and text. It contains a Global Positioning System that allows village farm cooperatives in India to obtain current produce prices.

Summary of Learning Goals

1 Distinguish between small and large businesses and identify the industries in which most small firms are established.
Small businesses can adopt many profiles, from part-time, home-based businesses to firms with several hundred employees. A small business is a firm that is independently owned and operated, is not dominant in its field, and meets industry-specific size standards for income or number of employees. Small businesses operate in every industry, but retailing, services, and construction feature the highest proportions of small enterprises.

2 Discuss the economic and social contributions of small business.
Small businesses create most of the new jobs in the U.S. economy and employ the majority of U.S. workers. They provide valuable outlets for entrepreneurial activity and often contribute to creation of new industries or development of new business processes. Women and minorities find small-business ownership to be an attractive alternative to opportunities available to them in large firms. Small firms may also offer enhanced lifestyle flexibility and opportunities to gain personal satisfaction.

3 Compare the advantages and disadvantages of small businesses.
Small firms can often operate with greater flexibility than larger corporations can achieve. This flexibility allows smaller businesses to provide superior customer service, develop innovative products, and fill small market niches ignored by large firms. However, small businesses also must operate with fewer resources than large corporations can apply. As a result, they may suffer from financial limitations and management inadequacies. Taxes and government regulation can also impose excessive burdens on small businesses.

4 Describe how the Small Business Administration assists small-business owners.
The U.S. Small Business Administration helps small-business owners to obtain financing through a variety of programs that guarantee repayment of their bank loans. The SBA also assists women and minority business owners in obtaining government purchasing contracts. It offers training and information resources, so business owners can improve their odds of success. Finally, the SBA advocates small-business interests within the federal government.

5 *Explain how franchising can provide opportunities for both franchisors and franchisees.*

A franchisor is a company that sells the rights to use its brand name, operating procedures, and other intellectual property to franchisees. Franchising helps business owners to expand their companies' operations with limited financial investments. Franchisees, the individuals who buy the right to operate a business using the franchisor's intellectual property, gain a proven business system, brand recognition, and training and other support from the franchisor.

6 *Summarize the three basic forms of business ownership and the advantages and disadvantages of each form.*

A sole proprietorship is owned and operated by one person. While sole proprietorships are easy to set up and offer great operating flexibility, the owner remains personally liable for all of the firm's debts and legal settlements. In a partnership, two or more individuals agree to share responsibility for owning and running the business. Partnerships are relatively easy to set up, but they do not offer protection from liability. Also, partnerships may experience problems by the death of a partner or when partners fail to communicate or establish effective working relationships. When a business is set up as a corporation, it becomes a separate legal entity. Individual owners receive shares of stock in the firm. Corporations protect owners from legal and financial liability, but double taxation reduces their revenues. Taxes paid on dividends were reduced to 15 percent by the 2003 federal tax cut.

7 *Identify the levels of corporate management.*

Stockholders, or shareholders, own a corporation. In return for their financial investments, they receive shares of stock in the company. The number of stockholders in a firm can vary widely, depending on whether the firm is privately owned or makes its stock available to the public. Shareholders elect the firm's board of directors, the individuals responsible for overall corporate management. The board has legal authority over the firm's policies. A company's officers are the top managers who oversee its operating decisions.

8 *Describe recent trends in mergers and acquisitions.*

Although slowed temporarily by the recent recession, the worldwide pace of mergers and acquisitions continues to grow. U.S. corporations are spending record amounts on mergers and acquisitions. These business combinations occur worldwide, and companies often merge with or acquire other companies to aid their operations across national boundaries. Vertical mergers help a firm to ensure access to adequate raw materials and supplies for production or to improve its distribution outlets. Horizontal mergers occur when firms in the same industry join in an attempt to diversify or offer expanded product lines. Conglomerate mergers combine unrelated firms, often as part of plans to spend cash surpluses that might otherwise make a firm a takeover target.

9 *Differentiate among private ownership, public ownership, and collective ownership (cooperatives).*

Managers or a group of major stockholders sometimes buy all of a firm's stock. The firm then becomes a privately owned company, and its stock is no longer publicly traded. Some firms allow workers to buy large blocks of stock, so the employees gain ownership stakes. Municipal, state, and national governments also own and operate some businesses. This public business ownership has declined, however, through a recent trend toward privatization of publicly run organizations. In a cooperative, individuals or companies band together to collectively operate all or part of an industry's functions. The cooperative's owners control its activities by electing a board of directors from their members. Cooperatives are usually set up to provide for collective ownership of a production, storage, transportation, or marketing organization that is important to an industry.

Business Terms You Need to Know

small business 157

business plan 168

Small Business Administration (SBA) 171

business incubator 172

franchising 176

sole proprietorship 180

partnership 181

corporation 182

stockholder 185

board of directors 185

merger 187

acquisition 187

Other Important Business Terms

home-based business 159	franchisee 177	alien corporation 183	vertical merger 187
overhead costs 164	franchisor 177	corporate charter 184	horizontal merger 187
microloans 171	S corporation 182	preferred stock 185	conglomerate merger 187
Small Business Investment Company (SBIC) 171	limited liability company (LLC) 183	common stock 185	joint venture 188
		employee ownership 186	public ownership 188
set-aside program 171	domestic corporation 183	not-for-profit corporation 186	cooperative 188

Review Questions

1. What is meant by the term *small business*? How do small businesses contribute to a nation's economy?

2. What are the advantages of a small business? What are the disadvantages?

3. What are the benefits of a good business plan? Identify the major components of a business plan.

4. What is the Small Business Administration? In what ways does it assist small businesses?

5. Why have Hispanic Americans become the nation's largest group of minority business owners? Why do economists predict that this growth of Hispanic-owned businesses will continue during the 21st century?

6. Describe a typical franchising agreement. What are the advantages and disadvantages of a franchising agreement?

7. What is a sole proprietorship? Why is this form of business ownership the most frequently used? What are its advantages and disadvantages?

8. Describe how small companies may enter foreign markets.

9. What is a corporation? What are the steps for creating a new corporation?

10. In what ways are mergers and acquisitions different? What type of merger does each of the following scenarios describe?
    a. A television station in one region merges with a television station in another.
    b. A large juice manufacturer merges with an orchard company.
    c. An Internet company merges with a chain of department stores.

Projects and Applications

1. Imagine that you are preparing to write a business plan for your own idea for a new company. First, choose one of the following ideas (or come up with one of your own):
   a. An Internet retailer for bicycles, skateboards, and scooters
   b. A shop that offers homemade heat-and-serve meals
   c. An online magazine
   d. A firm that provides people to do household chores such as yard work and grocery shopping
   Next, answer the questions for business owners in the Creating a Business Plan section on page 168. Once you have answered these questions, do you still think your business idea is viable? Why or why not?

2. Read the business page of your local or city newspaper and choose a small business that has been profiled or mentioned in the paper. What do you think makes this business successful?

3. Propose an idea for a business incubator in an industry that interests you. Describe where the incubator would be located, how it would function, and what it is intended to accomplish.

4. Livewire, a firm that provides electronic kiosks for ski lift-tickets, has made alliances with businesses such as ski resorts and sports retailers. Describe another type of company that Livewire might make an alliance with. How might this alliance benefit Livewire? What precautions should Livewire take in entering into the alliance?

5. Do you think that consumers benefit from public ownership of such functions as municipal water systems and the postal service? Why or why not?

Experiential Exercise

Background: Mergers between large firms seem to occur almost daily. Shareholders of the selling firm give, or tender, their shares to the acquiring firm in exchange for cash or shares of the acquiring firm. Sometimes selling firms will take actions to resist the merger. In other instances, the merger is a friendly deal. Mergers are generally categorized as one of three types: vertical, horizontal, or conglomerate. A vertical merger involves an acquiring firm buying a supplier. A horizontal merger is one in which the acquiring firms buys a competitor. A conglomerate merger, the third type, is a combination of seemingly unrelated firms.

Directions: Using the Internet or your college library, identify three recent mergers. Research each merger and answer the following questions:

1. Which firm was the buyer?
2. Which firm was the seller?
3. How did the acquiring firm pay for the merger (cash, stock, or a combination)?
4. What was the announced dollar value of the merger?
5. Did the selling firm resist the merger or was the deal a friendly one?
6. How would you classify the merger (vertical, horizontal, or conglomerate)?
7. What were some of the stated reasons for the merger?

NOTHING BUT NET

1. **Home-based businesses.** Assume you're considering starting a small home-based business. Visit the Web site listed below and click the "Work-at-home ideas" and "Business Opportunities" links. List the five businesses that interest you the most and prepare a brief business plan.

   http://www.wahm.com

2. **Franchising opportunities.** Several Web sites exist to help people evaluate the possibility of owning and operating a franchise. Visit the site listed, click on the "Franchise Directory" link, and choose from that menu. Prepare a report to your class describing the four types of franchising and the five steps involved in developing a successful franchise.

   http://www.betheboss.com

3. **Small-business statistics.** The U.S. Small Business Administration compiles and publishes extensive statistics on small business. One report, published each year, details small-business lending activity. Visit the SBA Web site listed, and click the most recent report on small-business lending activity.

   http://www.sba.gov/advo/stats/lending

   After reviewing the data, answer the following questions:
   a. What is a "micro-business loan"?
   b. In total, how much money did U.S. banks lend to micro-businesses?
   c. Which five U.S.-based banks made the most micro-business loans during the 12-month period covered by the report?
   d. Which states have the most micro-business friendly banks?

   Note: Internet Web addresses change frequently. If you do not find the exact sites listed, you may need to access the organization's or company's home page and search from there.

Case 5.1

Subway: The Nation's No. 1 Franchise

Move over Ronald McDonald. Make room for Jared Fogle, the former college student who lost 245 pounds on a diet of Subway's low-fat sandwiches. Subway is now the largest U.S. restaurant chain.

Subway Restaurants boasts more than 14,000 franchises in the U.S., 1,600 in Canada, and over 1,100 in other foreign countries (a total of more than 16,000 franchise locations in 74 countries around the globe). In fact, Subway also recently beat its own record for number of franchises sold in a single year—with more than 2,000 new stores opened worldwide in one 12-month period. Low start-up costs, flexibility in size, and simple equipment needs contribute to the attractiveness of Subway franchises.

Subway wasn't always the largest franchise. The firm had the same humble beginnings shared by many small businesses. In 1965, 17-year-old Fred DeLuca and a family friend, Peter Buck, opened Pete's Super Submarines in Bridgeport, Connecticut, with a $1,000 loan from Buck's family. DeLuca's goal was to earn enough to get through college. The shop limped along until 1974, when the founders changed its name to Subway and began franchising. Subway's simple premise was to offer a fresh, more healthful alternative to fast foods such as burgers and fries.

The last few years have shown how strong Subway's business model has remained. Despite stagnating business in the rival hamburger business (perhaps reflected by McDonald's drop in franchise ranking), Subway has leveraged the appeal of fresh ingredients and healthy meals into average per-store sales increases of nearly 18 percent, gains that were unaffected even by the business slowdown of a sluggish economy. Subway's executives have made it a policy to keep in touch with what customers want, continually researching and testing improved ingredients and better menus and then spending millions on clever, focused marketing campaigns designed to get the word out to many different market segments.

Dieters respond to the story of Subway's new spokesperson, Jared Fogle, while teens and nondieters like the chain's new combinations of condiments and sauces, as well as the upgraded meats, fresh flavored breads, and updated menus.

The firm is also responsive to its franchisees. When store owners expressed dissatisfaction with Subway's advertising in the late 1990s, the company revamped its campaign, turning same-store sales growth around. A few years later, Subway recognized the need to upgrade its image and switched ad agencies to make sure it got the right marketing message across. The successful "Eat Fresh" campaign and the popularity of Jared Fogle were the result.

Subway is determined to remain on top. Fred DeLuca attributes much of his company's success to his management team. "We have all the leadership working hard, working together as a team to improve the organization. It's kind of like getting everybody rowing in the same direction," says DeLuca. "That's provided me with a great assist—it's not really me running the company so much as a whole team working together to move things in the right direction."

QUESTIONS FOR CRITICAL THINKING

1. Subway has benefited greatly from its franchising strategy. However, franchising also poses challenges. Identify some of the problems that Subway might encounter as it grows through franchising here and abroad.

2. How has Fred DeLuca's approach to management helped the company stay on top?

Sources: Company Web site, http://www.subway.com, accessed January 6, 2004; "Top Ten Franchises for 2003," *Entrepreneur,* January 2003, http://www.entrepreneur.com; "Subway," *Entrepreneur,* January 2003, http://www.entrepreneur.com; "Landmark 16,000th Subway Restaurant Opens," March 2002; Jill Carroll and Shirley Leung, "Fries with That Burger? Fewer Consumers Say 'Yes,'" *The Wall Street Journal,* February 20, 2002, pp. B1, B4.

Video Case 5.2

Fresh Samantha: A Juicy Business

This video case appears on page 606. A recently filmed video, designed to expand and highlight the written case, is available for class use by instructors.

Chapter 6
Starting Your Own Business: The Entrepreneurship Alternative

Fanning the Entrepreneurial Flames at Apple with the iPod

Most of us probably think of entrepreneurs as lone geniuses, super-achievers perhaps working in a garage or basement workshop, struggling to fulfill a lifelong business dream. But one of the decade's biggest commercial successes, the tiny but powerful music player known as the iPod, was created through entrepreneurship within a major business.

An engineer named Tony Fadell was hired by Apple itself to create its new music player on a crash schedule. The product had to be very easy to use, it had to have a big capacity to hold music files, and it had to be the sort of sleek imaginative product Apple users had come to expect. With easy access to Apple employees at every level of the firm and freedom from hierarchical structure, Fadell was able to pull together technological and design innovations from various departments to come up with a product CEO Steve Jobs called "as Apple as anything Apple has ever done." Sales of the little device are skyrocketing, especially after Apple created an iPod that worked with Windows—the original had worked only with Macs—and licensed hundreds of thousands of songs for its online music store, which had already risen to a 70 percent share of the music downloading market.

© Lou Dematteis/Reuters/Landov

Other iPod innovations include a click wheel that replaces all the control buttons that the little device has no room for. Says Jobs, "The minute we experienced it we just thought, 'My God, why didn't we think of this sooner?'" A 50 percent increase in the life of the iPod battery was achieved with technology that conserves power, instead of with a bigger battery. New features such as three playback speeds and the ability to create several different playlists from a stock of up to 5,000 stored songs, even as the price drops appreciably with every new model, prove that the highly creative team that developed the iPod is still innovating. Nearly 4 million iPod owners approve the result, and Duke University is giving free iPods to its incoming classes to let students listen to lectures and practice foreign languages with tools downloaded from a special Web site.

Although the iPod story is not a tale of the classic "outside" entrepreneur (such as Apple's cofounders, Steve Jobs and Steven Wozniak, were), it exemplifies the intrapreneurial approach that brings entrepreneurial thinking into an established business, allowing innovators to think "outside the box" and come up with new products and new business methods that might otherwise be overlooked.[1]

Chapter Overview

Like millions of people, you'd probably love to start and run your own company. Perhaps you've spent time trying to come up with an idea for a business you could launch. If you've been bitten by the entrepreneurial bug, you're not alone. More than ever, whether on their own or within the embrace of an innovative firm, people like you, your classmates, and your friends are choosing the path of entrepreneurship for their careers.

How do you become an entrepreneur? Experts advise that aspiring entrepreneurs should learn as much as possible about business by completing academic programs such as the one in which you are currently enrolled and by gaining practical experience by working part- and full-time for business employers. In addition, invaluable insights about the pleasures and pitfalls of entrepreneurship can be obtained by reading newspaper and magazine articles and biographies of successful entrepreneurs. These inputs will help you learn how entrepreneurs handled the challenges of starting up their businesses. Advice you need to launch and grow a new venture is all around. Some resources to get you started are magazines like *Entrepreneur, Success, Black Enterprise, Hispanic,* and *Inc.* Entrepreneurship associations such as the Entrepreneurial Institute (614-895-1153), Association of African-American Women Business Owners (301-585-8051), and the Young Entrepreneurs' Organization (703-519-6700) also provide invaluable assistance. Finally, these Web sites should be familiar to any aspiring entrepreneur: Center for Entrepreneurial Leadership (http://www.celcee.edu/), Entrepreneur.com (http://www.entrepreneur .com), EntreWorld (http://www.entreworld.org), and the Small Business Administration (http://www.sba.gov).

In this chapter, we focus on pathways for entering the world of entrepreneurship, describing the increasingly important role that entrepreneurs play in the economy. The chapter explains why a growing number of people choose this way of participating in business. It discusses the characteristics that help entrepreneurs succeed and the ways they start new ventures. The chapter ends with a discussion of methods by which large companies try to incorporate the entrepreneurial spirit.

What Is an Entrepreneur?

entrepreneur person who seeks a profitable opportunity and takes the necessary risks to set up and operate a business.

You learned in Chapter 1 that an **entrepreneur** is a risk taker in the private enterprise system, a person who seeks a profitable opportunity and takes the necessary risks to set up and operate a business. Many entrepreneurs start their businesses from scratch, but you don't have to launch your own company to be considered an entrepreneur. Consider Sam Walton, founder of Wal-Mart. He started by purchasing a small dollar store, acquired one of the early discount retailers, and then launched his own store, which went by the simple name Wal-Mart. Forty years later, this small venture had grown into a multibillion-dollar global business that ranked as the largest company on earth.

They Said It

It's just paper. All I own is a pickup truck and a little Wal-Mart stock.

—*Sam Walton (1918–1992)*
American entrepreneur

Entrepreneurs differ from many small-business owners. Although many small-business owners possess the same drive, creative energy, and desire to become big-business owners, others may be content to operate a business that provides a comfortable living. By contrast, the typical entrepreneur tries to make the business grow. Entrepreneurs combine their ideas and drive with money, employees, and other resources to create a business that fills a market need. That entrepreneurial role can make something significant out of a small beginning. In preparing its annual list of the 500 fastest growing U.S. companies, *Inc.* magazine found that four in 10 began operations with $10,000 or less in the bank, and one-third of those started with less than $1,000. Yet 20 percent of the 500 CEOs on the list estimated their current net worth at more than $7.5 million.[2]

Entrepreneurs also differ from managers. Managers are employees who direct the efforts of others to achieve an organization's goals. In the case of small start-up firms, owners may find it necessary to serve as owner-managers to implement their plans for the business and to offset human resource limitations at the fledgling company. Entrepreneurs may also perform a managerial role, but their overriding responsibility is to use the resources of their organizations—employees, money, equipment, and facilities—to accomplish their goals. Particularly in the start-up stage of a new venture, entrepreneurs pursue their ideas for business success and take the initiative to find and organize the resources they need to start and build their ventures. Bill Gates recognized his own entrepreneurial role at Microsoft when he resigned from the chief executive post of his now-giant enterprise to take on the new position of "chief software architect." The change enables Microsoft's current CEO, Steve Ballmer, to focus on managing the company while Gates looks for new business opportunities. Also, Microsoft's growth has come not from Gates's talents as a programmer—most people agree that Microsoft's programs usually borrow existing ideas—but from his savvy in deploying resources to build a strong market for his products. The measure of Gates's success as an entrepreneur is the hugely profitable business he built by developing markets for operating systems and business software.

Courtesy of Hewlett Packard

take your small business to new heights

Jeff knows trees. Jeff wants people to know he knows trees.

Jeff and Lake Kowell operate Image Tree Service. Jeff works on the trees, Lake runs the business. Jeff doesn't just trim trees, he shapes them to complement and enhance homes and workplaces. He's an artist. That makes Image Tree Service different from most – an excellent selling point. But Jeff and Lake are so busy working, they don't have time to think about Image Tree's image. Ironic? Not to Jeff and Lake.

HP has a few ideas that might help...

Like so many entrepreneurs, Jeff Kowell is not equally skilled in all business specialties. Jeff is an artist at shaping trees and has a personality that attracts repeat business. His wife and partner, Lake, complements his skills with her own talents in managing the day-to-day operations of Image Tree Service.

On a smaller scale, Jeff Kowell has been dedicated to the success of his business, a Sonoma, California-based high-quality service called Image Tree Service. Kowell launched his business in 1988 with only a '69 pickup as a company asset—but with a dream to build a business a cut above the ordinary tree service competitors. With the help of a family loan, he was able to purchase entirely new equipment and set about creating an image of quality customer service. Although Image Tree Service offers a full line of services ranging from diagnosis and treatment to habitat restoration, view restoration, and shaping for workplaces and homes, he has specialized in serving the many nearby northern California vineyards as well as those in Oregon and Washington. This segment alone accounts for over 50 percent of annual revenues—revenues that have doubled annually during the past five years. But even though today Kowell counts among his clients such well-known names as Gallo, Kendall-Jackson, and Simi, he doesn't ignore small customers who helped him launch his business and continue to make up a sizable part of his client base. As he recalls, "One of my favorite customers is an 80-year-old gentleman. Once a year I drive out to his home to trim his lemon tree. It's a $30 job—and it may just be my favorite job."[3]

Studies of entrepreneurs have identified certain personality traits and behaviors common to them that differ from those required for managerial success. One of these traits is the willingness to assume the risks involved in starting a new venture. Some employees leave their jobs to start their own companies and become successful entrepreneurs. Others find that they lack the characteristics required to start and grow a business. Entrepreneurial characteristics are examined in detail in a later section of this chapter.

Concept Check

1. What tools do entrepreneurs use to create a new business?
2. How do entrepreneurs differ from managers?

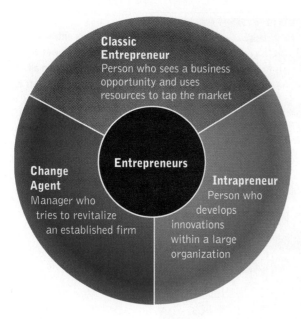

Classic Entrepreneur
Person who sees a business opportunity and uses resources to tap the market

Entrepreneurs

Change Agent
Manager who tries to revitalize an established firm

Intrapreneur
Person who develops innovations within a large organization

FIGURE 6.1
Categories of Entrepreneurs

classic entrepreneur
person who identifies a business opportunity and allocates available resources to tap that market.

Kimora, wife, mother, and full-time member of the Simmons entrepreneurial duo, models an outfit from the Baby Phat line with daughter Ming.

intrapreneur
entrepreneurially oriented person who develops innovations within the context of a large organization.

change agent manager who tries to revitalize an established firm to keep it competitive.

Categories of Entrepreneurs

Entrepreneurs apply their talents in different situations. These differences give rise to a set of distinct categories of entrepreneurs. As Figure 6.1 shows, three basic categories exist: classic entrepreneurs, intrapreneurs, and change agents.

Classic entrepreneurs identify business opportunities and allocate available resources to tap those markets. The story of Russell and Kimora Simmons exemplifies the actions of classic entrepreneurs. Russell, whom Sean "P. Diddy" Combs calls "the godfather of hip hop," dropped out of Manhattan's City College to launch a full-time venture booking hip-hop acts just as the music phenomenon was emerging. After promoting his younger brother Joey—"Run" in the rap act Run-DMC—he founded Def Jam, a talent management company that soon expanded with a start-up music label (Def Jam Recordings) and a movie production company (Def Pictures). Simmons had just launched Phat Fashions, his successful men's sportswear line with a Hamptons/hip-hop look that became a favorite of Eminem and Kobe Bryant, when he met his wife-to-be and future business partner Kimora, a stunningly beautiful supermodel who had been the face of Chanel. But Kimora proved to be much more than a trophy wife. She became actively involved in the Phat Fashions business, designed clothes for the new women's clothing, jewelry, and cosmetics lines (called Baby Phat), and played a major role in expanding distribution to more than 3,000 clothing outlets, as well as retail giants like Macy's and Bloomingdale's and two Phat Farm boutiques. The new lines, classified as "bodylicious," are frequently worn by singers like Alicia Keys and Pink. The

duo has worked well together as entrepreneurs, building a hip clothing empire to add to their entertainment base.[4]

Intrapreneurs are entrepreneurially oriented people who seek to develop new products, ideas, and commercial ventures within large organizations. For example, 3M Co. continues to develop innovative products by encouraging intrapreneurship among its personnel. Some of 3M's most successful products began as inspirations of intrapreneurs. Art Frey invented the Post-It Note, and intrapreneurs Connie Hubbard and Raymond Heyer invented the Scotch-Brite Never Rust soap pad. Intrapreneurship will be discussed later in this chapter.

Change agents, also called *turn-around entrepreneurs,* are managers who seek to revitalize established firms to keep them competitive in today's marketplace. Elisabeth Robert played this role at Vermont Teddy Bear Co. Ten years ago, the maker of furry bears in fancy costumes was enjoying fast growth, fueled by its Bear-Gram service, which delivers teddy bears nationwide. With millions of dollars pouring in, the company launched ambitious marketing plans, including three stores, a variety of bear-branded goods from knapsacks to books, and sponsorship of a NASCAR driver. Before long, this unfocused activity was causing the company to lose money. Vermont Teddy Bear promoted Robert, then its chief financial officer, to CEO and asked her to straighten out the mess. Using her background in finance, she began a careful evaluation of where the money was coming from and where it was going. Not only were the Teddy Bear stores expensive to operate, they were generating only half the sales the company had expected. So Robert shut them down.

Then she asked the big question: "What business are we in?" Half the people who had been visiting the stores were buying bears to ship elsewhere, and they were spending over $70 per bear. Clearly, they wanted more than just a stuffed animal. Robert concluded they were buying a special gift that conveyed a message, much as a person does by sending a gift of flowers. She determined that the company needed a fundamental change in its marketing strategy. Now offering a higher quality, tastefully packaged toy bear—one that Robert likes to call a "creative alternative to flowers"—Vermont Teddy Bear is again profitable.[5]

Although these categories of entrepreneurs involve different situations, they all offer the satisfaction of building a successful enterprise that provides jobs and meets a market need. Classic entrepreneurs Russell and Kimora Simmons focus on building the size of their business and applying their artistic and business creativity to launching new ventures. Don Todrin and Fred Seibert have combined similar ambitions with their talents as change agents to rebuild their chocolate and candy company, True Confections, by moving it away from being a direct competitor with deep-pockets giants Nestlé, Hershey, and Mars. Seibert used his contacts resulting from his experience as former head of Hanna-Barbera and Nickelodeon online to secure rights to feature entertainment icons ranging from Scooby Doo and Spider-Man to SpongeBob SquarePants and *Lord of the Rings* characters on True Confection wrappers. Today, the company doesn't have to compete with the giants. Its sweet treats are sold mostly in novelty, gift, and fashion chains at premium prices. "We're not really selling chocolate bars," says Todrin. "We're selling entertainment impulse items."[6]

> ## *They Said It*
>
> Ignore the stock market, ignore the economy, and buy a business you understand.
>
> *—Warren Buffett (b. 1930) CEO, Berkshire Hathaway, and one of America's richest entrepreneurs*

Concept Check

1. Do you think companies should encourage intrapreneurs? Why or why not?
2. What do intrapreneurs and change agents have in common?

Reasons to Choose Entrepreneurship as a Career Path

If you want to start your own company someday, you have plenty of company. Despite the ongoing threat of terrorism and the recent weakened economy, the Kauffman Center for Entrepreneurial Leadership's most recent research reported that one adult in 12 took part in a business start-up.[7] As Figure 6.2 illustrates, roughly one in 10 U.S. adults under the age of 45 is involved in starting a business with the expectation of owning at least part of it. A recent survey reported that about half of Americans expressed interest in starting a business. This interest is especially strong among young adults. Three of every 10 people between the ages of 18 and 29 want to run their own business.[8] Over the past 20 years, a heightened interest in entrepreneurial careers has been observed, spurred in part by publicity celebrating the successes of entrepreneurs like Pierre Omidyar, who

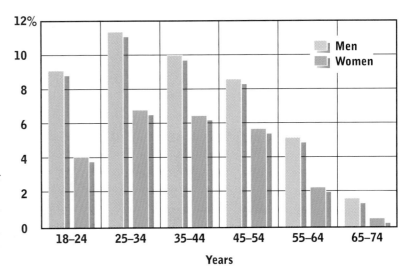

FIGURE 6.2
U.S. Adults Currently Engaged in Starting a Business

Source: Reprinted with permission of *The Wall Street Journal* from "Rewriting the Rules," by Paulette Thomas, May 22, 2000, Interactive Edition, copyright 2000; permission conveyed through Copyright Clearance Center, Inc.

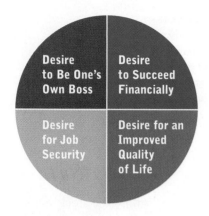

FIGURE 6.3
Why People Become Entrepreneurs

founded eBay; Oprah Winfrey, who has used her immensely popular television program as the springboard for ventures into magazine publishing and TV and film production; Michael Dell, who launched what would become personal computer giant Dell, Inc. following his freshman year at the University of Texas; and Bill Gates of Microsoft.

The popularity of entrepreneurship is evident on America's college campuses. Babson College is among several colleges that have set up business incubators to help students begin new ventures with guidance.

People choose to become entrepreneurs for many different reasons. Some are motivated by dissatisfaction with the organizational work world, citing desires to escape unreasonable bosses or insufficient rewards and recognition as motives to start their own firms. Other people start businesses because they believe their ideas represent opportunities to fulfill customer needs. Luis Espinoza founded a business to meet the unmet demand for Hispanic foods in his new home in northern Indiana. Espinoza had grown up in Texas, where his family enjoyed authentic Mexican foods. Although Espinoza found a significant, growing Hispanic community in Indiana, the local stores didn't know what products to offer these customers. One supermarket chain tried buying foods from a Texas distributor and stocked its shelves with items that appeal to Mexican tastes—in a neighborhood of Puerto Ricans, who prefer less spicy dishes. Espinoza knew he could do better. He learned about local tastes and set up Inca Quality Foods to provide canned goods and spices tailored to stores' local clientele. He convinced a Kroger manager to let him set up a display; when sales increased, he landed a contract to service Kroger's stores throughout the area.[9]

As pointed out in Figure 6.3, people become entrepreneurs for one or more of four major reasons: desire to be their own boss, desire to succeed financially, desire to attain job security, and desire to improve their quality of life. Each of these reasons is described in more detail in the following sections.

Liz Lange chose entrepreneurship to fill customer needs—and be her own boss—when she created Liz Lange Maternity.

Desire to Be Your Own Boss

Self-management is the motivation that drives many entrepreneurs. And no entrepreneur matches this portrait of the American independent professional as an individual who has control over when, where, and how she works more than Liz Lange, the 30-something founder and CEO of Liz Lange Maternity.

Lange recognized a real need back in 1996 while working as a designer's assistant. Expectant mothers seeking sophisticated maternity wear quickly discovered that they would have to make do with baby-doll dresses or pants with a hole cut in the front—and a lycra panel to accommodate their unborn child. Lange found herself offended by what was available. "[Nine months] is a fairly long period of time, and women are just too active today, too much a part of life to have to sit out nine months wearing a big tent, not feeling good about themselves."

Lange left her job to begin work designing a few basic items to show to retail buyers. They stated that pregnant women would not spend money on high-end maternity clothing. Undaunted, she borrowed $50,000 from family and friends and opened a small New York City office where she sold her made-to-order clothes by appointment. Word of the high-fashion maternity clothing spread like wildfire and led to an article in *The New York Times* Style section. Sales exploded after that, and Lange decided to bypass department stores in favor of selected high-fashion boutiques. Soon her slim pants, cashmere sweaters, and fitted slinky dress were attracting superstylish expectant moms, including such celebrities as Cindy Crawford and Catherine Zeta-Jones.

Today, Lange is running stores in Beverly Hills and on New York's Madison Avenue, as well as producing an online catalog (`http://www.lizlange.com`). Annual sales currently exceed $3 million, and the mother of two is considering new stores in London and Paris. Both Lange and her satisfied customers agree that her decision to be her own boss was a wise one.[10]

Financial Success

Entrepreneurs are wealth creators. Many start their ventures with the specific goal of creating a profitable business and reaping its financial rewards. They believe they won't get rich by working for someone else. During the 1990s—and prior to the burst of the dot.com bubble—the flood of money pouring into Internet start-ups encouraged the belief that launching a business—especially a high-tech business—was the most reliable path to wealth. After all, research shows that self-employed Americans are four times as likely to accumulate a million dollars than those who work for someone else.[11] And the business press publishes plenty of features about more dramatic successes. In one such story, college classmates and close friends Andy Stenzler and Nick Marsh, inspired by the slacker classic *Reality Bites,* decided to create a better day–night coffee shop than the one in which the film's characters skulked around. Raising $400,000 from loans and investments from friends up and down the East Coast, they opened their first Xandu Coffee Bar (with a motto of "From wake-up call to last call") in Hartford, Connecticut. To their delight, the coffee bars attracted the same young hipsters that the *Reality Bites* characters were based on—in addition to celebrities like Ethan Hawke, Julia Roberts, and Uma Thurman. The first store had expanded to 60 by the first years of the 21st century, and Stenzler and Marsh's purchase of Cosi Sandwich Co. added new revenues to their existing shops. Their original $400,000 has turned into a mini-coffee/sandwich shop empire with annual sales of $100 million.[12]

Although entrepreneurs often mention financial rewards as a motive for starting their businesses, the path to riches can be long and uncertain. Among the CEOs heading America's fastest-growing private companies (the so-called *Inc.* 500), almost one-fourth took no compensation at all from their business during its first five years of operation. Eric J. Ruff is an example of an entrepreneur who struggled financially during the early years. When he started his software business, PowerQuest, his first long-term goal was modest: to be able to afford to "supersize" his order of french fries when he took his family to McDonald's, without worrying whether he could afford the price. Ruff was surprised to discover that reaching this goal took four years. However, when that day arrived, he felt proud.[13]

Job Security

Although the demand for skilled employees remains high in many industries, the recent economic slowdown showed clearly how many workers lack job security. Over the last 10 years, large companies sought efficiency by downsizing, and they actually eliminated more U.S. jobs than they created. In addition, hundreds of companies have recently tried to improve their financial status through massive layoffs. Such well-known firms as Time Warner, JCPenney, DaimlerChrysler, Motorola, Sprint, and WorldCom have trimmed thousands of positions from their payrolls.[14] Six of the major transportation-related U.S. companies laid off at least 10,000 people—Boeing (20,000), American (20,000), United (20,000), Delta (13,000), Continental (13,000), and US Airways (11,000)—and each of them attributed the job losses to September 11. Other hard-hit industry sectors included computer manufacturers, information technology firms, and media companies.[15]

Among the hardest hit are the youngest and least experienced workers. When the unemployment rate hit 6 percent in 2003, the jobless rate among 20- to 24-year-olds was 61 percent higher at 9.7 percent. Even college graduates, stymied by gloomy hiring prospects, have accepted positions as contract workers to earn incomes.[16] In the wake of that trend, a growing number of the American workforce—both

Six years of facing the uncertainty of continuing work as a professional baseball player prompted Shawn Buchanan to become a successful entrepreneur. Not only did his efforts provide job security for him, but also for the 40 employees of All American Meats.

Courtesy of All American Meats, Inc.

first-time job seekers and laid-off long-term employees—decided to create their own job security by starting their own businesses. The U.S. Small Business Administration has found that the majority of new jobs created have been in the smallest companies, with a significant share of those jobs coming from the creation of new companies.[17]

Although working for others may not guarantee job security, lack of security is also an issue for entrepreneurs. An entrepreneur's job does not depend on the decisions of employers but rather on the decisions of customers and investors and on the cooperation and commitment of the entrepreneur's own employees. Thirty-four-year-old Shawn Buchanan learned the importance of teamwork and the contributions of others during his six years of professional baseball. But he made a career shift 10 years ago when he decided to learn the meat business.

Buchanan had saved most of his substantial baseball earnings and went to work selling Bill Hughes's Nebraska Beef products—but receiving no salary. Instead, Hughes taught him the business, a business he entered two years later. Today, All American Meats in Omaha, Nebraska, generates sales exceeding $35 million annually. Not only did the move pay off for Buchanan, his wife, and two daughters, but for the growing number of All American Meats employees. And in his words, that's just as satisfying. "It's not just about me and my family. I'm accountable for a minimum of 40 families now. That's what gives me the desire to continue and grow."[18]

Quality of Life

Entrepreneurship is an attractive career option for people seeking to improve their quality of life. Starting a business gives the founder some choice over when, where, and how to work. Roger Greene founded Ipswitch, a software company, with the ideal of moderation. His goal is moderate growth, and he encourages employees to take plenty of time off. In fact, each employee is expected to take at least five weeks off, a common employee benefit in many European firms but extremely unusual for a U.S. company. Greene's attitude is, instead of working hard to earn enough money to enjoy life, "live life as it goes along and do neat things while you're working and enjoy every year of your life." To protect this value, Ipswitch has not raised money through a stock offering or from venture capitalists because these outside investors would likely push management to achieve faster growth and profits. In addition, management avoids praising employees for working nights and weekends. In this environment, both Greene and his employees benefit from quality of work life, and employees know it. Ipswitch's employee turnover is about half the industry average.[19]

Despite the example of Ipswitch's Roger Greene, most entrepreneurs work long hours and at the whims of their customers. Adam Kanner, founder of an Internet business called Edu.com, says he typically works at least 90 hours a week. Much of that time, he is away from home looking for investors and customers.[20] As Heather Blease's technical support company, EnvisioNet, was making a transition from 3 to 1,500 employees, she was juggling business growth with the needs of her three children, all under the age of six. She says it was painful to hear one son ask her, as she flew off to a fund-raising meeting, "Mommy, do you love your company more than me?" But Sandra Kurtzig, founder of ASK Group, says the payoff can sometimes come when children are older. One of her children, now grown, wants Kurtzig to join him in his own start-up, putting a whole new and gratifying look on the prospect of the empty nest.[21] Ironically, Kurtzig had started ASK Group as a part-time occupation after leaving General Electric so that she could spend more time with her family.[22]

For other entrepreneurs, quality of life is defined in terms of their ability to fulfill broader social objectives through their ventures. Twenty-eight-year-old Darren Patrick founded San Antonio-based Rainbow Play Systems when he was 20. Three years later, he was a millionaire. Rainbow makes red-wood and red-cedar residential playground equipment and sells it in 14 stores in several south Texas cities and across the Rio Grande in Mexico. This year, the company will ring up more than $6 million in sales, making Rainbow one of the nation's largest consumers of redwood.

And that's what worried Patrick from the start. "Since the onset of our business, we have always been concerned about our lumber purchases and the mills that fulfill them," he states. Rainbow buys lumber only from mills participating in sustained-yield programs that protect the redwood population. The firm goes further by educating purchasers about the benefits offered by such programs. As a result, Patrick says, "Today, we have more redwood trees than ever before."[23]

Concept Check

1. Why are young adults particularly interested in starting their own businesses?

2. Why do you think entrepreneurs are more likely than employees to achieve financial success?

3. What factors affect the entrepreneur's job security?

The Environment for Entrepreneurs

If you are motivated to start your own company, a number of factors suggest that this first decade of the 21st century may be the right time to begin. First, the status of entrepreneurship as a career choice has been rising. The movement of entrepreneurship toward the business mainstream began in the early 1980s after Steve Jobs of Apple Computer and other high-tech entrepreneurs gained national attention by going public—that is, selling stock in their companies. Today's entrepreneurs are also reaping the benefits of financial interest among investors, as discussed later in the chapter, and the applications made possible by new technology. Along with those benefits comes respect for those who try, even if they fail. In Massachusetts, entrepreneur scientist Michael West is the biotech industry's self-appointed cloning advocate. His company, Advanced Cell Technology (ACT), is struggling financially, bringing in about $2 million a year from licensing patents and cloning prized cattle for farmers who hope the Food and Drug Administration will soon approve the sale of milk and meat from cloned animals. It's a controversial topic, and both President Bush and members of Congress have called for a complete ban on human cloning. But West says that, with FDA approval of cloned meat and milk sales, ACT could receive "millions of dollars' worth of orders" from farmers.[24]

In addition to favorable public attitudes toward entrepreneurs and the growing number of financing options, several other factors—identified in Figure 6.4—also support and expand opportunities for entrepreneurs: globalization, education, information technology, and demographic and economic trends. Each of these factors is discussed in the following section.

Globalization

The rapid globalization of business, described in the preceding chapters, has created many opportunities for entrepreneurs. Entrepreneurs are marketing their products abroad and hiring international talent. Among the fastest-growing small U.S. companies, almost two of every five have international sales. One entrepreneur who sees international opportunities is Bettye Pierce Zoller, who used her experience in teaching English to form ZWL Publishing, which sells her audiobook, *Speaking Effective English*. When the U.S. and China reached a free-trade agreement, Zoller was ready to tap this huge market's desire to learn to speak English correctly. Her plans include not simply selling the tapes but helping students through one-on-one instruction online, by mail, and in person.[25]

FIGURE 6.4

Factors Supporting and Expanding Opportunities for Entrepreneurs

In a more unusual move, William Heinecke "exported" his own entrepreneurial talents by moving to Thailand, borrowing $1,200, and opening two businesses: an office-cleaning service and a public relations firm. Before long, he had money to get into a third line of work: the fast-food industry. He bought a Pizza Hut franchise in spite of the common belief that Asian consumers wouldn't be interested in pizza because bread and cheese are not staples of the Asian diet. But Heinecke adapted toppings to Thai flavors, and before long, his franchise was profitable and growing. His operation has been greatly expanded since then, with the opening of more than 100 restaurants, including franchises with Mister Donut, Burger King, and Dairy Queen.[26]

Education

The past two decades have brought tremendous growth in the number of educational opportunities for would-be entrepreneurs. Today, hundreds of U.S. colleges and universities offer classes in starting and managing a business, and many of them offer entrepreneurship curricula. Some of these schools, including Alfred University, University of St. Thomas, and Miami University of Ohio, are adding entrepreneurship courses to programs outside the usual business curriculum on the assumption that people in other disciplines might eventually start a business. Alfred University offers a course on entrepreneurship and the arts to help artists make their work a viable means of securing enough income to support their full-time commitment to their art. A student with a rock band applied what he learned and wrote a business plan that has enabled the band to become profitable.[27]

Another way business schools are responding to the interest in entrepreneurship is by helping their students start businesses. Babson College has a program in which a few students are permitted to replace several of the usual classes with launching an actual business under coaching from an entrepreneur-turned-professor. Fordham University offers a class in which students interact with CEOs of high-tech start-ups. For Shannon Scherer, a marketing student who set up a business to market her father's sculptures online, the advantages of starting a business at school are as obvious as the school's high-quality faculty and facilities.

Besides schools, many organizations have sprouted up in recent years to teach entrepreneurship to young people. The Center for Entrepreneurial Leadership offers training programs for learners from kindergarten through community college. The center's Entreprep summer program teaches high school juniors how to start and manage a company. Students in Free Enterprise (SIFE) is a national not-for-profit organization in which college students, working with faculty advisors, teach grade school and high school students and other community members the value of private enterprise and entrepreneurship.[28] The Association of Collegiate Entrepreneurs has chapters on many college campuses in the U.S. and Canada.

And these outreach efforts to teenagers and young adults, coupled with a challenging job market, appear to be working. During the first three years of the 21st century, self-employment among 18- and 19-year-olds climbed 23 percent to 38,000, according to the U.S. Department of Labor.[29]

Information Technology

The explosion in information technology (IT) has provided one of the biggest boosts for entrepreneurs. As computer and communications technologies have merged, accompanied by dramatically falling costs, entrepreneurs have gained tools that help them compete with large companies. Information technology helps entrepreneurs work quickly and efficiently, provide attentive customer service, increase sales, and project professional images. Jackie Schwanberg, founder of Doggy Day Care, used the Internet to research the economics of the dog-care business, created a business plan with Excel spreadsheets, and set up payroll and tax systems using Quick Books. "Before computers," she says, "people were paying an accountant or everything went in a shoe box, and then at the end of the year it was, 'Gee, how did we do?' I can put my finger on the pulse of my business in two seconds."[30]

Advances in information technology have also created demand for new products, and entrepreneurs have risen to the challenge. Some have started businesses that directly apply information technology. Other entrepreneurs start businesses to support high-tech companies. TechBooks, formed in 1988 to do technical publishing, has since generated millions of dollars in business by preparing Internet versions of large publishers' printed works. Entrepreneurs have started other successful businesses to provide consulting or staffing in information technology.

The Internet is a challenge as well as an opportunity for entrepreneurs. Since customers can go online to check prices and buy from large or small companies anywhere in the world, entrepreneurs need to find a distinctive advantage over big competitors. Bruce Roberts, who runs Leesburg Pharmacy in the Virginia town of the same name, sees his advantage as serving special needs. With a growing number of patients filling routine prescriptions at big drugstore chains and over the Internet, Roberts specializes in custom prescriptions, such as for hospice patients who need strong pain relief or for animals that resist taking medicine. Down the road from Roberts's pharmacy, the Potomac Gallery uses the Internet to expand its range of customers and products. The gallery sells some of its lithographs at the Web site of Mill Pond Press, and owner Linda Callagy serves her clientele's interest in Civil War history by downloading information and prints about the era from the site of an art publisher, Hadley House.[31]

Demographic and Economic Trends

Demographic trends, such as the aging of the U.S. population, the emergence of Hispanic Americans as the nation's largest ethnic group, and the growth of two-income families, create opportunities for entrepreneurs to market new goods and services. Entrepreneurs take advantage of such trends to offer everything from retirement homes to grocery delivery services.

One trend that is likely to continue over the next few decades is the competition for talented workers. As noted in the previous section, many fast-growing start-ups are addressing the challenge of recruiting workers by offering specialists on a contract basis. The federal government has launched a program called 21st Century Skills for 21st Century Jobs to provide funding for organizations to train workers in skills that are especially needed. Entrepreneurs will undoubtedly find opportunities to help provide this training.

Entrepreneurship around the World

The growth in entrepreneurship is a worldwide phenomenon. The role of entrepreneurs is growing in most industrialized and newly industrialized nations as well as in the emerging free-market countries in Eastern Europe. However, the level of entrepreneurship varies considerably, even among industrialized nations. In a study of 10 countries, the U.S. had the highest level of entrepreneurship, with 1 of 12 people involved in starting or expanding a business. In contrast, the level of entrepreneurial activity in Finland was just 1 of 67 people. Figure 6.5 compares the amount of entrepreneurial activity in the 10 countries studied.

Entrepreneurs abroad struggle harder to start businesses than do their U.S. counterparts. Obstacles include government regulations, high taxes, and political attitudes that favor big business. In addition, cultural values in other countries may differ from those in the U.S., where high values are placed on seizing a business opportunity.

Davidi Gilo is a citizen from one country with a strong tradition of entrepreneurship: Israel. As digital processing boomed in the 1980s, Gilo founded DSP Group to produce microchips that convert

FIGURE 6.5

Levels of Entrepreneurial Activity in 10 Countries

Source: Data from Ewing Marion Kauffman Foundation, "Global Study on Entrepreneurship Reveals Direct Link between Rate of New Business Start-ups and Economic Growth," news release, June 21, 1999, accessed from the Kauffman Foundation Web site, http://www.emkf.org.

analog signals like voice communication into digital messages used in consumer electronics such as answering machines. At the time, most consumer electronics companies were in Japan, so DSP Group immediately became an exporter. The situation became more complex in the 1990s because answering machines were on the way out, to be replaced by popular cell phones. Gilo's company developed the microchips and software for this new technology, but selling these new products proved more difficult. Gilo moved to Tokyo to devote himself to building new customer relationships. He brought five chip designers and assigned each to one of the company's major customers. Eventually, his patience was rewarded with $16 million in business with his Japanese customers. DSP's next step has been to expand into other countries by developing products that meet their standards for cellular communications. DSP now has an office in California, and one-fourth of its sales are to U.S. customers.[32]

For young people well acquainted with the Internet, cyberculture may override differences in national culture. In Berlin, which has struggled to attract industry after the fall of the Berlin Wall, many Internet entrepreneurs have moved to vacant lofts and warehouses to set up businesses. People who are attracted to the revolutionary spirit of the Internet expansion also enjoy the spirit of change in Berlin, as the city adjusts to Western-style economic freedom. Recently, more than 400 Berlin start-ups were involved in Internet business or advertising. They included auction site Alando.de, later acquired by eBay. Alando's founders chose Berlin for its freewheeling atmosphere. The city's atmosphere also lured dooyoo.de, which offers a guide to online shopping. Dooyoo.de founder Felix Frohn-Bernau says, "We were convinced that the culture we want in the office could only be found here in Berlin."[33]

Concept Check

1. Identify the factors helping to expand current opportunities for entrepreneurs.
2. Describe current demographic trends that suggest new goods and services for entrepreneurial businesses.
3. Identify factors that affect entrepreneurial start-ups abroad.

Influence of Entrepreneurs on the Economy

From Thomas Edison's development of the phonograph to the birth of Apple Computer in Steve Jobs's garage, American entrepreneurs have given the world goods and services that have changed the way people live, work, and play. The list includes ballpoint pens, Netscape Navigator software, fiberglass skis, Velcro fasteners, the Yahoo! Internet directory, FedEx delivery service, and Big Mac hamburgers. As Figure 6.6 describes, entrepreneurs play a significant role in the economy by creating major innovations, increasing the number of jobs, and providing opportunities for women and minorities.

Innovation

Entrepreneurs create new products, build new industries, and bring new life to old industries. By one count, entrepreneurs are the force behind two-thirds of the inventions and 95 percent of major innovations made since World War II.[34] Amar V. Bhidé, in his widely acclaimed book *The Origin and Evolution of New Businesses*, states that this innovation rarely takes place in major leaps but moves in small steps, as entrepreneurs try out small modifications of the status quo and abandon any ideas the market rejects.[35] For example, Netscape Navigator was not the first Web browser, but it was the first to be relatively easy to use. This ease of use translated into market acceptance, and the World Wide Web went from an obscure government-sponsored technology to a major link among individuals and businesses.

Some innovations are born of personal experiences. Chuck Templeton watched his wife

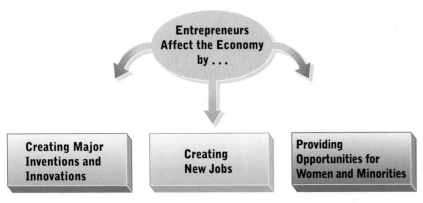

FIGURE 6.6
Influence of Entrepreneurs on the Economy

BUSINESS TOOL KIT

The Pros and Cons of Owning Your Own Business

Entrepreneurship is a mixed bag. On the one hand, you have a certain amount of freedom and autonomy; on the other, you are solely responsible for the success or failure of your livelihood. Owning your own business brings with it many joys and frustrations, but for the 10.1 million self-employed people in the United States (according to the U.S. Census Bureau), the pros and cons balance out in favor of entrepreneurship in spite of the challenges.

PROS

1. Instead of relying on a corporate job, you rely only on yourself to make a living. Downsizing and layoffs have convinced many that corporate life isn't what it's cracked up to be. Bad economic times usually see an increase in self-reliance due to corporate layoffs, scandals, and financial difficulties.

2. There is no race, gender, or age discrimination when you own your own business. Although more and more entrepreneurs are starting young, age has little to do with the success or failure of a venture.

3. When you start a business out of your home, you can balance your home life with your professional life. If you manage your time efficiently, working from home can offer many advantages: watching your kids grow up, being available for household needs such as broken pipes and deliveries, and being able to work in your sweatpants and bare feet. Self-employment can improve your quality of life while still offering a way to make a living.

CONS

1. According to the Small Business Administration, most small businesses fail within the first five years of operation. In addition, you must show a profit at least three out of every five years or the IRS may decide that your business is actually a hobby.

2. Maintaining cash flow during the start-up phase is difficult unless you plan ahead and save six months to a year's worth of salary to get you through the lean times. You must also handle your finances in a different way when you own your own business, especially if you have payroll, sales tax, and other financial requirements.

3. Your company's image depends on you. Despite the freedom you may have to operate your business the way you see fit, if you meet with clients or make sales calls, you need to work extra hard at projecting a professional image.

Sources: Damon Cline, "More Americans Opt for Post-Retirement Self-Employment," *Knight Ridder/Tribune Business News,* January 7, 2003; Frank Witsil, "Self-Employment Rises as People Try Turning Hobbies into Cash," *Knight Ridder/Tribune Business News,* December 30, 2002; Tammy Joyner, "More Workers Turn to Self-Employment, Avoid Scandal-Struck Corporations," *Knight Ridder/Tribune Business News,* August 19, 2002; Taimi Dunn Gorman, "The 10 Truths of Owning Your Own Business (Lessons I've Learned)," *Bellingham Business Journal,* June 2002, p. B10.

make last-minute dinner reservations over the phone and thought there must be an easier way to find a table at a good restaurant. He drew an analogy to online reservations for airline tickets and came up with the idea for OpenTable.com. The service signs up restaurants and provides the hardware and software to link them to its Web site. Diners go to the Web site to look for available tables, searching by neighborhood or cuisine or looking up restaurants by name. OpenTable.com indicates the times at which tables are available, and the hungry consumer clicks to select a preferred restaurant, table, and desired seating time.[36]

Other entrepreneurs identify better ways to serve business customers. Mini-Tankers was founded in Australia to provide superior service in the sale of diesel fuel. Construction firms or highway contractors sometimes work late into the evening, but if they run out of fuel at night, they can't buy from the major oil companies, which generally close in the evening. Mini-Tankers not only is open around the clock, but the company sends a truck right to the customer's site. In addition, each truck is equipped with a computer that generates a receipt containing information to help the customer analyze the efficiency of its diesel-burning machinery. This successful concept is now improving service in the U.S. market for diesel fuel, with Mini-Tankers trucks operating in Chicago, Portland, Seattle, and St. Louis.[37]

Job Generation

Entrepreneurs are a vital source of new jobs. Research on job generation and entrepreneurial activity has found that fast-growing start-ups—about 3 percent of all firms—have become the principal job creators in the U.S. These companies, frequently called **gazelles,** created about two-thirds of the new jobs in the U.S. during a recent three-year period.[38] Rapid growth by start-ups is also expected to be a significant source of future job creation.

Entrepreneurial job creation typically involves a small number of employees per firm but is spread over many, many companies. Strategic Communications Group more than tripled in size during a recent 12-month period, growing from 10 to 35 employees. The marketing and public relations firm struggled until a banker advised its founder, Marc Hausman, to hire a chief financial officer. Hausman found a recently retired financial officer willing to work for his company part time, freeing Hausman to develop many more client relationships. This new business enabled him to hire additional employees.[39]

Entrepreneurs sometimes find potential employees in locations where established businesses overlook them. Frank Tucker started Tucker Technology to install and maintain telecommunications equipment, and he located in an economically disadvantaged area of Oakland, California. Driving to work, Tucker says, "I'd see all the human resources on the street corner. Clearly, they had no jobs to go to." Recognizing that much of his installation and maintenance work required only basic skills, Tucker began to hire local people, teach them the job, and pay them a substantial $23 an hour—fair compensation for the grimy working conditions. In this way, Tucker can compete in the quest for workers, and his community also benefits by attracting a new business and increasing local job opportunities.[40]

FIGURE 6.7
Diversity of 21st-Century Entrepreneurs

Diversity and progress go hand in hand.

At Verizon, we do more than reach for diversity – we embrace it. That's why our employees, our suppliers and our solutions reflect the diverse communities we serve. Embracing our differences, as well as our shared goals, makes it possible for each of us to make progress in our own way. And that's something worth reaching for.

Make progress every day
verizon.com

verizon

Courtesy of Verizon

Diversity

Entrepreneurship offers excellent economic opportunities for women and minorities. As illustrated in Figure 6.7, today's entrepreneurial success stories have a colorful cast. This advertisement for telecommunications giant Verizon uses hands to reflect the diverse groups—different genders, different ethnic backgrounds, different ages—that make up the 21st-century business environment. It illustrates the reality of today: Barriers to making money have fallen, and a new generation of entrepreneurs has already made an indelible mark on American business.

The number of women- and minority-owned start-ups has grown tremendously in recent years. As noted in Chapter 5, the pace in growth of business start-ups is faster among Hispanics, African Americans, and Asian Americans than among the population at large, and much of that growth is among recent immigrants. Also, women are the entrepreneurs behind almost half of the millions of business start-ups in the U.S.

The range of businesses they operate defeats the usual stereotypes. Female entrepreneurs are engaged in service and manufacturing businesses ranging from Sheila Thompson's 70-employee firm that manufacturers wooden models of historic buildings and other collectibles to Ella D. Williams's systems engineering firm. Williams's company, Aegir Systems, also employs 70 people, including electrical engineers, computer scientists, and graphic designers.

Realizing the value of both women- and minority-owned start-ups in creating jobs and promoting diversity, many large companies have developed diversity programs that help these entrepreneurs get start-up capital, subcontracts, and other assistance. General Motors, Pacific Gas & Electric, and Toyota are just three of the large firms that offer supplier diversity programs. Large companies frequently advertise in magazines like *Black Enterprise* and *Hispanic,* encouraging readers to contact their directors of supplier diversity for information about their diversity programs.

Concept Check

1. Describe the link between personal experience and innovation.
2. Explain the process by which fast-growing start-ups create many of the new jobs in the U.S. today.
3. Among which demographic groups is the pace of start-ups fastest?

Characteristics of Entrepreneurs

The examples of entrepreneurship you've read about so far may give the impression that people who strike out on their own are a different breed. In addition to having similar motivations, successful entrepreneurs are more likely than other people to have parents who were entrepreneurs. They also tend to possess unique personality traits. Researchers who study successful entrepreneurs report that they are more likely to be inquisitive, passionate, self-motivated, honest, courageous, flexible, intelligent, and reliable people. The eight traits summarized in Figure 6.8 are especially important for people who want to succeed as entrepreneurs.

Vision

Entrepreneurs begin with a *vision,* an overall idea for how to make their business idea a success, and then they passionately pursue it. Bill Gates and Paul Allen launched Microsoft with the vision of a computer on every desk and in every home, all running Microsoft software. Their vision helped Microsoft to become the world's largest marketer of computer software. It guided the company and provided clear direction for employees as Microsoft grew, adapted, and prospered in an industry characterized by tremendous technological change.

Talk about vision, about the ability to think out of the box; talk about the Edison of the 21st century and you're not talking about Bill Gates, though. No, these descriptions are for wildly successful inventor and entrepreneur Dean Kamen. The tireless and gregarious father of the first portable insulin pump, heart stent (of which Vice President Cheney is a satisfied customer), and stair-climbing wheelchair certainly has vision, but he also keeps a close watch on the bottom line of the numerous successful companies that have resulted from his technological breakthroughs.

> *They Said It*
>
> In the end, a vision without the ability to execute is probably an hallucination.
>
> —*Stephen M. Case (b. 1958)*
> *Cofounder, America Online*

FIGURE 6.8
Characteristics of Entrepreneurs

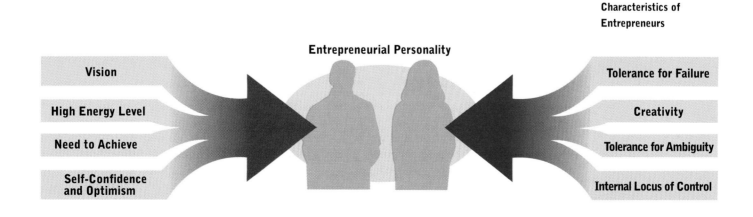

Entrepreneurial Personality

Vision

High Energy Level

Need to Achieve

Self-Confidence and Optimism

Tolerance for Failure

Creativity

Tolerance for Ambiguity

Internal Locus of Control

BUSINESS TOOL KIT

Creativity and the Creative Process

Creativity may be the best asset for an entrepreneur. When creative solutions are needed, you don't need a committee or a CEO. You need to be creative within the context of your own business and your own vision. One definition of *creativity* is to produce through imaginative skill. The term is usually used in the sense of creating a painting, but you can also effectively create solutions to business challenges. Creativity aids entrepreneurs by allowing them to think "outside the box."

Creativity often means relying on your intuition as much as it means accessing your right brain. Here are a few ways to develop creativity and intuition as an entrepreneur:

- **Listen.** Listening skills are very important, especially when you run your own business. Listen to your customers, your clients, your potential customers, your employees, your family, your neighbors, and your friends. Sometimes, seeing a problem through an outsider's eyes can be a great catalyst for innovative solutions. It is also very important to learn how to listen to yourself—use your intuition and think with your gut.
- **Brainstorm.** Be open to others' ideas, and start brainstorming with those around you. This technique is effective because no idea is thrown out or rejected during the brainstorming period; everything is initially recorded. Creativity calls for removing the

boundaries, and brainstorming is one of the best techniques to try when you need to open up the floodgates of ideas.

- **Shake things up.** Change your regular routine and you just may hit on a new way of thinking. We tend to be creatures of habit—driving the same routes, ordering the same meals, and repetitively performing the same tasks. When you alter your routine, you allow your mind to free itself, encouraging a different look at things. So go ahead and eat dinner for breakfast, watch cartoons with the kids, or walk a different path today. You will be amazed at how you view things differently.

The best part about the creative process is that there are no defined, correct ways to "be creative." Whatever works for you is the best approach, so don't be afraid to try new ways of thinking. As Albert Einstein once said, "Creativity is more important than knowledge."

Sources: Karen Kuebler, "Developing Your Personal Creativity—a Powerful Force!" http://www.betterbudgeting.com/articles/money/personal creativity.htm, accessed July 1, 2003; Scott Beagrie, "How to Manage Creativity," *Personnel Today*, February 18, 2003, p. 31; Debra Gerardi, "Developing Creativity and Intuition for Resolving Conflicts: The Magic of Improvisation," September 2001, http://www.mediate.com/articles/geradi.cfm, accessed July 1, 2003.

His latest creation has met with mixed success. The Segway Human Transporter is a two-wheeled self-balancing electric-powered superscooter that allows people to zip along sidewalks and in large business facilities at 8 to 12 miles per hour. Already 41 states have changed their laws to permit the vehicle on sidewalks, providing an environmentally friendly transportation alternative in overcrowded cities. But San Francisco banned them out of safety concerns. Kamen's launch of the Segway Human Transporter is the subject of the Hits & Misses box later in this chapter.[41]

High Energy Level

Entrepreneurs willingly work hard to realize their visions. Starting and building a company require an enormous amount of hard work and long hours. Some entrepreneurs work full time at their regular day jobs and spend weeknights and weekends launching their start-ups. Many devote 14-hour days seven days a week to their new ventures. In his 10-year study of entrepreneurs, author Amar Bhidé found that what distinguishes successful entrepreneurs from other business owners is that they "work harder, hustle for customers, and know that the opportunity may not last for more than six or eight months."[42]

A major reason entrepreneurship demands hard work is that start-up companies typically have a small staff and struggle to raise enough capital. Under these resource constraints, the entrepreneur has to make up the difference. When two engineers started Gilat Satellite Networks to build satellite systems, they had to work extremely hard to compete with giant corporations like EchoStar. They offered to do whatever was necessary to tailor a system to the client's needs. Gilat's first customer was Rite Aid, the drugstore chain. The company won the contract by agreeing to adapt its satellite system in significant ways. The two founders and four other members of the project's development team put in many nights and evenings to achieve their commitment. Co-founder Amiram Levinberg says simply, "In a high-tech start-up such as Gilat . . . it's a given that there will be some 12-hour days."[43]

The challenge for entrepreneurs is to balance the hard work with the rest, recreation, and family time that are so essential to good health, quality of life, and continued creativity. And this struggle continues with entrepreneur-inventor Dean Kamen. He typically handles business tasks during

© AP/Wide World Photos

Pompadoured and trim in Timberland boots, jeans, and denim shirt, Dean Kamen unveils the Segway Human Transporter at a media conference. But so far, the marketplace hasn't exactly received the $5,000 Segway with open arms. Only about 20,000 units have been sold to date. And the ability of prospective purchasers to actually try out the novel transporter is extremely limited. For months, customers could purchase it only on the Amazon Web site. Realizing this huge marketing problem in attempting to sell the relatively expensive item, Segway executives have opened about 20 retail outlets nationwide. But not every innovation proves a successful venture and, in Segway's case, it may prove an example of inadequate distribution that hindered product trials and service at a time when product excitement was at its peak.

the day and then heads for the engineering division of one of his companies by late afternoon. He dines with the engineers, at the same time urging them to "kiss the frog"—a reference to the many tries it takes to transform an amphibian into a prince. Kamen has no boundaries between life and work, referring to vacation as being able to "go from one project to another." Although his 30,000-square-foot mansion has two helicopters, a fully equipped machine shop, and a full-size baseball diamond in the back, there's no wife and family to greet his arrival. "I think getting in relationships is riskier [than business projects] and to me scarier," he ruefully admits.[44]

But most entrepreneurs manage to succeed at this work/life balancing act. Tom Melaragno routinely worked 12-hours days when he started Compri Consulting, a firm that provides consulting and staffing for information technology projects. As Melaragno's company has grown, he has become more able to delegate work, freeing time for his wife and children, workouts at a local health club, and his rock band, Orphan Boy.[45]

Need to Achieve

Entrepreneurs work hard because they want to excel. Their strong competitive drive helps them to enjoy the challenge of reaching difficult goals and promotes dedication to personal success. Entrepreneurship expert Amar Bhidé says successful entrepreneurs have "an almost maniacal level of ambition. Not just ambition to make a comfortable living, to make a few million dollars, but someone who wants to leave a significant mark on the world."[46]

To make ends meet, Maria de Lourdes Sobrino created a line of gelatin treats. Mexican immigrants were fond of these products, but had been unable to buy them in the U.S. and Lulu's Dessert Factory was born.

Courtesy of Lulu's Dessert Corporation

Maria de Lourdes Sobrino's dream was to find success in the U.S. A Mexican immigrant, Sobrino moved with her husband and daughter to Los Angeles, where she opened a travel business concentrating on travel between the U.S. and Mexico. But economic woes in Mexico ended demand for her services, and personal conflicts ended her marriage. Sobrino needed a new way to support herself, and an idea came to her: selling small cups of flavored gelatin, a common treat in Mexico that had not yet found its way to U.S. stores. Identifying retailers willing to take a chance on the new product required persistence. Store managers didn't understand the product, so Sobrino honed the marketing strategy for her company, Lulu's Dessert Factory. She identified Latino communities and visited independent stores. Finally, one allowed her to leave gelatin cups, with payment contingent on sales. When Sobrino returned to her spartan office, a message was waiting for her: "Please come back, Señora. Your gelatins are sold." That was the turning point for Lulu's. When her product became popular in local stores, a food broker began to carry it, and Sobrino borrowed money to expand her facilities. Paying off the loans was difficult and took years, but today Lulu's is a $12 million company with 45 products offered in West Coast stores. Through hard work and determination, Sobrino is achieving her goals. She says, "I enjoy my company, customers, and my 100 employees so much now because I fought hard for them."[47]

Self-Confidence and Optimism

Entrepreneurs believe in their ability to succeed, and they instill their optimism in others. Often, their optimism resembles fearlessness in the face of difficult odds. "People thought we were crazy to give up six-figure salaries at investment banking firms to reinvent the earmuff," says Brian LeGette of himself and his business partner Ron Wilson. "They laughed at us." LeGette and Wilson are the founders of Big Bang Products, a Baltimore company that got its start with a fleece-covered ear warmer that wraps around the back of the wearer's head. Despite not knowing anything about fabric or sewing, the two business school students put start-up expenses on their credit cards, built a prototype from items they bought at Wal-Mart, and went to work. Within a year, they were a successful start-up, selling their ear warmers for $20 each. Soon they were raising capital to finance growth, hiring additional employees, and adding products. The firm's innovative takes on ordinary products like sunglasses, beach chairs, and gloves have made Big Bang into a $35 million firm with 55 employees, and it's still growing. Says LeGette, "We have an inexhaustible desire to question the things that most people think have already been answered. And that's how we succeed in reinventing the wheel."[48]

Sometimes, though, a combination of overconfidence and questionable ethical standards can blind an entrepreneur and not only jeopardize the business but leave a bad taste about business in the mouths of millions. This is what happened with the ethical lapses of the entrepreneurs featured in the Solving an Ethical Controversy box.

Tolerance for Failure

On his first try, Edmund Hillary failed at climbing Mount Everest. But he always regaled audiences listening to him recount his experience by shouting, "Mount Everest, you beat me the first time, but I'll beat you the next time, because you've grown all you are going to grow, but I'm still growing!" He tried again, and again failed. But he kept at it, and on May 29, 1953, Hillary and his Sherpa companion, Tenzing Norgay, became the first humans to climb the world's tallest mountain. If Hillary, now in his mid-80s, had given up after his first try, he might still be an anonymous beekeeper in New Zealand.[49]

Like Hillary, entrepreneurs view setbacks and failures as learning experiences. They're not easily discouraged or disappointed when things don't go as planned. For Robert Luster, a major setback involved making a transition from his role as Army officer to civilian entrepreneur. His first construction management firm, Athena Management Engineers, failed after two years, as Luster got used to the subtleties of communication in the private sector. He then formed Luster Construction Management and won his first client by promising he could have someone on site the next day—even though his start-up company had no paid employees. While he was waiting for a reply, Luster began screening candidates, so when the client called and asked Luster to start the next morning, he was ready. Today, Luster's business is generating $10 million in sales and has over 100 employees.[50]

Creativity

Entrepreneurs typically conceive new ideas for goods and services, and they devise innovative ways to overcome difficult problems and situations. Kenny Kramm struggled in frustration and despair as he watched his infant daughter try to swallow bitter antiseizure medication four times a day. Often, Kramm and his wife had to rush their daughter to the emergency room for treatment for the seizures because she had not been able to take enough of the medicine. Kramm improvised at first, giving his daughter mashed banana to help her stomach her medication. Then inspiration struck: He guessed that he wasn't the only parent who had trouble feeding foul-tasting medications to his child. So Kramm concocted harmless additives in his parents' suburban Washington, DC, pharmacy, where he worked. The additives would sweeten the taste without diluting the medicine. From a banana flavor, he branched out to other flavors for liquids, pills, and powders. Soon his business FlavorX had agreements with major drugstore chains Kroger and Winn-Dixie, and he recently projected next-year sales of $5 million. Is Kramm finished innovating? Not yet. He has expanded into pet medications for vet clinics.[51]

Entrepreneurs often achieve success by making creative improvements, rather than single-handedly revolutionizing an industry. Amar Bhidé's research identified a substantial amount of creativity among entrepreneurs "at the tactical level"—in other words, in the ways entrepreneurs built their businesses, more so than in the product itself.[52]

Tolerance for Ambiguity

Entrepreneurs take in stride the uncertainties associated with launching a venture. Dealing with unexpected events is the norm for most entrepreneurs. For some, the endless variety of tasks and challenges is the fundamental allure. Corinna Lathan was on the verge of getting tenure in her teaching post at Catholic University when she left the academic world for good and returned to the company

SOLVING AN ETHICAL CONTROVERSY

Entrepreneurs Behaving Badly: What Can Be Done? What Should Be Done?

In the early years of the 21st century, "Another Business Scandal!" became the headline of daily newspapers and news telecasts, and unflattering images of successful entrepreneurs and modern-day descendants of earlier ones became fodder for both tabloids and prosecutors. The roster of accused entrepreneurial wrongdoers included:

1. Kenneth Lay, the entrepreneur who invented a new energy-trading industry with Enron Corp., saw it descend into the second-largest bankruptcy in U.S. history and cost thousands of employees both their jobs and most of their retirement savings. Lay, indicted for fraud and awaiting trial, admitted that he had received an annual salary of $104 million to preside over the firm's bankruptcy before being fired.

2. Telecommunications giant World-Com surpassed Enron as America's largest bankruptcy after accusations of "cooking the books" in a scheme to inflate profits led to plunging stock prices, pressure from lenders, and hundreds of lawsuits by investors and creditors. The deception was one that almost any Accounting 101 student would have detected. Former CEO Bernard J. Ebbers awaits trial on charges of conspiracy and fraud.

3. Enron auditor and consultant Arthur Andersen, a long-term entrepreneurial success story, was convicted of obstruction of justice following its shredding of Enron documents. Andersen had also served as WorldCom's auditor.

4. Dennis Kozlowski, who built Tyco in the image of General Electric as he acquired company after company to create a multibillion-dollar conglomerate, was fired following his indictment by the New York City

attorney general on charges of evading an estimated $1 million sales taxes. His first trial ended in a hung jury; he is being retried on charges of first-degree larceny and other crimes.

5. Samuel Waksal, who cofounded and led biotech powerhouse ImClone Systems, was arrested by the FBI on charges of insider trading—leaking information on a forthcoming negative FDA report to friends and family. He was sentenced to seven years in prison for securities fraud.

6. Home design and decorating diva Martha Stewart, a friend of ex-ImClone CEO Samuel Waksal, was convicted on obstruction of justice charges after it was shown that she impeded an investigation into her sale of ImClone stock a day before the negative FDA report was released. Stockholders of Martha Stewart Living, which runs a magazine, cable TV program, catalogs, online sites, and mass-market retail brands all emblazoned with Stewart's name, watched their shares crumble in value before recovering following the merger of Kmart and Sears.

Could entrepreneurial and managerial misdeeds break the public's trust in contemporary business?

PRO

1. Investment, the engine of business, relies on the public's being able to trust company founders and corporate leaders to use money honorably in search of financial return.

2. The public has made heroes of successful entrepreneurs and business

leaders who have then lost the money of many innocent people.

CON

1. Federal, state, and local governments continue to prosecute those who commit financial crimes, allowing the business system to function in spite of a few greedy executives.

2. Investigations into alleged misconduct traditionally bring reforms and new regulations where needed. Passage of the Sarbanes-Oxley Act of 2002 represented a swift and far-reaching government response to recent abuses.

SUMMARY

It would be naïve to think that additional financial or business scandals will not continue to be uncovered. But investors, and those who advise them, would be wise to encourage their government representatives to adopt additional laws to remedy these abuses.

Sources: Brooke A. Masters, "Prosecutors Say Ebbers Lied to Obtain Loans," *The Washington Post,* October 12, 2004, accessed at http://news.yahoo.com; April Vitello, "Stewart Begins Five-Month Prison Sentence," *Associated Press,* October 8, 2004, http://story.news.yahoo.com; Samuel Maull, "Top Count Is Withdrawn in Tyco Retrial," *Associated Press,* September 29, 2004, http://news.yahoo.com; Michael Freedman and Emily Lambert, "Will She Walk?" *Forbes,* July 7, 2004, pp. 46–47; Matthew Benjamin, "The Wages of Sin," *U.S. News & World Report,* June 23, 2003, p. 30; Amy Borrus and Mike McNamee, "Reform: Business Gets Religion," *BusinessWeek,* February 3, 2003, pp. 40–41; Robert Bryce, *Pipe Dreams, Greed, Ego, and the Death of Enron,* New York: Public Affairs, 2002; Susan Pullion et al., "Former WorldCom CEO Built an Empire on Mountain of Debt," *The Wall Street Journal,* December 31, 2002, p. A1; Marianne Lavelle, "The Actions of Corporate Honchos Horrified the Nation," *U.S. News & World Report,* December 30, 2002, http://www.usnews.com; Anthony Bianco, William Symonds, and Nanette Byrnes, "The Rise and Fall of Dennis Kozlowski," *BusinessWeek,* December 23, 2002, pp. 64–77.

she had founded the year before. AnthroTronix makes toys that help disabled kids to develop physical and language skills in a play environment. "I never wanted to do research on one thing for the rest of my life, which tends to be the academic model," says Lathan. "It's more fun as an entrepreneur because as a small company I get to do more hands-on research. I don't have to worry about being the best in one narrow area and doing the same experiments over and over with a twist. . . . It's the learning curve that turns me on."[53]

Tolerance for ambiguity is different from the love of risk taking that many people associate with entrepreneurship. Successful entrepreneurship is a far cry from gambling because entrepreneurs look for strategies that they believe have a good chance of success, and they quickly make adjustments when a strategy isn't working. Stanley Adelman has founded four companies, and he succeeds by investing small amounts of money to provide products for which a strong demand exists. Adelman's first business was Systems Strategies, a computer consulting company he started in the 1970s. He observed that little capital is needed to start a consulting firm: "You just go out there and sell services." Of course, even in the consulting business, success does require human talent coupled with entrepreneurial drive. Adelman had those resources, and he built a fast-growing enterprise. Then, while consulting with Citigroup, he realized that the hardware systems he was developing for securities trading would interest other companies. His second business, Systems Strategies Equipment Corp., sold the hardware. Adelman's third business offered software built to customer specifications—a very safe venture because the company was building something the customer had already asked for. He finally decided to sell all three companies, allowing him the funds and time needed to start his fourth business, Aegis Software, another consulting firm that has enjoyed rapid growth.[54]

An important way entrepreneurs manage ambiguity is by keeping close to customers so that they can adjust their offerings in keeping with customer desires. Sylvia Woods expanded from a Harlem restaurant into the packaged-foods business by listening to her customers. Patrons of Sylvia's Restaurant, famous for its soul food, loved her homemade barbecue sauce so much that they begged to buy some to take home. Around Christmastime, some would visit the restaurant with empty jars, asking to buy sauce for gifts. Even local firefighters showed up with gallon jugs and asked for sauce. Woods teamed up with her son Van and launched Queen of Soul Food, starting with bottles of barbecue sauce. They added other items customers praised, including bottled hot sauce and canned vegetables, and have gone on to open a second restaurant in Atlanta as well as lines of other food and beauty products.[55]

Internal Locus of Control

Entrepreneurs believe that they control their own fates, which means they have an internal locus of control. You won't find entrepreneurs gazing into a crystal ball, calling psychic helplines, or looking for a four-leaf clover; they take personal responsibility for the success or failure of their actions rather than believing in luck or fate. They neither make excuses for their shortcomings nor blame others for their setbacks and failures.

Mike Biddle's company, MBA Polymers, Inc., creates new manufacturing materials from the recycled plastics in so-called durable goods, including computers, appliances, and even cars. Biddle used to work on creating high-tech plastics for the aerospace industry. But he considered himself an environmentalist and even rode a bike to work. Several years ago, he realized that he hated the idea of creating tons of plastic that would never be reused, and MBA Polymers was born. Many technical problems had to be overcome, such as separating and sorting the kinds of plastics that go into durable goods and removing other materials like metal, glass, ink, and paper. But Biddle persevered. "I wanted to do something with my technical training that I could get excited about and feel good about," he says.[56]

After reading this summary of typical personality traits, maybe you're wondering if you have what it takes to become an entrepreneur. Take the test in Figure 6.9 to find out. Your results may help you determine whether you would succeed in starting your own company.

Concept Check

1. What is meant by an entrepreneur's vision?

2. Why is it important for an entrepreneur to have a high energy level and a strong need for achievement?

3. How do entrepreneurs generally feel about the possibility of failure?

ENTREPRENEUR POTENTIAL ASSESSMENT FORM

Answer each of the following questions:

Yes No

☐ ☐   1. Are you a first-generation American?

☐ ☐   2. Were you an honor student?

☐ ☐   3. Did you enjoy group functions in school—clubs, team sports, even double dates?

☐ ☐   4. As a youngster, did you frequently prefer to spend time alone?

☐ ☐   5. As a child, did you have a paper route, a lemonade stand, or some other small enterprise?

☐ ☐   6. Were you a stubborn child?

☐ ☐   7. Were you a cautious youngster, the last in the neighborhood to try diving off the high board?

☐ ☐   8. Do you worry about what others think of you?

☐ ☐   9. Are you in a rut, tired of the same routine every day?

☐ ☐   10. Would you be willing to invest your savings—and risk losing all you invested—to go it alone?

☐ ☐   11. If your new business should fail, would you get to work immediately on another?

☐ ☐   12. Are you an optimist?

Add up your total score. A score of 20 or more points indicates strong entrepreneurial tendencies. A score between 0 and 19 points suggests some possibility for success as an entrepreneur. A score between 0 and −10 indicates little chance of successful entrepreneurship. A score below −11 indicates someone who's not the entrepreneurial type.

Answers: 1. Yes = 1, No = −1; 2. Yes = −4, No = 4; 3. Yes = −1, No = 1; 4. Yes = 1, No = −1; 5. Yes = 2, No = −2; 6. Yes = 1, No = −1; 7. Yes = −4, No = 4 (if you were a very daring child, add another 4 points); 8. Yes = −1, No = 1; 9. Yes = 2, No = −2; 10. Yes = 2, No = −2; 11. Yes = 4, No = −4; 12. Yes = 2, No = −2.

FIGURE 6.9

Testing Your Entrepreneurial Potential

Source: Copyright Northwestern Mutual Life Insurance Company. Reprinted with permission.

Starting a New Venture

The examples of entrepreneurs presented so far have introduced many ways to start a business. This section discusses the process of choosing an idea for a new venture and transforming the idea into a working business. Success in a new business may not come instantly, as Dean Kamen knows well. The Hits & Misses box discusses the uncertain future of his latest invention, the Segway scooter.

Selecting a Business Idea

In choosing an idea for your business, the two most important considerations are (1) finding something you love to do and are good at doing and (2) determining whether your idea can satisfy a need in the marketplace. People willingly work hard doing something they love, and the experience will

HITS & MISSES

Segway: Has a "Sure Thing" Failed?

At what point does a good idea admit defeat? Originally intended to become a popular means of human transportation, the two-wheeled motorized scooter known as the Segway, brainchild of entrepreneur and inventor Dean Kamen, has been on the market only a few years. But it has already been banned from sidewalks as a safety hazard in San Francisco. Kamen says 41 states allow the use of motorized scooters on sidewalks, and with its gyroscopic stabilizers, highly responsive steering, and top speed of only 12 miles per hour, the Segway may not seem particularly dangerous to users or pedestrians, although a photograph of President Bush falling off a Segway was widely circulated.

But despite its apparent utility and quiet electric motor, the Segway has only about 10,000 users to date. It's expensive, costing $3,000 to $5,000 depending on the model. An early version was recalled, and distribution was at first limited to Amazon.com, which precluded test driving and may have limited sales. There are now 20 Segway retail outlets, and the company plans to expand that number and launch a new marketing campaign to reposition the scooter as "fun, smart transportation." But the general public doesn't seem that interested. Several local police departments and post offices have already tried the Segway, with mixed results. "You can't keep warm if you're not walking," says one postal worker. "You end up like a frozen Popsicle on a stick." Some consumer advocates worry that the Segway may cause accidents or encourage obesity. And it doesn't keep the rider dry, nor can it carry much besides the rider. Says one industry consultant, "I will be stunned if I ever look down the street and see 30 two-wheeled utility devices coming at me. But I could be wrong."

If it does not become a form of mainstream transport, however, the Segway may not be quite dead yet. It has some enthusiastic users among the elderly, who find it a boon for running errands and getting around town, and among the handicapped, who list many benefits in addition to increased mobility. Being at "human being height" instead of sitting in a wheelchair is one reason Disability Rights Advocates for Technology promotes use of the Segway. Improved digestion and circulation and the ability to focus on other things besides the struggle to walk are additional pluses. "There are people whose disabilities are rendered almost invisible by using the Segway," said Jerry Kerr, a disabled Segway user. Although the Segway has not been approved as a medical device, several hundred disabled users have already paid for the scooter and await an opinion from the U.S. Department of Transportation about permitted use under the Americans with Disabilities Act.

The disabled represent an "unsought market," according to Segway. Says one multiple sclerosis sufferer who rides his Segway to and from his office in Manhattan every day, "My life depends on that darn thing."

QUESTIONS FOR CRITICAL THINKING

1. Do you think the Segway is a failure? Why or why not? Does knowing that competing scooters are entering the market change your opinion? Why or why not?
2. What other unsought markets do you think the company could explore?

Sources: Rachel Metz, "Oft-Scorned Segway Finds Friends among the Disabled," *The New York Times,* October 14, 2004, http://www.nytimes.com; Jim Edwards, "With Competitor on Heels, Segway Says, 'Get Moving,'" *Adweek,* June 7, 2004, p. 8; "Disney Town Teems with Segways," *The New York Times,* February 9, 2003, http://www.nytimes.com; Faith Keenan, "Is Segway Going Anywhere?" *BusinessWeek,* January 27, 2003, p. 42; Angela Watercutter, "San Francisco Bans High-Tech Segway Scooters," *Mobile Register,* January 20, 2003, p. 9A.

---

bring personal fulfillment. The old adages "Do what makes you happy" and "To thine own self be true" are the best guidelines for deciding on a business idea.

Success also depends on customers, so would-be entrepreneurs must also be sure that the idea they choose has interest in the marketplace. The most successful entrepreneurs tend to operate in industries where a great deal of change is taking place and in which customers have difficulty pinpointing their precise needs. These industries, including advanced technology and consulting, allow entrepreneurs to capitalize on their strengths, such as creativity, hard work, and tolerance of ambiguity, to build customer relationships. Nevertheless, examples of outstanding success occur in every industry, from fast-growing companies with high-demand products like Krispy Kreme Donuts to retailers like upscale "cheap chic" discounter Target. According to one study, about 3 to 5 percent of the companies in any industry are growing exceptionally fast, so entrepreneurs do not need to limit their sights to industries characterized by rapid growth. The study advises entrepreneurs to be not only the best but also innovative and different.

The following guidelines may help you to select an idea that represents a good entrepreneurial opportunity:

- List your interests and abilities. Include your values and beliefs, your goals and dreams, things you like and dislike doing, and your job experiences.
- Make another list of the types of businesses that match your interests and abilities.
- Read newspapers and business and consumer magazines to learn about demographic and economic trends that identify future needs for products that no one yet offers.
- Carefully evaluate existing goods and services, looking for ways you can improve them.
- Decide on a business that matches what you want and offers profit potential.
- Conduct marketing research to determine whether your business idea will attract enough customers to earn a profit.
- Learn as much as you can about the industry in which your new venture will operate, your merchandise or service, and your competitors. Read surveys that project growth in various industries.

Like Kenny Kramm, whose medication-flavoring business was described earlier, many entrepreneurs start businesses to solve problems that they experienced either at work or in their personal lives. Others are more methodical in their search for business ideas. Cherrill Farnsworth actually studies government regulations to look for new business ideas. In the 1970s, she operated a bus franchise in Houston. After selling Suburban Transportation Co. to the city of Houston, Farnsworth evaluated her experience. She concluded that she had a talent for putting deals together, so she started and ran three different equipment-leasing businesses that profited from tax regulations, including investment tax credits. In the 1980s, Farnsworth identified an opportunity in a then-new medical technology, magnetic resonance imaging. Medicare did not yet reimburse hospitals for MRI scans, so hospitals didn't want to buy the equipment. Farnsworth launched a chain of centers providing MRI services. A decade later, she spotted another trend in medical care, a new interest in managed care. Building on her experience with the MRI centers, Farnsworth founded HealthHelp, which manages radiology services for HMOs and insurance companies. She has built Houston-based HealthHelp into one of the nation's fastest-growing small businesses, with almost $15 million in sales. Says Farnsworth of her skill at identifying and developing opportunities, "I used to think that entrepreneurship was more an art than a science, that it was a gift of something. I don't believe that anymore."[57]

An inventor-entrepreneur will need to protect the rights to the invention by securing a patent for it. At its Web site (http://www.uspto.gov), the U.S. Patent and Trademark Office provides information about this process, along with forms to apply for a patent. Since 2000, inventors have been able to apply for a patent online at this Web site.

Wayne Huizenga exemplifies an entrepreneur with a nose for a good business idea. He has started three ventures that ended up on the *Fortune* 1000 list, as described in the Best Business Practices box.

Buying an Existing Business   Some entrepreneurs prefer to buy established businesses rather than assume the risks of starting new ones. Buying an existing business brings many advantages: Employees already in place serve established customers and deal with familiar suppliers, the good or service is known in the marketplace, and the necessary permits and licenses have already been secured. Getting financing for an existing business also is easier than it is for most start-ups. Some sellers may even help the buyers by providing financing and offering to serve as consultants.

To find businesses for sale, contact your local Chamber of Commerce as well as professionals such as lawyers, accountants, and insurance agents. It is important to analyze the performance of businesses under consideration. Most people want to buy a healthy business so that they can build on its success. Masoud M. Anwarzai bought Marathon Runner Courier Service with the help of an SBA-guaranteed loan. The lender, Heller Financial, not only was willing to approve the loan for the purchase but also encouraged Anwarzai to borrow enough to establish a pool of working capital. Heller was impressed both with Anwarzai's own credit history and the business's solid finances.[58]

In contrast, turnaround entrepreneurs enjoy the challenge of buying unprofitable firms and making enough improvement in their operations to generate new profits. Pacific Cycles chose this route by recently purchasing bankrupt Schwinn/GT Bicycle Co. Success with a turnaround strategy requires that the entrepreneur have definite and practical ideas about how to operate the business more profitably.

BEST BUSINESS PRACTICES

Entrepreneur Creates Three Companies that Make the *Fortune* 1000

Wayne Huizenga is the first entrepreneur to put three companies, built from the ground up, on the *Fortune* 1000 list: Waste Management, a multinational trash-hauling firm that grew from a single truck; Blockbuster, which Huizenga later sold to Viacom for $8.4 billion worth of stock; and AutoNation, which unifies car dealerships under one management structure and earns nearly $20 billion a year. As a sideline, Huizenga bought the Florida Marlins—and watched them become World Series champions.

Huizenga's first move in creating each of his highly successful firms—and they are not the only businesses he has operated—was to identify unmet needs among a specific group of customers. When the video rental business was new, for example, it was served by thousands of individual "mom and pop" stores that were understocked and often poorly run. Unifying them, stocking them with thousands more tapes, and standardizing them to strengthen a recognizable brand seemed to Huizenga like an obvious untapped opportunity, and Blockbuster took off.

Speed matters, too. "We always try to move quickly to offer a service that no one else is providing," Huizenga says. How does an entrepreneur define speed? Of Blockbuster he says, "We opened a lot of stores in a short period. Over seven years, while I was there, we opened one store every 17 hours on average. The whole deal was to move quickly before our competition saw what we were doing."

Another hallmark of Huizenga's successful approach to creating new businesses was to concentrate on service businesses, because demand is often more stable than in a product-oriented or manufacturing business. His firms have also been built on rental income—from videos, trash containers, and so on. Although he notes that start-up costs are high, Huizenga says "the payoff can also be huge. At Blockbuster we were making, on average, 26 to 28 percent pretax profits in our stores."

But when it comes to pricing, Huizenga offers this advice: "It's better to have more customers than to raise the price. It all gets back to the notion that if you're going to do something and be successful, you have to be the low-cost provider."

QUESTIONS FOR CRITICAL THINKING

1. Which of Huizenga's entrepreneurial strategies do you think can apply to a small-business entrepreneur? Why or how?
2. Do you think being a low-cost provider always means offering the lowest dollar price? Explain.

Sources: "Huizenga Holdings, Inc. Company Profile," *Yahoo! Finance*, http://biz.yahoo.com/, accessed October 12, 2004; "H. Wayne Huizenga," Miami Dolphins Web site, www.miamidolphins.com/, accessed October 12, 2004; Dean Foust, "A Round with Wayne Huizenga," *BusinessWeek*, June 2, 2003, www.businessweek.com; Justin Martin, "Wayne's World," *Fortune*, May 12, 2003, pp. F144[B]–F144[D].

Buying a Franchise   Like buying an established business, a franchise offers a less risky way to begin a business than starting an entirely new firm. But as the previous chapter pointed out, franchising still involves risks. You must do your homework, carefully analyzing the franchisor's fees and capabilities for delivering the support it promises. Energetic preparation helps to ensure that your business will earn a profit and grow.

Creating a Business Plan

Traditionally, most entrepreneurs launched their ventures without creating formal business plans. Although planning is an integral part of managing in the world of 21st-century business, entrepreneurs typically seize opportunities as they arise and change course as necessary. Flexibility seems to be the key to business start-ups, especially in rapidly changing markets. Six in 10 of the most recent *Inc.* 500 CEOs did not create a formal written plan before launching their companies. Entrepreneurial researcher Amar Bhidé attributes that surprising fact to the types of businesses that today's entrepreneurs start. When businesspeople do not need a large amount of cash to start their businesses, they often do not need financing from outside sources—which almost always require plans. Also, the rapid pace of change in some industries reduces the benefit of writing a plan. He comments, "If [Bill Gates and Paul Allen of Microsoft] had tried to do a competitive analysis or a customer analysis, they wouldn't have known who their competitors were or been able to do the classic comparison of strengths and weaknesses vis-à-vis their competition. And they wouldn't have known who their customers were. . . .

When things are changing rapidly, there isn't data."[59] Still, when an entrepreneur needs additional funds to start or grow a business, a business plan is indispensable.

Although the planning process for entrepreneurs differs from a major company's planning function, today's entrepreneurs are advised to construct business plans following the guidelines presented in Chapters 5 and 8. Careful planning helps the entrepreneur prepare enough resources and stay focused on key objectives, and it also provides an important tool for convincing potential investors and employees that the enterprise has the ingredients for success. Entrepreneurial business plans vary depending on the type of start-up, but the basic elements of such a plan—stating company goals, outlining sales and marketing strategies, and determining financial needs and sources of funds—apply to all types of ventures. The Internet also offers a variety of resources for creating business plans. Table 6.1 lists some of these online resources.

Finding Financing

seed capital initial funding needed to launch a new venture.

A key issue in any business plan is financing. How much money will you need to start your business and where will you get it? Requirements for **seed capital**, funds used to launch a company, depend on the nature of your business and the type of facilities and equipment you need. Among the nation's fastest-growing small businesses, 41 percent launched their businesses with $10,000 or less. The amount of money at start-up was not related to the ultimate success of the company, but it did relate to the size of the company. Companies with seed capital of $100,000 or more employed on average 150 people and generated roughly $21 million in sales. Predictably, entrepreneurs starting with less than $1,000 ran smaller businesses, then grew them into larger businesses—employing an average of 56 people and generating $13 million in sales.[60]

The vast majority of entrepreneurs rely on personal savings, advances on credit cards, and money from partners, family members, and friends to fund their start-ups. After leaving a start-up with several partners, Lisa Johnson started a second business by opening Studio Elle, a Brookline, Massachusetts, fitness studio, with $3,000 in credit cards, a $7,000 bank loan, and $10,000 from her mother. Her passion was Pilates, an exercise first developed in the 1920s and recently made fashionable by celebrities like Julia Roberts. It quickly became a favorite of Brookline fitness enthusiasts, generating 2002 earnings of $215,000. And, yes, she paid back her mother.[61]

debt financing borrowed funds that entrepreneurs must repay.

Debt Financing   When entrepreneurs like Lisa Johnson use **debt financing**, they borrow money that they must repay. Loans from banks, finance companies, credit card companies, and family and friends are all sources of debt financing. Although many entrepreneurs charge business expenses to personal credit cards because they are relatively easy to obtain, high interest rates make this source of

Table 6.1	Online Resources for Preparing a Business Plan
Allbusiness.com http://www.allbusiness.com	The "Business Advice" page provides links to examples, templates, and tips for writing a plan.
American Express http://www.americanexpress.com	Click the "Small Businesses" tab, locate the "Inform Your Decisions" section, and access the "Explore business articles and tools" link, which provides information about business planning.
EntreWorld http://www.entreworld.org	The "Starting Your Business" section has links to information and resources for researching and writing a plan, as well as presenting it to lenders or investors.
Morebusiness.com http://www.morebusiness.com	To see a sample plan, select "Business & Marketing Plans" from the list of templates.

funding expensive. Annual interest charges on a credit card can run as high as 20 percent, while rates for a home equity loan (borrowing against the value of a home) currently run less than 5 percent. In exchange for a lower interest rate, borrowers with a home equity loan pledge the value of their home, so if the borrower does not repay the loan, he or she risks losing the home.

Still, credit card financing may be a viable option for entrepreneurs who expect to grow quickly and know that they can pay off their debt in a short time. Once the company has passed the start-up phase, entrepreneurs may continue to use credit cards for purchases they can pay off quickly. Herbert J. Mallet obtained an American Express card for his business, Broudy Printing. He uses the corporate card to buy paper and other supplies. Depending on the time of the month in which he purchases the supplies, this arrangement gives him up to 50 days before he has to pay the bill without incurring interest charges. Because the card enables Broudy Printing to pay its suppliers quickly, the company even gets a discount this way. But Mallet cautions entrepreneurs not to resort to a credit card unless they are sure they can pay on time: "If you don't have the cash flow to pay off your bills each month, and you get sucked into those [late-payment] penalties, you're going to wind up going down a dark, bleak road."[62]

Many banks turn down requests for loans to fund start-ups, fearful of the high risk such ventures entail. Only a small percentage of start-ups raise seed capital through bank loans, although some new firms can get SBA-backed loans, as discussed in Chapter 5. The challenge has historically been even greater for entrepreneurs who are women or ethnic minorities. As noted in the previous chapter, minority-owned businesses are less likely than white-owned businesses to have bank loans. Some simply wait to start their businesses until they can acquire enough capital without borrowing. Women, too, report that they have been taken less seriously than their male counterparts when they seek debt financing. Lisa Argiris was disappointed with her borrowing experiences as founder of International Musical Suppliers. She quickly secured a $50,000 line of credit to launch her mail-order musical instruments company, but the bank resisted when she wanted to borrow additional funds to expand her business into the more profitable realm of instrument rentals. After considerable frustration, Argiris concluded, "My bank was really just interested in supporting me because of my public-relations value to them—as a minority and female business owner—not because they really understood or believed in my business concept." She took her business elsewhere, eventually arranging $1 million in loans from Citibank.[63]

Like Argiris, persistent women and minorities are finding loans, as lenders begin to appreciate their significance as business founders. Some institutions, including First Union Bank, Fleet Bank, and Wells Fargo Bank, have even begun to tailor offerings to female entrepreneurs. Also, as noted in the preceding chapter, the Small Business Administration has programs designed to help female and minority entrepreneurs get financing.[64]

> ## *They Said It*
> The only thing tainted about money is it "taint mine" or "taint enough."
> —*Anonymous*

Applying for a bank loan requires careful preparation. Bank loan officers want to see a business plan and will evaluate the entrepreneur's credit history. Since a start-up has not yet established a business credit history, banks often base lending decisions on evaluations of entrepreneurs' personal credit histories. Banks are more willing to make loans to entrepreneurs who've been in business for a while, show a profit on rising revenues, and need funds to finance expansion. Some entrepreneurs have found that local community banks are more interested in their loan applications than the giant national banks are.

Equity Financing

To secure **equity financing,** entrepreneurs exchange a share of ownership in their company for money supplied by one or more investors. Entrepreneurs invest their own money along with funds supplied by other people and firms that become co-owners of the start-ups. An entrepreneur does not have to repay equity funds. Rather, the investors share in the success of the business. Sources of equity financing include family and friends, business partners, venture capital firms, and private investors.

Teaming up with a partner who has funds to invest may benefit an entrepreneur with a good idea and skills but little or no money. Investors may also have business experience, which they will be eager to share because the company's prosperity will benefit them.

Like borrowing, equity financing has its drawbacks. One is that investment partners may not agree on the future direction of the business, and in the case of partnerships, if they cannot resolve

equity financing funds invested in new ventures in exchange for part ownership.

disputes, one partner may have to buy out the other to keep operating. Thomas Santamorena, CEO of TLS Service Bureau, a company specializing in legal, corporate, and insurance investigations, faced that problem with his two partners. After initial strong growth, the company stalled, and Santamorena was worried that 80 percent of the firm's revenues came from only 20 percent of its clients. He thought it would be best to expand the company's client base, but his partners were happy with the status quo. He did manage to persuade one partner of the need for growth, but those two partners had to buy out the third partner's interest in the company after much conflict. Concerning partnerships, Santamorena says he would "look for another alternative" if he had to do it over again.[65]

venture capitalists business firm or group of individuals who invest in new and growing firms.

Venture capitalists are business organizations or groups of private individuals that invest in new and growing firms. These investors expect to receive high rates of return, typically more than 30 percent, within short time periods of five years or fewer. Consequently, until the recession of the first years of this century, they tended to concentrate their investments in firms in fast-growing industries such as technology and communications. Prior to the widespread failures of many dot.coms in the early years of the 21st century, a sizable portion of venture capital flowed into start-up Internet firms. Although venture capital firms have received a great deal of press coverage, the $30 billion invested during 2002 amounted to a 23 percent decline from the previous year.[66] The reason: Venture capital firms lost as much as one-third of the funds they invested that year. Even then, the $20 billion venture capitalists invest annually flows to a very limited number of businesses. Less than one-tenth of firms receiving funds from venture capitalists are start-ups, and most of the remainder are high-tech firms.[67]

angel investors wealthy individuals who invest directly in a new venture in exchange for an equity stake.

A larger source of investors in start-ups consists of angel investors. **Angel investors** are wealthy individuals willing to invest money directly in new ventures in return for equity stakes. They invest more capital in start-ups than do venture capitalists. In contrast to venture capitalists, angels focus primarily on new ventures. Many angel investors are themselves successful entrepreneurs who want to help aspiring business owners through the familiar difficulties of launching their businesses. Angel investors back a wide variety of new ventures. Some invest exclusively in certain industries, others invest only in start-ups with socially responsible missions, and still others prefer to back only women entrepreneurs.[68]

Because most entrepreneurs have trouble finding wealthy private investors, angel networks form to match business angels with start-ups in need of capital. WomenAngels.net targets female entrepreneurs. The Small Business Administration's Angel Capital Electronic Network (ACE-Net) provides online listings to connect would-be angels with small businesses seeking financing. Similar networks try to expand the old-boy network of venture capitalists to new investors and entrepreneurs as well. Venture capitalists that focus on women include the Women's Growth Capital Fund (http://www.wgcf.com) and Viridian Capital (http://www.viridian-capital.com).

As entrepreneurs start their businesses, they spend much of their time seeking and securing financing. Most company founders perform all the activities needed to operate their businesses because they don't have enough money to hire additional employees. The majority of entrepreneurs begin as sole proprietors working from their homes. After their initial start-up periods, however, entrepreneurs must make many management decisions as their companies begin to grow. They must establish legal entities, buy equipment, choose facilities and locations, assemble teams of employees, and ensure compliance with a host of government regulations. These challenges will be discussed in other chapters throughout this book.

Concept Check

1. What are the two most important considerations in choosing an idea for a new business?
2. What is the purpose of a patent?
3. What is seed capital?

Intrapreneurship

intrapreneurship process of promoting innovation within the structure of an existing organization.

Large, established companies try to retain the entrepreneurial spirit by encouraging **intrapreneurship,** the process of promoting innovation within their organizational structures. Today's fast-changing business climate compels large firms to innovate continually to maintain their competitive advantages.

Entrepreneurial environments created within companies such as 3M, Thermo Electron, Xerox, and Intuit can help these larger firms retain valuable employees who might otherwise leave their jobs to start their own businesses.

Large companies support intrapreneurial activity in varied ways. One leader in this area, 3M Corp., has established companywide policies and procedures that give employees personal freedom to explore new products and technologies. 3M allows its researchers to spend 15 percent of their time working on their own ideas without approval from management. The company's hiring process is designed to select innovative people. Using a personality profile of characteristics shared by its top creative scientists, 3M has crafted questions and scenarios that help company interviewers gauge the creative skills of job candidates. In addition to traditional product development, 3M implements two intrapreneurial approaches: skunkworks and pacing programs. A **skunkworks** project is initiated by an employee who conceives an idea and then recruits resources from within 3M to turn it into a commercial product. Pacing programs are company-initiated projects that focus on a few products and technologies in which 3M sees potential for rapid marketplace winners. The company provides financing, equipment, and people to support such pacing projects.

Intrapreneurship is not limited to giant firms. Elite Information Systems, a Los Angeles-based marketer of billing software, let its chief technology officer, Mark Goldin, switch from his managerial position to the role of intrapreneur. Goldin was planning to leave Elite to start a company offering access to time and billing software over the Internet. However, Elite agreed to let him stay on the payroll and start his business as an operation within Elite. Because Elite lacked the resources of a giant like 3M, it required Goldin to obtain approval for his strategy within two months. Offsetting that challenge, the company contributed managerial talent as well as office space and money. When Goldin obtained approval for Elite.com, management supplied needed funding to get his enterprise going in less than half a year. This time line reflected the start-up's distinctive culture within Elite; normally, the company spends two years developing new software. Under severe time pressure, Goldin benefited from his knowledge of the company's human resources and customers, as well as the free rein management has allowed him outside the time constraints. So far, Goldin has succeeded in bringing Elite.com online; the next step facing him is to make the company within a company profitable.[69]

Recognizing that entrepreneurial employees often leave to form their own start-ups, some companies actually encourage employees to take the plunge. The Walt Disney Co. is an icon of creativity, and many of its creative people leave to start businesses on their own. Among them is Jake Winebaum, formerly president of Walt Disney Magazine Publishing and intrapreneurial founder of Disney Online. While at Disney, he loved the climate of innovation in which he ran Disney.com, ABCNews.com, ESPN.com, and Go.com. He found the process of starting these operations inside Disney very similar to the process of starting a new company. In fact, the experience reminded him how much he loved being an entrepreneur, and he left to start a business incubator called eCompanies, with the goal of helping businesses move from ideas to operating businesses within a few months' time. Winebaum credits Disney with helping him learn how to identify business ideas with good potential.[70]

Concept Check
1. Why would large companies support intrapreneurship?
2. What is a skunkworks?
3. What are pacing programs?

What's Ahead

The next chapter turns to a realm of business in which many entrepreneurs have been active during the past decade: electronic commerce, or business use of the Internet. The chapter describes the technology behind electronic commerce. It introduces the challenges and opportunities available to entrepreneurs and other businesspeople who want to communicate with and sell to customers on the Internet. Not many years ago, Internet technology was a novelty except among high-tech firms and tech-savvy individuals. Today, it is an integral factor in starting and growing a business.

DID YOU KNOW?

1. U.S. entrepreneurs have even managed to sell snowplows to the desert dwellers of Saudi Arabia. The machines are used to remove sand from driveways.
2. Spike Lee financed his first film using his credit card.
3. A recent survey found that African Americans are more likely than Caucasians to try to start new companies.
4. Small businesses produce more than half of all innovations.
5. Despite the growth of Starbucks, the number of independent coffee shops has grown by nearly 8 percent since 2000.

Summary of Learning Goals

1 **Define the term *entrepreneur* and distinguish among entrepreneurs, small-business owners, and managers.**
Unlike many small-business owners, entrepreneurs typically own and run their businesses with the goal of building significant firms that create wealth and add jobs. Entrepreneurs are visionaries. They identify opportunities and take the initiative to gather the resources they need to start their businesses quickly. Both managers and entrepreneurs use the resources of their companies to achieve the goals of those organizations.

2 **Identify three different types of entrepreneurs.**
The three categories are classic entrepreneurs, intrapreneurs, and change agents. A classic entrepreneur identifies a business opportunity and allocates available resources to tap that market. An intrapreneur is an employee who develops a new idea or product within the context of an organizational position. A change agent is a manager who tries to revitalize an existing firm to make it a competitive success.

3 **Explain why people choose to become entrepreneurs.**
People choose this kind of career for many different reasons. Reasons most frequently cited include desires to be your own boss, to achieve financial success, to gain job security, and to improve one's quality of life.

4 **Discuss conditions that encourage opportunities for entrepreneurs.**
A favorable public perception, availability of financing, the falling cost and widespread availability of information technology, globalization, entrepreneurship education, and changing demographic and economic trends all contribute to a fertile environment for people to start new ventures.

5 **Describe the role of entrepreneurs in the economy.**
Entrepreneurs play a significant role in the economy as a major source of innovation and job creation. Entrepreneurship also provides many opportunities for women and minorities, who may encounter limits to their progress in established businesses.

6 **Identify personality traits that typically characterize successful entrepreneurs.**
Successful entrepreneurs share several typical traits, including vision, high energy levels, need to achieve, self-confidence and optimism, tolerance for failure, creativity, tolerance for ambiguity, and internal locus of control.

7 **Summarize the process of starting a new venture.**
Entrepreneurs must select an idea for their business, develop a business plan, obtain financing, and organize the resources they need to operate their start-ups.

8 **Explain how organizations promote intrapreneurship.**
Organizations encourage intrapreneurial activity within the company in a variety of ways. Hiring practices, dedicated programs such as skunkworks, access to resources, and wide latitude to innovate encourage intrapreneurship within established firms.

Business Terms You Need to Know

entrepreneur 196

classic entrepreneur 198

intrapreneur 198

change agent 198

seed capital 220

debt financing 220

equity financing 221

venture capitalist 222

angel investor 222

intrapreneurship 222

Other Important Business Terms

gazelles 208

skunkworks 223

Review Questions

1. What are the differences among entrepreneurs, small-business owners, and managers? What are the similarities?

2. Identify the three categories of entrepreneurs. How are they different from each other?

3. What are the four major reasons for becoming an entrepreneur?

4. How have globalization and information technology created new opportunities for entrepreneurs?

5. In what ways do entrepreneurs influence the overall economy?

6. Identify the eight characteristics that are attributed to successful entrepreneurs. Which trait or traits do you believe are the most important for success? Why?

7. What are the benefits and risks involved in buying an existing business or a franchise?

8. Why is creating a business plan an important step for an entrepreneur?

9. Describe the different types of financing that entrepreneurs may seek for their businesses. What are the risks and benefits involved with each?

10. What is intrapreneurship? How does it differ from entrepreneurship?

Projects and Applications

1. Think of an entrepreneur whom you admire or choose one of the following: Bill Gates of Microsoft, Jeff Bezos of Amazon.com, or Oprah Winfrey of Harpo Productions. Explain why you admire this entrepreneur, including ways in which the person has contributed to his or her industry as well as the economy.

2. Current demographic and economic trends support entrepreneurs who are creating new businesses. One of these trends is the willingness of Americans to spend more money on certain goods and services, such as pet care. On your own or with a classmate, brainstorm a trend that may be a good idea for a new business. Write one or two paragraphs describing the trend and how it could be applied to a business.

3. Review the eight characteristics of successful entrepreneurs. Which characteristics do you possess? Do you think

you would be a good entrepreneur? Why? Write a paragraph or two listing your strengths.

4. Think of an innovative product recently introduced by an existing company—a company that has used intrapreneurship. How does the new product fit within the scope of the company's existing products? Do some research in the library or on the Internet to see how successful the new idea is and how it was brought to life. Be ready to explain your findings.

5. Many entrepreneurs are motivated by working in an area they love. Think about something you love to do that you believe could be turned into a business. What aspect of the activity would actually be turned into a business? For example, if you love to play golf or shop at vintage clothing stores for 1970s-style attire, how would you shape this interest into a business?

Experiential Exercise

Background: As noted in the chapter, creating a business plan is an important step in creating or growing a successful new business. It helps convince potential investors, financial lenders, and company employees that the enterprise has the ingredients for success. The basic elements of a business plan include a statement of company goals, an outline of sales and marketing strategies, and an overview of financing needs and sources of needed funds.

Directions: Put yourself in the role of an aspiring entrepreneur who would like to start a business. Decide what goods or services the business will provide and write a general business plan for your new enterprise. Prepare a brief oral report and a two-page paper summarizing your plan. You can refer to one or more of the following online tools available to help you write your business:

http://www.americanexpress.com
(click "Small Businesses" tab)

http://www.entreworld.org
(go to the section "Starting Your Business")

http://www.inc.com/guides

http://www.morebusiness.com
(select "Business & Marketing Plans" from the list of templates)

NOTHING BUT NET

1. **Profiles of young entrepreneurs.** Check out the Web site listed below. It contains a vast amount of resources for would-be entrepreneurs, especially younger ones. Click the section labeled "Profiles" and read about some recent success stories. What did all of these entrepreneurs have in common?

   http://www.highschoolstartups.com

2. **Venture capital.** As the chapter points out, venture capital is an important source of funding for entrepreneurs. Visit the two Web sites listed below and answer the following questions:
   a. For the most recent year for which you can find data, what was the level of venture capital financing? What was the size of the average venture capital investment? What trends are evident from the data?
   b. Which industries currently have the heaviest concentration of venture capital financing? Have the favorite industries changed in recent years?

   http://www.nvca.org/ffax.html

   http://www.ventureeconomics.com

3. **Business-friendly cities.** Visit the Web site listed below. Read about the 50 best small and large cities for starting a new business. What are the top five small and large cities? What do these cities seem to have in common?

   http://www.inc.com

   Note: Internet Web addresses change frequently. If you do not find the exact sites listed, you may need to access the organization's or company's home page and search from there.

Case 6.1

Pita Chips on a Pittance: Business on a Budget

How does an entrepreneurial venture grow from $25,000 in annual sales to $1.3 million? All it takes is a great product, effective—and frugal—management, and hard work. Plus a little luck.

Cofounders and CEOs of tiny Stacy's Pita Chip Co., Mark and Stacy Andrus, were headed for careers in psychology and social work when both of them suddenly realized what they both really wanted to do: cook. The two started as pushcart hot dog vendors in their native New England but soon moved to Boston's financial district, where they changed their menu to fresh pita wraps with gourmet fillings. They sold out the first day and soon were selling 200 sandwiches a day in a brief two-hour time period around midday mealtime.

Oddly enough, it was customers waiting in lines of up to 40 people who inspired Mark with a winning idea. To keep them from wandering away, he began to recycle each day's leftovers, baking the extra pitas with toppings like cinnamon sugar or parmesan cheese and garlic to hand out the following day. Soon people were lining up for the crisp, low-fat chips.

Investors offered to help expand the sandwich business, but after doing some research, the couple decided their company would grow faster if they could mass-produce the chips and sell them in areas far beyond their Boston origins. Except for the ingredients, which were always top quality, chip production was low tech and low budget. A chance conversation led to cheap rented space in a bakery, where they sliced, seasoned, baked, bagged, and labeled pita chips by hand during the other tenant's downtime. After investing in packaging machinery one piece at a time, production became more efficient, and the Andruses gave up the pushcart to focus on the chip venture.

Money for expansion, new equipment, and a paint-it-yourself office space came from an SBA-backed loan program for women in business—the firm was registered in Stacy's name for that purpose—and from revenues plowed back into the company. When the Andruses needed an automatic slicer, rather than spend $100,000 for a custom design, they continued to cut pitas by hand and went to equipment auctions for a year until they found a 40-year-old carrot-cutting machine for $18,000. Mark retooled it, and every chip they make still goes through it.

Staff at Stacy's Pita Chip Co. has grown to 15, but operations are still frugal. Stacy's brother joined the firm and earns $7 an hour plus a share of profits. Stacy and Mark pay themselves minimal salaries despite earning two entrepreneurial awards, one from the White House. For business advice, they rely on a network of friends and unofficial mentors in the industry. Students at Babson College built and maintain the Stacy's Pita Chip Web site. Stacy travels to trade shows and cooking demonstrations to promote the chips in person instead of relying on expensive advertising, and Mark can often be found in supermarkets doing marketing research. The chips have been served at the Super Bowl and recommended by Weight Watchers, two strokes of luck the company could never have paid for. The company continues to thrive and grow, even after the founders' recent divorce.

QUESTIONS FOR CRITICAL THINKING

1. How has Mark and Stacy Andrus's attention to cost cutting contributed to the success of their firm? Do you think they should apply the same frugality to purchasing chip ingredients? Why or why not?

2. What else do you think Stacy's Pita Chips could do to promote its products? Be specific.

Sources: Stacy's Pita Chip Web site, http://www.pitachip.com, accessed January 23, 2004; "Metro South Chamber of Commerce Action Report," http://www.metrosouthchamber.com, accessed January 25, 2004; Anne Stuart, "The Pita Principle," *Inc.*, August 2001, pp. 58–64.

Video Case 6.2

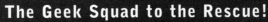

The Geek Squad to the Rescue!

This video case appears on page 607. A recently filmed video, designed to expand and highlight the written case, is available for class use by instructors.

Chapter 7
Electronic Commerce: The Internet and Online Business

Learning Goals

1 *Discuss how the Internet provides new routes to business success.*

2 *Describe the increasing diversity of Internet users.*

3 *Summarize the Internet's four functions and provide examples of each.*

4 *List the major forms of business-to-business (B2B) and business-to-consumer (B2C) e-commerce.*

5 *Describe some challenges associated with Internet selling.*

6 *List the steps involved in developing successful Web sites.*

7 *Identify methods for measuring Web site effectiveness.*

8 *Explain how global opportunities result from technological advances.*

Online Grocers Are Ready to Deliver

It's hard to disagree with the notion that people like convenience. But how much will they pay for it? Would you rather make a trip to the store for a dozen uncracked eggs, or order them online while you commute home with your laptop and receive a carton with at least half the eggs broken?

After several such experiences, online grocery shopper Betsy Cummings nearly gave up. "There is a huge tradeoff to pay for convenience," she says. But one Internet specialist persuasively points out that "people don't have time to shop or cook anymore. They're starting to catch on to how convenient it is to shop for food online. With a laptop you can shop from your office, car, school, wherever. Convenience is the No. 1 reason why people shop the Net."

Online grocers are more poised than ever to take advantage of that opportunity and make healthy inroads into the nearly $450 billion U.S. grocery market. The first attempt—by now-defunct Webvan—failed a few years ago, and even today online grocery shopping accounts for less than 1 percent of total grocery revenue in the U.S. and less than 6 percent of total online retail sales.

© Tim Boyle/Getty Images

More people have Internet access at home or at work than ever before. Three of four Americans can now shop online, and two of five Internet-connected homes in the U.S. have high-speed connections that make using the Internet an easier and faster experience. Notably, more and more women are surfing the Internet, and women already make most food and household purchases for their families. The majority of Internet shoppers now have few concerns about security and privacy when shopping, making them more willing to conduct personal business online, as the surge in online banking demonstrates. Finally, significant technology innovations have helped improve the services offered by online grocers can offer. Better Web site design, more highly automated warehouses, and increased investment in online businesses have all strengthened the incentive to shop online.

"We're about food at reasonable prices," says New York-based FreshDirect's marketing vice president. "We're not techies." That user-friendly attitude may be one reason FreshDirect has about 160,000 customers, mostly families and single professionals, placing 25,000 orders a week from its online assortment of 5,000 perishable and 3,000 packaged items.

With its fresh-baked breads and pies and home-roasted coffee, FreshDirect is only one of the online grocers striving to differentiate itself in this growing market. Peapod appeals to dual-income couples and young moms, and it brings them large quantities of fresh produce, as well as organic and low-carb items. Safeway's customers tend to order basics and nonperishables; its drivers undergo rigorous safety and customer-relations training.

Impromptu Gourmet is carving out a niche within a niche, selling prepared items such as prosciutto-wrapped chicken with Gouda cheese and Cajun precooked turkey to food lovers seeking restaurant-quality food to enjoy at home. Says its senior vice president of competing online grocers, "There's room for everyone. We have our niche, which is not the same as FreshDirect or Peapod." Other specialty retailers include GortonsFreshSeafood.com, which ships fresh seafood through FedEx within 24 hours of the order.

While most consumers still like the store experience—and online grocers don't intend to replace that—some observers feel it's only a matter of time before online grocers become a major force through continued quiet, but persistent, growth. Says the president of a research firm that monitors online customer satisfaction, "We're seeing increased consumer satisfaction across all online retail channels. And if [online jeweler] Blue Nile can sell a $14,000 diamond necklace online, surely Web grocers should be able to sell tomatoes and peas."[1]

Chapter Overview

Increasingly, executives are asking themselves, "What does the Internet, and related technology, mean to me and my business?" The Internet offers 21st-century businesspeople a source of information, a means of communication, and a channel for buying and selling all rolled into one. And the Internet offers tremendous opportunities for those who are willing to make the leap online.

In this chapter, we describe the ways that the Internet is revolutionizing the face of business. We begin with an overview of the Internet, including its origins, scope, and components. Then we describe how individuals and businesses use the Internet. Later, we review electronic commerce and its implications for both businesses and consumers, including how companies use Web sites to further their objectives. The Internet also drives the globalization of business, so we investigate how e-commerce is helping companies take advantage of opportunities around the world.

Internet (Net) worldwide network of interconnected computers that lets anyone with access to a personal computer send and receive images and data anywhere.

World Wide Web (Web) collection of resources on the Internet that offers easy access to text, graphics, sound, and other multimedia resources.

They Said It

The Net is a 10.5 on the Richter scale of economic change.

—*Nicholas Negroponte (b. 1945)*
American writer and director
of the MIT Media Laboratory

The Internet: A Key to Business Success

Want to find the cheapest price for a new car, computer, hotel room, or life insurance policy? Suppose you want to see which demographic groups in the U.S. are growing the fastest but don't know where to look. Just go online. With a few clicks of your mouse, you can find the answer to just about any question. Besides looking up information, you can trade messages with friends and colleagues, join an online discussion, watch previews of upcoming movies, or make purchases. No wonder that the average adult Internet user is expected to devote almost two years of his or her remaining life to online activities.

The Internet began in 1969 as a Department of Defense experiment that involved networking four computers to facilitate communications in the event of a nuclear war. Until the early 1990s, the **Internet** (or **Net**) remained an obscure computer network with few commercial applications. Today, however, this all-purpose, global network allows computer users anywhere to send and receive data, sound, and video content. Its growth has been phenomenal, with host computers more than doubling annually. Worldwide, approximately 500 million people use the Internet.[2] Over half of Americans are online, and this percentage is expected to increase to over 70 percent in the next few years.[3]

A major factor in the Internet's growth was the introduction of technology and software that provided point-and-click access to the **World Wide Web** (or **Web**). The

Web is an interlinked collection of graphically rich information sources within the larger Internet. Web documents are organized into **Web sites** composed of electronic pages that integrate text, graphics, audio, and video elements. The pages include hypertext links, highlighted words or images that, when clicked, whisk the user to other documents. Browsers are software programs that help users navigate the Web to locate, retrieve, and display information. By typing in search words or simply clicking hypertext links, users can explore the Web. The most widely used Web browsers are Netscape Navigator and Microsoft Internet Explorer.

Today, the Web is the most popular Internet resource. From just 100 Web sites in 1993, the scope of the Web has grown to almost 30 million registered domain names.[4] A **domain name** is a Web site address. Although not every domain name has an operating Web site, the incredible increase in only a few years shows that the scope and potential of the Web are enormous.

Online transactions generate hundreds of billions of dollars in revenues. In addition, many types of companies are selling the hardware and software required for Internet use as well as providing support services. Examples include telecommunications companies, computer and electronics manufacturers, software publishers, entertainment and media companies, and service businesses that offer Web site design and specialized software for electronic commerce.

> **Web site** integrated document composed of electronic pages that integrate text, graphics, audio, and video elements, as well as hyptertext links to other documents.

How the Internet Works

The Internet is a remarkable system of cooperating networks. In seconds, you can send e-mail from Pennsylvania to Hong Kong, search the archives of European newspapers, plan your next vacation, gather product information, or buy a best-selling novel.

To understand how this complex system of networks operates, follow the journey of an e-mail message that you send to a friend in a different state. In the example shown in Figure 7.1, your message begins its Internet journey at your personal computer (PC), where it travels through phone lines; modems convert digital data into analog form compatible with the phone lines. The data arrive at the modems of your **Internet service provider (ISP),** an organization that provides access to the Internet through its own series of local networks. Thousands of ISPs offer local Internet access to North American Web surfers.

This process is similar but faster if your friend has newer broadband technology, such as a **Digital Subscriber Line (DSL),** a cable modem, or a satellite link to the Internet. With DSL, data travel over standard telephone lines between computers and telephone switching stations, but a DSL router or modem makes the data move at higher frequencies and much faster speeds. This technology permits voice and DSL transmissions to be sent simultaneously over the same phone line, and the Internet connection is continuous, so the user does not have to dial up for Internet service. A cable connection uses the same line that supplies cable television programming. Satellite hookups have been slower to catch on in the U.S., where phone service is inexpensive and reliable. However, users in other countries have been faster to adopt satellite technology, which allows them to connect to the Internet from a cellular phone as well as a computer. In Finland, more than two-thirds of the people online use cell phones to

> **Internet service provider (ISP)** organization that provides access to the Internet, via a telephone or cable television network.

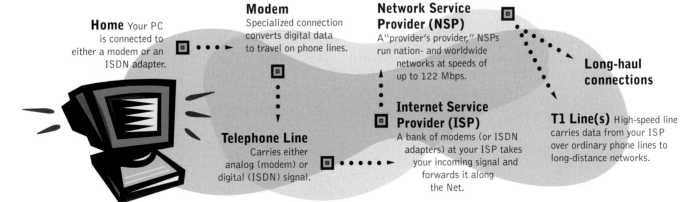

FIGURE 7.1

How Information Travels on the Internet

connect to the Internet and look up information, send e-mail, and even make purchases.[5] But wireless technology is catching on in the U.S. because it offers faster downloading than a standard phone hookup can deliver. Wireless capabilities enable new applications of the Internet, such as General Motors's OnStar dashboard communications system, which lets motorists access the Internet from their cars. Drivers with OnStar can use the Internet to find a local restaurant or the nearest ATM, or get driving directions. OnStar even calls for help if you have a flat tire along the way.

What happens when the message reaches the recipient's ISP network? The answer to this question requires a basic understanding of client/server systems. The message you sent is stored with the ISP's **server,** a larger, special computer that holds information and then provides it to clients on request. A **client** is another computer or device that relies on the resources of one or more servers for help with its own processing. Traditionally, clients have been desktop PCs, but Internet users are increasingly connecting from many other devices, including televisions and cell phones. Servers efficiently distribute resources to a network of client computers as needed. When your friend wants to check his or her e-mail, the message travels back through phone, DSL, or cable lines or via wireless transmission to his or her modem. The ISP functions as the intermediary for its customers. Monthly or hourly user fees cover the cost of equipment such as ISP modems, servers, related software, proprietary and leased networks, and in some cases, original content. The largest ISPs are America Online (AOL), Earthlink, and MSN.

Who's on the Net

Although the Internet was born in the U.S., its users now live on every continent. Today, about 40 percent of Internet users live in the U.S., but the share from other countries is growing. Within the next few years, three of every four Internet users will live outside the U.S.[6] As Figure 7.2 shows, of the world's total Internet users, the four nations with the largest concentration of Net users are the U.S., China, the United Kingdom, and Germany. Recent studies of U.S. Internet users reveal some major trends toward an increasingly diverse Net population:

- Women now make up more than half of U.S. Internet users and an estimated 45 percent of users worldwide. Female users are growing at an even faster rate in Europe and Asia than they are in the U.S.

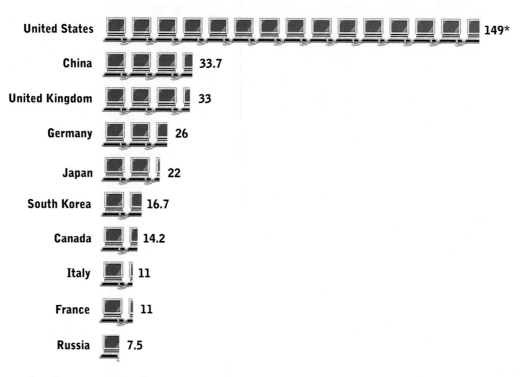

FIGURE 7.2
Top 10 Internet Users

United States	149*
China	33.7
United Kingdom	33
Germany	26
Japan	22
South Korea	16.7
Canada	14.2
Italy	11
France	11
Russia	7.5

*Number of Internet users in millions.

Source: Data from "The World's Online Populations," CyberAtlas Web site, http://www.cyberatlas.internet.com, March 21, 2002.

- U.S. Internet users are still predominantly white or Asian American, but percentages of African American and Hispanic American Internet users are rising.
- Net users tend to be more affluent and to attain higher levels of education than the general population.
- Seniors are the fastest-growing age group on the Internet.[7]

Just as the population of individuals using the Internet is becoming more like the overall population, so is the mix of businesses on the Internet. A Web site once set a company apart as "high tech," but virtually all large businesses have their own Web sites. Small businesses also see the Internet as a key to their success; in a recent poll of U.S. small businesses, two-thirds had integrated the Internet as a tool to help them run their businesses.[8]

Using the Net's Four Functions

As Figure 7.3 illustrates, the four primary functions performed on the Web are communication, information gathering and sharing, entertainment, and business transactions (e-commerce).

Communication   Most people go online to communicate. For both households and businesses, the most popular application of the Internet in the U.S. is **e-mail.** In fact, e-mails now outnumber regular mail by over 10 to one. Its popularity is easy to understand: E-mail is simple to use, travels quickly, and can be read at the receiver's convenience. Also, files—such as Microsoft Office documents—can be easily sent as attachments to e-mail messages.

e-mail electronic messages sent via the Internet.

A more recent adaptation of e-mail is **instant messaging.** With this application, when someone sends a message, it is immediately displayed on the recipient's computer screen. As sender and recipient reply to one another, they can communicate in real time. However, unlike regular e-mail messages, instant messages have to be relatively short—a few sentences at the most.

Other popular ways to communicate are chat rooms and bulletin boards. These methods provide a forum in which a group of people can share information. When someone sends a message, it is displayed for all to see. Users join chat sessions, or messages on bulletin boards, on topics that interest them. The resulting online communities are not only personally satisfying but an important force for business. Many companies participate in or even sponsor such communication. For instance, Symantec's Web site contains several bulletin boards. When a customer has a question or a problem with one of Symantec's products, he or she can send an e-mail directly to Symantec. A technician or customer support representative replies by e-mail to the customer. The original question, as well as the answer, is automatically posted on the appropriate bulletin board. Visitors to the Symantec Web site can search the bulletin boards by entering various key words.

Voice technology and videoconferencing have also come to the Web. Internet telephony allows users to use their computers to dial up and speak to friends and business associates alike. Voice messages and video

FIGURE 7.3
Four Functions of the Internet

images are divided into segments called *packets,* which move over the transmission lines and are reassembled at the receiving end. The quality of both voice and video can still be uneven but is improving.

Businesses also use the Internet to communicate promotional messages. Marketers use the Web to build brand relationships and offer products via e-mail, advertisements, sweepstakes, and more. Use of the Internet as a tool for marketing communications is discussed in Chapter 14.

Information   For many users, getting information is one of the main reasons they go online. Internet users meet their need for information at commercial sites—such as Google and AskJeeves—which search for information on topics entered by the user. Or they may visit online publications like *BusinessWeek, The New York Times,* and *USA Today.* Government sites provide a wealth of free data in the public domain. This information includes governments of foreign countries, such as Hong Kong, where Hewlett-Packard created a Web portal that provides 24-hour access to government services. At the site, Hong Kong citizens can even sign up for volunteer work or book a marriage date.

Newsgroups provide a forum for participants to share information on selected topics. Another fast-growing area of the Internet consists of sites providing online educational services. Over one-third of U.S. colleges now offer some sort of accredited degree online, and private investment in education-related Internet companies more than doubled every year during the past decade.[9]

With such an enormous variety of possibilities, some of the most popular Web sites are **portals,** sites designed to be a user's starting place when entering the World Wide Web. One popular portal is Yahoo!. All portals offer links to search engines, weather reports, news, yellow pages, maps, and other popular types of information, as well as e-mail, chat rooms, and the ability to bookmark favorite sites to click directly in the future. A **search engine** is software that scans the Web to find sites that contain data requested by a user. Three such engines are Google, Infoseek, and AltaVista. Currently, Google is the fourth most popular Web site in the world; about half of all Web searches worldwide are performed by Google, which is translated into 86 different languages. When a user types in a query for information, Google delivers an accurate answer in half a second.[10]

Many sites specialize in particular types of information. For example, Travelocity, Expedia, Orbitz, and a number of other sites search for airline flights, hotels, car rentals, or cruises that meet the user's criteria for date, city, and price. Visitors to the UPS Web site (http://www.ups.com) can check the delivery status of their packages. Other sites offer product reviews, maps and driving directions, stock prices, sports coverage, and much more.

Businesses turn to the Web to gather information about their rivals and to assess industry trends. Executives can visit competitors' Web sites to learn about new-product announcements and check financial reports. They can read trade and business publications online and visit the Web sites of pro-

Hewlett-Packard created a Web portal that provides 24-hour access to government services in countries like Hong Kong.

BUSINESS TOOL KIT

Conducting Online Research

One of the most important skills you will learn in college is how to conduct research. Although researching and writing papers, projects, and dissertations may not be your favorite way to spend an afternoon, the skills you learn *are* transferable to your future job search. Learning how to quickly and efficiently hunt down information about a particular career or company can be invaluable.

The first step is to define your research need. Are you looking for company information such as names, addresses, and telephone numbers? Or do you need to find information about the company's financial status? Have a clear objective before you get online, and be specific in what you are looking for.

Once you have an objective, your particular search strategy will follow. If you want information about the company with which you are interviewing next week, concentrate on recent media sources. If you want to know more about a company's CEO, enter his or her name into a search engine. The Internet contains a wealth of information; your strategy must allow for sifting through it to obtain the needed facts.

Search engines will become your best friends, so take some time to investigate each until you find one that works best for you. Yahoo!, Google, MSN, AltaVista, and Lycos are all good choices, and each will return different results. Most search engines provide categories to help you in your research, so some of the legwork has already been done.

As with all information found on the Internet, be sure you pay attention to the accuracy of your sources. Most reputable organizations such as Johnson & Johnson, IBM, or Ben & Jerry's will have accurate information on their site. The same goes for information found on dictionary and encyclopedia sites, government Web sites, and newspaper sites. When you start straying into personal home pages, special interest groups, and other similar sites, you will want to corroborate the information with other resources.

All in all, conducting research online is both convenient and fruitful once you learn a few simple strategies. And although it will be helpful to your job search later on, it will be even more helpful to your class projects right now!

Sources: Debbie Flanagan, "Researching Companies Online," June 17, 2003, http://home.sprintmail.com/~debflanagan/index.html; Alex Salkever, "The Web, According to Google; It's Becoming the Dominant Way to Search the Net, and That Worries Critics Who See Problems with Its Privacy Practices and Ranking Methods," *Business Week Online*, June 10, 2003; Debbie Flanagan, "Web Search Strategies," March 16, 2003, http://home.sprintmail.com/~debflanagan/main.html; Mary Panko and Jane Arlidge, "Online Information: The Spider's Sticky Web," *Academic Exchange Quarterly*, Spring 2003, p. 79; Judith Maginnis Kuster, "Don't Forget the Library! (Internet)" *ASHA Leader*, February 4, 2003, p. 18.

---

fessional organizations. Business-oriented Web portals offer links useful to businesspeople. The CEO Express Web site offers links to business publications, industry statistics, travel services, search engines, and other sites that can help with a manager's work. Other companies, including Yahoo! and Microsoft, set up portals tailored to the individual needs of their business customers. These business portals combine a company's data with information from the Internet.

Companies can also use the interactive technology of the Internet to gather information about their customers. For example, some sites ask visitors for personal information through registration or sweepstakes entry forms. To enter, visitors to this site provide their name, e-mail address, and other information. Sites that accept online orders gather the user-provided data, such as shipping addresses, along with purchase data. Even sites that do not ask for data can track the usage patterns of visitors to the site. With each type of data, marketers can adapt content, services, and advertising to their typical Web site users.

As an information source, the Internet is only as reliable as the individuals and companies that provide the information published there. Articles posted on Fox News, CNN, or MSNBC Web sites are likely to be more objective than Web sites put up by individuals to promote a particular viewpoint. Likewise, the ease of sending e-mail messages has markedly increased the speed with which people disseminate so-called *urban legends,* such as the story that the AIDS virus was on needles in gasoline pumps or flesh-eating viruses were found on banana peels. Because of the spread of misinformation, some practical cautions are essential for Web information gatherers:

- *Know your source.* Whenever you read information on the Web, make sure you have identified the provider of the information. Is it a reputable publication or news service, a known expert, or an organization or person with a position to promote? Some people have attempted to manipulate stock prices by posting misinformation on investment sites. The rumor spreaders then try to cash in on the wild swings in stock prices—and they hurt other investors in the process.[11] The moral? Check the accuracy of information on the Web before acting on it.
- *Investigate information by checking more than one source.* The old saying, "If it sounds too good to be true, it probably is" applies to the Internet just as it does in the rest of the world.
- *Don't believe all the e-mail announcements forwarded to you, especially those that have been forwarded to you and urge you to forward to your friends.* For one thing, e-mail is a common way to spread computer viruses. (Be especially careful when opening e-mail attachments unless you can verify the source.) Junk e-mail, or **spam,** is a growing problem. Spam is usually some sort of marketing message, but it may contain viruses or objectionable material. One study found that spam accounted for 40 percent of all e-mail sent during a recent year.[12] To verify certain sources, you can visit one of the Web sites that specialize in squelching misinformation. These include the U.S. Department of Energy's Computer Incident Advisory Capability (CIAC) and About.com's Web pages titled "Virus Hoaxes" and "Urban Legends and Folklore." These sites are not only informative, but highly entertaining.

Entertainment   Internet users are finding all kinds of entertainment online, including everything from concert Webcasts to online gaming. Online providers of entertainment can offer competitive prices, speed, and boundless services. Games, radio programming, short movies, and music clips are available online, sometimes for free, with the costs borne by advertising on the Web site. Sometimes entire songs, movies, and books are available on the Net. The availability of free content poses some ethical and business issues, including copyright issues, discussed later in the chapter. However, these issues are unlikely to chase entertainment off the Internet.

Business Transactions: E-Commerce   A newer application of Web technology, electronic business transactions are growing at lightning speed. Customers can not only learn about companies and their products on the Web but also complete purchases. This gives the Internet a key role in businesses' sales and distribution strategies. Organizations from major corporations like General Electric and Unilever to individuals have established a Web presence. Jeff Bradshaw, co-owner of TotalVac.com, which sells vacuum cleaner parts online, recently attended a business conference in Boston where many of the participants were small Internet companies. "Every one was a mom and pop," he notes.[13] Today, customers can go online to buy everything from toys and books to cars and business equipment. As growing numbers of companies sell their products on the Web, business success requires understanding the Web's advantages and its limitations and incorporating its use into a firm's overall business plans and strategies. Nordstrom managers decided to build the world's largest shoe store online, even though they operate brick-and-mortar retail outlets around the country and do a significant portion of business via mail-order catalog.

A Web presence builds awareness of a company's products and brands, provides the means for one-on-one communication with customers, and can allow customers to place orders from anywhere in the world, at any time of day. At the Web site of clothing retailer Lands' End, customers can check out what's new, what's on sale, and even "try" clothes on using a virtual model. These activities are the substance of **electronic commerce (e-commerce),** marketing products over the Internet by exchanging information between buyers and sellers.

electronic commerce (e-commerce) online marketing of goods and services, including product information, ordering, invoicing, payment processes, and customer service.

Concept Check

1. Which country is the top Internet user?
2. Of the Internet's four functions, which is the most popular?

The Scope of Electronic Commerce

Assume you're looking to buy a new espresso machine. Since you're computer savvy, you naturally want to look online, so you head for Amazon.com, which has an extensive selection of kitchen electronics. Since you've ordered from Amazon.com before, you're greeted with a personalized Web site that makes some recommendations based on your recent purchase history. A few mouse clicks later and you're reviewing the dozen or so espresso machines Amazon.com has for sale. You can compare features and read customer reviews of the various models. Once you make a selection, checkout involves only a few steps, such as entering a user name and password, since Amazon.com stores your address and credit card information. The entire process takes only a few minutes. Amazon.com uses e-mail to acknowledge your order and inform you of the shipment date. Links allow you to track your order online also. So, the Web not only enables Amazon.com and its customers to complete transactions, but it also provides speedy, effective customer service.

Companies around the world are discovering the advantages of e-commerce while in the process minimizing paperwork and simplifying payment procedures. As with other types of buyer–seller interaction, e-commerce involves a chain of events for customer and seller. It starts with product information; moves through the order, invoicing, and payment processes; and ends with customer service.

The first wave of e-commerce brought techniques such as charge card approval systems, point-of-sale terminals, scanners, and even early Internet selling—all activities focused mainly on lowering sellers' costs. As more firms discover the benefits of e-commerce, and as the Internet offers progressively more affordable services for almost any business, power begins to shift toward buyers, who gain access to a wider range of vendors.

A number of innovations promote both business-to-business and business-to-consumer e-commerce. One is encryption systems, which enable users to gather credit card numbers and other personal data required for completing transactions while protecting the security of purchasers. Another is the growing use of broadband technologies, which enable users to download more data at much faster speeds. Broadband makes technologies such as video and audio streaming more enjoyable and thus more attractive to users. With such developments, the number of businesses participating in e-commerce is growing fast. More than half of U.S. companies today have sold products online.[14]

The growth of e-commerce has attracted an army of specialized software firms and other service suppliers that provide expertise for firms taking their first steps into this competitive arena. Examples include Accenture, IBM, Microsoft, and Oracle.

> *They Said It*
>
> The question for us is, are you creating value? The Web and Internet is a great place for companies of all kinds that are creating genuine value for customers and it is a terrible place for companies that are not.
>
> —*Jeff Bezos (b. 1964) founder and CEO, Amazon.com*

Courtesy of Expedia, Inc.

Online travel sites such as Expedia have shifted power to buyers, who can now shop for and compare prices among several vendors. With a few clicks of a mouse, armchair travelers can get away from it all by selecting hotels, airline flights, rental cars, cruises—as well as learn about special deals.

IBM, for instance, offers its business customers both software and services designed to build virtual stores that go far beyond traditional Web sites. Although IBM was originally known as a producer of computer hardware, it now generates more than 25 percent of its revenue from sales related to e-commerce, and that percentage is growing rapidly. A huge staff of IBM consultants work on jobs ranging from designing Web sites to converting huge databases from old mainframe systems to Internet systems. IBM will even run e-commerce systems for companies that want to outsource this activity.[15]

E-Commerce and the Not-for-Profit Sector

E-commerce has also affected governments and others in the not-for-profit sector. For instance, MunicipalNet Inc. is a growing e-procurement business based in Boston. It focuses on services to states, local governments, and the businesses that supply them. The city of Evanston, Illinois, recently put its procurement process online using the services of MunicipalNet Inc. According to Chad Walton, the city's purchasing manager, one advantage of e-procurement is that "it lessens the cost of responding to solicitations from the city for businesses, which in turn should translate to lower costs for us as well." Both sides, he believes, can save time and money by cutting out some of the red tape from the process. MunicipalNet can also help governments set up Web sites at which citizens can register cars, pay taxes, or look for government jobs. By one estimate, 15 percent of federal, state, and local taxes will soon be collected online.[16]

Even the Girl Scouts are making use of the Internet to streamline their cookie sales. Though Scouts still sell cookies door to door, once the handwritten order forms are turned in, volunteers use Intuit's QuickBase system to tally orders and target where the cookies will be delivered. More than 300 Girl Scout councils nationwide are now processing cookie orders online.[17]

eBay is the most frequently visited e-commerce site on the Internet.

All the excitement of a live floor auction,

all the comfort of home.

eBay LiVE auctions™

The item you've been looking for is finally on the block. The first bid is in. Now it's your turn to jump in. And the competition begins. From works of art to fine jewelry or collector cars, eBay Live Auctions lets you experience the real-time bidding and excitement of a live floor auction without leaving your favorite chair. Unless you win, of course. Then you can jump around as much as you like.

Visit ebayliveauctions.com to bring the excitement of live auctions home.

© Copyright 2001 eBay Inc. eBay Live Auctions and the eBay Live Auctions logo are trademarks of eBay Inc. Designated trademarks and brands are the property of their respective owners.

eBay is a trademark of eBay Inc.

Profiting from E-Commerce

Not long ago, a minority of companies reported profits from their Web sites. Of sites catering to business customers, 36 percent were reported to be profitable, although 60 percent of companies expect their sites to be profitable soon.[18] But Web sites tailored to consumers are making steady progress in turning their red ink into black. Of the 208 publicly traded Net companies tracked by Pegasus Research International, more than 40 percent are now profitable—and the numbers are growing.[19]

Profitability is most common among online retailers and online finance companies. Companies such as Amazon.com and well-known retailers such as Eddie Bauer and JCPenney have had success in attracting online customers to generate their profits—not simply in cutting their costs. And they have made this progress despite a sluggish economy. LendingTree, an online loan site, also benefited from recent low mortgage interest rates to boost the percentage of its customers who close loans by 25 percent.[20]

As Figure 7.4 shows, the business potential of e-business involves more than sales transactions. Companies also establish an Internet presence to expand beyond their geographical boundaries to reach new markets, cut costs, and improve customer relationships. Putting massive business catalogs on the Web, for example, saves publishing and postage costs. With a few keystrokes, customers can send orders and service requests directly from their computers to the seller's computer—cutting the need for inbound telemarketing personnel and other customer service representatives.

The two main types of e-commerce are transactions between businesses and transactions between businesses and customers. Both are offering new opportunities, but business-to-business e-commerce is taking the lead. Business-to-business transactions are fueling the growth of e-commerce and forging new relationships along the way.

FIGURE 7.4
E-Commerce Is More Than Sales

Courtesy of IBM Corporation

Business-to-Business Transactions Lead the Way

One of the oldest applications of technology to business transactions is **electronic data interchange (EDI),** computer-to-computer exchanges of invoices, purchase orders, price quotations, and other sales information between buyers and sellers. EDI requires compatible hardware and software systems to exchange data over a network. Use of EDI cuts paper flow, speeds the order cycle, and reduces errors. In addition, by receiving daily inventory status reports from vendors, companies can set production schedules to match demand.

Wal-Mart was one of the first major corporations to adopt EDI in the early 1990s. In fact, the retailer refuses to do business with distributors and manufacturers that do not use compatible EDI standards. EDI is one of the major reasons Wal-Mart is able to operate with the efficiency that made it a market leader. It can buy just the merchandise its customers want, when it needs to restock its shelves, a system known as *quick response.*

From those early efforts to computerize business transactions, companies have taken the next technological leap—to the Internet—and are reaping rewards for doing so. **Business-to-business (B2B) e-commerce** is the use of the Internet for business transactions between organizations. Over one-quarter of all B2B transactions take place on the Internet, amounting to more than $3 trillion. This penetration of e-commerce is expected to increase to more than 40 percent of U.S. B2B sales.[21] Such sales are spread out across many businesses. The number of U.S. businesses engaged in B2B e-commerce is expected to grow to more than 90 percent by 2010.[22] Cisco Systems, IBM, and Intel are among the firms that generate billions of dollars in revenues online each year. As Chapter 5 pointed out, B2B e-commerce can also generate sales for small companies. For example, Neal Rothermel and Mandy Moore have established a well-grounded business based on virtual meetings. Their company, Virtual Meeting Strategies, sets up Internet meetings and events for other organizations. The firm was even able to ride out the recession by focusing on *Fortune* 500 companies and large pharmaceutical businesses as its main clients.[23]

They Said It

Within five years, the term "Internet Company" won't mean anything, because everyone will be an Internet company. The Internet becomes a fundamental part of your business.

—Kim Polese (b. 1962) founder, Marimba, Inc.

business-to-business (B2B) e-commerce electronic business transactions between organizations using the Internet.

In addition to generating sales revenue, B2B e-commerce also provides detailed product descriptions whenever they are needed and slashes order-processing expenses. Business-to-business transactions, which typically involve more steps than consumer purchases, can be much more efficient on the Internet. Orders placed over the Internet typically contain fewer errors than handwritten ones, and when mistakes occur, the technology can quickly locate them. So, the Internet is an attractive option for business buying and selling. In some industries, relying on the Internet to make purchases can reduce costs by almost 25 percent.[24]

Initially, companies used their own Web sites to conduct isolated B2B transactions. Today, the types of transactions and sites have become much more varied. The principal forms of B2B e-commerce include electronic exchanges, extranets, and private exchanges.

Electronic Exchanges   The earliest B2B e-commerce typically consisted of a company setting up a Web site and offering products to any buyer willing to make online purchases. More recently, businesses are buying and selling through **electronic exchanges,** Web-based marketplaces that cater to a specific industry's needs. An example of an electronic exchange is FreeMarkets, where suppliers compete for the business of organizational buyers who might be purchasing anything from gears to printed circuit boards; in other words, their online bidding events are hosted for a range of different sectors and industries. FreeMarkets was founded in 1995 by Glen Meakem, a former General Electric executive. Meakem understood that manufacturers spend roughly $5 trillion each year on industrial parts and business services and that the purchase process is usually very inefficient. He developed a new way of sourcing (or purchasing) whereby companies can negotiate for goods and services in an efficient manner using technology-based solutions. One such solution is an online market, in which suppliers use FreeMarkets's technology to compete online in real time for business. FreeMarkets consults with buyers and screens suppliers so that, when the online event takes place, each is familiar with the online negotiation process. The online event itself usually takes less than an hour. FreeMarkets's customers include large multinational companies across a range of industries. These companies regularly leverage FreeMarkets to source everything from gear services to accounting services. H. J. Heinz concluded that its relationship with FreeMarkets saved the packaged-foods company at least $50 million.[25] As the technology has evolved, FreeMarkets has developed additional products and services to address a much larger set of supply management challenges. Today, FreeMarkets's solutions support the entire sourcing (purchasing) process, from spend visibility and supply base rationalization to competitive negotiations, savings implementation, and contract compliance.

Extranets and Private Exchanges   Internet commerce also offers an efficient way for businesses to collaborate with vendors, partners, and customers through **extranets,** secure networks used for e-commerce and accessible through the firm's Web site by external customers, suppliers, or other authorized users. Extranets go beyond ordering and fulfillment processes by giving selected out-

Electronic exchanges offer streamlined purchasing for business customers. FreeMarkets has assisted such companies as General Motors, Carrier Aircon, and H. J. Heinz with their online purchasing activities.

Courtesy of FreeMarkets, Inc.

siders access to internal information. As with other forms of e-commerce, extranets provide additional benefits such as enhanced relationships with business partners. MasterCard created an extranet called Member Services Online for its member banks. The system gives banks quick access to market and customer research, forms, and transaction information. Currently, 87 percent of interactions are now done online—streamlining processes that used to take up to three days to a mere 10 seconds and slashing associated costs 67 percent.[26]

Security and access authorization remain critical issues, and most companies create virtual private networks that protect information traveling over public communications media. These networks control who uses a company's resources and what users can access. Also, they cost considerably less than leasing dedicated lines.

The next generation of extranets is the **private exchange,** a secure Web site at which a company and its suppliers share all types of data related to e-commerce, from product design through delivery of orders. A private exchange is more collaborative than a typical extranet, so this type of arrangement has sometimes been called *c-commerce.* The participants can use it to collaborate on product ideas, production scheduling, distribution, order tracking, and any other functions a business wants to include. Partners in a private exchange often form strategic alliances. IBM created a private exchange for its Personal Systems Group to use for product design, procurement, and logistics. The system permits IBM employees to identify qualified suppliers that can provide necessary components. The suppliers, in turn, can look up IBM's sales data and forecasts to manage their own inventory.[27]

Another variant of extranets is an **intranet,** which provides similar capabilities but limits users to an organization's employees. Intranets are discussed in more detail in Chapter 15.

Online Shopping Comes of Age

The area of e-commerce that has consistently grabbed news headlines and attracted new fans is Internet shopping. Known as **business-to-consumer (B2C) e-commerce,** it involves selling directly to consumers over the Internet. Driven by convenience and improved security for transmitting credit-card numbers and other financial information, online retail sales, sometimes called *e-tailing,* have hit $50 billion annually, with roughly 400 million online purchases.[28] Even with these increases, Internet retail sales are still only a tiny fraction of the overall retail market. Roughly 3 percent of all retail sales occur online.[29] However, in some product categories—computers, books, and audio and video recordings— online retailing has reached higher levels. Figure 7.5 lists the top five products purchased online. Other popular online purchases include entertainment services, computer hardware, and specialty gift items. Recently, online sales of shoes, watches, and various apparel items have increased dramatically.

B2C e-commerce got off to a rocky start. Not too long ago, few shoppers ventured online, most of them male, looking for videos and music CDs. Then a small wave of cybershoppers poured in, creating

business-to-consumer (B2C) e-commerce electronic business transactions between organizations and final customers using the Internet.

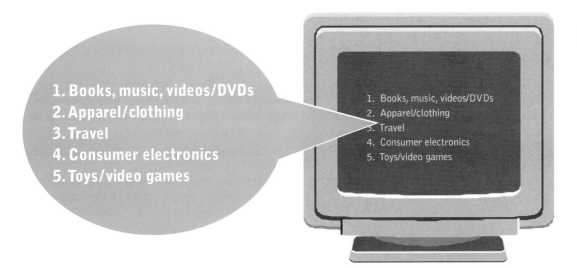

FIGURE 7.5
Top Products Sold Online

1. Books, music, videos/DVDs
2. Apparel/clothing
3. Travel
4. Consumer electronics
5. Toys/video games

Source: Data from Goldman Sachs, Harris Interactive, and Nielsen/Net Ratings, cited in Beth Cox, "Rising Tide Lifts E-Commerce Boats," CyberAtlas Web site, http://www.cybaratlas.internet.com, accessed January 13, 2003.

BEST BUSINESS PRACTICES

The Next Internet Business Targets

With Internet access getting faster, more reliable, and more secure, some feel the only question about e-commerce is, "What's next?" How many industries will face online competitors offering lower costs, lower prices, fewer middlemen, and the convenience consumers prize? With venture capitalists investing in survivors of the dot-com bust, more than half of which are making money again, the sky looks pretty high. Most analysts see six areas of e-commerce growth ahead: jewelry, bill payments, telecommunications, hotels, real estate, and software.

Amazon.com can make a profit selling diamonds below the prices charged by Tiffany and other established stores; online jeweler Blue Nile Inc. has already paved the way, making $27 million last year when it grew 12 times faster than the rest of the industry. Investments in Internet technology have allowed Verizon to respond to the threat posed by Internet phone service providers such as Vonage and Net2Phone.

Some hotel chains have tried to impose financial penalties on franchisees dealing with Internet partners that discount rooms. But Expedia, Travelocity, and other providers are accumulating market power from their huge numbers of loyal customers. In fact, their share of the lodging market is expected to more than double to 17 percent once antitrust challenges to the chains' restrictions move through the courts. Seven of every ten home buyers today have shopped online before their closing, almost double the number of a few years ago. With photos and floor plans a mouse click away, buyers have far more information than ever before.

Start-up real estate firms do too, and they use the Internet to cut their costs and commissions, pressuring traditional agents to do the same.

With software companies following in the open-source footsteps of firms such as Linux, giving software away as free downloadable files, traditional sellers like Microsoft and Oracle will be hard pressed to retain their customers and their profits in the $200 billion software business. "Open source shifts the balance of power to tech buyers," says an industry analyst.

Check-printing firms and community banks may soon feel the pinch as the number of written checks processed in the U.S. begins to decline, perhaps as much as 25 percent over the next few years. About $30 billion in revenue could be up for grabs as Internet firms that manage digital check services begin to proliferate. Banks, credit card companies, and retail merchants alike support the move, which promises to simplify an aging paper system that has dozens of middlemen.

QUESTIONS FOR CRITICAL THINKING
1. What can traditional companies do to compete with Internet start-ups?
2. Which business areas do you think might be next to face Internet competition?

Sources: Timothy J. Mullaney, "E-Biz Strikes Again!" *BusinessWeek*, May 10, 2004, pp. 80–90; Michael J. Russer, "Ask Mr. Internet: Bring Your Site Alive with Multimedia," *Realtor Magazine Online*, January 1, 2004, http://www.realtor.org; Robyn Greenspan, "Hotel Industry Makes Room for Online Bookings," *ClickZ Network*, January 9, 2003, http://www.clickz.com.

havoc with sites that weren't ready for the surge, and many holiday gifts weren't delivered on time, much to the frustration of parents who had to scramble at the last minute to buy gifts. Later, some of the first purely online retailers—such as Pets.com and eToys—began to fold. No one knew what to expect next. Today, e-tailing appears to be coming of age. In fact, in a number of industries, increased investment in successful start-ups that survived the early shakeout online seems to be paying off as consumers rediscover Internet shopping (see the Best Business Practices box).

A wide array of B2C e-commerce products are available. Industries such as investment and banking, online reservations and sales for travel and vacations, traditional retailing, and online auctions offer consumers a staggering array of products with just the click of a mouse. Expedia is the No. 1 Internet B2C travel service, with 19 percent of the online travel market. Visitors are able to book airline flights, make hotel reservations, and even purchase cruise packages. Expedia will search for the lowest airfare or the most direct flight. The site provides detailed driving directions, maps, and lists of attractions. In addition, the Web site supplies "insider" tips designed to resemble conversations with travelers who have recently visited the chosen destinations.[30]

E-Tailing and Electronic Storefronts   Major retailers are staking their claims in cyberspace. Many have set up **electronic storefronts,** Web sites where they offer items for sale to consumers. Wal-Mart received such a positive response to the launch of its electronic storefront that it expanded online product offerings from 2,500 to over 40,000 items. Macy's and Bloomingdale's department stores have put their bridal registry, personal shopping, and interior-decorating services online. The top 20 Web retailers, measured in terms of the number of buyers, include such well-known names as Amazon.com, Ticketmaster, Barnes & Noble, Sears, Staples, and JCPenney. Generally, retailers provide an online catalog where visitors click items they want to buy. These items are placed in a file called an **electronic shopping cart.** When the shopper indicates that he or she wants to complete the transaction, the items in the electronic shopping cart are listed on the screen, along with the total amount due, so that the customer can review the entire order and make any changes desired before making a payment.

Online retail selling works best for nontechnical products like flowers, books, compact discs, and travel and financial services. Even the sale of somewhat technical items, such as personal computers, has proven enormously successful through the combination of low prices, user-friendly Web sites, and 24-hour customer support offered by firms like Dell, Inc. and Gateway. In general though, cyber-shoppers like familiar goods that they can safely purchase without touching or trying out first. Marketing research firm Jupiter Communications predicts that the fastest growing categories of online sales to consumers will be groceries, housewares, toys, music, apparel, videos, and specialty gifts like gourmet food.[31]

A recent trend in online shopping is a hybrid that some call "click 'n pick shopping." Consumers visit electronic storefronts to order big-ticket items like digital cameras, washing machines, and computers online and then pick up the items at a nearby retail store. This method of shopping seems to offer the best of both worlds to many shoppers. They can avoid crowded stores, shipping charges, and a long wait to see the goods they've ordered. And if they decide they don't like the item once they see it, they can exchange it on the spot. Sears and Circuit City have set up such systems, and both claim success with it. Sears reports that 21 percent of customers who pick up an online order in a Sears store buy another item during the visit.[32]

Developing Safe Online Payment Systems   In response to consumer concerns about the safety of sending credit card numbers over the Internet, companies have developed secure payment systems for e-commerce. The most common forms of online payment are electronic cash, electronic wallets, and smart cards. Both Netscape and Microsoft Internet Explorer contain sophisticated encryption systems. **Encryption** is the process of encoding data for security purposes. When such a system is active, users see a special icon that indicates that they are at a protected Web site.

To increase consumer security, a group of companies, including Visa, MasterCard, and various technology suppliers, banded together to create Secure Electronic Transaction (SET), an industrywide standard for secure Internet payment transactions. Buyers using SET register with a bank and pay for purchases with **electronic cash** from their accounts using digital certificates that verify their identities. Adopting a standard technology provides consistency among merchants, card companies, software developers, and financial institutions.

An electronic wallet is another online payment method. An **electronic wallet** is a computer data file at an e-commerce site's checkout counter that contains not only electronic cash but credit card information, owner identification, and address. With electronic wallets, customers do not have to retype personal information each time they make a purchase at that site. Consumers simply click the electronic wallet after selecting items, and their credit card payment information, name and address, and preferred mailing method are transmitted instantly.

Besides using electronic cash or wallets, online consumers have other choices for making payments. **Smart cards**—plastic cards that store encrypted information on embedded computer chips rather than magnetic strips—are convenient and better protected. A smart card "reader" attaches to a shopper's computer, where the card is swiped for payment. In addition to storing e-cash, smart cards can also store data from several credit card companies and even a driver's license number. One example of a smart card is American Express's Blue credit card. Smart cards, however, have been slow to catch on in the U.S. and remain more popular in Asia and Europe. Other companies, including eBay's PayPal, Billpoint, and eMoneyMail, are offering online transfers of cash. When directed by the user, these programs send payments from a bank or credit card account to the recipient's account. Online bill paying

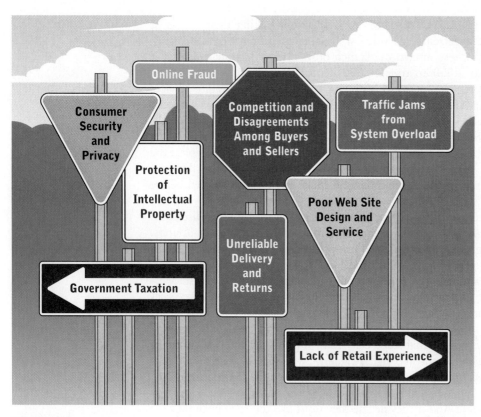

FIGURE 7.6
Roadblocks to E-Commerce

Signs in figure: Online Fraud; Consumer Security and Privacy; Competition and Disagreements Among Buyers and Sellers; Traffic Jams from System Overload; Protection of Intellectual Property; Poor Web Site Design and Service; Government Taxation; Unreliable Delivery and Returns; Lack of Retail Experience

has become one of the fastest growing Internet applications, with 12 million Americans paying some or all of their bills online.[33]

E-Commerce Challenges

As noted earlier, e-commerce has its challenges. Consumers are concerned about protecting their privacy and being victimized by Internet fraud, frustrated with hard-to-use Web sites, and annoyed over the inconveniences of scheduling deliveries and returning merchandise. Businesses are concerned about fair use of their trademarks and copyrights (see the Solving an Ethical Controversy box on page 246), conflicts with business partners, and difficulty in measuring the effectiveness of online promotion. Also, state and local governments are looking to e-commerce for increased sales tax revenue. The challenges to e-commerce are shown in Figure 7.6.

Privacy Issues Consumers worry that information about them will become available to others without their permission. In fact, marketing research indicates that privacy is the top concern of Internet users and may be an impediment to the growth of e-commerce.[34] As the earlier discussion of Internet payments explained, concern about the privacy of credit card numbers has led to the use of secure payment systems. To add to those security systems, e-commerce sites require passwords as a form of authentication—that is, to determine that the person using the site is actually the one authorized to have access to the account. More recently, **electronic signatures** have become a way to enter into legal contracts such as home mortgages and insurance policies online. With an e-signature, an individual obtains a form of electronic identification and installs it in his or her Web browser. Signing the contract involves looking up and verifying the buyer's identity with this software.

Thanks to cookies, the automatic data collection method introduced in Chapter 2, Web users leave electronic trails of personal information about their buying and viewing habits. The way that companies use cookies has the potential both to make visits to the Web site more convenient and to invade computer users' privacy. DoubleClick abandoned a plan to merge its data on Web use with a database of catalog orders, which would have given the company the ability to target online advertising to individual consumers based on their shopping habits.[35] Similarly, Amazon.com received such bad press over its plan to publicize customer shopping information by company or group, called Purchase Circles, that it now allows customers to request removal of their names. With over 23 million customers, Amazon's customer database is one of the largest, and keeping customers happy is critical to its success.[36]

Most consumers want assurances that any information they provide won't be sold to others without their permission. In response to these concerns, online merchants have been taking steps to protect consumer information. For example, many Internet companies have signed on with Internet privacy organizations like TRUSTe, shown in Figure 7.7. By displaying the TRUSTe logo on their Web sites, they indicate that they have promised to disclose how they collect personal data and what they do with the information. Prominently displaying a privacy policy is an effective way to build customers' trust.

A policy is only as good as the company implementing it, though. Online shoppers have no assurances about what happens if a company is sold or goes out of business. Now-defunct Toysmart.com promised customers that it would never share their personal data with a third party. But when the company landed in bankruptcy court, it considered selling its database, one of its most valuable assets. And Amazon.com has told customers openly that if it or part of its business is purchased at some point, its database would be one of the transferred assets.[37] With these concerns, it is no wonder that some companies are profiting by selling software designed to protect privacy. For example, a program called Freedom enables the user to set up an anonymous online identity. Another package called PersonaValet allows users to determine which personal data to reveal when they visit Web sites that have installed software that works with PersonaValet.[38]

Courtesy of TRUSTe

FIGURE 7.7
TRUSTe Logo

Such privacy features may become a necessary feature of Web sites if consumer concerns continue to grow. They also may become legally necessary. In the U.S., the **Children's Online Privacy Protection Act (COPPA)** requires that Web sites targeting children younger than 13 years of age obtain "verifiable parental consent" before collecting any data that could be used to identify or contact individual users, including names and e-mail addresses.[39] Congress has also begun considering laws to protect the privacy of adult users.

Security concerns are not limited to consumers. Employees are realizing that their employers can monitor their online behavior and e-mail messages at work. Some companies even specialize in helping employers use such information. Tacit Knowledge Systems builds a database from key terms in employees' e-mail. The primary objective is to help a company identify which employees have knowledge that they can contribute to the company—for example, knowledge about a particular competitor or type of product. Of course, many employees might be uncomfortable with their employer tracking what they write about. So, Tacit's software allows employees to decide which aspects, if any, of their personal profile they want to make public. In addition to e-mail, some companies track other Internet use by employees, particularly shopping. According to a survey conducted by ComScore Networks, 59 percent of U.S. Web purchases occurred in the workplace—on company time. Online access begins around 10 A.M. and continues until noon, actually dropping off during the traditional lunch hour.[40]

Companies, too, are concerned about the privacy of their data, and with good reason. Recently, a security flaw in an online registration system for Comdex, the world's largest computer trade show, exposed the personal data of some users. Those wishing to attend the trade show are allowed to register online. However, it was discovered that by slightly manipulating the login data sent in an e-mail confirming the registration, users were able to view the profiles of other users. These registrants included senior partners of a major law firm, the managing partner of a large venture capital firm, and the president of a midwestern manufacturing company. While the security flaw didn't expose attendees' credit card numbers or other financial information, the incident was an embarrassment for Key3Media, the producer of Comdex and other large computer trade shows. William Knowles, editor of InfoSec News, an online newsletter, put it this way, "You might expect the guys running the local Corvette show to make this kind of mistake. But Key3Media is supposed to be a cutting-edge IT show group. You'd think they would know better." Key3Media quickly patched the security flaw and implemented new procedures to keep it from happening again.[41]

To prevent such intrusions, companies install combinations of hardware and software called *firewalls* to keep unauthorized Net users from tapping into private corporate data. A **firewall** is an electronic barrier between a company's internal network and the Internet that limits access into and out of the network. However, an impenetrable firewall is difficult to find. A determined and skilled hacker can often gain access. So, it is important for firms to test their Web sites and networks for vulnerabilities and provide backups of critical data in case an intruder breaches security measures.

firewall electronic barrier between a company's internal network and the Internet that limits access into and out of the network.

Soon states may begin requiring companies to track and report any security breaches to their Web sites. A "cyber disclosure" law is being implemented in California, which mandates companies to report security intrusions that jeopardize customer information such as Social Security numbers and bank account data. Companies must notify customers if their information has been viewed without authorization. The impact of this law is still uncertain.[42]

Fighting File Sharing: Music and Movies

Will music lovers learn to pay for legitimately downloaded tunes? RealNetworks recently slashed the price of a song from 99 to 49 cents, a move expected to cost it $2 million in revenues. But with a federal appeals court allowing file-sharing companies to stay in business although their products can be used to commit piracy, music companies continue to feel the pinch from illegal free downloads. Legal downloading options are broadening as Microsoft and Yahoo! plan to enter the online music market. Napster adopted a subscription service, and Apple's iTunes online song sales have reached 2 million per week.

Kids have billions of free songs available for download, and the film industry is watching the music business closely as its own properties begin to show up illegally on the Internet. The Motion Picture Association of America has distributed a school lesson plan designed to prevent the drop-off in

sales that worries the music business. The lesson, formulated as a role-playing game, is called "What's the Diff?: A Guide to Digital Citizenship."

Should downloading copyrighted movie and song files for free be illegal?

PRO
1. Free downloads deprive the originating artists—singers, songwriters, actors, directors—of their well-earned livelihood.
2. Music prices are dropping so low that everyone should be prepared to pay for music and films.

CON
1. If technology makes songs and movies available at no cost, there's no reason to keep paying for them.
2. Most users eventually erase the free files they download; using them is no

different from borrowing a library book and hurts no one.

SUMMARY
After a long period of declining revenues, the music industry feels it may be nearing the end of its battle with piracy. The movie industry hopes to prevent the same kind of loss. It already estimates such losses amount to $3 billion a year, mostly through illegal copies of first-run films made by camcorders smuggled into theaters. Hidden cameras are being used to scan audiences for such rip-offs and technology that jams camcorders are being tested.

Sources: Nick Wingfield and Sarah McBride, "Green Light for Grokster," *The Wall Street Journal*, August 20, 2004, pp. B1, B3; Steve Knopper, "Lawsuits Fail," *Rolling Stone*, August 19, 2004, p. 32; Jeff Howe, "File-Sharing Is, Like, Totally Uncool," *Wired*, May 2004, pp. 133–135; Sarah McBride, "The Hunt for Movie Pirates," *The Wall Street Journal*, April 12, 2004, pp. B1, B3.

Internet Fraud   Fraud is another barrier to e-commerce. The Federal Bureau of Investigation and Department of Justice reported online auctions as the No. 1 source of fraud. They have logged more than 1,000 complaints a week and expect that rate to increase to 1,000 a day as the Internet Fraud Complaint Center becomes more widely used.[43] Auction fraud ranges from merchandise that does not match the description the bidder was given, such as art forgeries, to products that were purchased but never delivered. Because auction sites such as eBay might deal with thousands of sellers, it is difficult to monitor the activities of each one. However, if eBay becomes aware of fraud committed by a seller, the merchant is barred from selling on the site again.[44]

Investment scams are the second most common online crime. Unreliable company information posted anonymously on the Web by disgruntled employees or predators who want to cash in on a stock's rise or fall are the most common "cybersmears." The misinformation can vary from untrue reports of problems with company products to character attacks on executives—anything to change the public's view of a company. Law enforcement is gearing up to pursue online criminals, but untangling the layers of hidden online identities is proving difficult, though not impossible, to do. In the meantime, consumers and companies are being hurt by these fraudulent acts. As a result, online firms need to work harder to improve the image of the Internet as a safe place to conduct business. "Rather than assume [Web site] visitors understand a merchant is legitimate, merchants must assume the opposite and work from there," admits Chris Gwynn, president and founder of Fridgedoor Inc., an online retailer that specializes in novelty and custom magnets and magnetic supplies.[45]

Traffic Jams Caused by System Overload   After the 9/11 terrorist attacks, the Web site of the FBI experienced a surge in traffic, causing widespread delays and even outages. The FBI turned to Akamai Technologies, a leading provider of Web services and software. Akamai installed its EdgeSuite program to help the FBI Web site better manage traffic and ensure 100 percent uptime.[46] As the FBI discovered, the Internet's increasing popularity has also increased the likelihood of delays and service outages, even as more users depend on their links. In addition, hackers can tie up a Web site with programs that flood it with inquiries. Whatever the cause of these traffic jams, they are costly in terms of lost business and frustrated customers.

Solutions to these problems are on the way. Internet service providers have added capacity, and networking equipment manufacturers have introduced new technology capable of handling higher volumes of Internet traffic than older devices could manage. Many businesses also operate backup systems to ensure availability of Internet connections to customers. Companies like Akamai distribute content among thousands of computer servers so that traffic to a Web site can be rerouted if it becomes too heavy.

Poor Web Site Design and Service   For e-commerce firms to attract customers—and keep them—companies must meet buyers' expectations. Customers want to find what they want without frustration and have their questions answered. However, Web sites are not always well designed and easy to use. In fact, two-thirds of Web shopping carts are abandoned before a customer places an order.[47] In other words, among the people who start selecting items to buy online, most of them change their minds before making a purchase.

Unreliable Delivery and Returns   Another challenge to successful e-commerce is merchandise delivery and returns. Retailers sometimes have trouble making deliveries to on-the-go consumers. And consumers don't want to wait for packages to be delivered. Also, if customers aren't satisfied with products, they then have to arrange for pickup or send packages back themselves.

Retailers have begun to address these issues. Most have systems on their Web sites that allow customers to track orders from placement to delivery. Detailed directions on how to return merchandise, including preprinted shipping labels, are included in orders. A few, such as Nordstrom and Chef's Catalog, even pay the shipping cost for returns.

Lack of Retail Experience   Many of the so-called "pure play" dot-com retailers—those without traditional stores or catalogs—didn't survive very long. They had no history of selling and satisfying customers. Because of expertise in all parts of retailing, companies that combine their brick-and-mortar operations with e-commerce—such as Barnes & Noble and Talbots—have generally been more successful than those with little or no retail experience. However, even brick-and-mortar retailers have struggled to find the right place for themselves on the Internet.

The same lesson also applies to other service industries. To be successful at e-commerce, a firm must establish and maintain competitive standards for customer service. When it began offering customers the opportunity to check flight schedules and purchase tickets online, Southwest Airlines worked hard to make sure its Web site had the same high service standards the airline is known for. Its Web site has proved both very popular and profitable. Approximately one-third of all Southwest's passengers buy their tickets online. In a recent year, Southwest's online sales topped $1.7 billion. Not bad considering the Web site cost Southwest only $5 million to set up and $21 million annually to maintain.[48]

Competition and Disagreements among Buyers and Sellers   Companies spend time and money to nurture relationships with their partners. But when a manufacturer uses the Internet to sell directly to customers, it can compete with its usual partners. Retailers often have their own Web sites. So they don't want their suppliers competing with them for sales. As e-commerce broadens its reach, producers must decide whether these relationships are more important than the potential of selling directly on the Web.

Mattel, well-known for producing toys such as Barbie and Matchbox cars, sells most of its products in toy stores and toy departments of other retailers, such as Target and Wal-Mart. The company wants an Internet presence, but it would cut the retailers out of this important source of revenue if it sold toys online to consumers. Mattel cannot afford to lose the goodwill and purchasing power of giant retailers like Toys "R" Us and Wal-Mart. So the company sells only specialty products online, including pricey American Girl dolls.

BUSINESS TOOL KIT

Preparing an Electronic Résumé

Welcome to the Information Age. The days of mailing paper résumés, banking in person, and buying merchandise only in physical stores are gone thanks to the technology available to us. Many companies now ask you to submit an electronic résumé. The *electronic résumé* is an electronic copy of your résumé, usually in ASCII or plain text. Companies are using scanning software to quickly search résumés for applicable keywords, to enter your résumé into their database, and to reduce the amount of paper that enters their organization. Read the following tips before you prepare an electronic résumé.

1. Fancy formatting may look good on a piece of paper, but it has no place in the electronic version of your résumé. Bullets, lines, italics, boldface, or underlined text will only confuse the scanning software, reducing your chances of getting the right information to the right person. Format your résumé as if it was an e-mail or you were going to post it online; remember to keep it simple. Use asterisks, dashes, or capital letters for emphasis.

2. Use relevant keywords that relate to the specific job requirements. The scanning software will be more likely to pick up these keywords and ignore generic adjectives or phrases such as "organized," "works well with the public," or "good attitude." Use nouns rather than verbs ("project manager" rather than "managed several projects"), and check out the classified ads or online job boards for examples of relevant, industry-appropriate keywords.

3. In addition to sending an electronic résumé to organizations, you can also use the Internet in your job search by

posting your résumé online. Web sites such as Monster.com, CareerBuilder.com, and HotJobs.com allow you to post your electronic résumé online, making it searchable by hundreds of companies and recruiters. You can also post your résumé on your own Web page if you have the skills or know someone who does, and provide the link to interested parties for easy viewing.

4. Never send a document as an attachment unless specifically directed to do so. Too many organizations have been burned by computer viruses that spread as attachments, so many companies have filters to automatically delete files with attachments from unknown people. Include the text of your résumé within your e-mail to avoid this common problem.

5. Finally, as with all professional documents, remember to do a thorough review for spelling, punctuation, and grammatical errors. Regardless of the medium, accuracy and attention to detail still count, so invest a little time in the more mundane aspects of your résumé. If you need professional help in editing or proofreading your résumé, take the time to hire a professional editor. It could give you the upper hand in your job hunt!

Sources: "How to Format Your Electronic Résumé," *Knight Ridder/Tribune News Service,* April 1, 2003; J. Steven Niznik, "Résumés 101: Electronic Résumés" (1998) and "Submitting Your Résumé: Résumé Tips and Tricks, Part 1" (1999), About.com, http://jobsearchtech.about.com/library/weekly/aa070599-4.htm and http://jobsearchtech.about.com/library/weekly/aa112398.htm, accessed July 4, 2003.

Pricing is another potential area of conflict. In their eagerness to establish themselves as Internet leaders, some companies have sold merchandise at discount prices. American Leather sells custom leather furniture through upscale retailers, and each dealer serving a geographical area has an exclusive contract for the collections it offers in its area. But at least one dealer began offering American Leather furniture at a discount to customers outside its market area. Other dealers complained, so American Leather established a policy that dealers were not to advertise the company's products on the Internet. Instead, American Leather offered links to local dealers on its own Web site and made plans to allow buyers to order online, with the sale directed to the dealer serving the consumer's geographical area.[49]

Protection of Intellectual Property   Along with privacy, intellectual property is difficult to protect on the Internet. Intellectual property is a trademark; invention; or literary, musical, artistic, photographic, or audiovisual work. The open sharing of information online can conflict with the desire of organizations to protect the use of their brand names, copyrights, logos, patents, and other intellectual property. For instance, the entertainment industry has long complained that technology makes it too easy for consumers to make unauthorized copies of copyrighted works, such as movies and music. Copyright owners, the industry argues, will stop providing content online unless they are sure users can't make and distribute unauthorized copies. This, in turn, stunts the growth of high-speed Internet access and digital television. Under one plan, content providers would attach digital tags that would limit how the content could be played, viewed, or copied on devices such as computers and digital TVs. Consumer groups and the technology industry lined up in opposition to the bill. They argued that copyright owners would lose control over how consumers use technology and essentially give the entertainment industry power over the design of new technologies.[50]

Even the choice of domain names can cause headaches for companies that have spent millions of dollars to develop a good reputation and widespread recognition. When the Internet was new and few companies understood the value of a Web presence, some individuals registered domain names that used companies' brand names, as well as the names of celebrities. When the companies got ready to go online, they were surprised to find that someone else had the right to use their name in cyberspace. At first, trade name owners had little recourse but to buy these rights. Today, however, the Anti-Cybersquatting Consumer Protection Act imposes fines on people who in bad faith intend to profit from registering or using a domain name that is identical or similar to a company's trademark or an individual's name. The challenge for companies trying to protect their intellectual property is that the law requires them to show in court that the other party is using their name in bad faith to profit from it.

Companies have used a variety of approaches to protect themselves in the freewheeling world of the Internet. When a dissatisfied customer set up a Web site at **http://www.dunkindonuts.org** to post complaints about the food at Dunkin' Donuts, the doughnut chain initially threatened to sue him for misusing its trademarks. Instead, it arranged to buy the site and use it as a tool for obtaining consumer opinions, which brought a positive end to a difficult situation.

Lucasfilm worked with fan sites for *Attack of the Clones* to build excitement before the release of that Star Wars episode. The winners in cyberspace have to figure out how to participate in an environment where the flow of information is not always within their control. When information can zip around the globe within seconds, an after-the-fact lawsuit is not much protection.

Concept Check
1. What are the major functions of B2B e-commerce?
2. Name three of the top products purchased online.
3. Describe two concerns that consumers have about making purchases online.

Managing a Web Site

Web sites serve many purposes. They broaden customer bases, provide immediate accessibility to current catalogs, accept and process orders, and offer personalized customer service. As technology becomes increasingly easy to use, anyone with a computer equipped with a modem can open an Internet account and place a simple Web site on the Internet. How people or organizations use their sites to achieve their goals determines whether their sites will succeed. Figure 7.8 lists some key questions to consider in developing a Web site.

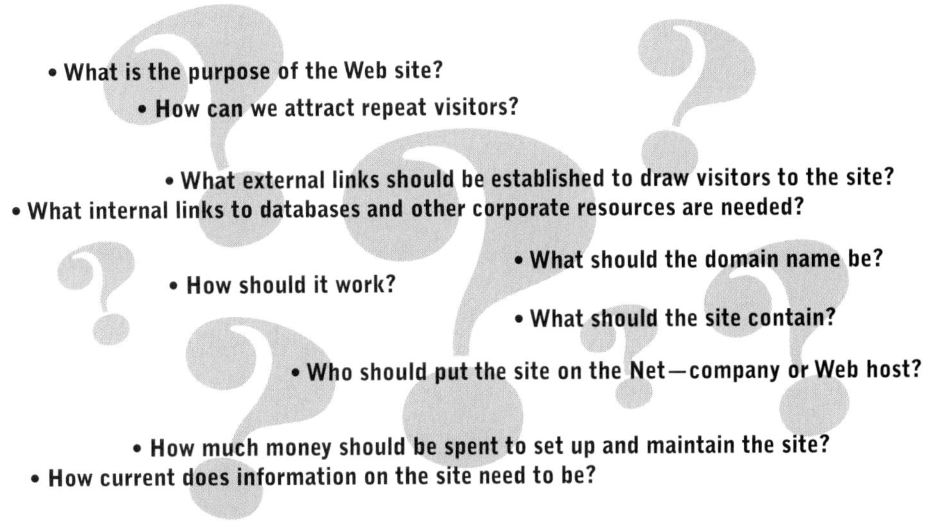

FIGURE 7.8
Questions to Consider in Developing a Web Site

• **What is the purpose of the Web site?**
• **How can we attract repeat visitors?**
• **What external links should be established to draw visitors to the site?**
• **What internal links to databases and other corporate resources are needed?**
• **What should the domain name be?**
• **How should it work?**
• **What should the site contain?**
• **Who should put the site on the Net—company or Web host?**
• **How much money should be spent to set up and maintain the site?**
• **How current does information on the site need to be?**

Developing Successful Web Sites

Most Web experts agree: "It is easier to build a bad Web site than a good one." When judging Web sites, success means different things to different businesses. One firm might feel satisfied by maintaining a popular site that conveys company information or reinforces name

HITS & MISSES

Business Discovers Blogs

By definition, a journal or diary is private, meant to be read by the writer only. But like so much else, journals have migrated to the Internet, where—as their writers are well aware—they can be read by almost anybody. That's the whole point. And along with their new audience and no-holds-barred content, they've added a new word, "blog," short for "Web log," to newly released dictionaries.

Marketers are taking increasing notice of blogs, which often center around a topic and generally express a particular point of view. Some blogs are written by well-known opinion leaders; others make their unknown writers famous because they attract thousands of readers, controversy, or discussion. Although most bloggers have tiny audiences, a few very popular blog sites are able to sell ad space—setting price as a per-week or per-site-visitors figure—and some are already earning a few thousand dollars a month from advertising related to their central topics. Since their audience tends to be upscale, and media savvy trendsetters between 26 and 35 (most of them male), blogs, however narrowly focused, may represent a broad future marketing opportunity.

But, the director of business development for Gawker Media, a popular blog publisher, emphasizes that blogging is "not a big business; it's a very small, niche, organic operation. It's nothing like the turnover of a restaurant or a shop. It's a pretty home-grown, family-styled business." In fact, few mainstream consumer companies have started buying ad space on blogs yet. Nike is a notable exception, with its recent Art of Speed blog. Some marketers might agree with Nike that reaching the right people is more efficient than reaching the widest possible audience. Says one marketing consultant, "Nike is talking to the right people—instead of

the most people—who happen to be the influencers. They will become the evangelizers and influence subsequent purchasers."

No one really knows yet how successful blog advertising can be. But perhaps the appeal of reaching influencers explains why political advertising has become one of the most popular forms of blog marketing. Thanks to an $80,000 media campaign, Ben Chandler won a seat in Congress in a recent special election. The TV spots and newspaper ads were paid for by funds Chandler's campaign manager raised with $2,000 worth of blog advertising.

"I don't think that the bloggers realized how much these ads are worth," says Paul Libman, a composer who sells his Christmas-humor CDs via blog ads. "Next year it will be much more expensive."

QUESTIONS FOR CRITICAL THINKING

1. Blogs are currently read by about 2 percent of the Internet's 70 million online households, and one observer doubts that blogs will increase significantly. Do you agree or disagree? Why?

2. Some mainstream advertisers are apprehensive about the uncensored nature of blogging and don't want to risk running their ads in an uncontrollable context. What advice would you give a company such as PepsiCo or Burger King about buying ad space on blogs? Support your suggestions with reasons.

Sources: Chris Seper, "Blogging for Dollars," *Mobile Register*, July 25, 2004, p. F3; Kris Oser, "Nike Assays Blog as Marketing Tool," *Advertising Age*, June 14, 2004, p. 26; Deanna Zammit, "In Blog Bonanza, Some See Fringe Benefits," *Adweek*, May 23, 2004, p. 12; Marcus Lillkvist, "Blogs Grow Up: Ads on the Sites Are Taking Off," *The Wall Street Journal*, March 15, 2004, pp. B1, B3.

recognition—just as a billboard or magazine ad does—without requiring any immediate sales activity. Web sites like those of *The Los Angeles Times* and *USA Today* draw many visitors who want the latest news, and Yahoo!, Netscape, CNet, and ESPN SportsZone are successful because they attract heavy traffic. Popular Web sites like these add to their success by selling advertising space to other businesses.

Internet merchants need to attract customers who transact business on the spot. Some companies find success by hosting Web sites that offer some value-added service to create goodwill for potential customers. Organizations like the Mayo Clinic provide useful information or links to related sites that people frequently visit. A Web site started by Florida immigration attorney Jose Latour, called usvisanews.com, provides a virtual encyclopedia of information on immigration and visas.[51] But to get people to stay at the site and complete a transaction, the site must also be secure, reliable, and easy to use. Marketers are also discovering the power of blogs, as described in the Hits & Misses box.

Planning and Preparation   What is the company's goal for its Web site? Answering this question is the first and most important step in the Web site development process. For discount brokerage firm Charles Schwab, the primary objective is to sign up new customers. So, the Web site designers put links called "Client Log In" and "Open an Account" prominently at the top of the home page.

Objectives for the Web site also determine the scope of its development. If the company's goal is to sell merchandise online, the site must incorporate a way for customers to place orders and ask questions about products, as well as links to the company's databases to track inventory and deliveries. The plan should include not only the appearance of the Web site but also the company's behind-the-scenes resources for making the Web site deliver on its promises.

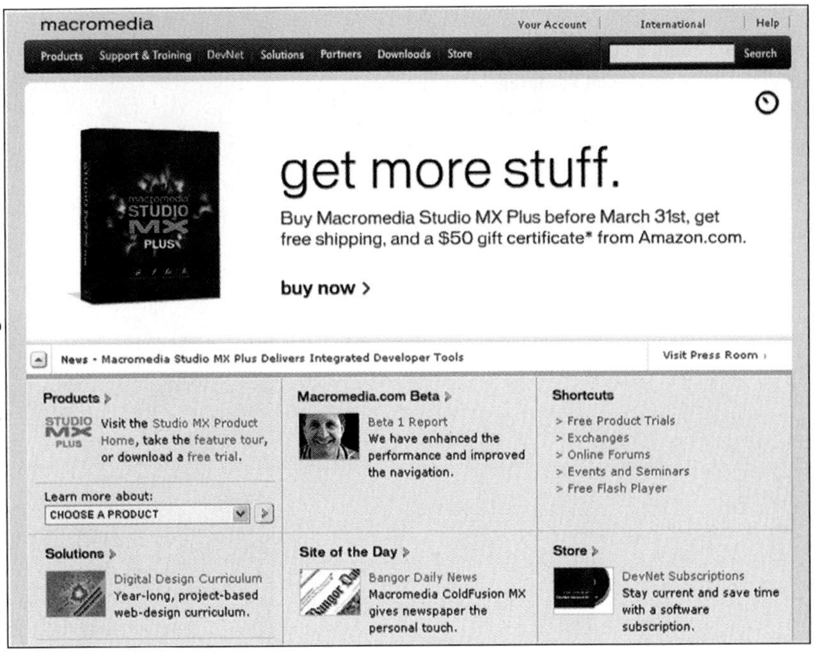

Other key decisions include whether to create and maintain a site in-house or to contract with outside experts. Some companies prefer to retain control over content and design by producing their own sites, using software such as Microsoft's FrontPage or Corel's HoTMetaL Pro. However, since acquiring the expertise to develop and maintain Web sites can be very time-consuming, hiring specialists may prove a more cost-effective option, especially if the site is critical to the functioning of the business. Often, companies like Macromedia are enlisted to provide both software and consulting services to clients for their Web sites, as illustrated in Figure 7.9.

FIGURE 7.9
Web Site Development Specialists: Help for Clients

Naming Your Web Site   Naming the Web site is another important early step in the planning process. A domain name should reflect the company and its products and be easy to remember. For U.S. companies, the last part of the domain name identifies an affiliation category. Examples include .com for businesses, .org for organizations, .gov for government sites, and .edu for educational institutions. For companies outside the U.S., the last part of the domain name identifies the country of origin, such as .ca for Canada and .jp for Japan. In addition to the original dot-com, dot-gov, and dot-org addresses, seven new suffixes have been added to the Internet's naming system. The new suffixes include .aero, .biz, .coop, .info, .museum, .name, and .pro. These suffixes were created to alleviate overcrowding in the .com domain and represent the first major addition of Internet addresses in more than a decade. With millions of dot-com names already registered, the search for a unique, memorable, and easily spelled name can be difficult. The Internet Corporation for Assigned Names and Numbers (ICANN; http://www.icann.org) is the nonprofit organization that coordinates assignment of Web domain names.

When Andrew Busey decided to create an e-commerce site for home furniture, he first thought of ForMyHome.com, which he was able to register, but it just wasn't catchy enough. So Busey and the design firm that was developing his site pondered the alternatives. Furniture.com was already taken, and its owner wanted $1 million for it. Eventually, they settled on Living.com because it was easy to spell and general enough in case the site broadened its offerings. However, the California Association of Realtors had already registered the name. Busey negotiated the right to use the name in exchange for more than $100,000. Furniture.com understood the importance of domain names, too. Furniture.com registered three misspellings of its competitor—Livng.com, Livign.com, and Lving.com—hoping to attract visitors with poor typing skills. Unfortunately, both Living.com and Furniture.com spent too much time choosing their domain names and not enough time with other aspects of their businesses, such as logistics. Most furniture items are too large to be shipped via FedEx or UPS. So, shipping charges for many of their products were prohibitively expensive. Neither dot-com entity stayed in business for long.[52]

What more could a cook want? Williams-Sonoma uses its Web site to maximum advantage, offering mouth-watering recipes and new cooking techniques—along with its vast array of colorful cookware, gleaming appliances, and timesaving gadgets.

© Terri L. Miller/E-Visual Communications Inc.

Content and Connections   Content is one of the most important factors in determining whether visitors return to a site. People obviously are more inclined to visit a site that provides material that interests them. Many e-commerce Web sites try to distinguish themselves by offering information or online communities along with a chance to buy. For example, Williams-Sonoma's Web site lures traffic to the site with weekly menu planners, printer-ready recipes, and features that convert menus between metric and U.S. measurement systems, adjust measurements for different numbers of servings, and create shopping lists for menus. Many sites offer links to other sites that may interest visitors.

Standards for good content vary for every site, but available resources should be relevant to viewers, easy to access and understand, updated regularly, and written or displayed in a compelling, entertaining way. A site should allow interactivity, including the ability to accept customer data and orders, keep up-to-the-minute inventory records, and respond quickly to customer questions and complaints. Also, today's Internet users are less patient about figuring out how to make a site do what it promises. They won't wait 10 minutes for a video clip to download or click through five different pages to complete a purchase. Jose Latour's usvisanews.com Web site, mentioned earlier, is a triumph of content. The site includes an extensive question-and-answer section about Immigration and Naturalization procedures, a glossary that defines visa designations, relevant news stories that are updated daily, live chat sessions on a biweekly basis, and regular columns on legal issues. What's the result of this rich content? Latour's $1.7 million law practice has recently gone national, with clients in 49 states. "We grew 26 percent in [a recent year], and we landed our biggest client ever, a $24-billion company," says Latour. He attributes his firm's successful growth to the Web site.[53]

After making content decisions and designing the site, the next step is connecting to the Internet by placing the required computer files on a server. Companies can have their own dedicated Web servers or contract to place their Web sites on servers at ISPs or other host companies. Most small businesses lack the necessary expertise to set up and run their own servers; they are better off outsourcing to meet their hosting and maintenance needs. They also need to draw business to their site. This usually requires a listing with the major search engines, like Google or Yahoo!.

Costs and Maintenance

As with any technological investment, Web site costs are an important consideration. The highly variable cost of a Web site includes not only development expenses but also the cost of placing the site on a Web server, maintaining and updating it, and promoting it. A reasonably tech-savvy employee with off-the-shelf software can create a simple piece of "brochureware" for a few hundred dollars. A Web site that can handle e-commerce will cost at least $10,000. Creating it requires an understanding of how to link the Web site to the company's other information systems.[54]

Although developing a commercial Web site with interactive features can cost tens of thousands of dollars, putting it online can cost as little as $20 a month for a spot on a **Web host**'s server such as America Online. And Web hosts deliver a huge audience. In a typical week, 30 million people visit the AOL site and another 25 million log on to Yahoo!.[55] Like so much new technology, the cost of putting a site on a server is falling. ISPs like America Online, Earthlink, and Prodigy host many commercial sites for basic monthly charges based on the number of Web pages. A number of e-commerce service providers are offering services for a few hundred dollars or even for free. Treadmill Doctor, which repairs treadmills, set up a Web site to answer common questions about that type of exercise equipment. The company used a template from Bigstep.com to create the site and pays Bigstep $14.95 monthly plus $0.20 per transaction to host the site. Bigstep allows the company to update the site at no charge.[56] Some e-commerce service providers also take care of listing the site with search engines, usually for an additional fee.

It's also important for a Web site to stay current. Visitors don't return to a site if they know the information never changes or that claims about inventory or product selection are not current. Consequently, updating design and content is another major expense. In addition, site maintenance should include running occasional searches to test that links to the company's Web site are still active.

Measuring Web Site Effectiveness

How does a company gauge the return from investing in a Web site? Measuring the effectiveness of a Web site is tricky, and the appropriate process often depends on the purpose of the Web site. Figure 7.10 lists several measures of effectiveness. Profitability is relatively easy to measure in companies that generate revenues directly from online product orders, advertising, or subscription sales. However, a telephone order resulting from an ad on a Web site still shows the sale as a phone sale, not a Web site sale, even though the order originated at the site.

For many companies, revenue is not a major Web site objective. Only about 15 percent of large companies use their Web sites to generate revenue; the rest use them to showcase their products and to offer information about their organizations. For such companies, success is measured by increased brand awareness and brand loyalty, which presumably translate into greater profitability offline.

Some standards guide efforts to collect and analyze traditional consumer purchase data, such as how many Ohio residents bought new Honda Accords the previous year, watched a boxing match on HBO, or tried Arby's deli-style sandwiches. Still, the Internet presents several challenges for marketers. Although information sources are getting better, it is difficult to be sure how many people use the Internet, how often, and what they actually do online. Some Web pages display counters that measure the number of visits. However, the counters can't tell whether someone has spent time on the page or skipped over it on the way to another site or whether that person is a first-time or repeat viewer.

Advertisers typically measure the success of their ads in terms of **click-through rates,** meaning the percentage of people presented with a banner ad who click it, thereby linking to a Web site or a pop-up page of information related to the ad. Recently, the average click-through rate has been declining to about half of 1 percent of those viewing an ad. This rate is much lower than the 1 to 1.5 percent response rate for direct-mail advertisements. Low click-through rates have made Web advertising less attractive than it was when it was novel and people were clicking just about anything online. Selling advertising has therefore become a less reliable source of e-commerce revenues.[57]

click-through rate percentage of people presented with a Web banner ad who click it.

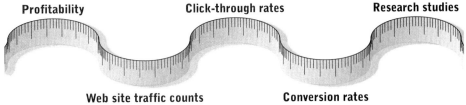

FIGURE 7.10
Measures of Web Site Effectiveness

conversion rate
percentage of visitors to a Web site who make a purchase.

As e-commerce gains popularity, new models for measuring its effectiveness are being developed. A basic measurement is the **conversion rate,** the percentage of Web site visitors who make purchases. A conversion rate of 3 to 5 percent is average by today's standards.[58] A company can use its advertising cost, site traffic, and conversion rate data to find out the cost to win each customer. E-commerce businesses are trying to boost their conversion rates by ensuring their sites download quickly, are easy to use, and deliver on their promises. For instance, Lexmark International turned to Web consultants WebCriteria to help it improve the overall performance of its Web site. Analysis of the traffic on Lexmark.com indicated that visitors used the site primarily for product and presales support. The site was large and difficult to navigate. WebCriteria assisted Lexmark.com by simplifying the site and better enabling customers to reach their goals. According to Patti Lybrook of Lexmark.com, "We're in constant change mode. We are constantly monitoring and updating the site design."[59]

Besides measuring click-through and conversion rates, companies can study samples of consumers. Research firms such as PC-Meter and Relevant Knowledge recruit panels of computer users to track Internet site performance and evaluate Web activity; this service works in much the same way that television rating firm AC Nielsen monitors television audiences. The WebTrends service provides information on Web site visitors, including where they come from, what they see, and the number of "hits," or visits to the site, during different times of the day. Other surveys of Web users investigate their brand awareness and their attitudes toward Web sites and brands.

Concept Check

1. What is the first question a company should ask itself when planning a Web site?
2. Identify two ways in which companies can measure the effectiveness of a Web site.

The Global Environment of E-Commerce

For many companies, future growth is directly linked to a global strategy that incorporates e-commerce. The U.S. leads the world in technology, communications infrastructure, and ownership of PCs and other consumer technology products, but as noted earlier in the chapter, Internet users live on every continent. Worldwide, people spend well over $600 million per year online and are soon expected to spend $6 billion.[60] Governments in developing countries such as India are working hard to bring the Internet to their people, which means that e-commerce is soon to follow. A government-sponsored program called Gyandoot, or "ambassador of knowledge," has installed 39 computer kiosks around the district of Dhar, whose residents earn an average of $270 a year. For the equivalent of a penny per visit, locals can obtain information such as current prices for produce, land records, and even the results of school exams. One villager figured out how to auction a cow through the Internet kiosk. Farmers have used the information obtained via Gyandoot to determine where to sell their produce, often boosting their incomes.[61]

With so many users and so much buying power, the Internet creates an enormous pool of potential customers. Companies can market their goods and services internationally and locate distribution sources and trading partners abroad. Customers can search for products at their convenience, browsing through online catalogs that always show current information. Many companies divide their Web sites internationally. For instance, when you visit Symantec's Web site, you are first asked your country of origin. After the information is entered, you are automatically taken to that country-specific portion of the Web site. A list of the products available for your country are listed, along with local distributors and service centers.

One practical implication of this global marketplace is the different languages that buyers and sellers speak. Reflecting the Internet's origins, more than half of users now communicate in English. However, the remainder use other languages, led by Japanese, German, Chinese, Spanish, and French.[62] As Figure 7.11 points out, Web site developers need to offer online information in more than one language. So far, however, three of every four Web pages are in English, slowing the adoption of the Internet in non-English-speaking countries.[63] Other international differences are important, too. Auction site eBay goofed in the United Kingdom by launching a site with

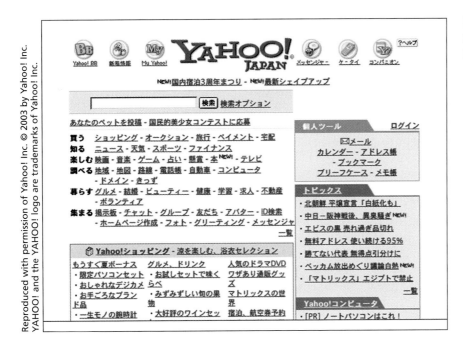

FIGURE 7.11

Importance of Considering the Internet's Global Population

prices given in U.S. dollars. After realizing that its British audience was offended, the company switched to local currency.[64]

E-commerce can heighten competition. In the virtual global marketplace, rivals can cross the oceans to enter your market. Many manufacturers use the Internet to search through online catalogs for the lowest priced parts. No longer can local suppliers assume that they have locked up the business of neighboring firms. And U.S. firms cannot expect that their earlier experience with the Internet gives them an edge in foreign markets. Yahoo!, which has been in Europe longer than any other U.S.-based portal, operates eight country-specific versions. They represent 15 percent of Yahoo!'s total traffic. Yahoo! enjoys the biggest slice of the market in the United Kingdom, but it lags in other countries. In France, for example, the top portal is Wanadoo, which is the default portal of the nation's biggest Internet service provider, France Telecom. Still, the Internet is a valuable way to expand a company's reach, especially for small businesses that would otherwise have difficulty finding customers overseas.

Concept Check

1. How do language differences around the world affect e-commerce?
2. How does e-commerce heighten global competition?

What's Ahead

The Internet is revolutionizing the way we communicate, obtain information, seek entertainment, and conduct business. It has created tremendous opportunities for B2B and B2C e-commerce. So far, B2B transactions are leading the way online. B2C e-commerce is still undergoing a shakeout: Companies that combine expertise in traditional retailing with the new online technology have gained a firmer foothold in cyberspace.

In upcoming chapters, we look at other trends that are reshaping the business world of the 21st century. For example, in Part 3, we explore the critical issues of how companies organize, lead, and manage their work processes; manage and motivate their employees; empower their employees through teamwork and enhanced communication; handle labor and workplace disputes; and create and produce world-class goods and services.

DID YOU KNOW?

1. The average AOL user will hear "You've Got Mail" 446,160 times.
2. Interested shoppers can actually purchase a kit online to build a do-it-yourself casket at http://www.mhp-casketkits.com.
3. Ninety-three percent of Internet users want to know how a site will use any personal information they provide as part of a purchase.
4. Web sites typically lose over half of their sales from would-be customers who click off because they are too difficult to use.

Summary of Learning Goals

1

Discuss how the Internet provides new routes to business success.

The Internet, a worldwide network of interconnected computers, removes limitations of time and place so that transactions can occur 24 hours a day between people in different countries. It creates opportunities that provide Internet infrastructure, access, and content, as well as for firms that use its resources in their business operations. The Internet offers a cost-effective way for managers to gather competitive intelligence; perform marketing research; showcase, sell, and in some cases, distribute products; and offer customer service and technical support.

2

Describe the increasing diversity of Internet users.

From its start as a U.S. military defense network, the Internet has grown to include users all over the world. An early gender gap has narrowed; women now represent more than half of all Internet users. Ethnic and racial diversity is also increasing with African American and Hispanic Americans going online in larger numbers. The average age of Internet users is also rising, reflecting the widespread acceptance of the Net.

3

Summarize the Internet's four functions and provide examples of each.

The Internet provides a means of communication, through e-mail, instant messaging, and electronic bulletin boards. Internet telephony and videoconferencing have also expanded online in recent years. The Net provides information services through search engines and portals, as well as online publications and newsgroups. Net entertainment is growing through online gaming, radio and television programming, electronic publishing, and music and movies. E-commerce, or online business transactions, makes up the fourth function. E-commerce

takes the form of electronic exchanges, extranets and private exchanges, electronic storefronts, online ticketing, and auctions.

4

List the major forms of business-to-business (B2B) and business-to-consumer (B2C) e-commerce.

Electronic data interchange (EDI) was an early use of technology to conduct business transactions. E-commerce is the process of selling goods and services through Internet-based exchanges of data. It includes product information; ordering, invoicing, and payment processes; and customer service. In a B2B context, e-commerce uses Internet technology to conduct transactions between two organizations via electronic exchanges, extranets, and private exchanges. After a rocky start, business-to-consumer (B2C) e-commerce is starting to mature. B2C uses the Internet to connect companies directly with consumers. E-tailing and electronic storefronts are the major forms of online sales to consumers. Payment methods include electronic cash, electronic wallets, smart cards, and online transfers of cash.

5

Describe some challenges associated with Internet selling.

The growth of Internet retailing has been hampered by consumer security and privacy concerns, fraud, and system overload. In addition, poor Web design and service, unreliability of delivery and returns, and lack of retail expertise has limited e-commerce success. The Internet can also generate conflict among buyers and sellers. Businesses also face challenges in protecting their intellectual property and proprietary data online.

6

List the steps involved in developing successful Web sites.

Businesses establish Web sites to expand their customer bases, increase buyer awareness of their products, improve consumer communications, and provide better service. Before designing a Web site, a company's decision makers must first determine what they want to achieve with the site. Other important decisions include who should create, host, and manage the site; how to promote it; and how much funding to allocate. Successful Web sites contain informative, up-to-date, and visually appealing content. Sites should also download quickly and be easy to use.

7 *Identify methods for measuring Web site effectiveness.*

The appropriate process for measuring the effectiveness of a Web site depends on the purpose of the site. Profitability, increased brand awareness, and loyalty are three such purposes. Measurement techniques include tallying click-through rates and conversion rates, as well as studying samples of consumers.

8 *Explain how global opportunities result from technological advances.*

Technology allows companies to compete in the global market and workplace. Even the smallest firms can sell products and find new vendors in international markets. Through its own Web site, a company can immediately reach customers all over the world. Improved communications among employees in different locations create new ways of collaborating on projects.

Business Terms You Need to Know

Internet (Net) 230

World Wide Web (Web) 230

Web site 231

Internet service provider (ISP) 231

e-mail 233

electronic commerce (e-commerce) 236

business-to-business (B2B) e-commerce 239

business-to-consumer (B2C) e-commerce 241

firewall 245

click-through rate 253

conversion rate 254

Other Important Business Terms

domain name 231

Digital Subscriber Line (DSL) 231

server 232

client 232

instant messaging 233

newsgroup 234

portal 234

search engine 234

spam 236

electronic data interchange (EDI) 239

electronic exchange 240

extranet 240

private exchange 241

intranet 241

electronic storefront 243

electronic shopping cart 243

encryption 243

electronic cash 243

electronic wallet 243

smart card 243

electronic signature 244

Children's Online Privacy Protection Act (COPPA) 245

Web host 253

Review Questions

1. What is the Internet? Explain briefly how the Internet works.

2. Using the statistics cited in the chapter, construct a profile of the "typical" Internet user. Explain how this profile is changing.

3. Identify the four functions of the Internet and give an example of each function.

4. Suppose you want to gather information from the Web for a school project, a job hunt, or some other reason. What precautions would you take to make sure you obtain accurate information?

5. Discuss how the Internet allows small companies to better compete with larger ones.

6. List the ways a company can generate revenue from its Web site. For what other purposes might a company set up a Web site?

7. Distinguish between B2B and B2C e-commerce. Why did B2C e-commerce get off to such a poor start?

8. Describe several of the challenges that face companies engaged in e-commerce. Which of these are B2C companies now overcoming and which do you think will be ongoing issues?

9. List the steps involved in developing a successful Web site. Why is the development of content so important?

10. What are the challenges and benefits of e-commerce in the global business environment?

Projects and Applications

1. Consider the following statement: "In order to remain competitive, all types of retailers will have to establish Web sites and be engaged in e-tailing." Do you agree or disagree with the statement? Why? If you disagree, name one or two types of retailers that you believe could succeed without doing business online.

2. Choose one of the following types of companies and describe how it could take advantage of online communication to market its goods or services:
   a. a travel agency that specializes in adventure travel
   b. financial advisor
   c. a firm that ships fresh gourmet foods—such as lobster, cheeses, or chocolates—nationwide
   d. a California winery
   e. a boutique specializing in trendy clothing

3. As described in the chapter, many companies have banded together to form exchanges that serve large segments of an industry, such as the auto industry. However, several large retailers, such as Wal-Mart and Home Depot, have decided not to follow this route. Do you think this is a wise decision? Why or why not?

4. Several large e-mail providers—such as Hotmail and Yahoo!—recently announced that they are going to begin charging for some of their services. How do you think these charges will affect e-mail usage?

5. Compared with brick-and-mortar retailers, what are the advantages and disadvantages of so-called pure-play e-commerce companies? Why have so many pure-play e-commerce companies failed?

Experiential Exercise

Background: The Internet is a powerful resource for businesses. As noted in the chapter, most businesses are online and around half are engaged in some form of B2B e-commerce.

Directions: Assume you work for Yvonne Williams, a small-business owner who is interested in developing a B2B e-commerce site on the Internet. Research the Web to find resources for your employer to use in developing her company's B2B Internet site. You may wish to use http://business .geoportals.com, an online directory with links to over 100 Web sites for a wide variety of information sources, including the following: Web-based business solutions; B2B auctions;

procurement services; sales force management; Web site design and hosting; supplier information; and business tools.

Print the home page for either GeoBiz2Biz.com or a similar site you found. Write a memo to Yvonne Williams that includes the home page printout of the Web site you recommend to get her started in B2B e-commerce. Summarize several links on the Web site you selected that you think are most important for her to visit. For each of the sites listed, include (1) the reason you recommend the link as particularly important and (2) any necessary explanations about the link that would be helpful to her.

NOTHING BUT NET

1. **B2B.** IBM offers extensive consulting services, software, and hardware for firms engaged in e-commerce. Assume you're an entrepreneur, and you'd like to expand your presence in the B2B market. Visit the IBM e-commerce Web site. Read about the services offered and review some of the case studies in which IBM has assisted firms in their B2B activities. Prepare a report on what you have learned.

    http://www.ibm.com

2. **Internet retailing experience.** Assume the role of an online shopper who wishes to purchase a pair of jeans over the Internet. Two leading online clothing retailers, Lands' End (http://www.landsend.com) and Eddie Bauer (http://www.eddiebauer.com) offer jeans through their Web sites. Visit both sites and learn enough so you can describe each to a friend, including which of the two you'd be most likely to purchase from and why.

3. **Rating e-commerce Web sites.** Gomez.com is one of the leading authorities on e-commerce. As such, it rates various e-commerce businesses. Go to the Web site (http://www.gomez.com) and read about its rankings of Internet mortgage companies. Which firm was ranked the highest? Why? What criteria does Gomez.com use when ranking e-commerce sites?

Note: Internet Web addresses change frequently. If you do not find the exact sites listed, you may need to access the organization's or company's home page and search from there.

Case 7.1

Sales Taxes Are Hitting the Internet

If nothing is certain but death and taxes, then it was inevitable that lawmakers, online and traditional merchants, and consumers would be locked in a struggle over whether Internet transactions should be subject to state sales tax. Until recently, shoppers have had a free ride on the Internet, which was exempt from collecting sales tax. But the 45 states—along with the District of Columbia—that levy sales taxes claim that they are losing about $13.5 billion a year in revenues that haven't been collected from Internet and other unrecorded out-of-state transactions. With tight budgets being cut even further, legislators believe that it is time to begin collecting sales taxes from the Internet. "Now there's a sense of urgency among governors and legislators to get this done," says Diane Hardt, tax administrator for the Wisconsin Department of Revenue and cochair of an organization called the Streamlined Sales Tax Project Steering Committee.

Tax and other government officials recognize that trying to collect 45 different sales taxes could be a real quagmire, especially for small online businesses. But it's even more complicated than that; currently, there are more than 7,000 different state and local tax jurisdictions nationwide. So officials from 34 states have joined together to form the Streamlined Sales Tax Project Steering Committee to accomplish just what the name of the committee suggests: streamlining. Once at least 10 states that represent 20 percent of the total national population have amended their laws to accommodate the program, state lawmakers could then approach Congress to pass a mandatory, nationwide online tax law. "We're doing everything we can to make it clear that the states can work together," notes R. Bruce Johnson, commissioner of the Utah state tax commission and cochair of the implementing states group. An online tax would level the playing field for brick-and-mortar retailers as well as catalog merchants, who currently are required to collect sales tax. "Our ultimate goal is that everybody will have to play by the same rules," remarks Maureen Riehl, counsel for the National Retail Federation.

In the meantime, some major retailers such as Wal-Mart, Toys "R" Us, and Target have voluntarily expanded the number of states in which they collect sales taxes from Web purchases. About 10 companies with both online and traditional sales began to collect taxes in 37 states and the District of Columbia. In exchange, the states promised not to try to collect back taxes from the merchants.

Although consumers may grumble about the new tax, a survey conducted by the Markle Foundation found—surprisingly—that 64 percent of Americans surveyed agreed that online purchases should be taxed the same as offline purchases. Would taxation slow down online shopping? Not likely, says Dan Hess of ComScore. "The Internet adds enormous convenience and time-saving benefits, and many consumers place a premium on that."

QUESTIONS FOR CRITICAL THINKING

1. Do you agree that online transactions should be subject to state and local sales tax? Why or why not?
2. Do you think certain types of businesses will be hurt by sales tax charges? Why or why not?

Sources: Nick Wingfield and Amy Merrick, "More Web Retailers Collect Sales Tax," *The Wall Street Journal,* February 10, 2003, p. B5; "Web Sales Taxes Spreading," *CBS News,* February 8, 2003, http://www.cbsnews.com; "Sales Tax Holiday," *Kiplinger's,* December 2002, pp. 19–20; Roy Mark, "End of the Beginning," *Internet.com,* November 13, 2002, http://ecommerce.internet.com; Brian Krebs, "State Coalition Approves Internet Sales Tax Plan," *Washington Post,* November 11, 2002, http://www.washingtonpost.com.

Video Case 7.2

Elderly Instruments

This video case appears on page 609. A recently filmed video, designed to expand and highlight the written case, is available for class use by instructors.

Part 2 Krispy Kreme Continuing Case

Krispy Kreme: The Entrepreneur's Dream

Vernon Carver Rudolph was an entrepreneur. He bought a little doughnut shop with a secret recipe as part of the deal and turned the company into a nationwide—and eventually, international—business. Of course, he didn't accomplish this feat overnight. It took decades of innovation and strategic planning before Krispy Kreme reached its current size and level of success.

Throughout Krispy Kreme's history, the driving engine for organization and growth has been franchising. Through its franchises, the company has managed to expand across the U.S. while maintaining the spirit of a small business. Krispy Kreme franchisees are entrepreneurs in their own right: people who want to run their own business and have a real shot at financial success beyond what they might achieve as part of a large corporation. These business owners are willing to take risks to achieve their goals and are optimistic about their chances for success. Eric Sigurdson, president of Sweet Traditions, one of the largest Krispy Kreme franchises, left a lucrative job at a large company to start his franchise business. "If I had a dollar for everybody who thought I had lost my mind for leaving the corporate world and going into doughnuts, I'd be on the beach somewhere," says Sigurdson.

Franchisees played a crucial role in one of Krispy Kreme's most important transformations. In 1976, food giant Beatrice Foods Co. acquired Krispy Kreme as a wholly owned subsidiary, subjecting Krispy Kreme to its own corporate culture and strategy, including product offerings—such as deli sandwiches—in Krispy Kreme shops. But in 1982, a group of Krispy Kreme franchisees led by Joseph A. McAleer, Sr., bought back the company from Beatrice. Krispy Kreme remained an independent company until it made its initial public offering (IPO) of stock on the NASDAQ in 2000 but has continued to focus on its signature product—great doughnuts. Krispy Kreme has since transferred to the New York Stock Exchange (NYSE), where its stock is traded today.

Krispy Kreme has been able to expand through franchises because franchisees share many of the costs in exchange for support from the franchisor. Franchisees pay an average fee of $40,000 per store, in addition to 4.5 percent of revenues per year. That's pennies compared with the $1 million required to build the store and purchase doughnut-making equipment and mix from Krispy Kreme. A potential franchisee—which is usually a group of businesspeople—must demonstrate a minimum net worth of $5 million, and Krispy Kreme does not offer financing. But Krispy Kreme franchisees have typically experienced a 100-percent return on their investment within the first year of business, compared with an average of 25 percent for most good restaurants. Still, the Krispy Kreme life isn't for everyone, and some franchisees have chosen to exit the business. In these cases, the company has opted to repurchase the franchise. Such buybacks have occurred in California, Louisiana, Michigan, and Texas. The accounting involved in these repurchases has caused Krispy Kreme some difficulties, but the firm remains confident of the outcome—both for the company and for its stockholders and franchisees.

Krispy Kreme has also managed to expand its organization through acquisition. In 2001, it acquired Digital Java, a small Chicago-based coffee company. This way, Krispy Kreme could not only broaden its beverage offerings but also control their quality. Revenues from coffee and other drinks hover between 12 and 15 percent at various Krispy Kreme shops, and the company is looking to increase that percentage by creating an atmosphere where customers can sit for awhile to sip coffee, eat doughnuts, and chat with friends, as they do in Starbucks and other coffeehouses. In addition, Krispy Kreme is boldly challenging Massachusetts-based Dunkin' Donuts's claim to the coffee turf on the East Coast. Krispy Kreme still offers fewer coffee varieties—at higher prices—than Dunkin' Donuts does, but the current No. 2 doughnut maker is no longer content to ride only on its doughnut wave. "At our core, and in our heart, we're a doughnut company," says company spokeswoman Brooke Smith. And in the wake of a recent flattening of sales—partly due to consumers' demand for healthier foods and partly due to rapid, aggressive expansion—Krispy Kreme is careful about where and how it plans to grow. But there's no doubt that company managers recognize that even the most passionate doughnut lovers want to wash their treats down with a tasty drink.

As mentioned earlier, in 2000 Krispy Kreme Doughnut Corp. made a bold organizational move: It made a public offering of stock—at first on the NASDAQ and later transfer-ring to the New York Stock Exchange (NYSE). As often happens with IPOs from companies with products that are already wildly popular, at first the stock was the sweetest buy investors could make. Since then, things have cooled somewhat as the firm reevaluates the way it spends its capital. One approach is to focus on developing smaller stores that use smaller—and less expensive—doughnut machines to churn out the same hot, delicious doughnuts.

Because of the nature of Krispy Kreme's best-loved product—its Hot Original Glazed doughnuts fresh from the glazing water-fall—the company primarily uses e-commerce for purposes other than selling directly to consumers. However, Krispy Kreme fans can find collectibles and memorabilia—T-shirts, mugs, hats, and even toys—at the company's Web site. The site itself is designed to enhance relationships with consumers as well as investors, providing information about the company's history, its products, franchise agreements, and revenues. Anyone who is interested can download the Krispy Kreme annual report.

The doughnut honeymoon is over—and yet Krispy Kreme continues to offer top-quality products to consumers, tailoring its offerings and its growth efforts to a changing business environment. The entrepreneurial spirit will always be central to Krispy Kreme's success.

QUESTIONS

1. In what ways does Krispy Kreme maintain a balance between being a small business and a large business?

2. In what ways can Krispy Kreme franchisees continue to improve the Krispy Kreme experience for consumers—and ultimately increase sales?

3. What entrepreneurial characteristics do you think Krispy Kreme franchisees should possess to help them achieve success?

4. How do you think Krispy Kreme could effectively expand its use of e-commerce?

Sources: Company Web site, http://www.krispykreme.com, accessed January 10, 2005; David Stires, "Krispy Kreme Is in the Hole—Again," *Fortune*, November 1, 2004, pp. 42–43; Robert Barker, "Why Krispy Kreme Is Worth a Bite," *BusinessWeek*, September 27, 2004, p. 130; Christopher Palmeri and Amy Borrus, "What's Really Inside Krispy Kreme?" *BusinessWeek*, August 16, 2004, p. 72; Mark Maremont and Rick Brooks, "Krispy Kreme Franchise Buy-backs May Spur New Concerns," *The Wall Street Journal*, May 25, 2004, pp. C1, C4; Andy Serwer, "The Hottest Brand in America: How Krispy Kreme Became the Hole Story," *Fortune*, July 7, 2003, pp. 52–62; Faith Arner, "Doughnut Détente about to End," *Mobile Register*, July 6, 2003, p. F3; Ellen Christenson and Geoffrey Gagnon, "Coffee Brew Ha Ha," *Newsweek*, October 7, 2002, p. 9.

Part 3

Management: Empowering People to Achieve Business Objectives

Chapter 8
Management, Leadership, and the Internal Organization

Leadership Lessons from—*The Apprentice?*

What is the seemingly magical quality that makes a leader? While the question consumes academic researchers and business managers alike, one television show thinks it has the answer. In its inaugural season, *The Apprentice*, hosted by the flamboyant tycoon Donald Trump, packed a huge weekly audience of

over 26 million viewers, making it the most popular show on TV. Even though ratings dropped somewhat during its second year on the air, it continued to attract not only wealthy, educated young fans who love its entertainment value but also business students, practicing managers, and business analysts who scrutinize it for what it might be telling us about business success.

The show's premise, familiar from the cutthroat reality shows that inspired it, pits 16 ambitious candidates against each other for 13 weeks of challenging business tasks presided over and judged by Trump. The winner gets a one-year $250,000 position as apprentice at the Trump Organization.

Although the show is a popular success, Trump's own business expertise has often been questioned; his hotel and casino empire recently filed for bankruptcy as its stock value plummeted, losing 95 percent of its original value. Appropriately enough for the host of a reality show, however, Trump is a survivor. Can *The Apprentice* shed light on the question of what makes a leader?

Some critics disparage the game show's flaws as a business primer, and others are dubious about its potential real-life application. Jonathan Estrin, dean of Drexel College of Media Arts & Design and a television producer, says the show celebrates "the American fantasy that you can achieve something

© Amanda Edwards/Getty Images

without actually having to work for it." Yale School of Management's associate dean Jeffrey Sonnenfeld called it "mindlessly cruel, but spellbindingly popular." But some business students find the show a popular discussion topic in their classes and watch the contestants avidly for cues. One student learned from the show that "there are going to be individual styles that work better in certain situations. You need to know when to lead and when to step back and support a teammate."

Employees at Long's Jewelers in Burlington, Massachusetts, are inspired enough by the show to have "a regular conversation about strategic alliances and how relationships are everything," said the company's vice president of sales and strategic planning. The talk gets quite specific. "It was really clear that Kwame, who was an impeccable candidate, was dragged down by Omarosa" on one show. "So we figured if we had any Omarosas, they needed to shape up or ship out."

Black Enterprise magazine recently took a close look at the show and drew four real-life leadership lessons from the fates of Kwame, Omarosa, and their competitors. They included the basic principles that planning is paramount; that successful leadership hinges on cultivating "a sincere interest in solving problems and meeting the needs of others"; that leaders earn their followers' trust and loyalty, they don't merely claim it; and that leaders "operate in a world of allies and opponents, knowing that anyone they encounter can be one or the other on any given day, and sometimes both at the same time."

These lessons are unquestionably true, and they help explain why some candidates on the show fare poorly on Trump's tasks and others succeed. Contestants who put their own needs first, who blamed teammates for their own failures, who planned for the short term or not at all, and who focused on others' personalities instead of their performance have been among the first to hear Trump's famous verdict, "You're fired."[1]

Chapter Overview

A management career brings challenges that appeal to many students in introductory business courses. When asked about their professional objectives, many students say, "I want to be a manager." You may think that the role of a manager is basically being the boss. But in today's business world, companies are looking for much more than bosses. They want managers who understand technology, can adapt quickly to change, skillfully motivate subordinates, and realize the importance of satisfying customers. Managers who can master those skills will continue to be in great demand because their performance strongly affects their firms' performance.

This chapter begins by examining how successful organizations use management to turn visions into reality. It describes the levels of management, the skills that managers need, and the functions that managers perform. The chapter explains how the first of these functions, planning, helps managers to meet the challenges of a rapidly changing business environment and to develop strategies that guide a company's future. Other sections of the chapter explore the types of decisions that managers make, the role of managers as leaders, and the importance of corporate culture. The chapter concludes by examining the second function of management—organizing.

What Is Management?

management process of achieving organization objectives through people and other resources.

Management is the process of achieving organizational objectives through people and other resources. The manager's job is to combine human and technical resources in the best way possible to achieve the company's goals.

Management principles and concepts apply to not-for-profit organizations as well as profit-seeking firms. A city administrator, a Salvation Army major, and a Boy Scout leader all perform the managerial functions described later in this chapter. Managers preside over organizations as diverse as Miami-Dade Community College, the New York Stock Exchange, and the Starbucks coffee shop down the street.

The Management Hierarchy

A local fast-food restaurant such as McDonald's typically works through a very simple organization that consists of an owner-manager and a few assistant managers. By contrast, large organizations develop more complex management structures. Southwest Airlines manages its activities through a chairperson of the board, a vice chairperson and chief executive officer, a president and chief operating officer, three executive vice presidents, a senior vice president, and 23 vice presidents, plus an array of managers and supervisors. All of these people are managers because they combine human and other resources to achieve company objectives. Their jobs differ, however, because they work at different levels of the organization.

A firm's management usually has three levels: top, middle, and supervisory. These levels of management form a management hierarchy, as shown in Figure 8.1. The hierarchy is the traditional structure found in most organizations. Managers at each level perform different activities.

The highest level of management is **top manage-ment.** Top managers include such positions as chief executive officer (CEO), chief financial officer (CFO), and executive vice president. Top managers devote most of their time to developing long-range plans for their organizations. They make decisions such as whether to introduce new products, purchase other companies, or enter new geographical markets. Top managers set a direction for their organization and inspire the company's executives and employees to achieve their vision for the company's future.

Michael Bloomberg once headed a media con-glomerate—Bloomberg LP—that primarily sells financial data via leased computer terminals. This business made Bloomberg a billionaire. Then he decided to move on to a new CEO position. Today, Michael Bloomberg has what is often called the sec-ond toughest job in the U.S.—mayor of New York City. Instead of building wealth, as mayor he works at rebuilding the city, resolving budget problems, and keeping firms from fleeing to the suburbs or else-where. Bloomberg still follows the leadership style he used in the corporate world. At Bloomberg LP, he sat in the corner of his TV studio. As mayor, Bloomberg operates out of an open cubicle in a big hall resem-bling the brokerage trading room where he got his

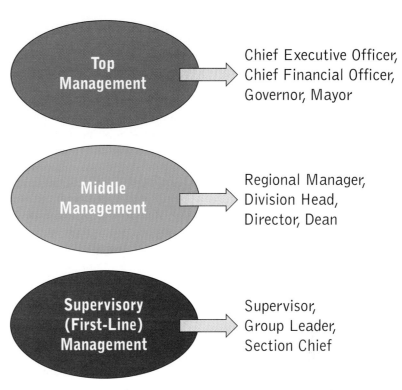

FIGURE 8.1
The Management Hierarchy

start. The official mayor's office is used only for interviews and similar events. Mayor Bloomberg is pro-viding hands-on direction to his staff—situated in nearby cubicles. The leadership pattern that proved successful at Bloomberg LP is now at work in New York's City Hall.[2]

Middle management, the second tier in the management hierarchy, includes positions such as gen-eral managers, plant managers, division managers, and branch managers. Middle managers' attention focuses on specific operations, products, or customer groups within an organization. They are respon-sible for developing detailed plans and procedures to implement the firm's strategic plans. If top man-agement decided to broaden the distribution of a product, a sales manager would be responsible for determining the number of salespeople required. If top management decided to institute a company-wide total quality management program, a quality control manager in the customer service department might design a survey to gather feedback on customer satisfaction. For example, 3M's CEO W. James McNerney has set a goal of double-digit earnings growth despite market uncertainties.[3] Middle man-agers are responsible for targeting the products and customers to the source of the sales and profit

As top manager for New York City, Mayor Michael Bloomberg is responsible for the smooth operation of the largest U.S. city. His leadership style, formed in the business world, is a no-nonsense, practical approach where communication is key. Bloomberg even prefers working from a cubicle in the "bullpen"—a room where his top aides work—to the official corner office where mayors traditionally sit.

growth expected by CEO McNerney. To achieve these goals, middle managers might budget money for product development, identify new uses for existing products, and improve the ways they train and motivate salespeople.

Supervisory management, or first-line management, includes positions such as supervisor, section chief, and team leader. These managers are directly responsible for assigning nonmanagerial employees to specific jobs and evaluating their performance. Managers at this first level of the hierarchy work in direct and continuing contact with the employees who produce and sell the firm's goods and services. They are responsible for implementing the plans developed by middle managers—motivating workers to accomplish daily, weekly, and monthly goals.

Sonic is the nation's biggest drive-in restaurant chain. It is also the fifth largest fast-food chain in the U.S. Pattye Moore, Sonic's president, outlines a unique Sonic plan to bring out new product ideas: "We encourage our employees to play with their food." A supervisor at an Oklahoma City location created the firm's grilled chicken wrap by experimenting in this way. Moore goes on to further describe how Sonic motivates managers and employees. "Our concept is fun. It is hard to be very serious when you're selling cherry lemonade and strawberry cheesecake shakes."[4]

Skills Needed for Managerial Success

Managers at every level in the management hierarchy must exercise three basic types of skills: technical, human, and conceptual. All managers must acquire these skills in varying proportions, although the importance of each category of skill changes at different management levels.

Technical skills are the manager's ability to understand and use the techniques, knowledge, and tools and equipment of a specific discipline or department. Technical skills lose relative importance at higher levels of the management hierarchy, but most top executives started out as technical experts. The résumé of a vice president for information systems probably lists experience as a computer analyst, and that of a vice president for marketing usually shows a background in sales. At Microsoft, Bill Gates's experience in developing a personal computer (PC) operating system helps him understand the challenges and opportunities for new kinds of software. He identified a need for an operating system that can turn cell phones into handheld computers. But the specifics of developing and marketing the software are primarily the responsibility of lower-level managers and employees.

Human skills are interpersonal skills that enable a manager to work effectively with and through people. Human skills include the ability to communicate with, motivate, and lead employees to accomplish assigned activities. Managers need human skills to interact with people both inside and outside the organization. It would be tough for a manager to succeed without such skills, even though they must be adapted to different forms today—for instance, mastering and communicating effectively with staff through e-mail, cell phones, pagers, faxes, and even instant messaging, which are widespread in offices.[5]

Conceptual skills determine a manager's ability to see the organization as a

Meg Whitman, CEO of the phenomenally successful Web auction site eBay, put her managerial skills to the test when she moved into the dot-com world. She had to polish her technical and conceptual skills when the site's computer server crashed on her first day on the job—and many times after that. Whitman spent several nights on an office cot as she learned about server technology—the key to keeping a Web site up and running.

© Kim Kulish/CORBIS

unified whole and to understand how each part of the overall organization interacts with other parts. These skills involve an ability to see the big picture by acquiring, analyzing, and interpreting information. Conceptual skills are especially important for top-level managers, who must develop long-range plans for the future direction of their organization. eBay was one of the few dot-com companies to survive the industry's shakeout period. CEO Meg Whitman is now moving her business plan to the global marketplace. According to Whitman, "Our vision is to create a global online marketplace where practically anyone can trade anything with anyone in any location."[6]

Managerial Functions

In the course of a typical day, managers spend time meeting and talking with people, reading, thinking, and sending e-mail messages. As they perform these activities, managers are carrying out four basic functions: planning, organizing, directing, and controlling. Planning activities lay the groundwork, and the other functions are aimed at carrying out the plans.

Planning

Planning is the process of anticipating future events and conditions and determining courses of action for achieving organizational objectives. Effective planning can help a business to crystallize its vision, described in the next section, as well as avoid costly mistakes and seize opportunities. Effective planning requires an evaluation of the business environment and a well-designed road map of the actions needed to lead a firm forward. For Michael Dell, founder and CEO of personal computer giant Dell, Inc., plans consist of answers to questions like these: "How many [new products] can you introduce at one time? Where are the big opportunities? What do customers most want us to do?"[7] In a later section of this chapter, we elaborate on the planning process.

planning process of anticipating future events and conditions and determining courses of action for achieving organizational objectives.

Organizing

Once plans have been developed, the next step in the management process typically is **organizing**—the means by which managers blend human and material resources through a formal structure of tasks and authority. This activity involves classifying and dividing work into manageable units by determining specific tasks necessary to accomplish organizational objectives, grouping tasks into a logical pattern or structure, and assigning them to specific personnel. Managers also must staff the organization with competent employees capable of performing the necessary tasks and assigning authority and responsibility to these individuals. Often, organizing involves studying a company's existing structure and determining whether to reorganize it so that the company can better meet its objectives. The organizing process is discussed in detail later in this chapter.

Directing

Once plans have been formulated and an organization has been created and staffed, the management task focuses on **directing,** or guiding and motivating employees to accomplish organizational objectives. Directing includes explaining procedures, issuing orders, and seeing that mistakes are corrected. Managers may also direct in other ways, such as getting employees to agree on how they will meet objectives and inspiring them to care about customer satisfaction or their contribution to the company.

The directing function is a vital responsibility of supervisory managers. To fulfill their responsibilities to get things done through people, supervisors must be effective leaders. In addition, middle and top managers must be good leaders and motivators, and they must create an environment that fosters such leadership. A later section of this chapter discusses leadership, and Chapter 9 discusses motivating employees and improving performance.

Controlling

Controlling is the function of evaluating an organization's performance to determine whether it is accomplishing its objectives. The basic purpose of controlling is to assess the success of the planning function. Controlling also provides feedback for future rounds of planning.

The four basic steps in controlling are to establish performance standards, monitor actual performance, compare actual performance with established standards, and take corrective action if required.

Concept Check
1. What is management?
2. How do the jobs of top managers, middle managers, and supervisory managers differ?
3. What is the relationship between the manager's planning and controlling functions?

Under the provisions of the 2002 Sarbanes-Oxley Act, for example, CEOs and CFOs must monitor the performance of the firm's accounting staff more closely. They must personally attest to the truth of financial reports filed with the Securities and Exchange Commission.

Setting a Vision and Ethical Standards for the Firm

vision perception of marketplace needs and methods an organization can use to satisfy them.

As Chapter 1 discusses, business success almost always begins with a **vision,** a perception of marketplace needs and the methods an organization can use to satisfy them. Vision serves as the target for a firm's actions, helping to direct the company toward opportunities and differentiating it from its competitors. Michael Dell's vision of selling custom-built computers directly to consumers helped distinguish Dell from many other computer industry start-ups. John Schnatter, founder of Papa John's Pizza, keeps his vision—and his menu—focused to satisfy his pizza-loving customers.

Vision must be focused and yet flexible enough to adapt to changes in the business environment. When PCs became commonplace, Microsoft had to switch its vision of a PC on every desk and in every home. The company's new vision refers to "great software, anytime, anyplace, and on any device."

Also critical to a firm's long-term success are the ethical standards that top executives set. As we saw in Chapter 2, a company's top managers can take an organization down a slippery slope to bankruptcy—and even criminal—court if they operate unethically. Avoiding that path requires executives to focus on the organization's success, not merely personal gain. Terry Hall, CEO of Sacramento-based GenCorp, put it this way: "Either you have honesty or you don't. . . . My reputation is not for sale. It doesn't matter what the executive compensation program is. It doesn't help you if you get it one year and the next year you go to jail."[8] Holding the welfare of the company's constituencies—customers, employees, investors, and society in general—as the top priority can build lasting success for a firm.

> *They Said It*
>
> Running a business is about identifying gaps between where we need to be and where we are, and the disciplined closing of gaps.
>
> —*Carly Fiorina (b. 1954)*
> *CEO, Hewlett-Packard Corp.*

The ethical tone that a top management team establishes can also reap nonmonetary rewards. Setting a high ethical standard does not merely restrain employees from doing evil, but it encourages, motivates, and inspires them to achieve goals they never thought possible. Such satisfaction creates a more productive, stable workforce—one that can create a long-term competitive advantage for the organization.

Still, a leader's vision and ethical conduct are only the first steps along an organization's path to success. Turning a business idea into reality takes careful planning and actions. The next sections take a closer look at the planning and implementation process.

Concept Check
1. What is meant by a vision for the firm?
2. Could a not-for-profit organization have a vision? Why or why not?
3. Why is it important for a top executive to set high ethical standards?

Importance of Planning

A Federal Appeals Court dealt Eli Lilly quite a blow when it ruled that Barr Laboratories could sell a generic Prozac-type drug two years earlier than expected. After all, Prozac, the firm's blockbuster antidepressant, accounted for close to 30 percent of Lilly's sales at the time and an even higher profit percentage. Despite the setback, Lilly CEO Sidney Taurel knew the importance of effective planning, and he was ready with a new strategy. During a conference call and various media interviews, he explained that Lilly had several new products in its late-stage drug pipeline. Taurel said that his company's margin would drop briefly and then quickly return to double-digit levels. When Taurel was asked about whether he had expected the court decision, the CEO smiled and replied, "We were ready with strategies and communications plans under various scenarios. This was one of the worst we could expect, but we were ready for it."[9] Let's take a closer look at the types of planning businesses do.

Types of Planning

Planning can be categorized by scope and breadth. Some plans are very broad and long range, focusing on key organizational objectives. Others specify how the organization will mobilize to achieve these objectives. Planning can be divided into the following categories: strategic, tactical, operational, and contingency. Each step in planning includes more specific information than the last. From the mission statement to objectives to specific plans, each phase must fit into a comprehensive planning framework. The framework also must include narrow, functional plans aimed at individual employees and work areas relevant to individual tasks. These plans fit within the firm's overall planning framework, allowing it to reach objectives and achieve its mission.

Strategic Planning   The most far-reaching level of planning is **strategic planning**—the process of determining the primary objectives of an organization and then acting and allocating resources to achieve those objectives. At Dell, Inc., managers maintain this long-range view. "You may have a great day today and the stock goes down, and you may have a horrible day tomorrow and the stock goes up," says CEO Michael Dell. "But over a long period of time you build a great company."[10] Strategic planning is what drives the transformation of a company's mission, as the Best Business Practices box describes.

Tactical Planning   **Tactical planning** involves implementing the activities specified by strategic plans. Tactical plans guide the current and near-term activities required to implement overall strategies. The Memphis Grizzlies' decision to hire Jerry West to run basketball operations was a tactical decision. West—a West Virginia University basketball great—was a longtime Los Angeles Laker as both a player and, more recently, as the team's general manager.

Operational Planning   **Operational planning** creates the detailed standards that guide implementation of tactical plans. This activity involves choosing specific work targets and assigning employees and teams to carry out plans. Unlike strategic planning, which focuses on the organization as a whole, operational planning deals with developing and implementing tactics in specific functional areas. Operational planning by Jerry West and others at the Memphis NBA franchise would be illustrated by their plans for an upcoming player draft.

Contingency Planning   Planning cannot foresee every possibility. Major accidents, natural disasters, and rapid economic downturns can throw even the best-laid plans into chaos. To handle the possibility of business disruption from events of this nature, many firms use **contingency planning,** which allows a firm to resume operations as quickly and as smoothly as possible after a crisis while openly communicating with the public about what happened. This planning activity involves two components: business continuation and public communication. Many firms have developed management strategies to speed recovery from accidents such as airline crashes, fires and explosions, chemical leaks, package tampering, and product failures.

> *They Said It*
>
> Great crises produce great men and great deeds of courage.
>
> —*John F. Kennedy (1917–1963)*
> *35th president of the United States*

A contingency plan usually designates a chain of command for crisis management, assigning specific functions to particular managers and employees in an emergency. Contingency planning also involves training workers to respond to emergencies, improving communications systems, and using advanced technology. Companies with well-defined disaster recovery plans generally fared better in the aftermath of the September 11 terrorist attacks than those that didn't develop and implement plans.

Planning at Different Organizational Levels

Although managers spend some time on planning virtually every day, the total time spent and the type of planning done differ according to the level of management. As Table 8.1 points out, members

BEST BUSINESS PRACTICES

Listening to Starbucks

"We are the most frequented retailer in the world. With hundreds of thousands of songs digitally filed and stored. . . . [Retail chain] Hear Music coffeehouses combined with our existing locations can become the largest music store in any city . . . . And because of the traffic, the frequency, and the trust that our customers have in the experience and the brand, we believe strongly that we can transform the retail record industry."

Those are the words of Howard Schultz, founder and CEO of Starbucks, as he describes his plan to invent his coffee chain after making it one of the best-known brands in the world. Schultz's firm purchased Hear Music in 1999 after he visited the CD store and realized that nothing goes together so well as the coffeehouse experience provided by Starbucks and music. Now, with 30 million customers enjoying not just their favorite coffee drink but also the carefully tailored ambiance of Schultz's 8,000 stores, Starbucks is poised to take a daring but well-planned risk.

Individual Hear Music listening stations, at which customers can burn their own custom-made CDs and even design their own cover art, are being installed in hundreds of Starbucks outlets across the country. Customers will be able to create their own take-home CDs while they sip their latte, surf the Internet, and soak up Starbucks's home-away-from-home ambiance. While some fear that its planned new focus on music will dilute Starbucks's brand, Schultz is confident. "Great companies are defined by their discipline and their understanding of who they are and who they are not," he says. "But also, great companies must have the courage to examine strategic opportunities that are transformational—as long as they are not inconsistent with the guiding principles and values of the core business." In fact, the CEO does see Starbucks's role evolving. Of the firm's first expansion into selling compiled music CDs in its stores, he said, "I began to understand that our customers looked to Starbucks as a kind of editor. It was like, 'We trust you. Help us choose.'"

QUESTIONS FOR CRITICAL THINKING

1. About planning the Hear Music expansion, Howard Schultz has said, "It's always best to surround yourself with people who've done it before, in some form or another." Do you agree or disagree? Why?
2. What kind of strategic, tactical, and operational decisions do you think Starbucks had to make in planning its expansion into the retail music business? Give an example of each.

Sources: Donna Rosato, "When It Pays to Pay Up," *Money,* August 2004, p. 124; Alison Overholt, "Listening to Starbucks," *Fast Company,* July 2004, pp. 50–56; Deborah Ball and Shirley Leung, "Latte versus Latte," *The Wall Street Journal,* February 10, 2004, pp. B1, B9; Andy Serwer, "Hot Starbucks to Go," *Fortune,* January 26, 2004, pp. 60–74.

Concept Check

1. Outline the planning process.
2. Describe the purpose of tactical planning.
3. Compare the kinds of plans made by top managers and middle managers. How does their focus differ?

of top management, including a firm's board of directors and CEO, spend a great deal of time on long-range planning, while middle-level managers and supervisors focus on short-term, tactical planning. Employees at all levels can benefit themselves and their company by making plans to meet their own specific goals.

Table 8.1   Planning at Different Management Levels

Primary Type of Planning	Managerial Level	Examples
Strategic	Top management	Organizational objectives, fundamental strategies, long-term plans
Tactical	Middle management	Quarterly and semiannual plans, departmental policies and procedures
Operational	Supervisory management	Daily and weekly plans, rules, and procedures for each department
Contingency	Primarily top management, but all levels contribute	Ongoing plans for actions and communications in an emergency

The Strategic Planning Process

Strategic planning often makes the difference between an organization's success and failure. Strategic planning has formed the basis of many fundamental management decisions:

- Hewlett-Packard's decision to acquire Compaq to improve its competitive position. One million hours were devoted to planning the integration of the two companies.[11]
- Altria's decision to sell Miller Brewing to concentrate on its food and tobacco units.
- Chicken king Tyson Foods's decision to reenter the beef and pork markets. Tyson implemented this strategic decision by acquiring IBP Corp.

Successful strategic planners typically follow the six steps shown in Figure 8.2: defining a mission, assessing the organization's competitive position, setting organizational objectives, creating strategies for competitive differentiation, implementing the strategy, and evaluating the results and refining the plan.

Defining the Organization's Mission

The first step in strategic planning is to translate the firm's vision into a mission statement. A **mission statement** is a written explanation of an organization's business intentions and aims. It is an enduring statement of a firm's purpose, possibly highlighting the scope of operations, the market it seeks to serve, and the ways it will attempt to set itself apart from competitors. A mission statement guides the actions of people inside the firm and informs customers and other stakeholders of the company's underlying reasons for existence. The mission statement should be widely publicized with employees, suppliers, partners, shareholders, customers, and the general public.

mission statement
written explanation of an organization's business intentions and aims.

The evolution of Microsoft's mission statement was outlined earlier in the section on establishing an organization's vision. Mission statements can vary in complexity and length.

- A Birmingham, Alabama, securities firm has a very straightforward mission statement: "The mission of Sterne, Agee, and Leach, Inc. is to build wealth for our clients."
- Software maker Adobe takes a somewhat different approach: "EVERYWHERE YOU LOOK Adobe is changing the way people do business, express their creativity, and connect with each other."
- Walgreen has a longer, more detailed mission statement: "Walgreen's mission is to offer customers the best drugstore service in America. We are guided by a century-old tradition of fairness, trust, and honesty as we continue to expand our store base and offer career opportunities to a fast-growing and diverse group of men and women. Our goal is to develop people who treat customers—and each other—with respect and dignity. We will support these efforts with the most innovative retail thinking, services, and technology. The success we achieve will allow us to reinvest in our future and build long-term financial security for our employees and our shareholders."[12]

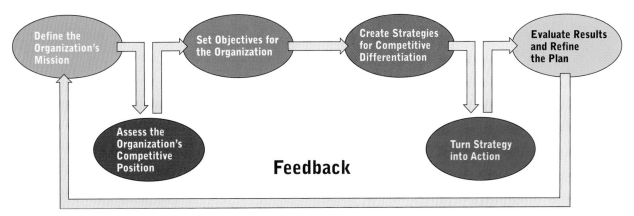

FIGURE 8.2

Steps in Strategic Planning Process

Developing a mission statement can be one of the most complex and difficult aspects of strategic planning. Completing these statements requires detailed considerations of a company's values and vision. Effective mission statements indicate specific, achievable, inspiring principles. They avoid unrealistic promises and statements.

Assessing Your Competitive Position

Once a mission statement has been created, the next step in the planning process is to assess the firm's current position in the marketplace. This phase also involves an examination of the factors that may help or hinder the organization in the future. A frequently used tool in this phase of strategic planning is SWOT analysis.

A **SWOT analysis** is an organized approach to assessing a company's internal strengths and weaknesses and its external opportunities and threats. SWOT is an acronym for strengths, weaknesses, opportunities, and threats. The basic premise of SWOT is that a critical internal and external reality check should lead managers to select the appropriate strategy to accomplish their organization's objectives. SWOT analysis encourages a practical approach to planning based on a realistic view of a firm's situation and scenarios of likely future events and conditions. Household Finance Corporation capitalized on its strengths and opportunities when it developed computer software to increase the efficiency with which it could process loan applications.[13] The framework for a SWOT analysis appears in Figure 8.3.

To evaluate a firm's strengths and weaknesses, the planners may examine each functional area such as finance, marketing, information technology, and human resources. Entrepreneurs may focus on the individual skills and experience they bring to a new business. Large firms may also examine strengths and weaknesses of individual decisions and geographical operations. Usually, planners attempt to look at their strengths and weaknesses in relation to those of other firms in the industry.

For Starbucks, a key strength is consumers' positive image of the company's brand, which gets them to stand in line to pay premium prices for coffee. The company's strategic plans have included various ways to build on its strong brand loyalty by attaching it to new products expanding into new markets.

FIGURE 8.3
Elements of SWOT Analysis

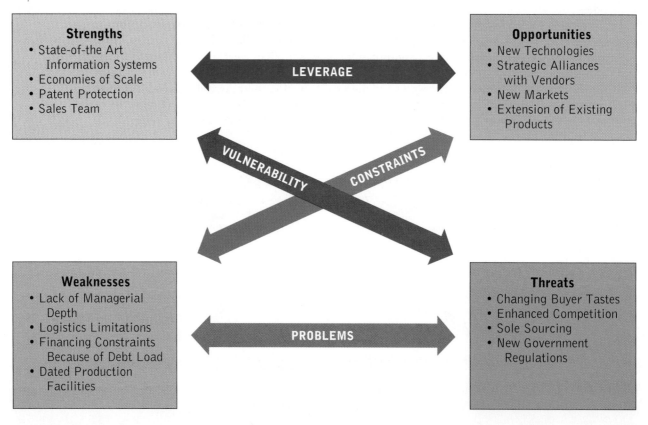

The expansion efforts have included a Web site, selling bottled Frappuccino iced coffee in supermarkets, and the opening of thousands of Starbucks outlets in Europe, Asia, and the Middle East.

SWOT analysis continues with an attempt to define the major opportunities and threats the firm is likely to face within the time frame of the plan. Possibilities include environmental factors such as market growth, regulatory changes, or increased competition. Starbucks saw an opportunity in the growth of the Internet and the interest in online shopping. Its Web site sells coffee and related accessories. In addition, Starbucks's experience in Japan, where its outlets' average sales top those in the U.S., suggested that international expansion presented a solid opportunity. A threat is that consumers could tire of paying $3 or so for cappuccinos and lattés and switch to something else. The company has begun addressing that threat with the introduction of gourmet tea products.

Some aspects of Starbucks's strategy have succeeded better than others. Initially, Starbucks tried selling gourmet foods, music, and even furniture on its Web site. Sales were disappointing, and the firm quickly dropped the least successful offerings. Recently, Starbucks has shifted more of its attention to its retail units, where sales remain strong.[14]

If a firm's strengths and opportunities mesh successfully, as at the Starbucks retail stores, it gains competitive leverage in the marketplace. On the other hand, if internal weaknesses prevent a firm from overcoming external threats, as in the case of the Starbucks Web site, it may find itself facing major difficulties. A SWOT analysis is a useful tool in the strategic planning process because it forces management to look at factors both inside and outside the organization. SWOT analysis examines not only the current picture but also necessary current actions to prepare for likely future developments.

The strength of Starbucks stems from its customers' devotion to its premium products. From frothy lattés, to iced frappuccinos, to rich ice creams, the company knows how to satisfy customer cravings. Starbucks recently expanded its sales channels by offering products in grocery stores so customers can enjoy their favorite products at home. Firms learn to assess their strengths when determining their competitive position in the marketplace via SWOT analysis.

© Terri L. Miller E-Visual Communications, Inc.

Establishing Objectives for the Organization

After defining the company's mission and examining factors that may affect its ability to fulfill that mission, the next step in planning is to develop objectives for the organization. **Objectives** set guideposts by which managers define the organization's desired performance in such areas as profitability, customer service, and employee satisfaction. The mission statement delineates the company's goals in general terms, but objectives are more concrete statements. More and more businesses are setting explicit objectives for performance standards other than profitability. As public concern about environmental issues mounts, many firms find that operating in an environmentally responsible manner pays off in good relations with customers. Others channel some of their profits into socially responsible causes, such as funding educational programs and scholarships.

At Continental Airlines, objectives include satisfying customers. Each month, the Department of Transportation tracks such airline performance measures as customer

objectives guideposts by which managers define the organization's desired performance in such areas as profitability, customer service, growth, and employee satisfaction.

satisfaction, on-time performance, and frequency of lost luggage. Several years ago, Continental ranked last in most of those measures, and late and canceled flights were costing the company $6 million a month. Continental's CEO Gordon Bethune declared that if Continental could achieve a ranking among the top three in any month, the company would split the $6 million with employees, amounting to about $65 per employee for the month. Employees began to collaborate on solutions to flight delays, and before long, they were earning the monthly bonuses. Today, Continental is usually ranked among the industry leaders in customer service.[15]

Creating Strategies for Competitive Differentiation

Developing a mission statement and setting objectives point a business toward a specific destination. To get there, however, the firm needs to map the strategies it will follow to compete with other companies pursuing similar missions and objectives. The underlying goal of strategy development is **competitive differentiation,** the unique combination of a company's abilities and approaches that places it ahead of competitors. Common sources of competitive differentiation include product innovation, technology, and employee motivation.

Product innovation, for instance, is a key part of the strategy at H. J. Heinz. The food giant recently introduced new variations of two of its most popular products—Ore-Ida french fries and ketchup. Funky Fries come in new flavors, shapes, and colors. John Carroll of Heinz describes the market for Funky Fries: "Kids will love new Funky Fries because they are a wild new way to enjoy french fries. . . . They can be enjoyed anytime—whether it's after school, during mealtime or as an evening snack." Heinz's other new product innovation is called KICK'RS, a line of flavored ketchup aimed at adults who want bolder flavors with meals. It is offered in three varieties: Zesty Garlic, Hot & Spicy, and Smokey Mesquite.[16]

The Implementation Phase of Planning

Once the first four phases of the strategic planning process are complete, managers face even bigger challenges. They must begin to put strategy into action by identifying the specific methods to do so and deploying the resources needed to implement the intended plans.

Capital One Financial—headquartered in Falls Church, Virginia—is a major player in the credit card industry. CEO Richard Fairbank and cofounder and President Nigel Morris decided to build their business by implementing some then-unique concepts. They decided to offer attractive credit card packages and then use the information generated to target products to specific customer segments. Morris revealed that the duo started to view credit cards "not as a banking business but as an information-management business." Capital One used Oracle software to build a huge database. The company offers lower interest rates to major borrowers, while giving riskier accounts lower credit limits and higher interest rates. Capital One was the first to offer balance transfers, teaser rates, and preapproved promotions. The implementation of Capital One's plan was clearly based on its massive database.

In a recent year, Capital One ran 64,000 tests on everything from the size and color of envelopes to the wording of promotions. CEO Fairbank summarizes the implementation of Capital One's planning this way: "Every customer takes a unique trip through Capital One. The product they're offered, the price it's offered at, the size of the credit lines, how we manage the account, what we do if you're delinquent—all of that is entirely customized."[17]

They Said It

Are you guys ready? Let's roll.

—*Todd Beamer (1969–2001)*
final words of one of the heroes of Flight 93

Monitoring and Adapting Strategic Plans

The final state in the strategic planning process, closely linked to implementation, consists of monitoring and adapting plans when actual performance fails to match expectations. Monitoring involves establishing methods of securing feedback about actual performance. Common methods include comparisons of actual sales and market share data with forecasts, information received from supplier and customer surveys, complaints received on the firm's customer hot line, and reports prepared by production, finance, marketing, and other company units.

Ongoing use of such tools as SWOT analysis and forecasting can help managers adapt objectives and functional plans as changes occur. An increase in the price of a key product component, for instance, could dramatically affect the firm's ability to maintain planned prices and still earn acceptable profits. An unexpected strike by UPS may disrupt shipments of products to retail and business customers. In each instance, the original plan may require modification to continue to guide the firm toward achievement of its objectives.

Concept Check

1. What is the purpose of a mission statement?
2. Which of the firm's characteristics does a SWOT analysis compare?
3. How do managers use objectives?

Managers as Decision Makers

In carrying out planning and the other management functions, executives must make decisions every day. **Decision making** is the process of recognizing a problem or opportunity and then dealing with it. The types of decisions that managers make can be classified as programmed and nonprogrammed.

Programmed and Nonprogrammed Decisions

Programmed and nonprogrammed decisions differ in whether they have unique elements. A **programmed decision** involves simple, common, and frequently occurring problems for which solutions have already been determined. Examples of programmed decisions include choosing the starting salary for a new marketing assistant, reordering raw materials needed in the manufacturing process, and setting a discount schedule for large-volume customers. For these types of decisions, organizations develop rules, policies, and detailed procedures that managers apply to achieve consistent, quick, and inexpensive solutions to common problems. Since such solutions eliminate the time-consuming process of identifying and evaluating alternatives and making new decisions each time a situation occurs, managers can devote their time to the more complex problems associated with nonprogrammed decisions. For example, satisfactory review of a staple item might allow the Wal-Mart buyer in this category more time to seek other merchandising opportunities.

A **nonprogrammed decision** involves a complex and unique problem or opportunity with important consequences for the organization. Examples of nonprogrammed decisions include entering a new geographical market, acquiring another company, or introducing a new product. Ted Waitt, whose computer company Gateway is engaged in costly market-share competitions with Dell and Apple, faces nonprogrammed decisions with major consequences. Waitt is waging a price war against Dell, and his company developed a product that Waitt hopes may compete against Apple's iMac, but with fewer features. Some observers believe Gateway could rise or fall on the results of the decisions Waitt makes as his company reaches a crisis point. Waitt, in turn, is banking on the recovery of the PC market.[18]

How Managers Make Decisions

In a narrow sense, decision making involves choosing among two or more alternatives; the chosen alternative becomes the decision. In a broader sense, decision making involves a systematic, step-by-step process that helps managers make effective choices. This process begins when someone recognizes a problem or opportunity; it proceeds with developing potential courses of action, evaluating the alternatives, selecting and implementing one of them, and assessing the outcome of the decision. The steps in the decision-making process are illustrated in Figure 8.4. This systematic approach can be applied to all decisions, with either programmed or nonprogrammed features.

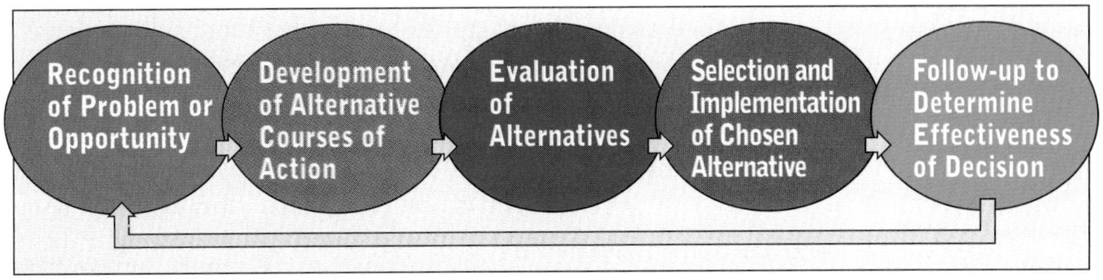

The decision-making process can be applied in both

decision making process of recognizing a problem or opportunity, evaluating alternative solutions, selecting and implementing an alternative, and assessing the results.

Recognition of Problem or Opportunity → Development of Alternative Courses of Action → Evaluation of Alternatives → Selection and Implementation of Chosen Alternative → Follow-up to Determine Effectiveness of Decision

FIGURE 8.4
Steps in the Decision-Making Process

SOLVING AN ETHICAL CONTROVERSY

Executive Pay: How Much Is Too Much?

CEO pay has reached staggering heights in the last 20 years. In 2000 the average CEO's pay package was 531 times the average worker's salary; in 1982 it was only 42 times as much. Charles Conway earned almost $23 million during his two-year stint as Kmart's CEO, and Dennis Kozlowski, scheduled for retrial in 2005 on allegations of fraud as CEO of Tyco Corp., received pay and perks totaling $446.7 million during his last year on the job. Until recently, CEO compensation was rarely scrutinized in public, but exorbitant packages that have come to light during recent SEC investigations have prompted overdue government regulations and public outcry.

Many are asking what CEOs are doing to earn so much money. CEOs often earn "stratospheric sums for mediocre performance," according to one analyst, who noted, "We have been surprised by the degree to which pay at many firms continues to be disconnected from performance." For example, compensation for the new CEO at drug giant Schering-Plough totaled $11 million, even though the firm lost $92 million that same year.

While some CEOs hold down their salaries—Continental Airlines's Gordon Bethune signed an agreement that capped his compensation at $1 million and eliminated bonus and stock options—others seem to feel they can never earn enough. Dick Grasso was fired as head of the New York Stock Exchange because of what was deemed excessive compensation. The issue is now in litigation.

Are CEOs and other top executives paid too much?

PRO
1. No one could possibly make a contribution to a firm's success that is worth more than 500 times the average worker's pay package.
2. Exorbitant salaries take money away from the employees and shareholders and reduce the value of the firm.

CON
1. High salaries are necessary to attract and retain the kind of talented executives who are willing to take high-risk jobs.

2. Keeping a company profitable is extraordinarily challenging in today's business environment, and executives who can do so deserve to be rewarded for it.

SUMMARY
Some forms of executive compensation, such as the granting of huge amounts of stock options in the firm, are no longer the norm because of shareholder revolts and because accounting requirements are changing so that such options must be recorded in the firm's financial statements as a business expense. All other forms of compensation are still rising, however, and it will likely be up to shareholders to become more active in voting down CEO salaries they feel are out of line.

Sources: Matthew Boyle, "When Will They Stop?" *Fortune*, May 3, 2004, pp. 123–128; Edward Iwata and Barbara Hansen, "Pay, Performance Don't Always Add Up," *USA Today*, April 30, 2004, pp. 1B–3B; Jesse Drucker, "As CEOs Miss Bonus Goals, Goalposts Move," *The Wall Street Journal*, February 7, 2004, p. C1.

for-profit and not-for-profit organizations. Consider how Michael Miller built the Portland, Oregon, Goodwill Industries retail business of selling donated items. Miller knew that he had to locate stores where Goodwill's donors and customers meshed. Surveys uncovered that the typical donor was a female, aged 35 to 44 with an income of $50,000. By contrast, Miller's customers were women aged 25 to 54 with two kids. Their average income was roughly $30,000. Miller then got some help from the locally based Fred Meyer supermarket chain (part of Kroger's). Fred Meyer's database contained gender and income demographics by neighborhood. Miller's decision to open stores was then based on where his two target clients intersected. To make customers more comfortable, Miller's 28 stores even feature bookstores and coffee bars.[19]

Making good decisions is never easy, however, because it involves taking risks that can influence a firm's success or failure. Often, decisions made by managers have complex legal and ethical dimensions.

Concept Check

1. Compare and contrast programmed and nonprogrammed decisions.
2. What are the steps in the decision-making process?

An executive research firm recently tested 1,400 managers to assess their integrity and found that one in eight "believe the rules do not apply to them" and they "rarely possess feelings of guilt."[20] The Solving an Ethical Controversy box describes one controversial issue about which managers and corporate directors must sometimes make decisions: their pay level and the amount of bonuses and perks they receive, in good times and bad.

Managers as Leaders

The most visible component of a manager's responsibilities is **leadership,** directing or inspiring people to attain organizational goals. *Worth* magazine annually picks the nation's best CEOs. A recent list included Meg Whitman of eBay, Henry McKinnell of Pfizer, David Pottruck of Charles Schwab, George David of United Technologies, and Steve Ballmer of Microsoft.[21] All are demanding leaders, yet they inspire their associates to reach their full potential.

Because effective leadership is so important to organizational success, a large amount of research has focused on the characteristics of a good leader. Great leaders do not all share the same qualities, but three traits are often mentioned: empathy, which is the ability to imagine yourself in another's position; self-awareness; and objectivity in dealing with others. Many great leaders share other traits, including courage, ability to inspire others, passion, commitment, flexibility, innovation, and willingness to experiment.

Leadership involves the use of influence or power. This influence may come from one or more sources. One source of power is the leader's position in the organization. A national sales manager has the authority to direct the activities of the sales force. Another source of power comes from a leader's expertise and experience. A first-line supervisor with expert machinist skills will most likely be respected by employees in the machining department. Some leaders derive power from their personalities. Employees may admire a leader because they recognize an exceptionally kind and fair, humorous, energetic, or enthusiastic person.

A well-known example is Herb Kelleher, the retired CEO of Southwest Airlines. Kelleher's legendary ability to motivate employees to outperform those at rival airlines came from his dynamic personality, boundless energy, love of fun, and sincere concern for his employees. Kelleher led by example, modeling the behavior he wanted to see in his employees. He pitched in to help serve snacks to passengers and load luggage. Employees, inspired by his example, now unload and reload a plane in 20 minutes—one-third of the average time for other airlines.

> **leadership** ability to direct or inspire people to attain organizational goals.

> ## They Said It
>
> A great leader is not one who does the greatest things. He's the one who gets the people to do the greatest things.
>
> —*Ronald Reagan (1911–2004)*
> *40th president of the United States*

Leadership Styles

The way a person uses power to lead others determines his or her leadership style. Researchers have identified a continuum of leadership styles based on the amount of employee participation allowed or invited. At one end of the continuum, **autocratic leadership** is centered on the boss. Autocratic leaders make decisions on their own without consulting employees. They reach decisions, communicate them to subordinates, and expect prompt implementation of instructions. An autocratic sales manager might assign quotas to individual salespeople without consulting them.

Democratic leadership involves subordinates in making decisions. Located in the middle of the continuum, this leadership style centers on employees' contributions. Democratic leaders delegate assignments, ask employees for suggestions, and encourage participation. An important trend that has developed in business during the past decade is the concept of **empowerment,** a practice in which managers lead employees by sharing power, responsibility, and decision making with them.

Sometimes the sharing of power is institutionalized, as in a company like Southwest Airlines. Southwest has the highest proportion of union members among all U.S. air carriers and is also the only one of the country's top eight airlines to post a profit coming out of the recent recession. Rules governing contract negotiations in unionized firms require labor and management to sit down together and discuss wages, hours, and benefits each time the contract is up for renewal. But Southwest's new CEO, Jim Parker, takes management participation a step further by personally leading most of the negotiations. A defender of the flexible policies that helped Southwest succeed, Parker has been known to take representatives of both sides in a conflict out to dinner. Says one of the company's pilots, "The biggest complaint in the industry is that management doesn't listen to employees. But you can't say that at Southwest. The top guy is in the room."[22]

At the other end of the continuum from autocratic leadership is **free-rein leadership.** Free-rein leaders believe in minimal supervision. They leave most decisions to their subordinates. Free-rein leaders communicate with employees frequently, as the situation warrants.

BUSINESS TOOL KIT

Managing Others:
How to Become a Good Manager

When you become a manager, the Golden Rule is most definitely applicable. Learning how to be a good manager requires time, patience, and some extraordinary people skills. You will need to learn how to motivate and communicate with many different types of people and, at the same time, keep an eye on the day-to-day running of the business and its bottom line. In short, the training it takes to become a good manager never ends. Here are some tips on becoming an effective manager.

1. Treat everyone the way you want to be treated. This is true regardless of your position or title in an organization. Respecting and listening to others not only gains you respect, it is also the key to effectively managing even the most unmanageable employee. Everyone has a need to be heard, so listen up and your employees will listen to you.

2. As the manager of a department, team, or business, you must set the tone at work. People will be more apt to follow your lead if you work diligently to create a positive environment for them to work in. It is also important to empower your employees and encourage them to use their own skills, ideas, and creativity when problem solving.

3. Communication skills are extremely important in management. To avoid misunderstandings, you must learn to be very specific when issuing tasks or directions. You will also learn that not everyone has the requisite people

skills—making eye contact, smiling, greeting customers—so it's up to you to teach your employees how to communicate effectively. Communicating your expectations is one of the most important tasks you'll accomplish as a manager. Let people know exactly what you expect of them and give them the tools to meet or exceed that expectation.

4. Establish and share your vision for your team and your company with everyone. Good managers know where they want to take their department or organization, and everyone benefits if everyone knows the game plan. Don't be shy about sharing your vision of success—as a manager, you will be expected to set and achieve personal and organizational goals, and the only way to meet them is to educate your employees.

5. Above all, have fun and allow others to have fun at their jobs. Fostering a pleasant environment and encouraging others to enjoy and succeed at their jobs is the hallmark of a good manager.

Sources: Richard L. Daft, *Management,* 6th ed. Mason, OH: South-Western/ Thomson Learning, 2003; Carol Radice, "Retraining the Trainers: Behind Every Good Employee, There's a Good Manager," *Grocery Headquarters,* October 2002, p. 24.

Which Leadership Style Is Best?

The most appropriate leadership style depends on the function of the leader, the subordinates, and the situation. Some leaders cannot work comfortably with a high degree of subordinate participation in decision making. Some employees lack the ability or the desire to assume responsibility. In addition, the specific situation helps to determine the most effective style of interactions. Sometimes managers must handle problems that require immediate solutions without consulting employees. When time pressure is less acute, participative decision making may work better for the same people.

Democratic leaders often ask for suggestions and advice from their employees but make the final decisions themselves. A manager who prefers the free-rein leadership style may be forced by circumstances to make a particular decision in an autocratic manner. A manager may involve employees in interviewing and hiring decisions but take complete responsibility for firing an employee.

After years of research intended to determine the best types of leaders, experts agree that they cannot identify any single best style of leadership. Instead, they contend that the most effective style

Management Lessons from the Best-Run Technology Company

Not long ago, a labor dispute shut ports all along the U.S. West Coast, preventing hundreds of commercial ships from unloading cargoes for 10 days. Without the raw materials and finished goods on which they depend, many U.S. businesses missed production targets and suffered lost sales. Most observers thought one of the biggest losers would be Dell, the computer company famous for relying on just-in-time production that keeps inventory at precariously low levels.

But Dell's supply chain manager knew that "when a labor problem or an earthquake or a SARS epidemic breaks out, we've got to react quicker than anyone else. There's no other choice. We know these things are going to happen; we must move fast to fix them. We just can't tolerate any kind of delay." Dell put into place a contingency plan it had worked out months before, based on information from its supply chain partners. It chartered more than a dozen planes from carriers all over the world, and it kept parts moving into its two factories in Austin and Nashville throughout the strike without delaying a single customer order. Dell had even anticipated the backlog of materials that would occur when the ports reopened and had workers on hand to unload the delayed containers and speed their contents to its factories.

In the aftermath of the strike, many companies that were caught short of parts and materials began looking for additional warehouse space so they could stock up on inventory. For Dell, however, its performance during the strike only reinforced how successful its most basic management principle is. Says its supply chain manager, "Speed is at the core of everything we do."

How does Dell remain the most profitable computer maker in the world, growing at nearly 20 percent a year on a revenue base of about $45 billion annually, when it assembles nearly 80,000 computers every 24 hours on two hours worth of inventory in its factories and maintains no warehouses? Its reliance on speed, and its determination to top its past performance, are maintained through adherence to a handful of straightforward management principles that filter down from founder-chairman Michael Dell and CEO Kevin Rollins. Described as someone who is "pleased but never satisfied" with meeting a challenge, Dell himself, known to be intensely shy, has painfully revamped his management style after performance reviews by his executives labeled him aloof and impersonal. Rollins similarly pledged to be less combative with employees. Dell's quarterly and annual performance reviews are designed to expose weaknesses such as overblown egos, poor teamwork, defensiveness about mistakes, and complacency about success as well as performance failures like missed cost or profit targets.

Saving money is paramount at Dell, and unprofitable or disappointing ventures are quickly shut down. Profits and growth are both stressed, and when a manager achieves them, the company's policy is to "celebrate for a nanosecond, then move on." Dwelling on success is discouraged. Says Michael Dell, "Museums are looking at the past." When a problem occurs, managers are expected to find it, admit to it, and solve it. On the other hand, they are also expected to speak up and challenge their bosses, being blunt and direct—like Dell himself—when criticism is warranted.

Dell managers are expected to make every product profitable from the start. The mandate to keep costs down has made itself felt outside the company, too, carried to Dell's vendors by supply-quality engineers who help parts makers meet Dell's exacting standards for quality, service, and delivery times. One maker of disk drives says that Dell "pushed all of us to streamline our processes and drive for maximum efficiency. Dell influenced the entire industry." Even suppliers are measured against expectations; a daily score for each vendor's performance is posted on a protected Dell Web site. Suppliers that don't measure up lose Dell's business.

QUESTIONS FOR CRITICAL THINKING

1. Dell is a proven leader in its industry. In what ways do you think its corporate management style is an outgrowth of Michael Dell's personal commitment to excellence?

2. What positive aspects do you see in Dell's management principles? Are there any negative aspects? What are they and how would you change them? What impact do you think your changes would have on the company's success?

Sources: Anne D'Innocenzio, "Grinchlike Gridlock," *Mobile Register,* November 14, 2004, pp. F1, F5; Bill Breen, "Living in Dell Time," *Fast Company,* November 2004, pp. 86–95; Andrew Park and Lauren Young, "Dell Outfoxes Its Rivals," *BusinessWeek,* September 6, 2004, p. 54; Andrew Park and Peter Burrows, "What You Don't Know about Dell," *BusinessWeek,* November 3, 2003, pp. 76–84.

1. How is leadership defined?
2. Identify the styles of leadership as they appear along a continuum of greater or less employee participation.

depends on the leader's base of power, the difficulty of the tasks involved, and the characteristics of the employees. Both extremely easy and extremely difficult situations are best suited to leaders who emphasize the accomplishment of assigned tasks. Moderately difficult situations are best suited to leaders who emphasize participation and good working relationships with subordinates. A good example of a distinctive management style that has helped revolutionize the computer industry is Dell, Inc., as discussed in the Hits & Misses box.

Corporate Culture

corporate culture
organization's system of values, principles, and beliefs.

The best leadership style to adopt often depends on the organization's **corporate culture,** its system of principles, beliefs, and values. Managerial philosophies, communications networks, and workplace environments and practices all influence corporate culture. At Home Depot, the corporate culture is based on the belief that employees should fully understand and be enthusiastic about the core business of serving do-it-yourselfers. All newly hired employees, including top managers, must spend their first two weeks working on the sales floor of a Home Depot store. Even CEO Robert Nardelli spends time at an Atlanta area store helping customers. By working at stores, all employees are exposed to the company's customers and, the company hopes, will soak up some of their can-do spirit. The company also encourages employees to get involved in service projects, like building homes for Habitat for Humanity, which brings them closer to their community while seeing the stores' products in use. In addition, Home Depot gets employees excited about the business by granting them stock options. This benefit has made millionaires of many Home Depot employees. Stories like that of Franc Gambatse, who started as a sales clerk and less than a decade later was managing a Home Depot store and enjoying prosperity he "never could have imagined," inspire other employees to give their all. The retailer even has a company cheer: "Gimme an H!" and on through the store's name, as the troops reply, ready to support the company's continued growth in stores, sales, and profits.[23]

Home Depot's corporate culture emphasizes the importance of employees' knowledge of the business and their enthusiasm. Here employees are working collaboratively to fulfill a customer order.

© Lon C. Diehl/Photo Edit

A corporate culture is typically shaped by the leaders who founded and developed the company and by those who have succeeded them. One generation of employees passes on a corporate culture to newer employees. Sometimes this transfer is part of formal training. New managers who attend sessions at McDonald's Hamburger University may learn skills in management, but they also acquire the basics of the organization's corporate culture. Employees can absorb corporate culture through informal contacts, as well as by talking with other workers and through their experiences on the job.

Managers use symbols, rituals, and ceremonies to reinforce corporate culture. Consider how the so-called "HP Way" got started. In

1957, Hewlett-Packard was a successful growing company about to sell its stock publicly. Still, cofounder David Packard worried that the firm would soon lose its "small company" atmosphere. Packard and his partner, Bill Hewlett, wanted to keep HP's record of innovation. After all, HP originated in a garage. The duo decided to hold one of American industry's first off-site company retreats. They took their top 20 employees to the California wine country. There at the Sonoma Mission Inn and Spa, Hewlett, Packard, and their associates decided to establish a corporate culture that would ensure innovation. By the end of the retreat, the participants had outlined values and objectives that became known as the HP Way. Today, HP's corporate culture is carried on by CEO Carly Fiorina.[24]

Corporate cultures can be changed. UPS was once known for its rigid and rule-oriented culture. Rules were needed, and still are, to ensure that this company of 330,000 employees achieves its goal of delivering 13.5 million packages on time every day. But in recent years, nearly 1,200 middle managers, most of them white, have completed the company's Community Internship Program (CIP), acquiring the flexibility they need to understand the needs of their increasingly diverse employees. Every summer, about 50 managers spend a month working on community service projects that help the urban poor. Assignments include building housing, collecting clothing for the Salvation Army, working in a drug rehab center, teaching business skills to prison inmates, and providing meals to the homeless. After participating in the Community Internship Program, manager Mark J. Colvard gave a valued employee two weeks off for a family illness, time to which the employee wasn't entitled. Colvard had to defend his actions, but he was able to keep the employee on board.[25]

In an organization with strong culture, everyone knows and supports the same objectives. A company with weak or constantly shifting culture lacks a clear sense of purpose. To achieve goals, a business must also provide a framework that defines how employees should accomplish their tasks. This framework is the organization structure, which results from the management function of organizing.

Concept Check

1. What is corporate culture?
2. What is the relationship between leadership style and corporate culture?

Organizational Structures

The management function of organizing is the process of blending human and material resources through a formal structure of tasks and authority. It involves arranging work, dividing tasks among employees, and coordinating them to ensure implementation of plans and accomplishment of objectives. The result of this process is an **organization,** a structured grouping of people working together to achieve common objectives. An organization features three key elements: human interaction, goal-directed activities, and structure. The organizing process should result in an overall structure that permits interactions among individuals and departments needed to achieve company goals.

organization structured grouping of people working together to achieve common goals.

The steps involved in the organizing process are shown in Figure 8.5. Managers must first determine the specific activities needed to implement plans and achieve goals. Next, they group these work activities into a logical structure. Then they assign work to specific employees and give the people the resources they need to complete it. Managers must coordinate the work of different groups and

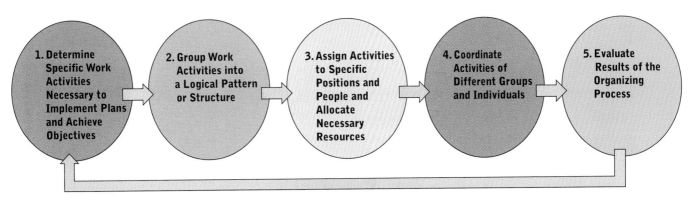

FIGURE 8.5
Steps in the Organizing Process

employees within the firm. Finally, they must evaluate the results of the organizing process to ensure effective and efficient progress toward planned goals. Evaluation often results in changes to the way work is organized.

Many factors influence the results of organizing. The list includes a firm's goals and competitive strategy, the type of product it offers, the way it uses technology to accomplish work, and its size. Small firms typically create very simple structures. The owner of a dry-cleaning business generally is the top manager, who hires several employees to process orders, clean the clothing, and make deliveries. The owner handles the functions of purchasing supplies such as detergents and hangers, hiring and training employees and coordinating their work, preparing advertisements for the local newspaper, and keeping accounting records.

As a company grows, its structure increases in complexity. With increased size comes specialization and growing numbers of employees. A larger firm may employ many salespeople, along with a sales manager to direct and coordinate their work, or organize an accounting department and hire employees to work as payroll clerks and cost accountants.

The organizing process should result in a well-defined structure so that employees know what expectations their jobs involve, to whom they report, and how their work contributes to the company's effort to meet its goals. To help employees understand how their work fits within the overall operation of the firm, managers prepare an **organization chart,** which is a visual representation of a firm's structure that illustrates job positions and functions. Figure 8.6 illustrates a sample organization chart. Each box in the chart would show a specific position. An organization chart depicts the division of a firm into departments that meet organizational needs.

Not-for-profit organizations also have specific structures. The Catholic Church, for example, is a hierarchy with clearly defined levels and a strict reporting structure. The head of the church is the pope, based at the Vatican in Rome. The pope is held to be preeminent in matters of church doctrine, but responsibility for administering the church's many other functions is dispersed downward in the hierarchy. Looking only at the U.S. church, we find 13 cardinals appointed by the pope. The cardinals advise the pope and are also responsible for electing a new pope when the current one dies. Reporting to the cardinals are 45 archbishops, who preside over major dioceses or congregational areas. Next in rank are 290 bishops, about half of whom head the country's dioceses. Bishops are teachers of doctrine and ministers of the church's government. Priests are the final level of the church hierarchy.[26]

They Said It

Reduce the layers of management. They put distance between the top of an organization and its customers.

—*Donald Rumsfeld (b. 1933)*
U.S. secretary of defense,
2001–2004

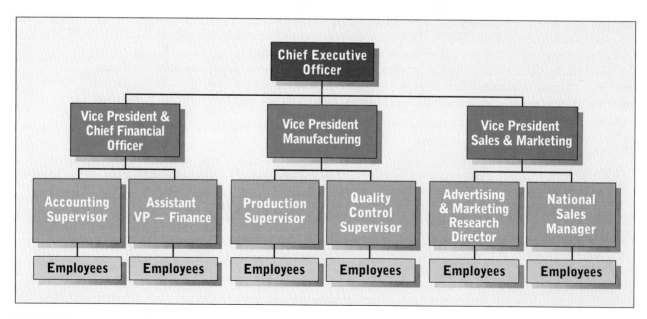

FIGURE 8.6
Sample Organization Chart

Departmentalization

Departmentalization is the process of dividing work activities into units within the organization. This arrangement lets employees specialize in certain jobs to promote efficient performance. The marketing effort may be headed by a sales and marketing vice president, who directs the work of salespeople, marketing researchers, and advertising and promotion personnel. A human resource manager may head a department made up of people with special skills in such areas as recruiting and hiring, employee benefits, and labor relations. The five major forms of departmentalization subdivide work by product, geographical area, customer, function, and process:

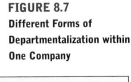

departmentalization
process of dividing work activities into units within the organization.

- *Product departmentalization.* This approach organizes work units based on the goods and services a company offers. Chrysler Group recently revamped its Product and Component teams into new teams organized around vehicle brands. Managers for Jeep, Dodge, and Chrysler now will manage the marketing and production of their vehicles, overseeing everything from product planning to pricing and showroom placement.[27]
- *Geographical departmentalization.* This form organizes units by geographical regions within a country or, for a multinational firm, by region throughout the world. Some retailers, such as Dillard's, are organized by divisions that serve different parts of the country. Railroads and gas and oil distributors also favor geographical departmentalization.
- *Customer departmentalization.* A firm that offers a variety of goods and services targeted at different types of customers might structure itself based on customer departmentalization. Management of 3M's 50,000 products is divided among six business units: health care; transportation, graphics, and safety; consumer and office; industrial; electro and communications; and specialty materials.[28]
- *Functional departmentalization.* Some firms organize work units according to business functions such as finance, marketing, human resources, and production. An advertising agency may create departments for creatives (say, copywriters), media buyers, and account executives.
- *Process departmentalization.* Some goods and services require multiple work processes to complete their production. A manufacturer may set up separate departments for cutting material, heat-treating it, forming it into its final shape, and painting it.

As Figure 8.7 illustrates, a single company may implement several different departmentalization schemes. The departments initially are organized by functions and then subdivided by geographical areas, which are further organized according to customer types. In deciding on a form of departmentalization, managers take into account the type of product they produce, the size of their company, their customer base, and the locations of their customers.

George Schaefer leads a Cincinnati-based banking chain with the unique name: Fifth Third Bank. The name resulted from the original merger of Third National Bank and Fifth National Bank. On Schaefer's decade-long watch, Fifth Third has made roughly 60 acquisitions. The bank now has 940 branches in seven states. Fifth Third has set up an organization structure with 16 regional affiliates. Each unit has its own CEO and president. The affiliates handle their own long-range planning as well as operational duties. Schaefer explains the rationale for Fifth Third's organization simply: "These people know their markets."[29]

FIGURE 8.7
Different Forms of Departmentalization within One Company

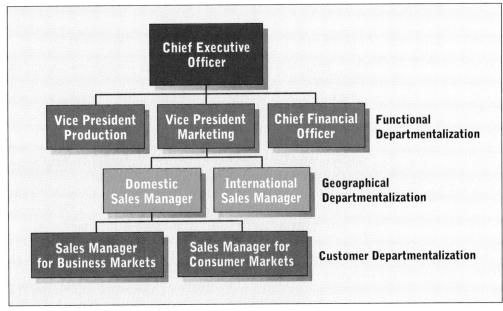

BUSINESS TOOL KIT

Behaving Like a Professional

Contrary to popular belief, learning how to behave like a professional does not necessarily come naturally to everyone. The business world can be vastly different from the college environment, so it's good to get a head start on life after graduation. Here are a few things to remember as you begin your new career as a professional.

- **First impressions are lasting ones.** From the beginning, act like a professional and your colleagues will think more favorably of you when you do happen to screw up (it happens to everyone!). Dress appropriately, learn to modulate your speaking voice, be nice to your colleagues, and listen carefully to learn from everyone. Your attitude is very important in developing positive relations in the business world, so bring a can-do attitude to work with you everyday.

- **Learn to work as a team player.** Getting along with your coworkers is one of the most valuable skills that you'll develop as an employee. In the college setting, you tend to compete and develop as an individual; once you begin working, you must adapt to the team concept. In a business environment, you must pull your own weight, contribute ideas and creative solutions, and always remember that every success is a team effort.

- **The basics: punctuality, writing and communication skills, and managing your time wisely.** Because meetings are a team effort, always be on time. Basics such as good grammar and spelling skills are rarely noticed when an employee

possesses them but are always noticed when they don't, so look over all documents, correspondence, and e-mails for errors. Your time management skills are apparent based on whether you meet your deadlines, so put some thought into project planning. If you need assistance with any of the basics, feel free to ask for help from your manager or mentor. Part of being a professional is being honest with yourself and your colleagues, so don't be afraid to own up to your shortcomings.

- **Always maintain a professional demeanor in spite of the circumstances.** Do not react emotionally to criticism or anger; stay on an even keel and keep your cool. Tempers may flare and personalities may clash as you approach hectic deadlines, but a professional always tries to maintain grace under pressure. If you do feel a negative emotion coming on, excuse yourself and take a few minutes to calm down in privacy. This one simple act will take you further in your career than you might imagine, because it shows tremendous restraint and maturity.

Sources: James Gregory, "Raw Talent: Looking for Eager, New Employees? Try Hiring a Recent College Grad," *Post*, April 2003, p. 44; Dave Johnson, "Tactics for Trying Times: How About Common Courtesy and Respect?" *Industrial Safety & Hygiene News*, May 2002, p. 8; "Dressing for an Interview, Expert Advice for College Grads Entering the Work Force from Men's Wearhouse," *PR Newswire*, April 29, 2002.

Delegating Work Assignments

delegation act of assigning work activities to subordinates.

After grouping activities into departments, managers assign this work to employees. The act of assigning activities to employees is called **delegation.** Managers delegate work to free their own time for planning and decision making. Subordinates to whom managers assign tasks thus receive responsibility, or obligations to perform those tasks. Along with responsibilities, employees also receive authority, or the power to make decisions and to act on them so they can carry out their responsibilities. Delegation of responsibility and authority makes employees accountable to their supervisor or manager. *Accountability* means that employees are responsible for the results of the ways they perform their assignments; they must accept the consequences of their actions.

Authority and responsibility tend to move downward in organizations, as managers and supervisors delegate work to subordinates. However, accountability moves upward, as managers assume final accountability for performance by the people they manage.

span of management number of subordinates a manager can supervise effectively.

Span of Management The **span of management,** or *span of control,* is the number of subordinates a manager supervises. The subordinates are often referred to as *direct reports.* For instance, former Citigroup CEO Sandy Weill had nine people who reported directly to him. First-line managers have wider spans of management, monitoring the work of many employees. The span of management varies considerably depending on many factors, including the type of work performed and employees' training. In recent years, a growing trend has brought ever wider spans of control, as companies have reduced their layers of management to flatten their organization structures, in the process increasing the decision-making responsibility they give employees.

Centralization and Decentralization   How widely should managers disperse decision-making authority throughout an organization? A company that emphasizes **centralization** retains decision making at the top of the management hierarchy. A company that emphasizes **decentralization** locates decision making at lower levels. A trend toward decentralization has pushed decision making down to operating employees in many cases. Firms that have decentralized believe that the change can enhance their flexibility and responsiveness in serving customers. At SAS Institute, decentralization and delegation are logical, given the company's high trust in its talented staff. Employee groups set project deadlines. Because of their input, project timetables and new-product announcements are usually on target.[30]

Types of Organization Structures

The four primary types of organization structures are line, line-and-staff, committee, and matrix structures. These terms do not specify mutually exclusive categories, though. In fact, most modern organizations combine elements of one or more of these structures.

Line Organizations   A **line organization,** the oldest and simplest organization structure, establishes a direct flow of authority from the chief executive to subordinates. The line organization defines a simple, clear **chain of command**—a set of relationships that indicates who gives direction to whom and who reports to whom. This arrangement helps to prevent buck passing. Decisions can be made quickly because the manager has authority to control subordinates' actions.

> **chain of command** set of relationships that indicates who directs which activities and who reports to whom.

A line organization has an obvious defect, though. Each manager must accept complete responsibility for a number of activities and cannot possibly be an expert in all of them. This defect is apparent in mid-size and large firms, where the pure line structure fails to take advantage of the specialized skills that are so vital to business today. Managers become overburdened with details and paperwork, leaving them little time for planning.

As a result, the line organization is an ineffective model in any but the smallest organizations. Hair-styling salons, so-called mom-and-pop grocery stores, and small law firms can operate effectively with simple line structures. Ford, Citigroup, and EDS cannot.

Line-and-Staff Organizations   A **line-and-staff organization** combines the direct flow of authority of a line organization with staff departments that support the line departments. Line departments participate directly in decisions that affect the core operations of the organization. Staff departments lend specialized technical support. Examples of staff departments include labor relations, legal counsel, and information technology. Figure 8.8 illustrates a line-and-staff organization. Accounting, engineering, and human resources are staff departments that support the line authority extending from the plant manager to the production manager and supervisors.

A line manager and a staff manager differ significantly in their authority relationships. A **line manager** forms part of the primary line of authority that flows throughout the organization. Line managers interact directly with the functions of production, financing, or marketing—the functions needed to produce and sell goods and services. A **staff manager** provides information, advice, or technical assistance to aid line managers. Staff managers do not have authority to give orders outside their own departments or to compel line managers to take action.

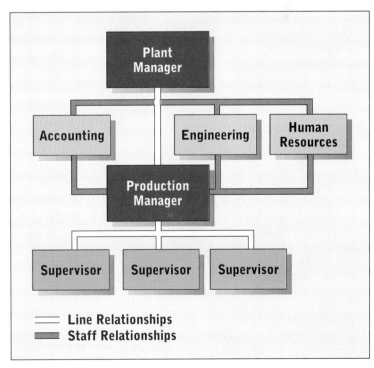

FIGURE 8.8
Line-and-Staff Organization

The line-and-staff organization is common in mid-size and large organizations. It is an effective structure because it combines the line organization's capabilities for rapid decision making and direct communication with the expert knowledge of staff specialists.

Committee Organizations   A **committee organization** is a structure that places authority and responsibility jointly in the hands of a group of individuals rather than a single manager. This model typically appears as part of a regular line-and-staff structure. Examples of the committee structure emerge throughout organizations at one point in time. Nordstrom, the department store chain, once had an "office of the co-presidency" in which six members of the Nordstrom family shared the top job.

Committees also work in areas such as new-product development. A new-product committee may include managers from such areas as accounting, engineering, finance, manufacturing, marketing, and technical research. By including representatives from all areas involved in creating and marketing products, such a committee generally improves planning and employee morale because decisions reflect diverse perspectives.

Committees tend to act slowly and conservatively, however, and they often make decisions by compromising conflicting interests rather than by choosing the best alternative. The definition of a camel as "a racehorse designed by committee" provides an apt description of some limitations of committee decisions. At Nordstrom, the six-person office of the co-presidency was eventually abandoned for a more traditional structure.

Matrix Organizations   Some organizations use the **matrix,** or project management, **structure.** This structure links employees from different parts of the organization to work together on specific projects. Figure 8.9 diagrams a matrix structure. For a specific project, a project manager assembles a group of employees from different functional areas. The employees retain their ties to the line-and-staff structure, as shown in the vertical white lines. As the horizontal gold lines indicate, however, employees are also members of project teams. Upon completion of a project, employees return to their "regular" jobs.

In the matrix structure, each employee reports to two managers: one line manager and one project manager. Employees who are selected to work on a special project, such as development of a new product, receive instructions from the project manager (horizontal authority), but they continue as employees in their permanent functional departments (vertical authority). The term *matrix* comes from the intersecting grid of horizontal and vertical lines of authority.

The matrix structure has become popular at high-technology and multinational corporations, as well as hospitals, consulting firms, and aerospace firms. Dow Chemical and P&G have both used matrix structures. The National Aeronautics and Space Administration used the matrix structure for its Mercury and Apollo space missions.

The major benefits of the matrix structure come from its flexibility in adapting quickly to rapid changes in the environment and its capability of focusing resources on major problems or products. It also provides an outlet for employees' creativity and initiative, giving them opportunities that their functional jobs may deny them. However, it challenges the project manager to integrate the skills of specialists from many departments into a coordinated team. Another disadvantage is that employees may be confused and frustrated in reporting to two bosses.

Concept Check

1. What is the purpose of an organization chart?
2. What are the five major forms of departmentalization?
3. What does span of management mean?

DID YOU KNOW?

1. Helene Curtis managers had to change the name of their Every Night shampoo line to Every Day when the firm expanded sales to Sweden because Swedes usually wash their hair in the morning.
2. KFC needed to make major adjustments when it expanded into Hong Kong. The Chinese typically use warm, damp towels to clean their hands after eating and were mystified by Kentucky Fried Chicken's "finger-lickin' good" slogan.
3. About a quarter of U.S. small-company owners are considering turning their business over to their daughters rather than their sons, according to a Babson College study.

What's Ahead

In the next chapter, we sharpen our focus on the importance of people—the human resource—in shaping the growth and profitability of the organization. We examine how firms recruit, select, train, evaluate, and compensate employees in their attempts to attract, retain, and motivate a high-quality workforce. The concept of motivation is examined, and we will discuss how managers apply theories of motivation in the modern workplace. The next chapter also looks at the important topic of labor–management relations.

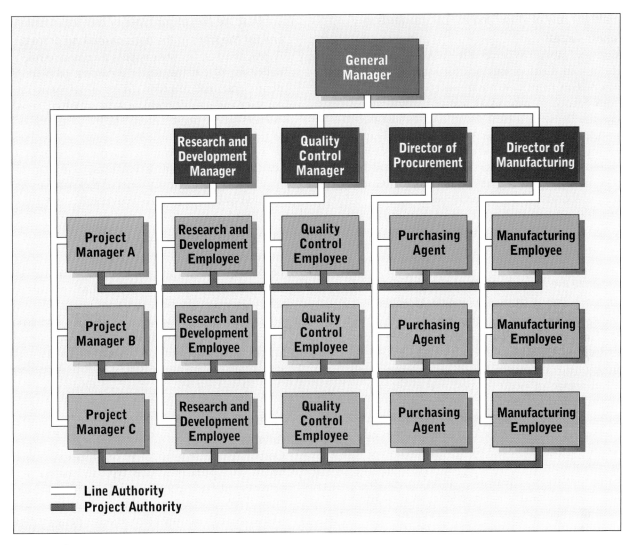

FIGURE 8.9
Matrix Organization

Summary of Learning Goals

1

Define management *and the three types of skills necessary for managerial success.*

Management is the process of achieving organizational objectives through people and other resources. The management hierarchy depicts the levels of management in organizations: Top managers provide overall direction for company activities, middle managers implement the strategies of top managers and direct the activities of supervi-

sors, and supervisors interact directly with workers. The three basic managerial skills are technical skills, or the ability to apply the techniques, tools, and knowledge of a specific discipline or department; human skills, which involve working effectively with and through people; and conceptual skills, or the capability to see an overall view of the organization and how each part contributes to its functioning.

2 *Explain the role of vision and ethical standards in business success.*

Vision is the ability to perceive the needs of the marketplace and develop methods for satisfying those needs. Vision helps new businesses to pinpoint the actions needed to take advantage of opportunities. In an existing firm, a clear vision of company purpose helps to unify the actions of far-flung divisions, keep customers satisfied, and sustain growth. Setting high ethical standards helps a firm survive and be successful over the long term. Behaving ethically places an organization's constituents—those to whom it is responsible—at the top of its priorities. It also goes beyond avoiding evil to encouraging, motivating, and inspiring employees.

3 *Summarize the major benefits of planning and distinguish among strategic planning, tactical planning, and operational planning.*

The planning process identifies organizational goals and develops the actions necessary to reach them. Planning helps a company to turn vision into action, take advantage of opportunities, and avoid costly mistakes. Strategic planning is a far-reaching process. It views the world through a wide-angle lens to determine the long-range focus and activities of the organization. Tactical planning focuses on the current and short-range activities required to implement the organization's strategies. Operational planning sets standards and work targets for functional areas such as production, human resources, and marketing.

4 *Describe the strategic planning process.*

The first step of strategic planning is to translate the firm's vision into a mission statement that explains its overall intentions and aims. Next, planners must assess the firm's current competitive position, using tools like SWOT analysis—which weighs the firm's strengths, weaknesses, opportunities, and threats—and forecasting. Based on this information, managers set specific objectives that elaborate what the organization hopes to accomplish. The next step is to develop strategies for reaching objectives that will differentiate the firm from its competitors. Managers then develop an action plan that outlines the specific methods for implementing the strategy. Finally, the results achieved by the plan are evaluated, and the plan is adjusted as needed.

5 *Contrast the two major types of business decisions and list the steps in the decision-making process.*

A programmed decision applies a company rule or policy to solve a frequently occurring problem. A nonprogrammed decision forms a response to a complex and unique problem with important consequences for the organization. The five-step approach to decision making includes recognizing a problem or opportunity, developing alternative courses of action, evaluating the alternatives, selecting and implementing an alternative, and following up the decision to determine its effectiveness.

6 *Define leadership and compare different leadership styles.*

Leadership is the act of motivating others or causing them to perform activities designed to achieve specific objectives. The basic styles are autocratic, democratic, and free-rein leadership. The best leadership style depends on three elements: the leader, the followers, and the situation. Today's leaders tend increasingly to involve employees in making decisions about their work.

7 *Discuss the meaning and importance of corporate culture.*

Corporate culture refers to an organization's values, beliefs, and principles. It is typically shaped by a firm's founder and perpetuated through formal programs such as training, rituals, and ceremonies, as well as through informal discussions among employees. Corporate culture can influence a firm's success by giving it a competitive advantage.

8 *Identify the five major forms of departmentalization and the four main types of organization structures.*

The subdivision of work activities into units within the organization is called *departmentalization*. It may be based on products, geographical locations, customers, functions, or processes. Most firms implement one or more of four structures: line, line-and-staff, committee, and matrix structures. Each structure has advantages and disadvantages.

Business Terms You Need to Know

management 266	objectives 275	organization 283	chain of command 287
planning 269	decision making 277	departmentalization 285	
vision 270	leadership 279	delegation 286	
mission statement 273	corporate culture 282	span of management 286	

Other Important Business Terms

top management 267	controlling 269	nonprogrammed decision 277	line organization 287
middle management 267	strategic planning 271	autocratic leadership 279	line-and-staff organization 287
supervisory management 268	tactical planning 271	democratic leadership 279	line manager 287
technical skills 268	operational planning 271	empowerment 279	staff manager 287
human skills 268	contingency planning 271	free-rein leadership 279	committee organization 288
conceptual skills 269	SWOT analysis 274	organization chart 284	matrix structure 288
organizing 269	competitive differentiation 276	centralization 287	
directing 269	programmed decision 277	decentralization 287	

Review Questions

1. What is a management hierarchy? In what ways does it help organizations to develop structure? In what ways could it be considered obsolete?

2. What are the three basic types of skills that managers must possess? Which type of skill is most important at each management level?

3. Identify and describe the four basic functions of managers.

4. Why is a clear vision particularly important for companies that have numerous operations around the country or around the world? Cite an example.

5. Which type of planning is most far-reaching? How does this type of planning affect other types of planning?

6. Suppose you planned a large cookout for your friends, but when you woke up on the morning of the party, it was pouring rain. What type of plan would allow you to cope with this situation? Specifically, what could you do?

7. As a student, you have a mission in school. Write your own mission statement for your education and program, including your goals and how you plan to accomplish them.

8. Identify each of the following as a programmed or nonprogrammed decision:
   a. reordering printer cartridges
   b. selecting a cell phone provider
   c. buying your favorite toothpaste and shampoo at the supermarket
   d. selecting a college to attend
   e. filling your car with gasoline

9. Identify the traits that are most often associated with great leaders. Which trait would be most important in the leader of a large corporation? A small company? Why?

10. Why is a strong corporate culture important to a company's success? Relate your answer to a specific firm.

Projects and Applications

1. Create a résumé for yourself, identifying your technical skills, human skills, and conceptual skills. Which set of skills do you think is your strongest? Why?

2. Think of a company with which you are familiar—either one you work for or one with whom you conduct business as a customer. Consider ways in which the organization

can meet the needs of its marketplace. Then write a sentence or two describing what you think the organization's vision is—or should be.

3. Conduct your own SWOT analysis for a company with which you are familiar. Visit the organization's Web site to learn as much about the company as you can before stating your conclusions. Be as specific as possible in identifying your perceptions of the company's strengths, weaknesses, opportunities, and threats.

4. Identify a classmate or college friend whom you think is a good leader. Describe the traits that you think are most important in making this person an effective leader.

5. Your school has its own organizational culture. Describe what you perceive to be its characteristics. Is the culture strong or weak? How does the culture affect you as a student?

Experiential Exercise

U.S. presidents are leaders of the free world. All have their own set of leadership traits. Interview five people and ask them their opinions of American presidents. Tell your respondents to ignore political opinion and concentrate on just leadership traits, both positive and negative. Develop a leadership profile modeled after the following chart.

President	Positive Leadership Traits	Factors Hindering This President's Leadership
George W. Bush		
Bill Clinton		
George H. W. Bush		
Ronald Reagan		
Jimmy Carter		

NOTHING BUT NET

1. **Company mission statements.** Most companies include their mission statements on their Web sites. Choose a company in which you have some interest and visit its Web site (if you can't find the Internet address, use a search engine such as Google; http://www.google.com). Make a note of the company's mission statement and strategic objectives. How do its strategic objectives relate to the company's mission statement? After a company establishes its mission statement, what's the next step in the strategic planning process?

2. **Effectiveness of a company's board of directors.** One issue that has received greatly increased attention in recent years is the effectiveness of a company's board of directors. Each year, *BusinessWeek* rates the effectiveness of boards of most major corporations. Visit the *BusinessWeek* Web site (http://www.businessweek.com) and review the most recent year's rankings. Which five companies have the most effective and least effective boards? What criteria does *BusinessWeek* use to rate the effectiveness of a company's board of directors?

3. **Dealing with adversity.** Often, one of the tests of a company's management is how well it responds to a crisis. In the late 1990s, several companies—such as Nike and Wal-Mart—came under criticism for labor practices at some Asian and South American factories that made products the companies were selling. Both Nike and Wal-Mart responded with a series of actions, including establishing a set of minimum working condition standards. Visit the following Web sites and review the actions both companies took. Were you favorably or unfavorably impressed? Explain your answer.

http://www.nike.com/nikebiz (click the "Responsibility" and then "Workers & Factories" links to find information on its manufacturing practices)

http://www.walmart.com/cservice/aw_index.gsp (click "Supplier Information" and then "Supplier Standards")

Note: Internet Web addresses change frequently. If you do not find the exact sites listed, you may need to access the organization's or company's home page and search from there.

Case 8.1

A New Generation of Women Makes It to the Top

More women fill the top ranks of corporations than ever before—chief financial officers, chief operations officers, chief information officers, and CEOs. Women held about 4 percent of the highest-paid jobs at 825 companies studied by *BusinessWeek*. While women are increasingly filling higher ranks, their numbers still lag behind males, and fewer than 1 percent of companies in the study had a female CEO.

One reason is that many women lack experience in operational positions that lead to CEO. Male-dominated social networks also still exclude them. "The more senior they get, the more subtle the barriers become, and the more profoundly they operate," according to Debra Meyerson, a professor who studies gender issues. Six of the seven female CEOs in the study also led Old Economy companies, which pay less across the board than their high-tech counterparts. Says Mary C. Mattis of women's business think tank Catalyst, "Generally speaking, the new industries are not level playing fields for women."

A study analyzing routine performance evaluations found that when rated by their peers, bosses, and subordinates, women scored higher than men in skills from producing high-quality work to setting goals and mentoring. These findings are echoed in a growing number of studies that looked at a wide variety of manufacturing and service companies nationwide.

The scoring differences were often small, but women were ahead overall. They collaborate better, are less self-interested, and think decisions through with greater care. And more companies are recognizing that they want exactly the skills women typically bring to the job. So why are CEOs like Carly Fiorina (Hewlett-Packard), Betsy Holden (Kraft Foods), Meg Whitman (eBay), and Andrea Jung (Avon Products) still so exceptional?

Some observers think women become too easily trapped in middle management jobs, which they leave in frustration, or get pigeonholed in areas like human resources and public relations, traditionally female-dominated and not on track to the executive suite. Perhaps Carly Fiorina was on to something when she objected to being introduced to an audience as "*Fortune* magazine's most powerful woman in American business for the fifth year in a row." "Please don't," she said. "Business shouldn't be like sports, separating the men from the women."

QUESTIONS FOR CRITICAL THINKING

1. Why do you think more women are not rising to the top in high-tech companies, and what can be done to improve the situation?
2. Do you believe that women are better suited to top jobs than men, or vice versa? Or do you think they each bring unique but different skills to management? Explain your answer.

Sources: "Executive Team Biography: Carleton S. Fiorina," Hewlett-Packard Web site, http://www.hp.com, accessed February 20, 2003; Adam Lashinsky, "Now for the Hard Part," *Fortune*, December 6, 2002, http://www.fortune.com; "Most Powerful Women in Business," *Fortune*, October 14, 2002, http://www.fortune.com; Louis Lavelle, "For Female CEOs, It's Stingy at the Top, *BusinessWeek*, April 23, 2001, http://www.businessweek.com; "The Highest Paid Women in America," *BusinessWeek*, April 23, 2001, http://www.businessweek.com.

Video Case 8.2

Buffalo Zoo's Leader Talks to the Animals—and People, Too

This video case appears on page 610. A recently filmed video, designed to expand and highlight the written case, is available for class use by instructors.

Chapter 9
Human Resource Management, Motivation, and Labor–Management Relations

1 *Explain the importance of human resource management, the responsibilities of human resource managers, and the role of human resource planning in an organization's competitive strategy.*

2 *Describe how recruitment and selection, training, and evaluation contribute to placing the right person in a job.*

3 *Outline the methods employers use to compensate employees through pay systems and benefit programs.*

4 *Discuss employee separation and the impact of downsizing and outsourcing.*

5 *Explain how Maslow's hierarchy of needs theory, job design, and managers' attitudes relate to employee motivation.*

6 *Summarize the role of labor unions and list their primary goals.*

7 *Outline the tactics of labor and management in conflicts between them.*

8 *Describe employee–management relations in nonunion organizations.*

"The Money's Too Good and the Need Is Too Great:" The Risk of Working Overseas

Not so long ago, an offer to work overseas was an exciting possibility for most workers. The idea of trying new foods, experiencing new cultures, and seeing new sights—not to mention a boost in salary—was enticing. Millions of Americans do work overseas. But today, an overseas assignment can very

© Karim Sahib/AFP/Getty Images

likely mean working in or near a war zone—or at least in an area that is risky to foreigners in general and Americans in particular. For years, Westerners flocked to Saudi Arabia, where high-paying jobs in industries ranging from oil to software were plentiful and housing was heavily guarded. But recent dangers have sent many of the 35,000 expatriates from the U.S. back home. In Iraq, 20,000 U.S. civilian workers are in constant physical danger as violence swirls around them. The danger isn't always life threatening, but it may involve serious health problems. A spokesperson for CIGNA International Expatriate Benefits warns newly-arriving U.S. workers about a risk that would ordinarily seem trivial: bites from sand flies, which are rampant in Iraq. If left untreated, these bites are likely to result in severe pain and illness in addition to producing painful lesions. These risks naturally inhibit the recruitment and motivation of qualified workers in these regions; they also threaten to undermine the entire effort to rebuild the infrastructure in Iraq and strengthen relationships with Saudi Arabia and other similar countries. Terrorist targets such as convoys assigned to deliver food, fuel, construction supplies, and other items are delayed or diverted, waiting for protection.

"We're in a lockdown," says Jack Herrmann, describing the entire situation.

But some workers are willing to take the risk. They may be drawn to excitement, or simply want to offer their skills during a moment in history. Many are motivated by need—they may have lost a job in the U.S. or have a family member with significant medical expenses. Others see it as an opportunity to make a lot of money in a short period of time. "Whether it's Colombia or Saudi Arabia or Iraq, there are always some people willing to bear those risks," notes Peter Singer, a scholar at the Brookings Institution. "If you were making $30,000 a year and you're out of work, $100,000 with $80,000 of that tax-free sounds very good." Even if a few candidates step up to take the risk, they may not receive the training they need—either for their jobs or for their daily lives. "Many people have been tempted by the lure of $350 to $1,500 a day for their services," explains Mary Hackman, a specialist with the Overseas Security Advisory Council. "And that doesn't necessarily guarantee that they're getting adequate training."

Adding to the quagmire is the fact that things are constantly changing in Iraq, Saudi Arabia, and other countries. In Iraq, a new government might decide to change taxes and tariffs, accept or reject assistance by foreign firms, or impose other policies that hamper progress. So the simple act of doing business may no longer be simple at all, and no one knows when the business environment will stabilize. "The answer to all these questions, unfortunately, is nobody knows," says William Reinsch, president of the National Foreign Trade Council.

Managing a workforce in these conditions is difficult at best and some days may seem nearly impossible. While many businesses and nonprofit organizations are sending employees home, the U.S. oil services firm Halliburton has more than 24,000 employees and subcontractors working in Iraq and Kuwait, and it continues to recruit more. "Our employees feel a great sense of pride in helping the United States bring freedom and democracy to a country [that was] ravaged," explains Wendy Hall, Halliburton's director of publications. "Without civilian contract efforts, Iraq would not be as far down the road to bringing a sense of normalcy back to its people." Not everyone agrees. "No matter how much money you make, you can't spend it if they cut your head off," remarks one former U.S. employee of the oil firm Saudi Aramco. That's a tough point for any company to argue.[1]

Chapter Overview

The importance of people to the success of any organization is the very definition of **management:** the use of people and other resources to accomplish organizational objectives. In this chapter, we address the critical issues of human resource management and motivation. We begin with a discussion of the ways organizations attract, develop, and retain employees. Then we describe the concepts behind motivation and the way human resource managers apply them to increase employee satisfaction and organizational effectiveness.

We also explore the reasons for labor unions and focus on legislation that affects labor–management relations. The process of collective bargaining is then discussed, along with tools used by unions and management in seeking their objectives.

Human Resource Management Is Vital to All Organizations

human resource management function of attracting, developing, and retaining enough qualified employees to perform the activities necessary to accomplish organizational objectives.

Most organizations devote considerable attention to **human resource management,** the function of attracting, developing, and retaining enough qualified employees to perform the activities necessary to accomplish organizational objectives. Human resource managers are responsible for developing specific programs and activities as well as creating a work environment that generates employee satisfaction and efficiency.

Relationships between employers and employees changed enormously during the past century. One hundred years ago, firms hired employees by posting notices at their sites stating that workers were needed and would be hired the following day. Such a notice might list required skills, such as carpentry or welding, or simply list the number of employees the firm required. People looking for work would line up at the employer's shop or factory the next day—a small number in prosperous times and a larger number in leaner times. Someone in authority made hiring decisions, often based on arbitrary criteria, after reviewing the candidates. Sometimes the first people in line were hired; sometimes the healthiest and strongest were hired. After being hired, the new employees were expected to work under a precise set of rules, such as the humorous list shown in Figure 9.1.

Today, flexibility and complexity characterize the relationship between employers and employees. Earlier, you learned that developing and sustaining a world-class workforce are essential for a firm to compete effectively. Human resource managers face challenges created by profound changes in the makeup of the labor force, a shortage of qualified job candidates, changes in the structure of the workplace, and employees' desires to balance their work and personal lives. These managers must also

They Said It

The best way to get what you want is to help other people get what they want.

—*Zig Ziglar (b. 1927)*
American motivational speaker

develop programs and policies that satisfy an increasingly diverse employee population while monitoring a growing number of employment-related laws that influence how they implement their firms' practices.

Midsize and larger organizations create human resource departments that systematically handle the tasks of attracting, training, and retaining employees. They often have people who specialize in individual areas of human resource management such as diversity training or employee benefits. In smaller companies, most human resource managers are generalists because they are responsible for several tasks.

Entrepreneurs and small-business managers usually assume most of the responsibility for human resource management. However, a growing number of small firms are outsourcing this function to **professional employer organizations (PEOs).** A PEO is a company that helps firms with a wide range of human resource services, including hiring and training employees, administering payroll and benefits programs, handling workers' compensation and unemployment insurance, and ensuring compliance with labor laws. These PEOs work in partnership with employers in these key decisions. Because the PEO typically negotiates benefits

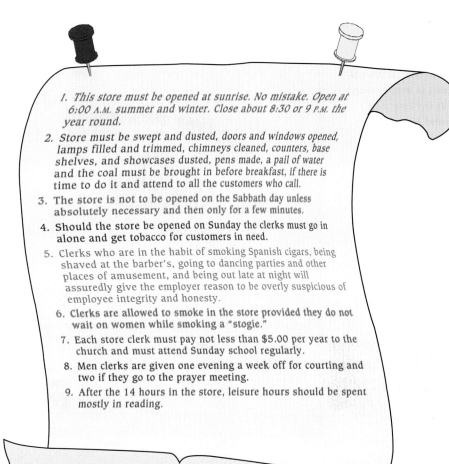

1. *This store must be opened at sunrise. No mistake. Open at 6:00 A.M. summer and winter. Close about 8:30 or 9 P.M. the year round.*

2. Store must be swept and dusted, doors and windows opened, lamps filled and trimmed, chimneys cleaned, counters, base shelves, and showcases dusted, pens made, a pail of water and the coal must be brought in before breakfast, if there is time to do it and attend to all the customers who call.

3. The store is not to be opened on the Sabbath day unless absolutely necessary and then only for a few minutes.

4. Should the store be opened on Sunday the clerks must go in alone and get tobacco for customers in need.

5. Clerks who are in the habit of smoking Spanish cigars, being shaved at the barber's, going to dancing parties and other places of amusement, and being out late at night will assuredly give the employer reason to be overly suspicious of employee integrity and honesty.

6. Clerks are allowed to smoke in the store provided they do not wait on women while smoking a "stogie."

7. Each store clerk must pay not less than $5.00 per year to the church and must attend Sunday school regularly.

8. Men clerks are given one evening a week off for courting and two if they go to the prayer meeting.

9. After the 14 hours in the store, leisure hours should be spent mostly in reading.

FIGURE 9.1
Rules for Clerks, 1905

for a large number of business clients, it can shop for better deals. And by handling a firm's human resource activities, a PEO enables a small firm to focus on production, marketing, and finance, as well as on motivating and leading employees. One such PEO, ADP TotalSource, helped Dogwood Golf and Country Club in Georgia find and keep the right staff. In such an organization, a skilled staff is needed to meet the needs of members and guests. However, turnover in the resort and country club business is very high, with competitors always ready to lure away key employees. ADP TotalSource designed an attractive benefits package that allowed Dogwood to recruit and retain skilled employees. In addition, the PEO handles every detail of the administrative responsibilities related to human resources. According to Dogwood's general manager, "ADP TotalSource is the human resources expert. When you run your business alone as I do, you want reassurance that your people are taken care of."[2]

Human resource management can be viewed in two ways. In a narrow sense, it includes the functions performed by human resource professionals. But in a broader sense, it involves the entire organization, even when a staff department assumes those responsibilities or a firm outsources the functions. Supervisors and general managers also participate in hiring, training, evaluating performance, and motivating employees. Since a company's success depends largely on the commitment and talents of its people, a growing number of firms are measuring and rewarding managers' performance in retaining employees and attracting qualified job candidates. Similarly, many companies consider workforce diversity to be a source of competitive advantage in serving various customer groups and thinking creatively. At these organizations, management goals may also include measures of employee diversity. In addition, some firms ask nonmanagement employees to participate in hiring decisions and evaluating their coworkers' performance.

Human resource managers are responsible for developing programs and policies to meet employee needs and keep them satisfied. Principal Financial Group offers retirement plans to help companies provide a secure financial future for their employees.

The core responsibilities of human resource management include planning for staffing needs, recruitment and selection, training and evaluating performance, compensation and benefits, and employee separation. In accomplishing these five tasks shown in Figure 9.2, human resource managers achieve their objectives of (1) providing qualified, well-trained employees for the organization, (2) maximizing employee effectiveness in the organization, and (3) satisfying individual employee needs through monetary compensation, benefits, opportunities to advance, and job satisfaction.

Human Resource Planning

Human resource managers develop staffing plans based on their organization's competitive strategies. They forecast the number of employees their firm will need and determine the types of skills necessary to implement its plans. Human resource managers are responsible for adjusting their company's workforce to meet the requirements of expanding in new markets; reducing costs, which may require laying off employees; or adapting to new technology. They formulate both long- and short-term plans to provide the right number of qualified employees.

Human resource managers also must plan how to attract and keep good employees with the right combination of pay, benefits, and working conditions. At Trilogy Software, this aspect of human resource planning is at the core of the company's strategy. Trilogy develops software that handles information processing related to sales and marketing, an industry in which only fast-moving, highly sophisticated companies can succeed. So the company has a strategy to continually expand its staff of software developers. Knowing that it is competing for talent with software giants like Microsoft and Cisco, Trilogy targets college campuses, recruiting the brightest, most energetic students it can find. As a substitute for work experience, the company sends these young recruits to an intense three-month orientation program called Trilogy University, where they work on the firm's products as they learn about the software industry and the company culture. Trilogy appeals to recruits by emphasizing that their contribution to the company matters. "By hiring great people and giving them mission-critical responsibilities from the first day on the

Concept Check

1. Why are flexibility and complexity part of today's relationship between employers and employees?

2. What is a professional employer organization (PEO)?

Concept Check

1. Why do human resource managers need to develop staffing plans?

2. How do human resource managers attract and keep good employees?

FIGURE 9.2
Human Resource Management Responsibilities

job, Trilogy ensures our ability to respond to competitive challenges, and to achieve the goal of building a high-impact company," states the company Web site.[3]

Recruitment and Selection

In recruiting and selecting employees, human resource managers strive to match applicants' skills with those the organization needs. To ensure that potential employees bring the necessary skills or have the capacity to learn them, most firms implement the recruitment and selection process shown in Figure 9.3.

Finding Qualified Candidates

Finding the right candidate for a job isn't as simple as it sounds, despite the number of layoffs in many industries in recent years. According to one estimate, the number of workers between the ages of 25 and 54 will dramatically decrease over the next 20 years, and the percentage of the labor force with a college degree who are age 25 and over will barely reach 32 percent.[4] So human resource managers must be creative in their search for qualified employees. Businesses access both internal and

We Have An Opening For A Chief People Person

If the most admired company in America offered you a job, would you take it?

What if it were a company that has a stated goal of becoming one of the best places in America to work!

HomeBanc is looking for a Chief People Person – someone who will help us attract, develop and support the people that make HomeBanc a great place to work.

HomeBanc is a company that seeks people with high moral character and exceptional talent. People who place ethics ahead of profits. People who serve their families, their co-workers and their communities. People who believe that "one nation, under God" provides the foundation for the best quality of life in the world.

HomeBanc helps Americans buy homes, achieve their dreams and support the strength of our nation. We are the leading home financing organization in the Southeast with over 800 associates in Georgia and Florida.

In the coming year we will open offices in North and South Carolina and we will add hundreds of new associates...associates who share our vision and our values.

If you are our new Executive Vice President of People and Culture, please email us at cposearch@homebanc.com and tell us about yourself. We look forward to meeting you.

The position is located in Atlanta, Georgia. For this and other opportunities at HomeBanc, visit us at:
www.homebanc.com/AboutHomeBanc/careers.asp

HomeBanc is an equal opportunity employer. Please do not call or fax resumés.

© 2002, HomeBanc Mortgage Corporation

homebanc.com

HOMEBANC MORTGAGE CORPORATION

Attracting and keeping good employees is important in any business, but especially so in firms where employees constantly interact with customers. HomeBanc recognizes the contributions its employees make to its bottom line.

external sources to find the best candidates for specific jobs. Policies of hiring from within emphasize internal sources, so many employers consider their own employees first for job openings. Internal recruiting is less expensive than external methods, and it helps boost employee morale. But if recruiters can find no qualified internal candidate, they must look for people outside the organization. Recruitment from external sources involves advertising in newspapers and trade magazines, placing radio and television ads, and working through state and private employment agencies, college recruiting and internship offices, retiree job banks, and job fairs. One of the most effective external sources is employee referrals, in which employers ask current employees to recommend applicants, rewarding them with bonuses or prizes for new hires.

Many firms are using the Internet as a recruiting tool. They have career sections on their Web sites, providing general employment information and listing open positions. Applicants may even be able to submit a résumé and apply for an open position online. As the Careers Prologue pointed out, some firms also post job openings at employment Web sites, such as Monster.com. Internet recruiting is a quick, efficient, inexpensive way to reach a large pool of job seekers. According to employers and career counselors, online recruiting has become a common method of finding qualified job candidates.

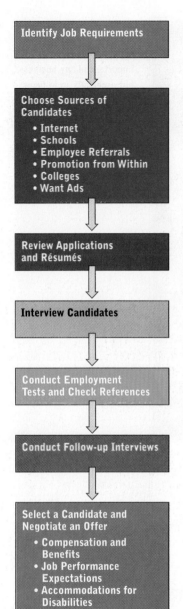

FIGURE 9.3

Steps in the Recruitment and Selection Process

Another recent trend for some businesses is to review the welfare rolls of people looking for work. Bank of America has been doing this for several years. The firm has a partnership with Goodwill Industries International, which trains welfare recipients for jobs such as cashiers and tax processors. Bank of America hired about 5,000 workers through the program during a recent five-year period and continues to recruit 150 per month. "We're mindful of the labor-shortage projections and see these populations as continuing to provide us with a wonderful source of labor and higher retention rates," says Karen B. Shawcross, a senior vice president at Bank of America.[5]

Selecting and Hiring Employees

In selecting and hiring employees, human resource managers must follow the requirements set out by federal and state laws. Title VII of the Civil Rights Act of 1964 prohibits employers from discriminating against applicants based on their race, religion, color, sex, or national origin. The Americans with Disabilities Act of 1990 prohibits employers from discriminating against disabled applicants. The Civil Rights Act created the Equal Employment Opportunity Commission (EEOC) to investigate discrimination complaints. The EEOC also assists employers in setting up affirmative-action programs to increase job opportunities for women, minorities, disabled people, and other protected groups. The Civil Rights Act of 1991 expanded the remedies available to victims of employment discrimination by including the right to a jury trial, punitive damages, and damages for emotional distress.

Failure to comply with equal employment opportunity legislation can expose an employer to fines and other penalties, negative publicity, and poor employee morale. The EEOC files hundreds of cases each year, with damages paid by businesses in the tens of millions annually. At the same time, opponents to such laws have launched initiatives to restrict affirmative-action standards and protect employers against unnecessary litigation. In one instance, California voters passed a proposition that prohibits the state from granting hiring preferences to minorities.

Increases in protected employees and discrimination lawsuits have elevated the importance of human resource managers in the hiring process. To prevent violations, human resource personnel must train managers involved in interviewing to make them knowledgeable about employment law. For example, the law prohibits asking an applicant any questions relating to marital

The Equal Employment Opportunity Commission is dedicated to eliminating discrimination in workplace hiring. Its award-winning Freedom to Compete public service campaign promotes a "level playing field" for today's workplace.

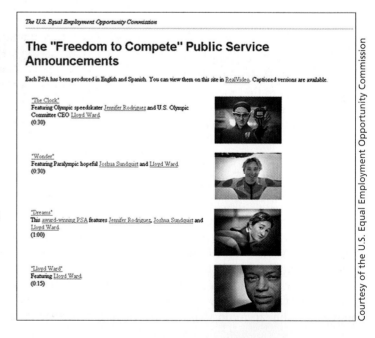

Courtesy of the U.S. Equal Employment Opportunity Commission

BUSINESS TOOL KIT

Interview Inquiries

Whether you end up on the management side of an organization or not, you need to know what questions can and cannot be asked of you during a job interview. Companies may ask you questions directly pertaining to the job itself and the skill set needed to perform the job. They cannot ask you about your gender, family, religion, national origin, or disabilities. Listen carefully for illegal questions during your interview and politely decline to respond to them. Here is a list of Do's and Don'ts pertaining to interview questions:

DO'S:
- What is your preferred management style?
- Describe what you think this job entails and what you might like and dislike about the work.
- Describe a conflict you've had with other staff members and how you resolved it.
- You have two bosses asking you to do conflicting tasks. How would you handle this dilemma?
- What database systems, spreadsheets, and software do you have experience with?

DON'TS:
- Do you have (or are you planning to have) a family?
- Where are you from or what is your ethnic origin?
- How many sick days did you take last year?
- What year were you born?
- What are your political views?
- What is your religion or which holidays do you observe/not observe?
- What is your sexual orientation/preference?
- What are your child care arrangements?
- Do you have any particular physical/mental traits or disabilities?
- Have you ever been arrested?

Sources: Peter Cardinal, "Questions You Should Ask When Hiring: Choosing the Best Candidate for Your Staff Depends a Lot on Selecting the Right Interview Questions," *Family Practice Management,* June 2003, p. 46; William J. Lynott, "How to Hire the Right Person and Stay Out of Trouble While You're Doing It: It's Important to Know What Questions to Ask and Not to," *Podiatry Management,* April–May 2003, p. 91; "Ask the Right Questions," *The Practical Accountant,* November 2002, p. 22; Deborah J. Myers, "Five Steps to Successful Hiring: Employers Have to Be Careful What They Ask Job Candidates During the Interview Process," *Alaska Business Monthly,* October 2002, p. 86.

status, number of children, race, nationality, religion, or age. Interviewers also may not ask questions about applicants' criminal records, mental illness histories, or alcohol-related problems. In addition, human resource managers can help organizations establish systems to promote fair employment practices. Several CBS-owned television stations were sued by the Equal Employment Opportunity Commission for sex discrimination. The EEOC alleged that these stations practiced discrimination against female technicians in regard to salary, training, and promotions. CBS and the EEOC settled the lawsuit, with CBS agreeing to pay $8 million to approximately 200 female employees. CBS also agreed to put in place extensive mechanisms to help prevent future discrimination.[6] For more information about employment-litigation issues, visit the Web sites of the Society for Human Resource Management (http://www.shrm.org) and the EEOC (http://www.eeoc.gov).

Employers must also observe various other legal restrictions governing hiring practices. Some firms try to screen out high-risk employees by requiring drug testing for job applicants, particularly in industries where employees are responsible for public safety, such as airlines and other public transportation. But drug testing is controversial because of concerns about privacy. Also, positive test results may not accurately indicate drug use, and traces of legal drugs, such as prescribed medications, may chemically resemble traces of illegal substances.

Recruitment and selection are expensive processes because a firm incurs costs for advertising job openings, interviewing applicants, and conducting background checks, employment tests, and medical exams. A bad hiring decision is even more expensive, though. A hiring mistake causes a firm to spend money to train and motivate a less than optimal employee, as well as risk the potential costs of poor decisions by that employee. Other costs resulting from a bad hiring decision may include lawsuits, unemployment compensation claims, recruiting and training a replacement, and reductions in productivity and employee morale.

To avoid the costly results of a bad hiring decision, many employers require applicants to complete employment tests. These tests help verify the skills that candidates list on their application forms or résumés to ensure that they meet the performance expectations of the job. A variety of tests are available to gauge applicants' knowledge of mechanical, technical, language, and computer skills. One example is the Wonderlic Basic Skills Test, which measures candidates' basic math and verbal skills. This test is intended to be a more objective and accurate way to measure qualifications than simply asking candidates about their educational background.

Following a hiring decision, a growing number of firms protect themselves from discrimination lawsuits by including explicit employment-at-will policies in their employee manuals. **Employment at will** means that the employment relationship can be terminated at any time by either the employee or the employer for any reason. Many people believe that the equal opportunity law prohibits employers from firing employees, but successful lawsuits must cite specific illegal practices such as discrimination in hiring based on sex, race, age, or disability. Although most state laws recognize the principle of employment at will, court decisions in firing disputes sometimes favor employees when their employers have failed to provide written proof of at-will policies and employees' acceptance of the policies. For further protection, some employers also publish policies that call for mandatory arbitration of employment disputes and waivers of the right to jury trials in such disputes.

Concept Check

1. What are some of the costs associated with recruitment and selection?
2. What is employment at will?

Orientation, Training, and Evaluation

Once hired, employees need information about what is expected of them and how well they are performing. Companies provide this information through orientation, training, and evaluation. A newly hired employee often completes an orientation program administered jointly by the human resource department and the department in which the employee will work. During orientation, employer representatives inform employees about company policies regarding their rights and benefits. Many organizations give new hires copies of employee manuals that describe benefits programs and working conditions and expectations. They also provide different types of training to ensure that employees get a good start at the company.

Training Programs

Employees are increasing their requests for training so they can build skills and knowledge that will prepare them for new job opportunities. Training is also a good investment from the employer's perspective. A firm should view employee training as an ongoing process throughout each employee's tenure with the company. Companies like Trilogy and Bank of America, both of which were mentioned earlier, make training a vital part of selecting and hiring employees, as well as developing their careers. Investment firm Edward Jones, rated the nation's top company to work for by *Fortune*, provides an average of 146 hours of training per year to its employees. Why so much time? "In order to grow you have to be trained," says managing partner John Bachmann, "or you get trapped in the present."[7]

On-the-Job Training   One popular instructional method is **on-the-job training,** which prepares employees for job duties by allowing them to perform tasks under the guidance of experienced employees. A variation of on-the-job training is apprenticeship training, in which an employee learns a job by serving for a time as an assistant to a trained worker. Patio Enclosures, a construction firm based in Ohio, made its employees more productive and more committed to the company by setting up an apprenticeship program. Apprenticeship programs are much more common in Europe than in the U.S. While American apprenticeships usually focus on blue-collar trades—such as lawn care, plumbing and heating services, and blacksmithing—in Europe many new entrants to white-collar professions complete apprenticeships.

Classroom and Computer-Based Training   Off-the-job training involves some form of classroom instruction such as lectures, conferences, audiovisual aids, computer instruction, and special machines to teach employees everything from basic math and language skills to complex, highly skilled tasks. Pharmaceutical giant Pfizer offers training at just about every level of the company, including self-paced courses through Harvard University and an on-site master's degree program.[8]

Many firms are replacing classroom training with computer-based training programs. These programs can save an employer money by reducing travel costs and employee time away from work. In addition, computer-based training offers consistent presentations, since the training content won't vary with the quality of the instructor. Audio and visual capabilities help these systems to simulate the work environment better than some classroom training could, and employees also benefit from greater control over the learning process. They can learn at their own pace and convenience, and they generally do not have to wait for the company to schedule a class before they can begin adding to their knowledge. Despite these advantages, firms also offer traditional classroom training because it usually provides more opportunities for employees to interact with the instructor and with one another. Some people learn better through human interaction, and some have difficulty disciplining themselves to complete a computer-based learning program on their own.

Off-the-job training frequently involves use of the Internet. The Web provides a convenient means of delivering text, audio, and video training materials to employees wherever they are located. Online training programs also can offer interactive learning, such as simulations in which employees see the results of their decisions.

When a firm decides to enter a foreign market, human resource managers must prepare employees who will work in overseas assignments by providing training in language skills, cultural practices, and adapting to the everyday living requirements abroad. Employees may begin an international assignment with the professional skills and job qualifications they need, but most benefit from additional cultural and language training to help them make successful transitions.

Management Development   A **management development program** provides training designed to improve the skills and broaden the knowledge of current and potential executives. The share of the workforce in their mid-20s to mid-30s, who traditionally have been the group developing management skills, is shrinking, and many members of the workforce are approaching retirement age. Without the luxury of developing executive talent slowly over the years, organizations instead provide programs that help managers quickly learn how to lead a fast-moving company through turbulent times.

The content of management development programs may involve reviews of issues facing the company, as well as *benchmarking*, or learning the best practices of the best companies so they can serve as performance standards to strive for. The teachers may be the company's own executives. At other times, managers may be encouraged to receive counseling from an outside management coach, who helps them improve their skills. Bob Nardelli, CEO of Home Depot, is trying to create a "coaching environment" throughout his company. "I absolutely believe that people, unless coached properly, never reach their maximum capabilities," he says. Nardelli also created a leadership institute at Home Depot's Atlanta headquarters. Here high-potential managers meet with Nardelli and other senior executives to complete courses in leadership, merchandising, store planning, and financial operations.[9]

Performance Appraisals

Organizations also help employees improve their performance by providing feedback about their past performance. A **performance appraisal** is an evaluation of an employee's job performance by comparing actual results with desired outcomes. Based on this evaluation, managers make objective decisions about compensation, promotions, additional training needs, transfers, or terminations. Rating employees' performance and communicating perceptions of their strengths and weaknesses are important elements in improving a firm's productivity and profits. Performance appraisals are not confined to business. Government agencies, not-for-profit organizations, and academic institutions also conduct them.

Some firms conduct peer reviews, in which employees assess the performance of coworkers, while other firms allow employees to review their supervisors and managers. One type of performance appraisal is the **360-degree performance review,** a process that gathers feedback from a review panel of

performance appraisal
evaluation of an employee's job performance by comparing actual results with desired outcomes.

eight to 12 people, including coworkers, supervisors, team members, subordinates, and sometimes customers. The idea is to get as much frank feedback from as many perspectives as possible. However, this approach to performance appraisal tends to generate considerable work for both employees and managers—each of whom may have to review 20 or more people—and volumes of paperwork. Also, since the evaluations are anonymous, staff members with an ax to grind might try to use the system to their advantage in personal disputes.

Still, the 360-degree system appears to be gaining in popularity. A survey of large U.S. firms found that a majority of them are using the multirater system, up from around 40 percent in 1995. At United Parcel Service (UPS), managers receive 360-degree reviews every six months. The managers' peers, employees, and supervisors rate them in such areas of performance as leadership, customer focus, people skills, and knowledge of business and financial issues. To ensure that the feedback is used constructively, the UPS human resource department first provides employees with training on the purpose and uses of performance reviews. Also, to simplify the process and reduce the amount of time devoted to performance reviews, the UPS system is automated.[10]

> **Concept Check**
>
> 1. Describe some aids in off-the-job training.
> 2. What is a management development program?
> 3. What is the main way an organization provides employees with feedback about their performance?

Compensation

Human resource managers work to develop an equitable compensation system spanning wages and salaries plus benefits. Because human resource costs represent a sizable percentage of any firm's total product costs, excessive wage rates may make its goods and services too expensive to compete effectively in the marketplace. Inadequate wages, however, lead to difficulty in attracting qualified people, high turnover rates, poor morale, and inefficient production.

wage compensation based on an hourly pay rate or the amount of output produced.

salary compensation calculated on a periodic basis, such as weekly or monthly.

The terms *wages* and *salary* are often used interchangeably, but they refer to different types of pay systems. **Wages** represent compensation based on an hourly pay rate or the amount of output produced. Firms pay wages to production employees, maintenance workers, and sometimes retail salespeople. **Salaries** represent compensation calculated periodically, such as weekly or monthly. Office personnel, executives, and professional employees usually receive salaries.

An effective compensation system should attract well-qualified workers, keep them satisfied in their jobs, and inspire them to succeed. Most firms base their compensation policies on the following five factors:

1. Salaries and wages paid by other companies that compete for the same people
2. Government legislation, including the federal, state, or local minimum wage
3. The cost of living
4. The firm's ability to pay
5. Worker productivity

Several cities have required businesses to pay a so-called living wage of as much as $11.75 per hour. A **living wage** is generally defined as one that allows a worker to support a family of four without having to receive any form of public assistance, such as food stamps. In some cities, living wage laws apply only to businesses with city contracts, but in other cities, the laws apply to all businesses. When Baltimore became the first city to adopt a living wage law, critics argued that the law would actually reduce employment and hobble businesses forced to pay higher wages. However, more than 60 municipalities have since passed living wage laws. From a human resource perspective, one study found that the slight job losses caused by these laws were more than offset by the decrease in family poverty.[11]

Many employers balance rewarding workers with maintaining profits by linking more of their pay to superior performance. They try to motivate employees to excel by offering some type of incentive compensation in addition to salaries or wages. Today, almost one-tenth of the compensation of salaried workers is some form of variable pay. These programs include:

- Profit sharing, which awards bonuses based on company profits
- Gain sharing, which awards bonuses based on surpassing predetermined performance goals

- Lump-sum bonuses and stock options, which reward one-time cash payments and the right to purchase stock in the company based on performance
- Pay for knowledge, which distributes wage or salary increases as employees learn new job tasks[12]

Figure 9.4 summarizes the four types of incentive compensation programs.

Some companies, such as Altria, Schering-Plough, and Anheuser-Busch, offer these programs to top and middle managers, as well as to employees with professional degrees. However, other companies believe that everyone should get a slice of the profit pie. Procter & Gamble, Freddie Mac, and Pfizer are some examples.[13] Of course, during slow economic times, benefits such as stock options are less desirable—and even disastrous—in certain cases. Also, controversy rages over top executives who continue to receive bonuses while lower-level employees are forced to accept pay cuts or reduced benefits. But at semiconductor manufacturer Xilinx, workers took a 6 percent pay cut—while the CEO's salary was slashed 20 percent.[14]

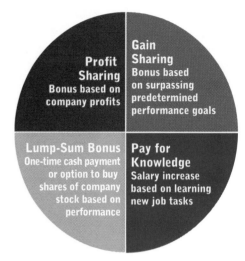

FIGURE 9.4
Four Forms of Incentive Compensation

Employee Benefits

In addition to wages and salaries, firms provide many benefits to employees and their families as part of the compensation they pay. **Employee benefits** are rewards, such as retirement plans, health and disability insurance, sick leave, child care and elder care, and tuition reimbursement, provided entirely or in part at the company's expense. Benefits represent a large component of an employee's total compensation. Although wages and salaries account for around 72 percent of the typical employee's earnings, the other 28 percent takes the form of employee benefits.[15]

The share of total compensation provided as benefits has grown over the years. General Motors spent $4.2 billion for health care recently; prescription drugs alone cost the company $1.3 billion.[16] And employees at UPS, Anheuser-Busch, and Pfizer pay relatively little for their health-care coverage, while retirees receive free coverage.[17]

But the increasing costs of health-care benefits have left some employers looking for ways to hold the line. One increasingly used, but highly controversial, technique involves collecting data about employees' weight, smoking and alcohol consumption rates, exercise habits, and medical test results to use as inputs in creating employee wellness programs. The companies use the information to predict which workers may become ill. At Logan Aluminum in Russellville, Kentucky, employees receive an additional $200 a year for voluntarily filling out the health risk assessment forms. Such programs raise privacy issues, however.[18]

Some benefits are required by law. U.S. firms are required to make Social Security and Medicare contributions as well as payments to state unemployment insurance and workers' compensation programs, which protect workers in case of job-related injuries or illnesses. The Family and Medical Leave Act of 1993 requires covered employers to offer up to 12 weeks of unpaid, job-protected leave to eligible employees. Firms voluntarily provide other employee benefits, such as child care and health insurance, to help them attract and retain employees. In 2003, California became the first state to sign *paid* family leave into law.[19]

In spite of the share of benefits that U.S. companies offer, they pale in comparison with European firms. Europeans, on average, get six weeks of paid vacation—double or triple what their American counterparts receive. And the length of the workweek has steadily dropped across Europe in the past two decades. A 35-hour workweek is commonplace in Germany, Italy, and France. In fact, the French government has mandated a 35-hour workweek for all companies. Such generosity has a cost, though. Multinational companies have moved work abroad because the cost of hiring a European worker for a shorter workweek is too expensive. Also, the European Union's goal of becoming the most competitive economy in the world by the end of the first decade of the 21st century is not likely to be met if trends continue. Growth per capita—a measure of a country's standard of living—is approximately 1 percent in Europe compared with the U.S.'s 3 percent. As one professor of labor economics at Humboldt University in Berlin put it, "You have to work to grow."[20]

> ## *They Said It*
>
> High motivation is as precious as talent. Barriers which must be hurdled bring highly motivated people to the top.
>
> —*John W. Gardner (1912–2002)*
> *American writer and public official*

employee benefits
rewards such as retirement plans, health insurance, vacation, and tuition reimbursement provided for employees either entirely or in part at the company's expense.

Benefits are an important component of employee compensation. Bright Horizons Family Solutions helps companies such as Microsoft, Cisco, and Toyota provide on-site day care for their employees' children. When employees know that their children are cared for, they can focus on their work.

© 2002 Shawn G. Henry

Pensions and other retirement plans have been another area of concern for U.S. companies. Some companies have reduced the amount of matching contributions they will make to workers' **401(k) plans,** retirement savings plans for which employees can make pretax contributions to retirement accounts. Some companies have been cutting back on cash contributions to their employees' plans and are contributing company stock instead. However, many companies and employees are uncomfortable with this practice in the wake of the collapse of Enron and other firms, which took employees' savings with them.[21] Still, plenty of firms—such as mortgage financer Freddie Mac and Anadarko Petroleum—continue to contribute to their employees' savings as generously as allowed by law.[22]

Many companies now recognize the importance of fulfilling employee requests for "family-friendly" benefits that help them care for children, aging parents, or other dependents. Such benefits—ranging from child-care facilities to paid time off and flexible work hours—help employees juggle responsibilities. Almost nine of 10 large U.S. companies offer dependent-care spending accounts to help pay for child care, and almost half offer some form of elder-care program. SAS Institute offers employees a superlative on-site child-care facility for a monthly fee of only $300, a cafeteria with pianist, an on-site health clinic, and a huge fitness center. Adobe Systems offers workers three-week paid sabbaticals every five years, while the Container Store provides domestic partner benefits.[23]

Flexible Benefits

In response to the increased diversity of the workplace, human resource managers are developing creative ways to tailor their benefit plans to the varying needs of employees. One approach sets up **flexible benefit plans,** also called *cafeteria plans.* Such a benefit system offers employees a range of options from which they can choose, including different types of medical insurance, dental and vision plans, and life and disability insurance. This flexibility allows one working spouse to choose his or her firm's generous medical coverage for the entire family, and the other spouse can allocate benefit dollars to purchasing other types of coverage. "Employees don't want all the same benefits," explains Jamie Berge, owner of a tax and financial services firm in Anchorage that administers cafeteria plans for small businesses. "With cafeteria plans, you pick and choose."[24] Typically, each employee receives a set allowance (called *flex dollars* or *credits*) to pay for purchases from the benefits menu. A healthy, single employee might choose to allocate less of his or her flex dollars to health insurance, say by choosing a higher deductible, and allocate more flex dollars to an optional dental or vision plan. By contrast, an older employee might allocate some of his or her flex dollars to pay for elder care for aging parents.

Contributions to cafeteria accounts are commonly made by both the employee and employer. Cafeteria plans also offer tax benefits to both employees and employers. Employee contributions are made

The Advantages and Disadvantages of Telecommuting

Many companies now allow employees to work remotely, or from home. This is not the same as being self-employed. Telecommuters still have to follow organizational guidelines for conducting business outside the office—usually these guidelines are established by your supervisor. Some telecommuters work two to three days from home, while others work from home as needed.

In addition to the technical requirements of telecommuting, there are a few characteristics that will ensure the situation works for you and your company. You should be flexible and able to multitask. You should possess good judgment and tenacity and have the self-discipline to stay on task when distractions arise. Here are the disadvantages and advantages of telecommuting:

- **Disadvantages.** Less human interaction than in an office; technical and managerial support is more difficult to administer; training and mentoring are more difficult for remote employees; promotion opportunities can be lessened due to the lack of office visibility;

and some employees work longer hours because of easier access to the office.

- **Advantages.** Helps the environment and air quality by decreasing vehicular traffic; saves time on commuting; increases employee productivity in many cases; decreases employee sick leave; improves employee retention; considered a reasonable accommodation for employees with disabilities; provides autonomy and self-management for motivated workers; increases scheduling flexibility; and provides a lack of distractions commonly associated with office life such as meetings and interruptions.

Sources: "Have Would-be Telecommuters Test Their Readiness," *HR Briefing*, June 1, 2003, p. 7; Richard W. Walker, "Teleworkers Add Up To, Well, More Work," *Government Computer News*, May 26, 2003, p. 23; Ross Bentley, "Missed Benefits for Home Workers," *Computer Weekly*, April 15, 2003, p. 44; Tish Hamilton, "Shower? Why Bother? The Pleasures and Perils of Working From Home," *AdWeek*, March 31, 2003, p. 34.

using so-called pretax dollars, meaning that employees don't pay taxes on their contributions. Also, employers don't have to pay unemployment taxes or Social Security and Medicare taxes on the amount deducted from employee paychecks.

Another way of increasing the flexibility of employee benefits involves time off from work. Instead of establishing set numbers of holidays, vacation days, and sick days, some employers give each employee a bank of **paid time off (PTO).** Employees use days from their PTO accounts without having to explain why they need the time. At Vision Service Plan, employees can convert unused sick time to cash or vacation. Home-mortgage originator Fannie Mae gives its workers a "healthy-living" day off and a day off to close on a home purchase.[25] One recent trend involves giving employees paid time off for volunteer service. Timberland is well-known for doing this. The boot and apparel maker gives every employee 40 hours of paid time a year for volunteer work, and its New Hampshire headquarters actually closes one day a year so Timberland employees can build playgrounds, work at the local SPCA, and assist the elderly. Employees are also eligible for six months of "social service leave" at full pay.[26]

Flexible Work

Another part of the trend toward responsiveness to employee needs is the option of **flexible work plans.** Flexible work plans are benefits that allow employees to adjust their working hours and places of work to accommodate their personal needs. Flexible work plan options include flextime, compressed workweeks, job sharing, and home-based work. By implementing these benefit programs, employers have reduced employee turnover and absenteeism and boosted productivity and job satisfaction.

Flextime is a scheduling system that allows employees to set their own work hours within constraints specified by the firm. Rather than requiring everyone to work the regular work hours of 8 A.M. to 5 P.M., an employer may require employees to be at work between the core hours of 10 A.M. and 3 P.M. but vary their start times. Outside the core hours, employees can choose when to start and end their workdays, opting either to arrive at work early, say at 6 A.M., and leave early, or to arrive later and work later. Flextime works well in jobs in which employees can work relatively independently, but not so well when they must work together in teams, such as in manufacturing, or must provide direct customer service. The practice is common in European countries; an estimated 40 percent of the Swiss workforce and 25 percent of German workers have flextime schedules. Growing numbers of U.S. firms—particularly those that are not involved in manufacturing—are offering flextime, and increasing numbers of employees are taking advantage of this benefit.

The **compressed workweek** is a scheduling option that allows employees to work the regular number of weekly hours in fewer than the typical five days. Employees might work four 10-hour days and then have three days off each week. Such arrangements not only reduce the number of hours employees spend commuting each week but can stretch out the company's overall workday, providing more availability to customers in other time zones. Hospitals, police and fire departments, and airlines often offer work schedules that allow several long days matched by several days off. At Boston-based Analytics Operations Engineering, employees choose their own schedules as well as the location from which they will work. "I judge an employee's value by what they create," says CEO Mitchell Burman. "It doesn't matter to me when they do it or even if they do it from Timbuktu." However, Analytics workers must meet company deadlines for completed projects.[27]

A **job sharing program** allows two or more employees to divide the tasks of one job. This plan appeals to a growing number of people who prefer to work part time rather than full time, such as older workers, students, working parents, and people of all ages who want to devote time to personal interests or leisure. Job sharing requires a high degree of cooperation and communication between the partners, but it can let a company benefit from the talents of people who do not want to work full time. Jennifer Keskikyla of IBM Canada is a strong proponent of job sharing. The mother of two believes that she and her partner are more productive than one person. Keskikyla comments: "I think IBM got more than 100% with our combined experience. It was like two minds for the price of one." She also observes that for a job sharing arrangement to work well, it is important to select a partner you can work well with, along with ongoing communication and a dedication to make the partnership work.[28]

A *home-based work program* allows employees to perform their jobs from home instead of at the workplace. Home-based workers are sometimes called *teleworkers* or **telecommuters** because many "commute" to work via telephones, e-mail, computers, and fax machines. Working from home has great appeal to employees with disabilities, older workers, and parents with small children. Almost 30 million U.S.-based teleworkers are currently employed, and their numbers are growing. In one recent year, the number increased 17 percent.[29]

Telecommuting is an increasingly attractive solution for businesses and employees. Today, companies such as Siemens provide Internet, cell phone, and other business communication services to enable employees to work from home.

energy & power • **information & communication** • medical systems & healthcare
financial services • lighting • transportation • industry & automation • building technologies

www.usa.siemens.com

Spacious corner office, redefined.

SIEMENS
Global network of innovation

©2003 Siemens Corporation

Courtesy of Siemens Corporation

Because telecommuters work with minimal supervision, they need to be self-disciplined and reliable employees. They also need managers who are comfortable with setting goals and managing from afar.

Concept Check

1. Explain the difference between wage and salary.
2. What is another name for cafeteria plan?
3. What types of organizations typically use a compressed workweek?

Employee Separation

Either employer or employee can take the initiative to terminate employment. Employees decide to leave firms to start their own businesses, take jobs with other firms, move to another city, or retire. Some firms ask employees who leave voluntarily to participate in *exit interviews* to find out why they decided to leave. These interviews give employers a chance to learn about problems in the workplace, such as unreasonable supervisors or unfair work practices.

Employers sometimes terminate employees because of poor job performance, negative attitudes toward work and coworkers, or misconduct such as dishonesty or sexual harassment. Terminating poor performers is necessary because they lower productivity and employee morale. Coworkers resent employees who receive the same pay and benefits as they do without contributing fairly to the company's work. But employers need to document reasons carefully for terminating employees. Protests against wrongful dismissal are often involved in complaints filed by the EEOC. After using an automatic performance-ranking system that resulted in laying off a specified percentage of employees, Ford Motor Company faced a class-action suit brought against it by those workers—who were mostly older, white, male middle managers. Ford settled the suit for $10.5 million.[30] Besides poor performance, reasons for terminating employees include downsizing, outsourcing, and the use of contingency workers.

Downsizing

During the early years of the 21st century, employers terminated thousands of employees, including many middle managers, through downsizing. **Downsizing** is the process of reducing the number of employees within a firm by eliminating jobs. Many downsizing firms have reduced their workforces by offering early retirement plans, voluntary severance programs, and opportunities for internal reassignment to different jobs. Employers who value their employees have helped them to find jobs with other companies and set up job counseling centers.

Companies downsize for many reasons. The two most common objectives of downsizing are to cut overhead costs and streamline the organizational structure. Some firms report improvements in profits, market share, employee productivity, quality, and customer service after downsizing. After Hewlett-Packard (HP) acquired Compaq Computer, the firm announced its intention to cut thousands of duplicate jobs created by the merger to reduce costs by several billion dollars.

Eliminating jobs through downsizing can have devastating effects on employee morale, though. Workers who remain after a downsizing worry about job security and become angry when they have to work harder for the same pay. As their feelings of commitment to their jobs wane, many employees leave the firm and seek employment offering greater job security. This situation has contributed to a shift in values away from loyalty to an employer in favor of concern for individual career success.

Employee surveys reveal that many workers are more interested in career security than job security. Specifically, the typical employee may seek opportunities for training to improve the skills needed for the next job. People are willing to work hard at their current jobs, but they also want to share in the success of their companies in the form of pay-for-performance and stock options. For human resource managers, the new employee–employer relationship requires developing continuous training and learning programs for employees.

Outsourcing

In their continuing efforts to remain competitive against domestic and international rivals, a growing number of firms choose to hold down costs by evolving into leaner organizations. A number of

downsizing process of reducing the number of employees within a firm by eliminating jobs.

SOLVING AN ETHICAL CONTROVERSY

Business Behind Bars: Is It Fair Play?

Unicor sounds like an average company name. But the name actually stands for Federal Prison Industries, a firm that operates computer-recycling facilities inside prisons and employs inmates who strip down old computers for salvage. This is a far cry from making license plates. It is a slowly growing trend—*Fortune 500* companies who manufacture or purchase goods and services made by prisoners. Home Depot and Lowe's are two examples of such firms, as is Anderson Hardwood Floors. What's the attraction? Prison labor is inexpensive, and quality can be monitored more easily than it could be in the private sector—either in the U.S. or overseas. Using the system, Anderson has been able to offer handcrafted hardwood floors to consumers that would otherwise be prohibitively expensive.

SHOULD PRIVATE BUSINESSES BE ALLOWED TO HIRE PRISON INMATES?

PRO

1. Hiring and paying U.S. workers, even if they are prison inmates, is better for the economy than outsourcing jobs overseas.

2. Despite the lower pay, these jobs provide useful training and experience for inmates once they are released from prison.

CON

1. Some critics charge that business facilities operating inside prisons have substandard working conditions.

2. Hiring lower-paid prison workers creates unfair competition for businesses who refuse to use prison labor and for job candidates in the outside world.

SUMMARY

Currently, about 2 million people in prison who are qualified for some type of contract work. One inmate who makes business-to-business telemarketing calls says, "I'm grateful for the opportunity. Many of us end up here [in prison] because we didn't have jobs and lacked communication skills." Another remarks that her call-center job has "brought self-esteem, order, skills and a stable income to my life." But critics argue that these businesses freely violate minimum-wage laws, as well as health-and-safety codes. "Quite literally, they're taking advantage of a captive audience," says Tony Daley, a research economist for the Communications Workers of America.

Sources: Jon Swartz, "Inmates vs. Outsourcing," *USA Today*, July 7, 2004, p. B1; K. Daniel Glober, "Prison Labor Program under Fire by Lawmakers, Private Industry," *Govexec.com*, April 12, 2004, http://www.govexec.com; Nicholas Stein, "Business Behind Bars," *Fortune*, September 15, 2003, pp. 161–165.

---

outsourcing practice of contracting out work previously performed by company employees.

functions that were performed previously by company employees may be contracted to other firms whose employees will perform them in a practice called **outsourcing.** Outsourcing began on a small scale, with firms contracting out services such as maintenance, cleaning, and delivery. Services commonly outsourced today include housekeeping; architectural design; grounds, building, utility, and furniture maintenance; food service; security; and relocation services. Today, outsourcing has expanded to include outside contracting of many tasks once considered fundamental internal functions. And in a recent twist, some firms are contracting for low-cost prison labor to produce their products. This practice is not without its critics, as the Solving an Ethical Controversy box explains.

Outsourcing complements today's focus on business competitiveness and flexibility. It allows a firm to continue performing the functions it does best, while hiring other companies to do tasks that they can handle more competently and cost-effectively than its own people can. Another benefit of outsourcing is the firm's ability to negotiate the best price among competing bidders and the chance to avoid the long-term resource costs associated with in-house operations. Firms that outsource also gain flexibility to change vendors at the end of contract periods if they desire. The key to successful outsourcing is a total commitment by both parties to form a partnership from which each derives benefits. The U.S. Army has begun to outsource more than 200,000 military and support jobs to trim costs and increase flexibility.[31]

Using Contingent Workers

The use of contingent workers, already about one-quarter of the workforce, is expected to grow. **Contingent workers** are employees who work part time, temporarily, or only the time required to fulfill a specific contract. Hiring contingent workers enables companies to maintain the efficiency of a pared-down workforce while being flexible enough to meet new and changing needs. Traditionally, contingent workers often earned less pay than full-time employees and did not receive benefits or have access to employer-sponsored pension plans. However, among highly skilled workers, contingent work may be a profitable alternative to traditional employment, as these workers can negotiate contracts that include benefits coverage or secure salaries large enough to cover self-paid benefits. In a survey of workers who often call themselves "free agents," six of 10 respondents said they earn more money as consultants than they did as employees, and over half said that their quality of life improved after they became consultants. Some people enjoy the variety and flexibility that can accompany contingent work. Others miss the continuing relationships with coworkers and the predictability of a regular paycheck.[32]

One corporate worker who turned to consulting for a career is Liz Ryan. Ryan worked for Chicago-based computer modem maker U.S. Robotics, but with four small children, she turned to human resource consulting to provide flexibility for her schedule. Ryan developed a global e-mail discussion site that provided information and contacts for people who wanted to return to the workforce. The site is called WorldWIT—for women in technology—and has spread to 52 communities in 19 countries.[33]

Still, companies need to be careful about their use of contingent workers. One major hospital chain claimed that use of contingent workers was saving it $5 million a year in staffing costs. The chief financial officer continually checked his rivals' staffing levels and reduced his chain's full-time staff to match their ratios. But the heavy use of part-timers—80 percent of the hospital staff—left the hospital with employees who were not able to function efficiently because they did not know their jobs as well as the full-time staff. Through further analysis, the hospital chain found that its heavy use of part-timers was actually costing it $25 million in reduced productivity—an amount totaling 3 percent of its annual revenues. When it reduced the contingent workforce to 63 percent of its staff, productivity rebounded 18 percent in two short months.[34]

> **contingent worker** employee who works part time, temporarily, or for the period of time specified in a contract.

They Said It

Contingency work can provide the flexible job opportunities many people are looking for.

—*Melvin R. Goodes (b. 1936) former chairman and CEO, Warner-Lambert*

Concept Check

1. What is the purpose of an exit interview?
2. What is downsizing?

Motivating Employees

Employee motivation is the key to effective management. And motivation starts with good employee morale. **Morale** is the mental attitude of employees toward their employer and jobs. It involves a sense of common purpose among the members of work groups and throughout the organization as a whole. High morale is a sign of a well-managed organization because workers' attitudes toward their jobs affect the quality of their work.

> **morale** mental attitude of employees toward their employer and jobs.

Courtesy of US Motivation

High morale is essential to motivation, and Mike Hadlow, CEO of Atlanta-based USMotivation, is an expert on both. His company helps other firms motivate their employees through special incentive programs—such as surprise bowling outings and other activities to foster communication and teamwork. He uses many of these incentives with his own employees.

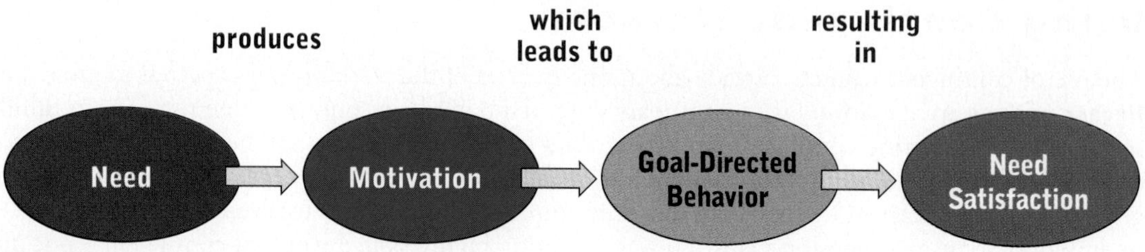

produces   which   resulting
                  leads to   in

Need → Motivation → Goal-Directed Behavior → Need Satisfaction

FIGURE 9.5
The Process of Motivation

One of the most obvious signs of poor manager–worker relations is poor morale. It lurks behind absenteeism, employee turnover, and strikes. It shows up in falling productivity and rising employee grievances.

In contrast, high employee morale occurs in organizations where employees feel valued and heard and where they are able to contribute what they do best. This climate reinforces a human tendency—that people perform best when they believe they are capable of succeeding. High morale also results from an organization's understanding of human needs and its success at satisfying those needs in ways that reinforce organizational goals. The Best Business Practices box describes how businesses' use of family-friendly policies can foster high morale.

Each person is motivated to take action designed to satisfy needs. A *need* is simply a lack of some useful benefit. It reflects a gap between an individual's actual state and his or her desired state. A *motive* is an inner state that directs a person toward the goal of satisfying a felt need. Once the need—the gap between where a person is now and where he or she wants to be—becomes important enough, it produces tension. The individual is then moved—the root word for motive—to reduce the tension and return to a condition of equilibrium. Figure 9.5 depicts the principle behind this process. A need produces a motivation, which leads to goal-directed behavior, resulting in need satisfaction.

Maslow's Hierarchy of Needs Theory

The studies of psychologist Abraham H. Maslow suggest how employers can motivate employees. **Maslow's hierarchy of needs** theory has become a widely accepted list of human needs based on these important assumptions:

- People's needs depend on what they already possess.
- A satisfied need is not a motivator; only needs that remain unsatisfied can influence behavior.
- People's needs are arranged in a hierarchy of importance; once they satisfy one need, at least partially, another emerges and demands satisfaction.

In his hierarchy of needs theory, Maslow proposed that all people have basic needs that they must satisfy before they can consider higher order needs. He identified five types of needs:

1. *Physiological needs.* These basic human needs include food, shelter, and clothing. In the workplace, employers satisfy these needs by paying salaries and wages and establishing comfortable working environments.
2. *Safety needs.* These needs refer to desires for physical and economic protection. Employers satisfy these needs by providing benefits such as retirement plans, job security, and safe workplaces.
3. *Social (belongingness) needs.* People want to be accepted by family and other individuals and groups. At work, employees want to maintain good relationships with their coworkers and managers and to participate in group activities.
4. *Esteem needs.* People like to receive attention, recognition, and appreciation from others. Employees feel good when they are recognized for good job performance and respected for their contributions.
5. *Self-actualization needs.* These needs drive people to seek fulfillment, realizing their own potential and fully using their talents and capabilities. Employers can satisfy these needs by offering challenging and creative work assignments and opportunities for advancement based on individual merit.

Maslow's hierarchy of needs theory of motivation proposed by Abraham Maslow. According to the theory, people have five levels of needs that they seek to satisfy: physiological, safety, social, esteem, and self-actualization.

BEST BUSINESS PRACTICES

How Family-Friendly Is Your Employer?

As you move along in your career and into other stages of your life—like parenthood—you think a lot more about the work/life balance. Company managers know this, and as a result, many businesses now offer a wide range of benefits designed to help their employees successfully juggle the demands of work and family. There's a strategy behind this practice. Businesses want to attract and keep its best employees, and if it means allowing them time off to take an aging parent to the doctor's office or letting them bring the kids to work, they'll try to accommodate.

One family-friendly benefit that has gained popularity for both large and small firms is on-site childcare. Experts believe that this is a win-win situation. "Fast-growing businesses that expect their employees to work long hours have to make that humanly possible," notes Nancy Ahlrichs Raichart, president of EOC Strategies, an HR consulting firm. "If they have Generation X or Generation Y employees, or are trying to attract them, this is a perfect magnet."

Flextime is another benefit that has worked its way into the mainstream. According to *Working Mother* magazine, all of the top 100 best companies for working moms offer flextime. The top 10 companies—which offer this and other family-friendly benefits—are Eli Lilly, Abbott Laboratories, Booz Allen Hamilton, Bristol-Myers Squibb, Fannie Mae, General Mills, IBM, Prudential Financial, S.C. Johnson and Sons, and Wachovia. "These companies are very committed to

work/life programs for their employees . . . ," praises Jill Kirschenbaum, the magazine's editor-in-chief.

These benefits and others, such as job sharing, adoption grants, paid family leave, and even telecommuting come at a cost. Some companies feel that these added benefits have failed to prove themselves worthy in terms of increased productivity or employee loyalty. Others say they simply can't survive if they continue to fund these benefits. "In an era when employers have the upper hand, there's little upside to family-friendly policies," remarks New York benefits attorney Steven Friedman. But other firms argue that family-friendly benefits are good business. "This is not a feel-good program from us," insists Ted Childs, vice president of global workforce diversity at IBM. "This is about getting the best talent and keeping them happy at our company."

QUESTIONS FOR CRITICAL THINKING

1. Do you think that family-friendly benefits should be the "new normal"? Why or why not?

2. When you are offered a job, will you ask about family-friendly benefits? Why or why not?

Sources: Stephanie Armour, "Moms Find it Easier to Pop Back into Workforce," *USA Today*, September 23, 2004, p. B1; Stephanie Armour, "Some Moms Quit as Offices Scrap Family-Friendliness," *USA Today*, May 4, 2004, pp. 1A, 2A; Nadine Heintz, "Can I Bring the Kids?" *Inc.*, June 2004, p. 40; Anusha Shrivastava, "Mother's Helpers," *Mobile Register*, September 28, 2003, pp. F1, F6.

According to Maslow, people must satisfy the lower order needs in the hierarchy (physiological and safety needs) before they are motivated to satisfy higher order needs (social, esteem, and self-actualization needs). Figure 9.6 elaborates on employers' efforts to motivate employees by satisfying each level of needs.

Job Design and Motivation

In their search for ways to improve employee productivity and morale, a growing number of firms are focusing on the motivation inherent in the job itself. Rather than simplifying the tasks involved in a job, employers are broadening tasks to add meaning and satisfaction to employees' work. Two ways employers are applying motivational theories to restructure jobs are job enlargement and job enrichment.

Job enlargement is a job design that expands an employee's responsibilities by increasing the number and variety of tasks they entail. Some firms have successfully applied job enlargement by redesigning the production process. A typical approach is to replace assembly lines where each worker repeats the same step on each product with modular work areas in which employees perform several tasks on a single item. Many companies have enlarged administrative assistants' jobs in areas such as communications.

Job enrichment is a change in job duties to increase employees' authority in planning their work, deciding how it should be done, and learning new skills that help them grow. Many companies have developed job enrichment programs that empower employees to take responsibility for their work. The Pampered Chef, a direct seller of kitchen products that is now owned by Berkshire Hathaway, gives its

job enlargement job design that expands an employee's responsibilities by increasing the number and variety of tasks assigned to the worker.

job enrichment change in job duties to increase employees' authority in planning their work, deciding how it should be done, and learning new skills.

Maslow's Hierarchy of Human Needs

Human Needs	Key Ingredients	Example
1. Physiological needs	Wages and working environment	Dallas-based Container Store has one of the highest pay scales in the retail industry. Entry-level sales professionals' salaries top $37,000, and entry-level hourly distribution center workers earn more than $20,000. Not surprisingly, the company enjoys low turnover.
2. Safety needs	Protection from harm, employee benefits	Florida Toyota distributor J. M. Family Enterprises has an on-site medical clinic staffed with two doctors and recently opened an on-site child-care center. Additional benefits include a lap pool, on-site hair salon, and recognition cruises on the company's yacht.
3. Social (belongingness) needs	Acceptance by other employees	Valassis Communications, which prints coupon inserts for newspapers, sends employees memos introducing new hires. The employees, including the president of the company, then write "welcoming" notes to the new employee. "On your first day on the job, you're so nervous and you feel uncomfortable, and it just really makes a difference and makes you feel comfortable," says one new employee.
4. Esteem needs	Recognition and appreciation from others	Entrepreneur Candace Bryan, chief executive of Kendle, a firm that designs clinical tests for drugs, keeps a photo gallery of her employees engaged in their favorite outside activities, from scuba diving to grandparenting. The recognition boosts employee morale and helps to make Bryan an inviting supervisor for prospective employees.
5. Self-actualization needs	Accomplishment, opportunities for advancement, growth, and creativity	Ohio-based J. M. Smucker allows its employees to take unlimited paid time off to volunteer and better their communities. Some of the programs with which employees are involved are the Orrville, Ohio, Heartland Education Community, which is focused on improving high school education; Adopt-a-School programs; Junior Achievement classroom volunteers; and Secondary Education Partnerships with local colleges.

FIGURE 9.6
Maslow's Hierarchy of Human Needs

managers and consultants the power to make decisions about many aspects of their work. Kitchen Consultants, who organize selling and demonstration parties at customers' homes, can choose how much or how little they want to work and receive various incentive rewards for performance. "Over the years, thousands of people from all walks of life have joined our Pampered Chef family. They've found a truly unlimited opportunity and life-changing possibilities," notes founder and chairman Doris Christopher.[35]

Managers' Attitudes and Motivation

The attitudes that managers display toward employees also influence worker motivation. Managers' traditional view of workers as cogs in the production process—much like lathes, drill presses, and other equipment—led them to believe that money was the best way to motivate employees. Maslow's theory has helped managers to understand that employees feel needs beyond those satisfied by monetary rewards.

Psychologist Douglas McGregor, a student of Maslow, studied motivation from the perspective of how managers view employees. After observing managers' interactions with employees, McGregor coined the terms *Theory X* and *Theory Y* as labels for the assumptions that different managers make about worker behavior and how these assumptions affect management styles.

Theory X assumes that employees dislike work and try to avoid it whenever possible. So managers must coerce or control them or threaten punishment to achieve the organization's goals. Managers who accept this view feel that the average person prefers to receive direction, wishes to avoid responsibility, has relatively little ambition, and can be motivated only by money and job security. Managers who hold these assumptions are likely to keep their subordinates under close and constant observation, hold out the threat of disciplinary action, and demand that they adhere closely to company policies and procedures.

Theory Y assumes that the typical person likes work and learns, under proper conditions, to accept and seek responsibilities to fulfill social, esteem, and self-actualization needs. Theory Y managers consider the expenditure of physical and mental effort in work as an ordinary activity, as natural as play or rest. They assume that most people are able to conceive of creative ways to solve work-related problems but that most organizations do not fully utilize the intelligence that most employees bring to their jobs. Unlike the traditional management philosophy that relies on external control and constant supervision, Theory Y emphasizes self-control and self-direction.

Theory Y requires a different management approach that includes worker participation in decisions that Theory X would reserve for management. If people actually behave in the manner described by Theory X, they may do so because the organization satisfies only their lower order needs. If the organization instead designs ways to satisfy their social, esteem, and self-actualization needs as well, employees may be motivated to behave in different ways.

Another perspective on management proposed by management professor William Ouchi has been labeled **Theory Z.** Organizations structured on Theory Z concepts attempt to blend the best of American and Japanese management practices. This approach views worker involvement as the key to increased productivity for the company and improved quality of work life for employees. Many U.S. firms have adopted the participative management style used in Japanese firms by asking workers for suggestions to improve their jobs and then giving them the authority to implement proposed changes.

> *They Said It*
>
> If you perform well, we're going to get along. If you don't, you've got to do push-ups.
>
> —*Colin Powell (b. 1937)*
> *American military leader and former U.S. secretary of state speaking to his employees*

Concept Check

1. In an organization, what conditions are likely to produce high morale?
2. Identify two ways employers restructure jobs for motivation.
3. Compare and contrast Theory X, Theory Y, and Theory Z.

Union–Management Relations

In nations throughout the world, employees have joined together to increase their power to achieve the goals of improved wages, hours, and working conditions. These efforts have succeeded to a considerable extent in the U.S.; today's workplace is far different from the one existing at the beginning of the previous century, where child labor, unsafe working conditions, and a 72-hour workweek (six 12-hour days a week) were common.

But conditions in the workplace vary considerably from one country to another, with more protections for workers in industrialized societies and generally fewer for those in developing countries. Today, the people who head organizations that provide needed goods and services, the people who do the work, and the government organizations that maintain societies make up various industrial relationships that stretch across the globe. With the growing interdependence among nations around the world and the increasing number of multinational corporations, it is critical for business students to gain an understanding of the basics of union-management relations. We look first at labor unions.

Development of Labor Unions

A **labor union** is a group of workers who have banded together to achieve common goals in the key areas of wages, hours, and working conditions. Workers gradually learned that bargaining as a unified group could bring them improvements in job security, wages, and working conditions. The organized efforts of Philadelphia printers in 1786 resulted in the first U.S. minimum wage—$1 a day. After 100 more years, New York City streetcar conductors were able to negotiate a reduction in their workday from 17 to 12 hours.

labor union group of workers who have banded together to achieve common goals in the areas of wages, hours, and working conditions.

Organized labor unions such as the United Auto Workers work to ensure that their members receive fair pay and safer working conditions. Unions use many tactics to draw attention to their cause including protesting, as shown in this illustration.

Labor unions can be found at the local, national, and international levels. A *local union* represents union members in a specific area, such as a single community, while a *national union* is a labor organization consisting of numerous local chapters. An *international union* is a national union with membership outside the U.S., usually in Canada. Large national and international unions in the U.S. include the United Auto Workers, National Education Association, Teamsters, International Brotherhood of Electrical Workers, International Association of Machinists and Aerospace Workers, United Steelworkers of America, and the American Federation of Teachers. Over half of U.S. union members belong to one of these giant organizations.

In the U.S., the governing body of most labor unions is the American Federation of Labor–Congress of Industrial Organizations (AFL–CIO), a federation of affiliated national and international unions that serves a mediation and political function. With 66 member unions and over 13 million union members, the AFL–CIO represents four of five organized American workers. They include hundreds of members of Local 40 of the Iron Workers of America who assisted rescue workers at the site of the World Trade Center within hours following the 9/11 terrorist attacks.

Almost 15 million U.S. workers—close to 17 percent of the nation's full-time workforce—belong to labor unions. Although only about 10 percent of workers in the private sector are unionized, over 40 percent of government workers belong to unions. The 1.5-million-member Service Employees International Union (SEIU) is the largest union in the U.S. In addition to a wide range of service workers (clerical staff, nurses' aides, and janitors), SEIU has also organized such professionals as nurses, doctors, engineers, and librarians.

After thousands of layoffs during the recent recession, interest in labor unions is growing among white-collar and service workers. Job security is the driving force. "After seeing so many jobs destroyed in the recession, Americans are looking for job protection," said Jared Bernstein, a senior economist at the Economic Policy Institute in Washington, DC.[36]

Labor Legislation

Government attitudes toward unions have varied considerably during the past century. These shifting attitudes influenced major pieces of legislation enacted during this period. Let's look at the major pieces of labor legislation:

- *Norris-La Guardia Act of 1932:* Reduced management's ability to obtain court injunctions to halt union activities. Before this act, employers could easily obtain court decrees—called *injunctions*—forbidding strikes, peaceful picketing, and even membership drives.
- *National Labor Relations Act of 1935 (Wagner Act):* Legalized collective bargaining and required employers to negotiate with elected representatives of their employees. Established the National Labor Relations Board (NLRB) to supervise union elections and prohibit unfair labor practices

such as firing workers for joining unions, refusing to hire union sympathizers, threatening to close if workers unionize, interfering with or dominating the administration of a union, and refusing to bargain with a union.

- *Fair Labor Standards Act of 1938:* Set the initial federal minimum wage (25 cents an hour, with exceptions for farm workers and retail employees) and maximum basic workweek for workers employed in industries engaged in interstate commerce. Outlawed child labor.
- *Taft-Hartley Act of 1947 (Labor–Management Relations Act):* Limited unions' power by prohibiting such practices as coercing employees to join unions; coercing employers to discriminate against employees who are not union members, except for failure to pay union dues under union shop agreements; discrimination against nonunion employees; picketing or conducting secondary boycotts or strikes for illegal purposes; featherbedding; and excessive initiation fees under union shop agreements.
- *Landrum-Griffin Act of 1959 (Labor–Management Reporting and Disclosure Act):* Amended the Taft-Hartley Act to promote honesty and democracy in running unions' internal affairs. Required unions to set up a constitution and bylaws and to hold regularly scheduled elections of union officers by secret ballot. Set forth a bill of rights for members. Required unions to submit certain financial reports to the U.S. secretary of labor.
- *Plant-Closing Notification Act of 1988:* Required employers with more than 100 employees to give workers and local elected officials 60 days' warning of a shutdown or mass layoff. Created the Worker Readjustment Program to assist displaced workers.

The Collective Bargaining Process

Labor unions work to increase job security for their members and improvement of wages, hours, and working conditions. These goals are achieved primarily through **collective bargaining,** the process of negotiation between management and union representatives for the purpose of arriving at mutually acceptable wages and working conditions for employees.

collective bargaining process of negotiation between management and union representatives for the purpose of arriving at mutually acceptable wages and working conditions for employees.

Issues covered in collective bargaining include wages, work hours, benefits, union activities and responsibilities, grievance handling and arbitration, layoffs, and employee rights and seniority. As is the case in all types of negotiations, the collective bargaining process involves demands, proposals, and counterproposals that ultimately result in compromise and agreement. The initial demands represent a starting point in negotiations. They are rarely, if ever, accepted by the other party without some compromise. The final agreement depends on the negotiating skills and relative power of management and union representatives.

Union contracts, which typically cover a two- or three-year period, are often the result of weeks or more of discussion, disagreement, compromise, and eventual agreement. Once agreement is reached, union members must vote to accept or reject the contract. If the contract is rejected, union representatives may resume the bargaining process with management representatives, or union members may strike to obtain their demands.

They Said It

When two teams are interested, you negotiate. When only one team is interested, you beg.

—Mark Schlereth
professional football player, Denver Broncos

Settling Union–Management Disputes

Although strikes make newspaper and television headlines, more than 19 of 20 union–management negotiations result in a signed agreement without a work stoppage. Approximately 140,000 union contracts are currently in force in the U.S. Of these, 133,000 were the result of successful negotiations with no work stoppage. The courts are the most visible and familiar vehicle for dispute settlement, but most disputes are settled by negotiations. Dispute resolution mechanisms, such as grievance procedures, mediation, and arbitration, are quicker, cheaper, and less complicated procedurally and receive less publicity.

The union contract serves as a guide to relations between the firm's management and its employees. The rights of each party are stated in the agreement. But no contract, regardless of how detailed, will eliminate the possibility of disagreement. Such differences can be the beginning of a **grievance,** a complaint—by a single employee or by the entire union—that management is violating some provision of the union contract. Almost all union contracts require these complaints to be submitted to a formal grievance procedure similar to the one shown in Figure 9.7.

grievance formal complaint filed by an employee or a union that management is violating some provision of a union contract.

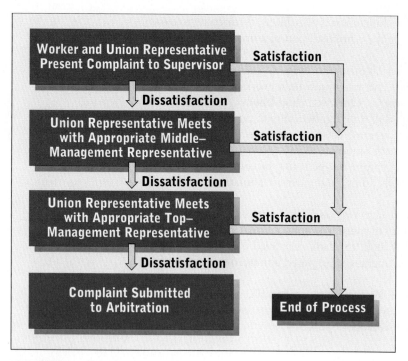

FIGURE 9.7
Steps in the Grievance Procedure

The procedure typically begins with the employee's supervisor and then moves up the company's chain of command. If the highest company officer cannot settle the grievance, it is submitted to an outside party for mediation or arbitration.

Mediation is the process of settling union–management disputes through recommendations of an impartial third party. Although the mediator does not serve as a decision maker, union and management representatives can be assisted by the mediator's suggestions, advice, and compromise solutions.

When disputes cannot be solved voluntarily through mediation, the parties can turn to **arbitration**—bringing in an impartial third party, called an *arbitrator,* who renders a legally binding decision. The arbitrator must be acceptable both to the union and to management, and his or her decision is legally enforceable. In essence, the arbitrator acts as a judge, making a decision after listening to both sides of the argument. The vast majority of union contracts call for the use of arbitration if union and management representatives fail to reach an agreement.

Competitive Tactics of Unions and Management

Although most differences between labor and management are settled through the collective bargaining process or through a formal grievance procedure, both unions and management occasionally resort to various tactics to make their demands known.

Union Tactics   The chief tactics of unions are strikes, picketing, and boycotts. The **strike,** or *walkout,* is one of the most effective tools of the labor union. It involves a temporary work stoppage by employees until a dispute has been settled or a contract signed. Although strikes are relatively rare, they do make headlines. In recent years, strikes have involved workers at Johnson Controls, Hershey Foods, and bus drivers for several private bus lines in New York City.

Although the power to strike represents unions' ultimate tactic, they do not wield it lightly because strikes can do damage in a number of ways, affecting not only one company but an entire industry as well as related businesses. A strike by Major League Baseball players affected not only the players, team owners, fans, and food and souvenir vendors but also the hotels, restaurants, and shops that were located near the stadiums. Strikes have diminished significantly over recent decades.

Picketing—workers marching at the entrances of the employer's business as a public protest against some management practice—is another effective form of union pressure. As long as picketing does not involve violence or intimidation, it is protected under the U.S. Constitution as freedom of speech. Picketing may accompany a strike, or it may be a protest against alleged unfair labor practices. Because members of other unions often refuse to cross picket lines, the picketed firm may be unable to obtain deliveries and other services. Unions occasionally stage "informational" picketing during contract negotiations to pressure management while still working. Union workers for Lockheed Martin engaged in informational picketing for several days after rejecting the company's contract offer. Both sides eventually came to an agreement without a strike.

A **boycott** is an organized attempt to keep the public from purchasing the products of a firm. Some unions have been quite successful in organizing boycotts, and some unions even fine members who defy a primary boycott. One of the most famous boycotts, a 16-year effort against California table grapes, made a folk hero of the late United Farm Workers representative Cesar Chavez. The boycott ended after the union persuaded farmers to eliminate or restrict the use of five pesticides.

HITS & MISSES

Wal-Mart and the Unions

The sheer size of Wal-Mart boggles the mind. The retail goliath is the nation's largest private employer, with 1.5 million workers. It sells $300 billion in merchandise annually, accounting for about 8.5 percent of all nonauto retail sales in the U.S. Consumers can get practically anything at Wal-Mart, from diapers to big-screen TVs. CEO Lee Scott quips, "We're a pretty good company." Perhaps because it is such a large firm, Wal-Mart has attracted both good and bad publicity. One area in which its image has struggled is its relationship to organized labor: basically, it doesn't have one. Or it has a relationship, but not the one that unions want.

Wal-Mart has resisted labor organization for years, but so have 74 percent of companies in the U.S. In general, the retail industry has one of the lowest rates of unionization in the country—about 5 percent—partly because many workers are part-time or seasonal. But organizing workers at Wal-Mart isn't just another challenge for the United Food and Commercial Workers (UFCW) union, which represents about 1.4 million grocery workers nationwide. It represents the Mt. Everest of organizing efforts. The firm is so large, "If we want to survive, labor has no choice but to organize Wal-Mart," warns Stewart Acuff, organizing director of the AFL-CIO. "What [Wal-Mart does] affects the standard of living across the globe," says Acuff, referring to Wal-Mart's ability to force its competitors to reduce their wages and prices in order to remain competitive. So individual unions are doing something they are not accustomed to—they are banding together in their drive to organize Wal-Mart workers.

Using a variety of tactics, union workers—some of them former Wal-Mart employees—are trying to recruit Wal-Mart's workforce around the country. The AFL-CIO has formed a committee of union presidents armed with several million dollars to coordinate the effort. But it isn't easy—Wal-Mart executives, including CEO Lee Scott, are dead set against the practice. "The UFCW has been successful in creating in people's minds the perception that we pay inadequate wages and benefits. I like the free-enterprise system in this country," says Scott. "We pay more than our competitors. We opened a store in Phoenix recently, and 5,000 people applied for 500 openings." The UFCW and other critics charge that employees who are interested in joining a union are ostracized by Wal-Mart management. "The first day I walked into Wal-Mart with a union button, everything changed," says Larry Allen, a former Wal-Mart associate. "In one day I went from being employee of the month to people not speaking to me." Clearly, this battle is far from over.

QUESTIONS FOR CRITICAL THINKING

1. Do you agree with Wal-Mart's position or the union's position on organizing Wal-Mart's employees? Why?

2. Do you believe that traditional union tactics such as picketing and boycotting are appropriate in this situation? Why or why not?

Sources: Ann Zimmerman, "Defending Wal-Mart," *The Wall Street Journal*, October 6, 2004, pp. B1, B10; Aaron Bernstein, "Up Against the Wal-Mart," *BusinessWeek*, August 2, 2004, p. 9; Cora Daniels, "Up Against the Wal-Mart," *Fortune*, May 17, 2004, pp. 112–120.

Management Tactics   Management also has tactics for dealing with organized labor. In the past, it has used the **lockout**—in effect, a management strike to bring pressure on union members by closing the firm. However, other than a few high-profile cases, the lockout is not commonplace unless a union strike has partially shut down a plant or engaged in a work slowdown. When members of the International Longshore and Warehouse Union engaged in a work slowdown because of failed contract talks with the Pacific Maritime Association, which represents shipping companies, the Pacific Maritime Association instituted a lockout, during which shipping containers piled up at West Coast ports and the goods inside them went nowhere. During the lockout, 181 million work hours were lost, 121 ships a day were anchored around Los Angeles-area ports, $693 million in tax revenues were lost, and 8.4 million pounds of Ecuadorian bananas, plantains, and yuccas had to be retrieved by produce importer Dole. U.S. retailers—and their customers—didn't receive the items they needed. President George W. Bush invoked the Taft-Hartley Act for the first time in 25 years to end the work stoppage.[37] Effects of the stoppage were felt by businesses and consumers for months afterward in the form of delivery delays and higher prices.

Managers at organizations ranging from Hormel to Caterpillar have resorted to replacing striking workers with *strikebreakers,* nonunion workers who cross picket lines to fill the jobs of striking workers.

Firms can easily recruit strikebreakers in high-status fields such as professional sports and in high-paying industries located in areas of high unemployment. Yet, even in favorable conditions, management frequently has difficulties securing sufficient numbers of replacement workers with required skills. Some employers use supervisory personnel and other nonunion employees to continue operations during strikes.

Management sometimes obtains an injunction—a court order prohibiting some practice—to prevent excessive picketing or certain unfair union practices. As noted earlier, firms frequently used injunctions to prohibit all types of strikes before passage of the Norris-La Guardia Act. Since then, court orders have been limited to restraining violence, restricting picketing, and preventing damage to company property.

Some employers have formed **employers' associations** to cooperate in their efforts and present a united front in dealing with labor unions. Employers' associations may even act as negotiators for individual employers who want to reach agreements with labor unions. In essence, major sports leagues, such as Major League Baseball and the NFL, act as employers' associations and negotiate with player unions. Although they do not negotiate contracts, the National Association of Manufacturers and the U.S. Chamber of Commerce are other examples of employers' associations. Both groups promote the views of their members on key issues.

Employee–Management Relations in Nonunion Organizations

Unions grew by giving industrial workers a voice in decisions about their wages and working conditions. As the U.S., Western Europe, and Japan have shifted from manufacturing economies to information and service economies, the makeup of the workforce has become less favorable for unions. Unions still retain their strength in manufacturing industries such as automotive, steel, and aerospace. They have been slower organizing employees in the high-tech computer and electronics industries and in service industries such as finance, but as mentioned earlier, interest in unions is growing among these workers after the recent recession.

Other factors contribute to the relatively small share of union members in today's workforce. Small businesses often employ nonunion workers. Another portion of the nonunionized segment consists of managerial employees. Other nonunion employees work in industries where unions have never developed strength. Still others have simply rejected attempts to establish unions in their workplaces.

At nonunion companies, management often chooses to offer a compensation and benefit structure comparable to those of unionized firms in the area. Willingness to offer comparable wages and working conditions coupled with effective communications, emphasis on promotions from within, employee empowerment, and employee participation in goal setting and grievance handling may help an employer avert unionization. Satisfied workers may conclude that they would receive few additional benefits for the union dues they would have to pay. In fact, many observers argue that the threat of joining a union gives nonunion employees an effective tool in securing desired wages, benefits, and working conditions.

For years, the United Food and Commercial Workers union has attempted to organize Wal-Mart employees (see the Hits & Misses box on page 319). Despite claims that Wal-Mart employees earn less than their counterparts at unionized stores and receive fewer benefits, the union has been unable to make headway. Wal-Mart has been accused of using aggressive antiunion tactics, including distributing a handbook to managers that states, "It is important you be constantly alert for efforts by a union to organize your associates." But many employees say that a union is unnecessary. "The union would hurt—sometimes it tells people not to shop here," explains one worker in Las Vegas. "I think our health plan is fantastic." And Wal-Mart managers believe that the company would rather take care of its employees by itself. "Our belief is that if we continue to manage our business in a positive way and take care of associates, they will see no need for third-party representation," notes one manager.[38]

Grievance Programs for Nonunion Employees
Even without a union, employees may have formal avenues for resolving grievances. Employees who believe they have suffered discrimination, sexual harassment, dismissal without cause, or inadequate promotion opportunities can file lawsuits against their employers or file charges with the EEOC or their state's human rights commission.

The need for labor union protection diminishes considerably in firms that encourage employees to communicate their complaints through programs designed to resolve grievances. A number of nonunion businesses establish formal grievance procedures similar to those used in unionized firms. An even larger number have instituted **alternative dispute resolution (ADR) programs.** These programs vary but usually include the following:

- *Open-door policies* designed to assure employees that they can discuss issues with supervisors, other managers, or human resource representatives.
- *An employee hot line* to give employees the right to call a phone number and air a complaint or get advice on how to file a formal complaint.
- *Peer-review boards* made up of both employee peers and management representatives who listen to employee complaints and make recommendations to management.
- *Mediation and arbitration,* which work in much the same way as in unionized firms, with mediation resulting in a nonbinding solution and arbitration in a binding solution.

Job Security in Nonunion Companies   Realizing that job security has always been a major motivation for workers to form labor unions, firms needing to reduce staffing levels use several alternatives to layoffs. Some offer incentives for early retirement and resignation. Although such programs may cost the employer some of its most highly qualified and experienced workers, the change often replaces older workers with younger employees who receive lower wages. At the same time, rewarding senior employees with early retirement bonuses is likely to enhance employee morale, in contrast to the destructive effects of a decision to lay off workers.

What's Ahead

Treating employees well by enriching the work environment will continue to gain importance as a way to recruit and retain a highly motivated workforce. In addition, managers can tap the full potential of their employees by empowering them to make decisions, leading them to work effectively as teams, and fostering clear, positive communication. The next chapter covers these three means of improving performance. By involving employees more fully through empowerment, teamwork, and communication, companies can benefit from their knowledge while the employees enjoy a more meaningful role in the company.

Concept Check

1. What is a labor union?
2. Identify the major issues covered in the collective bargaining process.
3. What is a boycott?

DID YOU KNOW?

1. Conducting personal interviews with job candidates from different countries requires special skills. While Americans value someone who "looks you in the eye," Japanese are taught never to look directly at a person with superior status.
2. Southwest Airlines displayed its sensitive side by changing the title of the employee who oversees personnel or employee relations to "vice president for people."
3. In 1980, the typical CEO was paid 43 times as much as his or her average worker. In 1990, it was 85 times as much. Today, it's 531 times as much.
4. Recently, one of the most popular employee benefits has been pet insurance. But employees usually foot the $12 to $16 monthly cost.
5. At Perkins Coie, a Seattle law firm, Happiness Committees perform random acts of kindness around the office to boost morale.

Summary of Learning Goals

1

Explain the importance of human resource management, the responsibilities of human resource managers, and the role of human resource planning in an organization's competitive strategy.
Organizations devote considerable attention to attracting, training, and retaining employees to help maintain their competitiveness. Human resource managers are responsible for recruiting, selecting, training, compensating, terminating, and motivating employees. They accomplish these tasks by developing specific programs and creating a work environment that generates employee satisfaction and efficiency. A human resource plan is designed to implement a firm's competitive strategies by providing the right number of employees, training them to meet job requirements, and motivating them to be productive and satisfied workers.

2 **Describe how recruitment and selection, training, and evaluation contribute to placing the right person in a job.**

Firms use internal and external methods to recruit qualified employees. For needs that the company cannot meet with existing employees, it may find candidates by encouraging employee referrals, advertising, accepting résumés at its Web site, and using job search Web sites. In selecting qualified candidates, human resource managers must follow legal requirements designed to promote equal employment opportunity. Human resource managers use a variety of training techniques, including on-the-job training, computerized training programs, and classroom methods. In addition, management development programs help managers make decisions and improve interpersonal skills. Companies conduct performance appraisals to assess employees' work, as well as their strengths and weaknesses.

3 **Outline the methods employers use to compensate employees through pay systems and benefit programs.**

Firms compensate employees with wages, salaries, and incentive pay systems, such as profit sharing, gain sharing, bonuses, and pay-for-knowledge programs. Benefit programs vary among firms, but most companies offer health-care programs, insurance, retirement plans, paid holidays, and sick leave. A growing number of companies are offering flexible benefit plans and flexible work plans, such as flextime, compressed workweeks, job sharing, and home-based work.

4 **Discuss employee separation and the impact of downsizing and outsourcing.**

Either an employer or an employee can decide to terminate employment. Downsizing reduces a company's workforce to reduce labor costs in an effort to improve the firm's competitive position. The company may transfer some responsibilities to contractors, a practice called outsourcing. The goals of outsourcing are to reduce costs by giving work to more efficient specialists and to allow the company to focus on the activities it does best. Another trend is the increasing use of contingent workers, such as consultants and temporary employees.

5 **Explain how Maslow's hierarchy of needs theory, job design, and managers' attitudes relate to employee motivation.**

Employee motivation starts with good employee morale. Maslow's hierarchy of needs theory states that all people have basic needs (physiological and safety) that they must satisfy before they can consider higher order needs (social, esteem, and self-actualization).

Job enlargement and job enrichment are two ways in which managers can motivate employees and satisfy various levels of needs. Managers' attitudes can also affect employee motivation. Theory X managers will likely keep their subordinates under close and constant observation. Theory Y managers emphasize workers' self-control and self-direction. Theory Z takes the approach that worker involvement is the key to increased productivity for a company and improved quality of work life for employees.

6 **Summarize the role of labor unions and list their primary goals.**

A labor union is a group of workers who have banded together to achieve common goals in the key areas of wages, working hours, and working conditions. Labor unions can be found at the local, national, and international levels. The governing body for most labor unions in the U.S. is the AFL–CIO, which is a federation of 66 member unions. The percentage of workers belonging to unions is much higher in the public sector than it is in the private sector. Government attitudes toward unions have varied considerably during the past century and are reflected in the major pieces of labor legislation enacted during this period.

7 **Outline the tactics of labor and management in conflicts between them.**

Labor unions work to achieve their goals of increased job security and improvements in wages, hours, and working conditions through a process known as collective bargaining. Most union–management negotiations result in a signed agreement without a work stoppage. Even after an agreement is signed, disputes can arise. A grievance is a complaint that management is violating some provision of the union contract. Mediation is the process of settling union–management disputes through recommendations of an impartial third party. Arbitration is a process in which an impartial third party renders a legally binding decision. Some of the tactics available to labor unions during disputes include strikes (walkouts), picketing, and boycotts. Tactics available to management include lockouts, hiring replacement workers (strikebreakers), obtaining court injunctions, and forming employer associations.

8 **Describe employee–management relations in nonunion organizations.**

Many nonunion companies offer a compensation and benefit structure comparable to those of unionized firms. Employees usually have formal avenues for resolving grievances, called alternative dispute resolution (ADR) programs. Nonunion firms usually try to use alternatives to layoffs when the need to reduce staff arises.

Business Terms You Need to Know

human resource
management 296

performance appraisal 303

wage 304

salary 304

employee benefits 305

downsizing 309

outsourcing 310

contingent worker 311

morale 311

Maslow's hierarchy of
needs 312

job enlargement 313

job enrichment 313

labor union 315

collective bargaining 317

grievance 317

Other Important Business Terms

management 296

professional employer
organization (PEO) 297

employment at will 302

on-the-job training 302

management development
program 303

360-degree performance
review 303

living wage 304

401(k) plan 306

flexible benefit plan 306

paid time off (PTO) 307

flexible work plan 307

flextime 308

compressed workweek 308

job sharing program 308

telecommuter 308

Theory X 315

Theory Y 315

Theory Z 315

mediation 318

arbitration 318

strike 318

picketing 318

boycott 318

lockout 319

employers' association 320

alternative dispute resolution
(ADR) program 321

Review Questions

1. What are the core responsibilities of human resource management? What are the three main objectives of human resource managers?

2. What methods do companies use to recruit and select employees? What types of training programs are popular today?

3. On what five factors are compensation policies usually based? Name at least three employee benefits that are required by law and three more that are provided voluntarily by many firms.

4. Describe four types of flexible work plans. Identify an industry that would be well suited to each type of plan and explain why.

5. Outline the major reasons for terminating employees. Why do companies downsize? What are some of the difficulties they may encounter in doing so?

6. What is a contingent worker? How are contingent workers used by firms? Name some industries that use contingent workers.

7. Explain Maslow's hierarchy of needs theory. How do companies attempt to satisfy employee needs at each level in the hierarchy?

8. How do companies use job design to motivate employees?

9. What are the chief tactics of unions and management in their contract negotiations? Are they usually effective? Why or why not?

10. In what ways are employee–management relations in nonunion organizations similar to those in unionized organizations? In what ways might they be different?

Projects and Applications

1. Choose one of the following organizations (or select one of your own) and write a memo outlining a plan for outsourcing some of the tasks currently performed by employees. Cite reasons for your choices.
   a. summer resort in Wisconsin
   b. regional high school in Arizona
   c. software development firm in California
   d. major hospital in Massachusetts
   e. manufacturing plant in Kentucky

2. Would you accept a job you didn't particularly like because the firm offered an attractive benefits package? Why or why not? Do you think your answer would change as you get older? Why or why not?

3. Not every unionized worker has the right to strike. All federal employees and many state and municipal employees—such as police officers and firefighters—cannot strike. Suppose you were a teacher or an airline pilot. Do you think members of your union should be allowed to strike? Why or why not?

4. Do you think the trend toward union–employee partnerships will continue to grow? In what ways might this trend change the relationship between companies and employees over the next decade?

5. Suppose you are a human resource manager and you have determined that your company would benefit from hiring some older workers. Write a memo explaining your reasons for this conclusion.

Experiential Exercise

Background: Every January, professional baseball players file for salary arbitration, which is followed by arbitration hearings during the first three weeks in February. The data indicate that the very act of filing for arbitration speeds up the salary negotiation process between the individual players and their clubs. Since 1990, only about 20 percent of the players who filed for arbitration went through the entire process, and the percentage appears to be declining. For instance, during one recent year, 94 players filed for arbitration. Of those 94, only five actually went through the entire arbitration process.

Directions: To learn more about the arbitration process, conduct research on a recent baseball arbitration case and report those findings in a brief oral presentation or a written report based on your instructor's directions. Select a case in which both parties went through the entire arbitration process. For your research, you can access the Major League Baseball Web site at http://www.mlb.com.

Sources: "Salary Arbitration Figures," Major League Baseball Web site, http://www.mlb.com, accessed June 29, 2002; Ken Gurnick, "Salary Arbitration: A Brief History," Major League Baseball Web site, http://www.mlb.com, accessed June 29, 2002.

NOTHING BUT NET

1. **Finding a job online.** Many companies advertise open positions on their Web sites. Some even allow candidates to submit applications online. Visit the company Web sites listed and explore their employment sections. Write a brief summary of the types of positions advertised, the application procedures, and other employment information—such as benefits—provided. Based on your visits to the three sites, would you be interested in working for any of these companies? Why or why not?

    http://www.amgen.com/career
    http://www.gecareers.com
    http://www.southwestairlines.com/careers

2. **Employee benefits.** The Bureau of Labor Statistics conducts regular surveys on employee benefits. Visit the Bureau's Web site and review the results of the most recent survey. Then respond to the following:
    a. List the benefits offered by a typical employer.
    b. Rank these benefits in terms of their importance to you individually.

    c. What percentage of employees enroll in employer-sponsored health care plans, retirement plans, and flexible spending plans?
    d. Are there any differences between the typical benefits package offered by large employers and the typical package offered by small employers? If so, explain.

    http://www.bls.gov/ncs/ebs/home.htm

3. **Union membership.** The AFL–CIO is the largest labor organization in the U.S. Visit the organization's Web site and click on the section "How & Why People Join Unions" within the "All About Unions" tub. Review the information and list five interesting facts you learned.

    http://www.aflcio.org

    Note: Internet Web addresses change frequently. If you do not find the exact sites listed, you may need to access the organization's or company's home page and search from there.

Case 9.1

Telecommuting Numbers Are on the Rise

Many of us genuinely like our jobs, but we'd be happy to skip the long commute, endless meetings, distracting phone calls, and bag lunches. Then there's that one colleague who always interrupts the workflow with a personal problem. Or perhaps we have children getting off the school bus at 3 when our workday doesn't end till 5. Working from home and telecommuting have become attractive alternatives for many office workers—and their employers. While workers enjoy the benefits of flexibility and avoid a commute, companies gain in increased productivity and reduced office-related costs. In a single decade, the number of workers who telecommute has gone from 4 million to nearly 24 million nationwide.

"I find that I get more done working at home," says Marcella Parsons, who now telecommutes from her home in Incline Village, Nevada, to VPacket Communications, a networking company near Los Angeles. "I don't have to be in as many meetings, and I can sit on phone conferences and look up at the mountain slopes lined with pine trees." Parsons also avoids sitting in an ever-increasing traffic jam. "People are getting more and more tired of the effects of traffic on their commutes and their lives," notes author Alan Pisarski. "We've reached a level of very high frustration." Of IBM's 320,000 employees worldwide, 80,000 feel the same way, and the company allows them to telecommute from their home offices, which saves IBM roughly $700 million in real estate costs, reports Jeanette Barlow, marketing manager for IBM Lotus.

Telecommuting can be a powerful motivator for some employees, whether it's a reduction in commuting, assistance in balancing family and work life, or a response to global events such as concern about potential terrorist attacks. But employees who telecommute must have certain qualities as workers. "Technology has facilitated this kind of work," says Vince Biviano, who is Marcella Parsons's boss at VPacket. "But it still has to be a special individual. They have to be able to work independently, have a proven track record within the company, be a hard worker, be in a certain discipline." In addition, a company has to be set up in such a way that the structure and culture support telecommuting. Managers and employees need written guidelines about the company's telecommuting program. Both managers and employees should receive training in telecommuting matters.

Finally, telecommuting isn't for everyone or every business—production supervisors, restaurant managers, and bank tellers obviously can't telecommute. Other businesses function well with part-time telecommuting arrangements so that these employees don't lose touch with colleagues and managers. Telecommuting doesn't answer all management questions about motivation and job satisfaction, but it does offer one attractive solution for some workers and their companies. Telecommuters can accomplish their work without losing time commuting, and employers can get productive, happier workers.

QUESTIONS FOR CRITICAL THINKING

1. Describe what you see as the downside to telecommuting. Do you think you would enjoy telecommuting? Why or why not?

2. Telecommuting has been a growing trend over the last decade. Do you think this trend will level off or reverse itself over the next decade? Why or why not?

Sources: "Frequently Asked Questions," Telework/Telecommuting Web site, U.S. General Services Administration, http://www.telework.gov, accessed March 13, 2003; Haya El Nasser, "Census: Home Is Where Work Is," *USA Today*, December 24, 2002, p. A1; L. A. Sorek, "Telecommuting Saves Businesses, Agencies Millions," *SiliconValley.com*, October 28, 2002, http://www.siliconvalley.com; "U.S. Telecommuting Population," *Office of Transportation*, May 13, 2002, http://www.ott.doe.gov/facts/archives/fotw216supp.shtml; Dave Carpenter, "Interest in Telecommuting Has Grown Since September 11," *Mobile Register*, December 16, 2001, p. F2; "Telecommuting: Making It Work," *HR Answers*, December 12, 2001, http://www.hranswers.com.

Video Case 9.2

Fannie Mae

This video case appears on page 611. A recently filmed video, designed to expand and highlight the written case, is available for class use by instructors.

Chapter 10
Improving Performance through Empowerment, Teamwork, and Communication

Learning Goals

1 Describe why and how organizations empower employees.

2 Distinguish between the two major types of teams in the workplace.

3 Identify the characteristics of an effective team and the roles played by team members.

4 Summarize the stages of team development.

5 Relate team cohesiveness and norms to effective team performance.

6 Describe the factors that can cause conflict in teams and how conflict can be resolved.

7 Explain the importance of effective communication skills in business.

8 Compare the different types of communication.

Teamwork—Whole Foods Style

When John Mackey cofounded Whole Foods Market in 1980, it was just a small store with a restaurant above it in Austin, Texas. Mackey jokes about living in tiny quarters on the third floor and using the dishwasher hose in the restaurant to take showers. At the time, he wasn't thinking about changing the

way Americans shop for groceries. But he has done that—and more. He has proved that what is now a good-sized public corporation can be run by teams of empowered employees who love their jobs.

Today, Whole Foods is the largest organic and natural foods grocer in the world. The firm operates 157 stores in 28 states, the District of Columbia, Canada, and Great Britain, with nearly $4 billion in annual revenues. While other grocery chains are losing money or struggling to break even—Safeway lost $1 billion in one recent two-year period, and Food Lion, which operates seven times as many stores as Whole Foods, cleared only $150 million—Whole Foods is virtually raking in the cash. So it's no wonder that industry watchers want to know Mackey's secret: the answer is, in part, Mackey's style of "no secrets management." The phrase comes from one of his original management decisions—to create a pay book that records everyone's salary and make it available to all employees. In general, Mackey wants to be sure that everyone in the organization has access to information about the company.

Teamwork is central to Whole Foods, which operates teams at every level of the organization, involving all 24,000 employees. There's a national team that deals with information technology issues, and the National Leadership Team, which is composed of 24 top executives. Stores have about eight or 10 work teams, including the seafood team, the prepared food team, and the cashier/front end team. Each new hire is assigned to a team; after four weeks, the worker must receive a two-thirds "yes" vote from team members to become a permanent team member and employee. But team members don't just vote "yes" for their best friends; they vote for workers who do the best job. That's

© Tim Boyle/Getty Images

because additional pay, beyond the base wage, is linked to team performance. Individual teams who meet or exceed their performance goals share in their store's profits.

At each Whole Foods store, team leaders and members are empowered to make a wide variety of decisions. Teams can decide to stock sushi or salmon, dinosaur kale or cabbage, beef or bison—as long as each item meets Whole Foods's quality standards. The average shopper is greeted with hundreds of choices, including a well-stocked salad bar and gourmet prepared foods such as pizza, Asian, Indian, and Latin specialties. Managing such a large menu of products may seem daunting, when you add the fact that some of the Whole Foods teams have as many as 150 members. The newest store in New York City has 468 team members, with 140 on the cashier team alone. But Mackey insists that even his largest teams reach consensus and find solutions to problems, often by breaking into subteams to accomplish tasks. At the highest level of the organization, the National Leadership Team makes decisions in much the same way as the store teams do. "We make decisions by majority vote," says Mackey. "I almost never overrule them."

People who work for Whole Foods tend to stay there for a long time, turning jobs into careers. The reason is simple, says one employee who is a member of the seafood team in New York: "They have a lot more respect for you as a person here." Doug Greene, founder and former editor of *Natural Foods Merchandiser*, believes that Whole Foods plays an even larger role in society. "If you look back 100 years from now," he predicts, "history will show that Whole Foods will be in the top five companies that changed the world."[1]

Chapter Overview

Top managers at most firms recognize that teamwork and communication are essential for encouraging employees and helping them improve organizational performance. Advances in information technology have given firms powerful tools to allow employees to make decisions, work in teams, and share information.

This chapter focuses on how organizations are involving employees by empowering them to make critical decisions, allowing them to work in teams, and fostering communication. We begin by discussing the ways managers are expanding their employees' decision-making authority and responsibility. Then we explain why and how a growing number of firms rely on teams of workers rather than individuals to make decisions and carry out assignments. Finally, we discuss how effective communication allows workers to share information that improves decision making.

Empowering Employees

empowerment giving employees authority and responsibility to make decisions about their work without traditional managerial approval and control.

An important component of effective management is **empowerment** of employees. Managers promote this goal by giving employees authority and responsibility to make decisions about their work without traditional managerial approval and control. Empowerment seeks to tap the brainpower of all employees to find improved ways of doing their jobs and executing their ideas. Empowering employees frees managers from hands-on control of subordinates. It also motivates workers by adding challenges to their jobs and giving them a feeling of ownership. Managers empower employees by sharing company information, sharing decision-making authority, and rewarding them based on company performance.

Anderson & Associates, an engineering firm, believes in empowering its employees through information. The company posts financial statements, training schedules, policy documents, and other information on its intranet.

Courtesy of Anderson & Associates

Sharing Information

One of the most effective methods of empowering employees is to keep them informed about the company's financial performance. Companies like Anderson & Associates provide regular reports to their employees on key financial information, such as profit and loss statements. Anderson, an engineering firm that designs roads, water and sewer lines, and water-treatment facilities, posts financial statements, training schedules, policy documents, and other information on the company's intranet. Any employee can visit the site and look up the company's cash flow, design standards, and photos of coworkers in other cities, as well as basic measures of financial performance. Like other companies that practice this strategy of open-book management, Anderson also trains its employees to interpret financial statements so they can understand how their work contributes to company profits. Anderson's policy is to hire engineers before they have completed their formal education and then help them develop their skills in one of the firm's offices following graduation. Once they have learned all facets of supervising a branch office, they are ready to open—and manage—a new branch office.[2]

In addition to sharing information about the company itself, top management can empower employees by communicating information about the business environment. Firms use intranets, meetings, and other tools to keep their employees posted about industry trends, competitive performance, suppliers and customers, and external opportunities and threats.

Employee empowerment has benefited from advances in information technology. Firms once needed multiple layers of management to analyze information and communicate it up and down their organizational hierarchies. But today, the Internet, internal company networks and databases, and communication tools such as e-mail and videoconferencing allow employees to carry out many activities on their own.

Using information technology to empower employees does carry some risks. One is that information may reach competitors. Although this problem was considered by Anderson & Associates, management decided that sharing information was essential to the company's strategy. Another risk of giving employees access to information and information technology is that they might use resources like the Internet for personal matters. Many large U.S. companies record and review employees' communications and Internet usage. Companies that market software for monitoring keystrokes and mouse clicks are doing a brisk business; some software even sends a signal to human resource personnel when it detects that a company computer is accessing an inappropriate Web site. Many observers, however, suggest that employer anxiety about Internet usage is misplaced. They point out that U.S. workers are putting in more hours than ever and that companies themselves are blurring the boundaries between work and personal time.

Sharing Decision-Making Authority

Companies empower employees when they give them broad authority to make workplace decisions that implement a firm's vision and its competitive strategy. Trust and freedom can be expressed in different ways. Bed Bath & Beyond lets individual store managers decide how much of each item to stock. The firm assumes that store managers know their customers better than anyone at headquarters. The results are sometimes unexpected. In Manhattan, the Bed Bath & Beyond store carries electric fans throughout the year, even during the cold winter months. Although the temperature outside may be frigid, many Manhattan residents live in stuffy apartments, so demand for fans doesn't end with the change of seasons. Thanks to such knowledge of local conditions, empowerment at Bed Bath & Beyond helps to keep sales per square foot high and turnover among store managers low.

Even among nonmanagement employees, empowerment extends to decisions and activities traditionally handled by managers. Employees might be responsible for such tasks as purchasing supplies, making hiring decisions, scheduling production or work hours, overseeing the safety program, and granting pay increases. Managers at Dana Corp., which produces truck parts for Toyota, rely on the knowledge and experience of their production-floor operators. "If you have a problem," says plant manager Tim Reed, "don't just sit in your office and try to figure it out yourself and make your own decision. Go ask the person who works in that area."[3] Employees are often empowered to make decisions as part of a team, an arrangement discussed later in this chapter.

Linking Rewards to Company Performance

To provide incentives for excellence, employers should reward their employees for contributing desirable ideas and actions. Compensation plans such as pay for performance, pay for knowledge, and gain sharing give employees a sense of ownership. (These plans are discussed in detail later in the chapter.) When celebrity chef Charlie Palmer was just beginning in his career, he asked the owner of the restaurant where he worked for a piece of the business. "I felt I was an integral part, and I wanted it to be my restaurant as well as the owner's," he said. The owner, however, wasn't interested. Palmer, now an author and the boss of a $36-million-a-year upscale food empire, decided early on to treat his employees differently. He gives his key people cash bonuses for performance. For instance, every day, his

Table 10.1	Employee Stock Ownership Plans and Stock Options	
ESOP	**Stock Options**
Company-sponsored trust fund holds shares of stock for employees	Company gives employees the option to buy shares of its stock
Usually covers all full-time employees	Can be granted to one, a few, or all employees
Employer pays for the shares of stock	Employees pay a set price to exercise the option
Employees receive stock shares (or value of stock) upon retiring or leaving the company	Employees receive shares of stock when (and if) they exercise the option, usually during a set period

Source: Based on "Employee Stock Options Fact Sheet," "How an Employee Stock Ownership Plan (ESOP) Works," and "A Comprehensive Overview of Employee Ownership," accessed at the National Center for Employee Ownership, http://www.nceo .org/library, March 6, 2003.

managers see up-to-date financial reports. Whenever one key ratio, the percentage of food cost to food sales, drops below 32 percent—35 percent is considered good—managers get a cash bonus based on the savings. Palmer also allows his managers and other key employees the chance to invest in any of his new ventures. He believes letting employees share in the prosperity of his business is the right thing to do. It also helps build loyalty, unique in an industry notorious for its high turnover.[4]

Perhaps the ultimate step in convincing employees of their stake in the continuing prosperity of their firm is worker ownership, which makes employees financial participants in company performance. Two widely used ways that companies provide worker ownership are employee stock ownership plans and stock options. Table 10.1 compares these two methods of employee ownership.

Employee Stock Ownership Plans   Around 8.8 million workers at 11,000 different companies participate in **employee stock ownership plans (ESOPs).**[5] These plans benefit employees by giving them ownership stakes in their companies, leading to potential profits as the value of their firm increases. Under ESOPs, the employer buys shares of the company stock on behalf of the employee as a retirement benefit. The accounts continue to grow in value tax-free, and when employees leave the company, they can cash in their stock shares. Employees are motivated to work harder and smarter than they would without ESOPs because, as part owners, they share in their firm's financial success. As retirement plans, ESOPs must comply with government regulations designed to protect pension benefits. Because ESOPs can be expensive to set up, they are more common in larger firms than in smaller ones. Public companies with ESOPs average around 14,000 employees.[6] Large firms with ESOPs include United Parcel Service and DynCorp.

Stock Options   Another popular way for companies to share ownership with their employees is through the use of **stock options,** or rights to buy a specified amount of the company stock at a given price within a given time period. In contrast to an ESOP, in which the company holds stock for the benefit of employees, stock options give employees a chance to own the stock themselves if they exercise their options by completing the stock purchase. Though options were once limited to senior executives and members of the board of directors, some companies now grant stock options to employees at all levels. Moreover, recent changes in federal labor laws allow stock options to be granted to hourly as well as salaried employees.[7] Stock options have turned hundreds of employees at firms such as Home Depot and Microsoft into millionaires.

Some argue, however, that to be most effective as motivators, stock options need to be granted to a much broader base of employees. About one-third of all stock options issued by U.S. corporations go to the top five executives at each firm. Much of the remainder goes to other executives and managers, who make up only about 2 percent of the U.S. workforce. Yet there is solid evidence that stock options

> *They Said It*
>
> Chief executives, who themselves own few shares of their companies, have no more feeling for the average stockholder than they do for baboons in Africa.
>
> —*T. Boone Pickens (b. 1928) American entrepreneur*

motivate regular employees to perform better. Employees at United Airlines, which has filed for bankruptcy, are disillusioned with their ESOP because they could not capitalize on their firm's success in the 1990s; they were not permitted to cash in their shares until they retired, by which time the carrier was struggling for survival.[8]

Concept Check

1. *What is empowerment?*
2. *What kinds of information can companies provide employees to help them share decision-making responsibility?*
3. *What are some of the risks of sharing this information?*

Teamwork

Teamwork is the cooperative effort by a group of workers acting together for a common cause. You have most likely experienced teamwork as a member of a class project, athletic team, band, or social or civic group. Teamwork is vital in business and in other areas. A team of workers cooperates to perform a certain function, such as developing the 2005 Toyota Camry, or solving a particular problem, such as improving methods of filling customer orders.

Teamwork is widely used in business and in many not-for-profit organizations such as hospitals, military units, police departments, and government agencies. Teamwork is one of the most frequently discussed topics in employee training programs, where individuals often learn team-building skills. Many firms emphasize the importance of teamwork during their hiring processes, asking job applicants about their previous experiences as team members. Companies want to hire people who can work well with other people.

Teamwork is an important consideration in employee recruitment and training because it encourages employees to pool their talents and ideas to achieve more together than they could achieve working as individuals. Teamwork is playing a critical role in the building of the new Joint Strike Fighter airplane. More than 80 suppliers, working in almost 200 different locations, are building components for the warplane. In addition, the U.S. Air Force, Navy, and Marines; Britain's Defense Ministry; and other U.S. allies are tracking the progress of the JSF, making changes if necessary. Lockheed Martin, the prime contractor for the project, has a 75-member team to link everyone together and coordinate the massive project. The Lockheed team uses a variety of Web-based software tools to share designs, track changes, and keep an eye on the schedule.[9]

teamwork cooperative effort by a group of workers acting together for a common cause.

What Is a Team?

A group of people with complementary skills who are committed to a common purpose, approach, and set of performance goals is referred to as a **team.** All team members hold themselves mutually responsible and accountable for accomplishing their objectives.

team group of employees who are committed to a common purpose, approach, and set of performance goals.

© AP/Wide World Photos

Lockheed Martin's Joint Strike Fighter team must coordinate a massive team of 80-plus suppliers in 200 different locations to design and build the new airplane.

BEST BUSINESS PRACTICES

Work Together, Closely—and Yet So Far

It is no secret that businesses have been trimming travel budgets. Travel is expensive, time-consuming, and disruptive of employees' personal lives. Add earlier check-in times and long security lines, and you can see why three U.S. corporations in five are reducing nonessential travel.

As the cost of technology drops, videoconferencing has proven an essential alternative to travel. "We cut our whole budget by 20 percent and our travel budget by 70 percent," says Michael Klein, spokesman for the American Forest and Paper Association, which substituted videoconferencing for its annual planning meeting. Whale Communications Ltd., a network-security firm in New Jersey, invested in Web and videoconferencing equipment that will pay for itself within a year by cutting travel to clients' offices by two-thirds. Video-conferencing can't replace a firm handshake or a smile. But it does let people exchange written documents in real time and collaborate in groups despite huge distances.

With Web technology, coworkers can share knowledge without even a long-distance phone call. IBM recently assembled over 50,000 employees online in a meeting it dubbed WorldJam, and State Farm Insurance set up regional sections of its intranet so agents could exchange information about state insurance legislation. State Farm also allocated a portion of its site for employees to post messages without restriction, and it became a "best practices" bulletin board to which many people contribute.

Telecommunications can also cut costs dramatically by reducing the inefficiency of institutional paper systems. American Express compared the cost of handling a typical expense account with paper systems—$36—to a fully automated system—$8. Instead of printing, mailing, approving, and signing paper documents, employees can work on more critical tasks.

Are business colleagues never to meet again? Hardly. Most firms use a combination of personal and virtual meetings to maintain that crucial human link. Better teamwork is often the result. As one expert put it, "You can still work together, even if you stay in place."

QUESTIONS FOR CRITICAL THINKING

1. List some advantages and disadvantages of virtual meetings.

2. In what situations might a face-to-face meeting be preferable?

Sources: Mie-Yun Lee, "Teleconferencing Puts Everyone on Same Page in Distance Meetings," *Pittsburgh Business Times,* November 8, 2002, http://www.pittsburgh.bizjournals.com; Rebecca Kumar, "Teleconferencing by Phone, Web Enjoying Rapid Growth," *Hotel Online,* September 2002, http://www.hotel-online.com; Anne Stuart, "Have Tech, Won't Travel," *Inc.,* January 2002, pp. 70–75; Joe Mathieu, "Travelers Still Wrestling with 9-11," *CBS MarketWatch,* January 25, 2002, http://cbs.marketwatch.com.

---

work team relatively permanent group of employees with complementary skills who perform the day-to-day work of organizations.

The trend in U.S. business toward developing teams began in the 1980s, when managers began to address quality concerns via the formation of quality circles, in which workers meet weekly or monthly to discuss ways to improve quality. This concept spread as the teams demonstrated their ability to help companies reduce output of defective products and the time wasted in reworking those units. Eventually, two-thirds of America's 1,000 largest firms operated quality circles. By the mid-1990s, the percentage of major firms implementing quality circles to solve minor quality problems had declined, primarily because their focus on activities with limited scope typically produced only modest increases in productivity.

With an eye on the bottom line, businesses continued to reduce the layers of management through downsizing, as they became increasingly involved in international business. These trends encouraged the formation of many different types of teams. As Figure 10.1 shows, the list includes work teams, problem-solving teams, management teams, quality circles, and virtual teams made up of geographically separated members who interact via computer. Virtual teams have become increasingly popular, as the Best Business Practices box explains. Today, there are two basic types of teams: work teams and problem-solving teams.

They Said It

Now an army is a team. It lives, eats, sleeps, fights as a team. This individuality stuff is a bunch of crap.

—*George C. Scott (1927–1999) American actor (in Franklin Schaffner's 1970 motion picture* Patton*)*

Work Teams   About two-thirds of U.S. firms currently use **work teams,** which are relatively permanent groups of employees. In this approach, people with complementary skills perform the day-to-day work of the organization. Most of Wal-Mart's major vendors maintain offices near its headquarters in Bentonville, Arkansas. Typically, the vendor offices operate as work teams, and the head of these vendor offices often has the title "team leader."

When a work team is empowered with authority to make decisions about how the members complete their daily tasks, it is called a *self-managed team.* A self-managed team works most effectively when it combines employees with a range of skills and functions. Members are cross-trained to perform each other's jobs as needed. Distributing decision-making authority in this way can free members to concentrate on satisfying customers.

As we saw in the opening vignette, Whole Foods Market has a structure based on self-managed work teams. Company managers decided that Whole Foods could be most innovative if employees made decisions themselves. Every employee is part of a team, and each store has about 10 teams handling separate functions, such as groceries, the bakery, and customer service. Each team handles responsibilities related to setting goals, hiring and training employees, scheduling team members, and purchasing goods to stock. Teams meet at least monthly to review goals and performance, solve problems, and explore new ideas. Whole Foods awards bonuses based on the teams' performance relative to their goals.[10]

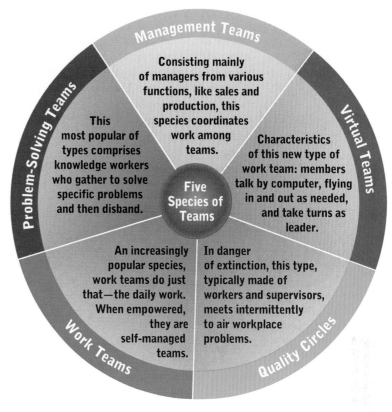

FIGURE 10.1
Five Species of Teams

Problem-Solving Teams In contrast to work teams, a **problem-solving team** is a temporary combination of workers who gather to solve a specific problem and then disband. Like work teams, problem-solving teams typically self-manage their work. They differ from work teams in important ways, though. Work teams are permanent units designed to handle any business problem that arises, but problem-solving teams pursue specific missions. These missions can be broadly stated, such as finding out why customers are satisfied, or narrowly defined, such as solving the overheating problem in Generator 4. Once the team completes its task by solving the assigned problem, it usually disbands.

problem-solving team
temporary combination of workers who gather to solve a specific problem and then disband.

When a team is made up of members from different functions, such as production, marketing, and finance, it is called a *cross-functional team.* Most often, cross-functional teams work on specific problems or projects, but they can also serve as permanent work-team arrangements. Lockheed Martin, for instance, created a cross-functional team to manage the Joint Strike Fighter project mentioned earlier. The value of cross-functional teams comes from their ability to bring many different perspectives to a work effort. General Electric's Bayamon, Puerto Rico, factory uses teams drawn from various departments to evaluate proposed changes. The team members discuss how each change will affect the different departments. This approach has reduced morale problems resulting from rumors about proposed changes and has contributed to improved productivity at the facility.[11]

One of the most innovative team approaches in business today involves vendor–client partnerships. In this type of arrangement, representatives from the vendor and client companies work together to identify client problems and outline solutions that the vendor can provide.

Concept Check

1. What is teamwork? What is a team?
2. When might a temporary team be more effective than a permanent one? Why?

Team Characteristics

Effective teams share a number of characteristics. They must be an appropriate size, have an understanding and acceptance of the roles played by members, and benefit from diversity among team members.

Team Size

Teams can range in size from as small as two people to as large as 150 people. In practice, however, most teams have fewer than 15 members. Although no ideal size limit applies to every team, research on team effectiveness indicates that they achieve maximum results with about six or seven members.[12] A group of this size is big enough to benefit from a variety of diverse skills, yet small enough to allow members to communicate easily and feel part of a close-knit group.

Certainly, groups smaller or larger than this ideal size can do effective work, but they can create added challenges for a team leader. Participants in small teams of two to four members often show a desire to get along with each other. They tend to favor informal interactions marked by discussions of personal topics, and they make only limited demands on team leaders. A large team with more than 12 members poses a different challenge for team leaders because decision making may work slowly and participants may feel limited commitments to team goals. Larger teams also tend to foster disagreements, absenteeism, and membership turnover. Subgroups may form, leading to possible conflicts among various functions. As a general rule, a team of more than 20 people should be divided into subteams, each with its own members and goals.

Team Roles

Team members tend to take on certain roles, as shown in Figure 10.2. They can be classified as task specialists or by socioemotional roles. People who assume the **task specialist role** devote time and energy to helping the team accomplish its specific goals. These team members are the ones who actively propose new ideas and solutions to problems, evaluate the suggestions of others, ask for more information, and summarize group discussions.

Team members who play the **socioemotional role** devote their time and energy to supporting the emotional needs of team members and to maintaining the team as a social unit. They encourage others to contribute ideas, try to reduce tensions that arise among team members, reconcile conflicts, and often change their own opinions in trying to maintain team harmony.

Some team members may assume *dual roles* by performing both task specialist and socioemotional activities. Those who can assume dual roles often are chosen as team leaders because they satisfy both types of needs. Finally, some members may fall into a *nonparticipative role*. These team members contribute little or nothing to accomplishing the task or satisfying social and emotional needs.

Managers work to form balanced teams, with members capable of performing both task-oriented and social roles. A team with too many task specialists may be productive in the short term but create an unsatisfying situation over a longer time period because team members may become unsupportive of each other. Teams with too many socioemotional types can be satisfying but unproductive because participants may hesitate to disagree with or criticize each other.

Some organizations, like audio systems maker Bose Corp., compare their team approach to the world of sports, whose team members each have specific roles to fill to ensure overall success. "We're a very collaborative company. When I watched the New England Patriots this season," said business administration manager Steve Devine, "it reminded me of us—it's a team approach."[13]

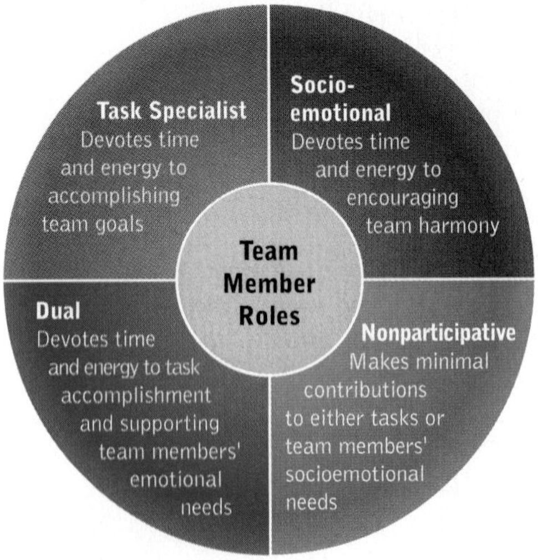

Team Diversity

Besides playing different roles, team members may bring to the team varied perspectives based on differences in their work experiences and age, gender, social, and cultural backgrounds. A cross-functional team establishes one type of diversity by bringing together the expertise of members from different functions in the organization. The team created by Lockheed Martin to manage the development and manufacture of the Joint Strike Fighter is made up of individuals with backgrounds in diverse areas like engineering, finance, and logistics. At Collins & Aikman's Tennessee plant, where parts for auto interiors are made, teams charged with monitoring lean manufacturing methods are made up of employees representing each of the company's product lines.[14]

FIGURE 10.2
Team Member Roles

Diversity can benefit a creative team. "It's great to work in an artistic environment where everybody is doing the same thing but has different interpretations," says Franklin Rowe of his experience working with others.

Teamwork in Small Organizations

The owner-manager of a small firm can cultivate the characteristics of successful teams. The manager can direct everyone's efforts toward the team's common purpose, empower team members, and ensure that the team includes a balance of task specialists and members comfortable playing a socioemotional role. The manager can also recruit team members with diverse backgrounds and encourage everyone to contribute to the team.

The concept of teamwork also applies to entrepreneurs. The key to success in managing the growth of a new venture often rests with the founder's ability to assemble a team of employees who bring skills and experience complementary to his or her own. Perhaps the greatest challenge for an entrepreneur who wants to encourage teamwork is to sit back and let the team generate ideas. Brainstorming, or gathering ideas spontaneously from group members, is a technique for generating new ideas that works particularly well for teams, including the product-development team at Cranium, Inc., maker of the innovative board game of the same name.[15]

FIGURE 10.3
Stages of Team Development

Stages of Team Development

Teams typically progress through five stages of development: forming, storming, norming, performing, and adjourning. These stages are summarized in Figure 10.3.

Stage 1: Forming   The first stage, forming, is an orientation period during which team members get to know each other and find out what behaviors are acceptable to the group. Team members begin with curiosity about expectations of them and whether they will fit in with the group. An effective team leader provides time for members to become acquainted.

Stage 2: Storming   The personalities of team members begin to emerge at the storming stage as members clarify their roles and expectations. Conflicts may arise, as people disagree over the team's mission and jockey for position and control of the group. Subgroups

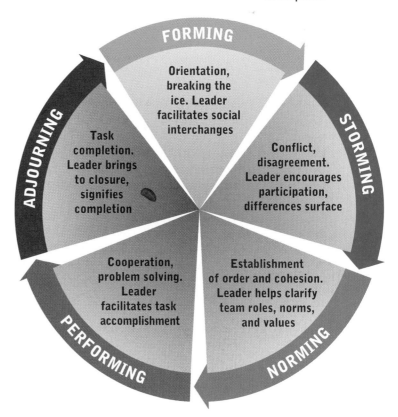

FORMING
Orientation, breaking the ice. Leader facilitates social interchanges

STORMING
Conflict, disagreement. Leader encourages participation, differences surface

NORMING
Establishment of order and cohesion. Leader helps clarify team roles, norms, and values

PERFORMING
Cooperation, problem solving. Leader facilitates task accomplishment

ADJOURNING
Task completion. Leader brings to closure, signifies completion

may form based on common interests or concerns. At this stage, the team leader must encourage everyone to participate, allowing members to work through their uncertainties and conflicts. Teams must move beyond this stage to achieve real productivity.

Step 3: Norming   During the norming stage, members resolve differences among them, accept each other, and reach broad agreement about the roles of the team leader and other participants. This stage is usually brief in duration, and the team leader should use it to emphasize the team's unity and the importance of its objectives.

Stage 4: Performing   Team members focus on solving problems and accomplishing tasks at the performing stage. They interact frequently and handle conflicts in constructive ways. The team leader encourages contributions from all members. He or she should attempt to get any nonparticipating team members involved.

Step 5: Adjourning   The team disbands at the adjourning stage after members have completed their assigned task or solved the problem. During this phase, the focus is on wrapping up and summarizing the team's experiences and accomplishments. The team leader may recognize the team's accomplishments with a celebration, perhaps handing out plaques or awards.

Team Cohesiveness and Norms

team cohesiveness extent to which team members feel attracted to the team and motivated to remain part of it.

Teams tend to maximize productivity when they form into highly cohesive units. **Team cohesiveness** is the extent to which team members are attracted to the team and motivated to remain part of it. This cohesiveness typically increases when members interact frequently, share common attitudes and goals, and enjoy being together. When cohesiveness is low, morale suffers.

Some firms try to promote interaction among team members through the design of work spaces. To foster teamwork in an office, the firm may have team members work in large rooms without walls dividing them. Chapter 8 noted that New York City Mayor Michael Bloomberg uses this approach in his management of the nation's largest city. Similarly, one of Wal-Mart's home office buildings is virtually windowless. The rows of cubicles in the building are given names like streets. Still, few employees really like open-office designs and working in cubicles. The Hits & Misses box describes what the future may hold for cubicle dwellers.

They Said It

The team that trusts—their leader and each other—is more likely to be successful.

—*Mike Krzyzewski (b. 1947) head basketball coach, Duke University*

To promote cohesiveness when team members work in different facilities, companies have to schedule opportunities for them to interact. Teams can schedule "virtual retreats"—Internet discussion groups or chat sessions during which they trade messages about personal and project-related matters. However, face-to-face meetings have the greatest potential to build cohesiveness, even though they require extensive travel for a geographically separated or international team.

team norm informal standard of conduct shared by team members that guides their behavior.

A **team norm** is a standard of conduct shared by team members that guides their behavior. Norms are not formal written guidelines; they are informal standards that identify key values and clarify team members' expectations. In a highly productive team, norms are consistent with working together constructively and accomplishing team goals.

Team Conflict

conflict antagonistic interaction in which one party attempts to thwart the intentions or goals of another.

Among all of a team leader's skills, none is more important than the ability to manage conflict. **Conflict** is an antagonistic interaction in which one party attempts to thwart the intentions or goals of another. A certain amount of conflict is inevitable in teams, but too much can impair the ability of team members to exchange ideas, cooperate with each other, and produce results.

Conflicts can stem from many sources. They frequently result in competition for scarce resources, such as information, money, or supplies. In addition, team members may experience personality clashes or differ in their ideas about what the team should accomplish. Poor communication also can cause misunderstandings or even resentment. Finally, conflict can result in the absence of clear job responsibilities or team roles. Levi Strauss, for instance, attempted to institute a teamwork-based production system. Instead of increasing productivity, though, conflict among team members seriously eroded productivity. Levi's gradually abandoned this system.[16]

HITS & MISSES

The Future of Cubicle Dwellers

Open-office designs, sometimes called bullpens or cubicles, are the norm today in American business. By one estimate, nearly three-quarters of U.S. and Canadian office workers toil in open-plan offices. The trend toward wide-open workplaces appears to have accelerated, with everyone from CEOs to unpaid interns sharing the same space. A door is now considered one of the ultimate status symbols in many offices. And as office plans have become more open, the average office space per person has shrunk steadily. Why? "The work culture is changing to be more collaborative," says Paul Groth, vice president of sales and design at office furniture firm M&M Office Interiors.

Businesses obviously like open-plan offices. They are cheaper to set up and are more flexible than traditional offices. Many managers argue that open-plan offices encourage teamwork and collaboration among employees. Open-plan offices are also more democratic, they say, since everyone has the same type of workplace—no more political infighting over who gets which private office.

Many office workers, however, grumble constantly about cubicles. Only 7 percent of employees surveyed by Steelcase, an office furnishings manufacturer, said that they preferred cubicles to any other type of work environment. Not surprisingly, cubicle jokes are popular. Scott Adams, creator of the popular Dilbert comic strip, once remarked that had he not been relegated to a tiny cubicle during his brief "corporate prison term"—as he calls the years he spent working for Pacific Bell—he never would have created Dilbert. Several Web sites, including http://www.dilbert.com, allow workers to share funny, and not so funny, cubicle stories. Workers can also find plenty of advice for learning to live without walls and doors.

One of the biggest gripes of cubicle dwellers is an almost total lack of privacy. Coworkers can often hear everything someone else is saying. Julie Nemitz, a cubicle dweller in New York, has learned to lower her chair and stick the phone under her desk whenever she wants to carry on a private conversation. "It's quieter down there," she comments. Joyce Saltzman, another cubicle dweller, leans into her cubicle walls to muffle her voice, though "for all I know, the sound is bouncing off more," she says. A lack of privacy is only one drawback to open-plan offices. Another is noise. A recent study found that even moderately open offices lead to higher stress levels and lower task motivation by employees.

Few predict that open-office designs and cubicles are going to disappear anytime soon; most believe that they are here to stay. However, employers are trying to make the lives of cubicle dwellers more tolerable. Some are installing extra-high walls and "visual privacy stackers." Others are putting sliding doors to seal off the entrance to cubicles. Other employers are setting up special offices, with actual doors, where cubicle dwellers can go when they need privacy or quiet work time. Furniture makers are getting into the act. New designs employ soft, warm colors and try to avoid the cookie-cutter look.

QUESTIONS FOR CRITICAL THINKING

1. Do you think open-office designs encourage teamwork? Why or why not?
2. One of the biggest gripes of cubicle dwellers is lack of privacy, but do employees really even have a right to privacy? Explain your answer.

Sources: Andrea Poe, "An Office Undivided," *HR Magazine,* http://www.shrm.org, accessed January 5, 2004; "Career Article 130: Working in Cubicle City," http://www.seekingsuccess.com, accessed January 22, 2003; Becca Mader, "Trends Changing Office Cubicles," *Milwaukee Business Journal,* October 4, 2002, http://www.milwaukee.bizjournals.com; "In Case You Haven't Heard," *Mental Health Weekly,* Free Articles Web site, http://www.freearticles.com, accessed July 16, 2002; Gwendolyn Bonds, "Open Offices Require Some Cubicle Etiquette," *The Morning News,* July 14, 2002, p. 6C; Larry Carson, "Designers Thinking Outside the Cubicle," *The Baltimore Sun,* May 17, 2002, p. 1B.

Styles of Conflict Resolution

No single method can resolve all conflicts. The most effective reaction depends on the situation. Conflict resolution styles represent a continuum ranging from assertive to cooperative responses:

- *The competing style.* This decisive, assertive approach might be summarized by the expression "We'll do this job my way." Although it does not build team rapport, the competing style can be useful for unpopular decisions or emergencies. This approach also helps to end conflict that escalates beyond hope of any other form of resolution.

BUSINESS TOOL KIT

Make Your Meetings Worthwhile

Just say the word *meeting* around any workplace and you'll hear a collective groan. Meetings have received such a bad rap as time wasters, sleep inducers, or gossip mills that most people have lost sight of their potential benefits. An effective meeting can foster creativity, generate decisions, and result in solutions to problems. Of course, if a meeting isn't necessary, don't hold one. But if your team or work group needs to gather, here are some tips from the experts on how to hold a successful meeting:

1. **Define the purpose of the meeting.** Is it to share information? Decide on a course of action? Write down the purpose.

2. **Decide who needs to attend.** This isn't a lunch date or a party, so the invitation isn't social. Based on the purpose of the meeting, decide who should be there.

3. **Set objectives for the meeting and provide an agenda.** Write down the concrete objectives you want to achieve at the meeting. Examples might be "delegate responsibilities for the upcoming project" and "create a schedule for the completion of tasks." If the meeting is formal, circulate an agenda to those who will be attending the meeting, including the objectives and a list of topics to be covered.

4. **Be prepared and be on time.** Whether the meeting is formal or informal, do your homework. Make sure you are prepared to discuss the topic at hand. Arrive at the meeting on time.

5. **Stay focused.** It's one thing to brainstorm and to discuss ideas, but it's another to allow a meeting to stray off on tangents or to gnaw on a single issue long after a decision has been made. One member of the meeting should be designated to make sure discussion sticks to the topic and wraps up efficiently.

6. **Listen to others.** Once you have presented your ideas, be sure to listen actively to others. Their information and insights are as valuable as yours.

7. **Wrap up and follow up in writing.** At meeting's end, recap the major points, such as who will take responsibility for certain tasks or any important decisions that have been made. Then write up a brief summary of the decisions, assigned responsibilities, deadlines, or any other pertinent information generated by the meeting, and circulate it to meeting members. That way, everyone is on the same page—literally.

Sources: "Six Tips for More Effective Meetings," *EffectiveMeetings.com*, http://www.effectivemeetings.com, accessed September 30, 2004; "Effective Meetings—Tips," *Meeting Wizard*, http://www.meetingwizard.com, accessed September 30, 2004; "Effective Meetings," *Toolpack Consulting*, http://www.toolpack.com, accessed September 30, 2004; Patrick J. Sauer, "What Time Is the Next Meeting," *Inc. Magazine*, May 2004, pp. 71–80.

- *The avoiding style.* Neither assertive nor cooperative, avoiding conflict is an effective response when the problem results from some trivial cause or creates a no-win situation, when more information is needed, or when open conflict would cause harm.
- *The compromising style.* This style blends both assertiveness and cooperation. It works well when conflict arises between two opposing and equally important goals, when combatants are equally powerful, or when the situation brings pressure to achieve an immediate solution.
- *The accommodating style.* Marked by active cooperation, this style can help to maintain team harmony. A team member may choose to back down in a disagreement on an issue that seems more important to others in the group than it does to that individual.
- *The collaborating style.* This style combines active assertiveness and cooperation. It can require lengthy, time-consuming negotiations but can achieve a win-win situation. It is useful when consensus from all parties is an important goal or when the viewpoints of all participants must be merged into a single, mutually acceptable solution.

A team leader can handle conflict by encouraging adversaries to negotiate an agreement between themselves. This method works well if the individuals deal with the situation in a businesslike, unemotional way. A stubborn disagreement may be turned over to a mediator, an outside party who will discuss the situation with both sides and bring the parties to a mutual decision. Ford Motor Company has socioemotional specialists called "team-effectiveness coaches," who are available to help teams when they have trouble resolving conflicts on their own.[17]

Perhaps the team leader's most important contribution to conflict resolution is to facilitate good communication. Ongoing, effective communication ensures that team members perceive each other accurately, understand what is expected of them, and obtain the information they need. Improved communication increases the chances of working cooperatively as a team. The remainder of this chapter discusses the importance of effective communication and the development of good communication skills.

Concept Check

1. Teams reach maximum effectiveness, diversity, and communication flow with how many members?
2. Compare and contrast the task specialist and socioemotional roles.
3. What is team cohesiveness?

The Importance of Effective Communication

Communication can be defined as a meaningful exchange of information through messages. Few businesses can succeed without effective communication. Managers spend about 80 percent of their time—six hours and 24 minutes of every eight-hour day—in direct communication with others, whether on the telephone, in meetings, via e-mail, or in individual conversations. The other 20 percent is typically spent on working at their desks, much of which also involves communication in the form of writing and reading.

communication
meaningful exchange of information through messages.

Communication skills are important throughout an organization—in every department and at all levels. Communications with consumers in the form of marketing research helps a company to learn what products people want and what changes they would like in existing offerings. Communication among engineers, marketers, and production employees enables a company to create products that satisfy customers. Communication through advertising and personal sales presentations creates a favorable image for the company and persuades customers to buy.

Well-planned communication is essential if a major company restructuring is going to succeed. Whenever a company restructures, such as during downsizing or moving into a new industry with a whole new culture, management should keep employees fully apprised of the company's plans. Once word of an impending restructuring gets out, employees naturally become anxious. Common employee concerns include what their new jobs will be, whom they'll report to, and whether their salaries and benefits will change. Ronnie Glaspie, a California human resources consultant, comments, "I have found that open communication is the best thing when it comes to these situations [corporate restructurings]. If you're honestly doing the restructuring for the betterment of the entire organization, there's no fear letting employees know about it." Michael Wolff, a partner at a New York consulting firm, also advises managers to meet with small groups of employees, allowing them to ask questions about the company's future, as well as their own. "Make them a part of the process," he recommends, "and you'll gain their trust."[18]

Companies have invested billions of dollars in communications technology—everything from telephone systems to sophisticated computer networks. One problem facing many organizations is employees using business phones and computers for personal communications. Employers have taken different approaches to the problem, as the Solving an Ethical Controversy box discusses.

FIGURE 10.4
The Communication Process

The Process of Communication

Every communication follows a step-by-step process that involves interactions among six elements: sender, message, channel, audience, feedback, and context. This process is illustrated in Figure 10.4.

In the first step, the *sender* composes the *message* and sends it through a communication carrier, or *channel*. Encoding a message means that the sender translates its meaning into understandable terms and a form that allows transmission through a

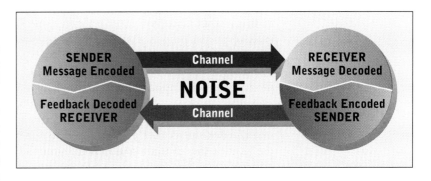

More than one-third of U.S. employees are electronically monitored at work, says a survey by the Privacy Foundation. Employers are increasingly checking workers' e-mail and Internet cruising, thanks to inexpensive technology that allows companies to monitor and reduce personal use of business phones and computers. Some firms report reductions of 40 to 60 percent in nonbusiness use of company telecommunications, with major cost savings. Monitoring reveals other problems with communications at work as well. ChevronTexaco settled a $2.2 million lawsuit brought by female employees over an offensive interoffice e-mail, and Dow Chemical fired more than 50 people for e-mailing pornography. "Almost every workplace lawsuit today, especially a sexual harassment case, has an e-mail component," according to Nancy Flynn, executive director of the ePolicy Institute.

But privacy advocates object to intrusive monitoring and insist that at the very least employers should put up warnings about surveillance. "The practice of keeping employees uninformed about the details of monitoring may be tantamount to entrapment," says the Privacy Foundation. Hiring those you can trust and providing reasonable guidelines for personal use of company property are suggested alternatives to monitoring.

Should firms monitor employee use of company telephones and Internet access?

PRO
1. Employers have a right to protect their communications from abuse and to guard themselves and their employees from messages that could prove embarrassing or even legally liable.
2. The cost savings and increased productivity and security outweigh the cost of monitoring and ultimately benefit all employees.

CON
1. Monitoring indicates a lack of faith and breaks down trust between employee and employer, creating a hostile and suspicious work environment.
2. It is only reasonable to expect that most people will spend a few minutes a day on personal business. Given sensible guidelines, they can monitor themselves.

SUMMARY
Privacy advocates continue to believe that monitoring is being forced on employees who have little choice in the matter, while surveillance becomes ever cheaper, easier, and more powerful. With so many potential employer concerns about corporate security and litigation arising from misuse of e-mail and the Internet, the debate is sure to continue.

Sources: Jerome D. Pinn, "Big Brother Is Watching," *East Tennessee Business Journal,* October 24, 2002, http://www.etbj.com; Monte Enbysk, "Should You Monitor Your Employees' Web Use?" *MSN Business,* http://www.bcentral.com, accessed July 2, 2002.

chosen channel. The sender can communicate a particular message through many different channels, including written messages, face-to-face conversations, and electronic mail. A promotional message to the firm's customers may be communicated through such forms as radio and television ads, billboards, magazines, and sales messages. The *audience* consists of the person or persons who receive the message. In decoding, the receiver of the message interprets its meaning. *Feedback* from the audience—in response to the sender's communication—helps the sender to determine whether the audience has correctly interpreted the intended meaning of the message.

Every communication takes place in some sort of situational or cultural context. The *context* can exert a powerful influence on how well the process works. A conversation between two people in a quiet office, for example, may be a very different experience from the same conversation held in a crowded and noisy restaurant. A request by an American to borrow a flashlight from an Australian friend might produce only confusion; what Americans call flashlights, Australians call torches.

Senders must pay attention to audience feedback, even soliciting it if none is forthcoming, since this response clarifies whether the communication has conveyed the intended message. Feedback can indicate whether the receiver paid attention to a message and was able to decode it accurately. Even when the receiver tries to understand, the communication may fail if the message was poorly encoded with difficult or ambiguous words. Managers sometimes become fond of using fuzzy language like *trans-*

parency, forward lending, and *paradigm shift.* Feedback can indicate whether the sender's audience succeeded in decoding this jargon—or even bothered to try.

Even with the best of intentions, sender and audience can misunderstand each other. Rob Wrubel, CEO of the online information service Ask Jeeves, constantly checks whether the people in his organization understand messages, and he is often surprised by the feedback. When the senior managers first began creating a yearlong plan of operations, Wrubel discovered that participants often interpreted phrases in different ways. If one person said, "I'll get it done by next week," one listener might decode "by next week" to mean "next Monday," while another might think "next Friday." Also, "get it done" meant "give me your thoughts" to one listener, while another decoded the phrase to mean the speaker would present a fully thought-out plan complete with a PowerPoint slide presentation.[19]

Noise during the communication process is some type of interference that influences the transmission of messages and feedback. Noise can result from simple physical factors such as poor reception of a cell-phone message or static that drowns out a radio commercial. It can also be caused by more complex differences in people's attitudes and perceptions. A message communicated by a manager may be interpreted differently by coworkers with different ethnic and cultural backgrounds. Jamie Dimon, president and COO of JPMorganChase, has a communication style that's described as "snappy and rude" by those who know him. While commonplace in Queens, New York, where Dimon is from, his communication style initially terrified people outside New York who were used to a more courtly communication style. Today, he is regarded as a great communicator. In one important speech, Dimon commented: "Winning isn't about your parents or your IQ or where you went to school. It's about one thing—how much you want it."[20]

Basic Forms of Communication

People communicate in many different ways. Some obvious methods include calling a meeting of team members or writing a formal mission statement. Other much less obvious methods include gestures and facial expressions during a conversation or leaning forward when speaking to someone. These subtle variations can significantly influence the reception of the message. As Table 10.2 points out, different communications can assume various forms: oral and written, formal and informal, and verbal and nonverbal.

Table 10.2   Forms of Communication

Form	Description	Examples
Oral communication	Communication transmitted through speech	Personal conversations, speeches, meetings, voice mail, telephone conversations, videoconferences
Written communication	Communication transmitted through writing	Letters, memos, formal reports, news releases, e-mail, faxes
Formal communication	Communication transmitted through the chain of command within an organization to other members or to people outside the organization	Internal—memos, reports, meetings, written proposals, oral presentations, meeting minutes; External—letters, written proposals, oral presentations, speeches, news releases, press conferences
Informal communication	Communication transmitted outside formal channels without regard for the organization's hierarchy of authority	Rumors spread informally among employees
Verbal communication	Transmission of messages in the form of words	Meetings, telephone calls, voice mail, videoconferences
Nonverbal communication	Communication transmitted through actions and behaviors rather than through words	Gestures, facial expressions, posture, body language, dress, makeup

Oral Communication   Managers spend a great deal of their time engaged in oral communication, both in person and on the phone. Some people prefer to communicate this way, believing that oral channels more accurately convey messages. Face-to-face oral communication allows people to combine words with such cues as facial expressions and tone of voice. Oral communication over the telephone lacks visual cues, but it offers some of the advantages of face-to-face communication, such as opportunities to hear the tone of voice and provide immediate feedback by asking questions about anything the receiver doesn't understand or raising new issues related to the message.

Home Depot's CEO Bob Nardelli strongly believes in the benefits of oral communication, especially when it is used to deliver bad news. For instance, he tells underperforming executives explicitly why they're not good enough. "I tell them all face to face, and I try not to tell them that I can't tell them why," he says.[21]

In any medium, a vital component of oral communication is **listening**—receiving a message and interpreting its genuine meaning by accurately grasping the facts and feeling conveyed. Although listening is the first communication skill that people learn and the one they use most often, it is also the one in which they receive the least formal training.

Listening may seem easy, since the listener makes no obvious effort. This apparent passivity creates a deceptive picture, however. The average person talks at a rate of roughly 150 words per minute, but the brain can handle up to 400 words per minute. This discrepancy can lead to boredom, inattention, and misinterpretation. In fact, immediately after listening to a message, the average person can recall only half of it. After several days, the proportion of a message that a listener can recall falls to 25 percent or less.

Certain types of listening behaviors are common in both business and personal interactions:

- *Cynical listening.* This defensive type of listening occurs when the receiver of a message feels that the sender is trying to gain some advantage from the communication.
- *Offensive listening.* In this type of listening, the receiver tries to catch the speaker in a mistake or contradiction.
- *Polite listening.* In this mechanical type of listening, the receiver listens to be polite rather than to communicate. Polite listeners are usually inattentive and spend their time rehearsing what they want to say when the speaker finishes.
- *Active listening.* This form of listening requires involvement with the information and empathy with the speaker's situation. In both business and personal life, active listening is the basis for effective communication.

Learning how to be an active listener is an especially important goal for business managers, since effective communication is essential to the manager's role.

Written Communication   Channels for written communication include reports, letters, memos, online chat sessions, and e-mail messages. Most of these channels permit only delayed feedback and create a record of the message. So it is important for the sender of a written communication to prepare the message carefully and review it to avoid misunderstandings.

Effective written communication reflects its audience, the channel carrying the message, and the appropriate degree of formality. When writing a formal business document, such as a complex report, a manager must plan in advance and carefully construct the document. The process of writing a formal document involves planning, research, organization, composition and design, and revision. Written communication via e-mail may call for a less formal writing style, including short sentences, phrases, and lists. Writers for electronic media often communicate through combinations of words, acronyms, and emoticons, which are symbols constructed with punctuation marks and letters.

E-mail can be a very effective communication channel. For marketers, it is an inexpensive way to reach thousands of customers, following up on recent sales and encouraging customers to buy again. However, using e-mail to communicate with customers is not without its pitfalls. Mass e-mailings, containing indiscriminate "buy me" messages, are rarely effective. Some recipients may consider mass e-mailings to be no more than *spam*—junk e-mail—ruining any chance of turning the recipient into a customer.

They Said It

Talk low, talk slow, and don't say too much.

—*John Wayne (1907–1979)*
American actor

listening skill of receiving a message and interpreting its intended meaning by grasping the facts and feelings it conveys.

They Said It

The difference between the right word and the almost right word is the difference between lightning and lightning bugs.

—*Mark Twain (1835–1910)*
American novelist

Another problem with e-mail is security. Because e-mail messages are often informal, senders occasionally forget that they are creating a written record. Also, even if the recipient deletes an e-mail message, other copies usually exist. Senders have at times embarrassed themselves, or worse. Merrill Lynch was forced to apologize and pay a monetary settlement recently when the New York Attorney General made public several e-mails sent between Merrill Lynch brokers and analysts. In these e-mails, Merrill Lynch employees made negative comments about several stocks that, in public, these same employees were recommending to their clients.

© AP/Wide World Photos

Today, meetings have taken on a whole new character. Cell phones and personal digital assistants (PDAs) allow instant communication but can also cause major headaches if employees have technical troubles.

Formal Communication

A **formal communication channel** carries messages that flow within the chain of command structure defined by an organization. The most familiar channel, downward communication, carries messages from someone who holds a senior position in the organization to subordinates. Managers may communicate downward by sending employees e-mail messages, presiding at department meetings, giving employees policy manuals, posting notices on bulletin boards, and reporting news in company newsletters.

Many firms also define formal channels for upward communications. These channels encourage communication from employees to supervisors and upward to top management levels. Some examples of upward communication channels are employee surveys, suggestion boxes, and systems that allow employees to propose new projects or voice complaints.

Informal Communication

Informal communication channels carry messages outside formally authorized channels within an organization's hierarchy. A familiar example of an informal channel is the **grapevine,** an internal channel that passes information from unofficial sources. Research shows that many employees cite the grapevine as their most frequent source of information. Grapevines rapidly disseminate information. A message sent through formal channels may take days to reach its audience, but messages that travel via grapevines can arrive within hours. Grapevines also are surprisingly reliable links. They pass on accurate information 70 to 90 percent of the time.[22] However, even a tiny inaccuracy can distort an entire message.

grapevine internal information channel that transmits information from unofficial sources.

The spontaneity of informal communication may diminish when a company's employees are spread among many locations. Employees who telecommute or travel frequently may miss opportunities to build smooth working relationships or exchange ideas. In those situations, communication technology can help firms to promote informal communication. Some companies establish online chat areas for employees, so they can visit each other during breaks. Some also encourage employees to create home pages that describe their interests and hobbies.

Verbal and Nonverbal Communication

So far, this section has considered different forms of verbal communication, or communication that conveys meaning through words. Equally important is **nonverbal communication,** which transmits messages through actions and behaviors. Gestures, posture, eye contact, tone of voice, and even clothing choices are all nonverbal actions that

FIGURE 10.5
Influence of Personal Space in Nonverbal Communication

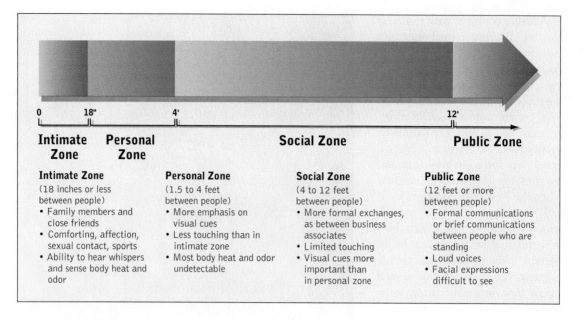

become communication cues. Nonverbal cues can strongly influence oral communication by altering or distorting intended meanings.

Nonverbal cues can have a far greater impact on communications than many people realize. One study divided face-to-face conversations into three sources of communication cues: verbal cues (the actual words spoken), vocal cues (pitch or tone of a person's voice), and facial expressions. The researchers found some surprising relative weights of these factors in message interpretation: verbal cues (7 percent), vocal cues (38 percent), and facial expressions (55 percent).[23]

Written communication can also be affected by nonverbal cues. For example, some believe that an e-mail message written in all caps is the electronic equivalent of screaming. Also, adding a short personalized sentence or two to a mass mailing can help make the recipient feel special.

Even personal space—the physical distance between people who are engaging in communication—can convey powerful messages. Figure 10.5 shows a continuum of personal space and social interaction with four zones: intimate, personal, social, and public. In the U.S., most business conversations occur within the social zone, roughly between 4 and 12 feet apart. If one person tries to approach closer than that, the other will likely feel uncomfortable or even threatened.

Interpreting nonverbal cues can be especially challenging for people with different cultural backgrounds. Concepts of appropriate personal space differ dramatically throughout most of the world. Latin Americans conduct business discussions in positions that most Americans and Northern Europeans would find uncomfortably close. Americans often back away to preserve their personal space, a gesture that Latin Americans perceive as a sign of cold and unfriendly relations. To protect themselves from such personal "threats," experienced Americans separate themselves across desks or tables from their Latin American counterparts—at the risk of challenging their colleagues to maneuver around those obstacles to reduce the uncomfortable distance.

People send nonverbal messages even when they consciously try to avoid doing so. Sometimes nonverbal cues convey a person's true attitudes and thoughts, which may differ from spoken meanings. Generally, when verbal and nonverbal cues conflict, receivers of the communication tend to believe the nonverbal content.

Concept Check

1. In the context of the communication process, what is noise?
2. What are four common listening behaviors? Characterize each.
3. What are some of the advantages of e-mail as a communication medium? What are some of its disadvantages?

Communication within the Organization

internal communication
system that sends messages through channels within an organization.

Internal communication consists of messages sent through channels within an organization. Examples include memos, meetings, speeches, phone conversations, and even a simple chat over lunch. When Carly Fiorina became CEO of Hewlett-Packard (HP), she wanted to foster a faster moving culture, so she launched a leadership campaign emphasizing internal communication. Fiorina traveled to 20 company sites in 10 countries, delivering impassioned speeches about the need for change and fielding questions from the audience. To continue this dialog, she composes a letter to employees for each issue of the company's quarterly magazine, reads thousands of e-mail messages from employees each month, and records occasional voice-mail messages to be broadcast companywide.[24] Fiorina's superb communication skills were evident in her successful battle to get stockholder approval of HP's purchase of Compaq.

Internal communication may be relatively simple in a small organization, since it often takes the form of face-to-face interactions. Unclear interpretations can be remedied by further conversation. Internal communication becomes increasingly difficult as the organization grows and adds employees. Messages, many of them transmitted via e-mail, often pass through several different layers of management in a typical large organization. The sender of a message must continually make certain that it is both clearly communicated orally or in writing and likely to be interpreted correctly.

Communication in Teams

Communication among team members can be divided into two broad categories: centralized and decentralized. In a **centralized communication network,** team members exchange messages through a single person to solve problems or make decisions. By contrast, in a **decentralized communication network,** members communicate freely with other team members and arrive at decisions together.

Which type of network supports more effective communications? The answer depends on the nature of the problem or decision facing the team. Research has shown that centralized networks usually solve straightforward problems more quickly and accurately than decentralized ones—an important consideration for life-or-death operations like the launch of an AC-130 gunship to protect members of the Army's Third Division or a British commando unit operating on the ground in Iraq. With a centralized network, members pass information along to a central decision maker, who issues the order. However, for complex problems, a decentralized network actually works faster and comes up with more accurate answers. This characteristic is important for task-oriented, creative groups. Team members pool their data, provide wide-ranging input into decisions, and emerge with high-quality solutions.

Although most researchers agree that organizations should establish centralized team networks to deal with straightforward problems, they also believe that these organizations should set up decentralized teams to handle complex issues. Members of decentralized teams should be encouraged to share information with each other and to generate as much input as possible to improve the quality of the final decision.[25]

Decentralized teams work well for the complex process of new-product development. Two important keys to success in this process are allowing all members of the team to voice concerns and working hard to get all of the members involved early in the project.

Centralized communication is critical to achieve quick decisions. In military conflicts, it can mean the difference between life and death.

© AP/Wide World Photos

Incentives that Inspire

There is a well-kept secret to employee retention: finding the incentives that inspire employees to work hard and remain loyal to the organization. There is even an annual Incentive Show in New York that presents unique and creative incentive ideas to replace the magnetic calendars or pens that are typically passed out in companies. Although incentive programs cannot compensate for poor hiring decisions, lack of training, or an unhealthy work environment, they can promote positive thinking and employee loyalty. Ready for a creative take on incentives? Here are a few examples.

- TechTarget, a Massachusetts-based interactive media company, allows its employees to come and go as they please (open-leave policy), setting their own work schedules.
- Marriott International offered Panasonic portable DVD players to meeting planners who booked a gathering of 75 or more. Past incentives have included PalmPilots and Kodak digital cameras.
- CheckFree, an electronic payments processing company based in Georgia, provides its employees with a

24/7 fitness center with a full-size basketball court and electronic scoreboard, racquetball courts, swimming pool, bowling alley, sauna, hot tub, and pro shop.
- Cognex, a computer manufacturer in Massachusetts, bought the field next to its facilities exclusively for its employees' Ultimate Frisbee games.
- Other incentives that inspire: flying lessons; dry-cleaning pickup and delivery; grocery-shopping services; hammocks in the lounge for midday naps; pet sitters; and reimbursement for classes in dream analysis, tai chi, and sculpture.

Sources: Patrick J. Sauer, "Open-Door Management," *Inc. Magazine*, June 2003, p. 44; "Juice Up: For an Energizing Incentive Program, It's Hard to Beat Electronics," *Incentive*, May 2003, p. 45; "Landmark Study on $27 Billion Incentive Industry Shows Incentives More Important than Ever in Motivating Employees: Incentives Play Critical Role in Employee Performance, Especially in Uncertain Times," press release for The Incentive Show 2003, March 8, 2002, http://www.piexpo.com/pressRoom/study.php.

Communication Outside the Organization

external communication
meaningful exchange of information through messages transmitted between an organization and its major audiences.

External communication is a meaningful exchange of information through messages transmitted between an organization and its major audiences, such as customers, suppliers, other firms, the general public, and government officials. Businesses use external communication to keep their operations functioning, to maintain their positions in the marketplace, and to build customer relationships by supplying information about topics such as product modifications and price changes. Delta Airlines uses its Web site to attract customers and build positive relationships with them. Visitors to the site can make reservations, check mileage in their frequent flyer accounts, and book vacation packages. Information on flights and weather delays is also available. The site receives and sends messages and invites visitors to send e-mail comments, suggestions, or complaints.

Every communication with customers—including sales presentations, customer orders, and advertisements—should create goodwill and contribute to customer satisfaction. Dee Electronics of Cedar Rapids, Iowa, relies on handheld computers and wireless communications that link all its warehouse and distribution employees. This new system has brought Dee close to its goal of 100 percent shipping accuracy, and it also inspired employees to come up with an e-mail function that automatically lets customers know when their orders are on the way.[26] External communications with other groups, such as investors and the general public, should be designed to put the company in a positive light. Royal Dutch Shell publishes *The Shell Report: People, Planet, and Profits* each year. The report outlines the company's goals and efforts in the economic, environmental, and social well-being of its stakeholders. It also explains how Shell manages its business with these goals in mind. In a recent report, Shell CEO Philip Watts writes, "Our commitment to sustainable development is today being integrated into the way Shell makes decisions. . . . I do not approve new investments unless they address the key sustainable development aspects of the project."[27]

Careless communication can produce doubt among customers, investors, and the public. A reporter for *Fortune* magazine once ordered a computer game from Mattel and was startled to receive a confirmation e-mail dated 10/19/1919. When she pointed out the error, the company representative worsened the situation by sending a form e-mail listing replies to eight frequently asked questions, none of which pertained to dates on e-mail messages. Two days later, a customer service representative wrote that the reporter's message would be forwarded to the company's technical department, but by then, the reporter had written a story about the incident and shared it with the world.[28]

Concept Check

1. To whom does an organization send external communications?
2. Why should organizations be concerned about routine communications like customer orders and advertisements?

International Business Communication

Communication can be a special challenge in the international business arena. An international message's appropriateness depends in part on an accurate translation that conveys the intended nuances of meaning. When PepsiCo marketers wanted to build sales in China, they created a promotional campaign based on the theme "Come Alive with Pepsi." Poor sales surprised them, until they discovered that the direct Chinese translation of their slogan was "Bring your ancestors back from the dead." Managers ordered a hasty rewrite of the theme. As this example shows, businesspeople who want to succeed in the global marketplace must ensure that they send only linguistically and culturally appropriate messages.

English is the primary language of business. One reason is that the strength and size of the U.S. economy have spread familiarity with U.S. products and media worldwide. Another is that the Internet originated in the U.S., so the English language currently dominates Internet usage. Public schoolchildren in Japan and Korea take between nine and 12 years of English. In over 75 nations, English is an official language. However, the English language is constantly expanding by borrowing words and expressions from other languages, so it varies radically from one country to another. The British, for example, call trucks *lorries,* and an elevator is a *lift.* In the U.S., *soccer* is played on a *field.* In Britain, *football* is played on a *pitch.* In English-speaking Nigeria, a traffic jam is a *go-slow;* Jamaicans refer to highway speed bumps as *sleeping policemen.* As the examples suggest, communication snafus may occur even among English-speaking countries.

Business communication improves when each party understands the cultural contexts that surround and influence every attempt at sending an international message. Translations have to consider not only the meanings of words but the audience's familiarity with elements of nonverbal communication. The mailbox that signals "You've Got Mail" on America Online is a familiar icon to many Americans, but to others it might look more like a loaf of bread.

Anthropologists classify cultures as low context and high context. Communication in **low-context cultures** tends to rely on explicit written and verbal messages. Examples include Switzerland, Austria, Germany, and the U.S. In contrast, communication in **high-context cultures**—such as those of Japan, Latin America, and India—depends not only on the message itself but also on the conditions that surround it, including nonverbal cues, past and present experiences, and personal relationships between the parties. Westerners must carefully temper their low-context style to the expectations of colleagues and clients from high-context countries. Although Americans tend to favor direct interactions and

Concept Check

1. Contrast communications in high-context and low-context cultures.
2. Why is English the primary language of business?

DID YOU KNOW?

1. To keep up with the rapidly expanding English language, a new edition of the *Oxford English Dictionary* has just been published. Among the nearly 6,000 new 21st-century words and phrases to be added were the frowner's favorite, *Botox;* passion-enhancing drug *Viagra; headcase,* referring to a person who exhibits irrational behavior; *screensaver;* and *bling,* referring to elaborate jewelry and clothing.
2. In the United Kingdom, outsourcing is called *contracting,* and employees would shudder at the thought of being empowered; they'd rather be *authorized.*
3. Kellogg's renamed its Bran Buds cereal in Sweden after learning the name translates into "burned farmer."
4. Three e-mail practices U.S. adults consider "downright rude" are, in ascending order of rudeness, resigning from a job via e-mail, using e-mail to reprimand an employee, and sending condolences via e-mail. Barely missing the top three was using e-mail to ask someone out on a date.

want to "get down to business" soon after shaking hands or sitting down to a business dinner, businesspeople in Mexico and Asian countries prefer to become acquainted before discussing details. When conducting business in these cultures, wise visitors allow time for relaxed meals during which business-related topics are avoided.

Workplace differences also influence the process of communication. For example, the open communication style in U.S. firms is foreign to workers in Russia, where employees have long expected specific directions about what to do and where asking questions was an invitation to trouble. Managers of foreign firms operating in Russia often encounter difficulties communicating with Russian employees, who are reluctant to ask for help and avoid giving feedback to messages. Success in this situation requires patience, as managers learn to be very specific in directing employees while also encouraging them to express their point of view. In general, learning about cultures of the countries in which they operate is essential for managers who want to communicate effectively.

What's Ahead

Today's consumers expect the products they buy to be of the highest value for the price. Firms ensure this value by developing efficient systems for producing goods and services, as well as maintaining high quality. The next chapter examines the ways in which businesses produce world-class goods and services.

Summary of Learning Goals

1 Describe why and how organizations empower employees.

By empowering employees, a firm finds better ways to perform jobs, motivates people by enhancing the challenges and satisfaction in their work, and frees managers from hands-on control so they can focus on other tasks. Employers empower workers by sharing information, distributing decision-making authority and responsibility, and linking rewards to company performance.

2 **Distinguish between the two major types of teams in the workplace.**

The two major types of teams are work teams and problem-solving teams. Work teams are permanent groups of coworkers who perform the day-to-day tasks necessary to operate the organization. Problem-solving teams are temporary groups of employees who gather to solve specific problems and then disband.

3 **Identify the characteristics of an effective team and the roles played by team members.**

Three important characteristics of a team are its size, member roles, and diversity. Effective teams typically combine between five and 12 members, with about six or seven members being the ideal size. Team members can play task specialist, socioemotional, dual, or nonparticipator roles. Effective teams balance the first three roles. Diverse teams tend to display broader ranges of viewpoints and produce more innovative solutions to problems than do homogeneous teams.

4 **Summarize the stages of team development.**

Teams pass through five stages of development: (1) Forming is an orientation period during which members get to know each other and find out what behaviors are acceptable to the group. (2) Storming is the stage during which individual personalities emerge as members clarify their roles and expectations. (3) Norming is a stage where differences are resolved, members accept each other, and consensus emerges about the roles of the team leader and other participants. (4) Performing is characterized by problem solving and a focus on task accomplishment. (5) Adjourning is the final stage, with a focus on wrapping up and summarizing the team's experiences and accomplishments.

5 **Relate team cohesiveness and norms to effective team performance.**

Team cohesiveness is the extent to which team members are attracted to the team and motivated to remain on it. Team norms are standards of conduct shared by team members that guide their behavior. Highly cohesive teams whose members share certain standards of conduct tend to be more productive and effective.

6 **Describe the factors that can cause conflict in teams and how conflict can be resolved.**

Conflict can stem from many sources: competition for scarce resources, personality clashes, conflicting goals, poor communication, unclear job responsibilities, or team role assignments. Conflict resolution styles range from assertive to cooperative measures. The most effective resolution style varies according to the situation. Resolution styles include the competing style, the accommodating style, and the collaborating style. A team leader can limit conflict by focusing team members on broad goals, clarifying participants' respective tasks and areas of authority, acting as mediator, and facilitating effective communication.

7 **Explain the importance of effective communication skills in business.**

Managers and employees spend much of their time exchanging information through messages. Communication helps all employees to understand the company's goals and values and the parts they play in achieving those goals.

8 **Compare the different types of communication.**

People exchange messages in many ways: oral and written, formal and informal, verbal and nonverbal communication. Although some people prefer oral channels because they accurately convey messages, nonverbal cues can distort meaning. Effective written communication reflects its audience, its channel, and the appropriate degree of formality. Formal communication channels carry messages within the chain of command. Informal communication channels, such as the grapevine, carry messages outside the formal chain of command. Nonverbal communication plays a larger role than most people realize. Generally, when verbal and nonverbal cues conflict, the receiver of a message tends to believe the meaning conveyed by nonverbal elements.

Business Terms You Need to Know

empowerment 328

teamwork 331

team 331

work team 332

problem-solving team 333

team cohesiveness 336

team norm 336

conflict 336

communication 339

listening 342

grapevine 343

internal communication 344

external communication 346

Other Important Business Terms

employee stock ownership plan (ESOP) 330

stock options 330

task specialist role 334

socioemotional role 334

formal communication channel 343

informal communication channel 343

nonverbal communication 343

centralized communication network 345

decentralized communication network 345

low-context culture 347

high-context culture 347

Review Questions

1. Describe the ways employers can empower their employees. Give a specific example of each.

2. Identify and briefly explain the approaches companies use to provide for worker ownership. What are the main differences between them?

3. What are the two major types of teams? How does each function? In what instances might a company use each type?

4. Identify the roles team members play. How do people in each of these roles operate?

5. What are the characteristics of an effective team? Why are these features so significant?

6. Identify and briefly describe the five stages of team development. At what stages might a team get "stuck" and not be able to move forward?

7. Describe the five different styles of conflict resolution. In what situations would you use each of these styles? Why?

8. What are the major elements in the communication process? Briefly define each element.

9. Outline the two channels for formal communication. Give an example of each.

10. What is the central focus of a company's external communication? List two or three examples of this type of communication.

Projects and Applications

1. Consider your current job or one you have held in the past. Did your employer practice any kind of employee empowerment? If so, what? If not, why not? Or think of your family as a company. Did your parents empower their children? If so, in what ways? In either scenario, what do you think were the consequences of empowerment or nonempowerment?

2. Identify a firm that makes extensive use of teams. Then interview someone from the firm to assess how their teams operate.

3. Do you consider yourself to be a good listener? First, identify which listening style you think you practice. Then describe the listening styles outlined in this chapter to a friend, family member, or classmate and ask that person what type of listening style he or she thinks you practice.

Finally, compare the two responses. Do they agree or disagree? *Note:* You can take this exercise a step further by asking more than one person what type of listening style you practice and then comparing all of the responses.

4. The grapevine is one of the strongest communication links in any organization, from large corporation to college classroom to family. Do you rely on information that travels along the grapevine? Why or why not?

5. Take a seat in the library or dorm lounge, in a mall, in a restaurant, or wherever there is a flow of people whom you can watch unobtrusively. For at least 15 minutes, observe and jot down the nonverbal cues that you see pass between people. Then try to interpret these cues. How would your interpretation affect any actual communication you might have with one of these people?

Experiential Exercise

Background: Customers don't have to look far to see companies using open and direct communications to develop personal relationships with customers. For example, Wal-Mart is well-known for its greeters, who provide a cheerful welcome to the stores and help personalize the shopping experience.

In the online world, Amazon.com was a pioneer in establishing personal relationships with its customers by studying the books they purchased and making recommendations based on what they're reading. Dell, Inc., which sells PCs built to order, remembers what customers have bought in the past and, with personalized Web pages, makes it easier for its customers

to add new equipment, upgrade what they already own, or troubleshoot technical problems.

Directions: Submit to your instructor a one-page paper in which you identify five or more examples similar to those already given that show how companies are communicating with customers on a one-on-one basis, as opposed to the mass marketing, mass communication approach. For each example you include, identify the source of the example: a personal experience, library or Internet research source, or a friend's or coworker's experience.

NOTHING BUT NET

1. **External communications.** One important external communication forum for a company is its annual report. Most firms whose stock is publicly traded also publish annual reports on their Web sites. Select two of the public companies mentioned in the chapter—such as Hewlett-Packard and Delta Airlines—and visit their Web sites. Review their most recent annual reports and make a list of the type of information presented.

2. **Employee stock ownership plans (ESOPs).** The chapter discussed the basics of employee stock ownership plans (ESOPs) and their growing importance. Visit the Web site listed here and review the current data on ESOPs. How many plans are there today compared with 1974 and 1990? List five interesting statistics about ESOPs.

http://www.nceo.org/esops/
(Select the "ESOP Articles Online" link.)

3. **Basics of team building.** The following Web site contains information about how to build an effective team. Review the material and write a brief report on the basics of designing and organizing an effective team.

http://www.mapnp.org/library/grp_skll/grp_skll.htm

Note: Internet Web addresses change frequently. If you do not find the exact sites listed, you may need to access the organization's or company's home page and search from there.

Case 10.1

The Pampered Chef: Performance through Empowerment

People enjoy getting together and sampling treats and sharing techniques for food preparation. Two decades ago, Doris Christopher decided to take that interest to another level and start her own business. She chose a new venture that would let her combine her love of cooking with her need to work out of her home and still have time for her two young daughters. So her husband, Jay, suggested that she host Tupperware-like parties. The difference was that Doris would do cooking demonstrations for customers, who would then sample the food and buy the utensils needed to make the appetizers, entrées, and desserts. Doris liked the idea. She borrowed $3,000 on her life insurance policy, bought some basic items for inventory, and set up business in her basement. Her first cooking demonstration was held at a friend's house, where Doris cooked for 15 people. Word of mouth resulted in more demonstrations, and within a year, the one-woman operation began to grow. Salespeople were recruited to keep up with demand. Doris taught her recruits how to do their own demonstrations, and in turn, they earned money both from sales and from their own recruits. Today, her company—The Pampered Chef—employs 1,100 corporate employees in two offices in Illinois. Some 60,000 independent sales consultants sell Pampered Chef products throughout the U.S., Canada, the United Kingdom, and Germany.

Doris Christopher relies on the performance of her independent sales organization for the ultimate success of her business. These people, called Kitchen Consultants, "organize, develop and maintain independent businesses according to their personal needs," says the company's Web site. Many of them work part time, while others choose to reap the added rewards of a full-time career. In addition, Kitchen Consultants who wish to advance within the organization can work toward management positions. For The Pampered Chef to succeed, its consultants and managers must be granted both the opportunity and the authority to make decisions about many aspects of their jobs. In other words, they must be empowered to think and act in ways that they believe will best reach their customers and benefit their business efforts.

The firm deliberately recruits individuals who enjoy independent decision making—but who also enjoy interacting with other people. In addition to conducting in-home demonstrations, Kitchen Consultants are encouraged to attend bridal expos and other events where potential customers may be located. The idea is for them to create new and different ways to find, entertain, educate, and sell to customers.

Because The Pampered Chef is a direct-selling organization, its products are available only through the Kitchen Consultants or at the company Web site. But the cornerstone of the firm's business is the in-home demonstration, where the consultants make the products come to life. After all, who wouldn't buy a set of high-quality knives after eating freshly sliced gourmet cheese? And who wouldn't want a pastry stone after sampling some warm, delicious tarts? Of course, this means that Kitchen Consultants must not only be skilled in cooking basics but also be able to present and serve meals attractively. It seems that Doris Christopher was right about their recipe for success. Twenty years after the first demonstration, The Pampered Chef was purchased by Warren Buffett, America's best-known investor.

QUESTIONS FOR CRITICAL THINKING

1. Why is employee empowerment such an important component of the success of The Pampered Chef?
2. In what ways does The Pampered Chef empower its employees?

Sources: "Our Company," The Pampered Chef Web site, http://www.pamperedchef.com, accessed January 3, 2004; Francine Knowles, "21st Century Company: Pampered Chef," *Chicago Sun-Times* Web site, http://www.suntimes.com, accessed July 17, 2002; Pamela Margoshes, "Queen of Hearths," in "Secrets of a Start-up," *Success,* September 1998.

Video Case 10.2

Le Meridien

This video case appears on page 612. A recently filmed video, designed to expand and highlight the written case, is available for class use by instructors.

Chapter 11
Production and Operations Management

1 Outline the importance of production and operations management.

2 Explain the roles of computers and related technologies in production.

3 Identify the factors involved in a plant location decision.

4 Explain the major tasks of production and operations managers.

5 Compare alternative layouts for production facilities.

6 List the steps in the purchasing process.

7 Outline the advantages and disadvantages of maintaining large inventories.

8 Identify the steps in the production control process.

9 Explain the benefits of quality control.

A Design Revolution Promises to Save Detroit

Here's the good news: The Big Three U.S. auto-makers are making progress in the quality and design of their new cars, trucks, and SUVs. *Consumer Reports* recently announced that the average number of quality problems per 100 new vehicles by General Motors, Ford, and Chrysler had dropped

from a high of 105 to 23. Here's the bad news: Market share of domestic automakers has also dropped, from 80 percent in 1975 to 62 percent today. But that slide could turn around soon—Detroit manufacturers are counting on it.

U.S. automakers have poured billions into improving the quality of their cars and trucks, reengineering production processes, and developing better designs. As a result, domestic cars that start to cough around the 60,000-mile mark and conk out around 100,000 miles—just when Toyotas and Hondas are hitting their stride—are increasingly rare. "The domestics are putting their money where their mouths are in terms of consistent long-term quality improvement," says Joe Ivers of J. D. Power & Associates, the firm that tests and ranks new vehicles. A recent Vehicle Dependability Study by Power, which rates vehicles after three years, rather than just as they come off the assembly line, placed the following U.S. vehicles at or near the top of the reliability list in their categories: Ford F-150 for pickup trucks, Chevy Tahoe for full-sized SUVs, and Chevy Malibu for entry-level midsize cars. And *Consumer Reports* recently named the Buick Regal, made by General Motors, the most reliable midsize sedan.

But here's the frustrating part: Auto shoppers have raised the bar. They want dependability, but they also want style. "Consumers have changed their minds about what defines quality—a shift that is making the uphill

© Joe Polimeni/Reuters/Landov

climb for U.S. automakers even more steep," says Aurobind Satpathy, head of consulting giant McKinsey & Co.'s Detroit office. Ford Motor Co. president Nicholas Scheele agrees. "Quality, previously, was freedom from defects," he says. "It has expanded to embrace a raft of subleties." Consumers want more than a car that doesn't break down by the side of the road. They want a smooth, comfortable ride, instruments that are easy to use, a decent sound system, and cup holders that are the right size. Defects "don't [necessarily] reflect technical failures, but failures to satisfy the consumer," explains Joe Ivers of J. D. Power.

So it's back to the drawing board—and all of the Big Three companies have come out with new, flashier, cooler models. One of the biggest hits so far has been the Chrysler 300, a bold, full-size sedan that looks like a muscle car and seats an entire family. Priced less than a luxury car, it offers buyers the performance and features of some luxury competitors. *Car and Driver* has proclaimed it a "mobster in pinstripes," and Wes Brown of auto consultant Iceology claims, "It makes the majority of vehicles on the road look like blobs." General Motors has decided to go after niche markets with its sports cars Solstice and Curve, as well as other models designed to take on rivals PT Cruiser and Mini Cooper. Ford has been working on several new performance models, as well.

By looking back to the future with another brand new design for it's ever popular Mustang, Ford hopes to capture the market share for those interested in affordable sports cars. Ford is also debuting a new GT muscle car aimed at those who want a one-of-a-kind collectible car. And with it's brand new Freestyle combination SUV, family sedan and the 500, Ford hopes to capitalize on those who are looking for family-friendly dependability but also style and affordability.

Automakers have now accepted the fact that style and quality are interconnected in consumers' minds. "The quality gap [among different brands] has narrowed to the point of being almost immaterial," says Robert Lutz of General Motors, "so the place to stand out with customers is in emotion-driven design and value." For some, that means cup holders that work.[1]

It remains to be seen how successful the Big Three American manufacturers will be in the next few years. But, one thing's for sure, from dependability and style in the automobiles themselves to friendly financing and good service, they're working hard to reach consumers and it's almost a guarantee that they'll continue doing whatever they can to gain your business.

Chapter Overview

By producing and marketing desired goods and services, businesses satisfy their commitment to society as a whole. They create what economists call *utility*—the want-satisfying power of a good or service. Businesses can create or enhance four basic kinds of utility: time, place, ownership, and form. A firm's marketing operation generates time, place, and ownership utility by offering goods and services to customers when they want to buy at convenient locations where ownership of the products can be transferred.

Production creates form utility by converting raw materials and other inputs into finished products. Auto manufacturers convert metal, rubber, fabric, plastic, glass, and other raw materials into cars, trucks, and SUVs, as described in the opening vignette. **Production** applies resources such as people and machinery to convert materials into finished goods and services. The task of **production and operations management** is to oversee the application of people and machinery in converting materials into finished goods and services. Figure 11.1 illustrates the production process.

People sometimes use the terms *production* and *manufacturing* interchangeably, but they ignore an important difference when they do so. *Production* is a broader term that spans both manufacturing and nonmanufacturing industries. For instance, companies in extractive industries such as fishing, lumber, and mining engage in production, and so do service providers. Services are intangible outputs of production systems. They include outputs as diverse as trash hauling, education, haircuts, tax accounting, dental care, mail delivery, transportation, and lodging. Figure 11.2 lists five examples of production systems for a variety of goods and services.

Whether the production process results in a tangible good or an intangible service, it always converts inputs into outputs. This conversion process may make major changes in raw materials or simply combine already finished parts into new products. A cabinetmaker combines wood, tools, and skill to create finished kitchen cabinets for a new home. A transit system combines buses, trains, and employees to create its output: passenger transportation. Both of these processes create utility.

This chapter describes the process of producing goods and services. It looks at the importance of production and operations management and discusses the new technologies that are transforming the production function. It then discusses the tasks of the production and operations manager, the importance of quality, and the methods businesses use to ensure high quality.

FIGURE 11.1
The Production Process: Converting Inputs to Outputs

Example	Primary Inputs	Transformation	Outputs
Pet Food Factory	Grain, water, fish meal, personnel, tools, machines, paper bags, cans, buildings, utilities	Converts raw materials into finished goods	Pet food products
Trucking Firm	Trucks, personnel, buildings, fuel, goods to be shipped, packaging supplies, truck parts, utilities	Packages and transports goods from sources to destinations	Delivered goods
Department Store	Buildings, displays, scanners, merchandise, personnel, supplies, utilities	Attracts customers, stores goods, sells products	Merchandise sold
Automobile Body Shop	Damaged autos, paints, supplies, machines, tools, buildings, personnel, utilities	Transforms damaged auto bodies into facsimiles of the originals	Repaired automobile bodies
County Sheriff's Department	Personnel, police equipment, automobiles, office furniture, buildings, utilities	Detects crimes and brings criminals to justice	Lower crime rates and peaceful communities

FIGURE 11.2
Typical Production Systems

production application of resources such as people and machinery to convert materials into finished goods and services.

production and operations management managing people and machinery in converting materials and resources into finished goods and services.

Strategic Importance of the Production Function

Along with marketing and finance, production is a vital business activity. Without a good or service to sell, a company cannot generate money to pay its employees, lenders, and stockholders. Without profits, the firm quickly fails. The production process is just as crucial in a not-for-profit organization, since the good or service it offers justifies the organization's existence. In short, the production function adds value to a company's inputs by converting them into marketable outputs. This added value comes from features of the outputs for which customers will pay money.

Clearly, effective production and operations management can lower a firm's costs of production, boost the quality of its goods and services, and allow it to respond dependably to customer demands. Skillful management of production can also promote flexibility, so an organization can respond quickly when customer demands change. Advances in production technology can enable a company to renew itself by providing new items for sale.

Consider this example of how production allows businesses to gain these advantages. Advances in production technology and management have allowed Boeing to shave the amount of time it takes to build landing gear supports for a passenger jetliner from 40 days to 12 days.[2]

Mass Production

From its beginnings as a colonial supplier of raw materials to Europe, the U.S. evolved into an industrial giant. Much of this remarkable change resulted from **mass production,** a system for manufacturing products in large amounts through effective combinations of employees with specialized skills, mechanization, and standardization. Mass production makes outputs available in large quantities at lower prices than individually crafted items would cost.

Mass production begins with specialization of labor, dividing work into its simplest components so that each worker can concentrate on performing one task. By separating jobs into small tasks, managers create conditions for high productivity through mechanization, in which machines perform much of the work previously done by people. Standardization, the third element of mass production, involves producing uniform, interchangeable goods and parts. Standardized parts simplify the replacement of defective or worn-out components. For instance, if your car's windshield wiper blades wear out, you can easily buy replacements at a local auto-parts store like AutoZone.

A logical extension of these principles of specialization, mechanization, and standardization led to development of the **assembly line.** This manufacturing technique moves the product along a conveyor belt past a number of workstations, where workers perform specialized tasks such as welding, painting, installing individual parts, and tightening bolts. Henry Ford's application of this concept revolutionized auto assembly. Before implementing the assembly line, Ford's workers assembled Model T cars at the rate of one per worker for each 12-hour workday. The assembly-line technique slashed the number of work hours per car to 1.5. Not surprisingly, dozens of other industries soon adopted the assembly-line technique.

assembly line
manufacturing technique that carries the product on a conveyor system past several workstations where workers perform specialized tasks.

Although mass production brings advantages for a firm, it imposes limitations, too. It is highly efficient for producing large numbers of similar products. However, mass production loses its efficiency advantage when production requires small batches of different items. The trade-off tempts some companies to focus on efficient production methods rather than on making what customers really want. In addition, specialization can lead to boring jobs, since each worker must keep repeating the same task. To improve their competitive capabilities, many firms are adopting increasingly flexible production systems, such as flexible production, customer-driven production, and the team concept. These techniques may not replace mass production altogether but may simply improve a company's use of mass production.

Flexible Production

While mass production efficiently creates large batches of similar items, flexible production can cost-effectively produce smaller batches. Flexible production can take many forms, but it generally involves using information technology to share the details of customer orders, programmable equipment to fulfill the orders, and skilled people to carry out whatever tasks are needed to fill a particular order. This arrangement is efficient when combined with lean production methods that use automation and information technology to reduce requirements for workers and inventory. Flexible production also requires a high degree of communication and cooperation among customers and employees throughout the organization.

Print-on-demand technology brings flexible production to the publishing industry. With print-on-demand, a book's contents are stored electronically and can be downloaded to fill orders as small as a dozen or fewer copies. For example, South-Western/Thomson Learning—the publisher of this text—offers a service that lets college instructors create customized textbooks for their classes. Instructors can mix and match chapters from multiple titles and even insert their own material, such as course notes and lecture outlines.[3]

Customer-Driven Production

A customer-driven production system evaluates customer demands to link what a manufacturer makes with what customers want to buy. Many firms have implemented this approach with great success. One method is to establish computer links between factories and retailers' scanners, using data about sales as the basis for creating short-term forecasts and designing production schedules to meet those forecasts.

Some companies make products to order. General Motors launched a successful customer-driven production program in Brazil. Here customers can visit a kiosk at a local dealership and order a new car directly from GM. They choose the color and options for their new car, and the order is sent electronically to the factory. If there's already a matching car in GM's inventory, it is shipped to the customer immediately. If not, the car is assembled and shipped a few days later. This arrangement benefits both the customer and GM. The customer gets the exact car he or she wants, along with a $1,000 discount. For the dealer and GM, customer-driven production means being able to reduce inventories, cutting costs by an estimated 3 to 5 percent. The arrangement also gives GM a better fix on customer demand.[4]

Team Concept

Some production methods challenge mass production's emphasis on specialized workers performing repetitive tasks. The team concept combines employees from various departments and functions such as design, manufacturing, finance, and maintenance to work together in designing and building products. Work teams—described in the previous chapter—may also include members from outside the firm, such as suppliers and customers. This kind of teamwork may include *concurrent engineering,* in which product development brings together engineers, designers, production staff, marketing personnel, and employees from other functions.

Pella Corporation uses the team approach to the production of windows and doors. For instance, by implementing the team concept, the production line for double-hung windows takes up only about half its previous amount of floor space. Instead of ordering necessary parts from a distant location within the large plant, team members make them right there, at the location where they are assembling the windows. The changes to Pella's production process also yielded an unexpected benefit. When windows are being manufactured, mounds of leftover wood chips, shavings, and sawdust are piled on the factory floor. In the past, these by-products of the process were simply considered waste and were discarded. Then team members and Pella managers found a way to convert this waste into a salable by-product. Today, this scrap is simply blown through a pipe directly to a new customer located next door—American Wood Fiber, a business that processes wood chips and shavings into pet and horse bedding.[5]

 Concept Check

1. What is specialization of labor and how does it differ from standardization?
2. What are the characteristics of flexible production?
3. Describe a customer-driven production system.

Production Processes

The methods by which firms produce goods and services differ according to their means of operating and time requirements involved. The means of operating may involve either an analytic or a synthetic system, and the time requirements call for either a continuous or an intermittent process.

An *analytic production system* reduces a raw material to its component parts in order to extract one or more marketable products. For example, petroleum refining breaks down crude oil into several marketable products, including gasoline, heating oil, and aviation fuel. When corn is processed, the resulting marketable products include animal feed and corn sweetener.

By contrast, a *synthetic production system* is the reverse of an analytic system. It combines a number of raw materials or parts or transforms raw materials to produce finished products. Dell's assembly line produces a personal computer by assembling the various components ordered by each customer. Ford's assembly line uses a variety of metal, plastic, and rubber components to produce cars and trucks. Other synthetic production systems make drugs, chemicals, computer chips, and canned soup.

A *continuous production process* generates finished products over a lengthy period of time. The steel industry provides a classic example. Its blast furnaces never completely shut down except for malfunctions. Petroleum refineries, chemical plants, and nuclear power facilities also practice continuous production. A shutdown can damage sensitive equipment, with extremely costly results.

An *intermittent production process* generates products in short production runs, shutting down machines frequently or changing their configurations to produce different products. Most services result from intermittent production systems. For instance, accountants, plumbers, and dentists traditionally have not attempted to standardize their services because each service provider confronts different problems that require individual approaches. However, some companies, including Jiffy Lube (auto service) and Terminix (pest control services), offer standardized services as part of a strategy to operate more efficiently and compete with lower prices. In contrast, McDonald's has moved toward a more intermittent production model. The fast-food chain invested millions in new cooking equipment to set up kitchens for preparing sandwiches quickly to order, rather than producing large batches ahead of time and then keeping them warm under heat lamps.

Concept Check

1. Explain how the four different production systems can be distinguished by comparing the operations and time requirements for production.
2. Which type of production system combines raw materials or parts into finished products?

Technology and the Production Process

Like other business functions, production has changed dramatically as computers and related technologies have developed. At Square D's facility in Lincoln, Nebraska, a fully automated production line makes approximately 100,000 circuit breakers in a day. Instead of 250 workers assembling these products the traditional way, the production line requires fewer than 50 operators, who earn around $20 an hour for their highly skilled work. The efficiency of automation allows the company to produce so many parts so fast that distributors can keep a lower stock on hand and place more frequent orders. This frees up funds so they can order a wider range of different Square D products. The factory is so efficient that the company moved some production to Lincoln from Mexico. And although Square D needs fewer assemblers for its automated facility, meeting the strong demand requires more skilled workers such as mold makers.[6]

In addition to boosting efficiency in the production process, automation and information technology allow firms to redesign their current methods to enhance flexibility. These changes allow a company to design and create new products faster, modify them more rapidly, and meet customers' changing needs more effectively than it could achieve with traditional methods. Important production technologies today include robots, computer-aided design and manufacturing, flexible manufacturing systems, and computer-integrated manufacturing.

Robots

robot reprogrammable machine capable of performing numerous tasks that require manipulations of materials and tools.

A growing number of manufacturers have freed people from boring, sometimes dangerous assignments by replacing them with robots. A **robot** is a reprogrammable machine capable of performing a variety of jobs that require manipulation of materials and tools. Robots can repeat the same tasks many times without varying their movements. In manufacturing the Civic, Honda uses robots to handle, move, and weld parts. Robots move pieces of sheet metal into fixtures and move parts around the end of the gun that sprays on a coating of sealant. A single general welder using 20 programmable electric robots to make about 130 welds attaches the floor, sides, and roof of each automobile. Not only are robots more efficient for these activities, but they are also more consistent than a human, who would grow tired after hours of lifting.[7]

Initially, robots were most common in automotive and electronics manufacturing, but growing numbers of industries are adding them to production lines, as improvements in technology bring progressively less expensive and more flexible alternatives. Firms operate many different types of robots. The simplest kind, a *pick-and-place robot,* moves in only two or three directions as it picks up something from one spot and places it in another. So-called *field robots* assist people in nonmanufacturing, often hazardous, environments such as nuclear power plants, the space station, and even battlefields.

A recent development called *nanotechnology* is enabling the use of production techniques that operate at the level of molecules. IBM researchers developed a process by which DNA powers a robot with fingers one-fiftieth the breadth of a single human hair. More sophisticated versions of this robot may be useful for destroying cancer cells. Nanotechnology is already being used to build

© 2002 David M. Russell

Plastic-parts manufacturer ABA-PGT, based in Vernon, Connecticut, relies on robotics to produce its gears, which are used in products ranging from lawn sprinklers to computer printers. The robots chug away in the fully automated factory—in the dark—producing the gears and plopping them into waiting boxes. Such manufacturing has been dubbed "lights-out manufacturing" because the robots don't need to see what they produce.

"read heads" for computer disk drives and to create tiny particles used to make extremely hard eyeglass lenses and car and floor waxes.[8]

Computer-Aided Design and Computer-Aided Manufacturing

A process called **computer-aided design (CAD)** enables engineers to design parts and buildings on computer screens faster and with fewer mistakes than they could achieve working with traditional drafting systems. Using an electronic pen, an engineer can sketch 3-D designs on an electronic drafting board or directly on the screen. The computer then provides tools to make major and minor design changes and to analyze the design for certain characteristics or problems. Engineers can put a new car design through a simulated road test to project its real-world performance. If they find a problem with weight distribution, for example, they can make the necessary changes on a computer terminal. Only when they satisfy themselves with all of the structural characteristics of their design will they build an actual model.

The process of **computer-aided manufacturing (CAM)** picks up where the CAD system leaves off. Computer tools enable a manufacturer to analyze the steps that a machine must take to produce a needed product or part. Electronic signals transmitted to processing equipment provide instructions for performing the appropriate production steps in the correct order. Both CAD and CAM technologies are now used together at most modern production facilities.

computer-aided design (CAD) system for interactions between a designer and a computer to design a product, facility, or part that meets predetermined specifications.

computer-aided manufacturing (CAM) electronic tools to analyze CAD output and determine necessary steps to implement the design, followed by electronic transmission of instructions to guide the activities of production equipment.

Flexible Manufacturing System

A **flexible manufacturing system (FMS)** is a production facility that workers can quickly modify to manufacture different products. The typical system consists of computer-controlled machining centers to produce metal parts, robots to handle the parts, and remote-controlled carts to deliver materials. All components are linked by electronic controls that dictate activities at each stage of the manufacturing sequence, even automatically replacing broken or worn-out drill bits and other implements.

Flexible manufacturing systems have been enhanced by powerful new software that allows machine tools to be reprogrammed while they are running. This allows the same machine to make hundreds of different parts without the operator having to shut the machine down each time to load new programs for making different parts. The software also connects to the Internet to receive updates or to control machine tools at other sites. And since the software resides on a company's computer network, engineers can use it to diagnose production problems anytime, from anywhere they can access the network.

Computer-Integrated Manufacturing

Companies integrate robots, CAD/CAM, FMS, computers, and other technologies to implement **computer-integrated manufacturing (CIM),** a production system in which computers help workers to design products, control machines, handle materials, and control the production function in an integrated fashion. This type of manufacturing does not necessarily imply more automation and fewer people than other alternatives. It does involve a new type of automation organized around the computer. The key to CIM is a centralized computer system running software that integrates and controls separate processes and functions. One software program, called Circuit-CAM, programs computer-controlled machinery, designs efficient production layouts, manages changes required when a process is revised, reports quality and cost performance, and prepares production-related documents.

Concept Check

1. List some of the reasons businesses are investing in research about robots.
2. What is nanotechnology?

The Location Decision

The decision of where to locate a production facility hinges on transportation, physical, and human factors as shown in Table 11.1. Transportation factors include proximity to markets and raw materials, along with availability of alternative modes for transporting both inputs and outputs. For instance, automobile assembly plants are located near major rail lines. Inputs—such as engines, plastics, and metal parts—arrive by rail, and the finished vehicles are shipped out by rail. Shopping malls are often located adjacent to major streets and freeways in urban and suburban areas, since most customers arrive by car.

Physical variables involve such issues as weather, water supplies, available energy, and options for disposing of hazardous waste. Theme parks, such as Walt Disney World, are often located in warm climates so they can be open, and attract visitors, year-round. A firm that wants to locate near a community often must prepare an **environmental impact study** that analyzes how a proposed plant would affect the quality of life in the surrounding area. Regulatory agencies typically require such studies to cover topics like the impact on transportation facilities; energy requirements; water and sewage treatment needs; natural plant life and wildlife; and water, air, and noise pollution. However, a plant location decision also involves many ethical considerations. The Solving an Ethical Controversy box debates the pros and cons of closing U.S. factories and moving production overseas.

Table 11.1   Factors in the Location Decision

Location Factor	Examples of Affected Businesses
Transportation	
Proximity to markets	Baking companies and manufacturers of other perishable products, dry cleaners, hotels, other services
Proximity to raw materials	Mining companies
Availability of transportation alternatives	Brick manufacturers, retail stores
Human Factors	
Labor supply	Auto manufacturers, software developers
Local regulations	Nightclubs, liquor stores
Community living conditions	All businesses
Physical Factors	
Water supply	Paper mills
Energy	Aluminum, chemical, and fertilizer manufacturers
Hazardous wastes	All businesses

Are Factory Closings a Bad Thing—or a Good Thing?

Just about everywhere in the U.S., factory doors are closing. In New Hampshire, it's the paper mills. In North Carolina, it's furniture factories. In Texas, it's the textile mills. Some of these companies are going out of business altogether. Others are moving production overseas to cut costs. U.S. factory output is down 2 percent from its peak several years ago, while imported goods are up 8 percent. Three million factory jobs have been lost over this same time period. Even as domestic productivity improves and these figures begin to turn around, European and Asian factories are moving faster. But U.S. business owners say that if they can't compete by moving production to lower-cost locations, they'll have to shut down completely—and workers would be better off with retraining in new, higher-paying fields.

Are some U.S. factory closings actually good for the economy and the workforce?

PRO

1. Many workers say they would rather retrain for new jobs in service or technology industries than get jobs in another new minimum-wage factory. "Those are the jobs of the past. We want jobs of the future," says the mayor of one town affected by the closing of a Fruit of the Loom plant in Texas.

2. Increased demand for certain products, such as specialized medical instruments, that require skilled labor will ensure that manufacturing will not die in the U.S.; ultimately, workers in those factories will be paid more.

CON

1. Many retailers argue that keeping production in the U.S. actually improves efficiency—like timely delivery of goods—and ultimately the bottom line.

2. Many American consumers prefer goods manufactured in the U.S.—and seek them out. "If Heinz Ketchup were ever bought by a foreign firm, I don't know what I'd do," laments one consumer who likes to buy American.

SUMMARY

While some believe that closing factories is a positive move, others disagree. "Our location [in Minnesota] is one of our competitive advantages," argues Wayne M. Fortun of Hutchinson Technology. "By going to China, and training them on precision toolmaking and our other processes, we'd stand the risk of disseminating a valuable technology that is one of the reasons we're able to compete worldwide."

Sources: Timothy Aeppel, "Still Made in the U.S.A.," *The Wall Street Journal*, July 8, 2004, pp. B1, B4; Clare Ansberry, "Why U.S. Manufacturing Won't Die," *The Wall Street Journal*, July 3, 2004, pp. B1, B2; Joellen Perry and Marianne Lavelle, "Made in America," *U.S. News & World Report*, May 17, 2004, pp. 50, 54; Michael Arndt and Adam Aston, "U.S. Factories: Falling Behind," *BusinessWeek*, May 24, 2004, pp. 94–95; Andy Serwer, "Good Riddance," *Fortune*, October 13, 2003, pp. 193–200.

Human factors include an area's labor supply, local regulations, and living conditions. Management considers local labor costs, as well as the availability of workers with needed qualifications. For example, some labor-intensive industries have located plants in rural areas with readily available labor pools and limited high-wage alternatives. Some firms with headquarters in the U.S. and other industrialized countries have moved production offshore in search of low wages. Apparel is a classic example.

In the U.S., this trend, coupled with automation, has shrunk manufacturing's share of the nation's gross domestic product. However, manufacturing continues to be an important segment of the U.S. economy, with total output greater than it ever has been. During the past 10 years, U.S. manufacturing output grew much faster than the number of people employed by manufacturing companies. One reason that many foreign companies locate facilities in the U.S. is that creative use of technology has made U.S. workers extremely productive. Output per hour has risen steadily and is higher than most other industrialized nations.

Concept Check

1. What is the purpose of an environmental impact study and how does it influence the location decision?
2. What human factors are relevant to the location decision?

Availability of qualified employees is a key factor in many location decisions. Software makers and other computer-related firms concentrate in areas with the technical talent they need, including Silicon Valley in and around San Jose, California; Boston; and Austin, Texas. But a downturn in the high-tech sector prompted investment banking firm Goldman Sachs to close its San Jose office. Goldman, like other firms, needs to watch its expenses, and consolidation of the office into its San Francisco office space saves the company money.[9]

The Job of Production Managers

Production and operations managers oversee the work of people and machinery to convert inputs (materials and resources) into finished goods and services. As Figure 11.3 shows, these managers perform four major tasks. First, they plan the overall production process. Next, they determine the best layout for the firm's facilities. Then they implement the production plan. Finally, they control the manufacturing process to maintain the highest possible quality. Part of the control process involves continuous evaluation of results. If problems occur, managers return to the first step and make adjustments.

Planning the Production Process

A firm's production planning begins with its choice of the goods or services to offer its customers. This decision is the essence of every company's reason for operating. Other decisions such as machinery purchases, pricing decisions, and selection of retail outlets all grow out of product planning.

Marketing research studies elicit consumer reactions to proposed products, test prototypes of new items, and estimate their potential sales and profitability levels. The production department concerns itself primarily with (1) converting original product concepts into final specifications and (2) designing the most efficient facilities to produce the new product. The product must not only win acceptance from consumers but also achieve production economies to ensure an acceptable financial return.

At DaimlerChrysler and other U.S. auto companies, the traditional approach to production planning has been to build enough cars to meet sales projections. Under this method, called *production push,* the company relies on its dealers to find buyers for all the vehicles. If sales are disappointing, the supplier has to offer discounts to move cars out of inventory. After Chrysler's combination with Daimler-Benz, it began losing money, and Daimler's management called for a shift to its own practice of *production pull,* in which production schedules are based on actual orders from customers. Production pull, however, requires greater flexibility and faster response, especially in the U.S., where customers are not used to waiting for the factory to build their new car.[10]

Determining the Facility Layout

FIGURE 11.3
Tasks of Production Managers

Once managers have established the activities needed in their firm's production process, they can determine the best layout for the facility. This decision requires them to consider all phases of production and the necessary inputs at each step. Figure 11.4 shows three common layout designs: process, product, and fixed-position layouts. It also shows a customer-oriented layout typical of service providers' production systems.

PRODUCTION MANAGEMENT TASKS

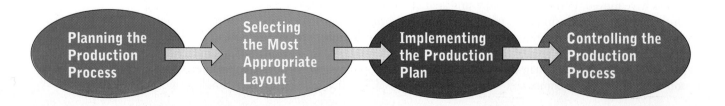

(A) Process Layout

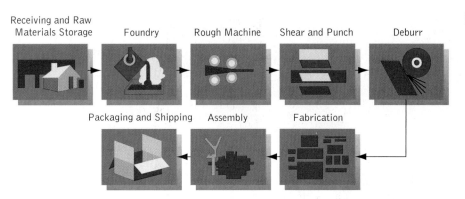

(B) Product Layout

(C) Fixed-Position Layout

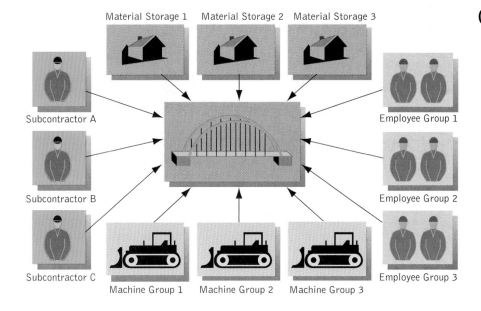

(D) Customer-Oriented Layout

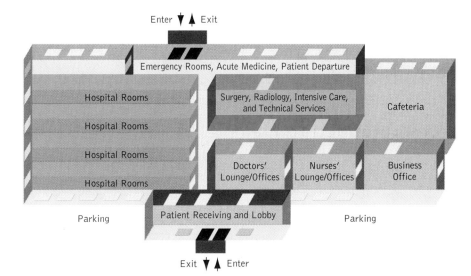

FIGURE 11.4
Basic Facility Layouts

In its Tuscaloosa, Alabama, plant, Mercedes-Benz continually fine-tunes its production process until it runs smoothly. Workers noticed that they were zigzagging through the production line, bumping into one another as they selected parts. Production supervisor Jack Duncan heard about the problem and worked with the team to reconfigure the placement of parts bins, shaving seconds off each worker's time. The payoff? The Tuscaloosa assembly line's M Class SUVs are among the company's most profitable vehicles.

Photograph by Patrick Witty

A process layout groups machinery and equipment according to their functions. The work in process moves around the plant to reach different workstations. A process layout often facilitates production of a variety of nonstandard items in relatively small batches. Honda also uses a version of a process layout to build its Civic. The company organizes into several workstations, or "zones" grouping together activities related to the interior, chassis, and wiring and tubing. At the end of each zone, workers perform an inspection before sending the car to the next zone. Nonstandard activities, such as preparing tanks for natural gas–powered vehicles, take place in a subassembly area.[11]

A product layout sets up production equipment along a product-flow line, and the work in process moves along this line past workstations. This type of layout efficiently produces large numbers of similar items, but it may prove inflexible and able to accommodate only a few product variations. Although product layouts date back at least to the Model T assembly line, companies are refining this approach with modern touches. In Saarlouis, Germany, the Ford Focus assembly plant uses a conveyor belt to move workers along the assembly line, rather than having them trudge from car to car. The resulting productivity increase allowed the company to transfer workers from the assembly line to other jobs. Based on the success of this idea, Ford has since installed similar conveyor belts in other factories.[12]

A fixed-position layout places the product in one spot, and workers, materials, and equipment come to it. This approach suits production of very large, bulky, heavy, or fragile products. An example is building a bridge. Airplanes were also traditionally assembled using the fixed-position layout approach. However, Boeing modified its Everett, Washington, production facility. Now giant jetliners move, albeit at the rate of one foot an hour, from workstation to workstation as the aircraft is assembled. This approach saves both time and money. For instance, workers used to spend up to two hours per shift walking around the huge plant gathering tools, parts, and other materials.[13]

Service organizations also must decide on appropriate layouts for their production processes. A service firm should arrange its facilities to enhance the interactions between customers and its services—a so-called *customer-oriented layout.* If you think of patients as inputs, the hospital implements a form of the process layout. In other service organizations, direct contact with the recipient of services is a less significant part of production. For example, much of a law or accounting firm's work takes place away from clients. Access to colleagues and the Internet, as well as a quiet environment, is often vital for such processes.

Implementing the Production Plan

After planning the manufacturing process and determining the best layout, a firm's production managers begin to implement the production plan. This activity involves (1) deciding whether to make, buy, or lease components; (2) selecting the best suppliers for materials; and (3) controlling inventory to keep enough, but not too much, on hand.

Make, Buy, or Lease Decision
One of the fundamental issues facing every producer is the **make, buy, or lease decision**—choosing whether to manufacture a needed product or component in house, purchase it from an outside supplier, or lease it. This decision is critical in many contemporary business situations.

BUSINESS TOOL KIT

Conflict Resolution at Work

Resolving conflict at work requires some delicate maneuvering and a host of interpersonal skills. While no one enjoys conflict, how you handle it in the workplace says a lot about your professionalism and your ability to work with others. Here are a few tips for when you find yourself at cross-purposes with a colleague.

1. **Always maintain your professionalism.** Regardless of who is escalating the situation, do not yell back or visibly get upset with that person. Keep your cool and suggest that you discuss the matter when both parties are calmer.

2. **Don't jump to conclusions.** Maintaining open and honest pathways to communications can help you clear up a simple misunderstanding. Always try to understand your colleagues' point of view and allow them time to adequately express themselves.

3. **Don't get personal.** Even if there is a major personality clash between you and a colleague, don't ever allow a conflict to escalate into a personal attack. Stick with the business-related issue at hand and keep returning to the issue that needs resolving. The bottom line is that unless you are prepared to tender your resignation, you will probably have to work with this person for a long while.

4. **Focus on common objectives and be honest.** Try to focus on commonalities when conflict arises, such as meeting a certain deadline or attaining a quality goal. Be honest and forthright with your colleague and work toward a mutually acceptable compromise.

5. **Conflicts are a normal aspect of the workplace.** Anytime you gather several unique individuals into a team environment, conflict is sure to be a part of the process. Learning how to deal with conflict sooner rather than later aids your growth as a professional and an employee. Recognize that not all conflicts are resolvable and learn to decide when it is worthwhile to keep trying and when it is time to walk away.

Sources: Max Messmer, "Building Better Rapport with Your Boss," *Strategic Finance,* May 2003, p. 15; Robert S. Adams, "Facing Up to Board Conflict: A Five-Pronged Path to Conflict Resolution," *Association Management,* April 2003, p. 56; Amy Alexander, "Simmer Down Now," *Greater Baton Rouge Business Report,* February 18, 2003, p. 24; William Cottringer, "Employee Conflict: Dealing with On-the-Job Employee Conflicts," *Supervision,* February 2003, p. 3.

Several factors affect the make, buy, or lease decision, including the costs of leasing or purchasing parts from outside suppliers compared with the costs of producing them in house. The decision sometimes hinges on the availability of outside suppliers that can dependably meet a firm's standards for quality and quantity. The need for confidentiality sometimes affects the decision, as does the short- or long-term duration of the firm's need for supplies.

Even when the firm decides to purchase from outside vendors, production managers should maintain access to multiple supply sources. An alternative supplier ensures that the firm can obtain needed materials despite strikes, quality assurance problems, or other situations that may affect inputs.

Selection of Suppliers   Once a company decides what inputs to purchase, it must choose the best vendors for its needs. To make this choice, production managers compare the quality, prices, dependability of delivery, and services offered by competing companies. Different suppliers may offer virtually identical quality levels and prices, so the final decision often rests on factors such as the firm's experience with each supplier, speed of delivery, warranties on purchases, and other services.

For a major purchase, negotiations between the purchaser and potential vendors may stretch over several weeks or even months, and the buying decision may rest with a number of colleagues who must say yes before the final decision is made. The choice of a supplier for an industrial drill press, for example, may require a joint decision by the production, engineering, purchasing, and quality control departments. These departments often must reconcile their different views to settle on a purchasing decision.

The Internet has given buyers powerful tools for finding and comparing suppliers. Buyers can log on to business exchanges to compare specifications, prices, and availability. FreeMarkets offers organizations software and other tools that allow them to source $35 billion worth of goods and services from suppliers around the world. FreeMarkets claims that it has saved customers over $7 billion.[14]

HITS & MISSES

Business Jet's Pieces Solve the Puzzle of Production

If you've ever built a model airplane, you have a pretty good idea how Bombardier Business Aircraft manufactures its newest eight-passenger business jet. The super-midsize Challenger 300, formerly known as the Continental, consists of about a dozen large parts, all manufactured elsewhere and assembled in a Wichita, Kansas, plant in just four days.

Nearly 70 feet long, with a wingspan of almost 64 feet, the Challenger 300 has engines from Phoenix, a nose and cockpit from Montreal, a midfuselage from Ireland, a tail from Taiwan, wings from Japan, and smaller parts such as landing gear and tail cone from suppliers in Canada, Austria, Australia, and the U.S. The company put the jet in service in 2003. Bombardier expects to manufacture nearly 60 Challenger 300 jets a year and already has orders for 115.

Managing the multicompany, multinational operation that produces the Challenger 300 is complex, and although the process isn't yet perfect, Bombardier is committed to the business partnerships that make it possible. In fact, relying on such partnerships has helped the company reduce the time between planning and delivery of all its new models.

But not even the closest partnership can replace in-house knowledge. As John Holding, in charge of engineering and

product development, says, "You can only manage a partner if you know what you're talking about. You have to have people who understand hydraulic systems and avionic systems—not to the detail of knowing exactly how you machine a valve, but you have to have the knowledge."

QUESTIONS FOR CRITICAL THINKING
1. How do you think Bombardier controls quality when parts of its new jet are made all over the world?
2. Bombardier hopes to work more closely with partners in the future, involving them earlier in the design and planning processes. What do you think are some of the benefits it wants to gain?

Sources: "Bombardier Challenger 300 Super Midsize Corporate Business Jet, Canada," *Aerospace Technology,* http://www.aerospace-technology.com/projects/bombardier, accessed March 11, 2003; "Bombardier Continental BD-100 Super Midsize Corporate Business Jet, Canada," *Aerospace-Technology.com,* http://www.aerospace-technology.com, accessed June 2, 2002; Philip Siekman, "The Snap-Together Business Jet," *Fortune,* January 21, 2002, pp. 104A–104H.

Firms often purchase raw materials and component parts on long-term contracts. If a manufacturer requires a continuous supply of materials, a one-year or two-year contract with a vendor helps to ensure availability. Today, many firms are building long-term relationships with suppliers and slashing the number of companies with which they do business. At the same time, they call on vendors to expand their roles in the production process. The Hits & Misses box outlines how Bombardier Business Aircraft uses outside suppliers to manufacture one of its latest business jet models.

Inventory Control   Production and operations managers' responsibility for **inventory control** requires them to balance the need to keep stocks on hand to meet demand against the costs of carrying inventory. Among the expenses involved in storing inventory are warehousing costs, taxes, insurance, and maintenance. A firm wastes money if it holds more inventory than it needs, but a shortage of raw materials, parts, or goods for sale often leads to delays and unhappy customers. Firms lose business when they consistently miss promised delivery dates or turn away orders. Managers must balance this threat against the cost of holding inventory to set acceptable stocking levels.

Efficient inventory control can save a great deal of money. In one common technique, many firms maintain **perpetual inventory** systems to continuously monitor the amounts and locations of their stocks. Such inventory control systems typically rely on computers, and many automatically generate orders at the appropriate times. Many supermarkets link their scanning devices to perpetual inventory systems that reorder needed merchandise without human interaction. As the system records a shopper's purchase, it reduces the inventory count stored in the computer. Once inventory on hand drops to a predetermined level, the system automatically reorders the merchandise.

Some companies go further and hand over their inventory control functions to suppliers. This concept is known as **vendor-managed inventory.** Audio equipment maker Bose Corporation has made arrangements with some of its vendors that effectively transfer control of its inventory to the sellers. An on-site representative is responsible for monitoring Bose's inventory and placing orders when needed with Bose's approval. Some firms—such as Wal-Mart—have modified vendor-managed inventory to an approach called **CPFaR** (collaborative planning, forecasting, and replenishment). CPFaR is a planning and forecasting technique involving collaborative efforts by both purchasers and vendors.

Just-in-Time Systems A **just-in-time (JIT) system** implements a broad management philosophy that reaches beyond the narrow activity of inventory control to influence the entire system of production and operations management. A JIT system seeks to eliminate all sources of waste—anything that does not add value—in operations activities by providing the right part at the right place at the right time. Compared with traditional production, this program reduces inventory and costs as it improves the quality of goods and services.

The inventory control function in a JIT system supplies parts to a production line or an entire company as they are needed. This action lowers factory inventory levels and carrying costs. The JIT system also lets firms respond quickly to changes in the market, retaining only the most essential personnel to handle inventory. It also better allows product customization. Nike recently began offering consumers the option of personalizing a Pegasus Air 2000 running shoe. A customer can select the color, the width, and the amount of cushioning. The personalized shoe costs about $10 more than buying it off the shelf. At Lands' End, consumers can customize jeans, dress pants, and men's dress shirts.[15] Not only do these systems give customers exactly what they want, but they also let firms such as Nike and Lands' End (now part of Sears) capture data that can be used in other product and production planning decisions.

Production using JIT shifts much of the responsibility for carrying inventory to vendors, which operate on forecasts and keep stocks on hand to respond to manufacturers' needs. Suppliers that cannot keep enough high-quality parts on hand often lose customers to vendors that can. Another risk of using JIT systems is what happens if manufacturers underestimate demand for a product. Strong demand will begin to overtax JIT systems, as suppliers and their customers struggle to keep up with orders with no inventory cushion to tide them over.

Materials Requirement Planning Besides efficiency, effective inventory control requires careful planning to ensure the firm has all the inputs it needs to make its products. How do production and operations managers coordinate all of this information? They rely on **materials requirement planning (MRP),** a computer-based production planning system that lets a firm ensure that it has all the parts and materials it needs to produce its output at the right time and place and in the right amounts.

Courtesy of Dell

just-in-time (JIT) system management philosophy aimed at improving profits and return on investment by minimizing costs and eliminating waste through cutting inventory on hand.

Dell is a master of just-in-time manufacturing systems. Its PCs are constructed one at a time to customer specifications—a system that has made it No. 1 in the competitive PC market.

materials requirement planning (MRP) computer-based production planning system by which a firm can ensure that it has needed parts and materials available at the right time and place in the correct amounts.

Production managers use MRP programs to create schedules that identify the specific parts and materials required to produce an item. These schedules specify the exact quantities required of each and dates on which to release orders to suppliers so deliveries will support the best timing within the production cycle. A small company might get by without an MRP system. If a firm makes a simple product with few components, a telephone call may ensure overnight delivery of crucial parts. For a complex product, however, such as a car or a joint-strike fighter, MRP becomes an invaluable tool.

Controlling the Production Process

The final task of production and operations managers is controlling the production process to maintain the highest possible quality. **Production control** creates a well-defined set of procedures for coordinating people, materials, and machinery to provide maximum production efficiency. Suppose that a watch factory must produce 80,000 watches during October. Production control managers break down this total into a daily production assignment of 4,000 watches for each of the month's 20 working days. Next, they determine the number of workers, raw materials, parts, and machines the plant needs to meet the production schedule. Similarly, a manager in a service business such as a restaurant must estimate how many dinners the outlet will serve each day and then determine how many people are needed to prepare and serve the food, as well as what food to purchase.

Figure 11.5 illustrates production control as a five-step process composed of planning, routing, scheduling, dispatching, and follow-up. These steps are part of the firm's overall emphasis on total quality management.

Production Planning   The phase of production control called **production planning** determines the amount of resources (including raw materials and other components) a firm needs to produce a certain output. The production planning process develops a bill of materials that lists all needed parts and materials. By comparing information about needed parts and materials with the firm's perpetual inventory data, purchasing personnel can identify necessary purchases. Employees or automated systems establish delivery schedules to provide that needed parts and materials arrive as required during the production process. Production planning also ensures the availability of needed machines and personnel. Although material inputs contribute to service-production systems, production planning for services tends to emphasize human resources more than materials.

Routing   Another phase of production control, called **routing,** determines the sequence of work throughout the facility and specifies who will perform each aspect of the work at what location. Routing choices depend on two factors: the nature of the good or service and the facility layouts discussed earlier in the chapter—product, process, fixed-position, or customer-oriented.

Observing production activities can improve routing decisions. At the Fenton, Michigan, factory of TRW Chassis Systems, a team of employees charged with improving work processes on an assembly line discovered that one worker's job consisted of simply moving parts from the end of a conveyor line to a test stand. The team moved the test stand, placing it next to the end of the assembly line so that the tester could unload the items. The unnecessary worker moved to another—probably more gratifying—job in a different part of the plant.[16]

scheduling development of timetables that specify how long each operation in the production process takes and when workers should perform it.

Scheduling   In the **scheduling** phase of production control, managers develop timetables that specify how long each operation in the production process takes and when workers should perform it. Efficient scheduling ensures that production will meet delivery schedules and make efficient use of resources.

FIGURE 11.5
Steps in Production Control

Planning → Routing → Scheduling → Dispatching → Follow-up

Scheduling is an extremely important activity for a manufacturer of a complex product with many parts or production stages. Think of all the component parts needed to make a CT or MRI scanner or other hospital equipment. Scheduling must make each one available in the right place at the right time and in the right amounts to ensure a smooth production process.

Scheduling practices vary considerably in service-related organizations. Printing shops or hair stylists may use relatively unsophisticated scheduling systems, resorting to such devices as "first come, first served" rules, appointment schedules, or take-a-number systems. They may call in part-time workers and use standby equipment to handle demand fluctuations. On the other hand, hospitals typically implement sophisticated scheduling systems similar to those of manufacturers.

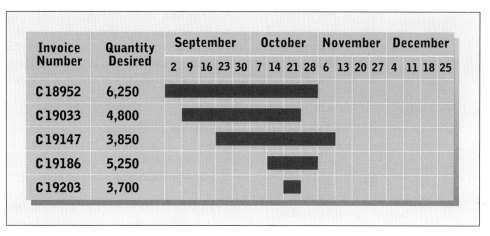

FIGURE 11.6
Sample Gantt Chart

Production managers use a number of analytical methods for scheduling. One of the oldest methods, the *Gantt chart*, tracks projected and actual work progress over time. Gantt charts like the one in Figure 11.6 remain popular because they show at a glance the status of a particular project. However, they are most effective for scheduling relatively simple projects.

A complex project might require a **PERT (Program Evaluation and Review Technique)** chart, which seeks to minimize delays by coordinating all aspects of the production process. First developed for the military, PERT has been modified for industry. The simplified PERT diagram in Figure 11.7 summarizes the schedule for construction of a house in a subdivision developed by a national home builder.

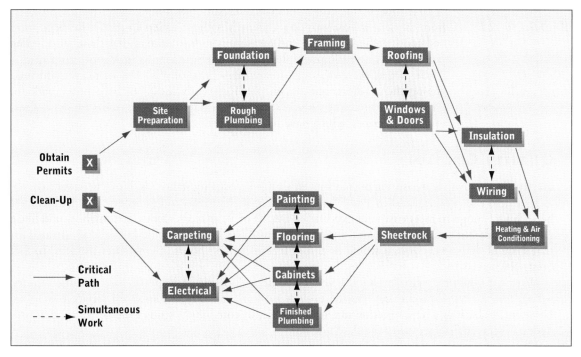

FIGURE 11.7
PERT Diagram for Building a Home

The red line indicates the **critical path**—the sequence of operations that requires the longest time for completion. The dotted line shows work that can be done simultaneously.

In practice, a PERT network may consist of thousands of events and cover months of time. Complex computer programs help production managers to develop such a network and find the critical path among the maze of events and activities. The construction of a huge skyscraper requires complex production planning of this nature.

Dispatching   The phase of production control in which the manager instructs each department on what work to do and the time allowed for its completion is called **dispatching.** The dispatcher authorizes performance, provides instructions, and lists job priorities. Dispatching may be the responsibility of a manager or a self-managed work team.

Follow-up   Because even the best plans sometimes go awry, production managers need to be aware of problems that arise. **Follow-up** is the phase of production control in which employees and their supervisors spot problems in the production process and determine needed changes. Problems take many forms: Machinery malfunctions, delayed shipments, and employee absenteeism can all affect production. The production control system must detect and report these delays to managers or work teams so they can adjust schedules and correct the underlying problems.

Concept Check

1. List the four major tasks of production and operations managers.
2. Differentiate between the three most common layout designs: process, product, and fixed-position.
3. What is a just-in-time inventory system and what are some of its advantages?

Importance of Quality

benchmarking identifying how leaders in certain fields perform and continually comparing and measuring performance against these outstanding performers.

Investing money up front in quality design and development ultimately decreases the cost of quality, measured by costs that result from failure to make the good or service right the first time. These costs average at least 20 percent of sales revenue for most companies. Some typical costs of poor quality include downtime, repair costs, rework, and employee turnover. Production and operations managers must set up systems to track and reduce such costs. If managers concentrate on making high-quality offerings that satisfy the needs of customers, they will reduce costs of quality as a by-product.

One process that companies use to ensure they produce high-quality products from the start is **benchmarking**—identifying how leaders in certain fields perform and continually comparing and measuring performance against these outstanding performers. The basic principle behind benchmarking is to identify a set of best practices that companies can follow. Benchmarking is used in many industries, among them automobile design. Audi currently seems to be a benchmark for Detroit's big three automakers. Their recent designs resemble Audi's rounded, sleek, minimal exteriors, which have been a hit with consumers.[17]

Quality Control

quality control measuring goods and services against established quality standards.

Quality control involves measuring output against established quality standards. Firms need such checks to spot defective products and to avoid delivering inferior shipments to customers. Standards should be set high enough to meet customer expectations. A 90 or 95 percent success rate might sound like a good number, but consider what your phone service or ATM network would be like if it operated for that share of time. Every year, it would be out of service for 438 hours (5 percent of the year) to 875 hours (10 percent).

Ways to monitor quality levels of a firm's output include visual inspections, electronic sensors, robots, and X-rays. Customer surveys can provide quality control information for service businesses. Negative feedback or a high rejection rate on a product or component sends a danger signal that production is not achieving quality standards.

Of course, a company cannot rely solely on inspections to achieve its quality goals. A typical American factory spends up to half its operating budget identifying and fixing mistakes, a costly and time-consuming process. Instead, quality-driven production managers identify all processes involved in pro-

BEST BUSINESS PRACTICES

Hyundai Makes a U-Turn

It wasn't long ago that the quality ratings for Hyundai autos were so low that J. D. Power & Associates gave them their own page—at the back. But times have changed. After five years of laserlike focus on quality, a push to design cars that U.S. consumers want to drive, a boost in manufacturing capacity, and a move toward globalization, Hyundai is in a new category. In fact, it occupies the front page of J. D. Power & Associates initial quality rankings—it is number 3, just behind Toyota and American Honda. How did the Korean carmaker get there so fast?

Traditionally, Hyundai hasn't been known for its quality vehicles—the firm was linked with low prices, and consumers got what they paid for. But in the past few years, Hyundai has radically improved the electrical systems in its cars, redesigned the automatic transmissions to be smoother and quieter, and improved body integrity. In addition, the company stands behind its cars with a 10-year, 100,000-mile warranty. Hyundai designers and engineers have been busily developing more stylish models like the new Sonata, which the company has positioned directly against Toyota's nearly legendary Camry; and the Santa Fe SUV, which looks a bit like Toyota's Highlander. As a result, prices are creeping upward—but Hyundai executives say that the quality and new styles match the prices. Choi Jong Min, chief designer of the Sonata, says "This will spearhead our efforts to boost our brand image and end Hyundai's reputation as a discount marque."

Hyundai increased its manufacturing capacity in one gulp by purchasing Kia Motors and has recently opened new plants in the U.S., China, India, and Europe. By 2010, Hyundai will have the capacity to produce 5 million cars a year. Exports now account for 64 percent of the automaker's sales of about 400,000 vehicles per year, an increase from 50 percent just five years ago. Hyundai's marketing chief, Lee Jae Wan, is thinking big. "Hyundai is gearing up to become a truly global player," he predicts.

QUESTIONS FOR CRITICAL THINKING

1. How might Hyundai use benchmarking to continue its quality improvements?

2. Would you buy a Hyundai? Why or why not?

Sources: Moon Ihlwan and Chester Dawson, "Building a Camry Fighter," *BusinessWeek*, September 6, 2004, pp. 62–63; Sholnn Freeman, "Hyundai Surges in Quality Rankings," *The Wall Street Journal*, April 29, 2004, p. A4; David Kiley, "Hyundai Pulls Off a Head-Spinning U-Turn," *USA Today*, April 28, 2004, pp. 1A, 2A.

ducing goods and services and work to maximize their efficiency. The causes of problems in the processes must be found and eliminated. If a company concentrates its efforts on improving processes, a high-quality product will result. Hyundai is one firm that has benefited from a focus on quality, as described in the Best Business Practices box.

General Electric, Ford, DuPont, Nokia, and Sony are just five of the growing number of major manufacturers using the so-called *Six Sigma* concept to achieve quality goals. Six Sigma means a company tries to make error-free products 99.9997 percent of time—a tiny 3.4 errors per million opportunities. At General Electric, the goal is to eliminate virtually all defects in its output, processes, and transactions. GE's Web site states: "Six Sigma has changed the DNA of GE. It is now the way we work on everything we do and is in every product we design."[18]

ISO Standards

For many goods, an important measure of quality is to meet standards of the **International Organization for Standardization,** known as **ISO** for short—not an acronym but a shorter name derived from the Greek word *isos,* meaning "equal." The organization uses ISO as an alternative to different acronyms for every member's language. Established in Europe in 1947, ISO includes representatives from over 140 nations. Its mission is to promote the development of standardized products to facilitate trade and cooperation across national borders. ISO standards govern everything from the format of banking and telephone cards to freight containers to paper sizes to metric screw threads. The U.S. member body of ISO is the American National Standards Institute.

International Organization for Standardization (ISO)
international organization whose mission is to promote the development of standardized products to facilitate trade and cooperation across national borders.

Concept Check

1. *What are some of the ways in which a company can monitor the quality level of its output?*
2. *What does Six Sigma mean?*
3. *List some of the benefits of acquiring ISO 9000 certification.*

DID YOU KNOW?

1. The production yield of a single acre of vineyard land is four tons of grapes, which can be used to make 2,400 bottles of wine.
2. Once the realm of science fiction, factories where products are entirely made by machines without the aid of human workers are now a reality.
3. Among the quality control issues for many service organizations such as banks, restaurants, and airline check-in counters is the amount of time customers must spend waiting in line, or queuing. Cheaper prices for matinees are an attempt to even out customer arrival times at theaters and reduce the length of queues.
4. To eliminate waste, in the early 1900s Henry Ford made the floor boards of his cars from the packing crates for the seats.
5. Thanks to increased quality, the average U.S. driver keeps a new car twice as long today as in the 1980s.

During the 1980s and 1990s, ISO developed standards not just for products themselves but for systems of management. The ISO 9000 family series of standards sets requirements for quality processes; these standards define how a company should ensure that its products meet customers' requirements. The ISO 14000 series sets standards for operations that minimize harm to the environment. ISO accredits organizations in member countries to evaluate performance against these standards. To receive an ISO 9000 family certification, a company must undergo an on-site audit. The audit ensures that documented quality procedures are in place and that all employees understand and follow the procedures. Production managers meet these requirements through an ongoing process involving periodic recertification.

Over 400,000 ISO 9000 family certificates have been awarded to companies around the world. Their numbers are growing rapidly, with the fastest growth occurring in China, Italy, and Japan. Over half the certificates have been awarded in Europe. In fact, ISO 9000 certification is a condition of doing business with many European firms, as well as with a significant number of corporations worldwide.[19]

What's Ahead

Maintaining high quality is an important element of satisfying customers. Product quality and customer satisfaction are also objectives of the business function of marketing. The next part consists of three chapters that explore the many activities involved in customer-driven marketing. These activities include product development, distribution, promotion, and pricing.

Summary of Learning Goals

1

Outline the importance of production and operations management.

Production and operations management is a vital business function. Without a quality good or service, a company cannot create profits, and it soon fails. The production process is also crucial in a not-for-profit organization, since the good or service it produces justifies the organization's existence. Production and operations management plays an important strategic role by lowering the costs of production, boosting output quality, and allowing the firm to respond flexibly and dependably to customers' demands.

2

Explain the roles of computers and related technologies in production.

Computer-driven automation allows companies to design, create, and modify products rapidly and produce them in ways that effectively meet customers' changing needs. Important design and production technologies include robots, computer-aided design (CAD), computer-aided manufacturing (CAM), and computer-integrated manufacturing (CIM).

3

Identify the factors involved in a plant location decision.

Criteria for choosing the best site for a production facility fall into three categories: transportation, human, and physical factors. Transportation factors include proximity to markets and raw materials, along with availability of transportation alternatives. Physical variables involve such issues as water supply, available energy, and options for disposing of hazardous wastes. Human factors include the area's labor supply, local regulations, and living conditions.

4

Explain the major tasks of production and operations managers.

Production and operations managers use people and machinery to convert inputs (materials and resources) into finished goods and services. Four major tasks are involved. First, the managers must plan the overall production process. Next, they must pick the best layout for their facilities. Then they implement their production plans. Finally, they are responsible for controlling the production process and evaluating results to maintain the highest possible quality.

5

Compare alternative layouts for production facilities.

Process layouts effectively produce nonstandard products in relatively small batches. Product layouts are appropriate for the production of a large quantity of relatively similar products. Fixed-position layouts are common when production involves very large, heavy, or fragile products. Customer-oriented layouts are typical for service facilities where success depends on interaction between customers and service providers.

6

List the steps in the purchasing process.

In the make, buy, or lease decision, production and operations managers determine whether to manufacture needed inputs in house, purchase them, or lease them from an outside supplier. Managers responsible for purchasing determine the correct materials to purchase, select appropriate suppliers, and develop an efficient ordering system. The objective is to buy the right materials in the right amounts at the right time and in the right place.

7

Outline the advantages and disadvantages of maintaining large inventories.

The task of inventory control is to balance the need to maintain adequate supplies against the need to minimize funds invested in inventory. Excessive inventory results in unnecessary expenditures for warehousing, taxes, insurance, and maintenance. Inadequate inventory may mean production delays, lost sales, and inefficient operations.

8

Identify the steps in the production control process.

The production control process consists of five steps: planning, routing, scheduling, dispatching, and follow-up. Quality control is an important consideration throughout this process. Coordination of each of these phases should result in high production efficiency and low production costs.

9

Explain the benefits of quality control.

Quality control involves evaluating goods and services against established quality standards. Such checks are necessary to spot defective products and to see that they are not shipped to customers. Devices for monitoring quality levels of the firm's output include visual inspection, electronic sensors, robots, and X-rays. Quality is just as vital in product development; investing money up front in quality design and development ultimately decreases the costs of quality.

Business Terms You Need to Know

production 356

production and operations management 356

assembly line 358

robot 360

computer-aided design (CAD) 361

computer-aided manufacturing (CAM) 361

just-in-time (JIT) system 369

materials requirement planning (MRP) 369

scheduling 370

benchmarking 372

quality control 372

International Organization for Standardization (ISO) 373

Other Important Business Terms

mass production 358

flexible manufacturing system (FMS) 361

computer-integrated manufacturing (CIM) 361

environmental impact study 362

make, buy, or lease decision 366

inventory control 368

perpetual inventory 368

vendor-managed inventory 369

CPFaR 369

production control 370

production planning 370

routing 370

PERT (Program Evaluation and Review Technique) 371

critical path 372

dispatching 372

follow-up 372

Review Questions

1. What is utility? Define and briefly describe the four different types of utility.

2. Distinguish between production and manufacturing. In what ways does each of the following perform a production function?
   a. delicatessen
   b. dentist
   c. local transit system
   d. Tower Records music store

3. Why is production such an important business activity? In what ways does it create value for the company and its customers?

4. How does mass production work? What are its benefits and limitations? Describe a good or service that would lend itself well to mass production and one that would not lend itself well to mass production.

5. Briefly describe the four different production systems. Give an example of a good or service that is produced by each.

6. Distinguish between computer-aided design (CAD) and computer-aided manufacturing (CAM).

7. What are the three categories that provide advantages for the best locations for companies? How does each function provide its advantage?

8. What would be the best type of facility layout for each of the following:
   a. card shop
   b. chain of economy motels
   c. car wash
   d. accountant's office
   e. large auto dealer's service facility

9. Identify and briefly describe the five steps involved in production control.

10. What are the benefits of producing a quality product? Briefly describe the International Organization for Standardization (ISO).

Projects and Applications

1. Think of an industry in which most companies currently use the push method in their production planning. How would the industry change if all companies began to shift more toward production pull?

2. Imagine that you have been hired as a management consultant for one of the following types of service organizations to decide on an appropriate layout for its facility. Select one and sketch or describe the layout that you think would be best.
   a. chain of dry-cleaning outlets
   b. doctor's office
   c. small, elegant lakeside restaurant
   d. coffee house

3. Imagine that you have been hired as production manager for a snowboard manufacturer (or choose another type of

manufacturer that interests you). What type of inventory control would you recommend for your company? Write a brief memo explaining why.

4. Nissan and Hyundai have built new auto assembly plants in Mississippi and Alabama, respectively. What factors do you think Nissan and Hyundai considered when making their plant location decisions?

5. Suggest two or three ways in which each of the following firms could practice effective quality control:
   a. pharmaceuticals manufacturer
   b. miniature golf course
   c. Internet florist
   d. agricultural packing house

Experiential Exercise

Background: As discussed in this chapter and throughout the text, quality is vital in all areas of business. One measure of a product's quality is the feedback a company receives from its customers.

Directions: Complete the following items to learn how companies solicit customer feedback about their products.

Select three food or personal care products you've recently purchased and complete the following chart. If no feedback options are provided on the packaging, list "none" in the right column.

Item Number	Product Name	Customer Feedback Option(s)
1.		
2.		
3.		

NOTHING BUT NET

1. **Customer-driven production.** Lands' End offers a service that allows customers to order custom-tailored clothing. Visit the Lands' End Web site and click one of the "custom clothing" options. Write a brief report on how the custom clothing program works and the benefits to customers.

   http://www.landsend.com

2. **Robotics.** The Web site listed here publishes statistics on the use of robots in the production of goods and services. Visit the site and review the most recent report on robotics industry statistics. Prepare an oral report on the current state and trends in robotics.

   http://www.robotics.org/public/articles/
   articles.cfm?cat=201

3. **Six Sigma.** As mentioned in the chapter, several companies use a technique called Six Sigma to improve product quality. Visit the Web site listed here and prepare a report summarizing the Six Sigma technique. Include a brief description of how it works and its overall objective. Be sure to cite several examples of where it has been successfully implemented.

   http://www.sixsigmasystems.com

   Note: Internet Web addresses change frequently. If you do not find the exact sites listed, you may need to access the organization's or company's home page and search from there.

Case 11.1

IBM Abandons the Industry It Created

A few years ago, IBM announced that it is getting out of the business of manufacturing desktop personal computers, servers, and workstations. Desktop PCs and other products will still carry the "IBM" name but will actually be made by another company, Sanmina-SCI of San Jose, California. The firm purchased manufacturing facilities in the U.S., Mexico, and Scotland from IBM. Sanmina-SCI is one of the world's largest contract electronics manufacturers, and it already had a major presence in the PC business. The company builds several personal computer models under contract for Hewlett-Packard and circuit boards for a number of PC makers.

IBM's announcement that it was quitting the desktop PC business was not entirely unexpected but was still a turning point in the history of the personal computer industry. After all, the computer giant practically invented the PC industry when it introduced the IBM PC in 1981. It was the first desktop PC based on Intel chips and running the disk operating system (DOS). The IBM PC quickly became the industry standard. Today, around 95 percent of all PCs are direct descendants of the original IBM design.

While IBM created the PC industry, it later had a difficult time competing in it. Its dominance of the PC industry ended sometime in the late 1980s or early 1990s. When IBM decided to exit the desktop business, it had only about a 15 percent share of the desktop market.

Not only has IBM continually lost market share over the past decade, but it has also lost a lot of money. In real terms, PC prices fell sharply over the last 10 years. IBM wasn't able to match the low costs of market leader Dell. In 1999, the company all but abandoned the consumer market when it stopped selling its PCs in retail stores. It continued selling PCs to business customers—at a loss. IBM claimed that PCs were an essential product offering when selling computer-related services and large machines to business and other "enterprise" cus-

tomers. Unfortunately, September 11 and a recession led to a drop in PC sales and a new wave of price cuts. IBM finally gave up and announced that it was exiting the desktop PC business. At the same time, however, IBM said that it would continue manufacturing and selling its highly regarded, and profitable, ThinkPad line of notebook computers.

IBM's decision to abandon the desktop market reflects a debate raging in the PC industry. In the industry's never-ending quest to cut costs, most major PC makers are either outsourcing the manufacturing of PCs to firms such as Sanmina-SCI or trying to mimic the efficient, low inventory, build-to-order approach that has made Dell, Inc. so successful. It is unclear yet which route will ultimately work best.

QUESTIONS FOR CRITICAL THINKING

1. Why did IBM finally decide to abandon the desktop PC business? Why did it have such a difficult time competing against firms like Dell, Inc.? Some industry analysts believe that IBM should have exited the PC business many years ago, concentrating instead on computer services and the sale of larger, more expensive computer systems. Do you agree or disagree?

2. Why is it often cheaper for a company to outsource the manufacturing of a product, such as a PC, to other firms? What other types of products are commonly outsourced?

Sources: Tom Krazit, "Sanmina-SCI Will Build IBM eServer, IntelliStation," *ComputerWorld,* January 7, 2003, http://www.computerworld.com; Mark Berniker, "IBM Outsourcing to Solectron, Sanmina-SCI," *Internetnews.com,* January 7, 2003, http://www.internetnews.com; "IBM Signs Agreement with Sanmina-SCI to Manufacture Its NetVista Desktop PCs in U.S. and Europe," IBM press release, June 10, 2002, http://www.ibm.com; John Spooner, "IBM to Outsource Desktop Manufacturing," *CNET News,* http://www.cnet.com, June 10, 2002; William Bulkeley, "As PC Industry Slumps, IBM Hands Off Manufacturing of Desktops," *The Wall Street Journal,* January 9, 2002, p. B1.

Video Case 11.2

Cannondale Bicycle Corporation

This video case appears on page 613. A recently filmed video, designed to expand and highlight the written case, is available for class use by instructors.

Krispy Kreme: The Magic Is in the Doughnut

"Krispy Kreme is about yesterday, today, and tomorrow," declares the Krispy Kreme Web site, which goes on to promise to "create magic moments" for customers who try its sweet, airy confections. The delicious taste of hot doughnuts and the nostalgic ambience of Krispy Kreme stores all evoke the past, allow customers to savor the present and send them off refreshed for the future. So, while Krispy Kreme has struggled in recent months with slumping sales from the low-carb craze, investigations into its accounting practices, and problems from its rapid expansion, this airy glazed confection, this magic of the Krispy Kreme doughnut, is why this company has so many loyal fans.

Quality in every single doughnut that passes through the hot waterfall of glaze is vital to Krispy Kreme's success. "We focus on what we do and try to make sure that we execute and make the best coffee and doughnuts we can for the customer," says senior vice president of marketing Stan Parker. The company's production process, which follows strict standards throughout all its fran-

chises, ensures that quality. Although ingredients are purchased in bulk from the company, Krispy Kreme doughnuts are made fresh on site every day. In fact, that's part of the magical experience: customers can watch the process because the doughnut-making apparatus—also purchased from Krispy Kreme—is located right in the center of the store, behind a viewing window. Krispy Kreme recently unveiled a new "Hot Doughnut Machine" that fits smaller spaces and requires less direct labor, allowing the company to enter markets in such locations as airports and shopping malls. Industry watchers anticipate that this innovation will be central to the company's future growth. As the firm experiments with new offerings, including lower-sugar and lower-carbohydrate products, they must meet Krispy Kreme's high standards for taste. And the acquisition of Digital Java, a high-quality manufacturer and distributor of coffee and equipment, means that Krispy Kreme can also control the quality of its coffee offerings.

Krispy Kreme management holds the view that simply producing the highest-quality doughnuts and coffee isn't enough. The company's success is "a natural result of the growth and success of its people." So the corporate culture is emphasized from the moment Krispy Kreme employees are hired, as well as throughout their training and daily management. "We have a culture that builds on its heritage and thrives on its ability to develop a team of people who share a common goal," notes the Web site. "That goal is to make the best doughnut we can while providing our customers service that exceeds their expectations, all while having fun in the process." The company believes that one of the best ways to motivate employees is to create an environment in which each individual feels valued, is respected, understands the job and expectations, is well trained, and has an opportunity to advance. Krispy Kreme currently employs about 5,000 workers in a variety of positions, ranging from retail management to district/regional management, supervisory, and, of course, doughnut production.

Krispy Kreme offers its management trainees a comprehensive course called Management 101, which combines two weeks of training at company headquarters in Winston-Salem, North Carolina, with 12 weeks of on-the-job training at one of Krispy Kreme's Certified Training Stores. Additional training materials include videos, workbooks, and computer-based training. The computer-based component uses graphics, video, and animation and is available in Krispy Kreme stores or through trainees' home computers. The Management 101 program not only standardizes the quality of training but also helps preserve Krispy Kreme's corporate culture and core values. As new technology becomes available, Krispy Kreme brings its employees into the loop in order to empower them while enhancing efficiency. Recently, the firm launched a portal that gives store managers, vendors, and employees access to all kinds of company information and allows them to pick products and ingredients from the warehouse electronically. "Our store employees should focus on serving customers," explains Chief Information Officer (CIO) Frank Hood. "We don't want people shuffling paper or reading faxes." As part of the company's commitment to its employees, the firm offers a full range of traditional benefits, from medical and dental insurance to tuition reimbursement and scholarship programs—and a discount on those warm, light Krispy Kremes.

How does leadership play a role in a company whose organization may seem to be fragmented through franchises? Krispy Kreme CEO Scott Livengood believes in the talent and dedication of the entrepreneurs who are franchisees, noting that giving people opportunities to be innovative is a cornerstone of the company. Livengood loves to tell the story about the Tennessee franchisee who bought a window shade, printed the message "Hot Doughnuts Now" on it, and hung the shade in the window of his store. Whenever hot doughnuts came out of the doughnut maker, he'd pull down the shade so passing customers would know when the warm doughnuts were available. Today, the "Hot Doughnuts Now" sign is standard at all Krispy Kreme stores.

Franchising does have its risks, and not every franchise has succeeded. As some franchisees have decided to exit the business, Krispy Kreme has bought back the stores, triggering a challenge to some of its accounting practices. Sales have slowed somewhat, resulting in a huge decline in the market price of Krispy Kreme's common stock, but CEO Livengood has remained firm in his conviction that Krispy Kreme would emerge tasting as sweet as ever. "We have faced tougher situations and come out stronger than before," he has stated. "I personally have never been more engaged and energized by Krispy Kreme's opportunities."

As Krispy Kreme continues to expand—no doubt more slowly than it has in the last few years—top managers will no doubt be monitoring every move carefully. Krispy Kreme fans are as loyal as they ever were, even if they are following the nationwide trend toward lower calories and carbs. "When Krispy Kremes are hot, they are to other doughnuts what angels are to people," writes humorist Roy Blount Jr. In other words, biting into a soft, sweet Krispy Kreme is still pure magic.

QUESTIONS

1. Based on what you've read and seen about Krispy Kreme so far, write a mission statement for the company.

2. How would you describe the Krispy Kreme corporate culture? How do you think the culture will handle the challenges that lie ahead?

3. In what ways is the development of human resources critical to Krispy Kreme? How might slower growth affect this?

4. How does Krispy Kreme use its production process to enhance its relationship with consumers?

Sources: Krispy Kreme Web site, http://www.krispykreme.com, accessed January 10, 2005; George Talbot, "Not Hot Now: Krispy Kreme Down Again," *Mobile Register,* November 23, 2004, p. B6; Rick Brooks and Mark Maremont, "Sticky Situation," *The Wall Street Journal,* , September 3, 2004, pp. A1, A5; "Glazed Diet? Krispy Kreme Plans Low-Sugar Doughnut," *USA Today,* March 12, 2004, http://www.usatoday.com; Ian Mount, "Krispy Kreme's Secret Ingredient," *Business 2.0,* September 2003, p. 36.

Part 4
Marketing Management

Chapter 12
Customer-Driven Marketing

Learning Goals

1 Summarize the ways in which marketing creates utility.

2 Explain the marketing concept and relate how customer satisfaction contributes to added value.

3 Describe the components of a market and distinguish between B2B and B2C marketing.

4 Outline the basic steps in developing a marketing strategy.

5 Describe the marketing research function.

6 Identify each of the methods available for segmenting consumer and business markets.

7 Distinguish between buyer behavior and consumer behavior.

8 Discuss the benefits of relationship marketing.

Customers to Companies: "Bring Home the Service!"

The strategy at first seemed to be brilliant: reduce the costs of customer service activities by moving them overseas to countries where wages are typically lower than in the U.S. Since customer service doesn't directly generate revenues, firms often look for ways to lower its associated expenses. Overseas

workers could be trained to answer customers' questions in shifts around the clock, the reasoning went, and no one would necessarily care where they were located. Dell Inc. was one of the first U.S. firms to move its call centers to India. "We put [local hires] through eight weeks of training—four weeks around accent and culture and another four weeks around Dell products," says M. D. Ramaswami, who helped set up Dell's Bangalore call center. "The biggest challenge was working on the accent and culture."

That challenge—among many others—remains. It seems that business customers and individual consumers were less than happy with the service they were receiving. They were frustrated when call center employees were unable to depart from a written script and could not solve individual problems. Within two years, customer complaints had tripled. Dell has since rerouted its large- and medium-business customer support back to Austin, Texas. But customer service operations for small businesses and consumers remain in India. During one recent year, the Internet firm Web.com decided to try moving its customer service function to India as well. Within months, as complaints and cultural misunderstandings skyrocketed, CEO Will Pemble pulled the whole department back to Connecticut. Pemble decided that outsourcing customer service was going to cost the company more in mistakes and lost customers than it would to pay U.S. workers the higher wages and benefits. GE had

© Sondeep Shankar/Bloomberg News/Landov

a similar experience. After several years of running its customer service department from a call center in India, the firm moved everything back to Phoenix when it learned that overseas workers simply couldn't relate to customers because they didn't own many appliances themselves. GE decided that U.S. workers were better equipped to answer questions from U.S. consumers.

Martin Kenney, a professor at University of California-Davis, is not surprised by these results. "Firms that just believe that this is going to be simple . . . very often get burned," he warns. "This is a very, very complicated business activity, and there are a thousand ways it can go wrong." In addition to miscommunication, legislators worry that in the health-care and financial industries, private information about customers could be compromised—and firms in these industries are under growing pressure to guarantee privacy. But this doesn't mean that customer service outsourcing is a disappearing fad; in fact, in some cases, outsourcing makes sense. But firms need to fine-tune their approach. "If it's a binary decision process—yes or no—then you should consider outsourcing," says Web.com's Will Pemble. "But if there's a maybe in there anywhere, then you can be sure all your customer-support difficulties will gravitate to that like iron filings to a magnet." Other experts advise that companies start small with a pilot program, gradually ironing out the kinks. Firms should determine exactly which tasks would be best moved overseas, then manage those functions tightly.

Between outsourcing call centers to Asian and European companies and relying on domestic companies, firms have a third option: *nearshoring.* Airline companies have begun nearshoring, which means routing calls to Canada. Companies are finding other ways to improve the performance of overseas call centers. Dell recently launched "Voice of the Customer," a program designed to make it easier to reach someone who is knowledgeable and fix problems more quickly. In the business environment, as boundaries surrounding countries continue to fade, firms will find new ways to connect their customer service with their customers.[1]

Chapter Overview

Business success in the 21st century is directly tied to a company's ability to identify and serve its target markets. In fact, all organizations—profit-oriented and not-for-profit, manufacturing and retailing—*must* serve customer needs to succeed, just as the companies described in the opening vignette are attempting to do. Marketing is the link between the organization and the people who buy and use its goods and services. It is the way organizations determine buyer needs and inform potential customers that their firms can meet those needs by supplying a quality product at a reasonable price. And it is the path to developing loyal, long-term customers.

Although final consumers who purchase goods for their own use and enjoyment or business purchasers seeking products to use in their firm's operation may seem to be massive, formless markets, marketers see different wants and needs for each group. To understand buyers, from huge manufacturers to Web surfers to shoppers in the grocery aisles, companies are gathering mountains of data on every aspect of lifestyles and buying behaviors. Marketers use the data to understand the needs and wants of both final customers and business buyers so that they can better satisfy them.

This chapter begins with an examination of the marketing concept and the way businesspeople develop a marketing strategy. We then turn to marketing research techniques, leading to an explanation of how businesses apply marketing research data to market segmentation and understanding customer behavior. The chapter closes with a detailed look at the important role played by customer relationships in today's highly competitive business world.

What Is Marketing?

marketing process of planning and executing the conception, distribution, promotion, and pricing of ideas, goods, services, organizations, and events to create and maintain relationships that satisfy individual and organizational objectives.

Every organization—from profit-seeking firms like BestBuy and Coach to such not-for-profits as Easter Seals and Make-A-Wish—must serve customer needs to succeed. Perhaps retail pioneer J. C. Penney best expressed this priority when he told his store managers, "Either you or your replacement will greet the customer within the first 60 seconds."

Marketing is the process of determining customer wants and needs and then providing the goods and services that meet or exceed expectations. In addition to selling goods and services, marketing techniques help people to advocate ideas or viewpoints and to educate others. The American Diabetes Association mails out questionnaires that ask, "Are you at risk for diabetes?" The documents help educate the general public about this widespread disease by listing its risk factors and common symptoms and describing the work of the association.

Department store founder Marshall Field explained marketing quite clearly when he advised one employee to "give the lady what she wants." The phrase became the company motto, and it remains a business truism that reflects the importance of a customer orientation to an organization. This orientation may permit marketers to respond to customer wants that the customers themselves have not yet identified. Moretti Polegato, founder of an Italian shoe company called Geox, identified a need for shoes that increase comfort by keeping feet dry. He developed a sole made of perforated rubber that allows air to circulate, combined with a membrane inside the sole to keep water out. Geox shoes, which combine this modern technology with sophisticated Italian design, are available at shops in Europe, North and South America, Asia, Australia, and South Africa. Geox informs customers about its products with a message that emphasizes the shoes' high-tech soles.[2]

Courtesy of WM. WRIGLEY JR. COMPANY. Photographer Darran Rees—Doug Brown, Agent.

FIGURE 12.1
The Exchange Process

As these examples illustrate, marketing is more than just selling. It is a process that begins with discovering unmet customer needs and continues with researching the potential market; producing a good or service capable of satisfying the targeted customers; and promoting, pricing, and distributing that good or service. Throughout the entire marketing process, a successful organization focuses on building customer relationships.

When two or more parties benefit from trading things of value, they have entered into an **exchange process.** If you decide to purchase the pack of Wrigley's Spearmint gum shown in Figure 12.1, you will engage in an exchange process. The other party may be a convenience food store clerk, a person operating the checkout counter at your local supermarket, a gas station attendant, or even a surrogate human in the form of a vending machine. In exchange for a few coins paid to the retail employee or inserted in the vending machine, you receive the gum. But the exchange process is more complex than that; it could not occur if Wrigley's did not market its product and if you were not aware of it and did not have the coins required to purchase it. Because of marketing, your need for a certain flavor—and brand—of gum is satisfied, and the manufacturer's business is successful. This example suggests how marketing can contribute to the continuing improvement of a society's overall standard of living.

How Marketing Creates Utility

Marketing is a complex activity that affects many aspects of an organization and its dealings with customers. The ability of a good or service to satisfy the wants and needs of customers is called **utility.** A company's production function creates *form utility* by converting raw materials, component parts, and other inputs into finished goods and services. But the marketing function creates time, place, and ownership utility. **Time utility** is created by making a good or service available when customers want to purchase it. **Place utility** is created by making a product available in a location convenient for customers. **Ownership utility** refers to an orderly transfer of goods and services from the seller to the buyer. Starbucks, which creates form utility by converting coffee plants into coffee beans and ground coffee, attempts to create time, place, and ownership utility by offering its gourmet coffee beans in selected

utility want-satisfying power of a good or service.

grocery stores. The upscale coffee marketer creates time utility by offering the coffee beans in a store where consumers can make their purchase while grocery shopping; place utility by offering them in a convenient location that consumers visit anyway; and ownership utility by making the transaction between consumer and seller a smooth, simple one. And there's an extra bonus: once consumers get the coffee beans home, they don't have to make an extra trip outside each time they want a cup of Starbucks coffee.

Concept Check

1. What is the exchange process?
2. What is utility?

Evolution of the Marketing Concept

Marketing has always been a part of business, from the earliest village traders to large 21st-century organizations producing and selling complex goods and services. Over time, however, marketing activities evolved through the four eras shown in Figure 12.2: the production, sales, and marketing eras, and now the relationship era. Note that these eras parallel some of the business eras discussed in Chapter 1.

For centuries, organizations of the *production era* stressed efficiency in producing quality products. Their philosophy could be summed up by the remark, "A good product will sell itself." Although this production orientation continued into the 20th century, it gradually gave way to the *sales era,* in which businesses assumed that consumers would buy as a result of energetic sales efforts. Organizations didn't fully recognize the importance of their customers until the *marketing era* of the 1950s, when they began to adopt a consumer orientation. This focus has intensified in recent years, leading to the emergence of the *relationship era* in the 1990s, which continues to this day. In the relationship era, companies emphasize customer satisfaction and building long-term relationships with customers.

marketing concept
companywide consumer orientation to promote long-run success.

Emergence of the Marketing Concept

The term **marketing concept** refers to a companywide customer orientation with the objective of achieving long-run success. The basic idea of the marketing concept is that marketplace success begins with the customer. In other words, a firm should analyze each customer's needs and then work backward to offer products that fulfill them. The emergence of the marketing concept can be explained best by the shift from a *seller's market*—one with a shortage of goods and services—to a *buyer's market*—one with an abundance of goods and services. During the 1950s, the U.S. became a strong buyer's market, forcing companies to satisfy customers rather than just producing and selling goods and services.

FIGURE 12.2
Four Eras in the History of Marketing

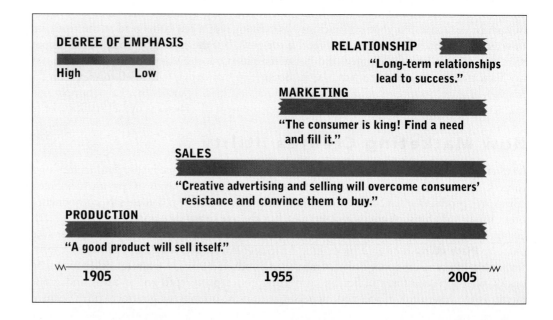

DEGREE OF EMPHASIS
High   Low

RELATIONSHIP
"Long-term relationships lead to success."

MARKETING
"The consumer is king! Find a need and fill it."

SALES
"Creative advertising and selling will overcome consumers' resistance and convince them to buy."

PRODUCTION
"A good product will sell itself."

1905   1955   2005

Delivering Added Value through Customer Satisfaction and Quality

What is the most important sale for a company? Some assume that it's the first, but many marketers argue that the second sale is the most important, since repeat purchases are concrete evidence of **customer satisfaction.** The concept of a good or service pleasing buyers because it has met or exceeded their needs and expectations is crucial to an organization's continued operation. A company that fails to match the customer satisfaction that its competitors provide will not stay in business for very long. In contrast, increasing customer loyalty by just 5 percent translates into significant increases in lifetime profits per customer. In the wake of unsettling times in the telecommunications industry, BellSouth set out to distinguish itself from competitors MCI and Qwest by launching a marketing campaign aimed at placing customer satisfaction first. "Listening. Answering" was the advertising slogan, as BellSouth described the kinds of services that real customers had requested—and that BellSouth was offering. Steve Centrillo, executive vice president and managing partner at BellSouth's advertising agency, dark-Grey, noted that the customer-first approach differed from those of BellSouth's largest rivals. "Usually I get the sense that [telcos] are saying, 'You should buy this because we have it,'" he explained. Bell-South, on the other hand, made an effort to find out what its customers wanted and tries to give it to them.[3]

> **customer satisfaction**
> result of a good or service meeting or exceeding the buyer's needs and expectations.

The best way to keep a customer is to offer more than just products. Customers today want value, their perception that the quality of goods or services is in balance with the prices charged. When a company exceeds value expectations by adding features, lowering its price, enhancing customer service, or making other improvements that increase customer satisfaction, it provides a **value-added** good or service. As long as customers believe they have received value—good quality for a fair price—they are likely to remain satisfied with the company and continue their relationships. Providing superior customer service can generate long-term success. FedEx, United Parcel Service, Hewlett-Packard, and Target are all firms noted for superior customer service. "When a company provides great service, its reputation benefits from a stronger emotional connection with its customers, as well as from increased confidence that it will stand behind its products," notes Joy Sever, a senior vice president at Harris Interactive Inc., which developed a survey of companies with the Reputation Institute.[4] Table 12.1 shows the 30 top-ranked companies for customer service in the annual Harris Interactive and Reputation Institute survey.

Table 12.1   The Top 30 Companies for Customer Service

Rank	Company	Rank	Company	Rank	Company
1	Johnson & Johnson	11	Disney	21	Target
2	Microsoft	12	General Electric	22	Honda
3	Coca-Cola	13	Dell	23	Boeing
4	Intel	14	Procter & Gamble	24	Southwest Airlines
5	3M	15	UPS	25	General Motors
6	Sony	16	Anheuser-Busch	26	Pfizer
7	Hewlett-Packard	17	Wal-Mart	27	Nordstrom
8	FedEx	18	Toyota	28	DuPont
9	Maytag	19	Home Depot	29	Merck
10	IBM	20	Cisco Systems	30	Nike

Source: Ronald Alsop, "Reputations Rest on Good Service," *The Wall Street Journal,* January 16, 2002, p. B4.

BUSINESS TOOL KIT

The Value of Customer Service

You read about it everywhere—customer service is king. But what exactly constitutes good customer service and how do you go about providing it? *Customer service* can be defined as providing the needed goods or services to the customer in an efficient manner. Good customer service goes beyond that, though; it involves doing it right the first time, communicating well, making on-time deliveries, responding to individual customer needs, and providing customers with knowledge. Customer service means being a team player in developing the appropriate goods and services. Here are three important principles to remember about customer service.

1. **Customer service is about establishing relationships.** Any store can offer a good deal on pricing to get customers in the door. Superior customer service means going beyond the price tag to establish an ongoing relationship with the customer. Some online companies do this by maintaining e-mail communications throughout the buying process. Other companies remember a customer's birthday and provide discount coupons as a gift. Amazon.com tracks customers' purchases and makes recommendations based on those purchases.

2. **Meet or exceed your customers' expectations.** Soliciting customer feedback, offering additional incentives for customers to return, and hosting special events or programs are a few ways to meet and exceed your customers' expectations. Competing on price alone is a very short-term strategy. To gain repeat customers, companies need to provide incentives that appeal to their customers' needs. Delta Air Lines now provides self-service check-in kiosks, virtual check-in via its Web site, and electronic gate-information screens to shorten the wait at the airport.

3. **Providing knowledge can be more valuable to customers than price savings.** The increased popularity of home improvement warehouses has demonstrated this principle. Businesses such as Lowe's or Home Depot don't just sell plumbing fixtures or tools; they sell knowledge, workshops, and expertise for every question the novice may have. Having your questions answered by a professional every time is great customer service.

Sources: Rob Hof with Peter Burrows, "Meet EBay's Auctioneer-in-Chief: Meg Whitman Has Taken the Site to the Top of the Net Heap by Listening to Customers—and Getting to Know the Selling Process from the Inside," *Business Week Online*, June 12, 2003; Terry G. Vavra, "The Advantages of Aftermarketing," *American Salesman*, June 2003, p. 24; Taimi Dunn Gorman, "Reality: Customers Are More Demanding Than Ever," *Bellingham Business Journal*, May 2003, p. B16; "Delta Air Lines Wins the Brand Keys Customer Loyalty Award for the Second Consecutive Year; Customer Poll Recognizes Delta for Exceeding Customer Expectations," *M2 Presswire*, July 1, 2002, p. 1.

They Said It

A sign at Dell headquarters reads "Think Customer." A full 90 percent of employees deal directly with customers. What are the universal attributes of the Dell brand? Customer advocacy.

—*Mike George*
chief marketing officer, Dell, Inc.

Quality—the degree of excellence or superiority of an organization's goods and services—is another way firms enhance customer satisfaction. Germany has long been associated with top-quality auto manufacturing, from luxury cars made by Mercedes-Benz to well-engineered workhorses produced by Volkswagen. These companies recently launched ultraluxury models with price tags of more than $300,000. Spokespeople for the firms note that they aren't worried about making a profit on these autos; rather, they are seeking to reinforce their reputation for superior quality.[5] While a reputation for high quality enhances a firm's competitiveness, a slip in quality can damage a firm's image. In addition to inroads made by competitors, McDonald's has suffered from quality slips in the past few years, despite its rank as the most recognizable corporate logo and one of the most socially responsible companies in the world. And the complaints haven't consisted solely of the drive-thru customer complaints of incorrect orders. A customer from upstate New York recently discovered his Big Mac was burgerless, just one of several service mishaps he experienced at his local McDonald's. "It's gotten so bad that we have to double check the bags before leaving the restaurant," he said.[6]

Courtesy of Hewlett Packard

Customer satisfaction is the goal of every marketing effort. It may be achieved through quality, customer service, or both.

Although quality relates to physical product traits, such as durability and reliability, it also includes customer service. A Boston-headquartered concierge service called Circles seeks to provide a level of service that makes the company indispensable, whether customers need help making restaurant reservations or, in one case, hunting for a circular staircase to fit a dollhouse. After receiving permission from its customers, Circles gathers as much data about its frequent purchasers as it can, from the types of car they drive to the food they eat for dinner. When a customer calls, employees can look up the data to help them tailor their services to individual tastes.[7]

Customer Satisfaction and Feedback

Successful companies share an important characteristic: They make every effort to ensure the satisfaction of their customers. Customer satisfaction is critical for building long-lasting relationships. One of the best ways to find out whether customers are satisfied with the goods and services provided by a company is to obtain *customer feedback* through toll-free telephone hot lines, customer satisfaction surveys, Web site message boards, or written correspondence. Some firms find out how well they have satisfied their customers by calling them or making personal visits to their businesses or residences.

Customer complaints are excellent sources of customer feedback, since they present companies with an opportunity to overcome problems and improve their services. Customers often feel greater loyalty after a conflict has been resolved than if they had never complained at all. Complaints can also allow firms to gather innovative ideas for improvement.

> *They Said It*
>
> We view a customer who is complaining as a real blessing in disguise. He or she is someone we can resell.
>
> —*Louis Carbone*
> *vice president, National Car Rental*

Concept Check

1. How does the relationship era of marketing differ from the sales era?
2. Why is customer satisfaction important to businesses?

Expanding Marketing's Traditional Boundaries

The marketing concept has traditionally been associated with products of profit-seeking organizations. Today, however, it is also being applied to not-for-profit sectors and other nontraditional areas ranging from religious organizations to political campaigns.

Not-for-Profit Marketing

Residents of every continent benefit in various ways from the approximately 20 million not-for-profit organizations currently operating around the globe. Some 1.5 million of them are located in the U.S., generating combined revenues of $1 trillion per year and all sharing a common bottom line—the lives they are able to change through their good works.[8] The largest not-for-profit organization in the world is the Red Cross/Red Crescent, but a multitude of others offer services for their members and clients. They range from the Salvation Army, Appalachian Mountain Club, Childreach, the Museum of Natural History, and the Audubon Society to Yellowstone National Park, the National Science Foundation, and the World Food Program. These organizations all benefit by applying many of the strategies and business concepts used by profit-seeking firms. They apply marketing tools to reach audiences, secure funding, improve their images, and accomplish their overall missions. Note the advertisement for the American Kennel Club (AKC) in Figure 12.3, which supplies a Web address where dog lovers can learn more about breeds, receive advice on how to choose a dog, get a schedule of AKC events, be informed about legislative issues—and, of course, join an AKC-affiliated club.

Marketing strategies are important for not-for-profit organizations because they are all competing for dollars—from individuals, foundations, and corporations—just as commercial businesses are. In the U.S., more than $200 billion is donated to not-for-profits each year. Religious causes and organizations receive the biggest share of the contributions, averaging about two of every five dollars donated to not-for-profits. Health and social services organizations rank second, receiving almost one in five dollars contributed. The other three organizations in the top five are, in order, education, gifts to foundations, and contributions to the arts.[9]

Not-for-profit organizations operate in both public and private sectors. Public groups include federal, state, and local government units as well as agencies that receive tax funding. A state's department of natural resources, for instance, regulates land conservation and environmental programs; the local animal-control officer enforces ordinances protecting people and animals; a city's public health board ensures safe drinking water for its citizens. The private not-for-profit sector comprises many different types of organizations, including labor unions, hospitals, California State University–Fullerton's baseball team, art museums, and local youth organizations. Although some private not-for-profits generate surplus revenue, their primary goals are not earning profits. If they earn funds beyond their expenses, they invest the excess in their organizational missions.

In some cases, not-for-profit organizations form a partnership with a profit-seeking company to promote the firm's message or distribute its goods and services. This partnership usually benefits both organizations. Figure 12.4 illustrates Toyota's partnership with the Kids Foundation for Developmental Disabilities, in which Toy-

FIGURE 12.3
Not-for-Profit Marketing

Courtesy of the American Kennel Club, http://www.akc.org. Photographer—David Radler

ota sponsors local "hole in one" golf tournaments to raise money for the foundation.

Nontraditional Marketing

Growth in the number of not-for-profit organizations has forced their executives to adopt business-like strategies and tactics to reach diverse audiences and successfully compete with other nontraditional organizations. Figure 12.5 summarizes the five major categories of nontraditional marketing. Although most involve not-for-profit organizations, profit-seeking organizations conduct special events like FanFests linked with major sporting events and person marketing involving celebrities.

Person Marketing   Efforts designed to attract the attention, interest, and preference of a target market toward a person are called **person marketing.** Campaign managers for a political candidate conduct marketing research, identify groups of voters and financial supporters, and then design advertising campaigns, fund-raising events, and political rallies to reach them. Celebrities ranging from Yankees third baseman Alex Rodriguez—arguably baseball's best player—to Grammy-winning songstress Norah Jones and rapper Eminem also engage in person marketing to expand their audiences; improve sales of tickets to games and concerts, books, licensed merchandise, and CDs; and enhance their images among fans.

Many successful job seekers apply the tools of person marketing. They research the wants and needs of prospective employers, and they identify ways they can meet them. They seek employers through a variety of channels, sending messages that emphasize how they can benefit the employer.

Place Marketing   As the term suggests, **place marketing** attempts to attract people to a particular area, such as a city,

FIGURE 12.4
Toyota Dealerships and The Kids Foundation for Developmental Disabilities: Partnership between Profit and Not-for-Profit Organizations

FIGURE 12.5
Categories of Nontraditional Marketing

HITS & MISSES

Home Retailers Focus on the Hispanic Market

It's official: According to the U.S. Census Bureau, Hispanic Americans are the largest minority group in the U.S., now making up 13 percent of the nation's population. Smart businesspeople are aware of this fact and are zeroing in on the market. Spanish television and radio broadcasts, ranging from news to NBA games, are already commonplace. Time Inc. launched its publication *People en Español* several years ago, and marketers of everything from automobiles to groceries are making huge efforts to attract Hispanic consumers as their purchasing power increases. However, it is important for businesses to beware of pitfalls. "The Hispanic community is made up of very different racial groups," warns Hilary Shelton of the NAACP. Within the Hispanic population are variations in language, food preferences, and traditions to which business owners must be sensitive.

Since Hispanic Americans now represent 13 percent of first-time U.S. home buyers, major home-product retailers—including IKEA, Lowe's, and The Home Depot—are focused on turning Hispanic consumers into loyal customers. Swedish furniture retailer IKEA has hired Anita Santiago Advertising, an agency specializing in the Hispanic market, to create the right message. "This is a real first step, getting into those markets to figure out a way to communicate," says Rich D'Amico of IKEA. The firm plans to work

such cultural practices as multigenerational living into its marketing efforts and to issue a Spanish version of its catalog soon. Lowe's has launched a multicultural advertising effort as well, while The Home Depot is placing bilingual signs and Spanish-speaking salespeople at key stores. "The U.S. has clearly become a multicultural country, and we're committed to meeting the needs of all our customers," notes John Costello of The Home Depot. Although most of the Hispanic marketing programs are based in California, where the concentration of population is the greatest, all three retailers see nationwide, targeted marketing efforts coming soon.

QUESTIONS FOR CRITICAL THINKING

1. What steps might these three retailers take to avoid the pitfalls of stereotyping and misunderstanding the Hispanic American market?

2. What additional steps might these retailers take to attract Hispanic American consumers to their stores?

Sources: "Past, Present, Future," *Hispanic Business,* June 2004, pp. 26–36; Mercedes M. Cardona, "Home Chains Focus on Hispanic Market," *Advertising Age,* March 22, 2004, p. 6; Haya el Nasser, "39 Million Make Hispanics Largest U.S. Minority Group," *USA Today,* June 18, 2003, www.usatoday.com.

---

state, or nation. It may involve appealing to consumers as a tourist destination or to businesses as a desirable business location. A strategy for place marketing often includes advertising.

Event Marketing   Marketing or sponsoring short-term events such as athletic competitions and cultural and charitable performances is known as **event marketing.** Event marketing often forges partnerships between not-for-profit and profit-seeking organizations. Many businesses sponsor fund-raising events like 10K runs to raise funds for health-related charities. These events require a marketing effort to plan the event and attract participants and sponsors. Fund-raising concerts, including singer Willie Nelson's annual Farm Aid concert, are another example of event marketing. Organizations also might combine event marketing and place marketing.

Cause Marketing   Marketing that promotes a cause or social issue, such as the prevention of child abuse, antilittering efforts, and antismoking campaigns, is **cause marketing.** Special fund-raising programs for charities and causes range from the annual Jerry Lewis Labor Day Telethon for the Muscular Dystrophy Association to the American Red Cross's "Fit for Life" relay races. Profit-seeking companies attempting to enhance their public images often join forces with charities and causes, providing financial, marketing, and human resources, as Toyota does with the Kids Foundation for Developmental Disabilities. The National Football League builds goodwill by airing advertisements for the United Way during its broadcasts and by encouraging its teams to support causes in their local communities. The San Diego Chargers have adopted Children's Hospital as the focus of their community. They also sponsor a blood drive considered to be the nation's largest. Similarly, well-known entertainers and individual athletes in various professional sports volunteer as banquet speakers and play in celebrity golf tournaments. The classic approach to a cause-related promotion ties a donation to a consumer purchase, such as a company's promise to donate $1 for each item it sells.

Organization Marketing   The final category of nontraditional marketing, **organization marketing,** influences consumers to accept the goals of, receive the services of, or contribute in some way to an organization. Many groups employ this practice, including mutual-benefit organizations like political groups, churches, and labor unions; service organizations such as community colleges, museums, and hospitals; and government organizations like police and fire departments, military services, and the U.S. National Park Service. Many charitable organizations mail greeting cards with donation requests enclosed to raise awareness of their groups and explain their objectives.

Concept Check

1. Why are marketing strategies and marketing tools used by not-for-profit organizations as well as by profit-seeking businesses?
2. What type of marketing do political candidates usually engage in?

Developing a Marketing Strategy

Decision makers in any successful organization, for-profit or not-for-profit, follow a two-step process to develop a *marketing strategy.* First, they study and analyze potential target markets (see the Hits & Misses box) and then choose among them. Second, they create a marketing mix to satisfy the chosen market. Figure 12.6 shows the relationship among the target market, the marketing mix variables, and the marketing environment. Later discussions will refer back to this figure as they cover each topic. This section describes the development of a marketing strategy.

Earlier chapters introduced many of the environmental factors that affect the success or failure of a firm's business strategy, including today's rapidly changing and highly competitive world of business, a vast array of social-cultural factors, economic challenges, political and legal factors, and technological innovations. Although these external forces frequently operate outside managers' control, marketers must still consider the impact of environmental factors on their decisions.

A marketing plan is a key component of the firm's overall business plan. The marketing plan outlines its marketing strategy and includes information about the target market, sales and revenue goals, the marketing budget, and the timing for implementing the elements of the marketing mix.

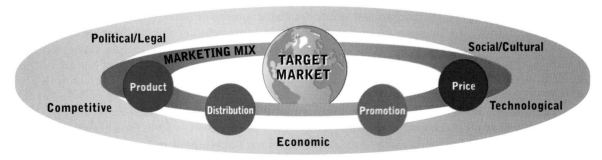

FIGURE 12.6

Target Market and Marketing Mix within the Marketing Environment

Selecting a Target Market

The expression "find a need and fill it" is perhaps the simplest explanation of the two elements of a marketing strategy. A firm's marketers find a need through careful and continuing study of the individuals and business decision makers in its potential market. A market consists of people with purchasing power, willingness to buy, and authority to make purchase decisions.

Markets can be classified by type of product. **Consumer products**—often known as business-to-consumer (B2C) products—are goods and services, such as DVDs, shampoo, and dental care, that are purchased by end users. **Business products**—or business-to-business (B2B) products—are goods and services purchased to be used, either directly or indirectly, in the production of other goods for resale. Some products can fit either classification depending on who buys them and why. A computer or checking account, for example, can be either a consumer or business product.

target market group of people toward whom an organization markets its goods, services, or ideas with a strategy designed to satisfy their specific needs and preferences.

An organization's **target market** is the group of potential customers toward whom it directs its marketing efforts. Customer needs and wants vary considerably, and no single organization has the resources to satisfy everyone. Music Playground is a music technology and entertainment company geared toward rock-star wannabes. With the company's technology, a musician can take a step beyond karaoke and become a "virtual guitarist, drummer, bassist, or form virtual bands with other players." Music Playground's system is often featured in pubs, restaurants, at outdoor events, and anywhere else music lovers who want to try performing might gather.[10]

Developing a Marketing Mix

Decisions about marketing involve strategies for four areas of marketing activity: product, distribution, promotion, and pricing. A firm's **marketing mix** blends the four strategies to fit the needs and preferences of a specific target market. Marketing success depends not on the four individual strategies but on their unique combination.

marketing mix blending the four elements of marketing strategy—product, distribution, promotion, and price—to satisfy chosen customer segments.

Product strategy involves more than just designing a good or service with needed attributes. It also includes decisions about package design, a brand name, trademarks, warranties, product image, new-product development, and customer service. Think, for instance, about your favorite fruit drink. Do you like it for its taste alone, or do other attributes, such as clever ads, attractive packaging, and overall image, also contribute to your brand preference? *Distribution strategy*, the second marketing mix variable, ensures that customers receive their purchases in the proper quantities at the right times and locations. *Promotional strategy*, the third marketing mix element, utilizes effective blending of advertising, personal selling, sales promotion, and public relations in achieving its goals of informing, persuading, and influencing purchase decisions.

Pricing strategy, the final mix element, is also one of the most difficult areas of marketing decision making in setting profitable and justifiable prices for the firm's product offerings. Such actions are sometimes subject to government regulation and considerable public scrutiny. They also represent a powerful competitive weapon and frequently produce responses by the other firms in the industry who match price changes to avoid losing customers.

Consider how the elements of the marketing mix allow one California firm to reach its target market. Mrs. Beasley's is a bakery business whose marketing strategy includes premium quality and prices to match, coupled with highly targeted promotion and convenient distribution. Mrs. Beasley's started as two sisters' home-based business in Tarzana, California. The women chose the name to sound homey, and they set high quality standards, insisting on top ingredients and plenty of human touches, like placing M&Ms on cookies by hand. Even though they built the business into a chain of stores with $2 million in sales, they were unable to turn a profit, so they sold it to another company. The new management then modified several elements to convert Mrs. Beasley's into a profitable marketing operation.

Mrs. Beasley's continues offering top quality at top prices—$30 to $200 for a basket of goodies. Instead of relying on advertising to reach individual consumers, marketers now focus on building relationships with corporate buyers who order gift baskets for their clients. Mrs. Beasley's places links to its Web site at sites such as 1-800-Flowers.com and Staples.com, where business buyers often are already making purchases. These sites provide the links in exchange for a share of Mrs. Beasley's sales generated through the links. The company also arranges links to its site from corporate intranets, offering discounts to employees at companies including Time Warner and Barnes & Noble.

Although corporate customers account for the biggest bite of Mrs. Beasley's total business, individual consumers can also find tasty treats at the company Web site, which offers a wide selection of gifts, wedding cakes, photo cookies, and gift baskets. Customers can order gifts by occasion—to say thank you, get well, congratulations on a new baby, welcome home, happy birthday, even I'm sorry. Particularly contrite individuals might want to send a basket of cookies with an FAO Schwarz teddy bear. Brides and grooms can order their wedding cake at Mrs. Beasley's, and the budget minded can shop the entire site according to price. Meanwhile, corporate customers can conveniently place multiple orders, sending orders to as many as 500 recipients. To back up the site, Mrs. Beasley's operates a call center located at its factory and uses an automated order-processing system to fill orders accurately and get them out the door on schedule.[11]

Developing a Marketing Mix for International Markets

Marketing a good or service in foreign markets means deciding whether to offer the same marketing mix in every market—*standardization*—or to develop a unique mix to fit each market—*adaptation*. The advantages of standardizing the marketing mix include reliable marketing performance and low costs. This approach works best with business goods, such as steel, chemicals, and aircraft, with little sensitivity to a nation's culture.

Adaptation, on the other hand, lets marketers vary their marketing mix to suit local competitive conditions, consumer preferences, and government regulations. Consumer tastes are often shaped by local cultures. Because consumer products generally tend to be more culture dependent than business products, they more often require adaptation. Nestlé S.A. is truly a global corporation, operating in dozens of countries as diverse as Australia, Argentina, Germany, China, South Africa, and Thailand. The company produces hundreds of food products, including baby foods, dairy goods, breakfast cereals, ice cream, bottled water, and chocolate products. Sometimes the products themselves are adapted for particular cultures; other times the packaging or advertising is adapted.[12] The advertisement for Nestlé's La Lechera in Figure 12.7 promotes a familiar product—condensed milk—adapted for U.S. Spanish-speaking consumers.

Increasingly, marketers are trying to build adaptability into the designs of standardized goods and services for international and domestic markets. Mass customization allows a firm to mass-produce goods and services while adding unique features to individual orders. This technique seeks to retain enough flexibility to satisfy a wide segment of the population without losing a product's identity and brand awareness. Oshkosh Truck Corp. applies mass customization to the business of making and marketing its construction, fire, and emergency trucks. Buyers of fire trucks can choose from among 19,000 options such as compartments, ladders, and foam systems for hard-to-extinguish fires. Buyers of concrete mixers can select options like the placement of the discharge

FIGURE 12.7
Adapting to a Spanish-Speaking Market

This advertisement reprinted by permission of Nestlé.

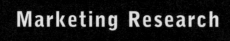

BUSINESS TOOL KIT

Marketing Research

Marketing research plays a valuable role in the development and marketing of goods and services. It focuses on understanding customers and their buying habits, and consists of both primary and secondary research. Primary research is research that doesn't exist yet—professional marketing research firms are often used to gather and analyze this data once an objective has been formulated by an organization. Here are a few common sources of secondary research that may be helpful to you in your marketing career.

- Federal, state, and local government agencies and publications
- Competitors' annual reports
- Competitors' employment ads
- Professional associations
- Newspaper, magazine, and journal reports
- Existing marketing research available online or in libraries

- Online marketing research databases such as Dialog/DataStar, Factiva, and LexisNexis
- Trade journals, associations, and trade fairs
- Public exhibitions, conferences, or seminars (search for published reports or papers)
- Statistics from nongovernmental organizations
- Trade literature, brochures, and newsletters
- Trade and industry publications
- Census and statistical information
- Industry directories and databases
- Internet sites of companies and organizations

Sources: Judy Guido, "Relief Is Spelled R-E-S-E-A-R-C-H: The Benefits of Market Research," *Landscape Management,* June 2003, p. 11; Sylvia James, "Compiling Global Market Research: A Tried and True Approach," *Business Information Alert,* April 2003, p. 1; Kate Maddox, "Marketers Re-Evaluate Research; Expensive Methods Such as Surveying Are First to Go," *B to B,* February 10, 2003, p. 1.

They Said It

We are all internationalists now, whether we like it or not.

—*Tony Blair (b. 1953)*
British prime minister

Concept Check

1. *Distinguish between consumer products and business products.*
2. *Define marketing mix.*
3. *What are the two methods for designing a marketing mix for international markets?*

marketing research
collection and use of information to support marketing decision making.

chute from which the concrete pours. By catering to customer needs, Oshkosh has tripled sales at a time when the industry as a whole has been slowing.[13]

Marketing Research for Improved Marketing Decisions

Marketing research involves more than just collecting data. Researchers must decide how to collect the data, interpret the results, convert the data into decision-oriented information, and communicate those results to managers for use in decision making. **Marketing research** is the process of collecting and evaluating information to help marketers make effective decisions. It links marketing decision makers to the marketplace by providing data about potential target markets that help them design effective marketing mixes. Marketers conduct research for five basic reasons:

1. To identify marketing problems and opportunities
2. To analyze competitors' strategies
3. To evaluate and predict customer behavior
4. To gauge the performance of existing products and package designs and assess the potential of new ones
5. To develop price, promotion, and distribution plans

Obtaining Marketing Research Data

Marketing researchers are concerned with both internal and external data. They generate *internal data* within their organizations. Financial records provide a tremendous amount of useful information, such as changes in unpaid bills, inventory levels, sales generated by different categories of customers or product lines, profitability of particular divisions, or comparisons of sales by territories, salespeople, customers, or product lines.

Researchers gather *external data* from sources outside their firms, including previously published data. Trade associations publish reports on activities in particular industries. Advertising agencies collect information on the audiences reached by various media. National marketing research firms offer information through subscription services. Some of these professional research firms specialize in specific markets, such as Teenage Research Unlimited, which recently reported that American teenagers spend $155 billion on goods and services each year—valuable information for firms interested in reaching these consumers.[14]

The low costs involved and easy access to previously published data lead marketing researchers to begin their search for needed information by exhausting all possible sources of previously collected *secondary data* before investing the time and money required to collect firsthand data. Federal, state, and local government publications are among the marketing researcher's most important data sources. The most frequently used government statistics include census data, containing such population characteristics as age, gender, ethnic background, education level, household size and composition, occupation, employment status, and income. Such information helps marketers assess the buying behavior of certain segments of the population, anticipate changes in the marketplace, and identify markets with above-average growth potential. Most government data can now be accessed over the Internet.

Even though secondary data represent a quick and inexpensive resource, marketing researchers often discover that previously published information gives insufficient insight into some marketing problems. In some cases, the secondary data may be too old for current purposes. Previously collected data may also be in an inappropriate format for a current marketing research investigation. A researcher may need data divided by city blocks but might find only data for the city as a whole. Other data—particularly data about consumer attitudes or intentions—may be difficult to find or not reflect actual behavior (see the Best Business Practices box). Facing these obstacles, researchers may conclude they must collect *primary data*—data collected for the first time through observation or surveys.

Marketing researchers sometimes collect primary data through observational studies, in which they view the actions of selected subjects either directly or through mechanical devices. Once Famous, a retail laboratory, observes the actions of shoppers in a "real" store setting. For other marketers, Internet sites measure traffic, typically by counting the number of unique visitors to a Web site during a given period. Web-based data collection can also track what links each visitor clicks while at a Web site, as well as what a visitor orders and how much money the visitor spends. But online data collection has its drawbacks, particularly in a global setting. For instance, the Internet is not readily accessible in many countries, including parts of Latin America and Central and Eastern Europe as well as much of Asia, so it is difficult to use online interviews to gain information about goods and services. "We can't send [consumers] an e-mail and expect them to participate," observes Van Terradot, general manager of Novatest, a marketing research firm based in Paris.[15]

Simply observing customers cannot provide some types of information. When researchers need information about attitudes, opinions, and motives, they must ask questions by conducting surveys. Survey methods include telephone interviews; mail, fax, and online questionnaires; personal interviews; and focus groups. A focus group brings together 8 to 12 people in a room or over the Internet to discuss a particular topic. Ideas generated during focus group interviews can be especially helpful to marketers in developing new products, improving existing products, and creating effective advertising campaigns. In the case of traditional phone interviews, marketers are discovering that they must find innovative ways to reach consumers, who are increasingly putting up barriers by using caller ID to screen their calls or who just hang up out of frustration with frequent calls from telemarketers. Veteran pollster Richard Wirthlin reports that 20 years ago, two-thirds of American citizens were willing to accept calls from interviewers and participate in surveys. Today, only about one-third are willing.[16]

McDonald's Gets Green

Consumers are bombarded with facts and figures about the nationwide epidemic of obesity related to poor diet and lack of exercise. One study says that a bad diet, coupled with inactivity, leads to conditions that kill 400,000 people per year—a figure very close to that of tobacco-related deaths. Diet experts, government agencies, and consumer advocates are quick to point the finger at the $144 billion fast-food industry, which feeds one-third of U.S. adults daily, for contributing to the decline in consumer health. In years past, fast-food restaurants have tried to introduce more healthful menu choices—often with dismal results. McDonald's tried a Lite Mac, but no one wanted it. About five years later, it introduced the McLean Deluxe burger, but that fell flat, too. It seems that although consumers *say* they want a more healthful diet, when they visit a fast-food restaurant, what they really want is a juicy burger and salty French fries.

Then a few years ago, McDonald's tried another tack: salads. True, the firm had introduced its first salad in 1986, but it was mostly a lump of iceberg lettuce with little nutritional value, and it proved to be a big-time failure. The new entrée salads are completely different. Made of romaine and other darker-leaf lettuces, they're also packed with cucumbers, tomatoes, and red onions—and can be ordered with grilled chicken, ground beef, low-calorie salsa, fruit, nuts, or other toppings. The first consumers to jump on McDonald's new green bandwagon were women—at $3.99, the fresh salads are a bargain, and they're served just as quickly as a burger and fries. And although they aren't as low-cal or low-carb as a salad you might fix at home, with dressing they still rack up only about 320 calories compared with a 600-calorie Big Mac or 520-calorie serving of fries. Salads aren't the core of McDonald's business—they never will be—but last year 150 million of them were sold. Perhaps the fast-food giant should start posting that number on the Golden Arches sign, just as it once did to report the number of burgers served.

QUESTIONS FOR CRITICAL THINKING

1. In the past, consumers have requested a more healthful fast-food menu, then rejected it. Do you think that McDonald's new entrée salads will meet the same fate? Why or why not?

2. What determinants of consumer behavior come into play in deciding whether to visit a fast-food restaurant?

Sources: Matthew Boyle, "Can You Really Make Fast Food Healthy?" *Fortune*, August 9, 2004, pp. 134–139; Michael Arndt, "McDonald's: Fries with that Salad?" *BusinessWeek*, July 5, 2004, pp. 82–84; Nanci Hellmich, "Obesity on Track as No. 1 Killer," *USA Today*, March 10, 2004, p. A1.

Applying Marketing Research Data

As the accuracy of information collected by researchers increases, so does the effectiveness of resulting marketing strategies. Heinz applied research data when it was looking for ways to expand sales of its ketchup, which already is the best-selling brand in a mature product category. The company talked to mothers and learned that many are reluctant to let their children handle bottles of ketchup for fear of a big, red mess. So Heinz researchers watched children wield bottles of ketchup, and they agreed that the traditional plastic bottles were difficult for small hands to manipulate. The company launched a new kid-friendly bottle called EZ Squirt, which is designed to be easy to hold with two little hands and offers a nozzle to aim at fries or a burger. Further research showed that kids like foods with different colors, so Heinz introduced its ketchup in two new colors—green and purple—but with the same flavor. Those colors were so successful that the company recently launched EZ Squirt Mystery Color ketchup—consumers won't know which color they've bought until they open the bottle. Choices include Passion Pink, Awesome Orange, and Totally Teal. The only potential drawback to this idea is that kids tend to have definite preferences and may refuse a color that they don't want. Why is Heinz fooling around with its traditional tomato red ketchup? "Kids love colorful things and things that turn colors," explains Lisa Allen, a spokeswoman for the Grocery Manufacturers of America. Interestingly, Phil Lempert, editor of *The Lempert Report* business newsletter, conducted his own survey of parents on his Web site to see if they liked the idea of alternative food colors; they didn't. "Parents were concerned about their kids' nutrition and felt the colored foods wouldn't benefit them," he reports.[17]

Computer-Based Marketing Research Systems

Computer technology helps many businesses create a strategic advantage in collecting and analyzing research data. Companies can gather detailed data with the *universal product code (UPC)* symbols that appear on most packaging. After scanning the information carried in the fine lines of the bar code, a computer identifies the product, its manufacturer, and its price. Managers use the data to schedule inventory, ordering, and delivery; track sales; and test the effectiveness of promotions and new-product introductions.

Marketing research firms, such as AC Nielsen and Data General, store consumer data in commercially available databases. AC Nielsen operates in more than 100 countries worldwide. Businesses subscribe to these databases to obtain data on sales and promotions of their products. Subscribing to the databases typically is more efficient than doing similar research in house. Using information from the databases, consulting firms such as Inter-Act Systems, Retail Systems Consulting, and Stratmar Systems work with firms to develop programs that reward their best customers.

Ice cream maker Ben & Jerry's uses an Oracle database and software from a company called Business Objects to conduct computer-based marketing research. Before a pint of ice cream leaves the plant, a special tracking number is stamped on its carton, and the number is logged into the Oracle database. From there, the research software tells the company's sales team which flavors are selling best—so far, Cherry Garcia is the No. 1 flavor. The consumer affairs staff can match pint numbers with the 225 phone calls and e-mails Ben & Jerry's receives each week and find out whether there are any complaints. If there are, they can even trace which suppliers contributed eggs, milk, or cherries to the pint to correct the problem.

The Business Objects software is a type of "business intelligence" software, which crunches enormous amounts of data looking for trends, problems, and even new opportunities for companies. Using the software, Ben & Jerry's learned that consumers thought its beloved Cherry Garcia ice cream pops had too few cherries. Once marketers traced the problem to its root—again, using the software—they discovered that the photo on the product box depicted frozen yogurt, not ice cream, and thus differed from what customers expected to find in the box. So they changed the photo on the box—and the complaints disappeared.[18]

data mining computer search of massive amounts of customer data to detect patterns and relationships.

Data Mining

Using a computer to search through massive amounts of customer data to detect patterns and relationships is referred to as **data mining.** These patterns may suggest predictive models of real-world business activities. Accurate data mining can help researchers forecast recessions, weed out credit card fraud, and pinpoint sales prospects.

Data mining uses **data warehouses,** which are sophisticated customer databases that allow managers to combine data from several different organizational functions. Wal-Mart's data warehouse, considered the largest in the private sector, contains over 500 terabytes (trillions of characters) of data. The retail giant uses data mining to assess local preferences for merchandise so that it can tailor the inventory of each store to the tastes of its neighborhood. The number of data warehouses containing at least a terabyte of data is only in the hundreds, but many companies are applying data-mining tools on a smaller scale.[19] By identifying patterns and connections, marketers can increase the accuracy of their predictions about the effectiveness of their strategy options. One researcher has demonstrated that data mining can show marketers how satisfied customers would be if certain changes were made in products.[20]

They Said It

Consumers are statistics.
Customers are people.

—Stanley Marcus (1905–2002)
American merchant

Concept Check

1. What is marketing research?
2. What is the difference between primary data and secondary data?
3. Explain how data warehouses are related to data mining.

Market Segmentation

The information collected by marketing researchers is valuable only when it helps managers make better decisions. Improving the accuracy of information being collected also increases the effectiveness of resulting marketing strategies. Marketing research can cover a broad range, perhaps an entire industry or nation, or it can focus on highly specific details, such as individual purchase patterns. Identifying the characteristics of a target market is a crucial step toward creating a successful marketing strategy. **Market segmentation** is the process of dividing a market into several relatively homogeneous groups. Both profit-seeking and not-for-profit organizations use market segmentation to help them reach desirable target markets.

The television broadcast industry is an excellent example of the process of market segmentation. During the 1960s, most American viewers watched programming from the three major television networks—ABC, CBS, and NBC—and only a few tuned in to the UHF stations. Today, cable networks and direct-broadcast satellites have increased the number of channels to the hundreds; soon, digital broadcasting services and Internet channels will offer more than 1,000 channels. This explosion in offerings means that broadcasters must find some way to target their markets, and they are doing so. Individuals who want to watch programs on cooking, gardening, gender issues, sports, and movies—to name just a few—may do so. There's even a cable TV channel called BirdSight, aimed at bird lovers, and channels called Classic Cars, Club Vegetarian, and Inside Weddings. These channels are all operated by Rainbow Media Group, which targets specific market segments.[21]

Market segmentation attempts to isolate the traits that distinguish a certain group of customers from the overall market. However, segmentation does not always promote marketing success. Table 12.2 lists several criteria that marketers should consider. The effectiveness of a segmentation strategy depends on how well the market meets these criteria. Once marketers identify a market segment to target, they can create an appropriate marketing strategy.

How Market Segmentation Works

An immediate segmentation distinction involves whether the firm is offering goods and services to customers for their own use (the consumer, or B2C, market) or to purchasers who will use them directly or indirectly in providing other products for resale (the business, or B2B, market). Depending on whether their firms offer consumer or business products, marketers segment their target markets differently. Four common bases for segmenting consumer markets are geographical segmentation, demographic segmentation, psychographic segmentation, and product-related segmentation. Business markets are segmented on only three criteria: customer-based segmentation, end-use segmentation, and geographical segmentation. Figure 12.8 illustrates the segmentation methods for these two types of markets.

Table 12.2   Criteria for Market Segmentation

Criterion	Example
A segment must be a measurable group.	Data can be collected on the dollar amount and number of purchases by preteens.
A segment must be accessible for communications.	A growing number of seniors are going online, so they can be reached through Internet marketing channels.
A segment must be large enough to offer profit potential.	In a small community, a store carrying only large-size shoes might not be profitable. Similarly, a specialty retail chain may not locate in a small market.

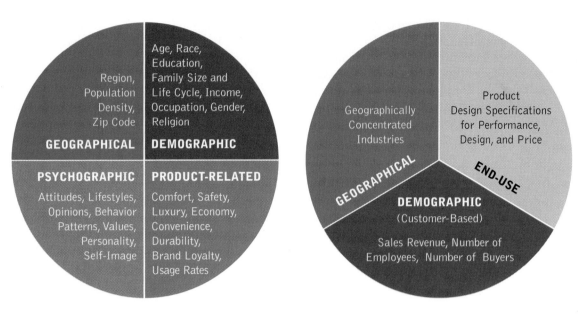

Consumer (B2C) Markets   **Business (B2B) Markets**

FIGURE 12.8
Methods of Segmenting Consumer and Business Markets

Segmenting Consumer Markets

Market segmentation has been practiced since people first produced surpluses and resold the unneeded products to others. Garment producers made some items for men and others for women. Some specialized in producing shoes or clothing for children. A millennium ago, Europeans fell in love with exotic spices and luxurious silk fabrics. Merchants began to serve this untapped market by bringing these precious items thousands of miles by land and sea from production sites in Asia and the Pacific islands to a waiting market in Europe. In addition to demographic and geographical segmentation, today's marketers also define customer groups based on psychographic criteria as well as product-related distinctions.

Geographical Segmentation   Perhaps the oldest segmentation method is **geographical segmentation**—dividing a market into homogeneous groups on the basis of population locations. While geographical location does not ensure that consumers in a particular area will always make the same kinds of buying decisions, this segmentation approach is useful when consumer preferences and purchase patterns for a good or service differ between regions. Suburbanites predictably purchase more lawn-care products than do their urban counterparts. Also, residents of northern states purchase snowblowers and car windshield ice scrapers and spray deicers, products generally not necessary in warmer climates. Besides looking at patterns of product use, marketers may base geographical segmentation on other regional differences such as the ethnicity of populations. For instance, larger U.S. cities such as New York, Los Angeles, and Chicago, as well as southwestern cities in general, have bigger Hispanic populations, so products targeted to Latinos work well there.

Population size, a common geographical segmentation factor, helps define target markets as urban, suburban, and rural. However, businesses also need to consider a wide variety of other variables, such as job growth and migration patterns, before deciding to expand into new areas. Some businesses may decide to combine areas or even entire countries that share similar population and product-use patterns instead of treating each as an independent segment.

Demographic Segmentation   By far the most common method of market segmentation, **demographic segmentation** distinguishes markets on the basis of various demographic or socioeconomic characteristics. Common demographic measures include income, age, occupation, household size, stage in the family life cycle, education, ethnic group, and gender. The U.S. Census Bureau is one of the best sources of demographic information for the domestic market.

Gender has traditionally been a simple way to define markets for certain products—perfume and cosmetics for women and hammers and drills for men. However, many products have spread beyond such gender stereotypes. Men no longer dominate purchases of sporting goods, exercise equipment, or automobiles. Women's participation in sports such as running and tennis has resulted in big revenues for smart marketers. Automobile manufacturers know that over half of all auto purchase decisions are made by women. In fact, women control an estimated 85 percent of the $7 trillion spent each year on personal consumption items.[22]

But rather than completely eliminating gender segmentation, marketers often develop different marketing mixes for their male and female customers. Home improvement retailer Home Depot has been running "Ladies Night" clinics at some of its stores, offering hands-on instruction for women in woodworking, laying ceramic tile, and repairing faucets or toilets. These events translate into real dollars because, according to the National Association of Realtors, women represent the second-largest group of homebuyers after couples. After taking a few of the Home Depot classes, Lawanda Green of Pensacola, Florida, says she is comfortable shopping for the tools she needs. "I've bought bits for my drill and some sawhorses," she reports. "Some day I'm going to get a router. I'd like to get into cabinetry."[23]

Some firms actually develop new products—or at least, new packaging—for women. Sherwin-Williams has designed a new Dutch Boy "Twist and Pour" paint can specifically for women. The Coca-Cola Co. has been researching a bottle that doesn't require drinkers to tilt their heads back while drinking—a position that marketing research has revealed makes women uncomfortable.

Seventeen was one of the first publications for teens. Recently many other publishers have created magazines for this rapidly growing market segment.

Gillette has launched a Venus women's razor, which is ergonomically designed to fit more easily in a woman's hand. Quaker Foods, a division of PepsiCo, now offers a line of cereals called Nutrition for Women, which contains ingredients such as calcium, soy, and folic acid.[24]

Age is perhaps the most volatile factor in demographic segmentation in the U.S., with our rapidly aging population. By 2020, one of every three Americans will be over 50 years old—still active and with money to spend—and smart companies will focus their attention on reaching this growing part of the market. According to Age Wave Impact, consultants on mature consumers, seniors control three-fourths of consumer wealth, wielding $1.7 trillion in annual buying power. They make 80 percent of luxury travel purchases, 48 percent of luxury auto purchases, and 77 percent of prescription drug purchases.[25] Recognizing this potential gold mine, firms as diverse as L'Oréal and Toyota have begun targeting seniors with advertising as well as new products. In one ad campaign, 80-something Sir Edmund Hillary, who made the first recorded ascent of Mt. Everest with his Nepalese partner Tenzing Norgay, touts the strength of Toyota trucks and SUVs. L'Oréal has developed an entire line of skin care called Age Perfect and hired 50-something Dale Haddon to represent the products in its ads.[26]

Teens are another rapidly growing market. According to Teenage Research Unlimited, the purchases that the average teen makes—or influences—add up to about $116 a week.[27] Note that this figure includes family purchases, such as a DVD player or a dinner out, that the teen may influence. Marketers are recognizing that this crop of teens, unlike the teens of a decade ago, actually likes to receive marketing messages. "They like being marketed to," notes Anne Zehren, publisher of *Teen People*. "They like that someone's paying attention to them." It's not surprising that companies like Old Navy, Abercrombie & Fitch, and the Gap—along with all the major snack and beverage manufacturers—have marketing campaigns aimed at teens. But so do Ford, DaimlerChrysler, General Motors, Honda, and Toyota—despite the fact that the legal driving age varies from state to state around the country and few teens can afford to purchase a car on their own. Why do these automakers sink millions into programs designed to attract this age group? "All brands recognize it's important to get them early because they're already starting to formulate their own opinions," explains Melisa Wolfson, president of Brains, Beauty, and BOB, a teen marketing agency based in Santa Monica, California.[28] Avon is another company traditionally associated with consumers over the age of 25, but it has recently made efforts to reach teens. Avon has come out with a new line of cosmetics called Mark for teens and is recruiting teens as sales reps for the products.[29]

Minority groups hold a combined purchasing power of more than $1 trillion a year in the U.S. alone, an amount that marketers must not overlook. The three largest minority groups—Hispanic Americans, African Americans, and Asian Americans—number almost one out of every three U.S. residents. The fastest-growing segment, Hispanic Americans, had grown to 40 million by 2005, and African Americans, historically the nation's largest ethnic group, ranked second in population at 37.5 million. Asian Americans, the third largest U.S. minority group, saw their numbers grow rapidly during the first years of this century, due largely to immigration.[30] Clearly, these populations represent important opportunities for marketers.

Although Hispanic Americans typically speak English as a first or second language, many view the Spanish language as part of their cultural identity. So companies like banking firm JP Morgan Chase are developing Spanish-language promotions for Hispanic TV, magazines, and newspapers. Morgan Chase, which focuses on relationship marketing, has translated its slogan, "The right relationship is everything," into Spanish and created a TV commercial featuring a 30-something couple talking in a cozy restaurant. The bank is planning a similar advertisement for the Asian American market.[31]

Entrepreneurs who are members of minority groups may start their own businesses out of frustration at not being able to find foods, clothing, entertainment, or other goods and services that fit their tastes and needs. Parry Singh did exactly that. He established a series of Web sites to cater to the demand for ethnic foods. The first site, Namaste.com, came about because of his sister's inability to find Indian groceries. Later sites have included Gongshee.com for Chinese products; QueRico.com for items from Mexico, Cuba, and South America; and EthnicGrocer.com, an English-language site that educates visitors about different international cuisines, offers recipes, and sells ingredients.[32]

Psychographic Segmentation   In recent years, marketing researchers have tried to formulate lifelike portraits of consumers. This effort has led to another strategy for segmenting target markets, **psychographic segmentation,** which divides consumer markets into groups with similar psychological characteristics, values, and lifestyles. Lifestyle is the sum of a person's needs, preferences, motives, attitudes, social habits, and cultural background.

Psychographic studies have evaluated motivations for purchases of hundreds of goods and services, ranging from soft drinks to health-care services. Using the resulting data, marketers tailor their marketing strategies to carefully chosen market segments. A frequently used method of developing psychographic profiles involves the use of *AIO statements*—verbal descriptions of various activities, interests, and opinions. Researchers survey a sample of consumers, asking them whether they agree or disagree with each statement. The answers are then tabulated and analyzed for use in identifying various

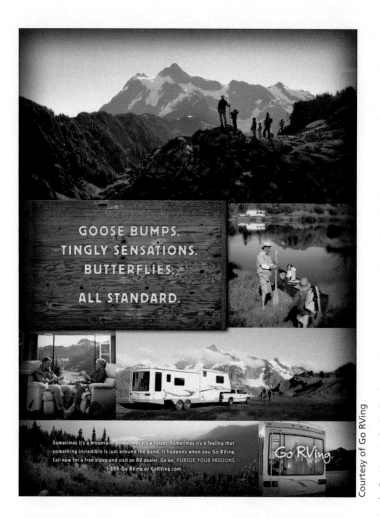

Recreational vehicle marketers are enjoying record sales as millions of baby boom generation adults grow older and begin to enjoy lifestyles impacted by income, increased leisure time, and concerns about foreign travel. An RV purchase permits them to enjoy seeing America in a safe and comfortable environment.

lifestyle categories. Procter & Gamble used a combination of psychographic and demographic data to identify consumers it calls "chatterers," shoppers who exert considerable influence on the purchase decisions of other people. To launch its Physique line of hair-care products, P&G targeted this segment, sending them samples and inviting them to a Web site that encouraged visitors to tell others about the product line. Within months, the effort had generated a million referrals to the Physique Web site.[33]

Although demographic classifications like age, gender, or income are relatively easy to identify and measure, researchers need to define psychographic categories. Often, marketing research firms conduct extensive studies of consumers and then share their psychographic data with marketers who sign up as clients. Ad agency Bulldog Drummond and research firm Radar Communications recently conducted a study of women consumers to find out more about their attitudes and lifestyles. Researchers were able to classify women by their life stages—not necessarily their ages—thus identifying some common attitudes, desires, values, and lifestyles. Common themes that surfaced were a desire to have more time and feel organized; a desire for the good life, which may or may not include material possessions; a need to express oneself freely; a desire for convenience, including one-stop shopping; and a desire for services that can solve challenging situations or questions.[34]

Psychographic segmentation can lead marketers to the right consumers for certain categories of products, such as those identified as luxury products. Luxury products may include high-priced autos, glamorous vacations, designer clothing, or gourmet foods. According to the U.S. Census Bureau, 15 million U.S. households have an annual income in excess of $100,000. Although affluence is relative—the cost of living continues to rise, along with incomes—marketers are keen to reach consumers who want to enhance their lives with luxury products. According to industry experts, doing so means offering superior customer service in addition to high-quality goods. "Invitation-only events, limited-edition products, and other types of experiential marketing are key to capturing the attention of today's affluent consumers," explains Marian Salzman, director of strategy and planning at Euro RSCG, New York.[35]

Product-Related Segmentation   Using **product-related segmentation,** marketers can divide a consumer market into groups based on buyers' relationships to the good or service. The three most popular approaches to product-related segmentation are based on benefits sought, usage rates, and brand loyalty levels.

Segmenting by *benefits sought* focuses on the attributes that people seek in a good or service and the benefits they expect to receive from it. The ad for Lexan resin hardening agent in Figure 12.9 emphasizes the product's strength and light weight for high-impact plastics—such as hockey helmets and goal-tenders' masks. Differences in benefits sought can also shape which products a customer selects or how customers use a given product. One person might buy a whitewater kayak from Current Designs to shoot rapids, while another might select a sea kayak from the same firm to cover a great distance along the ocean shoreline. Just about every household has a roll of duct tape stashed in a drawer or on a workbench—and people use it to fix everything from broken faucets to broken chair legs.

A consumer market can also be segmented according to the amounts of a product that different consumers buy and use. Segmentation by *product usage rate* usually defines such categories as heavy users, medium users, and light users. The 80/20 principle states that roughly 80 percent of a product's revenues come from only 20 percent of its buyers. Companies can now pinpoint which of their customers are the heaviest users—and even the most profitable customers—and direct their heaviest marketing efforts to those customers. Discount securities firm Charles Schwab segments customers who have at least $100,000 invested with Schwab or make at least 12 securities purchases and sales a year as "Signature Clients." These clients have a customer-service number with a wait time of 15 seconds or less, compared with a longer wait for other Schwab customers. The company can afford the higher level of service for Signature Clients because they are more profitable.[36]

FIGURE 12.9
Segmentation by Benefits Sought

The third technique for product-related segmentation divides customers by *brand loyalty*—the degree to which consumers recognize, prefer, and insist on a particular brand. Marketers define groups of consumers with similar degrees of brand loyalty. They then attempt to tie loyal customers to a good or service by giving away premiums, which can be anything from a logo-emblazoned T-shirt to a pair of free tickets to a concert or sports event.

Segmenting Business Markets

In many ways, the segmentation process for business markets resembles that for consumer markets. However, some specific methods differ. Marketers divide business markets through geographical segmentation; demographic, or customer-based, segmentation; and end-use segmentation.

Geographical segmentation methods for business markets resemble those for consumer markets. Many B2B marketers target geographically concentrated industries, such as aircraft manufacturing, automobiles, and oil-field equipment. Especially on an international scale, customer needs, languages, and other variables may require differences in the marketing mix from one location to another.

Demographic, or *customer-based, segmentation* begins with a good or service design intended to suit a specific organizational market. ITT, shown in Figure 12.10, serves a number of business segments, as well as such government segments as the U.S. military, with its global positioning satellite (GPS) technology. Online exchanges like DirectAg.com, Rooster.com, XSAg.com, and Farmbid.com specialize in linking suppliers with farmers. They serve this industry segment by offering products such as seeds, fertilizer, livestock, and farm machinery such as tractors.

To simplify the process of focusing on a particular type of business customer, the federal government has developed a system for subdividing the business marketplace into detailed segments. The six-digit

FIGURE 12.10
Segmentation for an
Organizational Market

He has no idea ITT Industries
helps track his missions.
But at Mach 1.2,
he knows exactly where he is.

Knifing through a mile of sky every five
seconds tightens tolerances. GPS responds
with positioning information accurate to the
foot. ITT satellite transmitters send GPS
information not just to fighter jets, but to
every receiver that flies, floats, rolls or walks
across the planet.
    ITT believes that technology should work
undetectably. In this case, keeping everybody
from jet pilots to hikers in the right place.
Out of the proverbial woods.

ITT Industries
Engineered for life
www.itt.com

DEFENSE ELECTRONICS AND SERVICES
ELECTRONIC COMPONENTS
FLUID TECHNOLOGY
MOTION AND FLOW CONTROL

Courtesy of ITT Industries

buyer behavior series of decision processes by individual consumers who buy products for their own use and organizational buyers who purchase business products to be used directly or indirectly in the sale of other items.

North American Industry Classification System (NAICS) provides a common classification system used by the member nations of NAFTA: the U.S., Canada, and Mexico. It divides industries into broad categories such as agriculture, forestry, and fishing; manufacturing; transportation; and retail and wholesale trade. Each major category is further subdivided into smaller segments (such as HMO medical centers and warehouse clubs) for more detailed information and to facilitate comparison among the member nations.

Another way to group firms by their demographics is to segment them by size based on their sales revenues or numbers of employees. Consolidated Freightways collects data from visitors to its Web site and uses the data to segment customers by size. Modern information processing enables companies to segment business markets based on how much they buy, not just how big they are. Government Computer Sales Inc. (GCSI), which provides computer hardware and software for government agencies, gathers data about each agency with which it interacts. It identifies customers with high purchase rates and focuses selling efforts on those customers. The targeted effort has significantly boosted GCSI's profits.

End-use segmentation focuses on the precise way a B2B purchaser will use a product. Resembling benefits-sought segmentation for consumer markets, this method helps small and mid-size companies to target specific end-user markets rather than competing directly with large firms for wider customer groups. A marketer might also craft a marketing mix based on certain criteria for making a purchase. A company whose owners are members of ethnic minorities might list its product on M-Xchange, an Internet exchange specializing in minority-owned companies. Participating in M-Xchange could support a strategy to target business customers who promote diversity among their suppliers. Other decision criteria that a marketer might target include companies that choose suppliers based on low price or ability to support just-in-time inventory management.

Concept Check

1. What is the oldest segmentation method in the consumer market?
2. What is currently the most common method of consumer market segmentation?
3. What is end-use segmentation in the B2B market?

consumer behavior actions of ultimate consumers directly involved in obtaining, consuming, and disposing of products and the decision processes that precede and follow these actions.

Buyer Behavior: Determining What Customers Want

A fundamental marketing task is to find out why people buy one product and not another. The answer requires an understanding of **buyer behavior,** the series of decision processes by individual consumers who buy products for their own use and organizational buyers who purchase business products to be used directly or indirectly in the sale of other items. In contrast, **consumer behavior** refers more specifically to the actions of ultimate consumers directly involved in obtaining, consuming, and disposing of products and the decision processes that precede and follow these actions.

Determinants of Consumer Behavior

By studying people's purchasing behavior, marketers can identify consumers' attitudes toward and uses of their products. This investigation also helps to improve the effectiveness of marketing strategies for reaching these target markets. Both personal and interpersonal factors influence the behavior of an ultimate consumer. Personal influences on consumer behavior include individual needs and motives, perceptions, attitudes, learned experiences, and their self-concepts. Marketers frequently apply psychological techniques to understand what motivates people to buy and to study consumers' emotional reactions to goods and services. For instance, today's busy consumers are constantly looking for ways to save time, so marketers for all kinds of companies try to fulfill that need with goods and services designed for convenience. Grocery manufacturers have gone all out to try to satisfy this need, offering everything from Hershey's pudding in a tube to Hormel's slow-roasted turkey breast that can be prepared in a reheated cooking bag in 30 minutes. One of Tyson's food product lines consists of fully cooked, marinated, and carved pork and beef roasts, which a harried consumer can serve in just 10 minutes. Betty Crocker's Hamburger Helper and Chicken Helper are still selling strong. And Campbell Soup has reduced its homey experience to cups of sippable soup that a commuter can hold in one hand.[37]

The interpersonal determinants of consumer behavior include cultural, social, and family influences. Because children often influence family purchases, marketers create messages aimed directly to them, which raises ethical questions, as discussed in the Solving an Ethical Controversy box. So marketers must navigate some tricky waters. In the area of convenience foods, cultural, social, and family influences come into play as much as an individual's need to save time. Understanding that many consumers value the time they spend with their families and want to care for them by providing good nutrition, marketers often emphasize these values in advertisements for convenience food products.

Sometimes external events influence consumer behavior. The 9/11 terrorist attacks, the recession that occurred around the same time, the brief 2003 war with Iraq, and the global SARS epidemic are four examples of these types of events. In fact, all of these events affected the decisions American consumers made about travel—whether to travel at all, whether to fly, and where to go. The outbreak of the deadly SARS (severe acute respiratory syndrome), a pneumonia-like virus that quickly infected thousands and claimed the lives of hundreds, affected business and vacation travel worldwide. A World Health Organization warning against travel to Beijing, Hong Kong, and Toronto left these destination cities virtually empty of tourists

Courtesy of Nestlé USA—Prepared Foods Division, Inc. Solon, Ohio 44139

A Family Tree

A Family Recipe

AMERICA'S FAVORITE* LASAGNA

Stouffers
Family *Style* Recipes

The lasagna recipe for a relaxing family dinner.

Start with a traditional tomato sauce mixed with ground beef. Add freshly made lasagna noodles, layered by hand, and a blend of real mozzarella, cottage and parmesan cheeses. You've got a perfect meal the whole family will enjoy.

Stouffers *Nothing Comes Closer to Home.*
www.stouffers.com

Personal and interpersonal needs influence consumer behavior. Stouffers addresses the personal need to save time and the interpersonal need to be with one's family.

and business visitors. Hong Kong tourist board ads using the slogan "Hong Kong will take your breath away" were quickly cancelled.[38] According to one report, attendance at theme parks such as Disney World in Florida and Dollywood in Tennessee declined significantly.[39]

Determinants of Business Buying Behavior

Because a number of people can influence purchases of B2B products, business buyers face a variety of organizational influences in addition to their own preferences. A design engineer may help to set the specifications that potential vendors must satisfy. A procurement manager may invite selected companies to bid on a purchase. A production supervisor may evaluate the operational aspects of the proposals that the firm receives, and the vice president of manufacturing may head a committee making the final decision.

Steps in the Consumer Behavior Process

Consumer decision making follows the sequential process outlined in Figure 12.11, with interpersonal and personal influences affecting every step. The process begins when the

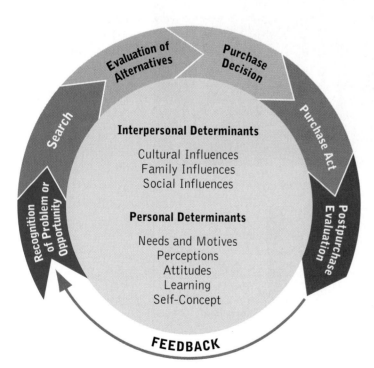

FIGURE 12.11
Steps in the Consumer Behavior Process

consumer recognizes a problem or opportunity. If someone needs a new pair of shoes, that need becomes a problem to solve. Should you receive a promotion at work and a 20 percent salary increase, that change may also become a purchase opportunity.

To solve the problem or take advantage of the opportunity, the consumer seeks information about the intended purchase and evaluates alternatives, such as available brands. The goal of this activity is to find the best response to the perceived problem or opportunity.

Eventually, the consumer reaches a decision and completes the transaction—the purchase act. Later, he or she evaluates the experience with the purchase by making a postpurchase evaluation. Feelings about the experience serve as feedback that will influence future purchase decisions. The various steps in the sequence are affected by both interpersonal and personal factors.

Concept Check

1. Distinguish between buyer behavior and consumer behavior.
2. What are some of the determinants of business buying behavior?

Creating, Maintaining, and Strengthening Marketing Relationships

The past decade has brought rapid change to most industries, as customers have become better informed and more demanding purchasers through closely comparing competing goods and services. They expect, even demand, new benefits from the companies that supply them, making it harder for firms to gain a competitive advantage based on product features alone. Meanwhile, most businesses have traditionally focused on **transaction marketing,** characterized by buyer and seller exchanges with limited communications and little or no ongoing relationships between the parties. In transaction marketing, the goal is simple: negotiate hard with suppliers to secure the least expensive raw materials and components; then build products and find customers to buy them at prices high enough to cover costs and still earn a profit.

In today's hypercompetitive era, however, businesses need to find new ways of relating to customers if they hope to maintain long-term success. Instead of keeping customers at arm's length, businesses are developing strategies and tactics that draw them into a tighter connection with their customers. Such webs may expand to include stronger bonds with suppliers and employees. As a result, many firms are turning their attention away from managing transactions to the broader issues of relationship marketing. **Relationship marketing** goes beyond an effort for making the sale to a drive for making the sale again and again. To keep particular customers coming back, firms must exceed customers' needs and wants so they will make repeat purchases. As its ultimate goal, relationship marketing seeks to achieve customer satisfaction.

Managing relationships instead of simply completing transactions often leads to creative partnerships. However, customers enter into relationships with marketing organizations only if they are assured that the relationship will be rewarding. As the intensity of commitment increases, so does the likelihood of a business continuing a long-term relationship with its customers. The following list reviews a few of the ways businesses are using relationships to reach corporate goals:

relationship marketing developing and maintaining long-term, cost-effective exchange relationships with individual customers, suppliers, employees, and other partners for mutual benefit.

- *Partnering with customers.* At its MasterCare Car Service Web site, Bridgestone/Firestone allows customers to set up their personal Web page called MyMasterCare. The site holds a customer's service history, schedules maintenance reminders via e-mail, and suggests maintenance services tailored to a person's driving habits. The site also has an extensive Customer Feedback link containing testimonials and a satisfaction survey. Customers receive coupons for upcoming services if they provide feedback on the survey.[40]
- *Partnering with suppliers.* Scott Paint buys ingredients for its paint from Gulf Coast Chemical. Gulf Coast won the contract by offering to do much more than ship products to Scott's factory. Gulf Coast provides Scott with just-in-time inventory management. It tracks Scott's needs, brings in raw materials from several suppliers, and consolidates them into four monthly shipments. For Scott, partnering with Gulf Coast means lower inventory costs, better prices for consolidated orders, and the ability to focus on paint production rather than inventory.
- *Partnering with other businesses.* Many of the largest pharmaceutical companies collaborate with small research firms that have expertise in a particular field, such as biotechnology. Such arrangements give the pharmaceutical giants access to innovation without requiring them to be leaders

State Farm seeks to build a relationship with its customers.

GET AN IRA ASAP FROM SOMEONE WHO HAS ALWAYS TREATED YOU LIKE A VIP. WE LIVE WHERE YOU LIVE.™

Agent Luz Thompson

April 15th will be here before you know it. Talk to your State Farm agent about the possible tax benefits of opening an IRA now. With a variety of funding options, a State Farm IRA could be A-OK. Call today or visit *statefarm.com.®*

LIKE A GOOD NEIGHBOR   STATE FARM IS THERE.™

Providing Insurance and Financial Services

Consult your tax or legal advisor for specific advice.
State Farm • Home Office: Bloomington, Illinois • statefarm.com®

in every kind of research. And colleges often partner with companies to lend their logos and colors to everything from polo shirts and sweatshirts to credit cards and custom license plates.

Benefits of Relationship Marketing

Relationship marketing helps all parties involved. In addition to mutual protection against competitors, businesses that forge solid links with suppliers and customers are often rewarded with lower costs and higher profits than they would generate on their own. Long-term agreements with a few high-quality suppliers frequently reduce a firm's production costs. Unlike one-time sales, these ongoing relationships encourage suppliers to offer customers preferential treatment, quickly adjusting shipments to accommodate changes in orders and correcting any quality problems that might arise.

Good relationships with customers can be vital strategic weapons for a firm. By identifying current purchasers and maintaining positive relationships with them, organizations can efficiently target their best customers. Studying current customers' buying habits and preferences can help marketers identify potential new customers and establish ongoing contact with them. Attracting a new customer can cost as much as five times more than keeping an existing one. Not only do marketing costs go down, but long-term customers usually buy more, require less service, refer other customers, and provide valuable feedback. Together, these elements contribute to a higher **lifetime value of a customer**—the revenues and intangible benefits (referrals and customer feedback) from the customer over the life of the relationship, minus the amount the company must spend to acquire and serve that customer.

Businesses also benefit from strong relationships with other companies. Purchasers who repeatedly buy from one business may find that they save time and gain service quality as the business learns their specific needs. Some relationship-oriented companies also customize goods and services based on customer preferences. Because many businesses reward loyal customers with discounts or bonuses, some customers may even find that they save money by developing long-term relationships. Alliances with other firms to serve the same customers also can be rewarding. The alliance partners combine their capabilities and resources to accomplish goals that they could not reach on their own. In addition, alliances with other firms may help businesses develop the skills and experience they need to successfully enter new markets or improve service to current customers.

Tools for Nurturing Customer Relationships

Although relationship marketing has important benefits for both customers and business, most relationship-oriented businesses quickly discover that not all customers justify equal treatment. Some customers generate more profitable business than others. If 20 percent of a firm's customers account for 80 percent of its sales and profits, a customer in this category undoubtedly has a higher lifetime value than a customer who buys only sporadically or in small amounts.

While businesses shouldn't ignore any customer, of course, their objectives and tactics for managing relationships with individual customers often reflect the overall value to the firm of the resulting business. A firm may choose to custom-manufacture goods or services for high-value customers while working to increase repeat sales of stock products to less valuable customers. An important task in developing relationship strategies is to differentiate between customer groups when seeking ways to pull each one closer to an intense commitment to the firm. The firm can then choose the particular tactics that suit each customer group.

Frequency Marketing and Affinity Marketing Programs Popular techniques through which firms try to build and protect customer relationships include frequent buyer and frequent user programs. Such a marketing initiative, commonly known as a **frequency marketing** program, rewards purchasers with cash, rebates, merchandise, or other premiums. For many years, the airline industry has relied on frequency marketing programs to build customer relationships. Frequent flyer programs have become standard at most carriers. But industry watchers say that frequent flyer programs no longer carry the weight they once did, when other services—such as in-flight meals and on-time schedules—have declined. "I've been an [elite-level frequent business traveler] for five years, and enjoyed it up until last year, when [an airline's] service became just horrible," complains one customer. Thus, frequent flyer programs create added value—and strengthen relationships—only when they are offered *in addition to* expected service.[41]

Affinity programs are another tool for building emotional links with customers. An affinity program is a marketing effort sponsored by an organization that solicits involvement by individuals who share common interests and activities. Affinity programs are common in the credit card industry. Under such a program, a person can sign up for a credit card emblazoned with the logo of a favorite charity, sports or entertainment celebrity, or photograph of his or her college. This type of arrangement typically calls for the company to donate a percentage of the person's charges to the organization displayed on the credit card. Other credit card affinity programs include ones like L. L. Bean's arrangement with Visa. Under this program, customers who apply for an L. L. Bean Visa card are entitled to special offers such as free shipping, free monogramming, and discount coupons from L. L. Bean.[42]

Many businesses also use comarketing and cobranding. In a **comarketing** deal, two businesses jointly market each other's products. Goodyear and NASCAR have teamed up to create humorous TV commercials promoting Goodyear tires that are used on cars at NASCAR races.[43] When two or more businesses team up to closely link their names for a single product, **cobranding** occurs. Some fast-food restaurants have joined forces to house more than one restaurant choice under one roof so customers can stop by for, say, Great American Bagels in the morning and Caffe Luna for a smoothie in the afternoon. Kolcraft Enterprises recently began offering a new line of baby strollers bearing the Jeep brand. The Jeep strollers, like their sport-utility vehicle counterparts, have all-terrain tires and cater to upscale families. Parents who wheel around in the top-of-the-line Grand Cherokee model cement their relationship with Jeep while baby plays with the toy steering wheel, key, and push-button radio mounted in front.[44]

One-on-One Marketing The ability to customize product offerings to individual needs and rapidly deliver goods and services has become increasingly dependent on investments in technology like computer-aided design and manufacturing. The Internet offers a way for businesses to connect with customers in a much more intimate manner than was previously available. Not only can companies take orders for customized products, but they can also gather data about customer characteristics and buying histories and then use the data to make predictions about what additional goods or services a given customer might want. Web sites or salespeople can tailor their messages based on those predictions. As long as customers are willing to share this information about themselves, the marketing possibilities are endless.

Computer databases provide strong support for effective relationship marketing. Marketers can maintain databases on customer tastes, price-range preferences, and lifestyles, and they can quickly obtain names and other information about promising prospects. Managers can then use the information in data warehouses to create a centralized, accurate profile of each customer's relationship with the firm as an aid to decision making. The Internet, with its capabilities for interactive electronic commerce, creates additional opportunities for firms to build close customer relationships.

Concept Check

1. What is the lifetime value of a customer?
2. Give an example of a frequency marketing program.

DID YOU KNOW?

1. In an effort to boost grapefruit sales, the Florida Citrus Department has hired a team of researchers to find out if the old grapefruit diet of the 1970s really works. They plan to serve grapefruit to overweight test subjects to see if they lose weight. Then they will market the results to women.
2. Fly fishing is now considered a luxury sport, so several companies are targeting wealthier consumers who want to visit exotic destinations, catch big fish, and stay in comfortable surroundings. Total spending on the sport is now nearly $700 million a year.
3. About 50 million dogs live in the U.S., accounting for an annual $6 billion food bill for their owners.
4. Hoover is such a well-known brand in the U.K. that the British use *hoover* as a verb for vacuuming. Similarly, many Middle Eastern shoppers call laundry detergents *tide*.
5. Want to save on gasoline? The Chase Freedom Card is a Visa card that gives a rebate of 3 percent on gas purchases, regardless of brand.

Service industries, such as the airlines, have been in the forefront of relationship marketing, since their employees often personally meet and interact with customers. However, manufacturing businesses also can apply this technology. By establishing a presence on Yahoo!'s Web site, Ford offers a variety of ways for customers to interact with the company throughout the time they own their car. At the same time, Ford can gather data about what kinds of information its customers look for at the Web page, as well as track service data that customers enter while on the site. These interactions help Ford understand what its customers want in terms of service and features on their autos.

The owners of the National Basketball Association's Portland Trail Blazers used Web-based customer relationship management to identify and respond to interest in a women's team, the Portland Fire. The Blazers used special software called Front Office to build a customer database. Whenever the team sold tickets, it entered sales and demographic data about the purchaser. Sales reps used the data to target customers that might be interested in additional tickets or attending games featuring special promotions. During the Fire's first season, they quickly surpassed their sales objectives. The teams continue to use the database to identify other marketing opportunities, including team merchandise purchases, group sales, and season ticket purchases.[45]

What's Ahead

The next two chapters examine each of the four elements of the marketing mix that marketers use to satisfy their selected target markets. Chapter 13 focuses on products and their distribution through various channels to different outlets. Chapter 14 covers promotion and the various methods marketers use to communicate with their target customers, along with strategies for setting prices for different products.

Summary of Learning Goals

1 *Summarize the ways in which marketing creates utility.*

Through an exchange, two or more parties give something of value to one another to satisfy felt needs. Marketing is closely linked with the exchange process. It creates utility—the want-satisfying power of a good or service—by making the product available when and where consumers want to buy and by arranging for orderly transfers of ownership. Production creates form utility; marketing creates time, place, and ownership utility.

2 *Explain the marketing concept and relate how customer satisfaction contributes to added value.*

The marketing concept refers to a companywide customer orientation with the objective of achieving long-run success. This concept is essential in today's marketplace, which is primarily a buyer's market, meaning buyers can choose from an abundance of goods and services. Customer satisfaction contributes to added value of a good or service by delivering more than buyers expect in the form of added features, reduced prices, enhanced customer service, a strengthened warranty, or other marketing mix improvements.

3 ***Describe the components of a market and distinguish between B2B and B2C marketing.***

A market consists of people with purchasing power and willingness and authority to buy. Markets can be classified by the types of products they handle. Consumer (or B2C) products are goods and services purchased by ultimate users. Business (or B2B) products are goods and services purchased to be used, directly or indirectly, in the production of other products for resale.

4 ***Outline the basic steps in developing a marketing strategy.***

All organizations, profit-oriented and not-for-profit, need to develop marketing strategies to effectively reach customers. This process involves analyzing the overall market, selecting a target market, and developing a marketing mix that blends elements related to product, distribution, promotion, and pricing decisions. Often, company marketers develop a marketing plan that expresses their marketing strategy.

5 ***Describe the marketing research function.***

Marketing research is the information-gathering function that links marketers to the marketplace. It provides the information about potential target markets that planners need as they construct effective marketing mixes. Marketers conduct research to identify marketing problems and opportunities, analyze competitors' strategies, evaluate and predict customer behavior, gauge the performance of existing products and package designs and assess the potential of new ones, and develop plans for pricing, promotion, and distribution. Besides collecting information, marketing research includes planning how to collect the information, as well as interpreting and communicating the results.

6 ***Identify each of the methods available for segmenting consumer and business markets.***

Consumer markets can be divided according to demographic characteristics, such as age and family size; geographical factors; psychographic variables, which involve behavioral and lifestyle profiles; and product-related variables, such as the benefits consumers seek when buying a product or the degree of brand loyalty they feel toward it. Business markets are segmented according to three criteria: geographic characteristics, customer-based specifications for products, and end-user applications.

7 ***Distinguish between buyer behavior and consumer behavior.***

Buyer behavior refers to the purchase processes of both individual consumers who buy goods and services for their own use and organizational buyers who purchase business products. Consumer behavior refers to the actions of ultimate consumers with direct effects on obtaining, consuming, and disposing of products, as well as the decision processes that precede and follow these actions. Personal influences on consumer behavior include an individual's needs and motives, perceptions, attitudes, learned experiences, and self-concept. The interpersonal determinants include cultural influences, social influences, and family influences. A number of people may participate in business purchase decisions, so business buyers encounter a variety of organizational influences in addition to their own preferences.

8 ***Discuss the benefits of relationship marketing.***

Relationship marketing is an organization's attempt to develop long-term, cost-effective links with individual customers for mutual benefit. Good relationships with customers can be a vital strategic weapon for a firm. By identifying current purchasers and maintaining a positive relationship with them, an organization can efficiently target its best customers, fulfill their needs, and create loyalty. Information technologies, such as computers, databases, and the Internet, support effective relationship marketing.

Business Terms You Need to Know

marketing 384

utility 385

marketing concept 386

customer satisfaction 387

target market 394

marketing mix 394

marketing research 396

data mining 399

market segmentation 400

buyer behavior 406

consumer behavior 406

relationship marketing 409

Other Important Business Terms

exchange process 385

time utility 385

place utility 385

ownership utility 385

value-added 387

person marketing 391

place marketing 391

event marketing 392

cause marketing 392

organization marketing 393

consumer (B2C) product 394

business (B2B) product 394

data warehouse 399

geographical segmentation 401

demographic
    segmentation 402

psychographic
    segmentation 403

product-related
    segmentation 404

end-use segmentation 406

transaction marketing 409

lifetime value of a
    customer 410

frequency marketing 411

affinity program 411

comarketing 411

cobranding 411

Review Questions

1. Define the four different types of utility and explain how marketing contributes to the creation of utility. Then choose one of the following companies and describe how it creates each type of utility with its goods or services:
   a. Krispy Kreme doughnuts
   b. Sea World
   c. Barnes & Noble bookstore
   d. H&R Block tax preparation service

2. What might be some good ways for a large food manufacturer like General Mills to obtain customer feedback?

3. What constitutes a market? Distinguish between the B2C market and the B2B market.

4. Identify the five types of nontraditional marketing and give an example of each.

5. Identify each of the following as a consumer product or a business product, or classify it as both:
   a. loaf of bread
   b. laptop computer
   c. electricity
   e. automobile license plates
   f. concert tickets
   g. lawn-mowing service

6. Explain each of the basic steps in developing a marketing strategy. What is a target market? Why is target market selection the first step performed in marketing strategy development?

7. What are the five basic reasons that marketers conduct research? Identify the basic methods used in collecting research data.

8. Explain each of the methods used to segment consumer and business markets. Which methods do you think would be most effective for each of the following and why? (Note that a combination of methods might be applicable.)
   a. supermarket featuring Mexican foods
   b. air conditioning units
   c. snow tires
   d. line of expensive golf clubs
   e. nursing home insurance
   f. laser eye surgery

9. Explain two ways that businesses use relationships to achieve corporate objectives.

10. What are the benefits, both to businesses and their customers, of relationship marketing?

Projects and Applications

1. Choose one of the following businesses and describe ways in which the owner might add value to the goods or services offered:
   a. tanning salon
   b. for-profit career placement service
   c. online apparel retailer
   d. supermarket

2. Choose a nonprofit organization that interests you, such as the Red Cross, the Nature Conservancy, National Park Service, or Smithsonian Institution. Research the organization online to learn more about it. Outline your proposed contents for a sample brochure based on the chapter discussion of nontraditional marketing, such as cause marketing or organization marketing.

3. Think of two situations in which you have been a customer: one in which you have been satisfied with the merchandise you received and one in which you have not. Make a list of the reasons you were satisfied in the first case and another list of the reasons you were not satisfied in the second case. Would you say that the failure was the result of marketers not understanding your needs?

4. Imagine that you are a marketer for Heinz, and you think your company has found a terrific new opportunity with its multicolored ketchups. How would you apply the information gained from marketing research conducted for the new ketchups to expand another food line—say, peanut butter, mustard, or mayonnaise?

5. Go online, pick up a magazine, or turn on the TV to search for a promotional effort that uses either comarketing or cobranding. Describe the ad, commercial, or special offer and explain whether you think it is effective—and why or why not.

Experiential Exercise

Background: This chapter has focused on the importance of building and maintaining relationships with customers. Two techniques for accomplishing this are frequency marketing programs and affinity programs.

Directions: Visit a so-called "big-box" retailer such as Wal-Mart, Target, or Lowe's. If you can't make the trip, access one of these firms online.

1. Make yourself familiar with the range of products your retailer offers, including any special services such as free delivery or gift wrapping.

2. Design a frequency marketing program or affinity program for the retailer that is designed to build relationships with the consumers who shop at the store.

3. Present your program to the class and ask your classmates whether it would encourage them to shop at the store—and why or why not.

NOTHING BUT NET

1. **Market segmentation.** Visit the Web site of a major firm that offers several products and prepare a report discussing how the company implements its market segmentation strategy. For instance, does it segment its markets by geography, demographics, psychographics, or a combination of techniques? Choose one of the following companies or select your own:

   http://www.mcdonalds.com
   http://www.microsoft.com
   http://www.eddiebauer.com
   http://www.harley-davidson.com
   http://www.dunkindonuts.com

2. **Census data.** Assume you are planning to start a small business, or buy a franchise, in your hometown (or in the town where your school is located). Visit the Census Bureau's Web site (http://www.census.gov) and make a list of the census data available that would help you in the development of a marketing strategy for your new business.

3. **Marketing higher education.** Today, virtually all colleges and universities have their own Web sites. Most use their sites to market the school to prospective students. Go to your institution's Web site and the Web sites of two other schools. Identify and evaluate the impact on you personally (positive, negative, or neutral) of the Web marketing strategies employed. What elements of the site made you react the way you did?

Note: Internet Web addresses change frequently. If you do not find the exact sites listed, you may need to access the organization's or company's home page and search from there.

Case 12.1

Marketing to Tweens

Tweens have come of age. Identified by many marketers as young people between the ages of 8 and 12, tweens may not be old enough to drive or vote, but they are old enough to buy, and today's tweens wield considerable purchasing power. Whether they have their own money, from allowances to cash earned from odd jobs, or influence adults who make the actual purchases, these 30 million consumers are now one of the most powerful groups in the country. They spend about $10 billion on their own each year and influence another $74 billion of family spending. Although they have much in common, they aren't all alike; one in every three American tweens is a member of a racial or ethnic minority. Marketers want to reach them all—or as many as possible. Creating a strong relationship with a tween, the thinking goes, may mean continuing a strong relationship for life. But to do so, firms must be able to offer goods and services that fulfill needs as people grow through different stages of life, which isn't always practical. Still, being able to reach tweens and influence their buying decisions represents a huge market.

Tweens clothing retailer Limited Too seems to have found a formula for success. Girls age 7 to 14 and their parents can shop for the retailer's trendy clothing in its shops, through its "catazine," or online. Fashions and colors change from season to season, keeping up with the rapidly changing tastes of tween girls. One season's collection might feature "retro" seventies-style peasant tops and crocheted sweaters; another might focus on lime green or aqua skorts. Limited Too has a variety of programs aimed at building a relationship with the girls and their shopping-weary parents—frequent buyer cards, a Birthday Club, a $5 discount when a tween presents a current report card with passing grades, and "Too Bucks," a program in which customers spend a certain amount to receive Too Bucks coupons. Of course, Limited Too tweens eventually outgrow the store's fashions; but they may have younger sisters who become customers.

Unilever's Bestfoods division is also searching for tween customers, launching Ragu Express, a line of microwavable pasta meals aimed at busy tweens and teens who want a quick, hot after-school snack. Ads for Ragu Express carry the tag line "Real pasta. Real food. Real fast." and show tweens engaged in typical activities like commuting to school, fixing a bicycle, and complaining about boring after-school snacks.

Other food and beverage firms are making bids for the tween market, attempting to influence their purchasing behavior by teaming up with media companies. Tony's Pizza partnered with Miramax and AMC/General Cinema theaters in promoting *Spy Kids II: Island of Lost Dreams.* The alliance offered tweens a chance to win lunch with the movie's cast. Tony's has shifted its marketing focus toward tweens since its marketing research has shown that pizza is the favorite food for 53 percent of tweens and 45 percent of tweens influence their family's choice of frozen pizza brands. "We knew all along that kids were the primary users of our brand," says Mark Rehborg, Tony's national brand group manager. "Now we want to communicate with them in their language."

QUESTIONS FOR CRITICAL THINKING
1. Marketers have identified tweens—consumers between the ages of 8 and 12—as a market segment. What characteristics other than age might marketers use to further segment this market?
2. What tools might Tony's Pizza use to nurture its relationship with tweens?

Sources: Limited Too Web site, http://www.limitedtoo.com, accessed February 1, 2004; Jim Kirk, "Generation $$," *The Mercury News,* January 4, 2003, http://www.bayarea.com/mld/mercurynews; Sonia Reyes, "Tony's Pizza Gives Tweens Assignment to Uncover 'Spy Kids II' Rewards," *Brandweek,* June 24, 2002, p. 6; "Keen on Tweens," *Brandweek,* May 6, 2002, pp. 26–34.

Video Case 12.2

Goya Foods
This video case appears on page 614. A recently filmed video, designed to expand and highlight the written case, is available for class use by instructors.

Chapter 13
Product and Distribution Strategies

Click: Kodak Reinvents Itself for the Digital Age

What does the inventor of the original Brownie and Instamatic cameras do for the digital age? Although the firm has been through some rough times in recent years as sales have dropped and layoffs have followed, managers at Eastman Kodak have no intentions of closing the shutters. To the contrary,

Kodak is now positioning itself for the new age of digital photos. In the U.S. and around the globe, traditional film is fading fast—consumers are buying fewer and fewer film cameras, opting instead for digital products. In fact, more than 30 percent of U.S. households have at least one digital camera. So, although Kodak has long been considered the gold standard in film—despite competition from Fuji—maintaining the top spot in film no longer matters.

It is ironic that Kodak actually produced the first digital camera in 1975. But the firm never pursued the technology, and 25 years later found itself behind competitors. Now, under the direction of CEO Antonio M. Perez, Kodak has begun vigorously to pursue digital imaging, focusing on products for the consumer, business, and health-care markets. Kodak recently acquired a division from National Semiconductor that develops and produces imaging sensors. This technology could help Kodak enter the market for cameras in cell phones and other handheld electronics. The company introduced six new digital cameras last year and has upgraded its photo-processing kiosks in CVS stores to process wirelessly photos from camera phones. The Kodak kiosks still walk consumers step by step through the printing process and accept memory cards.

With its long heritage of producing top-quality prints, focusing on prints from digital images is a natural for Kodak. A recent group of television ads featured the tag line, "the best part of photography is the prints." One version of the ad showed consumers using Kodak's kiosks and another showed them at their own EasyShare printer docks, at home. The EasyShare system, introduced several years ago, initially

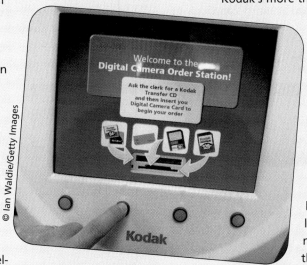

© Ian Waldie/Getty Images

included a digital camera that had to be hooked up to a computer to get prints. Now the system includes a portable printer dock. Consumers report that they keep it on the kitchen counter because they can return home from an outing, stick the camera on the dock, and out pop the prints.

CEO Perez is also dusting off a significant number of Kodak's more than 20,000 patents, looking for new ways to use them. "The intellectual property and knowhow is unbelievable in the company," he has reported. "There is no excuse not to succeed." One possible project stemming from these patents involves a change in inkjet printers that could mean new business for Kodak.

While film sales continue to decline steadily, Kodak's digital sales have jumped 44 percent during the last 12 months, and digital products now account for about 30 percent of the firm's revenues. Kodak is still behind Sony in market share for digital products. But Sony and Kodak appeal to different groups of consumers, and the longer Kodak stays in the digital market, the more ground it will cover. Sony's products are viewed as stylish and cutting edge, appealing to younger consumers who are eager to buy the latest goods. But Sony doesn't have the photographic history that belongs to Kodak, which appeals to more traditional consumers who want to take pictures that will last a lifetime. And despite the fact that 30 percent of U.S. households do have digital cameras, 70 percent do not—meaning that there are millions of consumers out there waiting to buy their first one. Kodak is ready to turn those consumers into loyal digital customers.[1]

Chapter Overview

In this chapter, we examine ways in which organizations design and implement marketing strategies that address customers' needs and wants and focus on the first two elements of the marketing mix: product and distribution. The creation of new products is the lifeblood of an organization. Since products do not remain economically viable forever, new ones must be developed to ensure the survival of an organization. The discussion of product strategy begins by describing the classifications of goods and services, customer service, product lines and the product mix, and the product life cycle. We also discuss product identification through brand names and distinctive packaging.

Distribution, the second mix variable discussed, focuses on moving goods and services from producers to buyers. It includes decisions such as where to offer products for sale and examines logistics, the process of physically moving information, goods, and services.

Product Strategy

product bundle of physical, service, and symbolic attributes designed to enhance buyers' want satisfaction.

Although most people respond to the question "What is a product?" by listing its physical features, marketers take a broader view. To them, a **product** is a bundle of physical, service, and symbolic attributes designed to satisfy consumer wants. The chief executive officer of a major tool manufacturer once startled his stockholders with this statement: "Last year our customers bought over 1 million quarter-inch drill bits, and none of them wanted to buy the product. They all wanted quarter-inch holes." *Product strategy* involves considerably more than just producing a good or service and focuses on benefits. It includes decisions about package design, brand name, trademarks, warranties, product image, new-product development, and customer service. Think, for instance, about your favorite soft drink. Do you like it for its taste alone, or do other attributes, such as clever ads, attractive packaging, ease of purchase from vending machines and other convenient locations, and overall image also attract you? These other attributes may influence your choice more than you realize.

Specialty products, like diamond jewelry, are those items consumers will make the most effort to purchase. Since such products are also usually quite expensive, consumers will often spend time and energy researching exactly what they want, finding the best source to buy it from, and traveling to make the purchase if necessary. This Hearts on Fire promotion emphasizes the fact that, like most other specialty goods, diamonds have no close substitute as far as the giver—and the recipient—are concerned.

"WOW"
Funny, everybody has the same reaction.

Available from $1,200 to $1,000,000

HEARTS ON FIRE®
THE WORLD'S MOST PERFECTLY CUT DIAMOND™

© AP/Wide World Photos

Classifying Goods and Services

Marketers have found it useful to classify goods and services as either B2C or B2B depending on the purchasers of the particular item. These classifications can be subdivided further, and each type requires a different competitive strategy.

Marketing Strategy Factor	Convenience Product	Shopping Product	Specialty Product
• **Purchase Frequency**	• Frequent	• Relatively infrequent	• Infrequent
• **Store Image**	• Unimportant	• Very important	• Important
• **Price**	• Low	• Relatively high	• High
• **Promotion**	• By manufacturer	• By manufacturer and retailers	• By manufacturer and retailers
• **Distribution Channel**	• Many wholesalers and retailers	• Relatively few wholesalers and retailers	• Very few wholesalers and retailers
• **Number of Retail Outlets**	• Many	• Few	• Very small number; often one per market area

FIGURE 13.1
Marketing Impacts of Consumer Product Classifications

Classifying Consumer Goods and Services   The classification typically used for ultimate consumers who purchase products for their own use and enjoyment and not for resale is based on consumer buying habits. **Convenience products** are items the consumer seeks to purchase frequently, immediately, and with little effort. Items stocked in 7-Eleven stores, vending machines, and local newsstands are usually convenience products—for example, newspapers, chewing gum, disposable diapers, and bread.

Shopping products are those typically purchased only after the buyer has compared competing products in competing stores. A person intent on buying a new sofa or dining room table may visit many stores, examine perhaps dozens of pieces of furniture, and spend days making the final decision. **Specialty products,** the third category of consumer products, are those that a purchaser is willing to make a special effort to obtain. The purchaser is already familiar with the item and considers it to have no reasonable substitute. The nearest Jaguar dealer may be 40 miles away, but if you have decided that you want one—and can afford it—you will make the trip.

Note that a shopping product for one person may be a convenience item for someone else. Each item's product classification is based on buying patterns of the majority of people who purchase it.

The interrelationship of the marketing mix factors is shown in Figure 13.1. By knowing the appropriate classification for a specific product, the marketing decision maker knows much about how the other mix variables will adapt to create a profitable, customer-driven marketing strategy.

Classifying Business Goods   *Business products* are goods and services like cell phones and personal computers used in operating an organization; they also include machinery, tools, raw materials, components, and buildings used to produce other products for resale. While consumer products are classified by buying habits, business products are classified based on how they are used and by their basic characteristics. Products that are long-lived and relatively expensive are called *capital items.* Less costly products that are consumed within a year are referred to as *expense items.*

Five basic categories of B2B products exist: installations, accessory equipment, component parts and materials, raw materials, and supplies. *Installations* are major capital items, such as new factories, heavy equipment and machinery, and custom-made equipment. Installations are expensive and often involve buyer and seller negotiations that may last for more than a year before a purchase actually is made. Purchase approval frequently involves a number of different people—production specialists, representatives from the purchasing department, and members of top management—who must agree on the final choice.

Although *accessory equipment* also includes capital items, they are usually less expensive and shorter lived than installations and involve fewer decision makers. Examples include hand tools and fax machines. *Component parts and materials* are finished business goods that become part of a final product, such as disk drives that are sold to computer manufacturers or batteries purchased by automakers. *Raw materials* are farm and natural products used in producing other final products. Examples include milk, iron ore, leather, and soybeans. *Supplies* are expense items used in a firm's daily operation that do not become part of the final product. Often referred to as MRO (maintenance, repair, and operating supplies), they include paper clips, light bulbs, and copy paper.

Classifying Services   Services can be classified as either B2C or B2B. Child- and elder-care centers and auto detail shops provide services for consumers, while the Pinkerton security patrol at a factory and Kelly Services' temporary office workers are examples of business services. In some cases, a service can accommodate both consumer and business markets. For example, when ServiceMaster cleans the upholstery in a home, it is a B2C service, but when it spruces up the painting system and robots in a manufacturing plant, it is a B2B service.

Like tangible goods, services can also be convenience, shopping, or specialty products depending on the buying patterns of customers. However, they are distinguished from goods in several ways. First of all, services, unlike goods, are intangible. In addition, they are perishable because firms cannot stockpile them in inventory. They are also difficult to standardize, since they must meet individual customers' needs. Finally, from a buyer's perspective, the service provider is the service; the two are inseparable in the buyer's mind.

Marketing Strategy Implications

The consumer product classification system is a useful tool in marketing strategy. As described in Figure 13.1, once a new desktop computer has been classified as a shopping good, marketers have a better idea of its promotion, pricing, and distribution needs.

> ### They Said It
>
> In all minor discussions between Statler employees and Statler guests, the employee is dead wrong.
>
> —*Ellsworth M. Statler (1863–1928)*
> *American hotel-chain owner*

Each group of business products, however, requires a different marketing strategy. Because most installations and many component parts frequently are marketed directly from manufacturer to business buyer, the promotional emphasis is on personal selling rather than on advertising. By contrast, marketers of supplies and accessory equipment rely more on advertising, since their products often are sold through an intermediary, such as a wholesaler. Producers of installations and component parts may involve their customers in new-product development, especially when the business product is custom made. Finally, firms marketing supplies and accessory equipment place greater emphasis on competitive pricing strategies than do other B2B product marketers, who tend to concentrate more on product quality and customer service.

Product Lines and Product Mix

Few firms operate with a single product. If their initial entry is successful, they tend to increase their profit and growth chances by adding new items to offer their customers. Some goods producers are even able to branch out into services. Dell, Inc., for instance, recently emerged from the slowdown in PC sales not only by adding printers, personal digital assistants, and a new low-price Axim pocket wireless e-mail device to its product line but also by marketing technical services to its business customers. Says founder and CEO Michael Dell, "[Suppose] you want to put in a network for an e-mail system. We'll do that. And we'll design our servers into it. . . . Since we're already selling the hardware, it's a natural extension to include services."[2]

A company's **product line** is a group of related products marked by physical similarities or intended for a similar market. Figure 13.2 shows various product lines that make up a **product mix,** the assortment of product lines and individual goods and services that a firm offers to consumers and business users. Although the Kellogg Co. first appeared in 1906 with a single product—Kellogg's Corn Flakes—

product line group of related products that are physically similar or are intended for the same market.

product mix company's assortment of product lines and individual offerings.

FIGURE 13.2
Kellogg's Product Mix

today its product mix has several product lines, including milk bars mixed with different cereals, Real Fruit Winders, Rice Krispies Squares, and Pop Tarts. Levi Strauss plans to extend its Dockers casual-clothing product line by moving into home furnishings.[3]

Marketers must assess their product mix continually to ensure company growth, to satisfy changing consumer needs and wants, and to adjust to competitors' offerings. To remain competitive, marketers look for gaps in their product lines and fill them with new products or modified versions of existing ones. A helpful tool that is frequently used in making product decisions is the product life cycle.

Concept Check

1. *Differentiate among convenience, shopping, and specialty products.*
2. *How do business products differ from consumer items?*

Product Life Cycle

Once a product is on the market, it usually goes through a series of four stages known as the **product life cycle:** introduction, growth, maturity, and decline. As Figure 13.3 shows, industry sales and profits will vary depending on the life-cycle stage of a product.

Product life cycles are not set in stone; not all products follow this pattern precisely, and different products may spend different periods of time in each stage. The concept, however, helps the marketing planner anticipate developments throughout the various stages of a product's life. Profits assume a predictable pattern through the stages, and promotional emphasis must shift from dispensing product information in the early stages to heavy brand promotion in the later ones.

product life cycle four basic stages—introduction, growth, maturity, and decline—through which a successful product progresses.

Stages of the Product Life Cycle

In the *introduction stage,* the firm tries to promote demand for its new offering, inform the market about it, give free samples to entice consumers to make a trial purchase, and explain its features, uses, and benefits. McDonald's, for instance, has used its stores around the country to test the introduction of new menu items like donuts, pizza slices, and higher-quality salads, as well as such services as Internet access, karaoke booths, and table service.[4] New-product development costs and extensive introductory promotional campaigns to acquaint prospective buyers with the merits of the innovation, though essential to later success, are expensive and commonly lead to losses in the introductory stage. Losses also occur due to the relatively low sales and high costs of promotions, establishing distribution channels, and training the sales force about the new product's advantages. It is not uncommon for firms to spend $30 million to introduce new packaged-goods products like detergents, bottled waters, and candies. But such expenditures are necessary if the firm is to profit later.

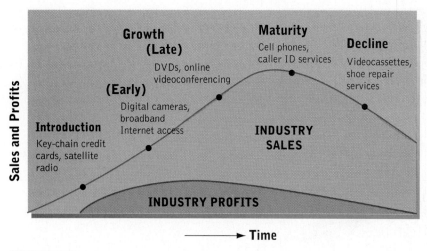

Sales and Profits

Growth (Late)
DVDs, online videoconferencing

(Early)
Digital cameras, broadband Internet access

Introduction
Key-chain credit cards, satellite radio

Maturity
Cell phones, caller ID services

Decline
Videocassettes, shoe repair services

INDUSTRY SALES

INDUSTRY PROFITS

→ **Time**

FIGURE 13.3
Stages in the Product Life Cycle

During the *growth stage,* sales climb quickly as new customers join early users who now are repurchasing the item. Word-of-mouth referrals and continued advertising and other special promotions by the firm induce others to make trial purchases. At this point, the company begins to earn profits on the new product. This success encourages competitors to enter the field with similar offerings, and price competition appears. Digital cameras are moving into the growth stage, and film suppliers like Eastman Kodak are struggling to continue their century-long record of sales and revenue growth in the wake of the greatest challenge ever to its market. One technology that is in the growth stage is radio-frequency identification devices (see the Hits & Misses box).

In the *maturity stage,* industry sales at first increase, but eventually, they reach a saturation level at which further expansion is difficult. Competition also intensifies, increasing the availability of the product. Firms concentrate on capturing competitors' customers, often dropping prices to further the appeal. Cell phones are moving into the maturity stage: Competitors compete not only on price but also on features such as calendars, e-mail and attachments, messaging capability, full-color screens, keyboards, and fax and word processing functions. A similar business environment also faces the world's largest personal computer marketers, who compete in an increasingly saturated U.S. market where 53 percent of all homes already have a PC and virtually all businesses are computerized.

Sales volume fades late in the maturity stage, and some of the weaker competitors leave the market.

Premium Salads, a recent menu addition to the McDonald's product offerings, represents an attempt to enhance food choices for adults preferring salads for their meals. The use of Newman's Own all-natural dressing adds to the image of the new offerings.

Pinch yourself.

Introducing
Premium Salads from
McDonald's.

What makes these new salads so surprising? A breast of warm, tender, grilled or crispy chicken that sits atop a sumptuous bed of premium greens. All tossed with delicious ingredients like hickory smoked bacon, real bleu cheese, or fresh parmesan and Newman's Own all-natural dressing. Choose California Cobb, Caesar or Bacon Ranch. For a taste that's almost too good to be true. At McDonald's.

Yeah,
McDonald's.

At participating McDonald's. ©2003 McDonald's Corporation.

During this stage, firms promote mature products aggressively to protect their market share and to distinguish their products from those of competitors.

Sales continue to fall in the *decline stage,* the fourth phase of the product life cycle. Profits decline and may become losses as further price-cutting occurs in the reduced overall market for the item. Competitors gradually exit, making some profits possible for the remaining firms in the shrinking market. The decline stage usually is caused by a product innovation or a shift in consumer preferences. Sometimes technology change can hasten the decline stage for a product. One of every three U.S. residences contains at least one DVD player, and DVDs have surpassed videocassettes in both sales and rental revenue. Releases of both new and older films on DVD are rapidly overtaking the VHS format, which some film studios—and a growing number of rental outlets—have abandoned.[5]

Used with permission from McDonald's Corporation.

HITS & MISSES

RFID: Improved Channel Efficiency

Bar codes may soon be a thing of the past, not that anyone will necessarily miss them. But there's a new code coming to your supermarket, and it's called RFID, for radio-frequency identification device. An RFID tag is a tiny computer chip with an antenna implanted somewhere on a product or its packaging. It uses a low-frequency radio signal to identify specific items, whereas a bar code simply identifies categories of products. The RFID doesn't require a line of sight for a scanner to identify it the way a bar code does, which means that items packed in cases and loaded onto trucks can still be identified by a handheld RFID reader.

If this technology still doesn't sound too exciting, consider this. With the most sophisticated technology, an RFID can contain as much as several pages of data about the product, where it has been in the supply chain, and where it ends up. The benefits include helping retailers manage inventories, reduce theft, and cut costs. And the technology itself isn't new: Drivers already use RFID tags to glide through the fast lane in toll booths, and veterinarians embed the chips beneath the skin of dogs and cats for easy tracking if they get lost.

Wal-Mart already requires its top suppliers to use RFID tags on pallets and containers of items. The tagging of individual products is not far off.

Critics warn that RFID technology may ultimately provide too much information about the habits of individual consumers, raising the question of privacy invasion. But those in favor say that channel efficiency will be improved to the benefit of consumers.

QUESTIONS FOR CRITICAL THINKING
1. Describe one place along the supply chain where the use of an RFID on a package of household batteries would be beneficial.
2. Do you agree with the use of RFID tags on individual products? Why or why not?

Sources: Kevin Maney, "RFID: Robot for Infinite Decluttering?" *USA Today,* October 6, 2004, p. 10B; "Wal-Mart Is Watching You," *Wired,* July 2004, p. 44; Andrea Coombes, "An Expansive Signal," *CBS MarketWatch,* July 6, 2004, http://cbs.marketwatch.com; Greg Griffin, "Bye-Bye Bar Codes?" *Mobile Register,* June 13, 2004, p. F3.

Marketing Strategy Implications of the Product Life Cycle

Like the product classification system, the product life cycle is a useful concept for designing a marketing strategy that will be flexible enough to accommodate changing marketplace characteristics. These competitive moves may involve developing new products, lowering prices, increasing distribution coverage, creating new promotional campaigns, or any combination of these strategies. In general, the marketer's objective is to extend the product life cycle as long as the item is profitable. Some products can be highly profitable during the later stages of their life cycle, since all of the initial development costs already have been recovered.

A commonly used strategy for extending the life cycle is to increase customers' frequency of use. Wal-Mart and Target have added grocery sections as major components of their giant discount-store locations, hoping to convince regular customers to stop in more frequently and pick up groceries.[6] Another strategy is to add new users. With cigarette sales in decline, Zippo Manufacturing is marketing a new Zippo Multi-Purpose Lighter for igniting candles, fireplaces, and grills. It boasts an advanced ignition system, a patented childproof safety lock, and a sturdy metal case.[7] Arm & Hammer used a third approach: finding new uses for its products. The original use of the firm's baking soda in baking has been augmented by its newer uses as a toothpaste, refrigerator freshener, and flame extinguisher. A fourth product life cycle extension strategy—changing package sizes, labels, and product designs— works well for White Castle, which introduced a new briefcase-size carton that holds 30 of its trademark tiny hamburgers, adding the value of convenience to its classic take-out menu. The Crave Case has been a hit, increasing sales for the chain at a time when profits at other fast-food restaurants have dipped.[8]

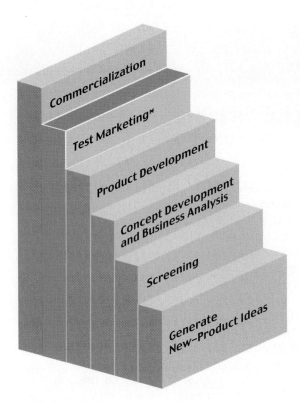

FIGURE 13.4
Process for Developing New Goods and Services
*Some firms skip this step and move directly from product development to commercialization.

Stages in New-Product Development

In one recent year, more than 32,000 new domestic products were introduced—over twice the number a decade ago.[9] New-product development is expensive, time-consuming, and risky, since only about one-third of new products become success stories. Products can fail for many reasons. Some are not properly developed and tested, some are poorly packaged, and others lack adequate promotional support or distribution or fail because they do not satisfy a consumer need or want. Even successful products eventually reach the end of the decline stage and must be replaced with new-product offerings.

Most of today's newly developed items are aimed at satisfying specific consumer demands. New-product development is becoming increasingly efficient and cost-effective because marketers use a systematic approach in developing new products. As Figure 13.4 shows, the new-product development process has six stages. Each stage requires a "go/no go" decision by management before moving on to subsequent stages. Since products that go through each development stage only to be rejected at one of the final stages involve significant investments in both money and time, the sooner that decision makers can identify a marginal product and drop it from further consideration, the less time and money will be wasted.

The starting point in the new-product development process is generating ideas for new offerings. Ideas come from many sources, including customer suggestions, suppliers, employees, research scientists, marketing research, inventors outside the firm, and competitive products. The most successful ideas are directly related to satisfying customer needs. Entrepreneur Stephanie Kellar was inspired to launch her innovative eyelash curler after the traditional model she used pinched her face.[10]

In the second stage, screening eliminates ideas that do not mesh with overall company objectives or cannot be developed given the company's resources. Some firms hold open discussions of new-product ideas with specialists who work in different functional areas in the organization.

During the concept development and business analysis phase, further screening is done. The analysis involves assessing the new product's potential sales, profits, growth rate, and competitive strengths and whether it fits with the company's product, distribution, and promotional resources. *Concept testing*—marketing research designed to solicit initial consumer reaction to new-product ideas before the products are developed—may be used at this stage. For example, potential consumers might be asked about proposed brand names and other methods of product identification.

Next, an actual product is developed, subjected to a series of tests, and revised. Functioning prototypes or detailed descriptions of the product may be created. These designs are the joint responsibility of the firm's development staff and its marketers, who provide feedback on consumer reactions to the proposed product design, color, and other physical features.

During the test marketing stage, the item is sold in a limited area while the company examines both consumer responses to the new offering and the marketing effort used to support it. Cities or television coverage areas that are typical of the targeted market segments are selected for such tests. Test market results can help managers determine the product's likely performance in a full-scale introduction. Some firms choose to skip test marketing, however, because of concerns that the test could reveal their product strategies to the competition. Also, the expense of developing limited production runs of complex products such as a new PDA (personal digital assistant), auto, or refrigerator is so high that the test marketing stage is skipped and the development process moves directly to the next stage.

In the final stage, commercialization, the product is made generally available in the marketplace. Sometimes this stage is referred to as a product launch. Considerable planning goes into this stage, since the firm's distribution, promotion, and pricing strategies must all be geared to support the new product offerings.

The need for a steady stream of new products to offer the firm's customers, the chances of product failure, and the $20 million to $50 million cost of completing a successful new-product launch make new-product development a vital process for 21st-century firms. However, as Table 13.1 illustrates, suc-

Table 13.1	The Five Worst Cars of the Millennium	
Rank	**Auto**	**Typical Owner Comment**
1	Yugo	"At least it had heated rear windows—so your hands would stay warm while you pushed."
2	Chevy Vega	"Burned so much oil, it was singlehandedly responsible for the formation of OPEC."
3	Ford Pinto	"The car would do 75 mph in 2nd gear, shaking apart and sounding like a bat out of hell. In 4th gear, the top speed was 70 mph. What's wrong with this picture? You do the math."
4	AMC Gremlin	"Calling it a pregnant roller skate would be kind."
5	Chevy Chevette	"If I got on the Interstate without being run over, the car would creep towards 55. About an hour later, I'd reach it. Then the shaking would begin."

Source: Reported in "Car Talk," downloaded from http://cartalk.cars.com, accessed August 11, 2003.

cess is not guaranteed until the new-product offering achieves customer acceptance. General Motors witnessed this principle when the company launched its much-ridiculed Aztek sport-utility vehicle. The design had started out as a smaller vehicle, like a tall station wagon meant to appeal to younger drivers. But for cost considerations, the design was adapted to fit GM's mini-van platform and then further modified to fit Pontiac's aggressive image. In testing, markets were divided in their opinion, but GM delivered a crushing blow to the Aztek by pricing it at the high end of what its younger target market could afford. Following the product launch, instead of taking to the back roads, Azteks sat quietly on dealers' lots.

Concept Check

1. Describe the four stages of the product life cycle.
2. Where do ideas for new products come from?

Product Identification

A major aspect of developing a successful new product involves methods used for identifying a product and distinguishing it from competing offerings. Both tangible goods and intangible services are identified by brands, brand names, and trademarks. A **brand** is a name, term, sign, symbol, design, or some combination thereof used to identify the products of one firm and to differentiate them from competitive offerings. Diet Coke, Fruitopia, and Nestea are all made by the Coca-Cola Co., but a unique combination of name, symbol, and package design distinguishes each brand from the others.

A **brand name** is that part of the brand consisting of words or letters included in a name used to identify and distinguish the firm's offerings from those of competitors. The brand name is the part of the brand that can be vocalized. Many brand names, such as Coca-Cola, McDonald's, American Express, and Nike, are famous around the world. Likewise, the "Golden Arches" brand mark of McDonald's also is widely recognized.

A **trademark** is a brand that has been given legal protection. The protection is granted solely to the brand's owner. Trademark protection includes not only the brand name but also design logos, slogans, packaging elements, and product features such as color and shape. A well-designed trademark can make a definite difference in how consumers perceive a brand.

brand name, term, sign, symbol, design, or some combination that identifies the products of a firm and distinguishes them from competitive offerings.

Selecting an Effective Brand Name

Good brands are easy to pronounce, recognize, and remember: Crest, Visa, and Avis are examples. Global firms face a real problem in selecting brand names, since an excellent brand name in one country may prove disastrous in another. Most languages have a short *a*, so Coca-Cola is pronounceable almost anywhere. But an advertising campaign for E-Z washing machines failed in the United Kingdom because the British pronounce *z* as "zed."

Brand names should also convey the right image to the buyer. One effective technique is to create a name that links the product with its positioning strategy. The name Dial reinforces the concept of 24-hour protection, EverReady batteries give an impression of dependability, and Taster's Choice instant coffee supports the promotional claim "Tastes and smells like ground roast coffee."

Brand names also must be legally protectable. Trademark law specifies that brand names cannot contain words in general use, such as *television* or *automobile*. Generic words—words that describe a type of product—cannot be used exclusively by any organization. On the other hand, if a brand name becomes so popular that it passes into common language and turns into a generic word, the company can no longer use it as a brand name. Once upon a time, aspirin, linoleum, and zipper were exclusive brand names, but today, they have become generic terms and are no longer legally protectable.

Brand Categories

A brand offered and promoted by a manufacturer is known as a **manufacturer's (**or **national) brand.** Examples are Tide, Jockey, Gatorade, Swatch, and Reebok. But not all brand names belong to manufacturers; some are the property of retailers or distributors. A **private (**or **store) brand** identifies a product that is not linked to the manufacturer but instead carries a wholesaler's or retailer's label. The Sears line of DieHard batteries and Wal-Mart's Old Roy dog food are examples.

Many retailers offer a third option, *generic products,* which have plain packaging and minimal labeling, enjoy little if any advertising, and meet only minimum quality standards. Intended to compete with well-known manufacturers' and private brands, generic products are typically priced considerably below these brands. Many consumer goods are available as generic products, such as paper towels, bathroom tissue, breakfast cereal, canned vegetables, and pasta.

This Heinz Ketchup ad reinforces the belief of diners that Heinz Ketchup is the only logical choice when they eat out as well as at home. The campaign's tag line, "A good meal out deserves a great ketchup. Insist on Heinz," is intended to extend the life cycle of this familiar product by building brand insistence for Heinz.

Must not be Heinz.

A good meal out deserves a great ketchup. Insist on

HEINZ TOMATO KETCHUP

H.J. Heinz Company

Another branding decision marketers must make is whether to use a family branding strategy or an individual branding strategy. A **family brand** is a single brand name used for several related products. KitchenAid, Johnson & Johnson, Hewlett-Packard, and Dole use a family name for their entire line of products. When a firm using family branding introduces a new product, both customers and retailers recognize the familiar brand name. The promotion of individual products within a line benefits all the products because the family brand is well known.

Other firms utilize an **individual branding** strategy by giving each product within a line a different name. For example, Procter & Gamble has individual brand names for its different laundry detergents, including Tide, Cheer, and Dash. Each brand targets a unique market segment. Consumers who want a cold-water detergent can choose Cheer over Tide or Dash, instead of purchasing a competitor's brand. Individual branding also builds competition within a firm and enables the company to increase overall sales.

Brand Loyalty and Brand Equity

Brands achieve varying consumer familiarity and acceptance. While a racing fan may insist on a Callaway Speedster when buying a car, the consumer buying a loaf of bread may not prefer any brand. Consumer loyalty increases a brand's value, so marketers try to strengthen brand loyalty. When a brand image suffers, marketers try to re-create a positive image (see the Solving an Ethical Controversy box).

Brand Loyalty   Marketers measure brand loyalty in three stages: brand recognition, brand preference, and brand insistence. *Brand recognition* is brand acceptance strong enough so that the consumer is aware of the brand, but not strong enough to cause a preference over other brands. Advertising, free samples, and discount coupons are among the most common ways to increase brand recognition.

Brand preference occurs when a consumer chooses one firm's brand over a competitor's. At this stage, the consumer is usually relying on previous experience in selecting the product. Automobiles and apparel fall into this category. Eight of ten owners of a Mercedes-Benz choose that brand again when they buy a new car. *Brand insistence* is the ultimate degree of brand loyalty, in which the consumer will accept no substitute for a preferred brand. If the desired product is not available, the consumer will look for it at another outlet, special order it from a dealer, order by mail, or search the Internet. Few firms can achieve brand insistence for their products, though cosmetics are one product that sometimes inspires this degree of loyalty.

Brand-building strategies were once limited to the consumer realm, but now they are becoming more important for B2B brands as well. Intel, Xerox, IBM, and service providers like Manpower and ServiceMaster are among the suppliers who have built brand names among business customers.

Brand Equity   Brand loyalty is at the heart of **brand equity,** the added value that a widely respected, highly successful name gives to a product in the marketplace. This value results from a combination of factors, including awareness, loyalty, and perceived quality, as well as any feelings or images the customer associates with the brand. High brand equity offers financial advantages to a firm, since the product commands a relatively large market share and sometimes reduces price sensitivity, generating higher profits. The world's 5 most valuable brands include Coca-Cola, Microsoft, IBM, Intel, and Nokia.[11]

Brand awareness means the product is the first one that comes to mind when a product category is mentioned. For instance, if someone says "diapers," you may instantly think of Pampers. *Brand association* is a link between a brand and other favorable images. When you think of getting together with friends over coffee, for example, you may associate that image with Starbucks.

Large companies have typically assigned the task of managing a brand's marketing strategies to a *brand manager,* who may also be called a *product manager* at some firms. This marketing professional plans and implements the balance of promotional, pricing, distribution, and product arrangements that leads to strong brand equity. A **category manager,** on the other hand, oversees a line of related products and assumes profit responsibility for his or her product group. Recently, companies have been reevaluating the effectiveness of brand management, and many consumer goods firms have adopted category management as part of their marketing strategy. Borders, a major retail book chain, revamped its cookbook section after analyzing sales data and selecting repeat buyers of cookbooks as its target market for the new category "Food and Cooking," which now includes nutrition books. The store's efforts to increase sales for this category faster than the store average include giving prominent display space to celebrity chefs and reducing the number of titles carried in certain subcategories.[12]

brand equity added value that a widely respected, highly successful name gives to a product in the marketplace.

Packages and Labels

Packaging and labels are important in product identification. They also play an important role in a firm's overall product strategy. Packaging affects the durability, image, and convenience of an item and is responsible for one of the biggest costs in many consumer products. As anyone who has struggled to open a newly purchased CD can attest, cost-effective packaging is one of industry's greatest needs.

SOLVING AN ETHICAL CONTROVERSY

Can America Improve Its Image Overseas?

Not everyone in the world is enamored with the U.S. People overseas often see unfavorable images of Americans. Photos of the wars in Afghanistan and Iraq, positioned along with lavish advertisements and TV programs depicting excessive lifestyles in the U.S., combine to create a view of Americans that is less than positive. Some people feel that the U.S. deserves the bad publicity; others don't understand why the country gets such a bad rap.

Can U.S. marketers rely on branding techniques to improve the nation's global image?

PRO

1. The nonprofit Business for Diplomatic Action (BDA) is creating programs designed to train U.S. businesspeople to become "good citizens" overseas. The BDA also plans to offer free English and technology classes in developing countries, and multicultural classes to students who plan to study overseas. The goal is to create good representatives of the U.S. overseas.
2. Marketers of multinational brands such as Coca-Cola, McDonald's, Nike, and Microsoft are shifting their focus from images like the American flag and focusing instead on local messages. "We try very hard to make our brands relevant regardless of what the political element might be," says Dick Detwiler of PepsiCo International. "We use local soccer stars. Local musicians. People with whom individuals in a particular market can identify."

CON

1. According to a poll by NOPWorld, "foreigners trust America less, like its brands less, and believe America is increasingly out of step with the values that the rest of the world holds dear."

2. The messages conveyed to U.S. consumers by marketers aren't effective overseas, and the total number of consumers who prefer American brands has declined, says polling firm NOPWorld.

SUMMARY

Many experts agree that the popularity of American goods and services overseas is tied to consumers' view of the country as a brand itself. They also believe that changes must be made. "We can't just throw in the towel and say, 'It's all about foreign policies,'" argues David Zucker of Porter Novelli, also a BDA board member.

Sources: Mandy de Wall and Janice Spark, "Brand America's Deteriorating Image Bad for Business," *Biz-Community,* September 17, 2004, www.biz-community.com; Hillary Chura, "Marketing Execs Try to Polish Brand USA," *Advertising Age,* May 17, 2004, p. 12; Jim Edwards, "Damn Americans," *Brandweek,* May 17, 2004, p. 24.

Choosing the right package is especially crucial in international marketing, since marketers must be aware of such factors as language variations and cultural preferences. Consumers in African nations often prefer bold colors, but flag colors may be preferred—or frowned upon—and red often is associated with death or witchcraft. Package size can vary according to the purchasing patterns and market conditions of a country. In countries with small refrigerators, people may want to buy their beverages one at a time rather than in six-packs. Package weight is another important issue, since shipping costs are often based on weight.

Labeling is an integral part of the packaging process as well. In the U.S., labeling must meet federal laws requiring companies to provide enough information to allow consumers to make value comparisons among competitive products and, in the case of food packaging, provide nutrition information on the label. Marketers who ship products to other countries have to comply with labeling requirements in these nations. This means knowing the answers to such questions as: Should the labels be in more than one language? Should ingredients be specified? Do the labels give enough information about the product to meet government standards? A recent lawsuit against McDonald's hinged on the amount of nutritional information the company provides about its products.

Another important aspect of packaging and labeling is the *Universal Product Code* (UPC), the bar code read by optical scanners that print the name of the item and the price on a receipt. For many stores, these identifiers are useful not

They Said It

Xenophobia doesn't benefit anybody unless you're playing high-stakes Scrabble.

—*Dennis Miller (b. 1953)*
American comedian

Concept Check
1. Differentiate between a brand, a brand name, and a trademark.
2. Define brand equity.

just for packaging and labeling but also for simplifying and speeding retail transactions and for evaluating customer purchases and controlling inventory.

Distribution Strategy

The next element of the marketing mix, **distribution strategy,** deals with the marketing activities and institutions involved in getting the right good or service to the firm's customers. Distribution decisions involve modes of transportation, warehousing, inventory control, order processing, and selection of marketing channels. Marketing channels typically are made up of intermediaries such as retailers and wholesalers that move a product from producer to final purchaser.

The two major components of an organization's distribution strategy are distribution channels and physical distribution. **Distribution channels** are the paths that products—and title to them—follow from producer to consumer or business user. They are the means by which all organizations distribute their goods and services. **Physical distribution** is the actual movement of these products from the producer to the user. Physical distribution covers a broad range of activities, including customer service, transportation, inventory control, materials handling, order processing, and warehousing.

distribution channel
path through which products—and legal ownership of them—flow from producer to consumers or business users.

physical distribution
actual movement of products from producer to consumers or business users.

Distribution Channels

In their first decision for distribution channel selection, marketers choose which type of channel will best meet both their firm's marketing objectives and the needs of their customers. As shown in Figure 13.5, marketers can choose either a **direct distribution channel,** which carries goods directly from producer to consumer or business user, or distribution channels that involve several different marketing intermediaries. A *marketing intermediary* (also called a *middleman*) is a business firm that moves goods between producers and consumers or business users. Marketing intermediaries perform various functions that help the distribution channel operate smoothly, such as buying, selling, storing, and transporting products; sorting and grading bulky items; and providing information to other channel members. The two main categories of marketing intermediaries are wholesalers and retailers.

The large number of goods and services distributed through so many different channels is enough to convince most observers that no one channel suits every product. The best choice depends on the circumstances of the market and on customer needs. The most appropriate channel choice may also change over time as new opportunities arise and marketers strive to maintain their

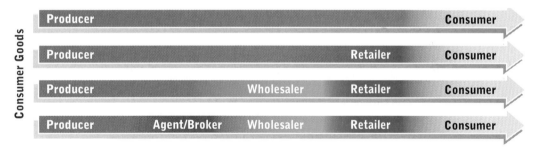

FIGURE 13.5
Alternative Distribution Channels

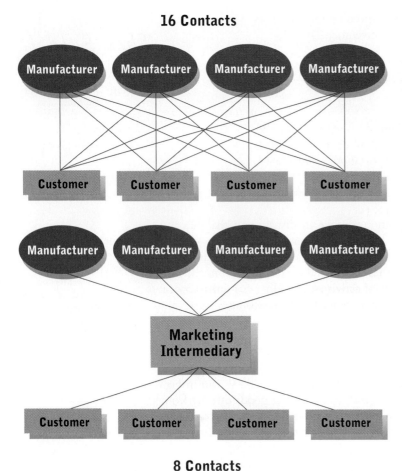

16 Contacts

8 Contacts

FIGURE 13.6
Reducing Transactions through Marketing Intermediaries

competitiveness. Dell, for instance, has launched a store-within-a-store trial by opening kiosks in selected Sears stores. Customers can select their computers at the store but will still place their orders online or over the phone, as Dell purchasers have always done. This decision allows Dell to avoid the costly strategy of keeping inventory at the stores. Of the kiosks, Dell senior vice president John Hamlin says, "We see it as another marketing vehicle to extend the direct [sales] model."[13]

Direct Distribution   The shortest and simplest means of connecting producers and customers is direct contact between the two parties. This approach is most common in the B2B market. It also serves consumers who buy fresh fruits and vegetables at rural roadside stands. Services ranging from banking and 10-minute oil changes to ear piercing employ direct distribution, as does Mary Kay Cosmetics.

Direct distribution is commonly found in the marketing of relatively expensive, complex products that may require demonstrations. Most major B2B products like installations, accessory equipment, component parts, business services, and even raw materials are typically marketed through direct contacts between producers and business buyers. The Internet has also made direct distribution an attractive option for many retail companies. Clinique sells its cosmetics at its own Web site as well as through department stores. Netflix allows movie enthusiasts to rent DVDs through its Web site; the discs arrive in the mail a few days later in a box that converts to a return mailer.[14]

Distribution Channels Using Marketing Intermediaries   Although direct channels allow simple and straightforward connections between producers and their customers, the list of channel alternatives in Figure 13.5 suggests that direct distribution is not the best choice in every instance. Some products sell in small quantities for relatively low prices to thousands of widely scattered consumers. Makers of such products cannot cost-effectively contact each of their customers, so they distribute products through specialized intermediaries called *wholesalers* and *retailers*.

Although you might think that adding intermediaries to the distribution process would increase the final cost of products, more often than not this choice actually lowers consumer prices. Intermediaries such as wholesalers and retailers often add significant value to a product as it moves through the distribution channel. They do so by creating utility, providing additional services, and reducing costs.

Marketing utility is created when intermediaries help ensure that products are available for sale when and where customers want to purchase them. If you want something warm to eat on a cold winter night, you don't call up Campbell Soup and ask them to sell and deliver a can of chicken noodle soup. Instead, you go to the nearest grocery store, where you find utility in the form of product availability. In addition, intermediaries perform such important services as transporting products to convenient locations. Finally, by representing numerous producers, a marketing intermediary can cut the costs of buying and selling. As Figure 13.6 shows, if four manufacturers each sold directly to four consumers, this would require 16 separate transactions. Adding a marketing intermediary, such as a retailer, to the exchange cuts the number of necessary transactions to 8.

> *They Said It*
>
> You can do away with the middleman, but you can't do away with the functions he or she performs.
>
> —*American business saying*

Concept Check

1. Define distribution channels.
2. What is a marketing intermediary?

Wholesaling

A **wholesaler** is a distribution channel member that sells primarily to retailers, other wholesalers, or business users. For instance, Sysco is a wholesaler that buys food products from manufacturers and then resells them to restaurants, hotels, and other institutions in the U.S. and Canada.

Wholesaling is a crucial part of the distribution channel for many products, particularly consumer goods and business supplies. Wholesaling intermediaries can be classified on the basis of ownership; some are owned by manufacturers, some by retailers, and others are independently owned. Most U.S. wholesalers are independent businesses, accounting for about two-thirds of all wholesale trade.

wholesaler distribution channel member that sells primarily to retailers, other wholesalers, or business users.

Manufacturer-Owned Wholesaling Intermediaries

A manufacturer's marketing manager may decide to distribute goods directly through company-owned facilities to maintain control of distribution or customer service. Firms operate two main types of manufacturer-owned wholesaling intermediaries: sales branches and sales offices.

Sales branches stock the products they distribute and fill orders from their inventories. They also provide offices for sales representatives. Sales branches are common in the chemical, petroleum products, motor vehicle, and machine and equipment industries.

A *sales office* is exactly what its name implies, an office for a producer's salespeople. Manufacturers set up sales offices in various regions to support local selling efforts and improve customer service. Some kitchen and bath fixture manufacturers maintain showrooms to display their products. Builders and decorators can visit these showrooms to see how the items would look in place. Unlike sales branches, however, sales offices do not store any inventory. When a customer orders from a showroom or other sales office, the merchandise is delivered from a separate warehouse.

Independent Wholesaling Intermediaries

An independent wholesaling intermediary is a business that represents a number of different manufacturers and makes sales calls on retailers, manufacturers, and other business accounts. These intermediaries account for about two-thirds of all wholesale trade. Independent wholesalers are classified as either merchant wholesalers or agents and brokers depending on whether they take title to the products they handle.

Merchant wholesalers are independently owned wholesaling intermediaries that take title to the goods they handle. Within this category, a *full-function merchant wholesaler* provides a complete assortment of services for retailers or industrial buyers, such as warehousing, shipping, and even financing. A subtype of full-function merchant is a *rack jobber.* This type of firm stocks, displays, and services particular retail products, such as paperback books or greeting cards in a drugstore or supermarket. Usually, the retailer receives a commission based on actual sales as payment for providing merchandise space to a rack jobber.

A *limited-function merchant wholesaler* also takes legal title to the products it handles, but it provides fewer services to the retailers to which it sells. Some limited-function merchant wholesalers only warehouse products but do not offer delivery service. Others warehouse and deliver products but provide no financing. One type of limited-function merchant wholesaler is a *drop shipper.* Drop shippers operate in such industries as coal and lumber, characterized by bulky products for which no single producer can provide a complete assortment. They give access to many related goods by contacting numerous producers and negotiating the best possible prices. Cost considerations call for producers to ship such products directly to the drop shipper's customers.

Another category of independent wholesaling intermediaries consists of *agents* and *brokers.* They may or may not take possession of the goods they handle, but they never take title, working mainly to bring buyers and sellers together. Stockbrokers and real estate agents perform functions similar to those of agents and brokers, but at the retail level. They do not take possession or title to the sellers' property; instead, they create time and ownership utility for both buyer and seller by helping to carry out transactions.

Manufacturers' reps act as independent sales forces by representing the manufacturers of related but noncompeting products. These agent intermediaries, sometimes referred to as *manufacturers' agents*, receive commissions based on a percentage of the sales they make.

Retailer-Owned Cooperatives and Buying Offices

Concept Check

1. Who are the customers of a whole-saler?
2. What are the functions of a sales branch? A sales office?
3. Differentiate between a merchant wholesaler and an agent or broker in terms of title to the goods.

Retailers sometimes band together to form their own wholesaling organizations. Such organizations can take the form of either a buying group or a cooperative. The participating retailers set up the new operation to reduce costs or to provide some special service that is not readily available in the marketplace. To achieve cost savings through quantity purchases, independent retailers may form a buying group that negotiates bulk sales with manufacturers. In a cooperative, an independent group of retailers may decide to band together to share functions like shipping or warehousing.

Retailing

retailer channel member that sells goods and services to individuals for their own use rather than for resale.

Retailers, in contrast to wholesalers, are distribution channel members that sell goods and services to individuals for their own use rather than for resale. Consumers usually buy their food, clothing, shampoo, furniture, and appliances from some type of retailer. The supermarket where you buy your groceries may have bought some of its items from a wholesaler like Sysco and then resold them to you.

Retailers are the final link—the so-called last three feet—of the distribution channel. Each of the five largest U.S.-based retailers—Wal-Mart, Kroger, Sears, Home Depot, and Albertson's—generates over $35 billion in sales every year, with global giant Wal-Mart registering annual sales that exceed *$250 billion*. Since they are often the only channel members that deal directly with consumers, it is essential they remain alert to changing shopper needs. It is also important that they keep pace with developments in the fast-changing business environment.

Nonstore Retailers

Two categories of retailers exist: nonstore and store. Although most retail transactions occur in stores, *nonstore retailers* currently account for almost $80 billion in sales, and that number is expected to continue to grow. As Figure 13.7 shows, nonstore retailing includes four forms: direct-response retailing, Internet retailing, automatic merchandising, and direct selling. *Direct-response retailing* reaches prospective customers through catalogs, telemarketing, and even magazine, newspaper, and television ads. Shoppers order merchandise by mail, telephone, computer, and fax machine and then receive home delivery or pick the merchandise up at a local store. Lands' End has long stood out as a highly successful direct-response retailer; its famous clothing catalog and stellar customer service have set the standard for this type of distribution channel. With the retailer's purchase by Sears, however, customers will now be able to see, feel and try on Lands' End's classic clothing at selected stores around the country.[15]

Internet retailing, the second form of nonstore retailing, has grown rapidly. Tens of thousands of retailers have set up shop online, with total sales surpassing $20 billion a year. A severe shakeout saw hundreds of Internet enterprises shut down during the first few years of the 21st century; firms that survived have stronger business models than those that failed. Two examples of success by pure dot-coms are Amazon and eBay.[16] A major shift in retailing has seen the tradi-

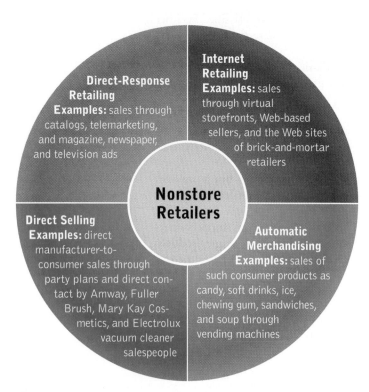

FIGURE 13.7
Types of Nonstore Retailing

tional brick-and-mortar retailer competing with pure dot-com start-ups by setting up their own Web sites as an option for shoppers. Such major retailers as Nordstrom, Toys "R" Us, JCPenney, and Wal-Mart report strong online sales, which are in fact growing faster than store sales. Shopping sites are among the most popular Internet destinations, and sales of clothing and DVDs in particular have risen.[17]

The last two forms of nonstore retailing are automatic merchandising and direct selling. *Automatic merchandising* provides convenience through the use of vending machines. ATMs may soon join the ranks of vending machines as banks find new ways to compete for customers. Some ATMs offer extra services such as check cashing and stamps, while others that are connected to the World Wide Web can accept bill payments, print checks and road maps, and sell everything from stocks to concert tickets. Future ATMs may be able to connect wirelessly to Palm Pilots and cell phones to allow downloading of games and music.[18] *Direct selling* includes direct-to-consumer sales by Kirby and Electrolux vacuum cleaner representatives and Avon and Amway salespeople. The party-plan selling methods of companies like Tupperware and Mary Kay also are forms of direct selling.

Companies that previously relied heavily on telemarketing in generating new customers encountered consumer resistance to intrusive phone calls. Among the growing barriers are caller-ID, call-blocking devices such as the TeleZapper, and the National Do Not Call registry created in 2003 that made it illegal for most companies to call people on that list. As a result, dozens of companies, including AT&T and regional utilities, have unleashed armies of door-to-door sales representatives to promote such services as phones, cable television, and natural gas. Comcast, the nation's largest cable TV company, registered 40,000 new customers last year with a door-to-door "win back" campaign aimed at luring customers away from such competitors as DirectTV and DISH satellite providers.[19]

Store Retailers

Although nonstore retailing methods—especially direct-response retailing and Internet selling—are rapidly growing, more than 95 percent of all retail sales take place in one of the nation's 2 million retail stores. Store retailers range in size from tiny newsstands to multistory department stores and multiacre warehouselike retailers such as Sam's Club. Table 13.2 lists the different types of store retailers, with examples of each type. Clearly, there are many approaches to retailing and a variety of services, prices, and product lines offered by each retail outlet.

The Wheel of Retailing   Retailers are subject to constant change as new stores replace older establishments. In a process called the **wheel of retailing,** new retailers enter the market by offering lower prices made possible through reductions in service. Supermarkets and discount houses, for example, gained their initial market footholds through low-price, limited-service appeals. These new entries gradually add services as they grow and ultimately become targets for new retailers.

As Figure 13.8 shows, most major developments over time in retailing appear to fit the wheel pattern. The low-price, limited-service strategy characterized supermarkets, catalog retailers, discount stores, and most recently, Internet retailers and giant "big-box" stores, such as PetsMart, Barnes & Noble, and Staples. Most of these retailers have raised price levels gradually as they added new services. Corner grocery stores gave way to supermarkets and then to warehouse clubs like Costco or discount supermarkets like Cub Foods. Department stores lost market share to discount clothing retailers like Target and T. J. Maxx. Independent bookstores have lost business to giant chains like Barnes & Noble, Books-A-Million, Borders, and more recently, to such online sellers as Amazon.com and Buy.com.

Even though the wheel of retailing does not fit every pattern of retail evolution—for example, automatic merchandising has always been a relatively high-priced method of retailing—it does give retail managers a general idea of what is likely to occur during the evolution of retailing. It also shows that business success involves the "survival of the fittest." Retailers that fail to change fail to survive.

How Retailers Compete

Retailers compete with each other in many ways. Nonstore retailers focus on making the shopping experience as convenient as possible. Shoppers at stores like the Nature Company, on the other hand,

> ### They Said It
> The question for us is are you creating value? The Internet is a great place for companies of all kinds that are creating genuine value for customers and it is a terrible place for companies that are not.
>
> —*Jeff Bezos (b. 1964)*
> *founder and CEO, Amazon.com*

> ### They Said It
> The universe is really big. It's even bigger than Wal-Mart.
>
> —*Richard Belzer (b. 1944)*
> *American comedian*

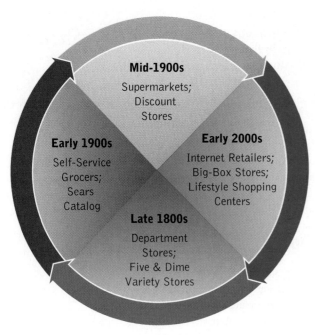

FIGURE 13.8
The Wheel of Retailing

enjoy maximum atmosphere in the form of soothing background music and ready access to environmentally oriented products like telescopes, globes, and books.

Like manufacturers, retailers must develop marketing strategies based on goals and strategic plans. Successful retailers convey images that alert consumers to the stores' identities and the shopping experiences they provide. To create that image, all components of a retailer's strategy must complement each other. After identifying their target markets, retailers must choose merchandising, customer service, pricing, and location strategies that will attract customers in those market segments. For an example of fierce retail competition, see the Best Business Practices box.

Identifying a Target Market The first step in developing a competitive retailing strategy is to select a target market. This choice requires careful evaluation of the size and profit potential of the chosen market segment and the current level of competition for the segment's business. Bargain stores like Family Dollar stores target consumers who are extremely price conscious, for example, while convenience stores target consumers who want an easy way to purchase items they buy frequently.

Selecting a Product Strategy Next, the retailer must develop a product strategy to determine the best mix of merchandise to carry to satisfy that market. Retail strategists must decide on the general product categories, product lines, and variety to offer. Seven of ten products carried in Home Depot stores were suggested by customers, for example.

Table 13.2 Types of Retail Stores

Store Type	Description	Example
Specialty store	Offers complete selection in a narrow line of merchandise	Bookstores, music stores, flower shops
Convenience store	Offers staple convenience goods, easily accessible locations, long store hours, and rapid checkouts	7-Eleven, QuikTrip, Shell Food Mart
Discount store	Offers wide selection of merchandise at low prices; off-price discounters offer designer or brand-name merchandise	Target, Wal-Mart, Nordstrom Rack, Marshall's
Warehouse club	Large, warehouse-style store selling food and general merchandise at discount prices to membership cardholders	Costco, Sam's Club, BJ's
Factory outlet	Manufacturer-owned store selling seconds, production overruns, or discontinued lines	Adidas, Reebok, Coach, Pottery Barn, Gap
Supermarket	Large, self-service retailer offering a wide selection of food and nonfood merchandise	Jewel, Whole Foods Market, Kroger, Albertson's
Supercenter	Giant store offering food and general merchandise at discount prices	Super Target
Department store	Offers a wide variety of merchandise selections (furniture, cosmetics, housewares, clothing) and many customer services	Marshall Field's, Dillard's, Nordstrom, JCPenney, Neiman Marcus

The Morphing of Malls: Changing to Satisfy Shopper Preferences

Imagine being able to live at the mall. You could shop, eat, sleep, see a movie, and do your banking without ever having to leave the boundaries of your favorite mall. If that sounds a little extreme even for the most dedicated shopper, the nation's mall developers don't think so. As the popularity of large, traditional shopping centers declines, developers are looking at new ways to attract consumers. One way is to create open-air shopping villages, or "lifestyle centers," that cater to the "lifestyle pursuits of consumers," according to the International Council of Shopping Centers (ICSC).

Mall developers across the country are responding to what they believe consumers want. Roofs are coming off, storefronts are now facing outward, and well-landscaped, open-air settings are becoming the new norm for malls. Convenient parking and security features are also part of the new scheme. "An outdoor mall is much more attractive to people," says Jerry Snyder, of J. H. Snyder, a developer in Los Angeles. The new open-air, lifestyle center approach is gaining popularity in cold climates as well. A large regional mall outside Detroit is now being demolished to make way for an outdoor shopping area that will feature large retailers.

Developers have learned that people want a sense of community where they do their shopping. "Many people live in communities where there's not a main street where they can walk, window-shop, and meet people," explains Ellen Greenberg of the Congress for the New Urbanism. "What we're learning is people value that and miss it, which is why it's being imitated in these lifestyle centers." In answer to this, the Paseo Colorado mall in Pasadena, California, creates a mixture of retail shops, offices, entertainment such as cinema multiplexes, restaurants, and even housing in a pedestrian-oriented setting. "These centers are designed very, very carefully," notes Ahsin Rasheed of the architecture firm Development Design Group. "We paced the country's greatest streets," he says, to determine just how to re-create them.

QUESTIONS FOR CRITICAL THINKING

1. How might retailers in a lifestyle center work together to attract and satisfy shoppers?
2. Do you think the new concept for shopping malls will be successful? Why or why not?

Sources: Sheila Muto, "A Breath of Fresh Air for Troubled Malls," *The Wall Street Journal*, August 4, 2004, p. B4; Julie Tamaki, "Malls Reborn as Community Centers," *Houston Chronicle*, June 27, 2004, p. D3; Jennifer Waters, "Lifestyle Centers Take Center Stage," *Mobile Register*, June 13, 2004, p. J1; R. J. King, "Retailers Bypass Malls for Lifestyle Centers," *The Detroit News*, January 2, 2004, www.detnews.com.

Shaping a Customer Service Strategy   A retailer's customer service strategy focuses on attracting and retaining target customers to maximize sales and profits. Some stores offer a wide variety of services, such as gift wrapping, alterations, returns, interior design services, and delivery. Other stores offer bare-bones customer service, stressing low price instead. Grocery shoppers, for instance, can find convenience online through a service like Peapod, which handles product selection, packing, and delivery. They can visit a supermarket and make their own selections. Or they can go to a discount supermarket like Cub Foods, where they not only assemble their orders but also bag their purchases.

Selecting a Pricing Strategy   Retailers base their pricing decisions on the costs of purchasing products from other channel members and offering services to customers. Pricing can play a major role in consumers' perceptions of a retailer. So pricing strategy must support the retailer's overall marketing objectives and policies. Pricing strategy is covered in more detail in Chapter 14.

Choosing a Location   A good location often makes the difference between success and failure in retailing. The location decision depends on the retailer's size, financial resources, product offerings, competition, and, of course, its target market. Traffic patterns, the visibility of the store's signage, parking, and the location of complementary stores also influence the choice of a retail location. One reason Target's in-store grocery departments are proving less successful than Wal-Mart's is that many of them are located in urban areas where heavy traffic tends to limit shopping trips and where rival grocery chains already dominate the market.[20]

A *planned shopping center* is a group of retail stores planned, coordinated, and marketed as a unit to shoppers in a geographical trade area. By providing single convenient locations with free parking, shopping centers have largely replaced downtown shopping in many urban areas. Each year, U.S. consumers spend over $1 trillion at the nation's 43,000 shopping centers. But time-pressed consumers are increasingly looking for more efficient ways to shop, including catalogs, Internet retailers, and one-stop shopping at large free-standing stores like Wal-Mart. In recent years, large regional malls have also witnessed a shift in shopping center traffic to smaller strip centers, name-brand outlet centers, and so-called "lifestyle" centers containing retailers focusing on specific shopper segments and product interests. To lure more customers, shopping centers are recasting themselves as entertainment destinations, with art displays, carousel rides, and musical entertainment. The giant Mall of America in Bloomington, Minnesota, features a seven-acre amusement park and an aquarium.[21]

Building a Promotional Strategy   A retailer designs advertisements and develops other promotions to stimulate demand and to provide information such as the store's location, merchandise offerings, prices, and hours. Nonstore retailers provide their phone numbers and Web site addresses. More recently, online retailers have scaled back their big advertising campaigns and worked to build traffic through word of mouth and clever promotions. Promotional strategy is also discussed in depth in Chapter 14.

Concept Check

1. What are the elements of a retailer's marketing strategy?
2. List some considerations in the location decision for a retailer.
3. What are store atmospherics?

Creating a Store Atmosphere   A successful retailer closely aligns its merchandising, pricing, and promotion strategies with *store atmospherics,* the physical characteristics of a store and its amenities, to influence consumers' perceptions of the shopping experience. Atmospherics begin with the store's exterior, which may use eye-catching architectural elements and signage to attract customer attention and interest. Interior atmospheric elements include store layout, merchandise presentation, lighting, color, sound, and cleanliness.

Distribution Channel Decisions and Physical Distribution

Every firm faces two major decisions when choosing how to distribute its goods or services: selecting a specific distribution channel and deciding on the level of distribution intensity. In deciding which distribution channel is most efficient, business managers need to consider four factors: the market, the product, the producer, and the competition. These factors are often interrelated and may change over time.

Selecting Distribution Channels

Market factors may be the most important consideration in choosing a distribution channel. To reach a target market with a small number of buyers or buyers concentrated in a geographical area, the most feasible alternative may be a direct channel. In contrast, if the firm must reach customers who are dispersed or who make frequent small purchases, then the channel may need to incorporate marketing intermediaries to make goods available when and where customers want them.

In general, products that are complex, expensive, custom made, or perishable move through shorter distribution channels involving few—or no—intermediaries. On the other hand, standardized products or items with low unit values usually pass through relatively long distribution channels. Levi's tried selling its basic jeans products through its Web site but quickly realized it was impractical to fill orders for a single order of pants available at local stores. Stelios Haji-Ioannou, however, finds the Internet the perfect channel for each of his multimillion-dollar firms: Easy Jet, a European airline; EasyCar rental; and the EasyInternetcafe chain. Each firm offers a no-frills service that consumers can order online with few choices. EasyCar, for instance, rents only one kind of car, and drivers must return it, clean, to the original rental location. Phil Jones, chief technology officer of parent company EasyGroup, says, "We don't aspire to be all things to all people. We do one thing very well at low cost."[22]

The Fine Art of Delegation

Delegation seems easy enough—you tell someone else what to do. Learning how to delegate *effectively* is a different matter. Throwing a project on an employee's desk with nothing more than a quick "It's due at 5 o'clock!" will not get you the results you want, and it won't build good working relationships with your colleagues. Delegating is a balancing act between having trust and providing direction. Here are a few tips on effective delegation.

1. **"No one can do it like I can."** If this is what you think, you aren't managing your resources efficiently. Managing means giving your employees responsibilities and letting them complete the tasks in their own way. If you insist on doing it all yourself, you are sending a message to your employees that you don't trust them to do *their* jobs.

2. **Clarify and communicate the task to the best of your ability.** Clarify the objective of the project in your own mind first, then give clear directions regarding what you are looking for to your employee. If necessary, write down or sketch out the end result. This helps clarify what you want and also helps you communicate more clearly what the employee must do.

3. **Always set a deadline when delegating projects.** Regardless of who works on the project, it has to be completed by a certain time. Be sure your employee understands the deadline or timeline required so that he or she has some leeway to ask for help *before* the deadline hits.

4. **Allow employees to develop their own work strategies.** You should concern yourself with the results, not with the process of how an employee accomplishes a task. Giving step-by-step instructions can be demoralizing and condescending, so don't offer too much advice unless asked. Let your employees use their own creativity and decision-making skills to accomplish a task.

5. **Always praise good work.** Be sure to praise your employee for a job well done, and be constructive in any criticisms to help improve performance the next time. Don't be negative; phrase your criticism in ways that will develop good working skills, not tear the employee down. Form a team with your employee to solve problems, make decisions, and complete tasks appropriately and on time.

Sources: Ted Pollock, "Secrets of Successful Delegation," *Electric Light & Power,* May 2003, p. 31; Anthony J. Urbaniak, "Delegating: Tips for Supervisors," *Supervision,* May 2003, p. 3; "18 Tips for Better Delegation," *HR Focus,* April 2003, p. 11.

Producers that offer a broad product line, with the financial and marketing resources to distribute and promote it, are more likely to choose a shorter channel. Instead of depending on marketing intermediaries, financially strong manufacturers with broad product lines typically use their own sales representatives, warehouses, and credit departments to serve both retailers and consumers.

In many cases, start-up manufacturers turn to direct channels because they can't persuade intermediaries to carry their products. Direct Focus launched production of an exercise bench called Bowflex, designed to be easier to store and use than competing products. But fitness and sporting goods stores, wary of the "fad of the month" mentality of their industry, passed on the product, forcing the company to offer it directly to consumers. Bowflex was promoted through thousands of television ads featuring product benefits and the company's toll-free telephone number. With this direct distribution combined with an effective promotion, Bowflex sales skyrocketed from $5 million to $138 million in just over five years.[23]

Competitive performance is the fourth key consideration when choosing a distribution channel. A producer loses customers when an intermediary fails to achieve promotion or product delivery. Channels used by established competitors as well as new market entries also can influence decisions.

Regardless of the channel, however, companies must work hand in hand with their channel partners or risk costly disruptions. Struggling to recover from a bankruptcy filing, Owens Corning decided to appeal directly to consumers of its building products by setting up kiosks in home-center stores that let customers choose Owens Corning as their home-improvement general contractor. The company would then route the sales leads to contractors on a preferred list. But local contractors perceived the move, which Owens Corning hadn't warned them about, as a competitive threat. The plan was soon dropped. Owens Corning still hopes to rely less on its channel partners, but this time through less drastic means, such as a franchised basement-finishing system promoting the company's famous Pink Panther icon.[24]

Selecting Distribution Intensity

A second key distribution decision involves *distribution intensity*—the number of intermediaries or outlets through which a manufacturer distributes its goods. Only one Mercedes-Benz dealership may be operating in your immediate area, but you can find Coca-Cola everywhere—in supermarkets, convenience stores, gas stations, vending machines, and restaurants. Mercedes-Benz has chosen a different level of distribution intensity than Coca-Cola. In general, market coverage varies along a continuum with three different intensity levels:

1. **Intensive distribution** involves placing a firm's products in nearly every available outlet. Generally, intensive distribution suits low-priced convenience goods such as chewing gum, newspapers, and soft drinks. This kind of market saturation requires cooperation by many intermediaries, including wholesalers and retailers, to achieve maximum coverage.
2. **Selective distribution** is a market-coverage strategy in which a manufacturer selects only a limited number of retailers to distribute its product lines. Selective distribution can reduce total marketing costs and establish strong working relationships within the channel. Godiva ice cream uses selective distribution. Its ads emphasize the fact that not every store can carry it by including the statement "Available wherever premium ice cream is sold."
3. **Exclusive distribution,** at the other end of the continuum from intensive distribution, limits market coverage to a single retailer or wholesaler in a specific geographical region. The approach suits relatively expensive specialty products. Retailers are carefully selected to enhance the product's image to the market and to make certain that well-trained sales and service personnel will contribute to customer satisfaction. Although producers may sacrifice some market coverage by granting an exclusive territory to a single intermediary, the decision usually pays off in developing and maintaining an image of quality and prestige.

Distribution intensity can have practical implications for a company's performance. Calvin Klein began as a prestigious designer brand, but as the designer's product mix grew, its distribution became more intensive, and the brand began to lose its exclusive image. Image deterioration accelerated following a decision to license its underwear and jeans to Warnaco, which promptly began selling them through mass merchandiser JCPenney and warehouse clubs like Costco. Other designer labels, including Gucci and Dior, have made similar blunders. Today, however, they have discontinued licensing

This B2B promotion features Menlo Worldwide, a company that specializes in helping businesses solve their distribution problems from start to finish. The firm provides physical distribution of its clients' products and oversees logistics, but it also helps manage the distribution channels from suppliers to producers, called the *supply chain*.

agreements and moved toward selling through their own boutiques—an exclusive strategy—rather than through department stores.

Logistics and Physical Distribution

A firm's choice of distribution channels creates the final link in the **supply chain,** the complete sequence of suppliers that contribute to creating and delivering a good or service to business users and final consumers. The supply chain begins when the raw materials used in production are delivered to the producer and continues with the actual production activities that create finished goods. Finally, the finished goods move through the producer's distribution channels to end customers.

The process of coordinating the flow of goods, services, and information among members of the supply chain is called **logistics.** The term originally referred to strategic movements of military troops and supplies. Today, however, it describes all of the business activities involved in managing movements through the supply chain with the ultimate goal of getting finished goods to customers.

Physical Distribution   A major focus of logistics management—identified earlier in the chapter as one of the two basic dimensions of distribution strategy—is *physical distribution,* the activities aimed at efficiently moving finished goods from the production line to the consumer or business buyer. As Figure 13.9 shows, physical distribution is a broad concept that includes transportation and numerous other elements that help to link buyers and sellers. An effectively managed physical distribution system can increase customer satisfaction by ensuring reliable movements of products through the supply chain. Wal-Mart even studies the speed with which goods can be shelved once they arrive at the store because strategies that look efficient at the warehouse, like completely filling pallets with goods, can actually be time-consuming or costly in the aisles.[25]

Warehousing is the physical distribution activity that involves the storage of products. *Materials handling* is moving items within factories, warehouses, transportation terminals, and stores. *Inventory control* involves managing inventory costs, such as storage facilities, insurance, taxes, and handling. The physical distribution activity of *order processing* includes preparing orders for shipment and receiving orders when shipments arrive.

The wide use of electronic data interchange and the constant pressure on suppliers to improve their response time have led to a new strategy called **vendor-managed inventory,** in which the producer and the retailer agree that the producer (or the wholesaler) will determine how much of a product a buyer needs and automatically ship new supplies when needed. Retailers like Sears, Wal-Mart, and Ford auto dealerships expect to save millions of dollars in inventory costs by working with their vendors in this way. Borders bookstores use this strategy with some publishers, such as HarperCollins.[26]

The form of transportation used to ship products depends primarily on the kind of product, the distance involved, and the cost. The physical distribution manager has a number of companies and modes of transportation from which to choose. As Table 13.3 shows, the five major transport modes are—in order of total expenditures—trucks (with about 75 percent of total expenditures), railroads (approximately 12 percent), water carriers (6 percent), air freight (4 percent), and pipelines (3 percent). The faster methods typically cost more than the slower ones. Speed, reliable delivery, shipment frequency, location availability, handling flexibility, and cost are all important considerations when choosing the most appropriate mode of transportation.

Roughly 80 percent of all finished goods sold in the U.S. are carried on a truck at some point on their way to the consumer.[27] But railroads, which compete with many truck routes despite their recent loss of market share, are trying to improve both their efficiency and their service by cutting costs, using tighter controls, and adding consulting services to help clients achieve efficient distribution and lower costs in their own businesses.[28]

Customer Service   Customer service is a vital component of both product and distribution strategies. *Customer service standards* measure the quality of service a firm provides for its customers. Managers frequently set quantitative guidelines—for

Marginal glossary

supply chain complete sequence of suppliers that contribute to creating and delivering a good or service to business users and final consumers.

logistics activities involved in controlling the flow of goods, services, and information among members of the supply chain.

FIGURE 13.9
Elements of a Physical Distribution System

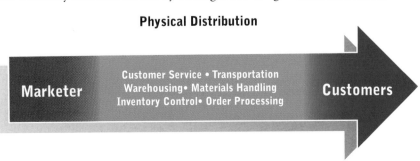

Physical Distribution

Marketer → Customer Service • Transportation • Warehousing • Materials Handling • Inventory Control • Order Processing → Customers

Table 13.3		Comparison of Transportation Modes				
Mode	**Speed**	**Dependability in Meeting Schedules**	**Frequency of Shipments**	**Availability in Different Locations**	**Flexibility in Handling**	**Cost**
Rail	Average	Average	Low	Extensive	High	Average
Water	Very slow	Average	Very low	Limited	Very high	Very low
Truck	Fast	High	High	Very extensive	Average	High
Pipeline	Slow	High	High	Very limited	Very low	Low
Air	Very fast	High	Average	Average	Low	Very high

example, that all orders be processed within 24 hours after they are received or that salespeople approach shoppers within two minutes after they enter the store. Sometimes customers set their own service standards and choose suppliers that meet or exceed them.

The customer service components of product strategy include warranty and repair service programs. *Warranties* are firms' promises to repair a defective product, refund money paid, or replace a product if it proves unsatisfactory. Repair services are also important. Consumers want to know that help is available if something goes wrong. Those who shop for home computers, for example, often choose retailers that not only feature low prices but also offer repair services and telephone "help lines." Products with inadequate service backing quickly disappear from the market as a result of word-of-mouth criticism.

Consumers' growing criticism of shoddy customer service practices of online marketers resulted in thousands returning to the familiar brick-and-mortar outlets, all equipped with service personnel and repair facilities. To combat this problem, dot-coms have taken a number of steps to "humanize" their customer interactions and deal with complaints. Many Web sites contain button help icons that link the visitor to a representative. Both Lands' End and Eddie Bauer have immediate customer feedback through chat rooms.

What's Ahead

This chapter covered two of the elements of the marketing mix: product and distribution. It introduced the key marketing tasks of developing, marketing, and packaging want-satisfying goods and services. It also focused on the three major components of an organization's distribution strategy: the design of efficient distribution channels; wholesalers and retailers who make up many distribution channels; and logistics and physical distribution. We turn to the remaining two—promotion and pricing—in Chapter 14.

Concept Check

1. What is distribution intensity?
2. Define supply chain.
3. What do customer service standards measure?

DID YOU KNOW?

1. Stickers on fruit—usually bananas—have been around since the 1960s. They are applied with some of the world's strongest adhesives, so removing them usually calls for a trip to the toolbox. But "don't worry," say the fruit marketers. Many of the stickers are made of rice paper and can be eaten.
2. The owl logo symbolizes wisdom in the U.S.—but not in India, where it is considered bad luck.
3. Feet are regarded as despicable in Thailand. Athletes' foot remedies with packages featuring a picture of feet will not be well received.
4. Many Japanese food stores are resupplied three times a day to ensure product freshness.
5. The nation's retailers sustain losses of $50 billion per year due to theft. An average of $130 in merchandise is taken in each shoplifting incident. Employee theft is much worse on a per-incident basis, amounting to an average $1,023 worth of goods lost.

Summary of Learning Goals

1
Explain the marketing conception of a product and list the components of a product strategy.

A product is a bundle of physical, service, and symbolic attributes designed to satisfy consumer wants. The marketing conception of a product includes the brand, product image, warranty, service attributes, packaging, and labeling, in addition to the physical or functional characteristics of the good or service.

2
Describe the classification system for consumer and business goods and services.

Goods and services can be classified as consumer (B2C) or business (B2B) products. Consumer products are those purchased by ultimate consumers for their own use. They can be convenience products, shopping products, or specialty products depending on consumer habits in buying them. Business products are those purchased for use either directly or indirectly in the production of other goods and services for resale. They can be classified as installations, accessory equipment, component parts and materials, raw materials, and supplies. This classification is based on how the items are used and product characteristics. Services can be classified as either consumer or business services.

3
Distinguish between a product mix and a product line.

A product mix is the assortment of goods and services a firm offers to individual consumers and B2B users. A product line is a series of related products.

4
Identify and briefly describe each of the four stages of the product life cycle.

Every successful new product passes through four stages in its product life cycle: introduction, growth, maturity, and decline. In the introduction stage, the firm attempts to elicit demand for the new product. In the product's growth stage, sales climb, and the company earns its initial profits. In the maturity stage, sales reach a saturation level. In the decline stage, both sales and profits decline. Marketers sometimes employ strategies to extend the product life cycle, including increasing frequency of use, adding new users, finding new uses for the product, and changing package size, labeling, or product quality.

5
List the stages of the new-product development process.

Six stages exist in the new-product development process for most products: idea generation, screening, business analysis, prototype or service process development, test marketing, and commercialization. At each stage, marketers must decide whether to continue to the next stages, modify the new product, or discontinue the development process. Some new products will skip the test marketing stage due to the desire to quickly introduce a new product with high marketplace potential, a desire not to reveal new-product strategies to competitors, and the high costs involved in limited production runs characteristic of expensive items.

6
Explain how firms identify their products.

Products are identified by brands, brand names, and trademarks, which are important elements of product images. Effective brand names are easy to pronounce, recognize, and remember, and they project the right images to buyers. Brand names cannot contain generic words. Under certain circumstances, companies lose exclusive rights to their brand names if common use makes them generic terms for product categories. Some brand names belong to retailers or distributors rather than to manufacturers. Some retailers offer a third option: no-brand generic products. Brand loyalty is measured in three degrees: brand recognition, brand preference, and brand insistence. Some marketers use family brands to identify several related items in a product line. Others employ individual branding strategies by giving each product within a line a different brand name.

7 Identify and briefly describe each of the major components of an effective distribution strategy and the impact of Internet commerce on distribution channels.

A firm must consider whether to move products through direct or indirect distribution. Once the decision is made, the company needs to identify the types of marketing intermediaries, if any, through which it will distribute its goods and services. The Internet has made direct distribution an attractive option for many retail companies. Another component is distribution intensity. The business must decide on the amount of market coverage—intensive, selective, or exclusive—needed to achieve its marketing strategies. Finally, attention must be paid to managing the distribution channel. It is vital to minimize conflict between channel members.

8 Identify the various categories of distribution channels and discuss the factors that influence channel selection.

Marketers can choose either a direct distribution channel, which moves goods directly from the producer to the consumer, or indirect distribution channels, which involve marketing intermediaries in the paths through which products—and legal ownership of them—flow from producer to the final customer. Ideally, the choice of a distribution channel should support a firm's overall marketing strategy. Before selecting distribution channels, firms must consider their target markets, the types of goods being distributed, their own internal systems and concerns, and competitive factors.

Business Terms You Need to Know

product 420

product line 422

product mix 422

product life cycle 423

brand 427

brand equity 429

distribution channel 431

physical distribution 431

wholesaler 433

retailer 434

supply chain 441

logistics 441

Other Important Business Terms

convenience product 421

shopping product 421

specialty product 421

brand name 427

trademark 427

manufacturer's (national) brand 428

private (store) brand 428

family brand 428

individual branding 428

category manager 429

distribution strategy 431

direct distribution channel 431

wheel of retailing 435

intensive distribution 440

selective distribution 440

exclusive distribution 440

vendor-managed inventory 441

Review Questions

1. Classify each of the following business-to-consumer (B2C) and business-to-business (B2B) products:
   a. *Time* or *Newsweek* magazine
   b. six-pack of bottled water
   c. notebook computer
   d. telecommunication system
   e. Whirlpool washing machine
   f. lumber
   g. Godiva chocolates
   h. living room carpet
   i. photocopy paper
   j. Cartier watch

2. What is the relationship between a product line and a product mix?

3. Identify and briefly describe the six stages of new-product development.

4. What are some strategies for extending the product life cycle?

5. What are the three stages of brand loyalty?

6. What are the advantages of direct distribution? When is a producer most likely to use direct distribution?

7. What is the wheel of retailing? How has the Internet affected the wheel of retailing?

8. Identify and briefly describe the four different types of nonstore retailers. Give an example of at least one type of good or service that would be suited to each type of nonstore retailer.

9. What are the three intensity levels of distribution? Give an example of two products for each level.

10. Describe the strengths and weaknesses of each transport mode and explain how companies can improve their competitiveness through effective distribution.

Projects and Applications

1. Suggest an appropriate brand name for each of the following goods. Defend your choices.
   a. laundry detergent
   b. sport-utility vehicle
   c. snowboard
   d. backpack
   e. outdoor boots
   f. pizza
   g. fresh-fruit drink

2. As a marketer, review your seven-brand list in question 1. What steps you would take to build brand loyalty for three of those products?

3. Which type of distribution intensity would best suit the following products?
   a. Ferrari sport cars
   b. Microsoft XP software
   c. facial tissue
   d. earth-moving equipment
   e. DKNY women's sportswear
   f. Altoid flavored mints

4. Think of your favorite store. If it is near where you live or go to school, stop by for a visit. If not, rely on your memory. Describe the store in terms of its atmospherics. What features contribute to your positive experiences and feelings about the store?

5. Suggest the best method for transporting each of the following goods. Explain your choices.
   a. natural gas
   b. dried pasta
   c. oranges and grapefruit
   d. teak furniture from Thailand
   e. redwood lumber from California
   f. industrial machine parts

Experiential Exercise

Background: You learned in this chapter the importance of packaging and labeling. This exercise will help you apply what you've learned about the characteristics of effective labeling.

Directions: Select two product labels—one you think is a highly effective label and a second that you regard as less effective.

1. Use the following chart to analyze your two labels based on the five functions of effective labeling.

2. In columns 2 and 3 of the chart, identify what was effective or ineffective for each of the functions.

3. Your second label does not have to be ineffective in every function of effective labeling, but it should be lacking in at least one of the functions.

4. Bring your two labels to class and be prepared to present your analysis during small-group discussions.

Functions of Effective Labeling	Label 1: Effective Labeling	Label 2: Ineffective Labeling
1. Attracts buyer's attention		
2. Describes package contents		
3. Conveys benefits of the product inside		
4. Provides information on warranties, warnings, and other consumer matters		
5. Gives an indication of price, value, and uses		

NOTHING BUT NET

1. **Product standards.** As noted in the chapter, many products must adhere to a prescribed set of standards. One example is ice hockey equipment. Visit the two Web sites listed and review the basic requirements ice hockey equipment must meet. How do these standards affect manufacturers of ice hockey equipment?

   http://www.usahockey.com

   http://www.iihf.com

2. **Trademarks and Internet domains.** The International Trademark Association is a worldwide not-for-profit organization of trademark owners and advisors. The association provides information and advice on trademarks, including the selection of an Internet domain name. Visit the association's Web site (http:// www.inta.org) and select "Information Center" and then "Learn the Basics." Prepare a brief oral report on the ins and outs of selecting and registering a domain name.

3. **Transportation statistics.** As noted in the chapter, two of the major transportation modes are pipelines and railroads. The Bureau of Transportation Statistics and Census Bureau provide detailed statistics on the transportation of goods. Go to the Web site listed and access the most recent Commodity Flow Survey you can find. Review the information and answer the following questions.

   a. In terms of volume, which transportation mode (pipelines or railroads) is growing faster?
   b. What types of goods are most commonly transported by rail?
   c. What types of goods are most commonly transported by pipeline?
   d. What is the average cost per mile of goods shipped by rail and by pipeline?

   http://www.bts.gov

   Note: Internet Web addresses change frequently. If you do not find the exact sites listed, you may need to access the organization's or company's home page and search from there.

Case 13.1

Hot Topic Succeeds by Attracting "Alternative" Teens

When teenager Aileen Valca walks out of the Hot Topic store in a Paramus, New Jersey, mall saying, "This is the only place I shop," it's music to management's ears. Catering to teens who see themselves as alienated and antifashion—and who hate malls—Hot Topic's densely packed stores, over 400 and growing, sell "alternative" fashions like red lace-up patent leather boots, fishnet stockings, blue hair dye, black nail polish, and that mainstay item, the rock-band T-shirt. In fact, much of Hot Topic's clothing is music-inspired, helping to further differentiate the chain from other retailers like Gap and Abercrombie & Fitch. Hot Topic customers, mainly 13 to 20 years old, like the convenience of finding weird items that used to be hard to locate; they don't seem to mind that by making them available in the mall where all the mainstream kids shop, the retail chain is slightly diluting their nonconformist angst.

Hot Topic's sales have risen rapidly in the last few years with profits reaching about $28 million, up from $2 million several years ago. Though some analysts believe that its "alternative" stores have no competition, at least in the malls, Betsy McLaughlin, Hot Topic's CEO, knows that success depends on savvy product strategies, like superfast restocking of popular items, and on managing the tricky task of staying just slightly ahead of the trends in the notoriously fickle teen market. How does the company do that? Hot Topic's buyers go to rock concerts and raves to report back on what performers and audiences are wearing. On every trip to the store, customers can fill out "report cards" listing the items they want to find on the shelves; those cards go directly to McLaughlin's desk. Even the chain's Web site polls potential customers on their personal image (everything from "Club" to "Gothic" to "Rockabilly" and back).

Anyone selling to teenagers knows that brand loyalty has to be won early. Teens "decide on their likes and dislikes very fast," says Greg Weaver, CEO of the teen clothing chain Pacific Sunwear, "and they spread the word." Brand names matter to Hot Topic's teen customers. T-shirts boasting the names and pictures of popular bands like Good Charlotte and Misfits are in big demand, as are an assortment of manufacturer's brands in Hot Topic's best-selling colors (red and black) emblazoned with grommets, spider webs, and death's heads. Care Bears pajamas are another big, if surprising, favorite. Quality is not as important as style; by the time a garment could begin to wear out, it has usually been consigned to the back of the closet.

QUESTIONS FOR CRITICAL THINKING

1. Why do you think Hot Topic's CEO Betsy McLaughlin feels comfortable saying, "Our merchandise is not functional; we're not selling jackets to keep you warm"? If not functionality, what is Hot Topic really selling?
2. In what sense can rock bands become brand names in the context of a market like Hot Topic's target audience?

Sources: Tracie Rozhon, "The Race to Think Like a Teenager," *The New York Times*, February 9, 2003, http://www.nytimes.com; Matthew Boyle, "Fortune's 100 Faster Growers Prove There Is Still Life in the Fast Lane," *Fortune*, August 12, 2002, http://www.fortune.com; Adelia Cellini Linecker, "Parents Beware: Hip Teens Love This Place," *Investor's Business Daily*, February 19, 2002, found at http://www.hottopic.com; Maureen Tkacik, "Hey Dude, This Sure Isn't the Gap," *The Wall Street Journal*, February 12, 2002, found at http://www.hottopic.com.

Video Case 13.2

Hasbro

This video case appears on page 615. A recently filmed video, designed to expand and highlight the written case, is available for class use by instructors.

Chapter 14
Promotion and Pricing Strategies

1 Discuss how integrated marketing communications relates to a firm's promotional strategy.

2 Explain the concept of a promotional mix and outline the objectives of promotion.

3 Summarize the different types of advertising and advertising media.

4 Describe the role of sales promotion, personal selling, and public relations in promotional strategy.

5 Identify the factors that influence the selection of a promotional mix.

6 Discuss the major ethical issues involved in promotion.

7 Outline the different types of pricing objectives and discuss how firms set prices in the marketplace.

8 Summarize the four alternative pricing strategies.

9 Discuss consumer perceptions of price.

How Promotion Is Responding to the Vanishing Mass Market

Mass marketing—like mass manufacturing—is disappearing. Marketers once created a single promotional campaign, with a single message, and launched it to all the consumers who might be remotely interested in the product. Just a decade ago, network TV viewers were a captive audience; they settled in for

the evening to watch their favorite programs, commercials and all. Visions of Ford trucks, McDonald's cheeseburgers, Tide detergent, Whiskas cat food, Bayer aspirin, Crest toothpaste, and other products flew past their eyes. Now these same viewers have hundreds of satellite and cable channels from which to choose, not to mention the option of recording their favorite shows to watch later and skipping over commercials or using TiVo, which lets them skip ads on the spot. In addition, consumers want products—and messages—tailored to meet their specific needs. They don't want to sort through unwanted junk mail to find the product information they need.

So how can marketers reach potential buyers and create some buzz about goods and services? More and more firms—large and small—are targeting promotional efforts at smaller groups of consumers. This doesn't mean they plan to sell fewer products; they are just individualizing their marketing messages. Even though Tide has been ranked the best-selling laundry detergent for 50 years, manufacturer Procter & Gamble now focuses on millions of individual customers instead of one giant mass of consumers. James R. Stengel, P&G's global marketing officer, explains, "Every one of our brands is targeted. You find the people. You are very focused on them. You become relevant to them."

Marketers may use different channels for their messages. They may advertise on closed-circuit sports programs or in targeted magazines like *Money* or *Traditional Home*. They can

© Tim Boyle/Getty Images

focus on working mothers through Web sites like iVillage or Oxygen. McDonald's advertises to active adults on Foot Locker's in-store video network. Then there are so-called guerilla tactics—the stunts that no one else thought of, that seem a little crazy, but definitely draw attention. BMW dismissed the idea of traditional advertising for its new Mini Cooper. Instead, the firm's ad agency put giant pay phones and trash cans in airport lobbies with Mini billboards beside them reading, "Makes everything else seem a little too big." Then they lifted a Mini on top of an SUV and drove it around San Francisco.

The fragmentation of TV channels actually works in favor of marketers who have moved away from the masses and toward fine-tuning their messages for specific customers. Black Entertainment Television, *Si* TV, Lifetime, and New England Cable News all serve targeted markets. Companies can create promotional efforts designed to attract these viewers. And don't forget direct response television advertising—once considered the poor cousin to network television advertising; it is now experiencing a surge in activity because of its ability to focus on individual consumers and get them to make a purchase immediately. Clorox, Merck, Sprint, American Airlines, Volkswagen, and even the U.S. Army are now using DRTV promotions. Just think—if you want to change your phone service, book a flight, buy a car, or join the army, all you have to do is watch TV. Then make that crucial phone call.[1]

Chapter Overview

This chapter focuses on the different types of promotional activities as well as the way prices are established for goods and services. **Promotion** is the function of informing, persuading, and influencing a purchase decision. This activity is as important to not-for-profit organizations such as the YMCA and National Public Radio as it is to profit-seeking companies like General Mills and the New York Yankees.

Some promotional strategies try to develop *primary demand,* or consumer desire for a general product category. The objective of such a campaign is to stimulate sales for an entire industry so that individual firms benefit from

this market growth. A popular example is the dairy industry's "Got Milk?" campaign. For the past several years, print and television messages about the nutritional benefits of milk show various celebrities, including Green Bay Packers quarterback Brett Favre and tennis stars Venus and Serena Williams, each wearing a milk moustache. Other promotional campaigns aimed at hiking per-capita consumption have been commissioned by the California Strawberry Commission and the National Cattlemen's Beef Association. For Hispanic consumers in California, the advertisements were modified to relate more closely to Hispanic culture. As Figure 14.1 illustrates, the goal of increasing milk consumption can be broadened by focusing on milk products—in this case, cheese.

Most promotional strategies, in contrast, seek to stimulate *selective demand*—desire for a specific brand. Actor James Earl Jones appears in advertisements for Verizon, which encourage consumers to select Verizon phone service over the services of competitors. Sales promotions that distribute discount coupons also encourage shoppers to purchase specific brands based on price.

Marketers choose among many promotional options to communicate with potential customers. Each marketing message a buyer receives—through a television or magazine ad, Web site, direct-mail ad, or sales call—reflects on the product, place, person, cause, or organization promoted in the content. In a process of **integrated marketing communications (IMC),** marketers coordinate all promotional activities—advertising, sales promotion, personal sales presentations, and public relations—to execute a unified, customer-focused promotional strategy. This coordination is designed to avoid confusing the consumer and to focus positive attention on the promotional message.

This chapter begins by explaining the role of IMC and then discusses the objectives of promotion and the importance of promotional planning. Next, it examines the components of the promotional mix: advertising, sales promotion, personal selling, and public relations. Finally, the chapter addresses pricing strategies for goods and services.

promotion communication link between buyer and seller that performs the function of informing, persuading, and influencing a purchase decision.

Integrated Marketing Communications

An integrated marketing communications strategy focuses on customer needs to create a unified promotional message in the firm's ads, its in-store displays, product samples, and presentations by company salespeople. To gain a competitive advantage, marketers who implement IMC need a broad view of promotion. Media options continue to multiply, and marketers cannot simply rely on traditional broadcast and print media and direct mail. Plans must include all forms of customer contact. Packaging, store displays, sales promotions, sales presentations, and online and interactive media also communicate information about a brand or organization. With IMC, marketers create a unified personality for and message about the good, brand, or service they promote. Coordinated activities also enhance the effectiveness of reaching and serving target markets.

Marketing managers set the goals and objectives for the firm's promotional strategy with overall organizational objectives and marketing goals in mind. Based on these objectives, marketers weave the various elements of the strategy—personal selling, advertising, sales promotion, publicity, and public relations—into an integrated communications plan. This document becomes a central part of the firm's total marketing strategy to reach its selected target market. Feedback, including marketing research and field reports, completes the system by identifying any deviations from the plan and suggesting improvements.

An excellent example of effective IMC in action can be found in the highly competitive world of sports equipment and attire. Nike Golf relies on a broad mix of promotional efforts in marketing its products, ranging from advertise-

FIGURE 14.1
Developing Primary Demand

Courtesy of Dairy Management Inc.

Ahh, the power of Cheese.

integrated marketing communications (IMC) coordination of all promotional activities—media advertising, direct mail, personal selling, sales promotion, and public relations—to produce a unified customer-focused message.

ments featuring champion golfers Tiger Woods and Nick Faldo to the Nike Golf Spring Swing, which includes television commercials and activities featured on Fox Sports Network, a national consumer sweepstakes, and promotional tie-ins with Starwood Hotels & Resorts. The consumer sweepstakes resulted in various prizes—one was a week-long golf vacation at Starwood's Princeville Resort in Hawaii, along with Nike Golf equipment and apparel. Entrants visited the company's Web site to view the results, which led them to other marketing activities. Celebrity golf interviews, tournament updates, and other giveaways were featured on Fox. "This is a good marketing test for us," said Chris Mike, marketing director for Nike Golf. "We've been a substantial advertiser on TV for awhile, but this is an integrated and different approach to see if we can boost business."[2]

Concept Check

1. What is the objective of an integrated marketing communications program?
2. What types of media are used in integrated marketing communications?

The Promotional Mix

Just as every organization creates a marketing mix combining product, pricing, distribution, and promotional strategies, each also requires a similar mix to blend the many facets of promotion into a cohesive plan. The **promotional mix** consists of two components—personal selling and nonpersonal selling activities—that marketers combine to meet the needs of their firm's target customers and effectively and efficiently communicate its message to them. **Personal selling** is the most basic form of promotion: a direct person-to-person promotional presentation to a potential buyer. The buyer–seller communication can occur during a face-to-face meeting or via telephone, videoconference, or interactive computer link.

promotional mix combination of personal and nonpersonal selling techniques designed to achieve promotional objectives.

personal selling interpersonal promotional process involving a seller's face-to-face presentation to a prospective buyer.

HITS & MISSES

Pop-Up Ads: How Marketers Snoop Online

When you go online, are you peppered with pop-up ads? If you are annoyed by them and find yourself chasing them around with your mouse until you can zap them off the screen, here's a new twist. The next generation of pop-ups may be implanted in your PC software. When you turn on your computer, a "silent" software program slips on also, tracking the Web sites you visit and collecting information about any purchases you make. Then, when you visit other Web sites, targeted ads pop up on your screen—ones for goods and services that you might be interesting in buying. Suppose you initially browse through a site for outdoor gear and buy a fleece jacket. Two days later, your screen might show pop-ups for adventure travel, airline tickets, outdoor clothing, and the like. You might not even be aware of it, but these pop-ups are the result of the embedded software that some people call *spyware*.

The largest creator of this software, Gator, recently teamed up with Yahoo! to send such pop-ups to 43 million computer screens worldwide. In one year the agreement generated $28 million in advertising fees that were split by the two companies, and industry experts expect that figure to increase. While Yahoo! insists that it is providing a service to its customers by offering more advertising choices, many consumers are less than pleased by the software—or the ads: Concerned about invasion of privacy, some who discover the programs on their PCs ask service technicians to remove it. Gator, whose advertising customers include Verizon and American Express, presents itself as a way for consumers to "find bargains." Marketing head Scott Eagle says that Gator's model of targeting ads to specific consumers is far more efficient than "spraying ads across everybody." However, companies such as Hertz and The Washington Post Inc. filed lawsuits against Gator for infringement of copyright and trademark laws, claiming that its ads were getting a "free ride" on their sites.

Not surprisingly, surveys focusing on the Internet experience typically list pop-up ads as the most annoying online experience. So marketers at Atlanta-based EarthLink came up with an idea: offer subscribers software to block them. Although EarthLink, the No. 3 U.S. Internet service provider with about five million subscribers, is small change in an industry dominated by industry giant AOL, the company has based its recent market growth strategy on offering a solution to the estimated 4.8 billion ads that pop up on computer screens worldwide every month.

Why do marketers continue to rely on such a disliked form of online advertising? The answer is cost. Pop-up ads are inexpensive to produce and cost nearly nothing to send. But they are so annoying to some computer users that dozens of special programs have been written to block them from appearing on the screen during Internet use. Even industry giant Microsoft has added some spyware-blocking capability to its most recent version of Windows XP, the Service Pack 2 for consumers who don't want marketers peering over their shoulders.

QUESTIONS FOR CRITICAL THINKING

1. As a potential marketer, do you agree with the use of spyware? How might it backfire?
2. Now consider the issue as a consumer. When you are using your computer, what is your response to pop-up ads? Why?

Sources: Stephen H. Wildstrom, "Windows: Security Is Suddenly Job One," *BusinessWeek*, August 30, 2004, p. 38; Ben Elgin, "Yahoo Gets You Coming and Going," *BusinessWeek*, August 30, 2004, p. 13; Melissa Campanelli, "A Pop-Up Victory," *Entrepreneur*, February 2004, p. 23; James R. Hagerty and Dennis K. Berman, "New Battleground in Web Privacy War: Ads That Snoop," *The Wall Street Journal*, August 27, 2003, pp. A1, A8.

Nonpersonal selling consists of advertising, sales promotion, direct marketing, and public relations. Advertising is the best-known form of nonpersonal selling, but sales promotion is about half of these marketing expenditures. Marketers need to be careful about the types of promotion they choose or risk alienating the very people they are trying to reach (see the Hits & Misses box).

Each component in the promotional mix offers its own advantages and disadvantages, as Table 14.1 demonstrates. By selecting the appropriate combination of promotional mix elements, marketers attempt to achieve their firm's promotional objectives. Allocations of funds within the promotional mix vary by industry. Manufacturers of business-to-business (B2B) products typically spend more on personal selling than on advertising, while consumer-goods marketers may focus more on advertising. Later sections of this chapter discuss how the parts of the mix contribute to effective promotions.

Table 14.1   Comparing the Components of the Promotional Mix

Component	Advantages	Disadvantages
Advertising	Reaches large consumer audience at low cost per contact Allows strong control of the message Message can be modified to match different audiences	Difficult to measure effectiveness Limited value for closing sales
Personal selling	Message can be tailored for each customer Produces immediate buyer response Effectiveness is easily measured	High cost per contact High expense and difficulty of attracting and retaining effective salespeople
Sales promotion	Attracts attention and creates awareness Effectiveness is easily measured Produces short-term sales increases	Difficult to differentiate from similar programs of competitors Nonpersonal appeal
Public relations	Enhances product or company credibility Creates a positive attitude about the product or company	Difficult to measure effectiveness Often devoted to nonmarketing activities

Objectives of Promotional Strategy

Promotional strategy objectives vary among organizations. Some use promotion to expand their markets, and others use it to defend their current positions. As Figure 14.2 illustrates, common objectives include providing information, differentiating a product, increasing sales, stabilizing sales, and accentuating a product's value.

Marketers often pursue multiple promotional objectives at the same time. To promote products aimed at children—such as clothing or snacks—marketers must convince kids and their parents that their products are superior. When the accounting industry's image took a plunge after accounting firm Arthur Andersen admitted to shredding Enron paperwork, and accounting irregularities were discovered at other companies, the American Institute of Certified Public Accountants (AICPA) hired a consultant to create a promotional campaign designed to help restore the public's trust in accountants as well as attract new business. "The profession has gotten a black eye as a result of these scandals," explained AICPA spokesperson Geoff Pickard. "We want to move ahead with the object of restoring confidence in the accounting profession and capital markets, in which we have a role to play."[3]

Providing Information   A major portion of U.S. advertising is information oriented. Credit card ads provide information about benefits and rates. Ads for over-the-counter and prescription drugs include information about benefits and potential side effects. Ads for breakfast cereals often contain nutritional information. When Philip Morris Companies decided to change its corporate name to better reflect its corporate structure of operating companies, which make brands such as Oscar Mayer, Oreo, and its highly successful line of Kraft products, it chose the name Altria. Prior to the change, highly successful product categories were less well-known than the firm's tobacco brands. To inform shareholders, the investment market, and its millions of customers, the company launched an eight-week promotional campaign, using metaphors like running

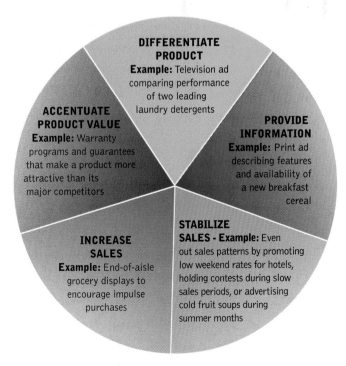

FIGURE 14.2
Five Major Promotional Objectives

water, a tree, a bridge, and columns to describe the new identity.[4] An example of this informative advertising is shown in Figure 14.3.

Differentiating a Product
Promotion can also be used to differentiate a firm's offerings from the competition. Applying a concept called **positioning,** marketers attempt to establish their own places in the minds of customers. The idea is to communicate to prospective purchasers meaningful distinctions about the attributes, price, quality, or use of a good or service, as in the following examples:

- *Attributes:* Procter & Gamble says Scope mouthwash tastes better than Listerine.
- *Price/quality:* Burger King says the Whopper tastes better and costs less than the Big Mac.
- *Use:* Yoplait markets Gogurt yogurt in squeezable tubes with images of kids who are too active to sit down and eat their yogurt with a spoon.

In the competitive arena of fashion, urban apparel has become an $86-billion-per-year industry. Current styles include large tunic-length T-shirts, ultrawide pants, and low-rise jeans. Designers and manufacturers of such clothing are constantly looking for ways to distinguish their fashions from those of competitors—and reach the widest audience possible. Sean John—founded and run by hip-hop star Sean "P. Diddy" Combs—targets men between the ages of 18 and 35 who live an urban lifestyle. "We want the cat wearing jeans to school during the day or a nice outfit to the club at night," says executive vice president Jeff Tweedy. Sean John designers keep the clothing logos small and the designs themselves as timeless as possible, including topcoats and leather jackets. But truly trendy consumers can purchase a pair of Sean John mink pants. Prices range from $32 for a T-shirt to $6,000 for a shearling coat. In addition, the company offers big and tall men's clothing, which many of its competitors do not. "It's been an underlooked business that other designers have treated like a stepchild, so we're bringing it to the forefront," notes Tweedy.[5]

Increasing Sales
Increasing sales volume is the most common objective of a promotional strategy. Naturalizer has employed a promotional strategy designed to increase shoe sales by broadening the appeal of its brand to a larger target market. Naturalizer became the third-largest seller of women's dress shoes by appealing to baby boomers. But as these women have grown older, they have been buying fewer pairs of shoes each year. To attract younger, freer spending women, the company developed a new line of fashionable shoes along with a promotional strategy that positions Naturalizer shoes as stylish and even sexy. The effort included ads in magazines read by younger women—such as *Elle* and *Marie Claire*—featuring young women in beach attire and Naturalizer shoes. The initial response to this strategy was a substantial increase in Naturalizer's sales through department stores.

FIGURE 14.3
Informative Advertising

Courtesy of Altria Group, Inc.

Stabilizing Sales
Sales stabilization is another goal of promotional strategy. Firms often use sales contests during slack periods, motivating salespeople by offering prizes such as vacation trips, TVs, cell phones, and cash to those who meet certain goals. Companies distribute sales promotion materi-

als—such as calendars, pens, and note pads—to customers to stimulate sales during off seasons. Jiffy Lube puts that little sticker on your windshield to remind you when to have your car's next oil change—the regular visits help stabilize sales.[6] A stable sales pattern brings several advantages. It evens out the production cycle, reduces some management and production costs, and simplifies financial, purchasing, and marketing planning. An effective promotional strategy can contribute to these goals.

Advertising supports other promotional efforts to stabilize sales. A common problem in the hotel industry occurs when hotels crowded on weekdays with business travelers become nearly empty on weekends. These hotels often advertise weekend packages to attract tourists, offering low rates and, occasionally, free meals or tickets to local attractions. Similarly, airlines may advertise special low airfares during off-peak periods. These deals often require travelers to stay through a Saturday night, when business travelers are most likely to be home.

Accentuating the Product's Value   Some promotional strategies enhance product values by explaining often unrecognized ownership benefits. Carmakers offer long-term warranty programs and promote the excellence of their repair services. Other promotional efforts focus on low-price aspects of value. As Figure 14.4 shows, Saab cleverly accentuates the fun drivers of its new auto model will have by comparing the driving experience with the exhilaration of parasailing.

The creation of brand awareness and brand loyalty also enhances a product's image and increases its desirability. Advertising with luxurious images supports the reputation of premium brands like Jaguar, Tiffany, and Rolex. Other promotional messages associate brands with desirable qualities such as fun, youthfulness, or even spirituality.

Promotional Planning

Today's marketers can promote their products in many ways, and the lines between the different elements of the promotional mix are blurring. In the practice of **product placement,** a growing number of marketers pay placement fees to have their products showcased in movies and television shows. Recent examples include Eastman Kodak and Royal Caribbean International, each of which paid $3 million to $5 million to have their products featured on a primetime CBS TV program. Snuggle fabric softener found its way onto NBC's *Friends.*[7] But classic examples include the Budget Rent-a-Truck used in the 1990 film *Home Alone* and the Reese's Pieces that appeared in the 1982 blockbuster *E.T.* (Sales of Reese's Pieces skyrocketed 65 percent. Mars, which makes M&Ms, had previously turned down the offer to have its candy appear in the movie.[8])

Guerrilla marketing, innovative, low-cost marketing efforts designed to get consumers' attention in unusual ways, represents an increasingly popular promotional tactic that marketers—especially those with limited promotional budgets—are using today. This approach is relatively new and began with companies that couldn't afford the huge costs of promoting their goods and services in the traditional

Sometimes it's hard to tell who's having

the most fun.

Introducing the new Saab 95
Starting at $32,995

© AP/Wide World Photos

FIGURE 14.4
Accentuating a Product's Value

media. Of necessity, they developed innovative, low-cost ways to reach their markets. Usually, that meant traveling to locations where potential customers would congregate—such as beaches, clubs, even street corners—and communicating with them in person. Today, bigger companies have caught on to the idea and engage in their own guerrilla marketing. Old Spice sent a roving team of "Old Spice Towel Girls" to several beaches in Florida during spring break, where they handed out sample packs of disposable Old Spice Cool Contact Refreshment Towels. The Towel Girls also hosted games of Twister on the beach. At some of the same beaches, Calvin Klein introduced its new line of swimwear. "These guys and girls don't shop in department stores," explained Kim Vernon, senior vice president of global marketing. "The trick is to reach them wherever they are."[9]

Entrepreneur Mark Vinci used guerrilla marketing to launch his own marketing business, K9 Billboards. Vinci lives in New York, and everywhere he takes his Akita puppy, Ling Ling, passersby seem to want to stop to pet her or talk with him. "So many people were drawn to her that it occurred to me that if I could put a brand banner on her, maybe people would be drawn to the brand," explains Vinci. He started with a banner for a local ski resort, which was a huge hit with skiers. When Pure Lip wanted to make more people aware of its cold sore lip balm, the firm hired Vinci to do the job, hitting such locations as Times Square and Rockefeller Center. K9 Billboards now has more dogs on its banner payroll—AT&T hired the firm's French poodles to tout its long-distance global plan on Bastille Day. Vinci is careful about choosing the dogs he hires. "We want them to wag their tails, give paw and kisses, but we're trying to build brand awareness. Tricks are distracting. The brand is the star," he says.[10]

The increasing complexity and sophistication of marketing communications require careful promotional planning to coordinate IMC strategies. General Motors's Chevrolet division had been losing ground for several years when GM decided to develop a major new promotional campaign based on a clever theme—rock 'n' roll songs that cite Chevy in their lyrics. "No other brand has inspired pop culture like Chevy has," explained Bill Ludwig, chief creative officer at Campbell-Ewald, the agency that developed the campaign, which was based on a previous Chevy billboard that read, "They don't write songs about Volvos." Researchers for the campaign came up with songs from Billy Joel, Iron Maiden, the Clash, Coolio, the Ramones, the Beach Boys, Meat Loaf, Elton John, Prince, and dozens of others. Television commercials and print ads featured current models as well as the classics, such as a yellow '57 and an old 409. In addition to evoking nostalgia, the promotional strategy included a focus on value—Chevys don't cost as much as other cars.[11]

From this overview of the promotional mix, we now turn to discussions of each of its elements. The following sections detail the major components of advertising, sales promotion, personal selling, and public relations.

> **Concept Check**
>
> 1. Which component of the promotional mix reaches the largest audience?
> 2. Which component of the promotional mix is the most expensive per contact?
> 3. On which objective is most promotion focused?

Advertising

advertising paid nonpersonal communication delivered through various media and designed to inform, persuade, or remind members of a particular audience.

Of the elements of the promotional mix, advertising is the most visible form of nonpersonal promotion—and the most effective for many firms. **Advertising** refers to paid nonpersonal communications usually targeted at large numbers of potential buyers. Although U.S. citizens often think of advertising as a typically American function, it is a global activity. As Figure 14.5 reveals, one-third of the top 15 advertisers in the U.S. are headquartered in other countries. Each of these companies spends billions of dollars a year on advertising in an attempt to build brand awareness and inform, persuade, or remind current and potential customers about its product offerings.

Advertising expenditures can vary considerably from industry to industry, from company to company, and from one advertising medium to another. For television, the top advertising spenders are manufacturers of cars and light trucks; automobile dealers spend the most on newspaper ads. On the radio, the leading industry is telecommunications, followed by advertising for broadcast and cable television. Among individual companies, giants like Ford and McDonald's have the financial resources needed to buy $2 million 30-second ads on the television broadcast of the annual Super Bowl. In contrast, small companies may be able to achieve their promotional objectives by spending a few thousand dollars on carefully targeted ads in local newspapers or coupon packages mailed to consumers or through guerrilla marketing tactics like those described earlier.

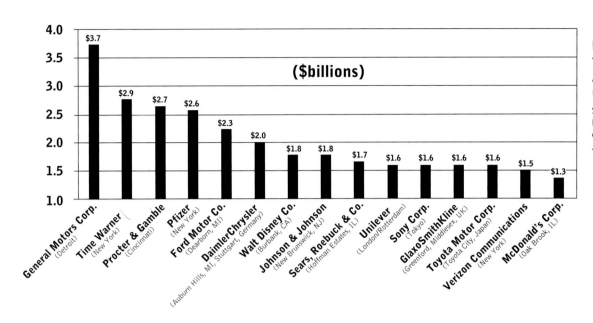

FIGURE 14.5
The 15 Largest Advertisers in the United States
Source: Data from "100 Leading National Advertisers," *Advertising Age*, June 23, 2003, p. S2.

Types of Advertising

The two basic types of ads are product and institutional advertisements. **Product advertising** consists of messages designed to sell a particular good or service. Advertisements for Snapple drinks, T-Mobile wireless phones, and Capital One credit cards are examples of product advertising. **Institutional advertising** involves messages that promote concepts, ideas, philosophies, or goodwill for industries, companies, organizations, or government entities. The Michigan Economic Development Corporation created the ad shown in Figure 14.6 in an effort to attract more technologically based businesses to the state. The ad features Howard Cash, creator of the Sequencher DNA sequencing standard, whose company, Gene Codes Corporation, is located in the state's Life Sciences Corridor.

A form of institutional advertising that is growing in importance, **advocacy advertising,** promotes a specific viewpoint on a public issue as a way to influence public opinion and the legislative process about issues such as America's homeless population, drug abuse, hunger, and efforts to reduce smoking and alcohol abuse. Both not-for-profit organizations and businesses use advocacy advertising, sometimes called *cause advertising.*

Courtesy of Michigan Economic Development Corporation.

FIGURE 14.6
Institutional Advertising

FIGURE 14.7
Comparative Advertising

PHILADELPHIA is a registered trademark used with the permission of Kraft Foods.

Advertising and the Product Life Cycle

Both product and institutional advertising fall into one of three categories based on whether the ads are intended to inform, persuade, or remind. A firm uses *informative advertising* to build initial demand for a product in the introductory phase of the product life cycle. Highly publicized new product entries attract the interest of potential buyers who seek detailed information about their superiority over existing products, warranties provided, prices, and locations where the new items can be seen and purchased.

Persuasive advertising attempts to improve the competitive status of a product, institution, or concept, usually in the growth and maturity stages of the product life cycle. One of the most popular types of persuasive product advertising, *comparative advertising,* compares products directly with their competitors—either by name or by inference. The ad for the Philadelphia cream cheese and bagel "to go" in Figure 14.7 combines persuasive and comparative advertising techniques by inviting consumers to say good-bye to breakfast bar products offered by other companies and try its new product instead. Advertisers need to be careful when they name competing brands in comparison ads because they might leave themselves open to controversy or even legal action by competitors.

Reminder-oriented advertising often appears in the late maturity or decline stages of the product life cycle to maintain awareness of the importance and usefulness of a product, concept, or institution. Reminder advertising can be used to breathe new life into products that have all but disappeared. One example is Maypo, a popular instant maple oatmeal product for children during the 1960s. Homestat recently bought the brand from ConAgra foods and is currently promoting it with new packaging along with radio, print, and television ads. The firm is also repositioning Maypo as a healthful food instead of oatmeal for kids.

Advertising Media

Marketers must choose how to allocate their advertising budgets among various media. All media offer advantages and disadvantages. Cost is an important consideration in media selection, but marketers must also choose the media best suited for communicating their message. As Figure 14.8 indicates, advertising on television and in

FIGURE 14.8
Carving Up the Advertising Media Pie

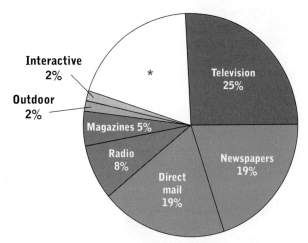

*An additional 20% is spent on such miscellaneous media as Yellow Pages listings, business papers, transit displays, point-of-purchase displays, cinema advertising, and regional farm papers.

Source: Universal McCann, New York.

newspapers and in the form of direct mail represent the three leading media outlets, in large part because of their flexibility. Online (Internet) advertising receives only about 2 percent of total advertising spending. Still, interactive advertising on the Internet is expected to grow far faster than the other media over the next decade. Other media expected to enjoy strong growth are cable television and outdoor advertising.

Newspapers   Daily and weekly newspapers continue to dominate local advertising. Marketers can easily tailor newspaper advertising for local tastes and preferences. Advertisers can also coordinate their newspaper messages with other promotional efforts. In fact, readers rank advertising as the third most useful feature in newspapers, after national and local news. A disadvantage comes from the relatively short life span; people usually discard their papers soon after reading.

The sheer volume of advertising in a typical newspaper produces intense competition for reader attention. Successful newspaper advertisers make newsworthy announcements in their ads, such as sales, the opening of new stores, or the launch of new products. Retailers and automobile dealers rank first among newspaper advertisers.

Newspaper publishers, originally concerned that the Web would erode their traditional role of providing news, advertising, and entertainment guides, have instead discovered that even frequent Web users are attracted to traditional print media to obtain more detailed reporting on news items and for coverage of local and regional events. Most newspapers now maintain Web sites to complement their print editions, some of which offer separate material and features.

Television   Television is America's leading national advertising medium. Television advertising can be classified as network, national, local, and cable ads. The four major national networks—ABC, CBS, NBC, and Fox—and relative newcomers Warner Brothers (WB) and United Paramount Network (UPN) broadcast about one fourth of all television ads. Despite a decline in audience share and growing competition from cable, network television remains the easiest way for advertisers to reach large numbers of viewers—10 million to 20 million with a single commercial. Among the heavy users of network television advertising are auto manufacturers, financial services companies, and fast-food chains.

Cable services continue to make inroads into the television sector; nearly two-thirds of the 106 million U.S. households with TVs now subscribe to cable.[12] Drawn to the dozens or even hundreds of channels available through cable or satellite services, many viewers have switched from network programming. Some experts predict that the number of cable subscribers may actually taper off as viewers switch to satellite for more channels.[13] As cable modems and satellite services broaden their offerings to Internet and interactive programming, their audience is expected to continue growing. The variety of channels on cable and satellite networks lets advertisers target specialized markets and reach selected demographic groups, often very small ones. This capability is drawing more and more ad dollars to cable, making it the second-fastest-growing advertising medium after the Internet. Based on ad revenues, the top five cable networks are ESPN (with ad revenues of more than $1 billion a year), Nickelodeon, MTV, Lifetime, and TNT.

Although television reaches the greatest number of consumers at once, it is the most expensive advertising medium. The price to air a 30-second ad during weeknight prime time on network television generally ranges from $100,000 to more than $500,000 for the most popular shows. Super Bowl ads have been known to command prices of over $2 million. So marketers want to be certain that their commercials reach the greatest number of viewers. Because of the high cost, advertisers may demand guarantees of audience size and receive compensation if a show fails to deliver the promised number of viewers.

Radio   The average U.S. household owns five radios—including those in cars—a market penetration that makes radio an important advertising medium. Advertisers like the captive audience of listeners as they commute to and from work. As a result, morning and evening drive time shows command top ad rates. In major markets, many stations serve different demographic groups with targeted programming. The potential of the Internet to deliver radio programming also offers opportunities for yet more focused targeting. Satellite transmission technology will also offer new opportunities for radio advertisers.

Magazines   Magazines include consumer publications and trade journals that serve as B2B links. *Time, Country Living,* and *Sports Illustrated* are consumer magazines, whereas *Advertising Age*

Traditional Home is a home decorating and furnishing magazine targeted for an upscale audience. Its advertisers include Orrefors crystal, Waverly fabric, Marvin windows, and Thibault wallpapers.

and the *Oil & Gas Journal* fall into the trade category.

Magazines often can customize their publications and target advertising messages to different regions of the country. One method places local advertising in regional editions of the magazine. Other magazines attach wraparounds—half-size covers on top of full-size covers—to highlight articles inside that relate to particular areas; different wraparounds appear in different parts of the country.

Magazines are a natural choice for targeted advertising. Media buyers study demographics of subscribers and select magazines that attract the desired readers. A company with a product geared to young women would advertise in *Glamour* and *Cosmopolitan;* one with a product that appeals to entrepreneurs might choose *Inc., Success,* or *Entrepreneur.*

Direct Mail The average American household receives about 550 pieces of direct mail each year, including 100 catalogs. The huge growth in the variety of direct-mail offerings combined with the convenience they offer to today's busy, time-pressed shoppers has made direct-mail advertising a multibillion-dollar business. Today this medium is tied with newspaper advertising in second place, trailing only television advertising, among the leading media alternatives. Although the cost per person reached via direct mail is high, a small business may be able to spend less on a limited direct-mail campaign than on a television or radio ad. For businesses with a small advertising budget, a carefully targeted direct-mail effort with a message that interests recipients can be highly effective.

Another way to minimize costs while maximizing the targeting of direct mail is to use e-mail, which bypasses the printing and postage costs. Marketers can target the most interested Internet users by offering Web site visitors an option to register to receive e-mail. They can gather names through their own Web site, as well as sites like Yesmail.com, which invite consumers looking for special offers to register to receive e-mail on subjects of interest to them. Marketers can then buy lists of names from Yesmail.com.

For both e-mail and postal campaigns, address lists are at the heart of direct-mail advertising. Using data-mining techniques to develop models for market segmentation, direct-mail marketers create profiles that show the traits of consumers who are likely to buy their products or donate to their organizations. Catalog retailers sometimes experiment by mailing direct-mail pieces randomly to people who subscribe to particular magazines. Next, they analyze the orders received from the mailings and develop profiles of purchasers. Finally, they rent lists of additional subscriber names that match the profiles they have developed.

Studies have shown that most U.S. consumers are annoyed by the amount of "junk mail" they receive every day, including catalogs, advertising post cards, and flyers. But in Asia, people receive only a few pieces of regular mail each week—and very little junk mail at all. So advertisers have begun to use more direct mail in Asian markets. When Heinz mailed little red packets of ketchup to 150,000 upper-income households in the Philippine capital city of Manila, 12,000 people responded to the invitation to join the company's mailing list. When Nestlé included back-to-school tips in a direct mailing to consumers in Malaysia, the firm received an emotional reply from one Malaysian mother. "I was shocked and excited because you really keep track of my family," she wrote.[14]

Among Internet users, a major pet peeve is *spam,* or unsolicited e-mail containing sales messages. Many states have outlawed such practices as sending e-mail promotions without legitimate return addresses. Other enterprising firms are working to perfect gadgets that screen out unwanted e-mail.[15] However, these laws are difficult to enforce and the messages keep coming. "It's an annoying, unwanted intrusion on consumers' lives," says Brian Huseman, a staff attorney with the Federal Trade Commission (FTC), which deals with consumer protection and online marketing. "The problem is growing."[16]

The Direct Marketing Association (DMA; http://www.the-dma.org) helps marketers combat negative attitudes by offering its members guidelines on ethical business practices. The DMA also provides consumer information at its Web site, as well as services that enable consumers to opt out of receiving unsolicited offers by mail, phone, or e-mail. In addition, the organization supports federal legislation that would track its guidelines, which state that its members may send promotional e-mail messages under these circumstances: (1) the messages are sent to the marketer's own customers; or (2) individuals have given consent to receive these messages; (3) individuals have not opted out when given the opportunity to do so; or (4) the marketer has received assurance from a third-party list provider (like Yesmail.com) that consumers have given their consent to receive promotional e-mails.[17]

Outdoor Advertising   Outdoor advertising, such as billboards and illuminated or animated signs or displays accounts for about 2 percent of total advertising expenditures. The majority of spending on outdoor advertising is for billboards, but spending for other types of outdoor advertising, such as signs in transit stations, stores, airports, and sports stadiums, is growing faster. Advertisers are exploring new forms of outdoor media, many of which involve technology: computerized paintings, video billboards, trivision that displays three revolving images on a single billboard, and moving billboards mounted on trucks. Other innovations include displaying ads on the Goodyear blimp, using an electronic system that offers animation and video. There's also K9 Billboards, described earlier in the chapter.

Outdoor advertising suffers from several disadvantages, however. The medium requires brief messages, and mounting concern for aesthetic and environmental issues is raising opposition. The Highway Beautification Act regulates placement of outdoor advertising near interstate highways. And debates still rage about whether billboards should be allowed at all. But they can be an effective way to reach a large number of people in one geographical location and can even promote important causes, such as providing information about missing children.

Online and Interactive Advertising   Ranging from Web sites and compact discs (CDs) to information kiosks in malls and financial institutions, interactive media are changing the nature of advertising. Although it currently commands only 2 percent of media spending, interactive advertising is the fastest-growing media segment.

Online advertising has changed dramatically in recent years. Companies first began experimenting with advertising on this medium in the mid-1990s. At that time, the Web was a novelty for most users. Today, successful interactive advertising adds value by offering the audience more than the product-related information contained in the early banner ads. Nike has embraced this type of advertising as one of its premier strategies. Within its Web site, consumers can visit dedicated sites tailored to each sport for which Nike has products. They can go to NikeLab.com for the company's most cutting-edge products—like its new running jacket that contains a built-in light, compass watch, and MP3 player. At the lab site, they can personalize a pair of shoes according to color, accent, and motto, play a virtual football game while wearing virtual Nike Air Max Q cross-trainers, run virtual races in various virtual Nike shoes, and create personalized digital music mixes to listen to during workouts. "We want to give consumers something unexpected," explains Brian Finke, Nike USA's director of digital brand marketing. "We realize that different consumers are going to connect with us in different ways. We want them to have a brand experience that's relevant to them."[18]

Just like spam, many consumers resent the intrusion of *pop-up* ads that suddenly appear on their computer screen. These ads can be difficult to ignore, remove, or pass by. Some Internet service providers, like Earthlink, have actually turned this problem into a marketing advantage by offering service that comes without pop-ups. "You'll never log-on and be greeted by an Earthlink pop-up ad. Your address comes with spam-reducing tools and eight mailboxes," its ads promise.

In addition to the Internet, technological advances are enabling other forms of interactive advertising. After years of hype, interactive television is making inroads into households and presenting new advertising opportunities. NBC has added interactive features to its broadcasts, such as merchandise offers related to its programs. Someone watching *The Tonight Show with Jay Leno* can use WebTV to order a CD by a musician he or she saw on the show or request more information from one of the show's advertisers. Other marketers are combining direct mail and interactive advertising by sending prospective customers computer discs or DVDs containing marketing messages with opportunities to respond. Unlike a simple brochure, a CD—like a mail-out videocassette—is frequently perceived as representing a significant value, so recipients are more likely to investigate its content.

Sponsorship   One of the hottest trends in promotion offers marketers the ability to integrate several elements of the promotional mix. **Sponsorship** involves providing funds for a sporting or cultural event in exchange for a direct association with the event. Sports sponsorships attract two-thirds of total sponsorship dollars in this $9 billion annual business in the U.S. alone. Entertainment, festivals, causes, and the arts divide up the remaining third of sponsorship dollars.[19]

NASCAR, the biggest spectator sport in the U.S., thrives on sponsorships. Because it can cost as much as $20 million a year to run a top NASCAR team, drivers depend on sponsorships from companies to keep the wheels turning. Firms ranging from Lowe's to General Mills pay fees to have their names and the logos of their products displayed prominently on the race cars and uniforms of the drivers. A primary sponsor may pay anywhere from $8 million to $20 million for its logo display on the hood and rear quarter-panel of its car. The front quarter-panel, meanwhile, may go for about $370,000. Drivers become marketers for their sponsors' products as their celebrity increases. "I saw [Jeff Gordon] at a function that Lowe's had for its store managers," says rookie driver Jimmie Johnson. "There's 1,200 people in the room, and he just worked them over. He's great at it."[20]

Sponsors receive two primary benefits: exposure to the event's audience and association with the image of the activity. Sponsors typically gain the rights to use the name of the person or event in their promotions, to advertise during media coverage of the event, to post promotional signs at the venue, to set up sales promotions, and to engage in personal selling to clients invited to attend the event. Event sponsors frequently set up hospitality tents where they entertain important distributors and potential customers. Sponsorships play an important role in relationship marketing, bringing together the event, its participants, and the sponsoring firms and allowing marketers to reach a narrow but highly desirable audience.

> *They Said It*
>
> There are two kinds of artists left: Those who endorse Pepsi, and those who simply won't.
>
> —*Annie Lennox (b. 1954)*
> *Scottish-born singer*

Other Media Options   As consumers filter out familiar advertising messages, marketers look for novel ways to catch their attention. In addition to the major media, firms promote through many other vehicles such as infomercials and specialized media. **Infomercials** are a form of broadcast direct marketing, also called *direct response television (DRTV)*. These 30-minute programs resemble regular television programs, but they are devoted to selling goods or services such as exercise equipment, skincare products, or kitchenware. The long format allows an advertiser to thoroughly present product benefits, increase awareness, and make an impact on consumers. Advertisers also receive immediate responses in the form of sales or inquiries because most infomercials feature toll-free phone numbers. Infomercial stars sometimes become celebrities in their own right, as in the case of Ron Popeil, founder of Ronco, and Billy Mays, well-known pitchman for OxiClean. Procter & Gamble recently entered the arena with a series of infomercials promoting its Swiffer WetJet floor-cleaning mop. "[Swiffer marketers are] seeing an increase in sales, shipments, and awareness," claims a P&G spokesperson. "They attribute that to their overall communications mix, of which DRTV is a piece."[21]

Other specialized media used for product promotions include advertising in movie theaters and on airline movie screens. Movie theaters show commercials for soft drinks like Coca-Cola, Pepsi, and Dr. Pepper before beginning feature presentations. Ads appear in printed programs of live-theater productions, and firms such as PepsiCo and DaimlerChrysler advertise on videocassettes of popular movies. Advertisers also place messages on subway tickets in New York City and toll receipts on the Massachusetts Turnpike. A more recent development is the use of ATMs for advertising. Some ATMs can play 15-second commercials on their screens, and many can print advertising messages on receipts. An ATM screen has a captive audience because the user must watch the screen to complete a transaction.

Directory advertising includes the familiar Yellow Pages listings in telephone books and thousands of other types of directories, most presenting business-related promotions. About 6 percent of total advertising revenue goes to Yellow Pages ads. Besides local and regional directories, publishers also have produced versions of the Yellow Pages that target ethnic groups.

A major advantage of Yellow Pages advertising is that most people who look in the Yellow Pages have already decided they want to locate a convenient restaurant, a nearby store carrying a needed item, or a service provider and are ready to make a purchase.

Concept Check

1. What are the two basic types of advertising?
2. Which advertising medium dominates local markets?
3. Why is outdoor advertising considered a controversial media outlet?

Sales Promotion

Traditionally viewed as a supplement to a firm's sales or advertising efforts, sales promotion has emerged as an integral part of the promotional mix. Promotion now accounts for close to half as many marketing dollars as are spent on advertising, and promotion spending is rising faster than ad spending. **Sales promotion** consists of forms of promotion such as coupons, product samples, and rebates that support advertising and personal selling.

Both retailers and manufacturers use sales promotions to offer consumers extra incentives to buy. Beyond the short-term advantage of increased sales, sales promotions can also help marketers to build brand equity and enhance customer relationships. Examples include samples, coupons, contests, displays, trade shows, and dealer incentives.

sales promotion
nonpersonal marketing activities other than advertising, personal selling, and public relations that stimulate consumer purchasing and dealer effectiveness.

Consumer-Oriented Promotions

The goal of a consumer-oriented sales promotion is to get new and existing customers to try or buy products. In addition, marketers want to encourage repeat purchases by rewarding current users, increase sales of complementary products, and boost impulse purchases. Figure 14.9 shows how marketers to consumers allocate their spending among the categories of promotions.

Premiums, Coupons, Rebates, and Samples
Two of every five sales promotion dollars are spent on *premiums*—items given free or at a reduced price with the purchase of another product. Cosmetics companies like Estée Lauder and Clinique offer gifts with purchases of special cosmetics and perfume sets. Fast-food restaurants are also big users of premiums. Often, McDonald's and Burger King give away a free toy with every children's meal—these toys are typically tie-ins to popular movies or television shows. Whenever possible, marketers should choose a premium that is likely to get consumers thinking about and caring about the brand and the product. The premiums given away by Estée Lauder and Clinique are usually samples of cosmetics and related accessories such as mirrors or cosmetics bags.

Customers redeem *coupons* for small price discounts when they purchase the promoted products. Such offers may persuade a customer to try a new or different product. Some retailers, including southern supermarket giant Winn-Dixie and West Coast competitors Ralph's and Von's, double the face values of manufacturer's coupons.

Coupons have the disadvantage of focusing customers on price rather than brand loyalty, and major consumer-products companies like Procter & Gamble tried to cut back on distributing coupons during the previous decade. However, discount stores like Wal-Mart have made that strategy difficult. Wal-Mart lures price-conscious shoppers with its own brands. Procter & Gamble has recently begun to offer more coupons for products like detergent and diapers to counter the everyday low pricing and national brands of discount retailers.

Rebates offer cash back to consumers who mail in required proofs of purchase. Rebates help packaged-goods manufacturers increase purchase rates, promote multiple purchases, and reward product users. Other types of companies also offer rebates, especially for electronics, computers and their accessories, and automobiles. Processing rebates gives marketers a way to collect data about their customers.

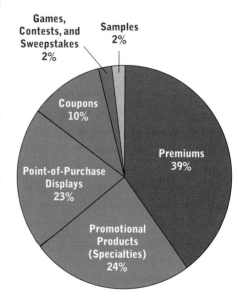

FIGURE 14.9
Spending on Consumer-Oriented Promotions

A *sample* is a gift of a product distributed by mail, door to door, in a demonstration, or inside packages of another product. America Online has widely distributed CDs providing free trials of its Internet service. After the sample period, users have the option to continue the service for a monthly fee. Although sampling is an expensive form of sales promotion, it generates a higher response rate than most other techniques. Three of every four consumers who receive samples will try them.

Games, Contests, and Sweepstakes   Contests, sweepstakes, and games offer cash, merchandise, or travel as prizes to participating winners. Firms often sponsor these activities to introduce new goods and services and to attract additional customers. Games and contests require entrants to solve problems or write essays and sometimes provide proof of purchase. Sweepstakes choose winners by chance and require no product purchase. Consumers typically prefer them since games and contests require more effort. Companies like sweepstakes, too, because they are inexpensive to run and determine the number of winners from the beginning. With games and contests, the company cannot predict the number of people who will correctly complete a puzzle or gather the right number of symbols from scratch-off cards. Sweepstakes, games, and contests can reinforce a company's image and advertising message, but consumer attention may focus on the promotion rather than the product.

In recent years, court rulings and legal restrictions have limited the use of games and contests. Companies must proceed carefully in advertising their contests and games and the prizes they award. Marketers must indicate the chances of winning and avoid false promises such as implying that a person has already won.

Promotional Products   Do you have any pens, T-shirts, or refrigerator magnets imprinted with a business name that you received for free? These offers are examples of **promotional products** (sometimes called *specialty advertising* or *advertising specialties*). This type of sales promotion involves the gift of useful merchandise carrying the name, logo, or slogan of a profit-seeking business or a not-for-profit organization. Because those products are useful and sometimes personalized with recipients' names, people tend to keep and use them, giving advertisers repeated exposure. Originally designed to identify and create goodwill for advertisers, promotional products now generate sales leads and develop traffic for stores and trade show exhibitors. Like premiums, these advertising specialties should reinforce the brand's image and its relationship with the recipient.

Trade-Oriented Promotions

Sales promotion techniques can also contribute to campaigns directed to retailers and wholesalers. **Trade promotion** is sales promotion geared to marketing intermediaries rather than to consumers. Marketers use trade promotion to encourage retailers to stock new products, continue carrying existing ones, and promote both new and existing products effectively to consumers. Successful trade promotions offer financial incentives. They require careful timing, attention to costs, and easy implementation for intermediaries. These promotions should bring quick results and improve retail sales. Major trade promotions include point-of-purchase advertising and trade shows.

Point-of-purchase (POP) advertising consists of displays or demonstrations that promote products when and where consumers buy them, such as in retail stores. Both Disney and Kodak place displays of their products—videos and film—near the check-out counters of supermarkets. A high-tech version of POP advertising is the use of kiosks that display product information and promotional offers. Whether cardboard or electronic, POP advertising takes advantage of many shoppers' tendencies to make purchase decisions in the store.

Manufacturers and importers often host or exhibit at *trade shows* to promote goods or services to members of their distribution channels. These shows are often organized by industry trade associations, typically during annual meetings or conventions. Each year, thousands of trade shows attract millions of exhibitors and hundreds of millions of attendees. Such shows are particularly important in fast-changing industries like those for computers, toys, furniture, and fashions. The annual electronics show, which is held in Las Vegas and attracts more than 100,000 visitors, is the nation's largest. These shows are especially effective for introducing new products and generating sales leads.

Concept Check

1. What is the greatest disadvantage of using coupons?
2. What is the benefit of POP advertising?

Personal Selling

Many companies consider *personal selling*—a person-to-person promotional presentation to a potential buyer—the key to marketing effectiveness. Unless a seller matches a firm's goods or services to the needs of a particular client or customer, none of the firm's other activities produce any benefits. Today, sales and sales-related jobs employ about 16 million Americans. Businesses often spend five to 10 times as much on personal selling as on advertising. Given the significant cost, businesses are very concerned with the effectiveness of their personal selling.

How do marketers decide whether to make personal selling the primary component of their firm's marketing mix? In general, firms are likely to emphasize personal selling rather than advertising or sales promotion under four conditions:

1. Customers are relatively few in number and geographically concentrated.
2. The product is technically complex, involves trade-ins, and requires special handling.
3. The product carries a relatively high price.
4. It moves through direct-distribution channels.

The sales functions of most companies are experiencing rapid change. Today's salespeople are more concerned with establishing long-term buyer–seller relationships and acting as consultants to their customers than in the past.

Personal selling can occur in several environments, each of which can involve business-to-business or business-to-consumer selling. Sales representatives who make sales calls on prospective customers at their homes or businesses are involved in *field selling*. Companies that sell major industrial equipment typically rely heavily on field selling. *Over-the-counter selling* describes sales activities in retailing and some wholesale locations, where customers visit the seller's facility to purchase items. *Telemarketing* sales representatives make their presentations over the phone. A later section reviews telemarketing in more detail.

> *They Said It*
>
> I learned something early in life. If you sell, you'll never starve. In any other profession, you can find yourself out on the street saying, "They don't want me anymore." But if you can sell, you'll never go hungry.
>
> —*George Foreman (b. 1949)*
> *American boxer and celebrity spokesman for the Lean Mean Grilling Machine*

Sales Tasks

All sales activities involve assisting customers in some manner. Although a salesperson's work can vary significantly from one company or situation to another, it usually includes a mix of three basic tasks: order processing, creative selling, and missionary selling.

Order Processing   Although both field selling and telemarketing involve this activity, **order processing** is most often related to retail and wholesale firms. The salesperson identifies customer needs, points out merchandise to meet them, and processes the order. Route sales personnel process orders for such consumer goods as bread, milk, soft drinks, and snack foods. They check each store's stock, report inventory needs to the store manager, and complete the sale. Most of these jobs include at least minor order-processing functions. A later section discusses sales force automation, showing how companies now use technology to simplify order processing.

Creative Selling   Sales representatives for most business products and some consumer items perform **creative selling,** a persuasive type of promotional presentation. Creative selling promotes a good or service whose benefits are not readily apparent or whose purchase decision requires a closer analysis of alternatives. Sales of intangible products such as insurance rely heavily on creative selling, but sales of tangible goods benefit as well.

Some store salespeople primarily process orders, but many consumers are looking for more in the form of customer service, which is where creative selling comes in. The women's clothing department of some department stores as well as smaller shops may hold "trunk shows" featuring specific clothing designers such as Eileen Fisher, inviting regular customers to attend. Trained sales staff at Talbots women's clothing stores hold seasonal wardrobe building workshops at the stores, helping customers select and purchase coordinating clothing, accessories, and shoes from the Talbots line—which they might not have purchased without the sales staff's advice.

Missionary Selling   Sales work also includes an indirect form of selling in which the representative promotes goodwill for a company or provides technical or operational assistance to the customer; this practice is called **missionary selling.** Many businesses that sell technical equipment, such as IBM and Xerox, provide systems specialists who act as consultants to customers. These salespeople work to solve problems and sometimes help their clients with questions not directly related to their employers' products. Other industries also use missionary selling techniques. Pharmaceutical company representatives—called *detailers*—visit physicians to describe the firm's latest products. The actual sales, however, are handled through pharmacies, which fill the prescriptions.

The Sales Process

The sales process typically follows the seven-step sequence shown in Figure 14.10: prospecting and qualifying, the approach, the presentation, the demonstration, handling objections, the closing, and the follow-up. Remember the importance of flexibility, though; a good salesperson is not afraid to vary the sales process based on a customer's responses and needs. The process of selling to a potential customer who is unfamiliar with a company's products differs from the process of serving a long-time customer.

Prospecting, Qualifying, and Approaching   At the prospecting stage, salespeople identify potential customers. They may seek leads for prospective sales from such sources as previous customers, friends, business associates, neighbors, other sales personnel, and other employees in the firm. The qualifying process identifies potential customers who have the financial ability and authority to buy. Those who lack the financial resources or who cannot make purchase decisions are not qualified prospects.

FIGURE 14.10
Seven Steps in the Sales Process

Companies use different tactics to identify and qualify prospects. Some companies rely on business development teams to do this legwork. They send direct mail and use the responses to provide leads to sales reps. Other companies believe in the paramount importance of personal visits from sales representatives.

Successful salespeople make careful preparations, analyzing available data about a prospective customer's product lines and other pertinent information before making the initial contact. They realize the importance of a first impression in influencing a customer's future attitudes toward the selling company and its products. They also learn to "read" customers and determine their needs.

Presentation and Demonstration   At the presentation stage, salespeople communicate promotional messages. Usually, they describe the major features of their products, highlight the advantages, and cite examples of satisfied consumers. A demonstration helps reinforce the message that the salesperson has been communicating—a critical step in the sales process. Visitors to almost any cosmetics counter in a department store may receive a free demonstration of certain products. Customers interested in buying new speakers for a music system may listen to them in the store. Of course, anyone looking to buy a car takes it for a test drive before deciding whether to purchase it.

Some products are too large to transport to prospective buyers or require special installation to demonstrate. Using laptop computers and multimedia presentations, sales representatives can demonstrate these products for customers.

Handling Objections   Some salespeople fear potential customers' objections because they view the questions as criticism. But a good salesperson can use objections as an opportunity to answer questions and explain how the product will benefit the customer. As a general rule, the key is to sell benefits, not features: How will this product help the customer?

Closing   The critical point in the sales process—the time at which the salesperson actually asks the prospect to buy—is the closing. If the presentation effectively matches product benefits to customer needs, the closing should be a natural conclusion. If there are more bumps in the process, the salesperson can try some different techniques, such as offering an alternative product, offering a special incentive for purchase, or restating the product benefits. Closing the sale—and beginning a relationship in which the customer builds loyalty to the brand or product—is the ideal outcome of this interaction. But even if the sale is not made at this time, the salesperson should regard the interaction as the beginning of a potential relationship anyway. The prospect might very well become a customer in the future.

Follow-up   A salesperson's actions after the sale may determine whether the customer will make another purchase. After closing, the seller should process the order quickly and efficiently and reassure the customer about the purchase decision. Follow-up is a vital activity for building a long-term relationship with customers to ensure that products satisfy them and to deliver service activities. By calling soon after a purchase, the salesperson provides psychological reinforcement for the customer's decision to buy. It also gives the seller a chance to correct any problems.

Proper follow-up is a logical part of the sales process. It involves not only continuing contact with customers but also a review of the sales process. Salespeople should ask themselves, "Why did I lose or close that sale? What could I have done differently to improve the outcome?"

Recent Trends in Personal Selling

Personal selling is taking on a new face. Companies are constantly looking for ways to reach existing and potential customers, meet their needs with goods and services, and build long-term relationships. To accomplish this, they are turning to telemarketing, relationship selling, consultative selling, team selling, and sales force automation—major personal selling trends that are changing the sales forces of companies of all sizes.

Telemarketing   **Telemarketing,** personal selling conducted entirely by telephone, provides a firm's marketers with a high return on their expenditures, an immediate response, and an opportunity for personalized two-way conversation. Many firms use telemarketing because expense or other obstacles prevent salespeople from meeting all potential customers in person. Telemarketers can use databases to target prospects based on demographic data. Telemarketing takes two forms. A sales representative who calls you is practicing *outbound telemarketing. Inbound telemarketing* occurs when you call a toll-free phone number to get product information or place an order.

As recently as 2003, the average telemarketer placed 104 calls a day to U.S. homes and businesses. Because not every consumer wants to receive unsolicited telemarketing calls, annoyed recipients of unsolicited—and unwanted—interruptions turned to unlisted numbers, phone-company services like caller ID and Privacy Manager, gadgets like Phone Butler and TeleZapper, and to state and the federal government for relief.[22] Today, outbound telemarketers must abide by the Federal Trade Commission's 1996 Telemarketing Sales Rule. Telemarketers must disclose that they are selling something and on whose behalf they call before they make their presentations. The rule also limits calls to between 8 A.M. and 9 P.M., requires sellers to disclose details on exchange policies, and requires them to keep lists of people who do not want to receive calls. In some states, it is also against the law for telemarketers to leave messages on consumers' answering machines. Despite opposition from the Direct Marketing Association, Congress enacted a new law in 2003 creating a national "do not call" list intended to help consumers block unwanted telemarketing calls. Telemarketers must check the list every three months and update their own lists or face stiff fines for each violation. Charities, surveys, and political campaign calls are exempt from these restrictions under the new law.[23]

Relationship Selling and Consultative Selling   As competitive pressures mount, a widening universe of firms is emphasizing **relationship selling,** in which a salesperson builds a mutually beneficial relationship with a customer through regular contacts over an extended period. When he took over as CEO of Newell Rubbermaid, Joe Galli realized that he needed to do something to get his company's products—plastic storage containers, as well as Levolor blinds, Graco car seats, and Calphalon cookware—back on the shelves of big customers like Wal-Mart, Home Depot, and Lowe's. So he came up with the Phoenix program, in which Rubbermaid recruited about 500 recent college graduates, trained them, and sent them into the stores where they did everything from stock shelves to demonstrate new products. They were at the stores every day. They talked with managers, staff, and customers. They sent ideas right up the corporate ladder to Galli—like a five-foot-high product display for Sharpie pens, which is now featured in 600 Lowe's stores. The result? Both retailers and consumers are returning to Rubbermaid products.[24]

Businesses often carry out relationship marketing by using consultative selling, which shifts the emphasis of the sales process from the product to the customer and often relies on creative selling. **Consultative selling** means meeting customers' needs by listening to them, understanding and caring about their problems, paying attention to details, suggesting solutions, and following through after the sale. Consultative selling is not cheap, however, because of the time one salesperson takes with one customer. But it can pay off in the form of customer loyalty.

Team Selling   **Team selling** joins salespeople with specialists from other functional areas of the

firm to complete the selling process. In this way, it complements relationship and consultative selling strategies. Teams can be formally assigned units or assembled for specific, temporary selling situations. Hewlett-Packard (HP) uses team selling to assess the needs of its biggest customers. The company brings together teams of employees representing its different products and assigns them to study each customer. Through the team approach, HP has substantially increased sales to its largest customers.

Many customers prefer the team approach, making them feel they receive exceptional service. Another advantage is the formation of relationships between companies rather than individuals.

Sales Force Automation   Recent advances in communications and information technol-

ogy have many applications to the sales process. These applications have produced a trend called **sales force automation (SFA).** This trend incorporates a broad range of tools, from e-mail, telecommunications devices such as pagers and cell phones, and notebook computers to increasingly sophisticated software systems that automate the sales process. These SFA software packages help sales managers develop account territories, plan sales campaigns, perform detailed analyses of sales trends, and forecast future sales. Sales personnel can use the system to analyze customer databases to develop leads, schedule sales campaigns, automatically file orders and expense reports, and tap into company databases for instant updates on prices and product availability.

Among its many benefits, SFA improves the consistency of the sales approach, speeds response times, and reduces the sales cycle. Salespeople can design product packages and close deals on the spot, instead of collecting information from customers and returning to their offices to prepare proposals.

Concept Check

1. Identify two environments in which personal selling takes place.
2. List the steps in the sales process.
3. Distinguish between inbound and outbound telemarketing.

Public Relations

A final element of the promotional mix, public relations (PR)—including publicity—supports advertising, personal selling, and sales promotion, usually by pursuing broader objectives. Through PR, companies attempt to improve their prestige and image with the public by distributing specific messages or ideas to target audiences. Cause-related promotional activities are often supported by PR and publicity campaigns. As such, PR is an important part of a company's promotional plan. In fact, some experts now believe that public relations can be as important to a company's marketing effort as much of its advertising is. That's because consumers are so bombarded with advertising messages that the messages lose either their impact or their credibility.[25]

public relations
organization's communications and relationships with its various audiences.

Public relations refers to an organization's nonpaid communications with its various public audiences, such as customers, vendors, news media, employees, stockholders, the government, and the general public. Many of these communication efforts serve marketing purposes. Public relations is an efficient, indirect communications channel for promoting products. It can publicize products and help to create and maintain a positive image of the company.

The PR department links a firm with the media. It provides the media with news releases and video and audio clips, as well as holding news conferences to announce new products, the formation of strategic alliances, management changes, financial results, and similar developments. Publications issued by the PR department include newsletters, brochures, and reports.

Publicity

The type of public relations that most closely approaches promoting a company's products is **publicity,** nonpersonal stimulation of demand for a good, service, place, idea, event, person, or organization by unpaid placement of information in print or broadcast media. Businesses generate publicity by engaging in unusual or significant activities that are picked up by local or national news. Although consumer demand for Dean Kamen's Segway human transporter system has lagged behind Kamen's goals, the initial publicity for the new invention created public awareness that no amount of advertising could match. Not-for-profit organizations benefit from publicity when they receive coverage of events such as the Boston Marathon, in which thousands of runners participate to raise money for 16 recognized charities, including the Doug Flutie Foundation for Autism.

While good publicity can promote a firm's positive image, negative publicity can cause problems. When home decorating and entertaining expert Martha Stewart was convicted of participating in a stock-trading scandal involving ImClone securities, the image of her own company—as well as that of Kmart, for whom she advertises and supplies a line of home products—suffered a loss.[26] The financial industry has suffered from bad publicity due to the unethical behavior of executives, accountants, financial advisors, and others. Many of these companies are now engaged in marketing campaigns designed to reinstill people's confidence in them. Negative publicity can cause a firm to lose credibility in the marketplace, which may be very difficult to reestablish.[27]

publicity stimulation of demand for a good, service, place, idea, person, or organization by disseminating news or obtaining favorable unpaid media presentations.

Concept Check
1. What function does a firm's PR department serve?
2. What is publicity?

Promotional Strategies

Many of this chapter's examples demonstrate the considerable overlap among the elements of the promotional mix. Clear boundaries no longer distinguish advertising from sales promotion. The Internet and other interactive media also change how marketers promote products. By blending advertising, sales promotion, personal selling, and public relations, marketers create an integrated promotional mix that reflects the market, product type, stage in the product life cycle, price, and promotional budget. Then they implement one of two promotional alternatives: pulling or pushing strategies. Finally, marketers must measure the effectiveness of their promotional strategies.

Selecting a Promotional Mix

Choosing the most appropriate promotional mix is one of the toughest tasks confronting a company's marketers. The following questions provide some general guidelines for allocating promotional efforts and expenditures among personal selling and advertising:

- *What is your target market?* The U.S. Department of Defense wanted to reconnect American adults with their military and remind them of the values and competencies that can be gained through military service and brought into professional life, so advertisements like the one in Figure 14.11 are part of the mix. The image of pro football defensive tackle Chad Hennings outfitted in his Dallas Cowboys uniform and the face mask he wore when flying A-10 "tank-buster" jets during his years in the Air Force and Air Force Reserves emphasizes the qualities that served him well in both careers: "Show up early. Study the threat. Visualize. Prepare. Focus."
- *What is the value of the product?* Although low-priced products like soda or toothpaste usually do well with advertising, high-priced products in both business and consumer markets require promotional mixes that include personal selling. Examples include commercial real estate and luxury automobiles.

FIGURE 14.11
Using Advertising, Toll-Free Telephone Numbers, and a Web Site to Communicate the Benefits of a Military Career

During his nine years as a defensive tackle for the Dallas Cowboys, Chad Hennings earned not only three Super Bowl rings, but the collective respect of players and coaches across the league. Not just as a result of rigorous physical conditioning and teamwork, but because his four years at the Air Force Academy and tour of duty flying A-10 Thunderbolt missions during Operation Provide Comfort provided him with a regimen they don't teach in training camp. Show up early. Study the threat. Visualize. Prepare. Focus.

TOTAL UNWAVERING COMMITMENT

–CHAD HENNINGS
U.S. AIR FORCE/RESERVE 1988-2005

The qualities you acquire while in the Military are qualities that stay with you forever.™

TODAY'S MILITARY
See it for what it really is.™
1.866.VIEW NOW
www.todaysmilitary.com
Active • Guard • Reserve

Dept. of Defense Joint Advertising, Market Research and Studies.

• *What time frame is involved?* Is the product something that will expire—like a ski vacation—within a certain time period? If so, advertising and sales promotions may be the preferred option.

Pushing and Pulling Strategies

Marketers can choose between two general promotional strategies: a pushing strategy or a pulling strategy. A **pushing strategy** relies on personal selling to market a product to wholesalers and retailers in a company's distribution channels. So marketers promote the product to members of the marketing channel, not to end users. Sales personnel explain to marketing intermediaries why they should carry a particular item, usually supported by offers of special discounts and promotional materials. Marketers also provide **cooperative advertising** allowances, in which they share the cost of local advertising of their firm's product or line with channel partners. All of these strategies are designed to motivate wholesalers and retailers to push the good or service to their own customers.

A **pulling strategy** attempts to promote a product by generating consumer demand for it, primarily through advertising and sales promotion appeals. Potential buyers will then request that their suppliers (retailers or local distributors) carry the product, thereby pulling it through the distribution channel.

Most marketing situations require combinations of pushing and pulling strategies, although the primary emphasis can vary. Consumer products usually depend more heavily on pulling strategies than do B2B products, which favor pushing strategies.

Concept Check

1. Give an example of a pushing strategy.
2. Give an example of a pulling strategy.

Bristol-Myers Squibb Co. uses a pulling strategy to stimulate demand for its cancer medications. This piece is also a good example of celebrity advertising, in which champion cyclist Lance Armstrong—a former cancer patient—appears.

"Don't give up. I didn't."

CYCLE OF HOPE
LANCE ARMSTRONG FOUNDATION
AND BRISTOL-MYERS SQUIBB

© AP/Wide World Photos

Ethics in Promotion

Of all the elements in a 21st-century business organization, promotion probably raises the most ethical questions. Many people view advertising with a cynical eye, criticizing its influence on consumers, its potential for creating unnecessary needs and wants, its overemphasis on sex and beauty, and its delivery of inappropriate messages to children.

This section examines three controversial issues related to the promotion element of the firm's marketing mix: puffery and deception, promotion to children and teens, and promotion in public schools and on college campuses.

Puffery and Deception

Legally as well as ethically, there are limits on the claims a marketer may make. Claims such as "bigger," "best," "most advanced," or "number 1" are example of **puffery,** exaggerated claims of a product's superiority or use of the doubtful, subjective, or vague statements. Puffery is actually legal because it doesn't imply a guarantee, but it certainly raises ethical questions. Is it ethical to make a boastful statement that has no objective basis? Can an advertiser be absolutely certain that every consumer knows the difference between exaggeration and reality? While advertisers argue that most people are not deceived by puffery, one critic responds this way: "Advertising people are smart. If puffery means nothing to consumers, why do they bother with it? If advertisers had the facts, they might use the facts and forget the puffs."[28]

The Uniform Commercial Code, which standardizes laws for business practices throughout the U.S., distinguishes puffery from specific or quantifiable statements about product quality or performance. Those statements amount to an "express warranty," for which the company must stand behind its claim. General boasts of product superiority and vague claims are considered puffery, not warranties. A marketer's quantifiable statement, on the other hand, implies a certain level of performance. Tests can establish the validity of a claim that one brand of batteries outlasts a rival brand.

Deception involves deliberately making promises that are untrue, such as guaranteed weight loss in five days, get-rich-quick schemes for would-be entrepreneurs, or promised return on investments. Today's climate of skepticism among consumers may actually present an opportunity for ethical companies to shine. "If corporations are not trying to promote, advertise, and sell their integrity through customers, employees, investors, and potential investors, then they are really missing a tremendous opportunity," notes W. Michael Hoffman, executive director of the Center for Business Ethics at Bentley College in Massachusetts.[29]

> *They Said It*
>
> Many a small thing has been made large by the right kind of advertising.
>
> —*Mark Twain (1835–1910)*
> *American author*

Promotion to Children and Teens

Marketers recognize the huge purchasing power that today's children and teens have, whether making their own purchases or influencing the buying decisions of their families. It is tempting for some marketers to try anything to influence these young consumers. Although today's children are certainly accustomed to promotional messages, they are not sophisticated at analyzing them. In addition, to woo young consumers, advertisers often make ads as unadlike as possible—designing messages that resemble entertainment. With modern media companies owning a variety of broadcast, print, Internet, and other outlets, children watching Saturday-morning cartoons are exposed to an integrated marketing effort that combines advertising for related videos, books, and video games, as well as licensed merchandise from toys to backpacks to T-shirts. And they often see advertisements for foods that most parents would prefer they eat only occasionally as a treat. By contrast, in Sweden, broadcasters may not direct advertising to children under the age of 12.

As children grow older and become more sophisticated, so does the marketing effort. The U.S. teen population is large, and marketers are working harder than ever to learn about them. In their search for insights into their market's special needs and wants, MTV marketers even borrowed the techniques of anthropology to visit teens and observe their lives firsthand.

BUSINESS TOOL KIT

Personal Selling Strategies

Developing effective personal selling strategies involves more than just presenting a product to the consumer. Personal selling is a direct person-to-person promotional presentation. This takes the form of business-to-business or business-to-consumer selling, but your personal selling strategy should remain the same in either case. Here are some tips to developing an effective personal selling strategy.

1. **Know your product.** The best way to make an impression when selling is to know your product backward and forward. Being extremely knowledgeable helps you sell your wares without having to say "I don't know" to a buyer's question. This not only applies to the products you represent; it also applies to the organization itself and its policies.

2. **Don't waste your customer's time.** Be prepared for every sales call, communicate the benefits quickly and efficiently, and try to establish an immediate rapport with your client. Businesspeople are busy people, and salespeople are sometimes seen as necessary evils. If you cultivate a positive attitude with businesslike strategies, you have a better chance of making the sale.

3. **Always follow up.** Sometimes your customer has to consult senior management, committees, boards, or his or her team before making a purchase, so be sure you have a plan for following up on each sales call. Don't wait for the phone to ring with an order—be proactive about finding out how long the committee usually takes to reach a decision, how many weeks to wait before calling your contact again, and the like.

4. **Be genuine with your customers.** Always be upbeat and friendly when making sales calls or presentations. Present yourself as a professional but relate as a consumer yourself if necessary. Don't try to fake kindness or concern; if you don't genuinely feel it, your customer won't either. Use the time to catch up on paperwork or lead generation instead!

Sources: Daryl Allen, "Sales Off? You Need a Personal Selling Plan," *Selling*, December 2001, p. 13; Christine Galea, "The Boldest Thing I Did to Make a Sale," *Sales & Marketing Management*, March 2000, p. 62.

Promotion in Public Schools and on College Campuses

A related ethical issue is the placement of promotional messages in schools, from kindergartens through university campuses. The idea of school as a place where students are free from marketing messages is long gone. In the public school district of Philadelphia, lunch menus are printed courtesy of the Cartoon Network. In addition to the daily specials, they feature the Turner network's logo, characters, and information about upcoming shows. Some schools are bringing in income by signing contracts that give certain brands exclusive access to their students. Wheeler High School in Marietta, Georgia, used some of the $50,000 it received in annual vending machine revenues to refinish the gym floor, install a new high-jump pit, and pay $7,000 for two buses. At a middle school in Seattle, a history lesson on the Civil War packaged by Procter & Gamble includes a page titled "Did You Know?" that informs students, among other things, that P&G was one of the suppliers of soap for the Union army.[30]

In-school promotions have begun to generate a backlash, however. Growing criticism of marketing snack foods and soft drinks on school campuses led to revisions in Coca-Cola's in-school marketing programs. The company decided to include healthier products—bottled water, juice, and other beverages—in school vending machines. In addition, Coke began to replace corporate logos on the machines with images of students exercising and playing. The timing couldn't have been better. Recent medical reports of greater obesity rates among children and teens who drank at least one soft drink a day and growing concerns about the rapid increase in the number of obese children have created negative publicity for the soft-drink industry.[31] Associating its name with healthy drinks may turn out to be a positive strategy for Coke.

Concept Check

1. Define puffery.
2. How are schools actually benefiting from advertising aimed at students?

Price in the Marketing Mix

The final variable of the marketing mix is made up of many major decisions that greatly influence the success of any organization. Price was first discussed in detail in Chapter 3, which focused on such economic concepts as determinants of demand and supply, equilibrium prices, impact of changes in price on customer behavior and company revenues, and the elasticity of demand and supply. All of these concepts influence the pricing decisions that business decision makers must make in formulating their overall marketing strategies.

Every successful product offers some utility, or want-satisfying power. However, individual preferences determine how much value a particular consumer associates with a good or service. One person may value leisure-time pursuits while another assigns a higher priority to acquiring property and automobiles. But all consumers have limited amounts of money and a variety of possible uses for it. So the **price**—the exchange value of a good or service—becomes a major factor in consumer buying decisions.

Businesspeople attempt to accomplish certain objectives through their pricing decisions. Pricing objectives vary from firm to firm, and many companies pursue multiple pricing objectives. Some try to improve profits by setting high prices; others set low prices to attract new business. As Figure 14.12 shows, the four basic categories of pricing objectives are (1) profitability, (2) volume, (3) meeting competition, and (4) prestige.

> *They Said It*
>
> Free is good—but read
> the fine print.
>
> —*Anonymous*

price exchange value of a good or service.

Profitability Objectives

Profitability objectives are perhaps the most common objectives included in the strategic plans of most firms. Marketers know that profits are the revenue the company brings in, minus its expenses. Usually, there is a big difference between revenue and profit. Every large automaker tries to produce at least one luxury vehicle for which they can charge $50,000 or more instead of relying entirely on the sale of $15,000 to $25,000 models, thus making a greater profit typical of luxury models. But the huge profits aren't always there. Jaguar recently lost $500 million in a single year in an unsuccessful effort to convince recession-worried auto buyers to buy its luxury vehicles instead of moderately priced sedans, minivans, and compact SUVs. Volkswagen recently sold only 2,000 of its luxury Passats in the U.S. during a year in which Ford sold almost 400,000 of its popular workhorse, the Explorer.[32]

Some firms try to maximize profits by reducing costs rather than through price changes. Companies can maintain prices and increase profitability by operating more efficiently or by modifying the product to make it less costly to produce. While maintaining a steady price, Frito-Lay has recently reduced the package weights for Tostitos and Cracker Jack snack foods, and Nestlé has done the same with its Poland Spring and Calistoga bottled waters.

Volume Objectives

A second approach to pricing strategy—**volume objectives**—bases pricing decisions on *market share*—the percentage of a market controlled by a certain company or product. One firm may seek to achieve a 25 percent market share in a certain industry, and another may want to maintain or expand its market share for particular products.

The market for the PC industry has shrunk over the last few years because so many consumers and businesses have already invested in PCs—and aren't willing or able to upgrade to newer models as quickly as the industry would like. So competitors like Dell, IBM, and Hewlett-Packard have had to rely on price to attract new customers or keep existing ones. One potential market is school districts, which might have as many as 14,000 computers needing service.[33]

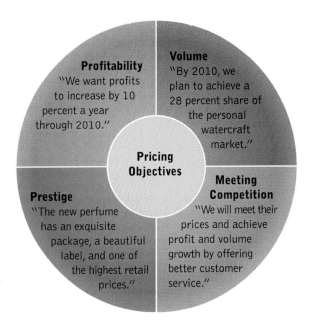

FIGURE 14.12
Pricing Objectives

How Much Should a CD Cost?

How much is a music CD worth to you—10 bucks, or 15, or 20? In recent years, CD prices have hovered around the $14 to $18 range, and the music industry would love to see them top $20. But consumers have been saying no to these price increases in a variety of ways. First, there was illegal downloading via Napster and other sites that contained unrestricted MP3 music files. Until Napster was shut down, music buffs could download thousands of songs onto their computers for free, meaning that artists and related businesses did not receive any revenues for their products. But the music industry was not guilt free, either. The states of New York and Florida sued the five largest music labels and several retail chains, alleging that CD prices had been fixed, a practice prohibited by federal law. The plaintiffs were ordered to pay $65 million in cash and distribute $75 million worth of CDs to nonprofit organizations in 50 states. Then came Rhapsody, a legal online music service that allowed consumers to download songs for a modest fee. Through its subscription service, music lovers can formulate

their own CDs for roughly half the retail price and continue to listen to the tunes—as long as they continue to pay for their subscriptions.

Should Rhapsody and other similar businesses continue to offer music online at reduced rates as a compromise between consumers and the music industry?

PRO
1. Discounting is part of the private enterprise system and provides a positive alternative to consumers downloading music for free.
2. Rhapsody's reduced rates should benefit consumers because to compete, traditional retailers—and music labels—will have to reduce their prices as well.

CON
1. Significantly reduced prices may further injure an industry that is already suffering from a severe decline.
2. Discounted prices available only to PC users may cause the music industry to raise prices in traditional outlets,

forcing consumers who shop there to pay higher prices.

SUMMARY
Competition in the music industry is legendary, and new technology has only increased the stakes. Recently, record companies have actually cut the prices on some of their CDs, such as those by new artists. And Apple recently opened its online music store in cooperation with the five largest record companies, where customers can download a single song for 99 cents or an entire album for about $9.99—all without subscribing. This partnership may help provide a solution to the clash between the music business and technology.

Sources: May Wong, "Apple Computer's Chief Pulls Off Coup in Music Industry," *Mobile Register,* May 10, 2003, p. B7; Laurie J. Flynn, "Apple Offers Music Downloads with Unique Pricing," *The New York Times,* April 29, 2003, http://www.nytimes.com; "Music Industry to Pay $67.4M in CD Price-fixing Case," *USA Today,* September 30, 2002, http://www.usatoday.com; Jenny Eliscu, "Do CDs Cost Too Much?" *Rolling Stone,* July 4–11, 2002, p. 34.

Pricing to Meet Competition

A third set of pricing objectives seeks simply to meet competitors' prices so that price essentially becomes a nonissue. In many lines of business, firms set their own prices to match those of established industry leaders. But companies may not legally work together to agree on prices or force retailers to sell at a set price, which is called *price fixing,* as described in the Solving an Ethical Controversy box.

Price is a highly visible component of a firm's marketing mix and an easily used and effective tool for obtaining an advantage over competitors. But sometimes the race to match competitors' prices can result in a *price war,* which has happened periodically in the airline and fast-food industries. The ability of competitors to match a price cut leads many marketers to try to avoid price wars by favoring other strategies, such as adding value, improving quality, educating consumers, and establishing relationships.

Concept Check
1. Define price.
2. Which pricing objective results in diverting consumer attention from price?

Prestige Objectives

The final category of objectives encompasses the effect of prices on prestige. **Prestige pricing** establishes a relatively high price to develop and maintain an image of quality and exclusiveness. Marketers set such objectives because they recognize the role of price in communicating an overall image for the firm and its products. People expect to pay more for prestigious brands like Rolls Royce, Gucci, Coach, or a Whistler ski vacation outside Vancouver.

Pricing Strategies

People from different areas of a company contribute their expertise to set the most strategic price for a product. Accountants, financial managers, and sales representatives provide relevant sales and cost data, along with customer feedback. Designers, engineers, and systems analysts all contribute important data as well.

Prices are determined in two basic ways: by applying the concepts of supply and demand discussed in Chapter 3 and by completing cost-oriented analyses. Economic theory assumes that a market price will be set at the point where the amount of a product desired at a given price equals the amount that suppliers will offer for sale at that price. In other words, this price occurs at the point where the amount demanded and the amount supplied are equal. Online auctions, such as those conducted on eBay, are a popular application of the demand-and-supply approach.

Price Determination in Practice

Economic theory might lead to the best pricing decisions, but most businesses do not have all the information they need to make those decisions, so they adopt **cost-based pricing** formulas. These formulas calculate total costs per unit and then add markups to cover overhead costs and generate profits.

Cost-based pricing totals all costs associated with offering a product in the market, including research and development, production, transportation, and marketing expenses. An added amount, the *markup*, then covers any unexpected or overlooked expenses and ensures a profit. The total becomes the price. Manufacturers, wholesalers, and retailers usually practice markup pricing. Although the actual markup used varies by such factors as brand image and type of store, the typical markup for clothing is determined by doubling wholesale price (the cost to the merchant) to arrive at the retail price for the item.

Breakeven Analysis

Businesses often conduct a **breakeven analysis** to determine the minimum sales volume a product must generate at a certain price level to cover all costs. This method involves a consideration of various costs

Used with permission from McDonald's Corporation.

For the price of this magazine, you could have bought 3 of these.

Dollar Menu

The Big N' Tasty,® McChicken® Sandwich, Snack-Sized Fruit 'n Yogurt® Parfait, McValue® Fries, Apple Pies and more. Each for $1. Every day on the Dollar Menu at McDonald's.®

Price wars are common in the fast-food industry. Both McDonald's and Burger King recently slashed their flagship brands—Big Mac and Whopper—in expensive moves to drive business. Although Wendy's offered a long menu of 99 cent offerings, the firm also sought to use nonprice mix variables by improving the quality of its offerings and adding a series of salad alternatives.

They Said It

The people of America have been overcharged. And on their behalf, I'm here asking for a refund.

—*George W. Bush (b. 1946)*
43rd president of the United States, explaining a recent tax cut

cost-based pricing practice of adding a percentage of specific amounts (markup) to the base cost of a product to cover overhead costs and generate profits.

breakeven analysis pricing technique used to determine the minimum sales volume a product must generate at a certain price level to cover all costs.

and total revenues. *Total cost* is the sum of total variable costs and total fixed costs. *Variable costs* change with the level of production, as labor and raw materials do, while *fixed costs* like insurance premiums and minimum utility rates charged by water, natural gas, and electric power suppliers remain stable regardless of the production level. *Total revenue* is determined by multiplying price by the number of units sold.

Finding the Breakeven Point   The level of sales that will generate enough revenue to cover all of the company's fixed and variable costs is called the breakeven point. It is the point at which total revenue just equals total costs. Sales beyond the breakeven point will generate profits; sales volume below the breakeven point will result in losses. The following formulas give the breakeven point in units and dollars:

$$\text{Breakeven point (in units)} = \frac{\text{Total Fixed Costs}}{\text{Contribution to Fixed Costs per Unit}}$$

$$\text{Breakeven point (in dollars)} = \frac{\text{Total Fixed Costs}}{1 - \text{Variable Cost per Unit/Price}}$$

A product selling for $20 with a variable cost of $14 per unit produces a $6 per-unit contribution to fixed costs. If the firm has total fixed costs of $42,000, then it must sell 7,000 units to break even on the product. The calculation of the breakeven point in units and dollars is as follows:

$$\text{Breakeven point (in units)} = \frac{\$42,000}{\$20 - \$14} = \frac{\$42,000}{\$6} = 7,000 \text{ units}$$

$$\text{Breakeven point (in dollars)} = \frac{\$42,000}{1 - \$14/\$20} = \frac{\$42,000}{1 - .7} = \frac{\$42,000}{.3} = \$140,000$$

Figure 14.13 illustrates this breakeven point in graphic form.

Marketers use breakeven analysis to determine the profits or losses that would result from several different proposed prices. Since different prices produce different breakeven points, marketers could compare their calculations of required sales to break even with sales estimates from marketing research studies. This comparison can identify the best price, one that would attract enough customers to exceed the breakeven point and earn profits for the firm.

Most firms add demand—determining whether enough customers will buy the number of units the firm must sell at a particular price to break even—by developing estimates of consumer demand through surveys of likely customers, interviews with retailers that would be handling the product, and assessments of prices charged by competitors. Then the breakeven points for several possible prices are calculated and compared with sales estimates for each price. This practice is referred to as *modified breakeven analysis*.

Alternative Pricing Strategies

The strategy a company uses to set its prices should grow out of the firm's overall marketing strategy. In general, firms can choose from four alternative pricing strategies: skimming, penetration, discount or everyday low pricing, and competitive pricing.

Skimming Pricing   A **skimming pricing** strategy sets an intentionally high price relative to the prices of competing

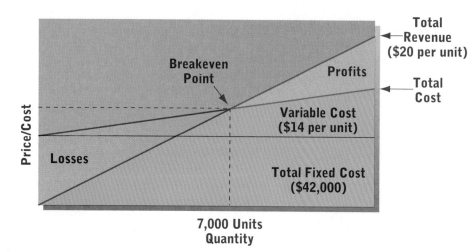

FIGURE 14.13
Breakeven Analysis

products. The term comes from the expression "skimming the cream." This pricing strategy often works for the introduction of a distinctive good or service with little or no competition, although it can be used at other stages of the product life cycle as well. A skimming strategy can help marketers to set a price that distinguishes a firm's high-end product from those of competitors. It can also help a firm recover its product development costs before competitors enter the field. This is often the case with prescription drugs such as the allergy medication Claritin. In its prescription form, Claritin sold for as much as $60 for a month's supply. When its manufacturer's patent expired and the drug began to sell without a prescription—facing more competitors—Claritin's retail price dropped 50 percent. Even so, the drug is still priced at about $1 per pill.[34]

Penetration Pricing
By contrast, a **penetration pricing** strategy sets a low price as a major marketing weapon. Businesses may price new products noticeably lower than competing offerings when they enter new industries characterized by dozens of competing brands. Once the new product achieves some market recognition through consumer trial purchases stimulated by its low price, marketers may increase the price to the level of competing products. However, stiff competition might prevent the price increase. When Microsoft introduced its Xbox at $299, the company claimed it lost an estimated $50 to $100 for each box sold. But Sony responded by offering its competing PlayStation 2 system for $199, meaning that Microsoft would have to take an even greater loss to undercut Sony.[35]

Everyday Low Pricing and Discount Pricing
Everyday low pricing (EDLP) is a strategy devoted to maintaining continuous low prices rather than relying on short-term price-cutting tactics such as cents-off coupons, rebates, and special sales. This strategy is used by retailers like Wal-Mart to consistently offer low prices to consumers; manufacturers also use EDLP to set stable prices for retailers.

With *discount pricing,* businesses hope to attract customers by dropping prices for a set period of time. The Gap marks its prices down every Wednesday, while Best Buy—featured in Figure 14.14— offers its CDs and DVDs at a discount for the first five days after their release. In recent years, many of the major automakers have attracted buyers by offering discounted financing: 0 percent for five years. Special pricing software is now available to help firms analyze the buying patterns of customers and then decide the best time to offer discounts. Because of this software, a few lucky consumers can buy a pair of Badgley-Mischka beaded pants at Saks Fifth Avenue for only $1,515—a thousand dollars off the original price.[36]

Competitive Pricing
Although many organizations rely heavily on price as a competitive weapon, even more implement **competitive pricing** strategies. They try to reduce the emphasis on price competition by matching other firms' prices and concentrating their own marketing efforts on the

FIGURE 14.14
Implementing a Discount Pricing Strategy

© AP/Wide World Photos

BEST BUSINESS PRACTICES

Best Buy Serves and Sells

He's called a "blueshirt," and there are lots more like him bustling around the store. Clad in royal blue shirts and rumpled khakis, with beepers clipped to their belts, Best Buy's sales staff are truly there to help consumers get the best buy on hundreds of products. They're on hand to help even the most technophobic consumer choose a computer, a digital camera, or a CD burner. Customers may come to Best Buy looking for a good price such as the regular discounts offered on new music CD releases. But they get service in the bargain, including someone to come to the house and set up the PC or home theater they've purchased and teach them how to use it—for a price, of course.

Although Best Buy has long been known for low priced, "grab-and-go" electronics such as videogames and software, the company is now turning toward higher-end deals. Blueshirts are trained to offer complete packages, not just individual items. So a customer might come in to buy a Canon digital camera that sells for $999 and end up purchasing accessories like a backup battery for $69, memory card for $119, memory card reader for $20, lens protector for $15, photo printer for $199 and photo paper for $40. In addition, some Best Buy stores offer try-and-buy opportunities. Customers can come into a store to burn a CD. They can watch—

or even make—movies. They can settle into a leather recliner. And if the 42-inch Zenith liquid-plasma, flat-panel TV costs $2,999, that's OK. Once they've watched a football game on it, they absolutely must have it—and the $1,299 recliner they were lounging in while they watched. And if they need their home wired for the appliance, Best Buy can arrange it. The Best Buy shopping experience may add up, but no one can say it isn't fun. Nearly every consumer will latch on to some gadget or gizmo that finds its way into the heart—and the shopping cart.

QUESTIONS FOR CRITICAL THINKING

1. Notice that Best Buy uses odd pricing for many of its items. Do you think this practice is more influential when an item is expensive—like the $2,999 liquid-plasma TV—or relatively inexpensive, like the $69 backup battery?

2. Do you think Best Buy will successfully balance its reputation for discount items with its new focus on higher-priced goods and services? Why or why not?

Sources: Michael V. Copeland, "Best Buy's Selling Machine," *Business 2.0*, July 2004, pp. 93–102; Mark Tatge, "Fun & Games," *Forbes*, January 12, 2004, pp. 138–144.

Concept Check

1. What is a cost-based pricing formula?

2. What is the breakeven point in a breakeven analysis?

product, distribution, and promotional elements of the marketing mix. In fact, in industries with relatively homogeneous products, competitors must match one another's price reductions to maintain market share and remain competitive. By pricing their products at the general levels of competing offerings, marketers largely negate the price variable in their marketing strategies.

Consumer Perceptions of Prices

In addition to costs and competitors, marketers must also consider how consumers perceive prices. If large numbers of potential buyers consider a price too high or too low, the marketer must correct the situation. Price-quality relationships and the use of odd pricing are important considerations, as discussed in the Best Business Practices box.

Price–Quality Relationships

Research shows that a consumer's perception of product quality is closely related to an item's price. Most marketers believe that this perceived price–quality relationship holds over a relatively wide range of prices, although consumers may view extreme prices as either too expensive or too cheap to consider paying. Businesspeople need to study and experiment with prices because the price–quality relationship can critically affect a firm's pricing strategy.

Some consumers are perfectly willing to pay more for foods that are certified to be organically grown, even when cheaper alternatives are readily available. Others will pay more for foods that are labeled "natural," regardless of what the word actually means. Home buyers are often willing to pay more for a house in one neighborhood than another, regardless of construction quality.

Odd Pricing

Have you ever wondered why retailers set prices like $1.99 instead of $2 or $9.99 instead of $10? Before the age of cash registers and sales taxes, retailers reportedly followed this practice of *odd pricing* to force clerks to make correct change as part of cash control efforts. But now **odd pricing** is commonly used because many retailers believe that consumers favor uneven amounts or amounts that sound less than they really are: It's easier to justify a purchase of $299 than one of $300. However, some retailers also use this method to identify items that have been marked down. Costco identifies markdowns with prices ending in $.77, while The Hayloft identifies its marked-down ladies clothing with prices ending in $.99.[37]

What's Ahead

The chapters in Part 4 have explained the main principles underlying marketing management and described how each fits a firm's overall business strategy. The next few chapters will help you understand how companies manage the technology and information that are available to businesses to create value for their customers and enhance their competitiveness in the marketplace. You'll also learn how firms manage their financial resources.

Concept Check

1. Give an example of the price–quality relationship.
2. Why is odd pricing used?

DID YOU KNOW?

1. Not realizing that Asian cultures view darkly stained teeth as attractive, Pepsodent lost sales in Asian countries by running ads showing the whitening benefits of its toothpaste.
2. Former boxing champion George Foreman's success as a celebrity spokesperson resulted in the sale of 50 million Lean Mean Grilling Machines and earned enough to make him the third-highest-paid sports-celebrity endorser, behind only Tiger Woods and Michael Jordan.
3. Although New York's Madison Avenue is virtually synonymous with advertising agencies, Tokyo is the world's major ad agency location.
4. If you shop at Sam's Club stores, try to spot the prices ending in $.91. Those are the items with the smallest markups.

Summary of Learning Goals

1 **_Discuss how integrated marketing communications relates to a firm's promotional strategy._**
In practicing integrated marketing communications, a firm coordinates all promotional activities to produce a unified, customer-focused message. IMC identifies consumer needs and then shows how a company's products meet those needs. Marketers select the promotional media that best target and reach customers. Teamwork and careful promotional planning to coordinate IMC strategy components are important elements of these programs.

2

Explain the concept of a promotional mix and outline the objectives of promotion.

A company's promotional mix integrates two components: personal selling and nonpersonal selling, which includes advertising, sales promotion, and public relations. By selecting the appropriate combination of promotional mix elements, marketers attempt to achieve the firm's five major promotional objectives: provide information, differentiate a product, increase demand, stabilize sales, and accentuate the product's value.

3

Summarize the different types of advertising and advertising media.

Advertising, the most visible form of nonpersonal promotion, is designed to inform, persuade, or remind. Product advertising promotes a good or service, while institutional advertising promotes a concept, idea, organization, or philosophy. Television, newspapers, and direct mail represent the largest advertising media categories. Others include magazines, radio, and outdoor advertising. Interactive media such as the Internet represent the fastest-growing type of advertising. Interactive advertising directly involves the consumer, who controls the flow of information.

4

Describe the role of sales promotion, personal selling, and public relations in promotional strategy.

Sales promotion accounts for greater expenditures than does advertising. Consumer-oriented sales promotions like coupons, games, rebates, samples, premiums, contests, sweepstakes, and promotional products offer an extra incentive to buy a product. Point-of-purchase advertising displays and trade shows are sales promotions directed to the trade markets. Personal selling involves face-to-face interactions between seller and buyer. The primary sales tasks are order processing, creative selling, and missionary selling. The seven-step sales process includes prospecting and qualifying, approach, presentation, demonstration, handling objections, closing, and follow-up. Public relations is nonpaid promotion that seeks to enhance a company's public image through press releases, news conferences, articles, and news broadcasts.

5

Identify the factors that influence the selection of a promotional mix.

Marketers begin by focusing on their company's target market, product value, time frame, and budget.

By analyzing these factors, they develop a promotional mix and allocate resources and expenditures among personal selling, advertising, sales promotion, and public relations.

6

Discuss the major ethical issues involved in promotion.

Many consumers believe that advertising exerts too much influence on buyers and that it deceives customers by exaggerating product claims and consciously blurring the line between promotion and entertainment. Many consumers also question the appropriateness of marketing to children and through schools.

7

Outline the different types of pricing objectives and discuss how firms set prices in the marketplace.

Pricing objectives can be classified as profitability, volume, meeting competition, and prestige. Although economic theory determines prices by the law of demand and supply, most firms use cost-based pricing, which adds a markup after costs. They usually conduct a breakeven analysis to determine the minimum sales volume a product must generate at a certain price in order to cover costs.

8

Summarize the four alternative pricing strategies.

These strategies include skimming, penetration, discounting, and competitive pricing. A skimming strategy sets a high price initially to recover costs and then lowers it; a penetration strategy sets a lower price to attract customers and then raises it later. Discounting offers a lower price for a certain period of time. Competitive pricing matches other firms' prices and emphasizes nonprice benefits of a product.

9

Discuss consumer perceptions of price.

Marketers must consider how consumers perceive the price–quality relationship of their products. Consumers may be willing to pay a higher price if they perceive a product to be of superior quality. However, extreme prices—either high or low—may turn consumers away. Marketers often use odd pricing to convey a message to consumers.

Business Terms You Need to Know

promotion 450

integrated marketing
communications
(IMC) 450

promotional mix 451

personal selling 451

advertising 456

sales promotion 463

public relations 468

publicity 469

price 473

cost-based pricing 475

breakeven analysis 475

Other Important Business Terms

nonpersonal selling 452

positioning 454

product placement 455

guerrilla marketing 455

product advertising 457

institutional advertising 457

advocacy (cause)
advertising 457

sponsorship 462

infomercial 462

promotional product 464

trade promotion 464

point-of-purchase (POP)
advertising 464

order processing 465

creative selling 465

missionary selling 466

telemarketing 467

relationship selling 467

consultative selling 468

team selling 468

sales force automation
(SFA) 468

pushing strategy 470

cooperative advertising 470

pulling strategy 470

puffery 471

profitability objectives 473

volume objectives 473

prestige pricing 475

skimming pricing 476

penetration pricing 477

everyday low pricing
(EDLP) 477

competitive pricing 477

odd pricing 479

Review Questions

1. Explain the concept of integrated marketing communications. Why do marketers use this process to develop their companies' promotional strategies?

2. What are the two major components of the promotional mix? What promotional mix might be appropriate for each of the following?
   a. six-pack of yogurt for kids
   b. wireless phone service
   c. specialty auto parts sold to car manufacturers
   d. JetBlue Airlines

3. Identify and define each of the three categories of advertising based on their purpose.

4. What are the benefits of television advertising? What are the drawbacks? What are the benefits of radio advertising? What are the drawbacks?

5. For each of the following, describe potential benefits of a sponsorship relationship:
   a. NASCAR and Krispy Kreme
   b. the Olympics and Visa
   c. the recent "Global Extremes" Mt. Everest expedition and Toyota
   d. the World Cup and Corona

6. If you were a marketer for General Mills, what kind of sales promotion might you use for your line of prepackaged chicken and pasta dinners?

7. What are some of the recent trends in personal selling? In what ways might these trends help build long-term relationships with customers?

8. Distinguish between pushing and pulling strategies. Under what conditions should each be used?

9. Identify and define the four basic categories of pricing objectives.

10. What are the four alternative pricing strategies used by marketers? Give an example of the circumstances under which each might be selected.

Projects and Applications

1. Choose a product that you purchased recently. Identify the various media that were used to promote the product and analyze the promotional mix. Do you agree with the company's marketing strategy, or would you recommend changes to the mix? Why? Create your own print ad for the product you chose using any business strategies or knowledge you have learned in this course so far.

2. As a consumer, what is your typical response to personal selling? Do you like personal attention or do you prefer to be left alone while making a decision? Does your preference change whether you are making a fairly routine purchase, such as a garden hose, or a large, complicated purchase, such as a computer?

3. You read in the chapter that some schools have received financial benefits by allowing companies to promote their goods and services to students within the school. Prepare a list of the major arguments for such practices. Create a similar list of reasons school administrators should avoid this practice.

4. Imagine that a mid-size city located near you has made an agreement with Major League Baseball to build and develop a new baseball stadium for a minor league team. The park will be small—about 7,500 seats. The town will be able to sell food and souvenirs at the park. As a marketer, what kind of approach would you take for establishing ticket prices?

5. Calculate the breakeven point for a baseball cap embroidered with a team logo, which sells for $20 with a variable cost of $12 per unit and produces a $4 per-unit contribution to fixed costs. The company that makes the cap has a total fixed cost of $40,000. What is the breakeven point in units? In dollars?

Experiential Exercise

Background: This exercise, which may be done either as an individual or a group project, will help you apply many of the chapter concepts to the promotion and pricing of a product that interests you.

Directions: Develop a promotional mix and choose a pricing strategy for an existing product that interests you or for a new product that you think could compete successfully with an existing product.

1. Identify your product and its target market.

2. Outline your firm's promotional objectives for the product.

3. Research the promotional mix for competing products by going online, looking at magazines and newspapers, and watching television. Then create a chart illustrating a competitor's promotional mix and your selection of promotional mix elements for your product.

4. Write a brief memo explaining the reasons for your choice of such elements as advertising or ways in which you think public relations could assist in your efforts.

5. Select the pricing strategy that you think would work best for your product and explain your choice.

NOTHING BUT NET

1. **Promotional products and specialty advertising.** The use of promotional products and specialty advertising is a form of marketing communication. Visit the Web sites listed here, review the material, and answer the following questions:
   a. What are promotional products?
   b. Which types of promotional products are the most popular? Why?
   c. What are the advantages of using promotional products?

   http://www.ppa.org
   http://www.saagny.org

2. **Ethics in advertising.** The American Association of Advertising Agencies (AAAA) is a professional organization whose members include many of the nation's largest ad agencies. Go to the association's Web site and prepare an oral report to your class outlining the associ-

ation's mission, its standards of practice, and its creative code. Find a recent newspaper or magazine ad that you believe adheres to AAAA standards.

http://www.aaaa.org

3. **Pricing strategy.** AT&T recently unveiled a new pricing plan for long-distance service. The plan allows unlimited calling to other AT&T customers for a fixed monthly rate. Visit the Web site listed here and prepare a brief report on how AT&T has applied some of the pricing concepts you learned in the chapter.

http://www.consumer.att.com/plans

Note: Internet Web addresses change frequently. If you do not find the exact sites listed, you may need to access the organization's or company's home page and search from there.

Case 14.1

Wow! It's Yao!

Yao Ming is the National Basketball Association's tallest player. That's saying a lot in a league where anyone under six feet five inches would be considered short. But Yao Ming (Yao is his surname) is seven feet five inches tall—a giant among giants. Just a couple of years ago, Yao left his home in China, where he played basketball for the Shanghai Sharks, to become the star center in his rookie year for the Houston Rockets. Just as quickly, he became a U.S. media celebrity—and a sought-after advertising spokesperson.

Yao, whose presence is hard to ignore, appeared in his first television commercial for Apple Computer, in which he promoted the firm's new PowerBook G4 computer. (His costar in the advertisement was the diminutive Verne Troyer, the actor who played Mini Me in the *Austin Powers* films.) Viewers loved him. But his slam dunk came in a commercial for Visa, which aired during a recent Super Bowl. In that ad, Yao sparred with a petite actress playing a clerk who wouldn't let him cash a check, saying, "Yo!" and pointing to a sign indicating no personal checks. A few months later, Yao signed an exclusive deal with Gatorade, for which he appeared in ads along with other sports celebrities like baseball player Derek Jeter and football star Peyton Manning.

Hiring sports celebrities as part of a promotional campaign is nothing new. But Yao is different. He speaks very little English, relying heavily on a translator to help him communicate. Yet, says Tom Fox, vice president of sports marketing for Gatorade, "What's truly exciting to us is Yao's ability to connect with American fans and transcend American culture. But Yao's international appeal and the NBA's international marketing strength present potential opportunities to also help grow our brand globally." Marketers view him as a global spokesperson rather than someone who reaches only the U.S. market. As they develop their promotional strategy, they can incorporate this strength into the overall plan. "Gatorade does have aspirations around the world, and there is application for Yao if we choose to go that way," notes Fox.

Companies such as Gatorade hope that Yao will help them gain a greater foothold in China in particular. Sorrent Inc. recently released a wireless game for mobile phones, called Yao Ming Basketball, which features his likeness. Yao is already popular in China, a fact that Sorrent hopes will give its sales a huge boost there. "[Yao is] a household name," says Jim Page, director of the Hong Kong sports marketing company JCP and Associates Inc. "He's probably the most popular athlete in China. Every game he plays in, they play live on TV in China. He's a marketer's dream." Even if Yao doesn't turn out to be the next Michael Jordan—on or off the basketball court—he's bound to help a few companies reach their promotional objectives. "I'm glad we got him before the wave started," comments Liz Silver, vice president of advertising for Visa.

QUESTIONS FOR CRITICAL THINKING
1. Do you think Yao would be as effective in radio advertising? In print advertising? As part of a direct-mail campaign? As part of a sponsorship? Explain your answers.
2. How might Yao contribute to positive publicity about a company?

Sources: Jim Kirk, "Gatorade Pact with Yao Ming Dunks PowerAde," *Chicago Tribune Online Edition,* February 7, 2003, http://www.chicagotribune.com; Theresa Howard, "Gatorade Gets Yao Factor," *USA Today,* February 6, 2003, http://usatoday.com; Adam Pasick, "NBA Rookie Yao Ming, Apple of Advertisers' Eyes," *Reuters Limited,* February 6, 2003, http://news.cnet.com; Theresa Howard, "Yao Ming's Super Deals," *USA Today,* January 23, 2003, p. B3; Tom Fowler, "Yao Ming's First TV Commercial Is for Apple," *Houston Chronicle,* January 7, 2003, http://www.chron.com; "Yao Ming Stars in Wireless Game," *GamePro,* January 7, 2003, http://www.gamepro.com.

Video Case 14.2

FUBU
This video case appears on page 617. A recently filmed video, designed to expand and highlight the written case, is available for class use by instructors.

Part 4 Krispy Kreme Continuing Case

Krispy Kreme Doughnuts Advertise Themselves

Chances are, you've heard of Krispy Kreme doughnuts. If you're lucky, a Krispy Kreme store is located somewhere near your campus or home. If not, maybe you will have the opportunity to sample the sweet, glazed confections while visiting family or friends. Or maybe a school group has held a Krispy Kreme fundraiser and you've bought a box of doughnuts to help students earn money for a trip or team uniforms. But you didn't learn about Krispy Kremes from a flashy TV commercial or magazine ad. That's because Krispy Kreme's marketing strategy contains no outlay for advertising. This doesn't mean that marketing is not important to the success of the company. In fact, Krispy Kreme is very good at practicing customer-driven marketing, but the promotional mix focuses heavily on publicity, public relations, and word-of-mouth from one consumer to another.

Every time a new Krispy Kreme shop opens, hundreds of fans line the streets to be among the first to taste those hot, glazed doughnuts fresh from the doughnut-making machine. When a team of middle-school soccer players holds a fundraiser to earn money for new uniforms, parents and other townspeople eagerly buy boxes of Krispy Kremes. Many times, local broadcasters and newspaper reporters cover both events. Marketers simply can't buy that kind of advertising. Field marketing coordinator Steve Baumgarner explains that his company prefers to focus on local causes, community events, and other opportunities to interact with consumers and their communities.

Instead of advertising, Krispy Kreme focuses on two key elements: the customer and the product. The famous "Hot Doughnuts Now" sign hanging in the window of every Krispy Kreme shop is the firm's signature marketing message. When the light comes on, consumers can literally watch the doughnuts pass through the glaze, then purchase them to eat hot. "Once someone's had a hot Krispy Kreme, it's done the job for us," quips Steve Baumgarner, the firm's field marketing coordinator. The hot doughnut light, as well as the setup of the stores, which includes the "Doughnut Theater" where customers can see how the doughnuts are made, are two of the firm's biggest

brand-building tools. "I think the brand is the store itself," explains Stan Parker, senior vice president of marketing. The retro-style white bakery boxes with red and green lettering also help strengthen the brand in consumers' minds.

Distribution and management of the supply chain also play an important part in developing relationships with customers. Location decisions, which greatly affect the success of a new outlet, are tightly controlled, and the final decision is usually based on careful marketing research. This is true not only of company-owned outlets and franchised shops but also of certain locations where Krispy Kreme has special operating agreements, such as the Loaf 'N Jug chain of convenience stores in Colorado and on the campuses of colleges such as UCLA. If consumers continue to buy the products, Krispy Kreme maintains the outlet. But if sales begin to decline, the firm may decide to move them to another location, as was the case in supermarkets in Ohio and North Carolina, where store-brand baked goods were taking a bite out of the sales of Krispy Kreme's boxed doughnuts. Despite a changing business environment, Krispy Kreme's management continues to look for suitable locations in the U.S. and overseas. "We remain excited about our growth prospects, both domestically and internationally," says CEO Scott Livengood.

Under the leadership of Chief Information Officer (CIO) Frank Hood, Krispy Kreme has built a formidable supply chain system. From any given store, software will send out orders for ingredients to radio-frequency stations in the warehouse that instruct workers which items to select, how to pack them, how to load the delivery truck, and where to deliver them. "Our portal is as useful as GM's or Boeing's," insists Hood. "On a store manager's PC, you'll see a near real-time window into the business. It has instructional streaming video on everything from store openings to how to calibrate a coffee grinder. It even provides weather forecasts, because people buy more doughnuts if it's rainy or when there's a temperature change from warmer to cooler," he explains. Store managers can use the forecast to order more or fewer ingredients to meet demand.

Even though Krispy Kreme wants everyone to fall in love with its treats, the company does practice market segmentation. College students are big fans, so franchisees try to locate outlets at or near universities. Race-car enthusiasts are also Krispy Kreme lovers. In Florida, there are two kosher Krispy Kreme shops, which use all kosher doughnut mix and preparations.

Pricing is another important part of the marketing strategy. Franchisees calculate their own costs and then add in a profit margin, so prices vary from region to region. The average Krispy Kreme Hot Original Glazed doughnut is priced at 70 cents, with a dozen doughnuts selling at a bargain for around $6.00. Scott Livengood likes to refer to his company's doughnuts as an "affordable luxury." Although competitors' doughnuts may sell for 15 cents less a piece, Krispy Kreme fans remain loyal. "I'm a diehard Krispy Kreme fan," declares one consumer who thinks nothing of standing outside the grand opening of a store at 5 A.M. Those are sweet words to members of the Krispy Kreme team.

QUESTIONS

1. In what ways does Krispy Kreme provide value-added goods?

2. In what ways does the target market for Krispy Kremes affect decisions about distribution?

3. Krispy Kreme can still be considered to be in the growth stage, but the firm has recently reduced the number of new stores it plans to open in the next year or two. What other steps might Krispy Kreme marketers take to strengthen their position in the marketplace?

4. In what ways does Krispy Kreme fit the criteria for an effective brand name?

Sources: Company Web site, http://www.krispykreme.com, accessed January 10, 2005; Rick Brooks and Mark Maremont, "Ovens Are Cooling at Krispy Kreme as Woes Multiply," *The Wall Street Journal,* September 3, 2004, pp. A1, A5; Paul Nowell, "Low-Carb Craze Catches up with Krispy Kreme," *USA Today,* May 26, 2004, p. 6B; Ian Mount, "Krispy Kreme's Secret Ingredient," *Business 2.0,* September 2003, p. 36.

Part 5
Managing Technology and Information

Chapter 15
Using Technology to Manage Information

Security Nation

We all know that the threat of terrorism is almost as great at home as abroad. Companies, consumers, and state and local governments are looking for ways to protect themselves. Firms that have been able to demonstrate their ability to solve terror-related problems, from airport security checks to the destruction of

data and loss of communications, have been received well in the business environment. In fact, experts estimate that government and private-sector spending on security measures may reach $180 billion a year by 2010.

Siemans Building Technologies Inc. is currently developing a video surveillance system that can detect cars that seem to stop for no apparent reason; pedestrians who turn up where they shouldn't be; or unattended purses, backpacks, shopping bags, and the like. Accenture recently landed a federal contract to design a new system for high-tech passports and visas, along with a database that tracks when and where travelers cross the U.S. border. The new system could take 10 years to perfect, but the contract is worth about $10 billion.

© Stephen Chernin/Getty Images

The Terrorism Risk Insurance Act of 2002 requires insurance companies to offer some type of terrorism coverage, and many firms are purchasing it. Tony Schmidtt, a managing director of the insurance services company Marsh Inc., explains, "A lot of it is driven by the banks. It is often required in the mortgage loan agreement." Depending on the type and amount of coverage, a policy might cover everything from building damage to business interruptions. Firms that offer data storage also provide security protection to businesses. For a monthly fee, these companies will store data and even back up an entire network of computers and all of their software, if necessary.

While travel-industry businesses such as airlines and hotels have suffered from rising costs associated with security and the continuing threat of terrorism, other companies have benefited. Luggage maker Tumi introduced a jacket for travelers with pockets and compartments to make it easier to reach documents as they navigate through various checkpoints during international travel. The jacket has so many pockets that a traveler can load it with keys, change, a cell phone, and CD player, then just pass the jacket and its contents through the X-ray machines. The Internet firm eBags offers a combination lock that can easily be unlocked by a Transportation Security Administration agent. "It's the only lock approved by TSA," says Peter Cobb of eBags.

All of these firms rely on technology to manage information—or to help their customers manage it. Bomb-screening technology, systems that identify people by their iris patterns, and fingerprint scanners are all examples of new technologies that help businesses, airports, and government evaluate the security risk of a given situation. Insurance coverage and data storage help businesses reduce the risk of losing valuable information and access to customers. New consumer products illustrate the ability of these firms to apply some simple technologies to challenges raised by heightened security.[1]

Chapter Overview

Information is the final frontier for organizations seeking to gain an edge over their competitors. In the past, managers focused on producing quality products, hiring and training the best workers, and finding ways to create value for their customers. As competition gets tougher and tougher in the global marketplace, businesses must look for opportunities to provide the quality goods and services that customers want and need but do it faster, better, and with greater customization than anyone else. To accomplish this feat, they need information and technology.

This chapter explores how businesses successfully manage information as a resource, particularly how they use technology to do so. It looks at ways to use information systems to organize and use information, including databases and information system programs. Because computers drive information systems, the chapter also discusses computer types and their applications in business settings. Today, specialized networks make information access and transmission function smoothly, so the chapter examines new types of networks to see how businesses are applying them for competitive advantage. Finally, the chapter explores the importance of protecting valuable information and recovering from information system disasters.

Management Information Systems

Every day, businesspeople ask themselves questions such as the following:

- How well is our brand selling in Seattle compared with Charlotte? How has the SARS epidemic affected sales in Singapore?
- If we raise the price of our products by 2 percent, how will the change affect sales in each city? In each country?
- What are the per-unit storage costs for our flagship model?
- If employees can access the benefits system through our network, will it increase or decrease benefits costs?

management information system (MIS) organized method for providing past, present, and projected information on internal operations as well as external intelligence to support decision making.

chief information officer (CIO) executive responsible for directing the firm's MIS and related computer operations.

An effective information system can help answer these and many other questions. *Data* consist of raw facts and figures that may or may not be relevant to a business decision. *Information* is the knowledge gained from processing those facts and figures. So, while businesspeople need to gather data about the demographics of a target market or the specifications of a certain product, the data are useless unless they are transformed into relevant information that can be used to make a competitive decision. Technology has advanced so quickly that all businesses, regardless of size or location, now have access to data and information that can make them competitive in a global arena. Figure 15.1 shows the increasingly rapid pace at which the U.S. adopts new technology.

A **management information system (MIS)** is an organized method for providing past, present, and projected information on internal operations as well as external intelligence to support decision making. A large organization typically assigns responsibility for directing its MIS and related computer operations to an executive called the **chief information officer (CIO).** Generally, the CIO reports directly to the firm's chief executive officer (CEO). But small companies rely just as much on an MIS as do large ones, even if they do not employ a manager assigned to this area on a full-time basis. The role of the CIO is both expanding and changing as the technology to manage information continues to develop. An effective CIO is someone who is capable of understanding and harnessing technology in such a way that the company can communicate internally and externally in one seamless operation.

Information systems can be tailored to assist many business functions and departments—providing reports for everything from marketing, to manufacturing, to finance and accounting. They can manage the overwhelming flood of information by organizing data in a logical and accessible manner. Through the system, a company

They Said It

You can give people responsibility and authority, but without information they are helpless.

—*Bill Gates (b. 1955)*
Microsoft founder and chairman

Telephone	Television	Radio	PCs	Internet
1876–1911 35 years*	1926–1952 26 years	1906–1928 22 years	1975–1991 16 years	1991–1998 7 years

*Number of years for new technology to be adopted by one-fourth of U.S. households.

FIGURE 15.1

Increasing Speed of Technology Acceptance

Source: The Media Management Group, "TimeLine of Music and Media Technology," http://www.classicthemes.com/technologyTimeline.html, accessed July 9, 2003.

can monitor all components of its business strategy, identifying problems and opportunities. Information systems gather data from inside and outside the organization; they then process the data to produce information that is relevant to all aspects of the organization. Processing steps could involve storing data for later use, classifying and analyzing it, and retrieving it easily when needed. Computerized location systems are a booming technology that has many applications (see the Best Business Practices box).

Many companies—and nations—use a combination of high-tech and low-tech solutions to manage the flow of information. E-mail and videoconferencing haven't totally replaced paper memos, phone conversations, and face-to-face meetings, but they are increasingly common. Information can make the difference between staying in business and going broke. Keeping on top of changing consumer demands, competitors' actions, and the latest government regulations will help a firm fine-tune existing products, develop new winners, and maintain effective marketing.

Databases

The heart of a management information system is its **database,** a centralized integrated collection of data resources. A company designs its databases to meet particular information processing and retrieval requirements that its decision makers encounter. A database serves as an electronic filing cabinet, capable of storing massive amounts of data and retrieving it within seconds. A database should be continually updated; otherwise, a firm may find itself with data that are outdated and possibly useless. One problem with

Courtesy of IBM Corporation

Databases are the heart of a business's information system. IBM sells its popular DB2 software to other firms so they can collect and manage data throughout their organizations.

database centralized integrated collection of data resources.

GPS: A High-Tech Problem Solver

You've seen the commercials. A driver breaks down on a lonely road at night but is saved from the predicament by a service that uses the global positioning system (GPS) to pinpoint his or her location and send out a tow truck. Or suppose you're hiking a nice mountain trail and realize you've become lost. No problem. You just pull out your GPS receiver and get yourself oriented, no compass needed. A golfer might use GPS technology to decide which club to use to deal with a particular stand of trees. And the U.S. military makes heavy use of GPS to ensure the precision of its operations. All of these uses of GPS involve the management of some type of information.

Here's how GPS technology works. A network of solar-powered satellites, deployed by the U.S. military, orbits the earth in a formation so that four satellites are always "visible" from any point on the planet. A GPS receiver locates the four satellites, calculates its distance to each, and then uses the information to determine its location on Earth.

Back to the car. Many new cars and trucks are equipped with GPS technology that includes digital maps and voice-automated driving cues that literally guide drivers turn by turn to their destinations. Televigation's TeleNav is one such

product. TeleNav provides drivers with voice-activated destination input, a Yellow Pages directory, and multilingual capabilities. Another firm, NAVTEQ, offers comprehensive digital map information for automotive navigation systems. Ryder, which delivers auto parts to local car dealerships, equips its trucks with mobile phones that have GPS capability. Ryder drivers and office staff use the technology developed by Xora Inc. to track trucks and pinpoint delivery destinations.

QUESTIONS FOR CRITICAL THINKING
1. How might the U.S. Postal Service use GPS technology?
2. Describe an industry that you think could benefit from GPS technology.

Sources: Marshall Brain and Tom Harris, "How GPS Receivers Work," *Howstuffworks*, http://electronics.howstuffworks.com, accessed January 14, 2005; "School Bags Equipped with GPS to Be Sold to Protect Kids from Crime," *Yahoo! News*, October 27, 2004, http://asia.news.yahoo.com; "Xora Boosts Ryder Performance," *TruckingInfo.com*, October 27, 2004, http://www.truckinginfo.com; "Pharos Selects NAVTEQ as Map Data Supplier," *PRNewswire*, October 25, 2004, http://www.prnewswire.com; "Televigation's TeleNav Steers Voters to Polls," *Business Wire*, October 26, 2004, http://home.businesswire.com; Lee Gomes, "Military's Use of GPS, A Civilian Mainstay, Is at Core of Its Might," *The Wall Street Journal*, March 24, 2003, p. B1.

They Said It

We are drowning in information, but starved for knowledge.

—*John Naisbitt (b. 1929)*
American social researcher and author

databases is that they can contribute to *information overload*—too much data for people to absorb or data that are not relevant to decision making. Since computer processing speed and storage capacity are both increasing rapidly, and as data have become more abundant, businesspeople need to be careful that their databases contain only the facts they need, so they do not waste time wading through unnecessary data.

Businesses create databases in a variety of ways. They can hire a staff person to build them on site, hire an outside source to do so, or buy database programs that are readily available. One of the largest databases is available from the U.S. Census Bureau. The census of population, conducted every 10 years, attempts to collect data on 120 million households across the country. Selected participants fill out forms containing questions about marital status, place of birth, ethnic background, citizenship, place of work, commute time, income, occupation, type of housing, number of telephones and vehicles, even grandparents as caregivers. Households receiving the most recent questionnaire could respond in English, Spanish, Chinese, Tagalog, Vietnamese, or Korean. Assistance was provided for other languages as well. Not surprisingly, sifting through all the collected data takes time. Although there are certain restrictions on how marketers can access and use specific census data, the general public may access the data via the American FactFinder on the Census Bureau's Web site (http://www.census.gov), as well as at state data centers and public libraries.

Decision makers can also look up online data. Online systems give access to enormous amounts of government data, such as the census and agency regulations. Another source of free information is company Web sites. Interested parties can visit the home pages to look for information about customers, suppliers, and competitors. Trade associations and academic institutions also maintain Web sites with information on topics of interest.

Companies also subscribe to commercial online services that provide fee-for-service databases on particular topics. In addition to broad-based online databases available through such services as Earthlink, Prodigy, and AOL, firms can access specialized databases geared to particular industries and functions. Many professional groups have set up bulletin board systems on the Internet where experts trade information. Businesspeople who gather data online should always try to verify the reliability of their sources, however.

Once a company has built a database, its managers need to be able to analyze the data in it. Data mining, described earlier, is the task of using computer-based technology to retrieve and evaluate data in a database to identify useful trends. Some consulting firms, such as Data Miners, Inc., specialize in data mining for their clients. Recently, Data Miners was asked to investigate transaction-level data from loyalty card holders of a New England health food supermarket. Data Miners found that 50 percent of the supermarket's customers were meat eaters, and this group spent more heavily than other customers. Even though only 5 percent of the supermarket's shoppers buy meat, they are among the store's most valuable customers. Had the supermarket eliminated meat, assuming that its customers were vegetarians, it would have had a significant negative impact on business.[2] As this example illustrates, successful data mining can help a business discover patterns in the sale of certain goods and services, find new customers, track customer complaints and requests, and evaluate the cost of materials.

Information Systems for Decision Making

So much data clog the Internet and other sources that the challenge for businesses has shifted from acquiring data to sorting through it to find the most useful elements, which can then be turned into valuable information.

New types of information system software are being developed all the time. These range from general tools that help users look up data on various topics to specialized systems that track costs, sales, inventory levels, and other data. Businesses can develop and implement their own systems or hire someone else to do so. They can even hire an outside service to manage data for them.

Decision Support System
A **decision support system (DSS)** is an information system that quickly provides relevant data to help businesspeople make decisions and choose courses of action. It includes software tools that help decision makers generate the type of information they need. These DSS tools may vary from company to company, but they typically include retrieval features that help users obtain needed information from a database, simulation elements that let decision makers create computer models to evaluate future company performance under different conditions, and presentation tools that help them create graphs and charts.

An information interface is a software program between the user and the underlying information system. Advances in information interfaces have simplified and synthesized data into useful information for a variety of users. For instance, visitors to the *Cooking Light* Web site (http://www.cookinglight.com) can access recipes through an easy-to-use interface. Visitors can search the magazine's vast database by main ingredient, cooking technique, ethnicity, and even special dietary requirements. Comments from users are also available. With a few mouse clicks visitors can create an entire menu, accompanied by a shopping list.[3] Such sophisticated interfaces make information retrieval more efficient.

decision support system (DSS) information system that quickly provides relevant data to help businesspeople make decisions and choose courses of action.

Executive Information Systems
Although the trend is increasingly toward employee empowerment and decision making at all levels of an organization, sometimes companies need to create specialized information systems to address the needs of executives. An **executive information system (EIS)** lets top managers access the firm's primary databases, often by touching the computer screen, pointing with a mouse, or even speaking via voice recognition. The typical EIS allows users to choose between many kinds of data, such as the firm's financial statements and sales figures as well as stock market trends for the company and for the industry as a whole. If they wish, managers can start by looking at summaries and then proceed toward more detailed information.

executive information system (EIS) system that allows top managers to access a firm's primary databases.

Expert Systems
An **expert system** is a computer program that imitates human thinking through complicated sets of "if . . . then" rules. The system applies human knowledge in a specific

subject area to solve the problem. Expert systems are used for a variety of business purposes: determining credit limits for credit card applicants, monitoring machinery in a plant to predict potential problems or breakdowns, making mortgage loans, or determining optimal plant layouts. They are typically developed by capturing the knowledge of recognized experts in a field whether within a business itself or outside it.

Trends in Information Systems

New information systems are being developed all the time. Today's computer networks help businesspeople obtain and share information in real time, across departments, across the country, and around the world.

Local Area Networks and Wide Area Networks

Many companies connect their offices and buildings by creating **local area networks (LANs),** computer networks that connect machines within limited areas, such as a building or several buildings near one another. LANs are useful tools because they link personal computers and allow them to share printers, documents, and information.

Wide area networks (WANs) tie larger geographical regions together by using telephone lines and microwave and satellite transmission. One familiar WAN is long-distance telephone service, and MCI, AT&T, and Sprint are telecommunications companies that provide WAN services to businesses and the general public. Firms also use WANs to conduct their own operations. Typically, companies own their own network systems at their operations sites and link to outside communications equipment and services for transmission across long distances. Later in the chapter, we cover other specialized networking systems.

Wireless Local Networks

One of the newest network innovations is wireless local networks, which allow computers, printers, and other devices to be connected without the hassle of stringing cables in traditional office settings. The most popular wireless network currently is Wi-Fi. **Wi-Fi**—short for *wireless fidelity*—is a wireless network that connects various devices and allows them to communicate with one another through radio waves. Wi-Fi allows high-speed wireless Internet connections when linked to a specially equipped modem. Any PCs with Wi-Fi receptors can wirelessly connect with the Internet wherever they are—provided they are within a range of approximately 300 feet, called a *hotspot.*[4] Industry groups are also working on two new telecommunications standards that would extend wireless connections from Wi-Fi's local hotspots to several miles and to mobile connections.[5]

Wi-Fi wireless network that connects various devices and allows them to communicate with one another through radio waves; short for *wireless fidelity.*

Enterprise Resource Planning

As information systems developed in organizations, they were at first contained within functional departments. Soon, managers noticed that the data collected about customers during order processing were reentered by inventory control and shipping. The same duplication was found in human resource management systems and finance and accounting. To avoid such rework, eliminate mistakes or inconsistencies in data, and streamline processes, businesses began to demand a system to unify these separate systems. An **enterprise resource planning (ERP)** system is a set of integrated programs designed to collect, process, and provide information about all business operations. Firms such as Microsoft, Oracle, and SAP offer enterprise software programs to help companies run factories, keep track of accounting, and assist in marketing efforts.

enterprise resource planning (ERP) information system that collects, processes, and provides information about an organization's various functions.

Oracle, for instance, offers an ERP system it calls E-Business Suite. It unifies separate systems in a variety of functional areas from customer relationship management to property management. The system works on a variety of different computer platforms. William Beaumont Hospitals, based in Royal Oak, Michigan, installed a recent version of Oracle's E-Business Suite. Among the benefits of using an ERP system noted by the hospital company include reduced administrative supply chain spending, a rapid increase in the turnaround of basic human resource tasks, and the adoption of a single set of computing standards for the entire organization.[6]

application service provider (ASP) specialist in providing both the computers and the application support for managing information systems of business clients.

Application Service Providers

Because of the increasing cost and complexity of obtaining and maintaining information systems, many firms choose to engage an **application service provider (ASP),** an outside supplier that provides both the computers and application support for man-

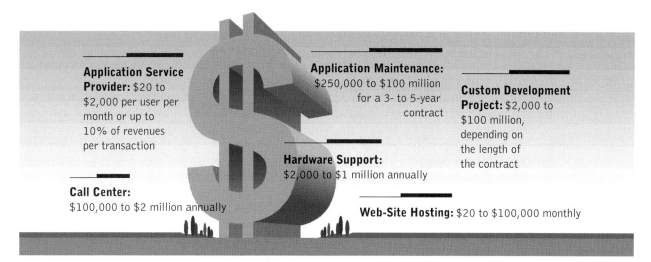

FIGURE 15.2

Costs of Outsourcing Information Systems

Source: Data from Ian S. Hayes, President, Clarity Consulting Inc., Hamilton, Massachusetts, in Jane Salodof MacNeil, "Tracking Tech Time," *Inc. Technology*, No. 4, 2000, p. 29.

aging an information system. An ASP can simplify complex software for its customers so it is easier for them to manage and use. When an ASP relationship is successful, the buyer can then devote more time and resources to its core businesses instead of struggling to manage its information systems. Other benefits include stretching the technology dollar farther and giving smaller companies the kind of information power that in the past has been available only to much larger organizations.

Companies that decide to use ASPs should check the backgrounds and references of these firms before hiring them to manage critical systems. In addition, customers should try to ensure that the service provider has taken appropriate measures to block computer hackers or other unauthorized access to the data, that its data centers are up and running consistently, and adequate backups are maintained. Figure 15.2 shows some of the costs associated with hiring an ASP as well as outsourcing other elements of information technology.

Although information systems can help a company run smoothly and efficiently, the firm must carefully plan and organize them. Otherwise, it can lose control of a critical function—and tremendous amounts of time and money. Issues of privacy and security also arise. Should everyone in the company be able to access all of the company's data? What about confidential human resource files or the corporation's payroll system? A later section of the chapter examines several of these issues.

Concept Check

1. *What is a management information system?*
2. *How are databases used?*
3. *Explain the role Wi-Fi is playing in contemporary business.*

Computer Hardware and Software

Just a few decades ago, computers were considered exotic curiosities, used only by scientists and the military. Today, they have become indispensable not only to businesses but to households as well. Who can imagine daily life without sending e-mails to friends, booking airline tickets over the Internet, preparing reports with a word processing program, or balancing a checkbook using a personal money management program?

Types of Computer Hardware

Hardware consists of all tangible elements of a computer system—the input devices, the components that store and process data and perform required calculations, and the output devices that present the results to information users. Input devices allow users to enter data and commands for processing, storage, and output. Common input devices include the keyboard, mouse, scanner, modem, microphone, and touch screen. Storage and processing components consist of the hard drive, diskette drive, Zip drive, and CD-ROM drive. The newer CD-RW and DVD-RW drives can write disks as well as read them. Another relatively new storage device is the USB bus drive. These small portable devices can store up to 128 MB of data and plug into a computer's USB port.

Output devices are the hardware elements that transmit or display documents and other results of a computer system's work. Examples include the monitor, printer, fax machine, modem, and audio system. Notice that some devices, such as the monitor and modem, can perform both input and output functions. And keep in mind that the monitor, once reserved for text and still graphics display, now commonly displays video.

Computer processing units incorporate widely varying memory capacities and processing speeds. As shown in Figure 15.3, these differences define three broad classifications: mainframes, minicomputers, and personal computers. A **mainframe** computer is the largest type of computer system with the most extensive storage capacity and the fastest processing speeds. Especially powerful mainframes called **supercomputers** can handle extremely rapid, complex calculations involving thousands of variables. They are most commonly found in scientific research settings. A **minicomputer** is an intermediate-size computer—more compact and less expensive than a mainframe but also slower and with less memory. These intermediate computers often toil in universities, factories, and research labs. Minicomputers also appeal to many small businesses that need more power than personal computers can offer to handle specialized tasks. Sun Microsystems is a large manufacturer of minicomputers.

Personal computers (PCs) are everywhere today—in homes, schools, businesses, nonprofit organizations, and government agencies. They have earned increasing popularity due to their ever-expanding capability to handle many of the functions that cumbersome mainframes performed only a few decades

FIGURE 15.3
Types of Computers

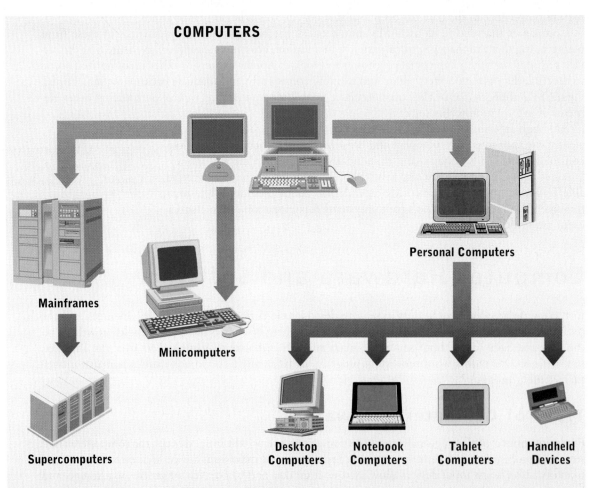

Courtesy of Microsoft Corporation. Photograph © Geof Kern.

Tablet PCs are the newest addition to portable computing. The screen detaches, allowing users to write or sketch directly on it with a special stylus. Diagrams and words are saved digitally. Best of all, tablet PCs can also run general-use applications.

ago. These advances were made possible by the development of powerful chips—thin silicon wafers that carry integrated circuits (networks of transistors and electronic circuits). A microprocessor is a fingernail-size chip that contains the PC's entire central processing unit. Intelligent functions of today's new cars, toys, watches, and other household items also rely on microprocessors. Additional chips provide instruction and memory to convert a microprocessor into a PC.

As technology continues to advance, computers have diminished in size. Desktop computers are the standard PCs that you see in offices and homes everywhere. **Notebook computers** are small enough to slip into a briefcase, yet are almost as powerful as desktop computers. Virtually all notebooks today have CD-RW or DVD-RW drives and often have "docking" capabilities that allow them to plug into a desktop PC to share data. In recent years, sales of notebook computers have grown more rapidly than sales of desktop computers. During one recent month, revenue from notebook PC sales actually surpassed that of desktop PCs. "You can't overestimate the appeal of a notebook to the consumer," according to one industry analyst.[7]

A recent innovation is the **tablet PC,** which looks like a notebook computer but with a difference. The screen is detachable. Users can write on the screen using a special-purpose pen. The handwriting is then digitized and can be converted into a format that can be read by word processing programs. The pen can also be used to edit existing documents.

Handheld devices—made by companies like Palm, Handspring, Sony, Toshiba, and Dell—are even smaller. They fit in a shirt pocket and run on rechargeable batteries. Handhelds can run common applications like word processing and database software as well as store documents and graphics created on a desktop computer. Most handheld devices can link up through wireless connections to a variety of other devices as well as the Internet.

The future will bring even smaller PCs that can perform even more functions. Industry technologists have been developing a credit card–size computer for storing and retrieving information such as phone numbers and appointments. And voice and data communications systems are merging. A recent batch of wireless telephones can also be used as PCs. Businesspeople can use certain cell phones to browse the Internet and send and receive e-mail messages from their phones. Most are Wi-Fi certified. This capability is especially helpful for those who are traveling, calling on customers, or working at remote sites.

Types of Computer Software

The software that controls the basic workings of a computer system is its **operating system. Software** is all of the programs, routines, and computer languages that control a computer and tell it how to operate. Over 80 percent of personal computers use a version of Microsoft's popular Windows operating system. Personal computers made by Apple use the Mac operating system. Handheld computers use either the Palm operating system or a special version of Windows called Pocket PC. Other operating systems include UNIX, which runs many minicomputers, and Linux, which is available for free in the public domain.

Operating-system designers have faced important challenges as businesses have shifted from stand-alone computers to networks, since computers running different operating systems may have difficulty sharing data. This problem is losing significance, however, thanks to a programming language called Java. Programs written in Java can run on any type of computer or operating system. As a result, Java applications are becoming increasingly popular for business databases and networks.

A program that performs the specific tasks that the user wants to carry out—such as writing a letter or looking up data—is called *applications software.* Examples of applications software include Microsoft Excel, Lotus Organizer, and Quick Books. Parents in a Pinch, Inc., located in Boston, provides babysitters and nannies to parents and to corporate clients for their employees. The firm uses Microsoft Access, Microsoft Excel, and Microsoft Word to manage the data about providers, jobs, and clients it needs to operate effectively. For instance, using Excel, Parents in a Pinch director Davida Manon creates charts of the company's income, volume of business, and number of jobs filled on a monthly basis. Using Microsoft Outlook, she communicates with providers and clients by e-mail. Manon couldn't imagine running her business without applications software.[8] The next section discusses the major categories of applications software used by business.

Concept Check

1. What are handheld devices and what can they do?
2. What does applications software do and what are some examples?

How Computers Help Business

Computers and their related technologies continue to revolutionize the methods by which businesses manage information. These technologies affect contemporary business in three important ways. First, the enhanced speed and quantity of information now available improves the speed and effectiveness of decision making. Second, computers make accurate, unbiased data available to all interested parties. Third, their information-sharing capabilities support team decision making at low levels of an organization's hierarchy. Every industry has felt at least some impact as computers and information systems have spread.

Consider the Great Harvest Bread Company, headquartered in Dillon, Montana, which operates over 180 franchised bakeries. Unlike other franchise operations, Great Harvest believes that its franchise operators should be free—after a one-year apprenticeship—to run their stores as they see fit. They aren't required to use the same bread recipe or paint their storefronts the same color. But they are required to share information with each other, which they do via computers. The Great Harvest internal Web site, called the Breadboard, contains announcements of equipment for sale, ongoing electronic charts among franchisees, new recipes, tips for maintaining certain ovens, and archives of other information. Computers help people manage information in an industry that has historically been considered low tech.[9]

Some of the most widely used business applications of computers include spreadsheets, word processing, electronic mail, presentation graphics, multimedia and interactive media, and groupware. Users once acquired applications such as these as individual software packages. Today, however, they normally buy *integrated software,* or *software suites,* which combine several applications into a single package that can share modules for data handling and processing. Parents in a Pinch, for instance, uses Microsoft's popular Office software suite, a package that includes word processing, database management, a spreadsheet, and electronic mail. Managers can import data from Access, a database program, into Excel to create needed reports and graphs. Some integrated software packages are designed to help businesses handle specific tasks. Palo Alto Software has several software packages that help business-people create customized advertising campaigns, marketing plans, and even overall business plans. These programs contain such features as ready-made formatting and spreadsheets, graphing, and the capability to evaluate a company's competitiveness in the marketplace.

Despite all the advantages of computers, it is important to keep in mind that they do have their limitations and should be used to serve the mission of the organization, not just for their own sake. Many businesses have found that their use of computers is actually enhanced by maintaining a human touch—or adding it—to the process. Computers will never replace such face-to-face interactions as phone conversations and meetings.

Word Processing

One of the original business applications—and currently one of the most popular—**word processing** uses computers to input, store, retrieve, edit, and print various types of documents. With word processing, users can revise sentences, check spelling, correct mistakes, and move copy around quickly and cleanly.

Word processing helps a company to handle huge volumes of correspondence, process numerous documents, and personalize form letters. Today, virtually all companies use general-purpose computers running word processing software. The most popular word processing software is Microsoft Word, part of the firm's Office suite. Other word processing programs include Corel's Word Perfect and Lotus's Word Pro. These three programs enable users to include graphics and spreadsheets from other programs in their documents and to create Web sites by translating documents into Hypertext Markup Language (HTML), the language of the World Wide Web.

As word processing capabilities have grown, a number of businesspeople have tried to create so-called paperless offices. They want to set achievable goals for electronically creating, transmitting, storing, and retrieving documents, eliminating any need to print them. In its attempt to create a paperless office, General Electric has embarked on a program to eliminate any machine that spits out paper and isn't shared by a group of people. So far GE has scrapped over 30,000 machines and reduced paper consumption by almost one-third. Although the idea appeals to both efficiency and environmentalist priorities, some people are naturally resistant to change. Comments Gary Reiner, the head of GE's Net strategy, "Big cultural shifts take time, and we're just at the beginning of this one."[10]

word processing software that uses a computer to input, store, retrieve, edit, and print various types of documents.

Desktop Publishing

Many businesses extend word processing capabilities to create sophisticated documents. **Desktop publishing** employs computer technology to allow users to design and produce attractively formatted printed material themselves rather than hiring professionals. Desktop publishing software combines high-quality type, graphics, and layout tools to create output that can look as attractive as documents produced by professional publishers and printers. Advanced equipment can scan photos and drawings and duplicate them on the printed page. Three popular desktop publishing programs are Microsoft Publisher, Adobe PageMaker, and QuarkXPress.

Many firms use desktop publishing systems to print newsletters, reports, and form letters. Advertising and graphic arts departments often use desktop publishing systems to create brochures and marketing materials. A good desktop publishing system can save a company money by allowing staff members to produce such documents, whether they are for internal or external use.

Ed Viesturs is in the business of climbing mountains. His current quest is to climb the 14 highest mountains on earth. He knows the importance of maintaining relationships with his sponsors and fans, so he created high-quality materials using Microsoft Publisher. One of Viesturs's most popular pieces is a fact sheet, which combines the story of his quest with his personal background and photos.[11]

Spreadsheets

An electronic **spreadsheet** is the computerized equivalent of an accountant's worksheet. This software permits businesspeople to manipulate decision variables and determine their impact on such outcomes as profits and sales. With a spreadsheet, a manager can have an accurate answer to a question in seconds and can often glance at the whole financial picture of a company on a single page. By far the most popular spreadsheet program is Microsoft Excel, part of the Office suite. Other spreadsheet programs include Lotus 1-2-3 and Corel Quattro Pro. Spreadsheet programs can also be used to create graphs and calculate a variety of statistics. Spreadsheets may seem daunting at first, but a good spreadsheet program is clear, even for the first-time user. When evaluating business software programs, reviewers often say how easy the spreadsheets are to navigate.

Figure 15.4 demonstrates how a manager uses a spreadsheet to set a price for a proposed product. Note that the manager can analyze alternative decisions using a spreadsheet. For instance, he or she can estimate the impact on sales given a change in the product's price. A more complex spreadsheet may stretch across many more columns, but the software still makes new calculations as fast as the manager can change the variables.

spreadsheet software package that creates the computerized equivalent of an accountant's worksheet, allowing the user to manipulate variables and see the impact of alternative decisions on operating results.

> With an $8 selling price, $4 in variable costs for each unit sold, and total fixed costs of $350,000, we have to sell 87,500 units just to break even. Now marketing suggests that we increase marketing expenses another $100,000 to stimulate additional sales. Let's see what the spreadsheet says.

> That extra $100,000 had better expand sales! The spreadsheet shows that we now have to sell 112,500 units just to break even. Maybe the second proposal would be better—the one to cut variable costs per unit to $3 and use the savings to shave $1.50 off the retail price. Let's run it through the spreadsheet.

Manu-facturing	Marketing	R&D	Fixed Cost	Per Unit Variable Cost	Sales Price	Breakeven Point in Units
	Fixed Costs					
$80,000	$100,000	$170,000	$350,000	$4	$8.00	87,500
$80,000	$200,000	$170,000	$450,000	$4	$8.00	112,500

Manu-facturing	Marketing	R&D	Fixed Cost	Per Unit Variable Cost	Sales Price	Breakeven Point in Units
	Fixed Costs					
$80,000	$100,000	$170,000	$350,000	$4	$8.00	87,500
$80,000	$200,000	$170,000	$450,000	$4	$8.00	112,500
$80,000	$100,000	$170,000	$350,000	$3	$6.50	100,000

FIGURE 15.4
How a Spreadsheet Works

Electronic Mail

Businesspeople need to communicate directly with associates as well as customers, suppliers, and others outside their organization. Increasingly, they turn to their computers for this function, replacing much of their regular mailings (so-called *snail mail*) by sending messages via *e-mail*. Popular e-mail programs include Microsoft Outlook, Outlook Express, Netscape Mail, and Eudora.

As discussed in Chapter 7, a popular adaptation of e-mail is *instant messaging*. Instant messaging allows users to create private chat rooms with other individuals on their private lists. The instant messaging system alerts a user whenever somebody on his or her list is online. The user can then initiate a chat session with that individual. There are several different instant messaging systems, including AOL Instant Messenger and Microsoft Windows Messenger. To communicate, however, all users must use the same instant messaging system.

E-mail and instant messaging are rapid ways to communicate both inside and outside the organization. As a means of internal communication, e-mail is especially useful in organizations with employees located in different parts of the country or in different countries altogether. Employees can typically access their organization's e-mail anytime, anywhere. All it takes is a Web connection.

Certainly, e-mail can help companies reduce paperwork, time wasted in playing telephone tag, and similar inefficiencies. But e-mail does have its limitations. It works best for short unemotional messages. Longer documents are best sent as attachments to e-mail or via fax. And e-mail users should be aware that messages are not private; employers may be monitoring messages, so employees should refrain from sending personal messages or jokes to each other. Some messages, such as those containing potentially emotional news or those that may need an explanation, are best transmitted by telephone or in person. Also, some of the benefits of e-mail have been undermined by the proliferation of spam, or junk e-mail, as described in the Solving an Ethical Controversy box.

They Said It

You'll be spammed if we do and spammed if we don't.

—*Federal Trade Commission spokesperson (on the agency's decision not to launch a do-not-spam registry out of fear spammers would target the list.)*

SOLVING AN ETHICAL CONTROVERSY

Spam and the Future of E-Mail

Even if you're on the national Do Not Call Registry prohibiting telemarketers from contacting you, you are probably receiving equally annoying messages from spammers on your computer. Despite a federal antispam law and some pretty sophisticated spam-blocking software, many unwanted e-mails find their way into consumers' in boxes. And a new practice called *phishing* has e-commerce experts worried about the future of e-mail as a medium. Phishing spammers attempt to steal personal financial data from consumers by posing as legitimate messages from banks, credit card companies, investment firms, and the like. "Spam, fraud, phishing schemes, all this other stuff is more than an annoyance," warns venture capitalist Steve Jurvetson. "The future of the medium is at stake."

Does spam threaten the future of e-mail?

PRO

1. Less than a year after the federal antispam law took effect, the percentage of junk e-mail screened by one e-mail security company increased from 70 percent to 92 percent. According to the Federal Trade Commission, 90 percent of all spam messages are untraceable, meaning that laws have little or no effect.

2. Businesses are already beginning to limit their use of e-mail, and some small business owners are considering abandoning it altogether.

CON

1. Software is being developed for authenticating domains, meaning that e-mail could be traced to the system that originated it. Microsoft has proposed software that would force spammers to solve a 10-second puzzle before being allowed entrance, thus slowing down literally billions of e-mails. IBM, Gateway, and Hewlett-Packard all offer security features.

2. Internet service providers such as Yahoo!, America Online, Earthlink, and Microsoft are taking major steps to block spammers, such as freezing infected e-mail accounts. "Finally, the Internet e-mail providers are taking more ownership for curbing spam at the source," notes Mitchell.

SUMMARY

A new communications medium has brought with it a quagmire of problems that no one could have anticipated. Just a few years ago, e-commerce companies were enthusiastically touting the promise of e-mail. Now, many are focusing on ways to offer e-mail security. "It shows how much things have changed," says Tim Chiu of Mirapoint, an e-mail security firm.

Sources: Margie Wylie, "Taking a Bite out of Spam," *Mobile Register*, September 26, 2004, p. F3; Jon Swartz, "Spammers Convicted; First Felony Case," *USA Today*, November 4, 2004, p. B1; Jon Swartz, "Spam Can Hurt in More Ways than One," *USA Today*, July 8, 2004, p. B1; Jon Swartz, "E-mail Carriers Sign on to Anti-Spam Efforts," *USA Today*, June 23, 2004, p. B1; Jon Swartz, "Is the Future of E-mail Under Cyberattack?" *USA Today*, June 15, 2004, p. B4.

Presentation Graphics

Analyzing columns of numbers can be a tedious task. But when people see data displayed as charts or graphs, they can often identify patterns and relationships that raw data do not reveal. Businesspeople once had to labor to create charts and graphs or send the data or rough sketches to professional artists and then wait for the results. Computer software has greatly simplified the process of creating graphics. As noted earlier, spreadsheet programs have the capability of creating dozens of high-quality graphs. **Presentation software,** the most popular of which by far is Microsoft PowerPoint, goes one step further. These programs create entire presentations. Users can create bulleted lists, charts, graphs, and pictures, like those shown in Figure 15.5. By combining these elements in ways that are easy to read, a user can prepare presentations and handouts for a business meeting. To persuade management to fund a new project, an employee might create a series of graphs and charts to illustrate how the project will benefit the organization over time.

Wireless e-mail technology has brought employees closer—no matter where they roam. This BlackBerry handheld device combines both e-mail and cell phone capabilities.

multimedia computing technologies that integrate two or more types of media, such as text, voice, sound, video, graphics, and animation into computer-based applications.

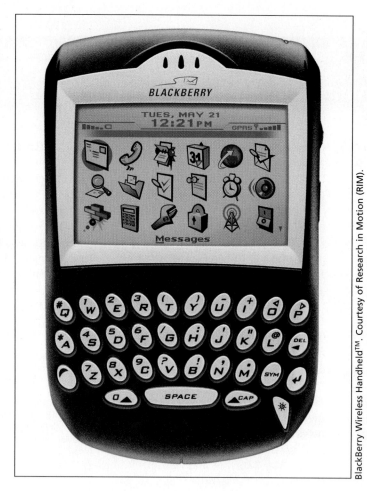

BlackBerry Wireless Handheld™. Courtesy of Research in Motion (RIM).

Multimedia and Interactive Media

Today's computers have leaped beyond numbers, text, and graphs to encompass multimedia and interactive media capabilities. **Multimedia computing** refers to technologies that integrate two or more types of media, such as text, voice, sound, full-motion video, still video, graphics, and animation into computer-based applications. Many popular business applications have multimedia computing capabilities. For example, Microsoft PowerPoint users can add audio and video clips into their presentations. Multimedia computing requires computers with fast processors and large storage capacities.

One of the growing business applications for multimedia computing is employee business presentations and conferences. And the Internet has made transmission of these meetings widely available. Many companies routinely provide multimedia Webcasts of their annual meetings for viewing on their Web sites. Salespeople use their notebook computers to make presentations to customers in the field.

Many applications of multimedia computing use *interactive media*—programs that allow users to interact with computer displays. Home Depot's Expo Design Centers user interactive software allows customers to plan and design home remodeling and building projects either online or at Home Depot stores. Customers can view a variety of 3-D products, enter their room dimensions, create orders, and track the installation of their projects on a computer screen.[12]

Groupware

groupware software that combines information sharing through a common database with communication via e-mail so that employees can collaborate on projects.

An especially useful interactive medium is **groupware,** computer software that combines information sharing through a common database with communication via e-mail or instant messaging. Using groupware, employees can work together on a single document at the same time, viewing one another's changes. They can also discuss ideas and check on another's calendars to schedule meetings or group efforts. Two of the most popular groupware packages are Lotus Notes and Domino. Microsoft recently added many groupware functions to its popular Office suite.

Intranets, Virtual Private Networks, and Broadband Technology

A previous section discussed the use of LANs and WANs to allow businesses to communicate, transmit and print documents, and share data. These networks require businesses to install special equipment and connections between office sites. But Internet technology has also been applied to internal company communications and business tasks, tapping a ready-made network. Among these new Internet-based applications are intranets, virtual private networks (VPNs), and broadband technologies. Each has contributed to the effectiveness and speed of business processes.

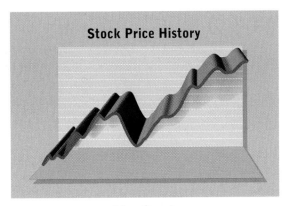

Line Graph

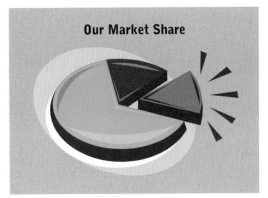

Pie Chart

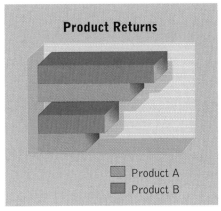

Map

Bar Graph

FIGURE 15.5
Examples of Visuals Created with Presentation Software

Intranets   A broad approach to sharing information in an organization is to establish a company network patterned after the Internet. Such a network, called an **intranet,** links employees through Internet tools like e-mail and searches using Web browsers. Intranets are similar to extranets, but they limit access only to employees or other authorized users. An intranet blocks outsiders without valid passwords from entering its network by incorporating software known as a **firewall.** Firewalls are available as off-the-shelf packages such as Firewall/Plus and On Guard. They limit data transfers to certain locations and log system use so managers can identify attempts to log on with invalid passwords and other threats to system security. Highly sophisticated packages will immediately alert system administrators about suspicious activities and permit authorized personnel to use smart cards to log on from remote terminals.

Intranets offer important advantages over more familiar, and now somewhat dated, computer networks. Perhaps most important, they solve problems of linking different types of computers. Like the Internet, intranets can integrate computers running all kinds of operating systems. In addition, intranets are relatively easy and inexpensive to set up because most businesses already have some of the required tools, such as PCs and Web browser software. Intranets also support teamwork among employees who travel or work from home. Any intranet member with the right identification, a PC, and some sort of network access (either dial-up or broadband) can access the intranet and gain access to group calendars, document managers, online conferencing rooms, bulletin boards, package tracing, and instant messaging.

Keller Williams Realty of Everett, Washington, uses an intranet to help its sales agents keep track of documents, calendars, listings, and other frequently needed information. Vicky Flick, the market center administrator, says that the intranet provides agents with a single location where they can access a wide variety of documents and information. This, in turn, allows the agents to better market themselves to prospective clients and sell their listings to potential buyers. "There are many different documents and materials that agents use on a regular basis," says Flick. "We keep all of this information on our intranet, so our people don't have to worry if the copy in their filing cabinet is the most up-to-date version of a given document."[13]

intranet a network that links employees and other authorized users through Internet tools like e-mail, hypertext links, and searches using Web browsers.

BUSINESS TOOL KIT

E-Mail Etiquette

Twenty years ago, electronic mail was new and used primarily by government and academic institutions. Now it's a necessity for everyone from grade school students to retirees, and it's here to stay. Sending e-mail within the confines of an organization is quite different from sending jokes and chatty notes to friends and family. Here are a few tips to keep your messages professional and to the point.

1. Communicating through e-mail requires the same skills as any other type of written communication. Make sure your message is clear and your audience is specifically targeted—and skip the fillers. Your objective is to exchange or seek out information from the other person.

2. Always provide an accurate subject line for your e-mails. This makes it easier for the recipient to prioritize reading and responding. Blank subject lines or random characters can also indicate unwanted "spam." These messages are often deleted unread.

3. Use complete sentences only, please. Spelling and grammar are important in business correspondence, which applies to e-mail as well. When responding to a question, restate the question so that the recipient won't need to scroll down to remember his or her original question. Always read over your response and run a spell-check before hitting Send.

4. In business, response times will vary, but replying within 24 hours is a good rule to follow. With some inboxes receiving more than 90 messages a day, e-mail is no longer "instant communication." If others do not respond to your e-mail within 24 to 48 hours, it is acceptable to resend the message. If there is still no response, you should pick up the phone.

5. Learn how to use your reply buttons correctly. *Reply* will send your reply to the individual who sent you the original e-mail. *Reply to All* sends your message to the original sender as well as all the other addresses listed in the original *To, CC* (carbon copy), and *BCC* (blind carbon copy) fields. This can be irritating and potentially embarrassing if you aren't careful, so always double-check before you hit Send.

6. Save the emoticons and smiley faces for your friends and family. They can sometimes make you appear less than professional when used in a business context, so use your words to convey your message and mind-set instead.

7. Finally, your employer has the right to monitor your e-mail usage and content. Jokes and personal messages should not be sent via your work e-mail account.

Sources: Peggy Post, "Peggy Post's Golden Rules of E-Mail Etiquette: The Right Way to Write—In the Office and at Home," *Good Housekeeping,* May 2003, p. 33; Dana May Casperson, "E-Mail Etiquette: How to Make Sure Your Message Gets Across," *American Salesman,* July 2002, p. 10; Suzy Guiard, "Was It Something I Typed?" *Success Magazine,* February/March 2001, p. 42; Ingrid Murro Botero, "E-Mail Etiquette: Think Before Sending Messages," *The Business Journal—Serving Phoenix & the Valley of the Sun,* July 21, 2000, p. 28.

In another cutting-edge application of intranets, two Ohio schools—Bluffton College and Cedarville University—have tied their intranets to the dorm laundry rooms. Students can log on to find out whether machines are currently being used and can receive e-mails to tell them their clothes have finished washing or drying. Payments are easier, too. Students can swipe their ID cards or enter codes on keypads, and the money is automatically deducted from their accounts. Additional schools plan to implement the new technology in coming years.[14]

Virtual Private Networks   To gain increased security for Internet communications, companies often turn to *virtual private networks (VPNs),* secure connections between two points on the Internet. These VPNs use firewalls and programs that encapsulate data to make them more secure during transit. Loosely defined, a VPN can include a range of networking technologies, from secure Internet connections to private networks from service providers like IBM and SBC Communications. A VPN is cheaper for a company to use than several leased lines, and while it can take months to install a leased line in some parts of the world, a new user can be added to a VPN in a day.

The Forum Corporation, a Boston-based global training and consulting firm, uses its VPN to network both internal and external users. The company's VPN links its offices in Boston with interna-

Table 15.1   Types of Broadband Technologies

Technology	Transmission Method
Digital Subscriber Lines (DSL)	Standard copper-wire phone lines
Cable modems	Coaxial cable (as used in cable television)
Fiber-optic network	Optical cables
Wireless network	Microwave or satellite transmission
Integrated Services Digital Network (ISDN)	Standard copper-wire phone lines and other media
T1 and T3 lines	Special dedicated phone connections

tional sites in Hong Kong, London, and Toronto. Initially, salespeople, consultants, and software developers used the VPN for e-mail, order processing, and financial tracking. Later, Forum added real-time collaboration, online learning, and videoconferencing. At the same time, the VPN also helped bring the company closer to its customers and suppliers. Several of Forum's customers and software development partners collaborate in real-time on the development of training software over the VPN.[15]

Broadband Technology   To maintain their competitive edge, companies want to be able to share larger chunks of information among employees and partners faster than ever before. To do so, they have turned to **broadband technology**—digital, fiber-optic, and wireless network technologies that compress data and transmit them at blinding speeds. Table 15.1 shows the different types of broadband technologies currently available. Most observers consider broadband to be the future of the Internet. Broadband technology can be thought of as a multilane communications highway in contrast to the single-lane country road represented by traditional phone transmission. With the digital data compression and bigger "lanes" of broadband technology, the same amount of information can travel faster from one destination to another. The Hits & Misses box on page 508 describes the amazing spread of wireless broadband networks.

> **broadband technology**
> digital, fiber-optic, and wireless network technology that compresses data and transmits them at blinding speeds.

Optical networks are one of the newest broadband technologies. They convert information into tiny bits of light that are transmitted over fiber-optic cables made of glass. Long-distance phone carriers are in the process of rapidly installing optical networks to increase the number of transmissions and the speed at which they travel. Optical networks have a million times the capacity of traditional phone networks because light particles are lighter than electrical impulses, they can be separated into different colors to create separate channels, and glass allows more rapid travel than copper.

Concept Check

1. What does integrated software do?
2. List two or three uses of electronic spreadsheets.
3. What is groupware?

Protecting Information Systems

As information systems become increasingly important business assets, they also become progressively harder to replace. When computers are connected to a network, a problem at any location can affect the entire network. Although many computer securities issues go beyond the scope of *Contemporary Business,* this section discusses three important security threats: computer crime, viruses, and disasters that may damage information systems.

Computer Crime

Computers provide efficient ways for employees to share information. But they may also allow people with more malicious intentions to access information. Or they may allow pranksters—who have no motive other than to see whether they can hack into a system—to gain access to classified information. Common computer crimes involve stealing or altering data in several ways:

- Employees or outsiders may change or invent data to produce inaccurate or misleading information.
- Employees or outsiders may modify computer programs to create false information or illegal transactions or to insert viruses.
- Unauthorized people can access computer systems for their own illicit benefit or knowledge or just to see if they can get in.

Computer crime is on the rise. The number of violations of Internet security as reported to the Computer Emergency Response Team Coordination Center, located on the Web at `http://www` `.cert.org`, has risen sharply in recent years. In 1988, only six incidents were reported. Recently, the number of reported incidents soared to over 82,000.[16] Of course, the statistics don't include the number of incidents that were not reported, so the total is probably much higher.

Individuals, businesses, and government agencies are all vulnerable to computer crime. Figure 15.6 shows the home page of the Federal Computer Incident Response Center (FedCIRC), which assists government agencies with computer security issues. Computer hackers—unauthorized users—sometimes work alone and sometimes in groups. One pair of hackers, nicknamed the "Deceptive Duo," once claimed that they hacked into Midwest Express Airlines's intranet. In an e-mail to several news organizations, the hackers said that their goal was to embarrass the airline and show how easy it is to gain access to supposedly secure networks. The hackers even posted evidence of their break-in on the Web site of the U.S. Space and Naval War Systems Command.[17]

In another incident, Best Buy abruptly shut off wireless cash registers at its stores. These registers use a wireless network that beams data, including credit card information, to a central computer located elsewhere in the store. Networked cash registers are an important part of most large retail operations, since they can more easily track inventory and let stores instantly change prices. Wireless networks offer added convenience, making cash registers easier to move and install. Best Buy shut down its wireless networks and switched to hardwired networks after it learned that a hacker could sit in a store's parking lot and access the data as they were sent.[18]

System administrators implement two basic protections against computer crime: They try to prevent access to their systems by unauthorized users and the viewing of data by unauthorized system users. To prevent access, the simplest method requires authorized users to enter passwords. The company may also install firewalls, described earlier. To prevent system users from reading sensitive information, the company may use **encryption** software, which encodes, or scrambles, messages. To read encrypted messages, users must use a key to convert them to regular text. But as fast as software developers invent new and more elaborate protective measures, hackers seem to break through their defenses. So security is an ongoing battle.

FIGURE 15.6

The Federal Computer Incident Response Center: Fighting Computer Crime

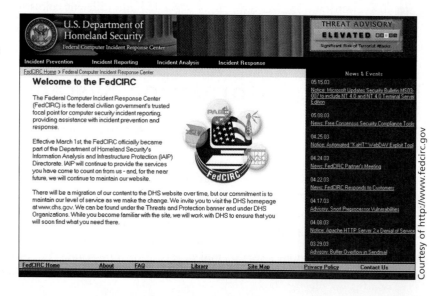

Courtesy of http://www.fedcirc.gov

Another form of computer theft is as old as crime itself: theft of equipment. As the size of computer hardware diminishes, it becomes increasingly vulnerable to theft. Handheld devices, for instance, can vanish with a pickpocket or purse snatcher. And since these machines may contain all kinds of important information for a business, employees need to be especially careful not to leave them unattended or out of reach. Many notebook computers and handheld devices now contain special security software that makes it difficult for a thief or any unauthorized person to access the data stored in the computer's memory.

Of growing concern to the entertainment industry is the ease with which consumers can use computer technology to "pirate" copyrighted works such as films and music and share them online.

Screen shots reprinted by permission from Apple Computer, Inc.

Apple Computer recently offered its own solution to the music piracy problem—opening its online music store and drastically reducing the price of online tunes at the same time. Through its AppleMusic.com site, fans can hear a preview of a song free and download it for a mere 99 cents.

Computer Viruses

Rather than directly tampering with a company's data or computers, computer hackers may create viruses to infect computers at random. **Computer viruses** are programs that secretly attach themselves to other programs or files and change them or destroy data. Viruses can be programmed to become active immediately or to remain dormant for a period of time, after which the infections suddenly activate themselves and cause problems.

A virus can reproduce by copying itself onto other programs stored in the same drive. It spreads as users install infected software on their systems or exchange files with others, usually by exchanging e-mail, accessing electronic bulletin boards, trading disks, or downloading programs or data from unknown sources on the Internet. With widespread data sharing in networks, including intranets and the Internet, viruses can do more damage today than ever before. According to Computer Economics, a company that assesses the financial impact of security threats and incidents, viruses cost organizations billions of dollars each year. The so-called "Love Bug" virus alone caused an estimated $8.75 billion in damage.[19] Some viruses, as with hacking incidents, result from pranks that get out of hand. But many involve outright vandalism or crime.

As viruses become more complex, the technology to fight them must increase in sophistication as well. The simplest way to protect against computer viruses is to install one of the many available antivirus software programs, such as Norton Anti-Virus and McAfee Virus Scan. These programs continuously monitor systems for viruses and automatically eliminate any they spot. Users should regularly update them by going online to download the latest virus definitions.

But management must begin to emphasize security at a deeper level: in software design, corporate servers, Web gateways, and Internet service providers. Because around 80 percent of the world's PCs run on Microsoft operating systems, a single virus can spread quickly among them. Individual computer users should carefully choose the files they load onto their systems, scan their systems regularly, make sure their antivirus software is up-to-date, and install software only from known sources. They should also be very careful when opening attachments to e-mails, since this is the way many viruses are spread. Both the Love Bug and more recent Klez viruses were both spread through attachments to e-mails.

computer virus program that secretly attaches itself to other computer programs or files and changes them or destroys data.

Wireless Networks Are Everywhere

When we lost the wires to our phones, we thought it was a big deal. Now we can pick up a laptop with built-in Wi-Fi for checking e-mail while we're sitting in the back yard or on the beach. What's next? Experts tell us that getting rid of the wires is only the beginning of a whole new age. Electronics makers are scrambling to come up with every device consumers could possibly want—free of wires. Their goal is to render all digital media, including music, photos, and video, accessible anywhere you are. "Wireless video—that's really the holy grail," enthuses Sean Wargo, an analyst with the Consumer Electronics Association.

Already, there are a number of cool gadgets. You can buy a Majicbike if you want to ride around with wireless Net connectivity. Want to network all your appliances? The technology is already here; it's called Zigbee. But the big picture is about connecting large chunks of previously unconnected civilization. The MIT Media Lab is working on a project through which it will install Wi-Fi base stations on local buses in rural India. When a bus stops to pick up or discharge passengers, any computer users in the area can use the signal to send or receive e-mail. Intel Research is working on a similar project. That might sound primitive to anyone who has constant connectivity; but think about the implications for remote, rural populations. The technology is lower in cost than broadband, and "doesn't require a big upfront infrastructure investment," explains Kevin Werbach, a former FCC counsel. This makes communication more accessible to nations that otherwise would remain isolated.

QUESTIONS FOR CRITICAL THINKING

1. Discuss at least two ways that Wi-Fi connectivity might change the way business is conducted in areas like rural India.
2. As a consumer, do you make regular use of Wi-Fi technology? Describe your experiences.

Sources: Nicholas Yulico, "Intel Targets Developing Countries," *Oakland Tribune*, October 25, 2004, http://www.oaklandtribune.com; David LaGesse, "Our Wireless World," *U.S. News & World Report*, September 27, 2004, pp. 48–52; Steven Levy, "Something in the Air," *Newsweek*, pp. 48–49; Maryanne Murray Buechner, "Wireless Made Easy," *Time*, June 21, 2004, p. 86; Edward C. Baig, "It's Here, It's There and Soon Everywhere," *USA Today*, March 29, 2004, http://www.usatoday.com.

Disaster Recovery and Backup

Natural disasters, power failures, equipment malfunctions, software glitches, human error, and terrorist attacks can disrupt even the most sophisticated computer systems. These disruptions can cost billions of dollars. For instance, the 9/11 terrorist attacks caused almost $16 billion in damage to information technology and communications systems. The banking and financial services industry was hit the hardest. The relocation of 100,000 people to temporary facilities and the replacement of thousands of computer servers, workstations, terminals, and printers cost over $8 billion.[20] Software glitches cost organizations billions of dollars each year. Recently, a software glitch allowed passengers booking flights on United Airlines's Web site to pay as little as $5 for Chicago–Denver flights. Another software glitch led to Starwood Hotel's Web site showing $85 a night rates—rather than $850—for its luxurious new resort on the island of Bora Bora.[21]

Concept Check

1. Name three common computer crimes.
2. What does encryption software do?
3. How does a password help protect an information system?

Disaster recovery planning—deciding how to prevent system failures and continue operations if computer systems fail—is a critical function of all organizations. Disaster prevention programs can avoid some of these costly problems. The most basic precaution is routinely backing up software and data—at the organizational and individual levels. Most financial service firms directly impacted by 9/11 were up and running within a few days thanks to backup systems.

Companies can now back up data at such online storage services as Iron Mountain or Network Associates. Technology planners may decide to respond to the possibility of a natural disaster such as an earthquake or flood by paying for extra hardware installation in a secure location, which can be accessed during an emergency. Advanced solutions include using integrated enterprise software from suppliers such as SAP and PeopleSoft, which tie a company's operations together in a single thoroughly tested suite. Another is for software manufacturers to reduce the complexity of programs.

Courtesy of Computer Associates International, Inc.

Companies need to prepare for all types of disasters. With the increasing reliance on information systems, they need to plan for recovery and backup of critical data and systems. Computer Associates provides backup storage, security systems, and infrastructure software to keep information systems humming.

What's Ahead

This is the first of two chapters devoted to managing technology and information. Chapter 16, "Understanding Accounting and Financial Statements," focuses on the functions of accounting, steps in the accounting process, functions and components of financial statements, and the role of budgets in an organization.

DID YOU KNOW?

1. Two of every three computers are located outside the U.S.
2. The average Internet user will send 304,200 electronic messages during his or her lifetime.
3. The average young adult will spend 9 years 11 months on the Internet during his or her lifetime.
4. Bell Canada has converted some public pay phones in Toronto and Montreal into terminals for Wi-Fi Internet connections.

Summary of Learning Goals

1 Distinguish between data and information.
It is important for businesspeople to know the difference between data and information. Data are raw facts and figures that may or may not be relevant to a business decision. Information is the knowledge gained from processing those facts and figures.

2 Explain the role of management information systems in business.
An effective information system can help answer many management questions. A management information system (MIS) is an organized method for providing past, present, and projected information

on internal operations as well as external intelligence to support decision making. The heart of an MIS is its database, which serves as an electronic filing cabinet for facts and figures.

3 *Identify and briefly describe the different types of information system programs.*

The key to a useful information system is the program that links users to data. Different types of information system programs include decision support systems (DSSs), which provide relevant data to help businesspeople make decisions and choose courses of action; executive information systems (EISs), which allow top managers to access the firm's primary databases; and expert systems, which imitate human thinking. Trends in information systems include local area and wide area networks (LANs and WANs); wireless local networks (Wi-Fi); enterprise resource planning (ERP) systems that integrate all computer systems within a business; and application service providers (ASPs), outside firms that provide both computers and application support for managing an information system.

4 *Describe the hardware and software used in managing information.*

Hardware consists of all the tangible elements of a computer system, including input and output devices. Major categories of computers include mainframes, supercomputers, minicomputers, and personal computers (PCs). Newer developments in PCs include notebooks, tablet PCs, and handheld devices. Computer software provides the instructions that tell the hardware what to do. The software that controls the basic workings of the computer is its operating system. Other programs, called *applications software,* perform specific tasks that users want to complete.

5 *Identify how different types of software can help businesspeople.*

Individual types of software can help businesses in a variety of ways. Word processing helps a company handle massive volumes of correspondence, reports,

and other documents. Desktop publishing allows users to design and produce attractively formatted printed material. Spreadsheets calculate and present information clearly. Electronic mail allows businesspeople to communicate rapidly anywhere in the world. Presentation graphics provide graphs and charts that help businesspeople see patterns in data. Multimedia integrates two or more types of media. Interactive media are programs that allow users to interact with computer displays. Integrated software combines several applications into a single package that can share modules for data handling and processing. Groupware lets businesspeople anywhere in the world work together on a single project.

6 *Explain the importance of special network technologies.*

Intranets allow employees to share information on a ready-made company network. Virtual private networks (VPNs) help save companies money by providing a secure Internet connection. Broadband technology allows a greater amount of information to flow through a network more quickly.

7 *List the ways that companies can protect themselves from computer crimes.*

Companies can protect themselves from computer crime by requiring users to enter passwords, installing firewalls or encryption software, and keeping up to date on new security methods. In addition, managers should install antivirus security programs on all computers and networks.

8 *Explain the steps that companies go through in anticipating, planning for, and recovering from information system disasters.*

Businesses can avoid the results of disaster by routinely backing up software and data, both at an organizational level and at an individual level. They can back up data at online storage services or pay for extra hardware installation in a secure location. They may also want to invest in extra hardware and software sites, which can be accessed during emergencies.

Business Terms You Need to Know

management information system (MIS) 490

chief information officer (CIO) 490

database 491

decision support system (DSS) 493

executive information system (EIS) 493

Wi-Fi 494

enterprise resource planning (ERP) 494

application service provider (ASP) 494

word processing 499

spreadsheet 499

multimedia computing 502

groupware 502

intranet 503

broadband technology 505

computer virus 507

Other Important Business Terms

expert system 493

local area network (LAN) 494

wide area network (WAN) 494

hardware 495

mainframe 496

supercomputer 496

minicomputer 496

personal (desktop) computer (PC) 496

notebook computer 497

tablet PC 497

handheld devices 497

operating system 497

software 497

desktop publishing 499

presentation software 501

firewall 503

encryption 506

disaster recovery planning 508

Review Questions

1. Distinguish between data and information. Why is the distinction important to businesspeople in their management of information?

2. Describe three different types of information system programs and give an example of how each might help a particular business.

3. Explain how computer hardware and software work together. Cite some examples.

4. How might a hotel chain use desktop publishing to manage its marketing program?

5. What is enterprise resource planning? How has it streamlined business processes?

6. What is an intranet? Give specific examples of benefits that result for firms that set up their own intranets.

7. Define broadband technology and describe the different broadband technologies currently in use.

8. What steps can organizations and individuals take to prevent computer crime?

9. How does a computer virus work? What can individuals and organizational computer users do to reduce the likelihood of a computer virus?

10. Why is disaster recovery important for businesses? Relate your answer to a hypothetical cyberattack.

Projects and Applications

1. Do you believe that information overload is a serious problem in your life? What steps do you (or can you) take to reduce this overload so that you can function more effectively in all areas of your life?

2. Suppose you were chief information officer for Great Harvest Bread Co. Describe the different parts of an integrated software package (in addition to the intranet described in the chapter) that would help your company manage its flow of information. Give an example of how each application you choose would help the company.

3. Wi-Fi technology is becoming more widespread. Its first applications were set up in Seattle-area Starbucks and in

some airports for travelers. Go online or to the library and find information about Wi-Fi's current uses. Prepare a short report on its current uses and its future for business computing.

4. Do you think computer hacking is a serious crime? Defend your answer.

5. What information-related technology lessons do you think businesses learned from 9/11? How will these lessons help businesses respond to other disasters—natural as well as those caused by humans?

Experiential Exercise

Background: Assume you're in the market for a new personal computer.

Directions: First, make a list of your needs. Needs represent the basic configuration that will meet your individual computing requirements. Next, make a list of your wants. Wants represent features you'd like to have in your new PC but don't necessarily need. Finally, decide between a notebook computer and a desktop computer. List the reasons why you chose a desktop or a notebook.

1. Visit the CNet (http://www.cnet.com) or ZDNet (http://www.zdnet.com) Web sites. Research different computer makes and models that meet your specifications. Make a list of the five top-rated systems. What criteria did CNet or ZDNet consider when developing the rankings?

2. Decide where you will buy your new computer. Will you order it from a direct seller, such as Dell, or will you buy it at a retail store, like Best Buy? What are the advantages and disadvantages of each option?

3. Finally, repeat the exercise assuming you're buying a computer for your job. Explain any differences between a computer purchased for personal and school use and one purchased for business use.

NOTHING BUT NET

1. **Computer viruses.** Computer viruses pose a major problem for computer users and systems. Software publishers constantly scramble to update their antivirus software programs in response to newly discovered viruses. Visit the Web sites listed here, review the material, and then answer the following questions:

   a. Approximately how many different computer viruses have been discovered?

   b. How many new viruses are discovered each month?

   c. What are the names of the most recently discovered viruses?

   d. What is the best way to protect a computer from viruses?

   http://www.symantec.com/avcenter
   http://vil.nai.com/vil/content/alert.htm

2. **Critical data backup and recovery.** After the terrorist attacks of September 11, 2001, interest in data backup and recovery software for critical computer data increased dramatically. Visit the Web sites listed and prepare a report on some of the key features of these programs.

   http://www.baymountain.com
   http://www.unitrends.com

3. **Shopping for handheld computers.** Assume you have been given the responsibility of buying new handheld computers for your company. Your manager wants you to compare and choose between handhelds that run Windows CE and those that run the Palm operating system. Visit the Web sites listed and write a brief report that compares the pros and cons of each handheld operating system. Which would you recommend and why?

   http://zdnetshopper.cnet.com
   http://www.microsoft.com/catalog/display.asp?subid=22&site=10578
   http://www.palmsource.com

   Note: Internet Web addresses change frequently. If you do not find the exact sites listed, you may need to access the organization's or company's home page and search from there.

Case 15.1

Cell Phones as PCs?

Cell phones are clearly getting smarter. New models offer a wide range of features from voice mail to call waiting. Many even allow users to check their e-mail and surf the Web. The next step in cell phone evolution has added features commonly found on personal digital assistants (PDAs) and other handheld computers. Samsung, Nokia, and other cell phone manufacturers have recently rolled out devices that combine traditional cell phones with PDAs. Samsung, for instance, offers a Sprint PCS cell phone that includes a PDA that runs on the popular Palm operating system. These devices are being marketed to businesspeople who commonly carry both a cell phone and PDA. It's one less device to carry, and important information, such as phone numbers, need to be entered only once.

The idea of cell phones as mini-PCs has caught the attention of the colossus of the PC industry, Microsoft. It teamed up with another tech heavyweight, Intel, to offer cell phone makers a blueprint of the innards of devices that would combine voice and data—literally, mini-PCs that double as cell phones. Intel supplies the chips and Microsoft supplies the software. The devices would run a version of Microsoft's Windows CE operating system, often called Pocket PC. Versions of popular Microsoft applications, such as Outlook, Internet Explorer, and Word, run on Windows CE. It would be up to the manufacturers, however, to decide what the handset will look like and how much of the Microsoft software it will contain.

So far several U.S. wireless operators have expressed an interest in the new devices from Microsoft and Intel. Audiovox Communications Corporation has begun making a new handset, called Thera, which is offered by prominent wireless operators Sprint PCS and Verizon. In addition, U.S.-based operator VoiceStream recently began offering devices based on the Microsoft and Intel plan.

Microsoft argues that its blueprint for Pocket PC wireless devices will vastly increase the versatility of cell phones. Because the insides will become standardized, cell phones will become much easier to make. Pamela Santos of Microsoft

says, "No one has ever brought this type of fully connected smart device to market. We have a comprehensive trial process in place with our partners to ensure that the devices not only work properly as mobile phones, but also as rich and comprehensive wireless data devices." Microsoft believes it will capture upwards of 25 percent of the cell phone market.

Other industry observers are skeptical, however. For one thing, Pocket PC handhelds are more expensive than standard cell phones. According to some industry insiders, many wireless consumers view cell phones as disposable commodities, and therefore, price is an important factor when they choose a handset. For another, Pocket PC handheld computers are still dominated by handhelds running the Palm operating system. Most users prefer the simplicity of the Palm operating system over the superior applications offered by Pocket PCs. Cell phone users may have similar reactions. Nokia's Timo Poikolainen states, "The mobile environment is not simply about downscaling the PC world."

Nevertheless, whenever Microsoft moves into a market, everyone sits up and takes notice. The future of this industry could look very different from what it does today.

QUESTIONS FOR CRITICAL THINKING

1. Why do you think Microsoft has entered the cell phone market? Will the business model it used to dominate PCs work in the wireless industry?

2. How will standardization benefit wireless consumers? Will standardization cause prices for wireless devices to fall? How well do you think Pocket PC wireless devices will sell? Would you consider buying such a device?

Sources: David Haskin, "Microsoft Notches Big Wireless Wins," *Wireless News,* Internet News Web site, http://www.internetnews.com, accessed January 24, 2003; Elisa Batista, "Cell World Awaits 500-Lb. Gorilla," *Wired News* Web site, http://www.wired.com, accessed January 24, 2003; Dan Richman, "Microsoft More Mobile," *Seattle Post-Intelligencer* Web site, http://www.seattlepi.nwsource.com, accessed May 17, 2002; "Turning Your Phone into a Mini-PC," *Time,* March 4, 2002, p. 48.

Video Case 15.2

Cannondale

This video case appears on page 618. A recently filmed video, designed to expand and highlight the written case, is available for class use by instructors.

Chapter 16
Understanding Accounting and Financial Statements

Plante & Moran Adopts People-Friendly Policies for the Employees

In an industry that has traditionally been dominated by men, 19 percent of the partners at Michigan-based accounting firm Plante & Moran are women. Plante & Moran isn't a small mom-and-pop operation, either. It is the 11th largest accounting firm in the nation. In addition, its percentage of women

partners is the greatest of the top 15 firms in the U.S. Just as important, Plante & Moran's employee turnover rate is extremely low for the accounting industry—around 14 percent. How do they do it, and why does it matter?

It matters because study after study reveals that a diverse workforce is more competitive than one that is not. So hiring and retaining women makes good business sense. In addition, high employee turnover is expensive and can undermine a firm's competitiveness. Plante & Moran's director of human resources, Bill Bufe, estimates that it costs his company $75,000 to replace a well-trained employee. And women may be more prone to leave the workforce because of conflicts between work and family. In the accounting profession, employees are expected to work long hours, including nights and weekends, during tax season. But it is almost impossible for a working mom to manage unless her firm has strong work-life programs in place.

Although most of the big accounting firms do recognize the need for benefits such as flexible work hours and on-site Saturday day care, Plante & Moran is different. Nearly 20 years ago, the firm launched a Personal Tightrope Action (PTA) Committee to deal with work-life issues—about a decade before most of its rivals. But a female-friendly work culture can be traced back even further, to the 1960s. Since then, every new hire has been assigned a "buddy" who helps the new employee learn the ropes of the firm and attends meetings with the new employee's formal mentor. Every effort is

© Jack Hollingsworth/Getty Images

made to encourage and advance womens' careers. Flexible work hours aren't just part of a program designed by the human resource department—they are part of the fabric of the firm. Frank Moran, one of the firm's cofounders, believed that professionals should work to meet the needs of their clients, not necessarily according to a set time schedule. So an accountant may arrive at the office and leave on a flexible schedule, as long as clients are being served. Other work-family initiatives include parenting buddies, in which every mother-to-be is teamed up with an experienced working mom to help smooth the transition out of work and back in. Plante & Moran's managing partners host breakfast clubs, in which each partner has breakfast with three employees at a time to talk about work, careers, and life in general. Unlike other major accounting firms, Plante & Moran bases only half of a partner's evaluation on developing new business. The rest depends on how well a partner manages and develops a team. This effort affects the bottom line, because partner's effectiveness is likely to be accompanied by low turnover among team members. Finally, Plante & Moran offers a paid, four-week sabbatical every seven years, during which employees can completely forget about the workplace and return refreshed.

"A lot of firms think [about work-life balance] and walk it and talk it, but Plante & Moran really lives it," notes Julie Lindy, editor of the publication *Bowman's Accounting Report*. Lindy emphasizes that while many of the major accounting firms have adopted such policies, Plante & Moran has had them from the beginning. It is a winning situation for everyone: clients are happy, women can balance their careers and family, they have opportunities to advance, and the firm retains top-notch employees. Plante & Moran has been named one of the "100 Best Companies to Work for in America" by *Fortune* magazine. Maybe that's because its work-life philosophy is so simple—to offer the best of both worlds to its clients and its professional employees.[1]

Chapter Overview

Accounting has been making headlines recently—and not for positive reasons. The scandals at Enron, WorldCom, HealthSouth, and Arthur Andersen focused a glaring spotlight on what can go wrong—terribly wrong—when accountants and executives fail to provide accurate and truthful financial information. Legal prosecutions to punish those responsible for ethical lapses and new regulations for the accounting profession are attempting to remedy the situation. Surviving accounting firms are trying to right the ship and move forward to a brighter future.

So who are accounting professionals and what do they do for businesses? Accountants are responsible for preparing the financial information that organizations present in their annual reports. Whether you begin your career by working for a company or by starting your own firm, you need to understand what accountants do and why their work is so important in contemporary business.

Accounting is the process of measuring, interpreting, and communicating financial information to enable people inside and outside the firm to make informed decisions. Accounting is the language of business. Accountants gather, record, report, and interpret financial information in a way that describes the status and operation of an organization and aids in decision making. In addition, accountants play fundamental roles not only in business but also in other aspects of society. Their work influences each of the business environments discussed earlier in this book. They contribute important information to help managers deal with the competitive and economic environments. Less obvious contributions help others to understand, predict, and react to the technological, regulatory, and social and cultural environments.

For example, Karen Stevenson Brown, a Normal, Illinois-based certified public accountant, provides accounting services to a variety of health-care providers. Brown also contributes to the understanding of a significant social concern: care of the elderly. She has combined her interest in computers and her concern for the welfare of older people in a Web site for those who need information related to elder care. Recognizing that elder care is growing in importance as the U.S. population ages, Brown designed ElderWeb, an online resource directory of articles and links to useful information that covers all aspects of the subject. Her site offers guidance to the elderly, their families, and caregivers on a wide variety of subjects, including financial, legal, medical, and spiritual. The site has won numerous awards from a variety of organizations.[2]

Millions of men and women throughout the world describe their occupations as accountants. In the U.S. alone, around 1 million accountants, more than half of whom are women, carry out these critical tasks. The number of accounting-related jobs is expected to increase by over 18 percent by the end of the decade. The availability of jobs and relatively high starting salaries for talented graduates—starting salaries for accounting graduates average over $40,000 per year—have made accounting a popular business major on college campuses.[3]

This chapter begins by describing who uses accounting information. It discusses business activities that involve accounting statements: financing, investing, and operations. It explains the accounting process and then discusses the development of accounting statements from information about financial transactions. It presents the methods of interpreting these statements and examines the role of budgeting in the planning and control of a business.

Users of Accounting Information

People both inside and outside an organization rely on accounting information to help them make business decisions. Figure 16.1 lists the users of accounting information and the applications they find for it.

Managers with a business, government agency, or not-for-profit organization are the major users of accounting information, since it helps them to plan and control daily and long-range operations. Business owners and boards of trustees of not-for-profit groups also rely on accounting data to determine how well managers are operating the organizations. Union officials use accounting data in contract negotiations.

To help employees understand how their work affects the bottom line, many companies share sensitive financial information with their employees and teach them how to understand and use financial statements. SAIC, a San Diego-based engineering company, shares financial information with all employees as part of a general policy of employee empowerment and ownership. Employees own a majority stake in the company, and managers want to ensure that employees understand the big picture of how their work contributes to everyone's success. "We're very concerned that people understand the whole story," comments Bill Roper, the firm's chief financial officer. SAIC has posted annual sales and profit increases for over three decades.[4]

Outside the firm, potential investors evaluate accounting information to help them decide whether to buy a firm's securities. Bankers and other lenders use accounting information to evaluate a potential borrower's financial soundness. The Internal Revenue Service (IRS) and state tax officials use it to determine a company's tax liability. Citizens' groups and government agencies use such information in assessing the efficiency of operations such as a charitable organization, a local school system, or a city museum.

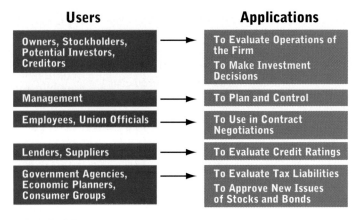

FIGURE 16.1
Users of Accounting Information

 Concept Check

1. How does accounting information help managers?
2. Why do some companies share sensitive financial information with their employees?

They Said It

Prosperity is only an instrument to be used, not a deity to be worshiped.

—*Calvin Coolidge (1872–1933)*
30th president of the United States

accounting practice of measuring, interpreting, and communicating financial information to support internal and external business decision making.

Business Activities that Involve Accounting

The natural progression of a business begins with financing. Subsequent steps, including investing, lead to operating the business. All organizations, profit-oriented and not-for-profit, perform these three basic activities, and accounting plays a key role in each one:

1. Financing activities provide necessary funds to start a business and expand it after it begins operating.
2. Investing activities provide valuable assets required to run a business.
3. Operating activities focus on selling goods and services, but they also consider expenses as important elements of sound financial management.

Dan Weinfurter performed these three activities during the start-up and growth of Parson Group LLC, a Chicago-based consulting firm specializing in accounting, finance, and corporate risk management. He financed his new company with $7.2 million of venture capital along with $800,000 of his own money. Weinfurter invested these funds in computer systems and other office equipment. His operating activities involved hiring professional and clerical staff and promoting the company's services to a variety of clients. The role of accounting has increased considerably since Parson Group began operating in 1995, driven by the firm's rapid growth. It was the fastest-growing private company for two consecutive years, according to *Inc.* magazine. Annual revenues have increased from $200,000 to more than $70 million, and the number of employees has risen from 5 to over 650.[5]

Accounting Professionals

Accounting professionals work in a variety of areas in and for business firms, government agencies, and not-for-profit organizations. They can be classified as public, management, government, and not-for-profit accountants.

Public Accountants

A **public accountant** provides accounting services to individuals or business firms for a fee. Most public accounting firms provide three basic services to clients: (1) auditing, or examining, financial records; (2) tax preparation, planning, and related services; and (3) management consulting. Since public accountants are not employees of a client firm, they are in a position to provide unbiased advice about the firm's financial condition.

The four largest U.S. public accounting firms are Deloitte & Touche, Ernst & Young, KPMG Peat Marwick, and PricewaterhouseCoopers. Together, these four giant firms collect around one-third of the more than $70 billion paid to accounting firms in the U.S. each year.

In recent years, public accounting firms came under sharp criticism for providing management consulting services to many of the same firms they audit. Critics argued that when a public accounting firm does both—auditing and management consulting—an inherent conflict of interest is created. Moreover, this conflict of interest may undermine confidence in the quality of the financial statements accounting firms audit. The bankruptcies of such high-profile firms as WorldCom, Enron, and Global Crossing increased pressure on the public accounting firms to end the practice. The Sarbanes-Oxley Act, and related federal regulation, also established strict limits on the types of consulting services auditors can provide to firms they audit, as discussed in the Solving an Ethical Controversy box. As a result, the four largest public accounting firms have either sold their consulting practices or spun them off into separate companies and now concentrate on providing auditing and tax services. PricewaterhouseCoopers, for instance, sold much of its consulting business to IBM. An example of the services provided by a public accounting firm is shown in Figure 16.2.

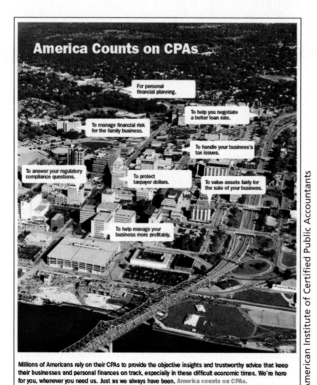

FIGURE 16.2
Services Provided by a Public Accounting Firm

Management Accountants

An accountant employed by a business other than a public accounting firm is called a **management accountant.** These individuals are responsible for collecting and recording financial transactions and preparing financial statements used by the firm's managers in decision making. Management accountants provide timely, relevant, accurate, and concise information that managers can use to operate their firms more effectively and more profitably than they could without this input. In addition to preparing financial statements, a management accountant plays a major role in interpreting them. In presenting financial information to managers, a management accountant should provide answers to many important questions: Where is the company going? What opportunities await it? Do certain situations expose the company to excessive risk? Does the firm's information system provide detailed and timely information to

SOLVING AN ETHICAL CONTROVERSY

Who's Accountable? The Story of Enron and Arthur Andersen

On February 14, 2002, Enron vice president Sherron Watkins stood before Congress to begin two days of testimony about the accounting practices of the company with which she had planned a long and dedicated career. Watkins explained how Enron, the giant Texas-based energy broker, had used accounting practices to conceal billions of dollars of debt within questionable partnerships. The testimony came after months of turmoil at Enron—Watkins had approached various senior executives with the problem, including former CEO Jeffrey Skilling, CFO Andrew Fastow, and chairman Kenneth Lay. Knowing it was in trouble, Enron began to lay off workers. As the Securities and Exchange Commission began investigating Enron, it was discovered that Enron's accounting firm, Arthur Andersen, had been shredding documents pertaining to the company's fraudulent practices. Enron ultimately filed for bankruptcy, wiping out the jobs and life savings of thousands of workers and individual investors. Arthur Andersen was charged with obstructing justice in the investigation of Enron.

Should Enron and Arthur Andersen be held equally accountable for the accounting practices that concealed billions of dollars of Enron debt?

PRO

1. If executives at both firms were aware of each other's transactions, then both should be held equally responsible. "Among the matters still under investigation are whether and to what extent Enron transactions were presented to Andersen for review and/or approval," stated the Department of Justice in its filing against Andersen.

2. If both companies engaged in illegal activities—together or separately—they must be held equally responsible.

CON

1. Andersen's role reached farther than Enron's. "Andersen's conduct in obstructing the Securities and Exchange Commission investigation of Enron, we submit, contributed to . . . the historic shaking of the foundations of our markets," stated prosecutor Sam Buell.

2. It is a felony for corporate executives to misrepresent important financial data to their auditors. In this case, if Enron's transactions were not reported correctly to Andersen, then Andersen should not be held responsible.

SUMMARY

Arthur Andersen lost the right to audit any public companies, was placed on five-year probation, and ordered to pay a fine of $500,000 for its role in the Enron scheme. Andersen clients fled to less controversial CPA firms, dropping Andersen from the list that once was called the Big Five accounting firms. The accounting profession has been dramatically altered by the passage of a new law and the creation of a special oversight board that imposed severe limitations on the activities auditors could perform—with the threat of huge penalties for future abuses.

Sources: Gary Silverman, "JP Morgan Likely to Face Charges over Enron," *Financial Times,* April 14, 2003, http://story.news.yahoo.com; Albert B. Crenshaw, "Testimony Casts Doubt on Enron Tax Deferrals," *Washington Post,* April 9, 2003, http://www.washingtonpost.com; Kristen Hayes, "2 Ex-Enron Broadband Execs Plead Innocent," *Associated Press,* April 2, 2003, http://story.news.yahoo.com; Edward Iwata, "Watkins Gets Frank about Days at Enron," *USA Today,* March 24, 2003, http://www.usatoday.com; Carrie Johnson, "SEC Accuses 4 Former Executives at Merrill of Aiding Enron Fraud," *Washington Post,* March 18, 2003, http://www.washingtonpost.com; Jodie Morse and Amanda Bower, "The Party Crasher," *Time,* December 30, 2002–January 6, 2003, pp. 53–56; Tom Fowler, "Delay Likely on Andersen Executive's Sentencing," *Houston Chronicle,* December 11, 2002, http://www.chron.com; Tom Fowler and Mary Flood, "Arthur Andersen Gets the Maximum Sentence," *Houston Chronicle,* October 16, 2002, http://www.chron.com.

all levels of management? **Certified public accountants (CPAs)** demonstrate their accounting knowledge by meeting state requirements for education and experience and successfully completing a number of rigorous tests in accounting theory and practice, auditing, law, and taxes. Other accountants who meet specified educational and experience requirements and pass certification exams carry the title *certified management accountant* or *certified internal auditor.*

   Management accountants frequently specialize in different aspects of accounting. A cost accountant, for example, determines the cost of goods and services and helps to set their prices. A tax accountant

certified public accountant (CPA)
accountant who met specified educational and experiential requirements and passed a comprehensive examination on accounting theory and practice.

works to minimize a firm's tax bill and assumes responsibility for its federal, state, county, and city tax returns. An internal auditor examines the firm's financial practices to ensure that records include accurate data and that its operations comply with federal, state, and local laws and regulations.

Government and Not-for-Profit Accountants

Federal, state, and local governments also require accounting services. **Government accountants** and those who work for not-for-profit organizations perform professional services similar to those of management accountants. Accountants in the public sector concern themselves with determining how efficiently organizations accomplish their objectives, rather than profits and losses. Among the many government agencies that employ accountants are the Environmental Protection Agency, the Federal Bureau of Investigation, the IRS, the Commonwealth of Pennsylvania, and the City of Fresno, California. Not-for-profit organizations, such as churches, labor unions, political parties, charities, schools, hospitals, and colleges, also hire accountants. In fact, the not-for-profit sector is one of the fastest-growing segments of accounting practice. An increasing number of not-for-profits are publishing financial information because contributors want to know how the groups spend the money that they donate.

Concept Check

1. Why do most public accounting firms no longer provide management consulting services to the firms they audit?
2. What is the major function of a government accountant?

The Accounting Process

Accounting deals with financial transactions between a firm and its employees, customers, suppliers, owners, bankers, and various government agencies. For example, payroll checks result in a cash outflow to compensate employees. A payment to a vendor results in receipt of needed materials for the production process. Cash, check, and credit purchases by customers generate funds to cover the costs of operations and to earn a profit. Prompt payment of bills preserves the firm's credit rating and its future ability to earn a profit. The procedural cycle in which accountants convert data about individual transactions into financial statements is called the **accounting process**. Figure 16.3 illustrates the activities involved in the accounting process: recording, classifying, and summarizing transactions to produce financial statements for the firm's management and other interested parties.

accounting process
set of activities involved in converting information about individual transactions into financial statements.

The Impact of Computers and the Internet on the Accounting Process

For hundreds of years, bookkeepers have recorded, or posted, accounting transactions through manual entries in journals. They then transferred the information, or posted it, to individual accounts listed in ledgers. Computers have simplified the process, making it faster and easier than the manual method. For instance, point-of-sale terminals perform a number of functions each time they record sales. These terminals not only recall prices

Basic Data

Transactions
Receipts, invoices, and other source documents related to each transaction are assembled to justify making an entry in the firm's accounting records.

Processing

Record
Transactions are recorded, usually electronically, in chronological order in books called journals, along with a brief explanation for each entry.

Classify
Journal entries are transferred, or posted, usually electronically, to individual accounts kept in a ledger. All entries involving cash are brought together in the ledger's cash account; all entries involving sales are recorded in the ledger's sales account.

Summarize
All accounts in the ledger are summarized at the end of the accounting period, and financial statements are prepared from these account summaries.

Financial Statements

| Balance Sheet | Income Statement | Statement of Cash Flows |

FIGURE 16.3
The Accounting Process

from computer system memory and maintain constant inventory counts of individual items in stock but also automatically perform accounting data-entry functions.

Accounting software programs are used widely in both large and small businesses today. They allow a do-it-once approach, in which a single input leads to automatic conversion of a sale into a journal entry, which is then stored until needed. Up-to-date financial statements and financial ratios then can be requested when needed by decision makers. Improvements in accounting software will continue to make the process even faster and easier than it is now.

Because the accounting needs of entrepreneurs and small businesses differ from those of larger firms, accounting software makers have designed programs that meet specific user needs. These programs are designed to run on personal computers. They include MYOB Accounting, Quick Books, and Peachtree Complete Accounting. Software programs designed for larger firms, and requiring more sophisticated computer systems, include products from Computer Associates, Oracle, and SAP.

For firms that conduct business worldwide, software producers have introduced new accounting programs that handle all of a company's accounting information for every country in which it operates. The software handles different languages and currencies as well as the financial, legal, and tax requirements of each nation in which the firm conducts business.

The Internet is also influencing the accounting process. Several software producers offer Web-based accounting products designed for small business. One company, Adminstaff Financial Management Services, has gone one step further. It provides Web-based bookkeeping and accounting services to fast-growing small and midsize businesses. Adminstaff Financial Management Services clients are companies that have outgrown off-the-shelf small-business accounting programs and need more sophisticated financial reports and services.

The Foundation of the Accounting System

To provide reliable, consistent, and unbiased information to decision makers, accountants follow guidelines, or standards, known as generally accepted accounting principles (GAAP). These principles encompass the conventions, rules, and procedures for determining acceptable accounting practices at a particular time. In the U.S., the Financial Accounting Standards Board (FASB) is primarily responsible for evaluating, setting, or modifying GAAP. Accountants adhere to GAAP to create uniform financial statements for comparison between firms. Using GAAP ensures a solid basis for sound business decision making. FASB carefully monitors changing business conditions, enacting new rules and modifying existing rules when necessary. Two examples include new rules on how losses resulting from the terrorist attacks of 9/11 were to be reported and a modification of rules regarding the reporting of stock option expenses.

In response to cases of accounting fraud, and questions about the

Courtesy of Softrax Corporation

With increasing concerns over reporting requirements, companies are looking for outside assistance. Softrax Corporation provides standardized automated revenue management systems that help software firms, online content providers, and Internet companies comply with regulatory requirements.

BEST BUSINESS PRACTICES

New Rules for Accountants

Allowing the fox to guard the henhouse just doesn't work. This is the conclusion that Congress reached in the wake of accounting scandals that caused corporate giants such as Enron—along with its accounting firm Arthur Andersen—and the former WorldCom (now MCI) to collapse, taking with them jobs, life savings, investments, and the trust of the general public. In addition, accounting firms Ernst &Young, KPMG, and PricewaterhouseCoopers faced lawsuits and fines by the IRS for their questionable practices.

Previously, the accounting profession regulated itself, much as the medical profession does. The Auditing Standards Board, which is part of the American Institute of Certified Public Accountants, was in charge of its own guidelines for accounting. The assumption was, of course, that accountants would be responsible for their own—and their colleagues'—professional practices. Some industry watchers have noted that accountants have been under undue pressure—perhaps coercion—to produce financial statements that reflect favorably on their companies. But the bottom line is that self-regulation just wasn't working.

So Congress passed the Sarbanes-Oxley Act in 2002, which requires companies with publicly traded stock to meet stricter requirements in reporting their financial activities. Under the act, a new agency designed to oversee accounting practices was formed, called the Public Company Accounting Oversight Board. Board members were appointed by the Securities and Exchange Commission, with the requirement that its five primary members serve full time and no more than two members be certified public accountants (CPAs). In addition, all members would be "prominent individuals of integrity and reputation who have a demonstrated commitment to the interests of investors and the public," according to the Sarbanes-Oxley Act. William J. McDonough, president

and chief executive of the Federal Reserve Bank of New York, was selected to head the board.

At the outset, the board was funded by taxpayers, which sparked controversy over board members' $452,000 to $556,000 annual salaries. Within months, the board voted to approve an alternative funding system under which companies themselves would pay fees on a sliding scale—according to size—to keep the board running.

The board's responsibilities include establishing auditing rules and regularly inspecting major accounting firms. It has the authority to revoke an auditing firm's professional registration and levy fines of up to $15 million. Naturally, time will tell whether the new board, as well as the Sarbanes-Oxley Act, has strong enough teeth to enforce new regulations. And some industry experts question whether this is the right move. But many believe that the board will go a long way toward establishing trust in the industry and ultimately polishing accounting's tarnished image. "We need to do business right," says Michael Haigh, a CPA with major accounting firm Deloitte & Touche. "And, I believe that this legislation is a giant step forward in accomplishing that."

QUESTIONS FOR CRITICAL THINKING

1. Do you agree with the formation of the Public Company Accounting Oversight Board? Why or why not?
2. What further steps might a large company take to monitor its accounting processes internally?

Sources: "Accounting Board Sets New Audit Standards," *Associated Press*, April 16, 2003, http://www.kansascity.com/mld/kansascity/business; "Update 1—New Board Takes Over Auditing Rule-making," *Reuters Limited*, April 16, 2003, http://reuters.com/; "Sarbanes-Oxley Bill Called Giant Step Toward Reform," *The Morning News*, December 15, 2002, pp. 1D, 2D.

Public Company Accounting Oversight Board five-member board created by the Sarbanes-Oxley Act of 2002 to set audit standards and to monitor accounting firms that certify the books of publicly traded firms; members of the board are appointed by the Securities and Exchange Commission to serve staggered five-year terms.

independence of auditors, the Sarbanes-Oxley Act of 2002 created the **Public Company Accounting Oversight Board.** As described in the Best Business Practices box, the five-member board has the power to set audit standards and to investigate, and sanction, accounting firms that certify the books of publicly traded firms. Members of the Public Company Accounting Oversight Board are appointed by the Securities and Exchange Commission—the chief federal regulator of the securities markets and the accounting industry—to serve staggered five-year terms. No more than two of the five members of the board can be certified public accountants.

Two financial statements form the foundation of the accounting system: the balance sheet and the income statement. The information found in these statements is calculated using the accounting equation and the double-entry bookkeeping system. A third statement, the statement of cash flows, is also prepared to focus specifically on the sources and uses of cash for a firm from its operating, investing, and financing activities.

The Accounting Equation

Three fundamental terms appear in the accounting equation: assets, liabilities, and owners' equity. An **asset** is anything of value owned or leased by a business. Assets include land, buildings, supplies, cash, accounts receivable (amounts owed to the business as payment for credit sales), and marketable securities.

Although most assets are tangible assets, such as equipment, buildings, and inventories, intangible possessions such as patents and trademarks are often some of a firm's most important assets. This kind of asset is especially essential for many firms involved in computer software, pharmaceuticals, and biotechnology. For instance, pharmaceutical company Merck has almost $7.5 billion in intangible assets, much of which consist of the value of the firm's drug patents. Similarly, computer networking firm Cisco Systems has around $4.4 billion in intangible assets.[6]

There are two claimants to the assets of a firm: creditors and owners. A **liability** of a business is anything owed to creditors—that is, the claims of a firm's creditors. When a company borrows money to purchase inventory, land, or machinery, the claims of creditors are shown as accounts payable, notes payable, or long-term debt. Wages and salaries owed to employees also represent liabilities (known as wages payable or accrued wages).

Owners' equity represents the owners' initial investment in the business plus retained earnings that were not paid out over time in dividends. A strong owners' equity position often is used as evidence of a firm's financial strength and stability.

The **basic accounting equation** states that assets equal liabilities plus owners' equity. This equation reflects the financial position of a firm at any point in time:

$$\text{Assets} = \text{Liabilities} + \text{Owners' Equity}$$

Since financing comes from either creditors or owners, the right side of the accounting equation also represents the business's financial structure.

The relationship expressed by the accounting equation underlies development of the balance sheet and income statement. These two statements reflect the firm's current financial position and the most recent report of its incomes, expenses, and profits for interested parties inside and outside the firm. They provide a fundamental basis for planning activities and help companies attract new investments, secure borrowed funds, and complete tax returns.

asset anything of value owned or leased by a business.

liability claim against a firm's assets by a creditor.

owners' equity all claims of the proprietor, partners, or stockholders against the assets of a firm, equal to the excess of assets over liabilities.

basic accounting equation relationship that states that assets equal liabilities plus owners' equity.

> **Concept Check**
> 1. How have computers had an impact on accounting?
> 2. What is the Public Company Accounting Oversight Board?

Financial Statements

Financial statements provide managers with essential information they need to evaluate the liquidity position of an organization—its ability to meet current obligations and needs by converting assets into cash, the firm's profitability, and its overall financial health. The balance sheet, income statement, and statement of cash flows provide a foundation on which managers can

Financial statements help managers set the course for their organizations. Robert Half Management Resources provides consulting services for its clients' financial projects. It offers assistance with tax planning, financial systems, audit preparation and cleanup, and business process reengineering.

base their decisions. By interpreting the data provided in these statements, the appropriate information can be communicated to internal decision makers and to interested parties outside the organization.

The Balance Sheet

balance sheet statement of a firm's financial position—what it owns and the claims against its assets—at a particular point in time.

A firm's **balance sheet** shows its financial position on a particular date. It is similar to a photograph of the firm's assets together with its liabilities and owners' equity at a specific moment in time. Balance sheets must be prepared at regular intervals, since a firm's managers and other internal units often request this information every day, week, or at least every month. On the other hand, external users, such as stockholders or industry analysts, may use this information less frequently, perhaps every quarter or once a year.

The balance sheet follows the accounting equation. On the left side of the balance sheet are the firm's assets—what it owns. These assets, shown in descending order of liquidity (in other words, convertibility to cash), represent the uses that management has made of available funds. On the right side of the equation are the claims against the firm's assets. Liabilities and owners' equity indicate the sources of the firm's assets and are listed in the order in which they are due. Liabilities reflect the claims of creditors—financial institutions or bondholders that have loaned the firm money, suppliers that have provided goods and services on credit, and others to be paid, such as federal, state, and local tax authorities. Although companies and their accountants are legally required to state liabilities, sometimes they do not, as described in the Hits & Misses box.

Owners' equity represents the owners' claims (those of stockholders, in the case of a corporation) against the firm's assets. Owners' equity can be viewed as the difference between total assets and total liabilities.

Figure 16.4 on page 526 shows the balance sheet for Golden Harvest, a chain of organic food stores based in San Diego. The basic accounting equation is illustrated by the three classifications of assets, liabilities, and owners' equity on the company's balance sheet. Total assets must equal the total of liabilities and owners' equity.

The Income Statement

income statement financial record of a company's revenues, expenses, and profits over a period of time.

Whereas the balance sheet reflects a firm's financial situation at a specific point in time, the income statement represents the flow of resources that reveals the performance of the organization over a specific time period. Resembling a video rather than a photograph, the **income statement** is a financial report summarizing a firm's financial performance in terms of revenues, expenses, and profits over a given time period.

In addition to reporting the firm's profit or loss results, the income statement helps decision makers to focus on overall revenues and the costs involved in generating these revenues. Managers of a not-for-profit organization use this statement to determine whether its revenues from contributions and other sources will cover its operating costs. Finally, the income statement provides much of the basic data needed to calculate the financial ratios managers use in planning and controlling activities. Figure 16.5 on page 527 shows the income statement for Golden Harvest.

An income statement (sometimes called a profit and loss, or P&L, statement) begins with total sales or revenues generated during a year, quarter, or month. Subsequent lines then deduct all of the costs related to producing the revenues. Typical categories of costs include administrative and marketing expenses, costs involved in producing the firm's good or service, interest, and taxes. After all of them have been subtracted, the remaining net income may be distributed to the firm's owners (stockholders, proprietors, or partners) or reinvested in the company as retained earnings. The final figure on the income statement—net income after taxes—is the so-called **bottom line.**

Keeping costs under control is an important part of running a business. Reducing costs will boost a firm's profits. Too often, however, companies concentrate more on increasing revenue than controlling costs.

The Statement of Cash Flows

In addition to the income statement and the balance sheet, many firms prepare a third accounting statement—the statement of cash flows. Public companies are required to prepare and publish a state-

HITS & MISSES

MCI Returns: The Company Formerly Known as WorldCom

Most of us would have a hard time imagining a decade-long spending spree involving buying entire companies. But that's what Bernard Ebbers, former CEO of WorldCom, did before the giant telecommunications firm collapsed into bankruptcy amid a federal investigation into questionable accounting practices. Everyone, from WorldCom employees to stockholders, from customers to the general public, asked, "What happened?"

Former WorldCom vice president Cynthia Cooper discovered the questionable move of $400 million from one account to another to boost WorldCom's reported income. Independent accounting firm Arthur Andersen was involved, just as it was in the case of Enron. This type of activity is hard to prove, yet Ebbers and former CFO Scott D. Sullivan were known to have consulted on most major company decisions. Under investigation by the Securities and Exchange Commission, WorldCom admitted that it found more than $11 billion in accounting fraud and errors, and both Sullivan and Ebbers were fired. A voicemail message left by Sullivan for Ebbers warned that the company's two sets of numbers could cause problems because investors would expect that the company was doing better than it really was. WorldCom filed for bankruptcy protection in 2002 and emerged a year later.

Amid the turmoil, WorldCom decided on a name change—to MCI, which the firm had acquired in 1998. New chairman and CEO Michael Capellas explained that the firm wanted to signal a new beginning with a name that already had an established reputation as a brand. Less than a year later, MCI announced that it would write down the value of its assets by $3.5 billion to reflect the decreased worth of its telephone network. On a brighter note, the firm entered into a $12 million agreement with the American Automobile Association (AAA) to deliver a wide range of communica-

tions solutions. "MCI is focused on helping customers like AAA put technology to work for them to heighten their customer experience," said Steve Young, senior vice president of MCI Commercial Services.

Meanwhile, facing fraud charges, Sullivan initially pleaded not guilty to wrongdoing, but later reversed his plea and agreed to cooperate with prosecutors in the trial of Bernard Ebbers, who was also charged with fraud, conspiracy, and making false regulatory filings. After a delay, Ebbers's trial was set to begin in early 2005. In turn, Ebbers's attorney indicated that Ebbers would be seeking reimbursement from MCI for his legal fees. And whistle-blower Cynthia Cooper was inducted into the American Institute of CPAs Business & Industry Hall of Fame.

QUESTIONS FOR CRITICAL THINKING

1. Do you believe that WorldCom should be allowed to emerge from bankruptcy, change its name, and reenter the marketplace? Do you think that a relationship with MCI will damage AAA's image in any way? Why or why not?

2. How can future accounting frauds best be prevented? Explain your answer.

Sources: "AAA Hits the Road with MCI in $12 Million Deal," *RedNova News*, October 25, 2004, http://www.rednova.com; "WorldCom Whistleblower among Those Chosen for Business & Industry Hall of Fame," *AccountingToday*, October 21, 2004, http://www.webcpa.com; Erin McClam, "Trial of WorldCom's Ebbers Is Delayed," *Associated Press*, October 19, 2004, http://news.yahoo.com; "MCI Takes $3.5 Billion Asset Charge," *Associated Press*, October 18, 2004, http://news.yahoo.com.

---

ment of cash flows. In addition, commercial lenders often require a borrower to submit this statement. The **statement of cash flows** provides investors and creditors with relevant information about a firm's cash receipts and cash payments for its operations, investments, and financing during an accounting period. Figure 16.6 on page 528 shows the statement of cash flows for Golden Harvest.

Companies often prepare a statement of cash flows due to the widespread use of **accrual accounting.** Accrual accounting recognizes revenues and costs when they occur, not when actual cash changes hands. As a result, there can be differences between what is reported as sales, expenses, and profits and the amount of cash that actually flows in and out of the business during a period of time. An example is depreciation. Companies depreciate fixed assets—such as machinery and buildings—over a specified

statement of cash flows statement of a firm's cash receipts and cash payments that presents information on its sources and uses of cash.

accrual accounting accounting method that records revenue and expenses when they occur, not necessarily when cash actually changes hands.

FIGURE 16.4
Balance Sheet for Golden Harvest, Inc.

① Current Assets: Cash and other liquid assets that can or will be converted to cash or used within one year.

② Fixed Assets: Plant, property, equipment, and other assets expected to last for more than one year. Accumulated depreciation represents the cumulative value of fixed assets that have been expensed, or depreciated.

③ Current Liabilities: Claims of creditors that are to be repaid within one year.

④ Long-Term Debt: Debts that come due one year or longer after the date on the balance sheet.

⑤ Owners' (Shareholders') Equity: Claims of the proprietor, partners, or stockholders against the assets of the firm; the difference between total assets and total liabilities.

GOLDEN HARVEST INC.

Balance Sheet
As of December 31

ASSETS	($000s)
① Current Assets	
Cash and Equivalents	$ 5,000
Accounts Receivable	4,800
Inventory	14,500
Total Current Assets	24,300
② Gross Fixed Assets	45,000
(Accumulated Depreciation)	(22,500)
Net Fixed Assets	22,500
Total Assets	$ 46,800

LIABILITIE S AND EQUITY	
③ Current Liabilities	
Notes Payable	$ 4,000
Accounts Payable	3,750
Accrued Expenses	3,000
Total Current Liabilities	10,750
④ Long-Term Debt	2,050
Total Liabilities	12,800
⑤ Shareholders' Equity	
Common stock (2,000 Shares Outstanding)	10,000
Retained Earnings	24,000
Total Shareholders' Equity	34,000
Total Liabilities and Equity	$ 46,800

period of time, meaning that they systematically reduce the value of the asset. Depreciation is reported as an expense on the firm's income statement—see Figure 16.5—but does not involve any cash. The fact that depreciation is a noncash expense means that what a firm reports as net income (profits after tax) for a particular period actually understates the amount of cash the firm took in, less expenses, during that period of time. Consequently, depreciation is added back to net income to obtain cash flow.

The fact that cash flow is the lifeblood of every organization is evidenced by the business failure rate. Many owners of firms that fail put the blame on inadequate cash flow. Proponents of the statement of

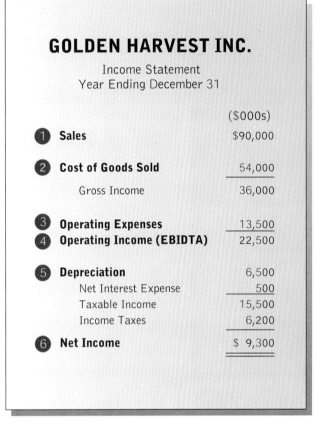

① **Sales:**
Funds received from the sale of goods and services over a specified period of time.

② **Cost of Goods Sold:**
Cost of merchandise or services that generate the firm's sales.

③ **Operating Expenses:**
Salaries, advertising, and other operational expenses not directly related to the acquisition, production, or sale of the firm's output.

④ **Operating Income (EBIDTA):**
Gross income minus operating expenses; also called EBIDTA (earnings before interest, depreciation, taxes, and amortization).

⑤ **Depreciation:**
Noncash expense that reflects the systematic reduction in the value of the firm's fixed assets.

⑥ **Net Income:**
Sales minus total expenses; profit after taxes.

GOLDEN HARVEST INC.

Income Statement
Year Ending December 31

		($000s)
①	Sales	$90,000
②	Cost of Goods Sold	54,000
	Gross Income	36,000
③	Operating Expenses	13,500
④	Operating Income (EBIDTA)	22,500
⑤	Depreciation	6,500
	Net Interest Expense	500
	Taxable Income	15,500
	Income Taxes	6,200
⑥	Net Income	$ 9,300

FIGURE 16.5
Income Statement for Golden Harvest

cash flows hope that its preparation and scrutiny by affected parties will prevent financial disaster for otherwise profitable firms, too many of which are forced to close their doors due to a lack of funds needed to continue day-to-day operations.

Even for firms for which failure is not an issue, the statement of cash flows can provide investors and other interested parties with vital information. For instance, assume a firm's income statement reports rising earnings. At the same time, however, the statement of cash flows shows that the firm's inventory is rising faster than sales—often a signal that demand for the firm's products is softening, which may in turn be a sign of impending financial trouble.

Today, many interested parties pay special attention to **free cash flow.** Free cash flow is defined as cash flow from operations minus capital expenditures. According to Figure 16.5, Golden Harvest had cash flow from operations of $14.25 million for the year shown and capital expenditures of $12.5 million. So the firm had free cash flow of $1.75 million. Investors and lenders like to see a company with positive, and rising, free cash flow.

Concept Check

1. How often is a balance sheet prepared?

2. Why is it so important for companies to have positive cash flow?

FIGURE 16.6
Statement of Cash Flows for Golden Harvest

① Operating Activities: The nuts and bolts, day-to-day activities of a company carrying out its regular business; in financially healthy firms, net cash flow from operating activities should be positive.

② Investing Activities: Transactions to accumulate or use cash in ways that affect operating activities in the future; often a use of cash.

③ Financing Activities: Ways to transfer cash to/from outsiders and/or owners; can be either positive or negative.

④ Net Cash Flow: A reconcilement of cash from the beginning to the end of the accounting period (one year in this example).

⑤ Free Cash Flow: Cash flow from operations minus capital expenditures.

GOLDEN HARVEST INC.

Statement of Cash Flows
Year Ending December 31

	($000s)
① Cash Flow from Operating Activities	
Net Income	$ 9,300
Depreciation	6,500
Cash Provided (Used) by Changes in:	
Accounts Receivable	(200)
Inventory	(2,000)
Accounts Payable	250
Accruals	400
Net Cash Flow from Operating Activities	14,250
② Cash Flow from Investing Activities	
Capital Investments	(12,500)
Net Cash Flow from Investing Activities	(12,500)
③ Cash Flow from Financing Activities	
Repayment of Short-Term Notes	(1,500)
Sale of Long-Term Debt	1,550
Cash Dividends to Shareholders	(1,300)
Net Cash Flow from Financing Activities	(1,250)
④ Net Cash Flow	500
Cash and Equivalents (Beginning of Year)	4,500
Cash and Equivalents (End of Year)	$ 5,000
⑤ Free Cash Flow	$ 1,750

Financial Ratio Analysis

Accounting professionals fulfill important responsibilities beyond preparing financial statements. In a more critical role, they help managers interpret the statements by comparing data about the firm's current activities to that for previous periods and to results posted by competitors. **Ratio analysis** is one of the most commonly used tools for measuring the firm's liquidity, profitability, and reliance on debt financing, as well as the effectiveness of management's resource utilization. This analysis also allows comparisons with other companies and with the firm's own past performance.

Ratios assist managers by interpreting actual performance and making comparisons to what should have happened. Comparisons with ratios of similar companies help managers to understand their firm's performance relative to competitors' results. These industry standards serve as important yardsticks and help to pinpoint problem areas as well as areas of excellence. Ratios for the current accounting period also may be compared with similar calculations for previous periods to spot developing trends. Ratios can be classified according to their specific purposes. The four major categories of financial ratios are summarized in Table 16.1.

Liquidity Ratios

A firm's ability to meet its short-term obligations when they must be paid is measured by **liquidity ratios.** Increasing liquidity reduces the likelihood that a firm will face emergencies caused by the need to raise funds to repay loans. On the other hand, firms with low liquidity may be forced to choose between default or borrowing from high-cost lending sources to meet their maturing obligations.

Two commonly used liquidity ratios are the current ratio and the acid-test ratio. The current ratio compares current assets to current liabilities, giving managers information about the firm's ability to pay its current debts as they mature. The current ratio of Golden Harvest can be computed as follows:

$$\text{Current ratio} = \frac{\$24.30 \text{ million}}{\$10.75 \text{ million}} = 2.26$$

Table 16.1   Financial Ratios and What They Measure

Ratio	What It Measures	Golden Harvest's Ratio
Liquidity Ratios	The ability of the firm to meet its short-term obligations	
Current ratio		2.26
Acid-test ratio		0.91
Profitability Ratios	The firm's ability to generate revenues in excess of expenses and earn an adequate rate of return	
Gross profit margin		40.0%
Net profit margin		10.3%
Earnings per share		$4.65
Return on assets		19.9%
Return on equity		27.4%
Leverage Ratios	The extent to which the firm relies on debt financing	
Total liabilities to total assets		27.4%
Activity Ratios	The effectiveness of the firm's use of resources	
Inventory turnover		4.00
Total asset turnover		2.12

In other words, Golden Harvest has $2.26 of current assets for every $1.00 of current liabilities. In general, a current ratio of 2 to 1 is considered to indicate satisfactory financial conditions. This rule of thumb must be considered along with other factors, such as the nature of the business, the season, and the quality of the company's management. Golden Harvest management and other interested parties are likely to evaluate this ratio of 2.26 to 1 by comparing it with ratios for previous operating periods and with industry averages.

The acid-test (or quick) ratio measures the ability of a firm to meet its debt payments on short notice. This ratio compares quick assets—the most liquid current assets—against current liabilities. Quick assets generally consist of cash and marketable securities and accounts receivable.

Golden Harvest's current balance sheet lists the following quick assets: cash and marketable securities ($5.0 million) and accounts receivable ($4.8 million). The firm's acid-test ratio is computed as follows:

$$\text{Acid-test ratio} = \frac{\$9.80 \text{ million}}{\$10.75 \text{ million}} = 0.91$$

Because the traditional rule of thumb for an adequate acid-test ratio is around 1 to 1, Golden Harvest appears to have a reasonable level of liquidity. However, the same cautions apply here as for the current ratio. The ratio should be compared with industry averages and data from previous operating periods in determining whether it is adequate for the firm.

Profitability Ratios

Some ratios measure the organization's overall financial performance by evaluating its ability to generate revenues in excess of operating costs and other expenses. These measures are called **profitability ratios.** To compute these ratios, accountants compare the firm's earnings with total sales or investments. Over a period of time, profitability ratios may reveal the effectiveness of management in operating the business. Five important profitability ratios are gross profit margin, net profit margin, earnings per share, return on assets, and return on equity:

$$\text{Gross profit margin} = \frac{\$36.0 \text{ million}}{\$90.0 \text{ million}} = 40.0\%$$

$$\text{Net profit margin} = \frac{\$9.3 \text{ million}}{\$90.0 \text{ million}} = 10.3\%$$

$$\text{Earnings per share} = \frac{\$9.3 \text{ million}}{2.0 \text{ million}} = \$4.65$$

$$\text{Return on assets} = \frac{\$9.3 \text{ million}}{\$46.8 \text{ million}} = 19.9\%$$

$$\text{Return on equity} = \frac{\$9.3 \text{ million}}{\$34.0 \text{ million}} = 27.4\%$$

All of these ratios support positive evaluations of the current operations of Golden Harvest. For example, the net profit margin indicates that the firm realizes a profit of about 10.3 cents on each dollar of products it sells. Although this ratio varies widely among business firms, Golden Harvest compares favorably with retailers in general, which have an average net profit margin of around 5 percent. However, this ratio, like the other profitability ratios, should be evaluated in relation to profit forecasts, past performance, or more specific industry averages to enhance the interpretation of results. Similarly, while the firm's return on equity of more than 27 percent appears to reflect excellent performance, the degree of risk in the industry also must be considered.

Profitability ratios are widely used indicators of business success. For example, over a 10-year period, the earnings per share of Johnson & Johnson rose by more than 250 percent. During the same period, the company's stock price rose by 350 percent.[7]

Leverage Ratios

Leverage ratios measure the extent to which a firm relies on debt financing. They provide vital information to potential investors and lenders. If management has assumed too much debt in financing the firm's operations, problems may arise in meeting future interest payments and repaying outstanding loans. Relying too heavily on debt financing can lead to failure. More generally, both investors and lenders may prefer to deal with firms whose owners have invested enough of their own money in their companies to avoid excessive borrowing. The total liabilities to total assets ratio helps analysts to evaluate these concerns:

$$\text{Total liabilities to total assets} = \frac{\$12.8 \text{ million}}{\$46.8 \text{ million}} = 27.4\%$$

A total liabilities to total assets ratio greater than 50 percent indicates that a firm is relying more on borrowed money than owners' equity. Since Golden Harvest's total liabilities to total assets ratio is 27.4 percent, the firm's owners have invested considerably more than the total amount of liabilities shown on the firm's balance sheet.

Activity Ratios

Activity ratios measure the effectiveness of management's use of the firm's resources. One of the most frequently used activity ratios, the inventory turnover ratio, indicates the number of times merchandise moves through a business:

$$\text{Inventory turnover} = \frac{\$54.0 \text{ million}}{\$13.5 \text{ million}} = 4.00$$

Average inventory for Golden Harvest is determined by adding inventory at the beginning of the year, assume it was $12.5 million, to inventory at the end of the year, $14.5 million, and dividing by 2.

Comparing the 4.0 inventory turnover ratio with industry standards gives a measure of efficiency. Furniture and jewelry retailers average an annual turnover of 1.5 times. A supermarket's annual inventory turnover can be as high as 30 times.

Another measure of efficiency is total asset turnover. It measures how much in sales each dollar in assets generates:

$$\text{Total asset turnover} = \frac{\$90.00 \text{ million}}{\$42.45 \text{ million}} = 2.12$$

Average total assets for Golden Harvest equal total assets at the beginning of the year (assume it was $38.1 million) plus total assets at the end of the year ($46.8 million) divided by 2.

Golden Harvest generates about $2.19 in sales for each dollar invested in assets. Although a higher ratio generally indicates that a firm is operating more efficiently, care must be taken when comparing firms that operate in different industries. For example, Southwest Airlines has a total asset turnover of around 0.90, low in comparison with some firms but high in comparison with other airlines.

The four categories of financial ratios relate balance sheet and income statement data to one another, assist management in pinpointing a firm's strengths and weaknesses, and indicate areas in need of further investigation. Large multiproduct firms that operate in diverse markets use their information systems to update their financial ratios every day or even hourly. Each company's management must decide on an appropriate review schedule to avoid the costly and time-consuming mistake of excessive monitoring.

In addition to calculating financial ratios, managers, investors, and lenders should pay close attention to how accountants applied a number of accounting rules when preparing financial statements. GAAP gives accountants leeway in reporting certain revenues and expenses. Public companies are required to disclose, in footnotes to the financial statements, how the various accounting rules were applied. Some firms have been accused of using so-called accounting gimmicks to boost reported profits.

Concept Check

1. What is the most commonly used tool for measuring a firm's financial health?
2. Which ratio measures a company's reliance on debt financing?

Budgeting

Although the financial statements discussed in this chapter focus on past business activities, they also provide the basis for planning in the future. A **budget** is a planning and controlling tool that reflects the firm's expected sales revenues, operating expenses, and cash receipts and outlays. It quantifies the firm's plans for a specified future period. Since it reflects management estimates of expected sales, cash inflows and outflows, and costs, the budget serves as a financial blueprint and can be thought of as a short-term financial plan. It becomes the standard for comparison against actual performance.

Budget preparation is frequently a time-consuming task that involves many people from various departments within the firm. The complexity of the budgeting process varies with the size and complexity of the organization. Large corporations such as Alcoa, General Motors, and Nokia maintain complex and sophisticated budgeting systems. Their budgets help managers to integrate their numerous divisions in addition to serving as planning and controlling tools. But budgeting in both large and small firms is similar to household budgeting in its purpose: to match income and expenses in a way that accomplishes objectives and correctly times cash inflows and outflows.

Since the accounting department is an organization's financial nerve center, it provides much of the data for budget development. The overall master, or operating, budget is a composite of many individual budgets for separate units of the firm. These individual budgets typically include the production budget, cash budget, capital expenditures budget, advertising budget, and sales budget.

Computers and the Internet have helped companies improve the efficiency of their budgeting process. For example, a company called FRx Forecaster—part of the Great Plains Business Solutions subsidiary of Microsoft—offers a Web-based budgeting application. Customers download all of their budget records directly to FRx's server. Nepco, a builder of power plants, found that using FRx cut several weeks off the firm's budgeting process and made it much less cumbersome. Kim Coates, Nepco's financial planning and reporting manager, also believes the Web-based system is more accurate and leads to better forecasts of project revenues and costs. That's an important consideration when large power plant projects can easily cost $800 million. ClosedLoop Solutions has developed a budgeting system that allows for more event-driven, collaborative budgeting.[8]

One of the most important budgets prepared by firms is the **cash budget.** The cash budget, usually prepared monthly, tracks the firm's cash inflows and outflows. Figure 16.7 illustrates a sample cash budget for Golden Harvest. Management has set a $2 million target cash balance. The cash budget indicates months in which the firm will need temporary loans (April and May in the case of Golden Harvest). The document also indicates months in which the firm can invest excess funds in

Budgeting is a critical task for organizations. FRx Forecaster offers Web-based tools for budgeting and forecasting, allowing companies to speed up these activities.

FRx Software Corporation, a Microsoft Company

marketable securities to earn interest rather than leaving them idle in a bank account (June in the case of Golden Harvest). Finally, the cash budget produces a tangible standard against which to compare actual cash inflows and outflows.

Concept Check

1. What function does a budget serve?
2. How have computers affected the budgeting process?

International Accounting

Today, accounting procedures and practices must be adapted to accommodate an international business environment. The Coca-Cola Company and McDonald's both generate over half their annual revenues from sales outside the U.S. Nestlé, the giant chocolate and food products multinational, operates throughout the world. It derives 98 percent of its revenues from outside Switzerland, its home country. International accounting practices for global firms must reliably translate the financial statements of the firm's international affiliates, branches, and subsidiaries and convert data about foreign-currency transactions to dollars. Also, the euro, Europe's relatively new single currency, will influence the accounting and financial reporting processes of firms operating in some European countries.

GOLDEN HARVEST INC.

Cash Inflows ($000s)	April	May	June
Cash Sales	3,000	4,500	6,000
Collections of Receivables	1,500	2,250	3,375
Other Cash Inflows	500	0	0
Total Cash Inflows	5,000	6,750	9,375
Cash Outflows ($000s)			
Cash Purchases	2,025	2,700	2,700
Payment of Credit Purchases	1,000	1,519	2,030
Cash Operating Expenses	1,125	1,125	1,125
Other Cash Outflows	1,500	1,500	0
Total Cash Outflows	5,650	6,844	5,855
Net Cash Flow	(650)	(94)	3,520
Beginning Cash Balance	2,000	2,000	2,000
Net Cash Flow	(650)	(94)	3,520
Ending Cash Balance	1,350	1,906	5,520
Target Cash Balance	2,000	2,000	2,000
Cash Surplus (Deficit)	(650)	(94)	3,520
Cumulative Surplus (Deficit)	(650)	(744)	2,776

FIGURE 16.7
Three-Month Cash Budget for Golden Harvest

Exchange Rates

As defined in Chapter 4, an exchange rate is the ratio at which a country's currency can be exchanged for other currencies. Currencies can be treated as goods to be bought and sold. Like the price of any good or service, currency prices change daily according to supply and demand. So exchange rate fluctuations complicate accounting entries and accounting practices.

Accountants who deal with international transactions must appropriately record their firms' foreign sales and purchases. Today's sophisticated accounting software helps companies handle all of their international transactions within a single program. An international firm's consolidated financial statements must reflect any gains or losses due to changes in exchange rates during specific periods of time. Financial statements that cover operations in two or more nations also need to treat fluctuations consistently to allow for comparison.

International Accounting Standards

The International Accounting Standards Committee (IASC) was established in 1973 to promote worldwide consistency in financial reporting practices. The IASC is recognized worldwide as the body with sole responsibility and authority to issue pronouncements on international accounting standards. The International Federation of Accountants supports the work of the IASC and develops international guidelines for auditing, ethics, education, and management accounting. Every five years, an

BUSINESS TOOL KIT

Careers for Accounting Professionals

Getting an accounting degree? Your options are wide open when it comes to deciding on where to take your accounting career. The communication of accurate accounting information is of great importance to people both inside and outside an organization. Based on information reported by accountants, decisions are made regarding the daily and long-range operations of a company, its financial status, and even who will invest in the company's stock.

You can work for a public accounting firm, the government, a corporation, or even yourself. Public accountants are not employees of the company to which they provide services, and they are limited in the types of consulting and auditing services that they can provide to publicly traded companies. Management accountants are responsible for gathering and recording financial transactions, preparing financial statements, and interpreting them so that managers can use the information to operate their own firms more effectively. Not-for-profit accountants provide functions similar to those of management accountants, but their emphasis is on the efficiency with which organizations achieve their objectives, not on profits and losses. Depending on your career path, you can work toward professional designation in a variety of areas. Here are the most common.

- Certified Public Accountant (CPA)
- Certified Management Accountant (CMA)
- Certified Financial Manager (CFM)
- Certified Fraud Examiner (CFE)
- Certified Financial Planner (CFP)
- Certified Internal Auditor (CIA)
- Certified Government Financial Manager (CGFM)
- Chartered Financial Analyst (CFA)
- Certified Business Manager (CBM)

In addition, there are several Web sites geared specifically to accounting professionals looking for a position. Check out these sites for more information and leads on jobs in your area.

- http://www.accounting.com
- http://www.accountemps.com
- http://www.accountingweb.com
- http://www.ajilonfinance.com
- http://www.cpajobs.com

Sources: "CPA TRACK: Education/Certification Info," http://www.cpatrack .com/educational_info/, accessed July 27, 2003; "Professional Designations," http://www.smartpros.com/x29668.xml, accessed July 27, 2003; Anthony J. Ridley, "Directory of International Professional Accounting & Business Certification Programmes," *Internal Auditor,* October 2001, p. 22.

Concept Check

1. *What is an exchange rate?*
2. *What function does the IASC serve?*

DID YOU KNOW?

1. More than half the ethical issues involved in recent business disasters focus on accountants and/or chief financial officers.
2. The accounting system used in Russia does not permit a manager to assess whether a product has made a profit or loss. Fixed and variable costs are not differentiated; direct and indirect costs are lumped together; and revenues are not matched with expenses.
3. Fifty-six percent of U.S. accountants are women.
4. Board members of the Public Company Accounting Oversight Board earn more than the president of the U.S.

international congress is held to judge progress in achieving consistency in standards and works toward increasing comparability among nations' financial data and currencies.

The European Union and NAFTA have led to widespread recognition of the necessity for comparability and uniformity of international accounting standards. An increasing number of investors are buying shares in foreign multinational corporations. In response to global investors' needs, more and more firms are beginning to report their financial information according to international accounting standards. This practice helps investors compare the financial results of firms in different countries.

What's Ahead

This chapter described the role of accounting in an organization. Accounting is the process of measuring, interpreting, and communicating financial information to interested parties both inside and outside the firm. The next chapter introduces the finance function of an organization. Finance deals with planning, obtaining, and managing the organization's funds to accomplish its objectives in the most efficient and effective manner possible.

Summary of Learning Goals

1 *Explain the functions of accounting and its importance to the firm's management, investors, creditors, and government agencies.*
Accountants measure, interpret, and communicate financial information to parties inside and outside the firm to support improved decision making. Accountants are responsible for gathering, recording, and interpreting financial information to management. They also provide financial information on the status and operations of the firm for evaluation by such outside parties as government agencies, stockholders, potential investors, and lenders.

2 *Identify the three basic business activities involved in accounting.*
Accounting plays key roles in financing activities, which help to start and expand an organization; investing activities, which provide the assets the firm requires; and operating activities, which focus on selling goods and services and paying expenses incurred in regular operations.

3 *Describe the roles played by public, management, government, and not-for-profit accountants.*
Public accountants are providers of accounting services to other firms or individuals for a fee. They are involved in such activities as tax statement preparation, management consulting, and accounting system design. Management accountants are responsible for collecting and recording financial transactions, preparing financial statements, and interpreting them for managers in their own firms. Government and not-for-profit accountants perform many of the same functions as management accountants, but their analysis emphasizes how effectively the organization or agency is operating rather than its profits and losses.

4 *Outline the steps in the accounting process.*
The accounting process involves recording, classifying, and summarizing data about transactions and then using this information to produce financial statements for the firm's managers and other interested parties. Transactions are recorded chronologically in journals, posted in ledgers, and then summarized in accounting statements. Today, much of this takes place electronically.

5 *Describe the impact of recent ethical scandals and the Sarbanes-Oxley Act on the accounting profession.*
In response to cases of accounting fraud and questions about the independence of auditors, the Sarbanes-Oxley Act of 2002 created the Public Company Accounting Oversight Board. The five-member board sets audit standards and investigates—and sanctions—accounting firms that certify the books of publicly traded firms. Members of the Public Company Accounting Oversight Board are appointed by the Securities and Exchange Commission—the chief federal regulator of the securities markets and the accounting industry.

6 *Explain the functions and major components of the three principal financial statements: the balance sheet, the income statement, and the statement of cash flows.*
The balance sheet shows the financial position of a company on a particular date. The three major classifications of balance sheet data represent the components of the accounting equation: assets, liabilities, and owners' equity. The income statement shows the results of a firm's operations over a specific period. It focuses on the firm's activities—its revenues and expenditures—and the resulting profit or loss during the period. The major

components of the income statement are revenues, cost of goods sold, expenses, and profit or loss. The statement of cash flows indicates a firm's cash receipts and cash payments during an accounting period. It shows the sources and uses of cash in the basic business activities of financing, investing, and operating.

7 *Discuss how financial ratios are used to analyze a firm's financial strengths and weaknesses.*

Liquidity ratios measure a firm's ability to meet short-term obligations. Examples are the current ratio and acid-test ratio. Profitability ratios assess the overall financial performance of the business. The gross profit margin, net profit margin, return on assets, and return on owners' equity are examples. Leverage ratios, such as the total liabilities to total assets ratio, measure the extent to which the firm relies on debt to finance its operations. Activity ratios, such as the inventory turnover ratio and total asset turnover ratio, measure how effectively a firm uses its resources. Financial ratios assist managers and outside evaluators in comparing a firm's current financial information with that of previous years and with results for other firms in the same industry.

8 *Describe the role of budgets in a business.*

Budgets are financial guidelines for future periods reflecting expected sales revenues, operating expenses, and/or cash receipts and outlays. They represent management expectations for future occurrences based on plans that have been made. Budgets serve as important planning and controlling tools by providing standards against which actual performance can be measured.

9 *Explain how exchange rates influence international accounting practices and the importance of uniform financial statements for global business.*

An exchange rate is the ratio at which a country's currency can be exchanged for other currencies. Daily changes in exchange rates affect the accounting entries for sales and purchases of firms involved in international markets. These fluctuations create either losses or gains for particular companies. Data about international financial transactions must be translated into the currency of the country in which the parent company resides. The International Accounting Standards Committee was established to provide worldwide consistency in financial reporting practices and comparability and uniformity of international accounting standards.

Business Terms You Need to Know

accounting 516

certified public accountant (CPA) 519

accounting process 520

Public Company Accounting Oversight Board 522

asset 523

liability 523

owners' equity 523

basic accounting equation 523

balance sheet 524

income statement 524

statement of cash flows 525

accrual accounting 525

Other Important Business Terms

public accountant 518

management accountant 518

government accountant 520

bottom line 524

free cash flow 527

ratio analysis 529

liquidity ratios 529

profitability ratios 530

leverage ratios 531

activity ratios 531

budget 532

cash budget 532

Review Questions

1. Define *accounting*. Who are the major users of accounting information?

2. What are the primary business activities in which accountants play a significant role? Give an example of each.

3. Explain the differences between a public accountant, a management accountant, and a government accountant. What services do public accounting firms provide for clients?

4. What does the term *GAAP* mean? Briefly explain the role of the Financial Accounting Standards Board.

5. List the three major financial statements. Explain the basic accounting equation.

6. What is the difference between a current asset and a long-term asset? Why is cash typically listed first on a balance sheet?

7. What is accrual accounting? Give an example of how accrual accounting affects a firm's financial statements.

8. List the four categories of financial ratios and give an example of each. What is the purpose of ratio analysis?

9. What is a cash budget? Briefly outline what a simple cash budget might look like.

10. What financial statements are affected by exchange rates for firms with global operations? What are the benefits of uniform international accounting standards?

Projects and Applications

1. Your grandmother sends you a large check for your birthday, suggesting that you use the money to buy shares of stock in a company. She recommends that you review the company's financial statements before investing. What can a company's financial statements tell you about the investment potential of its stock?

2. Suppose you work for a U.S. firm that has extensive European operations and owns several European businesses. You need to restate data from the various European currencies in U.S. dollars to prepare your firm's financial statements. Which financial statements and which components of these statements will be affected? Has the adoption of the euro made your job easier or more difficult?

3. The collapse of Enron, WorldCom, and other firms has raised a number of questions concerning the ethical standards of outside auditors. As a result, a number of new rules and laws were adopted. Research these new rules and laws and write a two-page report summarizing them. In your opinion, have the regulations adequately resolved the ethical issues and raised the ethical standards of outside auditors?

4. Suppose you are offered a job with a small private company. Since the company isn't required to publish its financial information—as public companies are—you ask the owner if you could review the financial statements prior to accepting the job. The owner refuses and says that only the firm's accountant and banker are allowed to see the statements. What could you say that might convince the company's owner to share financial information with employees?

5. You've been appointed treasurer of a local not-for-profit organization. You would like to improve the quality of the organization's financial reporting to existing and potential donors. Describe the kinds of financial statements you would like to see the organization's accountant prepare. Why do you think better-quality financial statements might help to reassure donors?

Experiential Exercise

Directions: Adapting the format of Figure 16.7, Three-Month Cash Budget for Golden Harvest, prepare on a separate sheet of paper your personal one-month cash budget for next month. Keep in mind the following suggestions as you prepare your budget.

1. *Cash inflows.* Your sources of cash would include your earnings, gifts, scholarship monies, tax refunds, and dividends and interest.

2. *Cash outflows.* When estimating next month's cash outflows, include any of the following that may apply to your situation:
   a. Household expenses (mortgage/rent, utilities, maintenance, home furnishings, telephone/cell phone, cable TV, household supplies, groceries)
   b. Education (tuition, fees, textbooks, supplies)
   c. Work (transportation, meals)
   d. Clothing (purchases, cleaning, laundry)
   e. Automobile (auto payments, fuel, repairs)
   f. Insurance (life, auto, homeowner's, renter's, health and dental)
   g. Taxes (income, property, Social Security, Medicare)
   h. Savings and Investments
   i. Entertainment/Recreation (health club, vacation/travel, dining, movies)
   j. Debt (credit card payments, installment loans)
   k. Miscellaneous (charitable contributions, child care, gifts, medical expenses)

3. *Beginning cash balance.* This amount could be based on a minimum cash balance you keep in your checking account and should include only the cash available for your use; therefore, money such as that invested in retirement plans should not be included.

NOTHING BUT NET

1. **Accounting reform.** The financial collapse of Enron, Global Crossing, and other firms highlighted a number of accounting issues and led to a number of proposals to improve the quality of accounting and financial disclosure. Using a search engine, type in the key words "accounting reform" and see how many hits you get. Visit three or four of the sites listed, along with the SEC's Web site (http://www.sec.gov); then prepare an oral report on the current status of accounting reform.

2. **Finding financial information on a company.** Select a public company in which you have some interest. Visit the company's Web site and one of the investment-oriented Web sites listed. Download the company's financial statements for the most recent year you can find. Calculate the financial ratios listed in the text. Briefly assess the financial strength and investment potential of your company.

http://moneycentral.msn.com/investor/home.asp
http://www.morningstar.com
http://www.quicken.com

3. **Accounting as a career.** As noted in the chapter, accounting is a popular business major. Ernst & Young—one of the largest public accounting firms in the world—includes an extensive section on accounting careers on its Web site. Visit the firm's Web site and prepare a report on the various career paths taken by actual Ernst & Young employees. Based on what you learned, do you think you'd be interested in a career in public accounting? Why or why not?

http://www.ey.com/global/content.nsf/US/Home

Note: Internet Web addresses change frequently. If you do not find the exact sites listed, you may need to access the organization's or company's home page and search from there.

Case 16.1

Joan Chen Prepares a Budget

The cash budget is an important planning tool for companies. But a budget is also an important financial planning tool for individuals like Joan Chen. Her budget is designed to monitor and control expenditures so that her short- and longer-term financial goals can be achieved. Budgets permit people like Joan to track past and current expenditures and plan new ones.

Joan decides to prepare her personal budget on a monthly basis. Most of her bills—such as her rent, Visa bill, utilities, and car payment—are due once a month. Joan, who is an assistant manager at a discount electronics store, is also paid once a month. The balance in her checking account always seems to get pretty low by the end of the month. She's hoping the monthly budget will help her better monitor and control her expenses.

Like a company's cash budget, Joan's personal budget is divided into two components: income (or cash inflows) and expenses (or cash outflows). She divides her expenses into two additional categories: fixed expenses (those that vary little if any from month to month) and variable expenses (those that vary from month to month). Examples of fixed expenses include her apartment rent, the car payment on her Volkswagen Beetle, insurance payments, and contributions to a Vanguard mutual fund. Variable expenses include Joan's food, electricity, and phone expenses. Her cash flow is simply the difference between cash inflows and outflows. The difference between her actual cash flows and estimated cash flows is referred to as *variance*.

Joan once took a personal finance course at American River College in Sacramento. She knows that you should keep your budget as simple as possible. So Joan limits the number of categories and rounds off to the nearest dollar. She also budgets some "personal spending money" each month. Joan is planning to get married within the next year. She and her fiancé have already discussed how they will budget their household income and expenses. They both know that arguments over money are a leading cause of divorce. Neither has any intention of getting caught in that financial trap.

QUESTIONS FOR CRITICAL THINKING

1. Explain the difference between a fixed expense and a variable expense. Why should "savings contribution" be considered a fixed expense?
2. Give an example of how a person's short- or long-term financial goals will influence his or her budget.
3. Now it is your turn to design a budget like Joan Chen did. Fill out the worksheet shown here.
4. How difficult will it be for you to stick to your budget? Do you think it is realistic?

Source: Adapted from Louis E. Boone, David L. Kurtz, and Douglas Hearth, *Planning Your Financial Future*, 3rd ed., Mason, Ohio: South-Western, 2003, pp. 75–79.

	Estimate	Actual	Variance
Cash inflows			
Salary (take-home)			
Other cash inflows			
Total cash inflows			
Cash outflows			
Fixed expenses			
Rent			
Auto loan			
Student loan			
Auto insurance premium			
Savings contribution			
Variable expenses			
Utilities			
Food & personal-care items			
Medical & dental			
Clothing & haircuts			
Entertainment			
Transportation expenses			
Gifts & contributions			
Personal spending money			
Total cash outflows			
Net cash flow			

Video Case 16.2

Chicago-Style Pizza Finds a Nationwide Market

This video case appears on page 619. A recently filmed video, designed to expand and highlight the written case, is available for class use by instructors.

Part 5 Krispy Kreme Continuing Case

Krispy Kreme: A Low-Tech Product in a High-Tech World

It's difficult to imagine anything more basic in its appeal than a fresh, hot, glazed doughnut. In fact, Krispy Kreme officials work hard to convey the message that Krispy Kremes are fresh from another, simpler era. The nostalgic atmosphere in the stores, from the staff's uniforms to the retro-style coffee mugs and doughnut boxes, transports visitors back to yesteryear. But Krispy Kreme relies on modern technology to get the message about its brand out to the public and to help employees communicate with one another.

A few years ago, the company launched an extranet called MyKrispyKreme designed to connect franchisees, vendors, and managers at corporate headquarters. Software lets store managers have direct access to enterprise applications such as the order entry system and retrieve their own daily sales numbers, which are automatically collected from the stores' point-of-sale systems and stored in a data warehouse. If a store manager needs more doughnut mix or other products, the information can be sent to radio-frequency stations at the warehouse, where workers select the products, pack them, and load the truck. "There's no paper generated, except for a physical signature on the bill of lading," explains Chief Information Officer (CIO) Frank Hood. "Short of having robots deliver the goods, it's as electronic as we can make it." The software also functions as an enterprise resource planning system, giving Krispy Kreme executives an overview of the company's business operations. Users can submit their financial reports electronically, and store managers can view any relevant corporate information they have approval to access.

How does a company get its employees—who signed on to make a low-tech product—to adopt new technology to serve their customers better? "We've tried to emulate Amazon," explains Frank Hood. "There's a single sign-on, so you don't have to remember multiple passwords. The system is intelligent enough that when a store manager is busy, it can be set to build and place an order automatically." Hood also notes that Krispy Kreme uses technology as a means to an end—serving customers—not as an end in itself.

Even before store managers become managers, they have used technology in their training. The managerial training materials now include Internet-based programs and testing, as well as components on CD-ROM. The Web-based materials include graphics, videos, and animation, and they are available through in-store computers connected to the extranet and employees' home computers for those who have preregistered for the courses. The results of computer-based testing are automatically transferred to corporate headquarters in North Carolina, where managers in the human resource department can review them. The system then refers trainees back to sections of the training program that may require more study. Of course, Internet education does not replace the hands-on training that employees receive in Krispy Kreme shops, but it is designed to complement the experience of actually running the doughnut machine. Once they take over a store, managers still receive training through their computers. "On a store manager's PC, you'll see a near real-time window into the business," says Frank Hood. "It has instructional streaming video on everything from store openings to how to calibrate a coffee grinder."

Running a Krispy Kreme business may seem simple on the surface: Turn on the doughnut machine, watch the doughnuts come out, serve the hungry customers, count the profits. Of course, it's not that simple at all. Company managers and franchise owners must have a clear understanding of their company's financing and operating activities. They must be able to record data such as operating expenses accurately and read financial statements. Potential franchisees must already be experienced businesspeople even to apply for a Krispy Kreme franchise, and there is no guarantee that they will succeed.

Accounting practices have received increased attention in the wake of such corporate scandals as Enron and Worldcom. Because of the methods the firm used to repurchase some franchises that were faltering and then report those transactions, Krispy Kreme has been under scrutiny by the SEC. But CEO Scott Livengood remains resolute. "We have faced tougher situations and come out stronger than before," he has declared. Meanwhile, Krispy Kreme keeps churning those low-tech doughnuts through the glaze waterfall. When asked what the firm's most important piece of technology is, CIO Frank Hood gives a sweet answer: "Our killer app is the glazed ring."

QUESTIONS

1. Describe a situation in which you think a decision support system (DSS) would be helpful either to a Krispy Kreme franchisee or to managers at Krispy Kreme headquarters.

2. In what ways do you think computer-based training can be helpful for new Krispy Kreme employees?

3. In what ways does technology help franchisees with their own accounting requirements?

4. Describe what you think are some of Krispy Kreme's most important assets, both tangible and intangible.

Sources: Krispy Kreme Web site, http://www.krispykreme.com, accessed January 10, 2005; Rick Brooks and Mark Maremont, "Ovens Are Cooling at Krispy Kreme as Woes Multiply," *The Wall Street Journal,* September 3, 2004, pp. A1, A5; Paul Nowell, "Low-Carb Craze Catches up with Krispy Kreme," May 26, 2004, p. 6B; Ian Mount, "Krispy Kreme's Secret Ingredient," *Business 2.0,* September 2003, p. 36.

Part 6
Managing Financial Resources

Chapter 17
Financial Management and Institutions

1 Identify the functions performed by a firm's financial managers.

2 Describe the characteristics a form of money should have and list the functions of money.

3 Explain each of the various measures of the money supply.

4 Explain how a firm uses funds.

5 Compare the two major sources of funds for a business.

6 Identify the likely sources of short- and long-term funds.

7 Describe the financial system and the major financial institutions.

8 Explain the functions of the Federal Reserve System and the tools it uses to control the money supply.

9 Describe the global financial system.

Credit Card Fees: Your Loss, Their Gain

America has become a plastic society. That's not a political statement; it's a financial one. Thirty years ago, only one in six U.S. households had a credit card; today, that number has tripled to 73 percent have an average of seven cards. A decade ago, consumers spent $724 billion each year using their cards;

today, that number has tripled to $2.2 trillion annually, with the average household spending about $15,000. Back then, credit cards were used sparingly—for emergency car repairs or to replace a broken washing machine. Now, credit and debit cards are the norm for nearly every type of payment, whether it involves groceries, a Big Mac, or visits to the doctor.

But as the use of these cards has increased, so have the fees charged by financial institutions. And the average household's credit card debt has soared as well, to about $6,300, according to Bankrate.com. Every year, the credit card industry bills more than $43 billion in penalty fees, including late fees, over-limit fees, fees by card issuers who are accepting bank transfers, and fees on large cash advances. The average late fee now hovers around $32, while the length of billing cycles shrink. Some credit card companies now send bills earlier in the cycle, leaving consumers a shorter period of time to respond. They have also reduced the "grace" (or leniency) period. Because companies are competing so hard with each other to attract consumers with low introductory—or even permanent—interest rates, they are turning to these penalty fees as a way to increase revenues.

Interest rates are subject to change as well, even on so-called fixed-rate cards. They can be adjusted by the card

© Susan Van Etten

issuer with 15 days' notice to the consumer. With total U.S. consumer debt topping $743 billion, rising interest rates mean higher interest payments. "We're in a position now in which close to 30 to 35 million households are either over their limit or behind on one of their cards," warns Chris Viale of Cambridge Credit Counseling. Amid rising fees, interest rates, and debt, why do credit card firms continue to raise credit limits and solicit new business from consumers? Three out of five credit cardholders roll their balances over each month, paying an average of 22 percent. These are the most profitable customers to banks and credit card firms.

As for consumers who still write checks or pay cash, "There are still trillions of dollars in cash and checks that are out there just waiting to be captured on plastic," says Bill Glenn, president of American Express's Merchant Network. As an enticement, American Express offers some glamorous rewards to consumers who use their cards regularly. How about earning a personal chef for a cooking lesson and dinner for eight? You'd have to charge $95,000 on your card. For a three-day polo lesson in Florida, it's a mere $180,000 in credit card charges. But if you want to take a suborbital space flight with Russian cosmonauts, you'll have to rack up $20 million in spending, in which case, you might as well buy your own rocket—and maybe put it on your card.[1]

Chapter Overview

Previous chapters discussed two essential functions that a business must perform. The organization must produce a good or service or contract with suppliers to produce it. Then the firm must market its product to prospective customers. This chapter introduces a third, equally important, function: A company's managers must ensure that it has enough money to perform its other tasks successfully in both the present and the future. Adequate funds must be available to buy materials and equipment, pay bills, purchase additional facilities, and compensate employees. This third business function is **finance**—planning, obtaining, and managing the company's funds to accomplish its objectives effectively and efficiently.

An organization's financial objectives include satisfying financial obligations to workers, suppliers, lenders, and the government. They also include maximizing the overall value of the firm, often determined by the worth of its common stock. Financial managers are responsible for raising funds, paying bills, and increasing profits to shareholders.

This chapter focuses on the role of financial managers, why businesses need funds, and the various types and sources of funds. It discusses the role of money and measures of the money supply. The chapter explains the purpose and structure of the financial system, the operations of financial institutions, and the functions of the Federal Reserve System. A discussion of the role of the financial system in the global business environment concludes the chapter.

finance business function of planning, obtaining, and managing a company's funds to accomplish its objectives in the most effective possible way.

financial manager employee responsible for developing and implementing the firm's financial plan and for determining the most appropriate sources and uses of funds.

chief financial officer (CFO) top finance executive of a corporation; usually reports directly to the firm's CEO.

The Role of the Financial Manager

Organizations are placing greater emphasis on measuring and reducing the costs of conducting business, as well as increasing revenues and profits. As a result, **financial managers**—executives responsible for developing and implementing their firm's financial plan and for determining the most appropriate sources and uses of funds—are among the most vital people on the corporate payroll.

The finance organization of a typical company might look like the structure shown in Figure 17.1. At the top is the **chief financial officer (CFO).** The CFO usually reports directly to the company's chief executive officer (CEO), or chief operating officer (COO) if the firm has one. In some companies, the CFO is also a member of the board of directors. Reporting directly to the CFO are often three senior managers. While titles can vary, these three executives are commonly called the **vice president for financial management** (or **planning**), the **treasurer,** and the **controller.** The vice president for financial management or planning is responsible for preparing financial forecasts and analyzing major investment decisions. Major investment decisions include new production facilities and acquisitions of other companies. The treasurer is responsible for all of the company's financing activities, including managing cash, the tax department, and shareholder relations. The treasurer also works on the sale of new security issues to investors. The controller is the chief accounting executive. The controller's functions include keeping the company's books, preparing financial statements, and conducting internal audits.

The growing importance of financial professionals is reflected in an expanding number of CEOs promoted from financial positions. By one estimate, around 20 percent of all newly appointed CEOs during a recent year spent time in the finance ranks. One example is Ralph F. Hake, CEO of Maytag. Prior to becoming Maytag's CEO, Hake held CFO positions at Whirlpool Corporation and Fluor. Another example is Harry Jansen Kraemer, CEO of drug giant Baxter. Prior to being named CEO, Kraemer served as the firm's CFO for several years. The importance of finance professionals is also reflected in how much CFOs earn today. According to one survey, total direct compensation for CFOs at major public companies averages around $2 million per year.[2]

While CFOs are well compensated, there is little doubt that the job has gotten tougher in recent years. According to one survey, 91 percent of CFOs said that their jobs are harder than two years earlier. During the same time period, the survey also revealed that over 60 percent of CFOs believe that their jobs have gotten more time consuming, and almost half are less satisfied with their jobs today. Carol Tomé, CFO of Home Depot, puts it this way: "For all my professional life, all I wanted was to be a CFO. But there are now days when I really ask myself if I signed up for all this."[3]

CFOs are subject to a wave of new laws and regulations stemming from the corporate scandals highlighted by the collapse of Enron, HealthSouth, and WorldCom. In many cases, CFOs were implicated in wrongdoing. The Sarbanes-Oxley Act created a number of obligations for CFOs of public companies. Among the best-known requirements, CFOs and CEOs must both certify a company's financial statements. However, Sarbanes-Oxley created numerous less known requirements for today's CFO.[4] Moreover, penalties for CFOs who knowingly make false statements to the SEC include fines of up to $5 million and up to 20 years in jail.

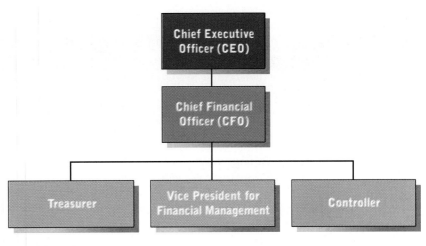

FIGURE 17.1
Organizational Structure of the Finance Function

In performing their jobs, financial professionals continually seek to balance risks with expected financial returns. Risk is the uncertainty of gain or loss; return is the gain or loss that results from an investment over a specified period of time. Financial managers strive to maximize the wealth of their firm's shareholders by striking the optimal balance between risk and return. This balance is called the **risk–return trade-off.** For example, a heavy reliance on borrowed funds may increase the return to shareholders, but at the same time, the more money a firm borrows, the greater the risks to shareholders. An increase in a firm's cash on hand reduces the risk of meeting unexpected cash needs. However, because cash does not earn any return, failure to invest surplus cash in an income-earning asset—such as in marketable securities—reduces a firm's potential return or profitability.

Every financial manager must perform this risk–return balancing act. For example, in the late 1980s, Boeing was wrestling with a major decision: whether to begin development of the 777 jetliner. The development costs were estimated to be over $5 billion. Before committing to such a huge investment, financial managers had to weigh the potential profits of the 777—the jetliner was expected to produce profits in excess of $50 billion over a 25-year period—with the risk that the profits would not materialize. With its future on the line, Boeing decided to go ahead with the development of the 777. The decision has turned out favorably for Boeing. Careful financial management helped to keep development costs well below the estimates, and sales have exceeded the original forecasts. At the present time, Boeing has sold over six hundred 777 jetliners to airlines throughout the world.[5]

The Financial Plan

Financial managers develop their organization's **financial plan,** a document that specifies the funds needed by a firm for a period of time, the timing of inflows and outflows, and the most appropriate sources and uses of funds. The financial plan is based on forecasts of production costs, purchasing needs, and expected sales activities for the period covered. Financial managers use forecasts to determine the specific amounts and timing of expenditures and receipts. They build a financial plan based on the answers to three questions:

financial plan document specifying the funds a firm will need for a period of time, the timing of inflows and outflows, and the most appropriate sources and uses of funds.

1. What funds will the firm require during the appropriate period of operations?
2. How will it obtain the necessary money?
3. When will it need more cash?

Some funds flow into the firm when it sells its products, but funding needs vary. The financial plan must reflect both the amounts and timing of inflows and outflows of funds. Even a profitable firm may

Western Union: Money Goes around the World

You know the saying, "Money makes the world go around." But Western Union makes money go around the world—literally. Western Union, which used to be known mainly for its telegraph and telegram services, is now functioning as a bank for millions of foreign workers, travelers, and others who want to send or receive money safely and electronically. With more than 200,000 locations in 195 countries and territories, Western Union has more outlets than McDonald's, Starbucks, and Wal-Mart combined. Without fanfare, Western Union has become one of the most profitable financial institutions in the world. Now a division of First Data Corp., which is the world's largest credit card processor, Western Union processes nearly a billion checks and money orders each year, and it is also the largest mortgage-payment processor in the U.S.

But the electronic money transfers form the foundation of Western Union's business. The firm accounts for nearly 80 percent of these transfers in the U.S. Perhaps its most lucrative customers are workers from other countries—legal or illegal—who send home part of their paychecks to relatives. A Ukranian citizen who is working in Germany stops by the local Western Union office to send half his paycheck home. "It's quick, easy, and reliable," says his wife. "There's no messing about, and they never lose the money." Mexican migrant workers in the U.S. sent home $2.74 billion over a 90-day period last year, much of it via Western Union, which operates more than 7,000 locations in Mexico. Western Union charges fees on a sliding scale for each transfer, which is how it makes its money. For an extra charge of around $10, a messenger will deliver the cash directly to the recipient's door.

Many of the workers who use Western Union never open traditional bank accounts, relying on Western Union for their needs instead. Consequently, competitors such as Bank of America, Citigroup, Wells Fargo, and others are making efforts to attract this market by emphasizing their greater variety of banking services. But Western Union isn't flinching. Instead, the firm recently launched a marketing campaign with a new slogan, "Uniting People with Possibilities."

QUESTIONS FOR CRITICAL THINKING

1. In many parts of the world, cash is still king. So, how can Western Union continue to maintain its competitive advantage?

2. What types of services might a traditional bank offer in order to compete with Western Union?

Sources: Company Web site: http://www.westernunion.com, accessed January 12, 2005; Mitchell Pacelle and John Lyons, "Citigroup Courts a New Clientele: Mexican Workers," *The Wall Street Journal,* July 27, 2004, pp. A1, A12; "Can Western Union Keep on Delivering?" *BusinessWeek Online,* December 22, 2003, http://www.businessweek.com; Julie Rawe, "The Fastest Way to Make Money," *Time,* July 2003, pp. A6–A10.

---

face a financial squeeze as a result of its need for cash when sales lag, when the volume of its credit sales increases, or when customers are slow in making payments.

The cash inflows and outflows of a business are similar to those of a household. The members of a household may depend on weekly or monthly paychecks for income, but their expenditures vary greatly from one pay period to the next. The financial plan should indicate when the flows of funds entering and leaving the organization will occur and in what amounts.

A good financial plan also involves financial control, a process of checking actual revenues, costs, and expenses and comparing them against forecasts. If this process reveals significant differences between projected and actual figures, it is important to discover them early and take timely corrective action.

At Hickory Farms of Ohio, the financial plan carefully monitors the cost of each item that the firm sells, breaking costs down into raw materials, direct labor, and overhead. This breakdown allows the company to see if its supply chain spending is too high. Cost control is important because Hickory Farms's cash receipts are very seasonal. The firm's 720 retail outlets are open only during the holiday season, while its wholesale and direct sales units operate year round. Consequently, its cash receipts exceed its cash disbursements only during November through February. The company relies on bank loans to operate between March and October.[6]

Concept Check

1. What do financial managers do?
2. Which three executives report directly to the CFO?
3. What is the purpose of the financial control process?

Characteristics and Functions of Money

Playwright George Bernard Shaw once said that the lack of money is the root of all evil. Added comedian Woody Allen, "Money is better than poverty, if only for financial reasons." Most businesspeople would agree because money is the lubricant of contemporary business. Most of Western Union's business involves the transfer of money, as described in the Hits & Misses box.

money anything generally accepted as payment for goods and services.

Characteristics of Money

Money is anything generally accepted as payment for goods and services. Most early forms of money imposed a number of serious disadvantages on users. For example, a cow is a poor form of money for an owner who wants only a loaf of bread and some cheese. Exchanges based on money permit economic specialization and provide a general basis for purchasing power. To do this efficiently, money must have certain characteristics. It must be divisible, portable, durable, and difficult to counterfeit, and it should have a stable value.

They Said It

Money is power, freedom, a cushion, the root of all evil, the sum of all blessings.

—*Carl Sandburg (1878–1967) American poet*

Divisibility   A U.S. dollar is divided into cents, nickels, dimes, and quarters. The Canadian dollar is divided similarly, with 1-cent, 5-cent, 10-cent, and 25-cent coins. Mexico's nuevo peso is broken down into centavos (100 centavos equal one nuevo peso). People can easily exchange these forms of money for products ranging from a cup of coffee to automobiles. Today, most economic activity involves making and spending money.

Portability   The light weight of modern paper currency facilitates the exchange process. Portability is an important characteristic of paper currency, since a typical dollar bill changes hands around 400 times during its lifetime, staying in the average person's pocket or purse fewer than two days. Also, think about how much $100 in coins would weigh in your pocket or purse versus, say, five $20 bills.

Durability   U.S. dollar bills survive an average of 12 to 18 months, and they can be folded an average of 4,000 times without tearing. Coins, on the other hand, can last 30 years or longer. Most countries have replaced small denomination paper currency with coins. For instance, Canada replaced its $1 and $2 bills with $1 and $2 dollar coins (nicknamed the "loonie" and "toonie"). In the U.S., several attempts have been made to get Americans to switch to dollar coins. The latest attempt was the Sacajawea dollar launched with great fanfare. Demand for the new dollar coins never materialized, and most are no longer in circulation. Americans, it appears, are reluctant to give up the dollar bill—the greenback is one of the great icons of American culture.

Difficulty in Counterfeiting   Widespread distribution of counterfeit money undermines a nation's monetary system and economy by ruining the value of legitimate money. For this reason, governments consider counterfeiting a serious crime and take elaborate steps to prevent it. Among counterfeiters, U.S. currency is the most popular. In fact, the original purpose of the Secret Service was to track down counterfeiters. To increase the difficulty of counterfeiting U.S. currency in this age of sophisticated computers and color printers, the U.S. Treasury has redesigned paper bills. The new design adds a letter to each bill's serial number along with the seal of the Federal Reserve, larger portraits that are off-centered, and polymer threads that run vertically through the bills and glow under ultraviolet light. Recently, the Treasury began adding a second color to bills, making them even more difficult to counterfeit.

The U.S. Treasury is in the process of redesigning all U.S. paper currency to make the growing international problem of counterfeiting more difficult. The first bill to be redesigned was the $20—the denomination most frequently counterfeited in the U.S. (Foreign counterfeiters think bigger. Outside the U.S., the $100 bill is most likely to be bogus.) Changes include new background colors, special inks that are hard to reproduce, and inks that shift color when viewed from different angles.

The New Color of Money: Series 2004
Safer, Smarter, More Secure $20 Note — Face

www.moneyfactory.com/newmoney

Stability   Money should also maintain a relatively stable value. If the value of money fluctuates too much, people hesitate to use it. They begin to abandon it and look for safer means of storing their wealth. Businesses start to demand that bills be paid in other more stable currencies.

As part of a broad economic reform program, Argentina pegged the value of its currency, the peso, to the U.S. dollar in the early 1990s (one peso equaled one dollar). This policy worked well for a while as inflation fell sharply and economic growth accelerated. However, a strong U.S. dollar meant a strong peso. This made Argentinean products more expensive and hurt exports. The country's economy started to unravel. The government was forced to close banks and limit cash withdrawals. Finally, Argentina allowed its currency to float independently of the dollar. The peso promptly lost 70 percent of its value relative to the dollar as Argentineans scrambled to convert their pesos into dollars.

Functions of Money

FIGURE 17.2
Basic Functions of Money

As Figure 17.2 shows, money performs three basic functions. First, it serves primarily as a medium of exchange—a means of facilitating economic transactions and eliminating the need for a barter system. Second, it functions as a unit of account—a common standard for measuring the value of goods and services. Third, money acts as a temporary store of value—a way of keeping accumulated wealth until the owner needs it to make new purchases. Money offers one big advantage as a store of value: Its high liquidity allows people to obtain it and dispose of it in quick and easy transactions. Money is immediately available for purchasing products or paying debts. See the Best Business Practices box for a look at plastic as a substitute for cash.

Concept Check

1. What does it mean to say that money should be divisible?
2. What are some of the U.S. Treasury's strategies for increasing the difficulty of counterfeiting?

The Money Supply

Ask someone on the street to define the money supply, and he or she might answer that the money supply is the total value of all currency and coins in circulation. That answer, however, is only half right. One

BEST BUSINESS PRACTICES

Is This Fast Enough for You?

Can fast food get any faster? McDonald's and other fast-food chains like What-a-Burger think so. They are now offering customers the opportunity to pay for their meals with credit cards in a time-saving strategy other big food chains are expected to copy.

McDonald's, which has over 13,000 locations, has been testing the concept, and once it's widely implemented, it should make both the burger giant and its customers happy. Customers will place their orders at the counter or the drive-through, swipe their cards, and get approval for the purchase in under five seconds with no signature required. That's faster than cash, which takes about eight to 10 seconds, and far faster than the usual credit card transaction, which takes 25 to 30 seconds, according to a credit card industry newsletter. Speedy service is one of the competitive advantages food chains use to win customers from each other, and since McDonald's aims to complete each customer transaction within 90 seconds, the time savings will really matter in determining its standards of customer service.

Customers who use their credit cards for accumulating perks should be happy not just with the time savings but also with the opportunity to add convenience—and frequent flier miles or other benefits associated with their cards—to their dining experience. The typical fast-food customer gets an average of 16 meals a month at McDonald's or one of its competitors, and there are even more loyal customers who eat fast food up to 27 times a month. That could add up to a few thousand airline miles a year.

Improved processing speeds that cut the time for each transaction are what finally led McDonald's to adopt the use of credit cards. Fears that it would slow service held the company back even though other fast-food sales made on credit cards recently tripled.

QUESTIONS FOR CRITICAL THINKING
1. Why do you suppose credit card transactions can be processed faster than cash?
2. If credit cards can be used to pay for food, earn frequent flier miles, and save time, are they money? Do you think cash will ever become obsolete? Why or why not?

Sources: "Charging Fast Food," Cardweb.com, http://www.cardweb.com, accessed March 31, 2003; "McDonald's to Start Accepting Credit Cards for Burgers and Fries," *News Tribune*, November 27, 2002, http://www.newstribune.com; Shirley Leung and Ron Lieber, "The New Menu Option at McDonald's: Plastic," *The Wall Street Journal*, November 26, 2002, pp. D1, D2; "McDonald's to Accept Plastic," *CNN Money*, November 26, 2002, http://www.cnnmoney.com.

measure of the U.S. money supply consists of coins and currency as well as financial assets that also serve as a medium of exchange: traveler's checks, bank checking accounts, and other so-called **demand deposits** (such as NOW accounts and credit union share draft accounts). Government reports and business publications use the term **M1** to refer to the total value of coins, currency, traveler's checks, bank checking account balances, and the balances in other demand deposit accounts. The current components of M1 are shown in Figure 17.3.

Another broader definition of the money supply is also widely used. Called **M2,** this measure of the money supply includes M1 plus a number of other financial assets that are almost as liquid as cash but do not serve directly as a medium of exchange. These assets include various savings accounts, certificates of deposit, and money market mutual funds. Users must complete some sort of transaction before these assets can fulfill the functions of money.

In recent years, the use of credit cards—often referred to as *plastic money*—has significantly increased. Over the past 20 years, the amount of outstanding credit card debt has increased by more than five times. American consumers now carry over 1 billion credit cards. Businesses also use credit cards. As noted in Chapter 6, some entrepreneurs rely on credit cards to finance their new businesses.

MasterCard and Visa, issued by banks, dominate the credit card market, though the Discover Card has made some inroads into the market. In addition, American Express offers several credit cards. However, its flagship green American Express card is not really a credit card but rather a charge

They Said It
When I was young I used to think that money was the most important thing in life; now that I am older, I know it is.
—*Oscar Wilde (1854–1900)*
Anglo-Irish humorist and playwright

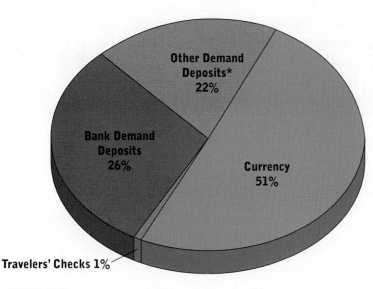

FIGURE 17.3
Components of M1

*Other demand deposits include accounts such as NOW accounts and share draft accounts (issued by credit unions).

Source: Federal Reserve, Federal Reserve Web site, http://www.federalreserve.gov, accessed March 24, 2003.

card; balances must be paid in full each month. Customers do not have the option of carrying a balance from month to month.

Even though all MasterCard and Visa credit cards are issued by banks, so-called *branded credit cards* have become popular in recent years. Corporations, not-for-profit organizations, and even college alumni associations have partnered with banks to issue branded credit cards. The partner receives a payment from the bank based on the amount charged. Branded cards often provide perks to the cardholder. For instance, holders of Shell Oil/Chase MasterCard receive a discount on purchases of Shell gasoline. An example of a branded credit card is shown in Figure 17.4.

In addition to offering branded credit cards, some retailers, such as Sears and Talbots, issue their own credit cards to customers. Typically, a retail credit card can be used to pay for purchases only at the retailer that issued the card; that is, a Talbots credit card can be used to pay only for purchases at a Talbots store, the Talbots catalog, or at Talbots.com. Credit cards are not only a means of stimulating retail sales, but they are often a retailer's best friend. During a recent recession, for instance, a number of well-known retailers generated a considerable portion of their profits from credit card interest and fees. In at least one case—electronics retail giant Circuit City—every cent of a recent year's earnings came from credit cards.[7]

Another recent trend has been the emergence of prepaid shopping cards. Consumers buy the cards in varying amounts and then use them to make purchases up to that amount. The cards are reusable, meaning that the consumer can put more money on them at any time. Some cards can even be used to make online purchases.

Although credit cards are convenient and easy to use, they are a very expensive source of business or consumer credit, with annual interest rates averaging over 16 percent. Another problem with credit cards is fraud. As discussed in Chapter 7, online purchases are especially vulnerable to fraud and cost credit card issuers and merchants billions of dollars each year. Several credit card issuers have

FIGURE 17.4
Branded credit cards provide benefits to the cardholder and to the organizations whose brands they carry. The holder of this card receives a discount on circus tickets.

begun issuing so-called "smart" credit cards. These cards contain a small microprocessor chip that stores information about the user, including the account number. The American Express Blue Card is one example of a smart card. Blue has an embedded computer chip that contains a unique digital certificate that acts much like a key. Those who want extra security when shopping on the Web swipe their cards through a special reader attached to their computers. After the cardholder enters his or her personal identification number, the certificate is read, and the necessary information to complete the purchase is transmitted securely.

Why Organizations Need Funds

Organizations require funds for many reasons. They need money to run day-to-day operations, compensate employees and hire new ones, pay for inventory, make interest payments on loans, pay dividends to shareholders, and purchase property, facilities, and equipment. A firm's financial plan identifies the amount and time of its specific cash needs. By comparing these needs with expenditures and expected cash receipts (from sales, payments made by credit purchasers, and other sources), financial managers determine precisely what additional funds they must obtain at any given time. If inflows exceed cash needs, financial managers invest the surplus. On the other hand, if inflows do not meet cash needs, they seek additional sources of funds. Figure 17.5 illustrates this process.

Generating Funds from Excess Cash

Many financial managers choose to invest the majority of their firms' excess cash balances in marketable securities. These financial instruments are very close to cash because they are, by definition, marketable and easy to convert into cash. Four of the most popular marketable securities are U.S. Treasury bills, commercial paper, repurchase agreements, and certificates of deposit.

Treasury bills are short-term securities issued by the U.S. Treasury and backed by the full faith and credit of the U.S. government. Treasury bills are sold with a maturity of either 30, 91, or 180 days and have a minimum denomination of $10,000. They are considered virtually risk-free and easy to resell. Commercial paper is securities sold by corporations, maturing anywhere from 1 to 270 days from the date of issue. Though slightly riskier than Treasury bills, commercial paper is generally still considered a low-risk security. Repurchase agreements, or repos, are an arrangement whereby one party sells a package of U.S. government securities to another party, agreeing to buy back, or repurchase, the securities at a higher price on a later date. Repos are also considered low-risk securities.

A certificate of deposit (CD) is a time deposit at a financial institution, such as a commercial bank, savings bank, or credit union. The sizes and maturity dates of CDs vary considerably and can often be tailored to meet the needs of purchasers. Assuming a depositor has less than $100,000 in total bank deposits, a CD is federally insured. CDs with denominations in excess of $100,000 are not federally insured but can be sold more easily prior to maturity.

Sources of Funds

To this point, the discussion has focused on only part of the definition of finance—the reasons organizations need funds and how they use them. A firm's financial plan must give equal importance, however, to the choice of the best sources of needed funds. Sources of funds fall into two categories: debt capital and equity capital.

Debt capital represents funds obtained through borrowing (referred to as debt financing in Chapter 6). **Equity capital** consists of funds provided by the firm's owners when they reinvest earnings, make additional contributions, liquidate assets, issue stock to the general public, or raise capital from venture capitalists and other investors (referred to as equity financing in Chapter 6). A firm also obtains equity capital whenever it makes a profit. For a look at the tax implications of these sources of cash, see the Solving an Ethical Controversy box.

Concept Check

1. Are savings accounts part of M1 or M2?
2. What is the difference between a charge card like the American Express card and a credit card?
3. What are two drawbacks of credit cards?

debt capital funds obtained through borrowing.

equity capital funds provided by the firm's owners when they reinvest earnings, make additional contributions, or issue stock to investors.

Concept Check

1. What are Treasury bills?
2. What is a certificate of deposit?

EXPENDITURES

- Day-to-Day Activities
- Inventory
- Dividends to Stockholders
- Purchases of Land, Facilities, and Equipment

If the firm has insufficient funds:
- Evaluate alternative sources for additional funds

CASH RECEIPTS

- Product Sales
- Payments from Credit Purchasers
- Sales of Stock
- Additional Funds from Venture Capitalists
- Private Placement Financing

If the firm has excess funds:
- Seek interest-producing investments

FIGURE 17.5
The Financial Planning Process

The Debate over Taxing Stock Dividends

Corporations pay taxes as high as 35 percent on their earnings. Until recently, when they paid dividends to shareholders from those earnings, the shareholders also paid income taxes on the dividends. Or if the company retained its earnings, shareholders were taxed when they sold their shares because the value of their shares had increased due to the retained earnings.

The result in either case was that corporate earnings were taxed twice, once at the corporate level and once at the shareholder level. The total tax paid added up to as much as 60 percent on dividend earnings and 48 percent on retained earnings.

The Bush administration believed this double taxation created a bias in financial markets, weighing against the payment of dividends and capital accumulation and leading companies to invest less, hold less capital stock, and pay lower wages. Under a recent $350 billion tax-cut bill President Bush

signed, taxes on income from dividends were cut to 15 percent (from as high as 38.6 percent) at the shareholder level, and the tax on capital gains from the sale of shares that have increased in value was also reduced to 15 percent (from 20 percent). The new capital gains rate applied to stocks held for over a year.

Was the corporate dividend tax cut a good idea?

PRO
1. Over half the U.S. population currently owns stock—either directly or indirectly through mutual funds and retirement plans.
2. Lowered taxes on dividends will put more money in consumers' hands and help stimulate the economy.

CON
1. The tax provided the government with up to $20 billion in needed annual revenue.

2. All provisions of the tax cut, taken together, reduced taxes proportionally more for the wealthy.

SUMMARY
Debates continue over the necessity and wisdom of dividend tax cuts. Opponents charge that deficits will skyrocket and the cuts favor wealthier Americans—who least need the money. Proponents argue that the cuts stimulated a sluggish economy, providing much-needed jobs. Time will tell on both counts.

Sources: Matt Krantz, "Dividend Tax Cut Not Luring Mob of Buyers," *USA Today,* July 7, 2003, p. B1; Dana Milbank and Jonathan Weisman, "Middle Class Tax Share Set to Rise," *Washington Post,* June 4, 2003, http://www.washingtonpost.com; Lisa Stein, "Top of the Week—Congress: Plump Paychecks?" *U.S. News & World Report,* June 2, 2003, http://www.usnews.com; "The President's Jobs and Growth Plan: Increasing Savings and Investment," http://www.whitehouse.gov/infocus/economy/save_investment.html, accessed May 5, 2003.

A company's cash needs vary from one time period to the next, and even an established firm may not generate sufficient funds from operations to cover all costs of a major expansion or a significant upgrade of equipment. In these instances, financial managers must evaluate the potential benefits and drawbacks of seeking funds by borrowing. As an alternative to borrowing, the firm may raise new equity capital. A financial manager's job includes determining the most cost-effective balance between equity and borrowed funds and the proper blend of short-term and long-term funds. Table 17.1 compares debt capital and equity capital on four criteria.

Different companies can take very different approaches to financing major investments. For example, both Wyeth (formerly known as American Home Products) and Johnson & Johnson have made a series of major investments in recent years. These include new products, joint ventures, and even acquiring other firms. Johnson & Johnson relies more on equity financing and internal funds to finance its large investments. For example, when Johnson & Johnson acquired biotech company Centocor for $5 billion, it used cash and stock to pay for the acquisition. On the other hand, Wyeth has tended to rely more heavily on debt financing. When it acquired American Cyanamid, for instance, Wyeth borrowed around $9 billion.

Short-Term Sources of Funds

Many times throughout a year, an organization may discover that its cash needs exceed its available funds. For example, retailers generate surplus cash for most of the year, but they need to build up inven-

Table 17.1   Comparison of Debt and Equity Capital

Criterion	Debt	Equity
Maturity	A contract specifies a date by which the borrower must repay the loan.	Securities specify no maturity dates.
Claim on assets	Lenders have prior claims on assets.	Stockholders have claims only after the firm satisfies the claims of lenders.
Claim on income	Lenders have prior claims on fixed interest payments, which must be paid before dividends can be paid to stockholders. Interest payments are a contractual obligation of the borrowing firm.	Stockholders have a residual claim after all creditors have been paid. Dividends are paid at the discretion of the board of directors; they are not a contractual obligation of the firm.
Right to a voice in management	Lenders are creditors, not owners. They have no voice in company affairs unless they do not receive interest payments.	Stockholders are the owners of the company, and most can voice preferences for its operation.

tory during the late summer and fall to get ready for the holiday shopping season. Consequently, they often need funds to pay for merchandise until holiday sales generate revenue. Then retailers use the incoming funds to repay the borrowed funds. In these instances, financial managers evaluate short-term sources of funds. By definition, short-term sources of funds are repaid within one year.

Three major sources of short-term funds exist: trade credit, short-term loans, and commercial paper. Trade credit is extended by suppliers when a firm receives goods or services, agreeing to pay for them at a later date. Short-term loans can be either unsecured (the borrower does not pledge any assets as collateral) or secured (specific assets such as inventory are pledged by the borrower as collateral). A major source of short-term loans is commercial banks. Commercial paper was briefly described earlier in the chapter. The interest cost on commercial paper is typically 1 or 2 percent lower than the interest rate on short-term bank loans, and firms can raise large amounts of money in the commercial paper market. However, only major firms with considerable financial strength and stability are able to sell commercial paper. GMAC—the financing subsidiary of General Motors—is the world's largest issuer of commercial paper.

Long-Term Sources of Funds

Funds from short-term sources can help a firm to meet current needs for cash or inventory. A larger need, however, such as acquiring another company or making a major investment in property or equipment, often requires funds for a much longer period of time. For instance, Freddie Mac (the Federal Home Loan Mortgage Corporation) recently raised around $3 billion in long-term funds to finance the purchase of home mortgage loans from banks and other lenders. Unlike short-term sources, long-term sources are repaid over many years.

Organizations acquire long-term funds from three sources. One is long-term loans obtained from financial institutions such as commercial banks, life insurance companies, and pension funds. A second source is **bonds**—certificates of indebtedness sold to raise long-term funds for firms and governments. A third source is equity financing acquired by selling stock in the company or reinvesting company earnings.

bonds certificates of indebtedness sold to raise long-term funds for a corporation or government agency.

Public Sale of Stocks and Bonds   Sales of stocks and bonds represent a major source of funds for corporations. Such sales provide cash inflows for the issuing firm and either a share in its ownership (for a stock purchaser) or a specified rate of interest and repayment at a stated time (for a bond purchaser). Because stock and bond issues of many corporations are traded in the securities

markets, stockholders and bondholders can easily sell these securities. Whether to issue stock or bonds to finance a firm's plans is an important decision discussed in more detail in Chapter 18.

Private Placements

Some new stock or bond issues may not be sold publicly but rather only to certain large investors such as pension funds and insurance companies. These sales are referred to as **private placements.** Most private placements involve corporate debt issues. In a typical year, about one-third of all new corporate debt issues are privately placed. It is often cheaper for a company to sell a security privately than publicly, and there is less government regulation with which to contend. Institutions buy private placements because they typically carry slightly higher interest rates than publicly issued bonds. In addition, the terms of the issue can be tailored to meet the specific needs of both the issuer and the institutional investors. Of course, the institutional investor gives up liquidity. Privately placed securities do not trade in securities markets.

Venture Capitalists

Venture capitalists are an important source of long-term financing, especially to new companies. **Venture capitalists** raise money from wealthy individuals and institutional investors and invest these funds in promising firms. Venture capitalists also provide management consulting advice as well as funds. In exchange for their investment, venture capitalists become part owners of the business. Should the business succeed, venture capitalists can earn substantial profits. For example, venture capital firm Benchmark Capital invested $5 million in eBay in exchange for 22 percent of the firm's stock. That investment is currently worth in excess of $7.5 billion.[8]

leverage technique of increasing the rate of return on an investment by financing it with borrowed funds.

Leverage

Raising needed cash by borrowing allows a firm to benefit from **leverage,** a technique of increasing the rate of return on funds invested through the use of borrowed funds. The key to managing leverage is ensuring that a company's earnings remain larger than its interest payments, which increases the leverage on the rate of return on shareholders' investment. Of course, if the company earns less than its interest payments, shareholders lose money on their original investments.

Table 17.2 shows two identical firms that choose to raise funds in different ways. Leverage Corporation obtains 90 percent of its funds from lenders who purchase company bonds. Equity Corporation raises all of its funds through the sale of company stock. Each company earns $30,000. Leverage Corporation pays $9,000 in interest to bondholders and earns a 210 percent return for its owners' $10,000 investment. By contrast, Equity Corporation provides only a 30 percent return on its shareholders' investment of $100,000.

As long as earnings exceed interest payments on borrowed funds, financial leverage allows a firm to increase the rate of return on its shareholders' investment. However, leverage also works in reverse. If, for example, Equity Corporation's earnings drop to $5,000, shareholders earn a 5 percent return on investment. Because Leverage Corporation must pay its bondholders $9,000 in interest, however, shareholders end up with a $4,000 loss. Another problem with borrowing money is that an overreliance on borrowed funds reduces management's flexibility in future financing decisions.

Concept Check

1. What are three sources of short-term funds?
2. What does a venture capitalist do?
3. What is leverage?

Table 17.2   How Leverage Works

Leverage Corporation		Equity Corporation	
Common stock	$ 10,000	Common stock	$100,000
Bonds (at 10% interest)	90,000	Bonds	0
	100,000		100,000
Earnings	30,000	Earnings	30,000
Less bond interest	9,000	Less bond interest	0
Net income/profit	21,000	Net income/profit	30,000
Return to stockholders	21,000 = 210%	Return to stockholders	30,000 = 30%
	$ 10,000		$100,000

The Financial System and Financial Institutions

Households, businesses, governments, financial institutions, and financial markets together form what is known as the financial system. The **financial system** is the process by which money flows from savers to users. A simple diagram of the financial system is shown in Figure 17.6.

On the left are savers—those with excess funds. For a variety of reasons, savers choose not to spend all of their current income, so they have a surplus of funds. Users are the opposite of savers; their spending needs exceed their current income, so they have a deficit. They need to obtain additional funds to make up the difference. Savings are provided by households, businesses, and governments. At the same time, borrowers also consist of households, businesses, and governments. Households need money to buy automobiles or homes. Businesses need money to purchase inventory or build new production facilities. Governments need money to build highways and new schools or to fund budget deficits.

Generally, in the U.S., households are net savers—meaning that in the aggregate they save more funds than they use—while businesses and governments are net users—meaning that they use more funds than they save. The fact that most of the net savings in the U.S. financial system are provided by households may be a bit of a surprise initially, since Americans do not have the reputation of being very thrifty. Yet, even though the savings rate of American households is low compared with those of other countries, American households still save hundreds of billions of dollars each year.

Two ways exist in which funds can be transferred between savers and users. One is through the financial markets. Whenever, for example, a company sells stocks or bonds publicly or privately, funds are being transferred between savers and users. Savers expect to receive some sort of return from the company for the use of their money. The role and functioning of the financial markets will be described in more depth in the next chapter.

The second way in which funds can be transferred is through financial institutions, such as commercial banks. For instance, whenever a consumer or business deposits money into a bank account, money is being transferred indirectly to users. The bank pools customer deposits and uses the funds to make loans to businesses and consumers. These borrowers pay the bank interest and it, in turn, pays depositors interest for the use of their money.

Financial institutions greatly increase the efficiency and effectiveness of the transfer of funds between savers and users. Because of financial institutions, savers earn more, and users pay less, than they would without financial institutions. Indeed, it is difficult to imagine how a modern economy could function without well-developed financial institutions. Think about how difficult it would be for a businessperson to obtain inventory financing, or a consumer to purchase a new home, without financial institutions. Prospective borrowers would have to identify and negotiate with each saver individually.

Traditionally, financial institutions have been classified into **depository institutions**—institutions that accept deposits that customers can withdraw on demand—and nondepository institutions. Examples of depository institutions include commercial banks, savings banks, and credit unions. Nondepository institutions include life insurance companies and pension funds.

financial system process by which funds are transferred from savers to users.

depository institutions financial institutions that accept deposits that can be converted into cash on demand.

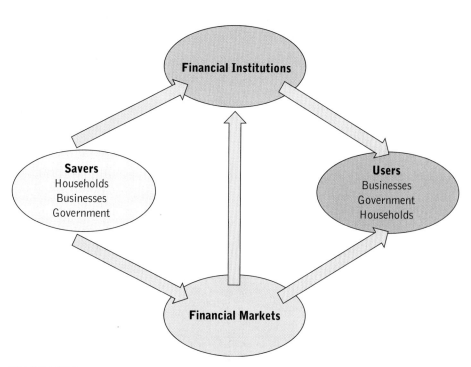

FIGURE 17.6

Overview of the Financial System and Its Components

Commercial Banks

Commercial banks are the largest and probably most important financial institution in the U.S. and in most other countries as well. In the U.S., the approximately 7,900 commercial banks have total assets of almost $7 trillion.[9] Examples of major U.S. commercial banks include Bank of America, Citibank, Fleet Financial, and Wells Fargo. Commercial banks offer the most services of any financial institution. These services include a wide range of checking and savings deposit accounts, consumer loans, credit cards, home mortgage loans, business loans, and trust services. Commercial banks also have permission to offer other products, including securities and insurance.

Although 7,900 may sound like a lot of banks, the number of banks has actually declined dramatically in recent years. At the same time, banks have gotten larger: Today, the typical commercial bank is about five times larger than it was 10 years ago. Both changes can be explained by the fact that larger banks are buying smaller banks. In a recent year, almost 700 banks were acquired by other banks. The consolidation of the banking industry is controversial. Larger banks, some contend, charge higher fees and offer a lower level of personal service than smaller banks. Others argue that larger banks are financially stronger and more efficient.

How Banks Operate   Banks raise funds by offering a variety of checking and savings deposits to customers. The banks then pool these deposits and lend most of them out in the form of a variety of consumer and business loans. Banks currently hold around $4.5 trillion in deposits and have almost $4 trillion in outstanding loans.[10] The distribution of outstanding loans is shown in Figure 17.7. As the figure shows, banks lend a great deal of money to both households and businesses for a variety of purposes. Commercial banks are an especially important source of funds for small businesses.

Banks make money primarily because the interest rate they charge borrowers is higher than the rate of interest they pay depositors. In one recent year, banks collected over $400 billion in interest from loans and other investments and paid out almost $200 billion to depositors. Banks also make money from other sources, such as fees charged to customers for checking accounts and using automated teller machines. In fact, the fees banks collect have risen sharply and now account for approximately 30 percent of bank profits.[11]

Electronic Banking   More and more funds each year move through **electronic funds transfer systems (EFTS),** computerized systems for conducting financial transactions over electronic links. Millions of businesses and consumers now pay bills and receive payments electronically. Most employers, for example, directly deposit employee paychecks in their bank accounts rather than issue employees paper checks. Today, nearly all Social Security checks and other federal payments arrive as electronic data rather than paper documents.

One of the original forms of electronic banking, the automated teller machine (ATM) continues to grow in popularity. ATMs allow customers to make banking transactions 24 hours a day, seven days a week by inserting an electronic card into the machine and entering a personal identification number. Networked systems enable ATM users to access their bank accounts in distant states and even throughout the world. In the U.S. alone, over 200,000 ATMs are in operation, processing in excess of 11 billion transactions annually.[12]

Most banks now offer customers debit cards—also called check cards—which allow customers to pay for purchases directly from their checking or savings account. A debit card looks like a credit card but acts like a check and replaces the customer's ATM card. Several large retailers—including Target, Wal-Mart, and Walgreen's—have installed special terminals that allow customers to use their ATM or debit cards to make purchases. Customers are required to enter their personal identification numbers and can often get cash back. Consumers enjoy the convenience of this feature, while at the same time, it eliminates the problem of bad checks for retailers.

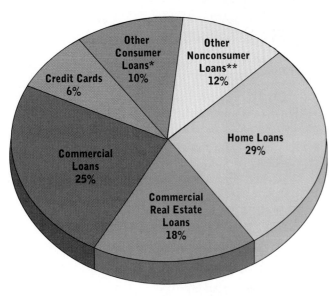

FIGURE 17.7

Types of Outstanding Bank Loans
*Other consumer loans include auto and student loans.
**Other nonconsumer loans include loans to governments and not-for-profit organizations.

Source: FDIC, FDIC Web site, http://www.fdic.gov, accessed March 24, 2003.

Online Banking Today, almost 1 out of every 5 U.S. households does some or all of its banking on the Internet. By 2010, these numbers will grow to 1 in 3 households. Over 80 percent of all U.S. banks offer some online services.[13] Two types of online banks exist: Internet-only banks (such as NetBank) and traditional brick-and-mortar banks with Web sites (such as First Union and Sun Trust). A major reason people are attracted to online banking is convenience. Customers can transfer money, check account balances, and pay bills 24 hours a day, seven days a week on their PCs.

Online banking offers conveniences such as 24-hour access to account information and the ability to transfer money to different accounts. Many banks now offer online bill paying as a convenience to their customers. Wells Fargo is a traditional bank that has expanded its services to include online banking.

Bank Regulation

Banks are among the nation's most heavily regulated businesses. The main purpose of bank regulation is to ensure public confidence in the safety and security of the banking system. Banks are critical to the overall functioning of the economy. In fact, many believe that one of the causes of the Great Depression was the collapse of the banking system starting in the late 1920s.

Who Regulates Banks? All banks are either state or federally chartered. The majority of banks are state chartered; however, federally chartered banks tend to be larger and control over 60 percent of banking assets. State chartered banks are regulated by the appropriate state banking authorities, while federally chartered banks are regulated by the Federal Reserve, the Federal Deposit Insurance Corporation, and the Comptroller of the Currency. Further, state banks that are federally insured—and virtually all are—are also subject to FDIC regulation.

Banks are subject to periodic examination by state and/or federal regulators. These audits are designed to ensure that the bank is following safe and sound banking practices and is complying with all applicable regulations. Bank examinations include the review of detailed reports on the bank's operating and financial condition, as well as on-site inspections.

Federal Deposit Insurance A cornerstone of bank regulation is deposit insurance. Deposits up to a set amount—currently $100,000 per depositor—are insured by the FDIC. Deposit insurance means that, in the event the bank fails, depositors are paid in full by the FDIC, up to $100,000. Federal deposit insurance was enacted by the Banking Act of 1933 as one of the measures designed to restore public confidence in the banking system. Before deposit insurance, so-called "runs" were common as people rushed to withdraw their money from a bank, often just on a rumor that the bank was in precarious financial condition. At some point, the bank was unable to meet withdrawal demands and closed its doors. Remaining depositors often lost most of the money they had in the bank. Deposit insurance shifts the risk of bank failures from individual depositors to the FDIC. While banks still fail today, those with insured deposits are paid in full by the FDIC.

Recent Changes in Banking Laws In addition to establishing the FDIC, Depression-era banking legislation also put restrictions on the kinds of activities in which banks could engage,

Online Banking Basics

Online banking is the fastest-growing Internet application around—there are more than 38 million users and counting. Online banking includes managing your money, paying your bills, and automatically keeping track of your bank accounts from the convenience of your own computer. If you haven't jumped into the river of online access yet, here are a few things to remember while banking online.

Most banks offer an online tutorial to get you started when you open an online account. Be sure to take this tutorial to familiarize yourself with the site and the features. Most online banking features include viewing your account, paying bills, transferring funds, and seeing images of your canceled checks. Additional features may include setting up automatic bill payments, applying for loans or credit cards, and using money management software such as Quicken with your online account.

Security is of utmost importance for the bank as well as for you. Most banks have security policies in place, so be sure to read them carefully. At the minimum, your bank should be using Secure Socket Layer (SSL) encryption technology. If the security policy is not readily available on the bank's Web site, be sure to ask your bank about its security measures and how they work; the steps you should take to protect your personal information; and their policy for any unauthorized activity.

Another way to keep your account secure is to select a randomly generated PIN code instead of something familiar such as a birth date or an anniversary date. Codes that combine numbers and letters are the hardest to crack, and be sure to change them often. In addition, regularly log in to your account and scan for unauthorized transactions. It's your money, and you are ultimately responsible for it, so keep an eye on all activity.

Depending on the bank, you may also be able to use a comprehensive service such as Yahoo!Finance, Quicken, or MSN Money to manage your banking business. These services allow you to manage your online activities (banking, e-mail, and paying bills) all in one place. "Check" it out!

Sources: David van den Berg, "Belleville, Ill., Customers Get Hooked on Online Banking Services," *Knight Ridder/Tribune Business News,* June 16, 2003; "Online Banking Adoption Still Stymied by Consumer Security Fears; TowerGroup ViewPoint Underscores Need for Banks to Educate Customers on Security Measures, Policies," *PR Newswire,* June 3, 2003; Robert Moritz, "Is Online Banking for You?" *Parade Magazine,* May 18, 2003, pp. 25–26; Richard Craver, "Consumers' Use of Online Banking Growing; 38 Million Pay Online, Studies Show," *Knight Ridder/Tribune Business News,* May 6, 2003; "Online Banking Use Up 164 Percent Since 2000," *Teller Vision,* April 2003, p. 4.

including restricting their role in the securities markets. Believing that some of these restrictions were outdated, Congress recently passed a law that allows banks to enter the securities and insurance businesses. In return, other financial services firms are now allowed to offer banking services. Some banks have begun to expand into the securities and insurance businesses, but it is still too early to tell what the ultimate outcome of these new regulations will be.

Savings Banks and Credit Unions

While commercial banks are by far the largest depository financial institution in the U.S., savings banks and credit unions are also important financial institutions. Today, savings banks and credit unions offer many of the same services as commercial banks.

Savings banks used to be called savings and loan associations or thrift institutions. They were originally established in the early 1800s to make home mortgage loans. Savings and loans raised funds by accepting only savings deposits and then lent these funds to consumers to buy homes. Today, there are slightly less than 1,500 savings banks with total assets of over $1.3 trillion.[14] While the typical savings bank offers many of the same services as a commercial bank, including checking accounts, savings banks are not major lenders to businesses. Over 70 percent of their outstanding loans are still home mortgage loans. Washington Mutual, the nation's largest savings bank with over $300 billion in assets, is also the nation's largest mortgage lender. Deposits in savings banks are now FDIC insured, and savings banks are regulated in much the same way as commercial banks.

Credit unions are unique financial institutions. They are cooperative financial institutions that are owned by their depositors, all of whom are members. Almost 80 million Americans belong to one of the nation's approximately 10,000 credit unions. Combined, credit unions have over $450 billion in assets.[15] By law, credit union members must share similar occupations, employers, or membership in certain organizations. This law effectively caps the size of credit unions. In fact, the nation's largest bank, Bank of America, has more assets than all credit unions combined. Four of every five credit union members belong to an occupational- or employer-based credit union. The Navy Federal Credit Union is the largest credit union in the country, with over 700,000 members.

Credit unions are designed to serve consumers, not businesses. Credit unions raise funds by offering members a number of demand and saving deposits—checking accounts at credit unions are referred to as share draft accounts—and then, in turn, lend these funds to members. Because credit unions are not-for-profit institutions, they often pay savers higher rates of interest, charge lower rates of interest on loans, and have fewer fees than other financial institutions. Credit unions can have either state or federal charters, and deposits are insured by a federal agency.

Nondepository Financial Institutions

Nondepository financial institutions accept funds from businesses and households, much of which they then invest. Generally, these institutions do not offer checking accounts or other types of demand deposits. Three examples of nondepository financial institutions are insurance companies, such as New York Life, pension funds, such as the California Public Employee Retirement Fund (CalPERS), and finance companies, such as Household Finance.

Insurance Companies   Households and businesses buy insurance to transfer risk from themselves to the insurance company. The insurance company accepts the risk in return for a series of payments, called *premiums*. In the insurance industry, **underwriting** is the process used by insurance companies to determine whom to insure and what to charge. During a typical year, insurance companies collect more in premiums than they pay in claims. After paying operating expenses, this difference is invested. Insurance companies are a major source of short- and long-term financing for businesses. Life insurance companies alone have total assets exceeding $3.3 trillion, much of which is invested in corporate securities and real estate.[16]

Pension Funds   Pension funds provide retirement benefits to workers and their families. They are set up by employers and are funded by regular contributions made by employers and employees. Because pension funds have predictable long-term cash inflows and very predictable cash outflows, they invest heavily in long-term assets, such as common stocks. By some estimates, over 25 percent of all common stocks are owned by pension funds. In total, pension funds have close to $6.5 trillion in assets.[17] CalPERS alone has total assets in excess of $133 billion, $83 billion of which is invested in common stocks. The giant retirement fund serves over 1.3 million current California state employees and around 350,000 retirees.[18]

Finance Companies   Consumer and commercial finance companies offer short-term loans to borrowers. A commercial finance company supplies short-term funds to businesses that pledge tangible assets such as inventory, accounts receivable, machinery, or property as collateral for the loan. A consumer finance company plays a similar role for consumers. GMAC does both. It finances dealer purchases of automobiles from General Motors and also finances consumer purchases of automobiles from dealers. Finance companies raise funds by selling securities or borrowing funds from commercial banks.

Federal Reserve System (Fed) central bank of the United States.

Concept Check

1. What is electronic funds transfer?
2. How does federal deposit insurance work?
3. What is the function of pension funds and how do they work?

The Federal Reserve System

Created in 1913, the **Federal Reserve System,** or **Fed,** is the central bank of the U.S. and is an important part of the nation's financial system. The Fed has four basic responsibilities: regulating commercial banks, performing banking-related activities for the U.S. Treasury, servicing member banks, and setting monetary policy. Not all banks belong to the Fed. Banks with federal charters are required to belong to the Fed, but membership is optional for state chartered banks. Because the largest banks in the country are all federally chartered, the bulk of banking assets is controlled by Fed members. The Fed acts as the banker's bank for members. It provides wire transfer facilities, clears checks, replaces worn-out currency, and even lends banks money.

Organization of the Federal Reserve System

The nation is divided into 12 federal reserve districts, each with its own federal reserve bank. Each district bank supplies banks within its district with currency and facilitates the clearing of checks. District banks are run by a nine-member board of directors, headed by a president.

The governing body of the Fed is the board of governors. The board consists of seven members, including a chair and vice chair, appointed by the president and confirmed by the Senate. The chair of the board of governors is a very important position. Some have commented, only half jokingly, that the Fed chair is the second most powerful person in the nation.

The Fed is designed to be politically independent. Fed governors are appointed to 14-year terms that are staggered in such a way that a president could not appoint a majority of members during a single term. The Fed also has its own sources of revenue and does not depend on congressional appropriations.

An important part of the Fed is the Federal Open Markets Committee (FOMC). The FOMC is responsible for setting most policies concerning monetary policy and interest rates. It consists of 12 members—the seven Fed board governors plus five representatives of the district banks who serve on a rotating basis. The Fed chair is also chair of the FOMC.

Check Clearing and the Fed

As mentioned earlier, one of the Fed's responsibilities is to help facilitate the clearing of checks. Even in this age of electronic and online banking, Americans still write billions of paper checks each year. The clearing of a check is the process by which funds are transferred from the check writer to the recipient.

Assume the owner of Gulf View Townhouses of Tampa buys a $1,000 lawn mower from the local Home Depot and writes a check. If Home Depot has an account at the same bank as Gulf View, the bank will clear the check in house. It will decrease the balance in the owner's account by $1,000 and increase the balance in Home Depot's account by $1,000. If Home Depot has an account at another bank in Tampa, the two banks may still clear the check directly with one another. This process is cumbersome, however, so it is more likely that the banks will use the services of a local check clearinghouse.

On the other hand, if Home Depot has its account with a bank in another state—perhaps in Atlanta where Home Depot is based—the check will likely be cleared through the Federal Reserve System. Home Depot will deposit the check in its Atlanta bank account. Its bank, in turn, will deposit the check in the Federal Reserve Bank of Atlanta. The Atlanta Federal Reserve Bank will present the check to Gulf View's bank for payment, which pays the check by deducting $1,000 from Gulf View's account. The journey of a check through the Federal Reserve System is shown in Figure 17.8. Regardless of the method used, it is Fed policy that all checks should clear within two business days.

Monetary Policy

monetary policy
managing the growth rate in the supply of money and credit, usually through the use of interest rates.

The Fed's most important function is controlling the supply of money and credit, or **monetary policy.** The Fed's job is to make sure that the money supply grows at an appropriate rate, allowing the economy to expand and inflation to remain in check. If the money supply grows too slowly, economic growth will slow, unemployment will rise, and the risk of a recession will increase. If the money supply grows too rapidly, inflationary pressures will build. The Fed uses its policy tools to push interest rates up or down. If the Fed pushes interest rates up, the growth rate in the money supply will slow, economic growth will moderate, and inflationary pressures will ease. If the Fed pushes interest rates down, the growth rate in the money supply will increase, economic growth will pick up, and unemployment will fall. The Fed has three major policy tools: reserve requirements, the discount rate, and open market operations.

The Fed requires that banks maintain reserves—defined as cash in their vaults plus deposits at district Federal Reserve banks or at other banks—equal to some percentage of what the banks hold in

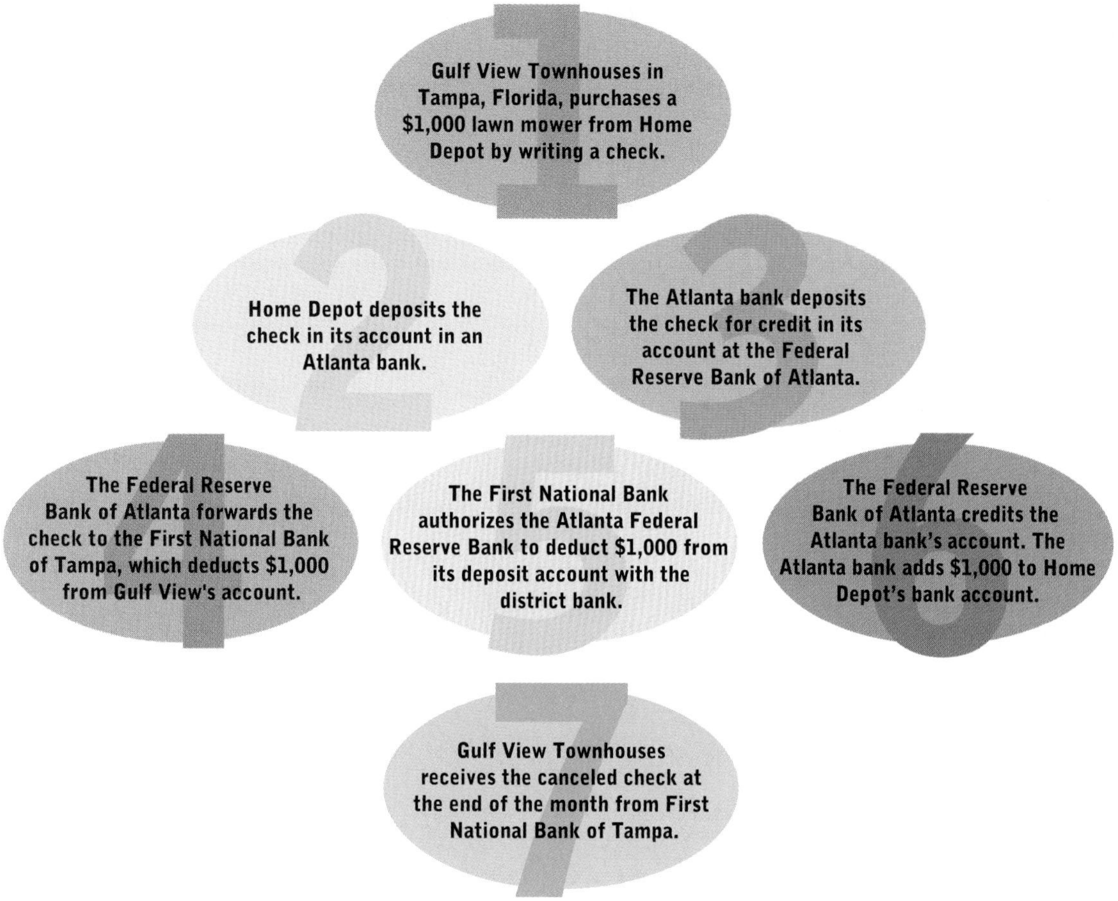

Gulf View Townhouses in Tampa, Florida, purchases a $1,000 lawn mower from Home Depot by writing a check.

Home Depot deposits the check in its account in an Atlanta bank.

The Atlanta bank deposits the check for credit in its account at the Federal Reserve Bank of Atlanta.

The Federal Reserve Bank of Atlanta forwards the check to the First National Bank of Tampa, which deducts $1,000 from Gulf View's account.

The First National Bank authorizes the Atlanta Federal Reserve Bank to deduct $1,000 from its deposit account with the district bank.

The Federal Reserve Bank of Atlanta credits the Atlanta bank's account. The Atlanta bank adds $1,000 to Home Depot's bank account.

Gulf View Townhouses receives the canceled check at the end of the month from First National Bank of Tampa.

FIGURE 17.8
A Check's Journey through the Federal Reserve System

deposits. For example, if the Fed sets the reserve requirement at 5 percent, a bank that receives a $500 deposit must reserve $25, so it has only $475 to invest or lend. By changing the reserve requirement, the Fed can affect the amount of money available for making loans. The higher the reserve requirement, the less banks can lend to consumers and businesses. The lower the reserve requirement, the more banks can lend. Because any change in the reserve requirement can have a sudden and dramatic impact on the money supply, the Fed rarely uses this tool. In fact, the Fed has not changed reserve requirements in over 10 years. Reserve requirements for demand deposit accounts range from 4 to 10 percent, depending on the size of the account.

Another policy tool is the so-called **discount rate,** the interest rate at which Federal Reserve banks make short-term loans to member banks. A bank might need a short-term loan if transactions leave it short of reserves. If the Fed wants to slow the growth rate in the money supply, it will increase the discount rate. This increase will make it more expensive for banks to borrow funds. Banks will, in turn, raise the interest rates they charge on loans to consumers and businesses. The end result will be a slowdown in economic activity. Lowering the discount rate will have the opposite effect.

The third policy tool, and the one most often used, is **open market operations,** the technique of controlling the money supply growth rate by buying or selling U.S. Treasury securities. If the Fed buys Treasury securities, the money it pays enters circulation, increasing the money supply and lowering interest rates. When the Fed sells Treasury securities, money is taken out of circulation and interest rates rise. When the Fed uses open market operations, it employs the so-called **federal funds rate**—the rate at which banks lend money to one another overnight—as its benchmark. Table 17.3 illustrates how the tools used by the Federal Reserve can stimulate or slow the economy.

Table 17.3   Federal Reserve Tools

General Tool	Action	Effect on Money Supply	Short-Term Effect on the Economy
Reserve requirement change	Increase reserve requirements	Reduces money supply	Boosts interest rates and slows economic activity
	Decrease reserve requirements	Increases money supply	Reduces interest rates and accelerates economic activity
Discount rate change	Increase discount rate	Reduces money supply	Boosts interest rates and slows economic activity
	Decrease discount rate	Increases money supply	Reduces interest rates and accelerates economic activity
Open market operation	Buy government securities	Increases money supply	Reduces interest rates and accelerates economic activity
	Sell government securities	Reduces money supply	Boosts interest rates and slows economic activity
Selective Credit Controls			
Margin requirement change	Increase margin requirements		Reduces credit purchases of securities with a negative impact on prices and trading activity on securities exchanges
	Decrease margin requirements		Increases credit purchases of securities with a positive impact on prices and trading activity on securities exchanges

The Federal Reserve also has the authority to exercise selective credit controls when it feels the economy is growing too rapidly or too slowly. These credit controls include the power to set margin requirements—the percentage of the purchase price of a security that an investor must pay in cash on credit purchases of stocks or bonds.

Transactions in international markets also affect the U.S. money supply. On the foreign exchange market, purchases and sales swap one nation's currency for that of another country. Billions of U.S. dollars are traded this way every day. The Fed can lower the exchange value of the dollar by selling dollars and buying foreign currencies, and it can raise the dollar's exchange value by doing the opposite—buying dollars and selling foreign currencies. When the Fed buys foreign currencies, the effect is the same as buying securities because it increases the U.S. banking system's reserves. Selling foreign currencies, on the other hand, is like selling securities because it reduces bank reserves.

Concept Check

1. How many federal reserve districts are there?
2. What is the governing body of the Fed?
3. What is meant by check clearing?

U.S. Financial Institutions: A Global Perspective

Financial institutions have become a global industry, and any review should consider U.S. financial institutions in their international context. Major U.S. banks—such as Fifth Third and J.P. Morgan Chase—have extensive international operations. They have offices, lend money, and accept deposits from customers throughout the world. According to recent statistics, U.S. banks have around $175 billion in outstanding loans to international customers.[19]

Only 3 of the 20 largest banks in the world (measured by total assets) are U.S. institutions: Bank of America, Citibank, and J.P. Morgan Chase. The other 17 are based in France, Germany, Holland,

© AP/Wide World Photos

Iraq's central banking system collapsed with the fall of Saddam Hussein. Its old central bank printed and distributed money at the dictator's bidding. The entire banking system is being rebuilt.

Japan, Switzerland, and the United Kingdom. The world's largest bank—Japan's Mizuko Group—has around $1.3 trillion in assets. These international banks also operate worldwide, including in the U.S.

Virtually all nations have some sort of a central bank, similar to the U.S. Federal Reserve. Canada's central bank, for example, is the Bank of Canada. Germany's central bank is the Bundesbank. These central banks play roles much like the Fed, such as controlling the money supply. Policymakers at other nations' central banks often respond to changes in the U.S. financial system by making similar changes in their own systems. For example, if the Fed pushes U.S. interest rates lower, central banks in Japan and Europe may also push their interest rates lower. These changes can influence events in countries around the world. Lower U.S. and European interest rates not only decrease the cost of borrowing for U.S. and European firms, but they also increase the amount of money available for loans to borrowers in Australia and Chile.

International banks and other providers of financial services play important roles in global business. They help to transfer purchasing power from buyers to sellers and from lenders to borrowers. They also provide credit to importers and reduce the risk associated with changes in exchange rates.

What's Ahead

This chapter introduced the finance function of contemporary business. Finance deals with the planning, obtaining, and managing of a company's funds to accomplish its objectives effectively and efficiently. The chapter also described the role of money, where and how firms obtain funds, and the financial system. The final chapter of *Contemporary Business* explores how securities—stocks and bonds—are bought and sold. It describes the investment characteristics of stocks and bonds and the methods investors use to choose specific securities. It outlines how securities' market regulations protect investors.

Concept Check

1. What are some of the functions of U.S. banks with international operations?

2. What are some international counterparts to the Fed and how do they operate?

DID YOU KNOW?

1. Items that have served as money include fishhooks, tea, shells, feathers, salt (from which came the word "salary" and the expression "being worth one's salt"), shark teeth, cocoa beans, and woodpecker scalps.

2. About 900 U.S. banks have failed since 1987.

3. About $7 billion in coins are out of circulation in the U.S.—almost $70 per household—because they are stashed away in people's homes. The U.S. Mint produces $52.5 million in coins every day just to keep up with circulation demands.

4. The rate of interest on your student loan is determined, in part, by bankers in Zurich and London.

5. Filings for personal bankruptcy have reached a record of 1.5 million annually, accounting for about 98 percent of all bankruptcies.

6. Prepaid cash cards from stores like Starbucks and 7-Eleven save retailers millions of dollars a year in bank fees for processing cash.

Summary of Learning Goals

1

Identify the functions performed by a firm's financial managers.

The major responsibility of financial managers is to develop and implement a financial plan for their organization. The firm's financial plan is based on forecasts of expenditures and receipts for a specified period and reflects the timing of cash inflows and outflows. Financial managers systematically determine their companies' need for funds during the period and the most appropriate sources from which it can obtain them. In short, the financial manager is responsible for both raising and spending money.

2

Describe the characteristics a form of money should have and list the functions of money.

Money should be divisible, portable, durable, stable in value, and difficult to counterfeit. Money used in modern economies has all of these characteristics. The functions of money are to serve as a medium of exchange; unit of account, or common standard for valuing goods and services; and store of value, or method of accumulating wealth.

3

Explain each of the various measures of the money supply.

The two most commonly used measures of the money supply are M1 and M2. M1 is defined as anything generally accepted in payment for goods and services, such as coins, paper money, and checks. M2 consists of M1 plus other assets that are almost as liquid as money but that do not function directly as a medium of exchange, such as savings deposits and money market mutual funds.

4

Explain how a firm uses funds.

Organizations use funds to run their day-to-day operations, pay for inventories, make interest payments on loans, pay dividends to shareholders, and purchase land, facilities, and equipment. If a firm finds itself with a surplus of cash, most financial managers choose to invest that excess cash in marketable securities.

5

Compare the two major sources of funds for a business.

Debt capital and equity capital are the two major sources from which businesses acquire funds. Debt capital represents funds obtained through borrowing. Equity capital comes from several sources, including the sale of stock, additional investments by the firm's owners, and previous earnings reinvested in the firm.

6

Identify the likely sources of short- and long-term funds.

Sources of short-term funds include trade credit (generated automatically through open-account purchases from suppliers), unsecured loans, secured loans (for which the firm must pledge collateral), and sales of commercial paper by large, financially sound firms. Sources of long-term funds include long-term loans repaid over one year or longer, bonds, and equity funds (ownership obtained from selling stock, accumulating additional contributions from owners, or reinvesting earnings in the firm).

7

Describe the financial system and the major financial institutions.

The financial system is the process by which funds are transferred between savers and users of funds. Funds can be transferred either through the financial markets or through financial institutions. Depository institutions—commercial banks, savings banks, and credit unions—accept deposits from customers that can be redeemed on demand. Depository institutions are closely regulated by state and federal authorities. Nondepository institutions include pension funds and insurance companies. Nondepository institutions invest a large portion of their funds in stocks, bonds, and real estate.

8 Explain the functions of the Federal Reserve System and the tools it uses to control the money supply.

The Federal Reserve System is the central bank of the U.S. The Federal Reserve regulates banks, performs banking functions for the U.S. Treasury, and acts as the banker's bank (clearing checks, lending money to banks, and replacing worn-out currency). It controls the supply of credit and money in the economy to promote growth and control inflation. The Federal Reserve's tools include reserve require-

ments, the discount rate, and open market operations. Selective credit controls and purchases and sales of foreign currencies also help the Federal Reserve manage the economy.

9 Describe the global financial system.

Large U.S. banks and other financial institutions have a global presence. They accept deposits, make loans, and have branches throughout the world. Foreign banks also operate throughout the world. The average European or Japanese bank is much larger than the average American bank. Virtually all nations have central banks that perform the same roles as the U.S. Federal Reserve System. Central bankers often act together raising and lowering interest rates as economic conditions warrant.

Business Terms You Need to Know

finance 546

financial manager 546

chief financial officer (CFO) 546

financial plan 547

money 549

debt capital 553

equity capital 553

bonds 555

leverage 556

financial system 557

depository institutions 557

Federal Reserve System (Fed) 561

monetary policy 562

Other Important Business Terms

vice president for financial management 546

treasurer 546

controller 546

risk–return trade-off 547

demand deposits 551

M1 551

M2 551

private placements 556

venture capitalists 556

electronic funds transfer systems (EFTS) 558

underwriting 561

discount rate 563

open market operations 563

federal funds rate 563

Review Questions

1. Define *finance*. Briefly explain the risk–return trade-off in finance.

2. What is a financial plan? When building a financial plan, what three questions have to be answered?

3. What characteristics should money have? List the three functions of money.

4. Explain the difference between M1 and M2. What is a demand deposit?

5. What are some of the reasons organizations need funds? What do many companies do if they find themselves having excess cash?

6. What is the difference between debt capital and equity capital? List several examples of each.

7. What is the financial system? By what two ways are funds transferred between savers and users?

8. Explain the difference between a depository and a nondepository financial institution. Give several examples of each type.

9. Briefly outline how a commercial bank operates. Why is deposit insurance so important?

10. How is the Federal Reserve System organized? What are the three policy tools the Fed can use to control the supply of money and credit?

Projects and Applications

1. Assume you would like to start a business. Put together a rough financial plan that addresses the three financial planning questions listed in the text.

2. Your business has really taken off but now needs a big infusion of new capital. A venture capital firm has agreed to invest the money you need. In return, the venture capital firm will own 75 percent of the business. You will be replaced as board chairman and CEO, though retaining the title of company founder and president, and the venture capital firm will hire a new CEO. Would you be willing to take the money but lose control of your business? Give your reasons.

3. The owner of your company is trying to decide how to raise an additional $1.5 million, and she has asked for your advice about whether the firm should use debt capital or equity capital. Prepare a brief memo to the owner outlining the advantages and disadvantages of both debt capital and equity capital. Be sure to explain the concept of leverage. Assume your company can borrow $1.5 million at an annual interest rate of 6 percent. It currently has $1.5 million in equity and no debt.

4. Compared to most businesses, is a bank more vulnerable to failure? Why or why not? Why does federal deposit insurance help protect the soundness of the banking system?

5. As noted in the chapter, the U.S. Federal Reserve System is politically independent. How is the Fed politically independent? Do you think it should remain so?

Experiential Exercise

Background: You learned in this chapter and in the previous one about investors, creditors, accountants, the accounting process, financial statements, budgeting, and other aspects of what's involved in a company's management of its financial assets. This chapter's exercise will test how much you know about the common denominator in all of these topics: money.

Directions: In the answer column, write the letter for the individual pictured on the front of each denomination of currency listed.

Number	Answer	Denomination	Letter	Picture
1.		$1	A.	Ulysses S. Grant (18th U.S. president)
2.		$2	B.	George Washington (1st U.S. president)
3.		$5	C.	Benjamin Franklin (American scientist and statesman)
4.		$10	D.	Abraham Lincoln (16th U.S. president)
5.		$20	E.	Thomas Jefferson (3rd U.S. president)
6.		$50	F.	Alexander Hamilton (1st U.S. treasury secretary)
7.		$100	G.	Andrew Jackson (7th U.S. president)

In the answer column, match the name of the currency with the country.

Number	Answer	Country	Letter	Name of Currency
1.		South Africa	A.	Real
2.		Brazil	B.	Dollar
3.		Kenya	C.	Shilling
4.		Sweden	D.	Zloty
5.		Thailand	E.	Krona
6.		New Zealand	F.	Baht
7.		Poland	G.	Rand

NOTHING BUT NET

1. **The board of governors of the Federal Reserve.** The board of governors is the governing body of the Federal Reserve System. Visit the Fed's Web site (http://www.federalreserve.gov) to learn more about the board of governors. Then answer the following questions:

   a.   How many board positions are currently vacant?

   b.   Who is the current chair and vice chair and how are they selected?

   c.   How long do board members serve?

   d.   When were each of the current board members appointed? When do their terms expire?

2. **Exchange rates.** An exchange rate is the rate at which one currency can be exchanged for another. Visit the Web site listed, or another similar site, and obtain the current exchange rate between the U.S. dollar and the following currencies:

   Canadian dollar
   Euro
   British pound
   Japanese yen
   Swiss franc

Compare the current exchange rate with the rate one year ago. Did the U.S. dollar get stronger or weaker relative to each currency?

http://finance.yahoo.com/m3?u

3. **Leverage.** Different companies have different degrees of leverage. Go to the two company Web sites listed. Access their financial statements and review current and historical balance sheets (look under "Investor Relations" or "Financial Information"). Which of the two companies is more leveraged? Has the amount of leverage employed by each company changed over time?

http://www.jnj.com/index.jsp
http://www.wyeth.com

Note: Internet Web addresses change frequently. If you do not find the exact sites listed, you may need to access the organization or company's home page and search from there.

Case 17.1

The Risks and Rewards of Subprime Lending

Capital One Bank is one of the nation's largest issuers of MasterCard and Visa bank credit cards and also offers a variety of other consumer lending products. Capital One has over 47 million accounts and close to $60 billion in outstanding loans.

Much of Capital One's past success has been attributed to the firm's sophisticated data-mining technology. The firm links its customer database to award-winning, proprietary information technology and analytics that allow Capital One to rigorously test ideas before taking them to market. This approach has also led to a risk management model that allows Capital One to come up with the best combination of rates, fees, and conditions for each individual customer. The result is a loss rate historically well below industry averages.

One of the few growth areas in consumer finance is the so-called "subprime" market, consisting of high-risk borrowers. When credit card companies that specialized in subprime borrowers, such as Providian Financial and NextCard, ran into trouble, Capital One aggressively moved in. The firm believed that its risk management model would allow it to cherry-pick the best customers. Capital One quickly added over 8 million new customers of which something like 40 percent were subprime. The company saw higher profits as a result. Interest rates for subprime cardholders are higher (15.9 percent versus 8.9 percent for lower risk cardholders), as are most fees.

Unfortunately, subprime lending also means higher risk, especially in a weak economy. Bad debts exploded. Nervous bank regulators ordered Capital One to boost reserves for bad debts. The market reacted to the news by sending the price of Capital One's stock down by 40 percent.

The firm insisted that its risk management model was not broken and that the higher risks associated with subprime lending were worth it. Capital One forecast annual increases in earnings of around 15 percent for the next couple of years. Investors, however, were not impressed, continuing to be spooked by the sharp increase in bad debts.

Aside from bad debts, Capital One faces further challenges. The company's CFO resigned in March 2003 after it was revealed that the SEC was investigating alleged insider trading (no other senior executives have been implicated, and Capital One is cooperating with the investigation). Moreover, federal banking regulators told all credit card companies to reduce some of the fees charged to customers. Many experts believe this action could have an adverse impact on Capital One's future earnings. Kathleen M. Shanley, a debt analyst with a bond rating and research firm, puts it this way: "It would be fair to say that I am skeptical the company can achieve its still-aggressive growth projections."

QUESTIONS FOR CRITICAL THINKING

1. Explain the decision by Capital One to move into the subprime market in the context of the tradeoff between risk and return. Did Capital One's risk management model fail as the firm moved into the subprime market? If so, what may have accounted for the failure?

2. Why did regulators require that Capital One boost reserves? How could a bank boost reserves for bad loans? What actions could Capital One take to replace lost fee income, restore investor confidence, and boost its stock price?

Sources: Stock prices obtained from MSN Web site, http://moneycentral.msn.com/investor, March 24, 2003; "Capital One Reports Record Earnings for 2002," News Release, Capital One Financial Corporation, Capital One Web site, http://www.capitalone.com, accessed March 24, 2003; "Cap One Financial CFO Resigns," *Dow Jones Business News,* Yahoo! Finance Web site, http://biz.yahoo.com, accessed March 24, 2003; Geoffrey Smith, "The Bill Comes Due for Capital One," *BusinessWeek* Web site, http://www.businessweek.com, accessed March 24, 2003.

Video Case 17.2

Developing a Financial Strategy for a Retail Chain

This video case appears on page 620. A recently filmed video, designed to expand and highlight the written case, is available for class use by instructors.

Chapter 18
Financing and Investing through Securities Markets

Learning Goals

1 Distinguish between the primary market for securities and the secondary market.

2 Compare money market instruments, bonds, and common stock and explain why particular investors might prefer each type of security.

3 Identify the five basic objectives of investors and the types of securities most likely to help them reach each objective.

4 Explain the process of buying or selling a security listed on an organized securities exchange.

5 Describe the information included in stock, bond, and mutual fund quotations.

6 Explain the role of mutual funds in securities markets.

7 Evaluate the major features of regulations designed to protect investors.

Microsoft Gives Back to Shareholders

Imagine receiving a $75-billion gift. That's what Microsoft's shareholders got in a giant payback from the company in which they had invested. After several years of accumulating cash profits, Microsoft had billions of dollars on hand but nowhere to spend it. So the firm decided to give $3 per share back to its

investors, in the form of a one-time dividend. In addition, Microsoft doubled the regular dividend on each share of its stock and bought back stock that had been languishing in the open market.

What was the reasoning behind this bold move? Normally, a rapidly-growing company will use most or all of its profits to develop new products and enter new markets. But Microsoft is already dominant in several sectors of the computer industry and has come under close scrutiny by regulators in both the U.S. and Europe who want to make sure the firm has not developed a monopoly that makes competition impossible.

© Ron Wurzer/Getty Images

With the exception of a new search engine targeted at Google, Microsoft sees limited emerging markets. "There aren't that many teams with great ideas worth investing in," notes Steve Domenik of Seven Rosen Funds, a venture capital firm that raises money to invest in businesses. So Microsoft and similar companies may have more cash on hand than they need—or want. Kirk Walden of PricewaterhouseCoopers notes "There is no Internet-like phenomenon to splurge on."

So, Microsoft gave the money back; and not only employees benefited in this situation. Recipients of the prize included everyone from founder Bill Gates, who owns 1.1 billion shares, to Fidelity Corp., which owns 432 million shares, to the average investor who may own 50 shares. Individual investors own about 30 percent of Microsoft's stock. The size of the giveback raised questions from speculators about whether or not the move would affect the United States overall economy or change consumer spending habits. Experts felt this was unlikely. They thought that most individual investors would probably reinvest the money or at least keep it in a cash account at their brokerage and since the dividend went to holders of Microsoft stock on November 15, 2004, it meant that they would also use some of it to pay the related 15% income tax rate. Corporate or institutional investors such as Fidelity would engage in other types of investment activity. What did Bill Gates do with his windfall? He contributed the $3.3 billion to his charitable foundation.

Meanwhile, Microsoft will look for ways to grow and increase profits even more. Thanks to revenues from its Windows and Office products, Microsoft rakes in about $1 billion each month. It has continued to invest in its Xbox video game console and MSN Web site and is looking to reap the rewards in coming months. Microsoft also continues to plow money into Business Solutions and .NET technologies, which the company feels have growth and earnings potential, which has not yet been realized. In addition, company executives are beginning to consider another option: acquiring a major competitor. "When we look out over the next several years, I'm confident we have some of the greatest dollar-growth prospects in front of us of any company in the world," says Microsoft CEO Steve Ballmer.[1]

Chapter Overview

The previous chapter discussed two sources of funds for long-term financial needs: debt capital and equity capital. Long-term debt capital takes the form of corporate bonds, U.S. government bonds, and municipal bonds. Equity capital consists of common and preferred stock—ownership shares in corporations. Stocks and bonds are commonly called **securities** because both represent obligations on the part of issuers and are purchased by investors seeking returns on the funds invested or loaned.

This chapter examines how securities are bought and sold in two markets—the primary market and the secondary market. The characteristics of stocks, bonds, and money market instruments (short-term debt securities), and how investors choose specific securities, are discussed. We also examine the role of organized securities exchanges in the financial sector and outline the information included in reports of securities transactions. Finally, we review the laws that regulate the securities markets and protect investors.

security stock, bond, or money market instrument that represents an obligation on the part of the issuer.

primary market market where new security issues are first sold to investors; the issuer receives the proceeds from the sale.

They Said It

Don't gamble! Take all your savings and buy some good stock and hold it till it goes up. If it don't go up, don't buy it.

—*Will Rogers (1879–1935) American humorist*

The Primary Market

In the **primary market,** firms and governments issue securities and sell them to the public. When a company needs capital to purchase inventory, expand a plant, make major investments, acquire another firm, or pursue other business goals, it may sell a bond or stock offering to the investing public. For example, General Electric periodically sells securities to raise funds to expand production facilities and make acquisitions. Similarly, when Michigan needs capital to build a new highway or a new community college, or to fulfill other public needs, its leaders may also decide to sell bonds.

A stock offering gives investors the opportunity to purchase ownership shares in a firm like well-known drug maker Amgen and to participate in its future growth in exchange for providing current capital. When a company offers stock for sale to the general public for the first time, it is called an **initial public offering (IPO).** The number of IPO issues tends to fluctuate up and down depending on economic conditions and the overall level of the stock market. In recent years, the number of IPOs has declined dramatically in the face of a weak economy and a declining stock market.

Both profit-seeking corporations and government agencies also rely on primary markets to raise funds by issuing bonds. For example, the federal government sells Treasury bonds to finance part of federal outlays such as interest on outstanding federal debt. State and local governments, such as the Commonwealth of Massachusetts and the city of San Diego, sell bonds to finance capital projects such as the construction of sewer systems, community colleges, streets, and fire stations. Announcements of new stock and bond offerings appear daily in business publications such as *The Wall Street Journal.* These announcements are in the form of a simple black-and-white ad called a *tombstone.*

There are two ways in which securities are sold to the investment public: in open auctions and through investment bankers. Virtually all securities sold through open auctions consist of U.S. Treasury securities. A week prior to an upcoming auction, the Treasury announces the type and number of securities it will be auctioning. Treasury bills are auctioned weekly, whereas longer-term Treasury securities are auctioned once a month or once a quarter. Prospective buyers submit competitive bids to the Treasury specifying how much they wish to purchase and the price they are willing to pay. The higher the price specified, the lower the return to the investor, and the lower the cost to the Treasury. In a typical auction, the Treasury accepts about half of the bids submitted. Competitive bids are submitted by large investment firms. Small individual investors may submit so-called *noncompetitive bids* to the Treasury. In it, the investor simply specifies the amount he or she wishes to purchase. The Treasury accepts all noncompetitive bids, and the investor pays the average price charged on accepted competitive bids.

The IPOs of most corporate and municipal securities are sold through financial specialists called **investment bankers.** Lehman Brothers, CS First Boston, and UBS Warburg are examples of well-known investment banking firms. An investment banker is a financial intermediary that purchases the issue from the firm or government and then resells the issue to investors. This process is known as **underwriting.**

Investment bankers underwrite stock and bond issues at a discount, meaning that they pay the issuing firm or government less than the price the firm charges investors. This discount is compensation for services rendered, including the risk investment bankers incur whenever they underwrite a new security issue. Although the size of the discount is often negotiable, it usually ranges between 4 and 8 percent of the public offering price. The size of the underwriting discount is generally higher for stock issues than it is for bond issues. For instance, when discount airline JetBlue went public, the investment bankers paid the airline $25.11 per share while charging investors $27 per share.

Corporations and federal, state, and local governments are willing to pay for the services provided by investment bankers because they are financial market experts. In addition to locating buyers for the issue, the underwriter typically advises the issuer on such details as the general characteristics of the issue, its pricing, and the timing of the offering. Typically, several investment banking firms participate in the underwriting process. The issuer selects a lead, or primary, firm, which in turn forms a syndicate consisting of other investment banking firms. Each member of the syndicate purchases a portion of the security issue, which it resells to investors.

Concept Check

1. What is an IPO?
2. What functions do investment bankers perform?

The Secondary Market

Media reports of stock and bond trading are most likely to refer to trading in the **secondary market,** a collection of financial markets where previously issued securities are traded among investors. The corporations or governments that originally issued the

Used with permission of Lincoln Financial Group

Market uncertainty.
Low consumer confidence.

Even in this environment, Lincoln can help find new opportunities for your clients.

MUTUAL FUNDS
ANNUITIES
LIFE INSURANCE
401(K)/403(B) PLANS
COLLEGE SAVINGS PLANS
MANAGED ACCOUNTS

Despite today's uncertainties, there's never been a better time to talk to your clients about balance and diversification. From small business retirement plans to top-rated, web-based tools—Lincoln's extensive range of financial solutions helps give your clients a potential hedge against an otherwise unpredictable world. For more information, see the adjacent page, or call 1-877-533-0003, or visit LFG.com/prepare. *Clear solutions in a complex world.*

Lincoln
Financial Group®

Investors often turn to professional firms for financial planning and investment advice. Lincoln Financial Group, which has been in business for nearly a century, offers a range of plans, funds, and services to help clients balance and diversify their portfolios.

secondary market
financial markets where previously issued securities are traded among investors.

Concept Check

1. *Give two examples of secondary markets.*

2. *Compare the sizes of the primary and secondary markets in terms of total dollar values.*

securities being traded are not directly involved in the secondary market. They neither make any payments when securities are sold nor receive any of the proceeds when securities are purchased. The NYSE and NASDAQ Stock Market are both secondary markets. In terms of the dollar value of securities bought and sold, the secondary market is four times larger than the primary market. During a typical trading day, tens of billions of dollars' worth of stock changes hands on the NYSE alone. The various elements of the secondary market are discussed later in the chapter.

Securities

Securities can be classified into three categories: money market instruments, bonds, and stock. Money market instruments and bonds are both debt securities, and stocks are units of ownership in corporations like Abbott Labs, General Electric, Boeing, and PepsiCo.

Money Market Instruments

money market instruments short-term debt securities issued by corporations, financial institutions such as banks, and governments.

Money market instruments are short-term debt securities issued by corporations, financial institutions such as banks, and governments. By definition, all money market instruments mature within one year from the date of issue. Investors are paid interest by the issuer for the use of their funds. Money market instruments are generally low-risk securities and are purchased by investors when they have surplus cash. As was noted in Chapter 17, financial managers often choose to invest surplus cash in money market instruments because they are low risk and are easily convertible into cash. For example, drug maker Merck has more than $1.5 billion invested in money market instruments. Examples of money market instruments include U.S. Treasury bills, commercial paper, repurchase agreements, and bank certificates of deposit. These securities were described in the prior chapter.

Bonds

Bondholders are creditors of a corporation. By selling bonds, a firm obtains long-term debt capital. Federal, state, and local governments also acquire funds in this way. Bonds are issued in various denominations (face values), usually between $1,000 and $25,000. Each issue indicates a rate of interest to be paid to the bondholder—stated as a percentage of the bond's face value—as well as a maturity date on which the bondholder is paid the bond's face value. Because bondholders are creditors, they have a claim on the firm's assets that must be satisfied before any claims of stockholders in the event of the firm's dissolution or bankruptcy. For instance, when US Airways came out of Chapter 11 bankruptcy, stockholders received virtually nothing. On the other hand, bondholders and other creditors received at least part of the amount they were owed.[2]

Types of Bonds

secured bond bond backed by specific pledge of a company's assets.

A prospective bond investor can choose among a variety of bonds. Major types of bonds are summarized in Figure 18.1. A **secured bond** is backed by a specific pledge of company assets. For example, mortgage bonds are backed by real property owned by the firm, such as machinery or office furniture, and collateral trust bonds are backed by stocks and bonds of other companies owned by the firm. In the event of default, bondholders may receive the proceeds from selling these assets.

Because bond purchasers want to balance their financial returns with their risks, bonds backed by pledges of specific assets are less risky than those without such collateral. Consequently, a firm can issue secured bonds at lower interest rates than it would have to pay for comparable unsecured bonds. However, many firms do issue unsecured bonds, called **debentures.** These bonds are backed only by the financial reputation and promises of the issuing corporation.

debenture bond backed by the reputation of the issuer rather than by a specific pledge of a company's assets.

Government bonds are issued by the U.S. Treasury. Because government bonds are backed by the full faith and credit of the U.S. government, they are considered the least risky of all bonds. **Municipal bonds** are issued by state or local governments. There are two types of municipal bonds. A revenue bond is a bond issue whose proceeds are used to pay for a project that will produce revenue—such as a toll road or bridge. The Oklahoma Turnpike Authority has issued such bonds. A general obligation bond is a bond whose proceeds are used to pay for a project that will not produce any revenue—such as a new state police post. General obligation bonds can be sold only by states like Oregon or local governmental units like Toledo, Ohio, or Bergen County, New Jersey, that have the power to levy taxes. An important feature of municipal bonds is the exemption of interest payments from federal income tax. Moreover, investors who purchase municipal bonds issued in their state of residence do not have to pay any state income tax on the interest received. Because of this attractive feature, municipal bonds generally carry lower interest rates than either corporate or government bonds.

Quality Ratings for Bonds

Two factors determine the price of a bond: its risk and its interest rate. Bonds vary considerably in terms of risk. One tool used by bond investors to assess the risk of a bond is its so-called **bond rating.** Two investment firms—Standard & Poor's (S&P) and Moody's—rate corporate and municipal bonds. The bonds with the least amount of risk are assigned a rating of either AAA (S&P) or Aaa (Moody's). The ratings descend as risk increases. Table 18.1 lists the S&P and Moody's bond ratings. Bonds with ratings below BBB (S&P) or Baa (Moody's) are classified as speculative, often called

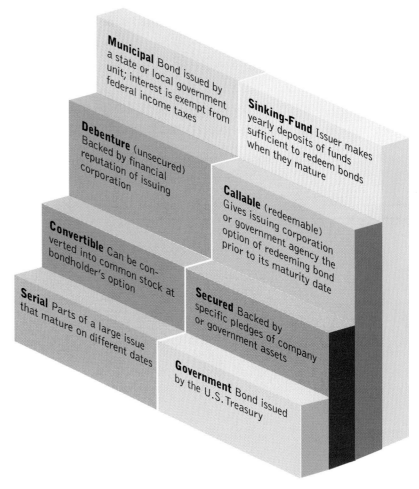

FIGURE 18.1
Types of Bonds and the Significant Features of Each

high-yield or *junk bonds.* Junk bonds attract investors by offering high interest rates in exchange for greater risk. Historically, junk bonds have paid around 5.5 percent higher annual interest rates than bonds issued by the U.S. government.

The second factor affecting the price of a bond is its interest rate. Other things being equal, the higher the interest rate, the higher the price of a bond. However, everything else usually is not equal; the bonds may not be equally risky, or one may have a longer maturity. Investors must evaluate the trade-offs involved.

Another important influence on bond prices is the market interest rate. Because bonds pay fixed rates of interest, as market interest rates rise, bond prices fall, and vice versa. For instance, when interest rates on 10-year U.S. government bonds fell a few years ago, the prices of these bonds rose by over 20 percent.

Retiring Bonds

Because bonds in an issue mature on a specific date, borrowers such as Bed Bath & Beyond or Harris County, Texas, must have the necessary funds available to repay the principal at that time. In some instances, this can create a cash flow problem. To ease the repayment problem, some borrowers issue serial bonds. A serial bond issue consists of bonds that mature on different dates. For example, assume a corporation issues $20 million in serial bonds for a 30-year period. None of the bonds mature during the first 20 years. However, beginning in the 21st year, $2 million in bonds mature each year until all the bonds are repaid at the end of the 30 years.

Table 18.1   Moody's and Standard & Poor's Bond Ratings

Moody's	Interpretation	Standard & Poor's	Interpretation
Aaa	Prime quality	AAA	Bank investment quality
Aa	High grade	AA	
A	Upper medium grade	A	
Baa	Medium grade	BBB	
		BB	
Ba	Lower medium grade or speculative	B	Speculative
B	Speculative	CCC	
		CC	
Caa	From very speculative to near or in default	C	
Ca			
C		DDD	In default (with a rating based on the issuer's relative salvage value)
		DD	
		D	

A variation of the concept of serial bonds is the sinking-fund bond, or prerefunded bond. Under this arrangement, an issuer like Duke Energy makes annual deposits to accumulate funds for use in redeeming the bonds when they mature. These deposits are made to the bond's trustee—usually a large bank—that is responsible for representing bondholders. The deposits must be large enough that their total, plus accrued interest, will be sufficient to redeem the bonds at maturity.

Most corporate and municipal bonds, and some government bonds, are callable. A **call provision** allows the issuer to redeem the bond prior to its maturity at a prespecified price. Not surprisingly, issuers tend to call bonds when market interest rates are declining or low by historical standards. For example, suppose York County, Pennsylvania, had $50 million in bonds outstanding with a 5.5 percent annual interest rate. If interest rates decline to 3 percent, it may decide to call the 5.5 percent bonds, repaying the principal from the proceeds of newly issued 3 percent bonds. Calling the 5.5 percent bonds and issuing 3 percent bonds will save the county $1.25 million a year in interest payments. The savings in annual interest expense should more than offset the cost of retiring the old bonds and issuing new ones.

Stock

common stock share of ownership in a company.

The basic form of corporate ownership is embodied in **common stock.** Purchasers of common stock are the true owners of a corporation. Holders of common stock vote on major company decisions, such as purchasing another company or electing a board of directors. In return for the money they invest, they expect to receive payments in the form of cash dividends. Dividends vary considerably from stock to stock. 3M, for instance, pays an annual dividend of $2.64 per share. By contrast, Microsoft's annual dividend is only 32 cents per share. Investors also hope to benefit from capital gains resulting from increases in the value of their stock holdings.

Common stockholders benefit from company success, and they risk the loss of their investments if the company fails. If a firm dissolves, claims of creditors must be satisfied before stockholders will receive anything. Because creditors have a senior claim to assets, holders of common stock are said to have a residual claim on company assets.

Sometimes confusion arises over the difference between book value and market value. Book value is determined by subtracting the company's liabilities from its assets. When this net figure is divided by the number of shares of common stock outstanding, the book value of each share is known.

The market value of a stock is the price at which the stock is currently selling. It is easily found by referring to the financial section of daily newspapers or on the Internet and may be more, or less, than the book value. Recently, for instance, ExxonMobil's market price was around three times its book value. What determines market value, however, is more complicated. Although many variables cause stock prices to fluctuate up and down in the short term, in the long run, stock prices tend to follow a company's profits. For instance, over the last 20 years, both the profits and stock price of Johnson & Johnson have increased by more than fivefold.

Preferred Stock   In addition to common stock, a few companies also issue **preferred stock—** stock whose holders receive preference in the payment of dividends. AEP is such a firm. Also, if a company is dissolved, holders of preferred stock have claims on the firm's assets that are ahead of the claims of common stockholders. On the other hand, preferred stockholders rarely have any voting rights, and the dividend they are paid is fixed, regardless of how profitable the firm becomes. Therefore, although preferred stock is legally equity, many investors consider it to be more like a bond than common stock.

Convertible Securities   Companies may issue bonds or preferred stock that contains a conversion feature. This feature gives the bondholder or preferred stockholder the right to exchange the bond or preferred stock for a fixed number of shares of common stock. For example, Lowe's has a convertible bond outstanding that its holder can exchange for 16.5 shares of Lowe's common stock. The value of the conversion feature depends on the price of Lowe's common stock. If the stock is selling for $50 per share, then the conversion feature is worth $825. Convertible bonds pay lower interest rates than those lacking conversion features, helping reduce the interest expense of the issuing firms. Investors are willing to accept these lower interest rates, since they value the potential for additional gains if the price of the firm's stock increases.

> **preferred stock** stock whose holders receive preference in the payment of dividends.

Concept Check

1. Who are bondholders?
2. Which factors determine the price of a bond?
3. What is the difference between book value and market value of a stock?

> *They Said It*
>
> Spend at least as much time researching a stock as you would choosing a refrigerator.
>
> —*Peter Lynch (b. 1944)*
> *American investment guru and vice chairman, Fidelity Investments*

Securities Purchasers

Two general types of investors buy securities: institutions and individuals. An institutional investor is an organization that invests its own funds or those it holds in trust for others. Institutional investors include insurance companies like New York Life, pension funds like the Retirement Systems of Alabama, T. Rowe Price mutual funds, and not-for-profit organizations such as the American Cancer Society. Many institutional investors are huge. As noted in the previous chapter, pension funds have almost $7 trillion in assets, and the total assets of life insurance companies exceed $3 trillion.[3]

Institutional investors buy and sell large quantities of securities, often in blocks of 10,000 or more shares per transaction. Such block trading represents about half of the total daily volume on the major securities exchanges.[4] By some estimates, institutional investors make up around half of the typical company's shareholders. For some stocks, institutional ownership is even more significant. For instance, over 73 percent of 3M's shares are owned by institutional investors.

Despite the importance of institutional investors, individual investors still play a vital role. Well over half of all American households now own stocks, either directly or by investing in stock mutual funds. In contrast, 30 years ago, less than one-third of American households owned stocks.[5] The Best Business Practices box discusses one firm that lets investors trade online.

> *They Said It*
>
> There are two times in a man's life when he should not speculate: when he can't afford it and when he can.
>
> —*Mark Twain (1835–1910)*
> *American author and humorist*

Investment Motivations

Why do individuals and institutions invest? What are their motivations for investing? In general, individuals and institutions have five primary motivations for investing: growth in capital, stability of

BEST BUSINESS PRACTICES

Ameritrade's Recipe for Success

Individual investors are getting the hang of it. They can log on to the Internet and trade stocks without the assistance of a full-service broker. They do most of their own research on companies and stock performances, and they make their own decisions about what to buy and sell. They like having control over their stock portfolios and in particular the low commissions offered by discount online brokers. One such broker stands out for the average U.S. investor, whose annual income is in the five figure range and who has up to $250,000 in assets: Ameritrade. Less than a decade ago, Ameritrade's major competitors were Charles Schwab and E*Trade. But after the stock market downturn several years ago, Schwab moved toward giving financial advice, and E*Trade decided to sell bank accounts and mortgages.

Because the firm has stuck by its initial philosophy and its original customers, its customers have remained loyal. Trading commissions remain at $10.99—admittedly not the industry's lowest. But Ameritrade customers like the site because they get exactly what they ordered, with so few surprises. "I look at it like the McDonald's of investing," explains one customer. "It's cheap, easy to use, and consistent. You know what you're getting, and you get it every single time." No hidden charges, no changes in the way trades are processed.

CEO Joe Moglia says that this focus on the online brokerage business and the individual investor are major ingredients in his company's recipe for success. The business is relatively straightforward compared with other types of investing. So, Ameritrade keeps its costs down, is subject to less regulation, and is exposed to fewer financial liabilities. "We are an Internet transaction processing company," says Moglia. "That's all we do." As a result, the firm's profits continue to rise while those of its competitors tend to be more volatile. "Ameritrade stuck to its knitting," says Matt Snowling, a senior analyst at Friedman Billings Ramsey, "and it's sitting pretty now."

QUESTIONS FOR CRITICAL THINKING

1. What are the advantages to the individual investor of trading stocks through Ameritrade? What are the disadvantages?

2. What steps might Ameritrade take to retain a competitive advantage over other firms?

Sources: Company Web site, http://www.ameritrade.com, accessed January 12, 2005; Kevin Kelleher, "The No-Service Broker," *Business 2.0*, July 2004, pp. 50–51; Rick Aristotle Munarriz, "A Cautious Ameritrade," *The Motley Fool*, June 10, 2004, http://www.fool.com.

principal, liquidity, current income, and growth in income. All investors must rank each motivation in terms of importance, and all investments involve trade-offs. For example, an investment that has the potential for substantial growth in capital may provide no current income. By contrast, an investment that has very stable principal may have little potential for capital growth. The bottom line is this: Some investments are more appropriate for certain investors than for others. Table 18.2 provides a useful guide for evaluating money market instruments, bonds, and stocks.

Growth in Capital   When it comes to potential growth in capital over time, especially over long periods of time, common stocks are the clear winner. For example, over a recent 25-year period, $1,000 invested in common stocks would have grown to over $24,000. A similar investment in bonds, made during the same period, would have grown to only a little over $8,700. This is not to imply, however, that the prices of all common stocks go up all the time, nor do they go up by the same amount. There is considerable variation in the performance of stocks. For instance, over the past decade, $10,000 invested in Procter & Gamble's common stock would have grown to over $42,000. Yet a $10,000 investment in The Coca-Cola Company's common stock would have grown to only $24,000 over the same period.

Table 18.2   Primary Investment Objectives by Type of Security

Investment Objective	Type of Security		
	Money Market Instruments	Bonds	Common Stock
Potential growth in capital	None	Little or none	Highest
Stability of principal	Highest	Good	Lowest
Liquidity	Highest	Good	Lowest
Current income	Variable	Highest	Good
Growth in income	Variable	Lowest	Highest

Stability of Principal   Treasury bills and other money market instruments are the clear winner when it comes to stability of principal. The odds that the price of a money market investment will fall below the price the investor originally paid are virtually zero. Furthermore, when an investor buys a Treasury bill or other money market instrument, the investor can be pretty sure the original investment will be returned. With stocks, there is no such guarantee.

Liquidity   Because the prices of stocks, and to a lesser extent bonds, can vary widely, investors cannot count on making profits whenever they decide or need to sell. Liquidity is a measure of the speed at which assets can be converted into cash. Since money market instruments such as a CD issued by Bank of America have short maturities and stable prices, they offer investors the highest amount of liquidity.

Current Income   Historically, bonds have provided the highest current income of any security. Interest rates on bonds are usually higher than money market interest rates or the dividends paid on common stocks. For instance, Lockheed Martin has a bond outstanding that yields around 4.1 percent. By contrast, the stock pays a dividend of only 1.1 percent. In addition, money market interest rates vary up and down while the interest rate on a bond remains constant. Traditionally, investors looking for high current income have invested a large portion of their funds in bonds.

Growth in Income   When you buy a bond, the interest you receive is fixed for the life of the bond. Interest rates on money market instruments can increase over time, but they can decrease as well. On the other hand, common stock dividends have historically risen at a rate that exceeds the rate of inflation. Over the past 20 years, for instance, Johnson & Johnson's common stock dividend has risen at an average annual rate of around 12 percent. There is, however, no guarantee that a company's common stock dividend will always increase. Several well-known companies, such as AT&T and Ford, have recently cut their common stock dividends.

Taxes and Investing

Taxes affect investment decisions, though more so for some investors than others. Investment returns come in two forms: income (bond interest and stock dividends) and realized capital gains (selling a security for more than its purchase price). These investment returns may or may not be taxable. Many institutional investors, such as pension funds, pay no taxes on investment returns. Individual investors, on the other hand, may owe taxes on investment returns resulting from either income or realized capital gains.

Concept Check

1. Who buys securities?
2. Name the two types of investment return.

Securities Exchanges

Stocks and bonds are traded in centralized marketplaces called *securities exchanges.* Most of the largest and best-known securities exchanges are commonly called **stock exchanges,** or *stock markets,* since the vast majority of securities traded are common stock issues. Stock exchanges are secondary markets. The securities have already been issued by firms, which received proceeds from the issue when it was sold in the primary market. Sales in a securities exchange occur between individual and institutional investors.

Stock exchanges exist throughout the world, and most countries today have at least one stock market. The two largest stock exchanges—measured by the value of securities traded—are the New York Stock Exchange and the NASDAQ Stock Market. Other large stock markets are located in London, Tokyo, Paris, and Frankfurt.

> ## They Said It
>
> Nothing tells in the long run like a good judgment, and no sound judgment can remain with the man whose mind is disturbed by the mercurial changes of the stock exchange. It places him under an influence akin to intoxication. What is not, he sees, and what he sees, is not.
>
> —*Andrew Carnegie (1835–1919)*
> *American industrialist and philanthropist*

The New York Stock Exchange

The New York Stock Exchange—sometimes referred to as the *Big Board*—is the largest and most famous stock market in the world. It is also one of the oldest, having been founded in 1792. Today, more than 3,000 common and preferred stock issues are traded on the NYSE. These stocks represent most of the largest, best-known companies in the U.S., with a total market value in excess of $10 trillion. For a company's stock to be traded on the NYSE, the firm must apply to the exchange for listing. Corporate bonds are also traded on the NYSE, but bond trading makes up less than 1 percent of the total value of securities traded there during a typical year.

Trading on the NYSE takes place face-to-face on a trading floor. Buy and sell orders are transmitted to 1 of 42 posts—each stock is assigned a post—on the floor of the exchange. Buyers and sellers then bid against one another in an open auction. Only investment firms that are members of the NYSE are allowed to trade, meaning that the firm owns at least 1 of 1,366 "seats." Seats are occasionally bought and sold. Currently, the asking price for an NYSE seat is around $2 million.[6]

Each NYSE stock is assigned to 1 of 42 specialist firms. Specialists are unique investment firms that are responsible for maintaining an orderly and liquid market in the stocks assigned to them. Specialists must be willing to buy when there are no other buyers and sell when there are no other sellers. Specialists also act as auctioneers and catalysts, bringing buyers and sellers together.

A number of observers portray the NYSE and its trading practices as somewhat old-fashioned, especially in this high-tech age. Even though the NYSE still retains a trading floor, the exchange has become highly automated in recent years. Its computer systems automatically match and route most

The New York Stock Exchange is the largest and most famous stock market in the world. Firms apply to be listed on its exchange and must meet high standards to do so.

© AP/Wide World Photos

orders, which are typically filled in a few seconds. In recent years, the NYSE has also moved aggressively to attract more firms and showcase its technological advances.

The terrorist attacks of September 11 challenged the NYSE technology. Located only a few blocks from the site of the Twin Towers, the NYSE was closed almost immediately after the attacks. It remained closed for the rest of the week as telephone, computer, and transportation systems were repaired. The exchange reopened on Monday, September 17. Trading was orderly, despite a big drop in stock prices, and trading volume soon returned to pre-9/11 levels.

The NASDAQ Stock Market

The world's second-largest stock market is the NASDAQ Stock Market. It is a very different market from the NYSE. NASDAQ—which stands for National Association of Securities Dealers Automated Quotation system—is a computerized communications network that links member investment firms. It is the world's largest intranet.[7] All trading on NASDAQ takes place through its intranet rather than on a trading floor. Buy and sell orders are entered into the network and executed electronically. All NASDAQ-listed stocks have two or more market makers—investment firms that perform essentially the same functions as NYSE specialists.

Around 4,000 companies have their stocks listed on NASDAQ. Compared with firms listed on the NYSE, NASDAQ-listed corporations tend to be smaller, less known firms. Some are relatively new businesses and cannot meet NYSE listing requirements. It is not uncommon for firms eventually to move the trading of their stocks from NASDAQ to the NYSE. Some recent examples include AirTran Holdings, E*Trade Financial, and Network Associates. However, there are dozens of companies currently trading on NASDAQ—such as Amgen, Cisco Systems, Dell, Intel, and Microsoft—that would easily meet NYSE listing requirements. For a variety of reasons, these firms have decided to remain on NASDAQ for the time being.

Other U.S. Stock Markets

In addition to the NYSE and NASDAQ Stock Market, there are several other stock markets in the U.S. The American Stock Exchange, or AMEX, is also located in New York. It focuses on the stocks of smaller firms as well as other financial instruments, such as options—instruments that give an investor the right to buy or sell stock at a fixed price for a fixed period of time. In comparison to the NYSE or NASDAQ, the AMEX is tiny. Daily trading volume is only around 25 million shares compared with the 1 billion-plus shares on each of the larger two exchanges.

Several regional stock exchanges also operate throughout the U.S. These include the Chicago, Pacific (San Francisco), Boston, Cincinnati, and Philadelphia stock exchanges. Originally established to trade the shares of small regional companies, the regional exchanges now list securities of many large

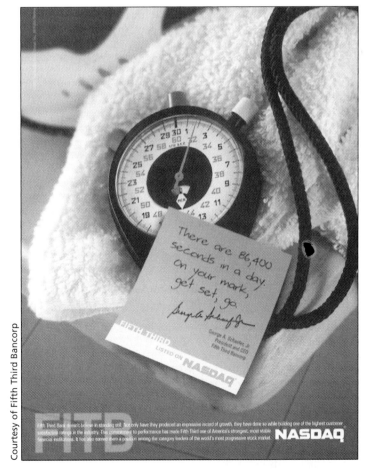

Courtesy of Fifth Third Bancorp

Cincinnati-based Fifth Third Bank is listed on the NASDAQ exchange, which is composed of a wide range of firms. The company has approximately $84 billion in assets, was recently ranked the No. 1 financial institution on the NASDAQ based on market value, and is recognized as an industry leader.

HITS & MISSES

Enron Teaches Every Investor a Lesson

The news was almost unbelievable. When Texas-based energy giant Enron reported more than $1 billion in losses a few years ago, its stock plummeted from over $90 to 26 cents per share, and when the firm finally filed for bankruptcy, hundreds of employees were not only out of their jobs, they were also out of their life savings. That's because they had entrusted all of their retirement savings to a retirement plan—all of it invested in Enron stock. Typically, an Enron employee saw his or her retirement savings slide from around $475,000 to $4,000. Even as they watched the disaster, employees couldn't sell their stock holdings because of rules that prohibited them from doing so. Meanwhile, top Enron executives, who were not forbidden to sell their holdings, did so—to the tune of about $1 billion as the company came crashing down.

The situation was devastating to employees, who felt they had nowhere to turn. Company founder Ken Lay tried to absolve himself by saying, "I didn't know what was going on." That statement has since been addressed by the Sarbanes-Oxley Act, which makes both the CEO and CFO personally accountable for all financial filings with the Securities and Exchange Commission. Eventually, the company's senior executives—including Lay, former CEO Jeffrey Skilling, former CFO Andrew Fastow and his wife Lea Fastow, and former chief accounting officer Richard Causey, among others—were indicted for crimes involving the collapse of the firm.

Charges included bank fraud and lying to banks, conspiracy, securities fraud and insider trading, along with various schemes designed to fool investors into thinking that Enron was a financially healthy company. Some executives pleaded guilty to charges and cooperated with the government; others maintained their innocence.

As Ken Lay continued to plead ignorance to what had been transpiring at the firm he founded, a federal judge announced that he would face two trials—one of his own and a joint one with Skilling and Causey. "The breadth of the indictment is staggering," remarked Skilling's lead trial lawyer, Daniel Petrocelli.

QUESTIONS FOR CRITICAL THINKING

1. What can employees of other firms learn from the Enron disaster?

2. The Sarbanes-Oxley Act now holds top executives fully accountable for accurately reporting the financial status of their companies. Do you agree or disagree with this new law? Why?

Sources: Carrie Johnson, "Enron's Lay to Have Two Trials," *Washington Post*, October 20, 2004, http://www.washingtonpost.com; Kristen Hays, "Skilling, Feds Fight over Trial Preps," *Associated Press*, October 20, 2004, http://news.yahoo.com; Kris Axtman, "Inside the Culture and Collapse of Enron," *The Christian Science Monitor*, October 12, 2004, http://www.csmonitor.com; Julie Rawe, "The Case against Ken Lay," *Time*, July 19, 2004, pp. 62–63.

corporations as well. In fact, over half the companies listed on the NYSE are also listed on one or more regional exchanges. The largest regional exchange, the Chicago, handles around 10 percent of all trades in NYSE-listed stocks.[8] It closes 30 minutes after the NYSE closes, giving investors a chance to take advantage of late-breaking news.

Foreign Stock Markets

As noted earlier, stock markets exist throughout the world. Virtually all developed, and many developing, countries have stock exchanges. Examples include Mumbai (Bombay), Helsinki, Hong Kong, Mexico City, Paris, and Toronto. One of the largest stock exchanges outside the U.S. is the London Stock Exchange. Founded in the early 17th century, the London Stock Exchange lists almost 3,000 stock and bond issues, more than 500 of which are shares of companies located outside the UK and Ireland. Trading on the London Stock Exchange takes place using a NASDAQ-type computerized communications network.

The London Stock Exchange is very much an international market. Around two-thirds of all cross-border trading in the world (for example, the trading of stocks of U.S. companies outside the U.S.) takes place in London. It is not uncommon for institutional investors in the U.S. to trade NYSE- or NASDAQ-listed stocks in London. These investors claim they often get better prices and faster order execution in London than they do in the U.S.

Direct Trading and ECNs

For years, a so-called *fourth market* has existed. The fourth market is the direct trading of exchange-listed stocks off the floor of the exchange, in the case of NYSE-listed stocks, or outside the network, in the case of NASDAQ-listed stocks. For the most part, trading in the fourth market was limited to institutional investors buying or selling large blocks of stock.

Now the fourth market has begun to open up to smaller, individual investors. Electronic Communications Networks (ECNs), such as Instinet, are part of the fourth market. Buyers and sellers meet in a virtual stock market where they trade directly with one another. No specialist or market maker is involved.

Concept Check
1. What is a stock exchange?
2. Name some of the foreign stock exchanges.

Buying and Selling Securities

Unless an investor is a member of one of the stock exchanges, the investor must use the services of a brokerage firm that is a member of one or more stock exchanges. A **brokerage firm** is a financial intermediary that buys and sells securities for individual and institutional investors. Examples include A. G. Edwards, Edward Jones, Quick and Reilly, and Salomon Smith Barney. Choosing a brokerage firm, and a specific stockbroker, is one of the most important decisions investors make.

brokerage firm financial intermediary that buys and sells securities for individual and institutional investors.

Placing an Order

An investor who wants to purchase shares of a stock would typically initiate the transaction by contacting his or her brokerage firm. The firm would transmit the order to the appropriate market, complete the transaction, and confirm the transaction with the investor—all within a few minutes.

An investor's request to buy or sell stock at the current market price is called a **market order.** A market order instructs the brokerage firm such as Charles Schwab to obtain the highest price possible—if the investor is selling—or the lowest price possible—if the investor is buying. By contrast, a **limit order** instructs the brokerage firm not to pay more than a specified price for a stock if the investor is buying or not to accept less than a specified price if the investor is selling. If Schwab is unable to fill a limit order immediately, it is left with either an NYSE specialist or NASDAQ market maker. If the price reaches the specified price, the order is carried out. Limit orders are often recommended during periods of extreme price volatility.

Concept Check
1. What is a brokerage firm?
2. How is an order initiated?

Costs of Trading

When investors buy or sell securities through a brokerage firm, they pay a fee for the related services. Today, these costs vary widely among brokerage firms. A trade that costs less than $20 using E*Trade might cost more than $75 using a full-service firm such as Merrill Lynch. Often, the cost depends on what type of brokerage firm the investor uses. A full-service firm—such as Morgan Stanley—provides extensive client services and offers considerable investment advice but charges higher fees. Brokers at full-service firms make recommendations and provide financial advice to investors.

By contrast, a discount firm—such as Charles Schwab or My Discount Broker—charges lower fees but offers fewer services. However, even discount firms usually provide research tools to customers to help them make better decisions. Moreover, many discount firms also offer fee-based

Reading a Financial Newspaper

Learning how to read a financial newspaper takes time and practice, but keeping abreast of financial news is beneficial to any professional. Aside from providing information about the financial markets, newspapers such as *Investor's Business Daily (IBD)*, *Barron's*, and *The Wall Street Journal (WSJ)* provide unbiased glimpses into general business news, emerging trends, stock research, market timing, and historical financial information. Here are some common elements to look for when glancing through a financial newspaper.

- **Company news.** Company news is reported throughout financial newspapers. *IBD* breaks the news down into brief capsules of information called "Business Briefs," "After the Close," and "Trends & Innovations" in its front section. In addition, there are longer articles throughout about the goings-on at different companies. How or what a company is doing relates to its financial condition or standing.
- **Financial markets/forecasts.** Financial markets are discussed, especially in light of significant global or political happenings. The *WSJ* has a column called "Ahead of the Tape: Today's Market Forecast," which discusses current financial forecasts for certain industries. Bar graphs, tables, and charts help illuminate the financial numbers throughout the papers.

- **Economic conditions.** Another area covered in financial newspapers is the economy. This information centers around the overall economic conditions of the country, certain industries, and businesses. Economic conditions play an important part in the financial world, of course, so this information is vital to smart investing.
- **General business news.** All papers include general business news. Usually this news relates to the financial markets and economic outlooks, but sometimes it's just good-to-know information about a particular business or industry.
- **Specific financial numbers** (such as American Exchange tables, NYSE tables, commodities, currency trading, treasury bonds/notes/bills, annuities, mutual funds, money rates, and NASDAQ stocks). This is the majority of the information you'll find in a financial newspaper. By following these numbers, you can determine the health of a stock or company, so it's important to take the time (and a magnifying glass!) to learn how to read and analyze this information.

Sources: *The Wall Street Journal,* July 28, 2003; *Investor's Business Daily,* July 28, 2003; "*Investor's Business Daily* Launches eIBD(TM); An Exact Digital Replica of the Newspaper Accessible Worldwide," *PR Newswire,* January 22, 2003.

investment planning services. All investors need to weigh the appropriate trade-off between cost, advice, and services when choosing a brokerage firm.

Online brokerage firms such as Ameritrade charge among the lowest fees of all brokerage firms. Investors enter buy and sell orders on their PCs or PDAs. Most online firms also give customers access to a wide range of investment information, though they do not directly provide advice to investors. According to recent statistics, about 10 percent of stock trades are conducted online today. In response, most discount and full-service brokerage firms have begun offering online trading services. Merrill Lynch, for instance, which once dismissed online trading as a passing fad, now offers a wide range of online trading services. In addition, the company's 15,000 brokers—called financial advisors—now offer clients more comprehensive personal financial planning advice.[9]

Direct Investing

A growing number of corporations—including Microsoft, Citigroup, Starbucks, and Hewlett-Packard—offer investors a direct way of purchasing stock. Hundreds offer dividend reinvestment plans (DRIPs). When an investor enrolls in a DRIP, the company uses the dividends paid on shares owned by the investor to buy more shares of the company's stock. The investor ends up buying more shares while avoiding brokerage fees. Another form of direct investing is the stock purchase program. Over 100 companies allow first-time investors to buy shares directly from the company, again avoiding brokerage fees. Firms offer direct investing programs because it gives them another source of long-term capital.

Companies offering direct investment programs charge one-time enrollment fees and perhaps a small fee on individual transactions. Most firms set a minimum purchase requirement starting as low as $50. To buy a stock directly, investors simply call the company and ask for an enrollment form. Information on direct investing is also available on most company Web sites. The Netstock Direct Web site (http://www.netstockdirect.com) lists firms offering direct investing and information on minimum purchase requirements and fees.

Reading the Financial News

At least four or five pages of most daily newspapers are devoted to reporting current financial news. This information is also available on countless Web sites. Much of the financial news coverage focuses on the day's securities transactions. Stocks and bonds traded on the various securities markets are listed alphabetically in the newspaper, with separate sections for each of the major markets. Information is provided about the volume of sales and the price of each security.

Today, all major stock markets throughout the world quote prices in decimals. In the U.S., stock prices are quoted in dollars and cents per share. In London, stock prices are quoted in pence, in Japan they are quoted in yen, and in Frankfurt prices are quoted in euros.

Stock Quotations

To understand how to read the stock tables found in newspapers, you need to understand how to interpret the symbols in the various columns. As Figure 18.2 explains, the symbol in Column 1 is the 52-week indicator. An arrow pointing up means that a stock hit its 52-week high during the day, and an arrow pointing down means that a stock hit its 52-week low. Column 2 gives the stock's highest and lowest trading prices during the past year. Column 3 contains the abbreviation for the company's name, footnotes that provide information about the stock (pf, for instance, refers to preferred stock), and the stock's ticker symbol. Column 4 lists the dividend, usually an annual payment based on the last quarterly declaration. Column 5 presents the yield, the annual dividend divided by the stock's closing price.

Column 6 lists the stock's **price-earnings (P/E) ratio,** the current market price divided by the annual earnings per share. The stock's trading volume in 100-share lots is in Column 7, and its highest and lowest prices for the day appear in

1	2		3		4	5	6	7	8		9	10
	52-Weeks					Yld		Vol				Net
	High	Low	Stock	Sym	Div	%	PE	(100s)	High	Low	Close	Chg
↑	50^{70}	29^{45}	AAAComp	AAC	1.00	2.00	20	15800	50^{70}	49^{50}	50^{00}	+ 50
	30^{00}	14^{00}	AAElec	AAE	...	...	26	510	22^{00}	19^{45}	21^{06}	-1^{34}
	78^{23}	65^{00}	AaronInc.	AAI	.25	.38	17	890	66^{56}	65^{00}	65^{00}	-1^{78}
↓	51^{55}	48^{00}	AaronInc. pf.		3.50	7.00	...	54	50^{10}	49^{75}	50^{00}	+ 05

(1) 52-Week Indicators: ↑ = Hit 52-week high during the day.   ↓ = Hit 52-week low.

(2) 52-Week High/Low: Highest and lowest per share trading prices in the past 52 weeks, adjusted for splits (dollars and cents—78.^{23} means $78.23 per share).

(3) Stock, Sym, and Footnotes: The company's name abbreviated. A capital letter usually means a new word. AAA-Comp, for example, is AAA Computer. The stock ticker symbol is expressed in capital letters. For AAA Computer, it is AAC. Stock footnotes include the following: **n**—new issue, **pf**—preferred stock, **rt**—rights, **s**—stock split within the past 52 weeks, **wi**—when issued, **wt**—warrant, **x**—ex-dividend.

(4) Div: Dividends are usually annual payments based on the most recent quarterly declaration. AAA Computer, for instance,

declared a dividend of $0.25 per share in the most recent quarter.

(5) Yld %: Percentage return from a dividend based on the stock's closing price.

(6) PE: Price-to-earnings ratio, calculated by taking the last closing price of the stock and dividing it by the earnings per share for the past fiscal year.

(7) Vol: Trading volume in 100-share lots. A listing of 510 means that 51,000 traded during the day. A number preceded by a "z" is the actual number of shares traded.

(8) High/Low: The high and low for the day (dollars and cents).

(9) Close: Closing price (dollars and cents).

(10) Net Chg: Change in price from the close of the previous trading day.

FIGURE 18.2
How to Read Stock Quote Tables

❶ **Bond:** Abbreviation of company name.

❷ **Annual Interest Rate:** Annual percentage rate of interest specified on the bond certificate.

❸ **Maturity Date:** Year in which the bond matures and the issuer repays the face value of each bond.

❹ **Cur Yld:** Annual interest payment divided by current price; **cv** means a convertible bond.

❺ **Vol:** Number of bonds traded during the day.

❶ ❷ ❸	❹	❺	❻	❼
Bond	**Cur Yld**	**Vol**	**Close**	**Net Chg**
AAA 9s20	7.8	15	$104^{3}/4$	$-1^{1}/8$
ABGasElec 6.5s10	6.6	10	$98^{1}/2$	$+^{3}/4$
AlbertoPharm 5s15	cv	20	$109^{1}/2$	$+^{1}/2$

❻ **Close:** Closing price.

❼ **Net Chg:** Change in the price from the close of the previous trading day.

FIGURE 18.3
How to Read Bond Quote Tables

Concept Check
1. What is direct investing?
2. Define price-earnings ratio.

Column 8. Column 9 gives the closing price for the day, and Column 10 summarizes the stock's net change in price from the close of the previous trading day.

Bond Quotations

To learn how to read corporate bond quotations, pick a bond listed in Figure 18.3 and examine the adjacent columns of information. Most corporate bonds are issued in denominations of $1,000, so bond prices must be read a little differently from stock prices. The closing price of the first AAA bond reads 104 3/4, but this does not mean $104.75. Because bond prices are quoted as a percentage of the $1,000 price stated on the face of the bond, the 104 3/4 means $1,047.50.

The notation following the bond name—such as 6.5s10 in the case of the AB Gas and Electric—indicates the annual interest rate stated on the bond certificate, 6.5 percent, and the maturity date of 2010. The s means that the bond pays half of its annual interest every six months, so the investor would receive $32.50 every six months. Since the bond is selling for slightly less than its face value, the bond would actually yield 6.6 percent. The price of a bond rises and falls to keep the current yield in line with market interest rates. The cv notation means that the AlbertoPharm bond is convertible.

The next column indicates the total trading volume for the day. The volume of 20 listed for the AlbertoPharm bond means that $20,000 worth of bonds were traded. The closing bond price is listed next, followed by the change in price since the previous day's closing price.

Stock Indexes

A feature of most financial news reports is the report of current stock indexes or averages. The most familiar is the Dow Jones Average (or Dow). Two other widely reported indexes on U.S. stocks are the Standard & Poor's 500 and NASDAQ Composite indexes. In addition, there are numerous indexes on foreign stocks including the DAX (Germany), the FT-100, or "Footsie" (London), and the Nikkei (Tokyo). All of these indexes have been developed to reflect the general activity of specific stock markets.

While there are several Dow Jones indexes, the most widely followed is the so-called *Dow Jones Industrial Average,* consisting of 30 stocks of large well-known companies. The S&P 500 is made up of 500 stocks, including industrial, financial, utility, and transportation stocks, and is considered to be a broader measure of overall stock market activity than the Dow. The NASDAQ Composite is an index made up of all the 5,000-plus stocks that trade on the NASDAQ Stock Market. Because technology companies—such as Oracle and Apple Computer—make up a substantial portion of the NASDAQ Stock Market, the NASDAQ Composite is considered to be a bellwether of the "tech" sector of the economy.

The Dow Jones Industrial Average has served as a general measure of changes in overall stock prices and a reflection of the U.S. economy since it was developed by Charles Dow, the original editor of *The Wall Street Journal,* in 1884. The term *industrial* is somewhat of a misnomer today because the index now combines industrial corporations such as Alcoa, General Motors, and United Technologies with such nonindustrial firms as American Express, McDonald's, and Wal-Mart.

Concept Check
1. What is the Dow Jones Industrial Average?
2. Which company is the only original member of the Dow that remains in the index today?

Changes in the composition of the Dow reflect changes in the U.S. economy. In fact, General Electric is the only original member of the Dow on the index today. Recent changes include adding American International Group, Home Depot, Intel, Microsoft, Pfizer, SBC Communications, and Verizon to the Dow, while dropping AT&T, Chevron, Eastman Kodak, Goodyear, International Paper Co., Sears, and Union Carbide. These changes were made to increase the representation of firms in communications, specialized retailing, and technology industries so that the index better reflects the overall stock market and U.S. economy.[10]

Mutual Funds

Many investors choose to invest through **mutual funds,** financial institutions that pool money from purchasers of their shares and use it to acquire diversified portfolios of securities consistent with their stated investment objectives. Investors who buy shares of a mutual fund become part owners of a large number of securities, thereby spreading their investment risk. Mutual funds also allow investors to purchase part of a diversified portfolio of securities for a relatively small investment, $1,000 to $3,000 in most cases. Mutual funds are managed by experienced investment professionals whose careers are based on success in analyzing the securities markets and choosing the right mix of securities for their funds. Mutual fund ads often stress performance or highlight the fund's investment philosophy. Most mutual funds are part of mutual families, a number of different funds sponsored by the same organization. The largest mutual fund families in the U.S. include Dreyfus, Fidelity, Janus, T. Rowe Price, and Vanguard.

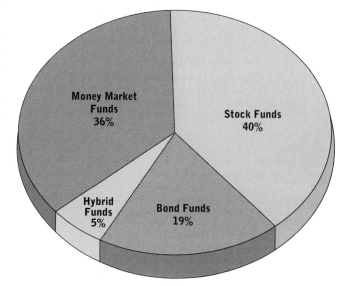

Source: The Vanguard Group, Inc. Reprinted with permission.

The Vanguard Group is one of the largest mutual fund firms in the U.S. It offers more than 100 funds, each with different investment objectives to meet varying client needs.

mutual fund financial institution that pools investment money from purchasers of its shares and uses the money to acquire diversified portfolios of securities consistent with the fund's investment objectives.

Mutual funds have become extremely popular in recent years. Today, U.S. mutual fund assets exceed $6.2 trillion. The number of American households owning mutual fund shares has increased from less than 5 million in 1980 to over 54 million today. Mutual funds are not limited to the U.S. either. Mutual funds in other countries have over $5 trillion in assets.[11]

Today's mutual fund investors choose among more than 8,000 mutual funds in the U.S. Some mutual funds invest only in stocks, some invest only in bonds, others invest in money market instruments. The approximate breakdown of mutual fund assets by stock, bond, hybrid (funds that invest in both stocks and bonds), and money market funds is shown in Figure 18.4. Most funds pursue more specific goals within these broad categories. Some stock funds concentrate on small companies, while others concentrate more on the shares of larger firms. Some bond funds limit their investments to municipal bonds, while other bond funds invest in only junk corporate bonds.

A number of mutual funds have been developed for investors who want their religious, social, or personal philosophies reflected in the management of the fund. For instance, there are funds designed for Catholics, conservative Christians, Lutherans, Mennonites, and Muslims. All attempt to follow investment philosophies that don't conflict with their religious teachings. Certain Muslim funds don't invest in bank stocks because banks charge interest, which some believe is contrary to Islamic teachings. Recently, many investors have been choosing funds that represent socially responsible investing. These

FIGURE 18.4

Distribution of Mutual Fund Assets by Type of Fund

Note: Hybrid funds invest in both stocks and bonds.
Source: Investment Company Institute, accessed at the ICI Web site,
http://www.ici.org, April 23, 2003.

SOLVING AN ETHICAL CONTROVERSY

Public or Private—Which Is Best?

After a flurry of initial public offerings (IPOs) that made a few people really rich, some companies are reconsidering whether going public is really the best course of action. Despite the obvious lure of ready cash, a public offering of stock means a whole host of new regulations and responsibilities, which some founders and executives of smaller firms are beginning to decide aren't necessarily worth the aggravation. Going public means opening company books and doors to the Securities and Exchange Commission (SEC), along with stricter regulations produced by the passage of the Sarbanes-Oxley Act.

Is going public really worth it for small companies?

PRO

1. It depends on the company. A bank, which is already accustomed to a high degree of financial scrutiny, is equipped to meet the requirements of the new regulations.

2. Being publicly traded carries a certain amount of prestige, say some banking experts, which can boost a company's image.

CON

1. Small companies aren't as visible in stock market listings as their larger counterparts. "If you have a market cap [or value] of under $200 million, no one will watch you," explains Dan T. Moore III, who sold his own small firm to General Electric.

2. The costs of going—and staying— public continue to rise, partly because of new regulations imposed by Sarbanes-Oxley and the SEC. In two years, these expenses doubled to an average of $2.3 million for companies with market caps under $900 million.

SUMMARY

Small public companies are investigating returning to private status, or "going dark" as industry watchers call it. Religious book and music publisher Integrity Media Group is one such firm. "The requirements of being a public company, especially for a small company like Integrity, are becoming increasingly expensive and time consuming," explains CEO Michael Coleman. With stock markets increasingly being dominated by institutional investors and a growing pile of investment capital available from private resources, the appeal of the flashy IPO is fading for many small companies.

Sources: Emily Thornton, "A Little Privacy, Please," *BusinessWeek*, May 24, 2004, pp. 74–75; Robert Barker, "When Companies 'Go Dark,' Investors Can Lose," *BusinessWeek*, May 24, 2004, p. 120; Lee Davidson, "Integrity Follows National Trend," *Mobile Register*, July 18, 2004, pp. 1F, 5F.

FIGURE 18.5
How to Read Mutual Fund Tables

	①	②	③	④
			Net	YTD
Issuer		NAV	Chg	% ret
Zardoz Funds:				
AggreGro		34.45	−0.37	+3.5
Gro		55.09	−0.45	+1.8
GroInc		20.17	+0.05	+6.9

① **Issuer:** Financial organization issuing and managing the mutual fund. Under the Zardoz family of funds are the different funds developed for investors with different objectives.

② **NAV:** Net asset value. Market value of fund's assets divided by the number of outstanding shares. Also the purchase price for no-load funds. (Load funds assess a sales charge on top of the NAV.)

③ **Net Chg:** The change in NAV from the previous day's close.

④ **YTD % ret:** The fund's total return for the year to date, from December 31 of the previous year. The percentage return assumes that all cash distributions were reinvested.

funds reflect many different social views, ranging from environmental protection to antidiscrimination.

Reading mutual fund tables is a relatively simple task. The first column in Figure 18.5 lists the organization issuing and managing the fund, the different types of funds offered for investors, and footnotes. The NAV column lists the fund's net asset value (the market value of fund assets divided by the number of outstanding shares), the price at which investors can buy shares if the fund is a no-load fund. Purchasers of shares of load funds pay a fee called a *load charge* on top of the NAV. The Net Change column shows gains or losses in the NAV from the previous day's close. The figures in the last column, the Year-to-Date Percentage Return, indicate each fund's total return from the beginning of the year.

Concept Check

1. Who typically manages a mutual fund?
2. What does the NAV column in a mutual fund table represent?

Legal and Ethical Issues in Securities Trading

As the number of Americans owning securities has increased, so too have concerns about illegal and unethical trading practices. Examples of unethical trading practices include brokers urging investors to buy high-risk investments and churning accounts (excessive trading) to generate higher commissions. Examples of illegal trading practices include broker theft from a client's portfolio and giving false or misleading information to investors. Even Internet chat rooms have come under increased scrutiny. The Internet is full of investment-oriented chat rooms where participants discuss various investment topics daily. The Securities and Exchange Commission (SEC) settled a lawsuit it had filed against a 17-year-old high school student in California. The SEC alleged that Cole Bartiromo posted false information about companies on several electronic bulletin boards in an attempt to inflate their stock prices. Once the prices rose, Bartiromo sold his block of shares at a profit. The settlement required that Bartiromo surrender almost $100,000 in ill-gotten investment profits.[12]

Government Regulation of the Securities Markets

Regulation of U.S. securities markets is primarily a function of the federal government, although states also regulate the securities markets. Federal regulation grew out of various trading abuses during the 1920s. During the Great Depression, in an attempt to restore confidence and stability in the financial markets after the 1929 stock market crash, Congress passed a series of landmark legislative acts that have formed the basis of federal securities regulation ever since.

As was noted earlier, the U.S. Securities and Exchange Commission, created in 1934, is the principal federal regulatory overseer of the securities markets. The SEC's mission is to administer securities laws and protect investors in public securities transactions, as discussed in the Solving an Ethical Controversy box. The SEC has broad enforcement power. It can file civil lawsuits against individuals and corporations, but actions requiring criminal proceedings are referred to the U.S. Department of Justice.

The SEC requires that virtually all new public issues of corporate securities be registered. Before offering securities for sale, an issuer must file a registration statement with the SEC. As part of the registration process for a new security issue, the issuer must prepare a prospectus. The typical prospectus gives a fairly detailed description of the company issuing the securities, including financial data, products, research and development projects, and pending litigation. It also describes the stock or bond issue and underwriting agreement in detail. The registration process seeks to guarantee full and fair disclosure. **Full and fair disclosure** means that the SEC does not rule on the investment merits of a registered security. Rather, it is concerned only that an issuer gives investors enough information to make their own informed decisions.

Besides primary market registration requirements, SEC regulation extends to the secondary markets as well, keeping tabs on trading activity to make sure it is fair to all participants. Every securities exchange, including NASDAQ, must, by law, follow a set of trading rules that have been approved by the SEC. In addition, the Market Reform Act of 1990 gave the SEC emergency authority to halt trading and restrict practices such as program trading (when computer systems are set to buy or sell securities if certain conditions arise) during periods of extreme volatility.

full and fair disclosure
requirement that investors should be told all relevant information by stock or bond issuers so they can make informed decisions.

insider trading use of material nonpublic information to make investment profits.

One area to which the SEC pays particular attention is so-called insider trading. **Insider trading** is defined as the use of material nonpublic information about a company to make investment profits. Examples of material nonpublic information could include a pending merger or a major oil discovery. The SEC's definition of insider trading goes beyond corporate insiders—people such as the company's officers and directors. It includes lawyers, accountants, investment bankers, and even reporters—anyone who uses nonpublic information to profit in the stock market at the expense of ordinary investors.

One well-known case of insider trading involved biotechnology company ImClone. Samuel Waksal, cofounder and former CEO of the firm, was charged with illegally tipping off several people that the Food and Drug Administration (FDA) was not going to approve for sale ImClone's principal product, the anticancer drug Erbitux. According to the SEC and Department of Justice, Waksal and others then sold thousands of shares of ImClone stock before the public learned of the FDA's decision. Once it was made public, the price of the company's stock plunged by over 50 percent. Waksal eventually pleaded guilty to several counts of criminal securities fraud. Others ensnared in the ImClone insider trading scandal included Waksal's father and daughter and lifestyle guru Martha Stewart. Stewart was convicted on federal charges of securities fraud and obstruction of justice and served her sentence in a minimum-security federal prison in West Virginia.[13]

Regulation FD requires that firms share information with all investors at the same time. It is designed to prohibit selective disclosure of information by companies to favored investment firms. Prior to regulation FD, many allege that clients of these firms often received the information sooner than other investors.

Securities laws also require every public corporation to file several reports each year with the SEC; the contents of these reports become public information. The best known, of course, is the annual report. Public corporations prepare annual reports for their shareholders, and they file another report containing essentially the same information, Form 10-K, with the SEC. The SEC requires additional reports each time certain company officers and directors buy or sell a company's stock for their own accounts (Form 4) or anytime an investor accumulates more than 5 percent of a company's outstanding stock (Form 13-d). All of these reports are available for viewing and download at the SEC's Web site (`http://www.sec.gov`, click on "Edgar").

Industry Self-Regulation

The securities markets are also closely monitored by professional associations and the major financial markets. The securities industry recognizes that rules and regulations designed to ensure fair and orderly markets will promote investor confidence to the benefit of all participants. Two examples of self-regulation are the rules of conduct established by the various professional organizations and the market surveillance techniques used by the major securities markets.

Professional Rules of Conduct   Prodded initially by federal legislation, the National Association of Securities Dealers (NASD) established, and periodically updates, rules of conduct for members—both individuals and firms. These rules try to ensure that brokers perform their basic functions honestly and fairly, under constant supervision. Failure to adhere to rules of conduct can result in disciplinary actions, including temporary or even permanent suspensions of brokerage licenses. The NASD also established a formal arbitration procedure through which investors can attempt to resolve disputes with brokers without litigation. In an arbitration proceeding, an impartial arbitrator reviews the facts of a case and attempts to render a decision that is acceptable to both parties. Arbitration is usually faster and cheaper than litigation.

Market Surveillance   All securities markets use a variety of market surveillance techniques to spot possible violations of trading rules or securities laws. For example, the NYSE continuously checks trading activity throughout the trading day. A key technical tool used by the NYSE is called *Stock Watch,* an electronic monitoring system that flags unusual price and volume activity. The NYSE then seeks explanations for unusual activity from the member firms and companies involved. In addition, all market participants must keep detailed records of every aspect of every trade. This is called an *audit trail.* The NYSE's enforcement division may impose a variety of penalties on members for rule violations, including fines and suspensions. Furthermore, the

Concept Check

1. *What function does the SEC serve?*
2. *What is full and fair disclosure?*

exchange turns over evidence to the SEC for further action if it believes that violations of federal securities laws may have occurred.

What's Ahead

Contemporary Business concludes with three appendixes. Appendix A examines risk management and insurance. It discusses the concept of risk, the alternative ways of dealing with it, and the various kinds of insurance available for businesses and individuals. Appendix B offers a guide to your own personal finances, as well as a stock market game. Finally, Appendix C outlines how to prepare a business plan.

DID YOU KNOW?

1. More than 60 million people directly own shares in publicly traded corporations. That's more than one out of every four U.S. households.
2. Major brokerage firms pay a total of $500 million for independent stock research to avoid conflicts of interest.
3. Seventy-three percent of participants in one poll said that if they observed wrongdoing at work (such as unethical accounting or insider trading), they would become whistleblowers. In the same poll, 57 percent said they believed whistleblowers face negative consequences at work.

Summary of Learning Goals

1 *Distinguish between the primary market for securities and the secondary market.*

The primary market for securities serves businesses and governments that want to sell new issues to raise funds. The secondary market handles transactions of previously issued securities between investors. The business or government that issued the security is not directly involved in secondary market transactions. In terms of the dollar value of trading volume, the secondary market is four times larger than the primary market.

2 *Compare money market instruments, bonds, and common stock and explain why particular investors might prefer each type of security.*

Money market instruments and bonds are debt instruments. Money market instruments are short-term debt securities and tend to be low-risk securities. Bonds are longer-term debt securities and pay a fixed amount of interest each year. Bonds are sold by the U.S. Treasury (government bonds), state and local governments (municipal bonds), and corporations. Most municipal and corporate bonds have risk-based ratings. Common stock represents ownership in corporations. Common stockholders have voting rights and a residual claim on the firm's assets.

3 *Identify the five basic objectives of investors and the types of securities most likely to help them reach each objective.*

The five basic objectives are growth in capital, stability of principal, liquidity, current income, and growth in income. Common stocks are the most likely to meet the objectives of growth in capital and growth in income. Historically, common stock investments have had higher returns on average than either bonds or money market instruments. Common stock dividends have also generally risen over time. Money market instruments are the most stable in price and rarely ever lose value. They are also the most liquid securities. Bonds tend to provide the highest current income of any security.

4 *Explain the process of buying or selling a security listed on an organized securities exchange.*

Investors use the services of a brokerage firm that is a member of one of the stock exchanges. After a broker receives a customer's order, it is sent electronically to the appropriate stock exchange for execution. A market order instructs the broker to obtain the best possible price, while a limit order places a ceiling or floor on the transaction price. Full-service brokers provide the most advice but charge the highest fees. Customers at discount firms have to make their own decisions but are charged lower fees. Online brokerage firms are popular today, and many full-service and discount firms have begun offering online trading services.

5 **Describe the information included in stock, bond, and mutual fund quotations.**

Information in a stock quote includes the 52-week indicator, the highest and lowest trading prices during the previous 52 weeks, the dividend, dividend yield, price-earnings ratio, trading volume, the stock's highest and lowest prices for the day, the closing price for that day, and the stock price's change from the close of the previous trading day. A bond quotation includes the maturity date and interest rate, the current yield, trading volume, and a comparison of the day's closing price with that of the previous day. Tables of mutual funds list each fund's general investment objective, net asset value (NAV), the change in NAV from the previous day, and the year-to-date total return.

6 **Explain the role of mutual funds in securities markets.**

Mutual funds are professionally managed investment companies that own securities consistent with their overall investment objectives. Investors purchase shares of a mutual fund, which make them part owners of a diversified investment portfolio. Investors can purchase shares of mutual funds for relatively small amounts. Mutual funds have become extremely popular in recent years. Mutual fund assets in the U.S. total over $6 trillion.

7 **Evaluate the major features of regulations designed to protect investors.**

U.S. financial markets are regulated at both the federal and state levels. Markets are also heavily self-regulated by the financial markets and professional organizations. The chief regulatory body is the federal Securities and Exchange Commission. It sets forth a number of requirements for both primary and secondary market activity, prohibiting a number of practices including insider trading. The SEC also requires that public companies disclose financial information regularly.

Business Terms You Need to Know

security 574
primary market 574
secondary market 575
money market instruments 576

secured bond 576
debenture 576
common stock 578
preferred stock 579

stock exchange 582
brokerage firm 585
mutual fund 589
full and fair disclosure 591

insider trading 592

Other Important Business Terms

initial public offering (IPO) 574
investment banker 575
underwriting 575

government bond 576
municipal bond 576
bond rating 577

call provision 578
market order 585
limit order 585

price-earnings (P/E) ratio 587
regulation FD 592

Review Questions

1. Explain the differences between a primary market and a secondary market. What two ways are securities sold in the primary market?

2. Outline the underwriting process. Why do corporations and state and local governments use investment bankers?

3. What are the major characteristics of money market instruments? How do money market instruments differ from bonds?

4. Distinguish between a corporate bond and a municipal bond. Explain the purpose of bond ratings.

5. What is common stock and how does it differ from preferred stock? Over the long run, what does a company's stock price tend to follow?

6. What are the primary investment motivations or objectives? Which security best meets each objective?

7. Explain the difference between a market order and a limit order. What are the differences among full-service, discount, and online brokerage firms?

8. How does the New York Stock Exchange operate? Compare the operations of the NYSE with those of the NASDAQ Stock Market.

9. Explain how a mutual fund operates. What are the benefits of investing in mutual funds?

10. Define and give an example of insider trading. List some ways in which the securities industries are self-regulated.

Projects and Applications

1. Assume you just inherited $50,000 from your uncle, and his will stipulates that you must invest all the money until you complete your education. Prepare an investment plan. What is (are) your primary investment objective(s)? How much would you invest in money market instruments, bonds, and common stocks?

2. Would you feel comfortable investing the $50,000 you inherited in Question 1 using an online broker, or would you use a full-service firm? Discuss the reasons behind your choice.

3. Many believe that conventional markets, such as the New York Stock Exchange, are fast becoming relics and eventually all securities markets will resemble Instinet. Do you agree with this assessment? Why or why not?

4. Assume you are considering buying shares of Merck. Describe how you would go about analyzing the stock and deciding whether or not now is a good time to buy it.

5. You've probably heard of U.S. savings bonds; you may even have received some bonds as a gift. What you may not know is that there are several different types of savings bonds. Do some research and compare and contrast the various types of savings bonds. What are their features? Their pros and cons? Assuming you were interested in buying savings bonds, which type do you find the most attractive?

Experiential Exercise

Background: Assume you receive $25,000 as a gift from a wealthy relative. As a condition of the gift, she expects you to invest the money. She also wants to review your investment plan and the securities you wish to purchase.

Directions:
a. Develop an investment plan, beginning with your investment objectives and goals. Make sure to consider your investment time horizon. Which of the five investment motivations (growth in capital, stability of principal, liquidity, current income, and growth in income) is emphasized by your investment plan? Why?

b. Assume you decide to purchase mutual fund shares with your relative's gift. What are some of the advantages of buying mutual fund shares rather than buying securities—such as stocks and bonds—directly? Next, go to the Morningstar Web site (http://www.morningstar.com). Based on your investment objectives and goals, select at least two Morningstar mutual fund categories. Make a list of the three top-performing funds in each category based on five-year performance. Research one of the top-performing funds in each category and prepare a brief summary. You should note the fund's investment objectives, its investment philosophy, its major holdings, and fund expenses.

NOTHING BUT NET

1. **Mutual fund information.** The Investment Company Institute compiles and publishes data on the mutual fund industry. Visit the Institute's Web site (http://www.ici.org) and review the most recent statistical release. Answer the following questions:

   a. What are the current net assets of U.S. mutual funds? Have net assets increased or decreased since the last reporting period?

   b. How many mutual funds are in operation? Has the number increased or decreased?

   c. Which type of mutual fund is the largest (measured in terms of both net assets and number of funds)?

2. **Purchasing Treasury securities.** As noted in the chapter, anyone may bid on Treasury securities when they are auctioned. Go to the Bureau of Public Debt's Web site and review the procedures for bidding on a Treasury security. Prepare an oral report outlining the bidding procedure, what the prospective buyer must specify, and how the Treasury decides which bids to accept. If you wanted to buy a newly issued Treasury security, would you have to go through a bank or brokerage firm?

   http://www.publicdebt.treas.gov

3. **Stock price quotations.** Choose five public companies mentioned somewhere in *Contemporary Business*. Visit one of the finance- or investment-oriented Web sites listed and obtain a current stock price quotation for each company, similar to the ones shown in the chapter.

   http://moneycentral.msn.com/investor
   http://finance.yahoo.com
   http://www.quicken.com
   http://www.morningstar.com

   Note: Internet Web addresses change frequently. If you do not find the exact sites listed, you may need to access the organization's or company's home page and search from there.

Case 18.1

Evaluating Alternative Stock Purchase Possibilities

Gina and Mario are a married couple in their mid-30s with two small children. Together, they earn around $90,000 per year. They have decided to begin investing in stocks and are most interested in stocks that promise growth with a steady return in the form of dividends. They have assembled the data in the following table from the past three years.

QUESTIONS FOR CRITICAL THINKING

1. Calculate the dividend yield and price-earnings ratio for each stock for each of the three years.

2. What is Gina and Mario's main investment objective (growth in capital, stability of principal, liquidity, current income, or growth in income)?

3. Based on your answer to the prior question, do you agree or disagree with Gina and Mario's main investment objective? Explain your answer.

4. Given your analysis of the data, and the couple's investment objective, recommend one of the five stocks.

		Price per Share	Earnings per Share	Dividends per Share
2004	A	$ 60	$ 5.12	$ 2.70
	B	268	13.35	10.00
	C	42	2.17	0.05
	D	6	0.12	0.08
	E	30	3.06	1.70
2005	A	59	7.98	2.80
	B	275	15.94	10.00
	C	45	2.74	0.06
	D	8	0.22	0.10
	E	29	3.20	1.80
2006	A	72	9.00	3.00
	B	320	17.50	10.00
	C	60	3.40	0.10
	D	11	0.80	0.12
	E	42	3.75	2.00

Video Case 18.2

Morgan Stanley

This video case appears on page 621. A recently filmed video, designed to expand and highlight the written case, is available for class use by instructors.

Investors Take a Bite Out of Krispy Kreme

Businesses need money to get started, to continue operating, and to grow. Vernon Rudolph sank his savings into his business when he purchased his first doughnut shop and its secret recipe from a French chef and opened the first Krispy Kreme shop in North Carolina in 1937. Company history says that Rudolph and two friends arrived in Winston-Salem "with $25 in cash, a few pieces of doughnut-making equipment, the secret recipe, and the name Krispy Kreme Doughnuts." Rudolph used the $25 to rent a building for the shop and then convinced local grocers to let him have the ingredients he needed to make his doughnuts on credit, promising they would be paid back as soon as he sold the first batches.

In 1976, Krispy Kreme became a wholly owned subsidiary of food giant Beatrice Foods, which gave the company access to Beatrice's resources—in return for running the business the Beatrice way. But the two cultures didn't match—Beatrice required Krispy Kreme shop owners to also serve their products, including deli sandwiches—and in the end, the influx of cash didn't necessarily guarantee success. So a group of ambitious franchisees led by Joseph A. McAleer, Sr., bought the company back from Beatrice in 1982 in a leveraged buyout worth about $22 million. Leveraged buyouts allow purchasers with limited funds to pay for a major portion of the acquisition cost with long-term notes, making it possible for the new owners to repay the balance over a period of years. Despite the amount of debt associated with the buyout, McAleer and his partners believed strongly that their profits would soon greatly outweigh any potential losses. However, the debt did slow the expansion of the company, which opened fewer than two dozen new stores between 1982 and 1995. Since then, Krispy Kreme's main avenue for growth has been through franchising, which places much of the risk squarely on the shoulders of franchisees, partly because Krispy Kreme does not offer financing to its franchisees. By around 1990, most of the buyout debt had been paid off, giving CEO Scott Livengood and then president Joseph "Mac" McAleer, Jr., the freedom to rethink the company's business model and find new ways to raise capital. (McAleer's father returned to Alabama to operate his own stores.) The executive team then focused on developing franchise deals for entire regions.

Another way companies raise cash is by offering an ownership share of the company to outside investors through the sale of shares of stock. Once companies have a good track record of sales and earnings growth, they can legitimately make an initial public offering (IPO) and bring financial success to themselves and their stockholders. By 2000, Livengood, now serving as president and CEO, had been working on Krispy Kreme's new business model for a decade. "Mac" McAleer returned to the South to run his own franchises, as had his father earlier. To continue its record of steady growth, Livengood and his executive team decided that they needed to raise additional funds. So, in April 2000, just when the dot-com stocks were beginning to tumble, Krispy Kreme issued its IPO to waiting investors. The stock, which was offered by the financial specialists who served as underwriters of the offering and had sold the shares to their clients at $21 per share, began trading on the NASDAQ at a price of $32 per share and more than doubled its offer price within a few months. In a little more than a year, the stock split twice. The money raised by the IPO was used to finance aggressive growth. During the following year, Krispy Kreme moved to the New York Stock Exchange (NYSE), where company officials celebrated by handing out 40,000 of its signature Hot Original Glazed doughnuts to anyone who wanted to try them.

Stocks, like those hot doughnuts, tend to cool off after awhile—which is exactly what Krispy Kreme's did. Despite the fact that during the first two years on the market, share prices increased 635 percent, changes in the marketplace, as well as other factors, resulted in a slide. As more and more consumers began to focus on counting the carbohydrates in their diets, fewer hot glazed doughnuts were sold. The firm decided to scale back its growth plans, focusing on smaller stores in carefully selected markets. Meanwhile, several operating franchises were faltering, and Krispy Kreme's management orchestrated a repurchase of those franchises. The high prices paid for some of these franchises—as well as the accounting methods used to report them—sparked an investigation by the SEC.

Still, industry watchers, investors, and Krispy Kreme managers remain upbeat about the future prospects for the company. "Krispy Kreme has no higher priority than the confidence of our shareholders, customers, and employees," declared CEO Scott Livengood.

QUESTIONS

1. How would you describe the risk–return tradeoff of Krispy Kreme's move into new markets?

2. List as many reasons as you can think of for why Krispy Kreme needs funds.

3. Why was Krispy Kreme's transfer from the NASDAQ to NYSE a significant business move?

4. Look at a stock table in one of the major newspapers to see how Krispy Kreme stock, shown under the ticker symbol KKD on the New York Stock Exchange (NYSE), is performing. What is today's price? Record also the P/E, 52-week high and low, and the net change.

Sources: Krispy Kreme Web site, http://www.krispykreme.com, accessed January 13, 2005; George Talbot, "Family Capitalizes on Company Success," *Mobile Register,* November 14, 2004, pp. 1A, 4A; George Talbot, "Doughnut Accounting Scrutinized," *Mobile Register,* October 9, 2004, pp. 1A, 4A; Rick Brooks and Mark Maremont, "Ovens Are Cooling at Krispy Kreme as Woes Multiply," *The Wall Street Journal,* September 3, 2004, pp. A1, A5; Paul Nowell, "Low-Carb Craze Catches Up with Krispy Kreme," *USA Today,* May 26, 2004, p. 6B; Christopher Palmeri, "What's Really Inside Krispy Kreme?" *BusinessWeek,* August 16, 2004, p. 72.

Video Case Contents

Video Case 1.2

Cannondale Keeps Satisfied Customers Rolling

You'll never forget your first real bicycle. Maybe it had stickers on the fenders, streamers from the handle-bars, and maybe even a bell or horn. The important point was that it didn't have training wheels—and it wasn't a tricycle. It was a bona fide bike. The people at Cannondale share your passion for that first bike, and they want you to enjoy cycling as an adult, preferably on one of their models.

The Connecticut-based company stresses quality and customer satisfaction from the ground up, from tires to seats to handlebars. Company management also understands that cyclists come in a variety of types, from recreational to racer. And satisfying the needs of a variety of cyclists means that Cannondale offers a broad product line made up of diverse models—including high-performance road bikes, sport road bikes, cross-country racing models, pack touring cycles, triathlon bikes, mountain bikes, "comfort" bikes, tandems, and even a recumbent cycle with a soft seat and backrest. For the truly persnickety customer, the bike maker also offers customized bike frames. And for cyclists who want to look and feel cool while they are riding, Cannondale can outfit riders with cycling apparel in high-tech fabrics. If that's not enough for the cycling enthusiast, there are hats, socks, shoes, seat and handlebar bags, and more.

It takes teamwork to produce Cannondale products, which are considered by both the cycling industry and their loyal customers to be of superior quality. If you could sit in on a research and development meeting for a particular model, you'd get a good sense of how dedicated Cannon-dale designers, engineers, and product managers are to their customers. Steve Metz, director of product management, oversees everything from decisions about how to meet customers' needs to selecting components for a bike and making sure the final product is manufactured to quality specifications and delivered promptly to customers. John Horton leads a team of project engineers who develop new models and improve currently popular models like the Jekyll. Designers and engineers meet frequently—and often informally—to discuss ways to add value by installing stronger or lighter components and increasing speed without driving up the price. They test different innovations, communicate with the manufacturing plant, and test them again. Once they have a prototype, they ride the bike. And to continually focus on customers, Cannondale designers use inputs from current and potential customers to guide every phase of the development process. After all, the world's highest quality bike is still a failure if it remains unsold in retail stores.

Technology also plays an important role in creating the lightweight, high-performance bikes for which Cannondale is so well-known. The company isn't hesitant to develop working relationships with outside firms capable of supplying technology not available in house. Several years ago, Cannondale reached an agreement with Genosys Technology Management under which Genosys would supply expertise in monitoring quality control and providing improved communication throughout the company. Cannondale has also pioneered such innovations as the electronic shock lockout system for mountain bikes. A traditional mountain bike is equipped with shock absorbers that reduce the amount of shock to a rider's leg, but the same mechanism also makes it harder to pedal uphill or make the most of sprints during a race. If a rider wants to "lock out" the shock absorber, he or she needs to remove one hand from the handlebar, a cumbersome maneuver for a cyclist on the move. The electronic Cannondale system works with the push of a button. One touch activates the lockout, and a second touch deactivates it. Riders love it. But the new system didn't come easily; Cannondale engineers tested and discarded several designs and prototypes before they had one that worked. The new system made its worldwide debut at the Sydney Olympics, where Swiss rider Christoph Sauser won a bronze medal.

The pursuit of quality requires that a firm must make ethical business decisions, even if that means admitting mistakes. Despite every effort to produce the best components, one year Cannondale discovered that the *stems*—part of the steering systems—on some of its $3,400 to $5,000 bicycles were breaking. The company responded quickly. After four reported instances and one minor injury, Cannondale issued a recall for the defective parts. Although a recall may have caused initial unwanted publicity, in the long run dealers and cyclists knew they could trust Cannondale to make the right decision. That's the mark of a company whose passion is perfection on wheels.

Like every business, Cannondale execs have made a few mistakes along the way. Their expansion into motorsports proved a failure. Worse yet, it ate up hordes of company funds and, coupled with the economic slowdown, forced founder Joe Montgomery to seek bankruptcy protection. In 2003, the firm was purchased by Pegasus Partners, which provided new funds for the cash-starved company and promised to make Cannondale even better. Pegasus representative David Uri voiced strong support for the company: "The fact that the bike division has remained profitable despite the . . . costs of its now closed motorsports business clearly demonstrates the strength of the brand. Our job now is to let Cannondale concentrate on what Cannondale does best—designing, manufacturing, and marketing lightweight, high-performance bicycles for the specialty retail market."

QUESTIONS FOR CRITICAL THINKING

1. Identify some of the types of capital that Cannondale uses in producing its bicycles.
2. In what ways do human resources at Cannondale contribute to value and customer satisfaction?

3. Describe how Cannondale can use relationship management to thrive and grow as a company.
4. Cannondale relies on teamwork to produce its bicycles. In what ways does this reflect the changing nature of today's workplace?

Sources: Cannondale Web site, http://www.cannondale.com, accessed January 9, 2005; Vernon Felton, "Cannondale Sold Off," *bikemag.com,* March 21, 2003; "CPSC, Cannondale Corp. Recall of Bicycles with Defective Systems," *U.S. Consumer Product Safety Commission,* August 15, 2002, http://www.cpsc.gov.

Video Case 2.2

Timberland Walks the Walk

We all know people who talk the talk of volunteerism and service. But do they walk the walk as well? Timberland is an extraordinary example of an entire company based on walking the walk of social responsibility—in its own boots. The Stratham, New Hampshire-based company has been making high-quality, durable work boots for decades under the name of Timberland, and prior to that under the name of the Abington Shoe Co., which Timberland's founder Nathan Swartz purchased in the 1950s. The firm is probably best known for its waterproof leather boots, but in recent years, it has added new lines of footwear that include casual fashion shoes, boat shoes, and hiking boots, as well as clothing and outerwear. While continuing to build its reputation as a brand that stands for durability, ruggedness, and the American outdoors, Timberland has been constructing a reputation for integrity and commitment to the community as well.

Ken Freitas, Timberland's vice president of social enterprise, loves to talk about the ways that his company has been able to build social responsibility right into its brand. "Doing good and doing well are *not* separate things," he says. "We're a business . . . part of our profits get put back into the community. Business and community should be joined together, and you have a more powerful enterprise *and* community."

Timberland implements this commitment through a series of programs in which its employees—including top managers—and corporate dollars participate. Through its Path of Service Program, employees receive up to 40 hours of paid time per year to participate in community service projects at

local schools, day-care centers, the S.P.C.A., food banks, and the like. They might clean up a nearby beach or help build a park. A few years ago, Timberland established its Service Sabbatical Program, in which three- to six-month sabbaticals are awarded to as many as four employees who wish to use their professional skills in assisting local nonprofit organizations full time. Then there's the Global Serv-A-Palooza, the annual worldwide, companywide celebration during which 2,000 employees, vendors, and community partners participate in a day of service.

Timberland's organized approach to community service began in 1989 following a phone call from a new volunteer program called City Year, which was based in Boston. As part of City Year, graduating high school students from diverse backgrounds would take a year off before starting work or college to participate in community service. Since many of the volunteer jobs involved outdoor work, City Year asked Timberland to donate 50 pairs of its work boots to the cause. Timberland agreed, and the next year City Year requested 70 pairs. A relationship was born during which both City Year and Timberland have grown nationwide. To date, Timberland has invested more than $10 million in the program and now outfits every City Year volunteer in boots, pants, shirts, jackets, and rain gear. "Yes, Timberland is helping to build City Year," notes Ken Freitas. "But City Year is helping to build Timberland."

How does Timberland measure the success of its community service programs? "One of the key challenges in a social responsibility program is measurement," admits Freitas. "How do you know if it is successful?" One way Timberland has been able to keep track of this is through joint marketing efforts with City Year. When a retailer in Philadelphia asked Timberland to make red boots to satisfy its younger customers (instead of the traditional tan work boots), Timberland balked at first. But then managers realized that red was the official color of City Year—and red boots might become the signature footwear of City Year volunteers. So Timberland made the boots and supplied them to the Philadelphia retailer as well as City Year participants—and all three organizations experienced growth in the Philadelphia area. This type of growth is reflected in Timberland's revenues, which currently reach more than $1 billion each year. But Freitas cautions against overdoing measurement. "What brings people to a brand isn't necessarily measurable," he explains. So Timberland adopts a "management and magic" philosophy that incorporates tangible results while leaving room for the unexpected or unexplainable.

At Timberland, social responsibility starts at the top. "Our company has a strong set of values that form the resolve for all that we do in the community—humanity, humility, integrity, and excellence," writes Jeff Swartz, president and CEO. "We strive to lead as responsible corporate citizens and to invest our resources, skills, ingenuity, and dedication to create positive change." If you happen to attend a Timber-

land national sales meeting, you'd better leave your golf clubs and swimsuit at home and wear your work boots instead. You might spend the day building a playground.

QUESTIONS FOR CRITICAL THINKING

1. In what ways does Timberland fulfill its responsibilities to consumers, employees, investors, and society as a whole?

2. In addition to a climate of social responsibility, do you think Timberland is likely to foster a climate of ethical awareness throughout its organization? Explain your answer.

3. In what ways does Timberland's Path of Service Program help develop the quality of its workforce?

4. Think of a small or large company in your hometown or in the town where you go to school. In what ways does the company serve its community? If it does not, describe ways in which it could.

Sources: Timberland Web site, http://www.timberland.com, accessed January 4, 2005; "Timberland's 5th Annual Serv-A-Palooza Goes Global for First Time," company press release, May 30, 2002, accessed January 4, 2005; "The Timberland Company Wins Business Ethics' Corporate Social Responsibility Report's Corporate Citizenship Award," company press release, November 2, 2001, accessed January 4, 2005.

Video Case 3.2

FedEx Hits the Ground Running

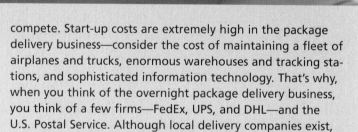

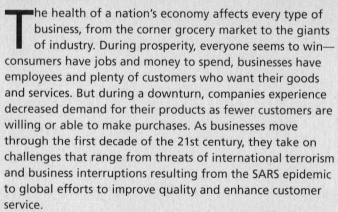

The health of a nation's economy affects every type of business, from the corner grocery market to the giants of industry. During prosperity, everyone seems to win—consumers have jobs and money to spend, businesses have employees and plenty of customers who want their goods and services. But during a downturn, companies experience decreased demand for their products as fewer customers are willing or able to make purchases. As businesses move through the first decade of the 21st century, they take on challenges that range from threats of international terrorism and business interruptions resulting from the SARS epidemic to global efforts to improve quality and enhance customer service.

FedEx has faced the challenges that come with swings in the business cycle as well as the unique conditions of the early 21st century. In addition, the firm is part of an oligopolistic market structure, in which relatively few companies

compete. Start-up costs are extremely high in the package delivery business—consider the cost of maintaining a fleet of airplanes and trucks, enormous warehouses and tracking stations, and sophisticated information technology. That's why, when you think of the overnight package delivery business, you think of a few firms—FedEx, UPS, and DHL—and the U.S. Postal Service. Although local delivery companies exist, they do not compete in the same market as the larger firms.

Several years ago, when the economy looked bleak and anthrax threats disrupted deliveries, demand for costly air delivery services was slipping (partly because the Internet could deliver documents faster and more cheaply), and prospects for growth appeared slim, FedEx did something unusual: It hit the ground. It spent $1.2 billion to build new shipping hubs, institute new sorting technology and package tracking systems, acquire several regional trucking companies, and hire independent (nonunion) drivers. Then FedEx was ready to enter the ground delivery business. Building its ground delivery system through acquisitions and contracts was less expensive—and faster—than starting from scratch. Start-up costs for an entirely new delivery system could easily have run as much as $3 billion. As demand for the new service increases, FedEx will spend an additional $1.8 billion to hire even more truckers. Because the FedEx truckers are essentially independent contractors, they are motivated by a pay system that rewards them for how much and how fast they deliver packages. "It's a system unique to the trucking business," notes Dan Sullivan, chief executive of the new subsidiary called FedEx Ground. Digital technology tracks every package and allows the firm to charge much less to deliver by ground than by air—$5 instead of $20.

With an 80 percent market share, UPS dominates the U.S. ground shipping market. FedEx is a distant second with about 15 percent. But FedEx is gaining ground more quickly than anyone anticipated as demand for its new delivery service increases. Although most of the firm's shipments have been business-to-business, FedEx has added such consumer-goods companies as Williams-Sonoma and L. L. Bean to its list of customers. By 2005, FedEx Ground accounted for 30 percent of the company's total revenues. FedEx has proved

that even in a slow economy, in a market structure that has expensive barriers to entering new markets, it can thrive. The company currently delivers more than 3 million packages per day, by ground and air, to 210 countries, in 24 to 48 hours. "FedEx is a different animal today," says transportation analyst James L. Winchester. "It's no longer a cyclical company, whipsawed in every downspin of the economy." Instead, FedEx is rolling down a whole new economic road.

QUESTIONS FOR CRITICAL THINKING

1. Describe some of the major factors driving demand for FedEx's business.
2. What kinds of restrictions might FedEx face if it were operating in a mixed market economy?
3. Why was the type of market structure in which FedEx operates an important consideration in the firm's strategy?
4. How might FedEx use a cycle of economic prosperity to further develop its ground shipping business?

Sources: FedEx Web site, http://www.fedex.com, accessed January 6, 2005; Charles Haddad, "FedEx: Gaining on the Ground," *BusinessWeek Online*, December 16, 2002, http://www.businessweek.com; David Shook, "FedEx Keeps Delivering," *BusinessWeek Online*, April 26, 2002, http://www.businessweek.com.

Video Case 4.2

ESPN Broadcasts Sports around the World

Bill Rasmussen made a big mistake in 1979. He had decided to launch a Connecticut-based cable TV station to broadcast local sports. So he and his partners leased a building and bought some satellite time. After they signed the agreement, they discovered that their satellite coverage was national, not local—and the idea for a regional cable sports station began to grow. New England, they thought, would be the perfect sports market for the new Entertainment and Sports Programming Network. Later, when business really got rolling, Rasmussen and his partners shortened the name to ESPN—and it stuck.

ESPN long ago leaped its New England borders into national coverage and ultimately extended its reach to covering sports and broadcasting them globally, although the company's headquarters remained in Bristol, Connecticut, where the original building was leased and where they still operate today. Headquarters now includes several buildings, 28 satellite dishes, and 3,200 employees. ESPN

operates 6 networks in the U.S. and 25 international networks, reaching between 150 and 155 million households globally. The company also produces ESPN Radio, ESPN Wireless, several Web sites including ESPN.com and ESPNSoccernet.com, magazines, and books, and it is exploring emerging technologies like video on demand and interactive TV. Spanish-speaking viewers can watch ESPN *Deportes* 24 hours a day. ESPN fans can eat at the ESPN Zone restaurant and buy merchandise at *TeamStore@ESPN*. Collectively, the ESPN media outlets offer coverage of local sporting events as well as major tournaments like the PGA Championship and the British Open for golf and the America's Cup sailing races—not to mention games of the NFL, NHL, MLB, WNBA, and various college sports. In addition to the game coverage, it offers sports news and analysis; information on scores, statistics, standings, and schedules; and just about any other sports-related content the enthusiast could want.

Reaching out for the global market was something that ESPN founders did "on gut feeling," says Willy Burkhardt, managing director of ESPN International. Because cable television was still new when ESPN was born, not much data existed on who was watching what around the world. But ESPNs executives had the idea that sports, like music and major news stories, had universal appeal. So they decided to try broadcasting American sports events in South America. Today, South and Central America—particularly Argentina, Brazil, and Mexico—represent 40 percent of ESPN's total business. And although the firm continues to broadcast American sports overseas, it now places much greater emphasis on local and regional programming based on the tastes and preferences of the host cultures. For example, says Burkhardt, in India "cricket is a total culture." While few Americans are familiar with the sport, millions of Indians are glued to the TV for cricket matches. In Argentina, rugby and polo occupy prime-time coverage. Major markets such as Argentina and India command their own ESPN offices and on-air announcing teams. In addition to South America and Asia, ESPN has a presence in Europe, Canada, Australia, and New Zealand—and even a station in Antarctica.

ESPN has used a variety of methods to enter international markets. In Europe, ESPN has had a long-standing partnership with EuroSport, which means that, although many European consumers watch sports on cable television, they are not necessarily aware of the ESPN name. However, recently ESPN did launch ESPN Classic Sport, a network dedicated to the greatest moments of European sporting history. ESPN operates in Canada through partnerships, as well. These arrangements are partly due to varying regulations in different countries and regions. But in Asia, ESPN has a large operation of its own, broadcasting to about 25 countries on the continent, including India, which is one of the firm's most important markets.

ESPN continues to grow in international markets because its managers believe they can bring "a new century of sport" to viewers around the world. "You learn by doing," says Burkhardt. ESPN wants viewers worldwide to watch what it is doing.

QUESTIONS FOR CRITICAL THINKING

1. Describe three barriers to ESPN as it expands in the global marketplace.
2. How might NAFTA and the European Union affect ESPN in those areas?
3. Describe the levels of involvement ESPN uses in its different international markets.
4. Does ESPN adopt a global business strategy or a multidomestic business strategy? Explain your answer.

Sources: ESPN Web site, http://www.international.espn.com, accessed January 14, 2005; "ESPN Executive from Waterbury, CT Leads High-Definition Television Venture," press release, http://www.hoovers.com; "ESPN to Be at the America's Cup," press release, February 12, 2003, http://hoovnews .hoovers.com.

Video Case 5.2

Fresh Samantha: A Juicy Business

Everyone loves a success story, especially when it involves ordinary people, an innovative product, a small business, and a dash of good luck. About a decade ago, Doug Levin and his wife, Abigail, decided to quit the fast life in New York City and move to rural Maine with their daughter, Samantha, to help Abby's parents run their alfalfa sprout farm. While he was delivering sprouts to local grocery stores, Levin kept encountering a product from another small business, a fresh carrot juice called 24 Carrot. He tried the juice and loved it so much he convinced his in-laws to buy the company. As they took over production of the juice, Abby—a children's book illustrator—designed a logo for the product, thought about their daughter, and chose the name Fresh Samantha for what would become a juice-based product line.

Like many small-business owners, the Levins didn't really have a business plan at first. They had a passion for their product and wanted to share it with the world. But consumers in rural Maine weren't enthusiastic about paying $2.50 to $3.50 for a single serving of juice, no matter how fresh and nutritious the ingredients were. Although they loved the taste, they decided the price was too high to make them switch from the much lower priced apple and orange juices they were accustomed to buying by the gallon. Still, the Levins knew they had an innovative product, and because the company was so small, they could shift their focus quickly. So they began looking for customers in the Boston area. "There's a bigger population in Boston," explains director of communications Betta Stothart. "It wasn't strategic, just a quest for the consumer," she recalls. They found their niche market on college campuses, starting with Tufts University in the Boston suburb of Somerville. Levin approached the Tufts food buyer with a bottle of Fresh

Samantha. The buyer liked the taste so much that he agreed to stock it at the university's various eateries. Fresh Samantha immediately clicked with college students: They liked the idea of fresh juice, they loved the taste, and they even liked the names of the different blends that Levin had begun to produce, including Desperately Seeking C and Mango Mama. It wasn't long before other schools—and then grocery stores and supermarkets—were stocking the fresh juice. Eventually, distribution of the juices spread up and down the eastern seaboard, from Maine to Florida.

Levin wasn't satisfied with simply fulfilling an isolated market niche, though. He was convinced that he could bring Fresh Samantha into the mainstream. "There's a place for this product in the mass market—I'm convinced of it." But expanding a small company that has enjoyed the flexibility of being able to develop new products at a relatively low cost is a challenge. From the beginning, the Levins and their employees could experiment with new juice blends right in their own kitchen. If a new flavor bombed—like Pumpkin Moonshine or Groovy Guava—they could move on. The company was entirely family owned, giving its founders complete control over everything from juice flavors to package design. Expanding might mean losing some of that control, as well as flexibility. But it could also mean greater financial resources, wider distribution, and a way to reach a general market as more consumers became conscious of nutrition.

In early 2000, they found an answer: Fresh Samantha agreed to a merger with California-based Odwalla, Inc., a publicly held premium juice producer with a philosophy similar to Fresh Samantha's. "Since our respective inceptions, Odwalla and Fresh Samantha's spirits have been aligned in our visions of delivering great-tasting nourishment," said Odwalla's chairman and CEO Steve Williamson. "Together, these two innovative brands have national leadership of this category." Doug Levin remained with the company as president.

Although the merger was successful, Fresh Samantha—like any small business—had to face further growing pains,

including the increased cost of developing new products. "It gets harder as you get bigger to have a flop because of the costs associated with it," notes Betta Stothart. "You eat the ingredients if it's a flop." One such case was Ginger Peach, which sounded great to everyone—except consumers. The company was stuck with a warehouse full of ginger. Another bittersweet experience was moving production of the juices from Maine to Florida to be closer to the fruit growers.

About a year after the merger with Odwalla, the big guns moved in: The new company was acquired by the Minute Maid division of The Coca-Cola Company. Would there be any major changes in the juices? Not likely, assured Minute Maid executives. But researchers have been examining ways to keep the juices fresh longer without compromising nutrition. Meanwhile, consumers can still enjoy their favorite flavors, including Desperately Seeking C, Get Smart, Mango Mama, and Oh Happy Day. Fresh Samantha, just like its namesake, has grown up.

QUESTIONS FOR CRITICAL THINKING

1. In what ways does a small business like Fresh Samantha contribute to the overall economy?

2. What are the advantages of running a small business like Fresh Samantha?

3. What are some of the challenges a small business like Fresh Samantha must face?

4. Fresh Samantha achieved growth through its merger with Odwalla and finally through Odwalla's acquisition by Minute Maid. Describe other ways in which the company might have achieved significant growth.

Sources: Fresh Samantha Web site, http://www.freshsamantha.com, accessed January 7, 2005; *Bevnet*, http://www.bevnet.com, accessed January 3, 2005; Dennis Rodkin, "Is It the Real Thing? Coca-Cola Buys Itself a Seat at the Juice Bar," *Conscious Choice*, The Kellogg School of Management, Northwestern University, March 2002, http://www.kellogg.northwestern.edu.

Video Case 6.2

The Geek Squad to the Rescue!

Who would have predicted that one day being a geek would be considered cool, much less heroic? Of course, heroic geekdom does have a few icons—Clark Kent, for one. But most people conjure up images of the Man of Steel—not the mild-mannered reporter—when they think about Clark Kent's fantastic deeds as Superman.

Entrepreneur Robert Stephens doesn't mind this perception. He also doesn't mind being called a geek, although he readily admits that he strives harder to emulate his own hero, James Bond, than he does Bill Gates, who transformed the world of computers with his company, Microsoft. But since Stephens does own a computer company—of sorts—he admits to his admiration to the geekish Gates as "having made everything easier for us."

Stephens is the epitome of an entrepreneur—so much so that associates joke that their dictionary definition of *entrepreneur* would read *See Robert Stephens.* A decade ago, he recognized an opportunity—a gap in the technical service provided by computer companies for individuals and small businesses—and made a business out of filling it. "No one wanted to make house calls [to repair people's computers]," he recalls. But Stephens was willing to be on call 24/7, and to drive to the homes or offices of people who ran small businesses, to diagnose any problems with their computers, fix the problem on the spot, and even upgrade their computers on request. It was a simple business idea, designed to take advantage of an opportunity. Stephens also had the vision to realize that the Internet, even though at the time in its infancy in commercial applications, would have a huge impact on the way companies conducted their business by allowing people to work from home. And computers had begun popping up in homes for personal use and entertainment. So Stephens quit his computer programming job at the University of Minnesota and launched his computer-repair business with an initial investment of $200.

Stephens didn't have much money. He also didn't have any employees. But he was blessed with liberal amounts of creativity, intelligence, humor, and energy. He thought hard about what to call his company, wanting the name to make a lasting impression on potential customers. Finally, he came up with The Geek Squad because he wanted to imply that he had a whole army of employees who could solve any computer-based trouble at a moment's notice. "The name is very important because it's what people think, say, and remember," Stephens explains.

When his customer base began to grow beyond his own service capabilities, he added his first employee, and then a few more. To support his company image, he designed badges identifying each employee as a member of The Geek Squad "intelligence network." He also designed uniforms for each serviceperson and provided a company car: a specially painted Volkswagen Beetle Geekmobile. Customers loved it—and so did The Geek Squad members.

For the most part, The Geek Squad serves customers operating home-based and other small businesses—ordinary people, such as lawyers who need fast repairs to their office computers. But sometimes glamour comes calling in the form of customers like U2 and the Rolling Stones. A few years ago, Geek Squad headquarters received an emergency call from U2's sound crew, who had encountered a host of computer problems in setting up the sound system for an Anaheim concert. They did such a bang-up job that the band called them in again during an appearance in Minneapolis.

Why did Stephens choose the entrepreneurial route for his career path? "I didn't want a boring job. I wanted to work for an international spy organization, and this is the closest I can get." He identified an important trend in the marketplace and built a business around it. His business model is based on his philosophy that he'd "rather be great at one thing than be mediocre at 15 things." The Geek Squad has progressed from a sole proprietorship begun in Minneapolis to a corporation with sizable offices in Chicago, Los Angeles, and San Francisco, as well as the Twin Cities. His intelligence network of service reps now numbers more than 50, and annual revenues have grown to several million dollars. His employees have job titles like "Dr. No" (the company's finance director) and "Counter Intelligence" (inside service representatives). He loves every minute of being a professional geek, even if he never did get his shot at being an international spy.

QUESTIONS FOR CRITICAL THINKING

1. Stephens identified two important trends in the environment—the need for on-site computer service and the growth of the Internet—that helped him predict his business would be a success. Identify at least one other factor in the environment that could be considered positive for The Geek Squad.

2. In what ways has Stephens and other entrepreneurs like him influenced the economy?

3. Describe some of the personal characteristics that probably contribute to Stephens's success.

4. Why was The Geek Squad a good business idea?

Sources: The Geek Squad Web site, http://www.geeksquad.com, accessed January 3, 2005; Kristin Davis, "This Geek for Hire," *Kiplinger Magazine,* December 2002, http://www.kiplinger.com.

Video Case 7.2

Elderly Instruments Stays Young on the Internet

If you are a musician, you've probably heard of them. If you've ever ordered a musical instrument (such as a guitar or banjo), accessories, or CDs online, you're probably a customer of Elderly Instruments. If you haven't heard of the company—and it's true that the name conjures up visions of a group of senior citizens in an orchestra—don't click past it so fast. Elderly Instruments is not your grandmother's band. It is a full-service music retailer offering new and vintage instruments—including a rare guitar for $25,000—along with accessories, CDs, books, and videos, all at a discount, online, by mail order, and in its flagship store in Lansing, Michigan.

Elderly Instruments was launched in 1972 by two guys who had just graduated from college, loved music, and wanted their own business. So they leased a 10- by 12-foot space, bought a bunch of used instruments at flea markets and yard sales, and set up shop to resell them. They quickly realized that there was money to be made and, within two years, decided to expand with a mail-order catalog. They also realized that offering price discounts gave them a great competitive advantage, something they still practice, says Stan Werbin, cofounder and CEO.

Two decades later, the firm developed a Web site and went online. In fact, becoming a New Economy business wasn't even Werbin's idea. One of his employees, Brian Hefferan, went to Werbin with the idea—and Stan gave him the go-ahead. Today, Hefferan is the firm's Web site network administrator, having shepherded the company through its initial stages of e-commerce to its current active involvement. At first, customers would access Elderly's Web site for information—facts about the company or to request a mail-order catalog. Today, however, "we have more [products] on the Web site than we have in the catalog because space is so easy to deal with," says Werbin. Transactions via the Internet move much more quickly as well. In the case of the $25,000 guitar, the firm would have had to wait weeks or maybe months after mailing a catalog before it got a response. But Brian Hefferan posted some photos of the guitar on Elderly's Web site, and the next morning the firm received an e-mail query from Japan. Before the day was out, the guitar was sold.

While other businesses struggle to figure out how to launch a successful Internet business, Werbin says it was pretty simple for Elderly Instruments because his company had already built a strong mail-order business on many of the same principles. "We already knew how to present things to people, and how to ship things to people," he says. "Going into the Internet business is just a mail-order business. It's just a different way of having a catalog. We already knew how to do that." But even Werbin concedes that there are some differences between the two. For instance, Web customers are more demanding in terms of time. "People who order on the Web want it yesterday," he grins. "You can't wait a couple of days, you have to process it right away." Werbin says he gets complaints if for some reason an item cannot be shipped within a day. So he strives to make sure orders go out immediately.

Another difference between mail-order and Internet business actually works to Elderly's advantage—information can be updated more quickly and more frequently. Instead of receiving an updated list of the vintage instruments Elderly has in its inventory every few months, music buffs can check the Web site for new products every day. This has translated to increased sales. In addition, Elderly keeps a log of its e-mail correspondence, requests or complaints from customers, purchase patterns, and other data that are useful in deciding which types of products to offer. So if you visit **http://www .elderly.com**, you won't be confronted by a group of retirees. Instead, you'll find yourself wandering through the offerings of a company that has music—and musical instruments—of every era.

QUESTIONS FOR CRITICAL THINKING

1. Describe two or three similarities between the Internet and mail-order selling, as well as two or three differences.
2. As Internet users become more diverse, how can Elderly Instruments capture a greater market?
3. How has the global reach of the Internet helped Elderly Instruments grow?
4. Identify two ways in which Elderly Instruments can measure the effectiveness of its Web site.

Source: Elderly Instruments Web site, **http://www.elderly.com**, accessed January 2, 2005.

Video Case 8.2

Buffalo Zoo's Leader Talks to the Animals— and People, Too

Being named head of an organization is a real honor. But leading and managing that organization effectively are huge responsibilities. Now try to imagine yourself in this position. But there's a twist because the organization's population is made up not only of humans but also snow leopards, rhinoceroses, and a lowland gorilla troop. That's the environment facing Donna Fernandes, chief executive officer of the Buffalo Zoo. Her domain is the nation's third-oldest zoo, located on 23 acres in beautiful Delaware Park and home to almost 1,000 wild and exotic animals. On any given day, she might observe the hand feeding of an infant tiger or lion and then speak to the zoo's board of directors about fund-raising to finance her master plan for the zoo's renovation.

When Fernandes arrived at the zoo, staff morale was low, the facilities needed immediate updating, and the zoo was in real danger of losing its accreditation. Both the zoo's staff and its board members were pessimistic about prospects of digging out of this financial and infrastructure hole. After all, they had heard grand plans for improvement from a succession of previous managers—and nothing ever happened. Because the zoo is a nonprofit organization whose board members are vital to any fund-raising efforts, Fernandes knew she had to establish her credibility—both with her staff and with the board—if she planned to succeed in accomplishing meaningful changes.

It didn't take long to win them over. Fernandes quickly developed a rapport with board members thanks to her enthusiasm, energy, and expertise. They also applauded her three-pronged mission of conservation, education, and recreation, as well as her comprehensive strategic plan for renovating the zoo. The plan included major construction of vastly improved natural settings for animals, with an emphasis on wildlife habitats rather than cages, along with enhanced education programs and increased access for children and visitors with disabilities.

Fernandes's democratic leadership style went a long way toward building trust among zoo employees. First, she had to get them to believe that her renovation plans weren't "pie in the sky" daydreams meant mainly for discussion: They were action plans. Second, she needed to convince them that their input and contributions were essential to the plan's completion and to the ultimate success of the Buffalo Zoo.

"I appreciate that collegial respect," notes Adair Saviola, director of development and marketing. "I never feel that I'm working for her, I'm working *with* her. She believes we know how to do our jobs." For instance, when a staff member or group comes up with an innovative way to attract additional funding for the zoo, that person or team participates in deciding how those funds will be used to improve the zoo. Darryl Hoffman, the elephant keeper and head of the animal training committee at the zoo, discovered this firsthand when he came up with a program called Art Gone Wild, in which elephants, primates, and big cats create "paintings" that the zoo sells to the public. When praised for her leadership style, Fernandes shrugs, "I appreciated it when my [previous] bosses listened to me and let me make my own decisions," she explains. She believes that empowerment is vital to enhancing the zoo and uses this philosophy to motivate her employees. Motivation, which is discussed in detail in the next chapter, is the key to success in almost any organization.

Fernandes's staff members also appreciate her managerial qualities. "As a manager, [she] is incredibly flexible," says Tiffany Vanderwerf, curator of education. "She's good at making sure there are two types of feedback: informational and emotional." Vanderwerf notes that Fernandes's informational feedback is clear and concrete, while the emotional feedback is positive whenever possible. Zoo marketing manager Heidi Henzler points out that Fernandes can be seen just about everywhere at the zoo, helping out whenever she can. "She gets down in the trenches with everyone. If there is a procedure that needs to be done, she wants to make sure it is done right," says Henzler. "She fosters a group environment, so we all get the same message." Fernandes even decided to undergo some training as an animal keeper so she could understand the job. She discovered that being a keeper can be pretty tedious at times, so she set up a program in which the different keepers could rotate jobs, as well as train others in their own areas of expertise.

The new millennium has seen the renaissance of the Buffalo Zoo under the leadership of its first female director. Nearly 400,000 visitors come to the zoo, a number that has steadily grown during the past five years. Lucky visitors might get the chance to wash an elephant or watch one paint; children can attend an on-site day camp; groups can take guided tours of habitats. The Buffalo Zoo's board, management, and staff members view the zoo as an important contributor to the preservation of wildlife through education. With Donna Fernandes at the helm, the zoo is bound to succeed.

QUESTIONS FOR CRITICAL THINKING

1. How did Donna Fernandes's leadership style help turn her strategic plan into action?
2. Imagine that you are a member of the Buffalo Zoo's board of directors. Write a brief statement of what you think the zoo's mission is.
3. Based on the information presented in the case, draw an organization chart of the Buffalo Zoo. Make any assumptions necessary.
4. How would you describe the corporate culture of the Buffalo Zoo under Donna Fernandes's leadership? Would you say that Donna Fernandes is good at delegating? Why or why not?

Sources: Buffalo Zoo Web site, http://www.buffalozoo.org, accessed January 3, 2005; "Can an MBA Help You Change Careers?" *ITworld.com*, February 22, 2005, http://www.itworld.com.

Video Case 9.2

Fannie Mae: Making Dreams Come True

Even though the U.S. Constitution doesn't guarantee American citizens the right to own their own homes, the idea of purchasing a home—whether it's a condo in the city, near the ski slopes, or at the beach; a four-bedroom Colonial in the suburbs; or a cottage by the ocean—has become a part of the American Dream. Further evidence is provided by the fact that the percentage of U.S. residents who own a home is one of the highest on earth. Buying a home is likely to be the greatest expense we will ever face as consumers. In addition, it is likely to be the largest financial asset for most of us. The Federal National Mortgage Association, also known as *Fannie Mae,* recognizes these facts. Fannie Mae is a private corporation that works with primary lenders like mortgage companies, banks, and credit unions to secure funds for mortgage loans so that more people can realize their dream of buying a home.

To achieve this goal, Fannie Mae operates like any other company in serving its customers. A key factor is its success in attracting, managing, motivating, and developing an effective workforce. The organization recognizes the value of diversity and strives to attract highly qualified recruits. Persons accepting employment offers receive thorough training designed to make them successful employees who have the ability and opportunity to move up the corporate ladder on their way toward fulfilling careers. Every new employee participates in the DREAM orientation program, which senior consultant Jane Shore describes as "a way of welcoming people and letting them know from the start that we are delighted to have them at Fannie Mae and we are going to do everything we can to gear them up for a productive and successful career at Fannie Mae." DREAM stands for *Discovering and Retaining Employees to Attain our Mission.* The

program is the beginning of Fannie Mae employee training designed to achieve their dream careers and to help the American dream come true for thousands of customers who want to buy homes.

A number of programs are used to help motivate Fannie Mae employees along a fulfilling career path. One is the mentoring program, which matches senior-level employees with newer recruits. The mentor helps guide his or her coworker up the career ladder by offering advice, asking and answering questions, and making sure that the individual is developing the right skills to achieve personal employment goals. The mentoring program identifies and develops talent among the workforce, which in turn helps Fannie Mae retain and encourage exceptional employees. Another motivating program is the ACE program, which provides tuition and expenses reimbursement and other benefits for advanced degrees in fields relevant to employee careers.

Ask Fannie Mae employees why they work there and many will rave about their company's benefits package. Along with the typical benefits like medical insurance, vacation time, and holidays, Fannie Mae offers such progressive benefit programs as elder care. Company employees with an aging or ill parent or other close relative can receive advice from an on-site consultant as well as time off to provide emergency and other necessary care. In addition, many Fannie Mae employees take advantage of flexible work schedules so they can balance family needs with job performance. Human resource director Emmanuel Bailey believes these programs benefit not only employees but the entire corporation. By reducing outside stress, these programs actually allow employees to "add value to the business." As he puts it, "The thing that impresses me the most is that these programs aren't created in a vacuum. They come from feedback from employees." He notes that while many companies preach that employees are their greatest asset, "Fannie Mae makes it a practice rather than a policy."

Naturally, the company wants to make sure that its employees have the opportunity to purchase their homes. It accomplishes this in a novel way. A special formula—both specific and easily understandable—is used to determine the amount of money each employee can borrow toward the purchase of a home, and if they stay with Fannie Mae over a period of time, the debt is gradually forgiven.

Because it deals with a great cross-section of the nation's customers, Fannie Mae is ahead of many other corporations in identifying demographic and workforce trends. And the diversity of its customers is also reflected in the firm's workforce. Christine Ladd, the company's general counsel, describes diversity as being much more than working with people from different cultural, ethnic, or economic backgrounds. Diversity "might mean different family statuses," she notes, such as the single working mother or grandpar-

ents raising grandchildren. So Fannie Mae uses its many human resource programs to provide flexible benefits and work schedules for its employees. You could say that Fannie Mae is in the business of making dreams come true.

QUESTIONS FOR CRITICAL THINKING

1. Why does Fannie Mae go to such great lengths to discover and retain the best workers for its staff?

2. How do Fannie Mae's training and education programs help build commitment to the organization?

3. In what ways does Fannie Mae motivate its workers?

4. Fannie Mae has already identified certain work/life trends such as the need for elder care. Describe at least one other work/life trend that you can identify in today's workplace, as well as a possible human resource solution.

Sources: Fannie Mae Web site, http://www.fanniemae.com, accessed January 7, 2005; "Fannie Mae," *Hoover's Online*, http://www.hoovers.com, accessed January 7, 2005; Laura Cohn, "Protecting Fannie's Franchise," *BusinessWeek*, December 9, 2002, pp. 94–98; "Best Places to Work in Technology," *Computerworld*, May 16, 2002, http://www.fanniemae.com.

Video Case 10.2

Communication Is Key at Le Meridien

Staying at a luxury hotel is a treat. Soft pillows, fluffy towels, and plush cushions on the couch all make for sweet dreams and comfortable stays. Creating the dream suite and maintaining it on a day-to-day basis is a continuing challenge for an entire team of hotel personnel, as Bob van den Oord, assistant general manager at Boston's Le Meridien, knows very well. Van den Oord and his staff are a finely tuned symphony as they orchestrate vacations, honeymoons, and business meetings for people who expect the very best.

Van den Oord knows that constant communication is the key to coordinating his team. He uses a mix of formal and informal, written and oral communications, but his favorite is what he calls "management by walkabout." This is literally what it sounds like—he takes a daily walk through the hotel to see how things are running, answer questions, help staff solve problems, and chat with guests. His daily tour "gives the staff a chance to talk to me," says van den Oord. "I think they like it that I'm present. They see that the manager is not just sitting in his office." Van den Oord believes that face-to-face interaction with his staff is vital. "All the one on

one with your people is good—it needs to happen on a [regular] basis," he notes. Van den Oord believes that this personal contact lets employees know that he is accessible and that they can come to him with questions or problems about their work—which facilitates a quicker solution.

In addition to his walkabout, van den Oord holds operational meetings each morning in which his team—his top managers—discusses each day's events, time line, and staffing requirements. "It's quite casual," van den Oord remarks. "Everyone has a cup of coffee and talks." In the 15 minutes allotted for the operational meeting, a great deal is accomplished because managers have learned how to present their messages clearly, listen well, and help each other find solutions to problems.

Although e-mails have become an ever-frequent form of written communication in the workplace, van den Oord and his managers use it sparingly. "E-mail facilitates a lot of communication processes, but it's not the solver of all problems," says Michiel Lugt, the hotel's room service and stewarding manager. Lugt notes that it's easy for someone who sends an e-mail to assume that the recipient actually read and understood the message, when in fact that person might not have checked his or her e-mail that day—or might not have understood the importance of a particular message.

Van den Oord agrees that e-mail is secondary to personal contact, particularly when conflicts exist with or among employees. "Some managers have difficulties confronting issues, so they send an e-mail," says van den Oord. He believes that a brief conversation in person or by phone is far more effective than e-mails in such instances.

Both Le Meridien managers are strong proponents of communicating by example. "Be present," says Lugt. "You are leading by example." This might mean filling a gap in service by pouring a cup of coffee for a guest, taking reservations or meal orders, or offering directions to a nearby theater in Boston. In performing these tasks, Lugt lets his staff know that he is part of their team—the team that is running the hotel.

In addition to constant internal communication, Bob van den Oord and his staff maintain ongoing external communi-

cation with a variety of others, including the media, any of the other 140 Le Meridien hotels around the world, the hotel's guests, and travel professionals. All of this communication leads back to one thing—a happy, motivated staff. "A happy staff equals happy guests," says van den Oord. "And happy guests help us meet our business objectives."

QUESTIONS FOR CRITICAL THINKING

1. Do you think that van den Oord's style of communication empowers his employees? Why or why not?

2. Describe the ways in which van den Oord exchanges information with his staff.

3. Is van den Oord likely to receive information through the grapevine? Why or why not?

4. Do you believe that van den Oord is an effective communicator? Why or why not?

Source: Le Meridien Web site, http://www.lemeridien.com, accessed January 8, 2005.

Video Case 11.2

Cannondale Produces World-Class Bicycles

Making and selling world-class products are continuing challenges for any manufacturer. Cannondale, which produces premium bicycles, is no different. The Connecticut-based company, whose origins are described on page 602, prides itself on rolling out the best bicycles for every type of rider, from recreational to racer. Cannondale keeps coming up with innovative designs and new technology to enhance the riding experience for its customers.

At Cannondale, the research and development team comes up with a particular vision for a new model or improvements to an existing model. Initial suggestions may come from customers, dealers, or from team members themselves. Components are selected, manufactured, and tested by staff, sometimes right on the grounds of company headquarters or in surrounding areas. If a component—say, the seat, handlebar, or pedals—doesn't meet the company's standards for quality, it goes back to the drawing board until it does. A new bike may be in development for a year or more, as was the recent Gemini freeride bike, designed for mountain bike competition. The Gemini features a special frame designed to withstand the shock of bumping and bouncing down a mountain trail at high speeds, and it is continually being updated to incorporate new technology.

At the other end of the riding spectrum is Cannondale's recumbent cycle, designed for riders who cannot—or prefer not to—ride a conventional bike. The design team, including designer Chris Dodman, worked on prototypes for three years before introducing the current model to the market. Dodman used advanced technology, including computer-aided design (CAD), to come up with the new recumbent. Cannondale's commitment to sophisticated—but user-friendly—design technology and testing gives the firm a great advantage when it comes to controlling production processes and quality. And Dodman is passionate about the design quality of his product. "You can only make a conventional bicycle so comfortable before the basic diamond frame becomes a limitation," Dodman explains. "A recumbent seats the rider in a far more natural position, so it's inherently more comfortable, especially to a recreational rider. And because it seats the operator in the same basic position as a car, a recumbent is more intuitive to ride than a conventional bicycle."

Computer technology also aids the production process on the factory floor at Cannondale. Workers use scanners and bar-code technology to track different stages in the manufacturing process. An employee can swipe a scanner across a bar code attached to a bicycle frame or other component, immediately updating a database that logs where every part in the process is located. This system not only tracks the actual production of every bicycle but also helps managers control the inventory of components and finished bicycles.

A few years ago, Cannondale updated its inventory system so that it could conduct materials requirement planning (MRP) in a little more than two minutes—as opposed to one to three weeks. This increased Cannondale's flexibility in designing and producing new or improved bicycle models and allowed its factory to reduce its inventory, which also reduced the amount of money that was tied up in inventory.

Cannondale prides itself on being able to satisfy even the most demanding customers, from the world's top racing cyclists to the most selective amateur riders. Meeting customers' needs means being able to accept an order for a custom cycle, manufacture it, and ship it in the shortest time possible. The factory can accomplish this in six weeks. Because it does small production runs of its regular models, Cannondale can also change paint colors or decals to meet a new demand or take advantage of a trend. In addition, the firm can incorporate other innovations, like its new electronic shock lockout system for mountain bikes, which features a push button that makes it much easier to use than other systems. And while Cannondale produces smaller runs

of bicycles than those of its larger competitors, it manages to produce a model for just about every type of rider, from triathlon competitors to urban commuters to tandem riders. "We devise flexible manufacturing processes that enable us to deliver those innovative, quality products to the market quickly and then back them with excellent customer service," notes the company's Web site. Cannondale makes manufacturing sound as easy as riding a bike.

QUESTIONS FOR CRITICAL THINKING
1. Cite three reasons Cannondale's successful production and operations management is an important business function.
2. How have computers contributed to Cannondale's production process?
3. Why would Cannondale want to reduce its inventory of finished products and components?
4. Why is quality control an important part of the production process at Cannondale?

Sources: Cannondale Web site, http://www.cannondale.com, accessed January 9, 2005; press release, "Cannondale Introduces New Freeride Model, with a Second One on the Way," September 30, 2001, http://www.cannondale.com; press release, "Cannondale's New Recumbent Lives Up to Its Name," September 12, 2001, http://www.cannondale.com.

Video Case 12.2
Goya Foods Serves Many Markets

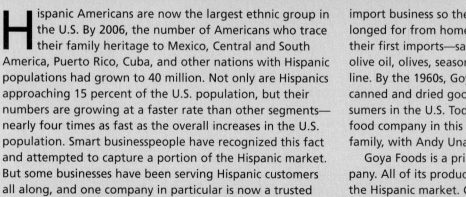

Hispanic Americans are now the largest ethnic group in the U.S. By 2006, the number of Americans who trace their family heritage to Mexico, Central and South America, Puerto Rico, Cuba, and other nations with Hispanic populations had grown to 40 million. Not only are Hispanics approaching 15 percent of the U.S. population, but their numbers are growing at a faster rate than other segments— nearly four times as fast as the overall increases in the U.S. population. Smart businesspeople have recognized this fact and attempted to capture a portion of the Hispanic market. But some businesses have been serving Hispanic customers all along, and one company in particular is now a trusted name throughout the Hispanic community, which includes people of varied backgrounds who come from such diverse countries such as Cuba, Mexico, Puerto Rico, Peru, and Spain.

Goya Foods was launched in 1936 when Spanish immigrant Don Prudencio Unanue and his wife opened a food

import business so they could enjoy the delicacies they longed for from home. From their earliest days with one of their first imports—sardines—over the years they added olive oil, olives, seasonings, and other food products to the line. By the 1960s, Goya was offering a wide range of canned and dried goods, from beans to rice, to Hispanic consumers in the U.S. Today, Goya Foods is the largest Hispanic food company in this country and is still run by the Unanue family, with Andy Unanue as chief operating officer.

Goya Foods is a prime example of a customer-driven company. All of its products are designed to meet segments of the Hispanic market. One of the keys to Goya's success is understanding the similarities and differences among those segments. Foods popular among Mexican Americans might be foreign to those from Peru. Cooking oils might vary in flavor from one country to another. Or standard foods like beans may come in different varieties—Mexicans like pinto beans, Cubans prefer black beans, while Nicaraguans want small chili beans. And the beans might be prepared differently, which means that Goya must offer them in a variety of ways. Shoppers can purchase Goya beans that are dried, canned, flavored, not flavored, recipe ready, or ready to serve. Goya tries to offer something for every Hispanic consumer—even niche products that are less profitable, such as Peruvian dried yellow hot peppers or the Salvadoran *pacaya*, a vegetable that's the blossom of a date palm tree. Doing so satisfies the needs of these consumers and begins building a long-term relationship as lovers of Hispanic foods look first to Goya when they seek an unusual item. According to Joe Perez, vice president of purchasing, the message to these consumers is, "We are the pre-eminent Hispanic company. We're there for you. We want you, and we will cater to your needs."

Goya also recognizes a difference between traditional Hispanic consumers and mainstream consumers. Traditional consumers want to be able to buy the right ingredients for traditional recipes, whether it is authentic flour for making tortillas or a certain flavor of cooking oil. Mainstream consumers, who have assimilated into the American culture, want the same quality but may prefer convenience foods such as ready-to-serve canned beans, canned tomato sauces, and frozen plantains. Goya offers foods in both of these categories. In addition, the firm reaches out to non-Hispanic consumers by making a special effort to market its Hispanic foods for recipes such as beef stew and spaghetti and meatballs.

Goya relies on family tradition for building a long-term relationship with its customers. As in many cultures, recipes are handed down from generation to generation in the Hispanic community, so when a grandmother begins to use Goya products and passes the tradition to her children, who then pass it to their children, the relationship is strengthened until it is built in to the family's tradition of cooking. "We're like the Goya-everything family," says frequent consumer Ricardo Los Melendez, a computer programmer in New York, whose wife, Wendy, is an assistant teacher. The couple, whose families are originally from the Dominican Republic, routinely fills their shopping cart with Goya frijoles (beans), fruit nectars, olives, rice, and other goods.

In addition, Goya has always worked to establish itself as part of the community it serves. It sponsors special events and works with nonprofit organizations to enhance the lives of Hispanic Americans. The company sponsors the annual Conference of the Organization of New Jersey Dominican Affairs, participates in the annual Puerto Rican Day parade in New York, recently sponsored an art exhibit by Puerto Rican painter Rafael Trufino at the Museo del Barrio in New York, and was recently showcased in a special exhibit at the Smithsonian during Hispanic Heritage Month.

"We make the community feel that we're part of them," Joe Perez explains. "We support them. We offer a quality product at a fair price." That's what every customer—from any culture—wants.

QUESTIONS FOR CRITICAL THINKING

1. What steps does Goya Foods take to increase customer satisfaction and create added value?
2. What advantages might Goya have over competitors such as Del Monte and Libby's in understanding the behavior of Hispanic American market consumers?
3. In what ways does Goya segment its market?
4. What are the benefits of Goya's efforts at relationship marketing?

Sources: Goya Web site, http://www.goya.com, accessed January 9, 2005; Haya El Nasser, "39 Million Make Hispanics Largest Minority Group," *USA Today*, June 19, 2003, pp. B1, B2; Emily Gersema, "Hispanic Foods Spice Up Marketing Ploys," *The Daily Texan*, May 5, 2003, http://www.dailytexan online.com; Al Sullivan, "Goya, Oh Boya!" *The Hoboken Reporter.com*, April 6, 2003, http://www.zwire.com; Gigi Anders, "More Than Rice and Beans," *Hispanic Trends.com*, Winter 2003, http://www.hispaniconline.com.

Video Case 13.2

Monopoly: America's Love of Rags-to-Riches Game Is Timeless

Maybe you've never been to Atlantic City, but if you've played Monopoly, the names Park Place, Boardwalk, and Atlantic Avenue are as familiar to you as the streets around your own hometown. Monopoly, invented in 1934 by entrepreneur Charles B. Darrow, is based on real streets in Atlantic City. When Darrow first showed his game to executives at Parker Brothers, they weren't interested. But the gamemaker's disinterest failed to discourage him. Darrow and a printer friend made 5,000 sets anyway and convinced a department store in Philadelphia to carry them. When all 5,000 quickly sold out, Darrow went back to Parker Brothers, who soon changed their minds after learning of the consumer response to the unknown—and untested—new game. Their decision to add it to their product line was perhaps the most important move in Parker Brothers' history. Within 12 months following its launch, Monopoly had become the best-selling game in the U.S. By 2005, Parker Brothers, now a division of Hasbro, Inc., had sold more than 200 million sets of Monopoly worldwide.

But the huge popularity of Monopoly poses a problem for its manufacturer: The game lasts, and repeat sales are difficult to secure. Once a family or an individual consumer buys a Monopoly set, there's no need to buy another. And if the idea of commerce—or rampant greed—doesn't appeal to someone, he or she is likely to pass on the game. Until recently, young children were left out of the game unless they had guidance from parents or older brothers and sisters, simply because the rules, concepts, and numbers were too complicated for them to follow. So Monopoly marketers began to evaluate ways to extend the product line. They examined new age groups, new socioeconomic groups likely to have market potential, and different interest groups and considered commemorative editions to mark or celebrate certain events in history. They also researched new platforms using interactive technology.

"Line extensions are all additives to Monopoly No. 9 [the official name of the original game]," explains Holly Riehl, director of marketing for Monopoly. The original game captures a universal truth that we all aspire to wealth, according to Riehl. In fact, Monopoly is such a universal game that, as Riehl says, "it has been adapted so thoroughly by every country that every country thinks it's their own." These ideas have combined to set the stage for a burst of new Monopoly editions targeted to different consumers.

Several years ago, Hasbro introduced a premium-priced Deluxe Monopoly with eye-catching new features for the collector—special tokens, title and deed carousels (making it easier to see and organize them during the game), and wooden houses and hotels. At around the same time, the company brought out Monopoly Junior for younger players. Based on an amusement park theme, in which game participants buy and sell amusement park rides and attractions, Monopoly Junior has attracted a younger generation of players ages 5 to 8. There's also the Dig'n Dinos edition for even younger children, and a Disney edition for players ages 8 to adult. Also in the product line are Monopoly 60th Anniversary and Monopoly Millennium, both developed to mark those anniversaries—and sold at a higher price of $39.95. If you are feeling particularly patriotic, pick up the America edition; if you speak Spanish, you can purchase the Spanish edition. And if you are a Star Wars or Pokemon fan, fear not—a Monopoly edition has been created for you, too.

Hasbro has also ventured into the interactive realm with a new subsidiary, Hasbro Interactive. The division sold 1 million copies of the first Monopoly CD-ROM, which became the fifth best-selling PC game of all time. "On the computer, Boardwalk and Park Place came to life," says Holly Riehl. Four years after the first release, an updated version hit the

market, in which players could customize the 3D board properties with their own street names and landmarks. Then came Monopoly PlayStation, Monopoly Hand-held, and Monopoly Nintendo, along with an e-mail version of the game.

Hasbro isn't trying to flood the market with Monopoly games, although certainly its marketers would like to see at least one edition in every household. But to reach as many consumers as possible, marketers conduct extensive product planning to make sure that each new version "makes sense," as Riehl puts it. "For instance, Monopoly Star Wars and Pokemon were a good fit," she says. The company tries to balance the basic concepts of the original Monopoly game with every one of its extensions, including such additions as a new token to the game. Several years ago, Hasbro conducted a search for a new Monopoly playing token, finally narrowing it down to three candidates: a biplane, a piggybank, and a sack of money. Then consumers were invited to vote for their favorite among the three. Over 2 million consumers cast their vote for the sack of money, which is now part of the game.

Riehl reports that Hasbro is planning even more extensions to attract new—and loyal—customers to the Monopoly experience. Monopoly slot machines are already very popular in Las Vegas, and game fanciers can watch for a Monopoly café as well as Monopoly books and other media. In short, Hasbro hopes Monopoly will eventually have a monopoly (of sorts) on all kinds of entertainment.

QUESTIONS FOR CRITICAL THINKING

1. How would you classify Monopoly as a consumer product? Why?
2. At what stage would you place Monopoly in the product life cycle? How does this relate to Hasbro's decision to extend the product line?
3. Monopoly marketing director Holly Riehl says that the idea for each new Monopoly edition goes through extensive planning before it is manufactured and brought to market. Even so, do you think that Hasbro is taking on more risk by introducing so many different types of Monopoly to the marketplace? Why or why not?
4. Visit the Monopoly Web site at http://www.monopoly.com or open up your own Monopoly game. Identify as many elements of the product image as you can. Do you think that Monopoly is a strong brand? Why or why not?

Sources: Monopoly Web site, http://www.monopoly.com, accessed January 9, 2005; "Hasbro, Inc.," *Hoover's Online*, http://www.hoovers.com, accessed January 9, 2005.

Video Case 14.2

FUBU: For Us, By Us

It's the American Dream: Four inner-city kids, steeped in hip-hop, start their own clothing business and make it big. Really big. It began when childhood friends Daymond John, Alexander Martin, Carl Brown, and Keith Perrin were looking for the tight-fitting tie-top hats that were popular among hip-hop fans. They left their Queens, New York, neighborhood and drove into downtown Manhattan in search of the hats. When they finally found them, the four realized quickly that they could easily make similar ones and sell them to their friends. So they bought fabric and made 40 hats, which sold right away. By then, they were thinking about starting a business. John was a homeowner, so he took out a mortgage to fund the business and turned half his house into a clothing factory for tie-top hats, T-shirts, and baseball caps—all with the logo FUBU embroidered on them. The name, which has a hip-hop ring to it, stands for the company philosophy: "For us, by us." The founders now laugh about those early beginnings. "Our entire business model was to get enough money to buy food to eat," they recall.

Selling some clothes to friends got their business off the ground, but the FUBU (pronounced *foo-boo*) founders needed more than that. Money was an obstacle. Even if they could place some socks in one retail store and some shirts and hats in another, they didn't have a way to promote them. And to be successful, they needed a way to promote their goods to get the message out to prospective customers. The messenger came in the form of rap artist and actor L. L. Cool J, who happened to be from Queens as well. Cool J liked FUBU's stuff, but he wasn't ready to wear it in a show or music video until the owners made some design and color changes. FUBU listened and came up with the right T-shirt for him, which resulted in Cool J becoming an early spokesperson for the brand. Since then, supporters have included Mariah Carey, Boys II Men, Will Smith, and Sean "P Diddy" Combs. Placements of FUBU clothing in music videos, feature films, and on stage have gone a long way toward building the brand's identity.

With the financing that came with a promotion and distribution agreement with Samsung, FUBU was able to open the doors to many of the 500 retailers who now stock FUBU clothing, including Macy's, Foot Locker, Champs, and Nordstrom. Eventually, the FUBU founders were able to afford a booth at the glamorous "Magic: The Business of Fashion" trade show in Los Angeles, where celebrities and department store buyers now flock to put in their orders as soon as possible—which generates sales as well as publicity for FUBU. And when the NBA approached FUBU about a licensing agreement, both sides realized immediately that it was the perfect match. The NBA's customers are often FUBU customers as well. NBA clothing by FUBU is expected to generate $25 to $50 million for FUBU, and potentially more. Each organization promotes the other, to the benefit of both.

Price has been an issue from the beginning for FUBU. The four founders wanted to produce high-quality clothing at prices somewhat lower than other manufacturers. Still, the clothes aren't cheap. Jeans run from $44.99 to $69.99, and a T-shirt with the official Harlem Globetrotters logo can be priced from $55 to $89. The company also has a women's line, where women can pick up a velour dress for $64.99, a stretch denim shirt dress for $55, and some graphic tees for $22.99. Clearly, consumers don't seem to be griping about price—today, FUBU is a $350 million global business, selling its products in countries as near as Canada and Mexico and as far away as Japan and Malaysia.

FUBU's relationship with customers is an important part of its promotional effort—all four founders say they are comfortable talking with anyone they meet on the street. They like to stop and listen to the experiences and ideas of the people who buy and wear their clothing, and they never forget their roots. Their personal presence gives them a connection with consumers that other designers and manufacturers simply can't achieve. When shoppers can't be near a FUBU store or the headquarters in New York, they can log on to the company's Web site at http://www.y2g.com to find out about company-sponsored parties, trips, and tours, and read celebrity interviews, all of which enhance their relationship with FUBU. "We're a lifestyle brand," say the founders. And shoppers seem to be happy to live their lives in FUBU clothes.

QUESTIONS FOR CRITICAL THINKING

1. FUBU has coordinated its promotional activities to produce a unified, customer-focused message. How would you state that message?
2. How would you characterize FUBU's promotional objectives?
3. Which advertising media would be the most effective for FUBU at its present stage? Why?
4. How do you think consumers perceive FUBU's pricing?

Sources: FUBU Web site, http://www.fubu.com, accessed January 10, 2005; Urban Clothing Web site, http://www.urbanclothing.net, accessed January 10, 2005 (for pricing information); "The Rumors Are True, FUBU & Snoop Dogg Set Their Sights on Hotlanta," *Business Wire*, January 23, 2003, accessed at http://www.findarticles.com; "FUBU," *CNN.com*, February 2002, http://www.cnn.com/SPECIALS/2002/black.history/stories/05.fubu.

Video Case 15.2

Cannondale Puts Technology and Information to Work

Technology and information are great if you know what to do with them. But all the bells and whistles in the world aren't worth a thing if you don't know how to use them. During the mid and late 1990s, many companies embraced technology without really understanding what it could do for them. Cannondale, on the other hand, has managed to integrate technology—including information technology—throughout the company in a strategic manner that benefits the entire firm, from the office to the factory floor.

Although there's no substitute for the actual test ride—when Cannondale staff members take the bikes out to see for themselves whether a new design or component works well—computer-aided design (CAD) helps designers and engineers get to that point. Using a 3D modeling program called Pro/Engineer, design engineers at company headquarters in Connecticut can input the information for an idea and immediately see the specs, parts, and other data required to build a prototype and eventually a mold for manufacturing. In addition, with Pro/Engineer, they can take a single model and automatically create the specs for different sizes to fit a variety of riders. As pointed out earlier in Video Case 1.2, Cannondale currently produces more than 80 bicycle models, so the CAD system can generate literally hundreds of different bikes to meet the requirements of cyclists of all different shapes, sizes, levels of riding ability, and interest.

One model that became reality with the help of CAD was the Super V Raven. For two years, special projects coordinator Todd Patterson and his team mulled the bike weight versus bike strength dilemma, searching for ideas that might make bikes stronger but lighter. When he happened to visit the nearby Sikorsky Helicopter plant, where he saw how the Blackhawk helicopter was built on a "skeleton" with layers of "skin" over it, Patterson knew he had the foundation for Cannondale's new frame. "From that moment on, I knew how I wanted to build the bike," he says. With Pro/Engineer, the design team was able to create the necessary shapes based on data for sizing, weight, and strength.

CAD continues to be used even after a bicycle is designed. The design engineers transmit the design electronically to production engineers at Cannondale's factory in Pennsylvania. The production engineers then use the software to generate the prototypes of a bicycle that can actually be ridden by staff on test rides. If the test rides uncover problems, Pro/Engineer can change the specs.

Pro/Engineer isn't the only form of technology used by Cannondale. The company has installed Web browsers on the factory floor so that the manufacturing process for each bicycle can be tracked. As a worker completes a step in assembling a bike, he or she swipes a scanner across a bar code label on the bike, which instantly updates a database. This system not only tracks the progress of the bicycle but also helps Cannondale manage its inventory of components and parts, which cuts the cost of holding inventory. Cannondale's inventory system now conducts materials requirements planning (MRP) in two minutes instead of one to three weeks. This means that the company can get bikes to the public much more quickly and efficiently.

Cannondale also uses technology to come up with specific models for its various racing teams, such as its line of Ironman bicycles, which were launched under a licensing agreement with Ironman Properties. "For years, we've sponsored some of triathlon's top athletes, and we've been producing some of the world's lightest, fastest, triathlon-specific bikes," explains Scott Montgomery, Cannondale's vice president of marketing. Using its system integration strategy—in which both frames and components are custom-designed to fit into an integrated whole using CAD—Cannondale came up with a specific design that maximized performance while saving weight.

Cannondale has won numerous design awards over the years and has continued producing award-winning bicycles even after its recent acquisition by Pegasus Partners. "We have no desire to disrupt a winning formula," says David Uri of Pegasus. The bicycles will keep rolling.

QUESTIONS FOR CRITICAL THINKING

1. Give two reasons Cannondale's use of technology has been strategically successful.
2. How does technology help Cannondale meet the needs of its customers?
3. How might Cannondale be vulnerable to computer crimes?
4. Suppose you are a sales rep for Cannondale. How might you use technology to showcase your products to dealers or individual consumers?

Sources: Cannondale Web site, http://www.cannondale.com, accessed January 16, 2005; "Cannondale Completes Chapter 11 Sale to Pegasus," press release, May 5, 2003, http://www.cannondale.com; "Cannondale Named Exclusive Licensee for Ironman Bicycles," press release, June 10, 2002, http://www.cannondale.com.

Video Case 16.2

Chicago-Style Pizza Finds a Nationwide Market

Pizzeria Uno started in downtown Chicago in 1943 when Ike Sewell opened his first pizza restaurant. Sewell believed that customers would flock to a place where traditional Chicago-style deep-dish pizza was served in a cozy, casual atmosphere—and he was right. In 1978, Sewell and partner Aaron Spencer made a deal to begin expanding the business, and the following year the first Pizzeria Uno opened in Boston, which would eventually become company headquarters.

Today, if you visit one of the 182 Pizzeria Uno restaurants located in 30 states and six foreign countries, you can order a deep-dish pizza with your choice of fresh toppings. Or you can select from a number of other favorites: gourmet thin-crust pizza, fresh salad, chicken, fajitas, a hamburger, pasta, ribs, and even steak. Costs associated with all of this food have to be managed carefully, from supplier to your table, for the company to stay in business and turn a profit. Here's how Uno does it.

"Margins in the restaurant business average three to four cents out of the dollar," says former CFO Craig Miller. "When you are managing pennies, you need to account for them." Cost management of food items, labor, and maintenance is important because it all adds up. So accounting professionals play a role in just about everything Pizzeria Uno does, from general financial management to menu planning. According to Miller, accounting starts at the store level. Recently, Pizzeria Uno installed computerized NCR point-of-sale systems in every restaurant to record daily data on types of meals customers bought, sales totals, number of employees on duty, amount of inventory in stock, and other operating details. Each night, those data are fed back to a computer system at company headquarters, where accounting employees analyze and interpret the information. The software program also provides information on what food should cost compared with what it does cost, which helps each store—and the company as a whole—establish food cost controls.

In another effort to improve its profit margins, Pizzeria Uno recently reviewed the design of its restaurants as well as the content of its menus. "Uno has been developing a new prototype," notes restaurant industry analyst Mathew McKay, "experimenting a lot with the look of the restaurant, new menu items, and expanding the menu away from deep dish and into other areas." Many of the restaurants have been remodeled to evoke the company's roots in the Chicago industrial scene, with black and white tile mixed with brick and open ceilings. "They're trying to get the same fun feeling but doing so by reinvesting less capital into each unit, thereby improving the return on investment," explains McKay.

Pizzeria Uno accountants use financial ratios to decide whether to borrow money, invest in future purchases of milk, or buy the land on which they plan to build a new restaurant. The company also relies on working capital. "The restaurant business is a cash business," comments Miller. He explains that if a restaurant buys a shipment of cheese, uses it in its cooking, and sells it the next day, the restaurant still has 30 days to use the money it received on the sale before it has to pay the supplier from which it bought the cheese. Pizzeria Uno also uses debt to build equity for the company. "The average Pizzeria Uno requires $1.7 million to build and open," says Miller. The company can borrow money, build the restaurant, and enjoy the 30 percent return that the restaurant generates. Whenever possible, Pizzeria Uno tries to buy the land on which the restaurant will be built, even if it involves a mortgage loan. "By buying land, we control our destiny and our future," explains Miller, because in general the value of real estate increases.

Because a tiny shift in costs can throw profits in the trash along with uneaten pizza crusts, Pizzeria Uno takes a conservative approach to its finances. "We take all the money we can and reinvest it in the business," comments Miller. That's sound financial practice for any business that plans to survive the ups and downs of the economy, not to mention the changing tastes of consumers who want to eat deep-dish pizza with the works on one day and thin-crust pizza with a salad the next.

QUESTIONS FOR CRITICAL THINKING

1. Why is the accounting function so important to a company like Pizzeria Uno?
2. How might activity ratios help accountants at Pizzeria Uno assess their company's performance?
3. Describe how the steps in the accounting process would be put into play by accounting staff who use the point-of-sale system at Pizzeria Uno.
4. Go to the Pizzeria Uno Web site at http://www.pizzeria uno.com to look for ways that the accounting function influences different aspects of the business. Write a brief memo describing the role that accounting would play in a particular aspect that interests you—say, building a new restaurant, setting up a franchise, or adding a new food item to the menu.

Sources: "All about Unos," Uno Restaurant Corporation, http://www.pizzeria uno.com, accessed January 3, 2005; "Uno Restaurant Corporation," Hoover's Online, http://www.hshbn.com, accessed February 3, 2005; "Profile: Uno Restaurant Corp.," *Yahoo! Market Guide*, http://www.biz.yahoo.com, accessed February 3, 2005; "Uno Restaurant Corp. to Install NCR Point-of-Sale System," Bizjournals.com, April 13, 2000, http://www.bizjournals.com.

Video Case 17.2

Developing a Financial Strategy for a Retail Chain

When asked what your favorite style of music is, you might answer rock, country, rap, folk, classical, or jazz. You can also name your favorite musical groups, composers, or performers almost without thinking. Chances are, you also have a sound system. Joe McGuire, CFO of Tweeter, hopes it was bought at one of his stores. But even if it wasn't, he is happy if you've heard of his company.

Tweeter, based in Cambridge, Massachusetts, is a retail chain that concentrates on selling mid- to high-priced audio and video equipment. In fact, McGuire isn't worried about selling younger customers their first stereo or television. Those lower priced items simply fail to generate the kind of revenue that Tweeter thrives on. Gross margin—the difference between a sound system's sales price and its purchase price—is the name of the game when it comes to making money, and high-end equipment generates a gross margin of about 28 percent for Tweeter. By contrast, gross margins for entry-level TV sets and stereos are only in the midteens. In other words, a 27-inch television that most electronics stores sell for around $350 generates less profit overall than a high-end big screen TV that sells for $1,500, even though a store is likely to sell many more of the smaller, less expensive sets.

McGuire explains that the most important task is "managing the pace of growth." Tweeter is a publicly held corporation whose shareholders expect regular growth in profits. McGuire and his fellow executives must look for creative yet financially sound ways to help the company grow. Making wise use of the funds that Tweeter generates not only from the sale of home entertainment equipment but also from investors is critical to the company's continued growth. Recently, the retail chain has used funds to make strategic acquisitions of smaller firms—companies that complement its business, such as Bryn Mawr Stereo & Video stores in the mid-Atlantic states and Douglas TV and United Audio Centers, both located around Chicago. Tweeter doesn't just plunk down cash for any store that's available. McGuire explains that, to be considered, a store "has to have a similar product mix." Stores that Tweeter acquires are usually privately owned and might not be profitable, but Tweeter executives must be able to see ways that the operation can be turned around. Acquiring another company naturally affects Tweeter's own earnings during the first year or two, but as in the case of the United Audio purchase, "We expect this acquisition to contribute to earnings per share growth as we further develop the greater Chicago market," notes

McGuire. Most of these transactions involve more complicated funding than the act of writing a big check. They are typically funded by taking on some debt and an exchange of stock if the company is already publicly held.

Of course, another way for Tweeter to grow is simply to open more stores. But that decision must also be carefully managed. For instance, if Tweeter has recently expanded an existing store in an area, grabbing an empty building to launch another store in a nearby town may not benefit the company in the long run—no matter how good an opportunity it may seem to be at the time. "Anything faster than 20 percent to 30 percent storefront growth in a year is dangerous," warns McGuire; "You can mess up what has been successful." The reason for such caution is that Tweeter has to make the investments required to support growth—such as training new employees and managing benefits.

Finally, McGuire bases many of his company's financial decisions on the niche that Tweeter has been so successful at filling. "We are a specialty retailer," he notes. Tweeter sells audio and video equipment only—no computers or telecommunications devices. And Tweeter operates relatively small stores—10,000 to 12,000 square feet—compared with the 30,000 to 50,000 square feet occupied by big discounters such as Best Buy and Circuit City.

Then there's the matter of store sales—or rather the lack of them. Tweeter doesn't hold promotional sales. Instead, it uses an everyday competitive pricing strategy that assures shoppers that they will find not only quality items in an intimate environment but also competitive prices that aren't going to change tomorrow.

Tweeter has come a long way from its 1970s beginnings as a tiny shop selling mostly speakers. The company now has over 3,700 employees working in 175 stores nationwide. Joe McGuire believes that this is because founder and chairman Sandy Bloomberg has never lost sight of the company's identity. That identity is supported by good financial decisions. "In order to be successful, it's very important that the back end of the house is in order," says McGuire in reference to the importance of finance. In the final analysis, he says, "the only thing that counts is how much money did you make." Those words are music to the ears of Tweeter's shareholders.

QUESTIONS FOR CRITICAL THINKING

1. Identify two ways that Tweeter could raise more cash if the company decided it was needed.

2. Explain how finance supports Tweeter's overall business strategy.

3. Discuss Tweeter's current financial status.

4. Go to the company's Web site, http://www.tweeter .com. What are the company's annual sales? List two or three other interesting financial facts about Tweeter.

Sources: "Corporate Overview," Tweeter Web site, http://www.tweeter .com, accessed January 7, 2005; "Tweeter Announces That It Has Completed the Acquisition of Douglas TV," company press release, Tweeter Web site, http://www.tweeter.com, accessed March 24, 2005.

Video Case 18.2

Morgan Stanley Fights the Battle of the Bulls and Bears

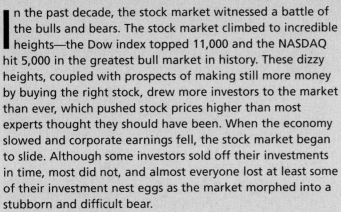

In the past decade, the stock market witnessed a battle of the bulls and bears. The stock market climbed to incredible heights—the Dow index topped 11,000 and the NASDAQ hit 5,000 in the greatest bull market in history. These dizzy heights, coupled with prospects of making still more money by buying the right stock, drew more investors to the market than ever, which pushed stock prices higher than most experts thought they should have been. When the economy slowed and corporate earnings fell, the stock market began to slide. Although some investors sold off their investments in time, most did not, and almost everyone lost at least some of their investment nest eggs as the market morphed into a stubborn and difficult bear.

Even if you were not directly involved in this recent market cycle, you can learn some good lessons about investing from the experiences of others. Chad Lombardi, a financial advisor for Morgan Stanley, outlines some basic principles of investing that are echoed by many experts in the industry—regardless of whether the bulls are running or the bears are hiding. Many new investors may take a more conservative approach by selecting one or more mutual funds that appear to match their specific objectives. Others may opt to buy individual stocks and bonds. Mutual funds offer the advantage of diversification; all of your financial eggs are not in one company's basket. With an individual stock, however, you have direct ownership in the company, and although the investment may be riskier, your return may be greater as well. With an individual bond, you have a better idea of what your return will be than you would with an individual stock.

Before you make an investment decision, says Lombardi, it's important to determine three things:

1. *What are your investment objectives?*
- are you saving for a car or a house?

- starting your own business?
- "growing" financial resources to help a child pay for a college education?
- and/or saving for retirement?

2. *What is your time horizon?*
- three years?
- five years?
- ten years or more?

3. *How risk-tolerant are you?*
- Answering this question is a major step in deciding the types of investments that are most appropriate for you.

Lombardi emphasizes that it's never too early to start investing, regardless of how much you earn, from your first job after college or even while you are in college. "Start off small," he says. The amount you accumulate will add up over time.

Lombardi is just one of the many people who work at Morgan Stanley whose job is to help people plan their financial lives. "Careful planning is key to achieving your financial goals," states the company's Web site. "Whatever your goals may be . . . our professionals will evaluate your situation and help you determine which strategies are right for you." The firm is a global financial services company and a major business in both investment banking and individual investing. Morgan Stanley offers a wide range of investment products from stocks and bonds, to mutual funds and annuities, to insurance and managed futures. Customers can trade bonds 24 hours a day or sign up for NetWorth, a customized program that gives them access online to all of their account information on a single, secure Web page. With Morgan Stanley's wireless server TradeRunner, they can trade anytime, anywhere in the world.

All of these services are both state of the art and a major aid for investors, provided consumers know how to use them. Part of Morgan Stanley's philosophy is that an educated consumer is the best kind of customer, so it provides a variety of support services, including a section of its Web site designed to teach people the fundamentals of planning and investing. There's even a glossary with terms like *maturity* and *interest rates.* The idea is to help the average person feel comfortable with the process of investing.

In the economic and business turmoil that rocked the economy during the early years of the new century, new standards for accounting, financial advising, and other business practices were established. Hardly a single major financial institution escaped fines and the loss of some executives, including Morgan Stanley. Yet the reform of the investment industry actually brought greater clarity to financial institutions and their customers.

Morgan Stanley continues to grow, having recently acquired a majority of Lend Lease Corporation Limited, which will allow the company to offer a broader range of investment products. "Morgan Stanley connects people, ideas and capital," says a company press release, "to help clients achieve their financial aspirations."

QUESTIONS FOR CRITICAL THINKING

1. Why is it important for Morgan Stanley clients to identify their investment objectives?

2. What combination of securities would you be likely to select in achieving the goal of starting your own business five years from now? Why?

3. Do stricter regulations on the investment industry make you feel more—or less—comfortable about becoming an individual investor? Why?

4. Visit Morgan Stanley's individual investment Web site at http://www.morganstanleyindividual.com and examine some of the investment products offered there. Which of these products do you think would be most suitable for students just graduating from college and beginning their careers?

Sources: Morgan Stanley Web site, http://www.morganstanleyindividual .com, accessed January 18, 2005; "Morgan Stanley Acquires a Majority of Lend Lease's U.S. Real Estate Equity Businesses," press release, *Hoover's Online,* June 17, 2003, http://www.hoovers.com; Dan Ackman, "For Wall Street, Fines Are a Day's Pay," *Forbes,* April 29, 2003, http://www.forbes.com.

Appendix A
Risk Management and Insurance

Is the U.S. facing an insurance crisis? Many believe so. As evidence, they point to dozens of doctors in states throughout the country who are moving or retiring as premiums for medical-malpractice insurance skyrocket. In Nevada, nearly one-third of the state's obstetricians have stopped accepting new patients in the face of premium increases of as much as 400 percent. One, Dr. Shelby Wilbourn, went even further. He moved his practice 3,000 miles, from Las Vegas to Maine. The move cut Dr. Wilbourn's annual malpractice insurance bill from $108,000 to less than $10,000.

Some physicians have even staged job actions to protest the high cost of medical-malpractice insurance. Surgeons in several states, including Texas, Nevada, West Virginia, and Pennsylvania, have abruptly resigned or gone on leave to protest the high cost of protecting themselves from lawsuits. Hundreds of patients have been affected by these job actions. According to one survey by the American Hospital Association, 20 percent of the nation's hospitals have curtailed or even discontinued some services because of rising insurance costs. Comments Dr. Donald Palmisano, president of the American Medical Association, "We consider it a crisis when a woman can't find a physician to deliver her baby. We consider it a crisis when a trauma center shuts down, and someone who has been seriously injured in an automobile accident has to be transferred to another hospital."

Doctors, hospitals, and patients aren't the only ones affected by the insurance crisis. Homeowners in many states are seeing their homeowners' insurance premiums double or even triple, assuming they can get coverage at all. Homeowners in Texas are especially hard hit. Mary Ann Selva of Dickinson, Texas, saw her annual homeowners' insurance premium jump from $1,400 to $2,100, for less coverage. Yet, she considered herself fortunate. "I feel incredibly lucky to get reduced coverage at increased rates," she noted. Real estate agents are now warning buyers to start shopping for insurance as soon as they sign a contract to buy a home. Deb Bryan, a real estate agent in Austin, said that she once had to contact over 100 insurance agents to find coverage for one buyer. State Farm—the nation's largest home insurer—has stopped writing new policies in Texas and several other states. Farmers Insurance, another large home insurer, even threatened to leave the state entirely.

What are the causes of the insurance crisis? In the case of medical-malpractice insurance, doctors and insurers blame the problem on trial lawyers and rising jury awards in liability lawsuits. Comments David Golden of the National Association of Independent Insurers, "The real sickness is people sue at the drop of a hat, judgments are going up and up and up, and the people getting rich out of this are the plaintiffs' attorneys." According to Jury Verdict Research, the median jury award for medical-malpractice cases rose nearly 175 percent over a recent six-year period.

When it comes to explanations for the rising cost of homeowners' insurance, many insurance companies cite the substantial rise in the number of claims involving mold and related water damage as a major culprit. In Texas alone, the top five home insurers saw their mold-related claims more than quintuple in only one year. In a recent two-year period, these companies paid out more than $1 billion in mold settlements. On top of that, a jury recently awarded a Texas homeowner $32 million in a mold-related lawsuit against Farmers Insurance.

While conceding that such factors as malpractice litigation and mold claims have contributed to rising insurance premiums, industry critics place some of the blame for the current insurance crisis squarely on the shoulders of the insurance industry itself. Insurance companies, they argue, relaxed underwriting standards throughout much of the 1990s in an attempt to keep or gain market share. (Underwriting is the process used by insurance companies to decide what, or whom, to insure and what to charge for insurance coverage.) Insurers sold thousands of policies with overly broad coverage and to higher-risk individuals and organizations. At the same time, however, insurance companies kept premiums artificially low. Consequently, many insurers actually lost money on underwriting—meaning that they paid out more in claims than they collected in premiums—throughout much of the 1990s.

Insurance companies were able to withstand these losses because they were earning very high rates of return on their investments, which more than offset underwriting losses. Unfortunately for insurers, investment returns have plunged in recent years, forcing sharp increases in premiums and decreases in coverage.

Whatever the reasons for the current insurance crisis, many types of insurance are very expensive, and they are getting more expensive each year. Nevertheless, few individuals or organizations can afford to go without insurance protection.[1]

Overview

Risk is a daily fact of life for both individuals and businesses. Sometimes it appears in the form of a serious illness. In other instances, it takes the form of property loss, such as the extensive damage to homes and businesses due to forest fires in Colorado or tornadoes in Alabama, Ohio, and Tennessee. Risk can also occur as the result of other people's actions—such as a pizza delivery driver's running a red light and striking another vehicle. In still other cases, risk may occur as a result of our own actions—we talk on a cell phone while driving or decline an extended service warranty on a new computer.

Businesspeople must understand the types of risk they face and develop methods for dealing with them. One approach to risk is to shift it to specialized firms called *insurance companies*. This appendix discusses the concept of insurance in a business setting. It begins with a definition of risk.

Concept of Risk

risk uncertainty about loss or injury.

Risk is uncertainty about loss or injury. Consider the risks faced by a typical business. A factory or warehouse faces the risk of fire, burglary, water damage, and physical deterioration. Accidents, judgments due to lawsuits, and customers failing to pay bills are other business risks. Risks can be divided into two major categories: speculative risk and pure risk.

Speculative risk gives the firm or individual the chance of either a profit or a loss. Purchasing shares of stock on the basis of the latest hot tip from an acquaintance at the local health club can result in profits or losses. Expanding operations into a new market may result in higher profits or the loss of invested funds.

Pure risk, on the other hand, involves only the chance of loss. Motorists, for example, always face the risk of accidents. Should they occur, both financial and physical losses may result. If they do not occur, however, drivers do not profit. Insurance often helps individuals and businesses protect against financial loss resulting from pure risk.

Risk Management

Since risk is an unavoidable part of business, managers must find ways of dealing with it. The first step in any risk management plan is to recognize what's at risk and why it's at risk. After that, the manager must decide how to handle the risk. In general, businesses have four alternatives in handling risk: avoid it, minimize it, assume it themselves, or transfer it to others.

Executives must consider many factors when evaluating the risks, both at home and abroad. These factors include a nation's economic stability; social and cultural factors, such as language; available technologies; distribution systems; and government regulations. International businesses are typically exposed to less risk in countries with stable economic, social and cultural, and political and legal environments.

Avoiding Risk

Some of the risks individuals face can be avoided by taking a conservative approach to life. Abstaining from smoking, exercising regularly and staying physically fit, and not driving during blizzards and other hazardous conditions are three ways of avoiding personal risk. By the same token, businesses can also avoid some of the risks they face. For example, a manufacturer can locate a new production facility away from a flood-prone area.

When deciding which risks to avoid, firms should also assess the benefits of taking a risk. For instance, introducing new products involves a substantial amount of risk, but it also offers high rewards. Although avoiding all risks may ensure a firm's profitability, it stifles innovation. As a result, most industry-leading companies are willing to take prudent amounts of risk.

> *They Said It*
>
> If the lion didn't bite the tamer every once in a while, it wouldn't be exciting.
>
> —*Darrell Waltrip (b. 1947)*
> *American race car driver*

Reducing Risk

Managers can reduce or even eliminate many types of risk by removing hazards or taking preventive measures. Many companies develop safety programs to educate employees about potential hazards and the proper methods of performing certain dangerous tasks. For instance, any employee who works at a hazardous waste site is required to have training and medical monitoring that meet the federal Occupational Safety and Health Administration (OSHA) standards. The training and monitoring not only reduce risk but pay off on the bottom line. Aside from the human tragedy, accidents cost companies time and money.

Although many actions can reduce the risk involved in business operations, they cannot eliminate risk entirely. Most major business insurers assist their clients in avoiding or minimizing risk by offering the services of loss-prevention experts to conduct thorough reviews of their operations. These health and safety professionals evaluate customers' work environments and recommend procedures and equipment to help firms minimize worker injuries and property losses.

Self-Insuring against Risk

Instead of purchasing insurance against certain types of pure risk, some companies accumulate funds to cover potential losses. So-called **self-insurance funds** are special funds created by periodically setting aside cash reserves that the firm can draw on in the event of a financial loss resulting from a pure risk. A firm makes regular payments to the fund, and it charges losses to the fund. Such a fund typically accompanies a risk-reduction program aimed at minimizing losses. Self-insurance is most useful in cases in which a company faces similar risks and the risks are spread over a broad geographical area.

One of the most common forms of self-insurance is in the area of employee health insurance. Most companies provide health insurance coverage to employees as a component of their benefits program. Some firms, especially large ones, find it more economical to create a self-insurance fund covering employee health-care expenses, as opposed to purchasing a health insurance policy from an insurance provider.

self-insurance fund special fund created by setting aside cash reserves periodically that can be drawn upon in the event of a loss.

Shifting Risk to an Insurance Company

Although a business or not-for-profit organization can take steps to avoid or reduce risk, the most common method of dealing with it is to shift it to others in the form of **insurance**—a contract by which an insurer, for a fee, agrees to reimburse another firm or individual a sum of money should a loss occur. The insured party's fee to the insurance company for coverage against losses is called a **premium.** Insurance

insurance contract by which the insurer, for a fee (the premium), agrees to reimburse another firm or individual a sum of money should a loss occur.

substitutes a small, known loss—the insurance premium—for a larger, unknown loss that may or may not occur. In the case of life insurance, the loss—death—is a certainty; the main uncertainty is the date it will occur.

It is important for the insurer to understand the customer's business, risk exposure, and insurance needs. Firms that operate in several countries usually choose to do business with insurance companies that maintain global networks of offices.

Basic Insurance Concepts

Figure A.1 illustrates how an insurance company operates. The insurer collects premiums from policyholders in exchange for insurance coverage. The insurance company takes some of these funds and uses them to pay current claims and operating expenses. What's left over is held in the form of reserves, which are in turn invested. Reserves can be used to pay for unexpected losses. The returns from insurance company reserves may allow the insurer to reduce premiums, generate profits, or both. By investing reserves, the insurance industry represents a major source of long-term financing for other businesses.

An insurance company is a professional risk taker. For a fee, it accepts risks of loss or damage to businesses and individuals. Three basic principles underlie insurance: the concept of insurable interest, the concept of insurable risks, and the law of large numbers.

Insurable Interest

insurable interest
demonstration that a direct financial loss will result if some event occurs.

To purchase insurance, an applicant must demonstrate an **insurable interest** in the property or life of the insured. In other words, the policyholder must stand to suffer a loss, financial or otherwise, due to fire, storm damage, accident, theft, illness, death, or lawsuit. A homeowner, for example, has an insurable interest in his or her home and its contents. In the case of life insurance coverage purchased for someone providing the bulk of a household's income, the policyholder's spouse and minor children have a clear insurable interest.

insurable risk
requirement that a pure risk must meet for the insurer to agree to provide protection.

A firm can purchase property and liability insurance on physical assets—such as offices and factories—to cover losses due to such hazards as fire and theft because the company can demonstrate an obvious insurable interest. Similarly, because top managers are important assets to a company, the firm can purchase key executive insurance on their lives. By contrast, a businessperson cannot collect on insurance to cover damage to property of competitors because that person cannot demonstrate an insurable interest.

Insurable Risk

Insurable risk refers to the requirements that a risk must meet for the insurer to provide protection. Only some pure risks, and no speculative ones, are insurable. Insurance companies impose five basic requirements for a pure risk to be considered an insurable risk:

1. The likelihood of loss should be reasonably predictable. If an insurance company cannot reasonably predict losses, it has no way of setting affordable premiums.
2. The loss should be financially measurable.
3. The loss should be accidental, or fortuitous.
4. The risk should be spread over a wide geographical area.
5. The insurance company has the right to set standards for accepting risk. The process of setting these standards is known as **underwriting.**

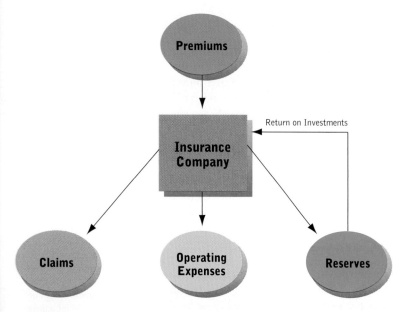

FIGURE A.1
How an Insurance Company Operates

Law of Large Numbers

Insurance is based on the law of averages, or statistical probability. Insurance companies have studied the chances of occurrences of deaths, injuries, property damage, lawsuits, and other types of hazards. Table A.1 is an example of the kind of data insurance companies examine. It shows the number of automobile accidents, by age of the driver, for a recent year. From their investigations, insurance companies have developed **actuarial tables,** which predict the number of fires, automobile accidents, or deaths that will occur in a given year. Premiums charged for insurance coverage are based on these tables. Actuarial tables are based on the **law of large numbers.** In essence, the law of large numbers states that seemingly random events will follow a predictable pattern if enough events are observed.

An example can demonstrate how insurers use the law of large numbers to calculate premiums. Previously collected statistical data on a city with 50,000 homes indicates that the city will experience an average of 500 fires a year, with damages averaging $30,000 per occurrence. What is the minimum annual premium an insurance company would charge to insure a house against fire?

To simplify the calculations, assume that the premiums would not produce profits or cover any of the insurance company's operating expenses—they would just produce enough income to pay policyholders for their losses. In total, fires in the city would generate claims of $15 million (500 homes damaged × $30,000). If these losses were spread over all 50,000 homes, each homeowner would be charged an annual premium of $300 ($15 million divided by 50,000 homes). In reality, though, the insurance company would set the premium at a higher figure to cover operating expenses, build reserves, and earn a reasonable profit.

Some losses are easier for insurance companies to predict than others. Life insurance companies, for example, can pretty accurately predict the number of policyholders who will die within a specified period of time. Losses from such hazards as automobile accidents and weather events are much more difficult to predict. The terrorist attacks of 9/11, for example, resulted in roughly $40 billion in insured losses.

actuarial table probability calculation of the number of specific events—such as deaths, injuries, fire, or windstorm losses—expected to occur within a given year.

law of large numbers concept that seemingly random events will follow a predictable pattern if enough events are observed.

Sources of Insurance Coverage

The insurance industry includes both private companies, such as Prudential, State Farm, and GEICO (part of famed investor Warren Buffet's Berkshire Hathaway), and a number of public agencies that provide insurance coverage for business firms, not-for-profit organizations, and individuals. Let's look at the primary features of this array of insurers.

Table A.1	Relationship between the Age of the Driver and the Number of Motor Vehicle Accidents	
Age Group	**Number of Licensed Drivers**	**Accidents per 100 Licensed Drivers**
19 and under	9,984,000	29
20 to 24	15,529,000	18
25 to 34	37,265,000	13
35 to 44	41,857,000	11
45 to 54	33,662,000	9
55 to 64	21,337,000	7
65 to 74	15,244,000	7
75 and older	10,570,000	7

Source: *Statistical Abstract of the United States,* Census Bureau Web site, http://www.census.gov, accessed January 9, 2003.

Public Insurance Agencies

A **public insurance agency** is a state or federal government unit established to provide specialized insurance protection for individuals and organizations. It provides protection in such areas as job loss (unemployment insurance) and work-related injuries (workers' compensation). Public insurance agencies also sponsor specialized programs, such as deposit, flood, and crop insurance.

Unemployment Insurance   Every state has an **unemployment insurance** program that assists unemployed workers by providing financial benefits, job counseling, and placement services. Compensation amounts vary depending on workers' previous incomes and the states in which they file claims. These insurance programs are funded by payroll taxes paid by employers.

Workers' Compensation   Under state laws, employers must provide **workers' compensation insurance** to guarantee payment of wages and salaries, medical care costs, and such rehabilitation services as retraining, job placement, and vocational rehabilitation to employees who are injured on the job. In addition, workers' compensation provides benefits in the form of weekly payments or single lump-sum payments to survivors of workers who die as a result of work-related injuries. Premiums are based on the company's payroll, the on-the-job hazards to which it exposes workers, and its safety record.

Social Security   The federal government is the nation's largest insurer. The Social Security program, established in 1935, provides retirement, survivor, and disability benefits to millions of Americans. **Medicare** was added to the Social Security program in 1965 to provide health insurance for persons 65 years or older and certain other Social Security recipients. More than nine of 10 workers in the U.S. and their dependents are eligible for Social Security program benefits. The program is funded through a payroll tax, half of which is paid by employers while the other half is paid by workers. Self-employed people pay the full tax.

New York Life is a mutual insurance company, which is owned by its policyholders. As the company points out in its ad, "Our policyholders are really buying a promise— that we'll be here to pay a claim, fund your retirement, or pay for nursing home costs."

Courtesy of New York Life Insurance Company

Private Insurance Companies

Much of the insurance in force is provided by private firms. These organizations provide protection in exchange for the payment of premiums. Some private insurance companies are stockholder owned, and therefore are run like any other business, and others are so-called *mutual associations*. Most, though not all, mutual insurance companies specialize in life insurance. Technically, mutual insurance companies are owned by their policyholders, who may receive premium rebates in the form of dividends. In spite of this, however, there is no evidence that an insurance policy from a mutual company costs any less than a comparable policy from a stockholder-owned insurer. In recent years, a number of mutual insurance companies have reorganized as stockholder-owned companies, including Prudential, one of the nation's largest insurers.

Types of Insurance

Individuals and businesses spend hundreds of billions of dollars each year on insurance coverage. All too often, however, both business firms and individual households make poor decisions when buying insurance. Several commonsense tips for buying insurance are offered in Table A.2. Although insurers offer hundreds of different policies, they all fall into three broad categories: property and liability insurance, health and disability insurance, and life insurance.

Property and Liability Insurance

Insurance that protects against fire, accident, theft, or other destructive events is called **property and liability insurance.** Examples of this insurance category include homeowners' insurance, auto insurance, business or commercial insurance, and liability insurance.

property and liability insurance general category of insurance that provides protection against financial losses due to a number of perils.

Homeowners' Insurance   Homeowners' insurance protects homeowners from damage to their homes due to various perils. If a home is destroyed by fire, for example, the homeowners' policy will pay to replace the home and its contents. Although standard policies cover a wide range of perils, most do not cover damage from widespread catastrophes such as floods and earthquakes. The federal government, through the National Flood Insurance Program, offers flood insurance as a supplement to a standard homeowners' policy. At an average cost of around $350 a year, flood insurance is often a wise purchase.

Homeowners in earthquake-prone areas can purchase earthquake insurance from a private insurer as an add-on to their homeowners' policy. However, earthquake coverage is expensive—the annual premium can exceed $1,000—and few homeowners have it—even in California. Following a recent Seattle quake that produced property damage topping the $2 billion mark, various states are studying the possibility of such coverage. The insurance industry is working closely with states to make earthquake insurance more affordable.

business interruption insurance insurance that protects firms from financial losses resulting from the interruption of business operations.

TABLE A.2
Some Commonsense Tips When Buying Insurance

Auto Insurance   With more than $130 billion in annual premiums, automobile insurance is the country's largest single type of property and liability insurance. Automobile insurance policies cover losses due to automobile accidents, including personal and property claims that result from accidents, fire, or theft. Virtually all states require drivers to have a minimum amount of auto insurance.

Commercial and Business Insurance   Commercial and business insurance protects firms from financial losses resulting from the interruption of business operations (**business interruption insurance**) or physical damage to property as a result of fires, accidents, thefts, or other destructive events. Commercial and business insurance policies may also protect employers from employee dishonesty or against losses resulting from the nonperformance of contracts.

Liability Insurance   **Liability insurance** protects an individual or business against financial losses to others for which the individual or business was responsible. If a driver runs a red light and hits another car, his or her liability insurance would pay to repair the damage to the other car. If a business sells a defective product, the firm's liability

- **Insure against big losses, not little ones.** Buy insurance to protect against big potential losses, but don't buy insurance to protect against small losses. A good example of this tip in action is to select the highest deductible you can afford on your property and liability insurance policies.

- **Buy insurance with broad coverage, not narrow coverage.** For example, it is much more cost-effective to buy a comprehensive health insurance policy, one that covers a wide range of illnesses and accidents, rather than several policies that cover only specific illnesses and accidents. It is extremely expensive to buy insurance coverage one disease at a time.

- **Shop around.** Insurance premiums for the same coverage can vary substantially. Insurance premiums also change frequently, so make sure to compare rates before renewing a policy.

- **Buy insurance only from financially strong companies.** Insurance companies occasionally go bankrupt. If this happens, you'll be left with no coverage and little chance of getting your premiums back. Several organizations—such as A. M. Best and Standard & Poor's—rate the financial strength of insurance companies.

Source: Louis E. Boone, David L. Kurtz, and Douglas Hearth, *Planning Your Financial Future,* 3rd edition, Mason, Ohio: South-Western College Publishing, p. 267.

insurance would pay for financial losses sustained by customers. A standard amount of liability coverage is usually attached to auto, homeowners', and commercial insurance policies. Additional amounts of liability insurance can be purchased if needed. Adequate liability insurance is critically important today. Wal-Mart, for example, requires all of its suppliers to have a minimum of $2 million in liability coverage.

Health and Disability Insurance

health insurance

insurance designed to provide coverage for losses due to illness or accidents.

Each of us faces the risk of getting sick or being injured in some way. Even a relatively minor illness can result in substantial health-care bills. To guard against this risk, most Americans have some form of **health insurance**—insurance that provides coverage for losses due to sickness or accidents. With soaring costs in health care, this type of insurance has become an important consideration for both businesses and individuals.

> ## They Said It
>
> My doctor gave me six months to live, but when I couldn't pay the bill he gave me six months more.
>
> —*Walter Matthau (1922–2000)*
> *American actor*

Sources of health insurance include private individual policies, private group policies, and the federal government, through Medicare and Medicaid (health insurance for the poor). Over 60 percent of Americans are covered by private group health insurance provided by their employer as an employee benefit. Four of every five U.S. employees work for businesses and not-for-profits that offer some form of group health insurance. Group policies resemble individual health insurance policies but are offered at lower premiums. Individual health insurance policies are simply too expensive for most people. Of every $10 spent by employers on employee compensation (wages, salaries, and employee benefits), almost $1 goes to cover the cost of health insurance. For example, General Motors spends several billion dollars a year on employee health care. As health insurance costs soared in recent years, employers have responded by cutting back on benefits, requiring employees to pay more of the premium or even dropping coverage altogether.

Private health insurance plans fall into one of two general categories: fee-for-service plans and managed-care plans. In a **fee-for-service plan,** the insured chooses his or her doctor and has almost unlimited access to specialists. Fee-for-service plans charge an annual deductible and copayments. By contrast, a **managed-care plan** pays most of the insured's health-care bills. In return, the program has a great deal of influence over the conditions of health care provided for the insured. Most managed-care plans, for example, place restrictions on the use of specialists and may specify which hospitals and pharmacies can be used. Some employers offer employees a choice between a fee-for-service and a managed-care plan. (Some may even offer multiple managed-care plans.) Table A.3 compares the pros and cons of both types of health-care plans.

Managed-care plans have become extremely popular in recent years. Over 150 million Americans are enrolled in some form of managed-care plan, and many fee-for-service plans have adopted some elements of managed care. A primary reason for the popularity of managed care is simply cost: Managed-care plans generally cost employers and employees less than fee-for-service plans. Managed care, however, is not without its critics. The effort to control costs has caused a backlash because of restrictions placed on doctors and patients. Managed care has now become a major public policy debate in the U.S.

Types of Managed-Care Plans
Two types of managed-care plans can be found in the U.S.: health maintenance organizations and preferred provider organizations. Although both manage health care, important differences exist between the two.

Health maintenance organizations (HMOs) do not provide health insurance; they provide health care. An HMO supplies all of the individual's health-care needs, including prescription drugs and hospitalization. The individual must use the HMO's own doctors and approved treatment facilities to receive benefits. Doctors and other health-care professionals are actually employees of the HMO. Individuals choose a primary care physician and cannot see a specialist without a referral. An HMO charges no deductibles and only a low fixed-dollar copayment.

The second type of managed-care plan is the **preferred provider organization (PPO).** Although PPOs may get less publicity than HMOs, they actually cover more people. A PPO is an arrangement in which an employer negotiates a contract between local health-care providers (physicians, hospitals, and pharmacies) to provide medical care to its employees at a discount. These plans have low fixed-dollar copayments. They are generally much more flexible than HMOs. Members can choose their primary care physician from a list of doctors. If a referral is given or hospitalization is required, the member again

Table A.3 Comparing Managed-Care Health Plans and Fee-for-Service Plans

	Fee-for-Service Plan	Managed-Care Plan
Pros	• Almost unlimited choice of health-care providers	• Little or no paperwork
	• Easy access to medical specialists	• Lower out-of-pocket expenses
	• Fewer limits on tests and diagnostic procedures	• No wait in getting reimbursed
		• Pays for routine physicals and immunizations
Cons	• Higher out-of-pocket expenses (deductible and copayment)	• Limited choice of health-care providers
	• Some plans involve more paperwork and delays in getting reimbursed	• More difficult to change doctors
	• Potentially more disputes with insurance company over charges	• Access to specialists restricted
	• Some plans do not pay for routine physicals and immunizations	• Limits on tests and diagnostic procedures

Source: Louis E. Boone, David L. Kurtz, and Douglas Hearth, *Planning Your Financial Future,* 3rd edition, Mason, Ohio: South-Western College Publishing, p. 302.

chooses from a list of approved health-care providers. A member who obtains treatment from a health-care provider outside the PPO network will likely be reimbursed for part of the cost.

Disability Income Insurance   Not only is disability income insurance one of the most overlooked forms of insurance, but many workers don't have enough coverage. The odds of a person developing a disability are considerably higher than most people realize. Take a group of five randomly selected 45-year-olds. There is approximately a 95 percent chance that one of the five will develop some form of a disability during the next 20 years. **Disability income insurance** is designed to replace lost income when a wage earner cannot work due to an accident or illness.

Two sources of disability income insurance exist: Social Security and private disability insurance policies. Social Security disability benefits are available to virtually all workers, but they have very strict requirements. Private disability insurance is available on either an individual or group basis. As with health insurance, a group policy is much cheaper than an individual policy. Many employers provide at least some disability coverage as an employee benefit. Employees often have the option of obtaining additional coverage by paying more.

Courtesy of CIGNA Corporation

Many people do not fully consider the consequences of disability or health problems. As part of its financial-planning services, CIGNA offers disability, life, health, and retirement plans.

disability income insurance insurance that replaces lost income when a wage earner cannot work due to accident or illness.

Life Insurance

life insurance insurance that protects people against the financial losses that occur with premature death.

Life insurance protects people against the financial losses that occur with premature death. Three of every four Americans own some form of life insurance. The main reason people buy life insurance is to provide financial security for their families in the event of their death. With assets totaling more than $2.5 trillion, life insurance is one of the nation's largest businesses.

key executive insurance life insurance designed to reimburse the organization for the loss of the services of an essential senior manager and to cover the executive search expenses needed to find a replacement.

Types of Life Insurance   As with health and disability insurance, both individual and group life insurance policies are available. Many employers offer life insurance to employees as a component of the firm's benefits program. However, unlike health and disability insurance, an individual life insurance policy is usually cheaper than a group policy for younger people.

The different types of life insurance fall neatly into two categories: term policies and cash value policies. **Term policies** provide a death benefit if the policyholder dies within a specified period of time. It has no value at the end of that period. **Cash value policies** combine life insurance protection with a savings or investment feature. The cash value represents the savings or investment portion of the life insurance policy. While there are arguments in favor of cash value policies, many experts believe that term insurance is a better choice for most consumers. For one thing, a term policy is much cheaper than a cash value policy, especially for younger people.

How Much Life Insurance Should You Have?   People can purchase life insurance policies for almost any amount. Life insurance purchases are limited only by the amount of premiums people can afford and their ability to meet medical qualifications. The amount of life insurance a person needs, however, is a very personal decision. The general rule of thumb is that a person needs life insurance if he or she has family members who financially depend on that person. A young parent with three small children could easily need $500,000 or more of life insurance. A single person with no dependents would reasonably see little or no need for a life insurance policy.

Businesses, as well as individuals, buy life insurance. The death of a partner or a key executive is likely to result in a financial loss to an organization. **Key executive insurance** is life insurance designed to reimburse the organization for the loss of the services of an essential senior manager and to cover the executive search expenses needed to find a replacement. In addition, life insurance policies may be purchased for each member of a partnership to be able to repay the deceased partner's survivors for his or her share of the firm and permit the business to continue.

Did You Know?

1. In the Caucasus Mountains dividing Russia and Georgia, people pay their doctor as long as they remain healthy. They stop payment when they get ill.
2. Most *Fortune* 500 U.S. companies have kidnap and ransom insurance for their top executives.
3. Malpractice premiums average $8,000 and up for physicians. Veterinarians pay premiums of about $240 per year.
4. In the Orient, two of every three adult males smoke. By contrast, only one in four adult males in the U.S. smokes.

Projects and Applications

1. Assume you're the owner of a small manufacturing facility. Make a list of some of the major risks you face. How should each risk be handled (avoided, reduced, assumed, or transferred)? What types of insurance will you likely need to have, including those required by law?

2. For many people, one frustrating aspect of insurance is deciphering insurance terminology. A Web site exists that provides a lexicon of insurance terms: http://www.insweb.com/learningcenter/glossary/general-a.htm. Visit the Web site and look up the following terms:

accommodation line
act of God
fortuitous
housekeeping
earned premium
non-admitted insurer
tickler

3. Many companies currently sell insurance online. Two prominent companies that sell auto insurance policies online are GEICO (http://www.geico.com) and Pro-

gressive (http://www.progressive.com). Visit both Web sites and write a brief report on your experience. Would you consider buying insurance online? What are the advantages and disadvantages?

4. Several insurance-oriented Web sites have interactive worksheets to help you determine whether you need life insurance and, if so, how much you need. Visit the MSN Money Central Web site listed below. Complete the interactive worksheet. If you need life insurance, what kind of policy should you buy? How much will it cost?

http://moneycentral.msn.com/investor/calcs/n_life/main.asp

5. Recently, some states have allowed insurance companies to sell auto insurance by the mile. Using a search engine, such as Google, compile a list of the states that allow the sale of auto insurance by the mile. Would you be interested? What are the pros and cons?

Appendix B

A Guide to Your Personal Finances

Will E-Billing Save You Money?

Everyone knows that paying bills late can affect a person's credit rating. And nearly three of four consumers take care to pay on time. But this means that about one-fourth of us pay at least one bill late each month.

That's the result of a survey by Opinion Research Corporation International and the Western Union SwiftPay service, which polled more than 1,000 consumers about their bill-paying habits. The survey also found that households with children are about 75 percent more likely to miss a payment than households with no children and that people over 55 years of age are least likely to be late payers. Those most often late are between 25 and 34 years. Also, with relatively less disposable income in general, 18- to 25-year-olds are most interested in managing their budgets.

Western Union believes the survey identifies two types of people who are late with their bills. Says spokesperson Wendy Carver-Herbert, "There's the budget-driven behavior—those consumers forced into a situation where they have to prioritize their bills and determine which are the most important to pay first. They tend to be folks most often living paycheck to paycheck." The second group, she believes, are "the business travelers, people who have extremely busy lifestyles whose payment date comes up and they realize, 'Oh my gosh. I still have to do that.'"

Prepayment of some bills—like cable, wireless phone, rent, and utility charges—is one way to avoid making late payments, but the number of consumers who take advantage of such services is still low. And cash is still the second-most preferred form of payment, after checks.

Many merchants expect that the common practice of using checks to pay bills will change in the near future. Electronic billing, though still in its early stages, holds the promise of cost savings and convenience, reduced paperwork and handling, and an easy way to remind consumers about their bills before payments begin to run late.

Research conducted by The Pew Internet and American Life Project found that more than three-fourths of all computer users say they use the Internet to gather hobby information, about two-thirds shop online, and half use the Internet for buying travel tickets. But online banking has the highest growth rate of any online activity: one in six did their banking online in 2000, but nearly one in three—32 percent—do so today. That adds up to about 37 million Americans, and about one in 10 of them is banking online every day. With the expansion of electronic banking in general, can e-billing be far behind? It's no surprise that merchants from wireless phone companies to car dealers to department stores are looking for similar growth in e-billing.

But is the trend toward online bill payments just about convenience for you and timely payments for them? Some industry experts believe that e-billing also offers sellers another opportunity to send targeted marketing messages to consumers who log on to their Web sites to settle their account. Product offers, gifts, and special deals can easily be communicated to consumers online, coupons and certificates can be printed out, and consumers can make immediate purchases on the spot.

Accessing financial information online provides the most current account information and allows consumers more direct control over their investments.

© John Riley/Index Stock Imagery

So, as always, the consumer should be wary. Does e-billing offer a way out of your late-payment habit or is it another way for you to run up your debt? As you read this appendix, you'll understand the role of such questions in your own personal financial planning and management.[1]

Overview

Although you enrolled in this course to study business, much of what you learn also applies to your personal life. For instance, you have learned about the important functions of a business from accounting to marketing, from finance to management. Learning about each business function helps you choose a career, and career choice is one of the most important personal financial decisions you will ever make. You also learned about how firms prepare budgets. Budgeting is another important aspect of your personal financial life.

Everyone, regardless of age or income, can probably do a better job managing his or her finances. As a group, Americans are much better at making money than they are at managing money. This appendix introduces you to personal financial management, a subject that deals with a variety of issues and decisions that affect a person's financial well-being. It includes basic money management, handling credit, tax planning, major consumer purchases, insurance, investing, and retirement planning. The appendix draws on many of the things you learned while studying business but introduces you to some new concepts as well. We hope that after completing the appendix, you are a better informed financial consumer and personal money manager—one who is motivated to learn more about personal finance. The rewards, in both monetary and nonmonetary terms, can be tremendous.

The Meaning and Importance of Personal Finance

personal finance study of the economic factors and personal decisions that affect a person's financial well-being.

standard of living lifestyle one seeks to obtain or to maintain.

Personal finance is the study of the economic factors and personal decisions that affect an individual's financial welfare. Personal finance affects, and is affected by, many things a person does and many decisions he or she makes throughout life.

On one level, personal finance involves money know-how. It is essential to know how to earn money as well as know how to save, spend, invest, and control it to achieve set goals. The reward of sound money management is an improvement in an individual's standard of living. The term **standard of living** refers to the necessities, comforts, and luxuries an individual seeks to obtain or maintain.

On another level, personal finance is intertwined with each person's **lifestyle**—the way you live your daily life. An individual's choice of careers, friends, hobbies, communities, and possessions is determined by personal finances, and yet an individual's personal finances can also be determined by his or her lifestyle. If you are a college student living independently on a shoestring budget, you likely have had to make many financial sacrifices as you work toward your educational goals. Where you live is determined by the school you attend and the amount you can afford to pay for rent. Your spring break vacation—if you are able to take one—is set by your academic schedule and the balance in your checkbook. Your clothing choices depend on both the climate and your budget. All these lifestyle decisions are at least partially determined by your personal finances.

lifestyle the way one lives one's daily life.

The Importance of Personal Finance Today

Good money management has always been important, but major changes in the external financial environment over the past couple of decades have made personal financial management even more important today. This growing importance of personal finance is true whether someone is a 20-year-old college student struggling to pay bills, a 40-year-old parent trying to save for a child's education, or a 60-year-old thinking about retirement. More specifically, there are three reasons personal finance is so important today.

Sluggish Growth in Personal Income
Over the past 20 years, average U.S. personal income, adjusted for taxes and inflation, has grown very slowly—slightly more than 2 percent per year. Also, many economists expect this trend to continue for the next 10 to 20 years. The sluggish growth in personal income makes sound money management very important. Simply put, you cannot count on a rising income to dramatically improve your standard of living. Rather, the keys to increasing your standard of living are saving and investing money, sticking to a budget, using credit properly, and making purchases wisely.

Changes in the Job Market
Job security and the notion of work have changed dramatically in recent years. The traditional model of an individual working for the same company for his or her entire career has become very rare. Most people entering the workforce today will change jobs, and probably employers, several times during their working careers. Some will end up working part time or on a contract basis, with little job security and few benefits. Others will take time off to care for small children or elderly parents. And a goal many people have today is to start their own businesses and work for themselves.

On average, one in four individuals entering the workforce today will be unemployed at some point during their working lives. A cold hard truth of the current job market is that you never know when your employer will decide to downsize, cutting your job along with costs.

Changes to the job market make sound personal financial management even more important. You need to keep your career skills up-to-date and accumulate sufficient financial resources to weather an unexpected crisis. Moreover, instead of relying on your employer to manage your retirement savings, you will likely need to make sure you have an adequate nest egg when you decide to retire.

More Choices
The number of choices in such areas as banking, credit, investments, and retirement planning can be bewildering. Today, you can do most of your banking online and then buy mutual fund shares or insurance at a brick-and-mortar bank. Even the simple checking account has become more complicated. The typical financial institution offers several different types of checking accounts, each with its own set of features and fees. Choosing the wrong account could easily cost you $100 or more each year in unnecessary fees.

One of the first things you do when you start a new job is make a number of benefit decisions. The typical employer offers choices in health insurance, disability insurance, group life insurance, and retirement plans. Unfortunately, you may receive only minimal guidance from your employer about which are the best choices for you. Pick the wrong health insurance plan, for example, and you may end up paying thousands of dollars more in out-of-pocket costs. Making the wrong decisions concerning retirement could make it difficult to accumulate a sufficient nest egg, even if you are still in your 20s.

In general, choice is good, and having more choice in the personal finance arena means consumers are likely to find what they are seeking. At the same time, however, a longer menu of choices means it is easier to make mistakes. The more informed you are, the better choices and fewer costly mistakes you are likely to make.

Personal Financial Planning: A Lifelong Activity

Personal financial planning is an important activity whether you are 20, 40, or 60; whether you are single, a single parent, or married with children; and whether your annual income is $30,000 or $300,000. The fact that sound financial planning is a lifelong activity, of course, does not mean that your financial goals will remain constant throughout your life—they will change. The major goals when you are young may be to pay off your college loans and begin saving to buy a new home. For older people, the major goal may be drawing up a sound estate plan or making sure that retirement savings last long enough.

In addition, the relative importance of the various personal planning areas will also change as you go through life. Right now, you may be more concerned with credit and basic money management but less concerned with investment or retirement planning. As you get older, the relative importance of investment and retirement planning will likely increase. Buying the right life insurance policy is a major decision for a 30-year-old parent but is a much less important decision for a 65-year-old grandparent. On the other hand, the 65-year-old is much more concerned with estate planning and long-term-care insurance than is the 30-year-old.

Do You Need Professional Help?

Many people believe they need professional help when it comes to managing their finances. The world is full of people and organizations willing to give you advice on everything from preparing a budget to estate planning. More than a few colleges and universities, for instance, offer credit counseling and other basic financial services to students who find themselves in financial trouble. Once you are older, you may find it prudent to use the services of a certified public accountant (CPA) when preparing your tax returns or a professional investment advisor when choosing the right investments to fund your retirement. There is also a great deal of financial information and advice available online today. Two of the better personal-finance Web sites are Quicken.com and MSN Money Central.

Be warned, though, that almost anyone can call him- or herself a financial planner, regardless of background or training. While financial planners must have certain federal and state licenses to sell most financial products, there are almost no other standards governing financial planners. However, a professional organization—called the Certified Financial Planner Board—certifies financial planners. Anyone who obtains the *certified financial planner (CFP)* designation has met a set of educational and professional requirements and passed a comprehensive examination.

The Certified Financial Planner Board ensures that financial planners who obtain CFP certification have met professional standards.

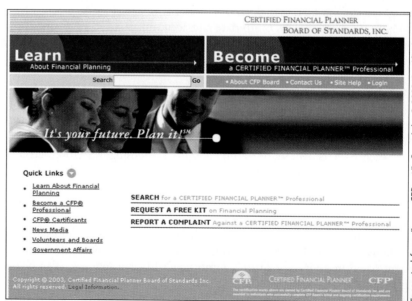

Getting Started: Your Financial Priorities

When it comes to personal financial management, one of the hardest things is to know where to begin. The proper way to get started is to establish some financial priorities. The worst thing you can do is procrastinate. According to the experts, people in their early 20s should do the following (in rough order of importance):

- *Figure out where you stand financially.* Most people, including those well beyond their 20s, have no clue about exactly what they own (assets) and what they owe (liabilities). While most people have a pretty good idea about how much they earn (income), many would have a hard time detailing how much they spend. So one of the first things you should do is prepare a set of financial statements (income statement and balance sheet) for yourself.
- *Put yourself on a budget.* Budget is not a four-letter word, nor does a budget merely imply sacrifice or always doing without. Instead, a budget is a tool that allows you to plan and monitor your expenses. People who stick to budgets are much less likely to experience a financial crisis of their own making. According to the authors of the popular book *The Millionaire Next Door,* the wealthy tend to be meticulous budgeters.
- *Insure yourself against financial ruin.* Insurance is not something most people like to think about. Insurance can be confusing, not to mention expensive. Still, you need to be properly insured. Being properly insured means having, at a bare minimum, health insurance, disability insurance (if you are working), auto insurance (if you own a car), and either renter's or homeowner's insurance. You need life insurance only if there are other people—such as a spouse or children—who depend on you financially.
- *Get your debts under control.* As the opening vignette points out, it is easy to allow your debts to get out of control, and the financial consequences can be severe. A good rule of thumb is to keep all your installment debt payments—credit cards, student loans, and auto loans—under 20 percent of your monthly income. In addition, the percentage of your income going to repay installment debt should decline over time.
- *Start saving for retirement.* To be able to retire—and live comfortably—you are going to need to save a lot of money while you are working. The earlier you start, the easier it is to meet your retirement savings goals. So sign up for your employer's retirement plan as soon as possible. These days, it is likely to be a so-called *defined contribution plan*—such as a 401(k). Retirement plans can also lower your taxes.
- *Set up a regular savings program.* The best way to save money is to treat it as a fixed expense—just like your rent or car payment—and have money automatically transferred from checking to savings. You need savings to help you through financial emergencies, to take advantage of opportunities, and to make major purchases.

> *They Said It*
>
> Someone's sitting in the shade today because someone else planted a tree a long time ago.
>
> —*Warren E. Buffett (b. 1930)*
> *American investor*

A Personal Financial Management Model

The starting point for developing a good financial plan is establishing a set of goals. They should reflect an honest assessment of your needs and wants in life, as well as your willingness and ability to achieve them. Personal financial decisions are guided by two types of goals: monetary and nonmonetary. A monetary goal might be paying off the outstanding balance on your Visa card, and a nonmonetary goal might be establishing and following a budget.

Because a variety of factors can affect decisions about securing, investing, and obtaining money, a financial plan considers both external and internal (personal) factors. External factors include general economic conditions and government actions that affect most personal financial decisions. For example, the outlook for interest rates affects everything from investment decisions to credit card behavior to major purchases. Personal factors include various aspects of individual and household financial behavior. Although individuals cannot change external factors, they can make personal decisions about savings, credit, major purchases, investments, and retirement.

FIGURE B.1
Personal Financial Model

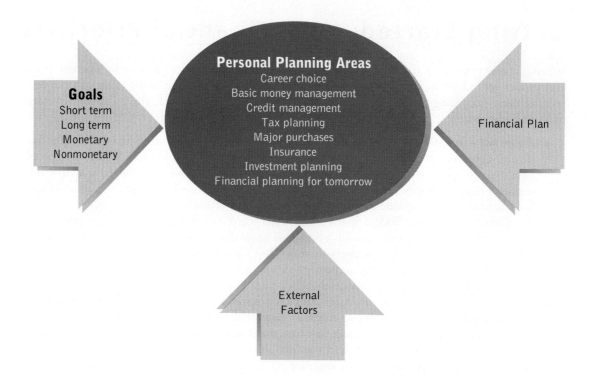

The model shown in Figure B.1 illustrates the basic components of personal financial plans and decisions. Each component influences the others. It would be foolish, for example, to make a decision about buying a home without considering the outlook for interest rates or your job security. Similarly, investment decisions should reflect your personal goals and lifestyle. Remember, financial planning is a lifelong activity. As your situation changes, so too should your financial plans.

Setting Personal Goals

Whatever your personal financial goals are, they should reflect your values. Values are a set of fundamental beliefs of what is important, desirable, and worthwhile in your life. Your values influence how you spend your money and, as a result, should be the foundation of your financial plan. Each person's financial goals are determined by his or her values because everyone has different priorities. Start by asking yourself some questions about your values—what is most important to you and what you would like to accomplish in your life?

Next, establish a series of financial goals based on your values. Separate your goals into short-term goals—those you would like to accomplish within the next year or so—and long-term goals—those you would like to accomplish within the next several years. An example of a short-term goal is "pay off the outstanding balance on my Visa card by this time next year." A long-term goal might be to buy a house by age 30. It is important, of course, that your short-term goals support your long-term goals. For instance, if your long-term goal is to buy a house, short-term goals should include starting a regular savings program and paying off credit card debt.

In addition, some of your goals will be monetary in nature—meaning you can put a price tag on them—while other goals will be nonmonetary. If you want to pay off the outstanding balance on your Visa card by this time next year, and the current balance is $1,000, that is an example of a monetary goal. A goal of constructing and following a monthly budget is an example of a nonmonetary goal.

Your financial goals should be defined as specifically as possible and focus on results. Goals should also be realistic and attainable. Paying off the $1,000 balance on your Visa card within the next 12 months may be realistic; paying it off in the next two months may not be. If your monthly take-home pay is $2,000, and your fixed monthly expenses—such as rent, utilities, transportation, and loan payments—amount to $1,000, setting a goal of saving $500 per month is probably not very realistic. On the other hand, a monthly savings goal of $250 may be much easier to attain.

Financial goals change throughout a person's lifetime, and for this reason, they should be written down and reviewed periodically. To be effective, goals should reflect changes in circumstances, such as education, family, career, the economy, and even your emotional and physical well-being.

Personal Financial Planning Areas

Your financial future is charted when you make decisions in such areas as career choice, credit, insurance, investments, spending, and tax planning. This section reviews the key elements of each of the major personal planning areas.

Career Choice

No factor exerts as strong an influence on your personal finances as does your career choice. After all, your job will likely provide most of your income. Through work, you acquire the income needed to build a lifestyle, to buy goods and services, to save and invest, and to plan for retirement. Your job is also the source of many important benefits, such as health and disability insurance and retirement plans.

A variety of factors go into a career choice. People pick careers based on financial considerations (income and financial security), job satisfaction, and the feeling that their work will contribute positively to society. How each person weighs these three factors is very much an individual decision. *Contemporary Business* contains material to help you choose a business career, look for a job, and even write a résumé. Additional resources can be found on the *Contemporary Business* Web site (`http://boone .swlearning.com`), on other Web sites such as Monster.com, or from your college's career center. One important fact to keep in mind, however, is that many people change careers, perhaps even several times, during their lives.

Basic Money Management

Another important component of sound financial planning is basic money management, which consists of preparing financial statements regularly, constructing and following a budget each month, and managing checking and savings accounts. In *Contemporary Business,* you learned about why and how firms prepare financial statements. Individuals should prepare financial statements for many of the same reasons. An individual's income statement is a record of how much money was earned and where money was spent during a period of time. As you recall, the balance sheet is a snapshot of what a person owns and owes at a point in time. The difference between what you own and what you owe is called **net worth.**

A set of financial statements for Anthony and LaToya is shown in Figure B.2. Notice that on their income statement Anthony and LaToya divide their expenses into major categories—such as housing, transportation, and child care. Anthony and LaToya spent less than they made during the year, so they added money to their savings and investments.

Anthony and LaToya prepared their balance sheet at the end of the year. They divided what they own into two major categories: financial assets and nonfinancial assets. They further divided their financial assets into subcategories based on the asset's liquidity (from the balance in their checking account to the balances in their retirement accounts). Also, they divided their liabilities into debts that are due within a short period of time—say, within the next month—and those that are due over a longer period of time. Try preparing a set of financial statements for yourself.

Individuals should prepare budgets for the same reasons firms do. A budget is an excellent tool for monitoring your expenditures and helping you achieve your financial goals. Most personal budgets are prepared monthly—many bills are paid monthly, and most workers are paid at least once a month. The budget is divided between cash inflows (income) and cash outflows (expenses). Expenses are then further divided into categories. A sample budget form is shown in Figure B.3.

The final element of basic money management involves managing checking and savings accounts. Properly managing these relatively simple assets is an important first step toward the proper management

They Said It

Why is there always so much month left at the end of the money?

—*Anonymous*

net worth difference between what a person owns (assets) and owes (liabilities).

FIGURE B.2

Financial Statements for Anthony and LaToya

Balance Sheet

Assets		Liabilities & Net Worth	
Current financial assets		**Current liabilities**	
Checking account	$2,500	Utilities	$200
Savings account	5,000	Insurance	250
Money market funds	4,500	Credit card	500
Total	$12,000	Other	0
Long-term financial assets		Total current liabilities	$950
Mutual funds	$12,000	**Long-term liabilities**	
Stocks and bonds	$0	Auto loan	$8,000
Pension	$0	Student loans	3,500
401(k)	30,000	Mortgage	130,000
IRAs	2,500	Other	0
Other	1,500	Total long-term liabilities	$141,500
Total	$46,000		
Nonfinancial assets		**Total Liabilities**	142,450
Home	$165,000		
Auto 1	13,000	**Net Worth**	**$127,050**
Auto 2	8,500		
Furniture	15,000		
Personal property	5,000		
Other	5,000		
Total fixed assets	$211,500		
Total Assets	**$269,500**		

Income Statement

Wages earned	
Anthony	38,500
LaToya	43,000
Other income	
Bonuses	2,500
Interest & dividends	1,000
Tax refunds	500
Other	0
Total income	$85,500
Income and FICA taxes	−16,000
Net income	**$69,500**
Expenditures	
Housing	
House payment or rent	12,000
Utilities	3,500
Property taxes	1,800
Maintenance	2,500
Insurance	500
Other housing	3,500
Total housing	$23,800
Transportation	
Car payments	3,600
Gas & repairs	1,500
Insurance	1,000
Registration	200
Other transportation	300
Total transportation	$6,600
Food & clothing	8,000
Medical & dental expenses	1,500
Child care	5,000
Vacation & entertainment	3,500
Student loan payments	2,000
Credit card interest	0
Life insurance premiums	1,500
Cash allowances	5,000
Other expenses	2,500
Total expenditures	**$59,400**
Amount available for savings	**$10,100**

Cash Inflows	Budget	Month _____ Actual	Difference	Budget	Month _____ Actual	Difference	Budget	Month _____ Actual	Difference	Cumulative Difference
Net salary										
Net salary										
Other										
Total cash inflows										

Cash Outflows **Fixed expenses**										
House payment or rent										
Auto loan										
Student loan										
Credit card payments										
Savings and investments										

Variable expenses										
Utilities										
Food										
Insurance payments										
Medical and dental										
Clothing and personal care										
Entertainment and recreation										
Transportation expenses										
Gifts and contributions										
Personal spending money										
Other expenses										
Total cash outflows										

Monthly Outcomes

Month				Three-month total
Cash inflows (actual				
− Cash outflows (actual)				
= Surplus (deficit)				

FIGURE B.3
Sample Budget Form

of more complicated assets such as investment and retirement accounts. You must choose a bank or other financial institution and then select the right checking account. As noted previously, most banks offer several different types of checking accounts, each with its own fees and services. Banking fees are a major issue today. The Best Business Practices box on bank fees lists some suggestions for controlling banking fees and getting the best deal on a checking account. Managing a savings account involves understanding the importance of savings, setting savings goals, and picking the best savings option. Major savings options include statement savings accounts, certificates of deposit, and money market mutual funds.

Credit Management

Not surprisingly, credit is the area of personal finance that gets the most people into trouble, including, as the opening vignette points out, many college students. **Credit** is a loan for a specified period of time with a specified rate of interest that allows a borrower to receive money, goods, or services. Credit is available from many sources today, but rates vary, so it pays to shop around. For instance, there are several thousand issuers of Visa and MasterCard credit cards. Some suggestions for picking the right credit card are listed in the Best Business Practices box.

There are two broad types of consumer credit: revolving (or open-end) credit and installment loans. **Revolving credit** is a type of credit arrangement that enables consumers to make a number of different purchases up to a credit limit, as specified by the lender. The consumer has the option of repaying some or all of the outstanding balance each month. If the consumer carries a balance from month to month, finance charges (interest) are levied. An example of revolving credit is a credit card such as Visa, MasterCard, or Discover. An **installment loan** is a credit arrangement in which the borrower takes out a loan

They Said It

About the same time we can make ends meet, somebody moves the ends.

—*Herbert Hoover (1874–1964)*
31st president of the United States

credit loan for a specified period of time with a specified rate of interest that allows a borrower to receive money, goods, or services.

BEST BUSINESS PRACTICES

Keeping Bank Fees under Control

Consumers can easily spend a couple of hundred dollars a year in banking fees. The following are some commonsense tips for keeping bank fees under control:

- *Make sure you have your bank's best deal, given the way you bank.* Banks today offer many different checking and savings accounts, each with its own fee structure. Given the way you bank, you may find certain accounts cheaper than others.
- *Consider credit unions or smaller banks.* Credit unions and smaller banks tend to charge less than larger banks. It pays to shop around.
- *Watch how you use your ATM card.* Make sure you know which ATMs you can use for free and how many free transactions you have each month.
- *Keep track of your daily account balance.* Make sure it doesn't drop below the minimum.
- *Keep track of the number of checks you write each month if you have a transaction limit.* Use a debit card or automated bill payments to reduce the number of checks you write each month.
- *Sign up for overdraft protection.* If you overdraw your account, you won't be charged.
- *Don't be afraid to beg.* The bank branch manager may have the power to waive certain fees—such as the fee for a bounced check. The worst the manager can say is no.
- *Read the fine print in your monthly statement.* See what your bank is charging for certain services and try to adjust your behavior accordingly. Remember, your bank can't change its fee structure without first informing you. That information will come after your monthly statement.

Source: Louis E. Boone, David L. Kurtz, and Douglas Hearth, *Tax Update of Planning Your Financial Future,* 3rd ed. Mason, OH: South-Western, 2005, p. 96.

---

for a specified amount, agreeing to repay the loan in regular installments over a specified period of time. The installments include the finance charge. Student loans, auto loans, and home mortgage loans are examples of installment loans.

There are good reasons for borrowing money, including purchasing large, important goods and services (cars, homes, or a college education); dealing with financial emergencies; taking advantage of opportunities; needing convenience; and establishing or improving your credit rating. All of these reasons are appropriate uses of credit if you can repay the loans in a timely manner.

But a wrong reason for borrowing money is using credit to live beyond your means. For instance, you want to go to Cancún for a vacation but really cannot afford to, so you charge the trip. Using credit to live beyond your means often leads to credit problems. Watch for these warnings signs:

- You use credit to meet basic living expenses.
- You use credit to make impulse purchases.
- You take a cash advance on one credit card to repay another; your unpaid balance increases month after month.

Consumers who think of credit purchases as a series of small monthly payments are fooling themselves. The average credit balance carried by college students today is around $2,700. The annual interest rate on credit cards carried by college students averages about 18 percent. How long would it take someone with the average balance to become debt-free, assuming he or she made only the minimum payment (typically $25 or 2.5 percent of the outstanding balance, whichever is greater) each month? The answer—13 years and five months, during which time the student would end up paying over $3,000 in interest. The scary details are shown in Table B.1 on page B-12. What's more, this example assumes that the person does not charge anything else while paying off the balance.

The simple quiz shown in Figure B.4 on page B-13 is one way of assessing whether you may have a credit problem. If you feel as though you have a problem with credit, or may be developing one, you should seek help as soon as possible. Your college or university may offer credit counseling services. If not, contact a local not-for-profit credit counseling service or the National Federation for Credit Counseling (800-388-2227 or http://www.nfcc.org).

BEST BUSINESS PRACTICES

Choosing the Right Credit Card

There are thousands of places where you can get a credit card. When it comes to selecting a credit card, consider the following four factors:

- *Annual and late payment fees.* Credit cards may charge an annual fee of up to $80 or $90. However, if you shop around, you can probably find a no-fee credit card. Also consider the cost of any late payment fees.
- *Annual percentage rate.* The annual percentage rate (APR) is the interest rate charged on cash advances and unpaid balances. If you faithfully pay off your balance each month and avoid taking cash advances, the APR is really not a consideration in choosing a card. If you carry a balance, find the card offering the lowest fixed APR. The national average APR on Visas and MasterCards is around 15 percent, but some cards offer much lower APRs. You can compare APRs at http://www.bankrate.com, and each issue of *Money* magazine lists the best deals on U.S. credit cards. Also, read the fine print. Some card issuers will

adjust rates up and down depending on your spending and payment pattern.
- *Credit limit.* The credit limit essentially caps your spending. The lender establishes the maximum credit limit. Of course, you can always request a lower credit limit than the lender is willing to grant.
- *Grace period.* The grace period is the amount of time you have to pay for new purchases without incurring any finance charges. Grace periods average between 25 and 30 days, but some credit cards have no grace period, meaning you pay interest from the date you make the purchase to the date you pay your balance. Also, many cards give you no grace period on new purchases if you carry a balance. Some credit card issuers have reduced the length of the grace period in recent years. Make sure to read any notices you receive from the issuer carefully.

Source: Adapted from Louis E. Boone, David L. Kurtz, and Douglas Hearth, *Tax Update of Planning Your Financial Future,* 3rd ed. Mason, OH: South-Western, 2005, pp. 138–140.

According to the experts, one of the keys to the wise use of credit is education. Learning about the pros and cons of borrowing money, as well as learning about responsible spending, can help people avoid future problems with credit. A new type of Visa card may help educate young people about responsible spending. Called Buxx, this Visa card is designed for high school and college students. Parents put a certain amount of money on the card, and the student can spend only that amount. He or she still has many of the advantages of a credit card, but without the risk of running up a large unpaid balance.

Tax Planning

Everyone pays a variety of taxes to federal, state, and local governments. The major taxes individuals pay include federal and state income taxes, Social Security and Medicare taxes, property taxes, and sales taxes. A family with median U.S. income paid almost 38 percent of that income in taxes during a recent year.[2] Think about your own situation and the taxes you pay. If you work, you have federal income taxes withheld from each paycheck. In addition, if you live in one of the 41 states with a state income tax, you have state tax withheld. The Social Security tax amounts to 7.65 percent of your wages (your employer pays the other 7.65 percent). Funding Medicare requires another payroll tax. If you rent an apartment, part of your monthly rent goes to pay the landlord's property tax bill. Every time you buy something, you likely pay sales tax to the state and local governments.

Unfortunately, there is very little you can do to reduce some of the taxes you pay. The only tax over which you have some control is the federal income tax. Even with the federal income tax, there are only a handful of ways the average person can legally reduce his or her income tax bill. Still, you need to understand the federal income tax system and know what kinds of tax records to keep. Even though millions of Americans pay someone else to prepare their taxes, many people have relatively simple returns, and preparing a tax return is one of the best ways of learning more about your personal

Table B.1   How Long It Takes to Pay Off a Credit Card Balance

Amount owed: $2,700
Annual percentage rate (APR): 18%
Interest owed: .015 × beginning balance
Payment: 2.5% of outstanding balance or $25 (whichever is greater)
Principal repaid: Payment minus interest
Ending balance: Beginning balance minus principal repaid

Payment Number	Beginning Balance	Interest Owed	Payment	Principal Repaid	Ending Balance	Cumulative Interest	Cumulative Principal
1	$2,700	$41	$68	$27	$2,673	$ 41	$ 27
2	2,673	40	67	27	2,646	81	54
3	2,646	40	66	26	2,620	120	80
4	2,620	39	65	26	2,594	160	106
5	2,594	39	65	26	2,568	198	132
6	2,568	39	64	26	2,542	237	158
7	2,542	38	64	25	2,517	275	183
8	2,517	38	63	25	2,491	313	209
9	2,491	37	62	25	2,466	350	234
10	2,466	37	62	25	2,442	387	258
11	2,442	37	61	24	2,417	424	283
12	2,417	36	60	24	2,393	460	307
60	1,492	22	37	15	1,477	1,834	1,223
120	766	11	25	14	753	2,832	1,947
161	9	0	9	9	0	3,089	2,700

They Said It

The taxpayer—that's someone who works for the federal government but doesn't have to take a civil service exam.

—*Ronald Reagan (b. 1911)*
40th president of the United States

finances. The Internal Revenue Service (IRS) has several excellent publications to help you prepare a federal income tax return. One of the best is IRS Publication 17 (You and Your Federal Income Tax). This and all other IRS publications are available free of charge from local IRS offices or the IRS Web site. If you have a personal computer, consider using one of the software programs—such as Turbo Tax—that helps prepare a federal income tax return.

Major Purchases

Even if you are a great budgeter and saver, you will still spend most of your income each year. Effective buying is an important part of your financial plan. Within personal budget limits, an individual exercises his or her rights as a consumer to select or reject the wide range of goods and services that are available. As you purchase an automobile, a home, or any other major item, you need to carefully evaluate alternatives, separate needs from wants, and determine how you are going to finance the purchase. Your goal is to make every dollar you spend count.

Americans spend over $500 billion annually on transportation, most of which goes to the purchase and maintenance of automobiles. Given that new vehicles average over $20,000 today and even a

True/False	1. You spend money in the expectation that your income will rise.
True/False	2. You take cash advances on one credit card to pay off another.
True/False	3. You spend more than 20 percent of your income on credit card bills.
True/False	4. You fail to keep adequate records of your purchases.
True/False	5. You regularly pay for groceries with a credit card because you don't have enough money in your checking account.
True/False	6. You have applied for more than five new cards in the past year.
True/False	7. You often hide your credit card purchases from your family.
True/False	8. Having several credit cards makes you feel richer.
True/False	9. You pay off your monthly credit card bills but let other bills slide.
True/False	10. You almost always make only the minimum payment on credit cards.
True/False	11. You like to collect cash from friends in restaurants and then charge the entire tab on your credit card.
True/False	12. You have trouble imagining your life without credit.

Scoring (number of "true" responses):

Less than 5: Green light—you are probably okay.
5 to 8: Yellow light—pay off your bills and examine your spending habits.
More than 8: Red light—you have or are developing a credit problem.

good used car can cost in excess of $12,000, buying an automobile is a substantial purchase. On top of that, most car purchases are financed. Buying a car involves weighing many factors, including whether you want a new or used car, the makes and models that appeal to you, and how much you can afford to pay.

For most people, housing consumes the largest share of their monthly budgets. About seven of every 10 Americans own their own homes, and home ownership is a goal of most people. Owning a home has a number of advantages, both financial and nonfinancial. Some of the financial benefits include tax savings (home mortgage interest and property taxes are both tax deductible) and the potential increase in the home's value. Nonfinancial benefits include pride of ownership. The major barrier to home ownership is the down payment required to get a mortgage loan. Even a modestly priced home requires a buyer to have $10,000 to $15,000 in cash.

Motor vehicles are a substantial purchase, and consumers must consider many factors in making a selection.

BEST BUSINESS PRACTICES

Are You Ready to Buy a Home?

Buying a home is one of the largest financial decisions you'll ever make. Too many people get caught up in emotion when buying a home and end up not making as reasoned a decision as they should. In fact, buying with your heart and not your head is a common mistake made by homebuyers. Answer the following questions and see whether you're really ready to buy a home.

- *How stable is your current job?* The stabler your job, the readier you are to buy a home.
- *What is your current rent?* Some people pay rents that are well below the prevailing rates. If you're one of them, it may not pay to buy a home.
- *How long do you plan on staying in the area?* The longer you plan on staying, the readier you are to buy a home.
- *Do you have a good credit record?* The better your credit record, the better your chances of getting a mortgage at a competitive interest rate.
- *What are your existing debts?* The more you currently pay for various types of consumer loans—such as auto loans and credit cards—the more difficult it will be to get a good mortgage loan.

- *Does the financial advantage of owning hinge on potential price appreciation?* If it does, think twice about buying.
- *Will you be able to take full advantage of all the housing tax deductions?* Given today's interest rates, you may not be able to.
- *Will your personal situation change in the coming years (will you get married, have children)?* Don't make a long-term decision based solely on your current situation.
- *Do you have the financial resources to afford a home with which you'll be satisfied?* Consider not only the down payment, monthly payment, and closing costs but also the cost of decorating, new furniture, landscaping, and so forth. Buying a home usually means buying a lot of other stuff.
- *Do you* really *want to own a home?* Owning a home means you'll be responsible for maintenance and repairs. Do you mind spending Saturday afternoon mowing the lawn?

Source: Louis E. Boone, David L. Kurtz, and Douglas Hearth, *Tax Update of Planning Your Financial Future,* 3rd ed. Mason, OH: South-Western, 2005, p. 229.

With mortgage rates at near-historic lows, many young Americans are opting to buy their own homes. Some have even found that it is cheaper than renting, and they can build equity for the future. Recent law school graduate Bradley Sanders searched for a house in an established neighborhood with a good resale value. "I feel like I'm in debt for the rest of my life," he joked. But he loves his neighborhood and doesn't think he'll have any problems selling his house when he's ready to move up.[3]

The other major housing option is renting. Renting also offers a number of advantages, including cost savings (the landlord takes care of maintenance and repairs) and mobility. It is much easier to move if you rent than if you own a home. People who plan on staying in an area for a short period of time are often better off renting.

The choice between buying and renting is obviously a major financial decision. It is one that needs to be approached rationally, not emotionally. This is especially true for first-time homebuyers. The Best Business Practices box lists some considerations for people thinking about buying their first home.

Insurance

Appendix A focused on another important personal planning area: insurance. Some of the basic principles of insurance, and the various types of insurance, were described in detail in that appendix. While the focus of the appendix was on business insurance, much of what was discussed applies to your personal insurance needs as well. Insurance is admittedly an expensive but necessary purchase. Americans spend over $100 billion each year on auto insurance alone.

Your goal is to have adequate and appropriate coverage in each of the major insurance types (life, health, disability, and property and liability). Insurance needs can vary substantially from individual to individual. For instance, consider the insurance needs of Maria (a single 25-year-old who rents an apartment) and Ben (a 40-year-old single parent who owns a home). Their individual insurance needs are listed in Figure B.5. Notice that they both need health, disability, and auto coverage, but only Ben needs life insurance. Ben's children are financially dependent on him, while Maria has no financial dependents. Maria should have renter's insurance, while Ben needs to have homeowner's insurance. What are your individual insurance needs? You can find out by filling out the worksheet shown in Figure B.6.

Some types of insurance will be provided by your employer as employee benefits. Most employers offer their workers group health insurance and basic disability coverage. Employers generally pay at least part of the premium, and some offer employees a choice of several health plans. Today, most people are covered by managed-care plans. A managed-care plan is an arrangement in which most of your health-care bills will be paid by the insurance company. In return, the insurance company has some control over your choice of health-care provider and your treatment. Appendix A described the different types of managed-care plans in more detail.

Investment Planning

Investing is a process by which money acquired through work, inheritance, or other sources is preserved and increased. Sound investment management is an important component of the financial plan and

Personal Characteristics	Ben	Maria
Age	40	25
Annual income	$70,000	$40,000
Marital status	divorced	single
Number of dependent children	2	0
Own automobile?	Yes	Yes
Homeowner?	Yes	No

Type of Insurance	Ben's Needs	Maria's Needs
Life	Needs life insurance amounting to several times his annual salary.	Needs no life insurance.
Health	Needs major medical plan that covers Ben and his children. Obtain from employer.	Should be covered by a major medical plan. Obtain from employer.
Disability	Should have a policy that pays an annual benefit of between $45,000 and $50,000. Obtain from employer.	Should have a policy that provides an annual benefit of between $30,000 and $33,000. Obtain from employer.
Auto	Should have substantial liability coverage and, depending on the age and value of his car, collision and comprehensive as well. Uninsured driver coverage is strongly recommended.	Should have as much liability coverage as she can afford. Collision and comprehensive are recommended, depending on the age and value of her car. Uninsured driver coverage is strongly recommended.
Homeowner's	Should have comprehensive, full replacement coverage on both the structure and contents of his home.	Should have a renter's policy covering her personal property.
Personal liability	Liability portions of auto and homeowner's policies probably sufficient. However, Ben might feel more comfortable with additional liability insurance.	Liability portions of auto and renter's policies probably sufficient.

FIGURE B.5
Comparing Ben's and Maria's Insurance Needs

FIGURE B.6
Your Insurance Needs

Personal Characteristics

Age	
Annual income	
Marital status	
Number of dependent children	
Own an automobile?	
Homeowner?	

Type of Insurance	Your Needs
Life	
Health	
Disability	
Auto	
Homeowner's	
Personal liability	

can make it easier to attain other personal goals, such as buying a home, sending children to college, starting a business, or retiring comfortably. It is very difficult today to substantially increase wealth without investing. Also, given changes to the external environment—such as reductions in employer-sponsored retirement plans—it is likely that everyone will have to make investment decisions at some point during their lives.

The investment process consists of four steps. The first step is to complete some preliminary tasks, including setting overall personal goals, having a regular savings program, and managing credit properly. The second step is to establish a set of investment goals—why you want to invest, what you want to accomplish, and what kind of time frame you have. Obviously, your investment goals should be closely related to your overall personal goals. Next, you need to assess risk and return. You invest because you expect to earn some future rate of return. At the same time, however, all investing exposes you to a variety of risks. You need to find the proper balance between risk and return because investments offering the highest potential returns also expose you to more risk. Your age, income, and whether you are a short- or long-term investor all have an impact on the risk–return trade-off.

The final step is to select the appropriate investments that match your individual needs. As we pointed out in Chapter 18, there are three general types of investments: money market instruments, bonds, and common stock. The proper mix of these three investments depends on such factors as your

BEST BUSINESS PRACTICES

Five Lessons of Saving for Retirement

Saving for retirement isn't as hard as you might think. Just follow these five lessons.

1. *Start early and stick with it.* The earlier you start, the easier it is to meet your retirement goals.
2. *Save as much as you can afford each month.* You'll build a substantial retirement nest egg in no time.
3. *Take advantage of all tax-deferred retirement savings plans to which you are entitled.* Retirement plans are a great tax shelter available to almost everyone.
4. *Don't be too conservative with your investments.* You should invest most of your retirement savings in stocks or

stock mutual funds if you're under 40. Even those in their 40s and early 50s should still invest a substantial portion of their retirement savings in common stocks.
5. *Diversify your investments.* Don't invest more than 20 percent of your retirement savings in your company's common stock. Mutual funds are an excellent choice for retirement savings.

Source: Louis E. Boone, David L. Kurtz, and Douglas Hearth, *Tax Update to Planning Your Financial Future,* 3rd ed. Mason, OH: South-Western, 2005, p. 457.

investment goals and investment time horizon. For instance, a 25-year-old investing for retirement should have close to 100 percent of his or her funds invested in common stocks because growth in capital is the overriding investment objective. Over longer periods of time, stocks tend to outperform money market instruments and bonds. On the other hand, if the 25-year-old is investing to have sufficient funds for a down payment on a house within the next couple of years, most of his or her funds should be invested in money market instruments and bonds. Liquidity, current income, and stability of principal are the most important investment objectives. Even after the investor selects the appropriate investments, he or she must monitor their performance and be prepared to make changes when necessary.

Financial Planning for Tomorrow

The last major personal financial planning area deals with retirement and estate planning. Most people eventually want to retire, and they need sufficient funds to ensure a degree of financial security. Social Security will provide only a fraction of what you will need, and you will be responsible for the rest. According to the experts, you will need to have a nest egg of at least $1 million by the time you retire. There are five important lessons when it comes to saving for retirement: start early, save as much as you can each month, take advantage of all tax-deferred retirement savings plans to which you are entitled, don't be too conservative with your investments, and diversify your investments. The Best Business Practices box elaborates on these five lessons.

Aside from Social Security, there are two other major sources of retirement income: employer-sponsored retirement plans and individual retirement plans. Most employers offer their workers a retirement plan, and many offer more than one plan. For most people, employer-sponsored retirement plans will likely provide the bulk of their retirement income. Essentially, two types of employer-sponsored retirement plans exist. A **defined benefit plan** guarantees a worker a certain retirement benefit each year. The size depends on a number of factors, including the worker's income and the length of time he or she worked for the employer. Pension plans are classified as defined benefit plans.

The other type of employer-sponsored retirement plan is the **defined contribution plan.** In this type of retirement plan, you contribute to your retirement account and typically so does your employer. You are given some latitude as to where your retirement funds can be invested. Often, you are given a list

> *They Said It*
>
> You can be young without money but you can't be old without it.
>
> —*Tennessee Williams (1914–1983)*
> *American dramatist*

of mutual funds where your money can be invested. A 401(k) is an example of a defined contribution plan. Defined contribution plans are becoming more and more common. By some estimates, nine of every 10 employers offer defined contribution plans. Many employers have partially or totally replaced their pension plans with defined contribution plans in recent years.

Millions of Americans have some sort of individual retirement plan. These plans are often set up and administered by individuals and are not tied to any employer. These workers may be self-employed or may merely want to supplement their retirement savings. Examples of individual retirement plans include regular individual retirement accounts (IRAs), Roth IRAs, Keogh plans, and simplified employee pension plans. To set up one of these retirement plans, you must meet certain eligibility requirements.

The other element of financial planning for tomorrow is estate planning. Of all the personal planning areas, estate planning is probably the least relevant for you, although your parents and grandparents probably face some estate planning issues. However, there are two documents that all adults need to have, regardless of age: a valid will (naming a guardian if you have any minor children) and a durable power of attorney (a document that gives someone else the power to make financial decisions if you are incapacitated).

Developing a Financial Plan

financial plan guide to help a person reach desired goals.

A previous section described personal financial statements. The income statement and balance sheet show where you are financially at a given point in time or where you have been historically. A **financial plan,** on the other hand, is a guide to help you reach future goals. All financial plans revolve around three themes: increasing wealth, using money more effectively, and monitoring expenditures.

Steps in Creating a Successful Financial Plan

The first step to developing a successful financial plan is to establish a set of goals based on your values. As described earlier, these goals—which can be both monetary and nonmonetary in nature—should be specific and realistic. They can help you visualize the gap between where you are now and where you want to be financially.

Goals are one thing, but to be effective, your financial plan must have consistent, logical, and realistic financial strategies. For instance, assume your goal is to retire comfortably by age 62. A financial strategy to meet this goal would be to make the maximum contribution to your employer's retirement plan each month and to invest the funds primarily in common stocks. Over time, stocks tend to produce much higher returns than other investments, so you will accumulate more money in your retirement account.

A financial plan cannot be developed in a vacuum. Your financial plan should take into account the resources you have available—especially salary and employee benefits. Your goals and strategies must be based on a realistic estimate of future income. If your financial goals cannot be reached through your present career path, you may need to consider switching careers or seek additional qualifications. Moreover, as you set goals and develop financial strategies, you are forced to make assumptions about the economy. If you are in the market for a new car and will finance the purchase, the outlook for interest rates could determine whether you accelerate or postpone your purchase.

Example of a Financial Plan

In Case 16.1 on page 539, Joan Chen learned about the importance of budgeting and preparing a budget. Now, she and her fiancé, Al, are preparing their first financial plan. Parts of it are shown in Figure B.7.

Several noteworthy items appear in Joan and Al's financial plan. First, they have divided the plan into categories—spending, debt, investments and savings, insurance, and other personal goals. This makes the plan easier to follow and generally more organized. Second, notice how Joan and Al have established a rough time frame for each of their goals. For instance, they would like to reduce their

Goal	Time Frame	Estimated Cost or Dollar Goal	Strategy
A. Spending			
1. Reduce nonessential spending by 5%	Ongoing	$1,500 to $2,000 annually	Review and revise budget quarterly; keep better track of cash ATM withdrawals
2. Buy new living room furniture	1 year	$3,000	Wait for sale; use money from savings
3. Buy a home	5 years	$15,000	Save $250 a month; save any bonuses
B. Debt			
1. Eliminate all credit card debt	1 year	$1,500	Reduce nonessential spending by around 10%; pay for new purchases using cash
2. Pay off student loans early	2–3 years	$5,000	Double up loan payments; make extra payments, if possible
C. Investments and Savings			
1. Build savings account	Ongoing	$5,000	Cut spending by 5%
2. Build retirement savings	Ongoing	$50,000 in 5 years	Make maximum contribution to employer-sponsored retirement accounts
D. Insurance			
1. Property and liability	Ongoing	Depends	Regularly review coverage; shop around for rates
2. Health and disability	Ongoing	Depends	Regularly review coverage
3. Life insurance	Ongoing	Depends	Review need for coverage
E. Other goals			
1. Start family	3–5 years	$15,000 in additional annual expenses	Build savings; budget for additional expenses

FIGURE B.7
Joan and Al's Financial Plan

combined credit card debt to zero within the next year. Third, Joan and Al have put a dollar value on each goal—reducing their credit card debt to zero will cost $1,500. Finally, a strategy, or strategies, is attached to each goal. Eliminating their credit card debt will require that Joan and Al cut their nonessential spending by about 10 percent per month.

Joan and Al's financial plan also reflects the couple's dreams. They eventually want to start a family and buy a home. Without sound planning today, their future dreams will be more difficult to achieve.

What's Ahead in Your Financial Future

This appendix just scratches the surface of personal financial planning. We hope it has encouraged you to learn more. There are dozens of helpful books, Web sites, and other resources available. If you can fit it into your academic schedule, consider taking a class in personal financial planning. Your institution probably offers one. Taking such a class may be one of the best decisions you make.

DID YOU KNOW?

1. Two of every three Americans do not balance their checkbooks on a regular basis.
2. You can expect to spend over $45,000 on ownership and operating expenses during the first five years that you own a typical new car.
3. There's a one in four chance that you will be unemployed at some point in your working career.
4. If both parents die without leaving a will, a court will decide who becomes the legal guardian of any minor children.

Projects and Applications

1. Prepare a current set of financial statements for yourself using the blank worksheets that follow. What do you think your financial statements will look like a year from now? Five years from now?

Financial Statement Worksheets

....

Balance Sheet

Assets	Liabilities & Net Worth
Current financial assets	Current liabilities
Checking account	Utilities
Savings account	Insurance
Money market funds	Credit card
Total	Other
	Total
Long-term financial assets	
Mutual funds	Long-term liabilities
Stocks and bonds	Auto loan
Pension	Student loans
401(k)	Mortgage
IRAs	Other
Other	Total
Total	
Fixed assets	
Home	Total liabilities
Auto 1	
Auto 2	Net worth
Furniture	
Personal property	
Other	
Total fixed assets	
Total assets	

Income Statement

Wages earned

Other income
    Bonuses
    Interest and dividends
    Tax refunds
    Other
Total income
(Income and FICA taxes)
Other income (proceeds from student loans, assistance from parents, etc.)
Net income

Expenditures
Housing
    House payment or rent
    Utilities
    Property taxes

Income Statement *(continued)*

Expenditures *(continued)*
Maintenance
Insurance
Other housing
Total housing
Transportation
Car payments
Gas and repairs
Insurance
Registration
Other transportation
Total transportation
College expenses
Tuition and fees
Books and school supplies
Total college
Food and clothing
Medical and dental expenses
Child care
Vacation and entertainment
Student loan payments
Credit card interest
Life insurance premiums
Cash allowances
Other expenses
Total expenditures
Amount available for savings

2. One of the most important tools for managing your personal finances is a budget. The earlier you learn to prepare and follow a budget, the better off you will be. If the budget worksheet shown in Figure B.3 looks a bit intimidating, there are a variety of interactive budget forms available on the Internet. Go to the following Web site, access the "Budget Worksheet" link, and fill out the budget worksheet. Compare your entries with the guidelines listed. Remember, a budget has to be realistic and must support your overall goals. How difficult will it be for you to follow the budget you prepared?

http://www.nelliemae.com/calculators

3. You have probably heard of credit files (or reports). In fact, if you have a credit card, a student loan, or some other form of credit, you already have a credit file. Visit the following Web site and review the material on credit files.

http://www.ftc.gov/bcp/conline/pubs/credit/bbcr.htm

Answer the following questions:
a. What is a credit report?
b. What information is in a credit file?
c. Who compiles the information in a credit file?
d. Who has access to a credit file?
e. Regarding your credit file, what rights do you have?

4. Even though you are still in college, you face a number of important financial issues—everything from paying college expenses to dealing with credit cards. Visit the following Web site and click the "Financial Fitness Tools" link. What are the 10 steps? Which of these will be the easiest for you to complete? Which will be the most difficult?

http://www.mapping-your-future.org

5. Using the worksheet on page B-22, analyze your current credit situation. What are your existing debts? How much are you paying each month? Did you borrow for the right reasons? List some steps you think you should start taking to improve your management of credit.

Worksheet
Summary of Outstanding Loans

Type of Loan	Amount Borrowed	Current Balance	Months Left	Annual Percentage Rate	Monthly Payment
Personal Loans 1. _____ 2. _____					
Car Loans 1. _____ 2. _____					
Student Loans 1. _____ 2. _____					
Credit Cards 1. _____ 2. _____ 3. _____ 4. _____					
Other Loans 1. _____ 2. _____					
				Total Monthly Payment	

Resources

The Web

Personal Finance Topics   Still have questions? Visit http://www.businessweek.com/investor/nonips_content/financenter.htm, where you'll find a selection of guides on personal finance topics like investing, banking, insurance, credit cards, and autos. Select a topic to explore and write a short paragraph describing what you found there.

Helpful Web Sites   Two excellent online sources of information and assistance on personal finance topics are:

> http://moneycentral.msn.com
> http://www.quicken.com

Visit each site and write a brief summary of some of the tools and other materials you found there. Do you prefer one site to the other? Why or why not?

Online Searches   Using a search engine, such as Yahoo (http://www.yahoo.com) or Google (http://www.google.com), type in the key words "personal finance" and see how many hits are returned (there will be dozens). Visit two sites that interest you, and write a brief summary of your reaction to the sites.

Stock Market Game

Have you ever invested in stocks? Perhaps you have or know someone who has. Historically, stocks have been marvelous investments, but investing in stocks is not without risk. During your introduction to business class, you learn a great deal about how businesses are organized and how they operate. You also learn about the financial system, including the stock market.

The *Contemporary Business* Web site offers a Stock Market Game in which you will learn about the risks and rewards of common stock and the different approaches to making the best stock selections. The purpose of the Stock Market Game is to give you some firsthand experience with investing in stocks without risking any real money. Everyone starts the game with the same amount of play money. But where everyone finishes—well, that's a story that hasn't been written yet. Good luck!

http://boone.swlearning.com

What You Will Learn

- Some of the risks and rewards of investing in common stocks
- How to obtain information and analysis about specific companies
- How to read and interpret corporate financial and nonfinancial information
- Different approaches to selecting stocks, including when to buy and sell stocks
- How stocks are bought and sold
- How to stay informed about any news that may affect the value of your stocks

How to Play

Objective

To increase the value of your stock portfolio more than any other student in your class by the end of the game. Your instructor will provide you with the dates the Stock Market Game officially starts and ends.

Rules

1. On the first day of the game, you will invest a total of $30,000 (play money, of course!) in any stocks listed on markets in the U.S. No transaction fees will be charged for your initial purchases, but fees will apply to any sales or purchases made during the game (see rule 3).
2. You must initially invest equal amounts of $10,000 in three different stocks.
3. You may sell any one of your stocks at any time and buy another stock in its place. However, you must pay a transaction fee of $10 per buy or sell order. Here's an example:

   After a month, you decide to sell one of your stocks that has declined in value from the original $10,000 to $8,000. After deducting $10 for the transaction fee to sell, $7,990 remains. You then purchase shares of another company valued at $7,980 ($7,990 minus $10 purchase transaction fee).
4. Maintain a file containing the following information on your stock portfolio:

   - Brief company profile for each stock you own during the game. Include a summary of the company's products, where it operates, strengths and weaknesses—especially in comparison with competitors—and copies of the most recent annual income statement and balance sheet (obtained from the company's annual report or other source).
   - Reasons for buying a stock, both initially and during the game.
   - Reasons for selling a stock during the game.
   - Number of shares of each stock you own at the close of the market each week.
   - Current stock price of each stock you own at the close of the market each week.
   - Detailed record of any buy or sell transactions: date of transaction, name of company for shares sold, number of shares sold, price per share sold, value of shares sold after deducting transaction fee, name of company for shares purchased, number of shares purchased, price per share purchased, and value of shares purchased after deducting transaction fee.
   - Summary statement at the end of the game stating the total value of your stock portfolio, including the number of shares in each stock and the price per share on the last day of the game.

Recommendation: Yahoo! offers a free service for tracking your stocks. You can set up an initial stock portfolio, add or remove stocks you buy or sell, and obtain printouts that display performance charts, total increases and decreases in stock value, and other useful information. It's easier than doing all the calculations yourself. Go to http://finance.yahoo.com to set up your portfolio.

How to Select Stocks

If you ask 100 experts what stocks to buy, you might get 100 different answers. In one experiment, someone picked stocks completely at random. These stocks often outperformed the choices of many experts. So there is no single method to recommend for making your selections. The best advice is to read expert opinions with caution and learn as much as you can about a company that interests you, including its recent financial performance, products, competitors, customers, and the industry in which it operates.

You may be wondering where to get started. There are actually many places to go for ideas. One approach is to keep up with the current business and financial news. Your college or university library has many current business publications. Perhaps you will read a story about a growing industry or consumer trend and find companies that are well positioned to take advantage of these opportunities.

The Internet contains a wealth of information you can use to help make your selections. Unfortunately, the quality of the information is very uneven, so it is recommended that you stick to well-known sites. Stay away from chat rooms. Some good places to start include the following:

Yahoo! (http://finance.yahoo.com)
MSN Investor (http://investor.msn.com)
CNNfn (http://www.cnnfn.com)
CNBC (http://www.cnbc.com)
Morningstar (http://www.morningstar.com)
Quicken (http://www.quicken.com)
Smart Money (http://www.smartmoney.com)
Money Magazine (http://www.money.com)

Annual reports and SEC filings can be obtained from the FreeEdgar Web Site (http://www.freeedgar.com). Most companies also publish current financial data on their own Web sites.

Don't forget! You can obtain more information about the Stock Market Game by visiting the *Contemporary Business* Web site (http://boone.swlearning.com).

Appendix C
Developing a Business Plan

From Car Parts to Capital

Growing up, Gus Conrades had no idea that his passion for cars and motorcycles would lead to a position as CEO of his own company. "Cars have always been so much more to me than something that takes you from one place to another," he said. At age 17, after mowing lawns and working summers at gas stations, he scraped together enough money to buy a 1957 Chevrolet Bel Air and then spent all of his free time rebuilding it.

With firsthand knowledge of auto parts under his belt, and now in his 30s, Conrades teamed up with his cousin, Bryan Murphy, and began discussing ideas for a new business: a Web site that sells auto parts to enthusiasts and professionals. Conrades already had extensive Internet experience to go with his exhaustive knowledge of cars, and Murphy mastered the financial side of the auto parts business by heading a traditional auto parts store in Detroit. Out of this collaboration came Wrenchead .com, an e-tail business based in White Plains, New York, that sells millions of auto parts and car-care products to consumers worldwide.

According to *Fortune* magazine, the secret to Wrenchead.com's success was Conrades and Murphy's business plan, which quickly made it clear why their idea would work. Although Conrades and Murphy were "newbies to the venture capital circuit when they dreamed up Wrenchead.com . . . they knew how to write a darn good business plan." Their business plan included a one-sentence statement that neatly summed up their idea for a multimillion-dollar business: "Wrenchead.com sells auto parts to consumers and professionals over the Internet." In other parts of the plan, the cousins-turned-partners made their huge market potential clear to investors. Car enthusiasts and specialists spend over $32 billion a year on auto parts. "If you have a clear, concise strategy, investors and consumers won't be confused," says Conrades.

Due in part to their outstanding, compelling business plan, Conrades and Murphy were able to channel their energies and raise an amazing $120 million in two appeals for venture capital from investors such as CBS, Yahoo!, Polaris Venture Partners, Goldman Sachs, and others. "We took our passion and turned it into a business," says Conrades. That passion, along with Conrades and Murphy's clearly articulated strategies and industry knowledge, made their company an enticing investment for venture capitalists. As described by Terry McGuire, a principal in Polaris Venture Partners, the venture capital firm who fronted the first institutional money ($15 million) for Wrenchead.com, the uniqueness of Conrades and Murphy's company "lies in creating a clear channel into both the consumer and the business-to-business market. Combine that with smart management, and it amounted to a great investment."

Wrenchead's clear mission is articulated on its Web site as well. "Wrenchead.com has put the power back in the hands of the consumer by giving him or her access to the same systems used by professional mechanics, a community of car enthusiasts and experts, and personalized shopping." Their business effectively filled a niche in the auto parts market. In just one year, the staff of Wrenchead.com expanded from two to about 100, and traffic on their site went up to 20,000 visitors each day.

If Conrades and Murphy didn't have such a clear, compelling business plan, venture capitalists would have had no reason to make note of them, especially considering the high volume of entrepreneurial activity in the U.S. According to the U.S. Small Business Administration, approximately 23 million small businesses were operating in the U.S. in a recent year. On the funding side of the coin, Suzanne King, a partner of California-based New Enterprise Associates, reports that of the 10,000 business plans the firm receives each year, between 20 and 30 get funded. "The ones that rise to the top," King says, "have one thing in common: opening sections that lay out the key points—the idea, the customer, how to sell it, how it'll make money, the management team, and the payback—in a scintillating, you-don't-want-to-miss-this-opportunity way."

If all of this sounds a little overwhelming, remember that success is not a fluke. It usually comes to those who work hard and have a keen sense of direction. It is up to the business owner to meticulously research and assess the business idea, which is usually achieved by developing a formal business plan.[1]

Overview

They Said It

Luck sometimes visits a fool, but never sits down with him.

—*German proverb*

Just as the owners of Wrenchead.com did, many entrepreneurs and small-business owners have written business plans to help them organize their businesses, get them up and running, and raise money for expansion. In this appendix, we cover the basics of business planning: what business plans are, why they're important, and who needs them. We also explain the steps involved in writing a good plan and the major elements it should contain. Finally, we offer additional resources to get you started with your own business plan—to help you bring your unique ideas to reality with a business of your own.

What Is a Business Plan?

business plan document that articulates a company's objectives, the methods by which these objectives will be achieved, the financing process, and the amount of revenue the company can expect to bring in.

With the millions and millions of different businesses operating in the U.S. and throughout the world today, you may wonder how they got their start. Often, it is with a formal business plan. A **business plan** is a written document that articulates what a company's objectives are, how these objectives will be achieved, how the business will be financed, and how much money the company expects to bring in. In short, it describes where a company is, where it wants to go, and how it intends to get there. Elizabeth Wasserman, writing in the magazine *MBA Jungle*, states that a business plan has to be "a compelling story with drama (a demonstrated need), hope (how your product can fill that need), heroes (the management team), and a happy ending (return on investment)."[2] A formal business plan will demonstrate whether a venture lacks these elements; it holds the proposal up to the light of day, revealing its strong points and flaws.

Why a Business Plan Is So Important

A well-written business plan can be used for many purposes, but it serves two key functions:

1. organizes the business and validates its central idea
2. summarizes the business and its strategy to obtain funding from investors

First, a business plan gives a business formal direction, whether it is just starting, going through a phase of growth, or struggling. The business plan forces the principals—the owners—through rigorous planning, to think through the realities of running and financing a business. In their planning, they will consider many details. How will inventory be stored, shipped, and stocked? Where should the business be located? How will I use the Internet? And most important how will I make enough money to make it all worthwhile?

A business plan also gives the owner a well-reasoned blueprint to refer to when daily challenges arise, and it acts as a benchmark by which successes and disappointments can be measured. Additionally, a solid business plan will sell the potential owner on the validity of the idea. In some cases, the by-product of developing the plan is demonstrating to a starry-eyed person that he is trying to start a bad business. Wasserman writes, "Investors today view the process of writing a business plan as necessary to help the entrepreneur—not just the investor—determine whether the venture has hope."[3] In other words, the process of writing a plan benefits a would-be businessperson as much as the final plan benefits potential investors.

Finally, a business plan articulates the business's strategy to financiers who can fund the business, and it is usually required to obtain a bank loan. Lenders and venture capitalists need to see that the business owner has thought through the critical issues and presented a promising idea before they will consider investing in it. They are, after all, interested in whether it will bring them significant returns.

> *They Said It*
>
> You can't have a better tomorrow if you are thinking about yesterday all the time.
>
> —*Charles F. Kettering (1876–1958)*
> *American electrical engineer and inventor*

Who Needs a Business Plan?

Some people mistakenly believe that they need a business plan only if it will land on the desk of a venture capitalist or the loan committee of the company's bank. Others think that writing a plan is unnecessary if their bank or lending institution doesn't require it. Such assumptions miss the point of planning, since a business plan acts as a road map to guide the way through the often tangled roads of running a business. The answer to the question of who needs a plan is: anyone who is serious about being successful. Every small-business owner should develop a business plan—even a freelancer working from home—because it empowers that person to take control.

> *They Said It*
>
> Plan your work and work your plan.
>
> —*Anonymous*

How Do I Write a Business Plan?

"Developing a business plan" should mean something different to everyone. Think of a business plan as a clear statement of a business's identity. A travel agency has a different identity from a newly launched magazine, which has yet a different identity from a restaurant hoping to expand its share of the market. Each business has unique objectives and processes, and each faces different obstacles.

At the same time, good business plans do contain some similar elements no matter who the business owner is, what he or she sells, or how far he or she is into the venture. A savvy business owner will mold the elements of a business plan into a personal and professional representation of the firm's needs and goals. The plan should also realistically assess the risks and obstacles specific to the business and present solutions for overcoming them.

Because the document is important, it takes time to collect needed information and organize it. Don't be misled into believing that you will simply sit down and begin writing. Before any writing begins, the business owner must become an expert in his or her field. Readying important information about the company and the market will make the writing easier and faster. Some critical pieces of information to have on hand are the following items:

- The company's name, legal form of organization, location, financial highlights, owners or shareholders (if any)
- Organization charts, list of key managers, consultants or directors, employee agreements
- Marketing research, customer surveys, and information about the company's key competitors
- Product information, including key goods and services; brochures; patents, licenses, and trademarks; research and development plans

Take a few minutes to read and answer these questions.
Don't worry about answering in too much detail at this point.
The questions are preliminary and
intended to help you think through your venture.

1. In general terms, how would you explain your idea to a friend?

2. What is the purpose or objective of your venture?

3. What service are you going to provide, or what goods are you going to manufacture?

4. Is there any significant difference between what you are planning and what already exists?

5. How will the quality of your product compare with competitive offerings?

6. What is the overview of the industry or service sector you are going to enter? Write it out.

7. What is the history, current status, and future of the industry?

8. Who is your customer or client base?

9. Where and by whom will your good or service be marketed?

10. How much will you charge for the product you are planning?

11. Where is the financing going to come from to initiate your venture?

12. What training and experience do you have that qualifies you for this venture?

13. Does such training or experience give you a significant edge?

14. If you lack specific experience, how do you plan to gain it?

FIGURE C.1
Self-Evaluation Questions

- Marketing plans and materials
- Financial statements and forecasts[4]

The business owner also must do a lot of soul-searching and brainstorming to answer important questions necessary to build the backbone of a healthy business. Figure C.1 lists some critical questions to ask yourself.

Once equipped with these answers, you can begin writing the document, which can be anywhere between 10 and 50 pages long. The length of the plan depends on the complexity of the company, whether the company is a start-up (established companies have a longer history to detail), and what the plan will be used for. Regardless of size, the document should be well organized and easy to use, especially if the business plan is intended for external uses, such as to secure financing. Number all pages, include a table of contents, and make sure the format is attractive and professional. Include two or three illustrative charts or graphs and highlight the sections and important points with headings and bulleted lists. Figure C.2 outlines the major sections of a business plan.

The following paragraphs discuss the most common elements of an effective business plan. When you need additional instruction as you write, refer to the Resources section at the end of this appendix.

Executive Summary

executive summary one- to two-page snapshot of what the overall business plan explains in detail.

The primary purpose of an executive summary is to entice readers sufficiently so that they want to read more about the business. An **executive summary** is a one- to two-page snapshot of what the overall business plan explains in further detail. Consider it a business plan within a business plan. Through its enthusiasm and quick momentum, the summary should capture the readers' imagination. Describe your strategy for succeeding in a positive, intriguing, and realistic way and briefly yet thoroughly answer the first questions anyone would have about your business: who, what, why, when, where, and how? Financiers always turn to the executive summary first. If it isn't well presented or lacks the proper information, they will quickly move on to the next business plan in the stack. The executive summary is just as important to people funding the business with personal resources, however, because it channels their motivations into an articulate mission statement. It is a good idea to write the summary last, since it will inevitably be revised once the business plan takes final shape.

To write a great executive summary, focus on the issues that are most important to your business's success and save the supporting matters for the body. The executive summary should describe the business's strategy and goals, the good or service it is selling, and the advantages it has over the competition. It should also give a snapshot of how much money will be required to launch the business, how it will be used, and how the lenders or investors will recoup their investment.

Introduction

The introduction follows the executive summary. After the executive summary has offered an attractive synopsis, the introduction should begin to discuss the fine details of the business. It should be crafted to include any material the upcoming marketing and financing sections do not cover. The **introduction** should describe the company, the management team, and the product in detail. If one of these topics is particularly noteworthy for your business, you may want to present that topic as its own section. Listen to what you write and respond as the plan takes shape.

Include basic information about the company—its past, present, and future. What are the company's roots, what is its current status, and what actions need to be taken to achieve its goals? If you are starting a company, include a description of the evolution of the concept. Be sure to tie all of the business's goals and plans to the industry in which it will operate, and describe the industry itself.

A business doesn't run itself, of course. People are the heart of a business, so write an appealing picture of the business's management team. Who are the key players and how does their experience resonate with the company's goals? Describe their—or your, if you are a sole proprietor—education, training, and experience, and highlight and refer to their résumés included later in the plan. Be honest, however—not all businesses are started by experts. If you lack demonstrated experience in a certain area, explain how you plan to get it.

Also describe the product, the driving force behind the venture. What are you offering and why is it special? What are the costs of the service or the price tag on the good? Analyze the features of the offering and the effect these features have on the overall cost.

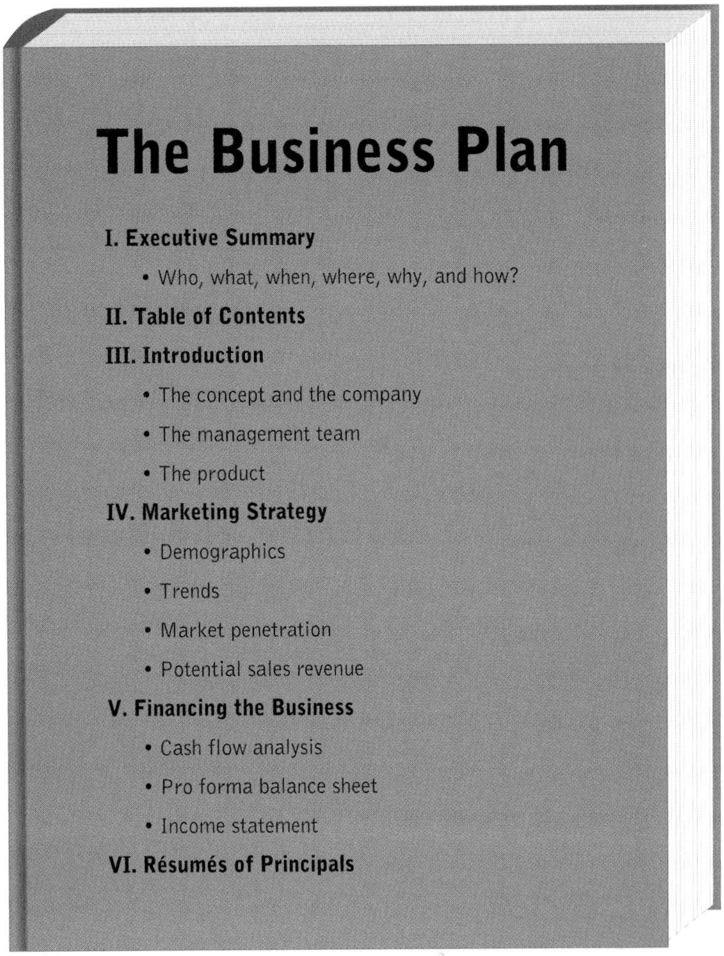

The Business Plan

I. Executive Summary
- Who, what, when, where, why, and how?

II. Table of Contents

III. Introduction
- The concept and the company
- The management team
- The product

IV. Marketing Strategy
- Demographics
- Trends
- Market penetration
- Potential sales revenue

V. Financing the Business
- Cash flow analysis
- Pro forma balance sheet
- Income statement

VI. Résumés of Principals

FIGURE C.2
Outline of a Business Plan

Marketing Strategy

Next comes the marketing strategy section. The **marketing strategy** presents information describing the market's need for the item and the ways the business will fulfill it. Marketing strategies are not based on informal projections or observations. They are the result of a careful market analysis. So formulating a marketing strategy allows the business owner to become familiar with every aspect of the particular market. If done properly, it will allow you to define your target market and position your business within that sector to get its share of sales.

The marketing strategy includes a discussion of the size of the customer base that will want to purchase your good or service and the projected rate of growth for the product or category. Highlight information on the demographics of your customers. **Demographics** are statistical characteristics of the segment of the market that might purchase a good or service, such as income, race, gender, and age. What types of people will purchase your product? How old are they and where do they live? What is their lifestyle like? For example, someone starting an interior design business will want to report how many homeowners there are within a certain radius of his or her business, what their median income is, and how much they have spent on home furnishings in the past. Of course, this section of the marketing analysis will be quite different for a company that conducts all of its business online. You will still want to know the types of people who will shop at your Web site, but your discussion won't be limited to one geographical area. It is also a good idea to describe the trends in your product category. **Trends** are consumer tendencies or patterns that business owners can exploit to gain market share in an industry.

The marketing strategy should also detail your distribution, pricing, and promotional goals. Discuss the average price of your offering and the reasons behind the price you have chosen. How do you

introduction section of a business plan that describes the company, the management team, and the product in detail.

marketing strategy section of a business plan that presents information describing the market's need for a product and the ways the business will go about satisfying it.

demographics statistical characteristics of the segment of the market that might purchase a product.

trends consumer and business tendencies or patterns that firms can exploit to gain market share in an industry.

market penetration
percentage of total
customers who have
purchased a company's
product.

potential sales revenue
total revenue of a company
if it captured 100 percent
market penetration.

financing section section
of a business plan that
specifies the cost of a
product, the company's
operating expenses, the sales
revenue and profit that can
be expected, and the amount
of the business owner's own
money that will be invested.

intend to let your potential customers know that you have a product to sell? How will you sell it—through a catalog, a retail location, online, or perhaps all three? The effectiveness of your distribution, pricing, and promotional goals determines the extent to which you will be able to garner market share.

Competitors are another important part of the marketing strategy. What companies are already selling products similar to yours? Include a list of your competitors to show that you know exactly who they are and what you are up against. Describe what you think are their major strengths and weaknesses and how successful they have been within your market.

Also include the **market penetration,** which is the percentage of total customers who have purchased a company's product. If there are 10,000 people in your market, and 5,000 have purchased your product, your market penetration is 50 percent. The **potential sales revenue,** also an important figure to include, is the total revenue of a company if it captured 100 percent market penetration. In other words, this figure represents the total dollar value of sales you would bring in if everyone who is a potential customer purchased your product.

Financing the Business

The goal of a business is to make money. Everything in the business plan lays the foundation for the financing section. Business owners should not skip this section even if they are not seeking outside money. While it is crucial to have an accurate financial analysis to get financing, it also is a necessary exercise for business owners funding the venture themselves. The **financing section** demonstrates the cost of the product, operating expenses, the sales revenue and profit that can be expected, and the amount of the business owner's own money that will be invested to get the business up and running. The financial projections should be compelling but accurate, and you should be able to defend them.

If you have made any assumptions in the body of your plan, tie them into the financial section. If you think you will need a staff of five, for example, your cash flow analysis should explain how you are going to pay them. A cash flow analysis is a mandatory component of a financial analysis, which shows how much money will flow through your business throughout the year. It helps you plan for staggered purchasing, for high-volume months, and for slow periods. Your business may be cyclical, so the cash flow projection lets you know if you need to arrange a line of credit to cover periodic shortfalls. In addition, an income statement is a critical component. The income statement is a statement of the gross income and expenses your company has accrued over a period of a year.

Remember that leaving out important details can certainly undercut your credibility, so be thorough. The plan must include assumptions you are making about the conditions under which your business will operate. It should cover details such as market health; date of start-up; sales buildup; gross profit margin; equipment, furniture, and fixtures required; and payroll and other key expenses that will affect the financial plan. In addition, a banker will want a pro forma balance sheet, which provides an estimate of the firm's worth. List the company's assets (what you own) and subtract the liabilities (what you owe), which will render the business's net worth. Refer to Chapters 16 and 17 of *Contemporary Business* for additional details on accounting, financial statements, and financial management.

Résumés of Principals

The final element of the business plan is the inclusion of the résumés of the principals behind the business: the management team. Each résumé should include detailed employment information and accomplishments. If applicable to your business, consider expanding on the traditional résumé by including business affiliations, professional memberships, hobbies, and leisure activities. Gus Conrades of Wrenchead.com might describe his strong passion for everything automotive, which would certainly complement his particular business plan.

However you choose to develop a business plan, make sure that *you* develop the plan. "I can see an entrepreneur's blood in every business plan," says Miles Spencer, a member of the venture fund Capital Express.[5] For this reason, he advises that the principals take primary responsibility for developing their business plan.

Resources

A tremendous amount of material is available to help business owners write an effective business plan. The biggest task is narrowing it down to which resources are right for you. The Internet delivers an abundance of sound business planning tools and advice, most of it free of charge. It allows you to seek diverse examples and opinions, which is important because no one source will match your business's situation exactly. Your school library and career center also have a wealth of resources. Following are some helpful resources for business planning.

Books

Three books with comprehensive coverage of business planning are:

David E. Gumpert, *How to Really Create a Successful Business Plan*, 4th ed. Lauson Publishing Co., 2003.
Joseph Covello and Brian J. Haselgren, *Your First Business Plan: A Simple Question and Answer Format Designed to Help You Write Your Own Plan*, 3rd ed. Sourcebooks Trade, 1998.
Romanus Wolter, *Kick Start Your Dream Business: Getting It Started and Keeping You Going*. Ten Speed Press, 2001.

The Web

Several Web sites offer advice, tips, and sample plans. Here are just a few that may be helpful.

Entrepreneur and *Inc.* magazines offer knowledgeable guides to writing a business plan at
`http://www.entrepreneur.com/open/archive/0,5994,300577,00.html`
`http://www.inc.com/guides/start_biz/20660.html`

Entrepreneur also offers a sample business plan at
`http://www.entrepreneur.com/Your_Business/YB_SegArticle/0,4621,287390,00.html`

Deloitte & Touche offers a useful document, "Writing an Effective Business Plan," that includes many helpful questions as a guide at
`http://www.deloitte.com/vc`

American Express offers a step-by-step business plan guide along with worksheets at
`http://home3.americanexpress.com/smallbusiness/tool/biz_plan/index.asp`

If you are hoping to obtain funding with your business plan, you may want to familiarize yourself with the perspective of venture capitalists, such as Crosspoint
`http://cpvp.com/submit/businessplan.html`

New Enterprise Associates
`http://www.nea.com/index.html`

Software

Business plan software can give initial shape to your business plan, but a word of caution should be issued about templates. Bankers and investors read so many business plans that those based on a template might sink to the bottom of their pile. Also, if you aren't looking for funding, using software can undercut a chief purpose of writing a plan—learning about your unique idea. So think twice before you deprive yourself of that experience. If you do choose to use a software package, make sure it includes a template tailored to your specific industry.

Associations and Organizations

Many government and professional organizations can provide assistance for would-be business owners. Here is a partial list:

The U.S. Small Business Administration offers planning materials, along with many other resources.

http://sba.gov/starting_business/planning/basic.html

The Ewing Marion Kauffman Foundation (http://www.emkf.org) encourages entrepreneurship across America. Their resources section, http://www.entreworld.com, is an online resource center for new and growing businesses.

http://www.entreworld.org/Channel/SYB.cfm?Topic=YouEPlan

Resources for Women and Minorities

Some resources specialize in assisting women and minorities in business planning.

The SBA's Women's Business Center

http://www.onlinewbc.gov/docs/starting/effective_bp.html

Minorities Pursuing the American Dream

http://new.blackvoices.com/business/bv-news-entrepreneurs021209,0,33493.story?coll=bv-business-headlines

Glossary

accounting (516) practice of measuring, interpreting, and communicating financial information to support internal and external business decision making.

accounting process (520) set of activities involved in converting information about individual transactions into financial statements.

accrual accounting (525) accounting method that records revenue and expenses when they occur, not necessarily when cash actually changes hands.

acquisition (187) procedure in which one firm purchases the property and assumes the obligations of another.

activity ratios (531) measures of the effectiveness of management's use of the firm's resources.

actuarial table (A-5) probability calculation of the number of specific events—such as deaths, injuries, fire, or windstorm losses—expected to occur within a given year.

advertising (456) paid nonpersonal communication delivered through various media and designed to inform, persuade, or remind members of a particular audience.

advocacy (cause) advertising (457) form of institutional advertising that promotes a specific viewpoint on a public issue as a way to influence public opinion and the legislative process.

affinity program (411) marketing effort sponsored by an organization that solicits involvement by individuals who share common interests and activities.

agency (145) legal relationship whereby one party, called a principal, appoints another party, called an agent, to enter into contracts with third parties on the principal's behalf.

alien corporation (183) firm incorporated in one nation and operating in another nation.

alternative dispute resolution (ADR) program (321) options for resolving grievances that include open-door policies, employee hot lines, peer review councils, mediation, and arbitration.

angel investors (222) wealthy individuals who invest directly in a new venture in exchange for an equity stake.

appellate courts (140) courts that hear appeals of decisions made at the general trial court level; both the federal and state systems have appellate courts.

application service provider (ASP) (494) specialist in providing both the computers and the application support for managing information systems of business clients.

arbitration (318) bringing in an impartial third party called an arbitrator to render a binding decision in the dispute.

assembly line (358) manufacturing technique that carries the product on a conveyor system past several workstations where workers perform specialized tasks.

asset (523) anything of value owned or leased by a business.

autocratic leadership (279) leaders make decisions on their own without consulting employees.

balance of payments (109) difference in money flows into or out of a country.

balance of trade (109) difference between a nation's exports and imports.

balance sheet (524) statement of a firm's financial position—what it owns and the claims against its assets—at a particular point in time.

balanced budget (94) situation in which total revenues raised by taxes and fees equal total proposed government spending for the year.

bankruptcy (148) legal nonpayment of financial obligations.

basic accounting equation (523) relationship that states that assets equal liabilities plus owners' equity.

benchmarking (372) identifying how leaders in certain fields perform and continually comparing and measuring performance against these outstanding performers.

board of directors (185) elected governing body of a corporation.

bond (555) certificate of indebtedness sold to raise long-term funds for a corporation or government agency.

bond rating (577) tool used by bond investors to assess the riskiness of a bond.

bottom line (524) overall profit or loss incurred by a firm over a period of time.

boycott (51, 318) effort to prevent people from purchasing a firm's goods or services.

brand (15, 427) name, term, sign, symbol, design, or some combination that identifies the products of one firm and differentiates them from competitors' offerings.

brand equity (429) added value that a widely respected, highly successful name gives to a product in the marketplace.

brand name (427) part of a brand consisting of words or letters that form a name that identifies and distinguishes an offering from those of competitors.

branding (15) process of creating an identity in consumers' minds for a good, service, or company; a major marketing tool of consumer-oriented firms.

breach of contract (145) violation of a valid contract.

breakeven analysis (475) pricing technique used to determine the minimum sales volume a product must generate at a certain price level to cover all costs.

broadband technology (505) digital, fiber-optic, and wireless network technology that compresses data and transmits them at blinding speeds.

brokerage firm (585) financial intermediary that buys and sells securities for individual and institutional investors.

budget (92, 532) organization's plan for how it will raise and spend money during a given period of time.

budget deficit (94) funding shortfall in which government spends more than the amount of funds raised through taxes and fees.

budget surplus (94) excess funding that occurs when government spends less than the amount of funds raised through taxes and fees.

business (5) all profit-seeking activities and enterprises that provide goods and services necessary to an economic system.

business (B2B) product (392) good or service purchased to be used, either directly or indirectly, in the production of other goods for resale.

business ethics (40)   standards of conduct and moral values involving right and wrong actions arising in the work environment.

business incubator (172)   organization that provides low-cost, shared facilities on a temporary basis to small start-up ventures.

business interruption insurance (A-7)   insurance that protects firms from financial losses resulting from the interruption of business operations.

business law (141)   aspects of law that most directly influence and regulate the management of business activity.

business plan (168, C-2)   written document that provides an orderly statement of a company's goals, the methods by which it intends to achieve those goals, and the standards by which it will measure achievements.

business-to-business (B2B) e-commerce (239) electronic business transactions between organizations using the Internet.

business-to-consumer (B2C) e-commerce (241)   electronic business transactions between organizations and final customers using the Internet.

buyer behavior (406)   series of decision processes by individual consumers who buy products for their own use and organizational buyers who purchase business products to be used directly or indirectly in the sale of other items.

call provision (578)   ability of an issuer to redeem a bond prior to its maturity at a prespecified price.

capital (7)   production inputs consisting of technology, tools, information, and physical facilities.

capitalism (10)   economic system that rewards businesses for their ability to perceive and serve the needs and demands of consumers; also called the *private enterprise system.*

cash budget (532)   accounting report that tracks the firm's cash inflows and outflows; usually prepared monthly.

cash value policies (A-10)   life insurance policies that combine a death benefit with some sort of a savings feature.

category manager (429)   person who oversees an entire product line and assumes profit responsibility for the product group.

cause marketing (392)   marketing that promotes a cause or social issue, such as the prevention of child abuse, antilittering efforts, and anti-smoking campaigns.

centralization (287)   decision making based at the top of the management hierarchy.

centralized communication network (345) exchange of messages through a single person to solve problems or make decisions.

certified public accountant (519)   accountant who met specified educational and experiential

requirements and passed a comprehensive examination on accounting theory and practice.

chain of command (287)   set of relationships that indicates who directs which activities and who reports to whom.

change agent (198)   manager who tries to revitalize an established firm to keep it competitive.

chief financial officer (CFO) (546)   top finance executive of a corporation; usually reports directly to the firm's CEO.

chief information officer (CIO) (490)   executive responsible for directing the firm's MIS and related computer operations.

Children's Online Privacy Protection Act (COPPA) (245)   federal law requiring Web sites targeting children younger than 13 to obtain "verifiable parental consent" before collecting any data that could be used to identify or contact individual users, including names and e-mail addresses.

classic entrepreneur (198)   person who identifies a business opportunity and allocates available resources to tap that market.

click-through rate (253)   percentage of people presented with a Web banner ad who click it.

client (232)   another computer or device that relies on the resources of one or more servers for help with its own processing.

cobranding (411)   cooperative arrangement in which two or more businesses team up to closely link their names on a single product.

code of conduct (48)   formal statement that defines how the organization expects and requires employees to resolve ethical issues.

collective bargaining (317)   process of negotiation between management and union representatives for the purpose of arriving at mutually acceptable wages and working conditions for employees.

comarketing (411)   cooperative arrangement in which two businesses jointly market each other's products.

committee organization (288)   organizational structure that places authority and responsibility jointly in the hands of a group of individuals rather than a single manager.

common law (141)   body of law arising out of judicial decisions, some of which can be traced back to early England.

common stock (185, 578)   shares of ownership in a corporation.

communication (339)   meaningful exchange of information through messages.

communism (82)   planned economic system in which private property is eliminated, goods are owned in common, and factors of production and production decisions are controlled by the state.

competition (10)   battle among businesses for consumer acceptance.

competitive differentiation (11, 276)   unique combination of organizational abilities and

approaches that sets a company apart from competitors in the minds of customers.

competitive pricing (477)   pricing strategy that tries to reduce the emphasis on price competition by matching other firms' prices and concentrating their own marketing efforts on the product, distribution, and promotional elements of the marketing mix.

compressed workweek (308)   scheduling option that allows employees to work the regular number of hours per week in fewer than the typical five days.

computer virus (507)   program that secretly attaches itself to other computer programs or files and changes them or destroys data.

computer-aided design (CAD) (361)   system for interactions between a designer and a computer to design a product, facility, or part that meets predetermined specifications.

computer-aided manufacturing (CAM) (361) electronic tools to analyze CAD output and determine necessary steps to implement the design, followed by electronic transmission of instructions to guide the activities of production equipment.

computer-integrated manufacturing (CIM) (361)   production system that integrates computer tools and human workers to design products, handle materials, and control production.

conceptual skills (269)   ability to see the organization as a unified whole and to understand how each part interacts with others.

conflict (336)   antagonistic interaction in which one party attempts to thwart the intentions or goals of another.

conflict of interest (45)   situation in which a business decision may be influenced by the potential for personal gain.

conglomerate merger (187)   combination of two or more unrelated firms, usually with the goal of diversification, spurring sales growth, or spending a cash surplus that might otherwise make the firm a tempting target for a takeover attempt.

consultative selling (468)   meeting customers' needs by listening to them, understanding and caring about their problems, paying attention to details, suggesting solutions, and following through after the sale.

consumer (B2C) product (392)   good or service, such as DVDs, shampoo, and dental care, that is purchased by end users.

consumer behavior (406)   actions of ultimate consumers directly involved in obtaining, consuming, and disposing of products and the decision processes that precede and follow these actions.

consumer orientation (15)   business philosophy incorporating the marketing concept of first determining unmet consumer needs and then designing a system for satisfying them.

Consumer Price Index (CPI) (89)   monthly measure of changes in retail price levels by comparisons of changes in the prices of a *market basket* of goods and services most commonly purchased by urban consumers.

consumerism (57)   public demand that a business consider the wants and needs of its customers in making decisions.

contingency planning (271)   plans that allow a firm to resume operations as quickly and as smoothly as possible after a crisis while openly communicating with the public about what happened.

contingent worker (311)   employee who works part time, temporarily, or for the period of time specified in a contract.

contract (145)   legally enforceable agreement between two or more parties regarding a specified act or thing.

controller (546)   chief accounting manager; the person who keeps the company's books, prepares financial statements, and conducts internal audits.

controlling (269)   the function of evaluating an organization's performance to determine whether it is accomplishing its objectives.

convenience product (421)   item the consumer seeks to purchase frequently, immediately, and with little effort.

conversion rate (254)   percentage of visitors to a Web site who make a purchase.

cooperative (188)   organization whose owners join forces to collectively operate all or part of the functions in their business.

cooperative advertising (470)   allowances provided by marketers in which they share the cost of local advertising of their firm's product or product line with channel partners.

copyright (147)   protection of written material such as textbooks, designs, cartoon illustrations, photos, and computer software.

corporate charter (184)   legal document that formally establishes a corporation.

corporate culture (282)   organization's system of values, principles, and beliefs.

corporate philanthropy (56)   act of an organization giving something back to the communities in which it earns profits.

corporation (182)   business that stands as a legal entity with assets and liabilities separate from those of its owner(s).

cost-based pricing (475)   practice of adding a percentage of specific amounts (markup) to the base cost of a product to cover overhead costs and generate profits.

countertrade (127)   bartering agreement whereby trade between two or more nations involves payment made in the form of local products instead of currency.

CPFaR (collaborative planning, forecasting, and replenishment) (369)   inventory planning and forecasting technique involving both purchasers and vendors.

creative selling (465)   personal selling involving situations in which a considerable degree of analytical decision making on the buyer's part results in the need for skillful proposals of solutions for the customer's needs.

creativity (28)   capacity to develop novel solutions to perceived organizational problems.

credit (B-9)   loan for a specified period of time with a specified rate of interest that allows a borrower to receive money, goods, or services.

critical path (372)   sequence of operations that requires the longest time for completion.

critical thinking (28)   ability to analyze and assess information to pinpoint problems or opportunities.

customer satisfaction (19, 387)   ability of a good or service to meet or exceed a buyer's needs and expectations.

damages (145)   financial payments to compensate for a loss and related suffering.

data mining (399)   computer search of massive amounts of customer data to detect patterns and relationships.

data warehouse (399)   customer database that allows managers to combine data from several different organizational functions.

database (491)   centralized integrated collection of data resources.

debenture (576)   bond backed by the reputation of the issuer rather than by a specific pledge of a company's assets.

debt capital (553)   funds obtained through borrowing.

debt financing (220)   borrowed funds that entrepreneurs must repay.

decentralization (287)   decision making based at lower levels of the organization.

decentralized communication network (345)   system whereby people communicate freely with other team members and arrive at decisions together.

decision making (277)   process of recognizing a problem or opportunity, evaluating alternative solutions, selecting and implementing an alternative, and assessing the results.

decision support system (DSS) (493)   information system that quickly provides relevant data to help businesspeople make decisions and choose courses of action.

defined benefit plan (B-17)   retirement plan which guarantees a worker a certain retirement benefit each year. The size depends on a number of factors, including the worker's income and the length of time he or she worked for the employer; example: pension plans.

defined contribution plan (B-17)   retirement plan in which individuals and typically their employers contribute to an employee's retirement account. Individuals often are given a list of mutual funds where the money can be invested; for example, a 401(k) plan.

deflation (89)   falling prices caused by a combination of reduced consumer demand and decreases in the costs of raw materials, human resources, and other factors of production.

delegation (286)   act of assigning work activities to subordinates.

demand (73)   willingness and ability of buyers to purchase goods and services.

demand curve (74)   graph of the amount of a product that buyers will purchase at different prices; generally slopes downward to reflect larger quantities likely to be purchased as prices decline.

demand deposits (551)   deposits held in banks, NOW accounts, and credit union share draft accounts.

democratic leadership (279)   management approach whereby leaders delegate assignments, ask employees for suggestions, and encourage their participation.

demographic segmentation (402)   dividing markets on the basis of various demographic or socioeconomic characteristics such as age, income, occupation, household size, stage in family life cycle, education, ethnic group, or gender.

demographics (C-5)   statistical characteristics of the segment of the market who might purchase a product.

departmentalization (285)   process of dividing work activities into units within the organization.

depository institutions (557)   financial institutions that accept deposits that can be converted into cash on demand.

deregulation (82)   regulatory trend toward elimination of legal restraints on competition in industries previously served by a single firm in an attempt to improve customer service and lower prices through increased competition.

desktop computer   *See* personal computer.

desktop publishing (499)   computer technology that allows users to design and produce attractively formatted printed material.

devaluation (111)   fall in a currency's value relative to other currencies or to a fixed standard.

Digital Subscriber Line (DSL) (231)   broadband technology; a high-speed cable modem or a satellite link to the Internet.

direct distribution channel (431)   marketing channel that moves goods directly from producer to ultimate user.

directing (269)   guiding and motivating employees to accomplish organizational objectives.

disability income insurance (A-9)   insurance that replaces lost income when a wage earner cannot work due to accident or illness.

disaster recovery planning (508)   deciding how to prevent system failures and continue operations should computer systems fail.

discount rate (563)   interest rate charged by the Federal Reserve on short-term loans to member banks.

dispatching (372)   phase of production control in which the manager instructs each department on what work to do and the time allowed for its completion.

distribution channel (431)   path through which products—and legal ownership of them—flow from producer to consumers or business users.

distribution strategy (431)   planning that ensures customers find their products in the proper quantities at the right times and places.

diversity (25)   blending individuals of different genders, ethnic backgrounds, cultures, religions, ages, and physical and mental abilities to enrich a firm's chances of success.

domain name (231)   string of letters and/or words that identify the owner of a Web site address.

domestic corporation (183)   firm operating in the state where it is incorporated.

downsizing (309)   process of reducing the number of employees within a firm by eliminating jobs.

dumping (120)   practice of selling products abroad at prices below production costs or at lower prices than the same products are sold in the home market in an effort to capture market share from domestic competitors.

economics (72)   social science that analyzes the choices made by people and governments in allocating scarce resources.

electronic cash (243)   buyers register with a bank to pay for purchases out of their accounts using digital certificates that verify their identities.

electronic commerce (e-commerce) (236)   online marketing of goods and services, including product information, ordering, invoicing, payment processes, and customer service.

electronic data interchange (EDI) (239)   computer-to-computer exchanges of invoices, purchase orders, price quotations, and other business documents between buyers and sellers.

electronic exchange (240)   online marketplace that caters to a specific industry's needs.

electronic funds transfer systems (558)   computerized systems for conducting financial transactions over electronic links.

electronic shopping cart (243)   file that holds items that the online shopper has chosen to buy.

electronic signature (244)   legal contracts such as home mortgages and insurance policies executed online.

electronic storefront (243)   Web sites where firms offer items for sale to consumers.

electronic wallet (243)   computer data file set up by an online shopper at an e-commerce site's checkout counter that contains not only elec-

tronic cash but credit card information, owner identification, and address.

e-mail (233)   electronic messages sent via the Internet.

embargo (120)   imposition of a total ban on importing specific products or a total halt to trading with a particular country.

employee benefits (305)   rewards such as retirement plans, health insurance, vacation, and tuition reimbursement provided for employees either entirely or in part at the company's expense.

employee ownership (186)   business in which workers purchase shares of stock in the firm that employs them.

employee stock ownership plan (ESOP) (330)   plan that benefits employees by giving them ownership stakes in the companies for which they work.

employers' association (320)   cooperative effort by employers to present a unified front in dealing with labor unions.

employment at will (302)   practice that allows the employment relationship to begin or end at any time at the decision of either the employee or the employer for any legal reason.

empowerment (279, 328)   giving employees authority and responsibility to make decisions about their work without traditional managerial approval and control.

encryption (243, 506)   the process of encoding data for security purposes; software that encodes, or scrambles, messages.

end-use segmentation (406)   marketing strategy that focuses on the precise way a B2B purchaser will use a product.

enterprise resource planning (ERP) (494)   information system that collects, processes, and provides information about an organization's various functions.

entrepreneur (12, 196)   person who seeks a profitable opportunity and takes the necessary risks to set up and operate a business.

entrepreneurship (9)   willingness to take risks to create and operate a business.

environmental impact study (362)   study that analyzes how a proposed plant would affect the quality of life in the surrounding area.

Equal Employment Opportunity Commission (EEOC) (62)   government agency created to increase job opportunities for women and minorities and to help end discrimination based on race, color, religion, disability, gender, or national origin in any personnel action.

equilibrium price (78)   prevailing market price; the point at which the quantity demanded of a product equals the quantity supplied.

equity capital (553)   funds provided by the firm's owners when they reinvest earnings, make additional contributions, or issue stock to investors.

equity financing (221)   funds invested in new ventures in exchange for part ownership.

European Union (EU) (123)   25-nation European economic alliance.

event marketing (392)   marketing or sponsoring short-term events such as athletic competitions and cultural and charitable performances.

everyday low pricing (EDLP) (477)   pricing strategy devoted to maintaining continuous low prices rather than relying on short-term price-cutting tactics such as cents-off coupons, rebates, and special sales.

exchange control (120)   administrative trade restriction that sets terms for currency transactions involving international product purchases and sales.

exchange process (385)   activity in which two or more parties give something of value to each other to satisfy perceived needs.

exchange rate (110)   value of one nation's currency relative to the currencies of other countries.

exclusive distribution (440)   distribution strategy involving limited market coverage by a single retailer or wholesaler in a specific geographical territory.

executive information system (EIS) (493)   system that allows top managers to access a firm's primary databases.

executive summary (C-4)   one- to two-page snapshot of what the overall business plan explains in detail.

expert system (493)   computer program that imitates human thinking through complicated sets of "if . . . then" rules.

exports (105)   domestically produced goods and services sold in other countries.

external communication (346)   meaningful exchange of information through messages transmitted between an organization and its major audiences.

extranet (240)   secure networks accessible from outside a firm, but only by trusted third parties such as familiar customers or suppliers; secure network accessible through a Web site by external customers or organizations for electronic commerce.

factors of production (7)   four basic inputs for effective operation: natural resources, capital, human resources, and entrepreneurship.

family brand (428)   brand name used to identify several different, but related, products.

family leave (61)   granting up to 12 weeks of unpaid leave annually for employees who have or adopt a child, who are becoming foster parents, or who are caring for a seriously ill relative or spouse, or who become seriously ill.

federal funds rate (563)   rate at which one bank lends reserves to another bank.

Federal Reserve System (Fed) (561)   central bank of the United States.

fee-for-service (A-8)   traditional form of health insurance; the insured chooses his or her doctor, pays for treatment, and is reimbursed by the insurance company; also called an indemnity plan.

finance (546)   business function of planning, obtaining, and managing a company's funds to accomplish its objectives in the most effective possible way.

financial manager (546)   employee responsible for developing and implementing the firm's financial plan and for determining the most appropriate sources and uses of funds.

financial plan (547, B-18)   document specifying the funds a firm will need for a period of time, the timing of inflows and outflows, and the most appropriate sources and uses of funds.

financial system (557)   process by which funds are transferred from savers to users.

financing section (C-6)   section of a business plan that specifies the cost of a product, the company's operating expenses, the sales revenue and profit that can be expected, and the amount of the business owner's own money that will be invested.

firewall (245, 503)   electronic barrier between a company's internal network and the Internet that limits access into and out of the network.

fiscal policy (91)   government spending and taxation decisions designed to control inflation, reduce unemployment, improve the general welfare of citizens, and encourage economic growth.

flexible benefit plan (306)   benefit system that offers employees a range of options from which they may choose the types of benefits they receive.

flexible manufacturing system (FMS) (361)   facility that workers can quickly modify to manufacture different products.

flexible work plan (307)   employment that allows personnel to adjust their working hours and places of work to accommodate their personal lives.

flextime (308)   scheduling system that allows employees to set their own work hours within constraints specified by the firm.

follow-up (372)   phase of production control in which employees and their supervisors spot problems in the production process and determine needed adjustments.

foreign licensing agreement (127)   international agreement in which one firm allows another to produce or sell its product, or use its trademark, patent, or manufacturing processes, in a specific geographical area in return for royalties or other compensation.

formal communication channel (343)   messages that flow within the chain of command defined by an organization.

401(k) plan (306)   retirement savings plan for which employees can make pretax contributions; sometimes, employers make additional contributions to the plan.

franchise (127)   contractual agreement in which a franchisee gains the right to produce and/or sell the franchisor's products under that company's brand name if it agrees to the franchisor's operating requirements.

franchisee (177)   small-business owner who contracts to sell the good or service of a supplier (the franchisor) in exchange for a payment (usually a flat fee plus a percentage of sales).

franchising (176)   contractual agreement that specifies the methods by which a dealer can produce and market a supplier's good or service.

franchisor (177)   business owner who permits the franchisee to sell the products and use its name, as well as providing a variety of marketing, management, and other services in return for the payment of fees and/or royalties based on sales by the franchisee.

free cash flow (527)   cash flow from operations minus capital expenditures.

free-rein leadership (279)   leaders believe in minimal supervision and leave most decisions to their subordinates.

frequency marketing (411)   marketing initiative that rewards frequent purchases with cash, rebates, merchandise, or other premiums.

full and fair disclosure (591)   requirement that investors should be told all relevant information by stock or bond issuers so they can make informed decisions.

gazelles (208)   fast-growing start-up companies that have become the primary job creators in the U.S.

General Agreement on Tariffs and Trade (GATT) (121)   international trade accord that substantially reduced worldwide tariffs and other trade barriers.

genetic engineering (55)   type of biotechnology that involves altering crops or other living things by inserting genes that provide them with a desirable characteristic, such as enhanced nutritional value or resistance to pesticides.

geographical segmentation (401)   dividing an overall market into homogeneous groups on the basis of population locations.

global business strategy (131)   offering a standardized, worldwide product and selling it in essentially the same manner throughout a firm's domestic and foreign markets.

government accountant (520)   accountant who performs professional services similar to those of management accountants and determines how efficiently government agencies accomplish their objectives.

government bond (576)   debt obligations issued by the U.S. Treasury; they are backed by the full faith and credit of the U.S. government.

grapevine (343)   internal information channel that transmits information from unofficial sources.

green marketing (54)   marketing strategy that promotes environmentally safe products and production methods.

grievance (317)   formal complaint filed by an employee or a union that management is violating some provision of a union contract.

gross domestic product (GDP) (23, 86)   sum of all goods and services produced within a country's boundaries during a specific time period, such as a year.

groupware (502)   software that combines information sharing through a common database with communication via e-mail so that employees can collaborate on projects.

guerrilla marketing (455)   innovative, low-cost marketing schemes designed to get consumers' attention in unusual ways.

handheld devices (497)   small computerized devices that operate on rechargeable batteries and run common applications like word processing and database software, as well as store documents and graphics created on a desktop computer.

hardware (495)   all the tangible elements of a computer system—the input devices, the machines that store and process data and perform required calculations, and the output devices that present the results to information users.

health insurance (A-8)   insurance designed to provide coverage for losses due to illness or accidents.

health maintenance organization (HMO) (A-8)   organization that, in return for a fixed monthly fee, provides all the insured's health care.

high-context culture (347)   communication within a society that depends not only on the message itself but also on nonverbal cues, past and present experiences, and personal relationships between the parties.

home-based business (159)   company operated from the residence of the business owner.

horizontal merger (187)   combination of two or more firms in the same industry that wish to diversify, increase their customer bases, reduce costs, or offer expanded product lines.

human resource management (296)   function of attracting, developing, and retaining enough qualified employees to perform the activities necessary to accomplish organizational objectives.

human resources (8)   production inputs consisting of anyone who works, including both the physical labor and the intellectual inputs contributed by workers.

human skills (268)   interpersonal skills that enable a manager to work effectively with and through people; the ability to communicate with, motivate, and lead employees to accomplish assigned activities.

imports (105) foreign goods and services purchased by domestic customers.

income statement (524) financial record of a company's revenues, expenses, and profits over a period of time.

individual brand (428) different brand names given to each product within a line.

inflation (87) rising prices caused by a combination of excess consumer demand and increases in the costs of raw materials, human resources, and other factors of production.

infomercial (462) form of broadcast direct marketing; 30-minute programs resemble regular TV programs, but they are devoted to selling goods or services.

informal communication channel (343) carries messages outside formally authorized channels within an organization's hierarchy.

infrastructure (115) basic systems of communication (television, radio, print media, telecommunications), transportation (roads and highways, railroads, and airports), and energy facilities (power plants, gas and electrical utilities).

initial public offering (IPO) (574) first sale of a firm's stock to the investing public.

insider trading (592) use of material nonpublic information to make investment profits.

installment loan (B-9) credit arrangement in which the borrower takes out a loan for a specified amount, agreeing to repay the loan in regular installments over a specified period of time. The installments include the finance charge.

instant messaging (233) a recent adaptation of e-mail whereby a message is immediately displayed on the recipient's computer screen.

institutional advertising (457) promotion of concepts, ideas, philosophies, or goodwill for industries, companies, organizations, or government entities.

insurable interest (A-4) demonstration that a direct financial loss will result if some event occurs.

insurable risk (A-4) requirement that a pure risk must meet for the insurer to agree to provide protection.

insurance (A-3) contract by which the insurer, for a fee (the premium), agrees to reimburse another firm or individual a sum of money should a loss occur.

integrated marketing communications (IMC) (450) coordination of all promotional activities—media advertising, direct mail, personal selling, sales promotion, and public relations—to produce a unified customer-focused message.

integrity (45) adhering to deeply felt ethical principles in business situations.

intensive distribution (440) distribution strategy that involves placing a firm's products in nearly every available outlet.

internal communication (344) system that sends messages through channels within an organization.

international law (141) regulations that govern international commerce.

International Monetary Fund (IMF) (122) organization created following the establishment of the World Bank to promote trade, eliminate barriers, and aid member nations that are unable to meet their budgetary expenses by providing short-term loans.

International Organization for Standardization (ISO) (373) international organization whose mission is to promote the development of standardized products to facilitate trade and cooperation across national borders.

Internet (16, 230) worldwide network of interconnected computers that, within limits, lets anyone with a PC or other computing device send and receive images and data anywhere.

Internet service provider (ISP) (231) organization that provides access to the Internet, via a telephone or cable television network.

intranet (241, 503) a network that links employees and other authorized users through Internet tools like e-mail, hypertext links, and searches using Web browsers.

intrapreneur (198) entrepreneurially oriented person who develops innovations within the context of a large organization.

intrapreneurship (222) process of promoting innovation within the structure of an existing organization.

introduction (C-5) section of a business plan that describes the company, the management team, and the product in detail.

inventory control (368) management effort to balance the priority of limiting costs of holding stocks with that of meeting customer demand.

investment banker (575) financial intermediary that purchases an issue or securities from the firm or government and then resells the issue to investors.

job enlargement (313) job design that expands an employee's responsibilities by increasing the number and variety of tasks assigned to the worker.

job enrichment (313) change in job duties to increase employees' authority in planning their work, deciding how it should be done, and learning new skills.

job sharing program (308) management decision that allows two or more employees to divide the tasks of one job.

joint venture (129, 188) in international business, an arrangement that allows companies to share risks, costs, profits, and management responsibilities with one or more host country nationals; a partnership between companies formed for a specific undertaking.

judiciary (140) branch of the government charged with deciding disputes among parties through the application of laws.

just-in-time (JIT) system (369) management philosophy aimed at improving profits and return on investment by minimizing costs and eliminating waste through cutting inventory on hand.

key executive insurance (A-10) life insurance designed to reimburse the organization for the loss of the services of an essential senior manager and to cover the executive search expenses needed to find a replacement.

labor union (315) group of workers who have banded together to achieve common goals in the areas of wages, hours, and working conditions.

law (141) standards set by government and society in the form of either legislation or custom.

law of large numbers (A-5) concept that seemingly random events will follow a predictable pattern if enough events are observed.

leadership (279) ability to direct or inspire people to attain organizational goals.

leverage (556) technique of increasing the rate of return on an investment by financing it with borrowed funds.

leverage ratios (531) measures of the extent to which a firm relies on debt financing.

liability (523) claim against a firm's assets by a creditor.

liability insurance (A-7) insurance that protects against financial losses to others for acts for which the insured was responsible.

life insurance (A-10) insurance that protects people against the financial losses that occur with premature death.

lifestyle (B-3) the way one lives one's daily life.

lifetime value of a customer (410) revenues and intangible benefits (referrals and customer feedback) from a customer over the life of the relationship, minus the amount the company must spend to acquire and serve that customer.

limit order (585) instructions that the brokerage firm is not to pay more than a specified price for a security if the investor is buying or not to accept less than a specified price if the investor is selling.

limited liability company (LLC) (183) special legal form of organization allowing business owners to secure the corporate advantage of limited liability while avoiding the double taxation characteristic of corporations.

line manager (287) executive involved with the functions of production, financing, or marketing.

line organization (287) organizational structure that establishes a direct flow of authority from the chief executive to subordinates.

line-and-staff organization (287) structure that combines the direct flow of authority of a line organization with staff departments that serve, advise, and support the line departments.

liquidity ratios (529) financial ratios measuring a firm's ability to meet its short-term obligations when they must be paid.

listening (342) skill of receiving a message and interpreting its intended meaning by grasping the facts and feelings it conveys.

living wage (304) legally mandated wage that allows a worker to support a family of four without any form of public assistance.

local area networks (LANs) (494) computer networks that connect machines within limited areas, such as one building or several buildings near each other; allow personal computers to share printers, documents, and information.

lockout (319) management decision to bring pressure on union members by closing the firm.

logistics (441) activities involved in controlling the flow of goods, services, and information among members of the supply chain.

low-context culture (347) communication within a society that tends to rely on explicit written and verbal messages.

M1 (551) total value of coins, currency, traveler's checks, bank checking account balances, and the balances in other demand deposit accounts.

M2 (551) measure of the money supply including M1 plus a number of other financial assets that are almost as liquid as cash but do not serve directly as a medium of exchange.

macroeconomics (73) study of a nation's overall economic issues, such as how an economy maintains and allocates resources and how government policies affect the standards of living of its citizens.

mainframe (496) computer system containing the most extensive storage capacity and the fastest processing speeds.

make, buy, or lease decision (366) choosing whether to manufacture a needed product or component in house, purchase it from an outside supplier, or lease it.

managed-care plan (A-8) form of health insurance in which most, if not all, of the insured's health-care bills are paid by the insurer; in return, the insured has less say in his or her treatment.

management (266, 296) process of achieving organization objectives through people and other resources.

management accountant (518) accountant employed by a business other than a public accounting firm and who is responsible for collecting and recording financial transactions and preparing financial statements used by the firm's managers in decision making.

management development program (303) training designed to improve the skills and broaden the knowledge of current and potential executives.

management information system (MIS) (490) organized method for providing past, present, and projected information on internal operations as well as external intelligence to support decision making.

manufacturer's (national) brand (428) brand offered and promoted by a manufacturer or producer; they are sometimes priced much higher than generic brands.

maquiladora **(123)** foreign-owned manufacturing facilities located along the U.S.–Mexican border that produce products for export.

market order (585) investor's request to buy or sell a security at the current market price.

market penetration (C-6) percentage of total customers who have purchased a company's product.

market segmentation (400) process of dividing a total market into several relatively homogeneous groups.

marketing (384) process of planning and executing the conception, distribution, promotion, and pricing of ideas, goods, services, organizations, and events to create and maintain relationships that satisfy individual and organizational objectives.

marketing concept (386) companywide consumer orientation to promote long-run success.

marketing mix (394) blending the four elements of marketing strategy—product, distribution, promotion, and price—to satisfy chosen customer segments.

marketing research (396) collection and use of information to support marketing decision making.

marketing strategy (C-5) section of a business plan that presents information describing the market's need for a product and the ways the business will go about satisfying it.

Maslow's hierarchy of needs (312) theory of motivation proposed by Abraham Maslow. According to the theory, people have five levels of needs that they seek to satisfy: physiological, safety, social, esteem, and self-actualization.

mass production (358) system for manufacturing products in large amounts through effective combinations of specialized labor, mechanization, and standardization.

materials requirement planning (MRP) (369) computer-based production planning system by which a firm can ensure that it has needed parts and materials available at the right time and place in the correct amounts.

matrix structure (288) project management structure that links employees from different parts of the organization to work together on specific projects.

mediation (318) dispute resolution process that uses a third party, called a mediator, to make recommendations for settling union-management differences.

Medicare (A-6) public insurance program that provides health-care benefits to people who are 65 or older.

merger (187) combination of two or more firms to form one company.

microeconomics (72) study of small economic units, such as individual consumers, families, and businesses.

microloans (171) Small Business Administration-guaranteed loans of less than $25,000 made to start-ups and other very small firms.

middle management (267) second tier in the management pyramid that focuses on specific operation within the organizations.

minicomputer (496) intermediate-size computer—more compact and less expensive than a mainframe but also slower and with less memory.

mission statement (273) written explanation of an organization's business intentions and aims.

missionary selling (466) indirect selling in which specialized salespeople promote the firm's goodwill among customers, often by assisting them in product use.

mixed market economy (83) economic system that combines characteristics of both planned and market economies in varying degrees, including the presence of both government ownership and private enterprise.

monetary policy (91, 562) government action to increase or decrease the money supply and change banking requirements and interest rates to influence bankers' willingness to make loans.

money (549) anything generally accepted as payment for goods and services.

money market instruments (576) short-term debt securities issued by corporations, financial institutions such as banks, and governments.

monopolistic competition (80) market structure, like that for retailing, in which large numbers of buyers and sellers exchange relatively well-differentiated (heterogeneous) products, so each participant has some control over price.

monopoly (81) market structure in which a single supplier dominates trade in a good or service for which buyers can find no close substitute.

morale (311) mental attitude of employees toward their employer and jobs.

multidomestic business strategy (131) developing and marketing products to serve different needs and tastes of separate national markets.

multimedia computing (502) technologies that integrate two or more types of media, such as text, voice, sound, video, graphics, and animation into computer-based applications.

multinational corporation (MNC) (129) firm with significant operations and marketing activities outside its home country.

municipal bond (576) credit instrument issued by state or local governments; they can be either revenue bonds or general obligation bonds.

mutual fund (589) financial institution that pools investment money from purchasers of its shares and uses the money to acquire diversified portfolios of securities consistent with the fund's investment objectives.

national debt (94) money owed by government to individuals, businesses, and government agencies who purchase Treasury bills, Treasury notes, and Treasury bonds sold as a result of trade deficits and other international expenditures.

natural resources (7) all production inputs that are useful in their natural states, including agricultural land, building sites, forests, and mineral deposits.

negotiable instrument (146) commercial paper such as checks that is transferable among individuals and businesses.

net worth (B-7) difference between what a person owns (assets) and owes (liabilities).

newsgroup (234) forum for online participants to share information on selected topics.

nonpersonal selling (452) promotion that includes advertising, sales promotion, direct marketing, and public relations—all conducted without face-to-face contact with the buyer

nonprogrammed decision (277) a complex and unique problem or opportunity with important consequences for the organization.

nonverbal communication (343) transmission of messages through actions and behavior.

North American Free Trade Agreement (NAFTA) (122) 1994 agreement among the U.S., Canada, and Mexico to break down tariffs and trade restrictions.

notebook computer (497) computer that is small enough to slip into a briefcase, yet more powerful than many desktop computers.

not-for-profit corporation (186) businesslike organization such as a charitable group, social welfare agency, or religious congregation that pursues objectives other than returning profit to its owners.

not-for-profit organization (6) businesslike establishment that has primary objectives, such as public service, other than returning a profit to its owners.

objectives (275) guideposts by which managers define the organization's desired performance in such areas as profitability, customer service, growth, and employee satisfaction.

odd pricing (479) pricing method based on the belief that consumers favor uneven amounts or amounts that sound less than they really are.

oligopoly (80) market structure, like those in the airline and steel industries, in which relatively few sellers compete and where high start-up costs form barriers that keep out most new competitors.

on-the-job training (302) training method that teaches an employee to complete new tasks by performing them under the guidance of an experienced employee.

open market operations (563) technique of controlling the money supply growth rate by buying or selling U.S. Treasury securities.

operating system (497) software that controls the basic workings of a computer's system.

operational planning (271) detailed standards that guide implementation of tactical plans.

order processing (465) form of selling, mostly at the wholesale and retail levels, that involves identifying customer needs, pointing them out to customers, and completing orders.

organization (283) structured grouping of people working together to achieve common goals.

organization chart (284) visual representation of a firm's structure that illustrates job positions and functions.

organization marketing (392) marketing strategy that influences consumers to accept the goals of, receive the services of, or contribute in some way to an organization.

organizing (269) process of blending human and material resources through a formal structure of tasks and authority; arranging work, dividing tasks among employees, and coordinating them to ensure implementation of plans and accomplishment of objectives.

outsourcing (25, 310) contracting with another business to perform tasks or functions previously handled by internal staff members.

overhead costs (164) business expenditures such as rent and utility expenses that are not directly related to providing specific goods and services.

owners' equity (523) all claims of the proprietor, partners, or stockholders against the assets of a firm, equal to the excess of assets over liabilities.

ownership utility (385) orderly transfer of goods and services from the seller to the buyer; also called *possession utility.*

paid time off (PTO) (307) bank of time that employees can use for holidays, vacation, and sick days.

partnership (18, 181) affiliation of two or more companies with the shared goal of assisting each other in the achievement of common goals; form of business ownership in which the company is operated by two or more people who are co-owners by voluntary legal agreement.

patent (147) guarantee to an inventor of exclusive rights to an invention for 17 years.

penetration pricing (477) pricing strategy that sets a low price as a major marketing weapon.

performance appraisal (303) evaluation of an employee's job performance by comparing actual results with desired outcomes.

perpetual inventory (368) system that continuously monitors the amounts and locations of a company's stocks.

person marketing (391) use of efforts designed to attract the attention, interest, and preference of a target market toward a person.

personal (desktop) computer (PC) (496) desktop computer used for both business and personal purposes.

personal finance (B-2) study of the economic factors and personal decisions that affect a person's financial well-being.

personal selling (451) interpersonal promotional process involving a seller's face-to-face presentation to a prospective buyer.

PERT (Program Evaluation and Review Technique) (371) chart that seeks to minimize delays by coordinating all aspects of the production process.

physical distribution (431) actual movement of products from producer to consumers or business users.

picketing (318) workers marching at a plant entrance to protest some management practice.

place marketing (391) attempt to attract people to a particular area, such as a city, state, or nation.

place utility (385) availability of a product in a location convenient for customers.

planned economy (82) economic system in which strict government controls determine business ownership, profits, and resource allocations to accomplish government goals rather than those set by individual businesses.

planning (269) process of anticipating future events and conditions and determining courses of action for achieving organizational objectives.

point-of-purchase (POP) advertising (464) displays or demonstrations that promote products when and where consumers buy them, such as in retail stores.

pollution (53) environmental damage caused by a company's products or operating processes; an important economic, legal, and social issue.

portal (234) site designed to be a user's starting place when entering the World Wide Web.

positioning (454) concept in which marketers attempt to establish their own places in the minds of customers by communicating to prospective purchasers meaningful distinctions about the attributes, price, quality, or use of a good or service.

potential sales revenue (C-6) total revenue of a company if it captured 100 percent market penetration.

preferred provider organization (PPO) (A-8) contract between local health-care providers and employers to provide employees medical care at a discount.

preferred stock (185, 579) stock whose holders receive preference over holders of common stock in the payment of dividends but have limited voting rights.

premium (A-3) payment made by insured in exchange for insurance coverage.

presentation software (501) computer program that includes graphics and tools to produce a variety of charts, graphs, and pictures.

prestige pricing (475) establishing a relatively high price to develop and maintain an image of quality and exclusiveness.

price (473) exchange value of a good or service.

price-earnings ratio (P/E) (587) investment ratio calculated by dividing current market price by the annual earnings per share.

primary market (574) market where new security issues are first sold to investors; the issuer receives the proceeds from the sale.

private (store) brand (428) product that is not linked to the manufacturer, but instead carries the label of a retailer or wholesaler.

private enterprise system (10, 79) economic system that rewards businesses for their ability to identify and serve the needs and demands of customers.

private exchange (241) secure Web site at which a company and its suppliers share all types of data related to e-commerce, from product design through delivery of orders.

private placement (556) new stock or bond issuance that may not be sold publicly but only to a small select group of large investors such as pension funds and life insurance companies.

private property (11) most basic freedom under the private enterprise system; the right to own, use, buy, sell, and bequeath land, buildings, machinery, equipment, patents, and various intangible kinds of property.

privatization (84) recent international trend to convert government-owned and operated companies into privately held businesses.

problem-solving team (333) temporary combination of workers who gather to solve a specific problem and then disband.

Producer Price Index (PPI) (90) monthly measure of changes in price at the producer and wholesale levels.

product (420) bundle of physical, service, and symbolic attributes designed to enhance buyers' want satisfaction.

product advertising (457) nonpersonal selling of a particular good or service.

product liability (57, 148) responsibility of manufacturers for injuries and damages caused by their products.

product life cycle (423) four basic stages—introduction, growth, maturity, and decline—through which a successful product progresses.

product line (422) group of related products that are physically similar or are intended for the same market.

product mix (422) company's assortment of product lines and individual offerings.

product placement (455) form of promotion in which marketers pay fees to have their products showcased in movies and television shows.

production (356) application of resources such as people and machinery to convert materials into finished goods and services.

production and operations management (356) managing people and machinery in converting materials and resources into finished goods and services.

production control (370) process that creates a well-defined set of procedures for coordinating people, materials, and machinery to provide maximum production efficiency.

production planning (370) phase of production control that determines the amount of resources (including raw materials and other components) a firm needs to produce a certain output.

productivity (22, 86) relationship between the number of units produced and the number of human and other production inputs necessary to produce them.

product-related segmentation (404) dividing a consumer market into groups based on benefits sought by buyers and usage rates.

professional employer organization (PEO) (297) a company that helps small and midsized firms with a wide range of human resources services.

profitability objectives (473) setting prices based on the amount of money the company brings in (its revenues), minus its expenses, thus generating a profit.

profitability ratios (530) ratios used to measure the organization's overall financial performance by evaluating its ability to generate revenues in excess of operating costs and other expenses.

profits (6) rewards for businesspeople who take the risks involved to offer goods and services to customers.

programmed decision (277) simple, common, and frequently occurring problem for which a solution has already been determined.

promotion (450) communication link between buyer and seller that performs the function of informing, persuading, and influencing a purchase decision.

promotional mix (451) combination of personal and nonpersonal selling techniques designed to achieve promotional objectives.

promotional product (464) promotional item that prominently displays a firm's name, logo, or business slogan.

property and liability insurance (A-7) general category of insurance that provides protection against financial losses due to a number of perils.

psychographic segmentation (403) dividing consumer markets into groups with similar psychological characteristics, values, and lifestyles.

public accountant (518) professional who provides accounting services to individuals or business firms for a fee.

Public Company Accounting Oversight Board (522) five-member board created by the Sarbanes-Oxley Act of 2002 to set audit standards and to investigate and sanction accounting firms that certify the books of publicly traded firms; members of the board are appointed by the Securities and Exchange Commission to serve staggered five-year terms.

public insurance agency (A-6) governmental agency that provides certain types of insurance protection.

public ownership (188) organization owned and operated by a unit or agency of government.

public relations (468) organization's communications and relationships with its various audiences.

publicity (469) stimulation of demand for a good, service, place, idea, person, or organization by disseminating news or obtaining favorable unpaid media presentations.

puffery (471) exaggerated claims of a product's superiority or the use of subjective or vague statements that may not be literally true.

pulling strategy (470) promotional effort by a seller to stimulate demand among final users, who will then exert pressure on the distribution channel to carry the good or service, pulling it through the distribution channel.

pure competition (80) market structure, like that of small-scale agriculture, in which large numbers of buyers and sellers exchange homogeneous products and where no single participant has a significant influence on price.

pure risk (A-2) risk with only the possibility of a loss.

pushing strategy (470) promotional effort by a seller to members of the distribution channel intended to stimulate personal selling of the good or service, thereby pushing it through the channel.

quality (19) degree of excellence or superiority of a firm's goods and services.

quality control (372) measuring goods and services against established quality standards.

quota (120) limit set by a nation on the amounts of particular products that can be imported during specified time periods.

ratio analysis (529) commonly used tools for measuring the firm's liquidity, profitability, and reliance on debt financing, as well as the effectiveness of management's use of its resources, compared to other firms and with the firm's own past performance.

recession (85) cyclical economic contraction that lasts for six months or longer.

recycling (54) reprocessing of used materials for reuse.

regulation FD (592) requirement that firms share information with all investors at the same time.

relationship management (18) collection of activities that build and maintain ongoing, mutually beneficial ties between a business and its customers and other parties.

relationship marketing (409) developing and maintaining long-term, cost-effective exchange relationships with individual customers, suppliers, employees, and other partners for mutual benefit.

relationship selling (467) regular contacts over an extended period to build and sustain a mutually beneficial buyer–seller relationship.

retailer (434) channel member that sells goods and services to individuals for their own use rather than for resale.

revolving credit (B-9) type of credit that enables consumers to make purchases up to a credit limit; if the consumer carries a balance from month to month, finance charges (interest) are levied.

risk (A-2) uncertainty about loss or injury.

risk–return trade-off (547) optimal balance between risk and return.

robot (360) reprogrammable machine capable of performing numerous tasks that require manipulations of materials and tools.

routing (370) phase of production control that determines the sequence of work throughout the facility and specifies who will perform each aspect of production at what location.

S corporation (182) modified form of the traditional corporate structure often used by firms with fewer than 75 shareholders; such businesses can elect to pay federal income taxes as partnerships while retaining the liability limitations typical of corporations.

salary (304) compensation calculated on a periodic basis, such as weekly or monthly.

sales force automation (SFA) (468) streamlining the sales process by incorporating a broad range of tools, from e-mail, telecommunications devices like pagers and cell phones, and laptop computers to increasingly sophisticated software systems.

sales law (146) law governing the sale of goods or services for money or on credit.

sales promotion (463) nonpersonal marketing activities other than advertising, personal selling, and public relations that stimulate consumer purchasing and dealer effectiveness.

Sarbanes-Oxley Act of 2002 (40) federal legislation designed to deter and punish corporate and accounting fraud and corruption and protect the interests of workers and shareholders through enhanced financial disclosures, imposing criminal penalties on CEOs and CFOs who defraud investors, protecting whistleblowers, and establishing a new regulatory body for public accounting firms.

scheduling (370) development of timetables that specify how long each operation in the production process takes and when workers should perform it.

search engine (234) software that scans the Web to find sites that contain data requested by a user.

secondary market (575) financial markets where previously issued securities are traded among investors.

secured bond (576) bond backed by specific pledge of a company's assets.

security (574) stock, bond, or money market instrument that represents an obligation on the part of the issuer.

seed capital (220) initial funding needed to launch a new venture.

selective distribution (440) strategy in which a manufacturer selects only a limited number of retailers to distribute its product lines.

self-insurance fund (A-3) special fund created by setting aside cash reserves periodically that can be drawn upon in the event of a loss.

server (232) large, special computer that holds information, then provides it to clients on request.

set-aside program (171) component of government contract specifying that certain government contracts (or portions of those contracts) are restricted to small businesses and/or to women- or minority-companies.

sexism (64) discrimination against members of either sex, but primarily affecting women.

sexual harassment (62) inappropriate actions of a sexual nature in the workplace.

shopping product (421) item typically purchased only after the buyer has compared competing products in competing stores.

skimming pricing (476) pricing strategy that sets an intentionally high price relative to the prices of competing products.

skunkworks (223) project initiated by a company employee who conceives the idea, convinces top management of its potential, and then recruits human and other resources from within the firm to turn it into a commercial project.

small business (157) firm that is independently owned and operated, not dominant in its field, and meets industry-specific size standards for income or number of employees.

Small Business Administration (SBA) (171) federal agency that assists small businesses by providing management training and consulting, financial advice, and support in securing government contracts.

Small Business Investment Company (SBIC) (171) business licensed by the Small Business Administration to provide loans to small businesses.

smart card (243) plastic card that stores encrypted information on embedded computer chips rather than magnetic strips; among the most popular methods of Internet payment.

social audit (51) formal procedure that identifies and evaluates all company activities that relate to social issues such as conservation, employment practices, environmental protection, and philanthropy.

social responsibility (30, 51) business acceptance of the obligation to consider societal well-being, consumer satisfaction, and profit of equal value in evaluating the firm's performance.

socialism (83) planned economic system characterized by government ownership and operation of major industries.

socioemotional role (334) devoting time and energy to supporting the emotional needs of team members and to maintaining the team as a social unit.

software (497) sets of instructions that tell the computer hardware what to do.

sole proprietorship (180) form of business ownership in which the company is owned and operated by one person.

spam (236) unsolicited e-mail messages; frequently called *junk e-mail.*

span of management (286) number of subordinates a manager can supervise effectively.

specialty product (421) item that a purchaser is willing to make a special effort to obtain.

speculative risk (A-2) executive risk that has both the possibility of a gain as well as the possibility of a loss.

sponsorship (462) providing funds for a sporting or cultural event in exchange for a direct association with the event.

spreadsheet (499) software package that creates the computerized equivalent of an accountant's worksheet, allowing the user to manipulate variables and see the impact of alternative decisions on operating results.

staff manager (287) executive who provides information, advice, or technical assistance to aid line managers; does not have the authority to give orders, outside his/her own department or to compel line managers to take action.

standard of living (B-2) lifestyle one seeks to obtain or to maintain.

statement of cash flows (525) statement of a firm's cash receipts and cash payments that presents information on its sources and uses of cash.

statutory law (141) written law, including state and federal constitutions, legislative enactments, treaties of the federal government, and ordinances of local governments.

stock exchange (582) centralized marketplace where primarily common stocks are traded.

stock options (330) rights to buy a specified amount of the company's stock at a given price within a given time period.

stockholder (185) person or organization who owns shares of stock in a corporation.

strategic alliance (19) partnership formed to create competitive advantages for the business involved; in international business, a business strategy in which a company finds a partner in the country where it wants to do business.

strategic planning (271) process of determining the primary objective of an organization and then adopting courses of action and allocating resources to achieve those objectives.

strike (318) temporary work stoppage by employees until a dispute is settled or a contract signed.

subcontracting (128) international agreement that involves hiring local companies to produce, distribute, or sell goods or services in a specific country or geographical region.

supercomputer (496) powerful mainframe that can handle extremely rapid, complex calculations involving thousands of variables, most commonly in scientific research settings.

supervisory management (268) first-line management; includes positions such as supervisor, line manager, and group leader; responsible for assigning nonmanagerial employees to specific jobs and evaluating their performance every day.

supply (73) willingness and ability of sellers to provide goods and services.

supply chain (441) complete sequence of suppliers that contribute to creating and delivering a good or service to business users and final consumers.

supply curve (77) graph of the amount of a product that suppliers will offer for sale at different prices; generally slopes upward to reflect larger quantities likely to be offered for sale as prices increase.

SWOT analysis (274) method of assessing a company's internal strengths and weaknesses and its external opportunities and threats.

tablet PC (497) computer that looks like a notebook computer but has a detachable screen, which users can write on with a special-purpose pen.

tactical planning (271) plans designed to implement the activities specified by strategic plans.

target market (394) group of people toward whom an organization markets its goods, services, or ideas with a strategy designed to satisfy their specific needs and preferences.

tariff (119) tax imposed on imported goods.

task specialist role (334) devoting time and energy to helping the team accomplish its specific goals.

tax (149) assessment by a governmental unit.

team (331) group of employees who are committed to a common purpose, approach, and set of performance goals.

team cohesiveness (336) extent to which team members feel attracted to the team and motivated to remain part of it.

team norm (336) informal standard of conduct shared by team members that guides their behavior.

team selling (468) selling situation in which several sales associates or other members of the organization work together with the lead sales representative in reaching all those who influence the purchase decision.

teamwork (331) cooperative effort by a group of workers acting together for a common cause.

technical skills (268) manager's ability to understand and use techniques, knowledge, and tools and equipment of a specific discipline or department.

technology (16) business applications of knowledge based on scientific discoveries, inventions, and innovations.

telecommuter (308) home-based employee.

telemarketing (467) personal selling conducted entirely by telephone, which provides a firm's marketers with a high return on their expenditures, an immediate response, and an opportunity for personalized two-way conversation.

term policies (A-10) life insurance containing only a death benefit.

Theory X (315) assumption that employees dislike work and will try to avoid it.

Theory Y (315) assumption that employees enjoy work and seek social, esteem, and self-actualization fulfillment.

Theory Z (315) assumption that employee involvement is key to productivity and quality of work life.

360-degree performance review (303) employee performance review that gathers feedback from coworkers, supervisors, managers, and sometimes customers.

time utility (385) availability of a good or service when customers want to purchase it.

top management (267) managers at the highest level of the management pyramid who devote most of their time to developing long-range plans for their organizations.

tort (148) civil wrong inflicted on another person or the person's property.

trade promotion (464) sales promotion geared to marketing intermediaries rather than to final consumers.

trademark (147, 427) brand with legal protection against another company's use, not only of the brand name but also of pictorial designs, slogans, packaging elements, and product features such as color and shape.

transaction management (17) traditional business practice of concentrating on building and promoting products in the hope that enough customers will buy them to cover costs and earn acceptable profits.

transaction marketing (409) marketing that is characterized by buyer and seller exchanges with limited communications and little or no ongoing relationships between the parties.

treasurer (546) executive responsible for all of the company's financing activities, including managing cash, the tax department, and shareholder relations.

trends (C-5) consumer and business tendencies or patterns that firms can exploit to gain market share in an industry.

trial courts (140) federal and state courts of general jurisdiction.

underwriting (561, 575, A-4) process used by insurance companies to determine whom to insure and what to charge; in finance, process of purchasing a stock or bond issue from a firm or government and then reselling it to investors.

unemployment insurance (A-6) benefits paid to workers who are currently unemployed.

unemployment rate (90) indicator of a nation's economic health, typically expressed as a percentage of the total workforce who are actively seeking work but are currently unemployed.

utility (385) want-satisfying power of a good or service.

value (19) customer's perception of the balance between the positive traits of a good or service and its price.

value-added (387) good or service that exceeds value expectation because the company has added features, lowered its price, enhanced customer service, or made other improvements that increase customer satisfaction.

vendor-managed inventory (369, 441) company's decision to hand over their inventory control functions to suppliers.

venture capitalists (222, 556) business firms or groups of individuals who invest in new and growing firms in exchange for an ownership share.

vertical merger (187) combination of two or more firms operating at different levels in the production and marketing process.

vice president for financial management (546) executive responsible for preparing financial forecasts and analyzing major investment decisions.

vision (26, 270) perception of marketplace needs and the methods an organization can use to satisfy them.

volume objectives (473) basing pricing decisions on market share—the percentage of a market controlled by a certain company or product.

wage (304) compensation based on an hourly pay rate or the amount of output produced.

Web host (253) Web site that allows commercial Web sites a spot on its server for a fee.

Web site (231) integrated document composed of electronic pages that integrate text, graphics, audio, and video elements, as well as hyptertext links to other documents.

wheel of retailing (435) theory explaining changes in retailing as a process in which new retailers gain a competitive foothold by offering low prices and limited services and then add services and raise prices, creating opportunities for new low-price competitors.

whistleblowing (46) employee's disclosure to government authorities or the media of illegal, immoral, or unethical practices committed by an organization.

wholesaler (433) distribution channel member that sells primarily to retailers, other wholesalers, or business users.

wide area networks (WANs) (494) computer networks that tie larger geographical regions together by using telephone lines and microwave and satellite transmission.

Wi-Fi (494) wireless network that connects various devices and allows them to communicate with one another through radio waves; short for *wireless fidelity.*

word processing (499) software that uses a computer to type, store, retrieve, edit, and print various types of documents.

work team (332) relatively permanent group of employees with complementary skills who perform the day-to-day work of organizations.

workers' compensation insurance (A-6) benefits paid to workers who are injured on the job.

World Bank (121) organization established by industrialized nations to lend money to less developed and developing countries.

World Trade Organization (WTO) (121) 135-member international institution that monitors GATT agreements and mediates international trade disputes.

World Wide Web (WWW or Web) (17, 230) collection of Internet resources that offers easy access to text, graphics, sound, and other multimedia resources.

Notes

Prologue

1. Laura Stevens, "A Promising Job Outlook for Graduating Seniors," *College Journal,* http://www.collegejournal.com, accessed November 4, 2004.
2. "U.S. Economy Grows 3.7 Percent in Third Quarter," *Agence France Presse,* October 29, 2004, http://story.news.yahoo.com.
3. Carlos Torres, "U.S. Economy: Productivity Rises at Slowest Rate in 2 Years," *Bloomberg News,* November 4, 2004, http://www.bloomberg.com.
4. Stevens, "A Promising Job Outlook for Graduating Seniors."
5. "Top Entry-Level Employers," *CollegeGrad.com,* http://ww.collegegrad.com, accessed November 4, 2004.
6. Raelyn Johnson, "Don't Blow Your Summer," *Black Enterprise,* June 2003, p. 8.
7. Adapted from Louis E. Boone, David L. Kurtz, and Douglas Hearth, *Planning Your Financial Future,* 3rd edition. Mason, OH: South-Western, 2003.
8. Burton Snowboards Web site, http://www.burton.com, accessed January 9, 2004; Kemba J. Dunham, "Frustrated Laid-Off Workers Take Risk of Entrepreneurship," *The Wall Street Journal,* July 8, 2003, p. B10.
9. Monster.com and HotJobs.com, accessed January 10, 2004.
10. Andrea Coombes, "Web Largely Untapped by Job Seekers," *CBS MarketWatch,* January 24, 2003, http://www.cbsmarketwatch.com.
11. Matthew Benjamin, "Jobs Built to Last," *U.S. News & World Report,* February 18, 2002, pp. 38–40.
12. William Poundstone, "Why Are Manhole Covers Round? (And How to Deal with Other Trick Interview Questions)," *Business 2.0,* July 2003, p. 118; Jeffrey Wood, "Recruiters Cite Résumé Pet Peeves, Offer Tips," *Northwest Arkansas Business Journal,* March 17, 2003, p. 23.
13. Résumé tips from Michelle Conlin, "The Résumé Doctor Is In," *Business Week,* July 14, 2003, pp. 115–117; Joann S. Lublin, "College Students Make Job-Hunting Tougher with Weak Résumés," *The Wall Street Journal,* April 29, 2003, p. B1; Wood, "Recruiters Cite Résumé Pet Peeves, Offer Tips"; Sonia Alleyne, "The Résumé, the Pitch, the Close," *Black Enterprise,* February 2003, pp. 80–82.
14. Wood, "Recruiters Cite Résumé Pet Peeves, Offer Tips."
15. "Interview Q&A," *USA Today Careers Network,* September 3, 2002, http://www.usatoday.com.
16. Alleyne, "The Résumé, the Pitch, the Close."
17. "Interview Q&A," *USA Today Careers Network.*
18. Stephanie Armour, "Classrooms Filled with Returning Adults," *USA Today,* June 13, 2003, pp. B1, B2.
19. Stephanie Armour, "Young Job Seekers Get Squeezed Out," *USA Today,* January 29, 2002, p. B1.
20. Cara Buckley, "E-Commerce's Second Wave," *Mobile Register,* January 7, 2001, p. 3F.
21. Mary Carmichael, "Beyond the Lab in Biotech," *Newsweek,* September 23, 2002, p. 53.
22. Phillip Longman and Adam Martin, "What Are You Worth?" *Business 2.0,* March 2003, p. 79.
23. Longman and Martin, "What Are You Worth?"
24. Jodi Schneider, "Search Clues," *U.S. News & World Report,* February 24–March 3, 2003, pp. 76–83.

Chapter 1

1. Scott Bowles, "'The Incredibles' Packs More Power for Pixar," *USA Today,* November 8, 2004, p. D1; Bruce Orwall and Pui-Wing Tam, "Freeze Frame: Pixar Still Lacks a Partner for Post-Disney," *The Wall Street Journal,* October 25, 2004, p. B1; Austin Bunn, "Welcome to Planet Pixar," *Wired,* June 2004, p. 126ff; Christine Y. Chen, "You Oughta Be in Pixar," *Fortune,* March 8, 2004, p. 196.
2. "About Meade," Meade Instruments Corp. Web site, http://www.meade.com, accessed January 27, 2004; Ronald Grover, "Meade Instruments: Back from a Black Hole," *BusinessWeek,* May 29, 2000, p. 186.
3. John Simons, "The $10 Billion Pill," *Fortune,* January 20, 2003, pp. 58–68.
4. "Finally, the Pot of Gold," *BusinessWeek,* June 24, 2002, p. 104.
5. "About WGBH" and "Ways to Support WGBH," WGBH Web site, http://main.wgbh.org, accessed January 26, 2004.
6. Report by Mont Fennel, *New England Cable News,* March 3, 2003.
7. Lee Gomes, "Military's Use of GPS, a Civilian Mainstay, Is at Core of Its Might," *The Wall Street Journal,* March 24, 2003, p. B1.
8. Bennett Voyles, "The Will to Survive," *Sales & Marketing Management,* May 2002, pp. 38–54.
9. Robert Levering and Milton Moskowitz, "100 Best Companies to Work For," *Fortune,* January 20, 2003, p. 152.
10. Company Web site, http://www.papagenos.com, accessed January 14, 2004.
11. Company Web site, http://commerceonline.com/, accessed January 14, 2004.
12. SCP Corp. company profile, http://www.scpool.com/, accessed January 27, 2004.
13. U.S. Census Bureau, http://www.uscensus.gov, accessed January 4, 2004.
14. G-vox Web site, http://www.gvox.com, accessed January 4, 2004.
15. Donna Fenn and John Case, "Ordinary People, Extraordinary Creativity," *Inc.,* October 2002, p. 84.
16. "Whatever Happened to Standard Oil?" http://www.us-highways.com/sohist.htm, accessed January 6, 2004; Daniel Gross, *Forbes' Greatest Business Stories of All Time.* New York: John Wiley & Sons, 1996, pp. 23–38 and 41–57.

17. Graniterock Web site, http://www.graniterock.com, accessed January 4, 2004.

18. Del, Inc. Web site, http://www.dell.com, accessed January 4, 2004.

19. Ron Harris, "High-Tech Discs Offer Glimpse of World without Late Fees," *Mobile Register,* November 28, 2002, p. B18.

20. Mark Henricks, "Net Meeting," *Entrepreneur,* February 2003, pp. 53–55.

21. Nick Wingfield, "Online Retailing Still Growing Despite Some Losses Last Year," *The Wall Street Journal,* June 12, 2002, p. B4.

22. "Evolution of Mongolia's Internet Service," March 26, 2002, Pan Asia Networking site, http://www.panasia.org.sg.

23. Elisa Williams, "Better Mousetrap," *Forbes,* June 10, 2002, pp. 81–82.

24. Company Web site, http://www.landsend.com, accessed January 5, 2004.

25. Karen Cummings, "American Skiing Co.—Still on the Skiers' Map," *The Mountain Ear,* December 26, 2002, http://www.mountainear.com.

26. Mike Leonard, "Man vs. Machine," *Inc.,* October 15, 2002, http://www.inc.com.

27. Brian Grow, "Excess Inventory? eBay to the Rescue," *BusinessWeek,* September 9, 2002, p. 8.

28. Fred Vogelstein, "Looking for a Dot-Com Winner? Search No Further," *Fortune,* May 27, 2002, p. 66.

29. Cummings, "American Skiing Co.—Still on the Skiers' Map."

30. Jim Collins, "Best Beats First," *Inc.,* August 2000, pp. 48–51.

31. Evelyn Roth, "Man vs. Machine," *Inc.,* October 15, 2002, http://www.inc.com.

32. Organization for Economic Cooperation and Development, "World Trade: Main Economic Indicators," OECD Web site, http://www.oecd.org, accessed January 12, 2004.

33. World Trade Organization, "International Trade Statistics 2002: Leading Exporters and Importers," http://www.wto.org, accessed January 12, 2004.

34. Jerry Useem, "One Nation under Wal-Mart," *Fortune,* March 3, 2003, pp. 66–78; Bill Saporito, "Can Wal-Mart Get Any Bigger?" *Time,* January 13, 2003, pp. 38–43.

35. J. Bradford DeLong, "The Show Countries," *Wired,* December 2002, http://www.wired.com.

36. DeLong, "The Show Countries."

37. "CDC: U.S. Senior Citizen Population to Double by 2030," *USA Today,* http://www.usatoday.com, accessed March 6, 2003.

38. "CDC: U.S. Senior Citizen Population to Double by 2030."

39. Ponchitta Pierce, "Interview with Kofi Annan," *AARP,* January/February 2003, p. 23.

40. Aaron Bernstein, "Too Many Workers? Not for Long," *BusinessWeek,* May 20, 2002, pp. 128–129.

41. Bernstein, "Too Many Workers? Not for Long," p. 130.

42. Company Web site, http://www.mastercard.com, accessed January 16, 2004.

43. Nelson D. Schwartz, "The Pentagon's Private Army," *Fortune,* March 17, 2003, pp. 99–108.

44. Company Web site, http://www.mastercard.com, accessed January 16, 2004.

45. Norm Brodsky, "Street Smarts: Peripheral Vision," *Inc.,* November 2002, pp. 52–54.

46. Stephanie N. Mehta, "Now the Honeymoon's Over," *Fortune,* January 20, 2003, pp. 95–98.

47. Julia Boorstin, "How Coach Got Hot," *Fortune,* October 28, 2002, pp. 131–134.

48. Richard Lacayo and Amanda Ripley, "Persons of the Year," *Time,* December 30, 2002–January 6, 2003, pp. 32–33.

49. Elizabeth Weise, "Priests, CEOs Fare Poorly in Ethics Poll," *USA Today,* December 5, 2002, p. D10.

50. Company Web site, http://www.patagonia.com, accessed January 18, 2004.

51. General Electric Web site, http://www.ge.com, accessed February 3, 2004; Michael Skapinker, "Different Game, Same Winners," *Financial Times,* January 17, 2003, http://www.ft.com; Justin Fox, "What's So Great about GE?" *Fortune,* March 4, 2002, pp. 66–67.

Chapter 2

1. Floyd Norris, "Halliburton Settles S.E.C. Accusations," *The New York Times,* August 4, 2004, http://ww.nytimes.com; Mike France, "The New Accountability," *BusinessWeek*, July 26, 2004, pp. 30–33; Jon Fine, "Martha Begs for Leniency, and Ads," *Advertising Age,* July 19, 2004, p. 1; Megan Barnett, "Reeling in a Big Fish," *U.S. News & World Report,* July 19, 2004, p. 26; Curt Anderson, "Prosecutions Change Corporate Landscape," *Mobile Register,* July 13, 2004, p. B6; Susan Pulliam, "The 'It Wasn't Me' Defense," *The Wall Street Journal,* July 9, 2004, p. B1.

2. Amy Borrus, Mike McNamee, et al., "Reform: Business Gets Religion," *BusinessWeek,* February 3, 2003, pp. 40–41; "Setting the Rules," *The Economist,* January 19, 2003, http://www.economist.com.

3. Elizabeth Weise, "Priests, CEOs Fare Poorly in Ethics Poll," *USA Today,* December 5, 2002, p. D10.

4. "MBAs Need More Than Ethics 101," *BusinessWeekOnline,* January 21, 2003, http://www.businessweek.com.

5. Nicholas Stein, "America's Most Admired Companies," *Fortune,* March 3, 2003, pp. 81–84; Johnson & Johnson Web site, http://www.jnj.com, accessed March 1, 2003.

6. "Business Ethics Statistics," white paper for Business for Social Responsibility, http://www.bsr.org, accessed February 3, 2003.

7. O. C. Ferrell, John Fraedrich, and Linda Ferrell, *Business Ethics.* Boston: Houghton Mifflin, 2002, pp. 10–11.

8. Jonathan D. Salant, "Ethics Officers Join Businesses," *The Morning News,* October 31, 2002, p. 1D.

9. Karyn-Siobhan Robinson, "Employees Engaging in Deceptive Behaviors at Alarming Rates," *HR News Online,* July 21, 2002, http://www.shrm.org.

10. Karen Lowry Miller, "The Pill Machine: How Much Money Should Big Drug Firms Have to Lose to Treat the World's Poorest Patients?" *Newsweek,* November 19, 2001, p. 46ff.

11. Salil Gutt, "A New Corporate Game: 'Janitor Insurance,'" KYW News-Radio 1060, Family Financial Report, January 11, 2003, http://www.kyw1060.com; Theo Francis and Ellen E. Schultz, "Many Banks Boost Earnings with 'Janitors' Life Insurance," *The Wall Street Journal,* April 26, 2002, pp. A1, A2; Theo Francis and Ellen E. Schultz, "Why Secret Insurance on Employees Pays Off," *The Wall Street Journal,* April 25, 2002, p. C1.

12. "Cendant: We Are . . . ," http://www.cendant.com, accessed January 19, 2004; Peter Elkind, "Cendant Case Scorecard: Government 3, Book-Cookers 0," *Fortune,* July 10, 2000, p. 42.

13. Richard Benke, "Energy Dept. Decries Los Alamos Firings," *Associated Press,* January 31, 2003.

14. "Many Whistleblowers Still Lack Legal Protection," *USA Today,* September 2, 2002, p. B1.

15. Nortel Networks Web site, http://www.nortelnetworks.com, accessed January 20, 2004.

16. "Ethics Programs Help Curb Employee Theft," *USA Today Magazine,* December 2002, p. 10.

17. Joshua Joseph, "Report Summary: National Business Ethics Survey," Ethics Resource Center, http://www.ethics.org, accessed March 20, 2003; Society for Human Resource Management, "Businesses Paying More Attention to Ethics; Management Support Essential, Report Says," *HR News Online,* June 14, 2000, http://www.shrm.org.

18. David Bank, "Red Cross Adjusts Procedures for its Disaster Fund-Raising," *The Wall Street Journal,* June 6, 2002, p. B2.

19. Nortel Networks Web site, http://www.nortelnetworks.com, accessed January 20, 2004.

20. "P&G Community Activity," http://www.pg.com, accessed January 20, 2004.

21. Intentional Communities Directory, "Council on Economic Priorities," http://www.ic.org/resources, accessed January 14, 2004; The Center for Science in the Public Interest Web site, http://www.cspinet.org, accessed January 14, 2004.

22. Mail Abuse Prevention System Web site, http://mail-abuse.org, accessed January 21, 2004.

23. Eric Lichtblau, "U.S. Seeks $289 Billion in Cigarette Makers' Profits," *The New York Times,* March 17, 2003, http://www.nytimes.com.

24. Michelle Kessler, "PC Makers Soon May Be Forced to Recycle," *USA Today,* February 26, 2001, p. B1.

25. Michelle Kessler, "PC Makers Soon May Be Forced to Recycle."

26. Stuart F. Brown, "Dude, Where's My Hybrid?" *Fortune,* April 28, 2003, pp. 112–118; Sholnn Freeman, "Hybrid Cars Attract More Buyers," *The Wall Street Journal,* March 13, 2003, p. D3; Paul Raeburn, "Hybrid Cars, Less Fuel, but More Costs," *BusinessWeek,* April 15, 2002, p. 107.

27. Nicholas D. Kristoff, "Our New Hydrogen Bomb," *The New York Times,* February 21, 2003, p. A27.

28. "This Is Dow: Social Responsibility," Dow Web site, http://www.dow.com, accessed January 4, 2004.

29. Christopher Tkaczyk, "Recycling," *Fortune,* April 1, 2002, p. 36.

30. Cathy L. Hartman and Edwin R. Stafford, "Enviro Groups Entering Marketing Fray," *Marketing News,* July 30, 2001, p. 15.

31. Geoffrey A. Fowler, "'Green' Sales Pitch Isn't Moving Many Products," *The Wall Street Journal,* March 6, 2002, p. B1.

32. Bill Lambrecht, "U.S. Goes on Offensive Against Europe's Resistance to Modified Foods," *Mobile Register,* May 25, 2003, p. A20; James Cox, "U.S. Challenges Europe's Biotech Crop Ban in Court," *USA Today,* May 14, 2003, p. B3.

33. David Stipp, "Is Monsanto's Biotech Worth Less Than a Hill of Beans?" *Fortune,* February 21, 2002, pp. 157–158.

34. U.S. Department of Labor Web site, http://www.dol.gov, accessed January 6, 2004.

35. Nortel Networks Web site, http://www.nortelnetworks.com, accessed January 13, 2004.

36. "Consumer Product Safety Commission, The Betesh Group Announce Recall of 'Busy Bug' Plush Toys," February 27, 2003, CPSC Web site, http://www.spsc.gov.

37. Howard Gleckman, "The Backlash Against Big Pharma," *BusinessWeek,* May 27, 2002, pp. 66–68.

38. "Fraud Protection Program," eBay Web site, http://pages.ebay.com/help, accessed January 14, 2004.

39. U.S. Department of Labor, Bureau of Labor Statistics, "Injuries, Illnesses, and Fatalities," http://www.bls.gov/iif/oshwc/osh/os/osnr0013.txt, accessed January 14, 2004.

40. Jewel-Osco Web site, http://www.jewelosco.com, accessed January 15, 2004.

41. U.S. Department of Labor Employment and Training Administration Final Rule, http://wdr.doleta.gov/readroom/FedReg/final/2000014801.htm, accessed January 14, 2004.

42. The U.S. Equal Employment Opportunity Commission Testimony of Cari M. Dominguez, Chair, U.S. Equal Employment Opportunity Commission, before the Senate Committee on Health, Education, Labor and Pensions United States Senate Hearing on Protecting against Genetic Discrimination, "The Limits of Existing Laws," February 13, 2002, http://www.eeoc.gov/coordination/dominguezspeech.html.

43. Stephanie Armour, "Largest Age Bias Settlement Hits $250M," *USA Today,* January 30, 2003, http://www.usatoday.com.

44. Alejandro Bodipo-Memba, "Lawyer to File Appeal in Ford Case," *Detroit Free Press,* August 27, 2002.

45. Del Jones, "Women Gain Corporate Slots," *USA Today,* November 19, 2002, p. B2; Toddi Gutner, "How to Shrink the Pay Gap," *Business-Week,* June 24, 2002, p. 151.

46. Wendy Zellner, "No Way to Treat a Lady?" *BusinessWeek,* March 3, 2003, pp. 63, 66.

Chapter 3

1. "DeBeers Pleads Guilty in Diamond Price-Fixing Case," *Mobile Register,* July 14, 2004, p. B6; Margaret Webb Pressler, "DeBeers Pleads to Price-Fixing," *Washington Post,* July 14, 2004, p. B1; "Diamond Price-Fixing Guilty Plea Seen," *CNNMoney,* July 11, 2004, http://money.cnn.com; John R. Wilke, "DeBeers Is in Talks to Settle Price-Fixing Charge," *The Wall Street Journal,* February 24, 2004, p. B1; Phyllis Berman and Lea Goldman, "The Billionaire Who Cracked DeBeers," *Forbes,* September 15, 2003, pp. 109–116.

2. Daniel Eisenberg, "Jail to the Chiefs?" *Time,* August 12, 2002, pp. 24–25; Paul Maco, "Don't Count on Laws to Restore Trust in Markets," *The Wall Street Journal,* August 6, 2002, p. B2.

3. WMUR local news report, March 20, 2003.

4. Bill Powell, "Iraq: We Win. Then What?" *Fortune,* November 25, 2002, pp. 61–70.

5. Lavelle, "Living without Oil."

6. Marianne Lavelle, "Power Overplay," *U.S. News & World Report,* April 22, 2002, pp. 44–46.

7. Jane Spencer, "States Relax Child Vaccine Laws," *The Wall Street Journal,* August 7, 2002, pp. D1, D2; Ira Carnahan, "Duh!" *Forbes,* March 18, 2002, p. 50.

8. "Investigators Look at Possible Illegal Feed in Mad Cow Case," *USA Today,* May 24, 2003, http://www.usatoday.com/news/world/2003-05-24-mad-cow_x.htm; Noelle Knox and Theresa Howard, "Anti-War Protesters Take Aim at American Brands," *USA Today,* April 4, 2003, pp. B1, B2.

9. Evan Thomas, "Women, Wine, and Weapons," *Newsweek,* January 13, 2003, http://www.msnbc.com/news/855119.asp.

10. Peter Fritsch, "A Cement Titan in Mexico Thrives by Selling to Poor," *The Wall Street Journal,* April 22, 2002, pp. A1, A12.

11. "History of the U.S. Postal Service: 1775–1993," U.S. Postal Service Web site, http://www.usps.com/history, accessed January 20, 2004; "Bush Creates Commission to Overhaul U.S. Postal Service," *USA Today,* December 11, 2002, http://www.usatoday.com.

12. Andrew Backover, "A Nickel Here, a Buck There Add Up to Big Local Bills," *USA Today,* February 28, 2003, pp. 1, 2.

13. Daniel Fisher, "Shell Game," *Forbes,* January 7, 2002, pp. 52–54; Jeremy Kahn, "One Plus One Makes What?" *Fortune,* January 7, 2002, pp. 88–90.

14. "The World Factbook," Central Intelligence Agency, http://www.cia.gov, accessed January 21, 2004.

15. Nick Wingfield, "If Times Are Tough, They Sell Their Stuff on Thriving eBay," *The Wall Street Journal,* August 6, 2002, p. A1.

16. Robert J. Samuelson, "Recovery or Recession?" *Newsweek,* October 7, 2002, p. 50; Daniel McGinn, "Betting on a Recovery," *Newsweek,* January 14, 2002, pp. 28–32.

17. Brian Bremner and Irene M. Kunii, "Deflation Nation," *BusinessWeek,* May 26, 2003, pp. 52–54.

18. Barbara Hagenbaugh, "Deflation? Not in This Household," *USA Today,* May 20, 2003, p. B2; John Waggoner, "Inflation? Deflation? Basic Knowledge Can Aid Investing," *USA Today,* May 16, 2003, p. B3;

Jeanne Aversa, "Economists Worry About Destabilizing Spiral of Price Drops," *Mobile Register,* May 16, 2003, p. B6.

19. Rachel Koning, "CPI Falls on Energy Drop; Core Flat," *CBS.MarketWatch.com,* May 16, 2003.

20. Bureau of Public Debt, "The Public Debt to the Penny and Who Holds It," *The Public Debt Online,* March 24, 2003, http://www.publicdebt.treas.gov.

21. William L. Watts, "White House Sees More Red Ink," *CBS.MarketWatch.com,* July 12, 2002, http://www.cbs.marketwatch.com.

22. "Employment Situation Summary," Bureau of Labor Statistics, September 2004, http://www.bls.gov; Justin Fox, "This Tunnel Has an End," *Fortune,* January 20, 2003, pp. 33–34; Anna Bernasek, "Is This Where the Economy Is Headed?" *Fortune,* September 2, 2002, pp. 85–90.

23. Nicholas Stein, "No Way Out," *Fortune,* January 20, 2003, pp. 102–106.

24. "Net Worth—PepsiCo," *Worth,* September 2002, p. 30.

Chapter 4

1. Alex Taylor III, "Shanghai Auto Wants to Be the World's Next Great Company," *Fortune,* October 4, 2004, pp. 103–110; Normandy Madden, "GM Prepares Way for Caddy in China," *Advertising Age,* September 27, 2004, pp. 4, 83; Frederik Balfour, "Letting Up on the Gas," *BusinessWeek,* September 20, 2004, p. 54.

2. "Why Trade Is Good for American Manufacturing," U.S. Trade Promotion Authority, http://www.tpa.gov, accessed January 19, 2004; "Table 1: U.S. International Trade in Goods and Services Balance of Payments (BOP) Basis," *Trade and Economy: Data and Analysis,* February 20, 2003, U.S. International Trade Administration Web site, http://www.ita.doc.gov.

3. "Oracle Increases Commitment to India," Oracle Corp. press release, http://www.oracle.com, accessed August 5, 2002.

4. Gautam Naik, Vanessa Fuhrmans, Jonathan Karp, Joel Millman, Farnas Fassihi, and Joanna Slater, "Global Baby Bust," *The Wall Street Journal,* January 24, 2003, p. B1.

5. *The World Factbook,* Central Intelligence Agency, http://www.cia.gov, accessed January 15, 2004.

6. "Saffron," *Spice Advice Encyclopedia,* http://www.spiceadvice.com, accessed January 17, 2004.

7. Martin Crutsinger, "U.S. 2002 Deficit Hit Record $435.2B," *Associated Press,* February 20, 2003.

8. http://www.getcustoms.com/gifts/latgifts.html, accessed January 11, 2004.

9. Hugh Rawson, "The Road to Freedom Fries," *American Heritage,* June/July 2003, p. 12; Bruce Horovitz, "Boycott Grinds on Against French Food, Wine, Travel," *USA Today,* May 1, 2003, p. B1; Christina Hoag, "French's Spreads the News: Its Mustard Born in USA," *Miami Herald,* March 27, 2003, http://www.miami.com/mld/miamiherald/business/5489025.htm; "In Quotes," *U.S. News & World Report,* March 31, 2003, p. 6; "Perspectives," *Newsweek,* March 31, 2003, p. 15.

10. "Better in Brazil," *U.S. News & World Report,* April 1, 2002, p. 28.

11. Larry Magid, "Talk to Your Kids about Cell Phone Use," *CBSNews.com,* March 14, 2003, http://www.cbsnews.com.

12. Associated Press, "Tech Show Emphasizes Ease of Use, Better Design," *USA Today,* March 13, 2003, http://www.usatoday.com.

13. Deborah L. Vence, "Match Game," *Marketing News,* November 11, 2002, pp. 1, 12.

14. Alex Rodriguez, "Despite Risks, Russia Again Tempting World's Investors," *Chicago Tribune,* February 24, 2003, Section 1, p. 3.

15. Organization for Economic Cooperation and Development, "Membership," January 19, 2004, http://www.oecd.org.

16. Andrew Dansby, "Stones to Rock China," *Rolling Stone,* April 17, 2003, p. 30; Leslie Chang, "China Get Satisfaction from the Stones," *The Wall Street Journal,* March 13, 2003, pp. B1, B2.

17. Geoffrey A. Fowler, "Copies 'R' Us," *The Wall Street Journal,* January 31, 2003, p. B1.

18. Neil King, Jr., and Robert Guy Matthews, "So Far, Steel Tariffs Do Little of What President Envisioned," *The Wall Street Journal,* September 13, 2002, p. A1; Angie Drobnic Holan, "Steel Tariffs Seep Across Economy," *Mobile Register,* July 7, 2002, Section F, pp. 1, 5.

19. Ira Carnahan, "Quota Factory," *Forbes,* April 14, 2003, p. 110.

20. Barbara Slavin, "U.S. Bans Imports from Huge Chinese Conglomerate," *USA Today,* May 27, 2003, p. B1.

21. Barbara Hagenbaugh, "U.S. Manufacturing Jobs Fading Away Fast," *USA Today,* December 13, 2002, pp. B1, B2.

22. David Sharp, "Major Shirt Plant Closes," *Mobile Register,* October 19, 2002, p. B9.

23. Pete Engardio et al., "Is Your Job Next?" *BusinessWeek,* February 3, 2003, pp. 50–59.

24. Dina Temple-Raston, "Protestors vs. Globalization, Part 2," *USA Today,* April 13, 2000, p. B3.

25. Pete Engardio and Rich Miller, "The IMF Mess," *BusinessWeek,* September 30, 2002, pp. 54–56.

26. Canadian, Mexican, and U.S. populations and gross domestic product data from Central Intelligence Agency, *CIA—The World Factbook,* http://www.civ.gov/cia/publications/factbook/geos, accessed January 16, 2004.

27. Barbara Hagenbaugh, "Between Two Economic Extremes," *USA Today,* August 15, 2002, p. B1.

28. Hagenbaugh, "Between Two Economic Extremes"; Geri Smith, "The Decline of the Maquiladora," *BusinessWeek,* April 29, 2002, p. 59.

29. Robert Taylor, "Mexico: NAFTA at 10—Growing Strains," *World Press Review Online,* February 2003, http://www.worldpress.org/Americas/880.cfm; United Nations Conference on Trade and Development, "Top Ten Foreign Direct Investment Host Economies," *UNCTAD World Investment Report 2002,* http://www.unctad.org, accessed January 19, 2004.

30. Geri Smith, "Farmers Are Getting Plowed Under," *BusinessWeek,* November 18, 2002, p. 53.

31. European Union population and GDP data from Economic Research Service, "Briefing Room: European Union Data," U.S. Department of Agriculture, http://www.ers.usda.gov, accessed January 19, 2004.

32. Brandon Mitchener, "Ten New Members to Weigh in on Future of EU," *The Wall Street Journal,* April 16, 2003, p. A16.

33. Howard Johnson Web site, http://www.hojo.com, accessed January 12, 2004.

34. Unilever Web site, http://www.unilever.com, accessed January 20, 2004; Michael Shari, "Indonesia: Consumer Heaven?" *BusinessWeek,* March 24, 2003, http://www.businessweek.com.

35. Bruce Einhorn and Andy Reinhardt, "Why Infineon Wants Asian Allies," *BusinessWeek,* March 24, 2003, http://www.businessweek.com.

36. "About Us," Gateway Web site, http://www.gateway.com, accessed January 20, 2004.

37. Chester Dawson et al., "The Americanization of Toyota," *BusinessWeek,* April 15, 2002, pp. 52–54.

38. Cris Prustay, "Selling to Singapore's Teens Is Tricky," *The Wall Street Journal,* October 4, 2002, p. B2.

39. Stanley Reed, "E-Commerce Starts to Click," *BusinessWeek,* August 26, 2002, p. 56.

Part 1 Appendix

1. Theresa Agovino, "Vioxx Battles Could Cost Merck Up to $18 Billion," *USA Today,* November 5, 2004, p. B7; Nancy Zuckerbrod, "Big Tobacco Disputes Conspiracy Claim," September 22, 2004, *Associated Press,* http://www.story.news.yahoo.com; Roger Parloff, "Welcome to the New Asbestos Scandal," *Fortune,* September 6, 2004, p. 186ff; "Pfizer to Settle Insulation Lawsuits for $430 Million," *Seattle Post-Intelligencer,* September 4, 2004, http://seattlepi.nwsource.com; Martin Kasindorf, "Robin Hood Is Alive in Court, Say Those Seeking Lawsuit Limits," *USA Today,* March 8, 2004, pp. A1, A4.

2. "By the Numbers," *Fortune,* March 3, 2003, p. 40.

3. Joan Biskupic, "Shop Wins Round in Victoria's Secret Case," *USA Today,* March 5, 2003, p. B5.

4. Steve Forbes, "Patently Good Idea," *Forbes,* March 31, 2003, p. 27.

5. Associated Press, "Winnie the Pooh Lawsuit Sent Back to State Court for Trial," *The Miami Herald,* May 20, 2003, http://www.miami.com/mld/miamiherald; Patrick Barrett, "Disney Loses Ground in Battle for Pooh," *The Guardian Unlimited,* February 21, 2003, http://media.guardian.co.uk.

6. "$5 Million Jury Verdict Largest in 2002," *North Carolina Lawyers Weekly,* January 13, 2003, http://www.nclawyersweekly.com.

7. Consumer Note, *Detroit Free Press,* May 18, 2003, http://www.freep.com.

8. Amy Merrick and Dennis K. Berman, "Kmart to Buy Sears for $11.5 Billion," *The Wall Street Journal,* November 18, 2004, pp. A1, A8; Anne D'Innocenzio, "An $11 Billion Gamble," *Mobile Register,* November 18, 2004, p. B6

9. Mary Ellen Podmolik, "Flawed Mega-Deals Shatter Promises," *Crain's Chicago Business,* 2001, http://www.chicagobusiness.com.

10. Patrick Jackson, "Tobacco Settlement Funds in Jeopardy," *The News Journal,* April 8, 2003, http://www.delawareonline.com; "States Will Lose in Philip Morris Bond Row," *Financial Review,* April 1, 2003, http://afr.com/worldbusiness.

Chapter 5

1. Nick Wingfield, "Auctioneer to the World," *The Wall Street Journal,* August 5, 2004, pp. B1, B6; Jarry R. Weber, "Middlemen Mine eBay," *Houston Chronicle,* June 27, 2004, p. D7; "iSold It Now Registered to Sell Franchises in 43 States," *Business Wire,* April 23, 2004, http://www.tmcnet.com; Lisa Baertlein, "eBay Drop-Off Stores Sprout on Main Street USA," *Reuters Limited,* January 14, 2004, http://www.forbes.com; David Steiner, "Drop-Off eBay Consignment Services: Poised to Pop or Flop?" *AuctionBytes.com,* January 4, 2004, http://www.auctionbytes.com; Monty Phan, "Easy eBay," *Newsday.com,* December 15, 2003, http://www.nyoasis.com.

2. U.S. Census Bureau, "Statistics about Small Businesses and Large Businesses from the U.S. Census Bureau," Census Bureau Web site, http://www.census.gov, January 6, 2004.

3. Office of Advocacy, U.S. Small Business Administration, "The Facts about Small Business," p. 1, SBA Web site, http://www.sba.gov/advo, January 6, 2004.

4. Office of Advocacy, U.S. Small Business Administration, "Minorities in Business," p. 27, SBA Web site, http://www.sba.gov, January 6, 2004.

5. Small Business Administration, "SBA Size Standards: Frequently Asked Questions," SBA Web site, http://www.sba.gov/size, January 6, 2004.

6. Thea Singer, "Man of Depth," *Inc.,* July 2002, p. 32.

7. "About Us," http://www.sanrise.com, January 27, 2004.

8. Jim Hopkins, "Big Business Can't Swallow These Little Fish," *USA Today,* March 27, 2002, p. B1.

9. Company Web site, http://www.powells.com, accessed January 6, 2004; "They Said It" quotation from "Michael Powell," *Inc.,* July 2001, p. 48.

10. U.S. Department of Agriculture, *Agriculture Fact Book,* pp. 20, 23, USDA Web site, http://www.usda.gov, January 7, 2004.

11. Bureau of the Census, "Increase in At-Home Workers Reverses Earlier Trend," Census Bureau Web site, http://www.census.gov, January 7, 2004.

12. Amanda C. Kooser, "Explore Your Auctions," *Entrepreneur,* January 2003, pp. 52–55.

13. Company Web sites, http://www.salemfive.com and http://www.directbanking.com, accessed January 14, 2004.

14. SBA, "The Facts about Small Business," p. 1.

15. SBA, "The Facts about Small Business," p. 2.

16. Stephanie Armour, "With Job Market Tight, Students Start Own Businesses," *USA Today,* March 5, 2002, p. B1.

17. SBA, "The Facts about Small Business," p. 1.

18. "iQuantic Buck at a Glance," http://www.hoovers.com, January 14, 2004; "iQuantic Acquired by Buck Consultants," *San Francisco Business Times,* http://www.sanfrancisco.bizjournals.com, January 14, 2004.

19. Erik Brady, "Cheerleading in the USA: A Sport and an Industry," *USA Today,* April 26, 2002, pp. A1, A2.

20. "The New Markets Initiative," http://www.i4sd.org/TCDDM.learningtodoit, January 14, 2004.

21. Ann Zimmerman et al., "Wal-Mart to Start Subscription Plan for Renting DVDs," *The Wall Street Journal,* October 16, 2002, p. D12; Ethan Zindler, "Low-Tech Twist: Rent DVDs by Mail," *Mobile Register,* August 25, 2002, p. F3; April Y. Pennington, "Tickets, Please," *Entrepreneur,* August 2002, p. 140.

22. "Interview with Thomas D'Ambra," http://www.tist.com/notes/articles/han616.html, January 21, 2004.

23. SBA, "The Facts about Small Business," p. 5.

24. Daren Fonda, "Plucky Little Competitors," *Time,* October 21, 2002, pp. 60–61.

25. "Reviving the Past, Creating the Future," http://www.schylling.com, January 17, 2004; Starbucks Web site, http://www.starbuckco.com, accessed January 17, 2004; Chris Penttila, "Still Playing with Toys?" *Entrepreneur,* August 2002, pp. 50–63; Kate O'Sullivan, "Licensing Wizardry," *Inc.,* August 2001, pp. 73–74.

26. SBA, "The Facts about Small Business," p. 9.

27. C. J. Prince, "Plastic Rap," *Entrepreneur,* January 2003, pp. 43–44.

28. "Precision Plastics: An Employee-Owned Company," http://www.pplastics.com, January 19, 2004.

29. David Worrell, "Our Little Angels," *Entrepreneur,* January 2003, pp. 45, 47.

30. Jeffrey H. Birnbaum, "Slowly but Surely," *Fortune,* December 9, 2002, pp. 218[A–H].

31. National Business Incubator Association Web site, http://www.nbia.org, accessed January 8, 2004.

32. "Drugstore.com—Online Pharmacy & Drugstore, Prescriptions Filled," http://www.drugstore.com, January 19, 2004.

33. "A Strategic Misalliance," *Inc. 500 Special Issue,* October 15, 2002, http://www.inc.com.

34. National Foundation for Women Business Owners, "Key Facts," NFWBO Web site, http://www.nfwbo.org, January 10, 2004; Alan Hughes, "Making Strides, but Losing Ground?," *Black Enterprise,* April 2002, p. 30.

35. Jim Hopkins, "Mars vs. Venus Extends to Entrepreneurs, Too," *USA Today,* May 19, 2003, pp. B1, B2; quotation from Aliza Pilar Sherman, "The Opposite Sex," *Entrepreneur,* July 2002, p. 36.

36. NFWBO, "Key Facts"; Aliza Pilar Sherman, "Wild, Wild, West," *Entrepreneur,* July 2002, p. 30.

37. Bridget McCrea, "Doing Her Part to Ensure the Safety of Children," *AdvancingChildren Network,* http://www.advancingwomen.com/business/entpr_8.html, January 8, 2004.

38. Sherman, "The Opposite Sex," p. 36.

39. Gina Holland, "Survey Reveals Entrepreneurial Side of America's Blacks," *The Morning News,* July 22, 2001, p. D7.

40. Eduardo Porter, "As Latinos Fan Out across America, Businesses Follow," *The Wall Street Journal,* November 26, 2002, p. A1.

41. Jim Hopkins, "Asian Business Owners Gaining Clout," *USA Today,* February 27, 2002, pp. A1, A2.

42. SBA, "The Facts about Small Business," pp. 3–5; SBA, "Minorities in Business," pp. iii, 1.

43. SBA, "Minorities in Business," pp. 4, 26.

44. "*Entrepreneur's* 24th Annual Franchise 500," *Entrepreneur,* January 2003, p. 161.

45. "The Fast & the Franchising," *Entrepreneur,* March 2002, p. 100.

46. SBA, "Minorities in Business," pp. 4, 26.

47. Alan Hughes, "How You Can Make $10,000 a Year from Home," *Black Enterprise,* September 2002, pp. 107–112.

48. "Franchising in the United States," McDonald's Web site, http://www.mcdonalds.com, accessed January 30, 2003; "Franchise Opportunities," Subway Web site, http://www.subway.com, accessed January 30, 2003.

49. "Welcome from Happy & Healthy Products Inc. and Our Fantastic Fruitfulls Franchisees!" http://www.fruitfull.com, January 18, 2004.

50. Alan Hughes, "Franchise to Go," *Black Enterprise,* July 2002, p. 46.

51. Michael Weinreb, "A Tarnished Ronald?" *Sales & Marketing Management,* February 2003, p. 9; Shirley Leung and Suzanne Vranica, "Happy Meals Are No Longer Bringing Smiles at McDonald's," *The Wall Street Journal,* January 31, 2003, pp. B1, B4; Bob Sperber, "A Mouse Divided," *Brandweek,* January 27, 2003, p. 3; "McDonald's to Close 175 Restaurants, Miss Earnings," *USA Today,* November 11, 2002, http://www.usatoday.com.

52. SBA, "Minorities in Business," p. 26. The data include only S corporations and businesses with at least $500 in receipts.

53. SBA, "The Facts about Small Business," p. 5.

54. "Drifting South," *Entrepreneur,* August 2002, p. 34.

55. Manjeet Kripalani and Pete Engardia, "Small Is Profitable," *Business-Week,* August 26, 2002, pp. 112–113.

56. "SerenaXChange," http://www.serenaxchange.com, January 19, 2003; Jim Kerstetter, "Serena Software: Keeping All Systems Go," *BusinessWeek,* May 29, 2000, p. 194.

57. "Introduction to the Fortune 500," *Fortune,* April 15, 2002, pp. 94–101.

58. Bobbie Gossage, "Own an S Corp? Take Note" and Ilan Mochari, "Tax News You Can Use Now," *Inc.,* January 2003, pp. 40–43.

59. The National Center for Employee Ownership, "Research and Statistics: A Statistical Profile of Employee Ownership," April 2002, http://www.nceo.org.

60. Information from Pennsylvania Ballet Web site, http://www.paballet.org, accessed January 18, 2004.

61. Robert Frank and Scott Hensley, "Pfizer to Buy Pharmacia for $60 Billion," *The Wall Street Journal,* July 15, 2002, pp. A1, A6.

62. Nerma Jelacis, "Diageo Sells Burger King Unit," *Financial Times Investor,* July 25, 2002; downloaded from http://www.ft.com, January 27, 2004.

63. "Report: Cendant to Buy Budget," *CBS.MarketWatch.com,* August 21, 2002, http://www.cbs.marketwatch.com.

64. David Henry, "Mergers: Why Most Big Deals Don't Pay Off," *Business-Week,* October 14, 2002, p. 63.

Chapter 6

1. Peter Burrows, "Can the iPod Keep Leading the Band?" *BusinessWeek,* November 8, 2004, p. 54; Beth Snyder Bulik, "The iPod Economy," *Advertising Age,* October 18, 2004, pp. 1, 37; Victoria Murphy, "The Song Remains the Same," *Forbes,* September 6, 2004, pp. 54–56; Nick Wingfield, "Online Music's Latest Tune," *The Wall Street Journal,* August 27, 2004, pp. B1, B2.

2. "Who's Running the *Inc.* 500?" *Inc. 500 Special Issue,* October 15, 2002, p. 32; "The Numbers Game," *Inc. 500 Special Issue,* October 15, 2002, p. 62.

3. Telephone interview with Jeff Kowell, CEO of Image Tree Service, January 23, 2004.

4. Galina Espinoza and Bob Meadows, "Phat Cats," *People,* July 1, 2002, pp. 97–98.

5. Vermont Teddy Bear Co. Web site, http://www.vermontteddybear.com, accessed January 30, 2004; Catherine Arnold, "Bear Hug," *Marketing News,* January 20, 2003, pp. 4, 7; Stephen D. Solomon, "Bear Feat," *Inc.,* October 17, 2000, pp. 167–168.

6. "Don Todrin & Fred Seibert," *Entrepreneur,* June 2002, p. 21.

7. Jim Hopkins, "Fewer Entrepreneurs Set Up Shop Last Year," *USA Today,* May 30, 2002, p. B2.

8. Hopkins, "Fewer Entrepreneurs Set Up Shop Last Year," p. B2.

9. Nancy J. Lyons, "Moonlight over Indiana," *Inc.com,* http://www.inc.com/magazine, accessed January 30, 2004.

10. Samantha Critchell, "Maternity Designer Liz Lange Loves Those Bulging Bellies," *Mobile Register,* April 28, 2003, p. D3; Debra Braggs, "Fashion Mother Lode," *Mobile Register,* April 28, 2003, pp. D1, D3; Nicole L. Torres et al., "Forever Young," *Entrepreneur,* November 2001, p. 60.

11. Tom Fetzer, "Never Say Die," *Success,* December–January 2001, p. 60.

12. "Andy Stenzler, 32," *Entrepreneur,* November 2001, p. 66.

13. PowerQuest Web site, http://www.powerquest.com, accessed January 24, 2004; Sara Callard, "'Supersize Those Fries!'" *Inc.,* October 17, 2000, p. 124.

14. "Sprint to Cut Jobs," *Mobile Register,* July 13, 2002, p. B7.

15. Louis E. Boone and David L. Kurtz, *The Impact of Terrorism.* Mason, OH: Thomson/South-Western, 2003, p. 42.

16. Stephanie Armour, "With Job Market Tight, Students Start Own Businesses," *USA Today,* March 5, 2002, p. B1.

17. Office of Advocacy, U.S. Small Business Administration, "The Facts about Small Business," SBA Web site, http://www.sba.gov/advo, January 15, 2004.

18. Torres, "Forever Young," p. 71.

19. "Welcome to Ipswitch," http://www.international.com, accessed January 26, 2004; Eleena de Lisser, "Start-up Attracts Staff with a Ban on Midnight Oil," *The Wall Street Journal,* August 23, 2000, pp. B1, B6.

20. Edu.com Web site, http://www.edu.com, accessed January 25, 2004; Leigh Buchanan, "Mother Is the Necessity of Invention," *Inc.,* January 2000, pp. 49, 51–52.

21. Marci McDonald, "A Start-Up of Her Own," *U.S. News & World Report,* May 15, 2000, pp. 34–38+.

22. "Women Pioneers in Technology," http://www.bren-bna.com/articles, January 25, 2004; Thaddeus Wawro, "Hero Worship," *Entrepreneur,* March 2000, pp. 114–121.

23. Rainbow Play Systems Web site, http://www.rainbowplay.com, accessed January 5, 2004; Joseph Conlin, "Natural Order," *Entrepreneur,* November 2001, pp. 72–74.

24. Faith Keenan, "Cloning: Huckster or Hero?" *BusinessWeek,* July 1, 2002, pp. 86–87.
25. ZWL Publishing Web site, http://www.business-china.com, accessed January 26, 2004; Moira Allen, "East Meets World," *Entrepreneur,* April 2000, p. 60.
26. "New Challenge for Thai 'Pizza King,'" *Taipei Times,* May 10, 2001, http://www.taipeitimes.com; Robert Horn, "Thailand's Big Cheese," *Time,* September 25, 2000, p. B13.
27. Thomas Melville, "Feeding the e-Frenzy," *Success,* December–January 2001, p. 58; Emily Barker, "The VC in My Dorm Room," *Inc.,* October 2000, pp. 42–45, 48.
28. Michelle Prather, "Child Stars," *Entrepreneur,* April 2002, p. 26.
29. Armour, "With Job Market Tight, Students Start Own Businesses," p. B1.
30. David Noonan, "Be Your Own Master," *Newsweek,* September 23, 2002, pp. 60–64.
31. Leesburg Pharmacy Web site, http://www.leesburgpharmacy.com, accessed January 23, 2004; Mill Pond Press Web site, http://www.millpond.com, accessed January 23, 2004; Lee Rainie, "MomandPop.com," *The Standard,* February 28, 2000, The Standard Web site, http://www.thestandard.com.
32. "Welcome to DSP Corporation," http://www.dspg.com, accessed January 26, 2004; Carleen Hawn, "Juggling Act," *Forbes,* November 1, 1999, pp. 242, 244.
33. Dooyoo.de Web site, http://www.dooyoo.de, accessed January 23, 2004; William Boston, "Berlin's 'Cool' Lifestyle Becomes a Magnet for Internet Start-up," *The Wall Street Journal,* February 29, 2000, pp. A17, A19.
34. National Commission on Entrepreneurship, "Fast Facts," Policy Makers Toolkit of the NCOE Web site, http://www.ncoe.org, January 25, 2004.
35. George Gendron, "The Origin of the Entrepreneurial Species," *Inc.,* February 2000, pp. 105–106+ (interview with Amar V. Bhidé).
36. "Welcome to OpenTable," http://www.metromix.opentable.com, accessed January 26, 2004.
37. Mini-Tankers International Web site, http://www.minitankers.com.au/, accessed January 27, 2003.
38. Kauffman Center for Entrepreneurial Leadership, "Entrepreneurship QuickFacts," http://www.celcee.edu/; NCOE, "Fast Facts." For more background on gazelles, see also the Cognetics Web site, http://www.cogonline.com.
39. Strategic Communications Group Web site, http://www.gotostrategic.com/aboutstrategic, accessed January 27, 2004; Sean M. Lyden, "Pass It On," *Business Start-ups,* February 2000, p. 62.
40. Tucker Technology Web site, http://www.innercity100.org, accessed January 27, 2004; Christopher Caggiano, "Insider Training," *Inc.,* May 1999, pp. 63–64.
41. Steven Levy, "Great Minds, Great Ideas," *Newsweek,* May 27, 2002, pp. 56–59.
42. Gendron, "The Origin of the Entrepreneurial Species," p. 106.
43. Gilat Satellite Network Web site, http://www.gilat.com, accessed January 27, 2004.
44. Levy, "Great Minds, Great Ideas," p. 58.
45. Kortney Stringer, "Time Out," *The Wall Street Journal,* March 27, 2002, p. B14; Thea Singer, "The Power of Balance," *Inc.,* October 17, 2000, pp. 105–108, 110.
46. Gendron, "The Origin of the Entrepreneurial Species," p. 110.
47. Lulu's Dessert Factory Web site, http://www.lulusdessert.com, accessed January 27, 2004; Michele Marrinan, "Stump the Slump," *Entrepreneur,* February 2002, pp. 90–94.
48. Mike Hofman, "Inside Innovative Minds," *Inc.,* September 2002, p. 78.
49. Geoff Williams, "Keep It Coming," *Entrepreneur,* April 2002, p. 100.
50. "Luster Organization," http://www.luster.com, accessed February 2, 2004.
51. Anne Stuart, "Where Do Great Ideas Come From?" *Inc. 500 Special Issue,* October 15, 2002, pp. 40, 42.
52. Gendron, "The Origin of the Entrepreneurial Species," pp. 109–110.
53. Hofman, "Inside Innovative Minds," p. 80.
54. "About Us," Aegis Software Web site, http://www.aegisoft.com, accessed January 24, 2004; Emily Barker, "When Creating Companies Is Habit-Forming," *Inc.,* October 17, 2000, p. 19.
55. Sylvia's Restaurant Web site, http://www.sylviassoulfood.com, accessed October 16, 2003; Wendy Beech, "Look before You Leap," *Black Enterprise,* September 1999, p. 96.
56. Hofman, "Inside Innovative Minds," p. 84.
57. "Corporate Leaders," HealthHelp Web site, http://www.hhni.com, accessed October 15, 2003; Emily Barker, "Red-Tape Brainstorms," *Inc.,* October 17, 2000, pp. 17–18; "Inc. 500: The List," *Inc.,* pp. 121, 123+.
58. Jill Andresky Fraser, "Seven Entrepreneurs in Search of a Deal," *Inc.,* April 2000, pp. 116–118, 120.
59. Sarah Bartlett, "Seat of the Pants," *Inc. 500 Special Issue,* October 15, 2002, pp. 38–40.
60. Ilan Mochari, "The Numbers Game," *Inc. 500 Special Issue,* October, 15, 2002, p. 62; Susan Greco, "A Little Goes a Long Way," *Inc. 500 Special Issue,* October 15, 2002, p. 66.
61. Williams, "Keep It Coming," pp. 101, 102.
62. "Welcome to Broudy Printing," http://www.broudyprinting.com, January 2, 2004; quotation from Jill Andresky Fraser, "How to Finance Anything," *Inc.,* March 1999, p. 39.
63. For an alternative source of financing, see Jim Hopkins, "Philanthropist Nurtures Tech Start-ups by Women," *USA Today,* January 22, 2002, p. B12.
64. Fraser, "Seven Entrepreneurs in Search of a Deal," p. 118; Martin Mayer, "A Borrower Be," *Inc.,* January 2003, pp. 86, 88.
65. Mochari, "The Numbers Game," p. 62.
66. Jim Hopkins, "Venture Capital Investments Plunge 23%," *USA Today,* May 1, 2002, p. B1.
67. Jim Hopkins, "Losses Grow for Venture Capitalists," *USA Today,* June 10, 2002, p. B1.
68. Russ Mitchell, "Too Much Ventured, Nothing Gained," *Fortune,* November 25, 2002, pp. 135–144; Nichole L. Torres, "Playing an Angel," *Entrepreneur,* May 2002, p. 130.
69. Elite.com Web site, http://www.elite.com, accessed January 2, 2004; Anne Marie Borrego, "Inside Play," *Inc.,* September 2000, pp. 74–76, 78–80.
70. "About Us" and "Management Team," eCompanies and Business.com Web sites, http://www.ecompanies.com and http://www.business.com, accessed January 23, 2004.

Chapter 7

1. "People Watching: Groceries with a Click," *Money,* July 2004, p. 33; Sonia Reyes, "FreshDirect Is Spreading the News of N.Y. Service," *Brandweek,* June 7, 2004, p. 35; Sonia Reyes, "Online Grocers: Ready to Deliver?" *Brandweek,* May 3, 2004, pp. 26–30; Jason Straziuso, "Internet Grocery Quietly Grows to $2.4 Billion Industry," *USA Today,* May 17, 2004, http://www.usatoday.com.
2. "The World's Online Populations," CyberAtlas Web site, http://cyberatlas.internet.com, March 21, 2002.
3. Mark Henricks, "Net Meeting," *Entrepreneur,* February 2003, pp. 53–55.

4. CyberAtlas, http://cyberatlas.internet.com, accessed March 28, 2002.
5. CyberAtlas Web site.
6. CyberAtlas Web site.
7. Henricks, "Net Meeting"; Robyn Greenspan, "Two-Thirds Hit the Net," CyberAtlas Web site, http://cyberatlas.internet.com, April 17, 2002.
8. Robyn Greenspan, "Small Biz Benefits from Internet Tools," CyberAtlas Web site, http://cyberatlas.internet.com, March 28, 2002.
9. Alessandra Bianchi, "E Is for E-School," *Inc.,* http://www.inc.com, accessed January 2004.
10. Steven Levy, "The World According to Google," *Newsweek,* December 16, 2002, pp. 47–51.
11. Gwendolyn Mariano, "Stock Fraud Spurs Regulators to Look Online," *CNET,* http://www.cnet.com, accessed January 2004.
12. Brad Stone, "Spammers ISO Respect," *Newsweek,* December 30, 2002–January 6, 2003, p.18.
13. Jill Lerner, "The Mom and Pop E-tailers Thrive," *Boston Business Journal,* January 31–February 6, 2003, pp. 1, 50.
14. Internet Indicators, http://www.internetindicators.com, accessed January 13, 2004.
15. IBM Web site, http://www.ibm.com, accessed January 13, 2004.
16. "Falling in Gov," *Entrepreneur,* March 2002, pp. 58–63.
17. Mark Hollmer, "Girl Scouts Take Cookie-Sales Operation High-Tech," *Boston Business Journal,* January 3–9, 2003, p. 6.
18. "CIO Web Business," *CIO,* http://www.cio.com, accessed March 29, 2002.
19. Timothy J. Mullaney, "The Web Is Finally Catching Profits," *BusinessWeek,* February 17, 2003; Jeff D. Opdyke, "Dot-Comeback: Internet Stocks Sizzle Again," *The Wall Street Journal,* February 18, 2003, pp. D1, D2.
20. Mullaney, "The Web Is Finally Catching Profits."
21. "CIO Web Business."
22. "CIO Web Business."
23. Amanda C. Kooser, "E-Biz Revisited," *Entrepreneur,* November 2002, p. 77.
24. "CIO Web Business."
25. "H. J. Heinz Company Case Study," *FreeMarkets.com,* http://www.freemarkets.com, accessed February 11, 2003.
26. Julie Hanson, "Online Services . . . Priceless," *CIO Magazine,* http://www.cio.com, February 1, 2003.
27. Steve Konicki, "Exchanges Go Private," *Information Week,* http://www.informationweek.com, March 29, 2002.
28. Robyn Greenspan, "2002 E-Commerce Holiday Wrap-up," CyberAtlas Web site, http://cyberatlas.internet.com, January 3, 2003.
29. Beth Cox, "Rising Tide Lifts E-Commerce Boats," CyberAtlas Web site, http://cyberatlas.internet.com, January 13, 2003.
30. Timothy J. Mullaney and Jay Greene, "Expedia: Changing Pilots in Mid-Climb," *BusinessWeek,* February 24, 2003, pp. 120–123.
31. Jupiter Media Metrix, http://www.jmm.com, March 28, 2002.
32. Jon Swartz, "More Buyers Click on Item on Web, Pick It Up at Store," *USA Today,* December 6, 2002, p. B1.
33. CNBC News, November 14, 2002.
34. Marcia Stepanek, "None of Your Business," *BusinessWeek Online,* http://www.bwonline.com, March 28, 2002.
35. Stepanek, "None of Your Business."
36. "Privacy Groups Ask for Investigation of Amazon.com," *ZDNET News,* http://www.zdnet.com, March 29, 2002; Nick Wingfield, "Amazon Clarifies Customer Info Policy," *The Wall Street Journal,* http://www.zdnet.com, March 29, 2002.
37. Wingfield, "Amazon Clarifies Customer Info Policy."
38. "PrivaSeek E-Wallet Protects Privacy," *PC World,* http://www.pcworld.com, March 21, 2002.
39. "How to Comply with the Children's Online Privacy Protection Rule," *Federal Trade Commission,* http://www.ftc.gov, accessed January 5, 2004.
40. Nick Wingfield, "The Rise and Fall of Web Shopping at Work," *The Wall Street Journal,* September 27, 2002, p. B1.
41. Brian McWilliams, "Comdex Attendees' Personal Data Exhibited on the Web," *Newsbytes,* http://www.newsbytes.com, March 18, 2002.
42. Alex Salkever, "The New Hurry to Foil Hackers," *BusinessWeek,* February 24, 2003, p. 16.
43. Federal Trade Commission, http://www.ftc.gov, accessed March 21, 2002; Internet Fraud Complaint Center, http://www1.ifccfbi.gov, accessed March 21, 2002.
44. Jon Swartz, "Fighting Back," *USA Today,* September 19, 2002, p. B3.
45. Melissa Campanelli, "Caught in the Web of Lies," *Tech,* January 2003, pp. 37–38.
46. Akamai Web site, http://www.akami.com, accessed January 16, 2004.
47. CyberAtlas, http://cyberatlas.internet.com, March 28, 2002.
48. "Sky High Performance," *CIO,* http://www.cio.com, March 27, 2002.
49. Bob Duncan, "First Do No Harm," *Inc. Technology,* http://www.inc.com, March 27, 2002.
50. Mike Musgrove, "Hollings Proposes Copyright Defense," *Washington Post,* http://www.washingtonpost.com, March 26, 2002.
51. "The Fourth Annual Inc. Web Awards," *Inc.,* December 2002, p. 94.
52. Nick Wingfield, "The Game of the Name," *The Wall Street Journal,* http://www.zdnet.com, March 29, 2002; "Fiercely Stupid," *Newsweek,* March 25, 2002, p. 2.
53. "The Fourth Annual Inc. Web Awards," *Inc.,* December 2002, p. 94.
54. Big Step Web site, http://www.bigstep.com, accessed January 16, 2004.
55. CyberAtlas, http://cyberatlas.internet.com, accessed March 29, 2002.
56. Big Step Web site.
57. CyberAtlas Web site, accessed March 29, 2002.
58. J. William Gurley, "The One Internet Metric That Really Matters," *Fortune,* http://www.fortune.com, March 29, 2002.
59. "Success Story: Lexmark International," *WebCriteria,* http://www.webcriteria.com, March 18, 2002.
60. CyberAtlas, http://cyberatlas.internet.com.
61. Manjeet Kripalani, "Wired Villages," *BusinessWeek,* October 14, 2002, p. 116.
62. CyberAtlas, http://cyberatlas.internet.com.
63. CyberAtlas Web site.
64. Katarzyna Moreno, "Global Pains," *Forbes,* http://www.forbes.com, March 29, 2002.

Chapter 8

1. James Brady, "In Step with Donald Trump," *Parade,* November 14, 2004, p. 30; Mark Burnett, "An Adventure with No Ending," *Brandweek,* October 11, 2004, pp. M58–M61; Alfred A. Edmond, Jr., "Make-or-Break Leadership Lessons from The Apprentice," *Black Enterprise,* May 2004, pp. 108–114; Daniel Roth, "The Trophy Life," *Fortune,* April 19, 2004, pp. 70–83; Jonathan Storm, "'Apprentice' Addiction: Why Have So Many Bought a Business Show?" *Mobile Register,* April 15, 2004, p. 4D.
2. Mark Grimlin, "Mayor Mogul," *Fortune,* April 1, 2002, pp. 96–104; Matt Bai, "Mayor Mike, Inc.," *Newsweek,* April 22, 2002, pp. 29–44; "The Other Bloomberg," *Fortune,* April 1, 2002, p. 100.
3. "3M Reports Higher Fourth Quarter, Calendar Year 2002 Sales and Earnings," 3M Worldwide press release, January 21, 2003, http://www.3m.com.

4. Jennifer L. Brown, "Sonic President Takes Job Personally," *The Morning News,* May 5, 2002, p. C8.

5. Yudhijit Bhattacharjee, "A Swarm of Little Notes," *Time,* Inside Business section, September 2002, pp. A4–A8.

6. Special Report: The 2002 E.Biz 25, "Meg Whitman's Bid for Growth," *BusinessWeek,* October 21, 2002, http://www.businessweek.com; Hillary Johnson, "Meg Whitman," *Worth,* June 2002, p. 59.

7. Del Jones, "Dell: Take Time to Build," *USA Today,* October 10, 2002, p. B6.

8. Loretta Kalb, Cathleen Ferraro, and Paul Schnitt, "Unmasking Corporate Greed," *The Sacramento Bee,* September 22, 2002, http://www.sacbee.com.

9. Michael Peltz, "Sidney Taurel," *Worth,* June 2002, p. 70.

10. Jones, "Dell: Take Time to Build."

11. HP advertisement, *USA Today,* May 7, 2002, p. A5.

12. "Our Company—Corporate Information," Walgreens Web site, http://www.walgreens.com, accessed January 5, 2004.

13. Derek Slater, "Loan Star," *CIO* Web site, http://www.cio.com, June 12, 2002.

14. Starbucks Corporation Annual Report, http://www.starbucks.com, accessed January 5, 2004; press releases, Starbucks Web site, http://www.starbucks.com, accessed June 13, 2002.

15. "Benefits and Incentives," "Awards," and press releases, Continental Airlines Web site, http://www.continental.com, accessed January 5, 2004.

16. "Heinz World," Heinz Web site, http://www.heinz.com, accessed January 6, 2004; H. J. Heinz press releases, http://www.heinz.com, accessed June 13, 2002.

17. Larry Kanter, "Richard D. Fairbank," *Worth,* June 2002, p. 77.

18. Arlene Weintraub, "Gateway: Picking Fights It Just Might Lose," *BusinessWeek,* September 9, 2002, p. 52.

19. Thomas Kellner, "One Man's Trash . . . ," *Forbes,* March 4, 2002, pp. 96–98.

20. Louis Lavelle, "Another Crop of Sleazy CEOs?" *BusinessWeek,* August 26, 2002, p. 12.

21. Edward Sussman, "The Best CEOs," *Worth,* June 2002, pp. 58–80.

22. Sally B. Donnelly, "One Airline's Magic," *Time,* October 28, 2002.

23. "Living Our Values," Home Depot Web site, http://www.careers.homedepot.com/values, accessed January 7, 2004; Lorrie Grant, "Home Depot's Chief Builds on Big Dreams," *USA Today,* June 14, 2002, pp. B1, B2; Daintry Duffy, "Cultural Evolution," *CIO Enterprise,* CIO Web site, http://www.cio.com, accessed June 14, 2002.

24. Mike Hofman, "From Boardroom to Steam Room," *Inc. Magazine,* April 2002, p. 132.

25. Jennifer Merritt, "For UPS Managers, a School of Hard Knocks," *BusinessWeek,* July 22, 2002, pp. 58–59.

26. "The State of the Church," *Time,* April 1, 2002, pp. 32–33.

27. Karl Greenberg, "No Missing Links: Chrysler Group Divides to Conquer," *BrandWeek,* June 24, 2002, p. 3.

28. Jerry Useem, "3M + GE = ?" *Fortune,* August 12, 2002, pp. 127–132.

29. Joan Raymond, "George Schaefer," *Worth,* June 2002, p. 69.

30. "100 Best Companies to Work For, SAS Institute," *Fortune,* January 20, 2003.

Chapter 9

1. Janet Guyon, "U.S. Workers Want out of the Kingdom," *Fortune,* July 12, 2004, p. 32; Ilana Ozernoy, "When Doctors Are the Victims," *U.S. News & World Report,* June 28–July 5, 2004, p. 30; Rick Hampson, "Many Accept Risks of Working Overseas," *USA Today,* June 21, 2004, http://www.usatoday.com; Michael Cowden, "Doing Businesss in a War Zone," *Medill News Service,* May 8, 2004, http://cbs.markewatch.com; Jeremy Kahn and Nelson D. Scwhartz, "Private Sector Soldiers," *Fortune,* May 3, 2004, pp. 33–36.

2. Client Stories, *ADP Total Source,* http://www.adptotalsource.com, accessed June 20, 2002.

3. Trilogy Web site, http://www.trilogy.com, accessed January 4, 2004.

4. Aaron Bernstein, "Too Many Workers? Not for Long," *BusinessWeek,* May 20, 2002, graph on p. 127.

5. Bernstein, "Too Many Workers? Not for Long," pp. 126–130.

6. "EEOC and CBS Settle Sex Bias Suit for $8 Million," EEOC news release, http://www.eeoc.gov, accessed June 21, 2002.

7. Robert Levering and Milton Moskowitz, "100 Best Companies to Work For," *Fortune,* February 2003, p. 128.

8. Levering and Moskowitz, "100 Best Companies to Work For," p. 130.

9. Patricia Sellers, "Something to Prove," *Fortune,* http://www.fortune.com, accessed June 21, 2002.

10. "Traveling Beyond 360-Degree Evaluations," *HR Magazine,* http://www.shrm.org, accessed June 22, 2002.

11. Daniel Wood, "Living Wage Laws Gain Momentum across the U.S.," *The Christian Science Monitor,* http://www.csmonitor.com, accessed June 22, 2002.

12. Leonard Wiener, "Paycheck Plus," *U.S. News & World Report,* February 24–March 3, 2003, p. 58.

13. "Best Benefits," *Money,* December 2002, pp. 160–161.

14. Levering and Moskowitz, "100 Best Companies to Work For," p. 128.

15. Ron Lieber and Barbara Martinez, "Companies Pass the Buck on Benefits," *The Wall Street Journal,* November 26, 2002, p. D1.

16. Lieber and Martinez, "Companies Pass the Buck on Benefits," pp. D1, D3.

17. "Best Benefits," p. 161.

18. Julie Appleby, "Employers Get Nosy about Workers' Health," *USA Today,* March 6, 2003, pp. B1–B2.

19. Chris Penttila, "First Family," *Entrepreneur,* January 2003, p. 29.

20. Christopher Rhoads, "Short Work Hours Undercut Europe in Economic Drive," *The Wall Street Journal,* August 8, 2002, pp. A1, A6.

21. Lieber and Martinez, "Companies Pass the Buck on Benefits," pp. D1, D3.

22. "Best Benefits," p. 161.

23. Levering and Moskowitz, "100 Best Companies to Work For," pp. 128–130.

24. Deborah Myers, "Cafeteria Plans Offer Flexible Insurance Options," *Alaska Business Monthly,* April 2002, p. 74.

25. Levering and Moskowitz, "100 Best Companies to Work For," p. 130.

26. Levering and Moskowitz, "100 Best Companies to Work For," p. 140.

27. "Keeping it Flexible," *Inc.,* October 15, 2002, http://www.inc.com.

28. Linda White, "Flex Time: A Win-Win Situation for Work and Home," *The Toronto Sun,* February 13, 2002, p. C1.

29. L. A. Lorek, "Telecommuting Saves Businesses, Agencies Millions," *SiliconValley.com,* October 28, 2002, http://www.siliconvalley.com.

30. Anne Fisher, "Do I Fire the Bottom 10% Just Because Jack Did?" *Fortune,* September 2, 2002, p. 210.

31. "Army Considers Outsourcing 214,000 Jobs," *USA Today,* November 3, 2002, http://www.usatoday.com.

32. Michelle Conlin, "And Now, the Just-in-Time Employee," *BusinessWeek,* http://www.businessweek.com, accessed June 25, 2002.

33. Wendy Cole, "Stay Connected," *Time Inside Business,* April 2003.

34. Michelle Conlin, "Now It's Getting Personal," *BusinessWeek,* December 16, 2002, pp. 90–92.

35. Pampered Chef Web site, http://www.pamperedchef.com, accessed January 6, 2004.

36. Joshua Kurlantzick, "United We Fall?" *Entrepreneur,* March 2003, p. 13.

37. Eryn Brown, "Fallout," *Fortune,* October 28, 2002, p. 32; Lisa Stein, "Ports of Call," *U.S. News & World Report,* October 21, 2002, p. 14.

38. Steven Greenhouse, "Labor Opens a Drive to Organize Wal-Mart," *The New York Times,* November 8, 2002, http://www.nytimes.com.

Chapter 10

1. Whole Foods Annual Report, *2003 Annual Report,* http://www.wholefoodsmarket.com/investor/annualreports.html, accessed November 18, 2004; Company Web site, http://www.wholefoods.com, accessed September 30, 2004; Chris Fishman, "The Anarchist's Cookbook," *Fast Company,* July 2004, pp. 70–78.

2. "About A&A," Anderson & Associates Web site, http://www.andassoc.com, accessed January 2, 2004.

3. Doug Bartholomew, "One Product, One Customer," *Industry Week,* October 2002, http://www.industryweek.com.

4. Francine Russo, "Palmer's People," *Time* Web site, http://www.time.com, accessed July 3, 2002.

5. National Center for Employee Ownership, "A Statistical Profile of Employee Ownership," April 2002, http://www.nceo.org.

6. "A Statistical Profile of Employee Ownership."

7. Tom Woodruff, "Punch a Clock and Still Earn Stock?" CNBC, MSN Investor Web site, http://investor.msn.com, accessed July 3, 2002.

8. David Leonhardt, "Option Math: Why So Many to So Few?" *The New York Times,* February 16, 2003, Section 3, pp. 1, 11; Corey Rosen, "Are We Stepping Away from Democratizing Capital?" *The Employee Ownership Report* (newsletter for NCEO members), January 2003, http://www.nceo.org; Joseph Blasi, Douglas Kruse, and Aaron Bernstein, "Stock Options: The Right Way to Go," adapted from *In the Company of Owners: The Truth About Stock Options,* New York: Basic Books, 2003, in *Business Week Online,* January 20, 2003, http://www.businessweek.com; Aaron Bernstein, "Stock Options: Fuel for United's Revival?" *BusinessWeek,* November 8, 2002, http://www.businessweek.com.

9. Faith Keenan and Spencer Ante, "The New Teamwork," *BusinessWeek e.biz,* February 18, 2002, pp. EB12–16.

10. "Whole Foods Market Makes *Fortune* Magazine's '100 Best Companies to Work For' List for Sixth Consecutive Year," company press release, January 21, 2003, http://www.wholefoods.com; "100 Best Companies to Work For," *Fortune,* January 20, 2003, http://www.fortune.com; Ed Carberry, "Hypergrowth Strategy: Create an Ownership Culture," *Inc.com* Case Study, December 1, 1999.

11. Bob Nelson, "Energizing Teams of Hourly Workers," *Bob Nelson's Rewarding Employees* (newsletter), *Inc.* Web site, http://www.inc.com, accessed July 17, 2002.

12. Mallory Stark, "The Five Keys to Successful Teams," *Working Knowledge from Harvard Business School,* PricewaterhouseCoopers Web site, http://www.pwcglobal.com, accessed January 22, 2003.

13. Mary Brandel, "Teamwork Buoys Big Audio at Bose," *ComputerWorld,* February 11, 2002, http://www.computerworld.com.

14. Jill Jusko, "Seeing Is Believing," *Industry Week,* October 2002, http://www.industryweek.com.

15. Julie Bick, "Inside the Smartest Little Company in America," *Inc.,* January 2002, p. 59.

16. "Levi Strauss & Co. Announces Fourth-Quarter and Fiscal 2001 Financial Results," press release, Levi Strauss Web site, http://www.levistrauss.com, accessed July 17, 2002; N. Munk, "How Levi's Trashed a Great American Brand," *Fortune* Web site, http://www.fortune.com, accessed July 17, 2002.

17. "What Makes Teams Work," *Fast Company* Web site, http://www.fastcompany.com, accessed July 17, 2002.

18. "Thriving after Restructuring," *BusinessWeek* Web site, http://www.businessweek.com, accessed July 9, 2002.

19. Rodes Fishburne, "More Survival Advice," *Forbes ASAP, Forbes* Web site, http://www.forbes.com, accessed July 17, 2002.

20. Shawn Tully, "The Jamie Dimon Show," *Fortune* Web site, http://www.fortune.com, accessed July 9, 2002.

21. Patricia Sellers, "Something to Prove," *Fortune* Web site, http://www.fortune.com, accessed July 10, 2002.

22. Traci Purdum, "Viewpoint—Dealing the Dirt," *IndustryWeek,* February 5, 2002, http://www.industryweek.com; Susan Bixler and Lisa Scherrer Dugan, "Being on the Grapevine Can Boost Your Career," *IT People,* December 10, 2001, http://www.expressitpeople.com.

23. Albert Mehrabian, *Silent Messages.* Belmont, California: Wadsworth, 1971; Albert Mehrabian, "Communication without Words," *Psychology Today,* September 1968, pp. 53–55.

24. Quentin Hardy, "All Carly, All the Time," *Forbes* Web site, http://www.forbes.com, accessed July 17, 2002.

25. Based on Richard Daft and Dorothy Marcic, *Understanding Management,* 3rd ed. Mason, Ohio: South-Western, 2001, pp. 456–457.

26. Anne Stuart, "Going Mobile," *Inc.,* December 2002, pp. 124–125.

27. Royal Dutch Shell, *The Shell Report: People, Planet, and Profits,* Shell Web site, http://www.shell.com, accessed July 12, 2002.

28. Jim Sterne, "At Your Service," *Inc.* Web site, http://www.inc.com, accessed July 17, 2002.

Chapter 11

1. Joann Muller, "Saving Chrysler," *Forbes,* August 16, 2004, pp. 58–64; David Kiley, "Big 3 Improve Dependability," *USA Today,* http://usatoday.com, accessed July 20, 2004; Jean Halliday, "Automakers Expand Their High-Power Niche," *Advertising Age,* June 28, 2004, p. S-8; Kathleen Kerwin, "Chrysler Puts Some Muscle on the Street," *BusinessWeek,* June 7, 2004, pp. 72, 74; David Kiley and James R. Healey, "GM Plans to Boldly Go after Niche Markets," *USA Today,* February 19, 2004, p. B3; Kathleen Kerwin, "When Flawless Isn't Enough," *BusinessWeek,* December 8, 2003, pp. 80–82.

2. Stephane Fitch, "The Progress of Change—Inch by Inch," *Forbes,* May 13, 2002, p. 88.

3. "TextChoice," Thomson Learning Custom Publishing, Thomson Publishing Web site, http://archive.thomson.com, accessed January 13, 2004.

4. "Better in Brazil," *U.S. News & World Report,* April 1, 2002, p. 28.

5. "Pella Corporation: Celebrating 75 years of Innovation," Pella Corporation Web site, http://www.pella.com, accessed January 13, 2004; "TBM Consulting Client Results," TBM Consulting Web site, http://www.tbmconsulting.com, accessed June 5, 2002; Philip Siekman, "Glass Act: How a Window Maker Rebuilt Itself," *Fortune* Web site, http://www.fortune.com, accessed June 5, 2002.

6. Gene Bylinsky, "America's Elite Factories," *Fortune* Web site, http://www.fortune.com, accessed June 5, 2002.

7. Gary S. Vasilash, "Honda's Hat Trick," Automotive Manufacturing and Production Web site, http://www.autofieldguide.com, accessed January 13, 2004.

8. Philip Longman, "The Next Big Thing Is Small," *U.S. News & World Report,* U.S. News Web site, http://www.usnews.com, accessed January 13, 2004.

9. Adam Lashinsky, "Another Valley Vacancy," *Fortune,* March 17, 2003, p. 38.

10. Micheline Maynard, "Amid the Turmoil, a Rare Success for Chrysler," *Fortune* Web site, http://www.fortune.com, accessed January 13, 2004; Jeffrey Ball and Scott Miller, "Zetsche to Cut Chrysler Incentives and Revamp Car Assembly Lines," *The Wall Street Journal* Web site, http://interactive.wsj.com, accessed June 7, 2002.

11. Vasilash, "Honda's Hat Trick."

12. Ford Motor Company press releases, Ford Web site, http://media .ford.com, accessed January 13, 2004; Jeff Rothfeder, "Know-It-Alls," *Executive Edge,* August–September 1999, pp. 39–43.

13. Fitch, "The Progress of Change—Inch by Inch"; Allison Linn, "Boeing Moving Right Along," *The Morning News,* April 12, 2002, p. 7C.

14. "About FreeMarkets," FreeMarkets press release, FreeMarkets Web site, http://www.freemarkets.com, accessed January 13, 2004.

15. Anne D'Innocenzio, "2nd Chance for Customizing," *The Morning News,* April 14, 2002, p. 3C.

16. Jeff Sabatini, "Turning Japanese," Automotive Manufacturing and Production Web site, http://www.autofieldguide.com, accessed January 13, 2004.

17. Robyn Meredith, "Accidental Audis," *Forbes,* January 20, 2003, p. 44.

18. "Making Customers Feel Six Sigma Quality," General Electric Web site, http://www.ge.com, accessed January 14, 2004.

19. "The ISO Survey of ISO 9000 and ISO 14000 Certificates," ISO Web site, http://www.iso.ch, accessed January 13, 2004.

Chapter 12

1. Pete Engardio, Josey Puliyenthuruthel, and Manjeet Kripalani, "Fortress India?" *BusinessWeek,* August 16, 2004, pp. 42–43; Elizabeth Corcoran, "Unoutsourcing," *Forbes,* May 10, 2004, pp. 50–51; Spencer E. Ante, "Shifting Work Offshore? Outsourcer Beware," *BusinessWeek,* January 12, 2004, pp. 36–37; Justin Fox, "Hang-ups in India," *Fortune,* December 22, 2003, p. 44; Barbara Hagenbaugh, "Moving Work Abroad Tough for Some Firms," *USA Today,* December 3, 2003, p. B1.

2. Company Web site, http://www.geox.com, accessed February 2, 2004; Mercedes M. Cardona, "Italian Shoemaker Moving into U.S.," *Advertising Age,* December 17, 2001, pp. 1, 22.

3. Todd Wasserman, "BellSouth Lends an Ear to Customer Concerns," *Brandweek,* July 29, 2002, p. 8.

4. Ronald Alsop, "Reputations Rest on Good Service," *The Wall Street Journal,* January 16, 2002, pp. B1, B4.

5. Alex Taylor, III, "Got $300,000?" *Fortune,* January 20, 2003, pp. 119–124.

6. Alsop, "Reputations Rest on Good Service."

7. "About Circles," http://www.circles.com, accessed January 18, 2004.

8. Frances Hesselbein, *Hesselbein on Leadership.* San Francisco: Jossey-Bass, 2002, p. 111.

9. Data from American Association of Fundraising Counsel Trust for Philanthropy, in "The Big Picture," *BusinessWeek,* July 20, 2002, p. 14.

10. Company Web site, http://www.musicplayground.com, accessed February 2, 2004.

11. Company Web site, http://www.mrsbeasleys.com, accessed February 3, 2004.

12. Company Web site, http://www.nestle.com, accessed February 3, 2004.

13. "Company," Oshkosh Truck Corp.'s Web site, http://www.oshkosh truck.com, accessed April 9, 2003.

14. Becky Ebenkamp, "Youth Shall Be Served," *Brandweek,* June 24, 2002, pp. 21–23.

15. Arundhati Parmar, "Net Research Is Not Quite Global," *Marketing News,* March 3, 2003, p. 51.

16. John Harwood and Shirley Leung, "Why Some Pollsters Got It So Wrong on Election Day," *The Wall Street Journal,* January 8, 2002, pp. A1, A6.

17. Nanci Hellmich, "Want Some Blue Fries with That Shake?" *USA Today,* March 21, 2002, http://www.usatoday.com.

18. Julie Schlosser, "Looking for Intelligence in Ice Cream," *Fortune,* March 17, 2003, pp. 114–120.

19. Owen Thomas, "Lord of the Things," *Business 2.0,* March 2002, http:// www.business2.com.

20. Michael S. Garver, "Try New Data-Mining Techniques," *Marketing News,* September 16, 2002, p. 31.

21. Marc Gunther, "The Future of Television," *Fortune,* April 1, 2002, pp. 105–112.

22. Hillary Chura, "Marketing Messages for Women Fall Short," *Advertising Age,* September 23, 2002, p. 4.

23. Pamela Sebastian Ridge, "Tool Sellers Tap Their Feminine Side," *The Wall Street Journal,* March 29, 2002, p. B1.

24. Chura, "Marketing Messages for Women Fall Short," pp. 4, 14.

25. Michael McCarthy, "Some Consumers Want Ads for a Mature Audience," *USA Today,* November 19, 2002, p. B1.

26. McCarthy, "Some Consumers Want Ads for a Mature Audience."

27. Diane Scharper, "Study Shows Young Generation's Brand-Name Playgrounds," *USA Today,* April 21, 2003, p. B6; Becky Ebenkamp, "Youth Shall Be Served," *Brandweek,* June 24, 2002, p. 21.

28. Ebenkamp, "Youth Shall Be Served"; Martin Lindstrom, *Brandchild: Remarkable Insights into the Minds of Today's Global Kids and Their Relationships with Brands.* New York: Kogan Page, 2003.

29. Sally Beatty, "Avon Is Set to Call on Teens," *The Wall Street Journal,* October 17, 2002, p. B1.

30. Karl Greenberg, "Respect," *Brandweek,* April 14, 2003, pp. 28–32; Genaro C. Armas, "Hispanics Outnumber Blacks as Largest Minority Group," *Mobile Register,* January 22, 2003, p. A3.

31. Todd Wasserman, "JP Morgan Chase Makes Major Move to Minorities," *Brandweek,* November 25, 2002, p. 5.

32. Company Web sites, accessed February 4, 2004.

33. "Consumer Products Firms Target Hair-Care Market for Growth," http://www.keratin.com/ar/ar036.shtml, accessed February 1, 2004.

34. "Work That's Never Done," *Brandweek,* March 3, 2003, pp. 30–36.

35. Sandra Dolbow, "Catering to the Well-Heeled," *Brandweek,* October 28, 2002, pp. 26–29.

36. "Schwab Signature Services," http://www.schwab-online.com, accessed February 1, 2004.

37. Sonia Reyes, "Marketers Get Creative to Fit Needs of Retailers, Time-Pressed Consumers," *Brandweek,* May 13, 2002, p. 13.

38. Peter Engardio, "Epidemics & Economics," *BusinessWeek,* April 28, 2003, pp. 44–47; Clay Chandler, "Masks Can't Stop This Virus," *Fortune,* April 28, 2003, p. 42; "Perspectives," *Newsweek,* April 21, 2003, p. 19; Barbara De Lollis, "Recession Changed Biz Travel Forever," *USA Today,* April 21, 2003, p. B1; Alan Wan, "SARS Infects Business Worldwide," *CBSMarketWatch.com,* accessed April 20, 2003.

39. "U.S. Theme Park Attendance Is Down," *Mobile Register,* December 24, 2002, p. B12.

40. MasterCare Car Service Web site, accessed February 9, 2004, http:// www.mastercare-usa.com.

41. Mike Beirne, "Up in the Air," *Brandweek,* December 16, 2002, p. 3.

42. L. L. Bean Catalog, Summer 2003.

43. Steve Kerch, "New Divas of Decorating: Man," http://www.CBS .marketwatch.com, accessed June 25, 2003; "News Roundup," *Brandweek,* March 18, 2002, p. 10.

44. "So You've Decided to Buy Kolcraft Jeep Strollers!" http://www .healthacres.com/childrenhealthsafety/Kolcraftjeepstrollers.shtml, accessed January 15, 2004.

45. "How Sports Teams Play One-on-One Marketing," http://www .alternetics.com/articles/, accessed January 16, 2004.

Chapter 13

1. "Kodak Digs into Digital," *BusinessWeek,* September 6, 2004, p. 56; Beth Snyder Bulik, "Sony, Kodak Lead U.S. Battle for Share in Digital Cameras," *Advertising Age,* May 31, 2004, p. 12; Faith Arner and Rachel Tipidy, "No Excuse Not to Succeed," *BusinessWeek,* May 10, 2004,

pp. 96–98; Stephen Manes, "Invasion of the Photo Kiosks!" *Forbes,* May 10, 2004, p. 160.

2. Kevin Maney, "Wireless E-Mail Likely to Get Boost from Dell," *USA Today,* May 5, 2003, p. B1; "CEO Speaks: Muscling into New Markets," *Money,* November 2002, pp. 49–50.

3. "Dockers Makes Its Move from Slacks to Sheets," *Brandweek,* October 21, 2002, p. 8.

4. "McMarketing," *BusinessWeek,* August 12, 2002, p. 8.

5. Peter M. Nichols, "Older Viewers Turn to DVDs," *The New York Times,* March 28, 2003, http://www.nytimes.com; Chris Sandlund, "Remember When," *Entrepreneur,* January 2003, p. 17.

6. Robert Berner et al., "Has Target's Food Foray Missed the Mark?" *BusinessWeek,* November 25, 2002, p. 76.

7. Cara B. DiPasquale, "Zippo: Rebel Has New Cause," *Advertising Age,* July 8, 2002, pp. 3, 40.

8. Bob Sperber, "Brand Builders: Little Burgers Bulk Up," *Brandweek,* March 3, 2003, pp. 20, 22.

9. Don Debelak, "Want Some of This?" *Entrepreneur,* June 2002, pp. 124–127.

10. Debelak, "Want Some of This?"

11. "Top 10 American Brands," April 4, 2003, p. B2; Gerry Kermouch, "The Best Global Brands," *BusinessWeek,* August 5, 2002, pp. 92–96.

12. Andrew Raskin, "Who's Minding the Store?" *Business 2.0,* February 2003, pp. 70–74.

13. Michael Krauss, "Dell Looks to Sears to Extend Buyer Reach," *Marketing News,* April 28, 2003, p. 8; Hamlin quotation from Gary McWilliams and Ann Zimmerman, "Dell Plans to Peddle PCs Inside Sears, Other Large Chains," *The Wall Street Journal,* January 3, 2003, pp. B1, B3.

14. Holly J. Morris, "You've Got DVD-Mail," *U.S. News & World Report,* September 9, 2002, p. 71.

15. Theresa Howard, "Sears Opens Shelves to Lands' End," *USA Today,* November 29, 2002, p. B3.

16. Carol Emert, "Vintage 1999 IPOs Sour at Record Rate," *San Francisco Chronicle,* September 19, 2002, http://www.sfgate.com.

17. Robyn Greenspan, "Apparel Sales Apparent Online," *CyberAtlas,* March 28, 2003, http://cyberatlas.internet.com.

18. Julie Rawe, "A Mini-Mall in Your ATM," *Time,* April 8, 2002, p. 61.

19. Jane Spencer, "Ignore That Knocking: Door-to-Door Sales Make a Comeback," *The Wall Street Journal,* April 30, 2003, pp. D1, D2.

20. Berner et al., "Has Target's Food Foray Missed the Mark?"

21. Maria Puente, "Mall of Them All Turns 10," *USA Today,* August 9, 2002, pp. D1, D6.

22. David Kirkpatrick, "How to Erase the Middleman in One Easy Lesson," *Fortune,* March 17, 2003, p. 122.

23. "Your Home Fitness Solution," http://www.bowflex.com, accessed January 20, 2004.

24. Dale Buss, "Crossing the Channel," *Sales & Marketing Management,* October 2002, pp. 43–48.

25. Virginia Postrel, "Lessons in Keeping Business Humming, Courtesy of Wal-Mart U.," *The New York Times,* February 28, 2002, http://www.nytimes.com.

26. Raskin, "Who's Minding the Store?"

27. "The Lifelong Lure of the Open Road," *U.S. News & World Report,* February 18, 2002, p. 48.

28. Tom Bemis, "For Railroads, It's All Aboard High Tech," *CBS Marketwatch.com,* February 20, 2003.

Chapter 14

1. Anthony Bianco, "The Vanishing Mass Market," *BusinessWeek,* July 12, 2004, pp. 61–72; Devin Leonard, "Nightmare on Madison Avenue," *Fortune,* June 28, 2004, pp. 93–108; Betsy Streisand, "TV Tuning Out," *U.S. News & World Report,* May 24, 2004, pp. 46–47; Robert Yallen, "Marketers: DRTV Can Be Your Friend," *Brandweek,* May 10, 2004, p. 24; Dean Foust and Brian Grow, "Coke: Wooing the TiVo Generation," *BusinessWeek,* March 1, 2004, pp. 77, 80.

2. Chuck Stogel, "Nike Golf Spring Swing Plays around with Sweeps, Fox Sports Net's BDSSP," *Brandweek,* February 24, 2003, p. 6.

3. Greg Farrell, "CPAs Look for an Ad Agency to Rebuild Image," *USA Today,* February 26, 2003, p. B2.

4. Jennifer Waters, "No Mo' Philip Morris; It's Altria Now," *CBSMarketWatch.com,* January 27, 2003.

5. Jeffrey McKinney, "Rags to Riches," *Black Enterprise,* September 2002, pp. 99–104.

6. Sean Carton, "Lessons from an Oil Change Sticker," *Small Business Computing,* April 17, 2003, http://www.smallbusinesscomputing.com.

7. Louis Chunovic, "Trying to Price Placement," *Advertising Age,* December 2, 2002, p. 4; Wayne Friedman, "Product Placements Rise at CBS," *Advertising Age,* September 23, 2002, p. 8.

8. Dale Buss, "A Product Placement Hall of Fame," *Business Week Online,* http://www.businessweek.com, accessed April 16, 2003.

9. Olivia Barker, "Dude, the Spring Break Beach Scene Is So Over," *USA Today,* March 22, 2002, p. D8.

10. Sonia Reyes, "Brand's Best Friend," *Brandweek,* December 9, 2002, p. 28.

11. Vanessa O'Connell, "GM to Sing the Songs Chevy Inspired," *The Wall Street Journal,* October 1, 2002, p. B10.

12. Joe Flint, "As Cable Gains in Prime Time, Broadcasters' Cachet Is at Stake," *The Wall Street Journal,* May 8, 2003, pp. A1, A8.

13. Chris Taylor, "To Dish or Not to Dish," *Time,* October 28, 2002, p. 70.

14. Geoffrey A. Fowler, "Junk Mailers Discover Asia Is Close to Heaven," *The Wall Street Journal,* March 5, 2003, p. B1.

15. Paul Davidson, "AOL Tech Army Goes on Hunt to Find, Zap Spam," *USA Today,* May 8, 2003, p. B3.

16. Stephen H. Wildstrom, "Hitting Spammers Where It Hurts," *BusinessWeek,* May 19, 2003, p. 20; John Swartz and Paul Davidson, "Spam Thrives Despite Effort to Screen It Out," *USA Today,* May 8, 2003, pp. A1, A2; Julie Creswell, "A New Way to Can E-mail Spam," *Fortune,* April 28, 2003, p. 34; David Lagesse, "That Damned Spam," *U.S. News & World Report,* April 28, 2003, pp. 50–51; Huseman quotation from Janet Kornblum, "Spam? No Thanks, We're Full," *USA Today,* January 13, 2003, p. D6.

17. Mylene Mangalindan, "Direct Marketers Help Fight Spam," *The Wall Street Journal,* February 25, 2003, p. D4.

18. Tobi Elkin, "Marketing beyond the Pop-up," *Advertising Age,* March 10, 2003, p. 40.

19. Amy Hernandez and Bill Thomas, "Research Studies Gauge Sponsorship ROI," *Marketing News,* May 12, 2003, pp. 16–17.

20. Chris Jenkins, "Wanted: Salesman, Must Drive," *USA Today,* July 12, 2002, pp. A1, A2.

21. Jack Neff, "Direct Response Getting Respect," *Advertising Age,* January 20, 2003, p. 4.

22. Perry Bacon, Jr., and Eric Roston, "Stop Calling Us," *Time,* April 28, 2003, pp. 56–58.

23. "'Do-Not-Call' List Becomes Law," *The Wall Street Journal,* March 12, 2003, p. D4.

24. Matthew Boyle, "Joe Galli's Army," *Fortune,* December 30, 2002, pp. 135–138.

25. Janine Gordon, "When PR Makes More Sense Than Ads," *BrandWeek,* April 21, 2003, p. 26.

26. Michael Freedman and Emily Lambert, "Will She Walk?" *Forbes,* July 2, 2003, pp. 46–47; Anita Kunz, "It's a Bad Thing," *Worth,* January/February 2003, pp. 62–65.
27. Jennifer Gilbert, "A Matter of Trust," *Sales & Marketing Management,* March 2003, pp. 31–36.
28. Barry Newman, "Ad Professor Huffs against Puffs, but It's a Quixotic Enterprise," *The Wall Street Journal,* January 24, 2003, pp. A1, A9.
29. Gilbert, "A Matter of Trust," p. 32.
30. Michael Applebaum, "Don't Spare the Brand," *BrandWeek,* March 10, 2003, pp. 21–26.
31. Nanci Hellmich, "Obesity Is the Target," *USA Today,* May 8, 2003, pp. D1, D2.
32. Jerry Flint, "Luxury: The Cure du Jour," *Forbes,* December 9, 2002, p. 88.
33. Jon Swartz, "Technology Recession Pushes Computer Giants into Slugfest," *USA Today,* November 14, 2002, pp. B1, B2.
34. Lauran Neergaard, "Claritin to Move across Counter," *Mobile Register,* November 28, 2002, p. B18.
35. Mike Snider, "Sony Slashes PS2's Price $100 before Electronics Expo," *USA Today,* May 14, 2002, p. D1.
36. Jane Spencer, "Beating Retailers at the Discount Game," *The Wall Street Journal,* November 27, 2002, p. D1.
37. Jane Bennett Clark, "Cheap Talk," *Kiplinger's,* March 2002, pp. 112–116.

Chapter 15

1. Lorrie Grant, "Fresh Products Help Air Travelers Navigate Security," *USA Today,* October 12, 2004, p. B6; Paul Magnusson et al., "Welcome to Security Nation," *BusinessWeek,* June 14, 2004, pp. 32–35; Gwendolyn Bounds, "To Survive a Disaster: Prepare Your Business," *The Wall Street Journal,* August 24, 2004, p. B7; William Kleinknecht, "More Companies Buy Terrorism Insurance," *Mobile Register,* July 20, 2004, p. B8.
2. "Retailing Case Study," Data Miners Web site, http://www.dataminers.com, accessed January 24, 2003.
3. *Cooking Light,* Cooking Light Web site, http://www.cookinglight.com, accessed January 24, 2004.
4. Heather Green, Steve Rosenbush, Roger O. Crockett, and Stanley Holmes, "Wi-Fi Means Business," *BusinessWeek,* April 28, 2003, pp. 86–92.
5. Scott Woolley, "Wider-Fi," *Forbes,* April 14, 2003, pp. 201–204.
6. "William Beaumont Hospitals Save Millions Using Oracle," Oracle Web site, http://www.oracle.com, accessed January 24, 2003.
7. Patrick Seitz, "Bigger Sales Now in Smaller Packages as Notebook PCs Surpass Desktop PCs," Yahoo? News, Yahoo! News Web site, http://news.yahoo.com, accessed July 9, 2003.
8. "Parents in a Pinch Case Study," Microsoft Web site, http://www.microsoft.com, accessed January 24, 2003.
9. "About Great Harvest Bread Company," Great Harvest Web site, http://www.greatharvest.com, accessed January 24, 2004.
10. Pamela Moore, "GE Embraces the Paperless Office," *BusinessWeek* Web site, http://www.businessweek.com, accessed May 15, 2002.
11. "How Ed Viesturs Uses Publisher Version 2002," Microsoft Web site, http://www.microsoft.com, accessed January 24, 2003.
12. "About Expo Design," Home Depot Web site, http://www.homedepot.com, accessed May 15, 2002.
13. "Customer Case Study," Intranets.com Web site, http:// www.intranets.com, accessed January 24, 2003.
14. "A New Spin on Laundry," *Kiplinger's,* May 2003, p. 32.
15. Polly Schneider, "The Bargain Hunter's Guide to Global Networks," *CIO* magazine Web site, http://www.cio.com, accessed May 15, 2002.
16. "Computer Emergency Response Team Coordination Center," CERT Web site, http://www.cert.org/statistics, accessed January 24, 2003.
17. Richard Thieme, "Midwest Express Hackers Cause a Stir," *The Business Journal of Milwaukee,* MSNBC Web site, http://www.msnbc.com, accessed May 16, 2002.
18. Bob Sullivan, "Best Buy Closes Wireless Registers," MSNBC Web site, http://www.msnbc.com, accessed May 16, 2002.
19. "The Computer Economics Security Review," *Computer Economics* Web site, http://www.computereconomics.com, accessed January 24, 2003.
20. "The Computer Economics Security Review."
21. Barbara De Lollis, "Internet Error Puts Starwood in a No-Win Situation," *USA Today* Web site, http://www.usatoday.com, accessed January 22, 2003.

Chapter 16

1. Company Web site, http://www.plante-moran.com, accessed January 4, 2005; Charles Fan and Kate Warren, "Philosophical Accounting 101: A Day in the Life of Plante & Moran," *The Monroe Street Journal,* http://ww.themsj.com, accessed October 27, 2004; Jena McGregor, "Balance and Balance Sheets," *Fast Company,* May 2004, pp. 96–97; Brian R. Ball, "Plante & Moran Putting Roots in Tower," *Columbus Business First,* January 23, 2004, http://columbus.bizjournals.com.
2. "About ElderWeb," ElderWeb site, http://www.elderweb.com, accessed January 4, 2004.
3. Bureau of Labor Statistics, BLS Web site, http://www.bls.gov, accessed February 3, 2003; American Institute of Certified Public Accountants, AICPA Web site, http://www.aicpa.org, accessed February 3, 2003.
4. Laird Harrison, "We're the Boss," *Time* magazine Web site, http://www.time.com, accessed February 3, 2003.
5. "Company Profile," Parson Group Web site, http://www.parsongroup.com, accessed January 4, 2004.
6. Merck and Cisco Systems financial statements, MSN Money Central Web site, http://moneycentral.msn.com, accessed February 3, 2003.
7. MSN Money Central, accessed from the MSN Money Central Web site, http://moneycentral.msn.com, accessed February 3, 2003.
8. Joseph Radigan, "Building Budgets on the Web," CFO.com Web site, http://www.cfo.com, accessed February 3, 2003; "Budget Software That Turns on a Dime," CFO.com Web site, http://www.cfo.com, accessed February 3, 2003.

Chapter 17

1. Dan Thanh Dang, "Most Consumers Are Now Choosing Plastic," *Mobile Register,* October 10, 2004, pp. 1F, 5F; Shaheen Pasha, "Your Fixed Credit-Card Rate Might Be Going Up," *The Wall Street Journal,* August 12, 2004, p. D2; Jathon Sapsford, "As Cash Fades, America Becomes a Plastic Nation," *The Wall Street Journal,* July 23, 2004, pp. A1, A6; Christine Dugas, "Credit Card Fees Become Cash Cow," *USA Today,* July 14, 2004, p. A1; Mitchell Pacelle, "Growing Profit Source for Banks: Fees from Riskiest Card Holders," *The Wall Street Journal,* July 6, 2004, p. A1.
2. CFO.com Web site, http://www.cfo.com, accessed January 15, 2004.
3. Joseph Weber, "CFOs on the Hot Seat," *BusinessWeek,* March 17, 2003, pp. 66–70.
4. David Katz, "What You Don't Know about Sarbanes-Oxley," CFO.com Web site, http://www.cfo.com, accessed March 15, 2003.
5. Boeing Corporation, Boeing Web site, http://www.boeing.com, accessed January 15, 2004.

6. Theresa Carey, "When Software Lets You Count Your Costs to the Penny," CFO.com Web site, http://www.cfo.com, accessed May 1, 2002.

7. David Stires, "Is Your Store a Bank in Drag?" *Fortune,* March 17, 2003, p. 38.

8. Linda Himelstein, "Benchmark's Venture Capitalists Take the Valley by Storm," *BusinessWeek* Web site, http://www.bwonline.com, accessed March 20, 2003.

9. Federal Deposit Insurance Corporation, FDIC Web site, http://www.fdic.gov, accessed March 20, 2003.

10. FDIC Web site, accessed March 20, 2003.

11. FDIC Web site, accessed March 20, 2003.

12. *Statistical Abstract of the United States,* Census Department Web site, http://www.census.gov, accessed March 21, 2003.

13. Online Banking Report, Online Banking Report Web site, http://www.onlinebanking.com, accessed March 21, 2003.

14. FDIC Web site, accessed March 21, 2003.

15. National Credit Union Administration, NCUA Web site, http://www.ncua.gov, accessed March 21, 2003.

16. Insurance Information Institute, Institute Web site, http://www.iii.org, accessed March 21, 2003.

17. Insurance Information Institute Web site, accessed March 21, 2003.

18. "About CalPERS," CalPERS Web site, http://www.calpers.ca.gov, accessed March 21, 2003.

19. FDIC Web site, accessed March 20, 2003.

Chapter 18

1. Steve Haamm, "A World Without Microsoft," *BusinessWeek,* November 8, 2004, p. 132; Adam Lashinsky, "Microsoft Shares the Wealth," *Fortune,* August 9, 2004, pp. 162–164; Olga Kharif, "Hallowed Hauls," *BusinessWeek,* August 9, 2004, p. 8; Elliot Blair Smith, Matt Krantz, and Jon Swartz, "Companies Flush, With Nothing to Splurge On," *USA Today,* July 22, 2004, pp. B1, B2; Byron Acohido and Adam Shell, "Microsoft Plans Big Dividend," *USA Today,* July 21, 2004, p. A1.

2. Frank Reeves, "US Airways Cleared to Emerge from Bankruptcy," *Pittsburgh Post-Gazette,* http://www.post-gazette.com, accessed April 21, 2003; "War Spreads Airline Industry Crash," *CBS News,* http://www.cbsnews.com, accessed April 21, 2003; "US Airways Reorganization Plan," US Airways Web site, http://www.usairways.com, accessed April 21, 2003.

3. *Financial Services Facts,* Insurance Information Institute, http://www.iii.org, accessed April 21, 2003.

4. New York Stock Exchange Web site, http://www.nyse.com, accessed April 21, 2003.

5. *Survey of Consumer Finances,* Federal Reserve Web site, http://www.federalreserve.gov, accessed April 21, 2003; Barbara Hagenbaugh, "Nation's Wealth Disparity Widens," *USA Today,* January 23, 2003, p. A1.

6. New York Stock Exchange Web site, http://www.nyse.com, accessed April 21, 2003.

7. NASDAQ Stock Market Web site, http://www.nasdaq.com, accessed April 21, 2003.

8. Chicago Stock Exchange Web site, http://www.chicagostockex.com, accessed April 21, 2003.

9. Merrill Lynch Web site, http://askmerrill.ml.com, accessed April 21, 2003.

10. Dow Jones Indexes Web site, http://www.dowjindexes.com, accessed April 21, 2003.

11. Investment Company Institute Web site, http://www.ici.org, accessed April 21, 2003.

12. "SEC Enters Partial Settlement with Cole A. Bartiromo," Litigation Release No. 17540, Securities & Exchange Commission Web site, http://www.sec.gov, accessed April 21, 2003.

13. Erin McClam, "Federal Grand Jury Indicts Martha Stewart," *Associated Press,* June 4, 2003, http://www.story.news.yahoo.com; Ben White and Justin Gillis, "ImClone's Waksal Pleads Guilty to 6 Charges," *Washington Post* Web site, http://www.washingtonpost.com, accessed April 16, 2003.

Appendix A

1. Rob Stein, "Increase in Physicians' Insurance Hurts Care," *Washington Post* Web site, http://www.washingtonpost.com, accessed January 8, 2003; Rochelle Sharpe, "Mold Getting a Costly Hold on Homes," *USA Today* Web site, http://www.usatoday.com, accessed January 8, 2003; Ray A. Smith, "Mold Problems Grow in Commercial Buildings," *Mobile Register,* December 8, 2002, p. 2J; Rachel Zimmerman and Christopher Oster, "Assigning Liability: Insurers' Missteps Helped Provoke Malpractice Crisis," *The Wall Street Journal,* June 24, 2002, p. A1.

Appendix B

1. John Korvin, "Unlocking the Real Benefits of E-Billing," SmartBiz.com, http://www.smartbiz.com, accessed January 14, 2003; Robyn Greenspan, "Users Bank on the Internet," *CyberAtlas,* December 16, 2002, http://cyberatlas.internet.com; Kristen Gerencher, "Routinely in Arrears," *CBS.MarketWatch.com,* October 15, 2002; "New Survey Uncovers Eye-Opening Facts about America's Bill-Paying Habits," *PR Newswire,* October 14, 2002; Robyn Greenspan, "Click-Banking Market Multiplies," *CyberAtlas,* October 7, 2002, http://cyberatlas.internet.com.

2. Tax Foundation, http://www.taxfoundation.org, accessed January 16, 2002. For more detail on personal financial planning, see Louis E. Boone, David L. Kurtz, and Douglas Hearth, *Planning Your Financial Future,* 3rd ed. Mason, OH: South-Western, 2003.

3. Kathy Jumper, "Low Rates Lure First-Timers," *Mobile Register,* June 1, 2003, pp. J1, J2.

Appendix C

1. Wrenchead.com Web site, http://www.wrenchead.com, accessed January 18, 2004; Bob Weinstein, "From Main Street to the Net," *Fortune Small Business,* May 26, 2003, http://www.fortune.com/fortune/; Elizabeth Wasserman, "A Simple Plan," *MBA Jungle,* February 2003, pp. 50–55; Phil Waga, "Wrenchead.com Is Gold Mine for Old Auto Parts," *Enquirer Business Coverage,* February 20, 2000, http://www.enquirer.com/editions/, accessed June 18, 2003.

2. Wasserman, "A Simple Plan."

3. Wasserman, "A Simple Plan," p. 52.

4. Deloitte & Touche, "Writing an Effective Business Plan," http://www.deloitte.com/vc, p. 3, accessed June 18, 2003.

5. C. J. Prince, "The Ultimate Business Plan," *Success,* January 2000, http://www.findarticles.com, accessed January 18, 2004.

Name Index

Subject Index

International Index

Nigeria
  population in, 106
Nike, 103, 129
Nikkei, 588
Nissan, 129
Nokia, 20, 21
Nontariff barriers, 120
Nonverbal communication
  cultural differences, 113, 114
Nonverbal cues, 344
North American Free Trade Agreement (NAFTA),
  122–123, 141
  international accounting standards, 534
North Korea. *See* Korea, North
Norway
  per-capita GDP of, 106
  technology and productivity, 23
NTT, 54

Office Depot, 110
Offset agreement, 127
Online business
  globalization and, 125
Online financial services, 132
Oracle, 105
Organization for Economic Cooperation and
      Development Anti-Bribery Convention, 117
Organization of Petroleum Export Countries (OPEC),
  72
Oshkosh Truck Corp., 395
Overseas division, 129
Ownership
  in various economic systems, 84

Pacific Rim
  as emerging market, 107
Packaging, 430
Pakistan
  population in, 106
Pak Mail, 177
Paraguay, 122
People's Republic of China. *See* China
PepsiCo, 96, 347
Per-capita GDP
  world's top ten nations based on, 106
Personal space, 344
Peso, 111, 123, 549
Philippines, 107
  abusive working conditions in, 96
Pier One Imports, 126
Pillsbury, 111
Pizza Hut, 127, 177
Poland, 107, 123
  political change and barrier to trade, 116
Political climate
  barriers to trade and, 116
Population
  world's top ten nations based on, 106
Pound, 111
Premier Hotels, 127
PriceSmart, 104
Procter & Gamble, 96
Productivity, 22–23
  globalization and, 22–23

Profit
  right to, in various economic systems, 84
Promotion
  sports celebrities as part of promotional campaign,
    484
Protective tariff, 119–120
Putin, Vladimir V., 116

Quality
  global economy and, 95–96
Quotas, 120

Rand, 111
Red Cross/Red Crescent, 390
Regulations
  international trade, 118–119
Religious attitudes
  as barrier to trade, 113–115
Restrictions
  on trade, 119–120
Revenue tariffs, 119–120
Richards, Keith, 119
Risk
  degree of, and globalization, 125
Roots, 126
Royal Dutch/Shell, 130
Ruble, 112
Rupee, 111
Russia
  corruption in, 117
  countertrade, 127
  Internet use in, 232
  open communication style of U.S. firms in, 348
  political change and barrier to trade, 116
  population in, 106
Ryanair, 327

Saffron
  difficulty in growing, 108
Samsung, 104, 129
San Marino
  per-capita GDP of, 106
Sanyo, 104
Saudi Arabia, 71
  barrier to trade and, 115
  working conditions in, 295
Securities exchange
  foreign stock markets, 584–585
Security (safety)
  airline industry and increased security, 489
Service industry
  in Canada, 123
ServiceMaster Clean, 177
Services
  U.S. exporters/importers, 109–100
7-Eleven, 177
Shortages, 83
Singapore, 107
Slovakia, 123
Slovenia, 123
Small businesses
  globalization and, 179
Soft Toy Concepts, 119

Software
  piracy of, in China, 119
Sony, 104, 129
South Africa, 107
South Korea. *See* Korea, South
Soviet Union, former
  as planned economy, 83
Sports celebrities
  promotional campaigns and, 484
St. Jude Medical, 112
Standardization strategy, 131
Starbucks, 137
STAT-USA, 125
Steel industry
  tariffs and, 120
Strategies
  global business strategies, 131
Subcontracting, 128
Sun Life, 21
Switzerland
  as low-context culture, 347
  per-capita GDP of, 106

Taiwan, 107
  GATT and, 121
  U.S. imports/exports of, 21
Target, 104
Tariffs, 118, **119**–120
Technology
  fighting terrorism with, 489
Telecommunications
  cell phone use, 115
Terrorism
  global economy and, 95–96
Thailand, 107
  abusive working conditions in, 96
The Coca-Cola Company, 20, 21, 96, 104, 118, 131,
    533
Toyota Motors, 130, 131
Trade. *See* International trade
Trade barriers. *See* Barriers to trade
Training
  diversity training, 126
TruGreenChemLawn, 177
Turkey, 107
  political change and barrier to trade, 116

Ukraine
  hyperinflation, 88
Unilever, 129
United Arab Emirates, 71
United Kingdom, 111, 118
  GDP of, 23
  Internet use in, 232
  level of entrepreneurial activity in, 205
  U.S. imports/exports of, 21
  U.S. trade with, 107
United States
  exports, 105, 109–100
  France and war in Iraq, 114
  GDP of, 23
  gross domestic product of, 105
  imports, 105, 109–100
  Internet use in, 232